Prepare, Apply, and Confirm

- **Auto-Graded Excel Projects**—Using proven, field-tested technology, MyAccountingLab's new auto-graded Excel Projects allow instructors to seamlessly integrate Excel content into their course without having to manually grade spreadsheets. Students have the opportunity to practice important Accounting skills in Microsoft Excel, helping them to master key concepts and gain proficiency in Excel. Students simply download a spreadsheet, work live on an accounting problem in Excel, and then upload that file back into MyAccountingLab, where they receive reports on their work that provide personalized, detailed feedback to pinpoint where they went wrong on any step of the problem. Available with select titles.

- **Enhanced eText**—The Pearson eText gives students access to their textbook anytime, anywhere. In addition to note-taking, highlighting, and bookmarking, the Pearson eText offers interactive and sharing features. Students actively read and learn through auto-graded practice, author videos, and more. Instructors can share comments or highlights, and students can add their own, for a tight community of learners in any class.

- Keep students engaged in learning on their own time, while helping them achieve greater conceptual understanding of course material through author-created solutions videos, opportunities to Try It!, and live exhibits.

- **Dynamic Study Modules**—With a focus on key topics, these modules work by continuously assessing student performance and activity in real time and, using data and analytics, provide personalized content to reinforce concepts that target each student's particular strengths and weakness.

Pearson

with MyAccountingLab®

- **Hallmark Features**—Personalized Learning Aids, like Help Me Solve This, Demo Docs, and instant feedback are available for further practice and mastery when students need the help most!

- **Learning Catalytics**—Generates classroom discussion, guides lecture, and promotes peer-to-peer learning with real-time analytics. Now, students can use any device to interact in the classroom.

- **Personalized Study Plan**—Assists students in monitoring their own progress by offering them a customized study plan based on Homework, Quiz, and Test results. Includes regenerated exercises with unlimited practice, as well as the opportunity to earn mastery points by completing quizzes on recommended learning objectives.

- **Worked Solutions**—Provide step-by-step explanations on how to solve select problems using the exact numbers and data that were presented in the problem. Instructors will have access to the Worked Out Solutions in preview and review mode.

ALWAYS LEARNING

Prepare, Apply, and Confirm with MyAccountingLab®

- **Algorithmic Test Bank**—Instructors have the ability to create multiple versions of a test or extra practice for students.

- **Reporting Dashboard**—View, analyze, and report learning outcomes clearly and easily. Available via the Gradebook and fully mobile-ready, the Reporting Dashboard presents student performance data at the class, section, and program levels in an accessible, visual manner.

- **LMS Integration**—Link from any LMS platform to access assignments, rosters, and resources, and synchronize MyLab grades with your LMS gradebook. For students, new direct, single sign-on provides access to all the personalized learning MyLab resources that make studying more efficient and effective.

Pearson

ALWAYS LEARN

ACCOUNTING in the headlines

Accounting in the Headlines.

One of the biggest challenges for accounting instructors is that students often feel disengaged from the course material, which can seem abstract and unrelated to their personal experiences. But by incorporating real-life examples, instructors can spark student interest and engagement, especially when teaching accounting at the introductory level.

Accounting in the Headlines, an award-winning blog by renowned author Wendy Tietz, does just that with stories about real companies and events that can be used in the accounting classroom to illustrate introductory financial and managerial accounting concepts.

Concise, tailorable, and updated on a weekly basis, these articles easily fit into the typical introductory accounting curriculum, whether the course is delivered in-person or online. **Accounting in the Headlines articles, along with multiple-choice and polling questions, can be assigned through MyAccountingLab and Learning Catalytics™. Instructors are also provided with discussion questions, PowerPoint slides, and handout files, to support learning initiatives.**

http://accountingintheheadlines.com

Managerial Accounting

Fifth Edition

Karen Wilken Braun, PhD, CPA, CGMA
Case Western Reserve University

Wendy M. Tietz, PhD, CPA, CGMA, CMA
Kent State University

New York, NY

Vice President, Business Publishing: Donna Battista
Director of Portfolio Management: Adrienne D'Ambrosio
Senior Portfolio Manager: Ellen Geary
Vice President, Product Marketing: Roxanne McCarley
Director of Strategic Marketing: Brad Parkins
Strategic Marketing Manager: Deborah Strickland
Product Marketer: Tricia Murphy
Field Marketing Manager: Natalie Wagner
Field Marketing Assistant: Kristen Compton
Product Marketing Assistant: Jessica Quazza
Vice President, Production and Digital Studio, Arts and Business: Etain O'Dea
Director of Production, Business: Jeff Holcomb
Managing Producer, Business: Ashley Santora
Content Producer: Daniel Edward Petrino
Operations Specialist: Carol Melville
Creative Director: Blair Brown
Manager, Learning Tools: Brian Surette
Content Developer, Learning Tools: Sarah Peterson
Managing Producer, Digital Studio, Arts and Business: Diane Lombardo
Digital Studio Producer: Regina DaSilva
Digital Studio Producer: Alana Coles
Digital Content Team Lead: Noel Lotz
Digital Content Project Lead: Martha LaChance
Full-Service Project Management and Composition: Kathy Smith, Cenveo® Publisher Services
Interior Design: Jerilyn Bockorick, Cenveo® Publisher Services
Cover Design: Cenveo® Publisher Services
Cover Art: style-photography/shutterstock & nikolae/shutterstock
Printer/Binder: LSC Communications
Cover Printer: Phoenix

Microsoft and/or its respective suppliers make no representations about the suitability of the information contained in the documents and related graphics published as part of the services for any purpose. All such documents and related graphics are provided "as is" without warranty of any kind. Microsoft and/or its respective suppliers hereby disclaim all warranties and conditions with regard to this information, including all warranties and conditions of merchantability, whether express, implied or statutory, fitness for a particular purpose, title and non-infringement. In no event shall Microsoft and/or its respective suppliers be liable for any special, indirect or consequential damages or any damages whatsoever resulting from loss of use, data or profits, whether in an action of contract, negligence or other tortious action, arising out of or in connection with the use or performance of information available from the services.

The documents and related graphics contained herein could include technical inaccuracies or typographical errors. Changes are periodically added to the information herein. Microsoft and/or its respective suppliers may make improvements and/or changes in the product(s) and/or the program(s) described herein at any time. Partial screen shots may be viewed in full within the software version specified.

Microsoft® and Windows® are registered trademarks of the Microsoft Corporation in the U.S.A. and other countries. This book is not sponsored or endorsed by or affiliated with the Microsoft Corporation.

Copyright © 2018, 2015, 2013 by Pearson Education, Inc. or its affiliates. All Rights Reserved. Manufactured in the United States of America. This publication is protected by copyright, and permission should be obtained from the publisher prior to any prohibited reproduction, storage in a retrieval system, or transmission in any form or by any means, electronic, mechanical, photocopying, recording, or otherwise. For information regarding permissions, request forms, and the appropriate contacts within the Pearson Education Global Rights and Permissions department, please visit www.pearsoned.com/permissions/.

Acknowledgments of third-party content appear on the appropriate page within the text.

PEARSON, ALWAYS LEARNING, and MYACCOUNTINGLAB® are exclusive trademarks owned by Pearson Education, Inc. or its affiliates in the U.S. and/or other countries.

Unless otherwise indicated herein, any third-party trademarks, logos, or icons that may appear in this work are the property of their respective owners, and any references to third-party trademarks, logos, icons, or other trade dress are for demonstrative or descriptive purposes only. Such references are not intended to imply any sponsorship, endorsement, authorization, or promotion of Pearson's products by the owners of such marks, or any relationship between the owner and Pearson Education, Inc., or its affiliates, authors, licensees, or distributors.

Cataloging-in-Publication Data is on file at the Library of Congress

ISBN 13: 978-0-13-412852-8
ISBN 10: 0-13-412852-4

BRIEF CONTENTS

1. Introduction to Managerial Accounting 1
2. Building Blocks of Managerial Accounting 48
3. Job Costing 104
4. Activity-Based Costing, Lean Operations, and the Costs of Quality 175
5. Process Costing 245
6. Cost Behavior 307
7. Cost-Volume-Profit Analysis 381
8. Relevant Costs for Short-Term Decisions 443
9. The Master Budget 507
10. Performance Evaluation 583
11. Standard Costs and Variances 653
12. Capital Investment Decisions and the Time Value of Money 710
13. Statement of Cash Flows 779
14. Financial Statement Analysis 838
15. Sustainability 894

Glossary/Index I-1

CONTENTS

1 Introduction to Managerial Accounting 1

What Is Managerial Accounting? 2
Managers' Three Primary Responsibilities 2
A Road Map: How Managerial Accounting Fits In 3
Differences Between Managerial Accounting and Financial Accounting 4

What Role Do Management Accountants Play? 6
The Role of Management Accountants 6
The Skills Required of Management Accountants 7
Managerial Accounting Is Important to All Careers 8
Accounting within the Organizational Structure 9
Professional Associations 10
Average Salaries of Management Accountants 12
Professional Ethics 12
Examples of Ethical Dilemmas 14

What Business Trends and Regulations Affect Management Accounting? 18
Big Data, Data Analytics, and Critical Thinking 18
Shifting Economy 20
Globalization 20
Lean Thinking and Focus on Quality 21
Sustainability, Social Responsibility, and the Triple Bottom Line 21
Integrated Reporting 22
The Sarbanes-Oxley Act of 2002 23
End of Chapter 27

2 Building Blocks of Managerial Accounting 48

What Are the Most Common Business Sectors and Their Activities? 49
Service, Merchandising, and Manufacturing Companies 49
Which Business Activities Make Up the Value Chain? 51
Coordinating Activities Across the Value Chain 52

How Do Companies Define Cost? 55
Cost Objects, Direct Costs, and Indirect Costs 55
Costs for Internal Decision Making and External Reporting 57
Merchandising Companies' Product Costs 58
Manufacturing Companies' Product Costs 60
Prime and Conversion Costs 61
Additional Labor Compensation Costs 62
Recap: Product Costs Versus Period Costs 62

How Are Product Costs and Period Costs Shown in the Financial Statements? 65
Service Companies 65
Merchandising Companies 65
Manufacturing Companies 67
Comparing Balance Sheets 70

What Other Cost Terms Are Used by Managers? 71
Controllable Versus Uncontrollable Costs 71
Relevant and Irrelevant Costs 71
Fixed and Variable Costs 72
How Manufacturing Costs Behave 73
Calculating Total and Average Costs 73
End of Chapter 78

3 Job Costing 104

What Methods Are Used to Determine the Cost of Manufacturing a Product? 105
Process Costing 105
Job Costing 106

How Do Manufacturers Determine a Job's Cost? 107
Overview: Flow of Inventory Through a Manufacturing System 107

Scheduling Production 108

Purchasing Raw Materials 109

Using a Job Cost Record to Keep Track of Job Costs 110

Tracing Direct Materials Cost to a Job 112

Tracing Direct Labor Cost to a Job 114

Allocating Manufacturing Overhead to a Job 116

Completing the Job Cost Record and Using It to Make Business Decisions 119

How Can Job Costing Information Be Enhanced for Decision Making? 121

Non-Manufacturing Costs 121

Direct or Variable Costing 123

How Do Managers Deal with Underallocated or Overallocated Manufacturing Overhead? 127

What Journal Entries Are Needed in a Manufacturer's Job Costing System? 129

APPENDIX 3A 143

How Do Service Firms Use Job Costing to Determine the Amount to Bill Clients? 143

What Costs Are Considered Direct Costs of Serving a Client? 143

What Costs Are Considered Indirect Costs of Serving a Client? 144

Finding the Total Cost of the Job and Adding a Profit Markup 145

Invoicing Clients Using a Professional Billing Rate 145

What Journal Entries Are Needed in a Service Firm's Job Costing System? 146

End of Chapter 147

4 Activity-Based Costing, Lean Operations, and the Costs of Quality 175

Why and How Do Companies Refine Their Cost Allocation Systems? 176

Simple Cost Allocation Systems Can Lead to Cost Distortion 176

Review: Using a Plantwide Overhead Rate to Allocate Indirect Costs 177

Using Departmental Overhead Rates to Allocate Indirect Costs 179

Using Activity-Based Costing to Allocate Indirect Costs 184

How Do Managers Use the Refined Cost Information to Improve Operations? 191

Activity-Based Management (ABM) 191

Passing the Cost-Benefit Test 193

What Is Lean Thinking? 198

The Eight Wastes of Traditional Operations 198

Characteristics of Lean Operations 200

Lean Operations in Service and Merchandising Companies 205

How Do Managers Improve Quality? 206

Costs of Quality (COQ) 206

Relationship Among Costs 207

Using Costs of Quality Reports to Aid Decisions 208

End of Chapter 213

5 Process Costing 245

Process Costing: An Overview 246

Two Basic Costing Systems: Job Costing and Process Costing 246

How Does the Flow of Costs Differ Between Job and Process Costing? 247

What Are the Building Blocks of Process Costing? 250

Conversion Costs 250

Equivalent Units 250

Inventory Flow Assumptions 251

How Does Process Costing Work in the First Processing Department? 252

Step 1: Summarize the Flow of Physical Units 254

Step 2: Compute Output in Terms of Equivalent Units 254

Step 3: Summarize Total Costs to Account For 256

Step 4: Compute the Cost per Equivalent Unit 256

Step 5: Assign Total Costs to Units Completed and to Units in Ending Work in Process Inventory 257

Average Unit Costs 257

What Journal Entries Are Needed in a Process Costing System? 259

How Does Process Costing Work in a Second or Later Processing Department? 264

Process Costing in SeaView's Insertion Department 264

Steps 1 and 2: Summarize the Flow of Physical Units and Compute Output in Terms of Equivalent Units 266

Steps 3 and 4: Summarize Total Costs to Account for and Compute the Cost per Equivalent Unit 267

Step 5: Assign Total Costs to Units Completed and to Units in Ending Work in Process Inventory 268

Unit Costs and Gross Profit 268

Production Cost Reports 269

Journal Entries in a Second Processing Department 270

End of Chapter 275

6 Cost Behavior 307

Cost Behavior: How Do Changes in Volume Affect Costs? 308

Variable Costs 308

Fixed Costs 311

Mixed Costs 314

Relevant Range 316

Other Cost Behaviors 317

How Do Managers Determine Cost Behavior? 322

Account Analysis 322

Scatterplots 322

High-Low Method 324

Regression Analysis 326

Data Concerns 330

What Are the Roles of Variable Costing and the Contribution Margin Income Statement? 331

Comparing Absorption Costing and Variable Costing 331

The Contribution Margin Income Statement 333

Comparing Operating Income: Variable Versus Absorption Costing 336

Reconciling Operating Income Between the Two Costing Systems 338

End of Chapter 346

7 Cost-Volume-Profit Analysis 381

How Does Cost-Volume-Profit Analysis Help Managers? 382

Data and Assumptions Required for CVP Analysis 382

The Unit Contribution Margin 383

The Contribution Margin Ratio 385

How Do Managers Find the Breakeven Point? 386

The Income Statement Approach 387

The Shortcut Approach Using the Unit Contribution Margin 388

The Shortcut Approach Using the Contribution Margin Ratio 388

How Do Managers Find the Volume Needed to Earn a Target Profit? 389

How Much Must We Sell to Earn a Target Profit? 389

Graphing CVP Relationships 391

How Do Managers Use CVP to Make Decisions When Business Conditions Change? 396

Changing the Sales Price and Volume 396

Changing Variable Costs 398

Changing Fixed Costs 399

Changing the Mix of Products Offered for Sale 402

What Are Some Common Indicators of Risk? 406

Margin of Safety 406

Operating Leverage 407

Choosing a Cost Structure 409

End of Chapter 415

Contents   ix

8 Relevant Costs for Short-Term Decisions   443

How Do Managers Make Decisions?   444
Relevant Information   444
Keys to Making Short-Term Special Decisions   445
Decision Pitfalls to Avoid   446

How Do Managers Make Pricing and Special Order Decisions?   448
Regular Pricing Decisions   448
Special Order Decisions   453

How Do Managers Make Other Special Business Decisions?   460
Decisions to Discontinue Products, Departments, or Stores   460
Product Mix Decisions When Resources Are Constrained   464
Outsourcing Decisions (Make or Buy)   467
Decisions to Sell As Is or Process Further   472

End of Chapter   477

9 The Master Budget   507

How and Why Do Managers Use Budgets?   508
How Are Budgets Used?   508
How Are Budgets Developed?   508
What Are the Benefits of Budgeting?   510
What Is the Master Budget?   511

How Are the Operating Budgets Prepared?   512
Sales Budget   512
Production Budget   513
Direct Materials Budget   515
Direct Labor Budget   516
Manufacturing Overhead Budget   517
Operating Expenses Budget   518
Budgeted Income Statement   519

How Are the Financial Budgets Prepared?   524
Capital Expenditures Budget   524
Cash Collections Budget   524
Cash Payments Budget   525
Combined Cash Budget   527
Budgeted Balance Sheet   528
Sensitivity Analysis and Flexible Budgeting   530

How Do the Budgets for Service and Merchandising Companies Differ?   531
Service Companies   531
Merchandising Companies   531
Impact of Credit and Debit Card Sales on Budgeting   533

End of Chapter   540

10 Performance Evaluation   583

How Does Decentralization Affect Performance Evaluation?   584
Advantages and Disadvantages of Decentralization   584
Performance Evaluation Systems   585

What Is Responsibility Accounting?   585
Types of Responsibility Centers   586
Responsibility Center Performance Reports   588
Evaluation of Investment Centers   590

What Is Transfer Pricing?   597
Strategies and Mechanisms for Determining a Transfer Price   598

How Do Managers Use Flexible Budgets to Evaluate Performance?   603
Creating a Flexible Budget Performance Report   604
Underlying Causes of the Variances   607

How Do Companies Incorporate Nonfinancial Performance Measurement?   609
The Balanced Scorecard   609

End of Chapter   617

11 Standard Costs and Variances 653

What Are Standard Costs? 654

Types of Standards 654

Information Used to Develop and Update Standards 655

Computing Standard Costs 655

How Do Managers Use Standard Costs to Compute DM and DL Variances? 658

Using Standard Costs to Develop the Flexible Budget 658

Direct Materials Variances 658

Direct Labor Variances 664

Summary of Direct Materials and Direct Labor Variances 666

Advantages and Disadvantages of Using Standard Costs and Variances 666

How Do Managers Use Standard Costs to Compute MOH Variances? 671

Variable Manufacturing Overhead Variances 671

Fixed Manufacturing Overhead Variances 673

Standard Costing Systems 675

APPENDIX 11A 679

Standard Costing 679

Standard Costing Income Statement 682

End of Chapter 683

12 Capital Investment Decisions and the Time Value of Money 710

What Is Capital Budgeting? 711

Four Popular Methods of Capital Budgeting Analysis 711

Focus on Cash Flows 712

Capital Budgeting Process 712

How Do Managers Calculate the Payback Period and Accounting Rate of Return? 714

Payback Period 714

Accounting Rate of Return (ARR) 717

How Do Managers Compute the Time Value of Money? 723

Factors Affecting the Time Value of Money 723

Future Values and Present Values: Points Along the Time Continuum 724

Future Value and Present Value Factors 725

Calculating Future Values of Single Sums and Annuities Using FV Factors 726

Calculating Present Values of Single Sums and Annuities Using PV Factors 727

How Do Managers Calculate the Net Present Value and Internal Rate of Return? 730

Net Present Value (NPV) 731

Internal Rate of Return (IRR) 736

How Do the Capital Budgeting Methods Compare? 739

APPENDIX 12A 743

Present Value Tables and Future Value Tables 743

Table A Present Value of $1 743

Table B Present Value of Annuity of $1 744

Table C Future Value of $1 745

Table D Future Value of Annuity of $1 746

APPENDIX 12B 747

Solutions to Chapter Examples Using Microsoft Excel 747

APPENDIX 12C 751

Using a TI-83, TI-83 Plus, TI-84, or TI-84 Plus Calculator to Perform Time Value of Money Calculations 751

End of Chapter 757

13 Statement of Cash Flows 779

What Is the Statement of Cash Flows? 780

Three Types of Activities That Generate and Use Cash 781

Two Methods of Presenting Operating Activities 783

How Is the Statement of Cash Flows Prepared Using the Indirect Method? 788

Information Needed to Prepare the Statement of Cash Flows   788

Preparing the Cash Flows from Operating Activities   788

Preparing the Cash Flows from Investing Activities   794

Preparing the Cash Flows from Financing Activities   796

Interpreting the Statement of Cash Flows   798

Recap: Steps to Preparing the Statement of Cash Flows Using the Indirect Method   798

How Is the Statement of Cash Flows Prepared Using the Direct Method?   799

Overview   799

Determining Cash Payments and Receipts   800

End of Chapter   808

14 Financial Statement Analysis   838

What Are the Most Common Methods of Analysis?   839

What Is Horizontal Analysis?   839

Horizontal Analysis of the Income Statement   841

Horizontal Analysis of the Balance Sheet   841

Trend Percentages   841

What Is Vertical Analysis?   843

How Do We Compare One Company with Another?   845

Using Microsoft Excel   845

What Are Some of the Most Common Financial Ratios?   849

Measuring Ability to Pay Current Liabilities   849

Measuring Ability to Sell Inventory and Collect Receivables   850

Measuring Ability to Pay Long-Term Debt   852

Measuring Profitability   853

Analyzing Stock Investments   857

Red Flags in Financial Statement Analysis   858

End of Chapter   865

15 Sustainability   894

What Is Sustainability, and How Does It Create Business Value?   895

Historical Overview   896

The Business Case for Sustainability   897

What Is Sustainability Reporting?   902

Current State of Sustainability Reporting   902

Reasons for Sustainability Reporting   903

Framework for Sustainability Reporting   903

What Is Environmental Management Accounting (EMA)?   908

EMA Systems   908

Uses of Environmental Management Accounting Information   909

Challenges to Implementing EMA Systems   911

Future of Environmental Management Accounting   912

End of Chapter   914

Glossary/Index   I-1

Visual Walk-Through

Technology Makes it Simple
Expanded to include several new topics, these features give students step-by-step directions on how to use Microsoft Excel 2016 to perform the accounting task with more efficiency. Examples include: scatterplots, regression analysis, capital budgeting, CVP graphs, budgeting, and sensitivity analysis.

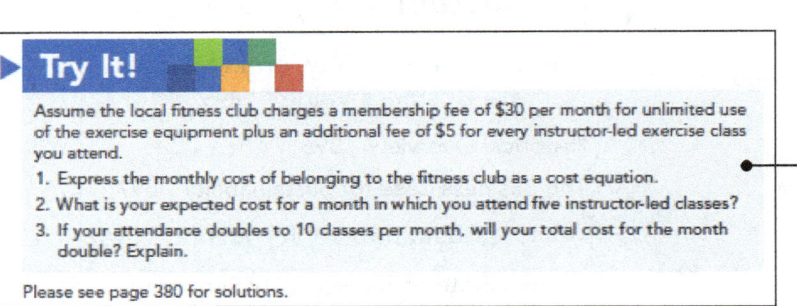

Try It! Interactive Questions
Found throughout the chapter, Try It interactive questions give students the opportunity to apply the concept they learned. Linking in the eText will allo students to practice in MyAccounting without interrupting their interaction the eText. Students' performance on questions creates a precise adaptive s plan for additional practice.

Video Solutions
Found in the eText and MyAccountingLab, the video solutions feature the author walking through the Try It! problems on a white board. Designed to give students detailed help when they need it.

Excel Exhibits
To give students a glimpse into the real world presentation of managerial accounting topics, financial statements and schedules are present in Excel. In the eText, a video link on selected exhibits will teach students how to create the same schedule using Excel.

...ainability

...n every chapter is a section on how sustain-...y relates to the main chapter topic.

Also included is a quick reference on which end-of-chapter problems correspond to the sustainability concept.

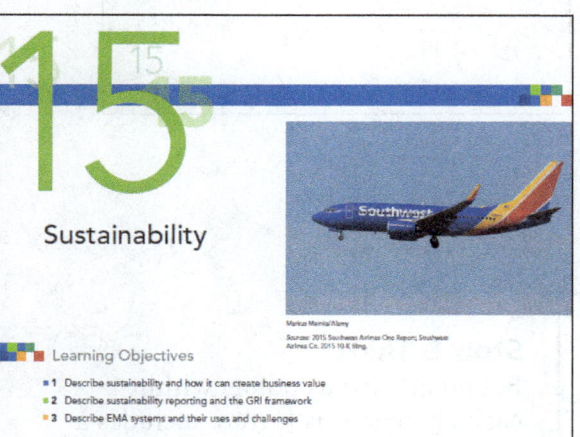

Sustainability Chapter

This chapter provides a deeper dive into how sustainability can generate business value. It also includes sections on sustainability reporting, the Sustainability Accounting Standards Board, and environmental management accounting systems.

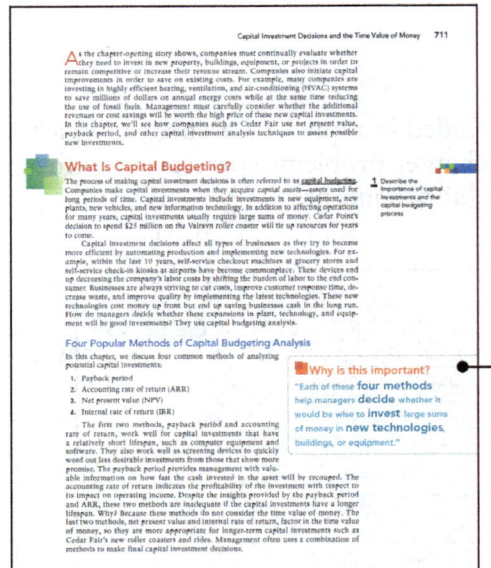

Why is this important?
Found throughout the chapter, this feature connects accounting with the business environment so that students can better understand the business significance of managerial accounting.

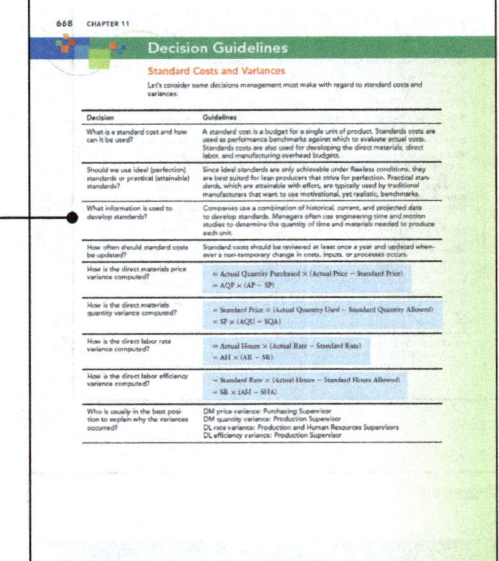

Decision Guidelines
Found at the midpoint and end of each chapter, this feature uses a business decision context to summarize key terms, concepts, and formulas from the chapter in question and answer format.

Stop & Think
Found at various points within each chapter, this feature includes a question-and-answer snapshot asking students to critically examine a concept they just learned.

End-of-Chapter Problems

The end-of-chapter content for short exercises, exercises, and problems has been refreshed for this edition. End-of-chapter items are structured to allow students to progress from simple to more rigorous as they move from item to item.

New short exercises based on real world situations have been added to every chapter to help students make the connection between the real world and the concepts being studied.

Case

A serial (continuing) case that focuses on one real world company has been added to the end-of-chapter material. The serial case consists of several small cases, one per chapter. These cases are meant to inspire critical thinking and connect the content with real life by following one company through all of the chapters in managerial accounting.

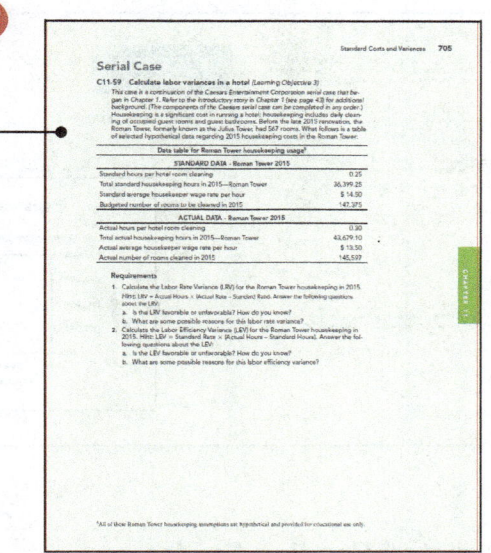

Critical Thinking

Problems are included to provide students with the opportunity for applied critical thinking. These problems include ethical topics, mini cases, and decision-making cases in real companies.

- Ethics Mini Cases based on the IMA Statement of Professional Practice are highlighted with an icon.

  ETHICS

- Real Life Mini Cases focusing on a real company and the decisions presented in business are highlighted with an icon.

  REAL LIFE

Excel in MyAccountingLab

- Students will download and complete problem in Microsoft Excel.
- Students receive personalized, detailed feedback upon uploading their completed spreadsheets.
- Questions will be auto-graded and reported to the grade book.

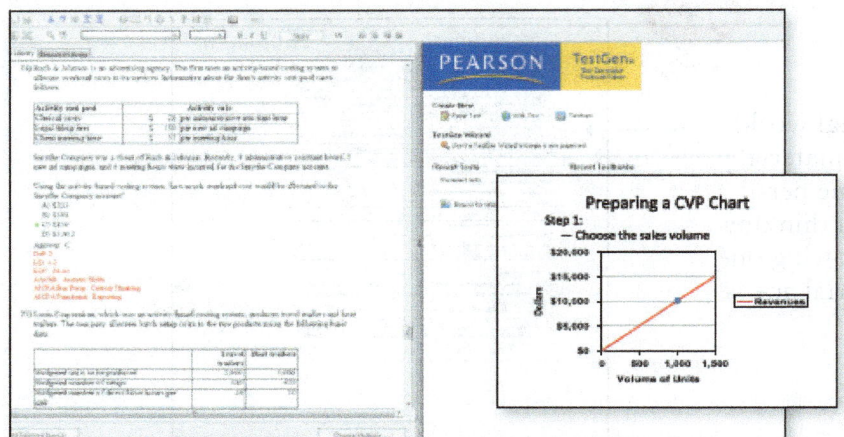

Test Bank and PowerPoints
Test bank includes algorithmic questions and 30% new material. PowerPoints have been updated and refreshed for the new edition. Worked-out problems contain the entire problem statement.

Directed Reading Guides
Directed reading guides, which have been prepared by the authors, help students take thorough while reading the text and glean the most important information from each chapter. Each chapter reading guide follows the text, paragraph-by-paragraph, asking students to answer questions and in the blanks, thereby keeping students actively engaged while preparing for class.

Accounting in the Headlines Blog
Accounting in the Headlines, www.accountingintheheadlines.com is a blog written by Wendy Tietz. N stories are added to the blog each week. The blog contains short stories about real-life companies and rent events that can be used in the accounting classroom to illustrate introductory accounting concepts blog posts contain discussion questions, PowerPoint slides, and handout files, making it a turnkey solu for instructors wanting to use real-life examples in their classes. All content is intended to be brief and ily into the typical introductory accounting class. In addition to the content found on the blog site, mu choice questions related to each blog post can be found in MyAccountingLab and in Learning Catalyti

Concept Videos for Students
Short videos focusing on key concepts are available in MyAccountingLab to further emphasize major cepts. These videos can be assigned in homework or used as part of a flipped classroom strategy.

CONTENT CHANGES TO THE FIFTH EDITION

Both students and instructors will benefit from a variety of new content in the fifth edition.

New and updated content within the text:

- Refreshed chapter opening stories attract student attention and lay the groundwork for the chapter using recognizable, real-world companies.
- Updated sustainability features in each chapter show how sustainability relates to the chapter content.
- Select modifications and enhancements were made to each chapter to make it easier for students to grasp difficult concepts. Some of these modifications include the following:

Chapter 1	Redesigned to focus on the professional nature of management accounting, including the American Accounting Association's Vision Model, IMA's definition of management accounting, technical and soft skills required by professionals, summary of CMA exam requirements, and a step-by-step model for critical thinking that can be referenced and used throughout the course. The chapter also includes a section on why management accounting is important to students majoring in other fields of study.
Chapter 2	Simplified language used for product costs (rather than inventoriable product costs) now used throughout the book; revised discussion of direct and indirect costs.
Chapter 3	Introduction and illustration of manufacturing overhead as a cost pool; Decision Guidelines now include job costing journal entries.
Chapter 5	Red arrows and speech bubbles on Exhibits help students better understand process costing calculations.
Chapter 7	Learning objective 3 expanded to illustrate the impact of changing business conditions on operating income as well as on the breakeven point.
Chapter 8	Streamlined introduction on relevant data; new company example for pricing, special order, and product discontinuation decisions; new "pitfalls to avoid" section with each decision; additional summary problem with worked out solution.

Chapter 10		To provide continuity between budgeting and performance evaluation, the flexible budgeting example now includes the entire income statement using the company featured in Chapter 9; updated PepsiCo data illustrates responsibility accounting.
Chapter 11		Company example tied to Chapters 9 and 10 to provide continuity between chapter topics; variance exhibits are more specifically labeled to better serve as references for students.
Chapter 14		Updated with the latest financial information from Target, Macy's, Kohl's, and Walmart; revised description of horizontal and vertical analysis; two additional profitability ratios included in the chapter.
Chapter 15		Updated for recent company examples and new data on sustainability reporting; new sections on the Sustainability Accounting Standards Board and inclusion of the landmark 2015 Paris Agreement.

New and updated content within the end-of-chapter material:

Quick Checks	Updated quick checks in each chapter. These questions are conceptual in nature.
Short Exercises	All short exercises have been updated. In addition, a new real world short exercise is included in every chapter.
Exercises	All exercises have been updated.
Problems	All problems have been updated.
Ethics Mini Cases	Updated case at the end of each chapter based on the IMA Statement of Professional Practice.
Real Life Mini Cases	Updated case at the end of each chapter focusing on a real company situation.
Serial Case	An all-new serial case has been added to the end-of-chapter material. All of these cases focus on the same real world company and continue throughout the text.

ABOUT THE AUTHORS

Karen Wilken Braun is a professor for the Department of Accountancy in the Weatherhead School of Management at Case Western Reserve University. Dr Braun is also the Beta Alpha Psi adviser and the director of the undergraduate accounting program. Professor Braun was on the faculty of the J.M. Tull School of Accounting at the University of Georgia before her appointment at Case Western Reserve University. She has received several student-nominated Outstanding Teacher of the Year awards at both business schools, and is regularly asked to speak to student clubs and organizations about personal financial planning.

Professor Braun is a Certified Public Accountant and holds membership in the American Accounting Association (AAA), the Institute of Management Accountants, and the American Institute of Certified Public Accountants. She also holds the Chartered Global Management Accountant designation, and is a member of the AAA's Management Accounting Section as well as the Teaching, Learning and Curriculum Section. Dr. Braun has has regularly held leadership positions with the AAA's Conference on Teaching and Learning in Accounting (CTLA) including co-chairing the 2015 and 2016 conferences. She was awarded the 2016 Bea Sanders/AICPA Teaching Innovation Award for her development of Excel-based active-learning resources for introductory managerial accounting courses. Dr. Braun's research and teaching interests revolve around lean operations, sustainability, corporate responsibility, and accounting education. Dr. Braun's work has been published in *Contemporary Accounting Research, Issues in Accounting Education*, and *Journal of Accounting Education*.

Dr. Braun received her Ph.D. from the University of Connecticut and her B.A., summa cum laude, from Luther College, where she was a member of Phi Beta Kappa. Dr. Braun gained public accounting experience while working at Arthur Andersen & Co. and accumulated additional business and management accounting experience as a corporate controller.

Professor Braun has two daughters who are both in college. In her free time, she enjoys biking, gardening, hiking, skiing, and spending time with family and friends.

*To my children, Rachel and Hannah, who are the joy of my life,
and to my students, who inspire me daily.*

Karen W. Braun

Wendy M. Tietz is a professor for the Department of Accounting in the College of Business Administration at Kent State University. She teaches introductory financial and managerial accounting in a variety of formats, including large sections, small sections, and web-based sections. She has received numerous college and university teaching awards while at Kent State University.

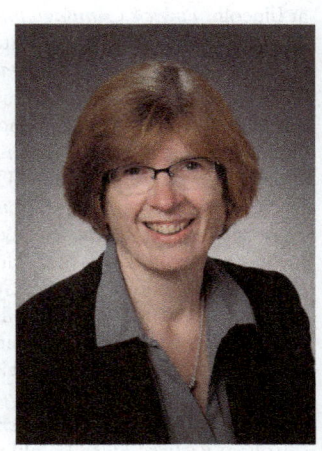

Dr. Tietz is a Certified Public Accountant, a Certified Management Accountant, and a Chartered Global Management Accountant. She is a member of the American Accounting Association (AAA), the Institute of Management Accountants and the American Institute of Certified Public Accountants. She is a member of the AAA's Management Accounting Section as well as the Teaching, Learning and Curriculum Section. She has published in *Strategic Finance, IMA Educational Case Journal, Issues in Accounting Education, Accounting Education: An International Journal*, and *Journal of Accounting & Public Policy*. She regularly presents at AAA regional and national meetings.

Dr. Tietz authors a blog, Accounting in the Headlines, which has real-world news stories and resources for use in the introductory accounting classroom. Dr. Tietz was awarded the Bea Sanders/AICPA Teaching Innovation Award for her blog in 2014 and the Jim Bulloch/IMA Award for Innovations in Management Accounting Education in 2016. She was also awarded the Best Educational/Case Award for the Teaching, Learning and Curriculum Section (AAA, Ohio Region) in 2016. Dr. Tietz earned her Ph.D. from Kent State University. She received both her M.B.A. and B.S.A. from the University of Akron. She worked in industry for several years, both as a controller for a financial institution and as the operations manager and controller for a recycled plastics manufacturer.

Dr. Tietz and her husband, Russ, have two grown sons. In her spare time, she enjoys walking, reading, and spending time with family and friends. She is also intensely interested in using technology and social media in education.

To my husband, Russ, who steadfastly and enthusiastically supports every new project.

Wendy M. Tietz

ACKNOWLEDGMENTS

We'd like to extend a special thank you to our reviewers who took the time to help us develop teaching and learning tools for Managerial Accounting courses to come. We value and appreciate their commitment, dedication, and passion for their students and the classroom:

Managerial Accounting, 5e and prior editions

Arinola Adebayo, University of South Carolina Aiken, *Nasrollah Ahadiat*, California State Polytechnic University, *Markus Ahrens*, St. Louis Community College, *Dave Alldredge*, Salt Lake Community College; *Natalie Allen*, Texas A&M University; *Vern Allen*, Central Florida Community College; *Lynn Almond*, Virginia Tech; *Felix E. Amenkhienan*, Radford University; *Arnold I. Barkman*, Texas Christian University; *Gary Barnett*, Salt Lake Community College; *Scott Berube*, University of New Hampshire; *Michael T. Blackwell*, West Liberty State College; *Phillip A. Blanchard*, The University of Arizona; *Charles Blumer*, St. Charles Community College; *Kevin Bosner*, SUNY Genesco; *Anna Boulware*, St. Charles Community College; *Ann K. Brooks*, University of New Mexico; *Molly Brown*, James Madison University; *Nina E. Brown*, Tarrant County College; *Helen Brubeck*, San Jose State University; *Janet B. Butler*, Texas State University–San Marcos; *Jennifer Cainas*, University of South Florida; *David Centers*, Grand Valley State University; *Sandra Cereola*, James Madison University; *Mike Chatham*, Radford University; *Julie Chenier*, Louisiana State University; *Robert Clarke*, Brigham Young University–Idaho; *Thomas Clevenger*, Washburn University; *Jay Cohen*, Oakton Community College; *Cheryl Copeland*, California State University Fresno; *Robert Cornell*, Oklahoma State University; *Deb Cosgrove*, University of Nebraska at Lincoln; *Patrick Cunningham*, Dawson Community College; *Alan B. Czyzewski*, Indiana State University; *Kreag Danvers*, Clarion University; *David L. Davis*, Tallahassee Community College; *Mike Deschamps*, MiraCosta College; *Patricia A. Doherty*, Boston University School of Management; *Jimmy Dong*, Sacramento City College; *Kevin Dooley*, Kapiolani Community College; *Jan Duffy*, Iowa State University; *Barbara Durham*, University of Central Florida; *Lisa Dutchik*, Kirkwood Community College; *Darlene K. Edwards*, Bellingham Technical College; *Robert S. Ellison*, Texas State University–San Marcos; *Anita Ellzey*, Harford Community College; *Gene B. Elrod*, The University of North Texas; *Jame M. Emig*, Villanova University; *Martin Epstei*, Central New Mexico Community College; *Diane Eure*, Texas State University; *Robert Everett*, Lewis & Clark Community College; *Dr. Kurt Fanning*, Grand Valley State University; *Amanda Farmer*, University of Georgia; *Janice Fergusson*, University of South Carolina; *Richard Filler*, Franklin University; *Jean Fornasieri*, Bergen Community College; *Ben Foster*, University of Louisville; *Faith Fugate*, University of Nevada, Reno; *Mary Anne Gaffney*, Temple University; *Karen Geiger*, Arizona State University; *Lisa Gillespie*, Loyola University–Chicago; *Shirley Glass*, Macomb Community College; *Marina Grau*, Houston Community College; *Timothy Griffin*, Hillsborough Community College; *Michael R. Hammond*, Missouri State University; *Michael R. Hammond*, Missouri State University; *Fei Han*, Robert Morris University; *Sheila Handy*, East Stroudsburg University; *Christopher Harper*, Grand Valley State University; *Sueann Hely*, West Kentucky Community & Technical College; *Pamela Hopcroft*, Florida State College at Jacksonville; *Audrey S. Hunter*, Broward College; *Frank Ilett*, Boise State University; *Ron Jastrzebski*, Penn State University–Berks; *Catherine Jeppson*, California State University, Northridge; *Nancy Jones*, California State University-Chico; *Mark T. Judd*, University of San Diego; *David Juriga*, St. Louis Community College; *Thomas Kam*, Hawaii Pacific University; *Ken Koerber*, Bucks County Community College; *Emil Koren*, Saint Leo University; *Ron Lazer*, University of Houston–Bauer College; *Pamela Legner*, College of DuPage; *Elliott Levy*, Bentley University; *Harold T. Little*, Western Kentucky University; *William Lloyd*, Lock Haven University *D. Jordan Lowe*, Arizona State University, West Campus; *Lois S. Mahoney*, Eastern Michigan University; *Diane Marker*, University of Toledo; *Linda Marquis*, Northern Kentucky University; *Lizbeth Matz*, University of Pittsburgh at Bradford; *David Mautz*, University of North Carolina–Wilmington; *Florence McGovern*, Bergen Community College; *Noel McKeon*, Florida State College at Jacksonville; *Mallory McWilliams*, San Jose State University; *Robert Meyer*, Parkland College; *Michael Newman*, University of Houston; *Kitty O'Donnell*, Onondaga Community College; *Mehmet Ozbilgin*, Baruch College, City University of New York; *Abbie Gail Parham*, Georgia Southern University; *Glenn Pate*, Palm Beach Community College; *Paige Paulsen*, Salt Lake Community College; *Deborah Pavelka*, Roosevelt University; *Sheldon Peng*, Washburn University; *Tamara Phelan*, Northern Illinois University; *Letitia Pleis*, Metropolitan State College of Denver; *Cindy Powell*, Southern Nazarene University; *Will Quilliam*, Florida Southern College; *Paulette A. Ratliff-Miller*, Grand Valley State University; *Donald Reynolds*, Calvin College; *Christina M. Ritsema*, University of Northern Colorado; *Doug Roberts*, Appalachian State University; *Amal Said*, University of Toledo; *Anwar Salimi*, California State Polytechnic University; *Kathryn Savage*, Northern Arizona University; *Christine Schalow*, California State University–San Bernadino; *Tony Scott*, Norwalk Community College; *Lloyd Seaton*, University of Northern Colorado; *David Skougstad*, Metropolitan State College of Denver; *John Stancil*, Florida Southern College; *Jenny Staskey*, Northern Arizona University; *Dennis Stovall*, Grand Valley State University; *Olin Scott Stovall*, Abilene Christian University; *Gloria Stuart*, Georgia Southern University; *Iris Stuart*, California State University, Fullerton; *Gracelyn V. Stuart-Tuggle*, Palm Beach State College, Boca Raton; *Jan Sweeney*, Baruch College, City University of New York; *Pavani Tallapally*, Slippery Rock University; *Lloyd Tanlu*, University of Washington; *Diane Tanner*, University of North Florida; *Linda Hayden Tarrago*, Hillsborough Community College; *Steven Thoede*, Texas State University; *Geoffrey Tickell*, Indiana University of Pennsylvania; *Don Trippeer*, SUNY Oneonta; *Igor Vaysman*, Baruch College; *John Virchick*, Chapman University; *Terri Walsh*, Seminole State; *Andy Williams*, Edmonds Community College; *Jeff Wong*, University of Nevada Reno; *Michael Yampuler*, University of Houston (Main Campus); *Jeff Jiewei Yu*, Southern Methodist University; *Judith Zander*, Grossmont College; *James Zeigler*, Bowling Green State University

Introduction to Managerial Accounting

Learning Objectives

- **1** Identify managers' three primary responsibilities
- **2** Distinguish financial accounting from managerial accounting
- **3** Describe the roles and skills required of management accountants within the organization
- **4** Describe the role of the Institute of Management Accountants (IMA) and apply its ethical standards
- **5** Discuss the business trends and regulations affecting management accounting

Pickture/Alamy

Sources: Starbucks 2015 10-K filing www.starbucks.com/about-us/company-information/starbucks-company-timeline; starbucks.com/responsibility

Starbucks Corporation, which began operations in 1971 as a sole coffee bean shop in Seattle's well-known Pike Street Market, now has over 23,000 company-owned and licensed stores in 68 countries around the world. The company's success can be attributed to innovative thinking, carefully disciplined expansion, and a focus on corporate responsibility. The company believes that its commitment to ethically sourced coffee, contributions to local communities, and superior employee benefits to part-time as well as full-time employees contribute to the company's objective of being one of the most recognized and respected brands in the world. Management accounting plays a role in implementing the company's strategy. Without information on the costs and benefits of different beverages, programs, distribution channels, and geographic areas, Starbucks would not be able to make responsible, yet profitable, decisions. Starbucks uses management accounting to make operating decisions that focus on corporate responsibility, while also keeping the company financially strong. Case in point: $100 invested in Starbucks's stock in 2010 would have been worth $480 at the end of fiscal 2015, a return well above the S&P 500.

As the Starbucks story shows, managers use accounting information for much more than preparing annual financial statements. They use managerial accounting information to guide their actions and decisions. For Starbucks, these decisions might include opening new stores, adding new products, or even providing new employee benefits, such as Starbucks's new tuition reimbursement plan. Management accounting information helps management decide whether any or all of these actions will help accomplish the company's ultimate goals. In this chapter, we'll introduce managerial accounting, describe how it differs from financial accounting, and discuss the skills and ethics management accountants need. We will also discuss the regulatory and business environment in which today's managers and management accountants operate.

What Is Managerial Accounting?

Managerial accounting, also referred to as management accounting, focuses on the financial insight needed for an organization to achieve success. In the words of the Institute of Management Accountants,

> <u>Management accounting</u> is a profession that involves partnering in management decision making, devising planning and performance management systems, and providing expertise in financial reporting and control to assist management in the formulation and implementation of an organization's strategy.[1]

As you will see throughout the book, managerial accounting is very different from financial accounting. Financial accounting focuses on providing stockholders and creditors with the information they need to make investment and lending decisions. This information takes the form of financial statements: the balance sheet, income statement, statement of shareholders' equity, and statement of cash flows. On the other hand, managerial accounting focuses on identifying, interpreting, analyzing, and implementing the financial information internal management needs to run the company efficiently, effectively, and profitably. This information takes many forms depending on management's needs.

To understand the kind of information managers need, let's first look at their primary responsibilities.

Managers' Three Primary Responsibilities

1 Identify managers' three primary responsibilities

Managerial accounting helps managers fulfill their three primary responsibilities, as shown in Exhibit 1-1: planning, directing, and controlling. Integrated throughout these responsibilities is <u>decision making</u> (identifying alternative courses of action and choosing among them).

EXHIBIT 1-1 Managers' Three Primary Responsibilities

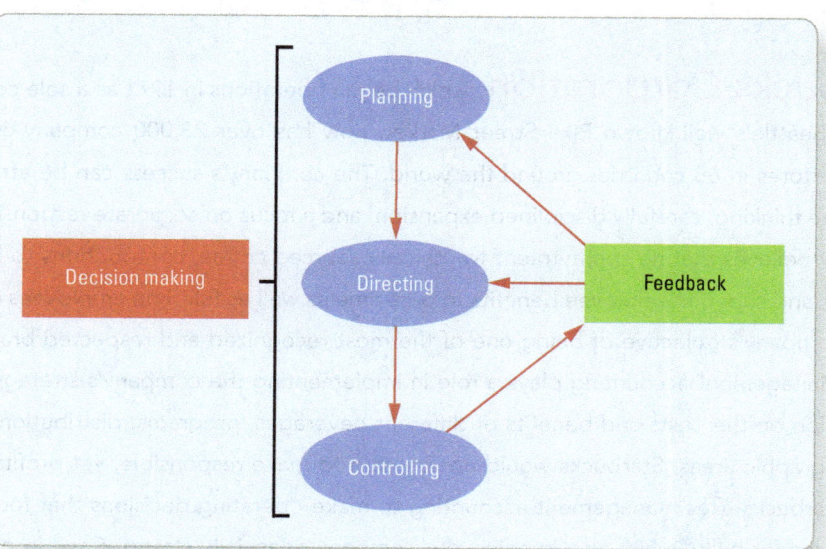

[1]Statement on Management Accounting, "Definition of Management Accounting," Institute of Management Accountants, 2008.

- **Planning** involves setting goals and objectives for the company and determining how to achieve them. For example, one of Starbucks's goals is to generate more sales. One strategy to achieve this goal is to open more retail locations. For example, the company opened 731 new company-operated stores in fiscal 2015, roughly half in the United States and half in China and the Asia-Pacific.[2] Another strategy is to develop new products and new distribution channels (such as selling coffee through grocery stores and warehouse clubs). Managerial accounting translates these plans into **budgets**—the quantitative expression of a plan. Management analyzes the budgets before proceeding to determine whether its expansion plans make financial sense.
- **Directing** means overseeing the company's day-to-day operations. Management uses sales and costs information by store, region, and distribution channel, to run daily business operations. For example, Starbucks managers use sales data to determine which beverages on the menu and products in the stores are generating the most sales. They use that information to adjust product offerings, marketing strategies, and retail expansion decisions.
- **Controlling** means evaluating the results of business operations against the plan and making adjustments to keep the company pressing toward its goals. Starbucks uses performance reports to compare each store's actual performance against the budget and then based on that *feedback* take corrective actions if needed. If actual costs are higher than planned, or actual sales are lower than planned, then management may revise its plans or adjust operations.

Management is continually making decisions while it plans, directs, and controls operations. Starbucks management must decide where to open new stores, which stores to refurnish, what prices to set for beverages and other products in the store, and so forth. Managerial accounting provides the financial insight needed to help make these decisions.

A Road Map: How Managerial Accounting Fits In

This book will show you how managerial accounting helps managers fulfill their responsibilities. The rest of the text is organized around the following themes:

1. **Managerial Accounting Building Blocks** Chapter 1 helps you understand more about the management accounting profession and today's business environment. Chapter 2 teaches you some of the language that is commonly used in managerial accounting. Just as musicians must know the notes to the musical scale, management accountants *and* managers must have a common understanding of these terms to communicate effectively with one another.

2. **Determining Unit Cost (Product Costing)** To run a business profitably, managers must be able to identify the costs associated with manufacturing its products or delivering its services. For example, Starbucks's managers need to know the cost of producing each beverage on the menu as well as the cost of operating each retail location. Managers must have this information so that they can set prices high enough to cover costs and generate an adequate profit. Chapters 3, 4, and 5 show you how businesses determine these costs. Chapter 4 also shows how managers can effectively control costs by eliminating wasteful activities and focusing on quality.

3. **Making Decisions** Before Harold Schultz opened the first Starbucks coffee house, he must have thought about the volume of sales needed just to break even—that is, just to cover costs. In order to do so, he had to first identify and estimate the types of costs the coffee house would incur, as well as the profit that would be generated on each beverage served. These topics are covered in Chapters 6 and 7. Chapter 6 shows how managers identify different types of cost behavior, while Chapter 7 shows how managers determine the profitability of each unit sold as well as the

[2]Starbucks 2015 10-K filing.

company's breakeven point. Chapter 8 continues to use cost behavior information to walk through common business decisions, such as outsourcing and pricing decisions. Finally, Chapter 12 shows how managers decide whether to invest in new equipment, new projects, or new locations.

4. **Planning** Budgets are management's primary tool for expressing its plans. Chapter 9 discusses all of the components of the master budget and the way companies like Starbucks use the budgeting process to implement their business goals and strategies.

5. **Controlling and Evaluating** Management uses many different performance evaluation tools to determine whether individual segments of the business are reaching company goals. Chapters 10 and 11 describe these tools in detail. Chapters 13 and 14 describe how the statement of cash flows and financial statement analysis can be used to evaluate the performance of the company as a whole. Finally, Chapter 15 discusses how companies are beginning to address the sustainability of their operations, by measuring, reporting, and minimizing the negative impact of their operations on people and the environment. As you saw in the opening story, some of Starbucks's primary business concerns are to use ethically sourced coffee, contribute to local communities, and provide superior employee benefits to part-time as well as full-time employees.

Differences Between Managerial Accounting and Financial Accounting

2 Distinguish financial accounting from managerial accounting

Managerial accounting information differs from financial accounting information in many respects. Exhibit 1-2 summarizes these differences. Take a few minutes to study the exhibit (on page 5), and then we'll apply it to Starbucks.

Starbucks's *financial accounting* system is geared toward producing annual and quarterly consolidated financial statements that will be used by investors and creditors to make investment and lending decisions. Since Starbucks is a publicly traded company, its financial statements can be easily found on the Internet by searching for its 10-K (annual) and 10-Q (quarterly) SEC filings. The financial statements, which must be prepared in accordance with Generally Accepted Accounting Principles (GAAP), objectively summarize the transactions that occurred between Starbucks and external parties during the previous period. The Securities and Exchange Commission (SEC) requires that the annual financial statements of publicly traded companies, such as Starbucks, be audited by independent certified public accountants (CPAs). Starbucks's financial statements are useful to its investors and creditors, but they do not provide management with enough information to run the company effectively.

Starbucks's *managerial accounting* system is designed to provide internal managers with the accounting information needed to plan, direct, and control operations. Since managerial accounting information is specifically designed to help *internal* management, it is confidential information that is generally *not* available to the public. There are no GAAP-type standards or audits required for managerial accounting. To provide Starbucks's management with the information needed to make good business decisions, managerial accounting reports focus on smaller segments of the company (such as individual retail locations, geographic areas, and specific beverages and products) rather than the company as a whole. Rather than preparing reports just once a year, Starbucks prepares managerial accounting reports as often as needed, which could be as frequently as daily or even hourly. Many companies even use "real-time performance dashboards" that constantly update so that managers have the financial information they need to control operations and make timely decisions. Since managerial accounting revolves around planning and decision making, much of it focuses on the *future* rather than on the past. Any information that is *relevant* to management will be included. Finally, since every company is different, managerial accounting systems will vary from company to company. In designing

EXHIBIT 1-2 Managerial Accounting Versus Financial Accounting

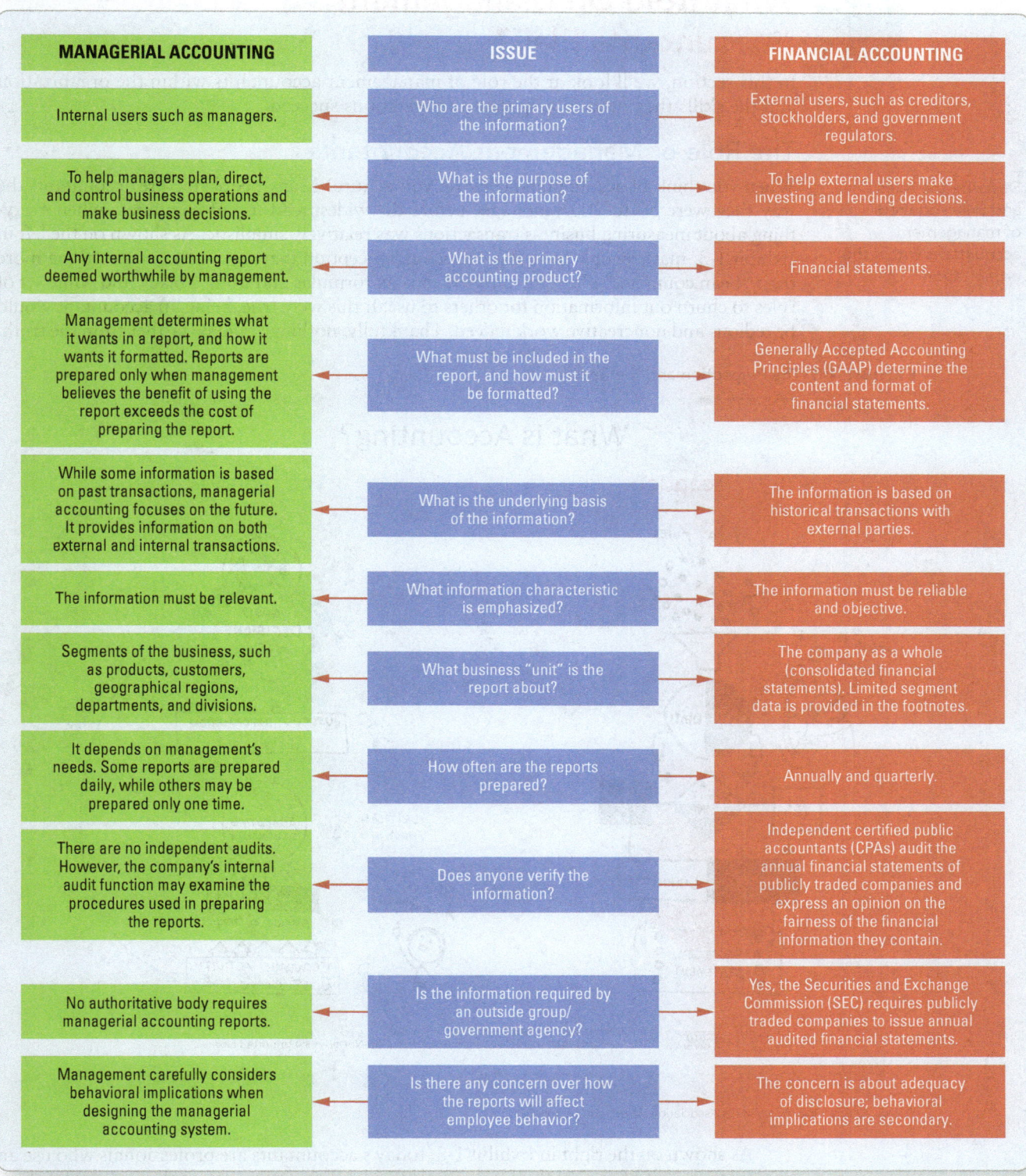

the system, management will weigh the costs of collecting and analyzing information with the benefits they expect to receive. Management will also consider how the system will affect employees' behavior. Employees try to perform well on the parts of their jobs that the accounting system measures and rewards.

What Role Do Management Accountants Play?

In this section, we'll look at the role of management accountants within the organization and the skills they need to help their organizations succeed.

The Role of Management Accountants

3 Describe the roles and skills required of management accountants within the organization

When you think of accountants, what do you picture? Many people picture accountants the way they were 50 to 100 years ago, before the widespread use of computers when everything about measuring business transactions was relatively simplistic. As shown on the left in Exhibit 1-3, many people have the erroneous conception that accountants are nothing more than "bean counters," plugging numbers into set formulas and using a black and white set of rules to churn out information for others to use. If this were true, being an accountant would be tedious and noncreative work indeed. Thankfully, nothing could be farther from the truth.

EXHIBIT 1-3 The Perception and the Reality

Source: © American Accounting Association. Used with permission.

As shown on the right in Exhibit 1-3, today's accountants are professionals who use an immense amount of critical thinking, insight, and judgment to capture the reality of today's complex economic events. As valued financial advisors, managerial accountants partner with management to make critical business decisions that have widespread and significant consequences for the business and for society. Let's face it: the business world is much more complex than it was in your grandparents' day. With rapidly changing technology and continual business innovation, the role of accountants has drastically changed from what it used to be. In fact, management accountants are rarely referred to by that name any more; instead, they are usually referred to as business advisors, analysts, or finance professionals.

As you go through each topic in this book, keep the blue picture in Exhibit 1-3 in mind, and ask yourself the following questions:

1. **What is the business issue, event, or problem, and how can accounting help to solve it?** Management accounting always begins with some relevant business issue that management is facing or some economic event that occurred in the past or might occur in the future. Management accounting is used to shed light on the issue and direct management's path.

2. **What are the "gray areas"?** In other words, what differences in methods, assumptions, estimates, measurement choices, and judgment calls might impact the information that is used for decision making? Because of the gray areas and judgment involved, accounting numbers are rarely as precise as they may seem.

3. **What are the implications for the business if the accounting information used in the decision is "wrong"?** Because of the gray areas, it's difficult to say that accounting information is ever "wrong." However, judgment in these gray areas could lead to financial estimates that are on the high side or on the low side. What are the consequences of numbers that are too high or too low? Would estimates that are "off" in one direction be worse than the other direction?

Since you are studying management accounting for the first time, the topics in the book may at first appear very straightforward and immutable. However, if you consider the three questions listed above, you'll begin to see the significance of the judgment calls that go into management accounting and the ramifications to the business decisions that are consequently made.

The Skills Required of Management Accountants

To understand the skills required of management accountants, let's go back to the definition of management accounting with which we started the chapter:

> *Management accounting is a profession that involves partnering in management decision making, devising planning and performance management systems, and providing expertise in financial reporting and control to assist management in the formulation and implementation of an organization's strategy.*[3]

First and foremost, management accounting is a profession (in a later section, we'll describe the professional organizations that represent management accountants). Since management accountants work in a professional advisory role, they need a vast array of

EXHIBIT 1-4 Technical and Nontechnical Competencies Needed by Management Accountants

Technical Competencies	Nontechnical Competencies
• Planning, budgeting, and forecasting	• Ethics
• Internal financial reporting	• Communication
• Performance management	• Customer service
• Cost management	• Adaptability
• Internal controls	• Strategic thinking
• Technology	• Process improvement
• Decision analysis	• Leadership
• Financial statement analysis	• Collaboration
• Investment decision making	• Business acumen
• Enterprise risk management	• Change management

[3]Statement on Management Accounting, "Definition of Management Accounting," Institute of Management Accountants, 2008.

skills. Some of these skills are technical, whereas others are nontechnical competencies, which are often referred to as "soft-skills." A recent survey of management accounting professionals revealed some of the top skills they need to help their organizations achieve success. Exhibit 1-4 summarizes some of these competencies.[4]

This book will introduce you to most of the technical competencies listed in Exhibit 1-4, as well as give you the opportunity to advance many of your nontechnical skills. As you can see in the exhibit, the ability to use technology and common software, such as Microsoft Excel, is a critical skill management accountants need to possess. Because Excel is used so pervasively in business, you will see many of the exhibits in this book featured in Excel. You will also see features in several chapters that teach you how to use Excel to perform various tasks. Regardless of your future career path, becoming as proficient as you can with Excel during this course will help you become more marketable and more valuable to your future employer.

Managerial Accounting Is Important to All Careers

As you can see, management accountants don't fit the stereotypical accountant portrayed in movies and shows. Because of their expanding role, management accountants have truly become trusted and valued internal business advisors. But what if you don't plan to major in accounting? How can this course be of use to you? Here are just a few specific ways this course can help you prepare for your future business career:

- **Entrepreneurs** If you are planning to be an entrepreneur, you'll first want to know if your business idea makes financial sense. How high will volume have to be for your business to at least break even? How high will it have to be for your business to earn the level of profit that you want to achieve? As you begin to implement your business plan, should you negotiate sales contracts that are more fixed (flat fee) or variable (fee per activity)? What about costs? Would having more fixed costs or variable costs be better? How sensitive will your profits be to changes in volume if the economy booms or if it takes a turn for the worse? How will you decide whether to invest in new equipment and technology? As your business grows in size, how will you divide it into manageable segments and relinquish oversight of day-to-day operations to others, while at the same time retain control? How can you design systems to ensure your managers will make decisions that are consistent with your goals? And if you decide to raise capital or sell your business, what will potential investors want to see when they analyze your financial statements and study your statement of cash flows? All of these topics are addressed in this book.

- **Business Management** If you are planning to be a general business manager, not a day will go by in which you don't consider the financial ramifications of your decisions. You'll need to have a firm grasp on the costs of obtaining or manufacturing every product you sell and/or every service you deliver. You'll also want to understand how costly every activity within the company is to perform and have specific strategies in hand for controlling and reducing those costs. You'll need to understand which costs will increase as your volume increases and which costs will be unaffected by changes in volume. Cost information will drive many, if not all, of your decisions about where to locate, what to produce, which suppliers to use, whether to outsource, which products to emphasize, whether to implement quality improvement initiatives, whether to automate some of your processes, how to price your products or bid for jobs, whether to discontinue certain products or operations, and so forth. Every business decision you make will be rooted in revenue and cost information, so it will be important for you to understand how those costs were obtained and what they include. Different costs will be used for different purposes. All of these topics are addressed in this book.

- **Marketing and Sales** If you are planning to be in marketing and sales, your marketing strategy, assumptions, and predictions will be the driving force behind the company's entire budget. As a result, you will be intimately involved with developing the budget. Product-line profitability reports will show you which products are most profitable and will guide your decisions about which products to emphasize. Cost information

---

[4]"The Skills Gap in Entry-level Management Accounting and Finance," Institute of Management Accountants and American Quality and Productivity Center, 2014.

will drive many of your pricing decisions, as well as decisions about whether to accept special orders at reduced sales prices or give volume discounts. The company's stance on sustainability may impact your ability to attract various customers and target different markets. All of these topics are addressed in this book.

- **Nonbusiness Majors** Even if you are planning to be a nurse, engineer, musician, or fashion designer, the information you learn in this course will be of consequence to you. All organizations, including nonprofits and governmental agencies, use cost and revenue information to guide their plans, actions, and decisions. No matter what your career path, every activity you engage in will impact the costs and revenues of your organization. That holds true, whether you are tending to sick patients, designing bridges, managing a symphony orchestra, or designing clothes. Management will expect you to operate under limited resources and will often look to you for revenue and expense estimates for specific projects or for specific periods of time. Management may also hand you budgets, cost data, and performance reports and expect you to understand it and use it for making decisions. The more you understand the underlying financial information, the better prepared you will be.

We've chosen to highlight just a few specific business career tracks here, but many of the same issues will pertain to all business careers, including those in logistics, supply chain management, production, and finance. There is such a huge overlap in business between managerial accounting and finance that both are often referred to as the "finance function," and the people who work in this function, regardless of whether they were accounting or finance majors, are often referred to as analysts. No matter what your eventual career, you will be using managerial accounting information. As is often said, accounting is the language of business, so the more you know about it, the more valuable you will be to your organization.

Accounting within the Organizational Structure

Most corporations are too large to be governed directly by their stockholders. Therefore, stockholders elect a **board of directors** to oversee the company. Exhibit 1-5 shows a typical organizational structure, with the green boxes representing employees of the firm and the orange and blue boxes representing nonemployees.

The board members meet only periodically, so they hire a **chief executive officer (CEO)** to manage the company on a daily basis. The CEO hires other executives to run various aspects

EXHIBIT 1-5 Typical Organizational Structure

of the organization, including the **chief operating officer (COO)** and the **chief financial officer (CFO)**. The COO is responsible for the company's operations, such as research and development (R&D), production, and distribution. The CFO is responsible for all of the company's financial concerns. The **treasurer** and the **controller** report directly to the CFO. The treasurer is primarily responsible for raising capital (through issuing stocks and bonds) and investing funds. The controller is usually responsible for general financial accounting, managerial accounting, and tax reporting. Many organizations have other C-Suite personnel not pictured in Exhibit 1-5, such as Chief Information Officer (in charge of the company's technology infrastructure) and the Chief Sustainability Officer (in charge of devising, implementing, and reporting on the company's sustainability initiatives). The CFO, controller, and others within the accounting function work closely with these individuals since technology plays a significant role in collecting managerial accounting information, and, as you'll see later in the chapter and book, managerial accounting both impacts, and is impacted by, sustainability initiatives.

Let's now turn our attention to the right side of Exhibit 1-5. The New York Stock Exchange requires that listed companies have an **internal audit function**. The role of the internal audit function is to ensure that the company's internal controls and risk management policies are functioning properly. The Internal Audit Department reports directly to a subcommittee of the board of directors called the **audit committee**. The audit committee oversees the internal audit function as well as the annual audit of the financial statements by independent CPAs. Both the Internal Audit Department and the independent CPAs report directly to the audit committee for one very important reason: to ensure that management will not intimidate them or bias their work. However, since the audit committee meets only periodically, it is not practical for the audit committee to manage the internal audit function on a day-to-day basis. Therefore, the internal audit function also reports to a senior executive, such as the CFO or CEO, for administrative matters.

> ### ■ Why is this important?
> "Management **accountants** act as internal business advisors. They provide the **financial** information and in-depth **analysis** needed to make good business **decisions**."

When you look at the organizational chart pictured in Exhibit 1-5, where do you think management accountants work? It depends on the company. Management accountants used to work in accounting departments and reported directly to the controller. Now, over half of management accountants are located throughout companies and work on cross-functional teams. **Cross-functional teams** consist of employees representing various functions of the company, such as R&D, design, production, marketing, distribution, and customer service. Cross-functional teams are effective because each member can address business decisions from a different viewpoint. These teams often report to various vice presidents of operations. Management accountants frequently take the leadership role in cross-functional teams since financial impact is the driving force in almost all business decisions.

Professional Associations

4 Describe the role of the Institute of Management Accountants (IMA) and apply its ethical standards

The **Institute of Management Accountants (IMA)** is the professional association for management accountants in the United States. Its mission is to provide a forum for research, practice development, education, knowledge sharing, and advocacy of the highest ethical and best practices in management accounting *and* finance. The IMA also educates society about the role management accountants play in organizations. According to the IMA, about 85 to 90% of accountants work in organizations, performing the roles discussed earlier. The IMA publishes a monthly journal called *Strategic Finance* that addresses current topics of interest to management accountants and helps them keep abreast of recent techniques and trends.

The IMA also issues the **Certified Management Accountant (CMA)** certification. Over 50,000 people around the globe have become CMAs. To become a CMA, you must pass a rigorous examination, gain two years of relevant professional experience, and maintain continuing professional education. You must also have a baccalaureate degree, although the degree does *not* need to be in accounting. One nice feature of the CMA exam is that you don't have to wait until you graduate from college to take it. Thus, you can start working on valuable credentials that will earn you a higher salary even before you graduate from college. A recent global survey conducted by the IMA revealed that, globally, CMAs earn 61% higher salaries than their non-CMA peers.

The CMA exam consists of two parts. Each part of the exam is 4 hours long and consists of 100 multiple-choice questions as well as two essay questions. As shown in the following, most of the topics on the exam are introduced in this textbook:

Part 1-Financial Reporting, Planning, Performance and Control—Financial Reporting (the financial statements, including the Statement of Cash Flows, Chapter 13); Planning, Budgeting and Forecasting (Chapters 9 and 6), Performance Management (Chapters 10 and 11); Cost Management (Chapters 2, 3, 4, 5, and 6); and Internal Controls.

Part 2-Financial Decision Making—Financial Statement Analysis (Chapter 14); Corporate Finance; Risk Management; Decision Analysis (Chapters 7 and 8); Investment Decisions (Chapter 12); and Professional Ethics (Chapter 1).

The CMA exam topics reinforce the technical skills, shown in Exhibit 1-4, that management accountants are expected to have. If you like the material in this course as well as in your finance course, you should strongly consider taking the CMA exam. You can also become a student member of the IMA for a significantly reduced annual fee, which will give you access to its job posting website as well as all of its publications. Finally, the IMA hosts an annual three-day student leadership conference at a different location in the United States each year. You can find out more about the IMA at its website: www.imanet.org.

In 2012, the **American Institute of Certified Public Accountants (AICPA)**, the world's largest association representing the accounting profession, joined forces with England's Chartered Institute of Management Accountants (CIMA) to launch a separate specialized credential geared toward members who work, or have worked, in accounting roles in business, industry, or government. The **Chartered Global Management Accountant (CGMA)** designation, which is available to qualifying AICPA and CIMA members, is meant to recognize the unique business and accounting skill set possessed by those certified public accountants (CPAs) who fill, or have filled, accounting roles within an organization, as opposed to strictly public accounting roles. The CGMA has issued a "Competency Framework" that covers many of the same technical and nontechnical skills shown in Exhibit 1-4. Currently, 36% of AICPA members work in management accounting rather than public accounting.[5] Qualification for the CGMA designation is based on examination and professional experience. You can find out more about the CGMA designation, qualifications, and benefits at www.CGMA.org.

Try It!

Throughout each chapter you will see several "Try It!" features. These features will allow you to see if you understand something you just learned about in the reading. Click the Try It! Icon to practice and get immediate feedback in the etext.

Determine whether each of the following statements is true or false:

1. Managers' three primary responsibilities are planning, directing, and controlling.
2. Management accounting is geared toward external stakeholders, such as investors and creditors.
3. Management accountants often work in cross-functional teams throughout the organization.
4. The internal audit function reports to the audit committee of the board of directors.
5. Management accountants are now more often looked upon as internal business advisors rather than "bean counters" recording historical transactions.
6. Management accountants should be technically proficient, but they don't need strong oral and written communication skills.
7. Management accountants should be proficient in Excel.
8. The AICPA (American Institute of Certified Public Accountants) issues the CMA (Certified Management Accountant) certification.

Please see page 47 for solutions.

[5]www.aicpa.org/About/Pages/About.aspx

Average Salaries of Management Accountants

The average salaries of management accountants reflect their large skill set. Naturally, salaries will vary with the accountant's level of experience, his or her specific job responsibilities, and the size and geographical location of the company. However, to give you a general idea, in 2015, the average base salary (before benefits, profit sharing, or bonuses) of *all* IMA members in the United States was $115,022, while the median base salary of IMA members in the United States with only one to five years of experience was $64,900. Those professionals in the United States with the CMA or CPA certification earned 31% more in total compensation than members with no certification, while those who held *both* the CMA and CPA certifications earned 45% more than noncertified members. You can obtain more specific salary information in the IMA's 2015 Salary Survey.[6]

Robert Half International, Inc., is another good source for salary information. Robert Half publishes a free yearly guide to average salaries for all types of finance professionals. The guide also provides information on current hiring trends. In addition, Robert Half offers a free online interactive salary calculator, which allows you to drill down to salary information by zip code, years of experience, job title, and company size. To explore salaries in the fields of accounting and finance, do a web search on the phrase, "Robert Half Salary Guide and Calculator."

Professional Ethics

Management accountants continually face ethical challenges. The IMA has developed principles and standards to help management accountants deal with these challenges. The principles and standards remind us that society expects professional accountants to exhibit the highest level of ethical behavior. The IMA's *Statement of Ethical Professional Practice* requires management accountants to do the following:

- Maintain their professional competence.
- Preserve the confidentiality of the information they handle.
- Uphold their integrity.
- Perform their duties with credibility.

These ethical standards are summarized in Exhibit 1-6, while the full *Statement of Ethical Professional Practice* appears in Exhibit 1-7.

EXHIBIT 1-6 Summary of Ethical Standards

[6]IMA 2015 U.S. Salary Survey, May 2016. http://www.imanet.org/resources-publications/thought-leadership-new/salary-survey

EXHIBIT 1-7 IMA Statement of Ethical Professional Practice

Members of IMA shall behave ethically. A commitment to ethical professional practice includes: overarching principles that express our values, and standards that guide our conduct.

Principles
IMA's overarching ethical principles include: Honesty, Fairness, Objectivity, and Responsibility. Members shall act in accordance with these principles and shall encourage others within their organizations to adhere to them.

Standards
A member's failure to comply with the following standards may result in disciplinary action.

I. Competence
Each member has a responsibility to:
1. Maintain an appropriate level of professional expertise by continually developing knowledge and skills.
2. Perform professional duties in accordance with relevant laws, regulations, and technical standards.
3. Provide decision support information and recommendations that are accurate, clear, concise, and timely.
4. Recognize and communicate professional limitations or other constraints that would preclude responsible judgment or successful performance of an activity.

II. Confidentiality
Each member has a responsibility to:
1. Keep information confidential except when disclosure is authorized or legally required.
2. Inform all relevant parties regarding appropriate use of confidential information. Monitor subordinates' activities to ensure compliance.
3. Refrain from using confidential information for unethical or illegal advantage.

III. Integrity
Each member has a responsibility to:
1. Mitigate actual conflicts of interest. Regularly communicate with business associates to avoid apparent conflicts of interest. Advise all parties of any potential conflicts.
2. Refrain from engaging in any conduct that would prejudice carrying out duties ethically.
3. Abstain from engaging in or supporting any activity that might discredit the profession.

IV. Credibility
Each member has a responsibility to:
1. Communicate information fairly and objectively.
2. Disclose all relevant information that could reasonably be expected to influence an intended user's understanding of the reports, analyses, or recommendations.
3. Disclose delays or deficiencies in information, timeliness, processing, or internal controls in conformance with organization policy and/or applicable law.

Institute of Management Accountants. Adapted with permission (2006).

Source: Courtesy of IMA (Institute of Management Accountants, www.imanet.org). Adapted with permission.

To resolve ethical dilemmas, the IMA suggests that management accountants first follow their company's established policies for reporting unethical behavior. If the conflict is not resolved through the company's procedures, the management accountant should:

- Discuss the unethical situation with the immediate supervisor unless the supervisor is involved in the unethical situation. If so, notify the supervisor at the next higher managerial level. If the immediate supervisor involved is the CEO, notify the audit committee or board of directors.
- Discuss the unethical situation with an objective advisor. The IMA offers a confidential "Ethics Hotline" to its members. Members may call the hotline and discuss their ethical dilemma. The ethics counselor will not provide a specific resolution but will clarify how the dilemma relates to the IMA's *Statement of Ethical Professional Practice* shown in Exhibit 1-7.
- Consult an attorney regarding legal obligations and rights.

Examples of Ethical Dilemmas

Because professional ethical behavior is so critical, we have included short exercises and cases related to ethical behavior in each chapter of the book. An ethics icon will mark each of these exercises so that they are readily identifiable to you and your instructor.

Unfortunately, the ethical path is not always clear. You may want to act ethically and do the right thing, but the consequences can make it difficult to decide what to do. Let's consider several ethical dilemmas in light of the IMA *Statement of Ethical Professional Practice*.

Dilemma #1

Sarah Baker is examining the expense reports of her staff, who counted inventory at Top-Flight's warehouses in Arizona. She discovers that Mike Flinders has claimed but not included hotel receipts for over $1,000 of accommodation expenses. Other staff, who also claimed $1,000, did attach hotel receipts. When asked about the receipts, Mike admits that he stayed with an old friend, not in the hotel, but he believes that he deserves the money he saved. After all, the company would have paid his hotel bill.

By asking to be reimbursed for hotel expenses he did not incur, Flinders violated the IMA's integrity standards (conflict of interest in which he tried to enrich himself at the company's expense). Because Baker discovered the inflated expense report, she would not be fulfilling her ethical responsibilities of integrity and credibility if she allowed the reimbursement.

Dilemma #2

As the accountant of Entreé Computer, you are aware of your company's weak financial condition. Entreé is close to signing a lucrative contract that should ensure its future success. To do so, the controller states that the company must report a profit this year (ending December 31). He suggests, "Two customers have placed orders that are really not supposed to be shipped until early January. Ask production to fill and ship those orders on December 31 so we can record them in this year's sales."

The resolution of this dilemma is less clear-cut. Many people believe that following the controller's suggestion to manipulate the company's income would violate the standards of competence, integrity, and credibility. Others would argue that because Entreé Computer already has the customer orders, shipping the goods and recording the sale in December is still ethical behavior. In this situation, you might discuss the available alternatives with the next managerial level or the IMA ethics hotline counselor.

Dilemma #3

As a new accounting staff member at Central City Hospital, your supervisor has asked you to prepare the yearly Medicare Cost Report, which the government uses to determine its reimbursement to the hospital for serving Medicare patients. The report requires specialized knowledge that you don't believe you possess. Your supervisor is busy planning for the coming year and cannot offer much guidance while you prepare the report.

This situation is not as rare as you might think. You may be asked to perform tasks that you don't feel qualified to perform. The competence standard requires you to perform professional duties in accordance with laws, regulations, and technical standards; but laws and regulations are always changing. For this reason, the competence standard also requires you to continually develop knowledge and skills. CPAs and CMAs are required to complete annual continuing professional education (about 40 hours per year) to fulfill this responsibility. However, even continuing professional education courses will not cover every situation you may encounter.

In the Medicare cost report situation, advise your supervisor that you currently lack the knowledge required to complete the Medicare report. By doing so, you are complying with the competence standard that requires you to recognize and communicate any limitations that would preclude you from fulfilling an activity. You should ask for training on the report preparation and supervision by someone experienced in preparing the report. If the supervisor denies your requests, you should ask him or her to reassign the Medicare report to a qualified staff member.

Dilemma #4

Your company is negotiating a large multiyear sales contract that, if won, would substantially increase the company's future earnings. At a dinner party over the weekend, your friends ask you how you like your job and the company you work for. In your enthusiasm, you tell them not only about your responsibilities at work, but also about the contract negotiations. As soon as the words pop out of your mouth, you worry that you've said too much.

> **Why is this important?**
>
> "At the **root** of all business relationships is **trust**. Would you put your **money** in a bank that you didn't trust, invest in a company you knew was '**cooking the books**,' or lend money to someone you thought would never pay you back? As a **manager**, your trust in the other party's **ethical** behavior, and vice versa, will be a vital component of the business **decisions** you make."

This situation is difficult to avoid. You may be so excited about your job and the company you work for that information unintentionally "slips out" during casual conversation with friends and family. The confidentiality standard requires you to refrain from disclosing information or using confidential information for unethical or illegal advantage. Was the contract negotiation confidential? If so, would your friends invest in company stock in hopes that the negotiations increase stock prices? Or were the negotiations public knowledge in the financial community? If so, your friends would gain no illegal advantage from the information. Recent cases in the news remind us that insider trading (use of inside knowledge for illegal gain) has serious consequences. Even seemingly mundane information about company operations could give competitors an advantage. Therefore, it's best to disclose only information that is meant for public consumption.

Unethical Versus Illegal Behavior

Finally, is there a difference between unethical and illegal behavior? Not all unethical behavior is illegal, but all illegal behavior is unethical. For example, consider the competence standard. The competence standard states that management accountants have a responsibility to provide decision support information that is accurate, clear, concise, and timely. Failure to follow this standard is unethical but in most cases not illegal. Now, consider the integrity standard. It states that management accountants must abstain from any activity that might discredit the profession. A management accountant who commits an illegal act is violating this ethical standard. In other words, ethical behavior encompasses more than simply following the law. The IMA's ethical principles include honesty, fairness, objectivity, and responsibility—principles that are much broader than what is codified in the law.

Decision Guidelines

Managerial Accounting and Management Accountants

Starbucks had to consider the following in designing its managerial accounting system.

Decision	Guidelines
What is the primary purpose and focus of managerial accounting?	Managerial accounting provides information that helps managers plan, direct, and control operations. By focusing on *relevant* information, managerial accounting assists managers in formulating and implementing the organization's strategy and making good business decisions.
What should managers take into consideration when designing managerial accounting systems?	Managers need to weigh the costs of the system (for example, collecting and analyzing data) with the benefits that are expected from using the information to make better decisions. Managers must carefully consider the behavioral effects of the system since employees tend to focus on those aspects of performance that are measured.
Where should management accountants be placed within the organizational structure?	In the past, most management accountants worked in accounting departments. Now, over 50% of management accountants work on cross-functional teams across the organization, where they serve in an advisory role.
What skills should management accountants possess?	Because of their expanding role within the organization, management accountants need both technical skills (such as managerial and financial accounting knowledge and technology skills) and nontechnical skills (such as ethics, communication, critical thinking, and leadership).
What professional associations advocate for management accountants in the United States?	The Institute of Management Accountants (IMA) is the premier organization advocating strictly for the advancement of the management accounting profession. The IMA also issues the CMA certification. In addition, the American Institute of Certified Public Accountants (AICPA) has launched a specialized credential (the CGMA) for CPAs who have experience in industry, business, and government.
By what ethical principles and standards should management accountants abide?	The IMA's overarching ethical *principles* include the following: • Honesty • Objectivity • Fairness • Responsibility The IMA's ethical *standards* include the following: • Competence • Integrity • Confidentiality • Credibility

SUMMARY PROBLEM 1

Requirements

1. Each of the following statements describes a responsibility of management. Match each statement to the management responsibility being fulfilled.

Statement	Management Responsibility
1. Identifying alternative courses of action and choosing among them	a. Planning
2. Running the company on a day-to-day basis	b. Decision making
3. Determining whether the company's units are operating according to plan	c. Directing
4. Setting goals and objectives for the company and determining strategies to achieve them	d. Controlling

2. Are the following statements more descriptive of managerial accounting or financial accounting information?
   a. Describes historical transactions with external parties
   b. Is not required by any authoritative body, such as the SEC
   c. Reports on the company's subunits, such as products, geographical areas, and departments
   d. Is intended to be used by creditors and investors
   e. Is formatted in accordance with GAAP

3. Each of the following statements paraphrases an ethical responsibility. Match each statement to the standard of ethical professional practice being fulfilled. Each standard may be used more than once or not at all.

Responsibility	Standard of Ethical Professional Practice
1. Do not disclose company information unless authorized to do so.	a. Competence
2. Continue to develop skills and knowledge.	b. Confidentiality
3. Don't bias the information and reports presented to management.	c. Integrity
4. If you do not have the skills to complete a task correctly, do not pretend that you do.	d. Credibility
5. Avoid actual *and* apparent conflicts of interest.	

■ SOLUTIONS

Requirement 1
1. (b) Decision making
2. (c) Directing
3. (d) Controlling
4. (a) Planning

Requirement 2
a. Financial accounting
b. Managerial accounting
c. Managerial accounting
d. Financial accounting
e. Financial accounting

Requirement 3
1. (b) Confidentiality
2. (a) Competence
3. (d) Credibility
4. (a) Competence
5. (c) Integrity

5 Discuss the business trends and regulations affecting management accounting

What Business Trends and Regulations Affect Management Accounting?

Business trends and regulations are continually changing. To remain competitive, companies need to be nimble and adaptable. In this section, we'll describe some of the business trends and regulations that are significantly affecting management accounting.

Big Data, Data Analytics, and Critical Thinking

The collection of data from sensors, social media, GPS signals, texts, pictures, customer reward cards, and so forth is increasing at an unprecedented rate. In fact, over 90% of the world's data has been created in the last two years.[7] Big, unstructured data, coupled with traditional business transaction data, are changing the ways in which companies operate. Although the power of much of this data still remains untapped, companies are using data visualization software, such as Tableau, and predictive modeling to become more cost-efficient, to better target their sales markets, to uncover fraud, and to innovate.

For business transaction data, many small businesses use ready-to-use accounting software packages, such as QuickBooks or Sage 50, to track their costs and to develop the information that owners and managers need to run the business. But large companies use **enterprise resource planning (ERP)** systems that can integrate all of a company's worldwide functions, departments, and data. ERP systems such as SAP and Oracle gather company data into a centralized data warehouse. The system feeds the data into software for all of the company's business activities, from budgeting and purchasing to production and customer service.

Advantages of ERP systems include the following:

- Companies streamline their operations before mapping them into ERP software. Streamlining operations saves money.
- ERP helps companies respond quickly to changes. A change in sales instantly ripples through the ERP's purchases, production, shipping, and accounting systems.
- An ERP system can replace hundreds of separate software systems, such as different software in different regions, or different payroll, shipping, and production software.

Gone are the days when decisions are made based on gut feelings. Data-driven decision making is here to stay. What can you do to prepare yourself for a data-driven business career? Data are only data, unless they are turned into useful information. The way to turn big data into information is to use critical thinking skills in conjunction with technological skills, such as competency in Excel, SAP, and Tableau. As mentioned earlier in the chapter, management accountants are expected to possess both technical *and* critical thinking skills. In other words, data cannot stand on their own; they require analysis and interpretation if they are to be of use to management.

Critical Thinking

You will need to use critical thinking throughout this course and throughout your career. But what does critical thinking really entail? **Critical thinking** can be described as improving the quality of thought by skillfully analyzing, assessing, and reconstructing it.[8] Critical thinking can be improved by asking yourself the following series of questions about any issue or problem you encounter:[9]

1. What is the purpose, goal, or objective? In other words, what am I trying to accomplish?
2. What is the specific question I'm trying to address? The question will guide your thought process.
3. What data will I need to answer the question? With the sheer magnitude of data available, you'll need to hone in solely on the data that will help you answer the question at hand.

---

[7] www-01.ibm.com/software/data/bigdata/what-is-big-data.html
[8] Criticalthinking.org
[9] www.criticalthinking.org/ctmodel/logic-model1.htm

4. What concepts am I using, and what assumptions might I be taking for granted? Make sure you clearly identify the concepts and assumptions you are using, since a change in assumption might impact your conclusions.
5. What conclusions am I coming to, and are my inferences logical? *Always* check for logic.
6. What are the implications and consequences of these conclusions? All decisions have repercussions. Think ahead to what the outcome might be.
7. What is my point of view or reference point through which I have viewed the problem? Could I look at the problem from another equally valid point of view? Recognize that your point of view, which is the lens through which you view an issue, might be only one of several equally valid viewpoints.

Often in business, school, and life, you may be faced with problems you don't feel you know how to attack. By asking yourself the series of questions listed above, you can put a thoughtful, intellectual framework around the problem that will help guide your journey toward a solution.

STOP & THINK

Companies are constantly faced with decisions about investing in technological innovations that could potentially save money. While Chapter 12 discusses investment decisions in more detail, we'll consider a simple one-year cost-benefit analysis here. Faced with rising pressure for a $15 per hour minimum wage rate, the fast-food industry is currently exploring the possible use of robotics for order-taking and food preparation tasks. Assume the following facts:

1. By investing in one robotic arm, a fast-food restaurant could potentially save $15 per hour plus 7.65% payroll tax. While the tasks performed by a human associate are more flexible and adaptable than those performed by a robot, assume the robot would replace 10 hours of human labor, 365 days per year.
2. The robotic arm is estimated to cost $35,000 plus $5,000 for installation. While the equipment itself may be in workable condition for up to five years, the company is viewing its implementation as a one-year experiment.
3. The annual cost of running the robotic arm, including utilities and servicing, is expected to be $1,500.

Perform a cost-benefit analysis for the first year of implementation to determine whether the robotic arm would be a financially viable investment if the minimum wage were to be raised to $15 per hour.

Answer:

	A	B	C
1	**Cost-Benefit Analysis**		**Total**
2	**Expected benefits (cost savings):**		
3	Wages: $15 per hour × 10 hours per day × 365 days per year	$ 54,750	
4	Payroll taxes: 7.65% of gross wages	4,188	
5	Total expected benefits		$ 58,938
6	**Expected costs:**		
7	Robotic arm and installation	$ 40,000	
8	Cost of operating and servicing	1,500	
9	Total expected costs		41,500
10	**Net expected benefit in first year**		$ 17,438
11			

Based on this one-year cost-benefit analysis, the fast-food restaurant would expect to benefit from investing in the robotic technology. This analysis is based on several key assumptions (hours of labor replaced, hourly wage rate, and equipment fully expensed in one year). As with most decisions, the projected financial impact would vary under different assumptions.

Shifting Economy

The U.S. economy is becoming a "knowledge economy" in which more and more people are being employed for their intellectual capital than for their ability to provide manual labor in agricultural and manufacturing roles. Outside of government, more people are now employed in the service sector of the U.S. economy (77 million) than in retail and wholesale merchandising (21 million); manufacturing, construction, and mining (19 million); and agriculture (2 million) combined.[10] Service companies provide health care, communication, transportation, banking, professional consulting, education, hospitality and leisure activities, and other important benefits to society. The critical thinking framework outlined earlier highlights the importance of these skills to knowledge workers in the new economy.

Many managerial accounting practices were first developed to meet the needs of manufacturers during the industrial age of the early twentieth century. However, since the U.S. economy has shifted away from manufacturing, managerial accounting has *expanded* to meet the needs of merchandising companies and service firms as well as manufacturers. For example, consider the following:

1. Manufacturers still need to know how much each unit of their product costs to produce. In addition to using this information for inventory valuation and pricing decisions, manufacturers also use cost information to determine whether they should outsource production to another company or to an overseas location, or even whether they should reshore (relocate) it back in the United States.

2. Because such a large percentage of goods are now produced overseas rather than domestically, retailers must now consider foreign currency translation, shipping costs, and import tariffs when determining the cost of imported products. Managers of merchandising companies also need cost and revenue information about operating their brick and mortar locations as well as their online sales platforms. All of this information helps managers make more strategic and profitable decisions.

3. Service companies also need cost information to make decisions. For example, health care providers need to know the cost of performing procedures and running lab tests; hotel managers need to know the cost of providing rooms and amenities to guests; cell phone carriers and Internet service providers need to know the cost of providing texts, data, and cloud computing services; and entrepreneurs that develop apps, such as Uber and Airbnb, need to have a good understanding of their cost structure and how they will monetize the site. No matter what the service, cost information helps managers make vital business decisions, such as pricing decisions, marketing decisions, decisions to invest in new technology, and market expansion decisions.

Globalization

The barriers to international trade have fallen over the past decades, allowing foreign companies to compete with domestic companies. Firms that are not highly efficient, innovative, and responsive to business trends will vanish from the global market. However, global markets also provide highly competitive domestic companies with great opportunities for growth.

Globalization has several implications for managerial accounting:

- Stiffer competition means managers need more accurate and timely information to make wise business decisions. Companies can no longer afford to make decisions by the "seat of their pants." Detailed, accurate, and real-time cost information has become a necessity for survival.

- Companies must decide whether to expand sales and/or production into foreign countries. To do so, managers need comprehensive estimates of the costs of running international operations and the benefits that can be reaped. They also need to be aware of regulations and laws in other countries that could impact their operations. For example, England

[10] www.bls.gov/emp/ep_table_201.htm

and Europe tend to have much stricter environmental protection laws than the United States.

- Companies can learn new management techniques by observing their international competitors. For example, lean thinking, which is discussed next, was developed in Japan by Toyota. Lean practice has now been adopted, expanded upon, and refined by U.S. companies.

Lean Thinking and Focus on Quality

To be competitive in the global market, companies need to be acutely aware of their costs, customer response time, and quality. Market share goes to any company that can do the same thing cheaper, faster, or better. To address these issues, many companies espouse **lean thinking**, which is both a philosophy and a business strategy of operating without waste. The more *wasteful activities* that can be eliminated, the lower the company's costs. The more *wasted time* that can be removed between receiving an order and delivering the product or service, the faster the customer response time. And the more *defects* that can be prevented or removed from the process, the less costly the production process and the higher the customer satisfaction. **Six Sigma**—the goal of producing near perfection (with less than 3.4 defects per million opportunities)—often goes hand in hand with lean thinking. In the second half of Chapter 4, we'll look at some of the unique characteristics of lean operations which companies in every sector of the economy are using with great success. We'll also show how companies analyze the costs associated with their current level of quality as well as make decisions about quality improvement initiatives.

> **Why is this important?**
> "To survive in the **global marketplace**, businesses must quickly respond to customer **demand**, providing high-quality products and **services** at a reasonable price."

Sustainability, Social Responsibility, and the Triple Bottom Line

Recent years have witnessed an increasing awareness and growing interest in sustainability and social responsibility by both consumers and corporations. The dictionary definition of **sustainability** refers to the ability of a system to maintain its own viability, endure without giving way, or use resources so that they are not depleted or permanently damaged.[11] In other words, it's the ability of a system to operate in such a manner that it is able to continue indefinitely. The United Nations has defined sustainability as "the ability to meet the needs of the present without compromising the ability of future generations to meet their own needs."[12] Others have defined sustainability as an expansion of the golden rule: "Do unto others, including future generations, as you would have done unto you."[13]

As pictured in Exhibit 1-8, sustainability has three pillars: environmental, social, and economic. A company will be viable in the long run only if all three of these factors are

EXHIBIT 1-8 The Three Pillars of Sustainability

[11] www.merriam-webster.com; http://dictionary.reference.com
[12] 1987 World Commission on Environment and Development, www.un.org/documents/ga/res/42/ares42-187.htm
[13] Gary Langenwalter, "Business Sustainability: Keeping Lean but with More Green for the Company's Long Haul," 2010, AICPA, Lewisville, Texas.

considered when making business decisions. For example, a company will not be able to survive in the long run if the natural resources (e.g., air, water, soil, minerals, plants, fuel supplies, etc.) or people (e.g., suppliers, customers, employees, communities) it relies on are put in jeopardy. Thus, sustainability is also viewed as the intersection of all three factors, as pictured in Exhibit 1-9. As a result, many companies are beginning to adhere to the notion of a triple bottom line. The **triple bottom line** recognizes that a company's performance should be viewed not only in terms of its ability to generate economic profits for its owners, as has traditionally been the case, but also in terms of its impact on people and the planet.

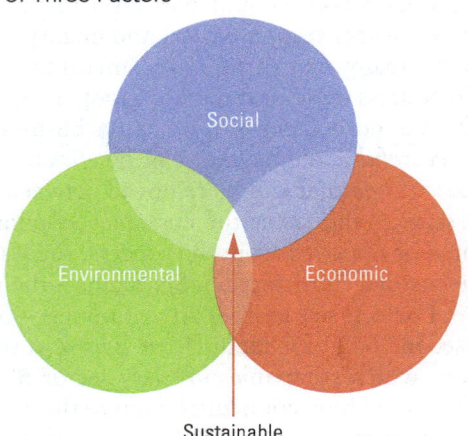

EXHIBIT 1-9 Sustainability as the Intersection of Three Factors

To move toward sustainability, companies are introducing "green initiatives"—ways of doing business that have fewer negative consequences for the earth's resources. They are innovating new products and manufacturing processes that use recycled materials to reduce the amount of waste going to landfills. The drive is toward a circular economy, where nothing goes to waste. Companies have also recognized the need to be socially responsible—carefully considering how their business affects employees, consumers, citizens, and entire communities. Many companies have introduced means of giving back to their local communities by supporting local schools, employee volunteerism, and charities. Most of the leading companies in the world are now issuing Corporate Social Responsibility (CSR) reports through which they communicate their social and environmental impacts. Businesses are now viewing sustainability and social responsibility as opportunities for innovation and business development. These initiatives not only allow a company to "do the right thing," but they also can lead to economic profits by increasing demand for a company's products and services and reducing costs.

In every chapter of this text, you will see a special section illustrating how management accounting can help companies pursue sustainable, socially responsible business practices. These sections will be marked with a green recycle symbol and will also point you to corresponding homework problems. In addition, Chapter 15 is devoted to sustainability, examining the reasons sustainability makes good business sense and the framework and methods companies use to measure and report on their social and environmental impact.

Integrated Reporting

The corporate reporting landscape is constantly changing. One of the most notable recent global movements is toward integrated reporting. According to the International Integrated Reporting Committee (IIRC), **integrated reporting** (symbolized as < IR >) "is a process that results in communication, most visibly a periodic 'integrated report,' about value creation over time. An integrated report is a concise communication about how an organization's strategy, governance, performance and prospects lead to the creation of value over the short, medium and long term."[14] As such, it is a

---

[14] www.theiirc.org

broader, more holistic, balanced, and future-looking report than traditional financial statements, which tend to focus on short-term financial measures of past performance. An integrated report essentially describes and measures all material elements of value creation, not just those relating to financial capital. In addition to financial capital, the report considers manufactured, intellectual, human, social, and natural (environmental) capital, which are often more difficult for investors to access through traditional financial reporting.

Integrated reporting, which is still in its infancy, is being driven by businesses and institutional investors who want more information for better decision making than that offered by traditional financial statements. Several well-known companies, including Microsoft, Prudential, and Coca-Cola, as well as the Big Four accounting firms, the Chartered Financial Analyst (CFA) Institute, and Goldman Sachs, are working closely with the IIRC to help further develop and refine the < IR > reporting framework. You may keep abreast of current developments in < IR > by visiting www.theiirc.org.

The Sarbanes-Oxley Act of 2002

As a result of corporate accounting scandals, such as those at Enron and WorldCom, the U.S. Congress enacted the **Sarbanes-Oxley Act of 2002 (SOX)**. The purpose of SOX is to restore trust in publicly traded corporations, their management, their financial statements, and their auditors. SOX enhances internal control and financial reporting requirements and establishes new regulatory requirements for publicly traded companies and their independent auditors. Publicly traded companies have spent millions of dollars upgrading their internal controls and accounting systems to comply with SOX regulations.

As shown in Exhibit 1-10, SOX requires the company's CEO and CFO to assume responsibility for their company's financial statements and disclosures. The CEO and CFO must certify that the financial statements and disclosures fairly present, in all material respects, the operations and financial condition of the company. Additionally, they must accept responsibility for establishing and maintaining an adequate internal control structure and procedures for financial reporting. The company must have its internal controls and financial reporting procedures assessed annually.

EXHIBIT 1-10 Some Important Features of SOX

> **Why is this important?**
>
> "**SOX** puts more pressure on companies, their **managers**, and their auditors to ensure that **investors** get financial information that **fairly reflects** the company's **operations**."

SOX also requires audit committee members to be independent; that is, they may not receive any consulting or advisory fees from the company other than for their service on the board of directors. In addition, at least one of the members should be a financial expert. The audit committee oversees not only the internal audit function but also the company's audit by independent CPAs.

To ensure that CPA firms maintain independence from their client company, SOX does not allow CPA firms to provide certain nonaudit services (such as bookkeeping and financial information systems design) to companies during the same period of time in which they are providing audit services. If a company wants to obtain such services from a CPA firm, it must hire a different firm to do the nonaudit work. Tax services may be provided by the same CPA firm if pre-approved by the audit committee. The audit partner must rotate off the audit engagement every five years, and the audit firm must undergo quality reviews every one to three years.

SOX also increases the penalties for white-collar crimes such as corporate fraud. These penalties include both monetary fines and substantial imprisonment. For example, knowingly destroying or creating documents to "impede, obstruct, or influence" any federal investigation can result in up to 20 years of imprisonment.[15]

SOX also contains a "clawback" provision in which previously paid CEO's and CFO's incentive-based compensation can be recovered if the financial statements were misstated due to misconduct. The Dodd-Frank Wall Street Reform and Consumer Protection Act of 2010 further strengthens the clawback rules, such that firms *must* recover all incentive compensation paid to *any* current or former executive, in the three years preceding the restatement, if that compensation would not have been paid under the restated financial statements. In other words, executives will not be allowed to profit from misstated financial statements, even if the misstatement was not due to misconduct.[16]

Since its enactment in 2002, SOX has significantly affected the internal operations of publicly traded corporations and their auditors. SOX will continue to play a major role in corporate management and the auditing profession.

Try It!

Determine whether each of the following statements is true or false:

1. The Sarbanes-Oxley Act of 2002 (SOX) imposes stricter requirements for financial reporting and internal controls and stricter consequences for those who engage in financial statement misconduct and other white-collar crimes.
2. Most business decisions are now based on gut feelings and hunches, rather than being data-driven.
3. Critical thinking can be improved by asking yourself a series of questions about any issue or problem you encounter. These questions, for example, include: What is the objective? What data will I need? What assumptions am I making? Is my conclusion logical?
4. The triple bottom line assesses company performance on three factors: people (social impact), planet (environmental impact), and profit (economic impact).
5. Manufacturing makes up the largest sector of the U.S. economy.
6. The globalization of business has little bearing on management accounting.
7. Computer systems that integrate all of a company's worldwide functions into one database are known as Integrated Worldwide Systems (IWSs).
8. Lean thinking focuses on eliminating waste from operations.

Please see page 47 for solutions.

---

[15] Go to www.AICPA.org to learn more about SOX.
[16] http://www.pwc.com/us/en/cfodirect/publications/in-brief/sec-dodd-frank-clawback-rule-954.html

Decision Guidelines

The Changing Business and Regulatory Environment

Successful companies have to respond to changes in the business and regulatory environment. Managers have many decisions to make as they adapt to current business trends.

Decision	Guidelines
What impact will big data and data analytics have on our organization?	The abundance of data allows managers to make data-driven decisions, rather than decisions that are made on a hunch. However, critical thinking is needed to turn data into useful information.
How can we use critical thinking to help solve business issues?	The following steps provide a framework for critically examining any issue or problem: 1. What is the purpose, goal, or objective? In other words, what am I trying to accomplish? 2. What is the specific question I'm trying to address? The question will guide your thought process. 3. What data will I need to answer the question? With the sheer magnitude of data available, you'll need to hone in solely on the data that will help you answer the question at hand. 4. What concepts am I using, and what assumptions might I be taking for granted? Make sure you clearly identify the concepts and assumptions you are using, since a change in assumption might impact your conclusions. 5. What conclusions am I coming to, and are my inferences logical? *Always* check for logic. 6. What are the implications and consequences of these conclusions? All decisions have repercussions. Think ahead to what the outcome might be. 7. What is my point of view or reference point through which I have viewed the problem? Could I look at the problem from another equally valid point of view? Recognize that your point of view, which is the lens through which you view an issue, might be only one of several equally valid viewpoints.
Is management accounting useful in the growing knowledge economy, or is it only applicable to manufacturers?	Managerial accounting has expanded to meet the needs of companies in all sectors of the economy. Managers in service industries need detailed cost and revenue data to plan, control, and direct operations just as much as manufacturers do.
How do companies compete in a global economy?	The globalization of business means more competition but more opportunity as well. To remain competitive, companies must constantly focus on costs, customer response times, and quality. Companies use lean thinking and Six Sigma to reduce wasted resources, reduce wasted time, and improve quality.
How does the concept of sustainability affect business?	Businesses will be viable in the long run only if they take a sustainable approach to operations, carefully considering the impact of the company's operations on people and the planet as well as on profit. Thus, company performance is often evaluated using a triple-bottom-line approach. Businesses are viewing sustainability as an opportunity to "do the right thing" while simultaneously increasing the company's value through innovation, risk minimization, and cost reduction.
Which companies need to comply with SOX?	Publicly traded companies must comply with SOX. To better ensure the legitimacy of companies' financial information, many of the law's specific requirements focus on implementing adequate internal controls, employing better financial reporting procedures, and maintaining independence from the company's auditors.

SUMMARY PROBLEM 2

EZ-Rider Motorcycles is considering whether to expand into Germany. If gas prices increase, the company expects more interest in fuel-efficient transportation such as motorcycles. As a result, the company is considering setting up a motorcycle assembly plant on the outskirts of Berlin.

EZ-Rider Motorcycles estimates that it will cost $850,000 to convert an existing building to motorcycle production. Workers will need training, at a total cost of $65,000. The additional cost to organize the business and to establish relationships is estimated to be $150,000.

The CEO believes the company can earn profits from this expansion (before considering the costs in the preceding paragraph) of $1,624,000.

Requirement

Use cost-benefit analysis to determine whether EZ-Rider should expand into Germany.

SOLUTION

The following cost-benefit analysis indicates that the company should expand into Germany because expected benefits exceed expected costs:

	A	B	C
1	**Cost-Benefit Analysis**		**Total**
2	**Expected Benefits:**		
3	Expected profits from increase in sales		$ 1,624,000
4	**Expected Costs:**		
5	Conversion of building	$ 850,000	
6	Workforce training	65,000	
7	Organizing and establishing relationships	150,000	
8	Total expected costs		1,065,000
9	**Net expected benefit**		$ 559,000
10			

END OF CHAPTER

Learning Objectives

- 1 Identify managers' three primary responsibilities
- 2 Distinguish financial accounting from managerial accounting
- 3 Describe the roles and skills required of management accountants within the organization
- 4 Describe the role of the Institute of Management Accountants (IMA) and apply its ethical standards
- 5 Discuss the business trends and regulations affecting management accounting

Accounting Vocabulary

American Institute of Certified Public Accountants (AICPA). (p. 11) The world's largest association representing the accounting profession; together with the Chartered Institute of Management Accountants (CIMA), offers the Chartered Global Management Accountant (CGMA) designation.

Audit Committee. (p. 10) A subcommittee of the board of directors that is responsible for overseeing both the internal audit function and the annual financial statement audit by independent CPAs.

Board of Directors. (p. 9) The body elected by shareholders to oversee the company.

Budget. (p. 3) Quantitative expression of a plan that helps managers coordinate and implement the plan.

Certified Management Accountant (CMA). (p. 10) A professional certification issued by the IMA to designate expertise in the areas of managerial accounting, economics, and business finance.

Chartered Global Management Accountant (CGMA). (p. 11) A designation available to qualifying American Institute of Certified Public Accountants (AICPA) members that is meant to recognize the unique business and accounting skill set possessed by those CPAs who work, or have worked, in business, industry, or government.

Chief Executive Officer (CEO). (p. 9) The position hired by the board of directors to oversee the company on a daily basis.

Chief Financial Officer (CFO). (p. 10) The position responsible for all of the company's financial concerns.

Chief Operating Officer (COO). (p. 10) The position responsible for overseeing the company's operations.

Controller. (p. 10) The position responsible for general financial accounting, managerial accounting, and tax reporting.

Controlling. (p. 3) One of management's primary responsibilities; evaluating the results of business operations against the plan and making adjustments to keep the company pressing toward its goals.

Cost-Benefit Analysis. (p. 19) Weighing costs against benefits to help make decisions.

Critical Thinking. (p. 18) Improving the quality of thought by skillfully analyzing, assessing, and reconstructing it.

Cross-Functional Teams. (p. 10) Corporate teams whose members represent various functions of the organization, such as R&D, design, production, marketing, distribution, and customer service.

Decision Making. (p. 2) Identifying possible courses of action and choosing among them.

Directing. (p. 3) One of management's primary responsibilities; running the company on a day-to-day basis.

Enterprise Resource Planning (ERP). (p. 18) Software systems that can integrate all of a company's worldwide functions, departments, and data into a single system.

Institute of Management Accountants (IMA). (p. 10) The professional organization that promotes the advancement of the management accounting profession.

Integrated Reporting. (p. 22) A process resulting in a report that describes how a company is creating value over time using financial, manufactured, intellectual, human, social, and natural capital.

Internal Audit Function. (p. 10) The corporate function charged with assessing the effectiveness of the company's internal controls and risk management policies.

Lean Thinking. (p. 21) A philosophy and business strategy of operating without waste.

Management Accounting (p. 2) A profession that involves partnering in management decision making, devising planning and performance management systems, and providing expertise in financial reporting and control to assist management in the formulation and implementation of an organization's strategy.

Planning. (p. 3) One of management's primary responsibilities: setting goals and objectives for the company and deciding how to achieve them.

Sarbanes-Oxley Act of 2002 (SOX). (p. 23) A congressional act that enhances internal control and financial reporting requirements and establishes new regulatory requirements for publicly traded companies and their independent auditors.

Six Sigma. (p. 21) The goal of producing near perfection with less than 3.4 defects per million opportunities.

Sustainability. (p. 21) The ability to meet the needs of the present without compromising the ability of future generations to meet their own needs.

Treasurer. (p. 10) The position responsible for raising the firm's capital and investing funds.

Triple Bottom Line. (p. 22) Evaluating a company's performance not only by its ability to generate economic profits, but also by its impact on people and on the planet.

Quick Check

1. *(Learning Objective 1)* Which of the following management responsibilities often involves evaluating the results of operations against the budget?
   a. Planning
   b. Directing
   c. Controlling
   d. None of the above

2. *(Learning Objective 2)* Managerial accounting differs from financial accounting in that managerial accounting
   a. tends to report on the company as a whole rather than segments of the company.
   b. emphasizes data relevance over data objectivity.
   c. is used primarily by external decision makers.
   d. is required by Generally Accepted Accounting Principles (GAAP).

3. *(Learning Objective 3)* Which of the following corporate positions is responsible for general financial accounting, managerial accounting, and tax reporting?
   a. Controller
   b. Treasurer
   c. Internal audit
   d. Chief operating officer (COO)

4. *(Learning Objective 3)* Of the following skills, which are needed by today's management accountants?
   a. Strategic thinking
   b. Cost management
   c. Decision analysis
   d. All of the above

5. *(Learning Objective 4)* Which of the following organizations is the professional association specifically for management accountants?
   a. FASB
   b. AICPA
   c. IMA
   d. IFRS

6. *(Learning Objective 4)* Which of the following professional standards requires management accountants to continually develop their knowledge and skills?
   a. Competence
   b. Confidentiality
   c. Integrity
   d. Credibility

7. *(Learning Objective 4)* Which of the following professional standards requires management accountants to not disclose private information about their organizations?
   a. Competence
   b. Confidentiality
   c. Integrity
   d. Credibility

8. *(Learning Objective 5)* Which of the following requires the company's CEO and CFO to assume responsibility for the company's financial statements and disclosures?
   a. Sarbanes-Oxley Act of 2002 (SOX)
   b. Institute of Management Accountants (IMA)
   c. Enterprise Resource Planning (ERP)
   d. Lean operations

9. *(Learning Objective 5)* Which of the following is *false*?
   a. Globalization has increased the necessity for more detailed and accurate cost information.
   b. The triple bottom line focuses on three items: net income, net assets, and return on investment.
   c. ERP systems integrate information from all company functions into a centralized data warehouse.
   d. Lean operations is a philosophy and business strategy of operating without waste.

10. *(Learning Objective 5)* All of the following are business trends affecting management accounting **except**:
    a. shifting economy.
    b. sustainability.
    c. big data.
    d. all of the above.

Quick Check Answers

1. c 2. b 3. a 4. d 5. c 6. a 7. b 8. a 9. b 10. d

Short Exercises

S1-1 Managers' responsibilities *(Learning Objective 1)*

Categorize each of the following activities as to which management responsibility it fulfills: planning, directing, or controlling. Some activities may fulfill more than one responsibility.

a. Management decides to increase sales growth by 20% next year.
b. Management analyzes the impact of a recent advertising campaign by comparing budgeted sales to actual sales.
c. Management reviews hourly sales reports to determine the level of staffing needed to staff the customer service desk.
d. Management uses information on product costs to determine sales prices.
e. To lower production costs, management moves production to China.

S1-2 Contrast managerial and financial accounting *(Learning Objective 2)*

Managerial accounting differs from financial accounting in several areas. Specify whether each of the following characteristics relates to managerial accounting or financial accounting.

a. Reports are usually prepared quarterly and annually.
b. Information is verified by external auditors.
c. Focus is on the past.
d. Main characteristic of information is that it must be relevant.
e. Reports tend to be prepared for the parts of the organization rather than the whole organization.
f. Primary users are internal (i.e., company managers).
g. It is governed by Generally Accepted Accounting Principles (GAAP) or International Financial Reporting Standards (IFRS).
h. The primary characteristics of information are that it must be reliable and objective.
i. Reports are prepared as needed.
j. It is not governed by legal requirements.
k. Primary users are external (i.e., creditors, investors).
l. Focus is on the future.
m. Reporting is based mainly on the company as a whole.

S1-3 Accounting roles in the organization *(Learning Objective 3)*

The following is a list of job duties or descriptions. For each item, specify whether it would be most likely to describe the duties or responsibilities of someone working for the treasurer, the controller, or the Internal Auditing Department.

a. Check to make sure that company risk management procedures are being followed.
b. Oversee accounts payable activities.
c. Report to the audit committee of the board of directors *and* to a senior executive, such as the CFO or CEO.
d. Ensure that the company's internal controls are functioning properly.
e. Issue company stock.
f. Perform cash counts at branch offices.
g. Work with various departments in preparing operating budgets for the upcoming year.
h. Create an analysis about whether to lease or buy a delivery truck.
i. Prepare journal entries for month-end closing.
j. Calculate the cost of a product.
k. Prepare company tax returns.
l. Invest company funds.
m. Issue company bonds.

S1-4 Role of internal audit function *(Learning Objective 3)*

The following table lists several characteristics. Place a check mark next to those items that pertain directly to the internal audit function and its role within the organization.

Characteristic	Check (✓) if related to internal auditing
a. Reports directly to the audit committee	
b. Reports to treasurer or controller	
c. Is part of the Accounting Department	
d. Helps to ensure that the company's internal controls are functioning properly	
e. Performs the same function as independent certified public accountants	
f. Usually reports to a senior executive (CFO or CEO) for administrative matters	
g. External audits can be performed by the Internal Auditing Department	
h. Required by the New York Stock Exchange (NYSE) if company stock is publicly traded on the NYSE	
i. Ensures that the company achieves its profit goals	

S1-5 Classify roles within the organization *(Learning Objective 3)*

Complete the following statements with one of the terms listed here. You may use a term more than once, and some terms may not be used at all.

Audit committee	Board of directors	CEO	CFO
Treasurer	Controller	Cross-functional teams	COO

a. The CEO is hired by the _____.
b. A subcommittee of the board of directors is called the _____.
c. Raising capital and investing funds are the direct responsibilities of the _____.
d. The _____ and the _____ report to the CEO.
e. Financial accounting, managerial accounting, and tax reporting are the direct responsibilities of the _____.
f. Management accountants often work on _____.
g. The internal audit function reports to the CFO or the _____ and the _____.
h. The company's operations are the direct responsibility of the _____.

S1-6 Professional organizations and certifications *(Learning Objective 4)*

Complete the following sentences:

1. The Institute of Management Accountants (IMA) issues the _____ _____ _____ certification.
2. The certification offered by IMA focuses on _____ and _____ topics.
3. The monthly professional magazine published by the Institute of Management Accountants is called _____.
4. The certification launched in 2012 jointly by the American Institute of Certified Public Accountants (AICPA) and the Chartered Institute of Management Accountants (CIMA) is called the _____ _____ _____ _____.
5. To earn CMA certification, a candidate must have a(n) _____ degree. The CMA exam can be taken, however, before finishing this degree.

Introduction to Managerial Accounting 31

S1-7 Violations of ethical standards *(Learning Objective 4)*

ETHICS

The IMA's *Statement of Ethical Professional Practice* (Exhibit 1–7) requires management accountants to meet standards regarding the following:
- Competence
- Confidentiality
- Integrity
- Credibility

Consider the following situations. Which guidelines are violated in each situation?

a. You do not provide top managers with the detailed job descriptions they requested because you fear they may use this information to cut a position from your department.

b. You tell your sister that your company will report earnings significantly above financial analysts' estimates.

c. You failed to read the detailed specifications of a new software package that you asked your company to purchase. After it is installed, you are surprised that it is incompatible with some of your company's older accounting software.

d. You see that other employees take office supplies for personal use. As an intern, you do the same thing, assuming that this is a "perk."

e. At a financial reporting seminar, you skip the afternoon session and go sightseeing. Your company paid for the registration fee, and you are getting paid for the day.

S1-8 Identify current competitive tools *(Learning Objective 5)*

Companies are facing a great amount of change in every facet of their operations today. To remain competitive, companies must keep abreast of current developments in several areas. You recently got together with a group of friends who work for different companies. Your friends share information about their current challenges in adopting new tools or complying with new regulations. Excerpts from the conversation are presented in the following section. Tell whether each excerpt describes data analytics, Six Sigma, sustainability, the Sarbanes-Oxley Act (SOX), or enterprise resource planning (ERP) systems.

a. Jordan: My company has a new initiative at work. All employees are encouraged to recycle paper and other materials. Employees are also given one work day a year to volunteer to help local nonprofit organizations. Employees are also urged to think outside the box to find ways to reduce the company's carbon footprint. The company has also begun an internal reporting system that reports on its triple bottom line.

b. Kate: I just started a new job in the Auditing Department. My new duties include assisting in the development of testing procedures and methods for determining internal controls effectiveness. I also oversee the testing for assurance of compliance with corporate policies. I am coordinating the review of SEC filings with our external auditors. I also am responsible for preparing periodic compliance status reports for management, the audit committee, and the external auditors.

c. Yiang: My company is working to demonstrate its commitment to continuous quality improvement. We are currently undergoing an extensive audit of our quality management processes and are striving to produce with a defect level of less than 3.4 defects per million parts produced. We hope to gain a competitive advantage through this process.

d. Christopher: We have just installed a system at our company that integrates all of our company's data across all systems. We have one central data warehouse that contains information about our suppliers, our customers, our employees, and our financial information. The software retrieves information from this single data warehouse and all systems are integrated. The process of implementing this system has been very expensive and time consuming, but we are reaping the benefits of being more streamlined, of being able to respond more quickly to changes in the market, and of not having several different software systems operating independently.

e. Emma: Our company is considering whether to set up a sales division in India where we feel there is untapped market potential. However, we have to carefully consider the costs of such an expansion against the increased sales we would see from the new division.

CHAPTER 1

ETHICS

S1-9 Identify ethical standards violated *(Learning Objective 4)*

For each of the situations listed, identify the primary standard from the IMA *Statement of Ethical Professional Practice* that is violated (competence, confidentiality, integrity, or credibility.) Refer to Exhibit 1–7 for the complete standard.

a. Jack, an accountant for a smartphone manufacturer, told his friends about a new model of smartphone being released by the company in the following quarter. For competitive reasons, the company keeps its models shrouded in secrecy until the release date.

b. The CFO directed that certain expenses be reclassified as assets, so that target profit could be achieved. The CFO rationalized that jobs would be saved by reaching the targeted income figures.

c. Even though Meagan's company is adopting a new ERP system that impacts the accounting system, Meagan (a management accountant) has not completed the required ERP training from the vendor.

d. Oliver provides an analysis of the profitability of a company-owned store that is managed by Oliver's best friend, Bob. Oliver neglects to include allocated fixed costs in Bob's report. If Oliver includes those allocated fixed costs, the store will show a loss and Bob's job could be in danger.

e. Yimeng, a purchasing agent for her company, received two tickets from a supplier to the upcoming Ohio State versus University of Michigan football game. These tickets sell for over $500 each.

S1-10 Define key terms *(Learning Objectives 1, 2, 3, 4, and 5)*

Complete the following statements with one of the terms listed here.

CEO	Economic	Planning
CFO	Environmental	Sarbanes-Oxley Act of 2002
Controlling	ERP	Six Sigma
Controller	Financial accounting system	Social
Critical thinking	Integrated report	Sustainability
Directing	Internal audit	Treasurer

a. The _____ is geared toward producing periodic financial statements that will be used by investors and creditors to make investment and lending decisions.

b. _____ improves the quality of thought by skillfully analyzing, assessing, and reconstructing initial thoughts.

c. The goal of producing near perfection with less than 3.4 defects per one million opportunities is called _____.

d. The _____ is the person responsible for raising the firm's capital and investing its funds.

e. The three pillars of sustainability are: _____, _____, and _____.

f. The _____ is the person responsible for general financial accounting, managerial accounting, and tax reporting.

g. The role of the _____ function is to ensure that the company's internal controls and risk management policies are functioning properly.

h. The _____ was enacted to restore trust in publicly traded corporations, their management, their financial statements, and their auditors.

i. _____ is a broad holistic report that describes all material elements of value creation, not just the financial elements.

j. _____ is the management process of evaluating the results of business operations against the plan and making adjustments to keep the company pressing toward its goals.

k. _____ is the management process of overseeing the company's day-to-day operations.

l. _____ serves the information needs of people in accounting as well as people in marketing and in the warehouse.

m. _____ is the ability to meet the needs of the present without compromising the ability of future generations to meet their own needs.

n. The _____ manages the company on a daily basis.

o. _____ is the management process of setting goals and objectives for the company and determining how to achieve them.

p. Typically, the treasurer and the controller report directly to the _____.

EXERCISES Group A

E1-11A Define key terms *(Learning Objectives 1 & 2)*

Complete the following statements with one of the terms listed here. You may use a term more than once, and some terms may not be used at all.

Budget	Creditors	Managerial accounting	Planning
Controlling	Financial accounting	Managers	Shareholders

a. Information on a company's past performance is provided to external parties by _____.

b. _____ systems are chosen by comparing the costs versus the benefits of the system and are not restricted by GAAP (or International Financial Reporting Standards, IFRS, in the case of companies headquartered in many countries outside of the United States).

c. _____ systems report on various segments or business units of the company.

d. Financial accounting develops reports for external parties such as _____ and _____.

e. When managers evaluate the company's performance compared to the plan, they are performing the _____ role of management.

f. CPAs audit the _____ statements of public companies.

g. Companies must follow GAAP (or International Financial Reporting Standards, IRFS, in the case of companies headquartered in many countries outside of the United States) in their _____ systems.

h. Choosing goals and the means to achieve them is the _____ function of management.

i. Decision makers inside a company are the _____.

E1-12A Identify skills needed by management accountants *(Learning Objective 3)*

Management accountants need a wide variety of skills for their roles in organizations. These skills can be classified as either technical or nontechnical.

Requirement

For each of the following skills, indicate whether it is a technical competency or a nontechnical competency for a management accountant.

a. Planning, budgeting, and forecasting
b. Leadership
c. Financial statement analysis
d. Adaptability
e. Strategic thinking
f. Change management
g. Investment decision making
h. Cost management
i. Technology
j. Internal financial reporting
k. Collaboration
l. Process improvement
m. Performance management
n. Customer service
o. Enterprise risk management
p. Decision analysis
q. Communication
r. Ethics
s. Internal controls
t. Business acumen

E1-13A Identify users of accounting information *(Learning Objective 3)*

For each of the following users of financial accounting information and managerial accounting information, specify whether the user would primarily use financial accounting information or managerial accounting information or both.

1. Reporter from *The Wall Street Journal*
2. Regional division managers
3. Potential investors
4. Bookkeeping Department
5. Manager of the Service Department
6. Wall Street analyst
7. Division controller
8. State tax agency auditor
9. External auditor (public accounting firm)
10. Loan officer at the company's bank
11. Board of directors
12. Internal auditor
13. SEC examiner
14. Current stockholders

ETHICS

E1-14A Classify ethical responsibilities *(Learning Objective 4)*

According to the IMA's *Statement of Ethical Professional Practice* (Exhibit 1–7), management accountants should follow four standards: competence, confidentiality, integrity, and credibility. Each of these standards contains specific responsibilities. Classify each of the following responsibilities according to the standard it addresses.

Responsibility:

1. Keep information confidential except when disclosure is authorized or legally required.
2. Disclose all relevant information that could reasonably be expected to influence an intended user's understanding of the reports, analyses, or recommendations.
3. Disclose delays or deficiencies in information, timeliness, processing, or internal controls in conformance with organization policy and/or applicable law.
4. Communicate information fairly and objectively.
5. Refrain from using confidential information for unethical or illegal advantage.
6. Inform all relevant parties regarding the appropriate use of confidential information. Monitor subordinates' activities to ensure compliance.
7. Mitigate actual conflicts of interest. Regularly communicate with business associates to avoid apparent conflicts of interest. Advise all parties of any potential conflicts.
8. Maintain an appropriate level of professional expertise by continually developing knowledge and skills.
9. Recognize and communicate professional limitations that would preclude responsible judgment or successful performance of an activity.
10. Perform professional duties in accordance with relevant laws, regulations, and technical standards.
11. Abstain from engaging in or supporting any activity that might discredit the profession.
12. Refrain from engaging in any conduct that would prejudice carrying out duties ethically.
13. Provide decision support information and recommendations that are accurate, clear, concise, and timely.

Introduction to Managerial Accounting

E1-15A Equipment purchase cost-benefit analysis *(Learning Objective 5)*

Faced with rising pressure for a $15 per hour minimum wage rate, the farming industry is currently exploring the possible use of robotics to replace some farm workers. The Lettuce Bot is one such robot; its job is to thin out a field of lettuce, removing the least promising buds of lettuce. By removing these weaker plants, the stronger lettuce plants have more room to grow. Assume the following facts:

1. One Lettuce Bot would do the work of 20 farm workers.
2. Each farm worker typically works 40 hours on the lettuce thinning process each year.
3. Each farm worker would earn $15 per hour plus 7.65% payroll tax.
4. The Lettuce Bot is estimated to cost $8,000 plus $500 for delivery.
5. Annual costs of operating the Lettuce Bot are expected to be $1,500.

While the Lettuce Bot itself may be in workable condition for up to five years, assume that the farm would view its implementation as a one-year experiment.

Requirement

Perform a cost-benefit analysis for the first year of implementation to determine whether the Lettuce Bot would be a financially viable investment if the minimum wage is raised to $15 per hour.

E1-16A Lean production cost-benefit analysis *(Learning Objective 5)*

McIntyre Industries manufactures iPhone case covers. Sarabeth Anderson, the CEO, is trying to decide whether to adopt a lean thinking model. She expects that adopting lean production would save $77,000 in warehousing expenses and $39,600 in spoilage costs. Adopting lean production will require several one-time up-front expenditures: $25,000 for an employee training program, $89,000 to streamline the plant's production process, and $7,000 to identify suppliers that will guarantee zero defects and on-time delivery.

Requirements

1. What are the total costs of adopting lean production?
2. What are the total benefits of adopting lean production?
3. Should the company adopt lean production? Why or why not?

E1-17A Identify sustainability efforts as impacting people, planet, or profit *(Learning Objective 5)*

SUSTAINABILITY

Sustainability involves more than just the impact of actions on the environment. The triple bottom line recognizes that a company has to measure its impact on its triple bottom line for its long-term viability. To follow are examples of green initiatives recently undertaken at PepsiCo., Inc. For each example, indicate whether this initiative would primarily impact environmental, social, or economic factors.

a. In 2015, PepsiCo increased its dividend to shareholders.
b. It created a new global ingredient standard in 2014 that helps to ensure ingredient safety and integrity.
c. In 2014, PepsiCo used 23% less water (considered to be a scarce resource) per unit of production than in 2006.
d. Almost 60% of beverage launches qualified as "Better-For-You" or "Good-For-You" products in 2014 (as opposed to PepsiCo's "Fun-For-You" category).
e. From 2008 to 2014, PepsiCo held its greenhouse gas emissions stable despite increasing production.
f. PepsiCo strengthened its Responsible Advertising to Children policy.
g. The return on PepsiCo's invested capital was above 13% for the fifth year in a row.
h. In 2014, PepsiCo increased its amount of recycled content in its packaging by 23%.
i. In 2014, 93% of PepsiCo's waste was not sent to landfills.
j. In 2014, approximately 20% of PepsiCo's net revenue came from its nutrition business since it has been making a concerted effort to promote more healthy food and beverage choices.
k. During 2014, 95% of PepsiCo's manufacturing sites underwent an independent food safety audit by the American Institute of Baking.
l. Since 2006, PepsiCo has reached more than 1.92 million children in 477 schools in India through its programs promoting nutrition and physical activity.
m. PepsiCo provided access to safe water for 6 million people.
n. Forty of PepsiCo's buildings have achieved LEED certification (LEED certification is a measure of energy efficiency).

EXERCISES Group B

E1-18B Define key terms *(Learning Objectives 1 & 2)*
Complete the following statements with one of the terms listed here. You may use a term more than once, and some terms may not be used at all.

| Budget | Creditors | Managerial accounting | Planning |
| Controlling | Financial accounting | Managers | Shareholders |

a. U.S. companies must follow GAAP (or International Financial Reporting Standards, IFRS, in the case of companies headquartered in many countries outside of the United States) in their _____ systems.
b. Financial accounting develops reports for external parties such as _____ and _____.
c. When managers evaluate the company's performance compared to the plan, they are performing the _____ role of management.
d. _____ are decision makers inside a company.
e. _____ provides information on a company's past performance to external parties.
f. _____ systems are not restricted by GAAP (or International Financial Reporting Standards, IFRS, in the case of companies headquartered in many countries outside of the United States) but are chosen by comparing the costs versus the benefits of the system.
g. Choosing goals and the means to achieve them is the _____ function of management.
h. _____ systems report on various segments or business units of the company.
i. _____ statements of public companies are audited annually by CPAs.

E1-19B Identify skills needed by management accountants *(Learning Objective 3)*
Management accountants need a wide variety of skills for their roles in organizations. These skills can be classified as either technical or nontechnical.

Requirement
For each of the following skills, indicate whether it is a technical competency or a non-technical competency for a management accountant.

a. Leadership
b. Communication
c. Collaboration
d. Internal controls
e. Change management
f. Cost management
g. Investment decision making
h. Technology
i. Customer service
j. Financial statement analysis
k. Business acumen
l. Performance management
m. Adaptability
n. Enterprise risk management
o. Planning, budgeting, and forecasting
p. Decision analysis
q. Internal financial reporting
r. Ethics
s. Process improvement
t. Strategic thinking

E1-20B Identify users of accounting information *(Learning Objective 3)*

For each of the following users of financial accounting information and managerial accounting information, specify whether the user would primarily use financial accounting information or managerial accounting information, or both.

1. Internal auditor
2. Potential shareholders
3. Loan officer at the company's bank
4. Manager of the Sales Department
5. Bookkeeping Department
6. Managers at regional offices
7. IRS agent
8. Current shareholders
9. Wall Street analyst
10. News reporter
11. Company controller
12. Board of directors
13. SEC employee
14. External auditor (public accounting firm)

E1-21B Classify ethical responsibilities *(Learning Objective 4)*

ETHICS

According to the IMA's *Statement of Ethical Professional Practice* (reproduced in the chapter), management accountants should follow four standards: competence, confidentiality, integrity, and credibility. Each of these standards contains specific responsibilities. Classify each of the following responsibilities according to the standard it addresses.

1. Communicate information fairly and objectively.
2. Recognize and communicate professional limitations that would preclude responsible judgment or successful performance of an activity.
3. Mitigate actual conflicts of interest. Regularly communicate with business associates to avoid apparent conflicts of interest. Advise all parties of any potential conflicts.
4. Provide decision support information and recommendations that are accurate, clear, concise, and timely.
5. Abstain from engaging in or supporting any activity that might discredit the profession.
6. Disclose all relevant information that could reasonably be expected to influence an intended user's understanding of the reports, analyses, or recommendations.
7. Inform all relevant parties regarding the appropriate use of confidential information. Monitor subordinates' activities to ensure compliance.
8. Perform professional duties in accordance with relevant laws, regulations, and technical standards.
9. Refrain from engaging in any conduct that would prejudice carrying out duties ethically.
10. Keep information confidential except when disclosure is authorized or legally required.
11. Disclose delays or deficiencies in information, timeliness, processing, or internal controls in conformance with organization policy and/or applicable law.
12. Refrain from using confidential information for unethical or illegal advantage.
13. Maintain an appropriate level of professional expertise by continually developing knowledge and skills.

E1-22B Equipment purchase cost-benefit analysis *(Learning Objective 5)*

Faced with rising pressure for a $15 per hour minimum wage rate, the farming industry is currently exploring the possible use of robotics to replace some farm workers. The Lettuce Bot is one such robot; its job is to thin out a field of lettuce, removing the least promising buds of lettuce. By removing these weaker plants, the stronger lettuce plants have more room to grow. Assume the following facts:

1. One Lettuce Bot would do the work of 25 farm workers.
2. Each farm worker typically works 50 hours on the lettuce thinning process each year.
3. Each farm worker would earn $15 per hour plus 7.65% payroll tax.
4. The Lettuce Bot is estimated to cost $9,500 plus $1,000 for delivery.
5. Annual costs of operating the Lettuce Bot are expected to be $2,500.

While the Lettuce Bot itself may be in workable condition for up to five years, assume that the farm would view its implementation as a one-year experiment.

Requirement
Perform a cost-benefit analysis for the first year of implementation to determine whether the Lettuce Bot would be a financially viable investment if the minimum wage is raised to $15 per hour.

E1-23B Lean production cost-benefit analysis *(Learning Objective 5)*

Pittinger Industries manufactures iPhone case covers. Jeanne Thompson, the CEO, is trying to decide whether to adopt a lean thinking model. She expects that adopting lean production would save $63,000 in warehousing expenses and $39,600 in spoilage costs. Adopting lean production will require several one-time up-front expenditures: $11,500 for an employee training program, $41,500 to streamline the plant's production process, and $7,500 to identify suppliers that will guarantee zero defects and on-time delivery.

Requirements
1. What are the total costs of adopting lean production?
2. What are the total benefits of adopting lean production?
3. Should the company adopt lean production? Why or why not?

SUSTAINABILITY

E1-24B Identify sustainability efforts as impacting people, planet, or profit *(Learning Objective 5)*

Sustainability involves more than just the impact of actions on the environment. The triple bottom line recognizes that a company has to measure its impact on its triple bottom line for its long-term viability. Following are examples of green initiatives recently undertaken at The Coca-Cola Company. For each example, indicate whether this initiative would *primarily* impact environmental, social, or economic factors.

a. Increased the number of countries where reduced-, low-, or no-calorie products represent more than 20% of the local product lineup.
b. For the twelfth consecutive year, improved overall water efficiency in manufacturing.
c. Achieved a 21% improvement in energy efficiency as compared to 2004.
d. Generated a profit for Coca-Cola's shareholders.
e. Worked with partners to recover and recycle the equivalent of 48% of bottles and cans used for finished beverages.
f. Exceeded the 2014 goal of 89% of direct suppliers' compliance with Coca-Cola's Supplier Guiding Principles (for human and workplace rights).
g. By 2014, Coca-Cola reduced the weight of its products sold by 15% since 2008.
h. By the end of 2014, 98% of Coca-Cola-owned facilities had achieved compliance with its Human Rights Policy.
i. Replaced a significant portion of the plastic used in its bottles with a plant-based material.
j. As of the end of 2014, 43% of Coca-Cola's U.S. workforce was multicultural.
k. Generated a positive economic benefit in every community in which Coca-Cola has facilities in the United States.
l. By the end of 2014, almost 80% of Coca-Cola's plants had achieved both the ISO 9001 Quality Management standard and the FSSC 22000 Food Safety Management System standard.
m. Reduced emissions from manufacturing in developed countries by 13% since 2004.
n. Lost-time incident (accident) rate fell from 4.1 incidents per 200,000 hours worked in 2010 to 1.9 incidents per 200,000 hours worked in 2014.

PROBLEMS Group A

P1-25A Management processes and accounting information (Learning Objectives 1 & 2)

Sarah Miracle has her own chain of music stores, Miracle Music. Her stores sell musical instruments, sheet music, and other related items. Music lessons and instrument repair are also offered through the stores. Miracle Music also has a website that sells music merchandise. The store has a staff of 80 people working in six departments: Sales, Repairs, Lessons, Web Development, Accounting, and Human Resources. Each department has its own manager.

Requirements

1. For each of the six departments, describe at least one decision/action for each of the three stages of management (planning, directing, and controlling). Prepare a table similar to the following for your answer:

	Planning	Directing	Controlling
Sales			
Repairs			
Lessons			
Web Development			
Accounting			
Human Resources			

2. For each of the decisions/actions you described in Part 1, identify what information is needed for that decision/action. Specify whether that information would be generated by the financial accounting system or the managerial accounting system at Miracle Music.

P1-26A Ethical dilemmas (Learning Objective 4)

Barb Perot is the new controller for EduTechno Software, which develops and sells educational software. Shortly before the December 31 fiscal year-end, Tony Cattrall, the company president, asks Perot how things look for the year-end numbers. He is not happy to learn that earnings growth may be below 15% for the first time in the company's five-year history. Cattrall explains that financial analysts have again predicted a 15% earnings growth for the company and that he does not intend to disappoint them. He suggests that Perot talk to the assistant controller, who can explain how the previous controller dealt with this situation. The assistant controller suggests the following strategies:

a. Persuade suppliers to postpone billing until January 1.
b. Record as sales certain software awaiting sale that is held in a public warehouse.
c. Delay the year-end closing a few days into January of the next year so that some of next year's sales are included as this year's sales.
d. Reduce the allowance for bad debts (and bad debts expense).
e. Postpone routine monthly maintenance expenditures from December to January.

Requirement

Which of these suggested strategies are inconsistent with IMA standards? What should Perot do if Cattrall insists that she follow all of these suggestions?

P1-27A ERP cost-benefit analysis *(Learning Objective 5)*

As CEO of Aqua Marine, Carrie Easton knows it is important to control costs and to respond quickly to changes in the highly competitive boat-building industry. When Rose Consulting proposes that Aqua Marine invest in an ERP system, she forms a team to evaluate the proposal: the plant engineer, the plant foreman, the systems specialist, the human resources director, the marketing director, and the management accountant.

A month later, management accountant Mark Cole reports that the team and Rose estimate that if Aqua Marine implements the ERP system, it will incur the following costs:

a. $435,000 in software costs
b. $95,000 to customize the ERP software and load Aqua Marine's data into the new ERP system
c. $105,000 for employee training

The team estimates that the ERP system should provide several benefits:

a. More efficient order processing should lead to savings of $105,000.
b. Streamlining the manufacturing process so that it maps into the ERP system will create savings of $125,000.
c. Integrating purchasing, production, marketing, and distribution into a single system will allow Aqua Marine to reduce inventories, saving $225,000.
d. Higher customer satisfaction should increase sales, which, in turn, should increase profits by $155,000.

Requirements

1. If the ERP installation succeeds, what is the dollar amount of the benefits?
2. Should Aqua Marine install the ERP system? Why or why not? Show your calculations.
3. Why did Easton create a team to evaluate Rose's proposal? Consider each piece of cost-benefit information that management accountant Cole reported. Which person on the team is most likely to have contributed each item? (*Hint:* Which team member is likely to have the most information about each cost or benefit?)

P1-28A Online order system cost-benefit analysis *(Learning Objective 5)*

Ferguson Gas wants to move its sales order system online. Under the proposed system, gas stations and other merchants will use a secure site to check the availability and current price of various products and place an order. Currently, customer service representatives take dealers' orders over the phone; they record the information on a paper form, then manually enter it into the firm's computer system.

CFO Stacey Wilson believes that dealers will not adopt the new online system unless Ferguson Gas provides financial assistance to help them purchase or upgrade their computer systems. Wilson estimates this one-time cost at $760,000. Ferguson Gas will also have to invest $160,000 in upgrading its own computer hardware. The cost of the software and the consulting fee for installing the system will be $220,000. The online system will enable Ferguson Gas to eliminate 25 clerical positions. Wilson estimates that the benefits of the new system's lower labor costs will have saved the company $1,340,000.

Requirement

Use a cost-benefit analysis to recommend to Wilson whether Ferguson Gas should proceed with the online ordering system. Give your reasons, showing supporting calculations.

P1-29A Continuation of P1-28A: revised estimates *(Learning Objective 5)*

Wilson revises her estimates of the benefits from the new system's lower labor costs as calculated in P1-28A. She now thinks the savings will be only $935,000.

Requirements

1. Compute the expected benefits of the online ordering system.
2. Would you recommend that Ferguson Gas accept the proposal?
3. Before Wilson makes a final decision, what other factors should she consider?

PROBLEMS Group B

P1-30B **Management processes and accounting information** (*Learning Objectives 1 & 2*)

Bryan Haas has his own electronics retail chain, TechnoGeek. His stores sell computer parts, audiovisual equipment, consumer electronics, and related items. Custom computer building and electronics repair are also offered. In addition, TechnoGeek has a website to sell its merchandise. The store has a staff of 90 people working in six departments: Sales, Customization, Repairs, Web Development, Accounting, and Human Resources. Each department has its own manager.

Requirements

1. For each of the six departments, describe at least one decision/action for each of the three stages of management (planning, directing, and controlling). Prepare a table similar to the following for your answer:

	Planning	Directing	Controlling
Sales			
Repairs			
Customization			
Web Development			
Accounting			
Human Resources			

2. For each of the decisions/actions you described in Part 1, identify what information is needed for that decision/action. Specify whether that information would be generated by the financial accounting system or the managerial accounting system at TechnoGeek.

P1-31B **Ethical dilemmas** (*Learning Objective 4*)

Maria Dees is the new controller for Harmony Tennis, a designer and manufacturer of tennis attire. Shortly before the December 31 fiscal year-end, Harmony Sapp (the company president) asks Dees how things look for the year-end numbers. Sapp is not happy to learn that earnings growth may be below 10% for the first time in the company's five-year history. Sapp explains that financial analysts have again predicted a 12% earnings growth for the company and that she does not intend to disappoint them. She suggests that Dees talk to the assistant controller, who can explain how the previous controller dealt with this situation. The assistant controller suggests the following strategies:

a. Postpone planned advertising expenditures from December to January.
b. Do not record sales returns and allowances on the basis that they are individually immaterial.
c. Persuade retail customers to accelerate January orders to December.
d. Reduce the allowance for bad debts (and bad debts expense).
e. Harmony Tennis ships finished goods to public warehouses across the country for temporary storage until it receives firm orders from customers. As Harmony Tennis receives orders, it directs the warehouse to ship the goods to nearby customers. The assistant controller suggests recording goods sent to the public warehouses as sales.

Requirement

Which of these suggested strategies are inconsistent with IMA standards? What should Dees do if Sapp insists that she follow all of these suggestions?

P1-32B ERP cost-benefit analysis (Learning Objective 5)

As CEO of Riverside Marine, Rachel Moore knows it is important to control costs and to respond quickly to changes in the highly competitive boat-building industry. When Gerbig Consulting proposes that Riverside Marine invest in an ERP system, she forms a team to evaluate the proposal: the plant engineer, the plant foreman, the systems specialist, the human resources director, the marketing director, and the management accountant.

A month later, management accountant Miles Cobalt reports that the team and Gerbig estimate that if Riverside Marine implements the ERP system, it will incur the following costs:

a. $390,000 in software costs
b. $85,000 to customize the ERP software and load Riverside Marine's data into the new ERP system
c. $112,000 for employee training

The team estimates that the ERP system should provide several benefits:

a. More efficient order processing should lead to savings of $185,000.
b. Streamlining the manufacturing process so that it maps into the ERP system will create savings of $255,000.
c. Integrating purchasing, production, marketing, and distribution into a single system will allow Riverside Marine to reduce inventories, saving $215,000.
d. Higher customer satisfaction should increase sales, which, in turn, should increase profits by $150,000.

Requirements

1. If the ERP installation succeeds, what is the dollar amount of the benefits?
2. Should Riverside Marine install the ERP system? Why or why not? Show your calculations.
3. Why did Moore create a team to evaluate Gerbig's proposal? Consider each piece of cost-benefit information that management accountant Cobalt reported. Which person on the team is most likely to have contributed each item? (*Hint:* Which team member is likely to have the most information about each cost or benefit?)

P1-33B Online order system cost-benefit analysis (Learning Objective 5)

Union Gas wants to move its sales order system online. Under the proposed system, gas stations and other merchants will use a secure site to check the availability and current price of various products and place an order. Currently, customer service representatives take dealers' orders over the phone; they record the information on a paper form, then manually enter it into the firm's computer system.

CFO Kate Bronson believes that dealers will not adopt the new online system unless Union Gas provides financial assistance to help them purchase or upgrade their computer network. Bronson estimates this one-time cost at $765,000. Union Gas will also have to invest $150,000 in upgrading its own computer hardware. The cost of the software and the consulting fee for installing the system will be $240,000. The online system will enable Union Gas to eliminate 25 clerical positions. Bronson estimates that the new system's lower labor costs will have saved the company $1,370,000.

Requirement

Use a cost-benefit analysis to recommend to Bronson whether Union Gas should proceed with the online ordering system. Give your reasons, showing supporting calculations.

P1-34B Continuation of P1-33B: revised estimates (Learning Objective 5)

Consider the Union Gas proposed entry into the online ordering system in P1-33B. Bronson revises her estimates of the benefits from the new system's lower labor costs. She now thinks the savings will be only $936,000.

Requirements

1. Compute the expected benefits of the online ordering system.
2. Would you recommend that Union Gas accept the proposal?
3. Before Bronson makes a final decision, what other factors should she consider?

Serial Case

C1-35 Discuss how managerial accounting can be used at Caesars Palace
(Learning Objectives 1, 2, 3, 4, and 5)

Note: This story is the first part of the Caesars Entertainment Corporation serial case contained in every chapter in this textbook.

Caesars Palace® Las Vegas, owned and operated by Caesars Entertainment Corporation (CZR), opened in 1966. The Nevada hotel-and-casino complex has been featured in several movies including *Rain Man*, *Iron Man*, and *The Hangover Part III*. Caesars Palace is the twelfth largest hotel in the world.[17] Caesars Palace® Las Vegas, at the start of 2015, included six towers (named Augustus, NOBU Hotel, Julius (formerly named Roman), Palace, Octavius, and Forum) containing almost 4,000 guest rooms. Beyond guest accommodations, the complex also included casinos, retail shops, restaurants, nightclubs, a 4,296-seat entertainment venue, and a large convention facility.

Caesars Palace® Las Vegas made headlines when it undertook a $75 million renovation. In mid-September 2015, the hotel closed its then-named Roman Tower, which was last updated in 2001, and started a major renovation of the 567 rooms housed in that tower. On January 1, 2016, the newly renamed Julius Tower reopened, replacing the Roman Tower. In addition to renovating the existing rooms and suites in the former Roman Tower, 20 guest rooms were added to the tower.

Each guest room in the Julius Tower features designer furniture, including beds boasting a custom-upholstered headboard, thick carpet, contemporary paint colors, a 55-inch flat-screen TV, and upscale artwork. Each guest room has a stocked minibar, likely offering such standard favorites as gummy bears, candy bars, beer, vodka, water, carbonated soft drinks, chips, and other assorted snacks and beverages. Each bathroom has a double-sink floating vanity, custom-lighted vanity mirrors, a stone shower with two glass sides, and both a rain shower and a hand-held showerhead. In-room toiletries boast the luxurious Gilchrist & Soames-branded soap and shampoo.

With the renovation completed, Caesars expects the Julius Tower room rate to average around $149 per night. This increase, a $25 or 20.2% increase, reflects, in part, the room improvements.

Requirement

What types of decisions might the management of Caesars Palace® Las Vegas need to make over the next several years? In other words, how might managerial accounting information be useful to the management of Caesars Palace® Las Vegas?

---

[17]Source: https://en.wikipedia.org/wiki/List_of_largest_hotels_in_the_world, as of January 8, 2016.

CRITICAL THINKING

Discussion & Analysis

A1-36 Discussion Questions

1. What are the three main areas of management's responsibility? How are these three areas interrelated? How does managerial accounting support each of the responsibility areas of managers?

2. What is the Sarbanes-Oxley Act of 2002 (SOX)? How does SOX affect financial accounting? How does SOX impact managerial accounting? Is there any overlap between financial and managerial accounting in terms of the SOX impact? If so, what are the areas of overlap?

3. Why is managerial accounting more suitable for internal reporting than for financial accounting?

4. How can what is taught in managerial accounting help you in other careers other than accounting?

5. A company currently has all of its managerial accountants reporting to the controller. What might be inefficient about this organizational structure? How might the company restructure? What benefits would the restructuring offer?

6. What skills are required of a management accountant? In what college courses are these skills taught or developed? What skills would be further developed in the workplace?

7. What is the Institute of Management Accountants (IMA)? What is the American Institute of Certified Public Accountants? How could being a member of a professional organization help a person's career?

8. How might a Certified Management Accountant (CMA) certification benefit a person in his or her career? What skills are assessed on the CMA exam?

9. What are the four ethical standards in the Institute of Management Accountants' *Statement of Ethical Professional Practice*? Describe the meaning of each of the four standards. How does each of these standards impact planning, directing, and controlling?

10. What business trends are influencing managerial accounting today? How do these trends impact management accountants' roles in the organization?

11. The effect of sustainability on the planet (environment) is probably the most visible component of the triple bottom line. For a company with which you are familiar, list two examples of its sustainability efforts related to the planet.

12. One controversial area regarding sustainability is whether organizations should use their sustainability progress and activities in their advertising. Do you think a company should publicize its sustainability efforts? Why or why not?

Application & Analysis

Mini Cases

A1-37 Accountants and Their Jobs

Basic Discussion Questions

1. When you think of an accountant, whom do you picture? Do you personally know anyone (family member, friend, relative) whose chosen career is accounting? If so, does the person "fit" your description of an accountant or not?

2. Before reading this chapter, what did you picture accountants doing, day-in and day-out, at their jobs? From where did this mental picture come (e.g., movies, first accounting class, speaking with accountants, etc.)?

3. What skills do employers value highly? What does that tell you about "what accountants do" at their companies?

4. Many accounting majors start their careers in public accounting. Do you think most of them stay in public accounting? Discuss what you consider to be a typical career track for accounting majors.

5. If you are not an accounting major, how do the salaries of accountants compare with those of your chosen field? How do the opportunities compare (i.e., demand for accountants)?

Introduction to Managerial Accounting 45

A1-38 Ethics at Enron

ETHICS

Watch the movie *Enron: The Smartest Guys in the Room* (Magnolia Home Entertainment, 2005, Los Angeles, California).

Basic Discussion Questions

1. Do you think such behavior is common at other companies, or do you think this was a fairly isolated event?
2. How important is the "tone at the top" (the tone set by company leadership)?
3. Do you think you could be tempted to follow along if the leadership at your company had the same mentality as the leadership at Enron, or do you think you would have the courage to "just say no" or even be a "whistle-blower"?
4. Why do you think some people can so easily justify (at least to themselves) their unethical behavior?
5. In general, do you think people stop to think about how their actions will affect other people (e.g., the elderly in California who suffered due to electricity blackouts) or do they just "do their job"?
6. What was your reaction to the psychology experiment shown in the DVD? Studies have shown that unlike the traders at Enron (who received large bonuses), most employees really have very little to gain from following a superior's directive to act unethically. Why then do some people do it?
7. Do you think people weigh the potential costs of acting unethically with the potential benefits?
8. You are a business student and will someday work for a company or own a business. How will watching this movie impact the way you intend to conduct yourself as an employee or owner?
9. The reporter from *Fortune* magazine asked the question, "How does Enron make its money?" Why should every employee and manager (at every company) know the answer to this question?
10. In light of the "mark-to-market" accounting that enabled Enron to basically record any profit it wished to record, can you understand why some of the cornerstones of financial accounting are "conservatism" and "recording transactions at historical cost"?
11. How did employees of Enron (and employees of the utilities company in Oregon) end up losing billions in retirement funds?

A1-39 Interviewing a local company about sustainability *(Learning Objective 5)*

SUSTAINABILITY

In this project, you will be conducting an interview about sustainability efforts at a local organization. Find a local company or organization with which you are familiar. Arrange an interview with a manager from that organization. Before the interview, do a search on the Internet about sustainability efforts of companies in that same industry so that you can ask related questions. Use the following questions to start your interview; add relevant questions related to what you discover through your Internet search about sustainability efforts at similar companies. After the interview, write up a report of what you found during the interview. Conclude your report with your overall assessment of that organization's sustainability efforts.

1. What is the company's primary product or service? (*Note:* You should be able to answer this question BEFORE your interview.)
2. Does your company have a stated policy on sustainability? (*Note*: The company might refer to "green" practices or use some other similar term rather than using the exact term of "sustainability.") What is the policy?
3. How would this manager define "sustainability"? Is the manager's definition similar to the definition of "sustainability" in this chapter?
4. Regardless of whether the company has a sustainability policy, what sustainability efforts does the company make with respect to the environment? For example, does the company recycle its waste? What specific types of waste are recycled? Does the company purchase recycled-content products?
5. Is the amount (or percentage) of waste that is recycled tracked in a reporting system? Who gets reports on the organization's recycling efforts?

6. How does the company measure its impact on the environment (if it does)? (For example, does it measure its carbon footprint in total? Does it measure the carbon footprint of individual projects?)
7. Does the company do any external reporting of sustainability? If so, how long has the company been reporting on its sustainability efforts? If the company does not do any sustainability reporting at the current time, does it anticipate starting to report on its sustainability efforts in the near future?
8. In the manager's opinion, is sustainability important within that organization's industry? Why or why not?

ETHICS

A1-40 Ethics and casual conversations *(Learning Objective 4)*

Jane is an accountant at Merelix, a large international firm where she works on potential acquisitions. When Merelix is preparing to acquire a company, Jane is involved in filing the necessary paperwork with the Securities and Exchange Commission (SEC).

Jane has been dating Tom for two years; they are now discussing marriage. Tom works as a salesperson for a golf equipment distributor.

Over the past two years, Jane has talked with Tom about what she's doing at work. She does not go into great detail, but does occasionally mention company names. Jane has given her phone passcode to Tom so he can answer calls for her or look things up for her when she's the one driving. Tom has read some of her emails by using the phone passcode. He has also eavesdropped on a few phone conversations she has had when a colleague calls her from work with a question.

Unbeknownst to Jane, Tom has been sharing the information he has gotten from her with his stockbroker friend, Allen. Tom will call Allen to give him a "heads up" that Jane's company is going to be acquiring another company soon. Allen will then place an order to buy the stock of the company and will later split the profits with Tom.

Jane has not shared any information intentionally, nor has she directly profited from it.

Requirements

Using the IMA Statement of Ethical Professional Practice as an ethical framework, answer the following questions:

1. What is (are) the ethical issue(s) in this situation?
2. What are Jane's responsibilities as a management accountant?
3. Has Jane violated any part of the IMA Statement of Ethical Professional Practice? Support your answer.

REAL LIFE

A1-41 Using managerial accounting information to manage a Broadway production *(Learning Objectives 1 and 2)*

The Shubert Organization operates 20 theaters, including 17 on Broadway. It has brought hundreds of shows to Broadway over the decades, including *The Phantom of the Opera*, *Cats*, and *Les Miserables*. Several of its shows have been in the news in recent years including:

Mamma Mia!

The Broadway musical *Mamma Mia!* moved from the Winter Garden Theatre to the Broadhurst Theatre, both of which are on Broadway in New York City. *Mamma Mia!* will save up to $100,000 per week[18] in operating costs due to the Broadhurst's smaller size; the Broadhurst seats 1,160, while the Winter Garden seats 1,530. Theatre experts estimate the show's weekly costs to be approximately $600,000 to $700,000, and its weekly ticket sales are usually in the mid- to high-six-figure range.

Once

Once is a Tony Award–winning show on Broadway also produced by the Shubert Organization. *Once* is a musical about an Irish musician and a Czech immigrant who are drawn together by their shared love of music. *Once* opened on Broadway in March 2012. The show earned back the amount that the Shubert Organization had invested in it after just 21 weeks (169 performances).[19] The show continues its run on Broadway.

---

[18] "'Mamma Mia!' to Move," *The New York Times*, April 18, 2013, retrieved from http://artsbeat.blogs.nytimes.com/2013/04/18/mamma-mia-to-move/ on July 1, 2013.

[19] http://evamere.com/screen-to-stage-musical-transfer-once-recoups-in-record-time/

Memphis

Another Shubert-produced musical, *Memphis*, is loosely based on the story of a Memphis disc jockey (DJ) who was one of the first white DJs to play black music in the 1950s. *Memphis* was composed by David Bryan, the keyboard player of the band Bon Jovi. The show opened on Broadway in the Shubert Theatre in October 2009 and won several awards, including four Tony Awards. The Shubert Organization had planned to run *Memphis* through November 2012, but closed the show in August 2012 because ticket revenues could not support the longer run. Instead of finding another show to use the Shubert Theatre between August 2012 and April 2013, when the show *Matilda* was scheduled to open, the Shubert Organization decided to use the time to renovate the theater.

Questions

1. For each show that the Shubert Organization produces, what type of financial accounting information would be generated or recorded?
2. What information would producers of *Mamma Mia!* have needed to make the decision to move the show to a different theatre? What information would be provided by the financial accounting system? What information would be provided by the management accounting system?
3. What information would the producers of *Once* have needed to calculate that the original investment of the show had been earned? What information would producers need to decide to keep the show open? What information would be provided by the financial accounting system? What information would be provided by the management accounting system?
4. What information would the producers of *Memphis* have needed to decide to close the show early? What information would the Shubert Organization management have needed to decide to renovate the theater rather than produce another show after *Memphis* closed its run? What information would be provided by the financial accounting system? What information would be provided by the management accounting system?

Try It Solutions

page 11:

1. True
2. False. Management accounting is geared toward helping internal managers run the company efficiently and effectively.
3. True
4. True
5. True
6. False. Management accountants must be able to effectively communicate with people throughout the organization. As a result, they need to have strong oral and written communication skills.
7. True
8. False. The IMA (Institute of Management Accountants) issues the CMA certification. However, the AICPA has recently instituted the CGMA designation for qualified CPAs who have experience in business and industry.

page 24:

1. True
2. False. Big data is driving most business decisions.
3. True
4. True
5. False. Service makes up the largest sector of the U.S. economy.
6. False. Globalization has several significant implications for management accounting.
7. False. These types of systems are known as enterprise resource planning (ERP) systems.
8. True

2 Building Blocks of Managerial Accounting

lev radin/Alamy

Source: http://www.toyota-global.com/company/vision_philosophy/toyota_global_vision_2020.html; http://www.statista.com/statistics/275520/ranking-of-car-manufacturers-based-on-global-sales/

Learning Objectives

- **1** Distinguish among service, merchandising, and manufacturing companies
- **2** Describe the value chain and its elements
- **3** Distinguish between direct and indirect costs
- **4** Identify product costs and period costs
- **5** Prepare the financial statements for service, merchandising, and manufacturing companies
- **6** Describe costs that are relevant and irrelevant for decision making
- **7** Classify costs as fixed or variable and calculate total and average costs at different volumes

As the world's largest automotive manufacturer, Toyota has been guided by a global vision designed "to lead the way to the future of mobility, enriching lives around the world with the safest and most responsible ways of moving people." In order to achieve this vision, company managers must focus on researching and developing new, safe, and environmentally friendly technologies, and on designing, marketing, and distributing new models that will appeal to a diverse array of global markets. Toyota must also produce vehicles in the most efficient manner possible and provide customers with exceptional post-sales service. All of these business activities, which cost money to perform, impact Toyota's bottom line by driving market share and sales revenue. Toyota's keys to financial success include its focus on performing these business activities as cost efficiently as possible and using cost and revenue information to make profitable business decisions. In this chapter, we discuss the costs incurred by these different business activities: costs that both managers and accountants must understand in order to make profitable business decisions.

So far, we have seen how managerial accounting provides information that managers use to run their businesses more efficiently. Managers must understand basic managerial accounting terms and concepts before they can use the information to make good decisions. This terminology provides the common ground through which managers and accountants communicate. Without a common understanding of these concepts, managers may ask for (and accountants may provide) the wrong information for making decisions. As you will see, different types of costs are useful for different purposes. Both managers and accountants must have a clear understanding of the types of costs that are relevant to the decision at hand.

What Are the Most Common Business Sectors and Their Activities?

Before we talk about specific types of costs, let's consider the three most common types of companies and the business activities they perform.

Service, Merchandising, and Manufacturing Companies

Recall from Chapter 1 that many companies are beginning to adhere to the notion of a **triple bottom line**, in which the company's performance is evaluated not only in terms of profitability, but also in terms of its impact on people and the planet. Even so, for a business to flourish and grow in the long run, it will need to generate economic profits that are sufficiently large to attract and retain investors, as well as fuel future business expansion. Companies typically generate profit through one of three basic business models: they provide a service, they sell merchandise, or they manufacture products.

1 Distinguish among service, merchandising, and manufacturing companies

Service Companies

Service companies are in business to sell intangible services—such as health care, insurance, banking, and consulting. Recall from Chapter 1 that service firms now make up the largest sector of the U.S. economy. Because these types of companies sell services, they generally don't carry inventory. Some service providers carry a minimal amount of supplies inventory; however, this inventory is typically used for internal operations—not sold for profit. Service companies incur costs to provide services, advertise, and develop new services. For many service providers, salaries and benefits make up the majority of their costs.

Merchandising Companies

Merchandising companies such as Walmart and Best Buy resell tangible products they buy from manufacturers and suppliers. For example, Walmart buys clothing, toys, and electronics and resells them to customers at higher prices than what it pays for these goods. Merchandising companies include retailers (such as Walmart) and wholesalers. **Retailers** sell to consumers like you and me. **Wholesalers**, often referred to as "middlemen," buy products in bulk from manufacturers, mark up the prices, and then sell those products to retailers.

Because merchandising companies are in business to sell tangible goods, they carry a substantial amount of inventory. The cost of inventory includes the cost merchandisers pay for the goods *plus* all costs necessary to get the merchandise in place and ready to sell, such as freight-in costs and any import duties or tariffs paid on merchandise purchased from overseas suppliers. A merchandiser's balance sheet has just one inventory account called "Inventory" or "Merchandise Inventory." Besides incurring inventory-related costs, merchandisers also incur costs to operate their retail stores and websites, advertise, research new products and new store locations, and provide customer service.

Manufacturing Companies

Manufacturing companies use labor, plant, and equipment to convert raw materials into new finished products. For example, Toyota converts steel, tires, and fabric into high-performance vehicles using production labor and advanced manufacturing equipment. The vehicles are then sold to car dealerships at a price that is high enough to cover costs and generate a profit.

As shown in Exhibit 2-1, manufacturers carry three types of inventory:

1. **Raw materials inventory**: *All raw materials that will be used in manufacturing.* Toyota's raw materials include steel, glass, tires, upholstery fabric, engines, and other automobile components. They also include other physical materials used in the plant, such as machine lubricants and janitorial supplies.

2. **Work in process inventory**: *Goods that are partway through the manufacturing process but not yet complete.* At Toyota, the work in process inventory consists of partially completed vehicles.

3. **Finished goods inventory**: *Completed goods that have not yet been sold.* Toyota is in business to sell completed cars, not work in process. Once the vehicles are completed, they are no longer considered work in process, but rather they become part of finished goods inventory.

EXHIBIT 2-1 Manufacturers' Three Types of Inventory

Exhibit 2-2 summarizes the differences among service, merchandising, and manufacturing companies.

EXHIBIT 2-2 Service, Merchandising, and Manufacturing Companies

	Service Companies	Merchandising Companies	Manufacturing Companies
Examples	Southwest Airlines Bank of America Progressive Insurance Goldman Sachs	Amazon.com Best Buy Walmart The Home Depot	Procter & Gamble General Mills Apple Toyota
Primary Output	Intangible services	Tangible products purchased from manufacturers and suppliers	New tangible products made using raw materials, labor, and production equipment
Type(s) of Inventory	None	Inventory (or Merchandise Inventory)	Raw materials inventory Work in process inventory Finished goods inventory

STOP & THINK

What type of company is Chipotle?

Answer: Some companies don't seem to fit nicely into one of the three categories previously discussed. For example, Chipotle has some elements of a service company (it serves hungry patrons), some elements of a manufacturing company (employees convert raw ingredients into finished meals), and some elements of a merchandising company (it sells ready-to-serve bottled drinks). Despite all of these different operating activities, restaurants are considered to be in the service sector.

As the "Stop & Think" feature shows, not all companies are strictly service, merchandising, or manufacturing firms. Recall from Chapter 1 that the U.S. economy is shifting more toward service-based companies. Many traditional manufacturers, such as General Electric (GE) and Ford, have developed profitable service segments that add additional profit to the company's bottom line. Even merchandising firms are getting into the "service game." For example, retailers often sell extended warranties on products ranging from furniture and major appliances to sporting equipment and consumer electronics. While the merchandiser recognizes a liability for these warranties, the price charged to customers for the warranties greatly exceeds the company's cost of fulfilling its warranty obligations, thus providing additional profit to the merchandiser.

> **Why is this important?**
> "All employees should have an **understanding** of their company's basic business model. The **Enron scandal** was finally brought to light as a **result** of someone seriously asking, "How does this company actually **make money?**" If the business model does not make **logical sense**, something fishy may be going on."

Which Business Activities Make Up the Value Chain?

Many people describe Toyota, General Mills, and Apple as manufacturing companies. But it would be more accurate to say that these are companies that *do* manufacturing. Why? Because companies that do manufacturing also do many other things. For example, even though Apple is a manufacturing company, it may be best known for its technological design innovations. Likewise, although Toyota is a manufacturer, it also conducts research to determine what type of new technology to integrate into next year's models. Toyota designs the new models based on its research and then produces, markets, distributes, and services the cars. These activities form Toyota's **value chain**—the activities that add value to the company's products and services. The value chain is pictured in Exhibit 2-3.

2 Describe the value chain and its elements

EXHIBIT 2-3 The Value Chain

The value chain activities also cost money. To set competitive, yet profitable selling prices, Toyota must consider all of the costs incurred along the value chain, not just the costs incurred in manufacturing vehicles. Let's briefly consider some of the costs incurred in each element of the value chain.[1]

---
[1] Toyota Motor Corp 2014 Annual report and Toyota.com.

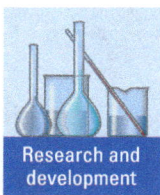

Research and Development (R&D): *Researching and developing new or improved products or services and the processes for producing them.* Toyota continually engages in researching and developing new technologies to incorporate in its vehicles (such as fuel cells, artificial intelligence, and pre-crash safety systems). Much of the R&D is aimed at safety and accessibility; improving how machines and humans work together. Toyota also researches and develops new technologies to use in its manufacturing plants (such as advanced manufacturing robotics). In 2014, Toyota spent 910.5 billion yen (approximately $7.7 billion) on R&D.

Design: *Detailed engineering of products and services and the processes for producing them.* Toyota's goal is to design vehicles that create total customer satisfaction, including satisfaction with vehicle style, features, safety, and quality. As a result, Toyota updates the design of older models (such as the Corolla) and designs new prototypes on a regular basis (such as the i-Road, a three-wheel electric commuter vehicle, and the Mirai, the first fuel cell vehicle for the mass market). Part of the design process also includes determining how to mass-produce the vehicles. Because Toyota produces over 8 million vehicles per year, engineers must design production plants that are efficient, yet flexible enough to allow for new features and models.

Production or Purchases: *Resources used by manufacturers to produce a product or by merchandising companies to purchase finished merchandise intended for resale.* For Toyota, the production activity includes all costs incurred to *make* the vehicles. These costs include raw materials (such as steel), plant labor (such as machine operators' wages), and manufacturing overhead (such as factory utilities and depreciation). As you can imagine, factories are very expensive to build and operate.

For a merchandiser such as Best Buy, this value chain activity includes the cost of purchasing the inventory that the company plans to sell to customers. It also includes all costs associated with getting the inventory to the store, including freight-in costs and any import duties and tariffs that might be incurred if the merchandise was purchased from overseas.

Marketing: *Promotion and advertising of products or services.* The goal of marketing is to create consumer demand for products and services. Toyota uses print advertisements in magazines and newspapers, billboards, television commercials, and the Internet to market its vehicles in both existing and emerging global markets. Some companies use star athletes and sporting events to market their products. Each method of advertising costs money but adds value by reaching different target customers.

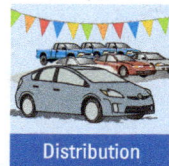

Distribution: *Delivery of products or services to customers.* On the one hand, Toyota sells most of its vehicles through traditional brick-and-mortar dealerships. On the other hand, Amazon sells and distributes its products almost entirely using a web-based sales platform and then ships the products directly to customers. Other industries use different distribution mechanisms, such as catalog sales and home-based parties.

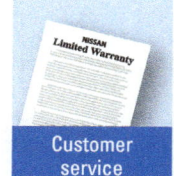

Customer Service: *Support provided for customers after the sale.* Toyota incurs substantial customer service costs, especially in connection with warranties on new car sales. Toyota generally warranties its vehicles for the first three years and/or 36,000 miles, whichever comes first. Historically, Toyota has had one of the best reputations in the auto industry for excellent quality. However, 2009–2010 proved to be costly and difficult years for the company, as recalls were made on over 14 million vehicles. In addition to the cost of repairing the vehicles, the company incurred millions of dollars in costs related to government fines, lawsuits, and public relations campaigns. However, as a result of the company's commitment to building safe and reliable vehicles, Toyota once again regained the title of the number-one carmaker in the world in 2012 and has continued to hold the number one position for the last four years, selling over 10 million vehicles per year.

Coordinating Activities Across the Value Chain

Many of the value chain activities occur in the order discussed here. However, managers cannot simply work on R&D and not think about customer service until after selling the car. Rather, cross-functional teams work on R&D, design, production, marketing, distribution, and customer service simultaneously. As the teams develop new model features, they also plan how to produce, market, and distribute the redesigned vehicles. They also consider how the new design will affect warranty costs. Recall from the last chapter that management accountants typically participate in these cross-functional teams. Even at the highest level of global operations, Toyota uses cross-functional teams to implement its business goals and strategy.

The value chain pictured in Exhibit 2-3 also reminds managers to control costs over the value chain as a whole. For example, Toyota spends more in R&D and product design to increase the quality of its vehicles, which in turn reduces customer service costs. Even though R&D and design costs are higher, the total cost of the vehicle—as measured throughout the entire value chain—is potentially lower as a result of this trade-off. Enhancing its reputation for safe, high-quality, innovative products has also enabled Toyota to increase its market share.

> **Why is this important?**
>
> "All activities in the **value chain** are important, yet each costs **money** to perform. Managers must understand how **decisions** made in one area of the value chain will **affect the costs** incurred in other areas of the value chain."

Sustainability and the Value Chain

Progressive companies will incorporate sustainability throughout every function of the value chain. However, experts estimate that 90% of sustainability occurs at the design stage. At the design stage, companies determine how the product will be used by customers, how easily the product can be repaired or eventually recycled, and the types of raw materials and manufacturing processes necessary to produce the product. Thus, good design is essential to the creation of environmentally friendly, safe products that enhance people's lives. For example, companies can integrate sustainability throughout the value chain by:

- **Researching and developing environmentally safe packaging.** Many companies are actively researching ways to reduce the amount of packaging used with their products as well as developing new types of packaging that are less harmful to the environment. In 2015, McDonald's achieved the goal of sourcing 100% of its packaging for its European operations from recycled sources or from forests certified by the Forest Stewardship Council. That same year, the company also pledged to end deforestation across the company's entire global supply chain.[2]

- **Designing products using life-cycle assessment and biomimicry.** <u>Life-cycle assessment</u> means the company analyzes the environmental impact of a product, from "cradle-to-grave," in an attempt to minimize negative environmental consequences throughout the entire lifespan of the product. For example, after studying the life cycles of its products, Procter & Gamble (P&G) discovered that about three-quarters of the energy used by consumers in washing their clothes comes from heating the water. As a result, the company developed Coldwater Tide, which is effective for laundering in cold water, thereby conserving energy. This product is a win–win for the environment and the company: the product is saving energy while also generating millions in annual sales revenue.[3]

    <u>Biomimicry</u> means that a company tries to mimic, or copy, natural biological features and processes. For example, Ford Motor Company and P&G are studying the gecko, nature's perfect example of a creature able to stick to surfaces without any liquids or adhesive substances, and then release from the surface, without any leaving sticky residue. The companies envision innovative adhesive applications from this research that will generate revenue, save money, and be more environmentally friendly.[4] Another aspect of biomimicry

---

[2]http://www.environmentalleader.com/2015/11/10/mcdonalds-achieves-100-sustainable-packaging-goal/
[3]http://www.nytimes.com/2011/09/17/business/cold-water-detergents-get-a-chilly-reception.html?pagewanted=1&_r=0
[4]http://www.environmentalleader.com/2015/10/21/ford-looks-to-lizards-to-increase-recyclability-improve-adhesives/

revolves around eliminating the concept of waste by creating "cradle-to-cradle" product life cycles. For example, Ricoh's copiers were designed so that at the end of a copier's useful life, Ricoh would collect and dismantle the product for usable parts, shred the metal casing, and use the parts and shredded material to build new copiers. The entire copier was designed so that nothing is wasted, or thrown out, except the dust from the shredding process. PT Tirta Marta has developed a "plastic" bag made from tapioca that can biodegrade in as little as two weeks,[5] whereas traditional plastic bags, according to the Environmental Protection Agency (EPA), can take as long as 1,000 years.[6]

- **Adopting sustainable purchasing practices.** Many of the world's largest companies, such as Walmart, Costco, and The Home Depot, are now actively assessing the sustainability level of potential suppliers as a factor in selecting suppliers. As leading retailers in the world, these companies' purchasing policies are forcing other companies to adopt more sustainable business practices.

- **Marketing with integrity.** Consumers are driving much of the sustainability movement by demanding that companies produce environmentally friendly products and limit or eliminate operational practices that have a detrimental impact on the environment and society. The LOHAS (Lifestyles of Health and Sustainability) market segment is estimated at $355 billion per year.[7] Thus, many companies are successfully spotlighting their sustainability initiatives in order to increase market share as well as attract potential investors and employees. However, <u>greenwashing</u>, the unfortunate practice of *overstating* a company's commitment to sustainability, can ultimately backfire as investors and consumers learn the truth about company operations. Hence, honesty and integrity in marketing are imperative.

- **Distributing using fossil-fuel alternatives and carbon offsets.** While the biofuel industry is still in its infancy, the production and use of biofuels, especially those generated from nonfood waste, are expected to grow exponentially in the near future. Companies whose business is heavily reliant upon fossil fuels, such as oil companies (Valero), airlines (United), and distribution companies (UPS), are especially interested in the development of sustainable fuel sources. In fact, many companies, such as UPS and Walmart, are investing in hybrid fleets in order to reduce energy consumption, which thereby reduces their costs. In addition, many companies are investing in carbon offsets through such measures as reforestation projects. For example, in 2013 UPS planted 1.3 million trees, and in 2014 it pledged to plant 2 million trees as part of its efforts to offset greenhouse gas emissions.[8] United Airlines offers a carbon-offset program that allows customers, as soon as they purchase their ticket, to offset the carbon emissions resulting from their air travel by donating to reforestation and renewable energy projects. The website automatically calculates the donation amount needed to offset the greenhouse gas emissions.

- **Providing customer service past the warranty date.** Environmentally conscious companies don't want customers discarding products that are in need of repair, or no longer serve the customer's needs or wants, thus, they provide the customer with other options. REI Co-op and Patagonia provide customers with free repair tips and offer repair services at a nominal charge. Best Buy recycles any electronic equipment regardless of where the customer bought it, and Apple buys back iPhones, iPads, and iPods by issuing credit toward the purchase of a new device.

If you are interested in learning more about what companies are doing to become more sustainable, visit the Environmentalleader.com website and sign up for its daily e-mail.

See Exercises E2-20A and E2-32B

---

[5] http://www.tirtamarta.com/green-plastic-solutions/about-us/
[6] http://www.nytimes.com/2007/04/01/weekinreview/01basics.html
[7] http://www.lohas.com/whos-changing
[8] http://compass.ups.com/how-ups-helps-turn-world-greener

How Do Companies Define Cost?

Now that you understand the most common types of companies and the primary business activities they perform, let's consider some of the specialized language that accountants use when referring to costs.

Cost Objects, Direct Costs, and Indirect Costs

A **cost object** is anything for which managers want to know the cost. Toyota's cost objects may include the following:

- Individual units (a specific, custom-ordered Prius)
- Different models (the Prius, Rav4, and Corolla)
- Alternative marketing strategies (television advertising, sponsorship of athletic events)
- Geographic segments of the business (United States, Europe, Japan)
- Departments (human resources, R&D, legal)
- Sustainability initiatives ("Toyota TogetherGreen" conservation programs)

Costs are classified as either direct or indirect with respect to the cost object.

- A **direct cost** is a cost that can be traced to the cost object, meaning the company can readily identify or associate the cost with the cost object. For example, say the cost object is one Prius. Toyota can easily trace, or associate, the cost of four tires with one specific Prius. Therefore, the tires are a direct cost of the vehicle.

- An **indirect cost**, in contrast, is a cost that relates to the cost object but cannot be traced specifically to it. Think of an indirect cost as a cost that is jointly used or shared by several cost objects. For example, Toyota incurs substantial cost to run a manufacturing plant, including utilities, property taxes, and depreciation. Toyota cannot build a Prius without incurring these costs, so the costs are related to the Prius. However, it's impossible to trace a specific amount of these costs to one Prius. These costs are shared by all of the vehicles produced in the plant during the period. Therefore, these costs are considered indirect costs of a single Prius.

Another example might help. Think about your university's football team. Direct costs of the football team would include their uniforms, footballs, coach's salary, and travel to away games. These costs are easily identifiable with and traceable to the football team, so they are considered direct costs of the football team. Indirect costs would include costs shared by the football team and other university athletic teams, such as the athletic director's salary, shared training facilities, and shared locker rooms. Since these resources are jointly used or shared by several athletic teams, not just the football team, they are considered indirect costs of the football team.

As shown in Exhibit 2-4, the same costs can be indirect with respect to one cost object, yet direct with respect to another cost object. For example, plant depreciation, plant property taxes, and plant utilities are indirect costs of a single Prius. However, if management wants to know how much it costs to operate the Prius manufacturing plant, the plant becomes the cost object; so the same depreciation, tax, and utility costs are direct costs of the manufacturing facility. Whether a cost is direct or indirect depends on the specified cost object. In this chapter, we'll be talking about a unit of product (such as one Prius) as the cost object.

If a company wants to know the *total* cost attributable to a cost object, it must **assign** all direct *and* indirect costs to the cost object. Assigning a cost simply means that you are "attaching" a cost to the cost object. For example, if Toyota wants to know the entire cost of manufacturing a Prius, it will need to assign both direct costs (such as the tires on the car) and indirect costs (such as

3 Distinguish between direct and indirect costs

> **Why is this important?**
> "As a manager **making decisions**, you'll need different types of **cost information** for different types of decisions. To get the **information** you really want, you'll have to **communicate** with the accountants using precise **definitions** of cost."

EXHIBIT 2-4 The Same Cost Can Be Direct or Indirect, Depending on the Cost Object

factory utilities) to the vehicle. Similarly, if the university wants to know the total cost of having a football team, it will have to consider both the direct and indirect costs related to the team.

The manner in which Toyota assigns costs depends on whether the costs are direct or indirect costs of the cost object. In our example, a specific vehicle is the cost object. Toyota can easily identify direct costs, such as tires, with specific vehicles. Therefore Toyota is able to **trace** direct costs to each vehicle manufactured in the plant. This results in a very precise cost figure, giving managers great confidence in the the amount of direct cost assigned to each vehicle. However, Toyota cannot trace indirect costs, such as utilities, to specific vehicles. Therefore, Toyota must **allocate** these indirect costs among all of the vehicles produced at the plant. The allocation process results in a less precise cost figure being assigned to each vehicle. We will discuss the allocation process in more detail in the following two chapters; but for now, think of allocation as dividing up the total indirect costs over all of the units produced, just as you might divide a pizza among friends. Exhibit 2-5 illustrates these concepts.

EXHIBIT 2-5 Assigning Direct and Indirect Costs to Cost Objects

> ### Try It!
> Assume a grocery store manager wants to know the cost of running the Produce Department. Thus, the Produce Department is the cost object. Which of the following would be considered direct costs of the Produce Department?
> 1. Wages of checkout clerks
> 2. Wages for workers in the Produce Department
> 3. Depreciation on refrigerated produce display cases
> 4. Cost of weekly advertisements in local newspaper
> 5. Cost of bananas, lettuce, and other produce
> 6. Baggies and twist ties available for shoppers in the Produce Department
> 7. Monthly lease payment for grocery store retail location
> 8. Cost of scales hanging in the Produce Department

Please see page 103 for solutions.

Costs for Internal Decision Making and External Reporting

Let's now consider how managers define the cost of one of their most important cost objects: their products. Managers need this information to determine the profitability of each product as well as to make other important business decisions. Managers define costs based on how the information will be used. Will the information be used for 1) internal decision making, or for 2) external reporting?

4 Identify product costs and period costs

Costs for Internal Decision Making

When making internal decisions, managers must consider all costs incurred across the value chain. For example, when determining a suitable selling price for a Prius, Toyota must consider the cost to research, design, manufacture, market, distribute, and service that model. A Prius's **total cost** includes the costs of *all resources used throughout the value chain*. For Toyota, the total cost of a particular model, such as the Prius, is the total cost to research, design, manufacture, market, distribute, and service that model. Before launching a new model, managers predict the total cost of the model to set a selling price that will cover *all costs* plus return a profit. By comparing each model's sales revenue with its total cost across the value chain, Toyota can determine which models are most profitable. Perhaps Rav4s are more profitable than Corollas. Marketing can then focus on advertising and promoting the most profitable models. We'll talk more about total costs in Chapter 8, where we discuss many common business decisions.

Costs for External Reporting

For external reporting purposes, management must follow Generally Accepted Accounting Principles (GAAP). For external reporting purposes, GAAP requires that certain costs of the company be attached, or assigned, to units of product in inventory, while other costs are treated as operating expenses of the period. Let's define each of these types of costs.

- **Product costs** are the costs incurred by *manufacturers to produce* their products or incurred by *merchandisers to purchase* their products. Notice how these costs relate to *obtaining inventory*, either through manufacturing the products or purchasing them. Thus, these costs are incurred in the production or purchases function of the value chain. For external financial reporting, GAAP requires that these costs be assigned to inventory until the related products are sold. When the products are sold, these costs are removed from the company's inventory and expensed as Cost of Goods Sold.

- **Period costs** are the costs incurred by the company that do *not* get treated as inventory, but rather, are expensed immediately in the period in which they are incurred. These costs do *not* relate to manufacturing or purchasing product. Rather, they include costs incurred in every other function of the value chain, including R&D, design, marketing, distribution, and customer service. In essence, any cost that is not treated as inventory, is treated as a period cost. While accountants refer to these costs as "period costs," most other people refer to them as "operating expenses" or "selling, general, and administrative expenses" (SG&A). These terms are essentially synonymous and arise from the fact that these are costs of operating the business over a specific period of time.

Keep the following two important rules of thumb in mind:

> Product costs are costs assigned to the company's inventory on the balance sheet. In essence, they are the costs of manufacturing or purchasing the company's products.
>
> Period costs are often called "operating expenses" or "selling, general, and administrative expenses" (SG&A) on the company's income statement. Period costs are always expensed in the period in which they are incurred and never become part of an inventory account.

Exhibit 2-6 shows that a company's total costs can be divided into two categories: product costs (those costs treated as part of inventory until the product is sold) and period costs (those costs expensed in the current period regardless of when inventory is sold). GAAP requires this distinction for external financial reporting. Study the exhibit carefully to make sure you understand how the two types of costs affect the income statement and balance sheet.

EXHIBIT 2-6 Total Costs, Product Costs, and Period Costs

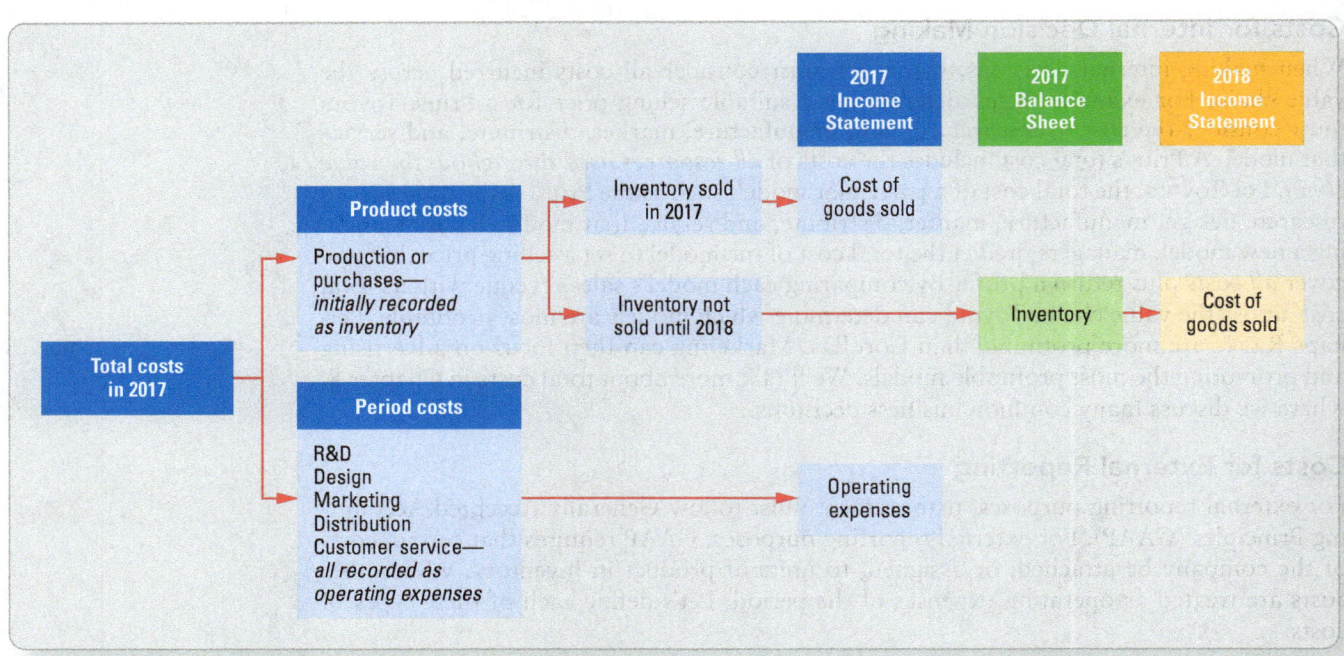

Now that you understand the difference between product costs and period costs, let's take a closer look at the specific costs that are treated as product costs in merchandising and manufacturing companies.

Merchandising Companies' Product Costs

Merchandising companies' product costs include *only* the cost of purchasing the inventory from suppliers plus any costs incurred to get the merchandise to the merchandiser's place of business and ready for sale. Typically, these additional costs include freight-in costs and import duties or tariffs, if the products were purchased from overseas. Why does the cost of the inventory include freight-in charges? Think of the last time you made a purchase from an online website, such as Amazon.com. The website may have shown the product's price as $15, but by the time you paid the shipping and handling charges, the product really cost you around $20. Likewise, merchandising companies pay freight-in charges to get the goods to their place of business. If they purchased the goods from overseas, there is a good chance they also had to pay import duties to bring the goods into the United States. As shown in Exhibit 2-7, these charges become part of the cost of their inventory.

EXHIBIT 2-7 Summary of a Merchandising Company's Total Costs

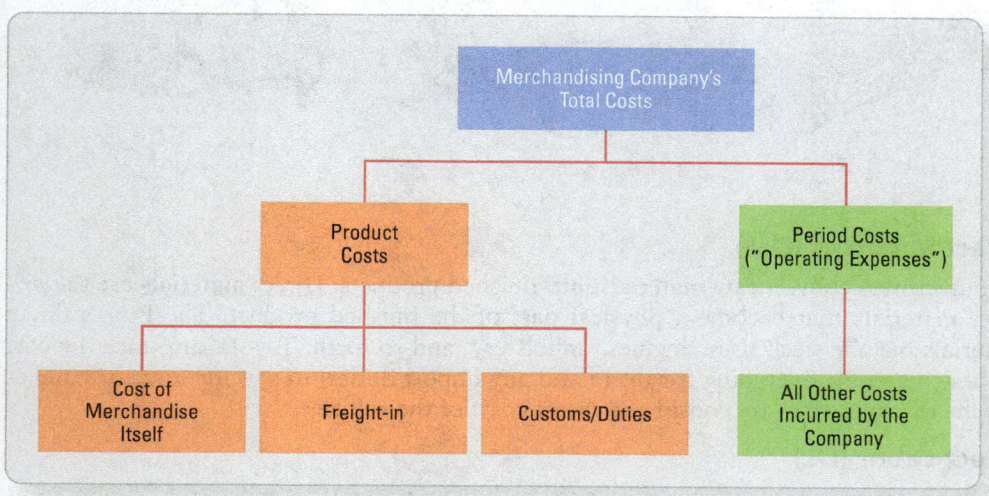

For example, The Home Depot's product costs include what the company paid for its store merchandise plus freight-in and import duties. The Home Depot records these costs in an asset account—Inventory—until it *sells* the merchandise. Once the merchandise is sold, it belongs to the customer, not The Home Depot. Therefore, The Home Depot takes the cost out of its inventory account and records it as an expense—the *cost of goods sold*. The Home Depot expenses all other costs incurred during the period, such as salaries, utilities, advertising, and property lease payments, as "operating expenses."

Try It!

Which of the following costs are treated as product costs by a *merchandising company*, such as Walmart? Which costs are treated as period costs?

1. Cost of leasing the retail locations
2. Cost of managers' and sales associates' salaries
3. Cost of merchandise purchased for resale
4. Cost of designing and operating the company's website
5. Cost of shipping merchandise to the store
6. Cost of providing free shipping to customers who buy product online
7. Cost of utilities used in running the retail locations
8. Cost of import duties paid on merchandise purchased from overseas suppliers
9. Depreciation on store shelving and shopping carts

Please see page 103 for solutions.

Manufacturing Companies' Product Costs

Manufacturing companies' product costs include *only* those costs related to producing, or manufacturing, their products. As shown in Exhibit 2-8, manufacturers such as Toyota incur three types of manufacturing costs when making a vehicle: direct materials, direct labor, and manufacturing overhead.

EXHIBIT 2-8 Summary of the Three Types of Manufacturing Costs

Direct Materials (DM)

Manufacturers convert raw materials into finished products. **Direct materials** are the *primary* materials that become a physical part of the finished product. The Prius's direct materials include steel, tires, engines, upholstery, and so forth. Toyota can trace the cost of these materials (including freight-in and any import duties) to specific units or batches of vehicles; thus, they are considered direct costs of the vehicles.

Direct Labor (DL)

Although many manufacturing facilities are highly automated, most still require some direct labor to convert raw materials into a finished product. **Direct labor** is the cost of compensating employees who physically convert raw materials into the company's products. At Toyota, direct labor includes the wages and benefits of machine operators and technicians who build and assemble the vehicles. Toyota can trace the time each of these employees spends working on specific units or batches of vehicles; thus, the cost of this labor is considered a direct cost of the vehicles.

Manufacturing Overhead (MOH)

The third production cost, **manufacturing overhead,** *includes all manufacturing costs other than direct materials and direct labor.* In other words, manufacturing overhead includes *all indirect manufacturing costs*. Manufacturing overhead is also referred to as factory overhead because all of these costs relate to the factory. Manufacturing overhead has three components: indirect materials, indirect labor, and other indirect manufacturing costs.

- **Indirect materials** include materials used in the plant that are not easily traced to individual units. For example, indirect materials often include janitorial supplies, oil and lubricants for the machines, and any physical components of the finished product that are very inexpensive. For example, Toyota might treat the invoice sticker placed on each vehicle's window as an indirect material rather than a direct material. Even though the cost of the sticker (roughly 10 cents) *could* be traced to the vehicle, it wouldn't make much sense to do so. Why? Because the cost of tracing the sticker to the vehicle outweighs the benefit management receives from the increased accuracy of the information.

- **Indirect labor** includes the cost of all employees working *in the plant* other than those employees directly converting the raw materials into the finished product. For example, at Toyota, indirect labor includes the salaries, wages, and benefits of plant forklift operators, plant security officers, plant janitors, and plant supervisors.

Building Blocks of Managerial Accounting 61

- **Other indirect manufacturing costs** include such *plant-related* costs as depreciation on the plant and plant equipment, plant property taxes and insurance, plant repairs and maintenance, and plant utilities. Indirect manufacturing costs have grown tremendously in recent years as manufacturers automate their plants with the latest advanced manufacturing technology.

Exhibit 2-9 summarizes how manufacturers classify their costs.

EXHIBIT 2-9 Summary of a Manufacturing Company's Total Costs

Prime and Conversion Costs

Managers and accountants sometimes talk about certain combinations of manufacturing costs. As shown in Exhibit 2-10, **prime costs** refer to the combination of direct materials and direct labor. Prime costs used to be the primary costs of production. However, as companies have automated production with expensive machinery, manufacturing overhead has become a greater cost of production. **Conversion costs** refer to the combination of direct labor and manufacturing overhead. These are the costs of *converting* raw materials into finished goods.

EXHIBIT 2-10 Prime and Conversion Costs

STOP & THINK

What is the difference between raw materials, direct materials, and indirect materials?

Raw materials are materials that have not yet been used. Once used, materials can be classified as direct or indirect. Direct materials are the primary physical components of a product. Indirect materials are materials used in the production plant that don't become part of the product (such as machine lubricants) or materials that do become part of the product but are insignificant in cost (such as the price sticker on a car).

Additional Labor Compensation Costs

The cost of labor, in all areas of the value chain, includes more than the salaries and wages paid to employees. The cost also includes company-paid fringe benefits such as health insurance, retirement plan contributions, payroll taxes, and paid vacations. These costs are very expensive. Health insurance premiums, which have seen double-digit increases for many years, often amount to $500–$1,500 per month for each employee electing coverage. Many companies also contribute an amount equal to 3% to 6% of their employees' salaries to company-sponsored retirement 401(k) plans. Employers must pay Federal Insurance Contributions Act (FICA) payroll taxes to the federal government for Social Security and Medicare, amounting to 7.65% of each employee's gross pay. In addition, most companies offer paid vacation and other benefits. Together, these fringe benefits usually cost the company an *additional* 35% beyond gross salaries and wages. Thus, an employee making a $40,000 salary actually costs the company about $54,000 to employ ($40,000 × 1.35). These fringe-benefit costs are expensed as period costs for all nonmanufacturing employees. However, they are treated as a product cost if they relate to employees working in the manufacturing plant. In Chapter 3 we'll discuss how these additional labor costs get assigned to products.

Recap: Product Costs Versus Period Costs

In this half of the chapter, you have learned about the activities and costs incurred by three different types of companies. You have also learned the difference between direct and indirect costs. Finally, you have learned the difference between product costs and period costs. Exhibit 2-11 summarizes some of these concepts for you.

EXHIBIT 2-11 Summary of Product Costs Versus Period Costs

	Total Costs Across the Value Chain	
	Product Costs	**Period costs**
Service Companies	None	All costs across value chain
Merchandising Companies	Cost of merchandise itself Freight-in Import duties and customs, if any	All costs across value chain except product costs
Manufacturing Companies	Direct materials Direct labor Manufacturing overhead	All costs across value chain except product costs
Accounting Treatment	Treat as inventory until product is sold. When sold, expense as "Cost of Goods Sold."	Expense in period incurred as "Operating Expenses" or "Selling, General, and Administrative Expenses."

Decision Guidelines

Building Blocks of Managerial Accounting

Dell engages in *manufacturing* when it assembles its computers, *merchandising* when it sells them on its website, and support *services* such as start-up and implementation services. Dell had to make the following types of decisions as it developed its accounting systems.

Decision	Guidelines

How do you distinguish among service, merchandising, and manufacturing companies? How do their balance sheets differ?	*Service companies:*
	• Provide customers with intangible services
	• Have no inventories on the balance sheet
	Merchandising companies:
	• Resell tangible products purchased ready-made from suppliers
	• Have only one category of inventory
	Manufacturing companies:
	• Use labor, plant, and equipment to transform raw materials into new finished products
	• Have three categories of inventory:
	  1. Raw materials inventory
	  2. Work in process inventory
	  3. Finished goods inventory

What business activities add value to companies?	All of the elements of the value chain, including the following: • R&D • Design • Production or purchases • Marketing • Distribution • Customer service
What costs should be assigned to cost objects such as products, departments, and geographic segments?	Both direct and indirect costs are assigned to cost objects. Direct costs are traced to cost objects, whereas indirect costs are allocated to cost objects.
Which costs are useful for internal decision making, and how are costs classified for external reporting?	Managers use *total costs* for internal decision making. However, GAAP requires companies to distinguish between product costs and period costs for external reporting purposes.
What costs are treated as product costs under GAAP?	• *Service companies:* Usually no product costs since they don't carry inventory • *Merchandising companies:* The cost of merchandise purchased for resale plus all of the costs of getting the merchandise to the company's place of business (for example, freight-in and import duties) • *Manufacturing companies:* Direct materials, direct labor, and manufacturing overhead
How are product costs treated on the financial statements?	Product costs are initially treated as an asset (inventory) on the balance sheet. These costs are expensed (as cost of goods sold) on the income statements when the products are sold.

SUMMARY PROBLEM 1

Requirements

1. Classify each of the following business costs into one of the six value chain elements:
   a. Costs associated with warranties and recalls
   b. Cost of shipping finished goods to overseas customers
   c. Costs a pharmaceutical company incurs to develop new drugs
   d. Cost of a 30-second commercial during the SuperBowl™
   e. Cost of making a new product prototype
   f. Cost of assembly labor used in the plant

2. For a manufacturing company, identify the following as either a product cost or a period cost. If it is a product cost, classify it as direct materials, direct labor, or manufacturing overhead.
   a. Depreciation on plant equipment
   b. Depreciation on salespeoples' automobiles
   c. Insurance on plant building
   d. Marketing manager's salary
   e. Cost of major components of the finished product
   f. Assembly-line workers' wages
   g. Costs of shipping finished products to customers
   h. Plant forklift operator's salary

SOLUTIONS

Requirement 1
a. Customer service
b. Distribution
c. Research and development
d. Marketing
e. Design
f. Production

Requirement 2
a. Product cost; manufacturing overhead
b. Period cost
c. Product cost; manufacturing overhead
d. Period cost
e. Product cost; direct materials
f. Product cost; direct labor
g. Period cost
h. Product cost; manufacturing overhead

How Are Product Costs and Period Costs Shown in the Financial Statements?

The difference between product costs and period costs is important because these costs are treated differently in the financial statements. All product costs remain in inventory accounts until the merchandise is sold; then, these costs become the cost of goods sold. In contrast, all period costs are expensed as "operating expenses" in the period in which they are incurred. Keep these differences in mind as we review the income statements of service firms (which have no inventory), merchandising companies (which purchase their inventory), and manufacturers (which make their inventory). We'll finish the section by comparing the balance sheets of these three different types of companies.

5 Prepare the financial statements for service, merchandising, and manufacturing companies

Service Companies

Service companies have the simplest income statement. Exhibit 2-12 shows the income statement of WSC Consulting, an e-commerce consulting firm. The firm has no inventory and thus, no product costs. Therefore, WSC Consulting's income statement has no Cost of Goods Sold. Rather, all of the company's costs are period costs, so they are expensed in the current period as "operating expenses."

EXHIBIT 2-12 Service Company Income Statement

	A	B	C	D
1	WSC Consulting			
2	Income Statement			
3	Year Ended December 31			
4				
5	Revenues		$ 160,000	
6	Less operating expenses:			
7	Salary expense	$ 106,000		
8	Office rent expense	18,000		
9	Depreciation expense	3,500		
10	Marketing expense	2,500		
11	Total operating expenses		130,000	
12	Operating income		$ 30,000	
13				

In this textbook, we will always be evaluating the company's "operating income" rather than its "net income." Why? Because internal managers are particularly concerned with the income generated through the company's ongoing, primary operations. To arrive at net income, we would need to add or subtract non-operating income and expenses, such as interest, and subtract income taxes. In general, **operating income** is simply the company's earnings before interest and income taxes.

Merchandising Companies

In contrast with service companies, a merchandiser's income statement features Cost of Goods Sold as the major expense. Exhibit 2-13 illustrates the income statement for Wholesome Foods, a regional grocery store chain. Notice how Cost of Goods Sold is deducted from Sales Revenue to yield the company's gross profit. Next, all operating expenses (*all period costs*) are deducted to arrive at the company's operating income.

EXHIBIT 2-13 Merchandiser's Income Statement

	A	B	C	D
1	**Wholesome Foods**			
2	**Income Statement**			
3	**For the Year Ended December 31**			
4	(all figures shown in thousands of dollars)			
5				
6	Sales revenues		$ 150,000	
7	Less: Cost of goods sold		106,500	
8	Gross profit		$ 43,500	
9	Less operating expenses:			
10	Salaries and wages	$ 5,000		
11	Rent and utilities	3,000		
12	Marketing	1,000		
13	Total operating expenses		9,000	
14	Operating income		$ 34,500	
15				

But how does a merchandising company calculate the Cost of Goods Sold?

- Most likely, the company uses bar coding to implement a **perpetual inventory** system during the year. If so, all inventory is labeled with a unique bar code that reflects (1) the sales price that will be charged to the customer, and (2) the "product cost" of the merchandise to the store. Every time a bar-coded product is scanned at the checkout counter, the company's accounting records are automatically updated to reflect (1) the sales revenue earned, (2) the cost of goods sold, and (3) the removal of the product from merchandise inventory.

- However, at the end of the period, merchandisers must also calculate Cost of Goods Sold using the **periodic inventory** method. Why? Because the company's accounting records only reflect those products that were scanned during checkout. Thus, the records would not reflect any breakage, theft, input errors, or obsolescence that occurred during the year. Exhibit 2-14 shows how to calculate Cost of Goods Sold using the periodic method.

EXHIBIT 2-14 Calculation of Cost of Goods Sold for a Merchandising Firm

	A	B	C	D
1	**Calculation of Cost of Goods Sold**			
2	Beginning inventory	$ 9,500		
3	Plus: Purchases, freight-in, and any import duties	110,000		
4	Cost of goods available for sale	$ 119,500		
5	Less: Ending inventory	13,000		
6	Cost of goods sold	$ 106,500		
7				

In this calculation, we start with the beginning inventory and add to it all of the company's *product costs* for the period: the cost of the merchandise purchased from suppliers, freight-in, and any import duties. The resulting total reflects the cost of all goods that were available for sale during the period. Then we subtract the cost of the products still in ending inventory to arrive at the Cost of Goods Sold.

Try It!

Compute Cost of Goods Sold for Ralph's Sporting Goods, a merchandising company, given the following information:

Advertising expense	$ 25,000
Purchases of merchandise	400,000
Salaries expense	80,000
Freight-in and import duties	20,000
Lease of store	75,000
Beginning inventory	35,000
Ending inventory	38,000

Please see page 103 for solutions.

Manufacturing Companies

Exhibit 2-15 shows the income statement for Proquest, a manufacturer of tennis balls. As you can see, the income statement for a manufacturer is essentially identical to that of a merchandising company. The only *real* difference is that the company is selling product that it has *made*, rather than merchandise that it has *purchased*. As a result, the calculation of Cost of Goods Sold is different from that shown in Exhibit 2-14.

EXHIBIT 2-15 Manufacturer's Income Statement

	A	B	C	D
1	Proquest			
2	Income Statement			
3	For the Year Ended December 31			
4	(all figures shown in thousands of dollars)			
5				
6	Sales revenues		$ 65,000	
7	Less: Cost of goods sold		40,000	
8	Gross profit		$ 25,000	
9	Less operating expenses:			
10	Selling and marketing expenses	$ 8,000		
11	General and administrative expenses	2,000		
12	Total operating expenses		10,000	
13	Operating income		$ 15,000	
14				

Calculating Cost of Goods Manufactured and Cost of Goods Sold

Exhibit 2-16 illustrates how the manufacturer's *product costs* (direct material used, direct labor, and manufacturing overhead) flow through the three inventory accounts before they become part of Cost of Goods Sold. In order to calculate Cost of Goods Sold, a manufacturer must first figure out the amount of direct materials *used* and the Cost of Goods Manufactured.

As you see in Exhibit 2-16, the **Cost of Goods Manufactured** represents the cost of those goods that were completed and moved to Finished Goods Inventory during the period.

EXHIBIT 2-16 Flow of Costs Through a Manufacturer's Financial Statements

Using Exhibit 2-16 as a guide, let's walk through the calculation of Cost of Goods Sold. We'll use three steps. Each step focuses on a different inventory account: Raw Materials, Work in Process, and Finished Goods.

STEP 1: **Calculate the cost of the direct materials used during the year**

Step 1 simply analyzes what happened in the *Raw Materials Inventory* account during the year. As shown in Exhibit 2-17, we start with the beginning balance in the Raw Materials Inventory account and add to it all of the direct materials purchased during the year, including any freight-in and import duties. This tells us the cost of materials that were available for use during the year. Finally, by subtracting out the ending balance of Raw Materials Inventory, we are able to back into the cost of the direct materials that were used.[9]

EXHIBIT 2-17 Calculation of Direct Materials Used

	A	B	C
1	**Calculation of Direct Materials Used**		
2	**(Analyze Raw Materials Inventory account)**		
3			
4	Beginning Raw Materials Inventory	$ 9,000	
5	Plus: Purchases of direct materials, freight-in, and import duties	27,000	
6	Materials available for use	$ 36,000	
7	Less: Ending Raw Materials Inventory	22,000	
8	Direct materials used	$ 14,000	
9			

[9]In this chapter, we'll assume that the Raw Materials account only contains direct materials because the company uses indirect materials as soon as they are purchased. In Chapter 3, we expand the discussion to include manufacturers who store both direct and indirect materials in the Raw Materials Inventory account.

STEP 2: **Calculate the cost of goods manufactured**

Step 2 simply analyzes what happened in the *Work in Process* account during the year. As shown in Exhibit 2-18, we start with the beginning balance in Work in Process and then add to it all three manufacturing costs that were incurred during the year (direct materials used, direct labor, and materials overhead). Finally, by subtracting out the goods still being worked on at year-end (ending Work in Process Inventory), we are able to back into the Cost of Goods Manufactured (CGM). This figure represents the cost of manufacturing the units that were *completed* and sent to Finished Goods Inventory during the year.

EXHIBIT 2-18 Calculation of Cost of Goods Manufactured

	A	B	C
1	Calculation of Cost of Goods Manufactured		
2	(Analyze Work in Process Inventory account)		
3			
4	Beginning Work in Process Inventory	$ 2,000	
5	Plus manufacturing costs incurred:		
6	Direct materials used	14,000	
7	Direct labor	19,000	
8	Manufacturing overhead	12,000	
9	Total manufacturing costs to account for	$ 47,000	
10	Less: Ending Work in Process Inventory	5,000	
11	Cost of goods manufactured (CGM)	$ 42,000	
12			

STEP 3: **Calculate the cost of goods sold**

Step 3 simply analyzes what happened in the *Finished Goods Inventory* account during the year. As shown in Exhibit 2-19, we start with the beginning balance of Finished Goods Inventory and add to it the product that was manufactured during the year (CGM) to arrive at the cost of the total goods available for sale. Finally, just like with a merchandiser, we subtract what was left in Finished Goods Inventory to back into the Cost of Goods Sold.

EXHIBIT 2-19 Calculation of Cost of Goods Sold

	A	B	C
1	Calculation of Cost of Goods Sold		
2	(Analyze Finished Goods Inventory account)		
3			
4	Beginning Finished Goods Inventory	$ 6,000	
5	Plus: Cost of goods manufactured (CGM)	42,000	
6	Cost of goods available for sale	$ 48,000	
7	Less: Ending Finished Goods Inventory	8,000	
8	Cost of goods sold	$ 40,000	
9			

By analyzing, step by step, what occurred in each of the three inventory accounts, we were able to calculate the Cost of Goods Sold shown on the company's Income Statement (see Exhibit 2-15). Some companies combine Steps 1 and 2 into one schedule called the Schedule of Cost of Goods Manufactured. Others combine all three steps into a Schedule of Cost of Goods Sold.

You may be wondering where all of the data come from. The beginning inventory balances were simply last year's ending balances. The purchases of direct materials and the incurrence of direct labor and manufacturing overhead would have been captured in the company's accounting records when those costs were incurred. Finally, the ending inventory balances come from doing a physical inventory count at the end of the year. In the coming chapters, we'll show you different systems manufacturers use to keep track of the product cost associated with the units still in the three inventory accounts.

Comparing Balance Sheets

Now that we've looked at the income statement for each type of company, let's consider their balance sheets. The only difference relates to how inventory is shown in the current asset section:

- Service companies show no Inventory.
- Merchandising companies show Inventory or Merchandise Inventory.
- Manufacturing companies show Raw Materials, Work in Process, and Finished Goods Inventory.

Sometimes manufacturers just show "Inventories" on the face of the balance sheet but disclose the breakdown of the inventory accounts (Raw Materials, Work in Process, and Finished Goods) in the footnotes to the financial statements.

Sustainability and Corporate Reporting

In addition to generating a full set of financial statements for external users, many companies are now preparing and issuing Corporate Social Responsibility, or CSR, reports. These reports provide sustainability-related information to a variety of stakeholders, including investors and creditors, customers, government regulators, nongovernmental organizations (NGOs), and the general public. Although these reports are still voluntary in the United States, the move toward providing stakeholders with more sustainability-related data is growing. For example, the following issued CSR reports:

- 92% of the world's 250 largest companies (2015)[10]
- 75% of the S&P 500 companies (2014)[11]

Although sustainability reporting is still in its infancy, the Global Reporting Initiative, or GRI, has become the dominant framework for sustainability reporting. The GRI report follows the triple-bottom-line approach (people, planet, profit) by specifying metrics that companies should report on related to each of the three pillars of sustainability:

- Social performance metrics—for example, fair labor and human rights practices
- Environmental performance metrics—for example, greenhouse gas emissions and total water use
- Economic performance metrics—for example, revenues, operating costs, and so forth.

Sustainability reporting is not just for external reporting; companies also use it as a tool for internal change management. The GRI reporting process helps an organization illuminate areas of social and environmental impact that need improvement. It also helps management track the company's social and environmental progress by comparing baseline performance metrics with those achieved over time. The old adage proves just as true for nonfinancial data as it does for financial data: "You can't manage what you don't measure."

Finally, in a 2014 survey, Verdantix found that the Big Four accounting firms dominated both the sustainability consulting and sustainability assurance services markets.[12] Thus, students who wish to enter the accounting profession should be aware of these reporting developments.

---

[10]KPMG, 2015 Survey of Corporate Responsibility Reporting.

[11]Governance and Accountability Institute, http://www.ga-institute.com/nc/issue-master-system/news-details/article/flash-report-seventy-five-percent-75-of-the-sp-index-published-corporate-sustainability-rep.html.

[12]http://research.verdantix.com/index.cfm/papers/Press.Details/press_id/105/verdantix-global-survey-finds-the-big-four-accounting-firms-continue-to-dominate-the-sustainability-brands-landscape/

What Other Cost Terms Are Used by Managers?

So far in this chapter, we have discussed direct versus indirect costs and product costs versus period costs. Now let's turn our attention to other cost terms that managers and accountants use when planning and making decisions.

6 Describe costs that are relevant and irrelevant for decision making

Controllable Versus Uncontrollable Costs

When deciding to make business changes, management needs to distinguish controllable costs from uncontrollable costs. In the long run, most costs are **controllable**, meaning management is able to influence or change them. However, in the short run, companies are often locked in to certain costs arising from previous decisions. These are called **uncontrollable costs**. For example, Toyota has little or no control over the property tax and insurance costs of its existing plants. These costs were locked in when Toyota built its plants. Toyota could replace existing production facilities with different-sized plants in different areas of the world that might cost less to operate, but that would take time. To see *immediate* benefits, management must change those costs that are controllable at the present time. For example, management can control costs of research and development, design, and advertising. Sometimes Toyota's management chose to *increase* rather than decrease these costs in order to successfully gain market share. However, Toyota was also able to *decrease* other controllable costs, such as the price paid for raw materials, by working with its suppliers.

Relevant and Irrelevant Costs

Decision making involves identifying various courses of action and then choosing among them. When managers make decisions, they focus on only those costs and revenues that are relevant to the decision.

Say you want to buy a new car and you have narrowed your decision to two choices: the Nissan Sentra or the Toyota Corolla. As shown in Exhibit 2-20, say the Sentra you like costs $18,480, whereas the Corolla costs $19,385. Because sales tax is based on the sales price, the Corolla's sales tax is higher. However, your insurance agent quotes you a higher price to insure the Sentra ($195 per month versus $149 per month for the Corolla). All of these costs are relevant to your decision because they differ between the two cars. The **differential cost**, is the difference in cost between two alternative courses of action.

EXHIBIT 2-20 Comparison of Relevant Information

	A	B	C	D
1	Relevant Costs	Sentra	Corolla	Differential Cost
2	Car's price	$ 18,480	$ 19,385	$ (905)
3	Sales tax (8%) (rounded)	1,478	1,551	(73)
4	Insurance*	11,700	8,940	2,760
5	Total relevant costs	31,658	$ 29,876	$ 1,782
6				

Over the five years (60 months) you plan to keep the car.

Other costs are not relevant to your decision. For example, both cars run on regular unleaded gasoline and have about the same fuel economy ratings, so the cost of operating the vehicles is about the same. Likewise, you don't expect cost differences in servicing the vehicles because they both carry the same warranty and have received excellent quality ratings. Because you project operating and maintenance costs to be the same for both cars, these costs are irrelevant to your decision. In other words, they won't influence your decision either way. Based on your analysis, the differential cost is $1,782 in favor of the Corolla. Does this mean that you will choose the Corolla? Not necessarily.

7 Classify costs as fixed or variable and calculate total and average costs at different volumes

The Sentra may have some characteristics you like better, such as a particular paint color, more comfortable seating, or more trunk space. When making decisions, management must also consider qualitative factors, such as effect on employee morale, in addition to differential costs.

Another cost that is irrelevant to your decision is the price you paid for the vehicle you currently own. Say you just bought a Ford F-150 pickup truck two months ago, but you've decided you need a small sedan rather than a pickup truck. The cost of the truck is a <u>sunk cost</u>. Sunk costs are costs that have already been incurred. Nothing you do now can change the fact that you already bought the truck. Thus, the cost of the truck is not relevant to your decision of whether to choose between the Sentra and the Corolla. The only thing you can do now is (1) keep your truck or (2) sell it for the best price you can get.

Managers often have trouble ignoring sunk costs when making decisions, even though they should. Perhaps they invested in a factory or a computer system that no longer serves the company's needs. Many times, new technology makes managers' past investments in older technology look like bad decisions, even though they weren't at the time. Managers should ignore sunk costs because their decisions about the future cannot alter decisions made in the past.

Fixed and Variable Costs

Managers cannot make good plans and decisions without first knowing how their costs behave. Costs generally behave as fixed costs or variable costs. We will spend all of Chapter 6 discussing cost behavior. For now, let's look just at the basics. **Fixed costs** stay constant in total over a wide range of activity levels. For example, let's say you decide to buy the Corolla, so your insurance cost for the year is $1,788 ($149 per month × 12 months). As shown in Exhibit 2-21, your total insurance cost stays fixed whether you drive your car 0 miles, 1,000 miles, or 10,000 miles during the year.

EXHIBIT 2-21 Fixed Cost Behavior

> ### Why is this important?
> "Most **business decisions** depend on how costs are **expected** to change at different volumes of **activity**. Managers can't make good decisions without first **understanding** how their costs **behave**."

However, the total cost of gasoline to operate your car varies depending on whether you drive 0 miles, 1,000 miles, or 10,000 miles. The more miles you drive, the higher your total gasoline cost for the year. If you don't drive your car at all, you won't incur any costs for gasoline. As shown in Exhibit 2-22, <u>variable costs</u>, such as your gasoline cost, change in total in direct proportion to changes in volume. To accurately forecast the total cost of operating your car during the year, you need to know which costs are fixed and which are variable.

EXHIBIT 2-22 Variable Cost Behavior

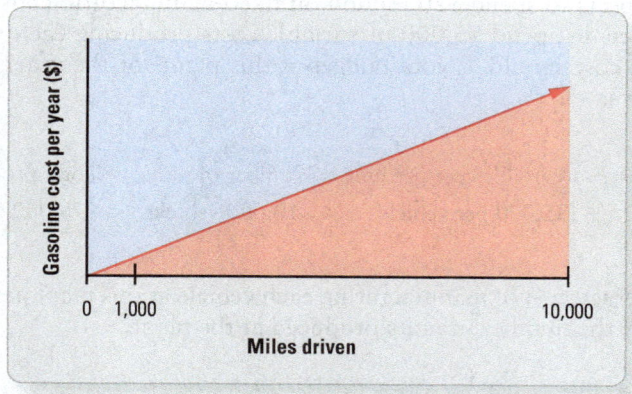

How Manufacturing Costs Behave

Most companies have both fixed and variable costs. At a manufacturer, materials are considered to be variable costs. The more cars Toyota makes, the higher its total cost for tires, steel, and parts. The behavior of direct labor is harder to characterize. Salaried employees are paid a fixed amount per year. Hourly wage earners are paid only when they work. The more hours they work, the more they are paid. Nonetheless, direct labor is generally treated as a variable cost because the more cars Toyota produces, the more assembly-line workers and machine operators it must employ. Manufacturing overhead includes both variable and fixed costs. For example, the cost of indirect materials is variable, while the cost of property tax, insurance, and straight-line depreciation on the plant and equipment is fixed. The cost of utilities is partially fixed and partially variable. Factories incur a certain level of utility costs just to keep the lights on. However, when more cars are produced, more electricity is used to run the production equipment. Exhibit 2-23 summarizes the behavior of manufacturing costs.

EXHIBIT 2-23 The Behavior of Manufacturing Costs

Direct materials	→	A variable cost
+		
Direct labor	→	Generally treated as a variable cost
+		
Manufacturing overhead	→	A mixture of fixed and variable costs
=		
Product cost	→	A mixture of fixed and variable costs

Calculating Total and Average Costs

Why is cost behavior important? Managers need to understand how costs behave to predict total costs and calculate average costs. In our example, we'll look at Toyota's total and average *production* costs, but the same principles apply to period costs.

Let's say Toyota wants to estimate the total cost of manufacturing 10,000 vehicles at one of its plants next year. To do so, Toyota must estimate (1) the total fixed manufacturing costs at the plant, and (2) the variable cost of manufacturing each vehicle. Let's say Toyota expects to spend $20 million on fixed manufacturing costs at the plant. In addition, it expects to spend $5,000 of variable costs producing each vehicle.[13] How much total product cost should Toyota budget at this plant for the year? Toyota would calculate it as follows:

$$\text{Total fixed cost} + (\text{Variable cost per unit} \times \text{Number of units}) = \text{Total product cost}$$
$$\$20,000,000 + (\$5,000 \text{ per vehicle} \times 10,000 \text{ vehicles}) = \$70,000,000$$

What is the **average cost** of manufacturing each vehicle at this plant next year? It's the total cost divided by the number of units produced at the plant:

$$\frac{\text{Total cost}}{\text{Number of units}} = \text{Average product cost per unit}$$
$$\frac{\$70,000,000}{10,000 \text{ vehicles}} = \$7,000 \text{ per vehicle}$$

If Toyota's managers decide they need to produce 12,000 vehicles at this plant instead, can they simply predict total product cost as follows?

$$\text{Average cost per unit} \times \text{Number of units} = \text{Total product cost???}$$
$$\$7,000 \times 12,000 = \$84,000,000???$$

No! They cannot! Why? *Because the average product cost per unit is NOT appropriate for predicting total costs at different levels of output.* Toyota's managers should forecast total product costs based on cost behavior:

$$\text{Total fixed cost} + (\text{Variable cost per unit} \times \text{Number of units}) = \text{Total product cost}$$
$$\$20,000,000 + (\$5,000 \text{ per vehicle} \times 12,000 \text{ vehicles}) = \$80,000,000$$

Why is the *correct* forecasted cost of $80 million less than the *faulty* prediction of $84 million? The difference stems from fixed costs. Remember, Toyota incurs $20 million of fixed manufacturing costs whether it makes 10,000 vehicles or 12,000 vehicles. As Toyota makes more vehicles, the fixed manufacturing costs are spread over more vehicles, so the average product cost per vehicle declines. If Toyota ends up making 12,000 vehicles, the new average product cost per vehicle decreases as follows:

$$\frac{\text{Total cost}}{\text{Number of units}} = \text{Average product cost per unit}$$
$$\frac{\$80,000,000}{12,000 \text{ vehicles}} = \$6,667 \text{ per vehicle (rounded)}$$

The average product cost per unit is lower when Toyota produces more vehicles because the company is using the fixed manufacturing costs more efficiently—taking the same $20 million of resources and making more vehicles with it.

---

[13] All references to Toyota in this hypothetical example were created by the author solely for academic purposes and are not intended in any way to represent the actual business practices of, or costs incurred by, Toyota-Motor Corporation.

Keep the following two important rules of thumb in mind:

- Managers like to operate near 100% capacity in order to spread fixed costs over more units. By doing so, they are able to reduce the average cost per unit.
- The average cost per unit is valid only at ONE level of output—the level used to compute the average cost per unit. NEVER use average costs to forecast costs at different output levels; if you do, you will miss the mark.

Finally, a **marginal cost** is the cost of making *one more unit*. Fixed costs will not change when Toyota makes one more vehicle unless the plant is operating at 100% capacity and simply cannot make one more unit. If that's the case, Toyota will need to incur additional costs to expand the plant. So, unless the plant is operating at 100% capacity, the marginal cost of a unit is simply its variable cost.

As you have seen, management accountants and managers use specialized terms for discussing costs. They use different costs for different purposes. To be able to communicate effectively with other people in the organization and get the correct cost information for different business decisions, managers and accountants need a solid understanding of these terms.

Decision Guidelines

Building Blocks of Managerial Accounting

Toyota also needs to know many characteristics about its costs in order to plan and make decisions. It also needs to know how to differentiate between product costs and period costs for external reporting. The following guidelines help managers with these types of decisions.

Decision	Guidelines

How do you compute cost of goods sold?	*Service companies:* No cost of goods sold because they don't sell tangible goods
	
	 • *Merchandising companies:*
	
	     Beginning inventory
	     + Purchases plus freight-in and import duties, if any
	     = Cost of goods available for sale
	     − Ending inventory
	     = Cost of goods sold
	
	 • *Manufacturing companies:*
	
	     Beginning finished goods inventory
	     + Cost of goods manufactured
	     = Cost of goods available for sale
	     − Ending finished goods inventory
	     = Cost of goods sold

How do you compute the cost of goods manufactured?	Beginning work in process inventory + Total manufacturing costs incurred during year (direct materials used + direct labor + manufacturing overhead) = Total manufacturing costs to account for − Ending work in process inventory = Cost of goods manufactured
How do managers decide which costs are relevant to their decisions?	Costs are relevant to a decision when they differ between alternatives and affect the future. Thus, *differential costs* are relevant, whereas *sunk costs* and costs that don't differ are not relevant.
How should managers forecast total costs for different production volumes?	Total cost = Total fixed costs + (Variable cost per unit × Number of units) Managers should *not* use a product's *average cost* to forecast total costs because it will change as production volume changes. As production increases, the average cost per unit declines (because fixed costs are spread over more units).

SUMMARY PROBLEM 2

Requirements

1. Show how to compute cost of goods manufactured. Use the following amounts: direct materials used ($24,000), direct labor ($9,000), manufacturing overhead ($17,000), beginning work in process inventory ($5,000), and ending work in process inventory ($4,000).
2. Auto-USA spent $300 million in total to produce 50,000 cars this year. The $300 million breaks down as follows: The company spent $50 million on fixed costs to run its manufacturing plants and $5,000 of variable costs to produce each car. Next year, it plans to produce 60,000 cars using the existing production facilities.
    a. What is the current *average product cost* per car this year?
    b. Assuming there is no change in fixed costs or variable costs per unit, what is the *total forecasted cost* to produce 60,000 cars next year?
    c. What is the *forecasted average product cost* per car next year?
    d. Why does the average product cost per car vary between years?

SOLUTIONS

Requirement 1
Cost of goods manufactured:

	A	B
1	**Calculation of Cost of Good Manufactured**	
2	Beginning Work in Process Inventory	$ 5,000
3	Plus manufacturing costs incurred:	
4	Direct materials used	24,000
5	Direct labor	9,000
6	Manufacturing overhead	17,000
7	Total manufacturing costs to account for	$ 55,000
8	Less: Ending Work in Process Inventory	4,000
9	Cost of goods manufactured (CGM)	$ 51,000
10		

Requirement 2

a.
Total cost ÷ Number of units = Current average product cost
$300 million ÷ 50,000 cars = $6,000 per car

b.
Total fixed costs + Total variable costs = Total projected product cost
$50 million + (60,000 cars × $5,000 per car) = $350 million

c.
Total cost ÷ Number of units = Projected average product cost
$350 million ÷ 60,000 cars = $5,833 per car

d. The average product cost per car decreases because Auto-USA will use the same fixed costs ($50 million) to produce more cars next year. Auto-USA will be using its resources more efficiently, so the average cost per unit will decrease.

END OF CHAPTER

Learning Objectives

- 1 Distinguish among service, merchandising, and manufacturing companies
- 2 Describe the value chain and its elements
- 3 Distinguish between direct and indirect costs
- 4 Identify product costs and period costs
- 5 Prepare the financial statements for service, merchandising, and manufacturing companies
- 6 Describe costs that are relevant and irrelevant for decision making
- 7 Classify costs as fixed or variable and calculate total and average costs at different volumes

Accounting Vocabulary

Allocate. (p. 56) To assign an *indirect* cost to a cost object.

Assign. (p. 55) To attach a cost to a cost object.

Average Cost. (p. 74) The total cost divided by the number of units.

Biomimicry. (p. 53) A means of product design in which a company tries to mimic, or copy, the natural biological process in which dead organisms (plants and animals) become the input for another organism or process.

Controllable Costs. (p. 71) Costs that can be influenced or changed by management.

Conversion Costs. (p. 61) The combination of direct labor and manufacturing overhead costs.

Cost Object. (p. 55) Anything for which managers want to know the cost.

Cost of Goods Manufactured. (p. 67) The cost of manufacturing the goods that were *finished* during the period.

Customer Service. (p. 52) Support provided for customers after the sale.

Design. (p. 52) Detailed engineering of products and services and the processes for producing them.

Differential Cost. (p. 71) The difference in cost between two alternative courses of action.

Direct Cost. (p. 55) A cost that can be traced to a cost object; a cost that is readily identifiable or associated with the cost object.

Direct Labor. (p. 60) The cost of compensating employees who physically convert raw materials into the company's products; labor costs that are directly traceable to the finished product.

Direct Materials. (p. 60) Primary raw materials that become a physical part of a finished product and whose costs are traceable to the finished product.

Distribution. (p. 52) Delivery of products or services to customers.

Finished Goods Inventory. (p. 50) Completed goods that have not yet been sold.

Fixed Costs. (p. 72) Costs that stay constant in total despite wide changes in volume.

Greenwashing. (p. 54) The unfortunate practice of *overstating* a company's commitment to sustainability.

Indirect Cost. (p. 55) A cost that relates to the cost object but cannot be traced specifically to it; a cost that is jointly used or shared by more than one cost object.

Indirect Labor. (p. 60) Labor costs that are difficult to trace to specific products.

Indirect Materials. (p. 60) Materials whose costs are difficult to trace to specific products.

Life-Cycle Assessment. (p. 53) A method of product design in which the company analyzes the environmental impact of a product, from cradle to grave, in an attempt to minimize negative environmental consequences throughout the entire lifespan of the product.

Manufacturing Company. (p. 50) A company that uses labor, plant, and equipment to convert raw materials into new finished products.

Manufacturing Overhead. (p. 60) All manufacturing costs other than direct materials and direct labor; also called factory overhead and indirect manufacturing cost.

Marginal Cost. (p. 75) The cost of producing one more unit.

Marketing. (p. 52) Promotion and advertising of products or services.

Merchandising Company. (p. 49) A company that resells tangible products previously bought from suppliers.

Operating Income. (p. 65) Earnings generated from the company's primary ongoing operations; the company's earnings before interest and taxes.

Other Indirect Manufacturing Costs. (p. 61) All manufacturing overhead costs aside from indirect materials and indirect labor.

Period Costs. (p. 57) The costs incurred by the company to operate the business that do *not* get treated as inventory, but rather are expensed immediately in the period in which they are incurred. These costs do *not* relate to manufacturing or purchasing product. Period costs are often called

Periodic Inventory. (p. 66) An inventory system in which Cost of Goods Sold is calculated at the end of the period rather than every time a sale is made.

Perpetual Inventory. (p. 66) An inventory system in which both Cost of Goods Sold and Inventory are updated every time a sale is made.

Prime Costs. (p. 61) The combination of direct material and direct labor costs.

Product Costs. (p. 57) The costs incurred by *manufacturers to produce* their products or incurred by *merchandisers to purchase* their products. For external financial reporting, GAAP requires that these costs be assigned to inventory until the products are sold, at which point, they are expensed as Cost of Goods Sold.

Production or Purchases. (p. 52) Resources used to produce a product or service or to purchase finished merchandise intended for resale.

Raw Materials Inventory. (p. 50) All raw materials (direct materials and indirect materials) not yet used in manufacturing.

Research and Development (R&D). (p. 52) Researching and developing new or improved products or services or the processes for producing them.

Retailer. (p. 49) Merchandising company that sells to consumers.

operating expenses or selling, general, and administrative expenses.

Service Company. (p. 49) A company that sells intangible services rather than tangible products.

Sunk Cost. (p. 72) A cost that has already been incurred.

Total Cost. (p. 57) The cost of all resources used throughout the value chain.

Trace. (p. 56) To assign a *direct* cost to a cost object.

Triple Bottom Line. (p. 49) Evaluating a company's performance not only by its ability to generate economic profits, but also by its impact on people and the planet.

Uncontrollable Costs. (p. 71) Costs that cannot be changed or influenced in the short run by management.

Value Chain. (p. 51) The activities that add value to a firm's products and services; includes R&D, design, production or purchases, marketing, distribution, and customer service.

Variable Costs. (p. 72) Costs that change in total in direct proportion to changes in volume.

Wholesaler. (p. 49) Merchandising companies that buy in bulk from manufacturers, mark up the prices, and then sell those products to retailers.

Work in Process Inventory. (p. 50) Goods that are partway through the manufacturing process but not yet complete.

MyAccountingLab Go to http://myaccountinglab.com/ for the following Quick Check, Short Exercises, Exercises, and Problems. They are available with immediate grading, explanations of correct and incorrect answers, and interactive media that acts as your own online tutor.

Quick Check

1. (*Learning Objective 1*) Which of the following types of companies would have work in process inventory?
    a. Service
    b. Merchandising
    c. Manufacturing
    d. All of the above

2. (*Learning Objective 2*) Which of the following is *not* an activity in the value chain?
    a. Marketing
    b. Customer Service
    c. Design
    d. Administration

3. (*Learning Objective 3*) A cost that can be traced to a cost object is known as a
    a. period cost.
    b. product cost.
    c. direct cost.
    d. indirect cost.

4. (*Learning Objective 4*) Period costs are often referred to as
    a. manufacturing expenses.
    b. operating expenses.
    c. direct costs.
    d. product costs.

5. (*Learning Objective 4*) Conversion costs consist of
    a. direct materials and manufacturing overhead.
    b. direct labor and manufacturing overhead.
    c. direct materials and direct labor.
    d. direct materials, direct labor, and manufacturing overhead.

6. (*Learning Objective 4*) Which of the following is *not* part of manufacturing overhead?
    a. Period costs, such as depreciation on office computers
    b. Indirect materials, such as machine lubricants
    c. Indirect labor, such as plant forklift operators' wages
    d. Other indirect manufacturing costs, such as plant utilities

7. (*Learning Objective 5*) Which of the following is a calculated amount, rather than a general ledger account?
   a. Finished goods inventory
   b. Cost of goods manufactured
   c. Sales revenue
   d. Cost of goods sold

8. (*Learning Objective 5*) Which of the following types of companies will always have the Cost of Goods Sold account on their income statements?
   a. Service and merchandising companies
   b. Merchandising and manufacturing companies
   c. Service and manufacturing companies
   d. Service, merchandising, and manufacturing companies

9. (*Learning Objective 6*) Which of the following is *false*?
   a. Uncontrollable costs are costs over which the company has little or no control in the short run.
   b. Sunk costs are costs that have already been incurred.
   c. Sunk costs are generally relevant to decisions.
   d. The difference in cost between two alternatives is known as a differential cost.

10. (*Learning Objective 7*) Which of the following is *true*?
    a. The average cost per unit can be used for predicting total costs at many different output levels.
    b. Manufacturing overhead is composed of only variable costs.
    c. Fixed costs stay constant in total over a wide range of activity levels.
    d. Direct materials are considered to be fixed costs.

Quick Check Answers

1. c 2. d 3. c 4. b 5. b 6. a 7. b 8. b 9. c 10. c

Short Exercises

S2-1 Identify types of companies and their inventories (*Learning Objective 1*)

Complete the following statements with one of the terms listed here. You may use a term more than once, and some terms may not be used at all.

Finished goods inventory	Inventory (merchandise)	Service companies
Manufacturing companies	Merchandising companies	Work in process inventory
Raw materials inventory	Wholesalers	

a. _____ report three types of inventory on the balance sheet.
b. _____ for a company such as Best Buy (consumer electronics) includes all of the costs necessary to purchase products and get them onto the store shelves.
c. Most for-profit organizations can be described as being in one (or more) of three categories: _____, _____, and _____.
d. _____ is composed of goods partially through the manufacturing process (not finished yet).
e. Forever 21, Target, and Kohl's are all examples of _____.
f. _____ typically do not have an inventory account.
g. Johnson & Johnson, a personal care products manufacturer, converts _____ into finished products.
h. A law office, an advertising agency, and a hospital are all examples of _____.
i. _____ buy products in bulk from producers, mark them up, and resell to retailers.

S2-2 Identify type of company from balance sheets (*Learning Objective 1*)

The current asset sections of the balance sheets of three companies follow. Which company is a service company? Which is a merchandiser? Which is a manufacturer? How can you tell?

Madison Company		Dean Company		Anderson Company	
Cash	$ 3,000	Cash	$ 2,400	Cash	$3,000
Accounts receivable	4,000	Accounts receivable	6,500	Accounts receivable	5,000
Raw materials inventory	2,000	Inventory	8,000	Prepaid expenses	600
Work in process inventory	900	Prepaid expenses	300	Total	$8,600
Finished goods inventory	4,000	Total	$17,200		
Total	$13,900				

S2-3 Classify costs by value chain function *(Learning Objective 2)*

Classify each of The J. M. Smucker Company's costs as one of the six business functions in the value chain.
a. Cost of a prime-time TV ad featuring Smucker's® Fruit & Honey™ Fruit Spreads
b. Salary of engineers who are designing the new plant's layout
c. Depreciation on Orrville, Ohio, plant
d. Depreciation on delivery vehicles
e. Transportation costs to deliver Folgers Coffee® to retailers such as Kroger, Walmart, and Save-A-Lot
f. Costs of a customer support center website
g. Plant manager's salary
h. Purchase of strawberries used in Smucker's® Strawberry Preserves
i. Depreciation on food research lab

S2-4 Classify costs as direct or indirect *(Learning Objective 3)*

Classify each of the following costs as a direct cost or an indirect cost, assuming that the cost object is the Juniors Department (clothing and accessories for teenage and young women) in the Stow Kohl's department store. (Kohl's is a chain of department stores and has stores located across the United States.)
a. Juniors Department sales clerks
b. Cost of Juniors clothing
c. Cost of hangers used to display the clothing in the store
d. Electricity for the building
e. Cost of radio advertising for the store
f. Juniors clothing buyers' salaries (these buyers buy for all the Juniors Departments of Kohl's stores)
g. Depreciation of the building
h. Cost of costume jewelry on the mannequins in the Juniors Department
i. Cost of bags used to package customer purchases at the main registers for the store
j. The Stow Kohl's store manager's salary
k. Cost of the security staff at the Stow store
l. Manager of Juniors Department

S2-5 Define cost terms *(Learning Objectives 3 & 4)*

Complete the following statements with one of the terms listed here. You may use a term more than once, and some terms may not be used at all.

Prime costs	Cost objects	Product costs
Assigned	Direct costs	Fringe benefits
Period costs	Assets	Cost of goods sold
Indirect costs	Conversion costs	Total costs

a. _____ are the costs of transforming direct materials into finished goods.
b. _____ include R&D, marketing, distribution, and customer service costs.
c. Direct material plus direct labor equals _____.
d. Steel, tires, engines, upholstery, carpet, and dashboard instruments are used in the assembly of a car. Since the manufacturer can trace the cost of these materials (including freight-in and import duties) to specific units or batches of vehicles, they are considered _____ of the vehicles.
e. Costs that can be traced directly to a(n) _____ are called _____.
f. _____ are initially treated as _____ on the balance sheet.
g. The allocation process results in a less precise cost figure being _____ to the _____.
h. _____ cannot be directly traced to a(n) _____.
i. _____ include the costs of all resources used throughout the value chain.

j. U.S. GAAP requires companies to use only _____ for inventory reported on external financial statements.

k. Company-paid _____ may include health insurance, retirement plan contributions, payroll taxes, and paid vacations.

l. When manufacturing companies sell their finished products, the costs of those finished products are removed from inventory and expensed as _____.

S2-6 Identify product costs and period costs *(Learning Objective 4)*

PEZ Candy Inc. produces the popular small candy that is dispensed in collectible flip-top dispensers. In the United States, PEZ candies are produced in a factory in Connecticut. The Connecticut location also houses PEZ's U.S. headquarters and a PEZ Visitors Center. PEZ candy is made from sugar, fruit flavoring, coloring, and corn syrup; the ingredients are put under pressure to form the hard tablets. About 95% of a PEZ tablet is sugar. The PEZ dispensers are popular with collectors; there are several PEZ collector conventions throughout the world.

In 2011, PEZ Candy Inc. opened a 6,000-square-foot Visitors Center in Connecticut. The Visitors Center houses the world's largest collection of PEZ memorabilia on public display. Visitors can also view the factory through special viewing windows. The center also has a touch-screen PEZ trivia game and interactive reviews of PEZ history. Birthday party packages are also offered in the Visitors Center; partygoers receive goodie bags that include a blank customizable PEZ dispenser, PEZ candy, a PEZ lanyard, and discount coupons.

Requirements

1. Is the cost of sugar in PEZ candies a product or a period cost? What about the wrappers that the candy is packaged in?
2. Is the cost of quality control testing in the manufacturing process for PEZ candies a product or a period cost?
3. Is the cost of the labor to make PEZ candy in the factory a product or a period cost? What about the cost of the benefits (i.e., health care, payroll taxes, vacation pay) for those workers?
4. Is the cost of staffing the PEZ Visitors Center a product or a period cost? What about the cost of the benefits (i.e., health care, payroll taxes, vacation pay) for those workers who work in the Visitors Center?
5. Assume that PEZ purchased the touch-screen PEZ trivia game from a custom video game developer. Is the cost of that game a product or a period cost? What about the costs of maintaining and updating the software and hardware for the game?
6. Is food cost for a birthday party in the PEZ Visitors Center a product or a period cost? What about the cost of the items included in the goodie bags?

S2-7 Classify product costs and period costs *(Learning Objective 4)*

Classify each of Ford Motor Company's costs as either product costs or period costs. Ford Motor Company is an automobile manufacturer headquartered in Detroit, Michigan.

a. Cost of chemical included in paint to inhibit rust
b. Life insurance for the CEO
c. Cost of electricity at the Lima Engine Plant in Ohio
d. Depreciation on the buildings at the Flat Rock Assembly Plant in Michigan
e. Cost of ad campaign and slogan called "By Design" to highlight the designs of Ford's cars
f. Purchase of aluminum to be used in car wheels
g. Salaries of Ford engineers researching ways to reduce CO_2 emissions
h. Cost of new software to schedule production
i. Salaries of Ford Motor Company's top executives

Building Blocks of Managerial Accounting

S2-8 Classify a manufacturer's costs *(Learning Objective 4)*

Classify each of the following costs as a period cost or a product cost. If you classify the cost as a product cost, further classify it as direct material (DM), direct labor (DL), or manufacturing overhead (MOH).

a. Property taxes—30% of building is used for sales, marketing, and administrative offices; 70% of building is used for manufacturing
b. Wages and benefits paid to assembly-line workers in the manufacturing plant
c. Depreciation on automated production equipment
d. Salaries paid to quality control inspectors in the plant
e. Repairs and maintenance on factory equipment
f. Standard packaging materials used to package individual units of product for sale (for example, cereal boxes in which cereal is packaged)
g. Lease payment on administrative headquarters
h. Telecommunications costs for the customer service call center

S2-9 Classify costs incurred by a dairy processing company *(Learning Objective 4)*

Each of the following costs pertains to Bailey Dairy Products Company, a dairy processing company. Classify each of the company's costs as a period cost or a product cost. Further classify product costs as direct material (DM), direct labor (DL), or manufacturing overhead (MOH).

Cost	Period Cost or Product Cost?	DM, DL, or MOH?
1. Television advertisements for Bailey's products		
2. Lubricants used in running bottling machines		
3. Research and development related to elimination of antibiotic residues in milk		
4. Gasoline used to operate refrigerated trucks delivering finished dairy products to grocery stores		
5. Company president's annual bonus		
6. Depreciation on refrigerated trucks used to collect raw milk from local dairy farmers		
7. Plastic gallon containers in which milk is packaged		
8. Property insurance on dairy processing plant		
9. Cost of milk purchased from local dairy farmers		
10. Depreciation on tablets used by sales staff		
11. Wages and salaries paid to machine operators at dairy processing plant		

S2-10 Determine total manufacturing overhead *(Learning Objective 4)*

McKay Frames manufactures picture frames. Suppose the company's January records include the items described below. What is McKay Frames' total manufacturing overhead cost in January?

Oil for manufacturing equipment	$ 250
Wood for frames	$46,000
Company president's salary	$26,500
Interest expense	$ 1,500
Plant supervisor's salary	$ 3,100
Depreciation expense on company cars used by sales force	$ 2,100
Plant janitor's salary	$ 1,800
Plant depreciation expense	$ 6,000
Glue for picture frames	$ 400

S2-11 Prepare a retailer's income statement *(Learning Objective 5)*

Salon Hair is a retail chain specializing in salon-quality hair-care products. During the year, Salon Hair had sales of $38,850,000. The company began the year with $3,500,000 of merchandise inventory and ended the year with $4,445,000 of inventory. During the year, Salon Hair purchased $23,975,000 of merchandise inventory. The company's selling, general, and administrative expenses totaled $7,100,000 for the year. Prepare Salon Hair's income statement for the year.

S2-12 Compute Cost of Goods Sold for a merchandiser *(Learning Objective 5)*

Given the following information for a retailer, compute the cost of goods sold.

Ending inventory	$ 5,900
Website maintenance	$ 7,700
Revenues	$67,000
Freight-in	$ 3,700
Import duties	$ 1,300
Marketing expenses	$12,000
Delivery expenses	$ 1,500
Purchases	$40,000
Beginning inventory	$ 3,800

S2-13 Calculate direct materials used *(Learning Objective 5)*

You are a new accounting intern at Mason Bikes. Your boss gives you the following information and asks you to compute the cost of direct materials used (assume that the company's raw materials inventory contains only direct materials).

Import duties	$ 1,300
Beginning raw materials inventory	$ 4,700
Ending raw materials inventory	$ 1,200
Freight-in	$ 400
Freight-out	$ 600
Purchases of direct materials	$16,000

S2-14 Compute Cost of Goods Manufactured *(Learning Objective 5)*

Robinson Manufacturing found the following information in its accounting records: $519,800 of direct materials used, $223,500 of direct labor, and $775,115 of manufacturing overhead. The Work in Process Inventory account had a beginning balance of $72,400 and an ending balance of $87,600. Compute the company's Cost of Goods Manufactured.

S2-15 Describe other cost terms *(Learning Objectives 6 & 7)*

Complete the following statements with one of the terms listed here. You may use a term more than once, and some terms may not be used at all.

Differential costs	Variable costs	Controllable costs
Marginal cost	Fixed costs	Average cost
Uncontrollable costs	Sunk costs	

a. A(n) _____ is the cost of making one more unit.
b. Gasoline is one of many _____ in the operation of a motor vehicle.
c. A product's _____ and _____, not the product's _____, should be used to forecast total costs at different production volumes.
d. Within the relevant range, _____ do not change in total with changes in production volume.
e. The _____ per unit declines as a production facility produces more units.
f. Costs that differ between alternatives are called _____.
g. In the long run, most costs are _____, meaning that management is able to influence or change the amount of the cost.
h. _____ are costs that have already been incurred.

S2-16 Classify costs as fixed or variable *(Learning Objective 7)*

Classify each of the following costs as fixed or variable:

a. Cost of French fries used at a McDonald's restaurant
b. Hourly wages paid to cashiers at The Home Depot
c. Monthly sugar costs for The Hershey Company
d. Cost of fuel used by Old Dominion Freight Line, a national trucking company
e. Shipping costs at Amazon.com
f. Monthly rent for Onyx Nail Bar, a nail salon in Dallas, Texas
g. Sales commissions at Tampa Honda in Florida
h. Monthly insurance costs for the building housing the administrative offices of Panera Bread in St. Louis, Missouri
i. Monthly depreciation of equipment used in the customer service department at Klaben Ford Lincoln, a car dealership in Kent, Ohio
j. Cost of rubber used to manufacture L.L.Bean boots
k. Cost of oranges sold at a Kroger's grocery store
l. Monthly office lease costs for the Portland office of E & Y, a global audit firm
m. Monthly cost of coffee at a Dunkin' Donuts store
n. Property taxes for an Applebee's Neighborhood Grill & Bar
o. Depreciation of exercise equipment at an LA Fitness club

S2-17 Identify ethical standards violated *(Learning Objectives 1, 2, 3, 4, 5, 6, & 7)*

ETHICS

For each of the situations listed, identify the primary standard from the IMA *Statement of Ethical Professional Practice* that is violated (competence, confidentiality, integrity, or credibility). Refer to Exhibit 1-7 for the complete standard.

1. To reduce the company's tax bill, Jack uses total cost to value inventory instead of using product cost as required by law.
2. Since Emilie works in the accounting department, she is aware that profits are going to fall short of analysts' projections. She tells her aunt to sell stock in the company before the earnings release date.
3. Veronica pays a Mexican official a bribe of $50,000 to allow the company to locate a factory in that jurisdiction so that the company can take advantage of the cheaper labor costs. Without the bribe, the factory cannot be located in that location.
4. There is a failure in the company's backup system after a system crash. Month-end reports will be delayed. Kayla, the manager of the division experiencing the system failure, does not report this upcoming delay to anyone since she does not want to be the bearer of bad news.
5. Taylor overhears a subordinate at a mutual friend's party tell others about a confidential deal with a supplier to get raw materials for a price lower than market price. Taylor does not do anything about the subordinate's indiscreet conversation.

EXERCISES Group A

E2-18A Classify costs along the value chain for a retailer *(Learning Objective 2)*

Suppose Motor Shack incurred the following costs at its Ann Arbor, Michigan, store:

Newspaper advertisements	$ 5,100
Payment to consultant for advice on location of new store	$ 2,700
Purchases of merchandise	$37,000
Freight-in	$ 3,700
Salespeople's salaries	$ 4,600
Depreciation expense on delivery trucks	$ 1,500
Research on whether store should sell satellite radio service	$ 250
Customer Complaint Department	$ 550
Rearranging store layout	$ 650

Requirements

1. Classify each cost as to which category of the value chain it belongs (R&D, Design, Purchases, Marketing, Distribution, or Customer Service).
2. Compute the total costs for each value chain category.
3. How much are the total product costs?

E2-19A Classify costs along the value chain for a manufacturer *(Learning Objectives 2 & 4)*

Suppose the smartphone manufacturer Kobo Electronics provides the following information for its costs last month (in millions):

Delivery expense to customers via UPS	$ 9
Salaries of salespeople	$ 4
Chipset (the set of chips used on a phone's motherboard)	$56
Exterior case for phone	$ 6
Assembly-line workers' wages	$ 8
Technical customer support hotline	$ 5
Depreciation on plant and equipment	$60
Rearrangement of production process to accommodate new robot	$ 3
1-800 (toll-free) line for customer orders	$ 1
Salaries of scientists who developed new model	$10

Requirements

1. Classify each of these costs according to its place in the value chain (R&D, Design, Production, Marketing, Distribution, or Customer Service). (*Hint:* You should have at least one cost in each value chain function.)
2. Within the production category, break the costs down further into three subcategories: Direct Materials, Direct Labor, and Manufacturing Overhead.
3. Compute the total costs for each value chain category.
4. How much are the total product costs?
5. How much are the total prime costs?
6. How much are the total conversion costs?

SUSTAINABILITY

E2-20A Value chain and sustainability efforts *(Learning Objective 2)*

Each of the following scenarios describes some cost item for organizations in recent years. For each scenario, identify which function of the value chain that cost would represent (R&D, Design, Purchasing/Producing, Marketing, Distributing, or Customer Service). *Note: The companies and products used in this exercise are real companies with a strong sustainable practices commitment.*

a. In recent years, the U.S. National Park Service approved the use of an erosion control system from GeoHay® for a roadway construction project in the Great Smoky Mountains National Park. GeoHay® erosion and sediment control products are produced from recycled carpet fibers. The cost of these erosion and sediment control products would fall into which function in the value chain?

b. Ford Motor Company's Rouge Center in Dearborn, Michigan, has a "living roof" on the Dearborn Truck Plant final assembly building. It is the largest living roof in the world, encompassing 10.4 acres. The living roof is made from living grass, and its primary purpose is to collect and filter rainfall as part of a natural stormwater management system. It also provides cooler surroundings and offers a longer roof life than a traditional roof. The cost of promoting the company's products and its sustainability efforts would fall into which function in the value chain?

c. Nike Products, an athletic apparel and shoe manufacturer, developed the Environmental Apparel Design Tool over a period of seven years. The Environmental Apparel Design Tool helps apparel and shoe designers to make real-time choices that decrease the environmental impact of their work. With the tool, the designers can see the potential waste resulting from their designs and the amount of environmentally preferred materials used by their designs. When designers make changes to the preliminary product design, they can see instantly the effect of those changes on waste and input usage. The $6 million investment used to develop the Environmental Apparel Design Tool would fall into which function in the value chain?

d. GreenShipping™ is a service that companies can use to purchase carbon offsets for the carbon generated by shipments to customers. Any shipments made with UPS, FedEx, or USPS can be tracked. The GreenShipping™ calculator uses weight, distance traveled, and mode of transport to calculate the carbon generated by that shipment. A carbon offset is then purchased so that the shipment becomes carbon neutral. The carbon offset helps to fund the development of renewable energy sources. The cost of these carbon offsets to the company making the shipment to the customer would fall into which function in the value chain?

e. The Red Wing Shoe Company manufactures work boots. The company has a philosophy that products should be repaired, not thrown away. After the 12-month warranty has expired on Red Wing boots, the company offers free oiling, free laces, low-cost replacement insoles, and low-cost hardware repairs. The cost of operating this shoe repair service would fall into which function in the value chain?

f. Nyloboard® produces decking materials made from recycled carpet. The cost of the research into how to create Nyloboard® from recycled carpet would fall into which function in the value chain?

E2-21A Classify and calculate a manufacturer's costs *(Learning Objectives 2 & 4)*

An airline manufacturer incurred the following costs last month (in thousands of dollars):

a. Airplane seats	$ 240
b. Production supervisors' salaries	$ 100
c. Depreciation on forklifts in factory	$ 40
d. Machine lubricants	$ 35
e. Factory janitors' wages	$ 15
f. Assembly workers' wages	$ 620
g. Property tax on corporate marketing office	$ 30
h. Plant utilities	$ 120
i. Cost of warranty repairs	$ 260
j. Machine operators' health insurance	$ 10
k. Depreciation on administrative offices	$ 60
l. Cost of designing new plant layout	$ 170
m. Jet engines	$1,400

Requirements

1. Assuming the cost object is an airplane, classify each cost as one of the following: direct material (DM), direct labor (DL), indirect labor (IL), indirect materials (IM), other manufacturing overhead (other MOH), or period cost. (*Hint:* Set up a column for each type of cost.) What is the total for each type of cost?
2. Calculate total manufacturing overhead costs.
3. Calculate total product costs.
4. Calculate total prime costs.
5. Calculate total conversion costs.
6. Calculate total period costs.

E2-22A Construct an income statement using product and period costs
(Learning Objectives 4 & 5)

Outdoor Amenities is a manufacturer of backyard and deck furniture. Its products are in high demand, and it carries no inventory. Following is a list of selected account balances from its trial balance for the most recent year ended December 31 (in no particular order.)

Salaries and wages (for administrative and sales staff)	$ 37,400
Stain (used in manufacturing furniture)	$ 12,700
Indirect labor costs (wages of maintenance workers in factory)	$ 21,300
Other manufacturing overhead (includes factory insurance and property taxes)	$ 9,800
Rent and utilities (for administrative offices)	$ 12,000
Utility costs (related to factory)	$ 11,200
Labor costs (wages of carpenters who build furniture)	$ 36,900
Accounts receivable	$ 27,100
Marketing costs	$ 17,300
Wood (used in manufacturing furniture)	$ 57,800
Sales revenues	$ 255,000
Accounts payable	$ 7,100

Requirements

Using the income statement accounts in the table, calculate:

1. Cost of goods sold. *Hint:* Cost of goods sold can be calculated by summing the total product costs since there is no inventory.
2. Operating expenses. *Hint:* Operating expenses are the company's period costs.
3. Gross profit
4. Operating income

E2-23A Work backward to find missing amounts *(Learning Objective 5)*

Gamma Electronics manufactures and sells a line of smartphones. Unfortunately, Gamma Electronics suffered serious fire damage at its home office. As a result, the accounting records for October were partially destroyed—and completely jumbled. Gamma Electronics has hired you to help figure out the missing pieces of the accounting puzzle. Assume that the Raw Materials Inventory contains only direct materials.

Revenues in October	$27,600
Work in process inventory, October 31	$ 1,700
Raw materials inventory, October 31	$ 3,200
Direct labor in October	$ 3,400
Manufacturing overhead in October	$ 6,300
Work in process inventory, October 1	0
Finished goods inventory, October 1	$ 4,900
Direct materials used in October	$ 8,600
Gross profit in October	$12,800
Purchases of direct materials in October	$ 9,200

Requirement

Find the following amounts:

a. Cost of Goods Sold in October
b. Beginning Raw Materials Inventory
c. Ending Finished Goods Inventory

E2-24A Prepare a retailer's income statement *(Learning Objective 5)*

Neil Webster is the sole proprietor of Prestigious Pugs, a business specializing in the sale of high-end pet gifts and accessories. Prestigious Pugs' sales totaled $1,105,000 during the most recent year. During the year, the company spent $55,000 on expenses relating to website maintenance, $30,500 on marketing, and $29,500 on wrapping, boxing, and shipping the goods to customers. Prestigious Pugs also spent $638,000 on inventory purchases and an additional $19,500 on freight-in charges. The company started the year with $16,250 of inventory on hand and ended the year with $16,000 of inventory. Prepare Prestigious Pugs' income statement for the most recent year.

E2-25A Compute direct materials used and Cost of Goods Manufactured
(Learning Objective 5)

Justine Industries is calculating its Cost of Goods Manufactured at year-end. The company's accounting records show the following: The Raw Materials Inventory account had a beginning balance of $17,000 and an ending balance of $12,000. During the year, the company purchased $55,000 of direct materials. Direct labor for the year totaled $121,000, while manufacturing overhead amounted to $151,000. The Work Process Inventory account had a beginning balance of $22,000 and an ending balance of $21,000. Assume that Raw Materials Inventory contains only direct materials. Compute the Cost of Goods Manufactured for the year. (*Hint:* The first step is to calculate the direct materials used during the year.)

E2-26A Compute Cost of Goods Manufactured and Cost of Goods Sold
(Learning Objective 5)

Compute the Cost of Goods Manufactured and Cost of Goods Sold for West Nautical Company for the most recent year using the amounts described next. Assume that the Raw Materials Inventory contains only direct materials.

	Beginning of Year	End of Year		End of Year
Raw materials inventory	$23,000	$25,000	Insurance on plant	$ 11,500
Work in process inventory	$35,000	$31,000	Depreciation—plant building and equipment	$ 13,400
Finished goods inventory	$20,000	$22,000	Repairs and maintenance—plant	$ 3,700
Purchases of direct materials		$74,000	Marketing expenses	$ 77,000
Direct labor		$86,000	General and administrative expenses	$ 28,500
Indirect labor		$42,000		

E2-27A Continues E2-26A: Prepare income statement *(Learning Objective 5)*

Prepare the income statement for West Nautical Company in E2-26A for the most recent year. Assume that the company sold 34,000 units of its product at a price of $12 each during the year.

E2-28A Determine whether information is relevant *(Learning Objective 6)*

Classify each of the following costs as relevant or irrelevant to the decision at hand and briefly explain your reason.

a. The fair market value of old manufacturing equipment when deciding whether to replace it with new equipment (old equipment will be sold if new equipment is purchased)

b. Cost of purchasing packaging materials from an outside vendor when deciding whether to continue manufacturing the packaging materials in-house

c. Depreciation expense on old manufacturing equipment when deciding whether to replace it with newer equipment

d. The total amount of the restaurant's fixed costs when deciding whether to add additional items to the menu

e. The cost of land purchased three years ago when deciding whether to build on the land now or wait two more years before building

f. The interest rate received on invested funds when deciding how much inventory to keep on hand

g. Cost of computers purchased six months ago when deciding whether to upgrade to computers with a faster processing speed

h. The property tax rates in different locales when deciding where to locate the company's headquarters

i. The type of fuel (gas or diesel) used by delivery vans when deciding which make and model of van to purchase for the company's delivery van fleet

j. Cost of operating automated production machinery versus the cost of direct labor when deciding whether to automate production

E2-29A Compute total and average costs *(Learning Objective 7)*

Bubbly Soda spends $2 on direct materials, direct labor, and variable manufacturing overhead for every unit (12-pack of soda) it produces. Fixed manufacturing overhead costs $7 million per year. The plant, which is currently operating at only 75% of capacity, produced 25 million units this year. Management plans to operate closer to full capacity next year, producing 35 million units. Management doesn't anticipate any changes in the prices it pays for materials, labor, and manufacturing overhead.

Requirements

1. What is the current total product cost (for the 25 million units), including fixed and variable costs?
2. What is the current average product cost per unit?
3. What is the current fixed cost per unit?
4. What is the forecasted total product cost next year (for the 35 million units), including fixed and variable costs?
5. What is the forecasted average product cost next year?
6. What is the forecasted fixed cost per unit?
7. Why does the average product cost decrease as production increases?

EXERCISES Group B

E2-30B Classify costs along the value chain for a retailer *(Learning Objective 2)*

Suppose Electronics Shack incurred the following costs at its Forest Lake, Minnesota, store.

Newspaper advertisements	$ 5,700
Payment to consultant for advice on location of new store	$ 2,100
Purchases of merchandise	$ 36,000
Freight-in	$ 3,500
Salespeople's salaries	$ 4,100
Depreciation expense on delivery trucks	$ 1,100
Research on whether store should sell satellite radio service	$ 500
Customer Complaint Department	$ 550
Rearrangement of store layout	$ 900

Requirements

1. Classify each cost as to which category of the value chain it belongs (R&D, Design, Purchases, Marketing, Distribution, Customer Service).
2. Compute the total costs for each value chain category.
3. How much are the total product costs?

E2-31B Classify costs along the value chain for a manufacturer *(Learning Objectives 2 & 4)*

Suppose the smartphone manufacturer Sabre Electronics provides the following information for its costs last month (in millions):

Delivery expense to customers via UPS	$10
Salaries of salespeople	$ 6
Chipset (the set of chips used on a phone's motherboard)	$60
Exterior case for phone	$ 4
Assembly-line workers' wages	$12
Technical customer-support hotline	$ 5
Depreciation on plant and equipment	$65
Rearrange production process to accommodate new robot	$ 1
1-800 (toll-free) line for customer orders	$ 3
Salaries of scientists who developed new model	$11

Requirements

1. Classify each of these costs according to its place in the value chain (R&D, Design, Production, Marketing, Distribution, or Customer Service).
2. Within the production category, break the costs down further into three subcategories: Direct Materials, Direct Labor, and Manufacturing Overhead.
3. Compute the total costs for each value chain category.
4. How much are the total product costs?
5. How much are the total prime costs?
6. How much are the total conversion costs?

E2-32B Value chain and sustainability efforts *(Learning Objective 2)*

Each of the scenarios to follow describes some cost item for organizations in the recycled carpet industry. For each scenario, identify which function of the value chain that cost would represent (R&D, Design, Purchasing/Producing, Marketing, Distributing, or Customer Service). *Note:* The companies and products used in this exercise are real companies with a strong sustainable practices commitment.

a. Flor®, a company that produces residential carpet tiles made from recycled carpet, has an R&R (return and recycle) Program. Homeowners can arrange to have old tiles picked up and shipped back to the plant for recycling. The cost of operating this R&R program would fall into which function in the value chain?

b. Los Angeles Fiber Company (LAFC) received the EPA/CARE award to recognize Los Angeles Fiber Company's sustainability efforts. Since 2000, LAFC has recycled more than 464 million pounds of post-consumer carpet. Its carpet brand, Reliance Carpet, is made entirely from post-consumer carpet fiber. The cost of promoting the company's products and its sustainability efforts would fall into which function in the value chain?

c. Ford Motor Company purchases cylinder head covers made from a nylon resin containing 100% recycled carpet in its Mustangs. The cost of the cylinder head covers would fall into which function in the value chain?

d. Axminster Carpets offsets the carbon emissions from its carpet distribution process by investing in renewable energy projects such as wind, power, and hydropower plants. This carbon offset is verified independently by the Voluntary Carbon Standard. The cost of these carbon offsets would fall into which function in the value chain?

e. Shaw Industries is a flooring manufacturer. It has created Cradle to Cradle Silver Certified carpet, which is carpet that can be recycled back into new carpet again and again at the end of its useful life, or it can go back into the soil. The costs to develop the production process for the Cradle to Cradle Silver Certified carpet would fall into which function in the value chain?

f. Fibre(B)lock® Flooring is manufactured using the waste generated from the manufacture of commercial nylon carpet. The cost of the research into how to create Fibre (B)lock® Flooring would fall into which function in the value chain?

E2-33B Classify and calculate a manufacturer's costs *(Learning Objectives 2 & 4)*

An airline manufacturer incurred the following costs last month (in thousands of dollars).

a.	Airplane seats..	$ 300
b.	Production supervisors' salaries	$ 110
c.	Depreciation on forklifts in factory..	$ 90
d.	Machine lubricants	$ 30
e.	Factory janitors' wages	$ 50
f.	Assembly workers' wages...	$ 630
g.	Property tax on corporate marketing offices...................................	$ 20
h.	Plant utilities...	$ 140
i.	Cost of warranty repairs...	$ 230
j.	Machine operators' health insurance...	$ 40
k.	Depreciation on administrative offices	$ 100
l.	Cost of designing new plant layout	$ 160
m.	Jet engines..	$ 1,400

Requirements

1. Assuming the cost object is an airplane, classify each cost as one of the following: direct material (DM), direct labor (DL), indirect labor (IL), indirect materials (IM), other manufacturing overhead (other MOH), or period cost. What is the total for each type of cost?
2. Calculate total manufacturing overhead costs.
3. Calculate total product costs.
4. Calculate total prime costs.
5. Calculate total conversion costs.
6. Calculate total period costs.

E2-34B Construct an income statement using product and period costs
(Learning Objectives 4 & 5)

Backyard Amenities is a manufacturer of backyard and deck furniture. Its products are in high demand, and it carries no inventory. To follow is a list of selected account balances from its trial balance for the most recent year ended December 31 (in no particular order).

Salaries and wages (for administrative and sales staff)	$ 38,100
Stain (used in manufacturing furniture)	$ 14,500
Indirect labor costs (wages of maintenance workers in factory)	$ 23,700
Other manufacturing overhead (includes factory insurance and property taxes)	$ 11,300
Rent and utilities (for administrative offices)	$ 13,200
Utility costs (related to factory)	$ 12,100
Labor costs (wages of carpenters who build furniture)	$ 33,700
Accounts receivable	$ 31,200
Marketing costs	$ 15,200
Wood (used in manufacturing furniture)	$ 59,100
Sales revenues	$ 267,000
Accounts payable	$ 8,200

Requirements

Using the income statement accounts in the table, calculate:

1. Cost of goods sold. *Hint:* Cost of goods sold can be calculated by summing the total product costs since there is no inventory.
2. Operating expenses. *Hint:* Operating expenses are the company's period costs.
3. Gross profit
4. Operating income

E2-35B Work backward to find missing amounts *(Learning Objective 5)*

Swift Electronics manufactures and sells smartphones. Unfortunately, the company recently suffered serious fire damage at its home office. As a result, the accounting records for October were partially destroyed and completely jumbled. Swift has hired you to help figure out the missing pieces of the accounting puzzle. Assume that Swift Electronics' Raw Materials Inventory contains only direct materials.

Work in process inventory, October 31	$ 1,900
Finished goods inventory, October 1	$ 4,300
Direct labor in October	$ 3,300
Purchases of direct materials in October	$ 9,700
Work in process inventory, October 1	0
Revenues in October	$27,500
Gross profit in October	$12,700
Direct materials used in October	$ 8,800
Raw materials inventory, October 31	$ 3,200
Manufacturing overhead in October	$ 6,300

Requirement

Find the following amounts:
a. Cost of Goods Sold in October
b. Beginning Raw Materials Inventory
c. Ending Finished Goods Inventory

E2-36B Prepare a retailer's income statement *(Learning Objective 5)*

Sam Peters is the sole proprietor of Charismatic Cats, a business specializing in the sale of high-end pet gifts and accessories. Charismatic Cats' sales totaled $1,060,000 during the most recent year. During the year, the company spent $53,000 on expenses relating to website maintenance, $33,200 on marketing, and $28,500 on wrapping, boxing, and shipping the goods to customers. Charismatic Cats also spent $636,000 on inventory purchases and an additional $19,500 on freight-in charges. The company started the year with $19,800 of inventory on hand and ended the year with $13,100 of inventory. Prepare Charismatic Cats' income statement for the most recent year.

E2-37B Compute direct materials used and Cost of Goods Manufactured *(Learning Objective 5)*

Laurel Industries is calculating its Cost of Goods Manufactured at year-end. The company's accounting records show the following: The Raw Materials Inventory account had a beginning balance of $14,000 and an ending balance of $19,000. During the year, the company purchased $63,000 of direct materials. Direct labor for the year totaled $133,000 while manufacturing overhead amounted to $162,000. The Work in Process Inventory account had a beginning balance of $25,000 and an ending balance of $24,000. Assume that Raw Materials Inventory contains only direct materials. Compute the Cost of Goods Manufactured for the year. (*Hint:* The first step is to calculate the direct materials used during the year.)

E2-38B Compute Cost of Goods Manufactured and Cost of Goods Sold *(Learning Objective 5)*

Compute the Cost of Goods Manufactured and Cost of Goods Sold for Golden Bay Company for the most recent year using the amounts described next. Assume that Raw Materials Inventory contains only direct materials.

	Beginning of Year	End of Year		End of Year
Raw materials inventory	$25,000	$33,000	Insurance on plant	$ 7,500
Work in process inventory	$42,000	$36,000	Depreciation—plant building and equipment	$13,100
Finished goods inventory	$21,000	$28,000	Repairs and maintenance—plant	$ 4,400
Purchases of direct materials		$79,000	Marketing expenses	$76,000
Direct labor		$84,000	General and administrative expenses	$26,500
Indirect labor		$46,000		

E2-39B Continues E2-38B: Prepare income statement *(Learning Objective 5)*

Prepare the income statement for Golden Bay Company using the data in E2-38B for the most recent year. Assume that the company sold 39,000 units of its product at a price of $15 each during the year.

E2-40B Determine whether information is relevant *(Learning Objective 6)*

Classify each of the following costs as relevant or irrelevant to the decision at hand and briefly explain your reason.

a. The cost of production when determining whether to continue to manufacture the screen for a smartphone or to purchase it from an outside supplier (old equipment will be sold if new equipment is purchased)
b. The cost of land when determining where to build a new call center
c. The average cost of vehicle operation when purchasing a new delivery van
d. Real estate property tax rates when selecting the location for a new order processing center
e. The purchase price of the old computer when replacing it with a new computer with improved features

f. The cost of renovations when deciding whether to build a new office building or to renovate the existing office building
g. The original cost of the current stove when selecting a new, more efficient stove for a restaurant
h. Local tax incentives when selecting the location of a new office complex for a company's headquarters
i. The fair market value (trade-in value) of the existing forklift when deciding whether to replace it with a new, more efficient model
j. Fuel economy when purchasing new trucks for the delivery fleet

E2-41B Compute total and average costs *(Learning Objective 7)*

Crackling Soda spends $1 on direct materials, direct labor, and variable manufacturing overhead for every unit (12-pack of soda) it produces. Fixed manufacturing overhead costs $3 million per year. The plant, which is currently operating at only 85% of capacity, produced 20 million units this year. Management plans to operate closer to full capacity next year, producing 30 million units. Management doesn't anticipate any changes in the prices it pays for materials, labor, or manufacturing overhead.

Requirements

1. What is the current total product cost (for the 20 million units), including fixed and variable costs?
2. What is the current average product cost per unit?
3. What is the current fixed cost per unit?
4. What is the forecasted total product cost next year (for the 30 million units), including fixed and variable costs?
5. What is the forecasted average product cost next year?
6. What is the forecasted fixed cost per unit?
7. Why does the average product cost decrease as production increases?

PROBLEMS Group A

P2-42A Classify costs along the value chain *(Learning Objectives 2 & 4)*

Ravenna Cola produces a lemon-lime soda. The production process starts with workers mixing the lemon syrup and lime flavors in a secret recipe. The company enhances the combined syrup with caffeine. Finally, the company dilutes the mixture with carbonated water. Ravenna Cola incurs the following costs (in thousands):

Plant janitors' wages	$ 1,100
Delivery truck drivers' wages	$ 305
Payment for new recipe	$ 1,260
Depreciation on delivery trucks	$ 250
Plant utilities	$ 450
Lime flavoring	$ 820
Rearrangement of plant layout	$ 1,600
Bottles	$ 1,040
Salt	$ 50
Sales commissions	$ 425
Production costs of "cents-off" store coupons for customers	$ 800
Lemon syrup	$ 18,000
Replacement of products with expired dates upon customer complaint	$ 30
Depreciation on plant and equipment	$ 3,400
Wages of workers who mix syrup	$ 8,300
Customer hotline	$ 210
Freight-in on materials	$ 1,100

Requirements

1. Classify each of the listed costs according to its category in the value chain (R&D, Design, Production, Marketing, Distribution, or Customer Service).
2. Further break down production costs into three subcategories: Direct Materials (DM), Direct Labor (DL), or Manufacturing Overhead (MOH).
3. Compute the total costs for each value chain category.
4. How much are the total product costs?
5. Suppose the managers of the R&D and design functions receive year-end bonuses based on meeting their unit's target cost reductions. What are they likely to do? How might this affect costs incurred in other elements of the value chain?

P2-43A Determine ending inventory balances *(Learning Objectives 5)*

Unique Displays designs and manufactures displays used in mobile devices. Serious flooding throughout the region affected Unique Displays' facilities. Inventory was completely ruined, and the company's computer system, including all accounting records, was destroyed.

Before the disaster recovery specialists clean the buildings, Louise Ditchey, the company controller, is anxious to salvage whatever records she can to support an insurance claim for the destroyed inventory. She is standing in what is left of the Accounting Department with Trent Parker, the cost accountant.

"I didn't know mud could smell so bad," Trent says. "What should I be looking for?"

"Don't worry about beginning inventory numbers," responds Louise. "We'll get them from last year's annual report. We need first-quarter cost data."

"I was working on the first-quarter results just before the storm hit," Trent says. "Look, my report's still in my desk drawer. But all I can make out is that for the first quarter, direct material purchases were $533,000 and that direct labor, manufacturing overhead (other than indirect materials), and total manufacturing costs to account for were $551,000; $218,000; and $1,491,000, respectively. Wait, and cost of goods available for sale was $1,615,000."

"Great," says Louise. "I remember that sales for the period were approximately $1.8 million. Given our gross profit of 30%, that's all you should need."

Trent is not sure about that but decides to see what he can do with this information. The beginning inventory numbers are as follows:

- Raw materials, $75,000
- Work in process, $226,000
- Finished goods, $213,000

He remembers several schedules he learned in college that may help him get started.

Requirement
Use exhibits in the chapter to determine the ending inventories of raw materials, work in process, and finished goods. Assume that Raw Materials Inventory contains only direct materials.

P2-44A Prepare income statements *(Learning Objective 5)*

Part One: In 2015, Patsy Jackson opened Patsy's Posies, a small retail shop selling floral arrangements. On December 31, 2016, her accounting records show the following:

Sales revenue	$53,000
Utilities for shop	$ 1,100
Inventory on December 31, 2016	$ 9,100
Inventory on January 1, 2016	$12,000
Rent for shop	$ 4,600
Sales commissions	$ 4,000
Purchases of merchandise	$36,000

Requirement
Prepare an income statement for Patsy's Posies, a merchandiser, for the year ended December 31, 2016.

Part Two: Patsy's Posies was so successful that Patsy decided to manufacture her own brand of floral supplies: Floral City Manufacturing. At the end of December 2017, her accounting records show the following:

Utilities for plant	$ 4,900
Delivery expense	$ 1,500
Sales salaries expense	$ 4,300
Plant janitorial services	$ 1,350
Work in process inventory, December 31, 2017	$ 5,000
Finished goods inventory, December 31, 2016	0
Finished goods inventory, December 31, 2017	$ 2,500
Sales revenue	$104,000
Customer service hotline expense	$ 1,400
Direct labor	$ 23,000
Direct material purchases	$ 30,000
Rent on manufacturing plant	$ 9,600
Raw materials inventory, December 31, 2016	$ 14,000
Raw materials inventory, December 31, 2017	$ 8,000
Work in process inventory, December 31, 2016	0

Requirements

1. Calculate the Cost of Goods Manufactured for Floral City Manufacturing for the year ended December 31, 2017.
2. Prepare an income statement for Floral City Manufacturing for the year ended December 31, 2017.
3. How does the format of the income statement for Floral City Manufacturing differ from the income statement of Patsy's Posies?

Part Three: Show the ending inventories that would appear on these balance sheets:
1. Patsy's Posies at December 31, 2016
2. Floral City Manufacturing at December 31, 2017

P2-45A Identify relevant information *(Learning Objective 6)*

You receive two job offers in the same big city. The first job is close to your parents' house, and they have offered to let you live at home for a year so you won't have to incur expenses for housing, food, or cable and Internet. This job pays $49,000 per year. The second job is far from your parents' house, so you'll have to rent an apartment with parking ($8,500 per year), buy your own food ($3,250 per year), and pay for your own cable and Internet ($650 per year). This job pays $54,000 per year. You still plan to do laundry at your parents' house once a week if you live in the city, and you plan to go into the city once a week to visit with friends if you live at home. Thus, the cost of operating your car will be about the same either way. In addition, your parents refuse to pay for your cell phone service ($670 per year).

Requirements

1. Based on this information alone, what is the net difference between the two alternatives (salary, net of relevant costs)?
2. What information is irrelevant? Why?
3. What qualitative information is relevant to your decision?
4. Assume that you really want to take Job #2, but you also want to live at home to cut costs. What new quantitative and qualitative information will you need to incorporate into your decision?

P2-46A Calculate the total and average costs *(Learning Objective 7)*

The owner of Marshall Restaurant is disappointed because the restaurant has been averaging 7,500 pizza sales per month, but the restaurant and wait staff can make and serve 10,000 pizzas per month. The variable cost (for example, ingredients) of each pizza is

$1.55. Monthly fixed costs (for example, depreciation, property taxes, business license, and manager's salary) are $12,000 per month. The owner wants cost information about different volumes so that some operating decisions can be made.

Requirements

1. Fill in the following chart to provide the owner with the cost information. Then use the completed chart to help you answer the remaining questions.

	6,000	7,500	10,000
Monthly pizza volume			
Total fixed costs	$	$	$
Total variable costs			
Total costs			
Fixed cost per pizza	$	$	$
Variable cost per pizza			
Average cost per pizza			
Selling price per pizza	$ 6.25	$ 6.25	$ 6.25
Average profit per pizza			

2. From a cost standpoint, why do companies such as Marshall Restaurant want to operate near or at full capacity?
3. The owner has been considering ways to increase the sales volume. The owner thinks that 10,000 pizzas could be sold per month by cutting the selling price per pizza from $6.25 to $5.75. How much extra profit (above the current level) would be generated if the selling price were to be decreased? (*Hint:* Find the restaurant's current monthly profit and compare it to the restaurant's projected monthly profit at the new sales price and volume.)

PROBLEMS Group B

P2-47B Classify costs along the value chain *(Learning Objectives 2 & 4)*

Crystal Cola produces a lemon-lime soda. The production process starts with workers mixing the lemon syrup and lime flavors in a secret recipe. The company enhances the combined syrup with caffeine. Finally, the company dilutes the mixture with carbonated water. Crystal Cola incurs the following costs (in thousands):

Delivery truck drivers' wages	$ 285
Lemon syrup	$16,000
Depreciation on delivery trucks	$ 175
Lime flavoring	$ 1,020
Payment for new recipe	$ 1,090
Customer hotline	$ 220
Sales commissions	$ 450
Production costs of "cents-off" store coupons for customers	$ 630
Rearrangement of plant layout	$ 1,200
Freight-in on materials	$ 1,300
Depreciation on plant and equipment	$ 2,900
Bottles	$ 1,490
Salt	$ 15
Plant utilities	$ 1,250
Wages of workers who mix syrup	$ 7,900
Plant janitors' wages	$ 1,000
Replacement of products with expired dates upon customer complaint	$ 40

Requirements

1. Classify each of the listed costs according to its category in the value chain (R&D, Design, Production, Marketing, Distribution, or Customer Service).
2. Further break down production costs into three subcategories: Direct Materials (DM), Direct Labor (DL), or Manufacturing Overhead (MOH).
3. Compute the total costs for each value chain category.
4. How much are the total product costs?
5. Suppose the managers of the R&D and design functions receive year-end bonuses based on meeting their unit's target cost reductions. What are they likely to do? How might this affect costs incurred in other elements of the value chain?

P2-48B   Determine ending inventory balances *(Learning Objective 5)*

Finney Displays designs and manufactures displays used in mobile devices. Serious flooding throughout the region affected Finney Displays' facilities. Inventory was completely ruined, and the company's computer system, including all accounting records, was destroyed.

Before the disaster recovery specialists clean the buildings, Heather Bailey, the company controller, is anxious to salvage whatever records she can to support an insurance claim for the destroyed inventory. She is standing in what is left of the Accounting Department with Tad Myers, the cost accountant.

"I didn't know mud could smell so bad," Tad says. "What should I be looking for?"

"Don't worry about beginning inventory numbers," responds Heather. "We'll get them from last year's annual report. We need first-quarter cost data."

"I was working on the first-quarter results just before the storm hit," Tad says. "Look, my report's still in my desk drawer. But all I can make out is that for the first quarter, direct material purchases were $524,000 and that direct labor, manufacturing overhead (other than indirect materials), and total manufacturing costs to account for were $545,000; $218,000; and $1,508,000, respectively. Wait, and cost of goods available for sale was $1,615,000."

"Great," says Heather. "I remember that sales for the period were approximately $1.6 million. Given our gross profit of 15%, that's all you should need."

Tad is not sure about that but decides to see what he can do with this information. The beginning inventory numbers are as follows:

- Raw materials, $85,000
- Work in process, $187,000
- Finished goods, $209,000

He remembers several schedules he learned in college that may help him get started.

Requirement

Use exhibits in the chapter to determine the ending inventories of raw materials, work in process, and finished goods. Assume that the Raw Materials Inventory contains only direct materials.

P2-49B   Prepare income statements *(Learning Objective 5)*

Part One: In 2015, Fran Lexa opened Fran's Flowers, a small shop selling floral arrangements. On December 31, 2016, her accounting records show the following:

Sales revenue	$53,000
Utilities for shop	$ 1,000
Inventory on December 31, 2016	$ 9,200
Inventory on January 1, 2016	$12,600
Rent for shop	$ 4,400
Sales commissions	$ 4,100
Purchases of merchandise	$38,000

Requirement

Prepare an income statement for Fran's Flowers, a merchandiser, for the year ended December 31, 2016.

Part Two: Fran's Flowers succeeded so well that Fran decided to manufacture her own brand of floral supplies: Floral Place Manufacturing. At the end of December 2017, her accounting records show the following:

Utilities for plant..	$ 4,300
Delivery expense...	$ 3,800
Sales salaries expense..	$ 4,800
Plant janitorial services..	$ 1,250
Work in process inventory, December 31, 2017..	$ 4,000
Finished goods inventory, December 31, 2016..	0
Finished goods inventory, December 31, 2017..	$ 4,500
Sales revenue	$ 109,000
Customer service hotline expense...	$ 1,700
Direct labor	$ 22,000
Direct material purchases..	$ 31,000
Rent on manufacturing plant	$ 9,400
Raw materials inventory, December 31, 2016..	$ 18,000
Raw materials inventory, December 31, 2017..	$ 7,500
Work in process inventory, December 31, 2016...	0

Requirements

1. Calculate the cost of goods manufactured for Floral Place Manufacturing for the year ended December 31, 2017.
2. Prepare an income statement for Floral Place Manufacturing for the year ended December 31, 2017.
3. How does the format of the income statement for Floral Place Manufacturing differ from the income statement of Fran's Flowers?

Part Three: Show the ending inventories that would appear on these balance sheets:

1. Fran's Flowers at December 31, 2016.
2. Floral Place Manufacturing at December 31, 2017.

P2-50B Identify relevant information *(Learning Objective 6)*

You receive two job offers in the same big city. The first job is close to your parents' house, and they have offered to let you live at home for a year so you won't have to incur expenses for housing, food, or cable and Internet. This job pays $42,000 per year. The second job is far away from your parents' house, so you'll have to rent an apartment with parking ($12,000 per year), buy your own food ($3,000 per year), and pay for your own cable and Internet ($800 per year). This job pays $47,000 per year. You still plan to do laundry at your parents' house once a week if you live in the city and plan to go into the city once a week to visit with friends if you live at home. Thus, the cost of operating your car will be about the same either way. Additionally, your parents refuse to pay for your cell phone service ($740 per year).

Requirements

1. Based on this information alone, what is the net difference between the two alternatives (salary, net of relevant costs)?
2. What information is irrelevant? Why?
3. What qualitative information is relevant to your decision?
4. Assume you really want to take Job #2, but you also want to live at home to cut costs. What new quantitative and qualitative information will you need to incorporate in your decision?

P2-51B Calculate the total and average costs *(Learning Objective 7)*

The owner of Yoders Restaurant is disappointed because the restaurant has been averaging 8,000 pizza sales per month but the restaurant and wait staff can make and serve 10,000 pizzas per month. The variable cost (for example, ingredients) of each pizza is $1.45. Monthly fixed costs (for example, depreciation, property taxes, business license, manager's salary) are $10,000 per month. The owner wants cost information about different volumes so that some operating decisions can be made.

Requirements

1. Fill in the chart to provide the owner with the cost information. Then use the completed chart to help you answer the remaining questions.

	$5,000	$8,000	$10,000
Monthly pizza volume			
Total fixed costs			
Total variable costs			
Total costs			
Fixed cost per pizza	$	$	$
Variable cost per pizza			
Average cost per pizza			
Selling price per pizza	$ 6.25	$ 6.25	$ 6.25
Average profit per pizza			

2. From a cost standpoint, why do companies such as Yoders Restaurant want to operate near or at full capacity?
3. The owner has been considering ways to increase the sales volume. The owner thinks that 10,000 pizzas could be sold per month by cutting the selling price from $6.25 per pizza to $5.75. How much extra profit (above the current level) would be generated if the selling price were to be decreased? (*Hint*: Find the restaurant's current monthly profit and compare it to the restaurant's projected monthly profit at the new sales price and volume.)

Serial Case

C2-52 Calculate operating income *(Learning Objective 5)*

This case is a continuation of the Caesars Entertainment Corporation serial case that began in Chapter 1. Refer to the introductory story in Chapter 1 (see page 43) for additional background. (The components of the Caesars serial case can be completed in any order.)

What follows is a table listing condensed revenue and expense figures for Caesars Entertainment Corporation for the years ending December 31, 2012 through 2014.

	2014	2013	2012
Food and beverage expenses	$ 694	$ 639	$ 634
Other revenues	369	73	(315)
Casino expenses	3,253	3,112	3,368
Food and beverage revenue	1,522	1,451	1,438
Rooms expenses	315	296	289
Miscellaneous expenses	4,706	6,199	3,761
Casino revenue	5,418	5,529	5,916
Rooms revenue	1,207	1,167	1,147

Requirements

1. Using the data provided, construct income statements for each of the three years; include the proper headings.
2. Did Caesars's operating income increase or decrease over the three-year period presented?
3. Which division, Food and Beverage, Casino, Rooms, or Other generated the most revenue for Caesars in 2014? Which division generated the most operating income in 2014?

CRITICAL THINKING

Discussion & Analysis

A2-53 Discussion Questions

1. Briefly describe a service company, a merchandising company, and a manufacturing company. Give an example of each type of company, but do not use the same examples as given in the chapter.

2. How do service, merchandising, and manufacturing companies differ from each other? How are service, merchandising, and manufacturing companies similar to each other? List as many similarities and differences as you can identify.

3. What is the value chain? What are the six types of business activities found in the value chain? Which type(s) of business activities in the value chain generate costs that go directly to the income statement once incurred? What type(s) of business activities in the value chain generate costs that flow into inventory on the balance sheet?

4. Compare direct costs to indirect costs. Give an example of a cost at a company that could be a direct cost at one level of the organization but would be considered an indirect cost at a different level of that organization. Explain why this same cost could be both direct and indirect (at different levels).

5. What is meant by the term *product costs*? What is meant by the term *period costs*? Why does it matter whether a cost is a product cost or a period cost?

6. Compare product costs to period costs. Using a product of your choice, give examples of product costs and period costs. Explain why you categorized your costs as you did.

7. Describe how the income statement of a merchandising company differs from the income statement of a manufacturing company. Also comment on how the income statement from a merchandising company is similar to the income statement of a manufacturing company.

8. How are the cost of goods manufactured, the cost of goods sold, the income statement, and the balance sheet related for a manufacturing company? What specific items flow from one statement or schedule to the next? Describe the flow of costs between the cost of goods manufactured, the cost of goods sold, the income statement, and the balance sheet for a manufacturing company.

9. What makes a cost relevant or irrelevant when making a decision? Suppose a company is evaluating whether to use its warehouse for storage of its own inventory or whether to rent it out to a local theater group for housing props. Describe what information might be relevant when making that decision.

10. Explain why "differential cost" and "variable cost" do *not* have the same meaning. Give an example of a situation in which there is a cost that is a differential cost but *not* a variable cost.

11. Greenwashing, the practice of overstating a company's commitment to sustainability, has been in the news over the past few years. Perform an online search of the term *greenwashing*. What examples of greenwashing can you find?

12. Ricoh is a company that has designed its copiers so that at the end of the copier's life, Ricoh will collect and dismantle the product for usable parts, shred the metal casing, and use the parts and shredded material to build new copiers. This product design can be called "cradle-to-cradle" design. Are there any other products you are aware of that have such a design? Perform an online search for "cradle-to-cradle design" or a related term if you need ideas.

Application & Analysis
Mini Cases

A2-54 Costs in the value chain at a real company and cost objects

Choose a company with which you are familiar that manufactures a product. In this activity, you will be making reasonable assumptions about the activities involved in the value chain for this product; companies do not typically publish information about their value chains.

Basic Discussion Questions

1. Describe the product that is being produced and the company that produces it.
2. Describe the six value chain business activities that this product would pass through from its inception to its ultimate delivery to the customer.
3. List at least three costs that would be incurred in each of the six business activities in the value chain.
4. Classify each cost you identified in the value chain as being either a product cost or a period cost. Explain your justification.
5. A cost object can be anything for which managers want a separate measurement of cost. List three different potential cost objects *other* than the product itself for the company you have selected.
6. List a direct cost and an indirect cost for each of the three different cost objects in question 5. Explain why each cost would be direct or indirect.

ETHICS

A2-55 Ethics involved with assigning costs to inventory *(Learning Objectives 4 & 5)*

Brandon is the production manager of a large manufacturing firm. He is worried about the prospect of bonuses for the upcoming year. The company has paid out bonuses for the past ten years, so Brandon has been counting on the bonus to help pay some debts he has accumulated over the year. In addition, Brandon and his wife are expecting their first baby in two months. Due to the unexpected downturn in sales, bonuses appear to be unlikely this year.

Ryan is the accounting manager for the company. He and Brandon are good friends. Over lunch one day, Brandon confides in Ryan about his financial difficulties. He is stressed out over the bills and the baby on the way. He really needs that bonus.

Ryan wants to help Brandon. Ryan has been with the company for many years and knows that fundamentally the company is strong. This year is just an unusual year. He thinks about ways that he can help Brandon. Brandon is a good employee, and the company does not want to lose him if he were to go to work for a competitor.

Ryan thinks about how he can best help Brandon. He thinks about a few different options, including the following:

Option #1: Ryan could increase income for the year by adding sales commission costs and advertising costs to the products. If he does this, the product cost will be higher. However, there is still a large inventory of units on hand. The units that are still in ending inventory will shield these costs from decreasing net income until the units are sold in a future year.

Option #2: Ryan could quietly make Brandon a loan from the company to help him get back on his feet. The company does not have a policy prohibiting loans to employees, but neither does it have a policy of allowing such loans to employees.

Ryan does not know what to do.

Requirements

Using the IMA *Statement of Ethical Professional Practice* as an ethical framework, answer the following questions:

a. If Ryan were to increase income by adding sales commission costs and advertising costs to product costs as described in Option #1, what ethical principles would be violated?
b. If Ryan were to make a company loan to Brandon (Option #2), what, if any, ethical principles would be violated?
c. What do you think Ryan should do in this situation?

Building Blocks of Managerial Accounting 103

A2-56 Cost definitions *(Learning Objectives 1, 2, 3, & 4)*

REAL LIFE

During 2015, the price that Starbucks paid its suppliers for its coffee decreased. Despite the decrease in coffee costs, Starbucks raised the prices of its brewed coffee across the United States by an average of about 1% in 2015.[14] Starbucks did not raise prices for its bagged coffee sold at grocery stores and at Starbucks stores.

In many of the regions in which Starbucks operates, laws have been passed to raise the minimum wage. In addition, the real estate market has recovered in several cities, causing the cost of retail space to increase. Starbucks also started an initiative in 2015 to cover the full cost of an online degree for its U.S. employees who work at least 20 hours per week.

Requirements

1. Would you consider Starbucks to be a service company, a merchandiser, a manufacturer, or some combination thereof? Support your answer with specific examples.

2. Describe the value chain for a cup of coffee at Starbucks. Use your imagination and brainstorm possible costs at each phase of the value chain. Where are the cost increases occurring in that value chain? Where are the cost decreases occurring in the value chain?

3. Think about a Starbucks café in Bellevue, Tennessee, and a cup of coffee served and consumed in that café.

    a. What costs would be included in the cost of a cup of coffee served in the café? Separate these costs into direct materials, direct labor, and overhead costs. Which type(s) of costs (direct materials, direct labor, or overhead costs) would have increased in 2015 for Starbucks? Which type(s) would have decreased in 2015?

    b. What are the direct costs of a cup of coffee, assuming that the cost object is the Bellevue location? What are the indirect costs of that same cup of coffee for the Bellevue location?

    c. Assume now that the cost object is the Starbucks corporation itself. What costs of that cup of coffee will now be reclassified as direct (as compared to using the Bellevue location as the cost object)?

4. Now think about a Starbucks café in Bellevue, Tennessee, and a pound of bagged ground coffee sold in that café (assume that the beans are ground in the store at the time of sale).

    a. What costs are included in the cost of a pound of bagged ground coffee sold at the Bellevue location? Separate these costs into direct materials, direct labor, and overhead costs.

    b. What are the direct costs of a pound of bagged ground coffee (to be sold to consumers), assuming that the cost object is the Bellevue location? What are the indirect costs of that same pound of bagged ground coffee for the Bellevue location?

    c. Assume now that the cost object is the Starbucks corporation itself. What costs of that bagged ground coffee will now be reclassified as direct (as compared to using the Bellevue location as the cost object)?

Try It Solutions

page 57:

Only those costs that can be traced directly to the Produce Department would be considered direct costs: 2, 3, 5, 6 and 8. All other costs (1, 4, and 7) would be considered indirect costs because they are part of the cost of selling produce at the store, yet cannot be traced directly to the Produce Department.

page 59:

The only costs that become inventoriable costs of the product are numbers 3, 5, and 8. All other costs are classified as period costs, which are shown as "operating expenses" on the income statement.

page 67:

Beginning inventory	$ 35,000
Plus: Purchases of merchandise	400,000
Freight-in and import duties	20,000
Cost of goods available for sale	455,000
Less: Ending inventory	38,000
Cost of goods sold	$ 417,000

[14]*Source:* "Starbucks Raises Prices Despite Declining Coffee Costs," *The Wall Street Journal*, July 6, 2015.

3
Job Costing

Nithid Memanee/Shutterstock

Sources: Brunswick Corp. 2015 10(k) filing; http://lifefitness.com

Learning Objectives

- **1** Distinguish between job costing and process costing
- **2** Understand the flow of production and how direct materials and direct labor are traced to jobs
- **3** Compute a predetermined manufacturing overhead rate and use it to allocate MOH to jobs
- **4** Determine the cost of a job and use it to make business decisions
- **5** Compute and dispose of overallocated or underallocated manufacturing overhead
- **6** Prepare journal entries for a manufacturer's job costing system
- **7** (Appendix) Use job costing at a service firm as a basis for billing clients

With annual sales of over $794 million, Life Fitness, a division of the Brunswick Corporation, is the world's largest manufacturer of commercial fitness equipment and a global leader in consumer fitness equipment. The company began in the 1970s by introducing the world's first-ever computerized stationary exercise bicycle. Since then, the company has grown to design and manufacture hundreds of different products, including treadmills, elliptical cross-trainers, stair climbers, strength equipment, and, of course, exercise bikes. While the company's growth has been propelled in part by consumers' ever-increasing zeal for personal fitness, the company has also grown through carefully analyzing the profit margins on each of its products and adjusting its operations accordingly.

How do managers determine the profit margins on each of the company's different models of fitness equipment? Managers first determine how much it costs to manufacture a batch of each model. Each batch of units produced is called a "job." The company's job costing system traces the cost of direct materials and direct labor used to each job. It also allocates some manufacturing overhead to each job. By adding up the direct materials, direct labor, and manufacturing overhead assigned to each job, the company can determine the cost of the job, as well as the average cost of each unit in the job. The company then uses this information to prepare the company's financial reports and make vital business decisions.

Job Costing

Whether you plan a career in marketing, engineering, production, general management, or accounting, you'll need to understand how much each of the company's products cost to produce. This chapter will show you the way companies determine their product costs when they make unique products or products made in relatively small batches.

What Methods Are Used to Determine the Cost of Manufacturing a Product?

1 Distinguish between job costing and process costing

Most manufacturers use one of two product costing systems in order to find the cost of producing their products:

- Process costing
- Job costing

The end goal of both product costing systems is the same: to find the cost of manufacturing one unit of the product. However, the manner in which this goal is achieved differs. Management chooses the product costing system that works best for its particular manufacturing environment. Let's go over the basics of each system and identify the types of companies that would be most likely to use them.

Process Costing

Process costing is used by companies that produce extremely large numbers of identical units through a series of uniform production steps or processes. Because each unit is identical, in theory, each unit should cost the same to make. In essence, process costing averages manufacturing costs across all units produced so that each identical unit bears the same cost.

For example, let's assume Pace Foods uses two processes to make picante sauce: (1) cleaning and chopping vegetables and (2) mixing and bottling the sauce. First, Pace accumulates all manufacturing costs incurred in the cleaning and chopping process over a period of time, such as a month. The costs incurred in this process include the cost of the vegetables themselves, as well as the cost of cleaning and chopping the vegetables. Next, the company averages the total costs of this process over all units passing through the process during the same period of time.

For example, let's say Pace spends $500,000 on purchasing, cleaning, and chopping the vegetables to make 1 million jars of picante sauce during the month. The average cost per jar of the cleaning and chopping process is as follows:

$$\text{Average cost per jar of the cleaning and chopping process} = \frac{\$500,000}{1,000,000 \text{ jars}} = \$0.50 \text{ per jar}$$

Now the cleaned and chopped vegetables go through the second production process, mixing and bottling, where a similar calculation is performed to find the average cost of that process. The cost of the second process would include any direct materials used, such as the cost of the glass jars, as well as the cost of mixing the sauce and filling the jars with the sauce. Let's say the average cost to mix and bottle each jar of sauce is $0.25.

Now Pace can determine the total cost to manufacture each jar of picante sauce:

Each jar of picante sauce is identical to every other jar, so each bears the same average cost: $0.75. Once managers know the cost of manufacturing each jar of sauce, they can use that information to help set sales prices and make other business decisions. To generate a profit, the sales price will have to be high enough to cover the $0.75 per jar product cost as well as the company's operating costs incurred in other areas of the value chain, including research and development (R&D), design, marketing, distribution, and customer service. We'll delve more deeply into process costing in Chapter 5. For now, just remember that any company that mass-produces identical units of product will most likely use process costing to determine the cost of making each unit.

Job Costing

Whereas process costing is used by companies that mass-manufacture identical units, **job costing** (also called job order costing) is used by companies that produce unique, custom-ordered products, or relatively small batches of different products. Each unique product or batch of units is considered a separate "job." Different jobs can vary considerably in direct materials, direct labor, and manufacturing overhead costs, so job costing tracks these costs separately for each individual job. For example, Life Fitness produces hundreds of different models of fitness equipment, including cross-trainers, bikes, stairclimbers, and strength equipment. Each model is produced in relatively small, separate batches. Each batch is considered a separate job. Job costing would also be used by Boeing (airplanes), custom-home builders (unique houses), high-end jewelers (unique jewelry), furniture manufacturers (sofas and chairs with different fabrics), and any other manufacturers that build relatively unique products in small batches.

Job costing is not limited to manufacturers. Professional service providers such as law firms, accounting firms, consulting firms, and marketing firms use job costing to determine the cost of serving each client. People working in trades, such as mechanics, plumbers, and electricians, also use job costing to determine the cost of performing separate jobs for clients. In both cases, the job cost is used as a basis for billing the client. The appendix to this chapter illustrates a complete example of how a law firm would use job costing to bill its clients.

In summary, companies use job costing when their products or services vary in terms of materials needed, time required to complete the job, and/or the complexity of the production process. Because the jobs are so different, it would not be reasonable to assign them equal costs. Therefore, the cost of each job is compiled separately. We'll spend the rest of this chapter looking at how companies compile, record, and use job costs to make important business decisions. Before moving on, take a look at Exhibit 3-1, which summarizes the key differences between job and process costing.

> ■ **Why is this important?**
>
> "Managers need the most accurate **cost information** they can get in order to make good **business decisions**. They will choose a costing system (usually **job costing** or **process costing**) based on which system best fits their operations."

EXHIBIT 3-1 Differences Between Job and Process Costing

	Job Costing	Process Costing
Cost object:	Job	Process
Outputs:	Single units or small batches with large differences between jobs	Large quantities of identical units
Extent of averaging:	Less averaging—costs are averaged over the small number of units in a job (often one unit in a job)	More averaging—costs are averaged over the thousands or millions of identical units that pass through each process

STOP & THINK

Do all manufacturers use job costing or process costing systems?

Answer: Some manufacturers use a hybrid of these two costing systems if neither "pure" system reflects their production environment very well. For example, clothing manufacturers often mass-produce the same product over and over (dress shirts) but use different materials on different batches (cotton fabric on one batch and silk fabric on another). Apple allows consumers to custom order computers with different choices on memory, storage, screen size, and so forth. **Mass customization** is large-scale production that allows manufacturers to meet a variety of consumer desires, while at the same time achieving the efficiencies of mass production (economies of scale) that drive down unit costs. A hybrid costing system suitable to mass customization would include some elements of a process costing system (averaging labor and manufacturing overhead costs across all units) and some elements of a job costing system (tracing different fabric costs to different batches; tracing different components to different build-to-order computers).

How Do Manufacturers Determine a Job's Cost?

2 Understand the flow of production and how direct materials and direct labor are traced to jobs

As we've just seen, manufacturers use job costing if they produce unique products or relatively small batches of different products. Life Fitness produces hundreds of different models in relatively small batches, so it considers each batch a separate job. In this section, we will show you how Life Fitness would determine the cost of producing Job 603, a batch of 50 identical X4 Elliptical Cross-Trainers.[1] The company's market for these cross-trainers includes health and fitness clubs, student fitness centers on college campuses, professional athletic teams, hotels, city recreation departments, and direct sales to customers for home fitness gyms. As we walk through the process, keep in mind that most companies maintain the illustrated documents in electronic, rather than hard copy, form. Even so, the basic information stored in the documents and the purpose for the documents remain the same.

Overview: Flow of Inventory Through a Manufacturing System

Before we delve into Life Fitness's job costing system, let's take a quick look at how the physical products, as well as costs, flow through the company. As you learned in Chapter 2, manufacturers such as Life Fitness maintain three separate types of inventory: raw materials, work in process, and finished goods. The cost of each of these inventories is reflected on the company's balance sheet.

As shown in Exhibit 3-2, the raw materials (RM) inventory is maintained in a storeroom in or near the factory until the materials are needed in production. As soon as these materials are transferred to the factory floor, they are no longer considered raw materials because they have become part of the work in process in the factory. The work in process (WIP) inventory consists of all products that are partway through the production process. As soon as the manufacturing process is complete, the products are moved out of the factory and into a finished goods (FG) inventory storage area, or warehouse, where they will await sale and shipment to a customer. Finally, when the products are shipped to customers, the cost of manufacturing those products becomes the Cost of Goods Sold (CGS) shown on the company's income statement.

---

[1] All references to Life Fitness in this hypothetical example were created by the author solely for academic purposes and are not intended, in any way, to represent the actual business practices of, or costs incurred by, Life Fitness, Inc.

EXHIBIT 3-2 Flow of Inventory Through a Manufacturing System

Keep the basic flow of inventory shown in Exhibit 3-2 in mind as we delve into Life Fitness's job costing system.

Scheduling Production

Job costing begins with management's decision to produce a batch of units. Sometimes companies produce a batch of units just to meet a particular customer order. For example, the Chicago Bears may custom order treadmills that have characteristics not found on other models. This batch of unique treadmills would become its own job. On the other hand, most companies also produce **stock inventory** for products they sell on a regular basis. They want to have stock available to quickly fill customer orders. By forecasting demand for the product, the manufacturer is able to estimate the number of units that should be produced during a given time period. As shown in Exhibit 3-3, the **production schedule** indicates the quantity and types of inventory that are scheduled to be manufactured during the period. Depending on the company, the types of products it offers, and the production time required, production schedules may cover periods of time as short as one day (Dell, producing customized laptops), several months (Boeing, manufacturing 737 airplanes), or several years (bridges, roads, large commercial buildings and stadiums).

EXHIBIT 3-3 Monthly Production Schedule

	Production Schedule For the Month of December				
Job	Model Number	Stock or Customer	Quantity	Scheduled Start Date	Scheduled End Date
603	X4 Cross-Trainer	For stock	50	12/2	12/6
604	T5 Treadmill	For stock	60	12/7	12/17
605	Custom T6-C Treadmill	Chicago Bears	15	12/18	12/21
606	Custom S3-C Stair-Climber	Chicago Bears	12	12/22	12/24
	FACTORY CLOSED FOR HOLIDAYS and ANNUAL MAINTENANCE			12/25	12/31

The production schedule is very important in helping management determine the direct labor and direct materials needed during the period. To complete production on time, managers must ensure they have the right amounts and types of raw materials and skilled labor available to meet production requirements. The next section shows how this is accomplished.

Purchasing Raw Materials

Production engineers prepare a **bill of materials** for each job. The bill of materials is like a recipe card: It simply lists all of the raw materials needed to manufacture the job. Exhibit 3-4 illustrates a partial bill of materials for Job 603:

EXHIBIT 3-4 Bill of Materials (Partial Listing)

Bill of Materials

Job: 603
Model: X4 Elliptical Cross-Trainer   Quantity: 50 units

Part Number	Description	Quantity Needed
HRM50812	Heart rate monitor	50
LCD620	LCD entertainment screen	50
B4906	Front and rear roller base	100
HG2567	Hand grips	100
FP689	Foot platform	100
	Etc.	

After the bill of materials has been prepared, the purchasing department checks the raw materials inventory to determine which raw materials needed for the job are currently in stock and which raw materials must be purchased. As shown in Exhibit 3-5, a **raw materials record** shows detailed information about each item in stock, including the number of units received, the number of units used, and the running balance of units currently in stock. Additionally, the raw materials record shows the cost of each unit purchased, the cost of each unit used, and the cost of the units currently in the raw materials inventory.

EXHIBIT 3-5 Raw Materials Record

Raw Materials Record

Item No.: HRM50812   Description: Heart rate monitor

Date	Received Units	Received Cost	Received Total	Requisition Number	Used Units	Used Cost	Used Total	Balance Units	Balance Cost	Balance Total
11-25	100	$60	$6,000					100	$60	$6,000
11-30				#7235	70	$60	$4,200	30	$60	$1,800

According to the raw materials record pictured in Exhibit 3-5, only 30 heart rate monitors are currently in stock. However, the bill of materials shown in Exhibit 3-4 indicates that 50 heart rate monitors are needed for Job 603. Therefore, the purchasing department will need to buy 20 more monitors. The purchasing department must also consider other jobs that will be using heart rate monitors in the near future, as well as the time it takes to obtain the monitors from the company's suppliers. According to the production schedule, Job 603 is scheduled to begin production on December 2; therefore, the purchasing department must make sure all necessary raw materials are on hand by that date.

Life Fitness's purchasing department will issue a **purchase order** to its suppliers for any needed parts. Incoming shipments of raw materials are counted and then recorded on a **receiving report**, as well as on the individual raw materials records. The receiving report is typically a duplicate of the purchase order, except it does not pre-list the quantity of parts ordered. The quantity ordered is intentionally left blank to ensure the receiving dock personnel will actually count and record the quantity of materials received. Progressive companies use bar-coding systems to electronically update the raw materials records as soon as incoming shipments are received.

Life Fitness's accounting department will not pay the **invoice** (bill from the supplier) unless the amount billed agrees with the quantity of parts both ordered *and* received. By matching the purchase order, receiving report, and invoice, Life Fitness ensures that it pays for only those parts that were ordered and received, *and nothing more*. This is an important control that helps companies avoid scams in which businesses are sent and billed for inventory that was not ordered.

In addition to tracking the current level of individual inventory items, the raw materials records also form the basis for valuing the Raw Materials Inventory account found on the balance sheet. On a given date, by adding together the balances in the individual raw materials records, the company is able to substantiate the total Raw Materials Inventory shown on the balance sheet. For example, as shown in Exhibit 3-6, on November 30, Life Fitness had $1,800 of heart rate monitors in stock, $24,000 of LCD entertainment screens, $1,200 of roller bases, and so forth. When added together, these individual balances sum to the Raw Materials Inventory balance shown on Life Fitness's November 30 balance sheet.

EXHIBIT 3-6 Individual Raw Materials Records Sum to the Raw Materials Inventory Balance

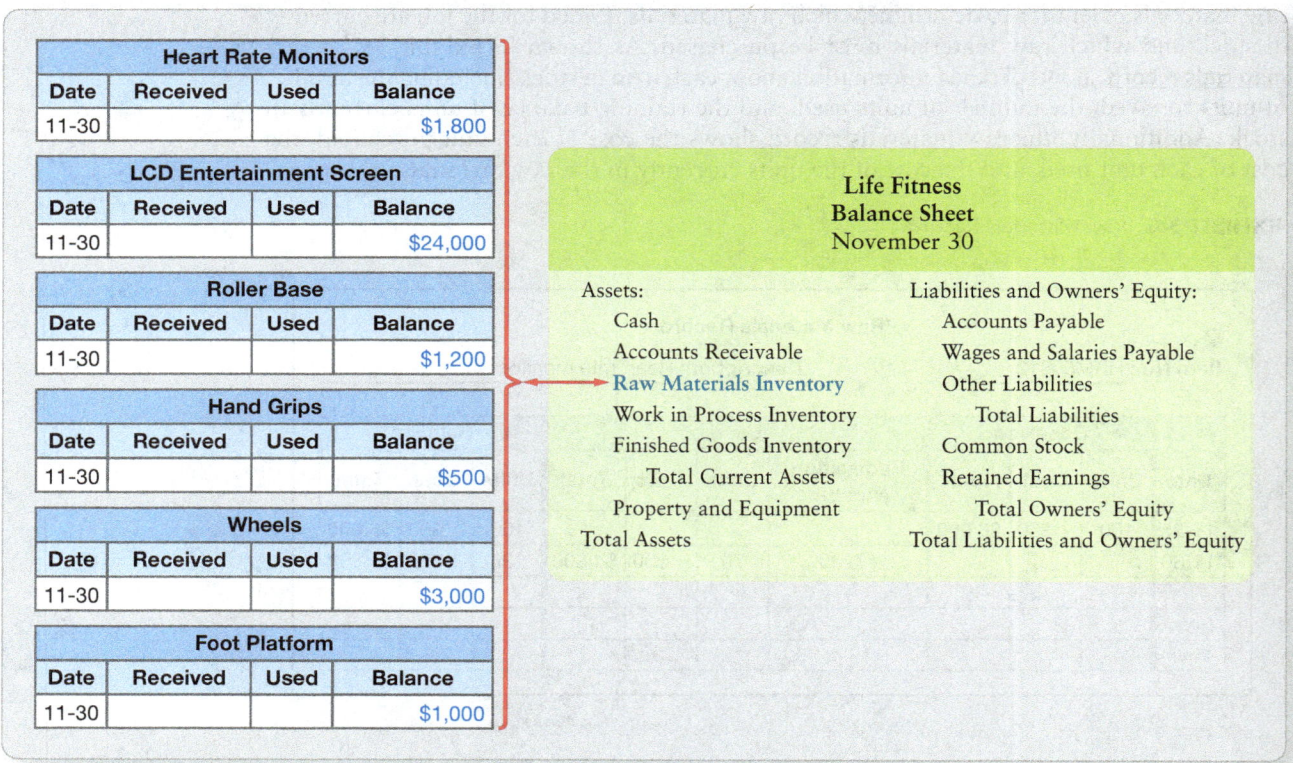

Using a Job Cost Record to Keep Track of Job Costs

Job 603 will be started when the scheduled production date arrives. A **job cost record**, as pictured in Exhibit 3-7, will be used to keep track of all the direct materials and direct labor used on the job, as well as the manufacturing overhead allocated to the job.

Try It!

Match the following concepts to their descriptions:

1. Document specifying when jobs will be manufactured
2. Product costing system used by mass manufacturers
3. Bill from supplier
4. Document specifying parts needed to produce a job
5. Product costing system used by manufacturers of unique products
6. Document containing the details and balance of each part in stock
7. Document for recording incoming shipments
8. Products normally kept on hand in order to fill orders quickly

a. Process costing
b. Stock inventory
c. Raw materials records
d. Production schedule
e. Receiving report
f. Invoice
g. Bill of materials
h. Job costing

Please see page 174 for solutions.

EXHIBIT 3-7 Job Cost Record

Job Cost Record

Job Number: 603

Customer: For stock

Job Description: 50 units of X4 Elliptical Cross-Trainers

Date Started: Dec. 2   **Date Completed:** _____

Manufacturing Cost Information:	Cost Summary	
Direct Materials		
	$	
Direct Labor		
	$	
Manufacturing Overhead		
	$	
Total Job Cost	$	
Number of Units	÷	50 units
Cost per Unit	$	

Shipping Information:			
Date	Quantity Shipped	Units Remaining	Cost Balance

112 CHAPTER 3

> **Why is this important?**
> "**Job cost records** keep track of **all manufacturing costs** assigned to **individual jobs** so that **managers** know the **cost** of making each product."

Each job will have its own job cost record. Note that the job cost record is merely a form (electronic or hard copy) for keeping track of the three manufacturing costs associated with each job:

- direct materials,
- direct labor, and
- manufacturing overhead.

The job cost records also show the number of units produced on the job, as well as the cost per unit.

As we saw in the last section, the individual raw materials records add up to the total Raw Materials Inventory account shown on the balance sheet. Likewise, as shown in Exhibit 3-8, the job cost records on *incomplete* jobs provide the supporting detail for the total Work in Process Inventory account shown on the balance sheet.

EXHIBIT 3-8 Job Cost Records on Incomplete Jobs Sum to the WIP Inventory Balance

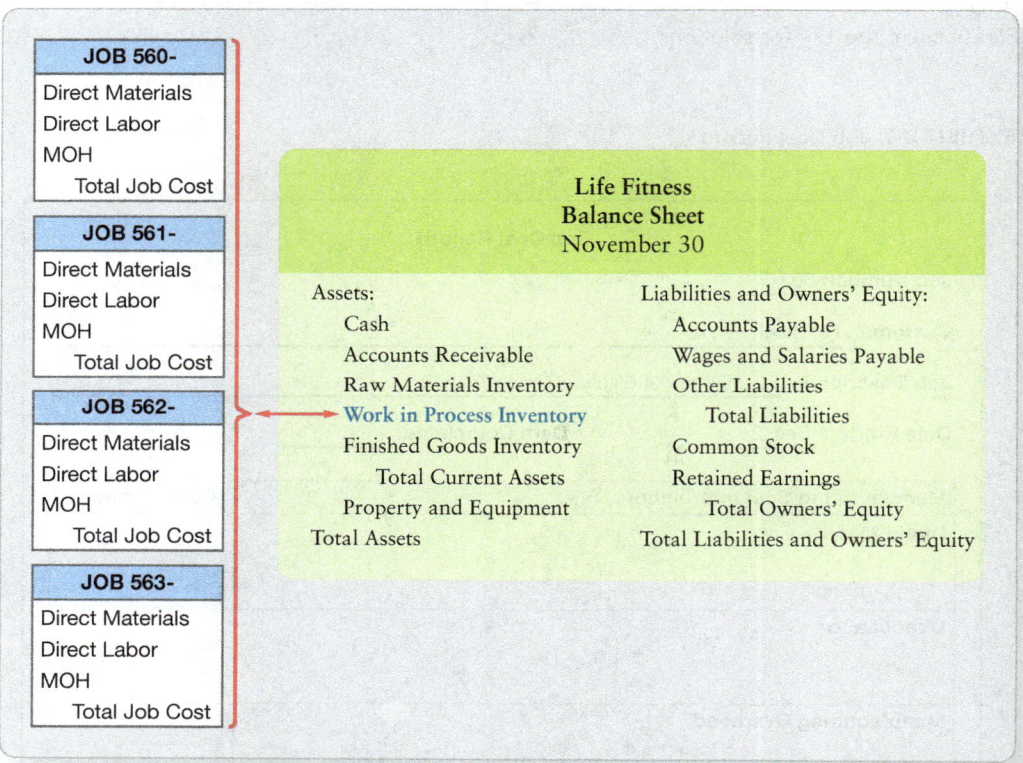

Once jobs are completed, the job cost records serve as a basis for valuing the Finished Goods Inventory account. As shown near the bottom of Exhibit 3-7, job cost records typically list the date and quantity of units shipped to customers, the number of units remaining in finished goods inventory, and the cost of those units. The balance of *unsold* units from *completed* job cost records add up to the total Finished Goods Inventory account shown on the balance sheet.

As you can see, the job cost records serve a vital role in a job costing system. Now let's take a look at how Life Fitness accumulates manufacturing costs on the job cost record. We'll begin by looking at how direct materials costs are traced to individual jobs.

Tracing Direct Materials Cost to a Job

Production will eventually need all of the parts shown on the bill of materials for Job 603 (Exhibit 3-4). However, according to the production schedule (Exhibit 3-3), this job is scheduled to take five days to complete, so the production crew may not want all of the raw materials at once. Each time materials are needed, production personnel will fill out a **materials requisition**. As shown in Exhibit 3-9, the materials requisition is a document itemizing the materials currently needed from the storeroom. Notice that the root word of *requisition* is *request*. In essence, production personnel use this document to *request* that certain materials be sent from the storeroom into the factory. Most progressive companies use electronic forms, but we show a hard copy here.

EXHIBIT 3-9 Materials Requisition

Materials Requisition

Date: 12/2 Number: #7568

Job: 603

Part Number	Description	Quantity	Unit Cost	Amount
HRM50812	Heart rate monitor	50	$60	$3,000
LCD620	LCD entertainment screen	50	$100	5,000
B4906	Front and rear roller base	100	$5	500
	Total			$8,500

As soon as the materials requisition is received by the raw materials storeroom, workers **pick** the appropriate materials and send them to the factory floor. Picking is just what it sounds like: storeroom workers pick the needed materials off of the storeroom shelves. The unit cost and total cost of all materials picked are posted to the materials requisition based on the cost information found in the individual raw materials records. The individual raw materials records are also updated as soon as the materials are picked, often using bar-coding systems to simplify the process and provide real-time information. For example, in Exhibit 3-10, we show how the raw material record for heart rate monitors is updated after requisition #7568 (Exhibit 3-9) has been picked.

EXHIBIT 3-10 Raw Materials Record Updated for Materials Received and Used

Raw Materials Record

Item No.: HRM50812   Description: Heart rate monitor

	Received			Used				Balance		
Date	Units	Cost	Total	Requisition Number	Units	Cost	Total	Units	Cost	Total
11-25	100	$60	$6,000					100	$60	$6,000
11-30				#7235	70	$60	$4,200	30	$60	$1,800
12-1	75	$60	$4,500					105	$60	$6,300
12-2				#7568	50	$60	$3,000	55	$60	$3,300

Finally, the raw materials requisitioned for the job are posted to the job cost record. As shown in Exhibit 3-11, each time raw materials are requisitioned for Job 603, they are posted to the direct materials section of the job cost record. Again, bar-coding systems allow this process to be completed with more efficiency. These materials are considered direct materials (rather than indirect materials), because they can be traced specifically to Job 603. By using this system to trace direct materials to specific jobs, managers know *exactly* how much direct materials cost is incurred by each job.

EXHIBIT 3-11 Posting Direct Materials Used to the Job Cost Record

Job Cost Record

Job Number: 603

Customer: For stock

Job Description: 50 units of X4 Elliptical Cross-Trainers

Date Started: Dec. 2   **Date Completed:** _____

Manufacturing Cost Information:	Cost Summary
Direct Materials	
Req. #7568: $ 8,500 (shown in Exhibit 3-9)	
Req. #7580: $14,000	
Req. #7595: $13,500	
Req. #7601: $ 4,000	$ 40,000
Direct Labor	
	$
Manufacturing Overhead	
	$
Total Job Cost	$
Number of Units	÷ 50 units
Cost per Unit	$

Tracing Direct Labor Cost to a Job

Now let's look at how direct labor costs are traced to individual jobs. All direct laborers in the factory fill out **labor time records**. As shown in Exhibit 3-12, a labor time record simply records the time spent by each employee on each job he or she worked on throughout the day. Often, these records are kept electronically. Rather than using old-fashioned time tickets and punch clocks, factory workers now "swipe" their bar-coded employee identification cards on a computer terminal and enter the appropriate job number. Based on each employee's unique hourly wage rate, the computer calculates the direct labor cost to be charged to the job. Companies that are even more progressive use biometric scanning devices to quickly capture information about how long individual employees work on each job.

For example, in Exhibit 3-12, we see that Hannah Smith, who is paid a wage rate of $20 per hour, worked on both Jobs 602 and 603 during the week. Hannah spent five hours working on Job 603 on December 2. Therefore, $100 of direct labor cost ($20 × 5) will be charged to Job 603 for Hannah's work on that date. On December 3, Hannah's eight hours of work on Job 603 resulted in another $160 ($20 × 8) of direct labor being charged to the job. The cost of each direct laborer's time will be computed using each employee's unique wage rate, just as was done with Hannah Smith's time. Then, as shown in Exhibit 3-13, the information from the individual labor time records is posted to the direct labor section of the job cost record. Again, this posting is normally done automatically, and often in real time, by the company's computer system.

As you can see, by tracing direct labor cost in this fashion, individual jobs are charged only for the exact amount of direct labor actually used in their production.

EXHIBIT 3-12 Labor Time Record

Labor Time Record

Employee: Hannah Smith
Hourly Wage Rate: $20

Week: 12/2 – 12/9
Record #: 324

Date	Job Number	Start Time	End Time	Hours	Cost
12/2	602	8:00	11:00	3	$60
12/2	603	12:00	5:00	5	$100
12/3	603	8:00	4:00	8	$160
12/4 etc.					

EXHIBIT 3-13 Posting Direct Labor Used to the Job Cost Record

Job Cost Record

Job Number: 603

Customer: For stock

Job Description: 50 units of X4 Elliptical Cross-Trainers

Date Started: Dec. 2   **Date Completed:** _____

Manufacturing Cost Information:		Cost Summary	
Direct Materials			
Req. #7568: $ 8,500			
Req. #7580: $14,000			
Req. #7595: $13,500			
Req. #7601: $ 4,000		$	40,000
Direct Labor			
No. #324 (30 DL hours): $100, $160, etc. (shown in Exhibit 3-12)			
No. #327 (40 DL hours): $240, $210, etc.			
No. #333 (36 DL hours): $80, $120, etc.			
Etc.			
(a total of 500 DL hours)		$	10,000
Manufacturing Overhead		$	
Total Job Cost		$	
Number of Units		÷	50 units
Cost per Unit		$	

What about employee benefits, such as employee-sponsored retirement plans, health insurance, payroll taxes, and other benefits? As discussed in Chapter 2, these payroll-related benefits often add another 30% or more to the cost of gross wages and salaries. Some companies factor, or load, these costs into the hourly wage rate charged to the jobs. For example, if a factory worker earns a wage rate of $10 per hour, the job cost records would show a loaded hourly rate of about $13 per hour, which would include all benefits associated with employing the worker. However, because coming up with an *accurate* loaded hourly rate such as this is difficult, many companies treat these extra payroll-related costs as part of manufacturing overhead, rather than loading these costs into the direct labor wage rates. Either method is acceptable. We'll next discuss how manufacturing overhead costs are handled.

Allocating Manufacturing Overhead to a Job

3 Compute a predetermined manufacturing overhead rate and use it to allocate MOH to jobs

So far we have traced the direct materials and direct labor costs to Job 603. Recall, however, that Life Fitness incurs many other manufacturing costs that cannot be directly traced to specific jobs. These indirect manufacturing costs, otherwise known as manufacturing overhead (MOH), include depreciation on the factory plant and equipment, utilities to run the plant, property taxes and insurance on plant, equipment maintenance, the salaries of plant janitors and supervisors, machine lubricants, and so forth. Because of the nature of these costs, we cannot tell exactly how much of these costs are attributable to producing a specific job. Therefore, we cannot trace these costs to specific jobs, as we did with direct materials and direct labor. Rather, we will have to allocate some reasonable amount of these costs to each job. Why bother? Generally Accepted Accounting Principles (GAAP) requires that manufacturing overhead *must* be treated as a product cost for external financial reporting purposes. The rationale is that these costs are a *necessary* part of the production process: Jobs could not be produced without incurring these costs, so they must become part of each job's stated product cost. Let's now look at how companies allocate manufacturing overhead costs to jobs.

What Does Allocating Mean?

Allocating manufacturing overhead[2] to jobs simply means that we will be "splitting up" or "dividing" the total manufacturing overhead costs among the jobs we produced during the year. There are many different ways we could split up the total manufacturing overhead costs among jobs. For example, there are a number of different ways you could split up a pizza pie among friends: You could give equal portions to each friend, you could give larger portions to the largest friends, or you could give larger portions to the hungriest friends. All in all, you have a set amount of pizza, but you could come up with several different reasonable bases for splitting it among your friends (based on number of friends, size of friends, or hunger level of friends).

Why is this important?

"Managers use the **predetermined MOH rate** as a way to **'spread'** (allocate) **indirect** manufacturing costs, such as factory utilities, **among all jobs** produced in the factory during the year."

Likewise, a manufacturer has a total amount of manufacturing overhead that must be split among all of the jobs produced during the year. Because each job is unique in size and resource requirements, it wouldn't be fair to allocate an equal amount of manufacturing overhead to each job. Rather, management needs some other reasonable basis for splitting up the total manufacturing overhead costs among jobs. In this chapter, we'll discuss the most basic method of allocating manufacturing overhead to jobs. This method has traditionally been used by most manufacturers, but more progressive companies are learning to use better, more accurate allocation systems, which we will discuss in Chapter 4. However, for now, we'll start with a basic allocation system.

Steps to Allocating Manufacturing Overhead

Manufacturers follow four steps to implement this basic allocation system. The first three steps are taken *before the year begins:*

STEP 1: **The company estimates its total manufacturing overhead costs for the coming year.**

This is the total "pie" to be allocated. For Life Fitness, let's assume management estimates total manufacturing overhead costs for the year to be $1 million.

---

[2] The term *applying* manufacturing overhead is often used synonymously with "allocating" manufacturing overhead.

STEP 2: **The company selects an allocation base and estimates the total amount that will be used during the year.**

This is the *basis* management has chosen for "dividing up the pie." For Life Fitness, let's assume management has selected direct labor hours as the allocation base. Furthermore, management estimates that 62,500 of direct labor hours will be used during the year.

Ideally, the allocation base should be the <u>cost driver</u> of the manufacturing overhead costs. As the term implies, a cost driver is the primary factor that causes, or drives, a cost. For example, in many companies, manufacturing overhead costs rise and fall with the amount of work performed in the factory. Because of this, most companies traditionally use either direct labor hours or direct labor cost as their allocation base. This information is also easy to gather from the labor time records or job cost records. However, for manufacturers that have automated much of their production process, machine hours is a more appropriate allocation base because the amount of time spent running the machines drives the utility, maintenance, and equipment depreciation costs in the factory. As you'll learn in Chapter 4, some companies use multiple allocation bases to more accurately allocate manufacturing overhead costs to individual jobs. The important point is that the allocation base selected should bear a strong, positive relationship to the manufacturing overhead costs.

STEP 3: **The company calculates its *predetermined* manufacturing overhead (MOH) rate using the information estimated in Steps 1 and 2:**

$$\text{Predetermined MOH rate} = \frac{\text{Total estimated manufacturing overhead costs}}{\text{Total estimated amount of the allocation base}}$$

For example, Life Fitness calculates its predetermined MOH rate as follows:

$$\text{Predetermined MOH rate} = \frac{\$1,000,000}{62,500 \text{ DL hours}} = \$16 \text{ per direct labor hour}$$

This rate will be used throughout the coming year. It is not revised unless the company finds that either the manufacturing overhead costs or the total amount of the allocation base being used in the factory (direct labor hours in our example) has substantially shifted away from the estimated amounts. If this is the case, management might find it necessary to revise the rate part way through the year.

Why does the company use a <u>predetermined MOH rate</u>, based on *estimated or budgeted data*, rather than an actual MOH rate based on actual data for the year? In order to get actual data, the company would have to wait until the *end of the year* to set its MOH rate. By then, the information is too late to be useful for making pricing and other decisions related to individual jobs. Managers are willing to sacrifice some accuracy in order to get timely information on how much each job costs to produce.

Once the company has established its predetermined MOH rate, it uses that rate throughout the year to calculate the amount of manufacturing overhead to allocate to each job produced, as shown in Step 4.

STEP 4: **The company allocates some manufacturing overhead to each individual job as follows:**

MOH allocated to a job = Predetermined MOH rate × Actual amount of allocation base used by the job

Let's see how this works for Life Fitness's Job 603. Because the predetermined MOH rate is based on direct labor (DL) hours ($16 per DL hour), we'll need to know how many direct labor hours were used on Job 603. From Exhibit 3-13, we see that Job 603 required a total of 500 DL hours. This information was collected from the individual labor time records and summarized on the job cost record. Therefore, we calculate the amount of manufacturing overhead to be allocated to Job 603 as follows:

> MOH to be allocated to Job 603 = $16 per direct labor hour × 500 direct labor hours
> = $8,000

The $8,000 of manufacturing overhead allocated to Job 603 is now posted to the job cost record, as shown in Exhibit 3-14.

EXHIBIT 3-14 Posting Manufacturing Overhead and Completing the Job Cost Record

Job Cost Record

Job Number: 603

Customer: For stock

Job Description: 50 units of X4 Elliptical Cross-Trainers

Date Started: Dec. 2   **Date Completed:** Dec. 6

Manufacturing Cost Information:	Cost Summary
Direct Materials	
Req. #7568: $ 8,500	
Req. #7580: $14,000	
Req. #7595: $13,500	
Req. #7601: $ 4,000	$ 40,000
Direct Labor	
No. #324 (30 DL hours): $100, $160, etc.	
No. #327 (40 DL hours): $240, $210, etc.	
No. #333 (36 DL hours): $80, $120, etc.	
Etc.	
(a total of 500 DL hours)	$ 10,000
Manufacturing Overhead	
$16/DL hour × 500 DL hours = $8,000	$ 8,000
Total Job Cost	$ 58,000
Number of Units	÷ 50 units
Cost per Unit	$ 1,160

When Is Manufacturing Overhead Allocated to Jobs?

The point in time at which manufacturing overhead is allocated to a job depends on the sophistication of the company's computer system. In most sophisticated systems, some manufacturing overhead is allocated to a job each time some of the allocation base is posted to the job cost record. In our Life Fitness example, every time an hour of direct labor is posted to a job, $16 of manufacturing overhead would also be posted to the same job. In less sophisticated systems, manufacturing overhead is allocated only once: as soon as the job is complete and the total amount of allocation base used by the job is known (as shown in Exhibit 3-14). However, if the balance sheet date (for example, December 31) arrives before the job is complete, Life Fitness would need to allocate some manufacturing overhead to the job based on the number of direct labor hours used on the job thus far. Only by updating the job cost records will the company have the most accurate Work in Process Inventory on its balance sheet.

STOP & THINK

Assume Life Fitness's managers had chosen direct labor cost as the MOH allocation base, rather than direct labor hours. Furthermore, assume management estimates $1,200,000 of direct labor cost for the year.

1. Calculate the company's predetermined MOH rate based on direct labor cost.
2. How much MOH would have been allocated to Job 603?

Answer:

1. Predetermined MOH rate = $\dfrac{\$1,000,000}{\$1,200,000 \text{ of DL cost}}$ = .8333 or 83.33% of direct labor cost

2. MOH allocated to Job 603 = 83.33% × $10,000 direct labor cost
   (from Exhibit 3-14)
   = $8,333

Note that this allocation differs from that shown in Exhibit 3-14 ($8,000). That's because the amount of MOH allocated to an individual job is highly dependent on the allocation base chosen by management as well as the amount of the allocation base used by the job. Although there is no one "correct" allocation, the most accurate allocation occurs when the company uses the MOH cost driver as its allocation base.

Completing the Job Cost Record and Using It to Make Business Decisions

As shown in Exhibit 3-14, now that all three manufacturing costs have been posted to the job cost record, Life Fitness can determine the total cost of manufacturing Job 603 ($58,000) as well as the cost of producing each of the 50 identical units in the job ($1,160 each). Let's look at a few ways management uses this information.

4 Determine the cost of a job and use it to make business decisions

REDUCING FUTURE JOB COSTS Management will use the job cost information to control costs. By examining the exact costs traced to the job, management might be able to determine ways of reducing the cost of similar jobs produced in the future. For example, are the heart rate monitors costing more than they did on previous jobs? Perhaps management can renegotiate the contracts with its primary suppliers, or identify different suppliers that are willing to sell the parts more cheaply, without sacrificing quality.

What about direct labor costs? By examining the time spent by various workers on the job, management may be able to improve the efficiency of the process so that less production time is required. Management will also examine the hourly wage rates paid to the individuals who worked on the job to determine if less skilled and therefore less costly workers could accomplish the same production tasks, freeing up the more highly skilled employees for more challenging work.

ASSESSING AND COMPARING THE PROFITABILITY OF EACH MODEL Management will also use job cost information to determine the profitability of the various models. Assume the X4 Elliptical Cross-Trainer is listed on the company's website at a sales price of $1,900. That means the company can expect the following gross profit on each unit sold:

Sales price per unit	$1,900
Cost of goods sold per unit (computed on job cost record in Exhibit 3-14)	1,160
Gross profit per unit	$ 740

This profit analysis shows that the company would generate a gross profit of $740 on each unit sold from this job. Although this may seem fairly high, keep in mind that companies incur many operating costs, outside of manufacturing costs, that must be covered by the gross profit earned by product sales. For example, in 2014, Life Fitness spent over $23 million on research and development in the fitness segment.[3] Managers will compare the gross profit on this model to the gross profit of other models to determine which products should be emphasized in sales effort. Obviously, management will want to concentrate on marketing those models that yield the higher profit margins.

DEALING WITH PRICING PRESSURE FROM COMPETITORS Management can also use job cost information to determine how it will deal with pricing pressure. Say a competitor drops the price of its similar elliptical cross-trainer to $1,500. The profit analysis shows that Life Fitness could drop its sales price to $1,500 and still generate $340 of gross profit on the sale ($1,500 − $1,160). In fact, Life Fitness could use a sales promotion to *undercut* competitors' prices. As long as Life Fitness charges at least $1,161 for each unit in this job, the company will be earning a positive gross profit on the sale.

ALLOWING DISCOUNTS ON HIGH-VOLUME SALES Customers will often expect discounts for high-volume sales. For example, say the City of Westlake wants to order 40 of these cross-trainers for the city's recreation center and has asked for a 25% volume discount off of the regular sales price. If Life Fitness won't agree to the discount, the city will take its business to the competitor. Can Life Fitness agree to this discount and still earn a profit on the sale? Let's see:

Discounted sales price per unit	$ 1,425
Cost of goods sold per unit	1,160
Gross profit per unit	$ 265
Multiplied by: Number of units	× 40
Total gross profit on sale	$ 10,600

These calculations show that the discounted sales price will still provide a gross profit. We'll talk more about special orders like this in Chapter 8.

BIDDING FOR CUSTOM ORDERS Management also uses product cost information to bid for custom orders. Let's say that the Atlanta Falcons training facility would like to order 15 custom treadmills and is accepting bids from various fitness equipment manufacturers. Management can use the job cost records from past treadmill jobs to get a good idea of how much it will cost to complete the custom order. For example, the custom treadmills may require additional components not found on the standard models. Life Fitness will factor in these additional costs to get an estimate of the total job cost before it is produced. Life Fitness will most likely use **cost-plus pricing** to determine a bid price for the custom job. When companies use cost-plus pricing, they take the cost of the job (from the estimated or actual job cost record) and add a markup to help cover operating expenses and generate a profit:

$$\text{Cost plus price} = \text{Cost} + \text{Markup on cost}$$

Usually, the markup percentage or final bid price is agreed upon in a written contract before the company goes ahead with production. For example, let's say that Life Fitness typically adds a 40% markup on cost to help cover operating costs and generate a reasonable profit. If the estimated total job cost for the 15 treadmills is $25,000, then the bid price would be calculated as follows:

> **Why is this important?**
>
> "Once managers know how much it **costs** to complete a **job**, they use that **information** to do the following:
>
> - Find **cheaper** ways of completing similar jobs in the future,
> - Determine which products are **most profitable**, and
> - Establish prices for **custom-ordered** jobs."

---

[3] Brunswick Corp., 2014 10-K filing. Life Fitness is a division of Brunswick Corporation.

$$\text{Cost-plus price} = \$25{,}000 + (40\% \times \$25{,}000)$$
$$= \$35{,}000$$

Once the management team of the Atlanta Falcons has received Life Fitness's bid as well as bids from other companies, the team will decide which bid to accept based on price, quality, reputation for service, and so forth.

PREPARING THE FINANCIAL STATEMENTS Finally, the job cost information is critical to preparing the company's financial statements. Why? Because the information is used to determine the total Cost of Goods Sold shown on the income statement, as well as the Work in Process and Finished Goods Inventory accounts shown on the balance sheet. Every time a cross-trainer from Job 603 is sold, its cost ($1,160) becomes part of the Cost of Goods Sold during the period. Likewise, every time a cross-trainer from the job is sold, the balance in Finished Goods Inventory is reduced by $1,160. As shown earlier (Exhibit 3-8), the cost-to-date of unfinished jobs remains in the company's Work in Process Inventory.

How Can Job Costing Information Be Enhanced for Decision Making?

We have just finished developing a traditional job cost record and have seen how managers use the information to make vital business decisions. With the help of today's advanced information systems, the job cost information can be further enhanced to help managers make even more informed decisions. This section describes just a few of these enhancements.

Non-Manufacturing Costs

Job costing has traditionally focused on assigning only manufacturing-related costs to jobs. The focus on manufacturing costs arises because GAAP requires that *only* direct materials, direct labor, and manufacturing overhead be assigned to units of inventory for external financial reporting purposes. Costs incurred by other activities in the value chain are not assigned to products for external financial reporting but instead are treated as operating expenses (period costs).

However, for setting long-term average sales prices and making other critical decisions, manufacturers must take into account the total costs of researching and developing, designing, producing, marketing, distributing, and providing customer service for new or existing products. In other words, *they want to know the total cost of the product across the entire value chain.* But how do managers figure this out?

> **Why is this important?**
> "**Job cost records** can provide managers with the detailed **environmental** and social **impact** information needed to develop more sustainable **products** and manufacturing processes."

The same principles of tracing direct costs and allocating indirect costs apply to all costs incurred in other activities of the value chain. Managers add these non-manufacturing costs to the production-related job costs to build the *total cost of the product across the entire value chain*. For example, say Life Fitness spent $2 million designing and marketing the X4 Elliptical Cross-Trainer. These costs are direct costs of the X4 Elliptical product line. On the other hand, the company may have spent $3 million researching basic technology for the video screen that is used on all of its products, making it an indirect cost of the X4 Elliptical, shared with other products that use the same video screen. Life Fitness may choose to add an additional cost section to the job cost record, indicating specific operating expenses associated with each job. By adding this information to the job cost record, managers have a more complete understanding of the total job costs, not just the job's manufacturing costs.

Keep in mind that these non-manufacturing costs are assigned to products *only* for internal decision making, never for external financial reporting, because GAAP does not allow it. For financial reporting, non-manufacturing costs must *always* be expensed on the income statement as operating expenses in the period in which they are incurred.

Sustainability and Job Costing

Job cost records serve a vital role for manufacturers who embrace sustainability. Because job cost records contain information about the direct materials, direct labor, and manufacturing overhead assigned to each job, they capture the essential resources required to manufacture a product. The summary information on the job cost records can be enhanced to provide management with further information about how the product or production process may affect the environment, employees involved in the manufacturing process, future consumers of the product, and future disposal of the packaging materials and product itself.

For example, the direct materials section of the job cost record can be broken down into subcategories that provide management with useful environmental information. Categories might include:

- percentage of material and packaging inputs that are post-consumer-use or recycled materials,
- percentage of materials sourced from local suppliers versus those sourced from geographically distant suppliers (thereby increasing the company's carbon footprint),
- amount of materials that will become waste as a result of the production process,
- percentage of the end-of-life product and packaging that can be recycled by the consumer.

See Exercises E3-22A and E3-36B

Likewise, the job cost record can help management track the extent of the company's fair-labor practices related to each job, such as:

- the percentage of labor paid at a rate greater than minimum wage as defined by law,
- the percentage of labor force receiving health-care benefits, and
- the diversity of labor force used on the job.

Finally, although MOH resources cannot be traced to specific jobs, the company can provide its potential customers with general information such as:

- percentage of factory utilities generated from renewable sources (wind, solar) versus fossil fuels, and
- percentage reclaimed and recycled water, versus potable water, used in the factory.

We'll discuss MOH and sustainability more in Chapter 4, but this should give you a basic idea of the types of sustainability-related data that can be measured and reported.

Once the company has tracked this information on job cost records, how is it used? First, it can be used by management to identify areas of weakness so that the company can move toward a more sustainable business model. Second, it can be used to provide information to potential customers, as part of their supply chain assessment.

Sustainability-related information is becoming increasingly important in supply chain management. Many of the world's largest companies, such as Walmart and Costco, are now assessing the environmental and social impact of the suppliers with whom they choose to do business. In fact, supply chain pressure has become a major driving force in corporate adoption of greener and more socially responsible practices.

Third, this information is useful for marketing and labeling. The Sustainability Consortium, a multi-stakeholder group of companies and organizations, is working on developing a standardized system for measuring and reporting the environmental and social impact of consumer products across their entire life cycles. The Consortium is in the process of developing a "sustainability profile" that would be shown on consumer products, somewhat akin to the nutrition labels currently found on food products. By accurately labeling consumer products with environmental and social impact information, consumers will be in a better position to make informed purchasing decisions.

Fourth, this information can be used to assess the risk of future environmental costs associated with each job. For example, **Extended Producer Responsibility (EPR)** laws, more commonly known as "take-back" laws, create future costs associated with the production of electronic devices and other problem waste, such as mattresses, paint, and batteries. EPR laws, which have been passed in over 25 states as well as several European countries, require manufacturers of electronic devices and other problem waste to take back a large percentage of their products at the end of the products' useful lives. For example, the Wisconsin E-waste Law requires electronics manufacturers to take back 80% of the products they have produced (by weight) in the previous three years; manufacturers that violate this law are subject to a fine.

The goal of EPR laws is to reduce the amount of potentially dangerous waste in landfills by shifting the end-of-life disposal cost back to the manufacturer. By bearing the disposal cost, manufacturers should be motivated to design products and components that are more easily repairable, reusable, and recyclable, and have a longer life cycle.

How do e-waste EPR laws work? Major electronics retailers, such as Best Buy and Staples, collect unused electronics from consumers free of charge, and then partner with responsible recyclers to ensure that the e-waste is dismantled and recycled rather than dumped in landfills or exported to developing nations. Electronics manufacturers partner with these retailers and recyclers by subsidizing their costs.

To put the size of e-waste into perspective, consider the following. In the first quarter of 2016, Apple sold over 74 million iPhones, 16 million iPads, and 5 million Macs.[4] And that's just for three months of sales! When you consider all of the other computer, TV, and smartphone producers, you begin to understand the size of the potential e-waste issue. In fact, a study funded by the EPA and carried out by MIT and others indicated that in 2010, approximately 258 million units of used electronics such as cell phones, TVs, and computers (equating to 1.6 million tons) were generated in the United States, but only 66% were collected.[5] As a result, many electronics producers, such as Apple, HP, and Dell, are supporting take-back policies and providing recycling options for their old products.

In addition to state EPR laws, the federal government is also considering a bill (the Responsible Electronics Recycling Act) that will restrict the export of toxic e-waste, which historically has been shipped to developing countries. This bill, if passed, will not only help with environmental and public health issues caused by e-waste but will also create even more incentive for manufacturers and recyclers to find alternative uses for outdated electronic equipment.

Direct or Variable Costing

Even though the job cost records contain information about all three manufacturing costs, managers base certain decisions on just the direct costs (direct materials and labor) or variable costs found on a job cost record. Why? For two reasons: (1) The simple allocation of MOH that we have described in this chapter results in a fairly arbitrary amount of MOH being allocated to jobs, and (2) because many MOH costs are fixed and will not be affected as a result of producing a job. Later in the book, we'll see how management accountants have addressed these issues. In Chapter 4, we'll show how managers can improve the allocation system so that the amount of manufacturing overhead assigned to the job is much more accurate. In Chapters 6 and 8, we'll discuss how direct costing or variable costing can be used to improve the decision-making process.

---

[4] www.apple.com; http://electronicstakeback.com/promote-good-laws/state-legislation

[5] December 2013, "Quantitative Characterization of Domestic and Transboundary Flows of Used Electronics: Analysis of Generation, Collection, Export in the United States." www.epa.gov/international-cooperation/cleaning-electronic-waste-e-waste

Decision Guidelines

Job Costing

Life Fitness uses a job costing system that assigns manufacturing costs to each batch of exercise machines that it makes. These guidelines explain some of the decisions Life Fitness made in designing its costing system.

Decision	Guidelines
Should we use job costing or process costing?	Managers use the costing system that best fits their production environment. Job costing is best suited to manufacturers that produce unique, custom-built products or relatively small batches of different products. Process costing is best suited to manufacturers that mass-produce identical units in a series of uniform production processes.
How do we determine the cost of manufacturing each job?	The exact amount of direct materials and direct labor can be traced to individual jobs using materials requisitions and labor time records. However, the exact amount of manufacturing overhead attributable to each job is unknown and therefore *cannot* be traced to individual jobs. To deal with this issue, companies *allocate* some manufacturing overhead to each job.
Should we use a predetermined manufacturing overhead rate or the actual manufacturing overhead rate?	Although it would be more accurate to use the actual manufacturing overhead rate, companies would have to wait until the end of the year to have that information. Most companies are willing to sacrifice some accuracy for the sake of having timely information that will help them make decisions throughout the year. Therefore, most companies use a predetermined overhead rate to allocate manufacturing overhead to jobs as they are produced throughout the year.
How do we calculate the predetermined MOH rate?	$$\text{Predetermined MOH rate} = \frac{\text{Total estimated manufacturing overhead cost}}{\text{Total estimated amount of the allocation base}}$$
What allocation base should we use for allocating manufacturing overhead?	If possible, companies should use the cost driver of manufacturing overhead as the allocation base. The most common allocation bases are direct labor hours, direct labor cost, and machine hours. Some companies use multiple bases in order to more accurately allocate MOH. This topic will be covered in Chapter 4.
How should we allocate manufacturing overhead to individual jobs?	The MOH allocated to a job is calculated as follows: = Predetermined MOH rate × Actual amount of allocation base used by the job
Can job cost records help companies in their journey toward sustainability?	Job cost records can be enhanced to provide more detail about the environmental and social impact of the resources used on the job. In addition to satisfying supply chain assessment, managers can use this information to determine how a product, or production process, can become more sustainable.
Can manufacturers also assign operating expenses to jobs?	Operating expenses can also be assigned to jobs, but *only* for *internal decision-making* purposes. Operating expenses are *never* assigned to jobs for external financial reporting purposes. Direct operating costs would be traced to jobs (such as the sales commission on a particular job or the design costs related to a particular job) whereas indirect operating costs (such as the R&D costs associated with several product lines) would be allocated to jobs.

SUMMARY PROBLEM 1

E-Z-Boy Furniture makes sofas, loveseats, and recliners. The company allocates manufacturing overhead based on direct labor hours. E-Z-Boy estimated a total of $2 million of manufacturing overhead and 40,000 direct labor hours for the year.

Job 310 consists of a batch of 10 recliners. The company's records show that the following direct materials were requisitioned for Job 310:

- Lumber: 10 units at $30 per unit
- Padding: 20 yards at $20 per yard
- Upholstery fabric: 60 yards at $25 per yard, sourced from a local manufacturer

Labor time records show the following employees (direct labor) worked on Job 310:

- Jesse Slothower: 10 hours at $12 per hour
- Becky Wilken: 15 hours at $18 per hour
- Chip Lathrop: 12 hours at $15 per hour

Requirements

1. Compute the company's predetermined manufacturing overhead rate.
2. Compute the total amount of direct materials, direct labor, and manufacturing overhead that should be shown on Job 310's job cost record.
3. Compute the total cost of Job 310, as well as the cost of each recliner produced in Job 310.
4. The company's customers are concerned about environmental responsibility and social justice and require additional sustainability-related information prior to making their purchasing decisions. To meet customer concerns, determine (a) which materials used for the product are sourced locally, and (b) the percentage of labor paid at a rate greater than minimum wage. Currently, the federal minimum wage is $7.25 per hour.

▪ SOLUTIONS

1. The predetermined MOH rate is calculated as follows:

$$\text{Predetermined MOH rate} = \frac{\text{Total estimated manufacturing overhead cost}}{\text{Total estimated amount of the allocation base}}$$

For E-Z-Boy:

$$\text{Predetermined MOH rate} = \frac{\$2{,}000{,}000}{40{,}000 \text{ direct labor hours}} = \$50 \text{ per direct labor hour}$$

2. The total amount of direct materials ($2,200) and direct labor ($570) incurred on Job 310 is determined from the materials requisitions and labor time records, as shown on the following job cost record. Because the job required 37 direct labor hours, we determine the amount of manufacturing overhead to allocate to the job is as follows:

   = Predetermined MOH rate × Actual amount of allocation base used by the job
   = $50 per direct labor hour × 37 direct labor hours used on Job 310
   = $1,850

These costs are summarized on the following job cost record:

Job Cost Record

Job Number: 310

Job Description: 10 recliners

Manufacturing Cost Information:	Cost Summary	
Direct Materials		
Lumber: 10 units × $30 = $300		
Padding: 20 yards × $20 = $400		
Fabric: 60 yards × $25 = $1,500	$	2,200
Direct Labor		
Slothower: 10 hours × $12 = $120		
Wilken: 15 hours × $18 = $270		
Lathrop: 12 hours × $15 = $180		
Total hours: 37 hours	$	570
Manufacturing Overhead		
37 direct labor hours × $50 = $1,850	$	1,850
Total Job Cost	$	4,620
Number of Units	÷	10 units
Cost per Unit	$	462

3. The direct materials ($2,200), direct labor ($570), and manufacturing overhead ($1,850) sum to a total job cost of $4,620. When the total job cost is averaged over the 10 recliners in the job, the cost per recliner is $462.

4. Supplemental sustainability information for Job 310:

   a. All fabric contained in the product was sourced locally.

   b. All labor used in the manufacturing was paid at a rate higher than minimum wage.

How Do Managers Deal with Underallocated or Overallocated Manufacturing Overhead?

In the first half of the chapter, we showed how managers find the cost of completing a job. Direct materials and direct labor are traced to each job using materials requisitions and labor time records, and manufacturing overhead is allocated to each job using a predetermined overhead rate. At the end of the period, all manufacturers will have a problem to deal with: Invariably, they will have either <u>underallocated manufacturing overhead</u> or <u>overallocated manufacturing overhead</u> to the jobs worked on during the period.

Recall that manufacturing overhead is allocated to jobs using a *predetermined rate* that is calculated using *estimates* of the company's total annual manufacturing overhead costs and *estimates* of the total annual allocation base (such as direct labor hours). By the end of the period, the *actual* manufacturing overhead costs incurred by the company will be known, and they will likely differ from the total amount allocated to jobs during the period.

For example, suppose Life Fitness incurred the following *actual* manufacturing overhead costs during the month of December:

> **"Why is this important?"**
>
> Because managers **allocate** MOH to jobs using a **predetermined** rate that is based on **estimates**, the amount of **MOH allocated** to jobs during the year will not be quite right. At the **end of the period**, managers find out whether the jobs have been allocated **too much** or **too little** MOH and then **fix** the error in the **financial** records.

Manufacturing Overhead Incurred	Actual MOH Costs
Indirect materials used (janitorial supplies, machine lubricants, etc.)	$ 2,000
Indirect labor (janitors' and supervisors' wages, etc.)	13,000
Other indirect manufacturing costs (Plant utilities, depreciation, property taxes, insurance, etc.)	10,000
Total actual manufacturing overhead costs incurred	$25,000

5 Compute and dispose of overallocated or underallocated manufacturing overhead

Now let's look at the total amount of manufacturing overhead that was *allocated* to individual jobs during the month using the predetermined manufacturing overhead rate of $16 per direct labor hour. For simplicity, we'll assume only two jobs were worked on during December.

Jobs	Amount of MOH Allocated to Job
603 (from Exhibit 3-14) ($16 per DL hour × 500 DL hours)	$ 8,000
604 (not shown) ($16 per DL hour × 1,000 DL hours)	16,000
Total MOH allocated to jobs ($16 per DL hour × 1,500 DL hours)	$24,000

Notice that we don't need to have the individual job cost records available to figure out the total amount of MOH allocated to jobs during the period. Rather, we can calculate the total amount of MOH allocated to jobs as follows:

> **Total MOH allocated** = Predetermined MOH rate × Actual *total* amount of allocation base used on all jobs
> = $16 per DL hour × 1,500 direct labor hours
> = $24,000 total MOH allocated to jobs during the period

To determine whether manufacturing overhead had been overallocated or underallocated, we simply compare the amount of MOH actually incurred during the period with the amount of MOH that was allocated to jobs during the same period. The difference between the *actual manufacturing overhead costs incurred* by the company and the amount of manufacturing overhead *allocated to jobs* shows that Life Fitness *underallocated* manufacturing overhead by $1,000 during December:

Actual manufacturing overhead costs **incurred**..	$25,000
Manufacturing overhead **allocated** to jobs	24,000
Underallocated manufacturing overhead..	$ 1,000

By underallocating manufacturing overhead, Life Fitness *did not allocate enough* manufacturing overhead cost to the jobs worked on during the period. In other words, the jobs worked on during the period should have had a total of $1,000 more manufacturing overhead cost allocated to them than the job cost records indicated. These jobs have been undercosted, as shown in Exhibit 3-15. If, on the other hand, a manufacturer finds that the amount of manufacturing overhead allocated to jobs is *greater* than the actual amount of manufacturing overhead incurred by the company, we would say that manufacturing overhead had been overallocated, resulting in overcosting these jobs.

EXHIBIT 3-15 Underallocated Versus Overallocated Manufacturing Overhead

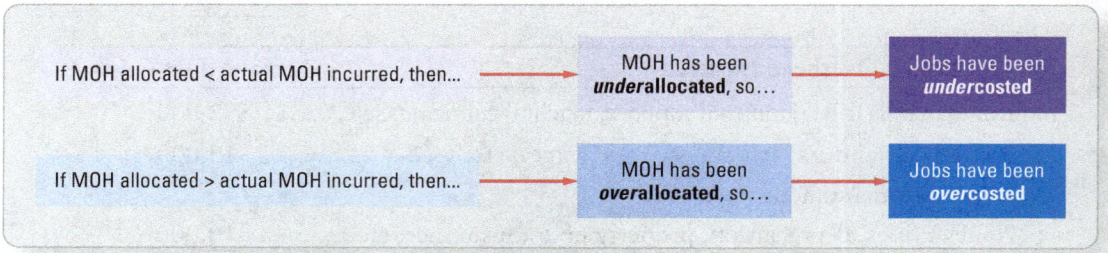

What do manufacturers do about this problem? *Assuming that the amount of underallocation or overallocation is immaterial, or that most of the inventory produced during the period has been sold*, manufacturers typically adjust Cost of Goods Sold for the total amount of the under- or overallocation. Why? Because (1) as a result of using a *predetermined* MOH rate, too much or too little MOH was originally recorded on the job cost records and (2) when the jobs were sold, the job cost records were used as a basis for recording Cost of Goods Sold. Hence, the Cost of Goods Sold account will be wrong unless it is corrected. As shown in Exhibit 3-16, by increasing Cost of Goods Sold when manufacturing overhead has been underallocated, or by decreasing Cost of Goods Sold when manufacturing overhead has been overallocated, the company actually corrects the error that exists in Cost of Goods Sold.

EXHIBIT 3-16 Correcting Cost of Goods Sold for Underallocated or Overallocated MOH

What if the amount of under- or overallocation is large, and the company has *not* sold almost all of the units produced during the period? Then the company will prorate the total amount of under- or overallocation among Work in Process Inventory, Finished Goods Inventory, and Cost of Goods Sold based on the current status of the jobs worked on during the period. For example, if 30% of the jobs are still in Work in Process, 20% are still in Finished Goods, and 50% were sold, then the total amount of underallocation ($1,000 in the case of Life Fitness) would be roughly allocated as follows: 30% ($300) to Work in Process Inventory, 20% ($200) to Finished Goods Inventory, and 50% ($500) to Cost of Goods Sold. The exact procedure for prorating is covered in more advanced accounting textbooks.

Try It!

Recall that Life Fitness had estimated $1,000,000 of MOH for the year and 62,500 DL hours, resulting in a predetermined MOH rate of $16/DL hour. By the end of the year, the company had actually incurred $975,000 of MOH costs and used a total of 60,000 DL hours on jobs. By how much had Life Fitness overallocated or underallocated MOH for the year?

Please see page 174 for solutions.

What Journal Entries Are Needed in a Manufacturer's Job Costing System?

Now that you know how manufacturers determine job costs and how those costs are used to make business decisions, let's look at how these costs are entered into the company's general ledger accounting system. We'll consider the journal entries needed to record the flow of costs through Life Fitness's accounts during the month of December. We'll use the same examples used earlier in the chapter. For the sake of simplicity, we'll continue to assume that Life Fitness only worked on two jobs during the month:

6 Prepare journal entries for a manufacturer's job costing system

- Job 603: 50 units of the X4 Elliptical Cross-Trainers
- Job 604: 60 units of the T5 Treadmill

You may wish to review the basic mechanics of journal entries, shown in Exhibit 3-17, before we begin our discussion.

EXHIBIT 3-17 Review of Journal Entry and T-account Mechanics

Additionally, keep in mind the flow of inventory that was first described in Exhibit 3-2. You may find this visual reminder helpful as we describe how the journal entries reflect the flow of inventory through the manufacturing system. In Exhibit 3-18, each arrow represents a journal entry that must be made to reflect activities that occur along the process: purchasing raw materials, using direct materials, using direct labor, recording actual MOH costs, allocating MOH to jobs, moving the jobs out of the factory after completion, and, finally, selling the units from a job. We'll now walk through journal entries associated with each of these activities.

EXHIBIT 3-18 Flow of Costs through a Manufacturing Plant

Purchase of Raw Materials

Assume that Life Fitness ordered and received $90,000 of raw materials during December. Once the materials are received and verified against the purchase order and the invoice received from the supplier, the purchase is recorded as follows:

(1)	Raw Materials Inventory	90,000	
	Accounts Payable		90,000
	(to record purchases of raw materials on account)		

These materials will remain in the raw materials storeroom until they are needed for production. The liability in Accounts Payable will be removed when the supplier is paid.

Use of Direct Materials

Recall that direct materials are the primary physical components of the product. Each time production managers need particular direct materials for Jobs 603 and 604, they fill out a materials requisition informing the storeroom to pick the materials and send them into the manufacturing facility. Once these materials are sent into production, they become part of the work in process on Jobs 603 and 604, so their cost is added to the job cost records, as follows:

Job Cost Record
Job Number: 603 (50 Cross-trainers)

Manufacturing Cost Information:	Cost Summary
Direct Materials	$40,000
Direct Labor	
Manufacturing Overhead	
Total Job Cost	

Job Cost Record
Job Number: 604 (60 Treadmills)

Manufacturing Cost Information:	Cost Summary
Direct Materials	$72,000
Direct Labor	
Manufacturing Overhead	
Total Job Cost	

From an accounting perspective, the cost of these materials must also be moved into Work in Process Inventory (through a debit) and out of Raw Materials Inventory (through a credit). The following journal entry is made:

(2)	Work in Process Inventory ($40,000 + $72,000)	112,000	
	Raw Materials Inventory		112,000
	(to record the use of direct materials on jobs)		

Recall from the first half of the chapter that the individual job cost records form the underlying support for Work in Process Inventory shown on the balance sheet.[6] Therefore, the amount posted to the general ledger account ($112,000) must be identical to the sum of the amounts posted to the individual job cost records ($40,000 + $72,000 = $112,000). Keep this important rule of thumb in mind:

> Whenever a cost is added to a job cost record, a corresponding journal entry is made to increase WIP Inventory.

Use of Indirect Materials

Indirect materials are materials used in the manufacturing plant that *cannot* be traced to individual jobs and therefore are *not* recorded on any job cost record. Examples include janitorial supplies used in the factory and machine lubricants for the factory machines. Once again, materials requisitions inform the raw materials storeroom to release these materials. However, instead of becoming part of the Work in Process account for a particular job, the indirect materials used in the factory (let's say $2,000) become part of the Manufacturing Overhead account. Therefore, the Manufacturing Overhead account is debited (to increase the account) and Raw Materials Inventory is credited (to decrease the account) as follows:

(3)	Manufacturing Overhead	2,000	
	Raw Materials Inventory		2,000
	(to record the use of indirect materials in the factory)		

All indirect manufacturing costs, including indirect materials, indirect labor, and other indirect manufacturing costs (such as plant insurance and depreciation), are accumulated, or gathered together, in the Manufacturing Overhead account. The Manufacturing Overhead account is a *temporary* account used to "pool" (gather together) indirect manufacturing costs until those costs can be allocated to individual jobs. In fact, the MOH account is sometimes referred to as the "MOH cost pool."

---

[6] The job cost records of unfinished jobs form the subsidiary ledger for the Work in Process Inventory account. Recall that a <u>subsidiary ledger</u> is simply the supporting detail for a general ledger account. Many other general ledger accounts (such as Accounts Receivable, Accounts Payable, and Plant & Equipment) also have subsidiary ledgers. The raw material inventory records form the subsidiary ledger for the Raw Materials Inventory account, whereas the job cost records on completed, unsold jobs form the subsidiary ledger for the Finished Goods Inventory account.

We can summarize the flow of materials costs through the T-accounts as follows:

Use of Direct Labor

The labor time records of individual factory workers are used to determine exactly how much time was spent directly working on Jobs 603 and 604. The cost of this direct labor is entered on the job cost records, as shown:

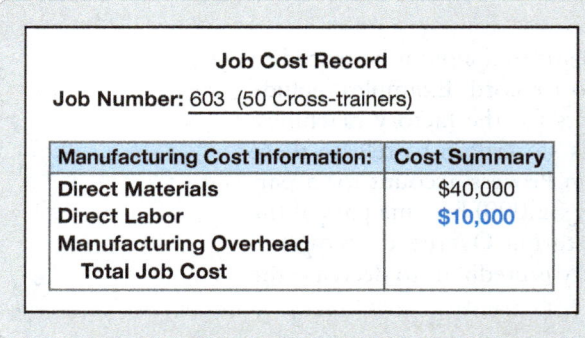

Again, because the job cost records form the underlying support for Work in Process Inventory, an identical amount ($10,000 + $20,000 = $30,000) must be debited to the Work in Process Inventory account. Wages Payable is credited to show that the company has a liability to pay its factory workers:

(4)	Work in Process Inventory ($10,000 + $20,000)	30,000	
	Wages Payable		30,000
	(*to record the use of direct labor on jobs*)		

The Wages Payable liability will be removed on payday when the workers receive their pay.

Use of Indirect Labor

Recall that indirect labor consists of the salary, wages, and benefits of all factory workers who are *not* directly working on individual jobs. Examples include factory janitors, supervisors, and forklift operators. Because their time cannot be traced to particular jobs, the cost of employing these factory workers during the month (let's say $13,000) cannot be posted to individual job cost records. Thus, we record the cost of indirect labor as part of Manufacturing Overhead, *not* Work in Process Inventory:

(5)	Manufacturing Overhead	13,000	
	Wages Payable		13,000
	(to record the use of indirect labor in the factory)		

Again, the Wages Payable liability will be removed on payday when the workers receive their pay.

We can summarize the flow of manufacturing labor costs through the T-accounts as follows:

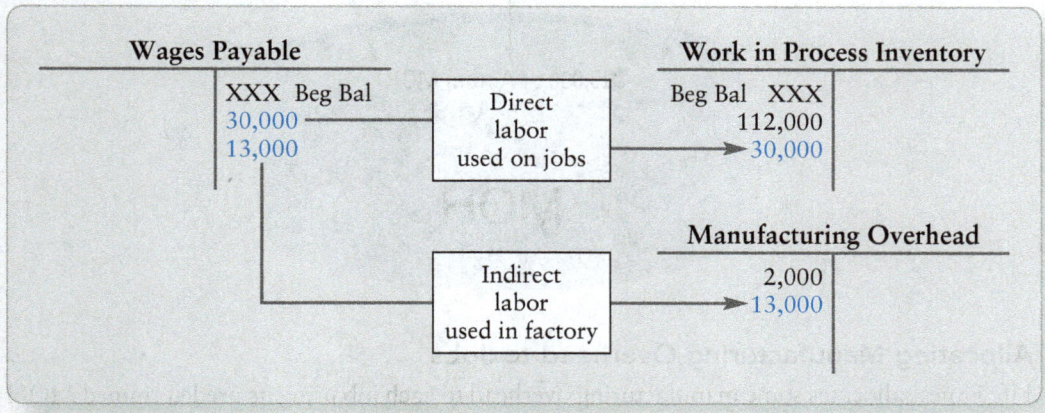

Incurring Other Manufacturing Overhead Costs

We have already recorded the indirect materials and indirect labor used in the factory during December by debiting the Manufacturing Overhead account. However, Life Fitness incurs other indirect manufacturing costs during the period, such as plant utilities ($3,000), plant and equipment depreciation ($4,000), plant insurance ($1,000), and plant property taxes ($2,000). All of these other costs of running the manufacturing plant during the month are also added to the Manufacturing Overhead account until they can be allocated to specific jobs:

(6)	Manufacturing Overhead	10,000	
	Accounts Payable (for electric bill)		3,000
	Accumulated Depreciation—Plant and Equipment		4,000
	Prepaid Plant Insurance (for expiration of prepaid insurance)		1,000
	Plant Property Taxes Payable (for taxes to be paid)		2,000
	(to record other indirect manufacturing costs incurred during the month)		

After recording all other indirect manufacturing costs, the Manufacturing Overhead account appears as follows:

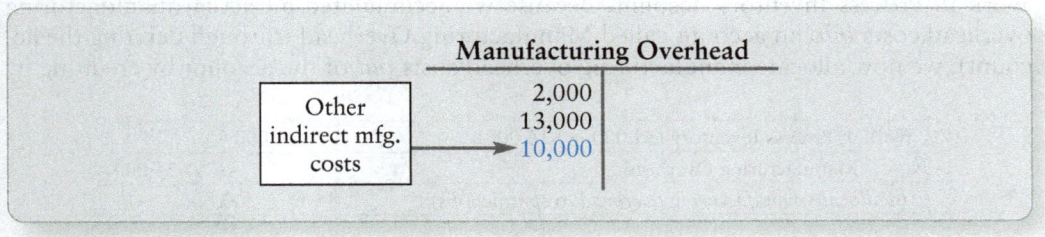

Since all MOH costs are combined, or "pooled together" into one account, the MOH account is sometimes referred to as a "cost pool." As shown in Exhibit 3-19, you might find it helpful to visualize a pool being filled with the actual MOH costs incurred during the year. In the next section, we'll see how the costs are removed from the pool and assigned to specific jobs.

EXHIBIT 3-19 Pooling Actual MOH Costs

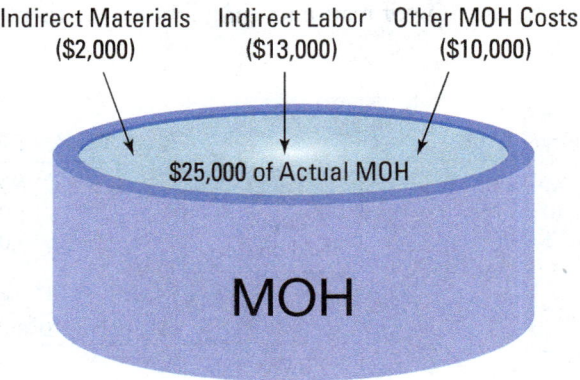

Allocating Manufacturing Overhead to Jobs

Life Fitness allocates some manufacturing overhead to each job using its predetermined MOH rate, calculated in the first half of the chapter to be $16 per direct labor hour. The total of direct labor hours used on each job is found on the labor time records and is summarized on the job cost records. Assume Job 603 used 500 DL hours and Job 604 used 1,000 DL hours. Then the amount of manufacturing overhead allocated to each job is determined as follows:

> Job 603: $16 per DL hour × 500 DL hours = $8,000
> Job 604: $16 per DL hour × 1,000 DL hours = $16,000

Job Cost Record
Job Number: 603 (50 Cross-trainers)

Manufacturing Cost Information:	Cost Summary
Direct Materials	$40,000
Direct Labor (500 DL hrs)	$10,000
Manufacturing Overhead	$ 8,000
Total Job Cost	

Job Cost Record
Job Number: 604 (60 Treadmills)

Manufacturing Cost Information:	Cost Summary
Direct Materials	$72,000
Direct Labor (1,000 DL hrs)	$20,000
Manufacturing Overhead	$16,000
Total Job Cost	

Again, because the job cost records form the underlying support for Work in Process Inventory, an identical amount ($8,000 + $16,000 = $24,000) must be debited to the Work in Process Inventory account. Because we accumulated all actual manufacturing overhead costs *into* an account called Manufacturing Overhead (through debiting the account), we now allocate manufacturing overhead costs *out* of the account by crediting it.

(7)	Work in Process Inventory ($8,000 + $16,000)	24,000	
	Manufacturing Overhead		24,000
	(to allocate manufacturing overhead to specific jobs)		

As shown in Exhibit 3-20, you might find it helpful to visualize the allocation process as removing, or ladling out, some of the MOH cost in the pool and allocating it to individual jobs worked on in the factory. In our example, we assumed only two jobs were worked on during the month (Jobs 603 and 604). However, if more jobs were worked on, the same allocation process would take place for each and every job. To recap, the MOH cost pool is increased through the addition of actual MOH costs as they are incurred, and decreased through the allocation of MOH to individual jobs. In the general ledger, the MOH cost pool is represented by the MOH account. Thus, the account is increased (debited) whenever an actual MOH cost is incurred, and it is credited whenever MOH costs are allocated to jobs.

EXHIBIT 3-20 Allocating MOH Costs to Individual Jobs

By looking at the Manufacturing Overhead T-account, you can see how actual manufacturing overhead costs are accumulated in the account through debits, and the amount of manufacturing overhead allocated to specific jobs is credited to the account:

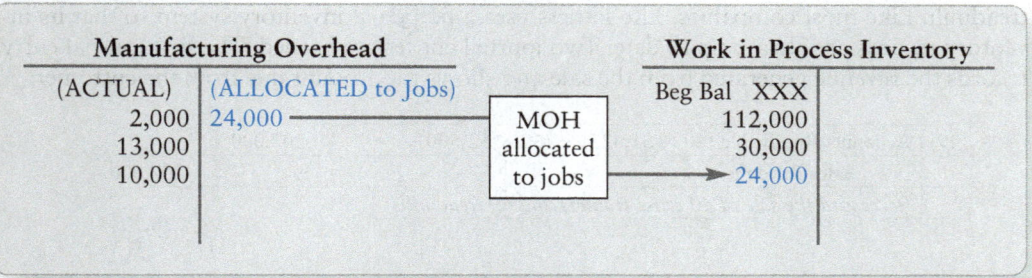

Completion of Jobs

Once the job has been completed, the three manufacturing costs shown on the job cost record are summed to find the total job cost. If the job consists of more than one unit, the total job cost is divided by the number of units to find the cost of each unit:

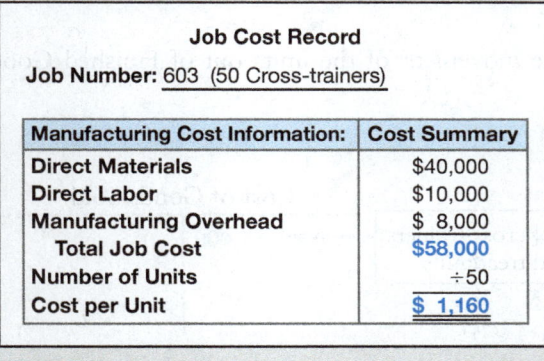

Job Cost Record	
Job Number: 603 (50 Cross-trainers)	
Manufacturing Cost Information:	**Cost Summary**
Direct Materials	$40,000
Direct Labor	$10,000
Manufacturing Overhead	$ 8,000
Total Job Cost	**$58,000**
Number of Units	÷50
Cost per Unit	**$ 1,160**

Job Cost Record	
Job Number: 604 (60 Treadmills)	
Manufacturing Cost Information:	**Cost Summary**
Direct Materials	$ 72,000
Direct Labor	$ 20,000
Manufacturing Overhead	$ 16,000
Total Job Cost	**$108,000**
Number of Units	÷60
Cost per Unit	**$ 1,800**

The units produced in the jobs are physically moved off of the plant floor and into the finished goods warehouse. Likewise, in the accounting records, the jobs are moved out of Work in Process Inventory (through a credit) and into Finished Goods Inventory (through a debit):

(8)	Finished Goods Inventory ($58,000 + $108,000)	166,000	
	Work in Process Inventory		166,000
	(to move the completed jobs out of the factory and into Finished Goods)		

The T-accounts show the movement of completed jobs off of the factory floor:

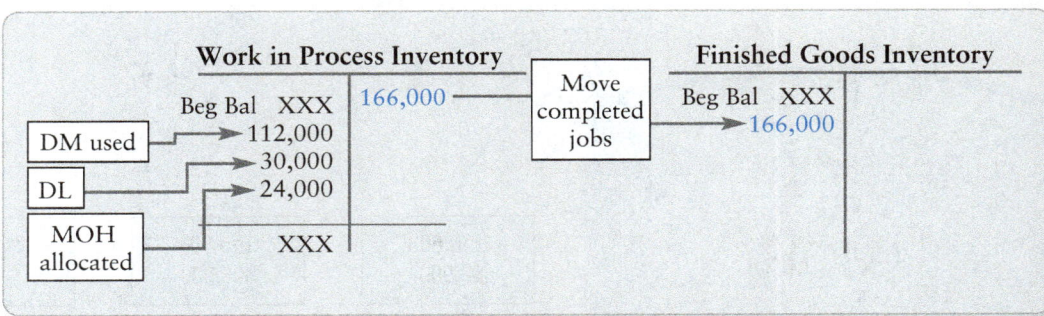

Sale of Units

For simplicity, let's assume that Life Fitness only had one sale during the month: It sold 40 cross-trainers from Job 603 and all 60 treadmills from Job 604 to the City of Westlake for its recreation centers. The sales price was $1,425 for each cross-trainer and $2,500 for each treadmill. Like most companies, Life Fitness uses a perpetual inventory system so that its inventory records are always up to date. Two journal entries are needed. The first journal entry records the revenue generated from the sale and shows the amount due from the customer:

(9)	Accounts Receivable (40 × $1,425) + (60 × $2,500)	207,000	
	Sales Revenue		207,000
	(to record the sale of 40 cross-trainers and 60 treadmills)		

The second journal entry reduces the company's Finished Goods Inventory and records the Cost of Goods Sold. From the job cost record, we know that each cross-trainer produced in Job 603 cost $1,160 to make, and each treadmill from Job 604 cost $1,800 to make. Therefore, the following entry is recorded:

(10)	Cost of Goods Sold (40 × $1,160) + (60 × $1,800)	154,400	
	Finished Goods Inventory		154,400
	(to reduce Finished Goods Inventory and record Cost of Goods Sold)		

The following T-accounts show the movement of the units out of Finished Goods Inventory and into Cost of Goods Sold:

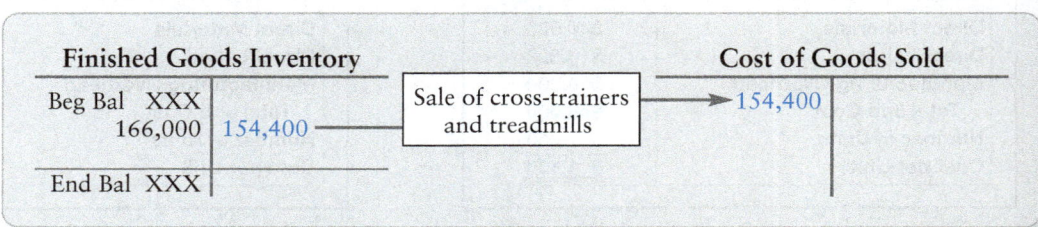

Operating Expenses

Let's assume Life Fitness also incurred $32,700 of operating expenses during the month to run its business. For example, Life Fitness incurred salaries and commissions ($20,000) for its salespeople, office administrators, research and design staff, and customer service representatives. It also needs to pay rent ($3,300) for its office headquarters. The company also received a bill from its advertising agency for marketing expenses incurred during the month ($9,400). *All costs incurred outside of the manufacturing function of the value chain* would be expensed in the current month as shown in the following journal entry:

(11)	Salaries and Commission Expense	20,000	
	Rent Expense	3,300	
	Marketing Expenses	9,400	
	Salaries and Commissions Payable		20,000
	Rent Payable		3,300
	Accounts Payable		9,400
	(to record all non-manufacturing costs incurred during the month)		

All non-manufacturing expenses (period costs) will be shown as "operating expenses" on the company's income statement, as shown in Exhibit 3-21 on the next page.

Closing Manufacturing Overhead

As a final step, Life Fitness must deal with the balance in the manufacturing overhead account. Because the company uses a *predetermined* manufacturing overhead rate to allocate manufacturing overhead to individual jobs, the total amount allocated to jobs will most likely differ from the amount of manufacturing overhead actually incurred.

Let's see how this plays out in the Manufacturing Overhead T-account:

1. All manufacturing overhead costs *incurred* by Life Fitness were recorded as *debits* to the Manufacturing Overhead account. These debits total $25,000 of actual manufacturing overhead incurred.

2. On the other hand, all manufacturing overhead *allocated* to specific jobs ($8,000 + $16,000) was recorded as *credits* to the Manufacturing Overhead account:

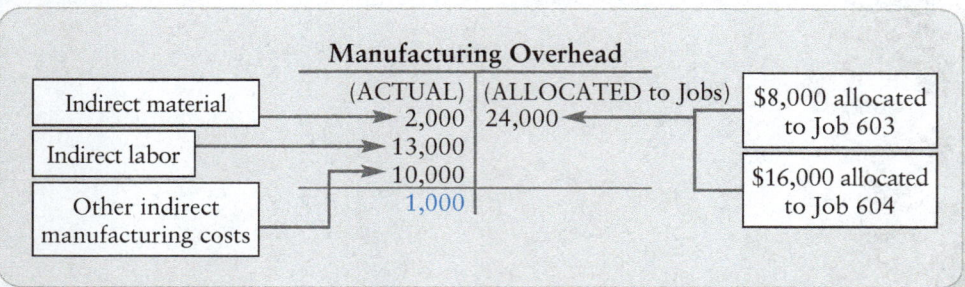

This leaves a debit balance of $1,000 in the Manufacturing Overhead account, which means that manufacturing overhead has been underallocated during the month. More manufacturing overhead costs were incurred than were allocated to jobs. Because Manufacturing Overhead is a temporary account not shown on any of the company's financial statements, it must be closed out (zeroed out) at the end of the period. Because most of the inventory produced during the period has been sold, Life Fitness will close the balance in Manufacturing Overhead to Cost of Goods Sold as follows:

(12)	Cost of Goods Sold	1,000	
	Manufacturing Overhead		1,000
	(to close the Manufacturing Overhead account)		

As a result of this entry, (1) the Manufacturing Overhead account now has a zero balance, and (2) the balance in Cost of Goods Sold has increased to correct for the fact that the jobs had been undercosted during the period.

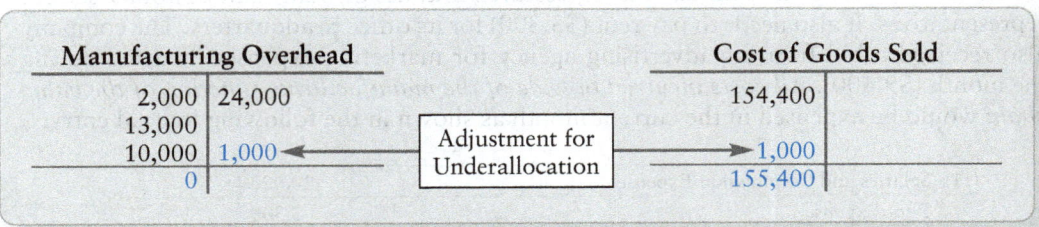

If, in some period, Life Fitness were to overallocate its overhead, the journal entry to close Manufacturing Overhead would be the opposite of that shown: Manufacturing Overhead would be debited to zero it out; Cost of Goods Sold would be credited to reduce it as a result of having overcosted jobs during the period.

Now you have seen how all of the costs flow through Life Fitness's accounts during December. Exhibit 3-21 shows the company's income statement that resulted from all of the previously shown journal entries.

EXHIBIT 3-21 Income Statement After Adjusting for Underallocated Manufacturing Overhead

	A	B	C	D
1	Life Fitness			
2	Income Statement			
3	For the Month Ended December 31			
4				
5	Sales Revenue	$ 207,000		
6	Less: Cost of Goods Sold	155,400		
7	Gross Profit	51,600		
8	Less: Operating Expenses	32,700		
9	Operating Income	$ 18,900		
10				

Decision Guidelines

Job Costing

The following decision guidelines describe the implications of over- or underallocating manufacturing overhead, as well as other decisions that need to be made in a job costing environment.

Decision	Guidelines
How does overallocating or underallocating MOH affect the cost of jobs manufactured during the period?	If manufacturing overhead has been *underallocated*, it means that not enough MOH was allocated to the jobs. The jobs have been undercosted as a result. On the other hand, if manufacturing overhead has been *overallocated*, it means that too much MOH was allocated to jobs. The jobs have been overcosted as a result.
What do we do about overallocated or underallocated manufacturing overhead?	Assuming most of the inventory produced during the period has been sold, manufacturers generally adjust the Cost of Goods Sold for the total amount of the under- or overallocation. If a significant portion of the inventory is still on hand, then the adjustment will be prorated between WIP Inventory, Finished Goods Inventory, and Cost of Goods Sold.
How do we know whether to increase or decrease Cost of Goods Sold (CGS)?	If manufacturing overhead has been overallocated, then Cost of Goods Sold (CGS) is too high and must be decreased through a credit to the CGS account. If manufacturing overhead has been underallocated, then Cost of Goods Sold is too low and must be increased through a debit to the CGS account.
How do we record the use of direct materials on a job?	Work in Process Inventory X Raw Materials Inventory X
How do we record the use of direct labor on a job?	Work in Process Inventory X Wages Payable X

How do we record actual MOH cost incurred in the factory?	Manufacturing Overhead X
	    Raw Materials Inventory (for indirect materials) X
	    Wages payable (for indirect labor) X
	    Accounts payable, etc. (for other MOH) X

How do we record the allocation of MOH costs to jobs?	Work in Process Inventory X Manufacturing Overhead X
How do we record the completion of the job?	Finished Goods Inventory X Work in Process Inventory X
How does job costing work at a service firm (Appendix)?	Job costing at a service firm is very similar to job costing at a manufacturer. The main difference is that the company is allocating operating expenses, rather than manufacturing costs, to each client job. In addition, because there are no Inventory or Cost of Goods Sold accounts, no journal entries are needed to move inventory through the system. All costs are simply expensed as period costs, but separate job cost records are maintained to keep track of the costs of serving each client.

SUMMARY PROBLEM 2

Fashion Fabrics makes custom handbags and accessories for high-end clothing boutiques. Record summary journal entries for each of the following transactions that took place during the month of January, the *first* month of the fiscal year.

Requirements

1. During January, $150,000 of raw materials was purchased on account.
2. During the month, $140,000 of raw materials was requisitioned. Of this amount, $135,000 was traced to specific jobs, while the remaining materials were for general factory use.
3. Manufacturing labor (both direct and indirect) for the month totaled $80,000. It has not yet been paid. Of this amount, $60,000 was traced to specific jobs.
4. The company recorded $9,000 of depreciation on the plant building and machinery. In addition, $3,000 of prepaid property tax expired during the month. The company also received the plant utility bill for $6,000 which will be paid at a later date.
5. Manufacturing overhead was allocated to jobs using a predetermined manufacturing overhead rate of 75% of direct labor *cost*. (*Hint:* Total direct labor cost is found in Requirement 3.)
6. Several jobs were completed during the month. According to the job cost records, these jobs cost $255,000 to manufacture.
7. Sales (all on credit) for the month totaled $340,000. According to the job cost records, the units sold cost $250,000 to manufacture. Assume the company uses a perpetual inventory system.
8. The company incurred operating expenses of $60,000 during the month. Assume that 80% of these were for marketing and administrative salaries and the other 20% were lease and utility bills related to the corporate headquarters. The expenses will be paid later.
9. In order to prepare its January financial statements, the company had to close its Manufacturing Overhead account.
10. Prepare the January income statement for Fashion Fabrics based on the transactions recorded in Requirements 1 through 9.

▪ SOLUTIONS

1. During January, $150,000 of raw materials was purchased on account.

Raw Materials Inventory		150,000	
Accounts Payable			150,000
(*to record purchases of raw materials*)			

2. During the month, $140,000 of raw materials was requisitioned. Of this amount, $135,000 was traced to specific jobs, while the remaining materials were for general factory use.

Work in Process Inventory		135,000	
Manufacturing Overhead		5,000	
Raw Materials Inventory			140,000
(*to record the use of direct materials and indirect materials*)			

3. Manufacturing labor (both direct and indirect) for the month totaled $80,000. It has not yet been paid. Of this amount, $60,000 was traced to specific jobs.

Work in Process Inventory (*for direct labor*)	60,000	
Manufacturing Overhead (*for indirect labor*)	20,000	
Wages Payable		80,000
(*to record the use of direct labor and indirect labor*)		

4. The company recorded $9,000 of depreciation on the plant building and machinery. In addition, $3,000 of prepaid property tax expired during the month. The company also received the plant utility bill for $6,000 which will be paid at a later date.

Manufacturing Overhead	18,000	
Accumulated Depreciation—Plant and Equipment		9,000
Prepaid Plant Property Tax (*for expiration of property tax*)		3,000
Accounts Payable (*for electric bill*)		6,000
(*to record other indirect manufacturing costs incurred during the month*)		

5. Manufacturing overhead was allocated to jobs using a predetermined manufacturing overhead rate of 75% of direct labor cost. (*Hint:* Total direct labor cost is found in Requirement 3.)

Work in Process Inventory (75% × $60,000 of direct labor)	45,000	
Manufacturing Overhead		45,000
(*to allocate manufacturing overhead to jobs*)		

6. Several jobs were completed during the month. According to the job cost records, these jobs cost $255,000 to manufacture.

Finished Goods Inventory	255,000	
Work in Process Inventory		255,000
(*to move the completed jobs out of the factory and into Finished Goods*)		

7. Sales (all on credit) for the month totaled $340,000. According to the job cost records, the units sold cost $250,000 to manufacture. Assume the company uses a perpetual inventory system.

Accounts Receivable	340,000	
Sales Revenue		340,000
(*to record the sales and receivables*)		

Cost of Goods Sold	250,000	
Finished Goods Inventory		250,000
(*to reduce Finished Goods Inventory and record Cost of Goods Sold*)		

8. The company incurred operating expenses of $60,000 during the month. Assume that 80% of these were for marketing and administrative salaries and the other 20% were lease and utility bills related to the corporate headquarters. The expenses will be paid later.

Salaries Expense ($60,000 × 80%)		48,000	
Lease and Utilities Expense ($60,000 × 20%)		12,000	
Salaries and Wages Payable			48,000
Accounts Payable			12,000
(*to record all non-manufacturing costs incurred during the month*)			

9. In order to prepare its January financial statements, the company had to close its Manufacturing Overhead account.

An analysis of the manufacturing overhead account *prior to closing* shows the following:

Manufacturing Overhead

(ACTUAL)	(ALLOCATED)
5,000	45,000
20,000	
18,000	
	2,000

Manufacturing Overhead		2,000	
Cost of Goods Sold			2,000
(*to close the Manufacturing Overhead account to CGS*)			

10. Prepare the January income statement for Fashion Fabrics based on the transactions recorded in Requirements 1 through 9.

	A	B	C	D
1	**Fashion Fabrics**			
2	**Income Statement**			
3	**For Month Ending January 31**			
4				
5	Sales Revenue	$ 340,000		
6	Less: Cost of Goods Sold**	248,000		
7	Gross Profit	92,000		
8	Less: Operating Expenses	60,000		
9	Operating Income	$ 32,000		
10				
11	(** $250,000 − $2,000 closing adjustment)			

Appendix 3A

How Do Service Firms Use Job Costing to Determine the Amount to Bill Clients?

So far in this chapter we have illustrated job costing in a manufacturing environment. However, job costing is also used by service firms (such as law firms, accounting firms, marketing firms, and consulting firms) and by tradespeople (such as plumbers, electricians, and auto mechanics). At these types of companies, the work performed for each individual client is considered a separate job. Service firms need to keep track of job costs so that they have a basis for billing their clients. As shown in Exhibit 3-22, the direct costs of serving the client are traced to the job, whereas the indirect costs of serving the client are allocated to the job.

7 Use job costing at a service firm as a basis for billing clients

EXHIBIT 3-22 Assigning Costs to Client Jobs

The amount billed to the client is determined by adding a profit markup to the total job cost. The main difference between job costing at a manufacturer and job costing at a service firm is that the indirect costs of serving the client are all *operating expenses* (period costs) rather than manufacturing (product) costs. In the next section, we will illustrate how job costing is used at the Bucaro & Associates law firm to determine how much to bill Client 367.

What Costs Are Considered Direct Costs of Serving a Client?

Professional labor is often the most significant direct cost at a service firm. It is considered a direct cost because professionals can use labor time records to keep track of the amount of time they spend performing work for individual clients. Because most professionals are paid an annual salary rather than an hourly wage rate, firms estimate the *hourly* professional labor cost based on the number of hours the professionals are expected to work during the year. For example, say Attorney Taylor Sweeney is paid a salary of $100,000 per year. The law firm she works for, Bucaro & Associates, expects her to spend 2,000 hours a year performing legal work for clients (50 weeks × 40 hours per week). Therefore, for job costing purposes, the law firm converts her annual salary to an hourly professional labor cost as follows:

$$\frac{\$100{,}000 \text{ annual salary}}{2{,}000 \text{ hours per year}} = \$50 \text{ per hour}$$

If the labor time record indicates that Sweeney has spent 14 hours on Client 367, then the direct professional labor cost traced to the client is calculated as follows:

$$14 \text{ hours} \times \$50 \text{ per hour} = \$700 \text{ of direct professional labor}$$

In addition to professional labor, any other costs that are readily identifiable with specific clients would be considered direct costs. For example, the law firm would be able to trace court filing fees to specific clients. Marketing firms would be able to trace the cost of placing print, billboard, and TV advertisements to specific clients. Plumbers, electricians, and auto mechanics would be able to trace materials (such as garbage disposals, lighting, and new tires) to specific clients. In summary, any cost that is traceable to a client would be considered a direct cost of serving the client.

What Costs Are Considered Indirect Costs of Serving a Client?

Service firms also incur general operating expenses, such as office rent, office supplies, and advertising. These costs are considered indirect because they can not be traced to individual clients. Rather, they are a joint cost of serving all clients. Since these costs cannot be traced to specific clients, they will be allocated among all clients using a *predetermined indirect cost allocation rate*. Service firms use the same four basic steps to allocate indirect costs as manufacturers use. The only real difference is that they are allocating indirect operating expenses, rather than indirect manufacturing costs (MOH).

STEP 1: Estimate the total indirect costs for the coming year.

Before the fiscal year begins, the law firm estimates the total indirect costs for the coming year:

Office rent	$190,000
Office supplies, telephone, internet access, and copier lease	10,000
Office support staff	70,000
Maintaining and updating law library for case research	25,000
Advertising	5,000
Total indirect costs	$300,000

STEP 2: Choose an allocation base and estimate the total amount that will be used during the year.

Next, the law firm chooses a cost allocation base. Service firms typically use professional labor hours as the cost allocation base. For example, Bucaro & Associates estimates that attorneys will spend a total of 10,000 professional labor hours working on client jobs throughout the coming year.

STEP 3: Compute the predetermined indirect cost allocation rate.

The predetermined indirect cost allocation rate is found as follows:

$$\text{Predetermined indirect cost allocation rate} = \frac{\text{Total estimated indirect costs}}{\text{Total estimated amount of the allocation base}}$$

$$= \frac{\$300,000 \text{ total indirect costs}}{10,000 \text{ professional labor hours}}$$

$$= \$30 \text{ per professional labor hour}$$

STEP 4: Allocate indirect costs to client jobs using the predetermined rate.

Throughout the year, indirect costs are allocated to individual client jobs using the predetermined indirect cost allocation rate. For example, assume Taylor Sweeney spent 14 hours working on Client 367 and she was the only attorney who worked on this job. The amount of indirect cost allocated to the job is computed as follows:

= Predetermined indirect cost allocation rate × Actual amount of allocation base used by the job
= $30 per professional labor hour × 14 professional labor hours
= $420

Finding the Total Cost of the Job and Adding a Profit Markup

Bucaro & Associates can now determine the total cost of serving Client 367:

Direct costs traced to Client 367 ($50 per hour × 14 hours)	$ 700
Indirect costs allocated to Client 367 ($30 per hour × 14 hours)	420
Total cost of serving Client 367	$1,120

Once the total job cost is known, Bucaro & Associates can determine the amount to bill the client. Let's assume that Bucaro & Associates bills clients at 25% over its costs. Bucaro & Associates would bill Client 367 as follows:

Job cost + Markup for profit = Amount to bill the client
$1,120 + (25% × $1,120) = $1,400

Invoicing Clients Using a Professional Billing Rate

When service firms and tradespeople bill their clients, they don't show the actual direct costs of providing the service, the allocation of indirect costs, or the profit they earned on the job. Rather, these individual figures are hidden from the client's view. How is this done? By incorporating these costs and profit components in the labor rate, often known as the **billing rate**, charged to the customer. Consider the last time you had your vehicle repaired. A typical mechanic billing rate exceeds $48 per hour, yet the mechanic employed by the auto repair shop does not actually earn a $48-per-hour wage rate.

Let's look at the calculations a service firm performs "behind the scenes" to determine its hourly billing rates. Bucaro & Associates determines Taylor Sweeney's billing rate as follows:

> **Why is this important?**
> "**Service** companies (such as **law firms**) and **tradespeople** (such as auto mechanics and plumbers) use **job costing** to determine how much to **bill** their clients."

Professional labor cost per hour	$ 50
Plus: Indirect cost allocation rate per hour	30
Total hourly cost	$ 80
Plus profit markup: (25% × $80 hourly cost)	+ 20
Hourly billing rate for Taylor Sweeney	$100

Whenever Taylor Sweeney performs legal work for a client, her time will be billed at $100 per hour. Remember, this is the *price* Bucaro & Associates charges its clients for any work performed by Taylor Sweeney. The actual invoice to Client 367 would look similar to Exhibit 3-23.

EXHIBIT 3-23 Invoice to Client

Bucaro & Associates Law Firm
Invoice: Client 367

Work performed the week of July 23: Researching and filing patent application

Attorney Taylor Sweeney: 14 hours × $100 hourly billing rate $1,400

What Journal Entries Are Needed in a Service Firm's Job Costing System?

The journal entries required for job costing at a service firm are much simpler than those used at a manufacturing company. That's because service firms typically have no inventory; hence, there is no need to record the movement of inventory through the system. Rather, all costs at a service company are treated as period costs, meaning they are immediately recorded as operating expenses in the period when they are incurred (for example, salary expense, rent expense, telephone expense, and advertising expense). The tracing of direct costs and the allocation of indirect costs is performed *only* on the client's job cost record, *not* through journal entries to the company's general ledger.

▶ Try It!

Sarah Haymeyer, CPA, pays her new staff accountant, Hannah, a salary equivalent to $25 per hour, while Sarah receives a salary equivalent to $40 per hour. The firm's predetermined indirect cost allocation rate for the year is $12 per hour. Haymeyer bills for the firm's services at 30% over cost. Assume Sarah works 5 hours and Hannah works 10 hours preparing a tax return for Michele Meckfessel.

1. What is the total cost of preparing Meckfessel's tax return?
2. How much will Sarah bill Meckfessel for the tax work?

Please see page 174 for solutions.

END OF CHAPTER

Learning Objectives

- 1 Distinguish between job costing and process costing
- 2 Understand the flow of production and how direct materials and direct labor are traced to jobs
- 3 Compute a predetermined manufacturing overhead rate and use it to allocate MOH to jobs
- 4 Determine the cost of a job and use it to make business decisions
- 5 Compute and dispose of overallocated or underallocated manufacturing overhead
- 6 Prepare journal entries for a manufacturer's job costing system
- 7 (Appendix) Use job costing at a service firm as a basis for billing clients

Accounting Vocabulary

Bill of Materials. (p. 109) A list of all of the raw materials needed to manufacture a job.

Billing Rate. (p. 145) The labor rate charged to the customer, which includes both cost and profit components.

Cost Driver. (p. 117) The primary factor that causes a cost.

Cost-Plus Pricing. (p. 120) A pricing approach in which the company adds a desired level of profit to the product's cost.

Extended Producer Responsibility (EPR). (p. 122) Laws that require product manufacturers to "take back" a large percentage of the products they manufacture at the end of the product's life in order to reduce the amount of waste ending up in landfills and the environment.

Invoice. (p. 110) Bill from a supplier.

Job Cost Record. (p. 110) A written or electronic document that lists the direct materials, direct labor, and manufacturing overhead costs assigned to each individual job.

Job Costing. (p. 106) A system for assigning costs to products or services that differ in the amount of materials, labor, and overhead required. Typically used by manufacturers that produce unique, or custom-ordered products in small batches; also used by professional service firms.

Labor Time Record. (p. 114) A written or electronic document that identifies the employee, the amount of time spent on a particular job, and the labor cost charged to a job.

Mass Customization. (p. 107) Large-scale production of customized product that allows manufacturers to meet a variety of consumer desires, while at the same time achieving the efficiencies of mass production that drive down unit costs.

Materials Requisition. (p. 113) A written or electronic document requesting that specific materials be transferred from the raw materials inventory storeroom to the production floor.

Overallocated Manufacturing Overhead. (p. 127) The amount of manufacturing overhead allocated to jobs is more than the amount of manufacturing overhead costs actually incurred; results in jobs being overcosted.

Pick. (p. 113) Storeroom workers remove items from raw materials inventory that are needed by production.

Predetermined Manufacturing Overhead Rate. (p. 117) The rate used to allocate manufacturing overhead to individual jobs; calculated before the year begins as follows: total estimated manufacturing overhead costs divided by total estimated amount of allocation base.

Process Costing. (p. 105) A system for assigning costs to a large number of identical units that typically pass through a series of uniform production steps. Costs are averaged over the units produced such that each unit bears the same unit cost.

Production Schedule. (p. 108) A written or electronic document indicating the quantity and types of inventory that will be manufactured during a specified time frame.

Purchase Order. (p. 110) A written or electronic document authorizing the purchase of specific raw materials from a specific supplier.

Raw Materials Record. (p. 109) A written or electronic document listing the number and cost of all units used and received, and the balance currently in stock; a separate record is maintained for each type of raw material kept in stock.

Receiving Report. (p. 110) A written or electronic document listing the quantity and type of raw materials received in an incoming shipment; the report is typically a duplicate of the purchase order without the quantity pre-listed on the form.

Stock Inventory. (p. 108) Products normally kept on hand in order to quickly fill customer orders.

Subsidiary Ledger. (p. 131) Supporting detail for a general ledger account.

Underallocated Manufacturing Overhead. (p. 127) The amount of manufacturing overhead allocated to jobs is less than the amount of manufacturing overhead costs actually incurred; this results in jobs being undercosted.

Quick Check

1. *(Learning Objective 1)* For which of the following would job costing *not* be appropriate?
   a. Electrician
   b. Manufacturer of mass-produced carbonated beverages
   c. Law firm
   d. Manufacturer of custom-ordered production equipment

2. *(Learning Objective 2)* Which of the following documents specifies the materials needed to produce a job?
   a. Bill of materials
   b. Raw materials records
   c. Receiving report
   d. Production schedule

3. *(Learning Objective 2)* Which of the following documents is used to accumulate all of the manufacturing costs assigned to a job?
   a. Labor time record
   b. Materials requisition
   c. Purchase order
   d. Job cost record

4. *(Learning Objective 3)* The amount of manufacturing overhead recorded on a job cost record for a particular job is found by
   a. tracing manufacturing overhead to the job.
   b. either tracing or allocating manufacturing overhead costs (management's choice).
   c. allocating manufacturing overhead to the job.
   d. None of the answers listed is correct.

5. *(Learning Objective 4)* Which of the following is *false*?
   a. Direct costing focuses on only the direct costs found on the job cost record.
   b. Job cost information is not useful for assessing the profitability of different products.
   c. A cost-plus price is determined by adding a markup to the cost.
   d. Non-manufacturing costs can be assigned to jobs only for internal decision making, never for external financial reporting.

6. *(Learning Objective 5)* Which of the following is *true*?
   a. If manufacturing overhead is underallocated, then jobs will be overcosted.
   b. If manufacturing overhead is overallocated, then jobs will be undercosted.
   c. Both of the statements are true.
   d. None of the statements is true.

7. *(Learning Objective 5)* Assuming the amount of manufacturing overhead overallocation or underallocation is not material, which account is adjusted at the end of the period?
   a. Sales Revenue
   b. Work in Process Inventory
   c. Raw Materials Inventory
   d. Cost of Goods Sold

8. *(Learning Objective 6)* Whenever direct material, direct labor, and manufacturing overhead are recorded on a job cost record, an associated journal entry is made to debit which of the following accounts?
   a. Sales Revenue
   b. Work in Process Inventory
   c. Cost of Goods Sold
   d. Finished Goods Inventory

9. *(Learning Objective 6)* When a job is completed, the total cost of manufacturing the job should be moved to which of the following general ledger accounts?
   a. Finished Goods Inventory
   b. Sales Revenue
   c. Cost of Goods Sold
   d. Work in Process Inventory

10. *(Learning Objective 7, Appendix)* Which of the following is *true* when using job costing at a service firm?
    a. Professional labor cost would be considered an indirect cost of serving the client.
    b. Office rent would be considered a direct cost of serving the client.
    c. Both direct and indirect costs are assigned to client jobs.
    d. The professional billing rate consists solely of the professionals' labor cost.

Quick Check Answers

1. b 2. a 3. d 4. c 5. b 6. d 7. d 8. b 9. a 10. c

Short Exercises

S3-1 Identify product costs, period costs, and product costing system *(Learning Objective 1)*

Smarties, the sugar candy that is packaged in rolls of 15 small candies, come in six flavors: white (orange crème), yellow (pineapple), pink (cherry), green (strawberry), purple (grape), and orange (orange). Smarties are gluten free and vegan and have 25 calories per roll of 15 candies. The main ingredient in Smarties is dextrose, a form of sugar.

The Smarties Candy Company, founded in 1949, makes its Smarties candy in a New Jersey plant. Its founder bought gunpowder pellet machines after World War I and repurposed them to make the tablet-shaped candies. Smarties are made by color in large batches and then dumped together to be sorted by machines into rolls and packs.

Three granddaughters of the original founder of Smarties now run the company and have been working to improve efficiency. Their chief mechanic designed a faster candy press and a new wrapper machine. Previously, 125 Smarties rolls could be wrapped per minute; now 200 rolls can be wrapped per minute. Smarties are produced 24 hours a day in continuous batches.

The Smarties Candy Company has its one main product that is likely to account for most of its sales, but recently it introduced Smarties 'n creme, which are tablets that are about the size of a quarter and have a flavor burst that is half fruit (strawberry, blueberry, raspberry, peach, or orange) and half cream (dairy-free).

Requirements

1. Give an example of each of the following types of costs at the Smarties Candy Company:
   a. Direct material
   b. Direct labor
   c. Manufacturing overhead
   d. Selling and administrative expense
2. Assume that only Smarties candies are made in the New Jersey plant. Do you think the Smarties Candy Company is likely to use job order costing or process costing? Explain.
3. If the New Jersey plant begins to produce Smarties 'n creme in addition to Smarties candy rolls, would this change be likely to impact whether the company uses job order costing or process costing? Why or why not?

S3-2 Decide on product costing system *(Learning Objective 1)*

Would the following companies use job costing or process costing?
a. A legal firm
b. An oil refinery
c. A commercial plumbing contractor
d. A cereal manufacturer
e. A custom-home builder

S3-3 Determine the flow of costs between inventory accounts *(Learning Objective 2)*

Kirkland Furniture is a manufacturing plant that makes a variety of tables, benches, and other furniture. Indicate which inventory account(s) would be affected by the following actions that occur at Kirkland's in the process of manufacturing its standard picnic tables. Also indicate whether the inventory account would increase or decrease as a result of the action.

a. Lumber is delivered by the supplier to the plant, where it is stored in a materials storeroom until needed.
b. Lumber is requisitioned from the storeroom to be used for tops and seats for the tables.
c. Factory workers cut the lumber for the tables.
d. Five tables are completed and moved to the inventory storage area to await sale.
e. A customer purchases a table and takes it home.

S3-4 Understanding key document terms in a job cost shop (Learning Objective 2)

Listed below are several document terms. Match each term with the corresponding statement in the list provided. Some terms may be used more than once and other terms may not be used at all.

Terms		
a. Bill of materials	b. Job cost record	c. Production schedule
d. Purchase orders	e. Raw materials record	f. Labor time record
g. Receiving report	h. Materials requisition	i. Invoice

1. A(n) _____ is used to accumulate all of the costs affiliated with each job.
2. All direct laborers in the factory fill out a(n) _____.
3. The accounting department will not pay a(n) _____ unless it agrees with the quantity of parts both ordered and received.
4. Each item in the raw materials storeroom has its own _____.
5. The _____ is a control for the materials stored in the storeroom. In order to get direct materials, a(n) _____ must be presented.
6. Before production begins, a manufacturer's purchasing department issues _____ to its supplier for needed direct materials.
7. A(n) _____ is typically a duplicate of the purchase order but without the quantity pre-listed on the form.
8. The _____ is like a list of ingredients in a recipe, stating the materials needed to produce a product.

S3-5 Compute a professional billing rate (Learning Objective 7)

Nicole Grandstone is a new staff accountant at James & Associates. She is paid a salary of $67,600 per year and is expected to work 2,600 hours per year on client jobs. The firm's indirect cost allocation rate is $25 per hour. The firm would like to achieve a profit equal to 20% of cost.

1. Convert Nicole's salary to an hourly wage rate for billing purposes.
2. Calculate the professional billing rate James & Associates would use for billing out Nicole's services.

S3-6 Compute various manufacturing overhead rates (Learning Objective 3)

Edmonton Pools manufactures swimming pool equipment. Edmonton estimates total manufacturing overhead costs next year to be $1,400,000. Edmonton also estimates it will use 50,000 direct labor hours and incur $1,000,000 of direct labor cost next year. In addition, the machines are expected to be run for 40,000 hours. Compute the predetermined manufacturing overhead rate for next year under the following independent situations:

1. Assume that the company uses direct labor hours as its manufacturing overhead allocation base.
2. Assume that the company uses direct labor cost as its manufacturing overhead allocation base.
3. Assume that the company uses machine hours as its manufacturing overhead allocation base.

S3-7 Continuation of S3-6: compute total allocated overhead (Learning Objective 3)

Use your answers from S3-6 to determine the total manufacturing overhead allocated to Edmonton's manufacturing jobs in the following independent situations:

1. Assume that the company actually used 51,700 direct labor hours.
2. Assume that the company actually incurred $1,020,000 of direct labor cost.
3. Assume that the company actually ran the machines 39,500 hours.
4. Briefly explain what you have learned about the total manufacturing overhead allocated to production.

S3-8 Continuation of S3-7: determine over- or underallocation *(Learning Objectives 3 & 5)*

Use your answers from S3-7 to determine the total overallocation or underallocation of manufacturing overhead during the year. Actual manufacturing costs for the year for Edmonton Pools totaled $1,425,000.

1. Assume that the company used direct labor hours as the allocation base.
2. Assume that the company used the direct labor cost as the allocation base.
3. Assume that the company used machine hours as the allocation base.
4. Were there any situations in which jobs were costed correctly? If not, when were they overcosted? When were they undercosted?

S3-9 Calculate rate and analyze year-end results *(Learning Objectives 3 & 5)*

Adam Industries manufactures wooden backyard playground equipment. Adam estimated $1,800,000 of manufacturing overhead and $2,000,000 of direct labor cost for the year. After the year was over, the accounting records indicated that the company had actually incurred $1,660,000 of manufacturing overhead and $2,650,000 of direct labor cost.

1. Calculate Adam's predetermined manufacturing overhead rate, assuming that the company uses direct labor cost as an allocation base.
2. How much manufacturing overhead would have been allocated to manufacturing jobs during the year?
3. At year-end, was manufacturing overhead overallocated or underallocated? By how much?

S3-10 Calculate job cost and billing at appliance repair service *(Learning Objectives 2, 4, & 7 (Appendix))*

Selle Appliance provides repair services for all makes and models of home appliances. Selle Appliance charges customers for labor on each job at a rate of $89 per hour. The labor rate is high enough to cover actual technician wages of $27 per hour, to cover shop overhead (allocated at a cost of $14 per hour), and to provide a profit. The company charges the customer "at cost" for parts and materials. A recent customer job consisted of $45 in parts and materials and 8 hours of technician time.

1. What was Selle Appliance's cost for this job? Include shop overhead in the cost calculation.
2. How much was charged to the customer for this repair job?

S3-11 Calculating overallocated or underallocated overhead *(Learning Objective 5)*

Well-Flow Company had estimated $1,053,000 of manufacturing overhead (MOH) for the year and 58,500 direct labor (DL) hours, resulting in a predetermined MOH rate of $18 per DL hour. By the end of that year, the company had actually incurred $1,005,000 of MOH costs and had used a total of 57,000 DL hours on various jobs.

1. By how much did the company overallocate or underallocate MOH for the year?
2. Was MOH overallocated or underallocated for the year? How do you know?

S3-12 Record purchase and use of materials *(Learning Objective 6)*

RitePacks manufactures backpacks. Its plant records include the following materials-related transactions:

Purchases of canvas (on account)	$70,000
Purchases of thread (on account)	$ 700
Material requisitions:	
Canvas	$60,000
Thread	$ 500

Make the journal entries to record these transactions. Post these transactions to the Raw Materials Inventory account. If the company had $37,000 of Raw Materials Inventory at the beginning of the period, what is the ending balance of Raw Materials Inventory?

S3-13 Record manufacturing labor costs *(Learning Objective 6)*

Bentley Glass reports the following labor-related transactions at its plant in Bryan, Ohio.

Plant janitor's wages	$ 610
Plant supervisor's wages	$ 900
Glassblowers' wages	$77,000

Record the journal entries for the incurrence of these wages.

S3-14 Recompute job cost at a legal firm *(Learning Objectives 3, 4, & 7)*

Irvin Associates, a law firm, hires Attorney Amanda Hiller at an annual salary of $207,000. The law firm expects her to spend 2,300 hours per year performing legal work for clients. Indirect costs are assigned to clients based on attorney billing hours. Firm attorneys are expected to work a total of 22,000 direct labor hours this year. Before the fiscal year begins, Irvin estimates that the total indirect costs for the upcoming year will be $660,000.

1. What would be the hourly (cost) rate to Irvin Associates of employing Hiller?
2. If Hiller works on Client 367 for 16 hours, what direct labor cost would be traced to Client 367?
3. What is the indirect cost allocation rate?
4. What indirect costs will be allocated to Client 367?
5. What is the total job cost for Client 367?

S3-15 Identify ethical standards violated *(Learning Objectives 1, 2, 3, 4, 5, & 6)*

ETHICS

For each of the situations listed, identify the primary standard from the IMA *Statement of Ethical Professional Practice* that is violated (competence, confidentiality, integrity, or credibility). Refer to Exhibit 1-7 for the complete standard.

1. Joe added in sales commissions to product costs on the financial statements because it seemed reasonable to include those costs.
2. At a neighborhood party, Megan talks about the upcoming bid her company is making for a city project. She shares specific cost estimates that are included in the bid.
3. Justin changed the way that manufacturing overhead is allocated to divisions on the monthly internal reports to better reflect resource usage. However, he did not note the change on any of the reports, nor did he inform any managers of the change.
4. Raquel does not disclose to her employer, Alpha Company, that her brother is the owner of a company that is bidding on a major contract with Alpha Company. Raquel is on the committee that evaluates the bids and makes a recommendation for which bid to select.
5. Anthony is asked to do an inventory count of a wide assortment of parts. Anthony does not know how to distinguish the various parts. He guesses when he enters the quantity. He does not ask for help because he does not want to look stupid.

S3-16 Understanding key terms *(Learning Objectives 1, 2, 3, & 4)*

Listed next are several terms. Complete the following statements with one of these terms. You may use a term more than once, and some terms may not be used at all.

Cost allocation	Cost driver	Job costing	Process costing
Cost tracing	Job cost record	Materials requisition	

a. _____ is used by companies that produce unique services and products.
b. Raw materials are stored in a storeroom until a _____ is received requesting the transfer of materials to the production area.
c. _____ is the assignment of direct costs to specific jobs.
d. Indirect costs cannot be traced to specific products, so they are divided up using a process called _____.
e. A custom-home builder would use a _____ system to determine product cost.
f. A _____ is any activity that causes a cost to be incurred.
g. _____ is used by companies that produce large numbers of identical units through a series of uniform production steps or processes.
h. The _____ is used to track and accumulate all of the costs for an individual job.
i. PepsiCo produces Ruffles potato chips; it would use a _____ system to determine product cost.

EXERCISES Group A

E3-17A Identify type of costing system *(Learning Objective 1)*

For each of the following companies, specify whether each company would be more likely to use job costing or process costing.

a. Janitorial services company
b. Soup manufacturer
c. Commercial plumbing contractor
d. Toothpaste manufacturer
e. Catering service
f. Shipbuilder
g. Company providing Web design services
h. Medical practice of six doctors and four physician assistants
i. Soft drink bottler
j. Movie studio
k. Plastic bottle manufacturer
l. Architect
m. Temporary staffing agency
n. Oil refinery

E3-18A Understand the flow of costs in a job cost shop *(Learning Objective 2)*

Gerbig Lighting manufactures a variety of lamps for lighting specialty stores. In September, Gerbig Lighting received an order from Zucca Decor for 32 mission-style table lamps (Model 5A). The order from Zucca Decor became Job Number 804 at Gerbig Lighting.

Materials requisition #1247 for Job 804 shows that a total of $147 of direct materials were used in manufacturing the job. In addition to the materials requisition, the labor time records show that a total of $68 of direct labor costs was incurred in producing these lamps; a total of 8 direct labor hours were worked on this job.

Job Cost Record

Job Number: 804

Customer: Zucca Decor

Job Description: 32 Model 5A - Mission-style table lamps

Date Started: Sep. 14   **Date Completed:** _____

Manufacturing Cost Information:	Cost Summary
Direct Materials	
Req. # :	
Direct Labor	
Manufacturing Overhead	
8 hours × $2 per direct labor hour	$ 16
Total Job Cost	
Number of Units	÷
Cost per Unit	

Requirement

Add direct materials and direct labor to the Job Cost Record for Job 804. Manufacturing overhead has already been added to the Job Cost Record for this job. Assume that the job was completed on September 19. Complete the Job Cost Record by calculating the total job cost and the cost per unit. Remember that this job consisted of 32 lamps (units).

E3-19A Determine the cost of a job and use it for pricing *(Learning Objectives 2, 3, & 4)*

Playtime Industries manufactures custom-designed playground equipment for schools and city parks. Playtime expected to incur $586,600 of manufacturing overhead cost, 41,900 of direct labor hours, and $1,592,200 of direct labor cost during the year (the cost of direct labor is $38 per hour). The company allocates manufacturing overhead on the basis of direct labor hours. During May, Playtime completed Job 304. The job used 190 direct labor hours and required $14,800 of direct materials. The City of Jonestown has contracted to purchase the playground equipment at a price of 28% over manufacturing cost.

Requirements

1. Calculate the manufacturing cost of Job 304.
2. How much will the City of Jonestown pay for this playground equipment?

E3-20A Compute a predetermined overhead rate and calculate cost of jobs based on direct labor hours *(Learning Objectives 3 & 4)*

Elkland Heating & Cooling installs and services commercial heating and cooling systems. Elkland uses job costing to calculate the cost of its jobs. Overhead is allocated to each job based on the number of direct labor hours spent on that job. At the beginning of the current year, Elkland estimated that its overhead for the coming year would be $61,500. It also anticipated using 4,100 direct labor hours for the year. In November, Elkland started and completed the following two jobs:

	Job 101	Job 102
Direct materials used	$15,000	$10,000
Direct labor hours used	155	72

Elkland paid a $24-per-hour wage rate to the employees who worked on these two jobs.

Requirements

1. What is Elkland's predetermined overhead rate based on direct labor hours?
2. Calculate the overhead to be allocated to each of the two jobs based on direct labor hours.
3. What is the total cost of Job 101? What is the total cost of Job 102?

E3-21A Compute a predetermined overhead rate and calculate cost of job based on direct labor costs *(Learning Objectives 3 & 4)*

Raymond Industries uses job costing to calculate the costs of its jobs with direct labor cost as its manufacturing overhead allocation base. The company manufactures a variety of engines for use in farm equipment. At the beginning of the current year, Raymond estimated that its overhead for the coming year would be $371,800. It also anticipated using 26,000 direct labor hours for the year. Raymond pays its employees an average of $22 per direct labor hour. Raymond just finished Job 371, which consisted of two engines for a farm equipment manufacturer. The costs and hours for this job consisted of $13,500 in direct materials used and 180 direct labor hours.

Requirements

1. What is Raymond's predetermined manufacturing overhead rate based on direct labor cost?
2. Calculate the manufacturing overhead to be allocated based on direct labor cost to Job 371.
3. What is the total cost of Job 371?

Job Costing 155

SUSTAINABILITY

E3-22A Sustainability and job costing *(Learning Objectives 2, 3, & 4)*

Lawrence Plastics manufactures custom park furniture and signage from recycled plastics (primarily shredded milk jugs). Many of the company's customers are municipalities that are required by law to purchase goods that meet certain recycled-content guidelines. (Recycled-content can include post-consumer waste materials, pre-consumer waste materials, and recovered materials). As a result, Lawrence includes two types of direct material charges in its job cost for each job: (1) virgin materials (non-recycled), and (2) recycled-content materials. Lawrence also keeps track of the pounds of each type of direct material so that the final recycled-content percentage for the job can be reported to the customer. Lawrence also reports on the percentage of recycled content as a total of total plastic used each month in its own internal reporting system to help encourage managers to use recycled content whenever possible.

Lawrence Plastics uses a predetermined manufacturing overhead rate of $14 per direct labor hour. Here is a summary of the materials and labor used on a recent job for Summit County:

Description	Quantity	Cost
Virgin materials	30 pounds	$ 3.80 per pound
Recycled-content materials	70 pounds	$ 3.50 per pound
Direct labor	18 hours	$19.00 per hour

Requirements

1. Calculate the total cost of the Summit County job.
2. Calculate the percentage of recycled content used in the Summit County job (using pounds). If items purchased by Summit County are required by county charter to contain at least 40% recycled content, does this job meet that requirement?

E3-23A Determine the cost of a job *(Learning Objectives 2, 3, & 4)*

Fontaine Furniture started and finished Job 310 during April. The company's records show that the following direct materials were requisitioned for Job 310:

  Lumber: 45 units at $4 per unit
  Padding: 13 yards at $14 per yard
  Upholstery fabric: 25 yards at $30 per yard

Labor time records show the following employees (direct labor) worked on Job 310:

  Penny Rawls: 12 hours at $13 per hour
  Mark Frizzell: 16 hours at $22 per hour

Fontaine allocates manufacturing overhead at a rate of $12 per direct labor hour.

Requirements

1. Compute the total amount of direct materials, direct labor, and manufacturing overhead that should be shown on Job 310's job cost record.
2. Job 310 consists of twelve recliners. If each recliner sells for $750, what is the gross profit per recliner?

E3-24A Compare bid prices under two different allocation bases *(Learning Objectives 3 & 4)*

Olney Recycling recycles newsprint, cardboard, and so forth, into recycled packaging materials. For the coming year, Olney estimates total manufacturing overhead to be $370,000. The company's managers are not sure if direct labor hours (estimated to be 10,000) or machine hours (estimated to be 14,800 hours) is the best allocation base to use for allocating manufacturing overhead. Olney bids for jobs using a 31% markup over total manufacturing cost.

After the new fiscal year began, Leftwich Paper Supply asked Olney Recycling to bid for a job that will take 2,020 machine hours and 1,650 direct labor hours to produce. The direct labor cost for this job will be $11 per hour, and the direct materials will total $25,400.

Requirements

1. Compute the total job cost and bid price if Olney Recycling decided to use direct labor hours as the manufacturing overhead allocation base for the year.
2. Compute the total job cost and bid price if Olney Recycling decided to use machine hours as the manufacturing overhead allocation base for the year.
3. In addition to the bid from Olney Recycling, Leftwich Paper Supply received a bid of $126,000 for this job from Drund Recycling. What are the ramifications for Olney Recycling?

E3-25A Analyze manufacturing overhead *(Learning Objectives 3 & 5)*

Smith Foundry in Columbus, Ohio, uses a predetermined manufacturing overhead rate to allocate overhead to individual jobs based on the machine hours required. At the beginning of the year, the company expected to incur the following:

Manufacturing overhead costs	$ 630,000
Direct labor cost	$1,650,000
Machine hours	90,000

At the end of the year, the company had actually incurred the following:

Direct labor cost	$1,230,000
Depreciation on manufacturing plant and equipment	$ 480,000
Property taxes on plant	$ 19,500
Sales salaries	$ 26,500
Delivery drivers' wages	$ 17,000
Plant janitors' wages	$ 8,500
Machine hours	56,500 hours

Requirements

1. Compute Smith's predetermined manufacturing overhead rate.
2. How much manufacturing overhead was allocated to jobs during the year?
3. How much manufacturing overhead was incurred during the year? Is manufacturing overhead underallocated or overallocated at the end of the year? By how much?
4. Were the jobs overcosted or undercosted? By how much?

E3-26A Record manufacturing overhead *(Learning Objectives 5 & 6)*

Refer to the data in Exercise 3-25A. Smith's accountant found an error in the expense records from the year reported. Depreciation on manufacturing plant and equipment was actually $364,000, not the $480,000 that had originally been reported. The unadjusted Cost of Goods Sold balance at year-end was $610,000.

Requirements

1. Prepare the journal entry (entries) to record manufacturing overhead costs incurred.
2. Prepare the journal entry to record the manufacturing overhead allocated to jobs in production.
3. Use a T-account to determine whether manufacturing overhead is underallocated or overallocated and by how much.
4. Record the entry to close out the underallocated or overallocated manufacturing overhead.
5. What is the adjusted ending balance of Cost of Goods Sold?

E3-27A Record journal entries *(Learning Objectives 2, 3, 5, & 6)*

The following transactions were incurred by Howe Fabricators during January, the first month of its fiscal year.

Requirements

1. Record the proper journal entry for each transaction.
   a. $215,000 of materials was purchased on account.
   b. $190,000 of materials was used in production; of this amount, $164,000 was used on specific jobs.
   c. Manufacturing labor and salaries for the month totaled $210,000. A total of $180,000 of manufacturing labor and salaries was traced to specific jobs, and the remainder was indirect labor used in the factory.
   d. The company recorded $15,000 of depreciation on the plant and plant equipment. The company also received a plant utility bill for $8,000 which will be paid at a later date.
   e. $70,000 of manufacturing overhead was allocated to specific jobs.
   f. The company received a bill for CAD design services for $9,000.
2. By the end of January, was manufacturing overhead overallocated or underallocated? By how much?

E3-28A Analyze T-accounts *(Learning Objectives 2, 3, 5, & 6)*

Crystale Displays produces screens for use in various smartphones. The company reports the following information at December 31. Crystale Displays began operations on January 31 earlier that same year.

Work in Process Inventory		Wages Payable		Manufacturing Overhead		Finished Goods Inventory		Raw Materials Inventory	
27,500	127,000	75,000	75,000	9,000	44,000	127,000	114,000	55,500	36,500
64,000				11,000					
44,000		Balance 0		42,500					

Requirements

1. What is the cost of direct materials used?
2. What is the cost of indirect materials used?
3. What is the cost of direct labor?
4. What is the cost of indirect labor?
5. What is the cost of goods manufactured?
6. What is the cost of goods sold (before adjusting for any under- or overallocated manufacturing overhead)?
7. What is the actual manufacturing overhead?
8. How much manufacturing overhead was allocated to jobs?
9. What is the predetermined manufacturing overhead rate as a percentage of direct labor cost?
10. Is manufacturing overhead underallocated or overallocated? By how much?

E3-29A Job cost and bid price at a consulting firm *(Learning Objective 7)*

Robert Consulting, a real estate consulting firm, specializes in advising companies on potential new plant sites. The firm uses a job cost system with a predetermined indirect cost allocation rate computed as a percentage of expected direct labor costs.

At the beginning of the year, managing partner DeeAnn Robert prepared the following plan, or budget, for the year:

Direct labor hours (professionals)	14,000 hours
Direct labor costs (professionals)	$2,150,000
Office rent	$ 240,000
Support staff salaries	$ 930,000
Utilities	$ 290,000

Chase Resources is inviting several consulting firms to bid for work. Robert estimates that this job will require about 210 direct labor hours.

Requirements

1. Compute Robert Consulting's (a) hourly direct labor cost rate and (b) indirect cost allocation rate.
2. Compute the predicted cost of the Chase Resources job.
3. If Robert Consulting wants to earn a profit that equals 25% of the job's cost, how much should the company bid for the Chase Resources job?

E3-30A Record journal entries *(Learning Objectives 2, 3, 5, & 6)*

The following transactions were incurred by Augustine Fabricators during January, the first month of its fiscal year.

Requirements

1. Record the proper journal entry for each transaction.
    a. $205,000 of materials was purchased on account.
    b. $158,000 of materials was used in production; of this amount, $155,000 was used on specific jobs.
    c. Manufacturing labor and salaries for the month totaled $250,000. $215,000 of the total manufacturing labor and salaries was traced to specific jobs, and the remainder was indirect labor used in the factory.
    d. The company recorded $19,000 of depreciation on the plant and plant equipment. The company also received a plant utility bill for $10,000 which will be paid at a later date.
    e. $62,000 of manufacturing overhead was allocated to specific jobs.
2. By the end of January, was manufacturing overhead overallocated or underallocated? By how much?

EXERCISES Group B

E3-31B Identify type of costing system *(Learning Objective 1)*

For each of the following companies, specify whether the company would be more likely to use job costing or process costing.

- a. Yacht builder
- b. Cereal manufacturer
- c. Landscaper
- d. Pet food processor
- e. Wallpaper installation service
- f. Aircraft builder
- g. Hospital
- h. Cement plant
- i. Dentist
- j. Advertising agency
- k. Custom-home builder
- l. Oil refinery
- m. House painter
- n. Computer chip manufacturer

E3-32B Understand the flow of costs in a job cost shop
(Learning Objective 2)

Hamilton Lighting manufactures a variety of lamps for lighting specialty stores. In September, Hamilton Lighting received an order from Rose Decor for 34 mission-style table lamps (Model 5A.) The order from Rose Decor became Job Number 951 at Hamilton Lighting.

Materials requisition #1298 for Job 951 shows that a total of $196 of direct materials were used in manufacturing the job. In addition to the materials requisition, the labor time records show that a total of $79 of direct labor costs was incurred in producing these lamps; a total of 8 direct labor hours were worked on this job.

Job Cost Record

Job Number: 951

Customer: Rose Decor

Job Description: 34 Model 5A Mission-style table lamps

Date Started: Sep. 14   Date Completed: _____

Manufacturing Cost Information:	Cost Summary
Direct Materials	
Req. # :	
Direct Labor	
Manufacturing Overhead	
8 hours × $3 per direct labor hour	$ 24
Total Job Cost	
Number of Units	
Cost per Unit	

Requirement

Add direct materials and direct labor to the Job Cost Record for Job 951. Manufacturing overhead has already been added to the Job Cost Record for this job. Assume that the job was completed on September 19. Complete the Job Cost Record by calculating the total job cost and the cost per unit. Remember that this job consisted of 34 lamps (units).

E3-33B Determine the cost of a job and use it for pricing
(Learning Objectives 2, 3, & 4)

Alltime Industries manufactures custom-designed playground equipment for schools and city parks. Alltime expected to incur $664,000 of manufacturing overhead cost, 41,500 of direct labor hours, and $1,577,000 of direct labor cost during the year (the cost of direct labor is $38 per hour). The company allocates manufacturing overhead on the basis of direct labor hours. During February, Alltime completed Job 302. The job used 160 direct labor hours and required $13,900 of direct materials. The City of Cooperstown has contracted to purchase the playground equipment at a price of 25% over manufacturing cost.

Requirements

1. Calculate the manufacturing cost of Job 302.
2. How much will the City of Cooperstown pay for this playground equipment?

E3-34B Compute a predetermined overhead rate and calculate cost of jobs
(Learning Objectives 3 & 4)

Peterson Heating & Cooling installs and services commercial heating and cooling systems. Peterson uses job costing to calculate the cost of its jobs. Overhead is allocated to each job based on the number of direct labor hours spent on that job. At the beginning of the current year, Peterson estimated that its overhead for the coming year would be $63,750. It also anticipated using 4,250 direct labor hours for the year. In October, Peterson started and completed the following two jobs:

	Job 101	Job 102
Direct materials used	$17,500	$13,000
Direct labor hours used	195	76

Peterson paid a $24-per-hour wage rate to the employees who worked on these two jobs.

Requirements

1. What is Peterson's predetermined overhead rate based on direct labor hours?
2. Calculate the overhead to be allocated to each of the two jobs based on direct labor hours.
3. What is the total cost of Job 101? What is the total cost of Job 102?

E3-35B Compute a predetermined overhead rate and calculate cost of job
(Learning Objectives 3 & 4)

Miskimen Industries uses job costing to calculate the costs of its jobs with direct labor cost as its manufacturing overhead allocation base. The company manufactures a variety of engines for use in farm equipment. At the beginning of the current year, Miskimen estimated that its overhead for the coming year will be $364,000. It also anticipated using 28,000 direct labor hours for the year. Miskimen pays its employees an average of $26 per direct labor hour. Miskimen just finished Job 371, which consisted of two engines for a farm equipment manufacturer. The costs and hours for this job consisted of $15,500 in direct materials used and 110 direct labor hours.

Requirements

1. What is Miskimen's predetermined manufacturing overhead rate based on direct labor cost?
2. Calculate the manufacturing overhead to be allocated based on direct labor costs to Job 371.
3. What is the total cost of Job 371?

E3-36B Sustainability and job costing *(Learning Objectives 2, 3, & 4)*

Lancaster Plastics manufactures custom park furniture and signage from recycled plastics (primarily shredded milk jugs). Many of the company's customers are municipalities that are required by law to purchase goods that meet certain recycled-content guidelines. (Recycled content can include post-consumer waste materials, pre-consumer waste materials, and recovered materials). As a result, Lancaster Plastics includes two types of direct material charges in its job cost for each job: (1) virgin materials (non-recycled), and (2) recycled-content materials. Lancaster Plastics also keeps track of the pounds of each type of direct material so that the final recycled-content percentage for the job can be reported to the customer. The company also reports on the percentage of recycled-content as a total of plastics used each month on its own internal reporting system to help encourage managers to use recycled content whenever possible.

Lancaster Plastics uses a predetermined manufacturing overhead rate of $8 per direct labor hour. Here is a summary of the materials and labor used on a recent job for Lyon County:

Description	Quantity	Cost
Virgin materials	80 pounds	$ 3.80 per pound
Recycled-content materials	120 pounds	$ 2.60 per pound
Direct labor	12 hours	$ 16.00 per hour

Job Costing

Requirements

1. Calculate the total cost of the Lyon County job.
2. Calculate the percentage of recycled-content used in the Lyon County job (using pounds.) If items purchased by Lyon County are required by county charter to contain at least 40% recycled-content, does the job meet that requirement?

E3-37B   Determine the cost of a job *(Learning Objectives 2, 3, & 4)*

Stonecreek Furniture started and finished Job 310 during November. The company's records show that the following direct materials were requisitioned for Job 310:

   Lumber: 45 units at $6 per unit
   Padding: 14 yards at $21 per yard
   Upholstery fabric: 32 yards at $27 per yard.

Labor time records show the following employees (direct labor) worked on Job 310:

   Holly Powers: 14 hours at $16 per hour
   Patrick Aaronson: 13 hours at $22 per hour.

Stonecreek Furniture allocates manufacturing overhead at a rate of $9 per direct labor hour.

Requirements

1. Compute the total amount of direct materials, direct labor, and manufacturing overhead that should be shown on Job 310's job cost record.
2. Job 310 consists of eight recliners. If each recliner sells for $725, what is the gross profit per recliner?

E3-38B   Compare bid prices under two different allocation bases
(Learning Objectives 3 & 4)

Nestor Recycling recycles newsprint, cardboard, and so forth, into recycled packaging materials. For the coming year, Nestor Recycling estimates total manufacturing overhead to be $369,260. The company's managers are not sure if direct labor hours (estimated to be 9,980) or machine hours (estimated to be 18,463 hours) is the best allocation base to use for allocating manufacturing overhead. Nestor bids for jobs using a 29% markup over total manufacturing cost.

After the new fiscal year began, Elliott Paper Supply asked Nestor Recycling to bid for a job that will take 1,975 machine hours and 1,600 direct labor hours to produce. The direct labor cost for this job will be $12 per hour, and the direct materials will total $25,600.

Requirements

1. Compute the total job cost and bid price if Nestor Recycling decided to use direct labor hours as the manufacturing overhead allocation base for the year.
2. Compute the total job cost and bid price if Nestor Recycling decided to use machine hours as the manufacturing overhead allocation base for the year.
3. In addition to the bid from Nestor Recycling, Elliott Paper Supply received a bid of $125,500 for this job from Kitson Recycling. What are the ramifications for Nestor Recycling?

E3-39B   Analyze manufacturing overhead *(Learning Objectives 3 & 5)*

Benson Foundry in Charleston, South Carolina, uses a predetermined manufacturing overhead rate to allocate overhead to individual jobs based on the machine hours required. At the beginning of the year, the company expected to incur the following:

Manufacturing overhead costs	$ 610,000
Direct labor cost	$1,500,000
Machine hours	76,250

At the end of the year, the company had actually incurred the following:

Direct labor cost	$1,220,000
Depreciation on manufacturing plant and equipment	$ 470,000
Property taxes on plant	$ 19,000
Sales salaries	$ 25,500
Delivery drivers' wages	$ 14,500
Plant janitors' wages	$ 8,000
Machine hours	55,500 hours

Requirements

1. Compute Benson Foundry's predetermined manufacturing overhead rate.
2. How much manufacturing overhead was allocated to jobs during the year?
3. How much manufacturing overhead was incurred during the year? Is manufacturing overhead underallocated or overallocated at the end of the year? By how much?
4. Were the jobs overcosted or undercosted? By how much?

E3-40B Record manufacturing overhead *(Learning Objectives 5 & 6)*

Refer to the data in Exercise E3-39B. Benson Foundry's accountant found an error in the expense records from the year reported. Depreciation on manufacturing plant and equipment was actually $415,000, not the $470,000 it had originally reported. The unadjusted Cost of Goods Sold balance at year-end was $560,000.

Requirements

1. Prepare the journal entry (entries) to record manufacturing overhead costs incurred.
2. Prepare the journal entry to record the manufacturing overhead allocated to jobs in production.
3. Use a T-account to determine whether manufacturing overhead is underallocated or overallocated, and by how much.
4. Record the entry to close out the underallocated or overallocated manufacturing overhead.
5. What is the adjusted ending balance of Cost of Goods Sold?

E3-41B Record journal entries *(Learning Objectives 2, 3, 5, & 6)*

The following transactions were incurred by Gregor Fabricators during January, the first month of its fiscal year.

Requirements

1. Record the proper journal entry for each transaction.
   a. $205,000 of materials was purchased on account.
   b. $170,000 of materials was used in production; of this amount, $152,000 was used on specific jobs.
   c. Manufacturing labor and salaries for the month totaled $255,000. $215,000 of the total manufacturing labor and salaries was traced to specific jobs, and the remainder was indirect labor used in the factory.
   d. The company recorded $25,000 of depreciation on the plant and plant equipment. The company also received a plant utility bill for $12,000 which will be paid at a later date.
   e. $79,000 of manufacturing overhead was allocated to specific jobs.
   f. The company received a bill for CAD design services for $1,000.
2. By the end of January, was manufacturing overhead overallocated or underallocated? By how much?

E3-42B Analyze T-accounts *(Learning Objectives 2, 3, 5, & 6)*

ClearDay Displays produces screens for use in various smartphones. The company reports the following information at December 31. ClearDay Displays began operations on January 31 earlier that same year.

Work in Process Inventory		Wages Payable		Manufacturing Overhead		Finished Goods Inventory		Raw Materials Inventory	
30,500	123,500	77,000	77,000	4,000	43,000	123,500	115,500	57,500	34,500
64,000				13,000					
43,000		Balance 0		40,500					

Requirements

1. What is the cost of direct materials used?
2. The cost of indirect materials used?
3. What is the cost of direct labor?
4. The cost of indirect labor?
5. What is the cost of goods manufactured?
6. What is the cost of goods sold (before adjusting for any under- or overallocated manufacturing overhead)?
7. What is the actual manufacturing overhead?
8. How much manufacturing overhead was allocated to jobs?
9. What is the predetermined manufacturing overhead rate as a percentage of direct labor cost?
10. Is manufacturing overhead underallocated or overallocated? By how much?

E3-43B Job cost and bid price at a consulting firm *(Learning Objective 7)*

Sayres Consulting, a real estate consulting firm, specializes in advising companies on potential new plant sites. The firm uses a job costing system with a predetermined indirect cost allocation rate computed as a percentage of direct labor costs. At the beginning of the year, managing partner Dana Sayres prepared the following plan, or budget, for the year:

Direct labor hours (professionals)	15,000 hours
Direct labor costs (professionals)	$ 2,250,000
Office rent	$ 250,000
Support staff salaries	$ 940,000
Utilities	$ 310,000

Granite Resources is inviting several consultants to bid for work. Sayres estimates that this job will require about 250 direct labor hours.

Requirements

1. Compute Sayres Consulting's (a) hourly direct labor cost rate and (b) indirect cost allocation rate.
2. Compute the predicted cost of the Granite Resources job.
3. If Sayres Consulting wants to earn a profit that equals 30% of the job's cost, how much should the company bid for the Granite Resources job?

E3-44B Record journal entries *(Learning Objectives 2, 3, 5, & 6)*

The following transactions were incurred by Mooney Fabricators during January, the first month of its fiscal year.

Requirements

1. Record the proper journal entry for each transaction.
    a. $210,000 of materials were purchased on account.
    b. $178,000 of materials were used in production; of this amount, $143,000 was used on specific jobs.
    c. Manufacturing labor and salaries for the month totaled $245,000. A total of $220,000 of manufacturing labor and salaries was traced to specific jobs, while the remainder was indirect labor used in the factory.
    d. The company recorded $16,000 of depreciation on the plant and plant equipment. The company also received a plant utility bill for $8,000 which will be paid at a later date.
    e. $74,000 of manufacturing overhead was allocated to specific jobs.
2. By the end of January, was manufacturing overhead overallocated or underallocated? By how much?

PROBLEMS Group A

P3-45A Analyze Manufacturing Overhead *(Learning Objectives 3 & 5)*

Hartley Uniforms produces uniforms. The company allocates manufacturing overhead based on the machine hours each job uses. Hartley Uniforms reports the following cost data for the past year:

	Budget	Actual
Direct labor hours	7,600 hours	6,100 hours
Machine hours	7,200 hours	6,300 hours
Depreciation on salespeople's autos	$23,000	$23,000
Indirect materials	$48,500	$50,500
Depreciation on trucks used to deliver uniforms to customers	$13,000	$11,000
Depreciation on plant and equipment	$70,000	$72,500
Indirect manufacturing labor	$40,000	$42,000
Customer service hotline	$19,000	$21,000
Plant utilities	$35,900	$38,400
Direct labor cost	$72,500	$85,500

Requirements

1. Compute the predetermined manufacturing overhead rate.
2. Calculate the allocated manufacturing overhead for the past year.
3. Compute the underallocated or overallocated manufacturing overhead. How will this underallocated or overallocated manufacturing overhead be disposed of?
4. How can managers use accounting information to help control manufacturing overhead costs?

P3-46A Use job costing at an advertising agency *(Learning Objectives 3, 4, & 7)*

Anderson & Little is an advertising agency. The firm uses a job cost system in which each client is a different "job." Anderson & Little traces direct labor, software licensing costs, and travel costs directly to each job (client). The company allocates indirect costs to jobs based on a predetermined indirect cost allocation rate based on direct labor hours.

At the beginning of the current year, managing partner Trang Anderson prepared a budget:

Direct labor hours (professional)	17,100 hours
Direct labor costs (professional)	$2,052,000
Support staff salaries	$ 160,000
Rent and utilities	$ 48,000
Supplies	$ 461,300
Lease payments on computer hardware	$ 66,000

During January of the current year, Anderson & Little served several clients. Records for two clients appear here:

	DreamVacation.com	Port Armour Golf Resort
Direct labor hours	750 hours	30 hours
Software licensing costs	$2,500	$150
Travel costs	$8,000	$ 0

Requirements

1. Compute Anderson & Little's predetermined indirect cost allocation rate for the current year based on direct labor hours.
2. Compute the total cost of each job.
3. If Anderson & Little wants to earn profits equal to 20% of sales revenue, how much (what total fee) should it charge each of these two clients?
4. Why does Anderson & Little assign costs to jobs?

P3-47A Use job costing at a consulting firm *(Learning Objectives 3, 4, & 7)*

Sierra Design is an interior design firm. The firm uses a job cost system in which each client is a different "job." Sierra Design traces direct labor, licensing costs, and travel costs directly to each job (client). It allocates indirect costs to jobs based on a predetermined indirect cost allocation rate computed as a percentage of direct labor costs.

At the beginning of the current year, managing partner Laurie Walker prepared the following budget:

Direct labor hours (professional)	10,000 hours
Direct labor costs (professional)	$ 1,100,000
Support staff salaries	$ 140,000
Computer lease payments	$ 46,000
Office supplies	$ 26,000
Office rent	$ 63,000

Later that same year in November, Sierra Design served several clients. Records for two clients appear here:

	Delightful Dining	DineNow.com
Direct labor hours	710 hours	40 hours
Licensing costs	$ 2,300	$300
Travel costs	$ 10,000	$ 0

Requirements

1. Compute Sierra Design's predetermined indirect cost allocation rate for the current year.
2. Compute the total cost of each of the two jobs listed.
3. If Sierra Design wants to earn profits equal to 20% of sales revenue, how much (what total fee) should the company charge each of these two clients?
4. Why does Sierra Design assign costs to jobs?

P3-48A Prepare job cost record *(Learning Objectives 2, 3, & 4)*

Chattanooga Tire manufactures tires for all-terrain vehicles. Chattanooga uses job costing and has a perpetual inventory system.

On June 22, Chattanooga received an order for 110 TX tires from ATV Corporation at a price of $90 each. The job, assigned number 298, was promised for July 10. After purchasing the materials, Chattanooga began production on June 30 and incurred the following direct labor and direct materials costs in completing the order:

Date	Labor Time Record No.	Description	Amount
6/30	1896	12 hours at $20	$240
7/3	1904	30 hours at $16	$480

Date	Materials Requisition No.	Description	Amount
6/30	437	60 pounds rubber at $10	$ 600
7/2	439	40 meters polyester fabric at $12	$ 480
7/3	501	100 meters steel cord at $14	$1,400

Chattanooga allocates manufacturing overhead to jobs on the basis of the relation between expected overhead costs ($490,000) and expected direct labor hours (17,500). Job 298 was completed on July 3 and shipped to ATV on July 5.

Requirements

1. Prepare a job cost record for Job 298.
2. Calculate the total profit and the per-unit profit for Job 298.

P3-49A Determine and record job costs *(Learning Objectives 2, 3, 4, & 6)*

Veon Homes manufactures prefabricated chalets in Colorado. The company uses a perpetual inventory system and a job cost system in which each chalet is a job. The following events occurred during May:

a. Purchased materials on account, $490,000.
b. Incurred total manufacturing wages of $115,000, which included both direct labor and indirect labor. Used direct labor in manufacturing as follows:

	Direct Labor
Chalet 13	$14,200
Chalet 14	$28,500
Chalet 15	$19,900
Chalet 16	$21,900

c. Requisitioned direct materials in manufacturing as follows:

	Direct Materials
Chalet 13	$41,400
Chalet 14	$56,700
Chalet 15	$62,400
Chalet 16	$66,500

d. Depreciation of manufacturing equipment used on different chalets, $6,300.
e. Other overhead costs incurred on Chalets 13–16:

Equipment rentals paid in cash	$10,600
Prepaid plant insurance expired	$ 8,000

f. Allocated overhead to jobs at the predetermined rate of 60% of direct labor cost.
g. Chalets completed: 13, 15, and 16.
h. Chalets sold on account: 13 for $92,000 and 16 for $141,000.

Requirements

1. Record the preceding events in the general journal.
2. Open T-accounts for Work in Process Inventory and Finished Goods Inventory. Post the appropriate entries to these accounts, identifying each entry by letter. Determine the ending account balances, assuming that the beginning balances were zero.
3. Summarize the job cost of the unfinished chalet and show that this equals the ending balance in Work in Process Inventory.
4. Summarize the job cost of the completed chalet that has not yet been sold and show that this equals the ending balance in Finished Goods Inventory.
5. Compute the gross profit on each chalet that was sold. What costs must the gross profit cover for Veon Homes?

P3-50A Determine flow of costs through accounts *(Learning Objectives 2 & 6)*

Stewart Engine reconditions engines. Its job cost records yield the following information. Stewart Engine uses a perpetual inventory system.

Job No.	Date Started	Date Finished	Sold	Total Cost of Job at June 30	Total Manufacturing Cost Added in July
1	5/26	6/7	6/9	$1,600	
2	5/3	6/12	6/13	$1,500	
3	6/29	6/30	7/3	$1,300	
4	6/30	7/1	7/1	$ 900	$ 300
5	7/8	7/12	7/14		$ 500
6	7/23	8/6	8/9		$1,400

Requirements

1. Compute Stewart Engine's cost of (a) Work in Process Inventory at June 30 and July 31, (b) Finished Goods Inventory at June 30 and July 31, and (c) Cost of Goods Sold for June and July.
2. Make summary journal entries to record the transfer of completed jobs from Work in Process Inventory to Finished Goods Inventory for June and July.
3. Record the sale of Job 5 on account for $1,900.
4. Compute the gross profit for Job 5. What costs must the gross profit cover?

PROBLEMS Group B

P3-51B Analyze Manufacturing Overhead *(Learning Objectives 3 & 5)*

Sloan Company produces uniforms. The company allocates manufacturing overhead based on the machine hours each job uses. Sloan Company reports the following cost data for the past year:

	Budget	Actual
Direct labor hours	7,600 hours	6,100 hours
Machine hours	7,000 hours	6,500 hours
Depreciation on salespeople's autos	$23,000	$23,000
Indirect materials	$50,500	$54,000
Depreciation on trucks used to deliver uniforms to customers	$16,000	$15,000
Depreciation on plant and equipment	$68,000	$69,000
Indirect manufacturing labor	$39,500	$42,500
Customer service hotline	$21,500	$22,500
Plant utilities	$38,000	$40,500
Direct labor cost	$72,500	$86,500

Requirements

1. Compute the predetermined manufacturing overhead rate.
2. Calculate the allocated manufacturing overhead for the past year.
3. Compute the underallocated or overallocated manufacturing overhead. How will this underallocated or overallocated manufacturing overhead be disposed of?
4. How can managers use accounting information to help control manufacturing overhead costs?

P3-52B Use job costing at an advertising agency *(Learning Objectives 3, 4, & 7)*

Unchil & Doshak is an advertising agency. The firm uses a job cost system in which each client is a different "job." Unchil & Doshak traces direct labor, software licensing costs, and travel costs directly to each job (client). The company allocates indirect costs to jobs based on a predetermined indirect cost allocation rate based on direct labor hours.

At the beginning of the current year, managing partner Anoop Unchil prepared a budget:

Direct labor hours (professional)	17,100 hours
Direct labor costs (professional)	$2,052,000
Support staff salaries	$ 305,000
Rent and utilities	$ 46,000
Supplies	$ 319,300
Lease payments on computer hardware	$ 65,000

During January of the current year, Unchil & Doshak served several clients. Records for two clients appear here:

	GoTrip.com	Port South Golf Resort
Direct labor hours	770 hours	65 hours
Software licensing costs	$2,100	$400
Travel costs	$7,000	$ 0

Requirements

1. Compute Unchil & Doshak's predetermined indirect cost allocation rate for the current year based on direct labor hours.
2. Compute the total cost of each job.
3. If Unchil & Doshak wants to earn profits equal to 20% of sales revenue, how much (what total fee) should it charge each of these two clients?
4. Why does Unchil & Doshak assign costs to jobs?

P3-53B Use job costing at a consulting firm *(Learning Objectives 3, 4, & 7)*

Thomas Design is an interior design firm. The firm uses a job cost system, in which each client is a different job. Thomas Design traces direct labor, licensing costs, and travel costs directly to each job (client). It allocates indirect costs to jobs based on a predetermined indirect cost allocation rate computed as a percentage of direct labor costs.

At the beginning of the current year, managing partner Sarah Miracle prepared the following budget:

Direct labor hours (professional)	10,000 hours
Direct labor costs (professional)	$1,400,000
Support staff salaries	$ 170,000
Computer leases	$ 49,000
Office supplies	$ 29,000
Office rent	$ 60,000

Later that same year in November, Thomas Design served several clients. Records for two clients appear here:

	Organic Foods	AllNews.com
Direct labor hours	730 hours	25 hours
Software licensing costs	$2,700	$400
Travel costs	$7,000	$ 0

Requirements

1. Compute Thomas Design's predetermined indirect cost allocation rate for the current year.
2. Compute the total cost of each of the two jobs listed.
3. If Thomas Design wants to earn profits equal to 30% of sales revenue, how much (what total fee) should the company charge each of these two clients?
4. Why does Thomas Design assign costs to jobs?

P3-54B Prepare job cost record *(Learning Objectives 2, 3, & 4)*

Durable Tire manufactures tires for all-terrain vehicles. Durable Tire uses job costing and has a perpetual inventory system. On November 22, Durable Tire received an order for 100 TX tires from ATV Corporation at a price of $60 each. The job, assigned number 298, was promised for December 10. After purchasing the materials, Durable Tire began production on November 30 and incurred the following direct labor and direct materials costs in completing the order:

Date	Labor Time Record No.	Description	Amount
11/30	1896	12 hours at $16	$192
12/3	1904	30 hours at $18	$540

Date	Materials Requisition No.	Description	Amount
11/30	437	60 pounds rubber at $14	$ 840
12/2	439	40 meters polyester fabric at $12	$ 480
12/3	501	100 meters steel cord at $8	$ 800

Durable Tire allocates manufacturing overhead to jobs on the basis of the relationship between expected overhead costs ($529,000) and expected direct labor hours (23,000). Job 298 was completed on December 3 and shipped to ATV on December 5.

Requirements

1. Prepare a job cost record for Job 298.
2. Calculate the total profit and the per-unit profit for Job 298.

P3-55B Determine and record job costs *(Learning Objectives 2, 3, 4, & 6)*

Red Canyon Homes manufactures prefabricated chalets in Colorado. The company uses a perpetual inventory system and a job cost system in which each chalet is a job. The following events occurred during May:

a. Purchased materials on account, $470,000.
b. Incurred total manufacturing wages of $115,000, which included both direct labor and indirect labor. Used direct labor in manufacturing as follows:

	Direct Labor
Chalet 13	$14,600
Chalet 14	$28,000
Chalet 15	$19,300
Chalet 16	$21,400

c. Requisitioned direct materials in manufacturing as follows:

	Direct Materials
Chalet 13	$41,500
Chalet 14	$56,700
Chalet 15	$62,700
Chalet 16	$66,000

d. Depreciation of manufacturing equipment used on different chalets, $6,500.
e. Other overhead costs incurred on Chalets 13–16:

Equipment rentals paid in cash	$10,000
Prepaid plant insurance expired	$ 6,000

f. Allocated overhead to jobs at the predetermined rate of 60% of direct labor cost.
g. Chalets completed: 13, 15, and 16.
h. Chalets sold on account: 13 for $93,000; 16 for $144,000.

Requirements

1. Record the events in the general journal.
2. Open T-accounts for Work in Process Inventory and Finished Goods Inventory. Post the appropriate entries to the T-accounts, identifying each entry by letter. Determine the ending account balances, assuming that the beginning balances were zero.

3. Summarize the job cost of the unfinished chalet, and show that this total amount equals the ending balance in the Work in Process Inventory account.
4. Summarize the job cost of the completed chalet that has not yet been sold and show that this equals the ending balance in Finished Goods Inventory.
5. Compute gross profit on each chalet that was sold. What costs must gross profit cover for Red Canyon Homes?

P3-56B Determine flow of costs through accounts *(Learning Objectives 2 & 6)*

Engine Pro reconditions engines. Its job costing records yield the following information. Engine Pro uses a perpetual inventory system.

Job No.	Date Started	Date Finished	Date Sold	Total Cost of Job at April 30	Total Manufacturing Cost Added in May
1	3/26	4/7	4/9	$1,800	
2	4/3	4/12	4/13	$1,300	
3	4/29	4/30	5/3	$1,500	
4	4/30	5/1	5/1	$ 300	$ 800
5	5/8	5/12	5/14		$ 500
6	5/23	6/6	6/9		$1,900

Requirements

1. Compute Engine Pro's cost of (a) Work in Process Inventory at April 30 and May 31, (b) Finished Goods Inventory at April 30 and May 31, and (c) Cost of Goods Sold for April and May.
2. Make summary journal entries to record the transfer of completed jobs from Work in Process to Finished Goods for April and May.
3. Record the sale of Job 5 on account for $2,300.
4. Compute the gross profit for Job 5. What costs must the gross profit cover?

Serial Case

C3-57 Job costing or process costing for wedding services *(Learning Objectives 1, 2, 3, 4, & 7)*

This case is a continuation of the Caesars Entertainment Corporation serial case that began in chapter 1. Refer to the introductory story in Chapter 1 (see page 43) for additional background. (The components of the Caesars serial case can be completed in any order.)

Caesars Palace® Las Vegas offers several wedding packages for on-site wedding ceremonies and/or receptions. Packages can include limousines, flowers, photographers, pianist/organist, and other services. Caesars charges a flat fee for the basic wedding package plus additional charges for a la carte or individually added-on items and services. Each wedding is facilitated by a Caesars wedding coordinator; assume that the planning services of a wedding coordinator are paid on an hourly basis.

1. Would Caesars be likely to use a job costing system or a process costing system for determining the costs and profit for each wedding? Explain.
2. If Caesars uses a job costing system for a wedding, describe what cost items might be included in each of the following categories:
   a. Direct material
   b. Direct labor
   c. Overhead

CRITICAL THINKING

Discussion & Analysis

A3-58 Discussion Questions

1. Why would it be inappropriate for a custom-home builder to use process costing?
2. For what types of products is job costing appropriate? Why? For what types of products is process costing appropriate? Why?
3. What product costs must be allocated to jobs? Why must these costs be allocated rather than assigned?
4. When the predetermined manufacturing overhead rate is calculated, why are estimated costs and cost driver levels used instead of actual dollars and amounts?
5. Why should manufacturing overhead be allocated to a job even though the costs cannot be directly traced to a job? Give at least two reasons.
6. Why does management need to know the cost of a job? Discuss at least five reasons.
7. Why is it acceptable to close overallocated or underallocated manufacturing overhead to Cost of Goods Sold rather than allocating it proportionately to Work in Process Inventory, Finished Goods Inventory, and Cost of Goods Sold? Under what circumstances would it be advisable to allocate the overallocated or underallocated manufacturing overhead to Work in Process Inventory, Finished Goods Inventory, and Cost of Goods Sold?
8. Describe a situation that may cause manufacturing overhead to be overallocated in a given year. Also, describe a situation that may cause manufacturing overhead to be underallocated in a given year.
9. Explain why the cost of goods sold should be lower if manufacturing overhead is overallocated. Should operating income be higher or lower if manufacturing overhead is overallocated? Why?
10. What account is credited when manufacturing overhead is allocated to jobs during the period? What account is debited when manufacturing overhead costs are incurred during the period? Would you expect these two amounts (allocated and incurred manufacturing overhead) to be the same? Why or why not?
11. How can job cost records help to promote sustainability efforts within a company?
12. Why should companies estimate the environmental costs of a given job? Why have EPR (extended producer responsibility) laws come into existence?

Application & Analysis

Mini Cases

A3-59 Unwrapped or How It's Made

Product Costs and Job Costing Versus Process Costing

Go to www.YouTube.com and search for clips from the show *Unwrapped* on the Food Network or *How It's Made* on the Discovery Channel. Watch a clip for a product you find interesting.

Basic Discussion Questions

1. Describe the product that is being produced and the company that makes it.
2. Summarize the production process that is used in making this product.
3. What raw materials are used to make this product?
4. What indirect materials are used to make this product?
5. Describe the jobs of the workers who would be considered "direct labor" in the making of this product.
6. Describe the jobs of the workers who would be considered "indirect labor" in the making of this product.

7. Define *manufacturing overhead*. In addition to the indirect materials and indirect labor previously described, what other manufacturing overhead costs would be incurred in this production process? Be specific and thorough. Make reasonable "guesses" if you do not know for sure.

8. Would a job-order costing system or a process costing system be used for this production process? Give specific reasons for your choice of which costing system would be most appropriate for this manufacturer.

ETHICS

A3-60 Ethics involved with choice of cost driver (Learning Objectives 2, 3, & 4)

Vicki Thornton is the controller for Jackson Manufacturing. It is a small company that manufactures plastic lumber and is run by the owner and CEO, Franklin Jackson. At the end of the year, Jackson is reviewing the projected operating income for the company for the year. He tells Thornton that the projected operating income is too low; if operating income is not at least $250,000, no holiday bonuses will be paid to employees, including Thornton.

Hoping to find an error, Thornton first rechecks the projected financial statements; she finds no errors. Since cost of goods sold is a large portion of Jackson's expenses, she next analyzes the components of cost of goods sold. The amount of direct material used ties directly to the physical inventory count, so there are no errors there. The direct labor dollars also tie directly to the payroll reports, eliminating another potential source of errors. She then looks at the way manufacturing overhead has been allocated to products.

Traditionally, manufacturing overhead has been allocated to products based on direct labor hours because the manufacturing process for plastic lumber is labor intensive. Thornton calculates manufacturing overhead based on machine hours used and finds that cost of goods sold will be $55,000 lower if manufacturing overhead is allocated based on machine hours rather than direct labor hours. The $55,000 difference, if booked, would cause net income to be $262,000, which means that bonuses would be paid to all employees. Thornton knows that several factory employees are struggling and the holiday bonus would be much appreciated. In addition, Thornton herself feels that she has earned the bonus over the past year because she has helped to implement several cost savings programs and has worked many long days without overtime pay.

Requirements

1. Using the IMA *Statement of Ethical Professional Practice* as an ethical framework, answer the following questions:

    a. What is(are) the ethical issue(s) in this situation?

    b. What are Thornton's responsibilities as a management accountant?

2. Discuss the specific steps Thornton should take to resolve the situation. Refer to the IMA *Statement of Ethical Professional Practice* in your response.

REAL LIFE

A3-61 Costs included in product cost (Learning Objectives 1, 2, 3, & 4)

A research firm, IHS (formerly known as iSuppli), did a teardown of the iPad Air 2 shortly after Apple refreshed the iPad in late 2014.[7] IHS estimated that the costs of the components in the 64-gigabyte (GB) model of the iPad Air 2 (Wi-Fi-only) add up to $295.25. See data table that follows.

Questions

1. Do you think that Apple uses a process costing system or a job costing system? Give reasons for your answer.

2. The iPad Air 2 is assigned a cost of $5 for "manufacturing cost." What specific costs do you think are included in that "manufacturing cost"?

3. In accounting terminology, what would Bill of Materials (BOM) be when discussing product cost?

4. The gross profit per iPad Air 2 is approximately $303.75, which is the difference between the retail price of $599 and its estimated cost (BOM + Manufacturing) of $295.25. Is Apple really making $303.75 for each iPad Air 2 sold? If not, what other types of costs would that gross profit have to go toward covering?

[7]Source: "Still Air: Apple iPad Air 2 Largely Holds the Line on Features and Costs, IHS Teardown Reveals" (Retrieved from https://technology.ihs.com/514553/still-air-apple-ipad-air-2-largely-holds-the-line-on-features-and-costs-ihs-teardown-reveals, on December 28, 2015.)

5. The BOM costs for the units sold would appear on Apple's income statement. In which income statement component would these BOM costs appear?

6. Apple has announced that it is going to start manufacturing some products in the United States rather than in China. If the iPad Air 2 were to be manufactured in the United States, which cost components would you expect to increase? Which cost components might you expect to decrease? What other factors would Apple consider when deciding where to manufacture its products?

Preliminary Bill of Materials (BOM) and Manufacturing Costs for the iPad Air 2 with 64GBytes of NAND Flash and Wi-Fi Only (Pricing in U.S. Dollars)

Components/Hardware Elements	Price
Retail Pricing (as of October 2014)	$599.00
Total BOM Cost	$290.25
Manufacturing Cost	$5.00
BOM + Manufacturing	$295.25
Major Cost Drivers	
Memory: 2GB LPDDR3 DRAM + 64GB NAND Flash	$45.00
Display & Touchscreen: 9.7" 2048 ×1536 IPS Mode LCD/GF2	$115.00
Processors: 64-Bit A8X Processor + M8 Co-Processor	$22.00
Camera(s): 8MP + 1.2 MP	$11.00
User Interface & Sensors & WLAN/BT/FM/GPS	$26.50
Power Management	$8.25
Battery: 27.6Wh Pack	$15.00
Mechanical/Electro-Mechanical/Other	$42.50
Box Contents	$5.00

Source: IHS iSuppli Research, October 2014.

A3-62 Issues with cost of job *(Learning Objectives 2, 3, & 4)*

Custom Cookies produces gourmet cookies with company logos for special promotions. The cookies are customized with the customer's choice of shape, color, flavor, and decorations. Custom Cookies uses a job cost system and allocates manufacturing overhead based on direct labor cost. At the beginning of the most recent year, Custom Cookies calculated the cost per batch of dozen cookies as:

Direct materials (flour, sugar, butter, eggs, baking soda, vanilla)	$1.50
Direct labor (shape and decorate cookies)	0.50
Manufacturing overhead	0.90
Total manufacturing cost per dozen cookies	$2.90

In September, Chesrown Motor Group ordered 400 dozen cookies to present to its clients as holiday gifts. Delivery of the cookies to Chesrown would occur in early December. At the time of Chesrown Motor Group's order, the selling price per dozen cookies was $7.25.

Chesrown Motor Group placed an order for an additional 100 dozen cookies in November, to be delivered with the original order of 400 dozen. However, since that original order, two events occurred that increased the cost of the cookies. First, the price of sugar skyrocketed due to bad weather in Brazil and India, two of the largest sugar suppliers in the world. Second, a new local cookie bakery is about to open in time for the holiday season and is aggressively trying to hire the cookie decorators from Custom Cookies. In response, Custom Cookies increased the hourly rate of the employees who decorate the cookies to keep those workers from going to work for the competition. *All other costs at Custom Cookies have remained the same.*

Because of these two events, Custom Cookies recalculated the cost of a dozen cookies as follows:

Direct materials (flour, sugar, butter, eggs, baking soda, vanilla)	$1.60
Direct labor (shape and decorate cookies)	0.65
Manufacturing overhead	1.17
Total manufacturing cost per dozen cookies	$3.42

Requirements

1. Do you agree with the cost analysis for the second order? Explain your answer.
2. Should the two orders be accounted for as one job or as two jobs in Custom Cookies' system?
3. What sales price per box should Custom Cookies set for the second order? Explain why you have selected this per-box price. What are the advantages and disadvantages of this price?

Try It Solutions

page 111: 1. d 2. a 3. f 4. g 5. h 6. c 7. e 8. b

page 129:

Actual MOH incurred during the year	$975,000
MOH allocated to jobs during the year ($16/DL hour × 60,000 DL hours)	960,000
Difference: Underallocated MOH	$ 15,000

Since the company allocated less MOH to jobs than was actually incurred during the year, it has underallocated MOH. Notice that the $1 million of estimated MOH at the beginning of the year is only used to calculate the predetermined MOH rate.

page 146:

1.

Direct cost: Sarah's time (5 hr × $40/hr) + Hannah's time (10 hr × $25/hr)	$450
Indirect cost: (15 hr × $12/hr)	180
Total cost of preparing tax return	$630

2.

Total cost of preparing tax return	$630
Plus profit markup ($630 × 30%)	189
Amount to bill Meckfessel	$819

Activity-Based Costing, Lean Operations, and the Costs of Quality

Andor Bujdoso/Alamy
Source: http://lifefitness.com

Learning Objectives

- **1** Develop and use departmental overhead rates to allocate indirect costs
- **2** Develop and use activity-based costing (ABC) to allocate indirect costs
- **3** Understand the benefits and limitations of ABC/ABM systems
- **4** Describe lean operations
- **5** Describe and use the costs of quality framework

When Life Fitness began, it only had one product: the Lifecycle exercise bike. With time, Life Fitness expanded its product lines to include treadmills, elliptical cross-trainers, stair climbers, and strength-training equipment. As a result of increased product diversity and competition, managers often found they needed better, more accurate product cost information to help guide their business decisions. While a traditional job costing system ensures that the direct materials and direct labor traced to each job is correct, it doesn't always do an adequate job of allocating manufacturing overhead, especially when a company produces multiple product lines that use different amounts of indirect manufacturing resources. In such cases, managers benefit from using a refined cost allocation system: one that isn't based on a single, predetermined manufacturing overhead rate. Refined costing systems not only help managers more accurately determine the cost of individual jobs but also highlight the cost of wasteful activities in the production process. Armed with this knowledge, managers are able to make more profitable business decisions.

As the chapter-opening story illustrates, successful companies experience increased competition over time. In addition, companies often seek to expand their customer base by offering a more diversified line of products. Both of these factors are good for consumers, who now enjoy more product options at very competitive prices. However, these factors also present unique challenges to business managers and the accounting systems that support them. To thrive in a globally competitive market, companies must provide value to the customer by delivering a high-quality product at an attractive price, while managing costs so that the company still earns a profit. This chapter will introduce several tools that today's managers use to make their companies as competitive as possible:

- Refined costing systems
- Lean operations
- Total quality management and the costs of quality

Why and How Do Companies Refine Their Cost Allocation Systems?

The traditional overhead cost allocation system we described in Chapter 3 may not be accurate enough for some compaies. Why? Because under certain conditions, the simple system doesn't do a good job of matching the cost of overhead resources with the products that consume those resources. The following example illustrates why simple systems can lead to less-than-acceptable results.

Simple Cost Allocation Systems Can Lead to Cost Distortion

David, Matt, and Marc are three college friends who share an apartment. They agree to split the following monthly costs equally:

Rent, Internet, and utilities	$570
Cable TV	50
Covered parking fee	40
Groceries	240
Total monthly costs	$900

Each roommate's share is $300 (=$900/3).

Things go smoothly for the first few months. But then David calls a meeting: "Because I started having dinner at Amy's each night, I shouldn't have to chip in for the groceries." Matt then pipes in: "I'm so busy studying and using the Internet that I never have time to watch TV. I don't want to pay for the cable TV anymore. And Marc, because your friend Jennifer eats here most evenings, you should pay a double share of the grocery bill." Marc replies, "If that's the way you feel, Matt, then you should pay for the covered parking since you're the only one around here who uses it!"

What happened? The friends originally agreed to share the costs equally. But they are not participating equally in watching cable TV, using the covered parking, and eating the groceries. Splitting these costs equally is not equitable.

The roommates could use a cost allocation approach that better matches costs with the people who participate in the activities that cause those costs. This means splitting the cable TV costs between David and Marc, assigning the covered parking cost to Matt, and allocating the grocery bill one-third to Matt and two-thirds to Marc. Exhibit 4-1 compares the results of this refined cost allocation system with the original cost allocation system.

No wonder David called a meeting! The original cost allocation system charged him $300 a month, but the refined system shows that a more equitable share would be only $215. The new system allocates Marc $375 a month instead of $300. David was paying for resources he did not use (covered parking and groceries), while Marc was not paying for all of the resources (groceries) he and his guest consumed. The simple cost allocation

EXHIBIT 4-1 More Refined Versus Less Refined Cost Allocation System

Allocation of Expenses	David	Matt	Marc	Total
More-refined cost allocation system:				
Rent, internet, and utilities	$190	$190	$190	$570
Cable TV	25	0	25	50
Covered parking	0	40	0	40
Groceries	0	80	160	240
Total cost allocated	$215	$310	$375	$900
Original cost allocation system:				
Equal allocation of expenses	$300	$300	$300	$900
Difference	($85)	$ 10	$ 75	$ 0

system the roommates initially devised had ended up distorting the cost that should be charged to each roommate: David was *overcharged* by $85 while Matt and Marc were *undercharged* by an equal, but offsetting, amount ($10 + $75 = $85). Notice that the total "pool" of monthly costs ($900) is the same under both allocation systems. The only difference is *how* the pool of costs is *allocated* among the three roommates.

Just as the simple allocation system had resulted in overcharging David, yet undercharging Matt and Marc, many companies find that the simple overhead cost allocation system described in the last chapter results in "overcosting" some of their jobs or products while "undercosting" others. **Cost distortion** occurs when some products are overcosted while other products are undercosted by the cost allocation system. As we'll see in the following sections, companies often refine their cost allocation systems to minimize the amount of cost distortion caused by the simpler cost allocation systems. By refining their costing systems, companies can more equitably assign indirect costs (such as manufacturing overhead) to their individual jobs, products, or services. As a result, less cost distortion occurs and managers have more accurate information for making vital business decisions.

In the following section, we will describe how refined cost allocation systems can be used to better allocate manufacturing overhead to specific products to reduce cost distortion. However, keep in mind that the same principles apply to allocating *any* indirect costs to *any* cost objects. Thus, even merchandising and service companies, as well as governmental agencies, can use these refined cost allocation systems to provide their managers with better cost information.

> **Why is this important?**
>
> "With better **cost information**, managers are able to make more **profitable** decisions. One company reported triple sales and a **five-fold increase** in profits after it implemented a **refined costing system**. By using better cost information for quoting jobs, **management** was able to generate a more **profitable mix** of job contracts."[1]

Review: Using a Plantwide Overhead Rate to Allocate Indirect Costs

In the last chapter, we assumed that Life Fitness allocated its manufacturing overhead (MOH) costs using one predetermined MOH rate ($16 per DL hour). This rate was based on management's estimate of the total manufacturing overhead costs for the year ($1 million) and its estimate of the total amount of the allocation base (62,500 DL hours) for the year.[2] The rate was calculated as follows:

$$\text{Predetermined MOH rate} = \frac{\$1,000,000}{62,500 \text{ DL hours}} = \$16 \text{ per direct labor hour}$$

---

[1] Douglas Hicks, "Yes, ABC Is for Small Business, Too," *Journal of Accountancy*, August 1999, p. 41.

[2] All references to Life Fitness in this hypothetical example were created by the authors solely for academic purposes and are not intended, in any way, to represent the actual business practices of, or costs incurred by, Life Fitness, Inc.

This rate is also known as a **plantwide overhead rate** because any job produced in the plant, whether it be treadmills, elliptical cross-trainers, or stair climbers, would be allocated manufacturing overhead using this single rate. It wouldn't matter whether the job was worked on in one department or many departments during the production process: The same rate would be used throughout the plant.

Let's see how this works for Life Fitness. Keep in mind that the company produces many different products and completes thousands of different jobs throughout the year. For simplicity of illustration, we will be following just two of those jobs:

- Job 101: One elliptical
- Job 102: One treadmill

In Chapter 3, we followed a job in which each elliptical cross-trainer required about 10 direct labor hours to make.[3] We'll continue to assume that each elliptical made by the company requires 10 direct labor hours to complete. Let's also assume that each treadmill requires 10 direct labor hours to complete. Exhibit 4-2 shows how manufacturing overhead would be allocated to a job in which one elliptical was made, and another job in which one treadmill was made, using the plantwide overhead rate.

EXHIBIT 4-2 Allocating Manufacturing Overhead Using a Plantwide Overhead Rate

	A	B C	D	E F	G	H
1	Job	Plantwide Overhead Rate		Actual Use of Allocation Base		MOH Allocated to Job
2	Job 101: One elliptical	$ 16 per DL hour	×	10 DL hours	=	$ 160
3	Job 102: One treadmill	$ 16 per DL hour	×	10 DL hours	=	$ 160
4						

NOTE: Arithmetic signs are only shown for illustrative teaching purposes. They are not typically displayed in spreadsheets.

The plantwide allocation system is illustrated in Exhibit 4-3.

EXHIBIT 4-3 Plantwide Allocation System

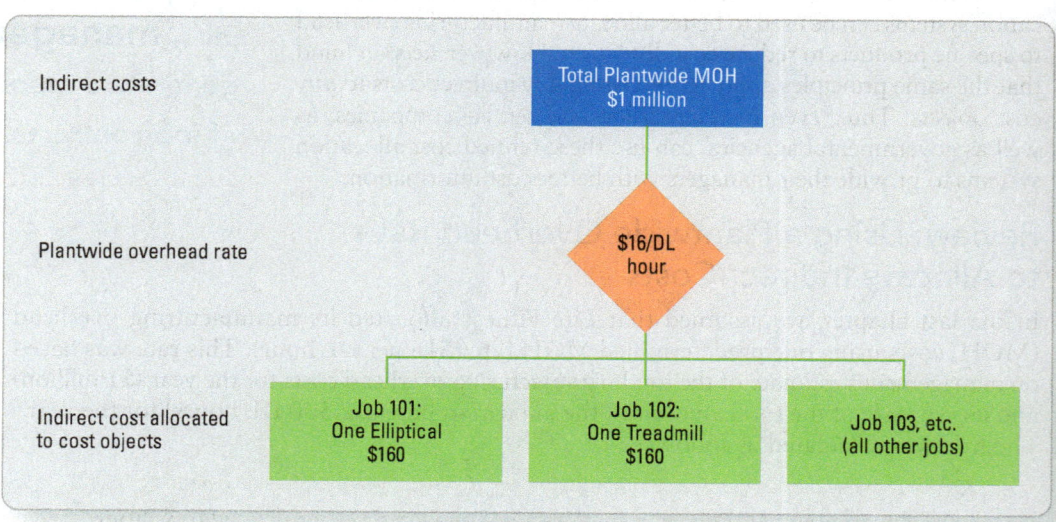

---

[3] Job 603, a batch of 50 elliptical cross-trainers, required 500 DL hours to complete. Thus, the average time spent on each unit was 10 DL hours.

Using Departmental Overhead Rates to Allocate Indirect Costs

The plantwide allocation system previously described works well for some companies but may end up distorting costs if the following conditions exist:

1. Different departments incur different amounts and types of manufacturing overhead.
2. Different jobs or products use the departments to a different extent.

If these circumstances exist, the company should strongly consider refining its cost allocation system. Let's see if these conditions exist at Life Fitness.

1 Develop and use departmental overhead rates to allocate indirect costs

CONDITION 1: DO DIFFERENT DEPARTMENTS HAVE DIFFERENT AMOUNTS AND TYPES OF MOH COSTS? As shown in Exhibit 4-4, let's assume Life Fitness has two primary production departments: Machining and Assembly. The Machining Department has a lot of machinery, which drives manufacturing overhead costs such as machine depreciation, utilities, machine lubricants, and repairs and maintenance. Let's say these overhead costs are estimated to be $400,000 for the year. On the other hand, the Assembly Department does not incur as many of these types of overhead costs. Rather, the Assembly Department's manufacturing overhead costs include more indirect labor for supervision, quality inspection, and so forth. These manufacturing overhead costs are expected to total $600,000 for the year.

Exhibit 4-4 shows that the first condition is present: Each department incurs different types and amounts of MOH. Life Fitness expects to incur a total of $1 million of manufacturing overhead: $400,000 relates to the Machining Department, while $600,000 relates to the Assembly Department.

EXHIBIT 4-4 Machining and Assembly Departments' Manufacturing Overhead

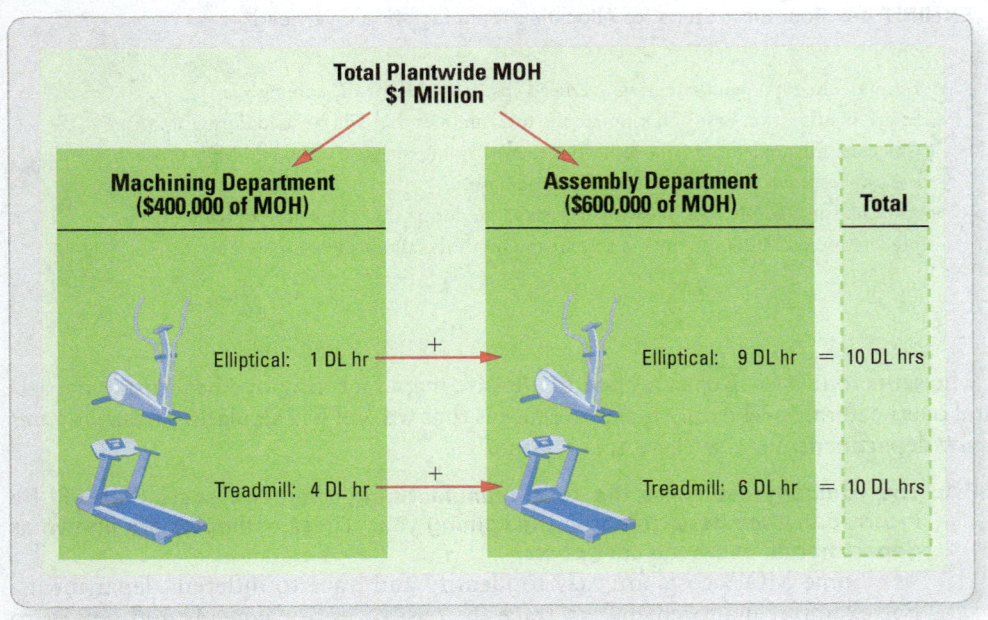

CONDITION 2: DO DIFFERENT PRODUCTS USE THE DEPARTMENTS TO A DIFFERENT EXTENT? Although both ellipticals and treadmills take 10 direct labor hours in total to make, Exhibit 4-4 also shows that ellipticals and treadmills spend *different* amounts of time in each production department. Each elliptical only requires 1 DL hour in the Machining Department but requires 9 DL hours in the Assembly Department. Contrast that with a treadmill, which spends more time in Machining to fabricate some of its components (4 DL hours) but less time in Assembly (6 DL hours). As a result of these

differences, the second condition is also present. The company's cost allocation system would be much more accurate if it took these differences into account when determining how much manufacturing overhead to allocate to each product.

Since both conditions are present, the company should consider "fine-tuning" its cost allocation systems by establishing separate manufacturing overhead rates, known as **departmental overhead rates**, for each department. That means that Life Fitness will establish one manufacturing overhead rate for the Machining Department and another overhead rate for the Assembly Department. These rates will then be used to allocate manufacturing overhead to jobs or products based on the extent to which each product uses the different manufacturing departments.

Exhibit 4-5 shows the circumstances favoring the use of departmental overhead rates rather than a single, plantwide overhead rate.

EXHIBIT 4-5 Circumstances Favoring Use of Departmental Overhead Rates

> Departmental overhead rates increase the accuracy of job costs when . . .
>
> - Each department incurs different types and amounts of manufacturing overhead.
> - Each product, or job, uses the departments to a different extent.

Four Basic Steps to Computing and Using Departmental Overhead Rates

In Chapter 3, we used four steps for allocating manufacturing overhead. These steps are summarized in Exhibit 4-6.

EXHIBIT 4-6 Four Basic Steps for Allocating Manufacturing Overhead

> 1. Estimate the total manufacturing overhead costs (MOH) for the coming year.
> 2. Select an allocation base and estimate the total amount that will be used during the year.
> 3. Calculate the predetermined overhead rate by dividing the total estimated MOH costs by the total estimated amount of the allocation base.
> 4. Allocate some MOH cost to each job worked on during the year by multiplying the predetermined MOH rate by the actual amount of the allocation base used by the job.

The same four basic steps are used to allocate manufacturing overhead using departmental overhead rates. The only real difference is that we will be calculating *separate rates* for *each* department. Let's see how this is done.

STEP 1: **The company estimates the total manufacturing overhead costs that will be incurred in *each department* in the coming year. These estimates are known as departmental overhead cost pools.**

Some MOH costs are easy to identify and trace to different departments. For example, management can trace the cost of lease payments and repairs to the machines used in the Machining Department. Management can also trace the cost of employing supervisors and quality control inspectors to the Assembly Department. However, other overhead costs are more difficult to identify with specific departments. For example, the depreciation, property taxes, and insurance on the entire plant would have to be split, or allocated, between the individual departments, most likely based on the square footage occupied by each department in the plant.

As shown in Exhibit 4-4, Life Fitness has determined that $400,000 of its total estimated MOH relates to its Machining Department, while the remaining $600,000 relates to its Assembly Department.

Department	Total Departmental Overhead Cost Pool
Machining Department	$ 400,000
Assembly Department	$ 600,000
TOTAL MOH	$1,000,000

STEP 2: **The company selects an allocation base for *each department* and estimates the total amount that will be used during the year.**

The allocation base selected for each department should be the cost driver of the costs in the departmental overhead pool. Often, manufacturers will use different allocation bases for the different departments. For example, machine hours might be the best allocation base for a very automated Machining Department that uses machine robotics extensively. However, direct labor hours might be the best allocation base for an Assembly Department.

Let's assume that Life Fitness's Machining Department uses a lot of human-operated machinery; therefore, the number of direct labor hours used in the department is identical to the number of hours the machines are run. While the number of machine hours is the real cost driver, direct labor hours will make an adequate surrogate. As a result, management has selected direct labor hours as the allocation base for both departments. Recall that Life Fitness estimates using a total of 62,500 direct labor hours during the year. Of this amount, management expects to use 12,500 in the Machining Department and 50,000 in the Assembly Department.

Department	Total Amount of Departmental Allocation Base
Machining Department	12,500 DL hours
Assembly Department	50,000 DL hours

STEP 3: **The company calculates departmental overhead rates using the information estimated in Steps 1 and 2:**

$$\text{Departmental overhead rate} = \frac{\text{Total estimated departmental overhead cost pool}}{\text{Total estimated amount of the departmental allocation base}}$$

Therefore, Life Fitness calculates its departmental overhead rates as follows:

$$\text{Machining Department overhead rate} = \frac{\$400,000}{12,500 \text{ DL hours}} = \$32 \text{ per DL hour}$$

$$\text{Assembly Department overhead rate} = \frac{\$600,000}{50,000 \text{ DL hours}} = \$12 \text{ per DL hour}$$

These first three steps are performed before the year begins, using estimated data for the year. Thus, departmental overhead rates are also "predetermined," just like the plantwide predetermined manufacturing overhead rate discussed in Chapter 3. The first three steps, performed before the year begins, are summarized in Exhibit 4-7.

EXHIBIT 4-7 Steps to Calculating the Departmental Overhead Rates

Department	Step 1: Total Departmental Overhead Cost Pool		Step 2: Total Amount of Departmental Allocation Base		Step 3: Departmental Overhead Rate	
Machining	$ 400,000	÷	12,500	DL hours	= $ 32	per DL hour
Assembly	$ 600,000	÷	50,000	DL hours	= $ 12	per DL hour

NOTE: Arithmetic signs are only shown for illustrative teaching purposes. They are not typically displayed in spreadsheets.

Once these rates have been established, the company uses them throughout the year to allocate manufacturing overhead to each job as it is produced, as shown in Step 4.

STEP 4: The company allocates some manufacturing overhead from each department to the individual jobs that use those departments.

The amount of MOH allocated from each department is calculated as follows:

MOH allocated to job = Departmental overhead rate × Actual amount of departmental allocation base used by job

Exhibit 4-8 shows how these departmental overhead rates would be used to allocate manufacturing overhead to a job in which one elliptical is produced.

EXHIBIT 4-8 Allocating MOH to One Elliptical Using Departmental Overhead Rates

Department	Departmental Overhead Rate (from Exhibit 4-7)		Actual Use of Departmental Allocation Base (from Exhibit 4-4)		MOH Allocated to Job 101: One Elliptical
Machining	$ 32 per DL hour	×	1	DL hours	= $ 32
Assembly	$ 12 per DL hour	×	9	DL hours	= $ 108
Total					$ 140

NOTE: Arithmetic signs are only shown for illustrative teaching purposes. They are not typically displayed in spreadsheets.

Exhibit 4-9 shows how the same rates would be used to allocate manufacturing overhead to another job in which one treadmill is produced. Because the treadmill spends more time in the Machining Department, but less time in the Assembly Department, the amount of MOH allocated to the treadmill differs from the amount allocated to the elliptical in Exhibit 4-8.

EXHIBIT 4-9 Allocating MOH to One Treadmill Using Departmental Overhead Rates

Department	Departmental Overhead Rate (from Exhibit 4-7)		Actual Use of Departmental Allocation Base (from Exhibit 4-4)		MOH Allocated to Job 102: One Treadmill
Machining	$ 32 per DL hour	×	4	DL hours	= $ 128
Assembly	$ 12 per DL hour	×	6	DL hours	= $ 72
Total					$ 200

NOTE: Arithmetic signs are only shown for illustrative teaching purposes. They are not typically displayed in spreadsheets.

Exhibit 4-10 illustrates the company's departmental cost allocation system.

EXHIBIT 4-10 Departmental Cost Allocation System

Had the Plantwide Overhead Rate Been Distorting Product Costs?

We have just seen that Life Fitness's refined cost allocation system allocates $140 of MOH to each elliptical and $200 of MOH to each treadmill (Exhibits 4-8 and 4-9). Does this differ from the amount that would have been allocated to each unit using Life Fitness's original plantwide rate? Yes. Recall from Exhibit 4-2 that if Life Fitness uses a plantwide overhead rate, $160 of manufacturing overhead would be allocated to both types of equipment, simply because both types of equipment require the *same total* number of direct labor hours (10 DL hours) to produce.

The plantwide allocation system does not pick up on the nuances of how many direct labor hours are used by the products in *each* department. Therefore, it was not able to do a very good job of matching manufacturing overhead costs to the products that use those costs. As a result, the plantwide rate would have overcosted each elliptical but undercosted each treadmill, as shown in Exhibit 4-11.

EXHIBIT 4-11 Cost Distortion Caused by Plantwide Overhead Rate

	Plantwide Overhead Rate MOH Allocation (from Exhibit 4-2)	Departmental Overhead Rates MOH Allocation (from Exhibits 4-8 and 4-9)	Amount of Cost Distortion
Job 101: One Elliptical	$160	$140	$20 *overcosted*
Job 102: One Treadmill	$160	$200	$40 *undercosted*

On the other hand, the refined cost allocation system recognizes the cost differences between departments and the usage difference between jobs. Therefore, the refined costing system does a *better job of matching* each department's overhead costs to the products that use the department's resources. This is the same thing we saw with the three roommates: The refined costing system did a better job of matching the cost of resources (cable, covered parking, groceries) to the roommates who used those resources. Because of this better matching, we believe that the departmental overhead rates *more accurately allocate* MOH costs than does a single plantwide overhead rate.

Try It!

Assume a job with one stair climber requires 5 direct labor (DL) hours to produce: 3 DL hours in the Machining Department and 2 DL hours in the Assembly Department. Use the plantwide overhead rate and departmental allocation rates computed in the chapter example to answer the following:

1. How much MOH would be allocated to the job using the plantwide overhead rate?
2. How much MOH would be allocated to the job using the departmental overhead rates?
3. Does the plantwide overhead rate overcost or undercost the job? By how much?

Please see page 244 for solutions.

STOP & THINK

Do companies always have separate production departments, such as Machining and Assembly, for each step of the production process?

Answer: No. Rather than basing production departments on separate processing steps, some companies have separate production departments for each of their products. For example, Life Fitness could have one department for producing treadmills, another department for producing ellipticals, and yet another department for producing stair climbers. Each department would have all of the machinery and equipment necessary for producing its unique product. Departmental overhead rates would be formulated using the same four basic steps just discussed to determine a unique departmental overhead rate for each department. The only difference is that each product (for example, a treadmill) would travel through *only one* department (the Treadmill Department) rather than traveling through separate production departments (Machining and Assembly). Always keep in mind that the accounting system should reflect the actual production environment.

Using Activity-Based Costing to Allocate Indirect Costs

2 Develop and use activity-based costing (ABC) to allocate indirect costs

We just saw how companies can refine their cost allocation systems by using departmental overhead rates. If a company wants an even more refined system, one that reduces cost distortion to a minimum, it will use activity-based costing (ABC). **Activity-based costing (ABC)** focuses on *activities*, rather than departments, as the fundamental cost objects. ABC recognizes that activities are costly to perform, and each product manufactured may require different types and amounts of activities. Thus, activities become the building blocks for compiling the indirect costs of products, services, and customers. Companies can use ABC to more accurately estimate the cost of resources required to produce different products, to render different services, and to serve different customers.

Think about the three roommates for a moment. The most equitable and accurate cost allocation system for the roommates was one in which the roommates were charged only for the *activities* in which they participated, and the *extent* to which they participated in those activities. Likewise, activity-based costing generally causes the *least* amount of cost distortion among products because indirect costs are allocated to the products based on the (1) *types* of activities used by the product and (2) the *extent* to which the activities are used.

Four Basic Steps to Computing and Using Activity Cost Allocation Rates

ABC requires the same four basic steps listed in Exhibit 4-6. The main difference between an ABC system and a plantwide or departmental cost allocation system is that ABC systems have *separate* cost allocation rates for *each activity* identified by the company.

STEP 1: The company first identifies its primary activities and then estimates the total manufacturing overhead costs associated with *each activity*. These are known as activity cost pools.

Let's assume Life Fitness has determined that the following activities occur in its plant: First, the machines must be set up to meet the particular specifications of the production run. Next, raw materials must be moved out of the storeroom and into the Machining Department, where some of the parts for the units are fabricated. Once the parts have been fabricated, they are moved into the Assembly Department, along with additional raw materials that are needed from the storeroom. The units are then assembled by direct laborers, while production engineers supervise the process. All units are inspected after assembly. Upon passing inspection, each unit is packaged so that it is not damaged during shipment. Finally, the units are moved to the finished goods warehouse where they await shipment to customers. These activities are pictured in Exhibit 4-12.

EXHIBIT 4-12 Primary Activities Identified in the Manufacturing Plant

As part of this step, management must determine how much of the total estimated $1 million of MOH relates to each activity. Exhibit 4-13 shows some of the specific MOH costs that management has identified with each activity, along with the total estimated amount of each activity cost pool.

EXHIBIT 4-13 Activity Cost Pools

Activity	MOH Costs Related to the Activity	Total Activity Cost Pool
Machine Setup	Indirect labor used to set up machines	$ 80,000
Materials Handling	Forklifts, gas, operators' wages	200,000
Fabricating Parts	Machine lease payments, electricity, repairs	300,000
Supervising Assembly	Production engineers' labor	150,000
Inspecting	Testing equipment, inspection labor	170,000
Packaging	Packaging equipment	100,000
	TOTAL MOH	$1,000,000

Keep in mind that all of the costs in the activity costs pools are MOH costs; direct labor costs and direct materials costs are *not included* because they will be directly traced to specific jobs and therefore do not need to be allocated. That is why we only include supervisory labor in the overhead cost pool for the assembly activity. The machine operators and assembly-line workers are considered direct labor, so their cost will be traced to individual jobs, not allocated as part of MOH.

STEP 2: **The company selects an allocation base for each activity and estimates the total amount that will be used during the year.**

When selecting an allocation base for each activity, the company should keep the following in mind:

- The allocation base selected for each activity should be the *cost driver* of the costs in that particular activity cost pool.
- The company will need to keep track of how much of the allocation base each job or product uses. Therefore, the company must have the means to collect usage information about each allocation base. Thankfully, bar coding and other technological advances have helped make data collection easier and less costly in recent years.

Let's assume that Life Fitness has identified a cost driver for each activity and has plans for how it will collect usage data. Exhibit 4-14 shows the selected allocation bases along with the total estimated amounts for the year.

EXHIBIT 4-14 Activity Allocation Bases and Total Estimated Amount of Each

Activity	Activity Allocation Base	Total Estimated Amount of Allocation Base
Machine Setup	Number of setups	8,000 setups
Materials Handling	Number of parts moved	400,000 parts
Fabricating Parts	Machine hours	12,500 machine hours
Supervising Assembly	Direct labor hours	50,000 DL hours
Inspecting	Number of inspections	34,000 inspections
Packaging	Cubic feet packaged	400,000 cubic feet

STEP 3: **The company calculates its activity cost allocation rates using the information estimated in Steps 1 and 2.**

The formula for calculating the activity cost allocation rates is as follows:

$$\text{Activity cost allocation rate} = \frac{\text{Total estimated activity cost pool}}{\text{Total estimated activity allocation base}}$$

Exhibit 4-15 shows how this formula is used to compute a unique cost allocation rate for each of the company's production activities.

EXHIBIT 4-15 Computing Activity Cost Allocation Rates

	A	B	C	D	E	F	G	H
1	Activity	Step 1: Total Activity Cost Pool (from Exhibit 4-13)		Step 2: Total Amount of Activity Allocation Base (from Exhibit 4-14)			Step 3: Activity Cost Allocation Rate	
2	Machine Setup	$ 80,000	÷	8,000	setups	=	$ 10.00	per setup
3	Materials Handling	200,000	÷	400,000	parts	=	$ 0.50	per part
4	Fabricating Parts	300,000	÷	12,500	machine hours	=	$ 24.00	per machine hour
5	Supervising Assembly	150,000	÷	50,000	DL hours	=	$ 3.00	per DL hour
6	Inspecting	170,000	÷	34,000	inspections	=	$ 5.00	per inspection
7	Packaging	100,000	÷	400,000	cubic feet	=	$ 0.25	per cubic foot
8	Total MOH	$ 1,000,000						
9								

NOTE: Arithmetic signs are only shown for illustrative teaching purposes. They are not typically displayed in spreadsheets.

Once again, these rates are calculated based on estimated, or budgeted, costs for the year. Hence, they too are "predetermined" before the year begins. Then, during the year, the company uses them to allocate manufacturing overhead to specific jobs, as shown in Step 4.

STEP 4: The company allocates some manufacturing overhead from each activity to the individual jobs that use the activities.

The formula is as follows:

> MOH allocated to job = Activity cost allocation rate × Actual amount of activity allocation base used by job

Exhibit 4-16 shows how these activity cost allocation rates would be used to allocate manufacturing overhead to Job 101, in which one elliptical was produced.

EXHIBIT 4-16 Allocating MOH to Job 101 (One Elliptical) Using ABC

	Activity	Activity Cost Allocation Rate (from Exhibit 4-15)		Actual Use of Activity Allocation Base (information collected on job cost record)		MOH Allocated to Job 101: One Elliptical
2	Machine Setup	$10.00	per setup	× 2	setups	= $ 20
3	Materials Handling	$ 0.50	per part	× 20	parts	= 10
4	Fabricating Parts	$24.00	per machine hour	× 1	machine hours	= 24
5	Supervising Assembly	$ 3.00	per DL hour	× 9	DL hours	= 27
6	Inspecting	$ 5.00	per inspection	× 3	inspections	= 15
7	Packaging	$ 0.25	per cubic foot	× 52	cubic feet	= 13
8	Total					$ 109

NOTE: Arithmetic signs are only shown for illustrative teaching purposes. They are not typically displayed in spreadsheets.

Exhibit 4-17 shows how the same activity cost allocation rates are used to allocate MOH to Job 102, in which one treadmill was produced.

EXHIBIT 4-17 Allocating MOH to Job 102 (One Treadmill) Using ABC

	Activity	Activity Cost Allocation Rate (from Exhibit 4-15)		Actual Use of Activity Allocation Base (information collected on job cost record)		MOH Allocated to Job 102: One Treadmill
2	Machine Setup	$10.00	per setup	× 4	setups	= $ 40
3	Materials Handling	$ 0.50	per part	× 26	parts	= 13
4	Fabricating Parts	$24.00	per machine hour	× 4	machine hours	= 96
5	Supervising Assembly	$ 3.00	per DL hour	× 6	DL hours	= 18
6	Inspecting	$ 5.00	per inspection	× 6	inspections	= 30
7	Packaging	$ 0.25	per cubic foot	× 60	cubic feet	= 15
8	Total					$ 212

NOTE: Arithmetic signs are only shown for illustrative teaching purposes. They are not typically displayed in spreadsheets.

Exhibit 4-18 illustrates the company's ABC system.

EXHIBIT 4-18 Illustration of the Company's ABC System

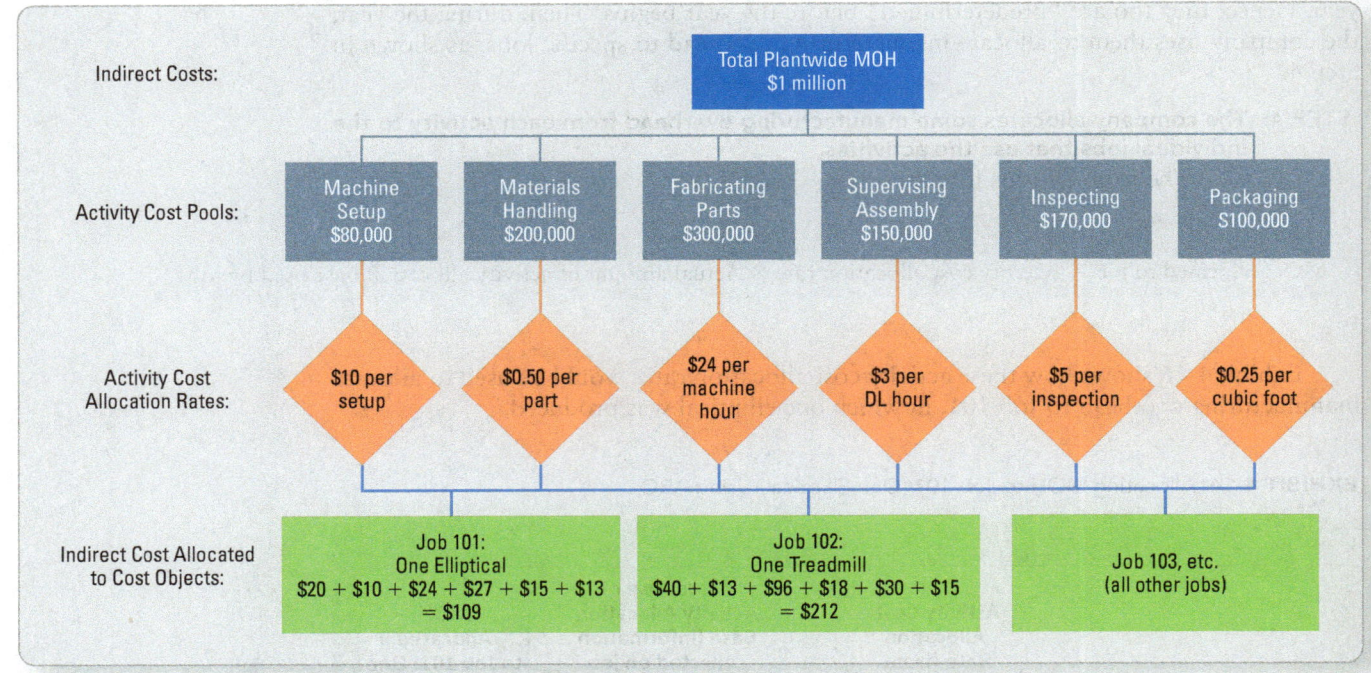

One Last Look at Cost Distortion: Comparing the Three Allocation Systems

Exhibit 4-19 compares the amount of manufacturing overhead that would have been allocated to each elliptical and each treadmill using the three cost allocation systems that we have discussed: (1) a single plantwide overhead rate, (2) departmental overhead rates, and (3) ABC.

EXHIBIT 4-19 Comparing the Three Cost Allocation Systems

	Plantwide Overhead Rate (Exhibit 4-2)	Departmental Overhead Rates (Exhibit 4-8 & 4-9)	Activity-Based Costing (Exhibit 4-16 & 4-17)
Job 101: One Elliptical	$160	$140	$109
Job 102: One Treadmill	$160	$200	$212

As you can see, each allocation system renders different answers for the amount of MOH that should be allocated to each elliptical and treadmill. Which is correct? Keep the following important rule of thumb in mind:

> ABC costs are generally thought to be the most accurate because ABC takes into account (1) the *specific resources* each product uses (for example, inspecting resources) and (2) the extent to which they use these resources (for example, each elliptical required *three* inspections, while each treadmill required *six* inspections.

Exhibit 4-19 shows that the plantwide rate had been severely distorting costs: The elliptical had been overcosted by $51 ($160 − $109), and the treadmill had been undercosted by $52 ($160 − $212). Here, we have only looked at two jobs produced during the year. However, the following rule of thumb holds true:

> If we consider all of the jobs and products the company produced during the year, we will see that the *total amount* by which some products have been *overcosted* will equal the total amount by which other products have been *undercosted*.

Why? Because $1 million of MOH is being allocated: If some products are allocated too much MOH, then other products are allocated too little MOH.

Keep in mind that cost distortion is solely a result of the way indirect costs (manufacturing overhead) are allocated. The direct costs of each product (direct materials and direct labor) are known with certainty because of the precise way in which they are traced to jobs.

STOP & THINK

If a company refines its costing system using departmental overhead rates or ABC, will manufacturing overhead still be overallocated or underallocated by the end of the year (as we saw in Chapter 3 when the company used a plantwide overhead rate)?

Answer: Yes. The use of *any predetermined* allocation rate will result in the over- or under-allocation of manufacturing overhead. That's because *predetermined* rates are developed using *estimated* data before the actual manufacturing overhead costs and actual cost driver activity for the year are known. Refined costing systems decrease cost distortion *between* products but do not eliminate the issue of over- or underallocating total manufacturing overhead.[4] As described in Chapter 3, the Cost of Goods Sold account will need to be adjusted at year-end for the *total* amount by which manufacturing overhead has been over- or underallocated.

Sustainability and Refined Costing Systems

Refined costing systems are almost always a necessity for companies that wish to move toward environmental sustainability. Why? Because jobs and product lines do not drive environmental overhead costs equally. Even a smaller manufacturing company with only two or three product lines will often find that environmental-related overhead costs, such as:

- solid waste disposal
- water use
- energy consumption
- hazardous materials handling and training
- air emissions

are not driven equally between each product line. If a company uses a single plantwide overhead rate, environmental and nonenvironmental overhead costs will be combined within one cost pool, where they will be allocated to each of the company's product lines using the same rate.

However, refined costing systems allow companies to identify the activities driving environmental costs and separately pool and allocate these costs to the appropriate products. As a result, management will have a clearer picture of the enviromental impact of its products and can use that information to work on reducing the company's environmental footprint. This information can also be used if the company is required to report environmental impact information to its customers upstream in the supply chain (for example, Walmart and Costco assess the environmental and social impact of their suppliers).

▶ See Exercises E4-21A and E4-32B

---

[4] In some cases, ABC may reduce the total amount of over- or underallocation of manufacturing overhead costs. How? Some activity cost pools may be overallocated, while others are underallocated, resulting in an offsetting total effect.

The Cost Hierarchy: A Useful Guide for Setting Up Activity Cost Pools

Some companies use a classification system, called the cost hierarchy, to establish activity cost pools. Companies often have hundreds of different activities. However, to keep the ABC system manageable, companies need to keep the system as simple as possible, yet refined enough to accurately determine product costs.[5] The cost hierarchy, pictured in Exhibit 4-20, helps managers understand the nature of each activity cost pool and what drives it.

EXHIBIT 4-20 The Cost Hierarchy

There are four categories of activity costs in this hierarchy, each determined by the underlying factor that drives its costs:

1. **Unit-level activities**—activities and costs incurred for every unit. Examples include inspecting and packaging *each* unit the company produces.

2. **Batch-level activities**—activities and costs incurred for every batch, regardless of the number of units in the batch. One example would be machine setup. Once the machines are set up for the specifications of the production run, the company could produce a batch of 1, 10, or 100 units, yet the company only incurs the machine setup cost once for the entire batch.

3. **Product-level activities**—activities and costs incurred for a particular product, regardless of the number of units or batches of the product produced. One example would be the lease payments on equipment used solely for manufacturing a particular product.

4. **Facility-level activities**—activities and costs incurred no matter how many units, batches, or products are produced in the plant. An example is facility upkeep: the cost of depreciation, insurance, property tax, and maintenance on the entire production plant.

By considering how the costs of different activities are consumed (at the unit, batch, product, or facility level), managers are often able to maintain a relatively simple, yet relatively accurate, ABC system. After initially identifying perhaps 100 different activities, managers may be able to settle on 5–15 cost pools by combining those activities that behave the same way into the same cost pools. For example, all batch-level costs might be combined into one cost pool that is allocated based on number of batches produced. Since facility-level costs do not have any particular cost driver, they are sometimes combined together in their own cost pool where they are allocated using a simple volume-based allocation base such as direct labor or machine hours, much like we saw in Chapter 3. Keep in mind that the cost hierarchy is simply a tool for helping managers think about costs and what drives them.

---

[5] When ABC system implementations fail, it is often due to managers' development of an overly complex system with too many cost pools and too many different cost drivers. After several redesigns of their ABC systems, Coca-Cola and Allied Signal both found that the simpler designs resulted in just as much accuracy. G. Cokins, "Learning to Love ABC," *Journal of Accountancy*, August 1999, pp. 37–39.

Activity-Based Costing, Lean Operations, and the Costs of Quality

STOP & THINK

Do the journal entries used to record job costing differ if a manufacturer uses a refined cost allocation system (departmental overhead rates or ABC) rather than a single, plantwide overhead rate?

Answer: The journal entries used for a refined costing system are essentially the same as those described in Chapter 3 for a traditional job costing system. The only difference is that the company will typically use *several* MOH accounts (one for each department or activity cost pool) rather than *one* MOH account. By using several MOH accounts, the manufacturer obtains more detailed information on each cost pool. This information may help managers make better estimates when calculating allocation rates the next year.

How Do Managers Use the Refined Cost Information to Improve Operations?

We've just seen how companies can increase the accuracy of their product costing systems by using departmental overhead rates or ABC. Now let's consider how managers use this improved cost information to run their companies more effectively and efficiently.

3 Understand the benefits and limitations of ABC/ABM systems

Activity-Based Management (ABM)

<u>Activity-based management (ABM)</u> refers to using activity-based cost information to make decisions that increase profits while satisfying customers' needs. Companies can use ABC information for pricing and product mix decisions, for identifying opportunities to cut costs, and for routine planning and control decisions.

Pricing and Product Mix Decisions

Earlier in the chapter, our ABC example showed managers that ellipticals cost *less* to make and treadmills cost *more* to make than indicated by the original plantwide cost allocation system. As a result, managers may decide to change pricing on these products. For example, the company may be able to reduce its price on ellipticals to become more price-competitive. Or the company may decide to capitalize on the extra profitability of the product by leaving the price where it is but increasing demand by placing more advertisements for ellipticals. On the other hand, managers will want to reevaluate the price charged for treadmills. The price must be high enough to cover the cost of producing and selling the treadmills while still being low enough to compete with other companies and earn Life Fitness a reasonable profit.

After implementing ABC, companies often realize they are overcosting their high-volume products and undercosting their low-volume products. Plantwide overhead rates based on volume-sensitive allocation bases (such as direct labor hours) end up allocating more cost to high-volume products and less cost to low-volume products. However, ABC recognizes that not all indirect costs are driven by the number of units produced. That is to say, not all costs are unit-level costs. Rather, many costs are incurred at the batch level or product level, where they can be spread over the number of batches or product lines. As shown in Exhibit 4-21, ABC tends to increase the unit cost of low-volume products (that have fewer units over which to spread batch-level and product-level costs), and decrease the unit cost of high-volume products.

As a result of using ABC, some companies have found that they were actually losing money on some of their products while earning much more profit than they had realized on other products! By shifting the mix of products offered away from the less profitable and toward the more profitable, companies are able to generate a higher operating income.

Cutting Costs

Most companies adopt ABC to get more accurate product costs for pricing and product mix decisions, but they often reap even *greater benefits* by using ABM to pinpoint opportunities to cut costs. For example, the ABC data calculated in Exhibit 4-15 showed

EXHIBIT 4-21 Typical Result of ABC Costing

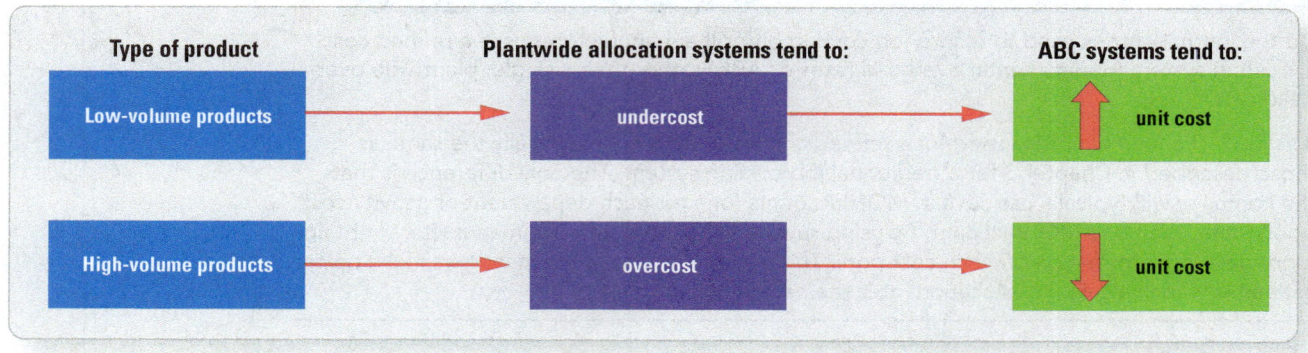

managers that each inspection costs $5, each machine setup costs $10, each part costs $0.50 to move, and so forth. This information gives production managers a starting place for cutting costs.

Once managers identify the company's activities and their related costs, managers can analyze whether all of the activities are really necessary. As the term suggests, **value-added activities** are activities for which the customer is willing to pay because these activities add value to the final product or service. In other words, these activities help satisfy the customer's expectations of the product or service. For example, fabricating component parts and assembling the units are value-added activities because they are necessary for changing raw materials into high-quality ellipticals and treadmills.

On the other hand, **non-value-added activities** (also referred to as **waste activities**), neither enhance the customer's image of the product or service nor provide a competitive advantage. These types of activities could be reduced or removed from the process with no ill effect on the end product or service. The primary goal of lean thinking, which is described in the second half of the chapter, is to make the company's processes as efficient as possible by eliminating all wasteful activities.

One way of determining whether an activity adds value is to ask if it could be eliminated or reduced by improving another part of the process. For example, could the movement of parts be eliminated or reduced by changing the factory layout? Could inventory storage be eliminated if the company only purchased the raw materials that were needed for each day's production run? Could inspection be reduced if more emphasis was placed on improving the production process, training employees, or using better-quality inputs? In the second half of the chapter we'll discuss tools that many companies have adopted to identify and eliminate these costly non-value-added activities.

Routine Planning and Control Decisions

In addition to pricing, product mix, and cost-cutting decisions, companies can use ABC in routine planning and control. Activity-based budgeting uses the costs of activities to create budgets. Managers can compare actual activity costs to budgeted activity costs to determine how well they are achieving their goals.

Using ABC Across the Value Chain and in Service and Merchandising Companies

Our chapter example revolved around using refined costing systems at a manufacturer to more accurately allocate manufacturing overhead costs. However, ABC can be used to identify the cost of *all* activities across the value chain associated with particular jobs, products, and services. For example, using ABC, a company can better determine the costs of designing or marketing new or existing products and services. It can also calculate the cost of providing customer service to different clients. The 80%/20% rule generally holds: 20% of clients often provide 80% of the company's profits once all the activities incurred on behalf of "needy" clients is taken into consideration. By more accurately allocating the cost of all activities across the value chain, businesses can focus on their most profitable products, services, and customers.

Merchandising and service companies also find ABC useful. For example, Walmart may use ABC to allocate the cost of store operating activities such as ordering, stocking, and customer service among its Housewares, Clothing, and Electronics Departments. An accounting firm may use ABC to allocate secretarial support, software costs, and travel costs between its tax, audit, and consulting clients. To implement ABC, these companies use the same four basic steps discussed earlier but apply them to indirect *operating* costs rather than indirect *manufacturing* costs (MOH). Once again, managers can use the data generated by ABC to determine which products or services to emphasize, to set prices, to cut costs, and to make other routine planning and control decisions.

STOP & THINK

Can governmental agencies use ABC/ABM to run their operations more efficiently?

Answer: Yes. ABC/ABM is not just for private-sector companies. The City of Indianapolis was able to save its taxpayers millions of dollars after using ABC to study the cost of providing city services (activities) to local citizens. Once the city determined the cost of its activities, it was able to obtain competitive bids for those same services from private businesses. As a result, the city outsourced many activities to private-sector firms for a lower cost.[6]

Passing the Cost-Benefit Test

Like all other management tools, managers must determine whether the cost of designing and implementing an ABC/ABM system is worth the benefits of having more precise information. The system should be refined enough to provide accurate product costs but simple enough for managers to understand. In our chapter example, ABC increased the number of allocation rates from the single plantwide allocation rate in the original system to six activity cost allocation rates. ABC systems are even more complex in real-world companies that have many more activities and cost drivers.

Circumstances Favoring ABC/ABM Systems

ABC and ABM pass the cost-benefit test when the benefits of adopting ABC/ABM exceed the costs.

The benefits of adopting ABC/ABM are higher for companies in competitive markets because

- accurate product cost information is essential for setting competitive sales prices that still allow the company to earn a profit.
- ABM can pinpoint opportunities for cost savings, which increase the company's profit or are passed on to customers through lower prices.

The benefits of adopting ABC/ABM are higher when the risk of cost distortion is high, for example, when

- the company produces many different products that use different types and amounts of resources. (If all products use similar types and amounts of resources, a simple plantwide allocation system works fine.)
- the company has high indirect costs. (If the company has relatively few indirect costs, it matters less how they are allocated.)
- the company produces high volumes of some products and low volumes of other products. (Plantwide allocation systems based on a volume-related driver, such as direct labor hours, tend to overcost high-volume products and undercost low-volume products.)

[6]H. Meyer, "Indianapolis Speeds Away," *The Journal of Business Strategy*, May/June 1998, pp. 41–46.

We have seen that ABC offers many benefits. However, the cost and time required to implement and maintain an ABC system are often quite high. Some companies report spending up to two to four years to design and implement their ABC systems. The larger the company, the longer it usually takes. Top management support is crucial for the success of such an expensive and time-consuming initiative. Without such support, ABC implementations might easily be abandoned for an easier, less costly accounting system. Because we know ABC systems are costly to implement, how can a company judge the costs involved with setting one up?

The costs of adopting ABC/ABM are generally lower when the company has

- accounting and information system expertise to develop the system. However, even "off-the-shelf" commercial accounting packages offer ABC modules. Small companies often find that Excel spreadsheets can be used to implement ABC, rather than integrating ABC into their general ledger software.
- information technology such as bar coding, optical scanning, Web-based data collection, or data warehouse systems to record and compile cost driver data.

Signs That the Old System May Be Distorting Costs

Broken cars or computers simply stop running. But unlike cars and computers, even broken or outdated costing systems continue to report product costs. How can you tell whether a costing system is broken and needs repair? In other words, how can you tell whether an existing costing system is distorting costs and needs to be refined by way of departmental rates or ABC?

A company's product costing system may need repair in the following situations:

Managers don't understand costs and profits:

- In bidding for jobs, managers lose bids they expected to win and win bids they expected to lose.
- Competitors with similar high-volume products price their products below the company's costs but still earn good profits.
- Employees do not believe the cost numbers reported by the accounting system.

The cost system is outdated:

- The company has diversified its product offerings since the allocation system was first developed.
- The company has reengineered its production process but has not changed its accounting system to reflect the new production environment.

Decision Guidelines

Refined Costing Systems

Several years ago, Dell decided that it needed to refine its costing system. Starting with an Excel spreadsheet, Dell developed a simple ABC system that focused on the 10 most critical activities. Here are some of the decisions Dell faced as it began refining its costing system.

Decision	Guidelines
How do we develop an ABC system?	1. Identify the activities and estimate the total MOH associated with each activity. These are known as the activity cost pools. 2. Select a cost allocation base for each activity and estimate the total amount that will be used during the year. 3. Calculate an activity cost allocation rate for each activity. 4. Allocate some MOH from each activity to the individual jobs that use the activities.
How do we compute an activity cost allocation rate?	$$\frac{\text{Total estimated activity cost pool}}{\text{Total estimated activity allocation base}}$$
How do we allocate an activity's cost to a job?	$$\text{Activity cost allocation rate} \times \text{Actual amount of activity allocation base used by job}$$
How can a refined costing system support environmental sustainability?	By creating separate cost pools for environmental related costs, managers are better able to identify those activities and products with larger environmental footprints.
What types of decisions would benefit from the use of ABC?	Managers use ABC data in ABM to make the following decisions: • Pricing and product mix • Cost cutting • Routine planning and control
What are the main benefits of ABC?	• More accurate product cost information. • More detailed information on costs of activities and associated cost drivers help managers control costs and eliminate non-value-added activities.
When is ABC most likely to pass the cost-benefit test?	• The company is in a competitive environment and needs accurate product costs. • The company makes different products that use different amounts of resources. • The company has high indirect costs. • The company produces high volumes of some products and lower volumes of other products. • The company has accounting and information technology expertise to implement the system.
How do we tell when a cost system needs to be refined?	• Managers lose bids they expected to win and win bids they expected to lose. • Competitors earn profits despite pricing high-volume products below the company's costs. • Employees do not believe cost numbers. • The company has diversified the products it manufactures. • The company has reengineered the production process but not the accounting system.

SUMMARY PROBLEM 1

Indianapolis Auto Parts (IAP) has a Seat Manufacturing Department that uses ABC. IAP's activity cost allocation rates include the following:

Activity	Allocation Base	Activity Cost Allocation Rate
Machining	Number of machine hours	$30.00 per machine hour
Assembling	Number of parts	0.50 per part
Packaging	Number of finished seats	0.90 per finished seat

Suppose Ford has asked for a bid on 50,000 built-in baby seats that would be installed as an option on some Ford SUVs. Each seat has 20 parts, and the direct materials cost per seat is $11. The job would require 10,000 direct labor hours at a labor wage rate of $25 per hour. In addition, IAP will use a total of 400 machine hours to fabricate some of the parts required for the seats.

Requirements

1. Compute the total cost of producing and packaging 50,000 baby seats. Also compute the average cost per seat.
2. For bidding, IAP adds a 30% markup to total cost. What price will the company bid for the Ford order?
3. Suppose that instead of an ABC system, IAP has a traditional product costing system that allocates manufacturing overhead at a plantwide overhead rate of $65 per direct labor hour. The baby seat order will require 10,000 direct labor hours. Compute the total cost of producing the baby seats and the average cost per seat. What price will IAP bid using this system's total cost?
4. Use your answers to Requirements 2 and 3 to explain how ABC can help IAP make a better decision about the bid price it will offer Ford.

SOLUTIONS

Requirements 1 and 2
Total Cost of Order, Average Cost per Seat, and Bid Price:

	A	B	C	D	E	F	G	H
1	**Manufacturing Costs**	**Usage of Activity**			**Cost Rate**			**Total**
2	Direct Material	50,000	seats	×	$ 11.00	per seat	=	$ 550,000
3	Direct Labor	10,000	DL hours	×	$ 25.00	per DL hour	=	250,000
4	MOH:							
5	Machining	400	machine hours	×	$ 30.00	per machine hour	=	12,000
6	Assembling	1,000,000*	parts	×	$ 0.50	per part	=	500,000
7	Packaging	50,000	seats	×	$ 0.90	per seat	=	45,000
8	Total Cost							$ 1,357,000
9	Divide by: Number of units							50,000
10	Average cost per unit							$ 27.14
11								
12	**Calculation of bid price:**							
13	Total job cost							$ 1,357,000
14	Multiply by: 100% + Markup							130%
15	Bid price							$ 1,764,100
16								

*1,000,000 = 50,000 seats × 20 parts per seat.
NOTE: Arithmetic signs are only shown for illustrative teaching purposes. They are not typically displayed in spreadsheets.

Requirement 3
Bid Price (Traditional System):

	A	B	C	D	E	F	G	H
1	**Manufacturing Costs**	**Usage of Activity**			**Cost Rate**			**Total**
2	Direct Material	50,000	seats	×	$ 11.00	per seat	=	$ 550,000
3	Direct Labor	10,000	DL hours	×	$ 25.00	per DL hour	=	250,000
4	MOH:	10,000	DL hours	×	$ 65.00	per DL hour	=	650,000
5	Total Cost							$ 1,450,000
6	Divide by: Number of units							50,000
7	Average cost per unit							$ 29.00
8								
9	**Calculation of bid price:**							
10	Total job cost							$ 1,450,000
11	Multiply by: 100% + Markup							130%
12	Bid price							$ 1,885,000
13								

NOTE: Arithmetic signs are only shown for illustrative teaching purposes. They are not typically displayed in spreadsheets.

Requirement 4
IAP's bid would be $120,900 higher using the plantwide overhead rate than using ABC ($1,885,000 versus $1,764,100). Assuming that the ABC system more accurately captures the costs caused by the order, the traditional plantwide overhead system overcosts the order. This leads to a higher bid price that reduces IAP's chance of winning the bid. The ABC system shows that IAP can increase its chance of winning the bid by bidding a lower price and still make a profit.

4 Describe lean operations

What Is Lean Thinking?

<u>Lean thinking</u> is a management philosophy and strategy focused on creating value for the customer by eliminating waste. Lean is often described by the Japanese word <u>Kaizen</u>, meaning "change for the better." Lean thinking is quickly becoming the dominant business paradigm; without it, a company has little chance of long-term survival in the highly competitive global marketplace. Since management accounting systems should be designed to reflect the company's operations, it's important for you to understand the key elements of lean operations and the costs that can be reduced by eliminating waste.

One key element of creating customer value is to emphasize a short <u>customer response time</u>: the time that elapses between receipt of a customer order and delivery of the product or service. To shorten this time, companies need to reduce their own internal processing time. Although lean thinking developed in the manufacturing industry (at Toyota, in particular), the concepts and tools are being applied with great success to all types of companies. For example, service companies, such as hospitals, car repair shops, and fast-food restaurants, must also focus on eliminating the waste in their operations. No matter the industry, the bottom line is clear: By eliminating wasteful activities, companies can reduce their costs and improve their customer response time.

The Eight Wastes of Traditional Operations

Advocates of lean thinking often talk about <u>eight wastes</u> that comprise much of the waste found in traditional organizations, including service and merchandising companies. As shown in Exhibit 4-22, these wastes are easy to remember using the acronym <u>DOWNTIME</u>.[7]

EXHIBIT 4-22 The Eight Wastes

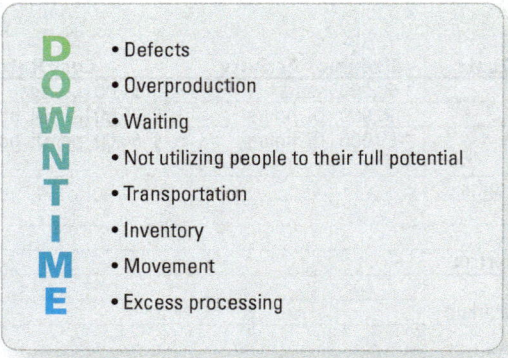

- **D** Defects
- **O** Overproduction
- **W** Waiting
- **N** Not utilizing people to their full potential
- **T** Transportation
- **I** Inventory
- **M** Movement
- **E** Excess processing

1. **Defects:** Producing defective products or services costs time and money. The product will either need to be repaired, at additional cost, or disposed of. In either case, resources are wasted. The final section of this chapter is devoted to discussing the various costs associated with poor quality of product or service.

2. **Overproduction:** Overproduction means that the company is making more product than needed or making product *sooner* than it is needed. Traditional manufacturers often make products in large batches because of long and costly machine setup times and to protect themselves against higher than expected demand for the product. Also, traditional manufacturers often make extra work in process inventory so that each department will have something to continue working on in the event production stops or slows in earlier departments. For example, in Exhibit 4-23, we see the series of production steps required to produce drill bits from bar stock. If the company keeps

[7] MAGNET (Manufacturing Advocacy and Growth Network), Cleveland, Ohio.

some work in process inventory between the grinding and smoothing operations, the smoothing operation can continue even if the shaping or grinding operations slow or come to a halt as a result of machine breakdown, absence of sick workers, or other production problems.

EXHIBIT 4-23 Sequence of Operations for Drill Bit Production

As you'll see next, overproduction can snowball into many problems, including extra wait time, extra transportation, and excess inventory build-up.

3. **Waiting:** Employees must often wait for parts, materials, information, or machine repairs before they can proceed with their tasks. In addition, because of overproduction and large batches, work in process inventory often waits in a queue for the next production process to begin. Whether it refers to people or product, wait time is wasted time. The company's customer response time could be much shorter if wait time were eliminated.

4. **Not utilizing people to their full potential:** By assuming that managers always know best, traditional companies have often underutilized their employees. In contrast, one of the key mantras of lean thinking is employee empowerment at all levels of the organization. Employees usually have excellent ideas on how their jobs could be done more efficiently and with less frustration.

5. **Transportation:** While movement of parts, inventory, and paperwork is necessary to some extent, any *excess* transportation is simply wasteful because of the equipment, manpower, energy, and time it requires. Excess transportation is often caused by poor plant layout, large centralized storage cribs, large batches, and long lead times that require product to be moved elsewhere until the next production process is ready to begin.

6. **Inventory:** Typically, traditional manufacturers buy more raw materials than they need "just in case" any of the materials are defective or the supplier is late with the next delivery. As noted earlier, they produce extra work in process inventory "just in case" something goes wrong in the production process. Also, they produce extra finished goods inventory "just in case" demand is higher than expected. In other words, large inventories are essentially a response to uncertainty. Uncertainty is a valid reason for keeping large inventories. So why are large inventories considered wasteful?

   ■ Inventories use cash. Companies incur interest expense from borrowing cash to finance their inventories or forgo income that could be earned from investing their cash elsewhere.

   ■ Large inventories hide quality problems, production bottlenecks, and obsolescence. Inventory may spoil, be broken or stolen, or become obsolete as it sits in storage and waits to be used or sold. Companies in high-tech and fashion industries are particularly susceptible to inventory obsolescence.

   ■ Storing and unstoring inventory is very expensive. Building space, shelving, warehouse equipment, security, computer systems, and labor are all needed to manage inventories.

7. **Movement:** In contrast to the waste of transportation, which refers to moving products and materials, the waste of movement refers to excess human motion, such as excess bending, reaching, turning, and walking. This waste is often caused by cluttered or unorganized work areas (where employees must search for the needed tools and supplies), poorly designed facilities (where employees must walk from one area of the building to another), and poorly designed workstations and work methods

(where employees must continually crouch, stretch, bend, and turn to do their tasks). Not only does excess movement take time, but also it can signal unsafe work conditions that can decrease employee morale and increase the company's exposure to workers' compensation claims.

8. **Excess processing:** This waste refers to performing additional production steps or adding features the customer doesn't care about. Often, this waste is caused when customer requirements are not clearly defined, when engineering changes are made without simultaneous process changes, or when additional steps are performed to make up for shortfalls in earlier production steps. For example, to keep its price point relatively low, IKEA flat packs all of its furniture and lets the customer perform the final assembly. By eliminating the final assembly process, IKEA gives customers what they want at a price that is affordable. Also, IKEA saves on related transportation and warehousing costs that would be incurred on bulkier, fully assembled furniture.

Characteristics of Lean Operations

One primary goal of a lean organization is to eliminate the waste of time and money that accompanies large inventories. Therefore, lean companies often adopt a **"just-in-time" (JIT)** inventory philosophy. As the name suggests, JIT inventory focuses on purchasing raw materials *just in time* for production and then completing finished goods *just in time* for delivery to customers. By doing so, companies eliminate the waste of storing and unstoring raw materials and finished goods, as pictured in Exhibit 4-24.

EXHIBIT 4-24 Traditional System Versus JIT System

Most companies that adopt lean thinking have several common characteristics that help minimize the amount of inventory that is kept on hand, yet enable the company to quickly satisfy customer demand. These characteristics are described next.

Value Stream Mapping

Companies need to understand their current state of operations before they can attempt to remove waste and improve operations. Each family of products or services the company offers is known as a value stream. Value stream maps (VSM) are used to identify and visually illustrate the flow of materials and information for each separate value stream, all the way from order receipt to final delivery. A *current state* VSM is used to illustrate the sequence of activities, communication of information, time elapsing, and build-up of inventories that is currently occurring. After identifying waste within the current state VSM, companies prepare a *future state* VSM, with waste removed, and use it as a goal for process improvement.

Production Occurs in Self-Contained Production Cells

One of the first wastes many companies identify on the current state VSM is the waste of time, transportation, and movement that occurs as a result of poor plant or office layout. On one hand, a traditional drill bit manufacturer would group all cutting machines in one area, all shaping machines in another area, all grinding machines in a third area, and all smoothing machines in a fourth area, as illustrated in Panel A of Exhibit 4-25. On the other hand, lean companies would group the machines in self-contained production cells as shown in Panel B of Exhibit 4-25. These self-contained production cells minimize the time and cost involved with physically moving parts across the factory to other departments.

EXHIBIT 4-25 Equipment Arrangement in Traditional and Lean Production Systems

Employee Empowerment: Broad Roles and the Use of Teams

To combat the waste of not utilizing people to their full potential, lean companies focus on employee empowerment. Employees typically hold broader roles than their counterparts at traditional companies. For example, employees working in production cells do more than operate a single machine. They also conduct maintenance, perform setups, inspect their own work, and operate other machines. For example, look at Panel B of Exhibit 4-25. A worker in the Drill Bit Production Cell 1 would be cross-trained to operate all of the machines (cutting, shaping, grinding, and smoothing) in that cell. This cross-training boosts morale, lowers costs, and creates a more flexible and versatile workforce. As a result, individual workloads become much more balanced, leading to a more equitable distribution of work and a more satisfied workforce.

Lean companies also empower employees by using small teams to identify waste and develop potential solutions to the problems identified. Problem solving at lean companies involves searching for and fixing the root cause of a problem, rather than making cosmetic changes to surface issues. To find the root cause of a problem, teams are encouraged to ask "Why?" at least five times. For example, say you received a "D" grade on an exam. Your initial response might be that you didn't understand the material. However, as you dig deeper by continually asking "Why?" you might find that the root cause was not a simple failure to understand the material, but having an overloaded schedule that didn't allow you sufficient time to study and practice the material. The solution might be to lighten your semester course load or not to participate in so many extracurricular activities. Without fixing the root cause of the problem, you are apt to run into similar problems in the future.

Often, lean companies institute profit-sharing plans so that employees at all levels of the company are compensated for improving the company's overall performance. Because of employee empowerment, lean companies typically report higher job satisfaction and better employee morale.

5S Workplace Organization

Lean companies use a workplace organization system called **"5S"** to keep their work cells clean and organized. The mantra of 5S is, "a place for everything and everything in its place." By having a clean, well-organized, ergonomic workplace, every employee within the work cell knows where to find the tools and supplies they need to do each job in the cell as efficiently as possible. A clean workplace also leads to fewer defects (due to fewer contaminants), a safer workplace, and fewer unscheduled machine repairs. The 5S stands for the following:

- **Sort:** Infrequently used tools and supplies are removed from the workplace.
- **Set in order:** Visual management tools, such as color-coding, are used to create a logical layout of tools, supplies, and equipment in the work cell so that anyone could walk into the cell and visually understand the current situation.
- **Shine:** All machines, floors, tools, and workstations are thoroughly cleaned.
- **Standardize:** Procedures are put in place to ensure the cleanliness and organization of the workplace does not deteriorate.
- **Sustain:** Daily upkeep of the workstations is maintained, and 5S inspections are routinely performed.

Continuous Flow

Lean organizations attempt to smooth the flow of production through the plant so that the rate of production is the same as the rate of demand, thus reducing the wastes of overproduction, waiting, and inventory. The goal is to make *only* as many units as needed by the next customer, whether that be the next machine operator or the final, external customer. **Takt time**, a critical concept in lean manufacturing, is the rate of production needed to meet customer demand, yet avoid overproduction. The term comes from a German word for *rhythm* or *beat*. For example, if a product line has a takt time of five minutes, it means that one unit needs to be produced every five minutes. By carefully monitoring takt time, lean companies are able to identify bottlenecks, balance the workloads of different processes, avoid inventory build-up, and satisfy customer demand.

Pull System

In a traditional production system, batches of product are "pushed" through production according to forecasted demand. However, in a lean production system, no products are made until a customer's order has been received. The customer order triggers the start of the production process and "pulls" the batch through production. Even the necessary raw materials are usually not purchased until a customer order is received. Obviously, for this to work, companies must employ various tactics that will allow the company to quickly satisfy the customer's order. We discuss these tactics next.

Shorter Manufacturing Cycle Times

Because products are not started until a customer order is received, lean companies must focus on reducing their **manufacturing cycle time**: the time that elapses between the start of production and the product's completion. According to most experts, the majority of manufacturing cycle time is spent on non-value-added activities. Shorter manufacturing times also protect companies from foreign competitors whose cheaper products take longer to ship. Delivery speed has become a competitive weapon.

Smaller Batches

Manufacturing cycle time is highly dependent on batch size. Large batch sizes cause wasted wait time. Therefore, one of the key elements of lean production is the use of smaller batches. For example, assume that a customer has ordered 10 units and that each unit requires three unique, sequential processes: A, B, and C. Furthermore, assume that each process takes *1 minute* to complete *on each unit*. The manufacturing cycle time is illustrated in Exhibit 4-26, where each "x" stands for one unit of the product, and the capital "X" stands for the first unit in the batch. Exhibit 4-26 shows that the entire order would take 30 minutes to complete if the manufacturer uses a batch size of 10. Exhibit 4-26 also shows that 21 minutes have elapsed before the first unit in the batch is completed.

EXHIBIT 4-26 Manufacturing Cycle Time with a Batch Size of 10

Alternatively, Exhibit 4-27 shows that the entire order could be completed in just 12 minutes if the manufacturer uses a batch size of 1. In addition, the first unit in the batch is completed after a mere 3 minutes has elapsed. Why the difference? With large batch sizes, each unit spends the bulk of the manufacturing cycle time *waiting*. Customer response time can be greatly reduced through the use of smaller batch sizes.

EXHIBIT 4-27 Manufacturing Cycle Time with a Batch Size of 1

Reduced Setup Times

One key component of manufacturing cycle time is the time required to set up a machine that is used to manufacture more than one product. Employee training and technology helped Toyota cut setup times from several hours to just a few minutes. As a result, the company became more flexible in scheduling production to meet customer orders.

Point-of-Use Storage

Point-of-use storage (POUS) is a storage system used to reduce the waste of transportation and movement. In essence, tools, materials, and equipment are stored in proximity to where they will be used most frequently, rather than in a centralized storage crib. In a similar vein, those items that are used infrequently are removed from the cells and stored elsewhere.

Emphasis on Quality

Lean companies focus on producing their products right the *first* time, *every* time. Why? First, they have no backup stock to give to waiting customers if they run into production problems. Second, defects in materials and workmanship can slow or shut down production. Lean companies cannot afford the time it takes to rework faulty products. Lean companies emphasize "building in" quality rather than relying on a final inspection point to catch defects. This approach to quality, called **quality at the source**, refers to shifting the responsibility for quality adherence to the operators at each step in the value stream, rather than relying on supervisors or quality assurance personnel to catch errors. Each operator checks the incoming work, as well as his or her own outgoing work, so that defective units do not get passed on to downstream production processes.

Many lean companies also pursue the dogma of **Six Sigma**, which is the goal of producing near perfection, with less than 3.4 defects per million opportunities. The name arises from its statistical probability: a defect that is six standard deviations from the mean is highly unlikely to occur. You may hear the term *Lean/Six Sigma* together because the two approaches often go hand in hand. Six Sigma was developed by Motorola in the 1980s but has been adopted by many successful companies. GE credits Six Sigma with saving the company over $10 billion in the first five years of its use.[8] Lean/Six Sigma companies use standardization tools, such as checklists and detailed step-by-step operating procedures, to ensure employees know how to complete each process correctly. They also use visual management, root cause analysis, and other tools to "mistake-proof" each process. "Poka-yoke" is the Japanese term used in lean companies for mistake-proofing a process. Let's look at an example: at gas stations, the nozzle for diesel gasoline is larger than the nozzle for regular unleaded gas, making it virtually impossible for absent-minded customers to accidentally put diesel fuel into a car that runs on regular fuel. The process of refueling has been mistake-proofed for owners of the majority of vehicles in the United States.

> **Why is this important?**
>
> "In order to **compete** and remain **profitable**, companies must cut costs by becoming as **efficient** as possible. **Lean** thinking helps **organizations** cut costs by **eliminating waste** from the system."

Supply-Chain Management

Because there are no inventory buffers, lean production requires close coordination with suppliers. These suppliers must guarantee *on-time delivery* of *defect-free* materials. *Supply-chain management* is the exchange of information with suppliers and customers to reduce costs, improve quality, and speed delivery of goods and services from the company's suppliers, through the company itself, and on to the company's end customers. Suppliers that bear the ISO 9001 certification have proven their ability to provide high-quality products and thus tend to be suppliers for lean manufacturers.

Backflush Costing

Due to the emphasis on JIT inventory (little to no raw materials or finished goods), short manufacturing cycle times, and a "pull" system (customer is awaiting production), many lean producers use a simplified accounting system, called backflush costing, that better mirrors their production environment and eliminates wasteful bookkeeping steps. In a **backflush costing** system, the production costs are not assigned to the units until they

---

[8] www.sixsigmadaily.com/why-six-sigma-certification-and-training-reduces-company-costs/

are finished, or even sold, thereby saving the bookkeeping steps of moving the product through the various inventory accounts. To get an accurate measurement of the inventory accounts and Cost of Goods Sold at the end of the period, the cost of any unfinished or unsold product is "flushed" out of Cost of Goods Sold and placed back in the Work in Process Inventory and Finished Goods Inventory accounts.

Are There Any Drawbacks to a Lean Production System?

While many companies credit lean thinking with saving them millions of dollars, the system is not without problems. With no inventory buffers, lean producers are vulnerable when problems strike suppliers or distributors. For example, natural disasters, such as the tsunamis in Japan, and man-made disasters, such as terrorist attacks, have caused production shutdown at several lean manufacturers.

Lean Operations in Service and Merchandising Companies

The eight wastes and lean principles discussed previously also apply to service and merchandising firms. In fact, lean practices have become extremely popular in service companies, such as banks and hospitals, as well as merchandising companies, such as IKEA. Entire books have been written on the subject of "lean health care" and "lean offices." Through the use of lean tools, offices have been able to identify the waste caused by excessive document processing, layers of unnecessary authorization, unbalanced workloads, poor office layouts, and unclear communication channels. Through streamlining their internal operations, hospitals, such as the world-renowned Cleveland Clinic, have found that they are able to decrease patient wait time, thereby creating higher levels of customer satisfaction while at the same time decreasing their own costs.

Try It!

Which of the following would you expect to see at a company that espouses lean thinking?
1. Larger inventories
2. Smaller batch sizes
3. More organized workstations
4. Longer setup times
5. Lower-level small-team problem solving
6. Centralized storage cribs
7. Pull system

Please see page 244 for solutions.

Sustainability and Lean Thinking

Sustainability and lean thinking have many similarities: both practices seek to reduce waste. However, lean operations focus on eliminating waste and empowering employees in an effort to increase economic profits. On the other hand, "lean and green" operations focus on eliminating waste and empowering employees not only to increase economic profits, but also to preserve the planet and improve the lives of *all* people touched by the company. Whereas lean practices tend to center on *internal* operational waste, green practices also consider the *external* waste that may occur as a result of the product. To become more sustainable, a lean company should be particularly cognizant of all waste that could harm the planet: packaging waste, water waste, energy waste, and emissions waste that would occur from both manufacturing the product *and* from consumers using and eventually disposing of the product.

See Exercises E4-21A and E4-32B

5 Describe and use the costs of quality framework

How Do Managers Improve Quality?

Because lean companies rarely hold extra inventory to fall back on in the event of errors or defects, they use the management philosophy of <u>total quality management (TQM)</u> to focus on consistently generating high-quality products. The goal of TQM is to provide customers with superior products and services. Each business function in the value chain continually examines its own activities to improve quality and eliminate defects.

Costs of Quality (COQ)

As part of TQM, many companies prepare costs of quality reports. <u>Costs of quality reports</u> categorize and list the costs incurred by the company related to quality. Once managers know the extent of their costs of quality, they can start to identify ways for the company to improve quality while at the same time controlling costs.

Quality-related costs generally fall into four different categories: prevention costs, appraisal costs, internal failure costs, and external failure costs. These categories form the framework for a costs of quality report. We'll briefly describe each next.

Prevention Costs

<u>Prevention costs</u> are costs incurred to *avoid* producing poor-quality goods or services. Often, poor quality is caused by the variability of the production process or the complexity of the product design. To reduce the variability of the production process, companies often automate as much of the process as possible. Employee training can help decrease variability in nonautomated processes. In addition, reducing the complexity of the product design or manufacturing process can prevent the potential for error: The fewer parts or processes, the fewer things that can go wrong. Frequently, companies need to literally "go back to the drawing board" (the R&D and design stages of the value chain) to make a significant difference in preventing production problems.

Appraisal Costs

<u>Appraisal costs</u> are costs incurred to *detect* poor-quality goods or services. Intel incurs appraisal costs when it tests its products. One procedure, called burn-in, heats circuits to a high temperature. A circuit that fails the burn-in test is also likely to fail in customer use. Nissan tests 100% of the vehicles that roll off the assembly lines at its plant in Canton, Mississippi. Each vehicle is put through the paces on Nissan's all-terrain test track. Any problems are identified before the vehicle leaves the plant.

Internal Failure Costs

<u>Internal failure costs</u> are costs incurred on defective units *before* delivery to customers. For example, if Nissan does identify a problem, the vehicle is reworked to eliminate the defect before it is allowed to leave the plant. In the worst-case scenario, a product may be so defective that it cannot be reworked and must be completely scrapped. In this case, the entire cost of manufacturing the defective unit, plus any disposal cost, would be an internal failure cost.

External Failure Costs

<u>External failure costs</u> are costs incurred because the defective goods or services are not detected until *after* delivery is made to customers. News reports are filled with stories of product recalls that damage a company's reputation and can significantly harm the company's future sales. Furthermore, consumers have harnessed the power of social media and online rating sites to "spread the word" to millions of potential customers about any unsatisfying experiences they have had with products or services. As a result, a company's reputation for either good or poor quality can increase at an exponential rate. To capture the extent of a reputation for poor quality, external failure costs should include an estimate of how much profit the company is losing due to having a bad reputation.

Relationship Among Costs

Exhibit 4-28 lists some common examples of the four different costs of quality. Prevention and appraisal costs are sometimes referred to as **conformance costs** since they are the costs incurred to make sure the product or service is not defective and therefore conforms to its intended design. On the other hand, internal and external failure costs are sometimes referred to as **nonconformance costs**. These costs are incurred when the product or service *is* defective and therefore does *not* conform to its intended design.

EXHIBIT 4-28 Four Types of Quality Costs

Prevention Costs	Appraisal Costs
Training personnel	Inspection of incoming materials
Evaluating potential suppliers	Inspection at various stages of production
Using better materials	Inspection of final products or services
Preventive maintenance	Product testing
Improved equipment	Cost of inspection equipment
Redesigning product or process	

Internal Failure Costs	External Failure Costs
Production loss caused by downtime	Lost profits from lost customers
Rework	Warranty costs
Abnormal quantities of scrap	Service costs at customer sites
Rejected product units	Sales returns and allowances due to quality problems
Disposal of rejected units	Product liability claims
Machine breakdowns	Cost of recalls

Most companies find that if they invest more in prevention costs at the front end of the value chain (R&D and design), they can generate even more savings in the back end of the value chain (production and customer service). Why? Because carefully designed products and manufacturing processes can significantly reduce the number of inspections, defects, rework, and warranty claims. Managers must make trade-offs between these costs. Companies that embrace TQM, such as Toyota, *design* and *build* quality into their products rather than having to *inspect* and *repair* later, as many traditional manufacturers do.

Costs of Quality at Service and Merchandising Companies

The costs of quality are not limited to manufacturers. Service firms and merchandising companies also incur costs of quality. For example, certified public accounting (CPA) firms spend a lot of money providing ongoing professional training to their staff. They also develop standardized audit checklists to minimize the variability of the audit procedures performed for each client. These measures help to *prevent* audit failures. Both audit managers and partners review audit work papers to *appraise* whether the audit procedures performed and evidence gathered are sufficient on each audit engagement. If audit procedures or evidence are deemed to be lacking (*internal failure*), the audit manager or partner will instruct the audit team to perform additional procedures before the firm will issue an audit opinion on the client's financial statements. This parallels the "rework" a manufacturer might perform on a product that isn't up to par. Finally, audit failures, such as those at Enron and WorldCom, illustrate just how expensive and devastating *external failure* can be to a CPA firm. The once-prestigious international CPA firm Arthur Andersen & Co. actually went out of business because of the reputation damage caused by its audit failure at Enron.

Using Costs of Quality Reports to Aid Decisions

Now that we have examined the four costs of quality, let's see how they can be presented to management in the form of a costs of quality report. Let's assume Global Fitness, another manufacturer of fitness equipment, is having difficulty competing with Life Fitness because it doesn't have the reputation for high quality that Life Fitness enjoys. To examine this issue, management has prepared the costs of quality report shown in Exhibit 4-29.

Notice how Global Fitness identifies, categorizes, and quantifies all of the costs it incurs relating to quality. Global Fitness also calculates the percentage of total costs of quality that is incurred in each cost category. This helps company managers see just how *little* they are spending on conformance costs (prevention and appraisal). Most of their costs are internal and external failure costs. The best way to reduce these nonconformance costs is to invest more in prevention and appraisal. Global Fitness managers can now begin to focus on *how* they might be able to prevent these failures from occurring.

> **Why is this important?**
>
> "Businesses **compete** with each other on the basis of price and quality. **Costs of Quality** reports help managers determine how they are **spending** money to ensure that consumers get the **best-quality** product for the price."

EXHIBIT 4-29 Global Fitness's Costs of Quality Report

	A	B	C	D
1	**Global Fitness Costs of Quality Report** Year Ended December 31	Costs Incurred	Total Costs of Quality	Percentage of Total COQ
2				
3	**Prevention Costs:**			
4	Employee training	$ 125,000		
5	Total prevention costs		$ 125,000	6.1%
6				
7	**Appraisal Costs:**			
8	Testing	$ 175,000		
9	Total appraisal costs		$ 175,000	8.5%
10				
11	**Internal Failure Costs:**			
12	Rework	$ 300,000		
13	Cost of rejected units	50,000		
14	Total internal failure costs		$ 350,000	17.0%
15				
16	**External Failure Costs:**			
17	Lost profits from lost sales due to poor reputation	$ 1,000,000		
18	Sales return processing	175,000		
19	Warranty costs	235,000		
20	Total external failure costs		$ 1,410,000	68.4%
21				
22	**Total costs of quality**		$ 2,060,000	100.0%
23				

NOTE: The percentage is calculated as the total cost of the category divided by the total costs of all categories combined.

After analyzing the costs of quality report, the CEO is considering spending the following amounts on a new quality program:

Inspect raw materials	$100,000
Reengineer the production process to improve product quality	750,000
Supplier screening and certification	25,000
Preventive maintenance on plant equipment	75,000
Total costs of implementing quality programs	$950,000

Although these measures won't completely eliminate internal and external failure costs, Global Fitness expects this quality program to *reduce* costs by the following amounts:

Reduction in lost profits from lost sales due to impaired reputation	$ 800,000
Fewer sales returns to be processed	150,000
Reduction in rework costs	250,000
Reduction in warranty costs	225,000
Total cost savings	$1,425,000

According to these projections, Global Fitness's quality initiative will cost $950,000 but result in total savings of $1,425,000—for a net benefit of $475,000. This cost-benefit analysis can also be organized using the costs of quality framework as shown in Exhibit 4-30. By spending $850,000 more on prevention costs and $100,000 more on appraisal costs, Global Fitness will be able to save $250,000 in internal failure costs and $1,175,000 in external failure costs. In total, Global Fitness expects a net benefit of $475,000 from this quality initiative. As is usually the case, Global Fitness will be able to reduce its *overall* costs of quality by spending more on conformance costs.

EXHIBIT 4-30 Cost-Benefit Analysis of Global Fitness's Proposed Quality Program

A	B	C	D
Global Fitness Quality Initiative Cost Benefit Analysis	(Costs) and Cost Savings	Total (Costs) and Cost Savings	
Prevention Costs:			
Reengineer the production process	$ (750,000)		
Supplier screening and certification	(25,000)		
Preventive maintenance on equipment	(75,000)		
Total additional prevention costs		$ (850,000)	
Appraisal Costs:			
Inspect raw materials	$ (100,000)		
Total additional appraisal costs		$ (100,000)	
Internal Failure Costs:			
Reduction of rework costs	$ 250,000		
Total internal failure cost savings		$ 250,000	
External Failure Costs:			
Reduction of lost profits from lost sales	$ 800,000		
Reduction of sales return	150,000		
Reduction of warranty costs	225,000		
Total external failure cost savings		$ 1,175,000	
Total savings (costs) from quality programs		$ 475,000	

The analysis shown in Exhibit 4-30 appears very straightforward. However, quality costs can be hard to measure. The largest external failure cost—profits lost because of the company's reputation for poor quality—does not even appear in the accounting records. This cost must be estimated based on the experiences and judgments of the Sales Department. Because these estimates may be subjective, TQM programs also emphasize nonfinancial measures such as defect rates, number of customer complaints, and number of warranty repairs that can be objectively measured.

Decision Guidelines

Lean Operations and the Costs of Quality

Toyota, the largest car manufacturer in the world, is famous for its complete commitment to both lean thinking and TQM. The following are several decisions Toyota's managers made when they helped develop and implement these two modern management techniques.

Decision	Guidelines
How will we begin to identify waste in our organization?	Most companies find that the majority of waste occurs in eight specific areas. The "eight wastes" can be remembered as DOWNTIME: • Defects • Overproduction • Waiting • Not utilizing people to their full potential • Transportation • Inventory • Movement • Excess processing
What operational features will help us become more lean?	Lean operations are typically characterized by many of the following features: • Just-in-time (JIT) inventory • Value stream mapping • Production in self-contained work cells • Employee empowerment through broader roles and use of small teams • 5S workplace organization • Point-of-use storage (POUS) • Continuous flow • Pull system • Shorter manufacturing cycle times • Reduced setup times • Smaller batches • Emphasis on quality and Six Sigma • Supply-chain management • Backflush costing
What are the four types of quality costs?	1. Prevention costs—costs incurred to avoid producing poor-quality goods and services. 2. Appraisal costs—costs incurred to detect poor-quality goods and services. 3. Internal failure costs—costs incurred on defective goods and services *before* they are delivered to the customer. 4. External failure costs—costs incurred because defective goods or services are not detected until *after* delivery is made to the customer.
How do we make trade-offs among the four types of quality costs?	Investment in prevention costs and appraisal costs reduces internal and external failure costs and usually reduces the overall costs of quality.

SUMMARY PROBLEM 2

The CEO of IAP is concerned with the quality of its products and the amount of resources currently spent on customer returns. The CEO would like to analyze the costs incurred in conjunction with the quality of the product.

The following information was collected from various departments within the company:

Warranty returns	$120,000
Training personnel	10,000
Litigation on product liability claims	175,000
Inspecting 10% of final products	5,000
Rework	10,000
Production loss due to machine breakdowns	45,000
Inspection of raw materials	5,000

Requirements

1. Prepare a costs of quality report. In addition to listing the costs by category, determine the percentage of the total costs of quality incurred in each cost category.
2. Do any additional subjective costs appear to be missing from the report?
3. What can be learned from the report?

SOLUTIONS

Requirement 1

IAP Costs of Quality Report	Costs Incurred	Total Costs of Quality	Percentage of Total COQ
Prevention Costs:			
Personnel training	$ 10,000		
Total prevention costs		$ 10,000	2.7%
Appraisal Costs:			
Inspecting raw materials	$ 5,000		
Inspecting 10% of final products	5,000		
Total appraisal costs		$ 10,000	2.7%
Internal Failure Costs:			
Rework	$ 10,000		
Production loss due to machine breakdown	45,000		
Total internal failure costs		$ 55,000	14.9%
External Failure Costs:			
Litigation from product liability claims	$ 175,000		
Warranty return costs	120,000		
Total external failure costs		$ 295,000	79.7%
Total costs of quality		$ 370,000	100.0%

Requirement 2

Because the company has warranty returns and product liability litigation, it is very possible that the company suffers from a reputation for poor-quality products. If so, it is losing profits from losing sales. Unsatisfied customers will probably avoid buying from the company in the future and may tell their friends and family not to buy from the company. Worse yet, unsatisfied customers may let their complaints be known to millions of potential customers through the use of social media and online customer satisfaction websites. As a result, this report should include an estimate of the lost profits arising from the company's reputation for poor-quality products.

Requirement 3

The costs of quality report shows that very little is being spent on prevention and appraisal, which is probably why the internal and external failure costs are so high. Management should use this information to develop quality initiatives in the areas of prevention and appraisal. Such initiatives should reduce future internal and external failure costs.

END OF CHAPTER

Learning Objectives

1. Develop and use departmental overhead rates to allocate indirect costs
2. Develop and use activity-based costing (ABC) to allocate indirect costs
3. Understand the benefits and limitations of ABC/ABM systems
4. Describe lean operations
5. Describe and use the costs of quality framework

Accounting Vocabulary

5S. (p. 202) A workplace organization system comprised of the following steps: sort, set in order, shine, standardize, and sustain.

Activity-Based Costing (ABC). (p. 184) Focusing on *activities* as the fundamental cost objects. The costs of those activities become building blocks for compiling the indirect costs of products, services, and customers.

Activity-Based Management (ABM). (p. 191) Using activity-based cost information to make decisions that increase profits while satisfying customers' needs.

Appraisal Costs. (p. 206) Costs incurred to *detect* poor-quality goods or services.

Backflush Costing. (p. 204) A simplified accounting system in which production costs are not assigned to the units until they are finished, or even sold, thereby saving the bookkeeping steps of moving the product through the various inventory accounts.

Batch-Level Activities. (p. 190) Activities and costs incurred for every batch, regardless of the number of units in the batch.

Conformance Costs. (p. 207) The combination of prevention and appraisal costs; the costs incurred to make sure a product or service is not defective and therefore conforms to its intended design.

Cost Distortion. (p. 177) Overcosting some products while undercosting other products.

Costs of Quality Report. (p. 206) A report that lists the costs incurred by the company related to quality. The costs are categorized as prevention costs, appraisal costs, internal failure costs, and external failure costs.

Customer Response Time. (p. 198) The time that elapses between receipt of a customer order and delivery of the product or service.

Departmental Overhead Rates. (p. 180) Separate manufacturing overhead rates established for each department.

DOWNTIME. (p. 198) An acronym for the eight wastes: defects, overproduction, waiting, not utilizing people to their full potential, transportation, inventory, movement, excess processing.

Eight Wastes. (p. 198) Defects, overproduction, waiting, not utilizing people to their full potential, transportation, inventory, movement, excess processing.

External Failure Costs. (p. 206) Costs incurred when the company does not detect poor-quality goods or services until *after* delivery is made to customers.

Facility-Level Activities. (p. 190) Activities and costs incurred no matter how many units, batches, or products are produced in the plant.

Internal Failure Costs. (p. 206) Costs incurred when the company detects and corrects poor-quality goods or services before making delivery to customers.

Just in Time (JIT). (p. 200) An inventory management philosophy that focuses on purchasing raw materials just in time for production and completing finished goods just in time for delivery to customers.

Kaizen. (p. 198) A Japanese word meaning "change for the better."

Lean Thinking. (p. 198) A management philosophy and strategy focused on creating value for the customer by eliminating waste.

Manufacturing Cycle Time. (p. 203) The time that elapses between the start of production and the product's completion.

Nonconformance costs. (p. 207) The combination of internal failure and external failure costs; the costs incurred when a product is defective and therefore does not conform to its intended design.

Non-Value-Added Activities. (p. 192) Activities that neither enhance the customer's image of the product or service nor provide a competitive advantage; also known as *waste activities*.

Plantwide Overhead Rate. (p. 178) When overhead is allocated to every product using the same manufacturing overhead rate.

Point of Use Storage (POUS). (p. 204) A storage system used to reduce the waste of transportation and movement in which tools, materials, and equipment are stored in proximity to where they will be used most frequently.

Prevention Costs. (p. 206) Costs incurred to *avoid* poor-quality goods or services.

Product-Level Activities. (p. 190) Activities and costs incurred for a particular product, regardless of the number of units or batches of the product produced.

Quality at the Source. (p. 204) A term that refers to shifting the responsibility for quality adherence to the operators at each step in the value stream, rather than relying on supervisors or a quality assurance department to catch errors.

Six Sigma. (p. 204) The goal of producing near perfection, with less than 3.4 defects per million opportunities.

Takt Time. (p. 202) The rate of production needed to meet customer demand, yet avoid overproduction.

Total Quality Management (TQM). (p. 206) A management philosophy of delighting customers with superior products and services by continually setting higher goals and improving the performance of every business function.

Unit-Level Activities. (p. 190) Activities and costs incurred for every unit produced.

Value-Added Activities. (p. 192) Activities for which the customer is willing to pay because these activities add value to the final product or service.

Waste Activities. (p. 192) Activities that neither enhance the customer's image of the product or service nor provide a competitive advantage; also known as non-value-added activities.

MyAccountingLab — Go to http://myaccountinglab.com/ for the following Quick Check, Short Exercises, Exercises, and Problems. They are available with immediate grading, explanations of correct and incorrect answers, and interactive media that act as your own online tutor.

Quick Check

1. *(Learning Objective 1)* Cost distortion is more likely to occur when
   a. departments incur different types of overhead and the products or jobs use the departments to a different extent.
   b. a company manufactures one type of product.
   c. all products require the same amount and type of processing activities.
   d. a company uses departmental overhead rates rather than a single plantwide overhead rate.

2. *(Learning Objective 2)* The first step in computing and using ABC is which of the following?
   a. Calculating activity cost allocation rates
   b. Identifying the company's primary activities
   c. Allocating some MOH to each job
   d. Selecting appropriate allocation bases

3. *(Learning Objective 2)* Activities incurred regardless of how many units, batches, or products are produced are called _____ activities.
   a. unit-level
   b. batch-level
   c. product-level
   d. facility-level

4. *(Learning Objective 3)* Which of the following is true?
   a. ABC is only applicable to manufacturers.
   b. Value-added activities are also referred to as waste activities.
   c. ABM refers to using activity-based cost information to make decisions.
   d. The goal of ABM is to decrease the amount of value-added activities.

5. *(Learning Objective 3)* The potential benefits of ABC/ABM are generally higher for companies that
   a. produce high volumes of some products and low volumes of other products.
   b. have low manufacturing overhead costs.
   c. are in noncompetitive markets.
   d. produce one product.

6. *(Learning Objective 4)* Lean operations are generally characterized by
   a. employee empowerment.
   b. JIT inventory systems.
   c. production in self-contained cells.
   d. all of the listed answers.

7. *(Learning Objective 4)* Which of the following is *not* one of the "eight wastes" included in the acronym DOWNTIME?
   a. Overproduction
   b. Transportation
   c. Inventory
   d. Neglect

8. *(Learning Objective 4)* Concerning lean operations, which of the following is *false*?
   a. Focus on internal and external waste
   b. Are quickly becoming the dominant business paradigm
   c. Can be found in all sectors, not just manufacturing
   d. Can leave companies vulnerable to supply-chain disruptions

9. *(Learning Objective 5)* Which of the following is *not* one of the costs of quality categories?
   a. Prevention costs
   b. Appraisal costs
   c. External failure costs
   d. Transportation costs

10. *(Learning Objective 5)* Which of the following would be considered an external failure cost?
    a. Rework costs
    b. Cost to train personnel
    c. Cost of inspecting incoming raw materials
    d. Warranty costs

Quick Check Answers

1.a 2.b 3.d 4.c 5.a 6.d 7.d 8.a 9.d 10.d

Short Exercises

S4-1 Understanding key terms *(Learning Objectives 1, 2, 3, 4, & 5)*

The following is a list of several terms. Complete each of the following statements with one of these terms. You may use a term more than once, and some terms may not be used at all.

Activity-based costing	External failure costs	Manufacturing cycle time	TQM
Activity-based management	Facility-level costs	POUS	Unit-level costs
Appraisal costs	Internal failure costs	Prevention costs	
Batch-level costs	Kaizen	Product-level costs	
DOWNTIME	Lean thinking	Takt time	

a. The time that elapses between the start of production and the product's completion is known as ____.

b. ____ is the management philosophy and strategy focused on creating value for the customer by eliminating waste.

c. The costs incurred for every batch, regardless of the number of units in the batch, are known as ____.

d. Costs incurred to avoid poor-quality goods or services are ____.

e. Using activity-based costing information to make decisions that increase profits while satisfying customers' needs is ____.

f. An acronym for the eight wastes is ____.

g. The costs incurred for a particular product, regardless of the number of units or batches of the product produced, are known as ____.

h. ____ focuses on activities as fundamental building blocks in compiling the indirect costs of products, services, and customers.

i. ____ are costs incurred when defects in poor-quality goods or services are corrected before making delivery to customers.

j. ____ are incurred for every single unit of product produced.

k. Costs incurred when the company does not detect poor-quality goods or services until after delivery is made to customers are ____.

l. ____ are costs incurred no matter how many units, batches, or products are produced.

m. ____ is a Japanese word meaning "change for the better."

n. Costs incurred to detect poor-quality goods or services are ____.

o. The rate of production needed to meet customer demand, yet avoid overproduction, is known as ____.

p. ____ is a storage system used to reduce the waste of transportation and movement, in which tools, materials, and equipment are stored in proximity to where they will be used most frequently.

q. ____ is a management philosophy of delighting customers with superior products and services by continually setting higher goals and improving every business function.

S4-2 Use departmental overhead rates to allocate manufacturing overhead
(Learning Objective 1)

Whitney Furniture uses departmental overhead rates (rather than a plantwide overhead rate) to allocate its manufacturing overhead to jobs. The company's two production departments have the following departmental overhead rates:

Cutting Department:	$9 per machine hour
Finishing Department:	$18 per direct labor hour

Job 484 used the following direct labor hours and machine hours in the two manufacturing departments:

JOB 484	Cutting Department	Finishing Department
Direct Labor Hours	2	7
Machine Hours	8	4

1. How much manufacturing overhead should be allocated to Job 484?
2. Assume that direct labor is paid at a rate of $24 per hour and Job 484 used $2,400 of direct materials. What was the total manufacturing cost of Job 484?

S4-3 Compute departmental overhead rates (Learning Objective 1)

Snyder Snacks makes potato chips, corn chips, and cheese puffs using three different production lines within the same manufacturing plant. Currently, Snyder uses a single plantwide overhead rate to allocate its $3,311,500 of annual manufacturing overhead. Of this amount, $2,070,000 is associated with the potato chip line, $763,000 is associated with the corn chip line, and $478,500 is associated with the cheese puff line. Snyder's plant is currently running a total of 17,900 machine hours: 11,500 in the potato chip line, 3,500 in the corn chip line, and 2,900 in the cheese puff line. Snyder considers machine hours to be the cost driver of manufacturing overhead costs.

1. What is Snyder's plantwide overhead rate?
2. Calculate the departmental overhead rates for Snyder's three production lines. Round all answers to the nearest cent.
3. Which products have been overcosted by the plantwide rate? Which products have been undercosted by the plantwide rate?

S4-4 Compute activity cost allocation rates (Learning Objective 2)

NatureMade Snacks produces different styles of sweet potato chips (ruffled, flat, thick-cut, gourmet) for different corporate customers. Each style of sweet potato chip requires different preparation time, different cooking and draining times (depending on desired fat content), and different packaging (single serving versus bulk). Therefore, NatureMade has decided to try ABC to better capture the manufacturing overhead costs incurred by each style of chip. NatureMade has identified the following activities related to yearly manufacturing overhead costs and cost drivers associated with producing sweet potato chips:

Activity	Manufacturing Overhead	Cost Driver
Preparation	$510,000	Preparation time
Cooking and draining	$928,000	Cooking and draining time
Packaging	$400,000	Units packaged

Compute the activity cost allocation rates for each activity assuming the following total estimated activity for the year: 8,500 preparation hours, 32,000 cooking and draining hours, and 4 million packages.

S4-5 Continuation of S4-4: Use ABC to allocate overhead
(Learning Objective 2)

NatureMade Snacks just received an order to produce 12,000 single-serving bags of gourmet, fancy-cut, sweet potato chips. The order will require 21 preparation hours and 36 cooking and draining hours. Use the activity rates you calculated in S4-4 to compute the following:

1. What is the total amount of manufacturing overhead that should be allocated to this order?
2. How much manufacturing overhead should be assigned to each bag?
3. What other costs will the company need to consider to determine the total manufacturing costs of this order?

S4-6 Calculate a job cost using ABC (Learning Objective 2)

Oliver Industries, a small, family-run manufacturer, has adopted an ABC system. The following manufacturing activities, indirect manufacturing costs, and usage of cost drivers have been estimated for the year:

Activity	Estimated Total Manufacturing Overhead Costs	Estimated Total Usage of Cost Driver
Machine setup	$161,650	3,050 setups
Machining	$1,100,000	5,000 machine hours
Quality control	$360,000	4,500 tests run

During May, Jeff and Arabella Oliver machined and assembled Job 557. Jeff worked a total of 10 hours on the job, while Arabella worked 4 hours on the job. Jeff is paid a $25 per hour wage rate, while Arabella is paid $28 per hour because of her additional experience level. Direct materials requisitioned for Job 557 totaled $1,250. The following additional information was collected on Job 557: the job required 2 machine setups, 6 machine hours, and 3 quality control tests.

1. Compute the activity cost allocation rates for the year.
2. Complete the following job cost record for Job 557:

Job Cost Record Job 557	Manufacturing Costs
Direct materials	?
Direct labor	?
Manufacturing overhead	?
Total job cost	$?

S4-7 Classifying costs within the cost hierarchy (Learning Objective 2)

Classify each of the following costs as either unit-level, batch-level, product-level, or facility-level.

a. Engineering costs for new product
b. Order processing
c. Depreciation on factory
d. Direct labor
e. Shipment of an order to a customer
f. Product line manager salary
g. Machine setup costs that are incurred whenever a new production order is started
h. Patent for new product
i. Factory utilities
j. Direct materials
k. Cost to inspect each product as it is finished
l. CEO salary

S4-8 Classifying costs within the cost hierarchy (Learning Objective 2)

Robbins Manufacturing produces a variety of plastic containers using an extrusion blow molding process. The following activities are part of Robbins Manufacturing's operating process:

1. Patents are obtained for each new type of container mold.
2. Each type of container has its own unique molds.
3. Routine maintenance is performed on the extrusion machines.
4. The sales force incurs travel expenses to attend various trade shows throughout the country to market the containers.
5. Plastic resins are used as the main direct material for the containers.
6. The extrusion machine is calibrated for each batch of containers made.
7. A plant manager oversees the entire manufacturing operation.
8. Rent is paid for the building that houses the manufacturing processes.
9. Each container product line has a product line manager.
10. Each container is cut from the mold once the plastic has cooled and hardened.

Classify each activity as either unit-level, batch-level, product-level, or facility-level.

S4-9 Determine the usefulness of refined costing systems in various situations (Learning Objective 3)

In each of the following situations, determine whether the company would be more likely or less likely to benefit from refining its costing system.

1. In bidding for jobs, managers lost bids they expected to win and won bids they expected to lose.
2. The company operates in a very competitive industry.
3. The company produces few products, and the products consume resources in a similar manner.
4. The company has very few indirect costs.
5. The company produces high volumes of some of its products and low volumes of other products.
6. The company has reengineered its production process but has not changed its accounting system.

S4-10 Determine the type of cost pool and utility of ABC/ABM (Learning Objectives 2 & 3)

In a *Wall Street Journal* article ("The Price You Pay for Water at the Airport," Scott McCartney, April 22, 2015), the cost of a bottle of water at various airports was compared to the cost of that same bottle of water at a convenience store. A 20-ounce bottle of Dasani water typically costs about $0.99 at a convenience store. At the JFK International airport in New York City, that bottle of Dasani water is $2.89.

An airport store operator interviewed for the *WSJ* story stated that the costs of operating airport shops are more expensive than other retail stores for a few reasons. Off-airport warehouses are needed due to limited inventory space. In addition, deliveries to stores inside airports are usually made during off-peak hours. Finally, deliveries must be made in small batches so that everything can go through airport security screening.

1. Would the cost of **an off-airport warehouse** be considered to be a unit-level, batch-level, product-level, or facility-level cost as it relates to:
    a. The airport store
    b. An individual bottle of water
2. Would the costs of **a delivery of two cases of Dasani water to the store inside the airport from the off-airport warehouse** be considered to be unit-level, batch-level, product-level, or facility-level costs as they relate to (consider each cost you listed in the first requirement separately):
    a. The airport store
    b. An individual bottle of water
3. Would the airport store be likely to use the ABC cost for water pricing? Why or why not?
4. Would activity-based costing or activity-based management be useful for the airport store? Why or why not?

S4-11 Identifying costs as value-added or non-valued-added
(Learning Objective 3)

Identify which of the following manufacturing overhead costs are value-added and which are non-value-added.

a. Costs of reworking of defective units
b. Cost of moving raw materials into production
c. Costs arising from backlog in production
d. Salary for supervisor on the factory floor
e. Wages of the workers assembling products
f. Costs of warehousing raw materials
g. Engineering design costs for a new product
h. Product inspection

S4-12 Identify lean production characteristics *(Learning Objective 4)*

Indicate whether each of the following is characteristic of a lean production system or a traditional production system.

a. There is an emphasis on building in quality.
b. The final operation in the production sequence "pulls" parts from the preceding operation.
c. Employees do a variety of jobs, including maintenance and setups as well as operation of machines.
d. Suppliers make frequent deliveries of small quantities of raw materials.
e. Each employee is responsible for inspecting his or her own work.
f. Suppliers can access the company's intranet.
g. Large stocks of finished goods protect against lost sales if customer demand is higher than expected.
h. The workflow is continuous to attempt to balance the rate of production with the rate of demand.
i. Setup times are long.
j. A workplace organization system called "5S" is frequently used to keep work spaces clean and organized.
k. The manufacturing cycle times are longer.
l. Management works with suppliers to ensure defect-free raw materials.
m. Products are produced in large batches.

S4-13 Identify the DOWNTIME activities at a manufacturer
(Learning Objective 4)

The following is a list of eight waste activities found at a furniture manufacturing plant. Classify each one as a type of waste as represented by the acronym DOWNTIME (Defects, Overproduction, Waiting, Not utilizing people to their full potential, Transportation, Inventory, Movement, and Excess processing).

a. The plant manager makes all decisions in the plant; employees follow directions.
b. Furniture is shipped fully assembled to customers, incurring extra shipping costs because of the additional bulk.
c. Employees must search for tools at the beginning of each work shift since there is no standard storage spot for each tool.
d. Because the drill press is broken, the furniture assembly workers cannot do any work until it is fixed.
e. The tables made yesterday need to have new umbrella holes drilled in them because the current holes are too small.
f. Tables are made in large batches because machine setup time is costly.
g. Raw materials are delivered to materials warehousing area; when production is ready for the raw materials, tow motor drivers drive the materials to the production area.
h. Twice as much raw material inventory as needed for current production is stocked in case defects are found in the raw material during production.

S4-14 Identifying waste activities in an office *(Learning Objective 4)*

The following is a list of waste activities found in an office. Classify each one as a type of waste as represented by the acronym DOWNTIME (Defects, Overproduction, Waiting, Not utilizing people to their full potential, Transportation, Inventory, Movement, and Excess processing).

a. The office is run by the office manager; employees do as they are told.
b. The computer system requires frequent restarting; restarting takes five minutes.
c. To retrieve inventory records, clerks must click through several menus in the program to get to the record needed.
d. Orders in the system are frequently missing information.
e. Paperwork (that might change) is printed before it is needed.
f. Sales orders are put into the computer by the sales people in the field, and paper reports are generated; these sales orders are then entered into the order processing system by clerks who type the orders based on the paper reports.
g. The files needed for loan approval are carried to and from the file storage office when the files are needed.
h. Approval of loans is done in batches once a week rather than as the loan paperwork is finished for each individual loan.
i. Pending vacation requests must be taken to the third floor offices to get the signature of the human resources manager.
j. Employees do not have the authority and responsibility to make routine decisions.

S4-15 Classifying costs of quality *(Learning Objective 5)*

Classify each of the following quality-related costs as prevention costs, appraisal costs, internal failure costs, or external failure costs.

1. Warranty repairs
2. Legal fees from customer lawsuits
3. Training employees
4. Cost incurred producing and disposing of defective units
5. Lost productivity due to machine breakdown
6. Inspecting products that are halfway through the production process
7. Inspecting incoming raw materials
8. Repairing defective units found during inspection
9. Incremental cost of using a higher-grade raw material
10. Redesigning the production process

S4-16 Quality initiative decision *(Learning Objective 5)*

Boswell manufactures high-quality speakers. Suppose Boswell is considering spending the following amounts on a new quality program:

Additional 20 minutes of testing for each speaker	$ 607,000
Negotiating with and training suppliers to obtain higher-quality materials and on-time delivery	$ 300,000
Redesigning the speakers to make them easier to manufacture	$1,402,000

Boswell expects this quality program to save costs as follows:

Reduced warranty repair costs	$205,000
Avoid inspection of raw materials	$403,000
Rework avoided because of fewer defective units	$652,000

It also expects this program to avoid lost profits from the following:

Lost sales due to disappointed customers	$853,000
Lost production time due to rework	$305,000

1. Classify each of these costs into one of the four categories of quality costs (prevention, appraisal, internal failure, external failure).
2. Should Boswell implement the quality program? Give your reasons.

S4-17 Assess the impact of a quality initiative *(Learning Objective 5)*

Dayton Industries is contemplating some operational changes to reduce its overall costs of quality. The company believes that if it upgrades one component of its product at an additional cost of $2.00 per unit, it will be able to decrease its current warranty repair rate by 90%. The company also believes it will be able to sell 1,000 more units over the next year due to an enhanced reputation for quality. Dayton currently has enough excess capacity to make the 1,000 extra units needed to meet the increased demand. The following data reflect current operations (*prior* to making the operational changes):

Current production and sales level (in units)	100,000
Sales price per unit	$150
Current variable cost of making and selling one unit	$ 80
Variable warranty repair costs per unit repaired	$ 30
Current warranty repair rate of units produced	10%

What is the anticipated annual effect on operating income from adopting this quality initiative? To answer this question, first calculate the total costs of quality before making the operational changes and then calculate the total costs of quality after making the operational changes. Compute the difference between the "before" and the "after."

S4-18 Identify ethical standards violated *(Learning Objectives 1, 2, 3, 4, & 5)* **ETHICS**

For each of the situations listed, identify the primary standard from the IMA *Statement of Ethical Professional Practice* that is violated (competence, confidentiality, integrity, or credibility). Refer to Exhibit 1-7 for the complete standard.

1. Alexandria receives an iPad from a salesperson at a lean consulting group. She keeps the iPad, even though she knows that her department will be responsible for selecting a consulting firm to come in to offer lean training sessions next year.
2. Bowes Company operates in a highly competitive environment and has developed some proprietary processes that allow it to maintain a market lead. Franklin, the CFO, does not have employees sign nondisclosure agreements because he feels that they are all family. He avoids talking about the topic.
3. Tammary Corporation has an activity-based costing system. Stephen prepares reports each month that are long and full of facts. The reports are hard to understand for anyone but Stephen.
4. Cliff, an accountant at the Wall Corporation, did not attend the training for the new activity-based costing system because he figures it will not be much different from the current allocation system.
5. Mack, the plant manager, does not disclose the quality issues he is aware of in the current production process. He figures that he can get them resolved in the next few months.

EXERCISES Group A

E4-19A Compare traditional and departmental cost allocations
(Learning Objective 1)

Sanderson's Fine Furnishings manufactures upscale custom furniture. Sanderson's currently uses a plantwide overhead rate based on direct labor hours to allocate its $1,000,000 of manufacturing overhead to individual jobs. However, Margaret Garmon, owner and CEO, is considering refining the company's costing system by using departmental overhead rates. Currently, the Machining Department incurs $660,000 of manufacturing overhead, while the Finishing Department incurs $340,000 of manufacturing overhead. Garmon has identified machine hours (MH) as the primary manufacturing overhead cost driver in the Machining Department and direct labor (DL) hours as the primary cost driver in the Finishing Department.

The Sanderson's plant completed Jobs 450 and 455 on May 15. Both jobs incurred a total of 5 DL hours throughout the entire production process. Job 450 incurred 3 MH in the Machining Department and 4 DL hours in the Finishing Department (the other DL hour occurred in the Machining Department). Job 455 incurred 4 MH in the Machining Department and 3 DL hours in the Finishing Department (the other two DL hours occurred in the Machining Department).

Requirements

1. Compute the plantwide overhead rate assuming that Sanderson's expects to incur 20,000 total DL hours during the year.
2. Compute departmental overhead rates assuming that Sanderson's expects to incur 15,000 MH in the Machining Department and 17,000 DL hours in the Finishing Department during the year.
3. If Sanderson's continues to use the plantwide overhead rate, how much manufacturing overhead would be allocated to Job 450 and Job 455?
4. If Sanderson's uses departmental overhead rates, how much manufacturing overhead would be allocated to Job 450 and Job 455?
5. Based on your answers to Requirements 3 and 4, does the plantwide overhead rate overcost or undercost either job? Explain. If Sanderson's sells its furniture at 125% of cost, will its choice of allocation systems affect product pricing? Explain.

E4-20A Compute activity rates and apply to jobs *(Learning Objective 2)*

Fuller Company uses ABC to account for its chrome wheel manufacturing process. Company managers have identified four manufacturing activities that incur manufacturing overhead costs: materials handling, machine setup, insertion of parts, and finishing. The budgeted activity costs for the upcoming year and their allocation bases are as follows:

Activity	Total Budgeted Manufacturing Overhead Cost	Allocation Base
Materials handling	$ 12,000	Number of parts
Machine setup	3,400	Number of setups
Insertion of parts	48,000	Number of parts
Finishing	80,000	Finishing direct labor hours
Total	$143,400	

Fuller Company expects to produce 1,000 chrome wheels during the year. The wheels are expected to use 3,000 parts, require 10 setups, and consume 2,000 hours of finishing time.

Job 420 used 200 parts, required 2 setups, and consumed 130 finishing hours.

Job 510 used 425 parts, required 4 setups, and consumed 350 finishing hours.

Requirements

1. Compute the cost allocation rate for each activity.
2. Compute the manufacturing overhead cost that should be assigned to Job 420.
3. Compute the manufacturing overhead cost that should be assigned to Job 510.

E4-21A Apply activity cost allocation rates *(Learning Objective 2)*

Holiday Industries manufactures a variety of custom products. The company has traditionally used a plantwide manufacturing overhead rate based on machine hours to allocate manufacturing overhead to its products. The company estimates that it will incur $970,000 in total manufacturing overhead costs in the upcoming year and will use 10,000 machine hours.

Up to this point, hazardous waste disposal fees have been absorbed into the plantwide manufacturing overhead rate and allocated to all products as part of the manufacturing overhead process. Recently, the company has been experiencing significantly increased waste-disposal fees for hazardous waste generated by certain products, and as a result, profit margins on all products have been negatively impacted. Company management wants to implement an activity-based costing system so that managers know the cost of each product, including its hazardous waste disposal costs.

Expected usage and costs for manufacturing overhead activities for the upcoming year are as follows:

Description of Cost Pool	Estimated Cost	Cost Driver	Estimated Activity for This Year
Machine maintenance costs	$ 400,000	Number of machine hours	10,000
Engineering change orders	$ 150,000	Number of change orders	3,000
Hazardous waste disposal	$ 420,000	Pounds of hazardous materials generated	1,500
Total overhead cost	$ 970,000		

During the year, Job 356 is started and completed. Usage for this job follows:

- 290 pounds of direct materials at $35 per pound
- 20 direct labor hours used at $20 per labor hour
- 60 machine hours used
- 9 change orders
- 60 pounds of hazardous waste generated

Requirements

1. Calculate the cost of Job 356 using the traditional plantwide manufacturing overhead rate based on machine hours.
2. Calculate the cost of Job 356 using activity-based costing.
3. If you were a manager, which cost estimate would provide you more useful information? How might you use this information?

E4-22A   Using ABC to bill clients at a service firm (Learning Objective 2)

Kushner & Company is an architectural firm specializing in home remodeling for private clients and new office buildings for corporate clients.

Kushner charges customers at a billing rate equal to 130% of the client's total job cost. A client's total job cost is a combination of (1) professional time spent on the client ($63 per hour cost of employing each professional) and (2) operating overhead allocated to the client's job. Kushner allocates operating overhead to jobs based on professional hours spent on the job. Kushner estimates its five professionals will incur a total of 10,000 professional hours working on client jobs during the year.

All operating costs other than professional salaries (travel reimbursements, copy costs, secretarial salaries, office lease, and so forth) can be assigned to the three activities. Total activity costs, cost drivers, and total usage of those cost drivers are estimated as follows:

Activity	Total Activity Cost	Cost Driver	Total Usage by Corporate Clients	Total Usage by Private Clients
Transportation to clients	$ 6,000	Round-trip mileage to clients	4,500 miles	10,500 miles
Blueprint copying	32,000	Number of copies	250 copies	750 copies
Office support	195,000	Secretarial time	2,500 secretarial hours	2,500 secretarial hours
Total operating overhead	$ 233,000			

Yimeng Li hired Kushner to design her kitchen remodeling. A total of 25 professional hours were incurred on this job. In addition, Li's remodeling job required one of the professionals to travel back and forth to her house for a total of 125 miles. The blueprints had to be copied four times because Li changed the plans several times. In addition, 15 hours of secretarial time were used lining up the subcontractors for the job.

Requirements

1. Calculate the current indirect cost allocation rate per professional hour.
2. Calculate the total amount that would be billed to Li given the current costing structure.
3. Calculate the activity cost allocation rates that could be used to allocate operating overhead costs to client jobs.
4. Calculate the amount that would be billed to Li using ABC costing.
5. Which type of billing system is more fair to clients? Explain.

E4-23A Compare traditional and ABC allocations at a pharmacy
(Learning Objective 2)

Dover Pharmacy, part of a large chain of pharmacies, fills a variety of prescriptions for customers. The complexity of prescriptions filled by Dover varies widely; pharmacists can spend between five minutes and six hours on a prescription order. Traditionally, the pharmacy has allocated its overhead based on the number of prescriptions.

The pharmacy chain's controller is exploring whether activity-based costing (ABC) may better allocate the pharmacy overhead costs to pharmacy orders. The controller has gathered the following information:

Cost Pools	Total Annual Estimated Cost	Cost Driver	Total Annual Estimated Cost Driver Activity
Pharmacy occupancy costs (utilities, rent, and other costs)	$ 102,000	Technician hours	85,000
Packaging supplies (bottles, bags, and other packaging)	$ 45,600	Number of prescriptions	24,000
Professional training and insurance costs	$ 180,000	Pharmacist hours	20,000
Total pharmacy overhead	$ 327,600		

The clerk for Dover has gathered the following information regarding two recent pharmacy orders:

Customer Order Number	Technician Hours	Number of Prescriptions	Pharmacist Hours
1247	0.5	4	1.0
1248	0.5	2	2.5

Requirements

1. What is the traditional overhead rate based on the number of prescriptions?
2. How much pharmacy overhead would be allocated to customer order number 1247 if traditional overhead allocation based on the number of prescriptions is used?
3. How much pharmacy overhead would be allocated to customer order number 1248 if traditional overhead allocation based on the number of prescriptions is used?
4. What are the following cost pool allocation rates?
   a. Pharmacy occupancy costs
   b. Packaging supplies
   c. Professional training and insurance costs
5. How much would be allocated to customer order number 1247 if activity-based costing (ABC) is used to allocate the pharmacy overhead costs?
6. How much would be allocated to customer order number 1248 if activity-based costing (ABC) is used to allocate the pharmacy overhead costs?
7. Which allocation method (traditional or activity-based costing) would produce a more accurate product cost? Explain your answer.

E4-24A Compare traditional and ABC allocations on a job (Learning Objective 2)

Radley Products has adopted an ABC costing system. The following manufacturing activities, indirect manufacturing costs, and cost drivers have been identified:

Activity	Total estimated MOH costs related to activity	Total estimated amount of allocation base activity
Machine setup	$ 120,000	2,000 setups
Machining	$1,050,000	6,000 machine hours
Polishing	$ 80,000	10,000 polishing cloths
Quality control	$ 280,000	4,000 tests run
Facility-level costs	$ 120,000	50,000 DL hours
Total manufacturing overhead (MOH)	$1,650,000	

The Job Cost Record for Job #624 revealed that direct materials requisitioned for the job totaled $1,050. The Job Cost Record also showed that direct labor for this job totaled 10 hours at a wage rate of $25 per hour.

Other data collected on the resources used by Job #624 included:

- 1 machine setup required
- 5 machine hours
- 2 polishing cloths
- 2 quality control tests run

Requirements

1. Calculate the activity cost allocation rate for each of the five pools listed in the table.
2. Calculate the total cost of Job #624 (use an ABC costing system).
3. Why would ABC provide a more accurate allocation of manufacturing overhead (MOH) than a plantwide rate?
4. Assume that Radley Products used a traditional costing system rather than an ABC system. Its plantwide MOH rate would have been determined using direct labor (DL) hours as the allocation base. How much cost distortion would have occurred on this job?

E4-25A Use ABC to allocate manufacturing overhead (Learning Objective 2)

Several years after reengineering its production process, Dettling Corporation hired a new controller, Alana Metzgar. She developed an ABC system very similar to the one used by Dettling's chief rival. Part of the reason Metzgar developed the ABC system was because Dettling's profits had been declining, even though the company had shifted its product mix toward the product that had appeared most profitable under the old system. Before adopting the new ABC system, the company had used a plantwide overhead rate based on direct labor hours that was developed years ago.

For the upcoming year, Dettling's budgeted ABC manufacturing overhead allocation rates are as follows:

Activity	Allocation Base	Activity Cost Allocation Rate
Materials handling	Number of parts	$ 4.50 per part
Machine setup	Number of setups	$325.00 per setup
Insertion of parts	Number of parts	$ 31.00 per part
Finishing	Finishing direct labor hours	$ 51.00 per hour

The number of parts is now a feasible allocation base because Dettling recently installed a plantwide computer system. Dettling produces two wheel models: Standard and Deluxe. Budgeted data for the upcoming year are as follows:

	Standard	Deluxe
Parts per wheel	4.0	6.0
Setups per 1,000 wheels	20.0	20.0
Finishing direct labor hours per wheel	1.0	3.0
Total direct labor hours per wheel	2.7	3.8

The company's managers expect to produce 1,000 units of each model during the year.

Requirements

1. Compute the total budgeted manufacturing overhead cost for the upcoming year.
2. Compute the manufacturing overhead cost per wheel of each model using ABC.
3. Compute the company's traditional plantwide overhead rate. Use this rate to determine the manufacturing overhead cost per wheel under the traditional system.

E4-26A Continuation of E4-25A: Determine product profitability
(Learning Objectives 2 & 3)

Refer to your answers in E4-25A. In addition to the manufacturing overhead costs, the following data are budgeted for the company's Standard and Deluxe models for next year:

	Standard	Deluxe
Sales price per wheel	$460.00	$630.00
Direct materials per wheel	$ 33.50	$ 48.00
Direct labor per wheel	$ 45.70	$ 52.00

Requirements

1. Compute the gross profit per wheel if managers rely on the ABC unit cost data computed in E4-25A.
2. Compute the gross profit per wheel if the managers rely on the plantwide allocation cost data.
3. Which product line is more profitable for the company?
4. Why might the controller have expected ABC to pass the cost-benefit test? Were there any warning signs that the company's old direct-labor-based allocation system was broken?

E4-27A Differentiate between traditional and lean operations *(Learning Objective 4)*

Categorize each of the following characteristics as being either more representative of a traditional organization or a lean organization.

1. Manufacturing plants tend to be organized with self-contained production cells.
2. Maintain greater quantities of raw materials, work in process, and finished goods inventories.
3. Setup times are longer.
4. High quality is stressed in every aspect of production.
5. Produce in smaller batches.
6. Emphasis is placed on shortening manufacturing cycle times.
7. Manufacturing plants tend to group like machinery together in different parts of the plant.
8. Setup times are shorter.
9. Produce in larger batches.
10. Strive to maintain low inventory levels.
11. Cycle time tends to be longer.
12. Quality tends to be "inspect-in" rather than "build-in."

E4-28A Classify costs and make a quality-initiative decision *(Learning Objective 5)*

Sinclair Corp. manufactures radiation-shielding glass panels. Suppose Sinclair is considering spending the following amounts on a new TQM program:

Strength-testing one item from each batch of panels	$63,000
Training employees in TQM	$27,000
Training suppliers in TQM	$39,000
Identifying preferred suppliers that commit to on-time delivery of perfect quality materials	$52,000

Sinclair expects the new program to save costs through the following:

Avoid lost profits from lost sales due to disappointed customers	$93,000
Avoid rework and spoilage	$64,000
Avoid inspection of raw materials	$52,000
Avoid warranty costs	$19,000

Requirements

1. Classify each item as a prevention cost, an appraisal cost, an internal failure cost, or an external failure cost.
2. Should Sinclair implement the new quality program? Give your reason.

E4-29A Prepare a Costs of Quality report *(Learning Objective 5)*

Goodchill Industries manufactures freezers. Here is some information about its "LX17" line of freezers over the past year:

Number of units manufactured and sold	5,000 units
Selling price per unit	$1,500
Variable manufacturing *and* selling costs per unit	$800
Hours spent by engineers improving design	1,000
Testing and inspection hours per unit	0.5 hours
Percentage of units reworked in the plant after inspection	10%
Average variable rework costs per freezer	$400
Percentage of units repaired under warranty at customers' homes	8%
Average variable repair costs at customers' homes per freezer	$450
Estimated lost sales due to quality reputation	300 units
Design engineer's labor rate (includes benefits and payroll taxes)	$75 per hour
Inspection costs per hour	$40 per hour

Requirements

1. Prepare a Cost of Quality (COQ) report. In addition to calculating the total costs of each category, calculate the percentage of each COQ category of the total COQ.
2. Why would the variable repair cost at the customers' home generally be higher than the "in factory" rework cost?
3. How can use of the COQ report lead to improvements in the production process or in the quality of the product itself?

EXERCISES Group B

E4-30B Compare traditional and departmental cost allocations
(Learning Objective 1)

Albertson's Fine Furnishings manufactures upscale custom furniture. Albertson's currently uses a plantwide overhead rate, based on direct labor hours, to allocate its $1,100,000 of manufacturing overhead to individual jobs. However, Debbie Howard, owner and CEO, is considering refining the company's costing system by using departmental overhead rates. Currently, the Machining Department incurs $740,000 of manufacturing overhead, while the Finishing Department incurs $360,000 of manufacturing overhead. Howard has identified machine hours (MH) as the primary manufacturing overhead cost driver in the Machining Department and direct labor (DL) hours as the primary cost driver in the Finishing Department.

Albertson's plant completed Jobs 450 and 455 on May 15. Both jobs incurred a total of 5 DL hours throughout the entire production process. Job 450 incurred 2 MH in the Machining Department and 4 DL hours in the Finishing Department (the other DL hour occurred in the Machining Department). Job 455 incurred 7 MH in the Machining Department and 3 DL hours in the Finishing Department (the other two DL hours occurred in the Machining Department).

Requirements

1. Compute the plantwide overhead rate, assuming Albertson's expects to incur 27,500 total DL hours during the year.
2. Compute departmental overhead rates, assuming Albertson's expects to incur 14,800 MH in the Machining Department and 18,000 DL hours in the Finishing Department during the year.

3. If the company continues to use the plantwide overhead rate, how much manufacturing overhead would be allocated to Job 450 and Job 455?
4. If the company uses departmental overhead rates, how much manufacturing overhead would be allocated to Job 450 and Job 455?
5. Based on your answers to Requirements 3 and 4, does the plantwide overhead rate overcost or undercost either of the jobs? Explain. If the company sells its furniture at 125% of cost, will its choice of allocation systems affect product pricing? Explain.

E4-31B Compute activity rates and apply to jobs *(Learning Objective 2)*

Farraway Company uses ABC to account for its chrome wheel manufacturing process. Company managers have identified four manufacturing activities that incur manufacturing overhead costs: materials handling, machine setup, insertion of parts, and finishing. The budgeted activity costs for the upcoming year and their allocation bases are as follows:

Activity	Total Budgeted Manufacturing Overhead Cost	Allocation Base
Materials handling	$ 13,200	Number of parts
Machine setup	5,200	Number of setups
Insertion of parts	49,500	Number of parts
Finishing	86,100	Finishing direct labor hours
Total	$154,000	

Farraway expects to produce 1,000 chrome wheels during the year. The wheels are expected to use 3,300 parts, require 20 setups, and consume 2,100 hours of finishing time.

Job 420 used 200 parts, required 2 setups, and consumed 150 finishing hours.
Job 510 used 400 parts, required 4 setups, and consumed 320 finishing hours.

Requirements

1. Compute the cost allocation rate for each activity.
2. Compute the manufacturing overhead cost that should be assigned to Job 420.
3. Compute the manufacturing overhead cost that should be assigned to Job 510.

E4-32B Apply activity cost allocation rates *(Learning Objective 2)*

Newman Industries manufactures a variety of custom products. The company has traditionally used a plantwide manufacturing overhead rate based on machine hours to allocate manufacturing overhead to its products. The company estimates that it will incur $1,440,000 in total manufacturing overhead costs in the upcoming year and will use 12,000 machine hours.

Up to this point, hazardous waste disposal fees have been absorbed into the plantwide manufacturing overhead rate and allocated to all products as part of the manufacturing overhead process. Recently, the company has been experiencing significantly increased waste-disposal fees for hazardous waste generated by certain products, and, as a result, profit margins on all products have been negatively impacted. Company management wants to implement an activity-based costing system so that managers know the cost of each product, including its hazardous waste-disposal costs.

Expected usage and costs for manufacturing overhead activities for the upcoming year are as follows:

Description of Cost Pool	Estimated Cost	Cost Driver	Estimated Activity for this Year
Machine maintenance costs	$ 840,000	Number of machine hours	12,000
Engineering change orders	20,000	Number of change orders	1,000
Hazardous waste disposal	580,000	Pounds of hazardous materials generated	2,000
Total overhead cost	$1,440,000		

During the year, Job 356 is started and completed. Usage data for this job are as follows:

> 250 pounds of direct materials at $45 per pound
> 60 direct labor hours used at $25 per labor hour
> 90 machine hours used
> 6 change orders
> 30 pounds of hazardous waste generated

Requirements

1. Calculate the cost of Job 356 using the traditional plantwide manufacturing overhead rate based on machine hours.
2. Calculate the cost of Job 356 using activity-based costing.
3. If you were a manager, which cost estimate would provide you more useful information? How might you use this information?

E4-33B Using ABC to bill clients at a service firm *(Learning Objective 2)*

Warren & Company is an architectural firm specializing in home remodeling for private clients and new office buildings for corporate clients.

Warren charges customers at a billing rate equal to 126% of the client's total job cost. A client's total job cost is a combination of 1) professional time spent on the client ($63 per hour cost of employing each professional) and 2) operating overhead allocated to the client's job. Warren allocates operating overhead to jobs based on professional hours spent on the job. Warren estimates its five professionals will incur a total of 10,000 professional hours working on client jobs during the year.

All operating costs other than professional salaries (travel reimbursements, copy costs, secretarial salaries, office lease, and so forth) can be assigned to the three activities. Total activity costs, cost drivers, and total usage of those cost drivers are estimated as follows:

Activity	Total Activity Cost	Cost Driver	Total Usage by Corporate Clients	Total Usage by Private Clients
Transportation to clients	$ 12,000	Round-trip mileage to clients	4,500 miles	10,500 miles
Blueprint copying	32,000	Number of copies	500 copies	500 copies
Office support	185,000	Secretarial time	2,900 secretarial hours	2,100 secretarial hours
Total operating overhead	$229,000			

Meredith Blaz hired Warren & Company to design her kitchen remodeling. A total of 20 professional hours were incurred on this job. In addition, Blaz's remodeling job required one of the professionals to travel back and forth to her house for a total of 140 miles. The blueprints had to be copied four times because Blaz changed the plans several times. In addition, 20 hours of secretarial time were used lining up the subcontractors for the job.

Requirements

1. Calculate the current operating overhead allocation rate per professional hour.
2. Calculate the total amount that would be billed to Meredith Blaz given the current costing structure.
3. Calculate the activity cost allocation rates that could be used to allocate operating overhead costs to client jobs.
4. Calculate the amount that would be billed to Meredith Blaz using ABC costing.
5. Which type of billing system is more fair to clients? Explain.

E4-34B Compare traditional and ABC cost allocations at a pharmacy
(Learning Objective 2)

Gracen Pharmacy, part of a large chain of pharmacies, fills a variety of prescriptions for customers. The complexity of prescriptions filled by Gracen varies widely; pharmacists can spend between five minutes and six hours on a prescription order. Traditionally, the pharmacy has allocated its overhead based on the number of prescriptions.

The pharmacy chain's controller is exploring whether activity-based costing (ABC) may better allocate the pharmacy overhead costs to pharmacy orders. The controller has gathered the following information:

Cost Pools	Total Annual Estimated Cost	Cost Driver	Total Annual Estimated Cost Driver Activity
Pharmacy occupancy costs (utilities, rent, and other costs)	$ 36,000	Technician hours	90,000
Packaging supplies (bottles, bags, and other packaging)	39,100	Number of prescriptions	23,000
Professional training and insurance costs	125,000	Pharmacist hours	25,000
Total pharmacy overhead	$ 200,100		

The clerk for Gracen Pharmacy has gathered the following information regarding two recent pharmacy orders:

Customer Order Number	Technician Hours	Number of Prescriptions	Pharmacist Hours
1102	0.5	3	2.0
1103	0.5	1	2.5

Requirements

1. What is the traditional overhead rate based on the number of prescriptions?
2. How much pharmacy overhead would be allocated to customer order number 1102 if traditional overhead allocation based on the number of prescriptions is used?
3. How much pharmacy overhead would be allocated to customer order number 1103 if traditional overhead allocation based on the number of prescriptions is used?
4. What are the following cost pool allocation rates?
   a. Pharmacy occupancy costs
   b. Packing supplies
   c. Professional training and insurance costs
5. How much would be allocated to customer order number 1102 if activity-based costing (ABC) is used to allocate the pharmacy overhead costs?
6. How much would be allocated to customer order number 1103 if activity-based costing (ABC) is used to allocate the pharmacy overhead costs?
7. Which allocation method (traditional or activity-based costing) would produce a more accurate product cost? Explain your answer.

E4-35B Compare traditional and ABC allocations on a job *(Learning Objective 2)*

Cornwell Products has adopted an ABC costing system. The following manufacturing activities, indirect manufacturing costs, and cost drivers have been identified:

Activity	Total estimated MOH costs related to activity	Total estimated amount of allocation base activity
Machine setup	$ 180,000	2,000 setups
Machining	$1,050,000	12,000 machine hours
Polishing	$ 100,000	5,000 polishing cloths
Quality control	$ 320,000	4,000 tests run
Facility-level costs	$ 150,000	50,000 DL hours
Total manufacturing overhead (MOH)	$1,800,000	

The Job Cost Record for Job #804 revealed that direct materials requisitioned for the job totaled $1,250. The Job Cost Record also showed that direct labor for this job totaled 12 hours at a wage rate of $30 per hour.

Other data collected on the resources used by Job #804 included:

- 1 machine setup required
- 6 machine hours
- 4 polishing cloths
- 3 quality control tests run

Requirements

1. Calculate the activity cost allocation rate for each of the five pools listed in the table.
2. Calculate the total cost of Job #804 (use an ABC costing system).
3. Why would ABC provide a more accurate allocation of manufacturing overhead (MOH) than a plantwide rate?
5. Assume that Cornwell Products used a traditional costing system rather than an ABC system. Its plantwide MOH rate would have been determined using direct labor (DL) hours as the allocation base. How much cost distortion would have occurred on this job?

E4-36B Use ABC to allocate manufacturing overhead *(Learning Objective 2)*

Several years after reengineering its production process, King Corporation hired a new controller, Christine Erickson. She developed an ABC system very similar to the one used by King's chief rival. Part of the reason Erickson developed the ABC system was because King's profits had been declining, even though the company had shifted its product mix toward the product that had appeared most profitable under the old system. Before adopting the new ABC system, the company had used a plantwide overhead rate, based on direct labor hours developed years ago.

For the upcoming year, King's budgeted ABC manufacturing overhead allocation rates are as follows:

Activity	Allocation Base	Activity Cost Allocation Rate
Materials handling	Number of parts	$ 4.00 per part
Machine setup	Number of setups	$375.00 per setup
Insertion of parts	Number of parts	$ 28.00 per part
Finishing	Finishing direct labor hours	$ 54.00 per hour

The number of parts is now a feasible allocation base because King recently purchased bar-coding technology. King produces two wheel models: Standard and Deluxe. Budgeted data for the upcoming year are as follows:

	Standard	Deluxe
Parts per wheel	8.0	10.0
Setups per 1,000 wheels	20.0	20.0
Finishing direct labor hours per wheel	2.0	3.5
Total direct labor hours per wheel	2.6	3.4

The company's managers expect to produce 1,000 units of each model during the year.

Requirements

1. Compute the total budgeted manufacturing overhead cost for the upcoming year.
2. Compute the manufacturing overhead cost per wheel of each model using ABC.
3. Compute the company's traditional plantwide overhead rate. Use this rate to determine the manufacturing overhead cost per wheel under the traditional system.

E4-37B Continuation of E4-36B Determine product profitability
(Learning Objectives 2 & 3)

Refer to your answers in E4-36B. In addition to the manufacturing overhead costs, the following data are budgeted for the company's Standard and Deluxe models for next year:

	Standard	Deluxe
Sales price per wheel	$575.00	$735.00
Direct materials per wheel	$ 33.00	$ 46.75
Direct labor per wheel	$ 45.90	$ 54.00

Requirements

1. Compute the gross profit per wheel if managers rely on the ABC unit cost data.
2. Compute the gross profit per unit if the managers rely on the plantwide allocation cost data.
3. Which product line is more profitable for the company?
4. Why might the controller have expected ABC to pass the cost-benefit test? Were there any warning signs that the company's old direct-labor-based allocation system was broken?

E4-38B Differentiate between traditional and lean production
(Learning Objective 4)

Categorize each of the following characteristics as being either more representative of a traditional organization or a lean organization.

1. High quality is stressed in every aspect of production.
2. Manufacturing plants tend to group like machinery together in different parts of the plant.
3. Setup times are longer.
4. Strive to maintain low inventory levels.
5. Setup times are shorter.
6. Produce in smaller batches.
7. Manufacturing plants tend to be organized with self-contained production cells.
8. Quality tends to be "inspect-in" rather than "build-in."
9. Maintain greater quantities of raw materials, work in process, and finished goods inventories.
10. Emphasis is placed on shortening manufacturing cycle times.
11. Produce in larger batches.
12. Cycle time tends to be longer.

E4-39B Classify costs and make a quality-initiative decision *(Learning Objective 5)*

Bradshaw Corp. manufactures radiation-shielding glass panels. Suppose the company is considering spending the following amounts on a new TQM program:

Strength-testing one item from each batch of panels	$62,000
Training employees in TQM	$21,000
Training suppliers in TQM	$31,000
Identifying preferred suppliers that commit to on-time delivery of perfect quality materials	$55,000

The company expects the new program would save costs through the following:

Avoid lost profits from lost sales due to disappointed customers	$89,000
Avoid rework and spoilage	$65,000
Avoid inspection of raw materials	$50,000
Avoid warranty costs	$25,000

Requirements

1. Classify each item as a prevention cost, an appraisal cost, an internal failure cost, or an external failure cost.
2. Should the company implement the new quality program? Give your reason.

E4-40B Prepare a Costs of Quality report *(Learning Objective 5)*

Frostline Industries manufactures freezers. Here is some information about its "LX17" line of freezers over the past year:

Number of units manufactured and sold	6,000 units
Selling price per unit	$1,800
Variable manufacturing *and* selling costs per unit	$700
Hours spent by engineers improving design	1,000
Testing and inspection hours per unit	1.0 hours
Percentage of units reworked in the plant after inspection	10%
Average variable rework costs per freezer	$600
Percentage of units repaired under warranty at customers' homes	8%
Average variable repair costs at customers' homes per freezer	$650
Estimated lost sales due to quality reputation	400 units
Design engineer's labor rate (includes benefits and payroll taxes)	$85 per hour
Inspection costs per hour	$45 per hour

Requirements

1. Prepare a Cost of Quality (COQ) report. In addition to calculating the total costs of each category, calculate the percentage of each COQ category of the total COQ.
2. Why would the variable repair cost at the customers' homes generally be higher than the "in factory" rework cost?
3. How can use of the COQ report lead to improvements in the production process or in the quality of the product itself?

PROBLEMS Group A

P4-41A Implementation and analysis of departmental rates *(Learning Objective 1)*

Hughes Products manufactures its products in two separate departments: Machining and Assembly. Total manufacturing overhead costs for the year are budgeted at $1,056,000. Of this amount, the Machining Department incurs $600,000 (primarily for machine operation and depreciation), while the Assembly Department incurs $456,000. The company estimates that it will incur 4,000 machine hours (all in the Machining Department) and 9,600 direct labor hours (1,600 in the Machining Department and 8,000 in the Assembly Department) during the year.

Hughes Products currently uses a plantwide overhead rate based on direct labor hours to allocate overhead. However, the company is considering refining its overhead allocation system by using departmental overhead rates. The Machining Department would allocate its overhead using machine hours (MH), but the Assembly Department would allocate its overhead using direct labor (DL) hours.

The following chart shows the machine hours (MH) and direct labor (DL) hours incurred by Jobs 500 and 501 in each production department:

	Machining Department	Assembly Department
Job 500	10 MH 2 DL hours	15 DL hours
Job 501	20 MH 2 DL hours	15 DL hours

Both Jobs 500 and 501 used $1,000 of direct materials. Wages and benefits total $30 per direct labor hour. Hughes Products prices its products at 120% of total manufacturing costs.

Requirements

1. Compute the company's current plantwide overhead rate.
2. Compute refined departmental overhead rates.
3. Which job (Job 500 or Job 501) uses more of the company's resources? Explain.
4. Compute the total amount of overhead allocated to each job if the company uses its current plantwide overhead rate.
5. Compute the total amount of overhead allocated to each job if the company uses departmental overhead rates.
6. Do both allocation systems accurately reflect the resources that each job used? Explain.
7. Compute the total manufacturing cost and sales price of each job using the company's current plantwide overhead rate.
8. Based on the current (plantwide) allocation system, how much profit did the company *think* it earned on each job? Based on the departmental overhead rates and the sales price determined in Requirement 7, how much profit did it *really* earn on each job?
9. Compare and comment on the results you obtained in Requirements 7 and 8.

P4-42A Use ABC to compute full product costs *(Learning Objective 2)*

Arnett Corp. manufactures computer desks in its White Bear Lake, Minnesota, plant. The company uses activity-based costing to allocate all manufacturing conversion costs (direct labor and manufacturing overhead). Its activities and related data follow:

Activity	Budgeted Cost of Activity	Allocation Base	Cost Allocation Rate
Materials handling	$ 330,000	Number of parts	$ 0.80
Assembling	$2,500,000	Direct labor hours	$12.00
Painting	$ 170,000	Number of painted desks	$ 4.90

Arnett produced two styles of desks in March: the Standard desk and the Unpainted desk. Data for each follow:

Product	Total Units Produced	Total Direct Materials Costs	Total Number of Parts	Total Assembling Direct Labor Hours
Standard desk	7,500	$178,950	118,500	6,000
Unpainted desk	1,500	$ 6,300	28,500	1,200

Requirements

1. Compute the per-unit manufacturing product cost of Standard desks and Unpainted desks.
2. Premanufacturing activities, such as product design, were assigned to the Standard desks at $6 each and to the Unpainted desks at $2 each. Similar analyses were conducted of post-manufacturing activities, such as distribution, marketing, and customer service. The post-manufacturing costs were $22 per Standard and $19 per Unpainted desk. Compute the full product costs per desk.
3. Which product costs are reported in the external financial statements? Which costs are used for management decision making? Explain the difference.
4. What price should Arnett's managers set for Standard desks to earn a $42 profit per desk?

P4-43A Comprehensive ABC implementation *(Learning Objectives 2 & 3)*

Durbin Pharmaceuticals manufactures an over-the-counter allergy medication called Breathe. Durbin is trying to win market share from Sudafed and Tylenol. The company has developed several different Breathe products tailored to specific markets. For example, the company sells large commercial containers of 1,000 capsules to health-care facilities and travel packs of 20 capsules to shops in airports, train stations, and hotels.

Durbin's controller, Katarina Hoffman, has just returned from a conference on ABC. She asks Bradley Williams, supervisor of the Breathe product line, to help her develop an ABC system. Hoffman and Williams identify the following activities, related costs, and cost allocation bases:

	Estimated Indirect Activity Costs	Allocation Base	Estimated Quantity of Allocation Base
Materials handling	$160,000	Kilos	20,000 kilos
Packaging	390,000	Machine hours	2,000 hours
Quality assurance	112,000	Samples	1,600 samples
Total indirect costs	$662,000		

The commercial-container Breathe product line had a total weight of 8,700 kilos, used 900 machine hours, and required 270 samples. The travel-pack line had a total weight of 4,450 kilos, used 300 machine hours, and required 370 samples. Durbin produced 3,000 commercial containers of Breathe and 20,000 travel packs.

Requirements

1. Compute the cost allocation rate for each activity.
2. Use the activity-based cost allocation rates to compute the indirect cost of each unit of the commercial containers and the travel packs. (*Hint:* Compute the total activity costs allocated to each product line and then compute the cost per unit.)
3. The company's original single-allocation-based cost system allocated indirect costs to products at $350 per machine hour. Compute the total indirect costs allocated to the commercial containers and to the travel packs under the original system. Then compute the indirect cost per unit for each product.
4. Compare the activity-based costs per unit to the costs from the original system. How have the unit costs changed? Explain why the costs changed as they did.

P4-44A Using ABC in conjunction with quality decisions *(Learning Objectives 2 & 5)*

Giant Construction Toys Corp. is using a costs-of-quality approach to evaluate design engineering efforts for a new toy robot. The company's senior managers expect the engineering work to reduce appraisal, internal failure, and external failure activities. The predicted reductions in activities over the two-year life of the toy robot follow. Also shown are the cost allocation rates for the activities.

Activity	Predicted Reduction in Activity Units	Activity Cost Allocation Rate per Unit
Inspection of incoming materials	390	$19
Inspection of finished goods	390	$33
Number of defective units discovered in-house	3,500	$17
Number of defective units discovered by customers	875	$43
Lost sales to dissatisfied customers	310	$61

Requirements

1. Calculate the predicted quality cost savings from the design engineering work.
2. The company spent $70,000 on design engineering for the new toy robot. What is the net benefit of this "preventive" quality activity?
3. What major difficulty would management have had in implementing this costs-of-quality approach? What alternative approach could it use to measure quality improvement?

P4-45A Comprehensive ABC *(Learning Objectives 2 & 3)*

Workflow Systems specializes in servers for work-group, e-commerce, and enterprise resource planning (ERP) applications. The company's original job cost system has two direct cost categories: direct materials and direct labor. Overhead is allocated to jobs at the single rate of $27 per direct labor hour.

A task force headed by Workflow's CFO recently designed an ABC system with four activities. The ABC system retains the current system's two direct cost categories. Thus, it budgets only overhead costs for each activity. Pertinent data follow:

Activity	Allocation Base	Cost Allocation Rate
Materials handling	Number of parts	$ 1.10
Machine setup	Number of setups	$ 470.00
Assembling	Assembling hours	$ 120.00
Shipping	Number of shipments	$1,280.00

Workflow Systems has been awarded two new contracts that will be produced as Job A and Job B. Budget data relating to the contracts follow:

	Job A	Job B
Number of parts	17,000	4,000
Number of setups	6	2
Number of assembling hours	1,700	400
Number of shipments	1	1
Total direct labor hours	9,900	880
Number of output units	100	20
Direct materials cost	$195,700	$100,640
Direct labor cost	$155,000	$25,000

Requirements

1. Compute the product cost per unit for each job using the original costing system (with two direct cost categories and a single overhead allocation rate).
2. Suppose Workflow Systems adopts the ABC system. Compute the product cost per unit for each job using ABC.
3. Which costing system more accurately assigns to jobs the costs of the resources consumed to produce them? Explain.
4. A dependable company has offered to produce both jobs for Workflow for $6,000 per output unit. Workflow may outsource (buy from the outside company) Job A only, Job B only, or both jobs. Which course of action will Workflow managers take if they base their decision on (a) the original system? (b) ABC system costs? Which course of action will yield more income? Explain.

PROBLEMS Group B

P4-46B Implementation and analysis of departmental rates *(Learning Objective 1)*

Powell Products manufactures its products in two separate departments: Machining and Assembly. Total manufacturing overhead costs for the year are budgeted at $1,050,000. Of this amount, the Machining Department incurs $650,000 (primarily for machine operation and depreciation) while the Assembly Department incurs $400,000. The company estimates it will incur 5,000 machine hours (all in the Machining Department) and 10,000 direct labor hours (2,000 in the Machining Department and 8,000 in the Assembly Department) during the year.

Powell currently uses a plantwide overhead rate based on direct labor hours to allocate overhead. However, the company is considering refining its overhead allocation system by using departmental overhead rates. The Machining Department would allocate its overhead using machine hours (MH), but the Assembly Department would allocate its overhead using direct labor (DL) hours.

The following chart shows the machine hours (MH) and direct labor (DL) hours incurred by Jobs 500 and 501 in each production department.

	Machining Department	Assembly Department
Job 500	4 MH 2 DL hours	10 DL hours
Job 501	8 MH 2 DL hours	10 DL hours

Both Jobs 500 and 501 used $1,000 of direct materials. Wages and benefits total $20 per direct labor hour. Powell prices its products at 110% of total manufacturing costs.

Requirements

1. Compute the company's current plantwide overhead rate.
2. Compute refined departmental overhead rates.
3. Which job (Job 500 or Job 501) uses more of the company's resources? Explain.
4. Compute the total amount of overhead allocated to each job if the company uses its current plantwide overhead rate.
5. Compute the total amount of overhead allocated to each job if the company uses departmental overhead rates.
6. Do both allocation systems accurately reflect the resources that each job used? Explain.
7. Compute the total manufacturing cost and sales price of each job using the company's current plantwide overhead rate.
8. Based on the current (plantwide) allocation system, how much profit did the company *think* it earned on each job? Based on the departmental overhead rates and the sales price determined in Requirement 7, how much profit did it *really* earn on each job?
9. Compare and comment on the results you obtained in Requirements 7 and 8.

P4-47B Use ABC to compute full product costs *(Learning Objective 2)*

Kimbro Furniture manufactures computer desks in its Austin, Texas, plant. The company uses activity-based costing to allocate all manufacturing conversion costs (direct labor and manufacturing overhead). Its activities and related data follow:

Activity	Budgeted Cost of Activity	Allocation Base	Cost Allocation Rate
Materials handling	$ 310,000	Number of parts	$ 0.90
Assembling	$2,400,000	Direct labor hours	$17.00
Painting	$ 190,000	Number of painted desks	$ 5.00

The company produced two styles of desks in March: the Standard desk and the Unpainted desk. Data for each follow:

Product	Total Units Produced	Total Direct Materials Costs	Total Number of Parts	Total Assembling Direct Labor Hours
Standard desk	7,500	$165,450	119,500	6,000
Unpainted desk	1,500	$ 21,350	29,500	800

Requirements

1. Compute the per-unit manufacturing product cost of Standard desks and Unpainted desks.
2. Premanufacturing activities, such as product design, were assigned to the Standard desks at $4 each and to the Unpainted desks at $2 each. Similar analyses were conducted of post-manufacturing activities such as distribution, marketing, and customer service. The post-manufacturing costs were $21 per Standard and $19 per Unpainted desk. Compute the full product costs per desk.
3. Which product costs are reported in the external financial statements? Which costs are used for management decision making? Explain the difference.
4. What price should management set for Standard desks to earn a $39 profit per desk?

P4-48B Comprehensive ABC implementation (Learning Objectives 2 & 3)

Percival Pharmaceuticals manufactures an over-the-counter allergy medication called Breathe. Percival is trying to win market share from Sudafed and Tylenol. The company has developed several different Breathe products tailored to specific markets. For example, the company sells large commercial containers of 1,000 capsules to healthcare facilities and travel packs of 20 capsules to shops in airports, train stations, and hotels.

Percival's controller, Donna Swanson, has just returned from a conference on ABC. She asks Carol Yost, supervisor of the Breathe product line, to help her develop an ABC system. Swanson and Yost identify the following activities, related costs, and cost allocation bases:

Activity	Estimated Indirect Activity Costs	Allocation Base	Estimated Quantity of Allocation Base
Materials handling	$180,000	Kilos	18,000 kilos
Packaging	460,000	Machine hours	2,600 hours
Quality assurance	116,000	Samples	1,500 samples
Total indirect costs	$756,000		

The commercial-container Breathe product line had a total weight of 8,500 kilos, used 1,200 machine hours, and 240 required samples. The travel-pack line had a total weight of 6,000 kilos, used 400 machine hours, and required 340 samples. The company produced 2,500 commercial containers of Breathe and 80,000 travel packs.

Requirements

1. Compute the cost allocation rate for each activity.
2. Use the activity-based cost allocation rates to compute the indirect cost of each unit of the commercial containers and the travel packs. (*Hint:* Compute the total activity costs allocated to each product line and then compute the cost per unit.)
3. The company's original single-allocation-based cost system allocated indirect costs to products at $350 per machine hour. Compute the total indirect costs allocated to the commercial containers and to the travel packs under the original system. Then, compute the indirect cost per unit for each product.
4. Compare the activity-based costs per unit to the costs from the simpler original system. How have the unit costs changed? Explain why the costs changed as they did.

P4-49B Using ABC in conjunction with quality decisions
(Learning Objectives 2 & 5)

Big Yellow Construction Toys Corporation is using a costs-of-quality approach to evaluate design engineering efforts for a new toy robot. The company's senior managers expect the engineering work to reduce appraisal, internal failure, and external failure activities. The predicted reductions in activities over the two-year life of the toy robot follow. Also shown are the cost allocation rates for the activities.

Activity	Predicted Reduction in Activity Units	Activity Cost Allocation Rate per Unit
Inspection of incoming materials	305	$22
Inspection of finished goods	305	$34
Number of defective units discovered in-house	3,100	$11
Number of defective units discovered by customers	825	$41
Lost sales to dissatisfied customers	280	$58

Requirements

1. Calculate the predicted quality cost savings from the design engineering work.
2. The company spent $65,000 on design engineering for the new toy robot. What is the net benefit of this "preventive" quality activity?
3. What major difficulty would management have had in implementing this costs-of-quality approach? What alternative approach could it use to measure quality improvement?

P4-50B Comprehensive ABC *(Learning Objectives 2 & 3)*

FirstServer Systems specializes in servers for work-group, e-commerce, and enterprise resource planning (ERP) applications. The company's original job cost system has two direct cost categories: direct materials and direct labor. Overhead is allocated to jobs at the single rate of $20 per direct labor hour.

A task force headed by FirstServer's CFO recently designed an ABC system with four activities. The ABC system retains the current system's two direct cost categories. Thus, it budgets only overhead costs for each activity. Pertinent data follow:

Activity	Allocation Base	Cost Allocation Rate
Materials handling	Number of parts	$ 1.10
Machine setup	Number of setups	$ 500.00
Assembling	Assembling hours	$ 80.00
Shipping	Number of shipments	$1,700.00

FirstServer Systems has been awarded two new contracts that will be produced as Job A and Job B. Budget data relating to the contracts follow:

	Job A	Job B
Number of parts	10,000	2,000
Number of setups	20	8
Number of assembling hours	1,000	200
Number of shipments	1	1
Total direct labor hours	9,200	500
Number of output units	100	10
Direct materials cost	$246,000	$46,900
Direct labor cost	$180,000	$18,000

Requirements

1. Compute the product cost per unit for each job using the original costing system (with two direct cost categories and a single overhead allocation rate).
2. Suppose FirstServer Systems adopts the ABC system. Compute the product cost per unit for each job using ABC.
3. Which costing system more accurately assigns to jobs the costs of the resources consumed to produce them? Explain.
4. A dependable company has offered to produce both jobs for FirstServer for $5,600 per output unit. FirstServer may outsource (buy from the outside company) Job A only, Job B only, or both jobs. Which course of action will FirstServer managers take if they base their decision on (a) the original system? (b) ABC system costs? Which course of action will yield more income? Explain.

Serial Case

C4-51 Calculate and interpret activity cost pool rates *(Learning Objective 2)*

This case is a continuation of the Caesars Entertainment Corporation serial case that began in Chapter 1. Refer to the introductory story in Chapter 1 (see page 43) for additional background. (The components of the Caesars serial case can be completed in any order.)
Caesars Entertainment Corporation (CEC) has several properties in Las Vegas, Nevada, which it owns or manages. The following list of selected property-related data is taken from CEC's 2014 Form 10-K, Item 2, pages 31–32.

Caesars Entertainment Corporation
Selected property data adapted from Form 10K, Item 2, pages 31–32
As of December 31, 2014

Property	Casino space-square feet	Slot machines	Table games	Hotel rooms & suites
Flamingo Las Vegas	72,300	1,110	120	3,460
Harrah's Las Vegas	90,600	1,280	90	2,720
Paris Las Vegas	95,300	1,020	100	2,920
Rio All-Suites Hotel & Casino	117,300	1,070	90	2,520
Bally's Las Vegas	66,200	1,000	70	2,810
The Cromwell	28,100	450	60	188
Planet Hollywood	64,500	1,100	90	2,500
The LINQ Hotel & Casino	62,200	750	70	2,250
Caesars Palace Las Vegas	123,700	1,300	170	3,960
Totals	720,200	9,080	860	23,328

Calculate a cost activity pool rate for each of the following pools. Use an activity measure for the denominator from the above table. Justify your choice of the cost driver for each of the cost pools. Please note that there may not be just one correct answer for one or more of these cost pools.

Item	Cost pool	Total
a.	Slot machine maintenance costs	$ 1,952,200
b.	Casino utilities expenses	$ 43,212,000
c.	Property taxes	$ 6,200,000
d.	Housekeeper wages and benefits	$ 12,947,040
e.	Casino dealer wages and benefits	$ 15,050,000

CRITICAL THINKING

Discussion & Analysis

A4-52 Discussion Questions

1. Explain why departmental overhead rates might be used instead of a single plantwide overhead rate.

2. Using activity-based costing, why are indirect costs allocated while direct costs are not allocated?

3. How can using a single predetermined manufacturing overhead rate based on a unit-level cost driver cause a high-volume product to be overcosted?

4. Assume a company uses a plantwide predetermined manufacturing overhead rate that is calculated using direct labor hours as the cost driver. The use of this plantwide predetermined manufacturing overhead rate has resulted in cost distortion. The company's high-volume products are overcosted, and its low-volume products are undercosted. What effects of this cost distortion will the company most likely be experiencing? Why might the cost distortion be harmful to the company's competitive position in the market?

5. A hospital can use activity-based costing (ABC) for costing its services. In a hospital, what activities might be considered to be value-added activities? What activities at that hospital might be considered to be non-value-added?

6. A company makes shatterproof, waterproof cases for the S-series of Samsung smartphones. The company makes only one model and has been very successful in marketing its cases; no other company in the market has a similar product. The only customization available to the customer is the color of the case. There is no manufacturing cost difference among the different colors of the cases. Since this company has a high-volume product, its controller thinks that the company should adopt activity-based costing. Why might activity-based costing not be as beneficial for this company as for other companies?

7. Compare a traditional production system with a lean production system. Discuss the similarities and the differences.

8. Think of a product with which you are familiar. Explain how activity-based costing could help the company that makes this product in its efforts to be "green."

9. It has been said that external failure costs can be catastrophic and much higher than the other categories. What are some examples of external failure costs? Why is it often difficult to arrive at the cost of external failures?

10. What are the four categories of quality-related costs? Name a cost in each of the four categories for each of the following types of organizations:

    a. Restaurant
    b. Hospital
    c. Law firm
    d. Bank
    e. Tire manufacturer
    f. University

11. What are the similarities between sustainability and lean thinking? What are the differences between sustainability and lean thinking?

12. Why might a company want to take lean thinking a step further by including operations and methods associated with sustainability?

Application & Analysis
Mini Cases

A4-53 ABC in Real Companies
Choose a company in any of the following categories: airline, florist, bookstore, bank, grocery store, restaurant, college, retail clothing shop, movie theater, or lawn service. In this activity, you will be making reasonable estimates of the types of costs and activities associated with this company; companies do not typically publish internal cost or process information. Be reasonable in your cost estimates and include your assumptions used in selecting costs.

Basic Discussion Questions

1. Describe the company selected, including its products or services.
2. List eight key activities performed at this company. Choose at least one activity in the areas of production, sales, human resources, and accounting.
3. For each of the key activities, list a potential cost driver for that activity and describe why this cost driver would be appropriate for the associated activity.

A4-54 Value-Added versus Non-Value-Added at a Restaurant
Go to a fast-food restaurant (or think of the last time you were at a fast-food restaurant). Observe the steps involved in providing a meal to a customer. You will be watching for value-added steps and non-value-added steps. Answer the following questions.

Basic Discussion Questions

1. Describe the steps involved with delivering the meal to the customer that you can observe.
2. Describe the "behind-the-scenes" processes that are likely in the restaurant, such as cleaning, stocking, and cooking activities.
3. With your answers for Questions 1 and 2, list all of the possible activities, materials, and information that you think might be included on a value stream map for the restaurant. Include all of the steps you can think of (not necessarily only those you can observe).
4. Make a list of the eight wastes as denoted by the acronym DOWNTIME (Defects, Overproduction, Waiting, Not utilizing people to their full potential, Transportation, Inventory, Movement, and Excess processing). Next to each waste category, list at least one possible non-value-added activity that might or might not be in the processes in that restaurant.
5. Go back to the list of items for the potential value stream map. Circle potential areas for improvement and explain which wastes might be involved in those areas.

ETHICS

A4-55 Ethics involved with ABC and hazardous waste costs
(Learning Objectives 2 & 3)

Sparkle Unlimited is a costume jewelry manufacturer located in the United States that uses electroplating. Electroplating is a process that involves applying a decorative metal coating to a base metal. The electroplating solution, or the water that is used in this process, becomes dirty over time and needs to be replaced. This used solution for electroplating is referred to as "spent" solution.

The spent solution contains dissolved metals such as gold, silver, platinum, copper, and other metals. Cyanide can also be present in the spent solution. Because of this content, spent solution is considered to be hazardous waste. This waste is more expensive to dispose of than regular waste.

Currently, Sparkle is using a traditional, volume-based costing system for its jewelry. Total manufacturing overhead for the period is allocated to the jewelry based on machine hours used.

Recently hired, Jacob is the controller for Sparkle. He previously worked at a manufacturer that produced custom furniture. At this prior job, he implemented an activity-based costing system that helped the company to determine the profitability of different product lines. He has been learning about Sparkle's operations and thinks activity-based costing might be a good tool for Sparkle's management to use to help to manage its operations.

Jacob's good friend, Michelle, is the division manager for the Silver line of jewelry at Sparkle. She runs an efficient production line and has earned bonuses for each of the past several years based on her division's productivity and profitability. Division managers are evaluated based on profits generated by their divisions as calculated by the internal reporting system.

If activity-based costing is used to allocate costs and hazardous waste costs are allocated to the products that generate spent solutions, the calculated internal profit from the Silver product line will decrease significantly. This decrease in profitability is because the cost of handling the spent solution is quite high, and this cost would be directly assigned to the Silver line if activity-based costing were to be used.

Michelle takes Jacob out to lunch at an expensive restaurant and steers the conversation toward the upcoming activity-based costing implementation. She is concerned that her division's profits will decrease due to the spent-solution costs charged to her division. Michelle asks Jacob if he can reduce the amount of hazardous waste costs allocated to her line.

Jacob values the working relationship he has with Michelle. She is one of the people who has input on his evaluation when it comes time for raises and promotions. He wants to keep her happy.

As a result, Jacob does not set up any cost pool for hazardous waste-disposal costs. Since the hazardous waste cost has always been part of the manufacturing process, he will continue to bury it in the other cost pools. His reasoning is that the activity-based costing system with hazardous waste-removal cost buried is still better than the traditional cost system; other costs are properly allocated and the costs are much more accurate than under the old system. He feels that no one is getting hurt. Since the activity-based costing cannot be used for external reporting, Jacob feels that what he is doing is not illegal.

Requirements

Using the IMA *Statement of Ethical Professional Practice* (Exhibit 1-7) as an ethical framework, answer the following questions:

1. What is(are) the ethical issue(s) in this situation?

2. Activity-based costing cannot be used for external financial reporting. Does this fact influence your analysis of whether Jacob has violated any ethical principles? Why or why not?

3. Do you agree that no one is hurt by the burying of the hazardous waste costs into general cost pools? Explain.

4. What are Jacob's responsibilities as a management accountant? What should he do now?

A4-56 Lean production costs and sustainability (Learning Objectives 4 & 5)

Cal-Maine Foods, Inc., is the largest producer of shell eggs in the United States. In 2012, it sold approximately 884.3 million dozen shell eggs, which was approximately 19% of shell eggs sold domestically.[9] Walmart and Sam's Club (owned by the same parent) combined account for almost one-third of Cal-Maine's net sales dollars in 2012.[10]

Per U.S. Department of Agriculture (USDA) regulations, every egg carton sold in the United States must be marked with information about the eggs inside the carton, including the eggs' grade, size, traceability code, and freshness date. The traceability code provides information about the egg farm, the region, and the specific building from which those eggs originate. This traceability information is necessary in case of health-related safety recalls (for example, salmonella outbreaks).

If one egg in a carton is broken or damaged, the entire carton must be discarded due to USDA regulations. The reason that the entire carton has to be thrown away rather than replacing just one egg with an unbroken one is that the eggs in the carton all must be from the same exact batch with identical traceability codes and freshness dates. The consumer would have no guarantee that the replacement egg matches the other eggs in the carton.

It is estimated that as many as one in every ten dozen eggs is broken and the carton thrown away.[11] This breakage ratio (10%) means that of the 884.3 million dozen eggs sold by Cal-Maine Foods in 2012, over 88.4 million dozen eggs, or over a billion individual eggs, were discarded.

---

[9] Cal-Maine Foods, Inc., 2012 Annual Report, www.calmainefoods.com/investor_relations/financial_reports.htm

[10] Ibid.

[11] "The Secret Lives of Bees," YouTube video produced by Walmart, https://www.youtube.com/watch?v=fat8ThBjofM

A Cal-Maine egg farm in Bushnell, Florida, in partnership with Walmart, two other suppliers, and the USDA, has developed a solution to significantly reduce the waste caused by egg breakage. Organic laser ink is used to mark each egg individually with its grade, size, traceability code, and freshness date. Now instead of throwing away the entire carton of eggs when a broken egg is discovered, the broken egg can be replaced with another egg that has the same grade, size, traceability code, and freshness date.

If this program is successful, Walmart alone will save over half a billion eggs from being thrown away each year (the broken or damaged eggs will still be discarded). Other egg sellers will have similar savings.

Requirements

1. Think about the value chain for a carton of eggs that is sold in the grocery store. (Start from the chicken and continue to the point of sale in the grocery store.) List as many steps in the value chain as you can imagine. At what points in the value chain does waste most likely occur?

2. In this chapter, the eight wastes of traditional operations were discussed. Which types of waste are in the value chain that you identified in Question 1?

3. Answer the following questions from the standpoint of Cal-Maine Foods, Inc., and its egg farms:
    a. What costs will be incurred to individually stamp each egg?
    b. What impact on revenue would the process of individually stamping each egg have?
    c. What wastes in the value chain occur at Cal-Maine Foods (and its egg farms)?

4. Now answer the following questions from the standpoint of Walmart:
    a. What costs might decrease as a result of purchasing eggs that are stamped individually with grade, size, traceability code, and freshness date information?
    b. What costs might increase as a result of purchasing individually stamped eggs?
    c. What wastes in the value chain occur at Walmart?

5. Who should bear the cost of the individual egg-stamping operations: Cal-Maine Foods, Walmart, or the consumer? Because of the tremendous amount of waste involved with the current system of discarding entire cartons, should individual egg stamping be mandated by the government? Why or why not?

Try It Solutions

page 184:

1. Plantwide: $16 per DL hour × 5 DL hours = $80

2. Machining Dept.: $32 per DL hour × 3 DL hours = $96

    Assembly Dept.: $12 per DL hour × 2 DL hours = $24

    Total MOH $120

3. The plantwide overhead rate undercosts the job by $40 (= $120 − $80).

page 205:

2, 3, 5, 7.

5

Wendy M. Tietz

Source: http://jellybelly.com

Process Costing

Learning Objectives

- **1** Distinguish between the flow of costs in process costing and job costing
- **2** Compute equivalent units
- **3** Use process costing in the first production department
- **4** Prepare journal entries for a process costing system
- **5** Use process costing in a second or later production department

What's your favorite Jelly Belly flavor? Chocolate Pudding? Peanut Butter? Or maybe Piña Colada? Have you ever wondered how these tasty gems are made? Each tiny Jelly Belly jelly bean spends seven to ten days going through eight different production processes: (1) Cooking the centers; (2) Shaping hot liquid centers into jelly beans; (3) Drying; (4) Sugar shower; (5) Shell-building; (6) Polishing; (7) Stamping the name of the company on each bean; and (8) Packaging. Since Jelly Belly mass produces its jelly beans, the accounting system it uses to find the cost of making each pound of jelly beans differs from the job costing system Life Fitness uses. Jelly Belly uses process costing to separately measure the manufacturing costs incurred in each of the eight production processes. Next, the company spreads these costs over the pounds of jelly beans that passed through each process during the month. By doing so, Jelly Belly is able to calculate the average cost of making a pound of jelly beans in each process, as well as the average cost of making a pound of jelly beans, from start to finish. Jelly Belly's managers use this information to measure profits and make business decisions. They also use this information to determine how efficiently each process is operating in order to control costs.

Process Costing: An Overview

Let's start by contrasting the two basic types of costing systems: *job costing* and *process costing*.

Two Basic Costing Systems: Job Costing and Process Costing

1 Distinguish between the flow of costs in process costing and job costing

We saw in Chapter 3 that Life Fitness and Boeing use job costing to determine the cost of producing unique goods in relatively small batches. Service companies such as law firms and hospitals also use job costing to determine the cost of serving individual clients. In contrast, companies such as Jelly Belly and Shell Oil use a series of steps (called *processes*) to make large quantities of identical units. These companies typically use *process costing* systems.

To simplify our discussion, we'll consolidate Jelly Belly's eight separate processes into three processes. We'll combine cooking, shaping, and drying the jelly bean centers into a single process called *Centers*. We'll also combine the sugar shower, shell-building, polishing, and stamping steps into a second process called *Shells*. The third and final process is *Packaging*.

Jelly Belly *accumulates* the costs of each process and then *assigns* these costs to the units (pounds of jelly beans) passing through that process.

Suppose the Centers process incurs $1,350,000 of costs to produce centers for 1,000,000 pounds of jelly beans, the Shells process incurs $800,000, and Packaging incurs $700,000. The total cost to produce a pound of jelly beans is the sum of the cost per pound for each of the three processes.

Jelly Belly's owners use the cost per pound of each process to help control costs. For example, they can compare the actual cost of producing centers for a pound of jelly beans (assumed to be $1.35 in our example) to the budget or plan. If the actual cost of the Centers process exceeds the budget, they can look for ways to cut costs in that process. Jelly Belly's owners also consider the total cost of making a pound of jelly beans (assumed to be $2.85 in our example) when setting selling prices. The price should be high enough to cover costs *and* to return a profit. Jelly Belly also uses the total cost of making a pound of jelly beans for financial reporting:

- To value the ending inventory of jelly beans for the balance sheet ($2.85 per pound still in ending inventory)
- To value the cost of goods sold for the income statement ($2.85 per pound sold)

The simple computation of the cost to make a pound of jelly beans is correct *only if there are no work in process inventories*, but it takes 7 to 10 days to complete all of the processes. So, Jelly Belly *does* have inventories of partially complete jelly beans. These inventories make the costing more complicated. In the rest of this chapter, you'll learn how to use process costing when there are work in process inventories.

How Does the Flow of Costs Differ Between Job and Process Costing?

Exhibit 5-1 compares the flow of costs in

- a job costing system for Life Fitness (Panel A), and
- a process costing system for Jelly Belly (Panel B).

EXHIBIT 5-1 Flow of Costs in Job Costing (Panel A) and Process Costing (Panel B)

Panel A shows that Life Fitness's job costing system has a single Work in Process Inventory control account supported by individual job cost records for each job that is being worked on. Life Fitness assigns direct materials, direct labor, and manufacturing overhead to individual jobs, as explained in Chapter 3. When a job is finished, its costs flow directly into Finished Goods Inventory. When the job is sold, the cost flows out of Finished Goods Inventory and into Cost of Goods Sold.

In contrast to Life Fitness's individual jobs, Jelly Belly uses a series of three *manufacturing processes* to produce jelly beans. The movement of jelly beans through these three processes is shown in Exhibit 5-2.

Take a moment to follow along as we describe Exhibit 5-2. In the first process (Centers process), Jelly Belly converts sugar and flavorings (the direct materials) into jelly bean centers using direct labor and manufacturing overhead, such as depreciation on the mixing vats. Once the jelly bean centers are made, they are transferred to the Shells process. In the Shells process, Jelly Belly uses different labor and equipment to coat the jelly bean centers with sugar, syrup, and glaze (the direct materials) to form the crunchy shells. Once that process is complete, the finished jelly beans are transferred to the Packaging process. In the Packaging process, Jelly Belly packages the finished jelly beans into various boxes and bags (direct materials), using other labor and equipment. The boxed and bagged jelly beans are then transferred to finished goods inventory until they are sold.

Now, let's see how Panel B of Exhibit 5-1 summarizes the flow of costs through this process costing system. Study the exhibit carefully, paying particular attention to the following key points:

1. Each process (Centers, Shells, and Packaging) has its own separate Work in Process Inventory account.

2. Direct materials, direct labor, and manufacturing overhead are assigned to *each* processing department's Work in Process Inventory account based on the manufacturing costs incurred by that process. Exhibit 5-2 shows that each of Jelly Belly's processes has different direct materials, direct labor, and manufacturing overhead costs.

3. Exhibit 5-2 shows that when the Centers process is complete, the jelly bean centers are physically *transferred out* of the Centers process and *transferred in* to the Shells process. Likewise, the *cost* of the centers is also *transferred out* of Work in Process Inventory—Centers and *transferred in* to Work in Process Inventory—Shells. The transfer of costs between accounts is pictured in Panel B of Exhibit 5-1 as a series of green *x*s. Keep the following important rule of thumb in mind:

> In process costing, the manufacturing costs assigned to the product must always follow the physical movement of the product. Therefore, when units are physically transferred out of one process and into the next, the *costs* assigned to those units must *also* be transferred out of the appropriate Work in Process Inventory account and into the next.

To simplify the accounting, the journal entry to record the transfer of costs between accounts is generally made once a month to reflect *all* physical transfers that occurred during the month.

4. When the Shells process is complete, the finished jelly beans are transferred out of the Shells process and into the Packaging process. Likewise, the *cost* assigned to the jelly beans thus far (cost of making the centers and adding the shells) is *transferred out* of Work in Process Inventory—Shells and *transferred in* to Work in Process Inventory—Packaging.

EXHIBIT 5-2 Flow of Costs in Production of Jelly Beans

Process Costing 249

5. When the Packaging process is complete, the finished packages of jelly beans are transferred to finished goods inventory. Likewise, the *cost* assigned to the jelly beans thus far (cost of making and packaging the jelly beans) is transferred out of Work in Process—Packaging and into Finished Goods Inventory. *In process costing, costs are transferred into Finished Goods Inventory only from the Work in Process Inventory of the last manufacturing process. The transferred cost includes all costs assigned to the units from every process the units have completed (Centers, Shells, and Packaging).* Finally, when the jelly beans are sold, their cost is transferred out of Finished Goods Inventory and into Cost of Goods Sold.

Keep the following rule of thumb in mind:

> Process costing is like rolling a snowball into a snowman. The product (snowball) keeps picking up cost (snow) as it rolls through each production process. Thus, the cost assigned to the product (snowball) keeps getting larger and larger as costs from each department are progressively added to it through the transfer of costs.

What Are the Building Blocks of Process Costing?

Before we illustrate process costing, we must first learn about the three building blocks of process costing: conversion costs, equivalent units, and inventory flow assumptions.

Conversion Costs

Chapter 2 introduced three kinds of manufacturing costs: direct materials, direct labor, and manufacturing overhead. Most companies, like Jelly Belly, that mass-produce a product use automated production processes. Therefore, direct labor is only a small part of total manufacturing costs. Companies that use automated production processes often condense the three manufacturing costs into two categories:

1. Direct materials
2. Conversion costs (= Direct Labor + MOH)

Recall from Chapter 2 that conversion costs are the combination of direct labor plus manufacturing overhead costs. Combining these costs in a single category simplifies the process costing procedures. We call this category *conversion costs* because it takes direct labor and manufacturing overhead to *convert* direct materials into new finished products—hence the name, conversion costs.

Equivalent Units

2 Compute equivalent units

Companies with work in process inventories use the concept of **equivalent units** to express the amount of work done during a period in terms of fully completed units of output.

To illustrate equivalent units, let's look at Callaway Golf, a manufacturer of golf balls and golf clubs. Let's assume that Callaway's golf ball production plant has 5,000 partially completed balls in ending work process inventory. Each ball is 80% of the way through the production process. If conversion costs are incurred evenly throughout the process, then getting each of 5,000 balls 80% of the way through the process takes about the same amount of work as getting 4,000 balls (5,000 × 80%) all the way through the process.

Equivalent units are calculated as follows:

> Number of physical units × Percentage of completion = Number of equivalent units

So, the number of equivalent units of conversion costs in Callaway's ending work process inventory is calculated as follows:

$$5{,}000 \times 80\% = 4{,}000$$

Conversion costs are usually incurred *evenly* throughout production. However, direct materials are often added at a particular point in the process. For example, Exhibit 5-3 shows that Callaway adds rubber at the *beginning* of the production process but doesn't add packaging materials until the *end*. How many equivalent units of rubber and packaging materials are in the ending inventory of 5,000 balls?

EXHIBIT 5-3 Callaway Production Plant Time Line

All 5,000 balls are 80% complete, so they all have passed the point at which rubber is added. Each ball has its full share of rubber (100%), so the balls have 5,000 equivalent units of rubber. In contrast, the time line in Exhibit 5-3 shows that *none* of the 5,000 balls has made it to the end of the process, where the packaging materials are added. The ending inventory, therefore, has *zero* equivalent units of packaging materials.

To summarize, the 5,000 balls in ending work in process inventory have the following:

- 5,000 equivalent units of rubber (5,000 units × 100% of rubber)
- 0 equivalent units of packaging materials (5,000 units × 0% of packaging materials)
- 4,000 equivalent units of conversion costs (5,000 units × 80% converted)

Try It!

Dairymaid makes organic yogurt. The only ingredients, milk and bacteria cultures, are added at the very beginning of the fermentation process. At month end, Dairymaid has 100,000 cups of yogurt that are only 25% of the way through the fermentation process. Use the equivalent unit formula to answer the following:

a. How many equivalent units of direct materials are in ending work in process?
b. How many equivalent units of conversion costs are in ending work in process?

Please see page 306 for solutions.

Inventory Flow Assumptions

Firms compute process costing using either the weighted-average or first-in, first-out (FIFO) method. Throughout the rest of the chapter, we will use the **weighted-average method of process costing**. *The two costing methods differ only in how they treat beginning inventory.* The FIFO method requires that any units in beginning inventory be costed *separately* from any units started in the current period. The weighted-average method *combines* any beginning inventory costs with the current period's costs to get a weighted-average cost. Many firms prefer to use the weighted-average method because it is simpler and the differences between the two methods' results are usually immaterial.

How Does Process Costing Work in the First Processing Department?

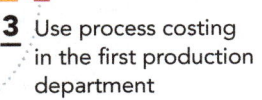

3 Use process costing in the first production department

To illustrate process costing, we'll be following SeaView, a manufacturer that mass-produces swim masks. We'll see how SeaView uses the weighted-average method of process costing to measure (1) the average cost of producing each swim mask and (2) the cost of the two major processes it uses to make the masks (Shaping and Insertion).

Exhibit 5-4 illustrates SeaView's production process. The Shaping Department begins with plastic and metal fasteners (direct materials) and uses labor and equipment (conversion costs) to transform the materials into shaped masks. The direct materials are added at the *beginning* of the process, but conversion costs are incurred *evenly* throughout the process. After shaping, the masks move to the Insertion Department, where the shaped masks are polished and then the clear faceplates are inserted.

EXHIBIT 5-4 SeaView's Production Process

Let's assume that the Shaping Department begins October with no work process inventory. During October, the Shaping Department incurs the following costs while working on 50,000 masks:

Beginning work in process inventory		$ 0
Direct materials		140,000
Conversion costs:		
Direct labor	$21,250	
Manufacturing overhead	46,750	
Total conversion costs		68,000
Total costs to account for		$208,000

How did SeaView arrive at these costs? SeaView traces direct materials and direct labor to each processing department using materials requisitions and labor time records (just as we used these documents to trace direct materials and direct labor to individual *jobs* in Chapter 3). SeaView allocates manufacturing overhead to each processing department using either a plantwide rate, departmental overhead rates, or ABC (just as we allocated manufacturing overhead to individual *jobs* in Chapters 3 and 4).

If, at the end of October, all 50,000 masks have been completely shaped and transferred out of the Shaping Department and into the Insertion Department, the entire $208,000 of manufacturing cost associated with these masks should *likewise* be transferred out of Work in Process—Shaping and into Work in Process—Insertion. In this case, the unit cost for *just* the shaping process is $4.16 per mask ($208,000/50,000 masks).

But what if only 40,000 masks are completely through the shaping process? Let's say that at October 31, the Shaping Department still has 10,000 masks that are only one-quarter of the way through the shaping process. How do we split the $208,000 between the following?

- 40,000 completely shaped masks transferred to the Insertion Department
- 10,000 partially shaped masks remaining in the Shaping Department's ending work in process inventory

In other words, how do we determine the cost of making the *completely* shaped masks versus the cost of making the *partially* shaped masks? We can't simply assign $4.16 to each mask because a partially shaped mask does *not* cost the same to make as a completely shaped mask. To figure out the cost of making a *completely* shaped mask versus a *partially* shaped mask, we must use the following five-step process costing procedure:

STEP 1: Summarize the flow of physical units.

STEP 2: Compute output in terms of equivalent units.

STEP 3: Summarize total costs to account for.

STEP 4: Compute the cost per equivalent unit.

STEP 5: Assign total costs to units completed and to units in ending Work in Process inventory.

> **Why is this important?**
>
> "Most food and consumer products are **mass-produced**. Managers need to know (1) the **cost** of each **manufacturing** process, to make each one as **cost-efficient** as possible; and (2) the cost of **each unit**, to aid in **pricing** and other business decisions."

Step 1: Summarize the Flow of Physical Units

Step 1 tracks the physical movement of swim masks into and out of the Shaping Department during the month. Follow along as we walk through this step in the first column of Exhibit 5-5. The first question addressed is this: *How many physical units did the Shaping Department work on during the month?* Recall that the Shaping Department had no masks in the beginning work in process inventory. During the month, the Shaping Department began work on 50,000 masks. Thus, the department needs to account for a *total* of 50,000 masks.

EXHIBIT 5-5 Step 1: Summarize the Flow of Physical Units
Step 2: Compute Output in Terms of Equivalent Units

	A	B	C	D
1	Sea View Shaping Department	Step 1:	Step 2: Equivalent Units	
2	Month Ended October 31 Flow of Production	Flow of Physical Units	Direct Materials	Conversion Costs
3	**Units to account for:**			
4	Beginning work in process, October 1	0		
5	Plus: Started in production during October	50,000		
6	Total physical units to account for	50,000		
7				
8	**Units accounted for:**			
9	Completed and transferred out during October	40,000	40,000	40,000
10	Plus: Ending work in process, October 31	10,000	10,000	2,500
11	Total physical units accounted for	50,000		
12	**Total equivalent units**		50,000	42,500
13				

These two lines must be equal. (lines 6 and 11)

Notes about calculating equivalent units in ending WIP:
DM = 10,000 units × 100% complete = 10,000
Conversion = 10,000 units × 25% complete = 2,500

The second question addressed is this: *What happened to those masks?* The Shaping Department reports that it completed and transferred out 40,000 masks to the Insertion Department during October. The remaining 10,000 partially shaped masks are still in the Shaping Department's ending work in process inventory on October 31. Notice that the *total physical units to account for* (50,000) must equal the *total physical units accounted for* (50,000). In other words, the Shaping Department must account for the whereabouts of every mask it worked on during the month.

Step 2: Compute Output in Terms of Equivalent Units

Step 2 computes all of the Shaping Department's output for the month in terms of equivalent units. Step 2 is shown in the last two columns of Exhibit 5-5. First, let's consider the 40,000 masks that were *completed and transferred out* to the Insertion Department during October. These units have been fully completed in the Shaping Department; therefore, they are 100% complete with respect to both direct materials and conversion. Equivalent units for these physical units are calculated as follows:

Number of Physical Units	×	Percentage of Completion	= Equivalent units
40,000	×	100%	= 40,000 equivalent units of direct materials
40,000	×	100%	= 40,000 equivalent units of conversion costs

Now, let's consider the 10,000 masks still in ending work in process. These masks are only 25% of the way through the shaping process on October 31. The time line in Exhibit 5-6 reminds us that all direct materials are added at the *beginning* of the shaping process.

Therefore, the partially shaped masks have made it past the point where direct materials are added. As a result, the equivalent units for direct materials are as follows:

Number of Physical Units	×	Percentage of Completion	=	Equivalent units
10,000	×	100%	=	10,000 equivalent units of direct materials

Unlike direct materials, the conversion costs are incurred *evenly* throughout the shaping process. For these partially shaped masks, the equivalent units of conversion costs are calculated as follows:

Number of Physical Units	×	Percentage of Completion	=	Equivalent units
10,000	×	25%	=	2,500 equivalent units of conversion costs

Our last step is to calculate the Shaping Department's output in terms of *total equivalent units* for the month. We must calculate totals separately for direct materials and conversion costs because they will differ in most circumstances. To find the totals, we simply add the equivalent units of all masks worked on during the month. As shown in Exhibit 5-5, the *total equivalent units of direct materials* (50,000) is simply the sum of the 40,000 equivalent units completed and transferred out *plus* the 10,000 equivalent units still in ending work in process (WIP). Likewise, the *total equivalent units of conversion costs* (42,500) is the sum of the 40,000 equivalent units completed and transferred out plus the 2,500 equivalent units still in ending work in process.

EXHIBIT 5-6 SeaView's Shaping Department Time Line

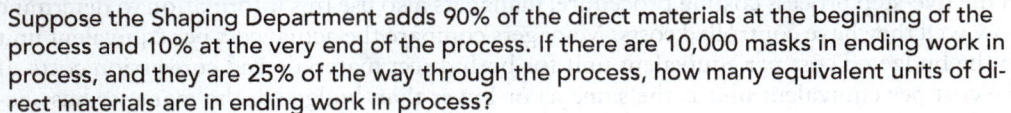

Suppose the Shaping Department adds 90% of the direct materials at the beginning of the process and 10% at the very end of the process. If there are 10,000 masks in ending work in process, and they are 25% of the way through the process, how many equivalent units of direct materials are in ending work in process?

Answer: Because the masks are only 25% of the way through the process, they have not reached the point where 10% of the materials is added. They have only received the 90% of materials added at the beginning of the process. Therefore, there are 9,000 (= 10,000 × 90%) equivalent units of direct materials in ending work in process.

Step 3: Summarize Total Costs to Account For

Step 3, as shown in Exhibit 5-7, summarizes all of the production costs the Shaping Department must account for. These are the production costs associated with beginning inventory (if any existed) plus the production costs that were incurred during the month.[1]

EXHIBIT 5-7 Step 3: Summarize Total Costs to Account For

	A	B	C	D
1	Sea View Shaping Department Month Ended October 31 Step 3: Total Costs to Account For	Direct Materials	Conversion Costs	Total
2	Beginning work in process, October 1	$ 0	$ 0	$ 0
3	Plus: Costs added during October	140,000	68,000	208,000
4	Total costs to account for	$ 140,000	$ 68,000	$ 208,000
5				

Total costs to account for must ALWAYS equal Total costs accounted for in Step 5. This is the total cost in the WIP inventory account.

Note: Conversion costs of $68,000 = $21,250 of direct labor plus $46,750 of MOH

Once again, we must show separate totals for each of the two cost categories: direct materials and conversion costs. Because the Shaping Department did not have any beginning inventory of partially shaped masks, the beginning balance in the Work Process Inventory—Shaping account is zero. As shown on page 253, during the month, the Shaping Department used $140,000 of direct materials and $68,000 of conversion costs ($21,250 of direct labor plus $46,750 of manufacturing overhead).

Step 4: Compute the Cost per Equivalent Unit

Remember that one of the primary goals of process costing is to average the cost of the production process over the units that pass through the process during the month. Step 4 does this by calculating the cost per equivalent unit. The word *per* means "divided by," so the *cost per equivalent unit* is the *total costs to account for* (from Step 3) divided by the *total equivalent units* (from Step 2). Because the total equivalent units for direct materials (50,000) and conversion costs (42,500) differ, we must compute a separate cost per equivalent unit for each cost category. Exhibit 5-8 shows the computations.

EXHIBIT 5-8 Step 4: Compute the Cost per Equivalent Unit

	A	B	C	D
1	Sea View Shaping Department Month Ended October 31 Step 4: Cost per Equivalent Unit	Direct Materials	Conversion Costs	
2	Total costs to account for (from Step 3)	$ 140,000	$ 68,000	
3	Divided by: Total equivalent units (from Step 2)	50,000	42,500	
4	Cost per equivalent unit	$ 2.80	$ 1.60	
5				

This is the average cost of making one unit in this department.

What do these figures mean? During October, SeaView's Shaping Department incurred an average of $2.80 of direct materials cost and $1.60 of conversion costs to completely shape the equivalent of one mask. In addition to using the cost per equivalent unit in the five-step process costing procedure, managers also use this information to determine how well they have controlled costs. Managers compare the actual cost per equivalent unit to the budgeted cost per equivalent unit for both direct materials and conversion costs. If the cost per equivalent unit is the same as or lower than budgeted, the manager has successfully controlled costs.

---

[1] The Shaping Department did not have a beginning inventory. Summary Problem 1 illustrates a department that does have a beginning inventory. As long as we assume the weighted-average method of process costing, we include the beginning balance to arrive at total costs to account for, as shown in Exhibit 5-7.

Step 5: Assign Total Costs to Units Completed and to Units in Ending Work in Process Inventory

The goal of Step 5 (Exhibit 5-9) is to determine how much of the Shaping Department's $208,000 total costs should be assigned to (1) the 40,000 completely shaped masks transferred out to the Insertion Department and (2) the 10,000 partially shaped masks remaining in the Shaping Department's ending work in process inventory. Exhibit 5-9 shows how the equivalent units computed in Step 2 (Exhibit 5-5) are multiplied by the cost per equivalent unit computed in Step 4 (Exhibit 5-8) to assign costs to units.

First, consider the 40,000 masks completed and transferred out. Exhibit 5-5 shows 40,000 equivalent units for both direct materials and conversion costs. In Exhibit 5-8 we learned that the company spent $2.80 on direct materials for each equivalent unit and $1.60 on conversion costs for each equivalent unit. Thus, the total cost of these completed masks is (40,000 × $2.80) + (40,000 × $1.60) = $176,000, as shown in Exhibit 5-9. We've accomplished our first goal—now we know how much cost ($176,000) should be assigned to the completely shaped masks transferred to the Insertion Department.

EXHIBIT 5-9 Step 5: Assign Total Costs to Units Completed and to Units in Ending Work in Process Inventory

	A	B	C	D
1	Sea View Shaping Department Month Ended October 31 Step 5: Assigning Total Costs	Direct Materials	Conversion Costs	Total
2	**Completed and transferred out:**			
3	Equivalent units completed and transferred out (from Step 2)	40,000	40,000	
4	Multiplied by: Cost per equivalent unit (from Step 4)	$ 2.80	$ 1.60	
5	Cost assigned to units completed and transferred out	$ 112,000	$ 64,000	$ 176,000
6				
7	**Ending work in process:**			
8	Equivalent units in ending WIP (from Step 2)	10,000	2,500	
9	Multiplied by: Cost per equivalent unit (from Step 4)	$ 2.80	$ 1.60	
10	Cost assigned to units in ending WIP	$ 28,000	$ 4,000	$ 32,000
11	**Total costs accounted for**			$ 208,000
12				

This cost must be transferred out of the department to go with the units that were transferred out.

Total costs accounted for must ALWAYS equal Total costs to account for (Step 3).

Next, consider the 10,000 masks still in ending work in process. These masks have 10,000 equivalent units of direct materials (which cost $2.80 per equivalent unit), so the direct material cost is $28,000 (= 10,000 × $2.80). These masks also have 2,500 equivalent units of conversion costs, which cost $1.60 per equivalent unit, so the conversion costs are $4,000 (= 2,500 × $1.60). Therefore, the total cost of the 10,000 partially completed masks in the Shaping Department's ending work in process inventory is the sum of these direct material and conversion costs: $28,000 + $4,000 = $32,000. Now, we've accomplished our second goal—we know how much cost ($32,000) should be assigned to the partially shaped masks still in ending work in process inventory.

In summary, Exhibit 5-9 has accomplished our goal of splitting the $208,000 *total cost to account for* between the 40,000 masks completed and transferred out to the Insertion Department and the 10,000 partially shaped masks remaining in Work in Process Inventory.

Average Unit Costs

How does this information relate to unit costs? The average cost of making one *completely shaped* unit is $4.40 ($176,000 transferred to Insertion ÷ 40,000 completely shaped masks transferred to Insertion). This average unit cost ($4.40) is the sum of the direct materials cost per equivalent unit ($2.80) and the conversion cost per equivalent unit ($1.60). The average cost of one *partially* shaped unit that is 25% of the way through the production process is $3.20 ($32,000 in ending inventory of Shaping ÷ 10,000 partially shaped masks). We needed the five-step process costing procedure to find these average costs per unit. If the Shaping Department manager ignored the five-step process and simply spread the entire production cost over all units worked on during the period, each unit would be assigned a cost of $4.16 ($208,000 ÷ 50,000 masks)—whether completely shaped or not. That would be wrong. The average cost per unit should be (and is) higher for completely shaped units transferred to the Insertion Department than it is for partially shaped units remaining in the Shaping Department's ending work in process inventory.

Recall that once the masks are shaped, they still need to have the faceplates inserted. In the second half of the chapter, we will discuss how the second process—Insertion—uses the same five-step procedure to find the *total* unit cost of making a completed mask, from start to finish.

STOP & THINK

Assume that the Shaping Department manager incorrectly assigned all of October's production costs ($208,000) to the 40,000 completely shaped masks rather than using the five-step process to divide the costs between the 40,000 completely shaped and 10,000 partially shaped masks. What would be the results of this error?

Answer: If the manager incorrectly assigned all production costs to the completely shaped masks, the unit cost of completely shaped masks would be too high ($208,000 ÷ 40,000 = $5.20). In addition, the unit cost of the partially shaped masks would be too low ($0.00). In essence, the manager would be saying that the partially shaped units were "free" to make because he or she assigned all of the production costs to the completely shaped units. To assign production costs properly, managers must use the five-step process.

Sustainability and Process Costing

As we have seen, process costing is suitable for manufacturers that produce large volumes of product using a set of standardized production processes. These manufacturing environments are conducive to employing lean practices, which eliminate economic waste from the manufacturing process, and green practices, which minimize or eliminate harmful environmental consequences.

Management should study each of the production processes to discover the quantities and types of solid waste, airborne emissions, and waste water that are generated, as well as the types and quantities of energy used. Solid waste and scrap can be identified simply by studying the contents of the company's trash. These studies are known as **waste audits** (or **trash audits**). After conducting waste audits, many companies have discovered they can reclaim and repurpose the waste and scraps into new products, or sell them to a third-party recycler. What was previously considered "waste" is now being considered a potential resource that helps companies avoid costly landfilling fees and generate new streams of revenue. In other words, "waste = wasted cash."

For example:

- In 2015, Unilever, maker of such diverse products as Lipton Tea, Ben & Jerry's Ice Cream, and Dove soap, achieved its goal of "zero-waste to landfill" at all 240 of its factories in 67 countries around the world. In the process, the company has saved over 200 million euros (about $223 million) and has created hundreds of jobs.[2] The reduction in waste, despite the growth in sales volume, has occurred primarily from innovative ways of reducing, recovering, recycling, and reusing what was previously considered waste. For example, the company now sells the scraps of fabrics, known as offcuts, from cutting tea bags to other companies, which then use it for making wallpaper and animal bedding.[3]

- General Mills began burning the oat hull waste remaining from the production of its Cheerios brand cereal to generate power. In doing so, the cereal manufacturing plant decreased its natural gas consumption by 90%, thereby saving about

---

[2] https://www.unilever.com/news/press-releases/2015/15-01-30-Unilever-achieves-zero-waste-to-landfill-across-global-factory-network.html

[3] http://www.environmentalleader.com/2013/01/24/unilever-moves-zero-waste-goal-five-years-closer/#.UQF0vje6g6o.email

$350 million in energy costs, and also reduced its carbon footprint by 21%. In addition, the company generates revenue by selling excess oat hull waste to a local energy company, as well as a nearby state university.[4] Likewise, the company turns waste from its Greek yogurt plant into biofuel, saving about $2.4 million each year and reducing carbon emissions by 14%.[5]

- In 2015, Ford Motor Company announced that it had cut the waste-per-vehicle by 50% over the past five years, with plans to further reduce waste to 13.4 pounds per vehicle by the end of 2016. Ford says it is using lean manufacturing strategies, as discussed in Chapter 4, to eliminate waste.[6]

While switching to environmentally friendly production equipment, energy sources, and production processes may be costly in the short run, companies may recognize long-term economic benefits as a result. For example, as carbon-trading schemes (otherwise known as "cap and trade") become more prevalent across the globe, those companies that manage to reduce their carbon emissions may be able to profit from selling their carbon credits. In searching for greener ways to manufacture and recycle their products, some companies may eventually profit from developing, patenting, and selling their own environmentally neutral production systems and technologies.

See Exercises E5-34A and E5-48B

What Journal Entries Are Needed in a Process Costing System?

The journal entries used in a process costing system are very similar to those in a job costing system. The basic difference is that the manufacturing costs (direct materials, direct labor, and manufacturing overhead) are assigned to *processing departments* rather than *jobs*. In addition, at the end of the month, a journal entry must be made to transfer cost to the next processing department. Let's now look at the journal entries that would have been made in October for the Shaping Department.

During October, $140,000 of direct materials was requisitioned for use by the Shaping Department. In the following journal entry, notice how these costs are recorded specifically to the Shaping Department's Work in Process Inventory account. In process costing, each processing department maintains a separate Work in Process Inventory account.

4 Prepare journal entries for a process costing system

Work in Process Inventory—Shaping		140,000	
Raw Materials Inventory			140,000
(To record direct materials used by the Shaping Department in October)			

Labor time records show that $21,250 of direct labor was used in the Shaping Department during October, resulting in the following journal entry:

Work in Process Inventory—Shaping		21,250	
Wages Payable			21,250
(To record direct labor used in the Shaping Department in October)			

---

[4] http://www.youtube.com/watch?v=hYLK4lPq0SM
[5] http://www.environmentalleader.com/2015/11/04/why-general-mills-dell-unilever-care-about-the-cop-21-climate-talks/
[6] http://www.environmentalleader.com/2013/02/28/ford-to-cut-vehicle-waste-40-percent-by-2016/

Manufacturing overhead (MOH) is allocated to the Shaping Department using the company's predetermined overhead rate(s). Just as in a job costing environment, the company may use a single plantwide rate, departmental overhead rates, or ABC to allocate its manufacturing overhead costs. For example, let's say that the Shaping Department's overhead rate is $50 per machine hour and the department used 935 machine hours during the month. That means $46,750 ($50 × 935) of MOH should be allocated to the Shaping Department during October:

Work Process Inventory—Shaping	46,750	
Manufacturing Overhead		46,750
(To record manufacturing overhead allocated to the		
Shaping Department in October)		

After making these journal entries during the month, the Work in Process Inventory—Shaping T-account appears as follows:

Work in Process Inventory—Shaping

Balance, October 1	0
Direct materials	140,000
Direct labor $208,000	21,250
Manufacturing overhead	46,750

Notice how the sum of the costs currently in the T-account is $208,000. This is the *same total costs* to account for summarized in Exhibit 5-7. By performing the five-step process at the end of the month, SeaView was able to determine how much of the $208,000 should be assigned to units still being worked on ($32,000) and how much should be assigned to the units completed and transferred out to the Insertion Department ($176,000). The company uses this information (pictured in Exhibit 5-9) to make the following journal entry:

> This entry transfers costs (found in Step 5) to the next department.

Work in Process Inventory—Insertion	176,000	
Work in Process Inventory—Shaping		176,000
(To record transfer of cost out of the Shaping Department		
and into the Insertion Department)		

After this journal entry is posted, the Work in Process Inventory—Shaping account appears as follows. Notice that the new ending balance in the account—$32,000—agrees with the amount assigned to the partially shaped masks in Exhibit 5-9.

Work in Process Inventory—Shaping

Balance, October 1	0	Transferred to Insertion	176,000
Direct materials	140,000		
Direct labor	21,250		
Manufacturing overhead	46,750		
Balance, October 31	32,000		

In the next half of the chapter, we'll look at the journal entries made by the Insertion Department to record the completion and sale of the swim masks.

Decision Guidelines

Process Costing—First Processing Department

Here are some of the key decisions SeaView made in setting up its process costing system.

Decision	Guidelines
Should SeaView use job or process costing?	SeaView mass-produces large quantities of identical swim masks using two production processes: Shaping and Insertion. It uses *process costing* to: 1. Determine the cost of each production process. 2. Determine the average direct materials cost and conversion cost incurred on each unit passing through the production process.
How many Work in Process Inventory accounts does SeaView's process costing system have?	SeaView uses a separate Work in Process Inventory account for each of its two major processes: Shaping and Insertion.
How does SeaView account for partially completed units?	SeaView uses equivalent units. SeaView computes equivalent units separately for direct materials and conversion costs because it adds direct materials at specific points in the production process but incurs conversion costs evenly throughout the process.
How does SeaView compute equivalent units of conversion costs?	SeaView's *conversion costs* are incurred evenly throughout the production process, so the equivalent units are computed as follows: $$\text{Equivalent units} = \text{Number of physical units} \times \text{Percentage of completion}$$
How does SeaView compute equivalent units of direct materials?	Equivalent units of direct materials are computed using the same equivalent unit formula shown directly above. However, SeaView's *materials* are added at specific points in the production process, so the equivalent units are computed using the following percentages: • If physical units have passed the point at which materials are added, then the units are 100% complete with respect to materials. • If physical units have not passed the point at which materials are added, then the units are 0% complete with respect to materials. • If physical units have received a portion, but not all, of the direct materials (say 25%), then equivalent units of direct materials are calculated using that particular percentage.
How does SeaView compute the cost per equivalent unit?	For each category (direct materials and conversion), SeaView divides the total cost to account for by the total equivalent units. The resulting information tells management the average cost of making one unit in each processing department. This information can then be compared to the budget to the help managers control costs.
How does SeaView split the total costs of the shaping process between the following? • Swim masks completed and transferred out • Partially completed swim masks in ending work in process inventory	SeaView multiplies the cost per equivalent unit by the following: • Number of equivalent units completed and transferred out • Number of equivalent units in the ending work in process inventory

SUMMARY PROBLEM 1

Florida Tile produces ceramic tiles using two sequential production departments: Tile-Forming and Tile-Finishing. The following information was found for Florida Tile's first production process, the Tile-Forming Department.

FLORIDA TILE
TILE-FORMING DEPARTMENT
Month Ended May 31

Information about units:

Beginning work in process, May 1	2,000 units
Started in production during May	18,000 units
Completed and transferred to Finishing Department during May	16,000 units
Ending work in process, May 31 (25% complete as to direct materials, 55% complete as to conversion cost)	4,000 units

Information about costs:

Beginning work in process, May 1 (consists of $800 of direct materials cost and $4,000 of conversion costs)	$ 4,800
Direct materials used in May	$ 6,000
Conversion costs incurred in May	$32,400

Requirement

Use the five steps of process costing to calculate the cost that should be assigned to (1) units completed and transferred out and (2) units still in ending work in process inventory. Then prepare the journal entry needed at month-end to transfer the costs associated with the formed tiles to the next department, Tile-Finishing.

▪ SOLUTION

Step 1: Summarize the flow of physical units.
Step 2: Compute output in terms of equivalent units.

	A	B	C	D
1	**Florida Tile: Tile-Forming Department**	**Step 1:**	**Step 2: Equivalent Units**	
	Month Ended May 31	Flow of Physical	Direct	Conversion
2	Flow of Production	Units	Materials	Costs
3	**Units to account for:**			
4	Beginning work in process, May 1	2,000		
5	Plus: Started in production during May	18,000		
6	Total physical units to account for	20,000		
7				
8	**Units accounted for:**			
9	Completed and transferred out during May	16,000	16,000	16,000
10	Plus: Ending work in process, May 31	4,000	1,000	2,200
11	Total physical units accounted for	20,000		
12	**Total equivalent units**		17,000	18,200
13				

Notes about calculating equivalent units in ending WIP:
DM = 4,000 units × 25% complete = 1,000
Conversion = 4,000 units × 55% complete = 2,200

Step 3: Summarize total costs to account for.

	A	B	C	D
1	**Florida Tile: Tile-Forming Department** **Month Ended May 31** **Step 3: Total Costs to Account For**	**Direct Materials**	**Conversion Costs**	**Total**
2	Beginning work in process, May 1	$ 800	$ 4,000	$ 4,800
3	Plus: Costs added during May	6,000	32,400	38,400
4	Total costs to account for	$ 6,800	$ 36,400	$ 43,200
5				

Step 4: Compute the cost per equivalent unit.

	A	B	C	D
1	**Florida Tile: Tile-Forming Department** **Month Ended May 31** **Step 4: Cost per Equivalent Unit**	**Direct Materials**	**Conversion Costs**	
2	Total costs to account for (from Step 3)	$ 6,800	$ 36,400	
3	Divided by: Total equivalent units (from Step 2)	17,000	18,200	
4	Cost per equivalent unit	$ 0.40	$ 2.00	
5				

Step 5: Assign total costs to units completed and to units in ending WIP.

	A	B	C	D
1	**Florida Tile: Tile-Forming Department** **Month Ended May 31** **Step 5: Assigning Costs**	**Direct Materials**	**Conversion Costs**	**Total**
3	**Completed and transferred out:**			
4	Equivalent units completed and transferred out (from Step 2)	16,000	16,000	
5	Multiplied by: Cost per equivalent unit (from Step 4)	$ 0.40	$ 2.00	
6	Cost assigned to units completed and transferred out	$ 6,400	$ 32,000	$ 38,400
7				
8	**Ending work in process:**			
9	Equivalent units in ending WIP (from Step 2)	1,000	2,200	
10	Multiplied by: Cost per equivalent unit (from Step 4)	$ 0.40	$ 2.00	
11	Cost assigned to units in ending WIP	$ 400	$ 4,400	$ 4,800
12				
13	**Total costs accounted for**			$ 43,200
14				

The journal entry needed to transfer costs is as follows:

	Work in Process Inventory—Tile-Finishing	38,400	
	Work in Process Inventory—Tile-Forming		38,400

The cost of making one completely formed tile in the Tile-Forming Department is $2.40. This is the sum of the direct materials cost per equivalent unit ($0.40) and the conversion cost per equivalent unit ($2.00). The completely formed tiles must still be finished in the Tile-Finishing Department before we will know the final cost of making one tile from start to finish.

5 Use process costing in a second or later production department

How Does Process Costing Work in a Second or Later Processing Department?

Most products require a series of processing steps. Recall that Jelly Belly uses eight processing steps to make its jelly beans. In the last section, we saw how much it costs SeaView to *shape* one mask. In this section, we consider a second department, SeaView's Insertion Department. After units pass through the *final* department (Insertion, in SeaView's case), managers can determine the *entire* cost of making one unit—from start to finish. In the second or later department, we use the same five-step process costing procedure that we used for the Shaping Department, with one major difference: We separately consider the costs *transferred in* to the Insertion Department from the Shaping Department when calculating equivalent units and the cost per equivalent unit. <u>Transferred-in costs</u> are incurred in a previous process (the Shaping Department, in the SeaView example) and are carried forward as part of the product's cost when it moves to the next process.

To account for transferred-in costs, we will add one more column to our calculations in Steps 2–5. Let's walk through the Insertion Department's process costing to see how this is done.

Process Costing in SeaView's Insertion Department

The Insertion Department receives the shaped masks and polishes them before inserting the faceplates at the end of the process. Exhibit 5-10 shows the following:

- Shaped masks are transferred in from the Shaping Department at the beginning of the Insertion Department's process.
- The Insertion Department's conversion costs are incurred evenly throughout the process.
- The Insertion Department's direct materials (faceplates) are not added until the *end* of the process.

> **Why is this important?**
>
> "Most products are **manufactured** through a **series** of production processes. To find the **total cost** of making one unit—from **start to finish**—managers must perform the five-step process costing procedure in **each** production department."

EXHIBIT 5-10 SeaView's Insertion Department Time Line

Keep in mind that *direct materials* in the Insertion Department refer *only* to the faceplates and not to the materials (the plastic and metal fasteners) added in the Shaping Department. Likewise, *conversion costs* in the Insertion Department refer to the direct labor and manufacturing overhead costs incurred *only* in the Insertion Department.

Exhibit 5-11 lists SeaView's Insertion Department data for October. The top portion of the exhibit lists the unit information, while the lower portion lists the costs. Let's walk through this information together.

EXHIBIT 5-11 SeaView's Insertion Department Data for October

Information about units:		
Beginning work in process, October 1		
(0% complete as to direct materials, 60% complete as to conversion)		5,000 masks*
Transferred in from Shaping Department during October (from Exhibit 5-5)		40,000 masks
Completed and transferred out to Finished Goods Inventory during October		38,000 masks
Ending work in process, October 31		
(0% complete as to direct materials, 30% complete as to conversion)		7,000 masks
Information about costs:		
Beginning work in process, October 1		
Transferred-in costs	$ 22,000*	
Conversion costs	1,100*	
Beginning balance		$ 23,100
Transferred in from Shaping Department during October (from journal entry on page 260)		$176,000
Direct materials added during October in Insertion Department		$ 19,000
Conversion costs incurred during October in Insertion Department:		
Direct labor	$ 3,710	
Manufacturing overhead	9,225	
Total conversion costs		$ 12,935
Total costs to account for		$231,035

*This information would have been obtained from Step 5 of the process costing procedure from September. The September 30 balance in work in process becomes the October 1 balance.

Exhibit 5-11 shows that SeaView's Insertion Department started the October period with 5,000 masks that had made it partway through the insertion process in September. During October, the Insertion Department started work on the 40,000 masks received from the Shaping Department. By the end of the month, the Insertion Department had completed 38,000 masks, while 7,000 remained partially complete.

Exhibit 5-11 also shows that the Insertion Department started October with a beginning balance of $23,100 in its Work in Process Inventory account, which is associated with the 5,000 partially completed masks in its beginning inventory. During the month, $176,000 was transferred in from the Shaping Department (recall the journal entry on page 260 for the 40,000 masks transferred into the department from Shaping). Additionally, the Insertion Department incurred $19,000 in direct materials costs (faceplates) and $12,935 in conversion costs during the month.

Just as in the Shaping Department, our goal is to split the total cost in the Insertion Department ($231,035) between the following:

- The 38,000 masks that the Insertion Department completed and transferred out (this time, to finished goods inventory)
- The 7,000 partially complete masks remaining in the Insertion Department's ending work in process inventory at the end of October

After splitting the total cost, we'll be able to determine the cost of making one complete mask—from start to finish. We use the same five-step process costing procedure that we used for the Shaping Department.

Steps 1 and 2: Summarize the Flow of Physical Units and Compute Output in Terms of Equivalent Units

Step 1: Summarize the Flow of Physical Units

Step 1 tracks the movement of swim masks into and out of the Insertion Department, just as we did in the Shaping Department. The data in Exhibit 5-11 show that the Insertion Department had a beginning work in process inventory of 5,000 masks. Then, during October, the Insertion Department received 40,000 masks from the Shaping Department. Thus, Exhibit 5-12 shows that the Insertion Department has 45,000 masks to account for (5,000 + 40,000).

Where did these 45,000 masks go? Exhibit 5-11 shows that the Insertion Department completed and transferred 38,000 masks out to finished goods inventory while the remaining 7,000 masks were only partway through the insertion process on October 31. Thus, Exhibit 5-12 shows that the department has accounted for all 45,000 masks.

Step 2: Compute Output in Terms of Equivalent Units

As mentioned earlier, process costing in a second or later department separately calculates equivalent units for transferred-in costs, direct materials, and conversion costs. Therefore, Step 2 in Exhibit 5-12 shows *three* columns for the Insertion Department's *three* categories of equivalent units: transferred-in, direct materials, and conversion costs. Let's consider each in turn.

Exhibit 5-10 shows that transferred-in masks are added at the very *beginning* of the insertion process. You might think of the shaped masks transferred in as raw materials added at the very *beginning* of the insertion process. All masks worked on in the Insertion Department—whether completed or not by the end of the month—started in the department as a shaped mask. Therefore, they are *all 100% complete with respect to transferred-in work and costs*. So, the "Transferred-in" column of Exhibit 5-12 shows 38,000 equivalent units completed and transferred out (38,000 physical units × 100%)

EXHIBIT 5-12 Step 1: Summarize the Flow of Physical Units
Step 2: Compute Output in Terms of Equivalent Units

	A	B	C	D	E
1	Sea View Insertion Department	Step 1:	Step 2: Equivalent Units		
2	Month Ended October 31 Flow of Production	Flow of Physical Units	Transferred-in	Direct Materials	Conversion Costs
3	**Units to account for:**				
4	Beginning work in process, October 1	5,000			
5	Plus: Transferred in during October	40,000			
6	Total physical units to account for	45,000			
7					
8	**Units accounted for:**				
9	Completed and transferred out during October	38,000	38,000	38,000	38,000
10	Plus: Ending work in process, October 31	7,000	7,000	0	2,100
11	Total physical units accounted for	45,000			
12	**Total equivalent units**		45,000	38,000	40,100
13					

(New Column points to column C)

Notes about calculating equivalent units in ending WIP:
Transferred-in = 7,000 units × 100% complete = 7,000
DM = 7,000 units × 0% complete = 0
Conversion = 7,000 units × 30% complete = 2,100

and 7,000 equivalent units still in ending inventory (7,000 physical units × 100%). Keep the following important rule of thumb in mind:

> All physical units, whether completed and transferred or still in ending work in process, are considered 100% complete with respect to transferred-in work and costs.

The Insertion Department calculates equivalent units of direct material the same way as in the Shaping Department. However, in the Insertion Department, the direct materials (faceplates) are added at the *end* of the process rather than at the beginning of the process. The 38,000 *finished* masks (completed and transferred out) contain 100% of their direct materials. On the other hand, the 7,000 *unfinished* masks in ending work process inventory have *not* made it to the end of the process, so they *do not* contain faceplates. As we see in Exhibit 5-12, these unfinished masks have zero equivalent units of the Insertion Department's direct materials (7,000 physical units × 0%).

Now, consider the conversion costs. The 38,000 *finished* masks are 100% complete with respect to the Insertion Department's conversion costs. However, the 7,000 *unfinished* masks are only 30% converted (see Exhibits 5-10 and 5-11), so the equivalent units of conversion costs equal 2,100 (7,000 × 30%).

Finally, the equivalent units in each column are summed to find the *total* equivalent units for each of the three categories: transferred-in (45,000), direct materials (38,000), and conversion costs (40,100). We'll use these equivalent units in Step 4.

Steps 3 and 4: Summarize Total Costs to Account for and Compute the Cost per Equivalent Unit

Exhibit 5-13 accumulates the Insertion Department's total costs to account for based on the data in Exhibit 5-11.

EXHIBIT 5-13 Step 3: Summarize Total Costs to Account For
Step 4: Compute the Cost per Equivalent Unit

	A	B	C	D	E
1	Sea View Insertion Department Month Ended October 31	Transferred-in	Direct Materials	Conversion Costs	Total
2	Steps 3 and 4				
3	Beginning work in process, October 1 (Exhibit 5-11)	$ 22,000	$ 0	$ 1,100	$ 23,100
4	Plus: Costs added during October	176,000	19,000	12,935	207,935
5	Total costs to account for	$ 198,000	$ 19,000	$ 14,035	$ 231,035
6	Divided by: Total equivalent units (from Step 2)	45,000	38,000	40,100	
7	Cost per equivalent unit	$ 4.40	$ 0.50	$ 0.35	

In addition to direct material and conversion costs, the Insertion Department must account for transferred-in costs ($176,000 in our example). Recall that transferred-in costs are incurred in a previous process (the Shaping Department) and are carried forward as part of the product's cost when the physical product is transferred to the next process.

If the Insertion Department had bought these shaped masks from an outside supplier, the cost would have been included as part of direct materials. However, the Insertion Department receives the masks from an *internal* supplier—the Shaping Department. Thus, the Insertion Department must account for the costs the Shaping Department incurred to provide the shaped masks ($176,000) as well as the Insertion Department's own direct materials ($19,000 for faceplates purchased from an outside supplier) and conversion costs ($12,935 for labor and overhead to insert the faceplates).

Exhibit 5-13 shows that the Insertion Department's total costs to account for ($231,035) consist of the costs associated with beginning work process inventory ($23,100) plus the costs added during the month ($207,935).

Exhibit 5-13 also shows Step 4: the calculation of cost per equivalent unit. For each category of cost, SeaView simply divides the total costs by the corresponding number of total equivalent units that were found in Step 2 (Exhibit 5-12).

Step 5: Assign Total Costs to Units Completed and to Units in Ending Work in Process Inventory

Exhibit 5-14 shows how SeaView finishes the five-step process by assigning costs to (1) units completed and transferred out to finished goods inventory and (2) units remaining in the Insertion Department's ending work process inventory. SeaView uses the same approach as it used for the Shaping Department in Exhibit 5-9. SeaView multiplies the number of equivalent units from Step 2 (Exhibit 5-12) by the cost per equivalent unit from Step 4 (Exhibit 5-13).

EXHIBIT 5-14 Step 5: Assign Total Costs to Units Completed and to Units in Ending Work in Process Inventory

This cost must be transferred out of the department to go with the units that were transferred out. (→ row 6)

Total costs accounted for must ALWAYS equal Total costs to account for (Step 3). (→ row 13)

	A	B	C	D	E
1	Sea View Insertion Department Month Ended October 31	Transferred-in	Direct Materials	Conversion Costs	Total
2	Step 5: Assigning Total Costs				
3	**Completed and transferred out:**				
4	Equivalent units completed and transferred out (from Step 2)	38,000	38,000	38,000	
5	Multiplied by: Cost per equivalent unit (from Step 4)	$ 4.40	$ 0.50	$ 0.35	
6	Cost assigned to units completed and transferred out	$ 167,200	$ 19,000	$ 13,300	$ 199,500
7					
8	**Ending work in process:**				
9	Equivalent units in ending WIP (from Step 2)	7,000	0	2,100	
10	Multiplied by: Cost per equivalent unit (from Step 4)	$ 4.40	$ 0.50	$ 0.35	
11	Cost assigned to units in ending WIP	$ 30,800	$ 0	$ 735	$ 31,535
12					
13	**Total costs accounted for**				$ 231,035
14					

Unit Costs and Gross Profit

SeaView's managers can now compute the cost of manufacturing one swim mask, from start to finish. Step 5 shows that $199,500 should be transferred to the Finished Goods Inventory account for the 38,000 masks completed during the month. Therefore, SeaView's cost of making one completed mask is $5.25 ($199,500 ÷ 38,000 finished masks). Exhibit 5-14 shows that this cost includes the costs from both processing departments:

- $4.40 per unit from the Shaping Department[7]
- $0.85 per unit from the Insertion Department ($0.50 for direct materials and $0.35 for conversion costs)

Going back to our earlier snowball analogy on page 250, we see that each unit of the product picked up $4.40 of cost in the first department (Shaping), and then picked up another $0.85 of cost in the second department (Insertion). Therefore, the cost of making one mask, from start to finish, is $5.25 ($4.40 + $0.85).

---

[7] This is the same $4.40 per unit we saw the Shaping Department transfer out to the Insertion Department in the first half of the chapter. Notice how the transferred-in cost carries through from one department to the next. The weighted-average method of process costing *combines* the current period's costs ($176,000) with any costs in beginning inventory ($22,000) to yield a weighted-average cost per unit ($4.40). Therefore, the weighted-average cost could be different than $4.40 if the beginning inventory had cost more or less than $4.40 per unit to make in September.

SeaView's managers use this information to help control costs, set prices, and assess the profitability of the swim masks. Let's assume SeaView is able to charge customers $10 for each mask. If so, the gross profit on the sale of each of these masks will be as follows:

Sales Revenue (per mask)	$10.00
Less: Cost of Goods Sold (per mask)	5.25
Gross Profit (per mask)	$ 4.75

For SeaView to be profitable, the total gross profit (gross profit per mask × number of masks sold) will need to be high enough to cover all of SeaView's operating expenses, such as marketing and distribution expenses, incurred in the non-manufacturing activities of the value chain. In addition to using the unit cost for valuing Cost of Goods Sold, SeaView will also use it to value Finished Goods Inventory ($5.25 for each mask still in finished goods inventory at the end of October).

Try It!

Dairymaid's yogurt goes through two sequential processes in two departments: Fermenting and Packaging. Assume that in the Packaging Department, Step 4 of the process costing procedure indicated the following costs per equivalent unit (cases of yogurt):

	Transferred-in	Direct Materials	Conversion Costs
Cost per equivalent unit	$6.50	$1.15	$1.25

a. How much did each case of yogurt cost to make, from start to finish?
b. If each case sells for $20, what is the gross profit per case?

Please see page 306 for solutions.

Production Cost Reports

Most companies prepare a **production cost report**, which summarizes the entire five-step process on one schedule. Notice how the production cost report for the Insertion Department shown in Exhibit 5-15 simply brings together all of the steps that we showed separately in Exhibits 5-12, 5-13, and 5-14. The top half of the schedule focuses on *units* (Steps 1 and 2), while the bottom half of the schedule focuses on *costs* (Steps 3, 4, and 5). Each processing department prepares its own production cost report each month. The transferred-in costs, direct materials cost, and conversion costs assigned to the units in *ending* work process inventory become the *beginning* work in process inventory balances on the next month's cost report.

SeaView's managers monitor the production costs found on this report by comparing the actual direct materials and conversion costs—particularly the equivalent-unit costs—with expected amounts. If actual costs are higher than expected, managers will try to uncover the reason for the increase and look for ways to cut costs in the future without sacrificing quality.

EXHIBIT 5-15 Production Cost Report

	Sea View Insertion Department Month Ended October 31 Flow of Production	Step 1 Flow of Physical Units	Step 2: Equivalent Units			
			Transferred-in	Direct Materials	Conversion Costs	
	Units to account for:					
	Beginning work in process, October 1	5,000				
	Plus: Transferred in during October	40,000				
	Total physical units to account for	45,000				
	Units accounted for:					
	Completed and transferred out during October	38,000	38,000	38,000	38,000	
	Plus: Ending work in process, October 31	7,000	7,000	0	2,100	
	Total physical units accounted for	45,000				
	Total equivalent units		45,000	38,000	40,100	
	Total Costs to account for and Cost per Equivalent Unit: **Steps 3 and 4**		Transferred-in	Direct Materials	Conversion Costs	Total
	Beginning work in process, October 1		$ 22,000	$ 0	$ 1,100	$ 23,100
	Plus: Costs added during October		176,000	19,000	12,935	207,935
	Total costs to account for		$ 198,000	$ 19,000	$ 14,035	$ 231,035
	Divided by: Total equivalent units (from Step 2)		45,000	38,000	40,100	
	Cost per equivalent unit		$ 4.40	$ 0.50	$ 0.35	
	Assignment of total costs: Step 5					
	Completed and transferred out:					
	Equivalent units completed and transferred out (from Step 2)		38,000	38,000	38,000	
	Multiplied by: Cost per equivalent unit (from Step 4)		$ 4.40	$ 0.50	$ 0.35	
	Cost assigned to units completed and transferred out		$ 167,200	$ 19,000	$ 13,300	$ 199,500
	Ending work in process:					
	Equivalent units in ending WIP (from Step 2)		7,000	0	2,100	
	Multiplied by: Cost per equivalent unit (from Step 4)		$ 4.40	$ 0.50	$ 0.35	
	Cost assigned to units in ending WIP		$ 30,800	$ 0	$ 735	$ 31,535
	Total costs accounted for					$ 231,035

Journal Entries in a Second Processing Department

The Insertion Department's journal entries are similar to those of the Shaping Department.

The following summary entry records the manufacturing costs incurred in the Insertion Department during the month of October (data from Exhibit 5-11):

Work Process Inventory—Insertion		31,935	
Raw Materials Inventory			19,000
Wages Payable			3,710
Manufacturing Overhead			9,225
(To record manufacturing costs incurred in the Insertion Department during October)			

In addition to this journal entry, which records the the Insertion Department's October costs, recall that a journal entry was made to transfer $176,000 of cost out of the Shaping Department and into the Insertion Department (see page 260). As a final step, the Insertion Department must now transfer cost out of its department into Finished Goods Inventory. The fifth step of the process costing procedure (Exhibit 5-14) showed that $199,500 should be assigned to the completed masks, while $31,535 should be assigned to the units still being worked on. Thus, the following journal entry is needed to transfer cost out of the Insertion Department and into Finished Goods Inventory:

Finished Goods Inventory	199,500	
Work in Process Inventory—Insertion		199,500
(To record transfer of cost out of the Insertion Department and into Finished Goods Inventory)		

After posting, the key accounts appear as follows:

Work in Process Inventory—Shaping

Balance, September 30	0	Transferred to Insertion	176,000
Direct materials	140,000		
Direct labor	21,250		
Manufacturing overhead	46,750		
Balance, October 31	32,000		

Work in Process Inventory—Insertion

Balance, September 30	23,100	Transferred to Finished	
Transferred in from Shaping	176,000	Goods Inventory	199,500
Direct materials	19,000		
Direct labor	3,710		
Manufacturing overhead	9,225		
Balance, October 31	31,535		

Finished Goods Inventory

Balance, September 30	0	
Transferred in from Insertion	199,500	

STOP & THINK

Assume that SeaView sells 36,000 of the masks on account for $10 each. Assuming that SeaView uses a perpetual inventory system, what journal entries would SeaView make to record the sales transaction?

Answer: The unit cost of making one mask from start to finish is $5.25 ($199,500 transferred to Finished Goods ÷ 38,000 finished masks). SeaView will make one journal entry to record the sales revenue, and a second journal entry to record the cost of goods sold:

Accounts Receivable (36,000 × $10.00)	360,000	
Sales Revenue		360,000

Cost of Goods Sold (36,000 × $5.25)	189,000	
Finished Goods Inventory		189,000

Decision Guidelines

Process Costing—Second Process

Let's use SeaView's Insertion Department to review some of the key process costing decisions that arise in a second (or later) process.

Decision	Guidelines
At what point in the insertion process are transferred-in costs (from the shaping process) incurred?	Transferred-in costs are incurred at the *beginning* of the insertion process. The masks must be completely shaped before the insertion process begins.
What percentage of completion is used to calculate equivalent units in the "Transferred-in" column?	All units, whether completed and transferred out or still in ending work in process, are considered 100% complete with respect to transferred-in work and costs.
What checks and balances does the five-step process costing procedure provide?	The five-step procedure provides two important checks: 1. The total physical units to account for (beginning WIP inventory + units started or transferred in) *must equal* the total physical units accounted for (units completed and transferred out + units in ending WIP inventory). 2. The total costs to account for (cost of beginning WIP inventory + costs incurred in the current period) *must equal* the total costs accounted for (cost of units completed and transferred out + cost of ending WIP inventory).
What are the main goals of the Insertion Department's process costing?	One goal is to determine the cost of operating the department during the month. This information is used by managers to control production costs. Another goal is to determine the cost of making each swim mask—from start to finish. The final goal is to split total costs between swim masks completed and transferred out to finished goods inventory and the masks that remain in the Insertion Department's ending work in process inventory.
What is a production cost report, and how do managers use the information found on it?	A production cost report simply summarizes all five steps on one schedule. SeaView's managers use the cost per equivalent unit to determine the cost of producing a swim mask. These costs provide a basis for setting selling prices, performing profitability analysis to decide which products to emphasize, and so forth. These costs are also the basis for valuing inventory on the balance sheet and cost of goods sold on the income statement. Managers also use the cost per equivalent unit to control material and conversion costs and to evaluate the performance of production department managers.

SUMMARY PROBLEM 2

This problem extends the Summary Problem 1 to a second department. During May, Florida Tile Industries reports the following in its Tile-Finishing Department:

Tile-Finishing Department Data for May

Information about units:
- Beginning work in process, May 1 (20% complete as to direct materials, 70% complete as to conversion work).. 4,000 units
- Transferred in from Tile-Forming Department during May................................. 16,000 units
- Completed and transferred out to Finished Goods Inventory during May... 15,000 units
- Ending work in process, May 31 (36% complete as to direct materials, 80% complete as to conversion work).. 5,000 units

Information about costs:
- Work in process, May 1 (transferred-in costs, $10,000; direct materials costs, $488; conversion costs, $5,530).. $16,018
- Transferred in from Tile-Forming Department during May (page 263)......... 38,400
- Tile-Finishing Department direct materials added during May..................... 6,400
- Tile-Finishing Department conversion costs incurred during May................ 24,300

Requirements

1. Complete the five-step process costing procedure to assign the Tile-Finishing Department's *total costs to account for* to units completed and to units in ending work in process inventory.
2. Make the journal entry to transfer the appropriate amount of cost to Finished Goods Inventory.
3. What is the cost of making one unit of product from start to finish?

▪ SOLUTION

Steps 1 and 2: Summarize the flow of physical units; compute output in terms of equivalent units.

	Florida Tile Tile-Finishing Department Month Ended May 31 Flow of Production	Step 1: Flow of Physical Units	Step 2: Equivalent Units		
			Transferred- in	Direct Materials	Conversion Costs
Units to account for:					
	Beginning work in process, May 1	4,000			
	Plus: Transferred in during May	16,000			
	Total physical units to account for	20,000			
Units accounted for:					
	Completed and transferred out during May	15,000	15,000	15,000	15,000
	Plus: Ending work in process, May 31	5,000	5,000	1,800	4,000
	Total physical units accounted for	20,000			
Total equivalent units			20,000	16,800	19,000

Notes about calculating equivalent units in ending WIP:
Transferred-in = 5,000 units × 100% complete = 5,000
DM = 5,000 units × 36% complete = 1,800
Conversion = 5,000 units × 80% complete = 4,000

Steps 3 and 4: Summarize total costs to account for; compute the cost per equivalent unit.

	Florida Tile Tile-Finishing Department Month Ended May 31 Steps 3 and 4	Transferred-in	Direct Materials	Conversion Costs	Total
3	Beginning work in process, May 1	$ 10,000	$ 488	$ 5,530	$ 16,018
4	Plus: Costs added during May	38,400	6,400	24,300	69,100
5	Total costs to account for	$ 48,400	$ 6,888	$ 29,830	$ 85,118
6	Divided by: Total equivalent units	20,000	16,800	19,000	
7	Cost per equivalent unit	$ 2.42	$ 0.41	$ 1.57	

Step 5: Assign total costs to units completed and to units in ending work process inventory.

	Florida Tile Tile-Finishing Department Month Ended May 31 Step 5: Assigning Total Costs	Transferred-in	Direct Materials	Conversion Costs	Total
3	**Completed and transferred out:**				
4	Equivalent units completed and transferred out	15,000	15,000	15,000	
5	Multiplied by: Cost per equivalent unit	$ 2.42	$ 0.41	$ 1.57	
6	Cost assigned to units completed and transferred out	$ 36,300	$ 6,150	$ 23,550	$ 66,000
7					
8	**Ending work in process:**				
9	Equivalent units in ending WIP	5,000	1,800	4,000	
10	Multiplied by: Cost per equivalent unit	$ 2.42	$ 0.41	$ 1.57	
11	Cost assigned to units in ending WIP	$ 12,100	$ 738	$ 6,280	$ 19,118
12					
13	**Total costs accounted for**				$ 85,118

Requirement 2
Journal entry:

Finished Goods Inventory	66,000	
Work Process Inventory—Tile-Finishing Department		66,000
(To record the transfer of cost out of the Tile-Finishing		
Department and into Finished Goods Inventory)		

Requirement 3
The cost of making one unit from start to finish is $4.40 ($66,000 transferred to Finished Goods Inventory divided by the 15,000 completed tiles). This consists of $2.42[8] of cost incurred in the Tile-Forming Department and $1.98 of cost incurred in the Tile-Finishing Department ($0.41 of direct materials and $1.57 of conversion costs).

---

[8] In Summary Problem 1, we saw that the average cost per unit in May was $2.40. The weighted-average method combines the current period's costs (May's costs) with any costs in beginning inventory to yield a weighted-average cost of $2.42 per unit.

END OF CHAPTER

Learning Objectives

- 1 Distinguish between the flow of costs in process costing and job costing
- 2 Compute equivalent units
- 3 Use process costing in the first production department
- 4 Prepare journal entries for a process costing system
- 5 Use process costing in a second or later production department

Accounting Vocabulary

Equivalent Units. (p. 250) Express the amount of work done during a period in terms of fully completed units of output.

Production Cost Report. (p. 269) Summarizes a processing department's operations for a period.

Transferred-In Costs. (p. 264) Costs incurred in a previous process that are carried forward as part of the product's cost when it moves to the next process.

Waste Audit. (p. 258) Studying the contents of a company's trash in order to identify solid waste and scraps that could potentially be recycled, repurposed, or sold to create a new revenue stream. Also known as *trash audit* or *waste sort*.

Weighted-Average Method of Process Costing. (p. 251) A process costing method that *combines* any beginning inventory units (and costs) with the current period's units (and costs) to get a weighted-average cost.

MyAccountingLab   Go to http://myaccountinglab.com/ for the following Quick Check, Short Exercises, Exercises, and Problems. They are available with immediate grading, explanations of correct and incorrect answers, and interactive media that acts as your own online tutor.

Quick Check

1. *(Learning Objective 1)* Which of the following is *false* concerning process costing?
   a. It accumulates production costs by activities.
   b. It transfers costs from one processing department to the next.
   c. It is well suited for a company whose products are indistinguishable from each other.
   d. It uses multiple WIP accounts, one for each processing department.

2. *(Learning Objective 2)* Conversion costs consist of
   a. direct materials + direct labor + manufacturing overhead.
   b. direct materials + direct labor.
   c. direct labor + manufacturing overhead.
   d. direct materials + manufacturing overhead.

3. *(Learning Objective 2)* Which of the following is true?
   a. FIFO is always used for process costing.
   b. Units in ending WIP are expressed in terms of equivalent units.
   c. A partially completed product whose direct materials are added at the beginning of the process would be 0% complete with respect to direct materials.
   d. The weighted-average method is always used for process costing.

4. *(Learning Objective 3)* Which of the following is the first step in completing the five-step process costing procedure?
   a. Summarize total costs to account for.
   b. Compute output in terms of equivalent units.
   c. Summarize the flow of physical units.
   d. Compute the cost per equivalent unit.

5. *(Learning Objective 3)* Assume 100 units were completed and transferred out during the period. The 40 units left in ending WIP are 20% complete with respect to conversion costs. The total equivalent units for conversion costs would be
   a. 100.
   b. 140.
   c. 108.
   d. 8.

6. *(Learning Objective 4)* The journal entry needed to record direct labor used but unpaid in the Finishing Department during the month would be
   a. Debit Finished Goods Inventory; Credit Wages Payable
   b. Debit Wages Payable; Credit Finished Goods Inventory
   c. Debit Wages Payable; Credit WIP-Finishing Dept.
   d. Debit WIP-Finishing Dept.; Credit Wages Payable

7. *(Learning Objective 4)* A company has two sequential processing departments: Mixing and Forming. In the Mixing Department, Step 5 of the process costing procedure assigned $10,000 to units in ending WIP and $80,000 to units completed and transferred out. What journal entry is needed as a result of these calculations?
   a. Debit WIP—Mixing Department: $80,000; credit WIP—Forming Department: $80,000
   b. Debit WIP—Forming Department: $80,000; Credit WIP—Mixing Department: $80,000
   c. Debit WIP—Forming Department: $10,000; Credit WIP—Mixing Department: $10,000
   d. Debit WIP—Mixing Department: $10,000; credit WIP—Forming Department: $10,000

8. *(Learning Objective 5)* In the second processing department, the percentage of completion assigned to units transferred in is always:
   a. 0%.
   b. 100%.
   c. dependent on the percentage of completion at month end.
   d. None of the listed choices are correct.

9. *(Learning Objective 5)* The schedule used to summarize the entire five-step process costing procedure is called a
   a. processing report.
   b. process costing schedule.
   c. production cost report.
   d. job cost record.

10. *(Learning Objective 5)* A company sells each unit of its product for $90. The final department showed the following costs per equivalent unit: $40 transferred-in, $21 direct materials, $13 conversion. What is the gross profit on each unit sold by the company?
    a. $16
    b. $56
    c. $74
    d. $90

Quick Check Answers

1. a 2. c 3. b 4. c 5. d 6. c 7. b 8. b 9. c 10. a

Short Exercises

S5-1 Compare job costing and process costing *(Learning Objective 1)*

Compare and contrast the primary differences between the job costing and process costing using the following table:

	Job costing	Process costing
Most suitable manufacturing environment		
Cost object used for accumulating costs		
Primary document for tracking costs		
Manufacturing cost categories		
Flow of costs through accounts		

S5-2 Flow of costs through Work in Process Inventory *(Learning Objective 1)*

Jelly Treats produces jelly beans in three sequential processing departments: Centers, Shells, and Packaging. Assume that the Shells processing department began April with $18,500 of unfinished jelly bean centers. During April, the Shells process used $42,200 of direct materials, used $12,500 of direct labor, and was allocated $17,200 of manufacturing overhead. In addition, $126,400 was transferred out of the Centers processing department during the month and $196,500 was transferred out of the Shells processing department during the month. These transfers represent the cost of the jelly beans transferred from one process to another.

1. Prepare a T-account for the Work in Process Inventory—Shells showing all activity that took place in the account during April.
2. What is the ending balance in the Work in Process Inventory—Shells on April 30? What does this figure represent?

S5-3 Compare job costing and process costing *(Learning Objective 1)*

PEZ Candy Inc. produces the popular small candy that is dispensed in collectible flip-top dispensers. In the United States, PEZ candies are produced in a factory in Connecticut. Over 3 billion of the small brick-shaped candies are consumed in the U.S. each year. PEZ candy is made from sugar, fruit flavoring, coloring, and corn syrup; the ingredients are put under pressure to form the hard tablets. About 95% of a PEZ tablet is sugar. The Connecticut location also houses PEZ's US headquarters and the PEZ Visitor Center. The Visitor Center offers birthday parties that include a staff member to host the party, goodie bags, pizza, soft drinks, and other options. When a family wants to have a birthday party, the family will work with PEZ staff to customize the birthday party.

1. Would PEZ Candy Inc. be more likely to use job costing or process costing for the manufacture of its PEZ candies? Why?
2. Give an example of each of the following types of costs that PEZ Candy Inc. would be likely to incur in the manufacture of its PEZ candies:
   a. Direct material
   b. Direct labor
   c. Manufacturing overhead
      i. Indirect materials
      ii. Indirect labor
      iii. Other manufacturing overhead
3. Would PEZ Candy Inc. be more likely to use job costing or process costing to calculate the cost of one particular birthday party hosted at the PEZ Visitor Center? Why?

S5-4 Determine the physical flow of units (process costing Step 1) *(Learning Objective 3)*

Lundeen Soda's Bottling Department had 15,000 units in the beginning inventory of Work in Process on September 1. During September, 125,000 units were started into production. On September 30, 29,000 units were left in ending inventory of Work in Process. Summarize the physical flow of units in a schedule.

S5-5 Compute equivalent units (process costing Step 2) *(Learning Objectives 2 & 3)*

Klein's Packaging Department had the following information at January 31. All direct materials are added at the *end* of the conversion process. The units in ending work in process inventory were only 32% of the way through the conversion process.

	A	B	C	D
1			Equivalent Units	
2		Flow of Physical Units	Direct Materials	Conversion Costs
3	**Units accounted for:**			
4	Completed and transferred out	119,000		
5	Plus: Ending work in process, January 31	18,000		
6	Total physical units accounted for	137,000		
7	**Total equivalent units**			
8				

Complete the schedule by computing the total equivalent units of direct materials and conversion costs for the month.

S5-6 Compute equivalent units (process costing Step 2) *(Learning Objectives 2 & 3)*

The Frying Department of Ripple Chips had 110,000 partially completed units in work in process at the end of July. All of the direct materials had been added to these units, but the units were only 70% of the way through the conversion process. In addition, 1,050,000 units had been completed and transferred out of the Frying Department to the Packaging Department during the month.

1. How many equivalent units of direct materials and equivalent units of conversion costs are associated with the 1,050,000 units completed and transferred out?
2. Compute the equivalent units of direct materials and the equivalent units of conversion costs associated with the 110,000 partially completed units still in ending work in process.
3. What are the total equivalent units of direct materials and the total equivalent units of conversion costs for the month?

S5-7 Summarize total costs to account for (process costing Step 3)
(Learning Objective 3)

Kushner Company's Work in Process Inventory account had a $61,000 beginning balance on March 1 ($36,000 of this related to direct materials used during February, while $25,000 related to conversion costs incurred during February). During March, the following costs were incurred in the department:

Direct materials used	$107,000
Direct labor	$ 18,000
Manufacturing overhead allocated to the department	$150,000

Summarize the department's "Total costs to account for." Prepare a schedule that summarizes the department's total costs to account for by direct materials and conversion costs.

S5-8 Compute the cost per equivalent unit (process costing Step 4)
(Learning Objective 3)

At the end of October, Cranston Bottling's mixing department had "Total costs to account for" of $739,731. Of this amount, $271,596 related to direct materials costs, while the remainder related to conversion costs. The department had 52,230 total equivalent units of direct materials and 45,450 total equivalent units of conversion costs for the month.

Compute the cost per equivalent unit for direct materials and the cost per equivalent unit for conversion costs.

S5-9 Assign costs (process costing Step 5) *(Learning Objective 3)*

Pharma-True Company produces its product using a *single* production process. For the month of March, the company determined its "cost per equivalent unit" to be as follows:

	Direct Materials	Conversion Costs
Cost per equivalent unit:	$3.80	$3.00

During the month, Pharma-True completed and transferred out 370,000 units to finished goods inventory. At month end, 82,000 partially complete units remained in ending work in process inventory. These partially completed units were equal to 70,000 equivalent units of direct materials and 53,000 equivalent units of conversion costs.

1. Determine the total cost that should be assigned to the following:
   a. Units completed and transferred out
   b. Units in ending work in process inventory
2. What were the total costs accounted for?
3. What was Pharma-True's average cost of making one unit of its product?

S5-10 Flow of costs through Work in Process Inventory *(Learning Objective 4)*

Samson Tile produces its product in two processing departments: Forming and Finishing. The following T-account shows the Forming Department's Work in Process Inventory at August 31 prior to completing the five-step process costing procedure:

Work in Process Inventory—Forming Department	
Beginning balance	$ 53,700
Direct materials used	78,400
Direct labor	14,800
Manufacturing overhead allocated	126,100

1. What is the Forming Department's "Total costs to account for" for the month of August?
2. Assume that after using the five-step process costing procedure, the company determines that the "cost to be assigned to units completed and transferred out" is $243,800. What journal entry is needed to record the transfer of costs to the Finishing Department?
3. After the journal entry is made in Requirement 2, what will be the new ending balance in the Forming Department's Work in Process Inventory account?

S5-11 Assign total costs in a second processing department
(Learning Objective 5)

After completing Steps 1–4 of the process costing procedure, Peterson Corporation arrived at the following equivalent units and costs per equivalent unit for its *final* production department for the month of July:

	A	B	C	D
1			Equivalent Units	
2		Transferred-in	Direct Materials	Conversion Costs
3	Units completed and transferred out during July	72,000	72,000	72,000
4	Plus: Ending work in process, July 31	9,000	7,900	3,500
5	Total equivalent units	81,000	79,900	75,500
6	Cost per equivalent unit	$ 2.34	$ 0.75	$ 1.56
7				

1. How much cost should be assigned to the
   a. units completed and transferred out to Finished Goods Inventory during July?
   b. partially complete units still in ending work in process inventory at the end of July?
2. What was the "Total cost accounted for" during July? What other important figure must this match? What does this figure tell you?
3. What is Peterson Corporation's average cost of making *each unit* of its product from the first production department all the way through the final production department?

S5-12 Find unit cost and gross profit on a final product *(Learning Objective 5)*

Gallagher Counter Co. produces quartz countertops in two sequential production departments: Forming and Polishing. The Polishing Department calculated the following costs per equivalent unit (square feet) on its May production cost report:

	Transferred-in	Direct Materials	Conversion Costs
Cost per equivalent unit:	$2.94	$0.90	$1.46

During May, 135,000 square feet were completed and transferred out of the Polishing Department to Finished Goods Inventory. The countertops were subsequently sold for $13.50 per square foot.

1. What was the cost per square foot of the finished product?
2. Did most of the production cost occur in the Forming Department or in the Polishing Department? Explain how you can tell where the most production cost occurred.
3. What was the gross profit per square foot?
4. What was the total gross profit on the countertops produced in May?

The following data set is used for S5-13 through S5-17:

Arctic Springs Data Set: Filtration Department

Arctic Springs produces premium bottled water. Arctic Springs purchases artesian water, stores the water in large tanks, and then runs the water through two processes:
- Filtration, where workers microfilter and ozonate the water
- Bottling, where workers bottle and package the filtered water

During December, the filtration process incurs the following costs in processing 200,000 liters:

Wages of workers operating the filtration equipment	$ 9,380
Wages of workers operating ozonation equipment	$ 9,300
Manufacturing overhead allocated to filtration	$ 24,000
Water	$120,000

Arctic Springs has no beginning inventory in the Filtration Department.

S5-13 Compute cost per liter *(Learning Objective 1)*

Refer to the Arctic Springs Filtration Department Data Set.

1. Compute the December conversion costs in the Filtration Department.
2. If the Filtration Department completely processed 200,000 liters, what would be the average filtration cost per liter?
3. Now, assume that the total costs of the filtration process listed in the previous chart yield 160,000 liters that are completely filtered and ozonated, while the remaining 40,000 liters are only partway through the process at the end of December. Is the cost per completely filtered and ozonated liter higher, lower, or the same as in Requirement 2? Why?

S5-14 Summarize physical flow and compute equivalent units
(Learning Objective 2)

Refer to the Arctic Springs Filtration Department Data Set. At Arctic Springs, water is added at the beginning of the filtration process. Conversion costs are incurred evenly throughout the process, and in December, 160,000 liters have been completed and transferred out of the Filtration Department to the Bottling Department. The 40,000 liters remaining in the Filtration Department's ending work in process inventory are 85% of the way through the filtration process. Recall that Arctic Springs has no beginning inventories.

1. Draw a time line for the filtration process.
2. Complete the first two steps of the process costing procedure for the Filtration Department: summarize the physical flows of units and then compute the equivalent units of direct materials and conversion costs.

S5-15 Continuation of S5-14: Summarize total costs to account for and compute cost per equivalent unit *(Learning Objective 3)*

Refer to the Arctic Springs Filtration Department Data Set and your answer to S5-14. Complete Steps 3 and 4 of the process costing procedure: Summarize total costs to account for and then compute the cost per equivalent unit for both direct materials and conversion costs.

S5-16 Continuation of S5-14 and S5-15: Assign costs *(Learning Objective 3)*

Refer to the Arctic Springs Filtration Department Data Set and your answer to S5-14 and S5-15. Complete Step 5 of the process costing procedure: Assign costs to units completed and to units in ending inventory. Prepare a schedule that answers the following questions.

1. What is the cost of the 160,000 liters completed and transferred out of the Filtration Department?
2. What is the cost of 40,000 liters remaining in the Filtration Department's ending work in process inventory?

S5-17 Continuation of S5-16: Record journal entry and post to T-account
(Learning Objective 4)

Refer to the Arctic Springs Filtration Department Data Set and your answer to S5-16.

1. Record the journal entry to transfer the cost of the 160,000 liters completed and transferred out of the Filtration Department and into the Bottling Department.
2. Record all of the transactions in the "Work in Process Inventory—Filtration" T-account.

The following data set is used for S5-18 through S5-21:

Arctic Springs Data Set: Bottling Department

Arctic Springs produces premium bottled water. The preceding Short Exercises considered the first process in bottling premium water—Filtration. We now consider Arctic Springs' second process—Bottling. In the Bottling Department, workers bottle the filtered water and pack the bottles into boxes. Conversion costs are incurred evenly throughout the Bottling process, but packaging materials are not added until the end of the process.

December data from the Bottling Department follow:

Beginning work in process inventory (45% of the way through the process) ...	9,000 liters
Transferred in from Filtration	160,000 liters
Completed and transferred out to Finished Goods Inventory in December	147,000 liters
Ending work in process inventory (85% of the way through the bottling process)	22,000 liters

Costs in beginning work in process inventory		Costs added during December	
Transferred in	$4,100	Transferred in	$148,000
Direct materials	0	Direct materials	30,870
Direct labor	650	Direct labor	35,000
Manufacturing overhead	2,025	Manufacturing overhead	25,291
Total beginning work in process inventory as of December 1	$6,775	Total costs added during December	$239,161

The Filtration Department completed and transferred out 160,000 liters at a total cost of $148,000.

S5-18 Compute equivalent units in second department *(Learning Objectives 2 & 5)*

Refer to the Arctic Springs Bottling Department Data Set.

1. Draw a time line.
2. Complete the first two steps of the process costing procedure for the Bottling Department: summarize the physical flow of units and then compute the equivalent units of direct materials and conversion costs.

S5-19 Continuation of S5-18: Compute cost per equivalent unit in second department *(Learning Objective 5)*

Refer to the Arctic Springs Bottling Department Data Set and your answer to S5-18. Complete Steps 3 and 4 of the process costing procedure: Summarize total costs to account for and then compute the cost per equivalent unit for both direct materials and conversion costs.

S5-20 Continuation of S5-18 and S5-19: Assign costs in second department *(Learning Objective 5)*

Refer to the Arctic Springs Bottling Department Data Set and your answers to S5-18 and S5-19. Complete Step 5 of the process costing procedure: Assign costs to units completed and to units in ending inventory.

S5-21 Continuation of S5-20: Record journal entry and post to T-account *(Learning Objective 4)*

Refer to the Arctic Springs Bottling Department Data Set and your answer to S5-20.

1. Prepare the journal entry to record the cost of units completed and transferred to finished goods.
2. Post all transactions to the Work in Process Inventory—Bottling T-account. What is the ending balance?

ETHICS

S5-22 Identify ethical standards violated *(Learning Objectives 1, 2, 3, 4, & 5)*

For each of the situations listed, identify the primary standard from the IMA Statement of Ethical Professional Practice that is violated (competence, confidentiality, integrity, or credibility). Refer to Exhibit 1-6 for the complete standard.

1. At a party, Eric gets carried away with bragging about the production process that he has helped to develop at his company. A party-goer who works for a competitor overhears.
2. Process costing has always confused Courtney, an accountant for Murdock Corporation. At the end of the year, she just accepts the bookkeeper's numbers for ending inventory and cost of goods sold even though the bookkeeper does not have formal training in process costing.
3. Lauren works in the Accounting Department at Blue Moon Consulting. She does not disclose that one of the companies bidding on a contract to provide payroll services for Blue Moon employs her daughter.
4. Cassidy Ritter is a bubbly, fun person. She continually makes recommendations one day after the recommendations were needed. She figures that the managers will tolerate the tardiness of the recommendations because the recommendations are well researched and she gets along with everyone.
5. This quarter, the company switched from using the FIFO method of process costing to the weighted-average method of process costing. Andrew, the chief accountant, did not disclose the change in methods in the reports because he did not want to have to justify the change.

EXERCISES Group A

E5-23A Analyze flow of costs through inventory T-accounts *(Learning Objective 1)*

Golden Sun Bakery mass-produces bread using three sequential processing departments: Mixing, Baking, and Packaging. The following transactions occurred during April:

1. Direct materials used in the Packaging Department	$ 34,000
2. Costs assigned to units completed and transferred out of Mixing	$227,000
3. Direct labor incurred in the Mixing Department	$ 11,400
4. Beginning balance: Work in Process Inventory—Baking	$ 15,800
5. Manufacturing overhead allocated to the Baking Department	$ 78,000
6. Beginning balance: Finished Goods	$ 4,600
7. Costs assigned to units completed and transferred out of Baking	$308,000
8. Beginning balance: Work in Process Inventory—Mixing	$ 12,100
9. Direct labor incurred in the Packaging Department	$ 8,900
10. Manufacturing overhead allocated to the Mixing Department	$ 68,000
11. Direct materials used in the Mixing Department	$156,000
12. Beginning balance: Raw Materials Inventory	$ 23,200
13. Costs assigned to units completed and transferred out of Packaging	$385,000
14. Beginning balance: Work in Process Inventory—Packaging	$ 8,000
15. Purchases of Raw Materials	$179,000
16. Direct labor incurred in the Baking Department	$ 4,200
17. Manufacturing overhead allocated to the Packaging Department	$ 40,000
18. Cost of goods sold	$386,000

Note: No direct materials were used by the Baking Department.

Requirements

1. Post each of these transactions to the company's inventory T-accounts. You should set up separate T-accounts for the following:
   - Raw Materials Inventory
   - Work in Process Inventory—Mixing Department
   - Work in Process Inventory—Baking Department
   - Work in Process Inventory—Packaging Department
   - Finished Goods Inventory
2. Determine the balance at month end in each of the inventory accounts.
3. Assume that 3,025,000 loaves of bread were completed and transferred out of the Packaging Department during the month. What was the cost per unit of making each loaf of bread (from start to finish)?

E5-24A Summarize physical units and compute equivalent units (process costing Steps 1 and 2) *(Learning Objective 3)*

Patty's Pumpkin Pies collected the following production information relating to November's baking operations:

	Physical Units	Direct Materials (% complete)	Conversion Costs (% complete)
Beginning work in process	203,000	—	—
Ending work in process	153,000	75%	80%
Units started during the month	995,000		

Requirements

Complete the first two steps in the process costing procedure:

1. Summarize the flow of physical units.
2. Compute output in terms of equivalent units.

E5-25A Compute equivalent units in a second processing department *(Learning Objectives 2 & 5)*

Boswell's Hot Sauce uses a process costing system to determine its product's cost. The last of the three processes is packaging. The Packaging Department reported the following information for the month of July:

	A	B	C	D	E
1	**Boswell's Hot Sauce Packaging Department**	Step 1:		Step 2: Equivalent Units	
2	Month Ended July 31 Flow of Production	Flow of Physical Units	Transferred-in	Direct Materials	Conversion Costs
3	**Units to account for:**				
4	Beginning work in process, July 1	24,000			
5	Plus: Transferred in during July	226,000			
6	Total physical units to account for	(a)			
7					
8	**Units accounted for:**				
9	Completed and transferred out during July	(b)	(d)	(g)	(j)
10	Plus: Ending work in process, July 31	29,000	(e)	(h)	(k)
11	Total physical units accounted for	(c)			
12	**Total Equivalent Units**		(f)	(i)	(l)
13					

The units in ending work in process inventory were 90% complete with respect to direct materials but only 60% complete with respect to conversion.

Requirement

Summarize the flow of physical units and compute output in terms of equivalent units in order to arrive at the missing figures (a) through (l).

E5-26A   Complete five-step procedure in first department *(Learning Objective 3)*

The Color World Paint Company prepares and packages paint products. The company has two departments: (1) Blending and (2) Packaging. Direct materials are added at the beginning of the blending process (dyes) and at the end of the packaging process (cans). Conversion costs are incurred evenly throughout each process. Data from the month of August for the Blending Department are as follows:

Gallons:	
Beginning work in process inventory	0
Started production	9,000 gallons
Completed and transferred out to Packaging in August	6,500 gallons
Ending work in process inventory (30% of the way through the blending process)	2,500 gallons
Costs:	
Beginning work in process inventory	$ 0
Costs added during August:	
Direct materials (dyes)	5,670
Direct labor	800
Manufacturing overhead	2,100
Total costs added during August	$8,570

Requirements

1. Draw a time line.
2. Summarize the physical flow of units and compute total equivalent units for direct materials and for conversion costs.
3. Summarize total costs to account for and find the cost per equivalent unit for direct materials and conversion costs.
4. Assign total costs to units (gallons):
   a Completed and transferred out to the Packaging Department
   b In the Blending Department ending work in process inventory
5. What is the average cost per gallon transferred out of the Blending Department to the Packaging Department? Why would the company's managers want to know this cost?

E5-27A   Continuation of E5-26A: Journal entries *(Learning Objective 4)*

Return to the Blending Department for the Color World Paint Company in E5-26A.

Requirements

1. Prepare the journal entry to record the use of direct materials and direct labor and the allocation of manufacturing overhead to the Blending Department. Also, give the journal entry to record the costs of the gallons completed and transferred out to the Packaging Department. Assume the wages are unpaid.
2. Post the journal entries to the Work in Process Inventory—Blending T-account. What is the ending balance?

E5-28A Complete the production cost report in first department
(Learning Objective 3)

Woodson Dairy produces an organic butter that is sold by the pound. The production of the butter begins in the Churning Department.

Data for the Churning Department for January follows:

Units in beginning Work in Process (WIP) inventory	100,000 units
Units started during the month (all direct materials, including cream and salt, are added at the **beginning** of the churning process)	1,500,000 units
Units in ending Work in Process (WIP) inventory (40% of the way through the process)	200,000 units

Cost information is as follows:

WIP–Churning Department balance as of January 1:

Direct material cost included in beginning WIP balance	$110,000
Conversion cost included in beginning WIP balance	24,000
Beginning balance, WIP, January 1	$134,000

Manufacturing costs incurred during January:

Direct materials used	$1,730,000
Direct labor	10,000
Manufacturing overhead	558,000
Total manufacturing costs entered into production during January	$2,298,000

Requirements
1. Prepare a production cost report for January for the Churning Department.
2. How much did it cost to make one pound of butter in the Churning Department?
3. How much did it cost to make a *partially completed* pound of butter in the Churning Department? Does this make sense? Why or why not?

E5-29A Prepare journal entries for first production department
(Learning Objective 4)

Refer to the Churning Department information for Woodson Dairy in E5-28A.

Requirements
1. What journal entry(s) would have been made *during the month* to record manufacturing costs? (Use Wages Payable as the credit for the direct labor costs.)
2. What journal entry is needed at the *end of the month* to transfer the cost of the butter out of the Churning Department and into the next department, the Forming Department?
3. Post the journal entries to the Work in Process Inventory—Churning Department T-account.

E5-30A Analyze costs and gross profit in a process costing environment
(Learning Objective 5)

Refer to E5-28A and E5-29A. Assume the Woodson Dairy Forming Department has the following costs per equivalent unit (EU) on its own production cost report for the month of January:

Cost per EU transferred in from Churning Department (see your answer from E5-28A)
Cost per Direct Materials EU = $0.10
Cost per Conversion Costs EU = $0.15

Requirements
1. What is the total cost, *from start to finish*, of producing one pound of butter during January?
2. If the company sells all 1,400,000 pounds of the butter made in January, at a selling price of $2.55 per pound, what is the total gross profit for the month?

E5-31A Record journal entries *(Learning Objective 4)*

Record the following process costing transactions in the general journal:
a. Purchase of raw materials on account, $9,300
b. Requisition of direct materials to

   Assembly Department, $4,300

   Finishing Department, $2,400
c. Incurrence and payment of direct labor, $10,500 (these costs should be debited to WIP Inventory—Assembly)
d. Incurrence of manufacturing overhead costs (unpaid):

   Property taxes—plant, $1,800

   Utilities—plant, $4,800

   Insurance—plant, $1,700

   Depreciation—plant, $3,800
e. Assignment of conversion costs to the Assembly Department:

   Direct labor, $5,000

   Manufacturing overhead, $2,600
f. Assignment of conversion costs to the Finishing Department:

   Direct labor, $4,700

   Manufacturing overhead, $6,600
g. Cost of goods completed and transferred out of the Assembly Department to the Finishing Department, $10,500
h. Cost of goods completed and transferred out of the Finishing Department into Finished Goods Inventory, $15,600

E5-32A Compute equivalent units and assign costs *(Learning Objectives 2, 3, & 4)*

The Assembly Department of Easton Motors began September with no work in process inventory. During the month, production that cost $41,352 (direct materials, $12,532, and conversion costs, $28,820) was started on 28,000 units. Easton completed and transferred to the Testing Department a total of 22,000 units. The ending work in process inventory was 35% complete as to direct materials and 70% complete as to conversion work.

Requirements

1. Compute the equivalent units for direct materials and conversion costs.
2. Compute the cost per equivalent unit.
3. Assign the costs to units completed and transferred out and ending work in process inventory.
4. Record the journal entry for the costs transferred out of the Assembly Department to the Testing Department.
5. Post all of the transactions in the Work in Process Inventory—Assembly T-account. What is the ending balance?

E5-33A Complete five-step procedure in first department *(Learning Objective 3)*

Paulson Winery in Albany, New York, has two departments: Fermenting and Packaging. Direct materials are added at the beginning of the fermenting process (grapes) and at the end of the packaging process (bottles). Conversion costs are incurred evenly throughout each process. Data from the month of March for the Fermenting Department are as follows:

Gallons:	
Beginning work in process inventory	2,100 gallons
Started production	5,860 gallons
Completed and transferred out to Packaging in March	6,560 gallons
Ending work in process inventory (80% of the way through the fermenting process)	1,400 gallons
Costs:	
Beginning work in process inventory ($2,500 of direct materials and $3,715 of conversion cost)	$ 6,215
Costs added during March:	
Direct materials	$ 9,440
Direct labor	600
Manufacturing overhead	1,829
Total costs added during March	$11,869

Requirements

1. Draw a time line for the Fermenting Department.
2. Summarize the flow of physical units and compute the total equivalent units.
3. Summarize total costs to account for and compute the cost per equivalent unit for direct materials and conversion costs.
4. Assign total costs to units (gallons):
    a. Completed and transferred out to the Packaging Department
    b. In the Fermenting Department ending work in process inventory
5. What is the average cost per gallon transferred out of Fermenting into Packaging? Why would the company's managers want to know this cost?

E5-34A Sustainability and process costing *(Learning Objective 3)*

Revol Industries manufactures plastic bottles for the food industry. On average, Revol pays $76 per ton for its plastics. Revol's waste-disposal company has increased its waste-disposal charge to $57 per ton for solid and inert waste. Revol generates a total of 500 tons of waste per month.

Revol's managers have been evaluating the production processes for areas to cut waste. In the process of making plastic bottles, a certain amount of machine "drool" occurs. Machine drool is the excess plastic that drips off the machine between molds. In the past, Revol has discarded the machine drool. In an average month, 180 tons of machine drool is generated.

Management has arrived at three possible courses of action for the machine drool issue:

1. Do nothing and pay the increased waste-disposal charge.
2. Sell the machine drool waste to a local recycler for $18 per ton.
3. Reengineer the production process at an annual cost of $55,000. This change in the production process would cause the amount of machine drool generated to be reduced by 50% each month. The remaining machine drool would then be sold to a local recycler for $18 per ton.

Requirements

1. What is the annual cost of the machine drool currently? Include both the original plastic cost and the waste-disposal cost.
2. How much would the company save per year (net) if the machine drool were to be sold to the local recycler?
3. How much would the company save per year (net) if the production process were to be reengineered?
4. What do you think the company should do? Explain your rationale.

E5-35A Complete five-step procedure and journalize result
(Learning Objectives 3 & 4)

The following information was taken from the ledger of Cleveland Foundry:

Work in Process—Forming			
Beginning inventory, October 1	$ 46,930	Transferred to Finishing	$?
Direct materials	196,746		
Conversion costs	161,100		
Ending inventory	?		

The Forming Department had 10,150 partially complete units in beginning work in process inventory. The department started work on 71,050 units during the month and ended the month with 8,200 units still in work in process. These unfinished units were 60% complete as to direct materials but 20% complete as to conversion work. The beginning balance of $46,930 consisted of $21,430 of direct materials and $25,500 of conversion costs.

Requirement

Journalize the transfer of costs to the Finishing Department. (*Hint:* Complete the five-step process costing procedure to determine how much cost to transfer.)

E5-36A Complete five-step procedure in second department
(Learning Objective 5)

Alpha Semiconductors experienced the following activity in its Photolithography Department during December. Materials are added at the beginning of the photolithography process.

Units:	
Work in process, December 1 (80% of the way through the process)	6,000 units
Transferred in from the Polishing and Cutting Department during December	29,000 units
Completed during December	? units
Work in process, December 31 (70% of the way through the process)	7,000 units

Costs:	
Work in process, December 1 (transferred-in costs, $21,600; direct materials costs, $20,350; and conversion costs, $27,690)	$69,640
Transferred in from the Polishing and Cutting Department during December	97,400
Direct materials added during December	63,650
Conversion costs added during December	90,750

Requirements

1. Summarize flow of physical units and compute total equivalent units for three cost categories: transferred-in, direct materials, and conversion costs.
2. Summarize total costs to account for and compute the cost per equivalent unit for each cost category.
3. Assign total costs to (a) units completed and transferred to Finished Goods Inventory and (b) units in December 31 Work in Process Inventory.

EXERCISES Group B

E5-37B Analyze flow of costs through inventory T-accounts *(Learning Objective 1)*

Early Start Bakery mass-produces bread using three sequential processing departments: Mixing, Baking, and Packaging. The following transactions occurred during February:

1. Direct materials used in the Packaging Department	$ 30,000
2. Costs assigned to units completed and transferred out of Mixing	$228,000
3. Direct labor incurred in the Mixing Department	$ 11,200
4. Beginning balance: Work in Process Inventory—Baking	$ 15,900
5. Manufactured overhead allocated to the Baking Department	$ 70,000
6. Beginning balance: Finished Goods Inventory	$ 4,900
7. Costs assigned to units completed and transferred out of Baking	$301,000
8. Beginning balance: Work in Process Inventory—Mixing	$ 12,100
9. Direct labor incurred in the Packaging Department	$ 8,800
10. Manufacturing overhead allocated to the Mixing Department	$ 67,000
11. Direct materials used in the Mixing Department	$151,000
12. Beginning balance: Raw Materials Inventory	$ 23,500
13. Costs assigned to units completed and transferred out of Packaging	$380,000
14. Beginning balance: Work in Process Inventory—Packaging	$ 8,200
15. Purchases of Raw Materials	$177,000
16. Direct labor incurred in the Baking Department	$ 4,600
17. Manufacturing overhead allocated to the Packaging Department	$ 46,000
18. Cost of goods sold	$381,000

Requirements

1. Post each of these transactions to the company's inventory T-accounts. You should set up separate T-accounts for the following:
   - Raw Materials Inventory
   - Work in Process Inventory—Mixing Department
   - Work in Process Inventory—Baking Department
   - Work in Process Inventory—Packaging Department
   - Finished Goods Inventory
2. Determine the balance at month-end in each of the inventory accounts.
3. Assume 3,375,000 loaves of bread were completed and transferred out of the Packaging Department during the month. What was the cost per unit of making each loaf of bread (from start to finish)?

E5-38B Summarize physical units and compute equivalent units (process costing Steps 1 and 2) *(Learning Objective 3)*

Paul's Pies collected the following production information relating to November's baking operations:

	Physical Units	Direct Materials (% complete)	Conversion Costs (% complete)
Beginning work in process	207,000	—	—
Ending work in process	157,000	70%	80%
Units started during the month	985,000		

Requirements

Complete the first two steps in the process costing procedure:

1. Summarize the flow of physical units.
2. Compute output in terms of equivalent units.

E5-39B   Compute equivalent units in a second processing department
(Learning Objectives 2 & 5)

Wendell's Hot Sauce uses a process costing system to determine its product's cost. The last of the three processes is packaging. The Packaging Department reported the following information for the month of August:

	A	B	C	D	E
1	**Wendell's Hot Sauce Packaging Department** **Month Ended August 31** **Flow of Production**	**Step 1:** **Flow of Physical Units**	**Step 2: Equivalent Units**		
2			**Transferred-in**	**Direct Materials**	**Conversion Costs**
3	**Units to account for:**				
4	Beginning work in process, August 1	25,000			
5	Plus: Transferred in during August	229,000			
6	Total physical units to account for	(a)			
7					
8	**Units accounted for:**				
9	Completed and transferred out during August	(b)	(d)	(g)	(j)
10	Plus: Ending work in process, August 31	30,000	(e)	(h)	(k)
11	Total physical units accounted for	(c)			
12	**Total Equivalent Units**		(f)	(i)	(l)
13					

The units in ending work in process inventory were 90% complete with respect to direct materials, but only 40% complete with respect to conversion.

Requirement

Summarize the flow of physical units and compute output in terms of equivalent units in order to arrive at the missing figures (a) through (l).

E5-40B   Complete five-step procedure in first department *(Learning Objective 3)*

The Bright Day Paint Company prepares and packages paint products. The company has two departments: (1) Blending and (2) Packaging. Direct materials are added at the beginning of the blending process (dyes) and at the end of the packaging process (cans). Conversion costs are incurred evenly throughout each process. Data from the month of June for the Blending Department are as follows:

Gallons:	
Beginning work in process inventory	0
Started production	9,600 gallons
Completed and transferred out to Packaging in June	6,800 gallons
Ending work in process inventory (45% of the way through the blending process)	2,800 gallons
Costs:	
Beginning work in process inventory	$ 0
Costs added during June:	
Direct materials (dyes)	$6,240
Direct labor	950
Manufacturing overhead	1,871
Total costs added during June	$9,061

Requirements

1. Fill in the time line for the Blending Department.
2. Summarize the physical flow of units and compute total equivalent units for direct materials and for conversion costs.
3. Summarize total costs to account for and find the cost per equivalent unit for direct materials and for conversion costs.
4. Assign total costs to units (gallons):
   a. Completed and transferred out to the Packaging Department
   b. In the Blending Department ending work in process inventory
5. What is the average cost per gallon transferred out of the Blending Department to the Packaging Department? Why would the company's managers want to know this cost?

E5-41B Continuation of E5-40B: Journal entries *(Learning Objective 4)*

Return to the Blending Department for The Bright Day Paint Company in E5-40B.

Requirements

1. Prepare the journal entry to record the use of direct materials and direct labor and the allocation of manufacturing overhead to the Blending Department. Also, give the journal entry to record the costs of the gallons completed and transferred out to the Packaging Department. Assume the wages are unpaid.
2. Post the journal entries to the Work in Process Inventory—Blending T-account. What is the ending balance?

E5-42B Complete the production cost report in first department
(Learning Objective 3)

Landon Dairy produces an organic butter that is sold by the pound. The production of the butter begins in the Churning Department.

Data for the Churning Department for January follows:

Units in beginning Work in Process (WIP) inventory	35,000 units
Units started during the month (all direct materials, including cream and salt, are added at the *beginning* of the churning process)	385,000 units
Units in ending Work in Process (WIP) inventory (60% of the way through the process)	20,000 units

Cost information is as follows:

WIP–Churning Department balance as of January 1:

Direct material cost included in beginning WIP balance	$122,500
Conversion cost included in beginning WIP balance	14,000
Beginning balance, WIP, January 1	$136,500

Manufacturing costs incurred during January:

Direct materials used	$1,347,500
Direct labor	25,000
Manufacturing overhead	290,600
Total manufacturing costs entered into production during January	$1,663,100

Requirements

1. Prepare a production cost report for January for the Churning Department.
2. How much did it cost to make one pound of butter in the Churning Department?
3. How much did it cost to make a *partially completed* pound of butter in the Churning Department? Does this make sense? Why or why not?

E5-43B Prepare journal entries for first production department
(Learning Objective 4)

Refer to the Churning Department information for Landon Dairy in E5-42B.

Requirements

1. What journal entry(s) would have been made *during the month* to record manufacturing costs? (Use Wages Payable as the credit for the direct labor costs.)
2. What journal entry is needed at the *end of the month* to transfer the cost of the butter out of the Churning Department and into the next department, the Forming Department?
3. Post the journal entries to the Work in Process Inventory–Churning Department T-account.

E5-44B Analyze costs and gross profit in a process costing environment
(Learning Objective 5)

Refer to E5-42B and E5-43B. Assume the Landon Dairy Forming Department has the following costs per equivalent unit (EU) on its own production cost report for the month of January:

> Cost per EU transferred in from Churning Department (see your answer from E5-42B)
> Cost per Direct Materials EU = $0.10
> Cost per Conversion Costs EU = $0.15

Requirements

1. What is the total cost, *from start to finish*, of producing one pound of butter during January?
2. If the company sells all 400,000 pounds of the butter made in January, at a selling price of $5.50 per pound, what is the total gross profit for the month?

E5-45B Record journal entries *(Learning Objective 4)*

Record the following process costing transactions in the general journal:

a. Purchase of raw materials on account, $9,900
b. Requisition of direct materials to:

   Assembly Department, $4,500
   Finishing Department, $2,200

c. Incurrence and payment of manufacturing labor, $10,900 (these costs should be debited to WIP Inventory—Assembly)
d. Incurrence of manufacturing overhead costs (unpaid):

   Property taxes—plant, $1,200
   Utilities—plant, $4,300
   Insurance—plant, $1,000
   Depreciation—plant, $3,600

e. Assignment of conversion costs to the Assembly Department:

   Direct labor, $5,200
   Manufacturing overhead, $2,200

f. Assignment of conversion costs to the Finishing Department:

   Direct labor, $4,400
   Manufacturing overhead, $6,400

g. Cost of goods completed and transferred out of the Assembly Department to the Finishing Department, $10,200
h. Cost of goods completed and transferred out of the Finishing Department into Finished Goods Inventory, $15,600

E5-46B Compute equivalent units and assign costs *(Learning Objectives 2, 3, & 4)*

The Assembly Department of Thomas Motors began September with no work in process inventory. During the month, production that cost $35,282 (direct materials, $8,242, and conversion costs, $27,040) was started on 23,000 units. Thomas completed and transferred to the Testing Department a total of 12,000 units. The ending work in process inventory was 35% complete as to direct materials and 80% complete as to conversion work.

Requirements

1. Compute the equivalent units for direct materials and conversion costs.
2. Compute the cost per equivalent unit.
3. Assign the costs to units completed and transferred out and ending work in process inventory.
4. Record the journal entry for the costs transferred out of the Assembly Department to the Testing Department.
5. Post all of the transactions in the Work in Process Inventory—Assembly T-account. What is the ending balance?

E5-47B Complete five-step procedure in first department *(Learning Objective 3)*

Newton Winery in Newton, Massachusetts, has two departments: Fermenting and Packaging. Direct materials are added at the beginning of the fermenting process (grapes) and at the end of the packaging process (bottles). Conversion costs are incurred evenly throughout each process. Data from the month of March for the Fermenting Department are as follows:

Gallons:	
Beginning work in process inventory	2,900 gallons
Started production	4,770 gallons
Completed and transferred out to Packaging in March	6,420 gallons
Ending work in process inventory (80% of the way through the fermenting process)	1,250 gallons
Costs:	
Beginning work in process inventory ($2,100 of direct materials and $1,409 of conversion cost)	$ 3,509
Costs added during March:	
Direct materials	$ 10,172
Direct labor	1,000
Manufacturing overhead	1,301
Total costs added during March	$ 12,473

Requirements

1. Draw a time line for the Fermenting Department.
2. Summarize the flow of physical units and compute the total equivalent units.
3. Summarize total costs to account for and compute the cost per equivalent unit for direct materials and conversion costs.
4. Assign total costs to units (gallons):
    a. Completed and transferred out to the Packaging Department
    b. In the Fermenting Department ending work in process inventory
5. What is the average cost per gallon transferred out of Fermenting into Packaging? Why would the company's managers want to know this cost?

E5-48B Sustainability and process costing *(Learning Objective 3)*

Sandler Industries manufactures plastic bottles for the food industry. On average, Sandler pays $72 per ton for its plastics. Sandler's waste-disposal company has increased its waste-disposal charge to $54 per ton for solid and inert waste. Sandler generates a total of 500 tons of waste per month.

Sandler's managers have been evaluating the production processes for areas to cut waste. In the process of making plastic bottles, a certain amount of machine "drool" occurs. Machine drool is the excess plastic that drips off the machine between molds. In the past, Sandler has discarded the machine drool. In an average month, 140 tons of machine drool are generated.

Management has arrived at three possible courses of action for the machine drool issue:

1. Do nothing and pay the increased waste-disposal charge.
2. Sell the machine drool waste to a local recycler for $15 per ton.
3. Reengineer the production process at an annual cost of $70,000. This change in the production process would cause the amount of machine drool generated to be reduced by 40% each month. The remaining machine drool would then be sold to a local recycler for $15 per ton.

Requirements

1. What is the annual cost of the machine drool currently? Include both the original plastics cost and the waste disposal cost.
2. How much would the company save per year (net) if the machine drool were to be sold at the local recycler?
3. How much would the company save per year (net) if the production process were to be reengineered?
4. What do you think the company should do? Explain your rationale.

E5-49B Complete five-step procedure and journalize result
(Learning Objectives 3 & 4)

The following information was taken from the ledger of Denver Foundry:

Work in Process—Forming			
Beginning inventory, October 1	71,110	Transferred to Finishing	?
Direct materials	171,930		
Conversion costs	162,800		
Ending inventory	?		

The Forming Department had 10,470 partially complete units in beginning work in process inventory. The department started work on 67,530 units during the month and ended the month with 9,000 units still in work in process. These unfinished units were 60% complete as to direct materials but 20% complete as to conversion work. The beginning balance of $71,110 consisted of $21,510 of direct materials and $49,600 of conversion costs.

Requirement

Journalize the transfer of costs to the Finishing Department. (*Hint*: Complete the five-step process costing procedure to determine how much cost to transfer.)

E5-50B Complete five-step procedure in second department
(Learning Objective 5)

Brookman Semiconductors experienced the following activity in its Photolithography Department during May. Materials are added at the beginning of the photolithography process.

Units:	
Work in process, May 1 (80% of the way through the process)	9,000 units
Transferred in from the Polishing and Cutting Department during May	23,000 units
Completed during May	? units
Work in process, May 31 (70% of the way through the process)	2,000 units
Costs:	
Work in process, May 1 (transferred-in costs, $1,600; direct materials costs, $20,450; and conversion costs, $37,890)	$59,940
Transferred in from the Polishing and Cutting Department during May	97,600
Direct materials added during May	53,150
Conversion costs incurred during May	90,850

Requirements

1. Summarize flow of physical units and compute total equivalent units for three cost categories: transferred-in, direct materials, and conversion costs.
2. Summarize total costs to account for and compute the cost per equivalent unit for each cost category.
3. Assign total costs to (a) units completed and transferred to Finished Goods Inventory and (b) units in May 31 Work in Process Inventory.

PROBLEMS Group A

P5-51A Process costing in a single processing department
(Learning Objectives 1, 2, & 3)

Decker Cosmetics produces a lip balm used for cold-weather sports. The balm is manufactured in a single processing department. No lip balm was in process on May 31, and Decker Lips started production on 20,000 lip balm tubes during June. Direct materials are added at the beginning of the process, but conversion costs are incurred evenly throughout the process. Completed production for June totaled 15,000 units. The June 30 work in process was 30% of the way through the production process. Direct materials costing $5,800 were placed in production during June, and direct labor of $3,400 and manufacturing overhead of $560 were assigned to the process.

Requirements

1. Draw a time line for Decker Cosmetics.
2. Use the time line to help you compute the total equivalent units and the cost per equivalent unit for June.
3. Assign total costs to (a) units completed and transferred to Finished Goods and (b) units still in process at June 30.
4. Prepare a T-account for Work in Process Inventory to show activity during June, including the June 30 balance.

P5-52A Process costing in a first department *(Learning Objectives 1, 3, & 4)*

The Timberbrook Furniture Company produces dining tables in a three-stage process: Sawing, Assembly, and Staining. Costs incurred in the Sawing Department during September are summarized as follows:

Work in Process Inventory—Sawing	
September 1 balance	0
Direct materials	1,830,000
Direct labor	144,900
Manufacturing overhead	165,300

Direct materials (lumber) are added at the beginning of the sawing process, while conversion costs are incurred evenly throughout the process. September activity in the Sawing Department included sawing of 12,000 meters of lumber, which were transferred to the Assembly Department. Also, work began on 3,000 meters of lumber, which on September 30 were 70% of the way through the sawing process.

Requirements

1. Draw a time line for the Sawing Department.
2. Use the time line to help you compute the number of equivalent units and the cost per equivalent unit in the Sawing Department for September.
3. Show that the sum of (a) cost of goods transferred out of the Sawing Department and (b) ending Work in Process Inventory—Sawing equals the total cost accumulated in the department during September.
4. Journalize all transactions affecting the company's sawing process during September, including those already posted. Assume the wages are unpaid.

P5-53A Five-step process: Materials added at different points
(Learning Objectives 1, 2, & 3)

Grammer Chicken produces canned chicken a la king. The chicken a la king passes through three departments: (1) Mixing, (2) Retort (sterilization), and (3) Packing. In the Mixing Department, chicken and cream are added at the beginning of the process, the mixture is partly cooked, and chopped green peppers and mushrooms are added at the end of the process. Conversion costs are incurred evenly throughout the mixing process. November data from the Mixing Department are as follows:

Gallons		Costs	
Beginning work in process inventory	0 gallons	Beginning work in process inventory	$ 0
Started production	14,300 gallons	Costs added during November:	
Completed and transferred out to Retort in November	13,600 gallons	Chicken	21,740
		Cream	4,000
Ending work in process inventory (60% of the way through the mixing process)	700 gallons	Green peppers and mushrooms	5,440
		Direct labor	11,200
		Manufacturing overhead	9,830
		Total costs	$52,210

Requirements

1. Draw a time line for the Mixing Department.
2. Use the time line to help you summarize the flow of physical units and compute the equivalent units. (*Hint:* Each direct material added at a different point in the production process requires its own equivalent-unit computation.)
3. Compute the cost per equivalent unit for each cost category.
4. Compute the total costs of the units (gallons):
   a. Completed and transferred out to the Retort Department
   b. In the Mixing Department's ending work in process inventory

P5-54A Prepare a production cost report and journal entries
(Learning Objectives 4 & 5)

Vintage Accessories manufactures auto roof racks in a two-stage process that includes shaping and plating. Steel alloy is the basic raw material of the shaping process. The steel is molded according to the design specifications of automobile manufacturers. The Plating Department then adds an anodized finish.

At March 31, before recording the transfer of cost from the Plating Department to Finished Goods Inventory, the Vintage Accessories general ledger included the following account:

Work in Process Inventory—Plating	
March 1 balance	30,480
Transferred-in from Shaping	36,000
Direct materials	24,200
Direct labor	21,732
Manufacturing overhead	35,388

The direct materials (rubber pads) are added at the end of the plating process. Conversion costs are incurred evenly throughout the process. Work in process of the Plating Department on March 1 consisted of 1,200 racks. The $30,480 beginning balance of Work in Process—Plating includes $18,000 of transferred-in cost and $12,480 of conversion cost. During March, 2,400 racks were transferred in from the Shaping Department. The Plating Department transferred 2,200 racks to Finished Goods Inventory in March, and 1,400 were still in process on March 31. This ending inventory was 50% of the way through the plating process.

Requirements

1. Draw a time line for the Plating Department.
2. Prepare the March production cost report for the Plating Department.
3. Journalize all transactions affecting the Plating Department during March, including the entries that have already been posted. Assume the wages are unpaid.

P5-55A Cost per unit and gross profit *(Learning Objective 5)*

Bradley Wilmer operates Bradley's Cricket Farm in Fairview, Georgia. Bradley's raises about 18 million crickets a month. Most are sold to pet stores at $10.26 for a box of 1,000 crickets. Pet stores sell the crickets for $0.05 to $0.10 each as live feed for reptiles.

Raising crickets requires a two-step process: incubation and brooding. In the first process, incubation, employees place cricket eggs on mounds of peat moss to hatch. In the second process, employees move the newly hatched crickets into large boxes filled with cardboard dividers. Depending on the desired size, the crickets spend approximately two weeks in brooding before being shipped to pet stores. In the brooding process, Bradley's crickets consume about 16 tons of food and produce 12 tons of manure.

Wilmer has invested $375,000 in the cricket farm, and he had hoped to earn a 60% annual rate of return, which works out to a 5% monthly return on his investment. After looking at the farm's bank balance, Wilmer fears he is not achieving this return. To get more accurate information on the farm's performance, Wilmer bought new accounting software that provides weighted-average process cost information. After Wilmer input the data, the software provided the following reports. However, Wilmer needs help interpreting these reports.

Wilmer does know that a unit of production is a box of 1,000 crickets. For example, in June's report, the 7,000 physical units of beginning work-in-process inventory are 7,000 boxes (each one of those boxes contains 1,000 immature crickets). The finished goods inventory is zero because the crickets ship out as soon as they reach the required size. Monthly operating expenses total $8,250 (in addition to the costs that follow).

	A	B	C	D	E
1	Bradley's Cricket Farm—Brooding Department Month Ended June 30 Production Cost Report (part 1 of 3)	Step 1: Flow of Physical Units	Step 2: Equivalent Units		
2			Transferred-in	Direct Materials	Conversion Costs
3	Flow of Production				
4	Units to account for:				
5	Beginning work in process, June 1	7,000			
6	Plus: Transferred in during June	30,000			
7	Total physical units to account for	37,000			
8					
9	Units accounted for:				
10	Completed and transferred out during June	27,000	27,000	27,000	27,000
11	Plus: Ending work in process, June 30	10,000	10,000	8,000	3,000
12	Total physical units accounted for	37,000			
13	Total equivalent units		37,000	35,000	30,000
14					

	A	B	C	D	E
1	Bradley's Cricket Farm—Brooding Department Month Ended June 30 Production Cost Report (part 2 of 3)	Transferred-in	Direct Materials	Conversion Costs	Total
3	Beginning work in process, June 1	$ 16,000	$ 34,000	$ 8,000	$ 58,000
4	Plus: Costs added during June	50,970	162,000	55,000	267,970
5	Total costs to account for	$ 66,970	$ 196,000	$ 63,000	$ 325,970
6	Divided by: Total equivalent units	37,000	35,000	30,000	
7	Cost per equivalent unit	$ 1.81	$ 5.60	$ 2.10	
8					

	A	B	C	D	E
1	Bradley's Cricket Farm—Brooding Department Month Ended June 30 Production Cost Report (part 3 of 3)	Transferred-in	Direct Materials	Conversion Costs	Total
3	Assignment of total cost:				
4	Completed and transferred out:				
5	Equivalent units completed and transferred out	27,000	27,000	27,000	
6	Multiplied by: Cost per equivalent unit	$ 1.81	$ 5.60	$ 2.10	
7	Cost assigned to units completed and transferred out	$ 48,870	$ 151,200	$ 56,700	$ 256,770
8					
9	Ending work in process:				
10	Equivalent units in ending WIP	10,000	8,000	3,000	
11	Multiplied by: Cost per equivalent unit	$ 1.81	$ 5.60	$ 2.10	
12	Cost assigned to units in ending WIP	$ 18,100	$ 44,800	$ 6,300	$ 69,200
13					
14	Total costs accounted for				$ 325,970
15					

Requirements

Bradley Wilmer has the following questions about the farm's performance during June:

1. What is the cost per box of crickets sold? (*Hint:* This is the cost of the boxes completed and shipped out of brooding.)
2. What is the gross profit per box?
3. How much operating income did Bradley's Cricket Farm make in June?
4. What is the return on Wilmer's investment of $375,000 for the month of June? (Compute this as June's operating income divided by Wilmer's investment, expressed as a percentage.)
5. What monthly operating income would provide a 5% monthly rate of return? What price per box would Bradley's Cricket Farm have had to charge in June to achieve this target monthly rate of return?

PROBLEMS Group B

P5-56B Process costing in a single processing department
(Learning Objectives 1, 2, & 3)

Cool Balm produces a lip balm used for cold-weather sports. The balm is manufactured in a single processing department. No lip balm was in process on May 31, and Cool Balm started production on 20,900 lip balm tubes during June. Direct materials are added at the beginning of the process, but conversion costs are incurred evenly throughout the process. Completed production for June totaled 15,700 units. The June 30 work in process was 45% of the way through the production process. Direct materials costing $5,225 were placed in production during June, and direct labor of $3,360 and manufacturing overhead of $248 were assigned to the process.

Requirements

1. Fill-in the time line for Cool Balm.
2. Use the time line to help you compute the total equivalent units and the cost per equivalent unit for June.
3. Assign total costs to (a) units completed and transferred to Finished Goods and (b) units still in process at June 30.
4. Prepare a T-account for Work in Process Inventory to show activity during June, including the June 30 balance.

P5-57B Process costing in a first department *(Learning Objectives 1, 3, & 4)*

The Weaver Furniture Company produces dining tables in a three-stage process: Sawing, Assembly, and Staining. Costs incurred in the Sawing Department during September are summarized as follows:

Work in Process Inventory—Sawing	
September 1 balance	0
Direct materials	1,848,000
Direct labor	142,000
Manufacturing overhead	173,000

Direct materials (lumber) are added at the beginning of the sawing process, while conversion costs are incurred evenly throughout the process. September activity in the Sawing Department included sawing of 14,000 meters of lumber, which were transferred to the Assembly Department. Also, work began on 2,500 meters of lumber, which on September 30 were 70% of the way through the sawing process.

Requirements

1. Draw a time line for the Sawing Department.
2. Use the time line to help you compute the number of equivalent units and the cost per equivalent unit in the Sawing Department for September.
3. Show that the sum of (a) cost of goods transferred out of the Sawing Department and (b) ending "Work in Process Inventory—Sawing" equals the total cost accumulated in the department during September.
4. Journalize all transactions affecting the company's sawing process during September, including those already posted. Assume the wages are unpaid.

P5-58B Five-step process: Materials added at different points
(Learning Objectives 1, 2, & 3)

Tastee Foods produces canned chicken a la king. The chicken a la king passes through three departments: (1) Mixing, (2) Retort (sterilization), and (3) Packing. In the Mixing Department, chicken and cream are added at the beginning of the process, the mixture is partly cooked, then chopped green peppers and mushrooms are added at the end of the process. Conversion costs are incurred evenly throughout the mixing process. November data from the Mixing Department are as follows:

Gallons		Costs	
Beginning work in process inventory	0 gallons	Beginning work in process inventory	$ 0
Started production	14,000 gallons	Costs added during November:	
Completed and transferred out to Retort in November	13,200 gallons	Chicken	22,300
		Cream	4,300
Ending work in process inventory (70% of the way through the mixing process)	800 gallons	Green peppers and mushrooms	6,600
		Direct labor	11,500
		Manufacturing overhead	10,516
		Total costs	$55,216

Requirements

1. Draw a time line for the Mixing Department.
2. Use the time line to help you summarize the flow of physical units and compute the equivalent units. (*Hint:* Each direct material added at a different point in the production process requires its own equivalent-unit computation.)
3. Compute the cost per equivalent unit for each cost category.
4. Compute the total costs of the units (gallons):
   a. Completed and transferred out to the Retort Department
   b. In the Mixing Department's ending work in process inventory

P5-59B Prepare a production cost report and journal entries
(Learning Objectives 4 & 5)

Antique Accessories manufactures auto roof racks in a two-stage process that includes shaping and plating. Steel alloy is the basic raw material of the shaping process. The steel is molded according to the design specifications of automobile manufacturers. The Plating Department then adds an anodized finish.

At March 31, before recording the transfer of cost from the Plating Department to Finished Goods Inventory, the Antique Accessories general ledger included the following account:

Work in Process Inventory—Plating	
March 1 balance	26,370
Transferred-in from Shaping	28,800
Direct materials	28,600
Direct labor	20,867
Manufacturing overhead	36,763

The direct materials (rubber pads) are added at the end of the plating process. Conversion costs are incurred evenly throughout the process. Work in process of the Plating Department on March 1 consisted of 600 racks. The $26,370 beginning balance of Work in Process—Plating includes $14,400 of transferred-in cost and $11,970 of conversion cost. During March, 3,000 racks were transferred in from the Shaping Department. The Plating Department transferred 2,200 racks to Finished Goods Inventory in March and 1,400 were still in process on March 31. This ending inventory was 50% of the way through the plating process.

Requirements

1. Draw a time line for the Plating Department.
2. Prepare the March production cost report for the Plating Department.
3. Journalize all transactions affecting the Plating Department during March, including the entries that have already been posted. Assume the wages are unpaid.

P5-60B **Cost per unit and gross profit** *(Learning Objective 5)*

Anthony Zelinski operates Anthony's Cricket Farm in Atlanta, Georgia. Anthony's raises about 18 million crickets a month. Most are sold to pet stores at $9.23 for a box of 1,000 crickets. Pet stores sell the crickets for $0.05 to $0.10 each as live feed for reptiles.

Raising crickets requires a two-step process: incubation and brooding. In the first process, incubation, employees place cricket eggs on mounds of peat moss to hatch. In the second process, employees move the newly hatched crickets into large boxes filled with cardboard dividers. Depending on the desired size, the crickets spend approximately two weeks in brooding before being shipped to pet stores. In the brooding process, Anthony's crickets consume about 16 tons of food and produce 12 tons of manure.

Zelinski has invested $420,000 in the cricket farm, and he had hoped to earn a 53.4% annual rate of return, which works out to a 4.45% monthly return on his investment. After looking at the farm's bank balance, Zelinski fears he is not achieving this return. To get more accurate information on the farm's performance, Zelinski bought new accounting software that provides weighted-average process cost information. After Zelinski input the data, the software provided the following reports. However, Zelinski needs help interpreting these reports.

Zelinski does know that a unit of production is a box of 1,000 crickets. For example, in June's report, the 7,000 physical units of beginning work in process inventory are 7,000 boxes (each one of these boxes contains 1,000 immature crickets). The finished goods inventory is zero because the crickets ship out as soon as they reach the required size. Monthly operating expenses total $19,050 (in addition to the costs that follow).

	A	B	C	D	E
1	Anthony's Cricket Farm—Brooding Department Month Ended June 30 Production Cost Report (part 1 of 3)	Step 1: Flow of Physical Units	Step 2: Equivalent Units		
2			Transferred-in	Direct Materials	Conversion Costs
3	Flow of Production				
4	Units to account for:				
5	Beginning work in process, June 1	7,000			
6	Plus: Transferred in during June	37,000			
7	Total physical units to account for	44,000			
8					
9	Units accounted for:				
10	Completed and transferred out during June	34,000	34,000	34,000	34,000
11	Plus: Ending work in process, June 30	10,000	10,000	6,000	3,000
12	Total physical units accounted for	44,000			
13	Total equivalent units		44,000	40,000	37,000
14					

	A	B	C	D	E
1	Anthony's Cricket Farm—Brooding Department Month Ended June 30 Production Cost Report (part 2 of 3)	Transferred-in	Direct Materials	Conversion Costs	Total
3	Beginning work in process, June 1	$ 15,000	$ 41,000	$ 5,460	$ 61,460
4	Plus: Costs added during June	51,000	169,000	53,000	273,000
5	Total costs to account for	$ 66,000	$ 210,000	$ 58,460	$ 334,460
6	Divided by: Total equivalent units	44,000	40,000	37,000	
7	Cost per equivalent unit	$ 1.50	$ 5.25	$ 1.58	
8					

	A	B	C	D	E
1	**Anthony's Cricket Farm—Brooding Department**	Transferred-in	Direct Materials	Conversion Costs	Total
2	**Month Ended June 30** **Production Cost Report (part 3 of 3)**				
3	**Assignment of total cost:**				
4	**Completed and transferred out:**				
5	Equivalent units completed and transferred out	34,000	34,000	34,000	
6	Multiplied by: Cost per equivalent unit	$ 1.50	$ 5.25	$ 1.58	
7	Cost assigned to units completed and transferred out	$ 51,000	$ 178,500	$ 53,720	$ 283,220
8					
9	**Ending work in process:**				
10	Equivalent units in ending WIP	10,000	6,000	3,000	
11	Multiplied by: Cost per equivalent unit	$ 1.50	$ 5.25	$ 1.58	
12	Cost assigned to units in ending WIP	$ 15,000	$ 31,500	$ 4,740	$ 51,240
13					
14	**Total costs accounted for**				$ 334,460
15					

Requirements

Anthony Zelinski has the following questions about the farm's performance during June:

1. What is the cost per box of crickets sold? (*Hint:* This is the cost of the boxes completed and shipped out of brooding.)
2. What is the gross profit per box?
3. How much operating income did Anthony's Cricket Farm make in June?
4. What is the return on Zelinski's investment of $420,000 for the month of June? (Compute this as June's operating income divided by Zelinski's investment, expressed as a percentage.)
5. What monthly operating income would provide a 4.45% monthly rate of return? What price per box would Anthony's Cricket Farm have had to charge in June to achieve this target monthly rate of return?

Serial Case

C5-61 Calculate and interpret activity cost pool rates *(Learning Objectives 1 & 2)*

This case is a continuation of the Caesars Entertainment Corporation serial case that began in Chapter 1. Refer to the introductory story in Chapter 1 (see page 43) for additional background. (The components of the Caesars serial case can be completed in any order.)

For several years running, the Bacchanel Buffet, a Caesars Palace® Las Vegas all-you-can-eat attraction, has been voted the best buffet by "USA Today" and other publications. The Bacchanal Buffet offers a seemingly unlimited selection of food. Menu items include fried chicken and waffles, Japanese curry, a seafood station, prime rib, truffle scalloped potatoes, made-to-order dessert crepes, and hundreds of other choices. The price paid by customers varies according to the time of day. Brunch is approximately $52 per customer, while dinner is approximately $62 per customer.

Questions

1. Suppose Caesars wants to know how much profit it earns per buffet customer. Would Caesars use a job costing system or a process costing system when determining the cost of the buffet per customer? Explain.
2. Why does Caesars need to know the cost of the buffet per customer? Do you think the buffet cost per customer will vary depending on the time of day and the buffet options offered with the brunch or dinner shifts?

CRITICAL THINKING

Discussion & Analysis

A5-62 Discussion Questions

1. What characteristics of the product or manufacturing process would lead a company to use a process costing system? Give two examples of companies that are likely to be using process costing. What characteristics of the product or manufacturing process would lead a company to use a job costing system? Give two examples of companies that are likely to be using job costing.

2. How are process costing and job costing similar? How are they different?

3. What are conversion costs? In a job costing system, at least some conversion costs are assigned directly to products. Why do all conversion costs need to be assigned to processing departments in a process costing system?

4. Why not assign all costs of production during a period to only the completed units? What happens if a company does this? Why are the costs of production in any period allocated between completed units and units in work in process? Is there any situation where a company can assign all costs of production during a period to the completed units? If so, when?

5. What information generated by a process costing system can be used by management? How can management use this process costing information?

6. Why are the equivalent units for direct materials often different from the equivalent units for conversion costs in the same period?

7. Describe the flow of costs in a process costing system. List each type of journal entry that would be made and describe the purpose of that journal entry.

8. If a company has very little or no inventory, what effect does that lack of inventory have on its process costing system? What other benefits result from having very little to no inventory?

9. How does process costing differ between a first processing department and a second or later processing department?

10. "Process costing is easier to use than job costing." Do you agree or disagree with this statement? Explain your reasoning.

11. Think of a business or an organization that would use process costing. What types of waste are likely to be generated during the manufacturing process? Are there ways to avoid this waste or minimize it? How might managerial accounting support the efforts to reduce waste in the production process?

12. Provide an example of how a company may change its processes to make its manufacturing more efficient or environmentally sustainable. How will the company benefit?

Application & Analysis
Mini Cases

REAL LIFE

A5-63 Process Costing in Real Companies

Go to YouTube.com and search for clips from the show *Unwrapped* on Food Network or *How It's Made* on Discovery Channel. Watch a clip for a product that would use process costing. For some of the questions, you may need to make assumptions about the production process (i.e., companies may not publicize their entire production process). If you make any assumptions, be sure to disclose both the assumption and your rationale for that assumption.

Basic Discussion Questions

1. Describe the product selected.
2. Summarize the production process.
3. Justify why you think this production process would dictate the use of a process costing system.
4. List at least two separate processes that are performed in creating this product. What departments would house these processes?
5. Describe at least one department that would have ending work in process. What do the units look like as they are "in process"?

ETHICS

A5-64 Ethics and physical inventory counts *(Learning Objectives 1, 2, 3, 4, & 5)*

Sheldon Products produces plastic containers through a blow-molding process. The company uses process costing because its products are generally homogeneous and are produced in large batches.

Mitchell Jackson is the controller at Sheldon Products. It is December 31, 2017, and Jackson is supervising a physical count of all the inventory on hand. He knows it will be a tough year because of a sharp decline in sales near the end of the year.

In early December 2017, an earthquake struck in the southwestern Sichuan province in China. A major supplier of Sheldon Products sustained considerable damage in the earthquake, preventing this supplier from delivering critical parts to Sheldon Products in December. This shortage of raw materials has caused a decline in sales revenue for the last month in the year since production at Sheldon Products has stalled due to the lack of the critical parts from this supplier. Sheldon Products' income will therefore be lower than projected for 2017.

If annual income targets are not met, the company will not be paying bonuses to its employees. Jackson feels that this decline in sales revenue is a temporary situation due entirely to the earthquake. It appears likely that the supplier for these parts will be able to supply Sheldon Products with all of the parts it needs by the end of February 2018.

As Jackson is supervising the physical count on the last day of the year, he edits some inventory records to show more inventory items on the floor on December 31, 2017, than are actually in inventory.

Jackson justifies his action by thinking that the missed sales will actually be made up in January and February (of 2018) when the supplier gets back on track with shipments. The decrease in sales revenue the company experienced in December is only a temporary timing difference. He is concerned that if bonuses are not paid to employees because of this timing difference, Sheldon Products could lose some of its best employees to competitors that are offering higher wages. Sheldon Products has always used the bonuses as a key component of its talent recruiting and retention strategy. Jackson himself has verbally promised bonuses to key employees he has recruited during 2017, as have other managers.

Requirements

1. Using the IMA *Statement of Ethical Professional Practice* (refer to Exhibit 1-7) as an ethical framework, answer the following questions:
    a. What are the ethical issue(s) in this situation?
    b. What are Jackson's responsibilities as a management accountant?
2. How would recording more units than are actually in inventory impact the 2017 balance sheet and income statement? How would it impact the 2018 balance sheet and income statement?
3. Discuss the specific steps Jackson should take in this situation. Refer to the IMA *Statement of Ethical Professional Practice* in your response.

A5-65 Process costing and hybrid costing issues *(Learning Objectives 1, 2, 3, 4, & 5)*

Polly Products is a recycled plastics manufacturer located in Mulliken, Michigan. It makes plastic "lumber" called Polly Planks from 100% recycled plastics. It also builds park benches, picnic tables, and other outdoor amenities from the Polly Planks it produces.

Plastic lumber like that made by Polly Products is typically manufactured using an extrusion process. Post-consumer plastics (milk jugs, bottles, and other plastics) are purchased from municipalities and other recyclers. Much of plastic lumber is produced from post-consumer milk jug material. At the recycler, the milk jugs are crushed into giant cubes, weighing 800 to 1,000 pounds per pallet. When an extrusion manufacturer receives the milk jug, the manufacturer puts the milk jug through a powerful shredder that cuts the milk jug into small pieces resembling confetti. The shredded milk jug is stored in large cardboard boxes called gaylords.

When production begins, gaylords containing shredded plastic are brought to the extrusion line. The shredded plastic is dumped into a large hopper. Other materials are added to the hopper at the initial start of manufacture, including oils, colorants, other plastics, and foaming agents. All of the ingredients are stirred in the hopper until thoroughly mixed. The materials then go into the extrusion machine. The extrusion machine melts the plastic into a hot liquid form. That liquid plastic is pushed through the extrusion machine through a screw mechanism into molds that give the plastic lumber its final shape.

Polly Planks can be sold as dimensional lumber in similar sizes as natural wood lumber, including 2" × 4", 2" × 6", and other sizes. The lengths of the Polly Planks can be 8', 10', or a custom length.

Polly Products also uses its Polly Planks to produce park benches, picnic tables, trash receptacles, and other outdoor amenities. Polly Products' employees fabricate these outdoor amenities both for stock inventory and for special orders. Custom orders are likely to comprise a significant portion of Polly Products' sales.

A manufacturer such as Polly Products would use a hybrid costing system rather than a pure process costing system or a pure job costing system. A hybrid costing system includes elements of both a process costing system and a job costing system and is unique to each manufacturer since it reflects each manufacturer's specific processes and products.

Requirements

1. Which product(s) manufactured by Polly Products would use elements of a process costing system? Give a detailed description of why you think that product (or those products) would require a process costing system.
2. Within the process costing portion of the hybrid system at Polly Products, what costs would be considered to be direct materials? What costs are likely to be in conversion costs in the process costing system? (Use your imagination to brainstorm about potential conversion costs at Polly Products since these costs were not directly addressed in the case.)
3. Which products manufactured by Polly Products would be likely to use elements of a job costing system? Again, explain your reasoning and be specific.
4. Within the job costing portion of the hybrid system at Polly Products, what are the direct materials? What would be direct labor? What costs are likely to be in manufacturing overhead? (Again, use your imagination to brainstorm about potential direct labor and manufacturing overhead costs.)
5. In addition to manufacturing costs, Polly Products has sales, engineering, and general administrative support costs. Are these costs relevant in the hybrid costing system? Why or why not?
6. What major issues do you see in a hybrid costing system?

Try It Solutions

page 251:

1. 100,000 units × 100% of direct materials = 100,000 equivalent units of direct materials.

2. 100,000 units × 25% of the way through fermentation process = 25,000 equivalent units of conversion costs.

page 269:

a. The total cost of making each unit can be found by looking at Step 4 of the process costing procedure in the final production department. The total cost is the sum of the cost per equivalent unit transferred in from earlier departments and the costs per equivalent unit incurred in the final department. In this example, those figures add up to $8.90 per case ($6.50 + $1.15 + $1.25).

b. The gross profit per case is $11.10, which is the sales price per case ($20.00) minus the cost to manufacture each case ($8.90).

6

Cost Behavior

Learning Objectives

- **1** Describe key characteristics and graphs of various cost behaviors
- **2** Use cost equations to express and predict costs
- **3** Use account analysis and scatterplots to analyze cost behavior
- **4** Use the high-low method to analyze cost behavior
- **5** Use regression analysis to analyze cost behavior
- **6** Describe variable costing and prepare a contribution margin income statement

Karen W. Braun

Source: embassysuites3.hilton.com/en/about/index.html

Embassy Suites by Hilton™ differentiates itself from competing hotel brands by providing all guests with two-room suites, featuring separate bedroom and living areas, complimentary made-to-order breakfasts, and a complimentary evening reception. The evening reception provides guests with free refreshments including drinks, appetizers, and snacks. All of these amenities cost money for the hotel to provide but generate customer loyalty among travelers who have come to relish the unique and enjoyable hospitality provided by Embassy Suites.

How do hotel managers set prices high enough to cover all of these costs and earn a profit, but low enough to fill most rooms each night? They know how their costs behave. Some hotel costs, such as the complimentary morning breakfast and evening reception, rise and fall with the number of guests. But many hotel costs, such as depreciation on the building and furniture, stay the same whether the hotel is fairly vacant or 100% occupied each night. In this chapter, we'll learn more about how costs behave and how managers can use that knowledge to make better business decisions.

Up to this point, we have focused our attention on product costing. We have discussed how managers use job costing or process costing to figure out the cost of making a product or providing a service. Product costs are useful for valuing inventory and calculating cost of goods sold. Product costs are also used as a starting place for setting sales prices. However, product costs are not very helpful for planning and making many business decisions. Why? Because they contain a mixture of fixed and variable costs. Some of these costs change as volume changes, but other costs do not. To make good decisions and accurate projections, managers must understand how the company's costs will react to changes in volume.

Cost Behavior: How Do Changes in Volume Affect Costs?

1 Describe key characteristics and graphs of various cost behaviors

In order to make good decisions and accurate projections, managers must understand **cost behavior**—that is, how costs change as volume changes. Embassy Suite's managers need to understand how the hotel's costs will be affected by the number of guests staying at the hotel each night. Our chapter example will revolve around one Embassy Suites hotel, namely, the 525-room hotel overlooking Niagara Falls.

We first consider three of the most common cost behaviors, some of which were introduced in Chapter 2.

- Variable costs
- Fixed costs
- Mixed costs

> **■ Why is this important?**
>
> "Cost behavior is a **key** component of most **planning** and operating decisions. Without a thorough understanding of **cost behavior**, managers are apt to make less **profitable** decisions."

Variable Costs

Variable costs are costs that are incurred for every unit of volume. As a result, total variable costs change in direct proportion to changes in volume. For example, every guest at Embassy Suites is entitled to a complimentary morning breakfast and evening refreshment hour (drinks and snacks). Guests also receive complimentary toiletries (shampoo, soap, lotion, and mouthwash) that they typically use or take with them. These costs are considered to be variable because they are incurred for every guest. In addition, the hotel's total cost for the complimentary breakfast, evening refreshments, and toiletries will increase as the number of guests increases.

Let's assume that the toiletries cost the hotel $3 per guest and that the breakfast and refreshment hour costs the hotel $10 per guest.[1] Exhibit 6-1 graphs these costs in relation to the number of guests staying at the hotel. The vertical axis (*y*-axis) shows total variable costs, while the horizontal axis (*x*-axis) shows total volume of activity (thousands of guests, in this case).

Notice a few things about these graphs:

- Graphs of variable costs always begin at the *origin*, the point that represents zero volume and zero cost. For example, if the hotel has no guests for the night, it will not incur any costs for complimentary toiletries or breakfasts.

- The *slope* of the variable cost line represents the *variable cost per unit of activity*. For example, the slope of the toiletry cost line is $3 per guest, while the slope of the breakfast and refreshment hour cost line is $10 per guest. As a result, the slope of the line representing the breakfast and refreshment hour cost is steeper than that of the toiletry cost.

---

[1] All reference to Embassy Suites in this hypothetical example were created by the author solely for academic purposes and are not intended, in any way, to represent the actual costs incurred by an Embassy Suites by Hilton hotel.

Cost Behavior 309

EXHIBIT 6-1 Variable Costs

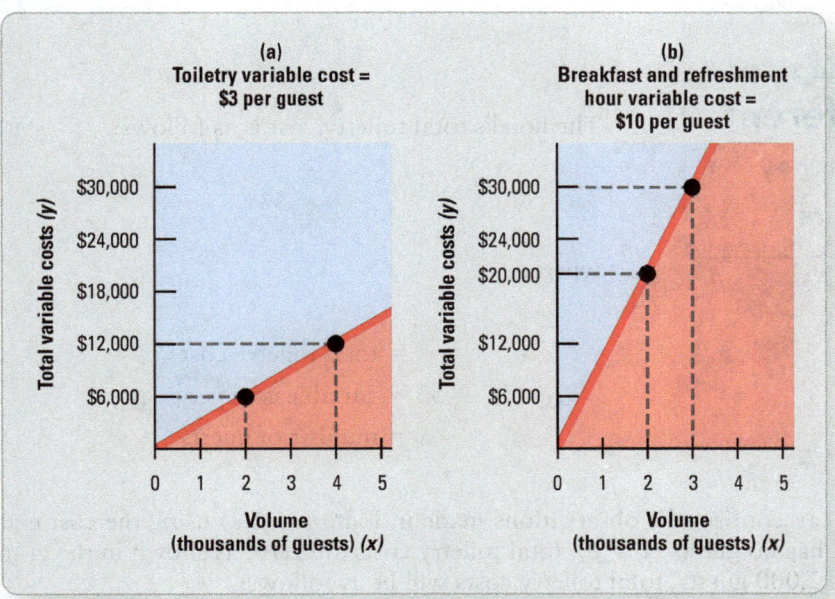

- Total variable costs change in *direct proportion* to changes in volume. In other words, if volume doubles, then total variable cost doubles. If volume triples, then total variable cost triples. For example, Exhibit 6-1(a) shows that if the hotel serves 2,000 guests, it will spend $6,000 on toiletries. However, doubling the number of guests to 4,000 likewise doubles the total variable cost to $12,000.

Managers do not need to rely on graphs to predict total variable costs at different volumes of activity. They can use a **cost equation**, a mathematical equation for a straight line, to express how a cost behaves. On cost graphs like the ones pictured in Exhibit 6-1, the vertical (y-axis) always shows total costs, while the horizontal axis (x-axis) shows volume of activity. Therefore, any variable cost line can be mathematically expressed as follows:

2 Use cost equations to express and predict costs

Total variable cost (y) = Variable cost per unit of activity (v) × Volume of activity (x)

> **Why is this important?**
>
> "Cost **equations** help managers predict **total costs** at **different** operating **volumes** so that they can **better** plan for the future."

Or simply:

$$y = vx$$

The hotel's total toiletry cost is as follows:

$$y = \$3x$$

where,

y = total toiletry cost
$\$3$ = variable cost per guest
x = number of guests

We can confirm the observations made in Exhibit 6-1(a) using the cost equation. If the hotel has no guests ($x = 0$), total toiletry costs are zero, as shown in the graph. If the hotel has 2,000 guests, total toiletry costs will be as follows:

$$y = \$3 \text{ per guest} \times 2{,}000 \text{ guests}$$
$$= \$6{,}000$$

If the hotel has 4,000 guests, managers will expect total toiletry costs to be as follows:

$$y = \$3 \text{ per guest} \times 4{,}000 \text{ guests}$$
$$= \$12{,}000$$

STOP & THINK

How much will the hotel spend on complimentary toiletries if it serves 3,467 guests?

Answer: You would have a hard time answering this question by simply looking at the graph in Exhibit 6-1(a), but cost equations can be used for any volume. We simply multiply the variable cost per guest by the expected volume:

$$y = \$3 \text{ per guest} \times 3{,}467 \text{ guests}$$
$$= \$10{,}401$$

Complimentary toiletries will cost approximately $10,401.

Now, consider Exhibit 6-1(b), the total variable costs for the complimentary breakfast and refreshment hour. The slope of the line is $10, representing the cost of providing each guest with the complimentary breakfast and refreshments. We can express the total breakfast and refreshment hour cost as follows:

$$y = \$10x$$

where,

y = total breakfast and refreshment hour cost
$10 = variable cost per guest
x = number of guests

The total cost of the breakfast and refreshment hour for 2,000 guests is as follows:

y = $10 per guest × 2,000 guests
 = $20,000

Both graphs in Exhibit 6-1 show how *total* variable costs vary with the number of guests. *But note that the variable cost per guest (v) remains constant in each of the graphs.* That is, Embassy Suites incurs $3 in toiletry costs and $10 in breakfast and refreshment hour costs for each guest no matter how many guests the hotel serves. Some key points to remember about variable costs are shown in Exhibit 6-2.

EXHIBIT 6-2 Key Characteristics of Variable Costs

- *Total* variable costs change in *direct proportion* to changes in volume
- The *variable cost per unit of activity* (v) remains constant and is the slope of the variable cost line
- Total variable cost graphs always begin at the origin (if volume is zero, total variable costs are zero)
- Total variable costs can be expressed as follows:

  $y = vx$

  where,

  y = total variable cost
  v = variable cost per unit of activity
  x = volume of activity

Fixed Costs

Fixed costs are costs that do not change in total despite wide changes in volume. Many of Embassy Suites' costs are fixed because the same total cost will be incurred regardless of the number of guests that stay each month. Some of the hotel's fixed costs include the following:

- Property taxes and insurance
- Straight-line depreciation and maintenance on parking ramp, hotel, and furnishings
- Lease payments on fitness room equipment
- Cable TV and wireless Internet access for all rooms
- Salaries of hotel department managers (housekeeping, food service, special events, etc.)

Most of these costs are **committed fixed costs**, meaning that the hotel is locked in to these costs because of previous management decisions. For example, as soon as a hotel is built, management becomes locked in to a certain amount of property taxes and depreciation, simply because of the location and size of the hotel, and management's choice of furnishings and amenities (pool, fitness room, restaurant, and so forth). Management has little or no control over these committed fixed costs in the short run.

However, the hotel also incurs **discretionary fixed costs**, such as advertising expenses, that are a result of annual management decisions. Companies have more control over discretionary fixed costs.

Suppose the hotel incurs $100,000 of fixed costs each month. In Exhibit 6-3, the vertical axis (*y*-axis) shows total fixed costs, while the horizontal axis (*x*-axis) plots volume of activity (thousands of guests). The graph shows total fixed costs as a *flat line* that intersects the *y*-axis at $100,000 (this is known as the vertical intercept) because the hotel will incur the same $100,000 of fixed costs regardless of the number of guests that stay at the hotel during the month.

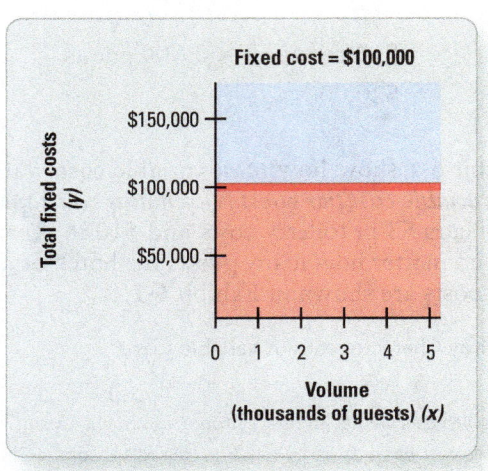

EXHIBIT 6-3 Fixed Costs

The cost equation for a fixed cost is as follows:

$$\text{Total fixed cost } (y) = \text{Fixed amount over a period of time } (f)$$

Or simply,

$$y = f$$

Embassy Suites' *monthly* fixed cost equation is as follows:

$$y = \$100{,}000$$

where

$$y = \text{total fixed cost per month}$$

In contrast to the *total fixed costs* shown in Exhibit 6-3, the *fixed cost per guest* depends on the number of guests that stay at the hotel during the month. If the hotel only serves 2,000 guests during the month, the fixed cost per guest is as follows:

$$\$100{,}000 \div 2{,}000 \text{ guests} = \$50/\text{guest}$$

If the number of guests *doubles* to 4,000, the fixed cost per guest is *cut in half*:

$$\$100{,}000 \div 4{,}000 \text{ guests} = \$25/\text{guest}$$

Notice that the fixed cost per guest is *inversely proportional* to the number of guests. When volume *increases*, not only does the fixed cost per guest *decrease*, but it also *decreases in a proportional fashion*. For example, if volume triples, then the cost per unit will be one-third of what it was at the original volume. If volume quadruples, then the cost per unit will be one quarter of what it was at the original volume. The opposite is also true: When volume *decreases*, the fixed cost per guest *increases in a proportional fashion*. In our example, cutting the number of guests in half (from 4,000 to 2,000) will double the cost per unit (from $25 per guest to $50 per guest).

Keep the following important rule of thumb in mind:

Companies like to operate near full capacity because it drives down their fixed costs per unit. A lower cost per unit gives businesses the flexibility to decrease sales prices, which makes them more competitive.

Key points to remember about fixed costs appear in Exhibit 6-4.

EXHIBIT 6-4 Key Characteristics of Fixed Costs

- *Total* fixed costs stay *constant* over a wide range of volume
- Fixed costs *per unit of activity* vary *inversely* in proportion to changes in volume:
    - Fixed cost per unit of activity *increases* when volume *decreases* (*If volume is cut in half, the fixed cost per unit will double*)
    - Fixed cost per unit of activity *decreases* when volume *increases* (*If volume doubles, the fixed cost per unit will be cut in half*)
- Total fixed cost graphs are always flat lines with no slope that intersect the y-axis at a level equal to total fixed costs
- Total fixed costs can be expressed as $y = f$
    where,
        y = total fixed cost
        f = fixed cost over a given period of time

Try It!

Compute the (a) total fixed cost and (b) fixed cost per guest if the hotel has 16,000 guests next month. Compare the fixed cost per guest at the higher occupancy rate to the fixed cost per guest when only 2,000 guests stay during the month.

Please see page 380 for solutions.

Mixed Costs

Mixed costs contain both variable and fixed cost components. Embassy Suites' utilities are mixed costs because the hotel requires a certain amount of utilities just to operate. However, the more guests that stay at the hotel, the more water, electricity, and gas required. Exhibit 6-5 illustrates mixed costs.

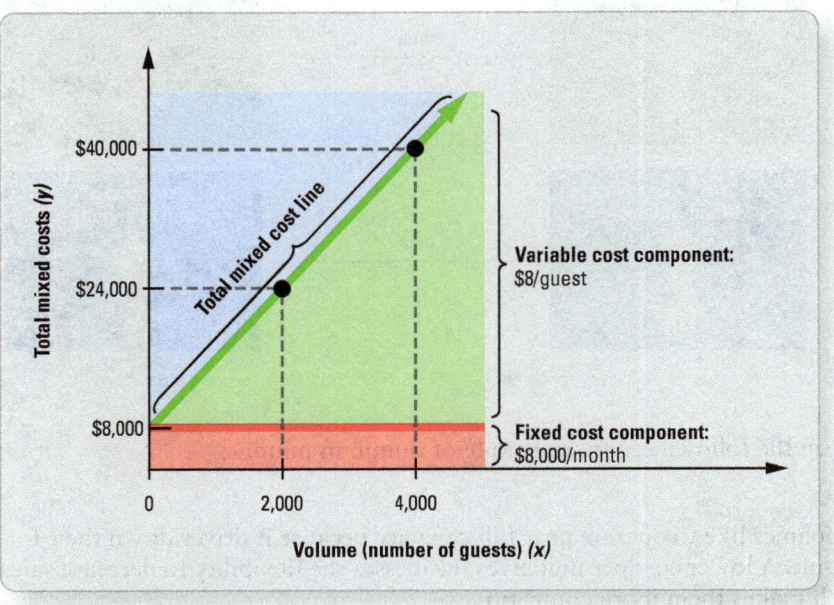

EXHIBIT 6-5 Mixed Costs

For example, let's assume that utilities for the common areas of the hotel and unoccupied rooms cost $8,000 per month. In addition, utilities increase by $8 per guest as each guest cools or heats his or her room, takes showers, turns on the TV and lights, and uses freshly laundered sheets and towels.

Notice the two components—variable and fixed—of the mixed costs in Exhibit 6-5. Similar to a variable cost, the total mixed cost line increases as the volume of activity increases. However, *the line does **not** begin at the origin*. Rather, it intersects the y-axis at a level equal to the fixed cost component. Even if no guests stay this month, the hotel will still incur $8,000 of utilities cost.

Managers can once again use a cost equation to express the mixed cost line so that they can predict total mixed costs at different volumes. The mixed costs equation simply *combines* the variable cost and fixed cost equations:

$$\text{Total mixed costs} = \text{Variable cost component} + \text{Fixed cost component}$$
$$y = vx + f$$

Embassy Suites' monthly utilities cost equation is as follows:

$$y = \$8x + \$8{,}000$$

where

y = total utilities cost per month
x = number of guests

If the hotel serves 2,000 guests this month, it expects utilities to cost:

$$y = (\$8 \text{ per guest} \times 2,000 \text{ guests}) + \$8,000$$
$$= \$24,000$$

If the hotel serves 4,000 guests this month, it expects utilities to cost:

$$y = (\$8 \text{ per guest} \times 4,000 \text{ guests}) + \$8,000$$
$$= \$40,000$$

Total mixed costs increase as volume increases, *but not in direct proportion to changes in volume*. The total mixed costs did *not* double when volume doubled. This is because of the fixed cost component. Additionally, consider the mixed costs *per guest*:

If the hotel serves 2,000 guests: $24,000 total cost ÷ 2,000 guests = $12.00 per guest
If the hotel serves 4,000 guests: $40,000 total cost ÷ 4,000 guests = $10.00 per guest

The mixed costs per guest did *not* decrease by half when the hotel served twice as many guests. This is because of the variable cost component. Mixed costs per unit decrease as volume increases, but *not in direct proportion* to changes in volume. Because mixed costs contain both fixed cost and variable cost components, they behave differently than purely variable costs and purely fixed costs. Key points to remember about mixed costs appear in Exhibit 6-6.

EXHIBIT 6-6 Key Characteristics of Mixed Costs

- *Total* mixed costs increase as volume increases because of the variable cost component
- Mixed costs *per unit* decrease as volume increases because of the fixed cost component
- Total mixed costs graphs slope upward but do *not* begin at the origin—they intersect the y-axis at the level of fixed costs
- Total mixed costs can be expressed as a *combination* of the variable and fixed cost equations:

    Total mixed costs = variable cost component + fixed cost component
    $$y = vx + f$$
    where,
    y = total mixed costs
    v = variable cost per unit of activity (slope)
    x = volume of activity
    f = fixed cost over a given period of time (vertical intercept)

Try It!

Assume the local fitness club charges a membership fee of $30 per month for unlimited use of the exercise equipment plus an additional fee of $5 for every instructor-led exercise class you attend.

1. Express the monthly cost of belonging to the fitness club as a cost equation.
2. What is your expected cost for a month in which you attend five instructor-led classes?
3. If your attendance doubles to 10 classes per month, will your total cost for the month double? Explain.

Please see page 380 for solutions.

Relevant Range

Managers always need to keep their **relevant range** in mind when predicting total costs. The relevant range is the band of volume where the following remain constant:

- *Total fixed costs*
- *Variable cost per unit*

In other words, it's the range of volume in which costs behave a certain way. A change in cost behavior means a change to a different relevant range.

Let's consider how the concept of relevant range applies to Embassy Suites. As shown in Exhibit 6-3, the hotel's current fixed costs are $100,000 per month. However, because of the hotel's popularity, the percentage of rooms occupied each night (room occupancy rate) continues to increase. To keep customer satisfaction high, management may decide to add more capacity to the common areas of the hotel, such as a new elevator bank and additional breakfast and fitness areas. This expansion, if carried out, will increase the hotel's fixed costs because of depreciation on the new fixed assets. The same sort of situation often occurs with manufacturers and merchandising companies that must expand their capacity to keep up with growing sales volume. Exhibit 6-7 illustrates different relevant ranges for the hotel's fixed costs.

EXHIBIT 6-7 Examples of Different Relevant Ranges for Fixed Costs

The concept of relevant range also applies to variable costs. As shown in Exhibit 6-1, the hotel's current variable cost for toiletries is $3 per guest. However, as room occupancy rates continue to grow, management hopes to negotiate greater volume discounts on the toiletries from its suppliers. These volume discounts will decrease the variable toiletries cost per guest (for example, down to $2.75 per guest). Exhibit 6-8 illustrates different relevant ranges for the hotel's variable toiletries cost.

Why is the concept of relevant range important? Managers can predict costs accurately only if they use cost information for the appropriate relevant range. For example, think about smartphone plans. Many smartphone plans offer unlimited talk and texting and a large block of data for a fixed fee each month. If the customer exceeds the allotted amount of data, the company charges an additional per-MB fee. Exhibit 6-9 shows a smartphone plan in which the first 5 GB of data each month costs $50. After 5 GB are used, the customer must pay an additional 1.5 cents per MB. This smartphone plan has two relevant ranges. The first relevant range extends from 0 to 5 GB. In this range, the $50 fee behaves strictly as a fixed cost. The customer could use 0 MB, 800 MB, or 5 GB of data and still pay a flat $50 fee that month. The second relevant range starts after 5 GB and extends indefinitely. In this relevant range, the cost is mixed: $50 plus 1.5 cents per MB of data in excess of 5 GB. To accurately predict costs, customers need to know in which relevant range they plan to operate. The same holds true for businesses.

EXHIBIT 6-8 Examples of Different Relevant Ranges for Variable Costs

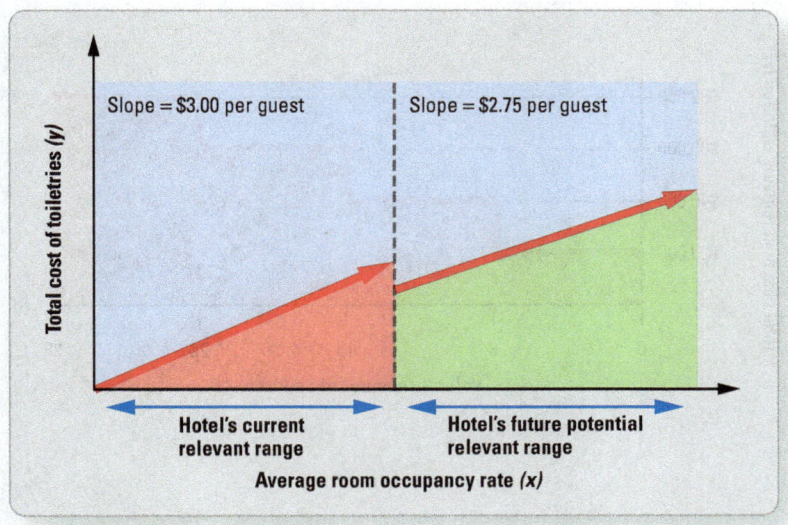

EXHIBIT 6-9 Example of Relevant Ranges

Other Cost Behaviors

While many business costs behave as variable, fixed, or mixed costs, some costs do not neatly fit these patterns. We'll briefly describe other cost behaviors you may encounter.

Step costs resemble stair steps: They are fixed over a small range of activity and then jump up to a new fixed level with moderately small changes in volume. Hotels, restaurants, hospitals, and educational institutions typically experience step costs. For example, states usually require day-care centers to limit the caregiver-to-child ratio to 1:7—that is, there must be one caregiver for every seven children. As shown in Exhibit 6-10, a day-care center that takes on an eighth child must incur the cost of employing another caregiver. The new caregiver can watch the eighth through fourteenth child enrolled at the day-care center. If the day-care center takes on a fifteenth child, management will once again hire another caregiver, costing another $20,000 in salary. The same step cost patterns occur with hotels (maid-to-room ratio), restaurants (server-to-table ratio), hospitals (nurse-to-bed ratio), and schools (teacher-to-student ratio).

EXHIBIT 6-10 Step Costs

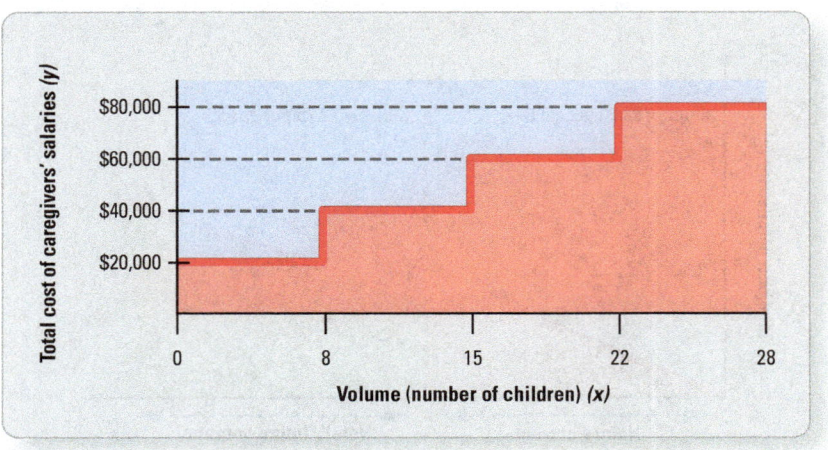

Step costs differ from fixed costs only in that they "step up" to a new relevant range with relatively small changes in volume. Fixed costs hold constant over much larger ranges of volume.

As shown by the red lines in Exhibit 6-11, **curvilinear costs** are not linear (not a straight line) and, therefore, do not fit into any neat pattern that we have discussed thus far.

EXHIBIT 6-11 Curvilinear Costs and Straight-Line Approximations

As shown by the straight green arrow in Exhibit 6-11(a), some businesses *approximate* these types of costs as mixed costs, knowing that they will have an estimation error at particular volumes. Sometimes managers also approximate step costs the same way: they simply draw a straight mixed cost line through the steps.

As shown in Exhibit 6-11(b), however, if managers need more accurate predictions, they can simply break these types of costs into smaller relevant ranges and make their predictions based on the particular relevant range. For example, the day-care center may want to predict total caregiver salaries if it enrolls 26 children. The manager knows this enrollment falls into the relevant range of 22 to 28 children, where he or she needs to employ four caregivers. The manager can then predict total caregiver salaries to be $80,000 (four caregivers × $20,000 salary per caregiver).

Sustainability and Cost Behavior

Many companies adopting sustainable business practices experience changes in the way their costs behave. For example, most banks, credit card companies, and utilities now promote the use of paperless e-banking and e-billing as a preferable alternative to sending traditional paper statements and bills through the mail. Why? Because e-banking and e-billing drives down a company's variable costs since they don't have to spend money on the paper, envelopes, printing, and postage associated with sending out paper statements. Likewise, when a customer pays electronically, rather than sending in a check, the company doesn't incur the variable cost associated with opening the mail, recording the payment to the customer's account, and processing the bank deposit. All of this is accomplished electronically by the company's software.

On the other hand, the company must incur additional fixed costs to develop and operate secure online banking and billing websites. However, we know that the variable cost savings is greater than the increase in fixed costs because many companies are either (1) offering customer incentives to switch to e-billing or (2) charging customers an additional fee for receiving paper-based bills and statements in the mail. Whether using the carrot or the stick approach, companies are shifting consumer behavior as a means to decrease total costs.

The environmental consequences of e-billing and e-banking are tremendous if you consider the entire production and delivery cycle of the bills and statements, all of the way from logging the trees in the forest to delivery of the bill at the customer's doorstep. Not only are fewer trees cut down, but also less energy is consumed in transportation of the timber, processing of the paper, distribution of the paper, delivery of the statements via the U.S. Postal Service, and final disposal of the paper at landfills or recycling centers. In addition, less waste water is generated and fewer greenhouse gas emissions are produced. The downside, from a triple-bottom-line perspective, is the loss of jobs in associated industries, such as the U.S. Postal Service.

Adoption of e-billing and e-banking services provides one means for households to embrace a greener lifestyle. For example, the average household that receives e-bills and makes electronic bill payments reduces paper consumption by 6.6 pounds and prevents 29 pounds of greenhouse gas emissions each year. Water and gasoline are also saved in the process.[2] According to the U.S. Postal Service, in 2014, 19.5 billion bills and statements (equating to approximately 900 million pounds of paper) were delivered across the country. Because of the increasing popularity of e-billing, the annual volume is actually down by over 5.5 billion pieces, or about 22%, when compared with 2008. Whereas 2010 marked the first year in history that more bills were paid electronically than by the mail, by 2014, only 34% of bills were paid by mail.[3] Thus, the huge shift toward adoption of electronic bill payment by the general public could have a significant positive impact on the environment.

▶ See Exercises 6-24A and E6-45B

We have just described the most typical cost behaviors. In the next part of the chapter, we will discuss methods managers use for determining how their costs behave.

---

[2] www.payitgreen.org/consumer/get-the-facts
[3] The Household Diary Study: Mail Use and Attributes in FY 2014 (and 2010). U.S. Postal Service.

Decision Guidelines

Cost Behavior

Suppose you manage a local fitness club. To be an effective manager, you need to know how the club's costs behave. Here are some decisions you will need to make.

Decision	Guidelines
How can you tell if a *total* cost is variable, fixed, or mixed?	• Total variable costs increase in *direct proportion* to increases in volume. • Total fixed costs stay *constant* over a wide range of volumes. • Total mixed costs increase but *not* in direct proportion to increases in volume.
How can you tell if a *per-unit* cost is variable, fixed, or mixed?	• On a per-unit basis, variable costs stay constant. • On a per-unit basis, fixed costs decrease in proportion to increases in volume (that is to say, they are inversely proportional). • On a per-unit basis, mixed costs decrease but not in direct proportion to increases in volume.
How can you tell by looking at a graph if a cost is variable, fixed, or mixed?	• Variable cost lines slope upward and begin at the origin. • Fixed cost lines are flat (no slope) and intersect the *y*-axis at a level equal to total fixed costs (this is known as the vertical intercept). • Mixed cost lines slope upward but do *not* begin at the origin. They intersect the *y*-axis at a level equal to their fixed cost component.
How can you mathematically express different cost behaviors?	• Cost equations mathematically express cost behavior using the equation for a straight line: $$y = vx + f$$ where y = total cost v = variable cost per unit of activity (slope) x = volume of activity f = fixed cost (the vertical intercept) • For a variable cost, *f* is zero, leaving the following: $$y = vx$$ • For a fixed cost, *v* is zero, leaving the following: $$y = f$$ • Because a mixed cost has both a fixed cost component and a variable cost component, its cost equation is: $$y = vx + f$$

SUMMARY PROBLEM 1

The previous manager of Fitness-for-Life started the following schedule but left before completing it. The manager wasn't sure but thought the club's fixed operating costs were $10,000 per month and the variable operating costs were $1 per member. The club's existing facilities could serve up to 750 members per month.

Requirements

1. Complete the following schedule for different levels of monthly membership, assuming the previous manager's cost behavior estimates are accurate:

	A	B	C	D
1	Monthly Operating Costs	100 Members	500 Members	750 Members
2	Total variable costs			
3	Plus: Total fixed costs			
4	Total operating costs			
5				
6	Variable cost per member			
7	Plus: Fixed cost per member			
8	Average cost per member			
9				

2. As the manager of the fitness club, why shouldn't you use the average cost per member to predict total costs at different levels of membership?

▪ SOLUTIONS

Requirement 1

As volume increases, fixed costs stay constant in total but decrease on a per-unit basis. As volume increases, variable costs stay constant on a per-unit basis but increase in total in direct proportion to increases in volume:

	A	B	C	D
1	Monthly Operating Costs	100 Members	500 Members	750 Members
2	Total variable costs	$ 100	$ 500	$ 750
3	Plus: Total fixed costs	10,000	10,000	10,000
4	Total operating costs	$ 10,100	$ 10,500	$ 10,750
5				
6	Variable cost per member	$ 1.00	$ 1.00	$ 1.00
7	Plus: Fixed cost per member	100.00	20.00	13.33
8	Average cost per member	$ 101.00	$ 21.00	$ 14.33
9				

Requirement 2

The average cost per member should not be used to predict total costs at different volumes of membership because it changes as volume changes. The average cost per member decreases as volume increases due to the fixed component of the club's operating costs. Managers should base cost predictions on cost equations, not on the average cost per member.

How Do Managers Determine Cost Behavior?

Managers need to figure out how their costs behave before they can make predictions and good business decisions. In this section, we discuss the most common ways of determining cost behavior.

3 Use account analysis and scatterplots to analyze cost behavior

Account Analysis

When performing <u>**account analysis**</u>, managers use their judgment to classify each general ledger account as a variable, fixed, or mixed cost. For example, by looking at invoices from his or her supplier, the hotel manager knows that every guest packet of toiletries costs $3. Because guests use or take these toiletries, the total toiletries cost rises in direct proportion to the number of guests. These facts allow the manager to classify the complimentary toiletries expense account as a variable cost.

Likewise, the hotel manager uses account analysis to determine how the depreciation expense accounts behave. Because the hotel uses straight-line depreciation on the parking ramp, building, and furnishings, the manager would classify the depreciation expense accounts as fixed costs. Thus, the manager can use this knowledge of cost behavior and his or her judgment to classify many accounts as variable or fixed.

Scatterplots

The hotel manager also knows that many of the hotel's costs, such as utilities, are mixed costs. But how does the manager figure out the portion of the mixed cost that is fixed and the portion that is variable? In other words, how does the manager know from looking at the monthly utility bills that the hotel's utilities cost about $8,000 per month plus $8 more for every guest? One way of figuring this out is by collecting and analyzing historical data about costs and volume.

For example, let's assume that the hotel's manager has collected the information shown in Exhibit 6-12 about last year's guest volume and utility costs.

EXHIBIT 6-12 Historical Information on Guest Volume and Utility Costs

Month	Guest Volume (x)	Utility Costs (y)
January	13,250	$114,000
February	15,200	136,000
March	17,600	135,000
April	18,300	157,000
May	22,900	195,400
June	24,600	207,800
July	25,200	209,600
August	24,900	208,300
September	22,600	196,000
October	20,800	176,400
November	18,300	173,600
December	15,420	142,000

Once the data have been collected, the manager creates a <u>**scatterplot**</u> of the data.

A scatterplot, which graphs the historical cost data on the y-axis and volume data on the x-axis, helps managers visualize the relationship between the cost and volume of activity (number of guests, in our example). If there is a fairly strong relationship (correlation) between the cost and volume, the data points will fall in a linear pattern, meaning they will resemble something close to a straight line. However, if there is little or no relationship between the cost and volume, the data points will appear almost random.

Exhibit 6-13 shows a scatterplot of the data in Exhibit 6-12. Scatterplots are simple to create using Microsoft Excel (see the "Technology Makes It Simple" feature on the next page). Notice how the data points fall in a pattern that resembles something *close* to a straight line. This shows us that there is a strong relationship between the number of guests and the hotel's utility costs. In other words, the number of guests could be considered a driver of the hotel's utilities costs (recall from our discussion of ABC in Chapter 4 that cost drivers are activities that cause costs to be incurred). On the other hand, if there were a *weaker* relationship between the number of guests and the utility costs, the data points would not fall in such a tight linear pattern. They would be more loosely scattered. If there were *no* relationship between the number of guests and the utility costs, the data points would appear almost random.

> **Why is this important?**
>
> "Scatterplots **help managers** easily **visualize** the **relationship** between cost and volume. Scatterplots are fast and easy to prepare using Excel."

EXHIBIT 6-13 Scatterplot of Monthly Data

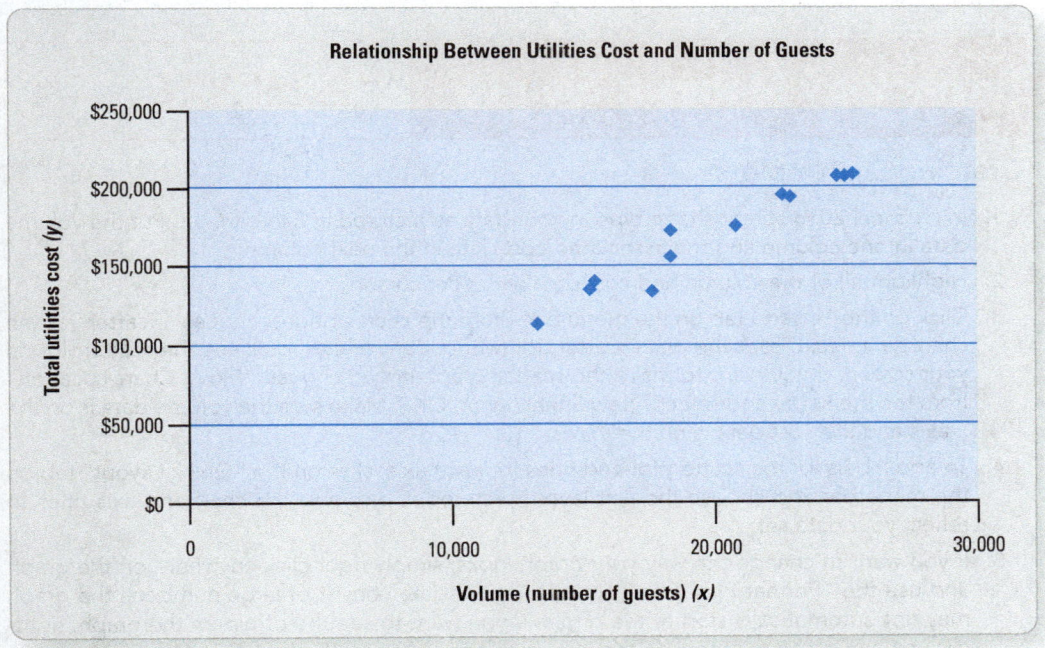

Why is this important? If the data points suggest a fairly weak relationship between the cost and the volume of the chosen activity, any cost equation based on that data will not be very useful for predicting future costs. If this is the case, the manager should consider using a different activity for modeling cost behavior. For example, many hotels use "occupancy rate" (the percentage of rooms rented) rather than number of guests as a basis for explaining and predicting variable and mixed costs.

Scatterplots are also very useful because they allow managers to identify **outliers**, or abnormal data points. Outliers are data points that do not fall in the same general pattern as the other data points. Since all data points in Exhibit 6-13 fall in the same basic pattern, no outliers appear to exist in our data. However, if a manager sees a potential outlier in the data, he or she should first determine whether the data are correct. Perhaps a clerical error was made when gathering or inputting the data. However, if the data are correct, the manager will use his or her judgment to determine whether to keep the data point in the analysis or whether to delete it.

Once the scatterplot has been prepared and examined for outliers, the next step is to determine the cost behavior that best describes the historical data points pictured in the scatterplot. Take a moment and pencil in the cost behavior line that you think best represents the data points in Exhibit 6-13. Where does your line intersect the *y*-axis? At the origin or above it? In other words, does the utilities cost appear to be a purely variable cost or a mixed cost? If it's a mixed cost, what portion of it is fixed?

Instead of guessing, managers can use one of the following methods to estimate the cost equation that describes the data in the scatterplot:

- High-low method
- Regression analysis

The biggest difference between these methods is that the high-low method *uses only two* of the historical data points for this estimate, whereas regression analysis uses *all* of the historical data points. Therefore, regression analysis is theoretically the better of the two methods.

We'll describe both of these methods in the next sections. Before continuing, check out the "Technology Makes It Simple" feature. It shows you just how easy it is to make a scatterplot using Microsoft Excel.

Technology Makes It Simple — Excel 2016

Creating Scatterplots

1. In an Excel 2016 spreadsheet, type in your data as pictured in Exhibit 6-12. Put the volume data in one column and the associated cost data in the next column.
2. Highlight all of the volume and cost data with your cursor.
3. Click on the "Insert" tab on the menu bar. From the chart options, choose "Scatter" as the chart type. Next, click the plain scatterplot (without any lines). You'll see the scatterplot on your screen. If you want to make the scatter graph larger, choose "Move Chart Location" from the menu bar and select "New Sheet" and "OK." Make sure the volume data is on the *x*-axis and the cost data is on the *y*-axis.
4. To add labels for the scatterplot and titles for each axis, click on the "Quick Layout" tab on the menu bar and choose the first layout pictured. Customize the chart and axis titles to reflect your data set.
5. If you want to change the way your graph looks, simply right click anywhere on the graph and use the "Format Plot Area" options. If your data consist of large numbers, the graph may not automatically start at the origin. If you want to see the origin on the graph, right-click on any of the numbers on the *x*- or *y*-axis and choose "Format Axis." Then, insert "0" (zero) as the minimum bound.

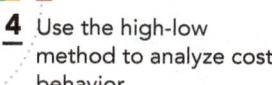

4 Use the high-low method to analyze cost behavior

High-Low Method

The **high-low method** is an easy way to estimate the variable and fixed cost components of a mixed cost. The high-low method basically fits a mixed cost line through the highest and lowest *volume* data points, as shown in Exhibit 6-14, hence the name *high-low*. The high-low method produces the cost equation describing this mixed cost line.

To use the high-low method, we must first identify the months with the highest and lowest volume of activity. Looking at Exhibit 6-12, we see that the hotel served the *most* guests in July and the *fewest* guests in January. *Therefore, we use the data from only these two months in our analysis. We ignore data from all other months.* Even if a month other than July had the highest utility cost, we would still use July. Why? Because we choose

EXHIBIT 6-14 Mixed Cost Line Using High-Low Method

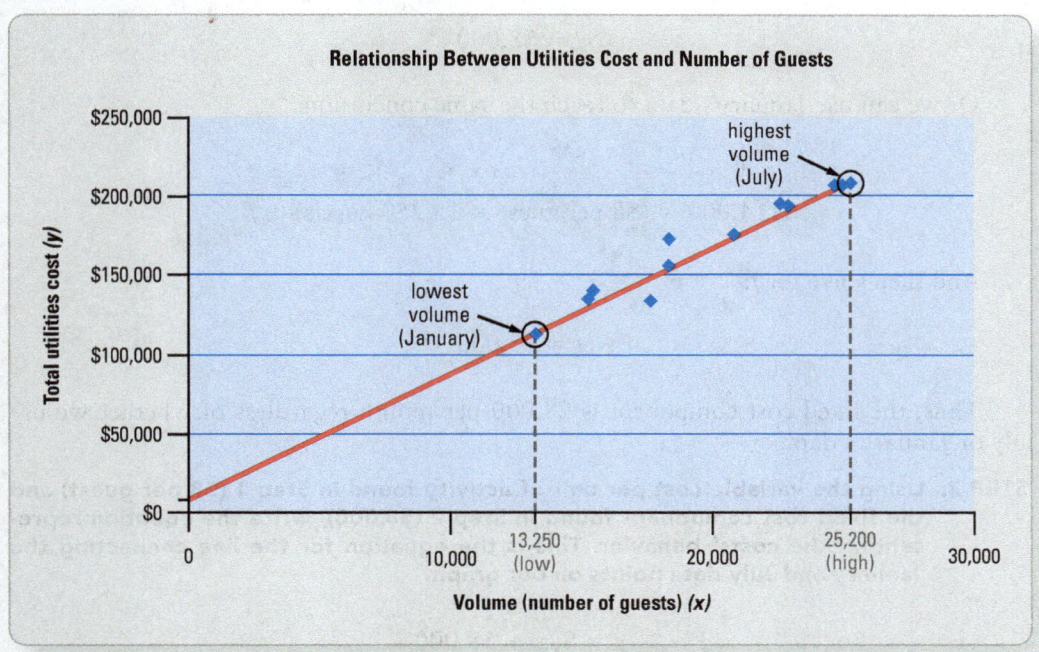

the "high" data point based on the month with the highest volume of activity (number of guests)—not the highest cost. We choose the "low" data point in a similar fashion.

STEP 1: The first step is to find *the slope of the mixed cost line* that connects the January and July data points. The slope is the variable cost per unit of activity. We can determine the slope of a line as "rise over run." The *rise* is simply the difference in cost between the high and low data points (July and January in our case), while the *run* is the difference in *volume* between the high and low data points:

$$\text{Slope} = \text{Variable cost per unit of activity } (v) = \frac{\text{Rise}}{\text{Run}} = \frac{\text{Change in cost}}{\text{Change in volume}} = \frac{y \text{ (high)} - y \text{ (low)}}{x \text{ (high)} - x \text{ (low)}}$$

Using the data from July (as our high) and January (as our low), we calculate the slope as follows:

$$\frac{(\$209,600 - \$114,000)}{(25,200 \text{ guests} - 13,250 \text{ guests})} = \$8 \text{ per guest}$$

The slope of the mixed cost line, or variable cost per unit of activity, is $8 per guest.

STEP 2: The second step is to find the vertical intercept—the place where the line connecting the January and July data points intersects the y-axis. This is the fixed cost component of the mixed cost. We insert the slope found in Step 1 ($8 per guest) and the volume and cost data from *either* the high or low month into a mixed costs equation:

$$\text{Total mixed costs} = \text{Variable cost component} + \text{Fixed cost component}$$
$$y = vx + f$$

For example, we can insert July's cost and volume data as follows:

$$\$209,600 = (\$8 \text{ per guest} \times 25,200 \text{ guests}) + f$$

And then solve for *f*:

$$f = \$8,000$$

Or we can use January's data to reach the same conclusion:

$$y = vx + f$$
$$\$114,000 = (\$8 \text{ per guest} \times 13,250 \text{ guests}) + f$$

And then solve for *f*:

$$f = \$8,000$$

Thus, the fixed cost component is $8,000 per month regardless of whether we use July or January's data.

STEP 3: Using the variable cost per unit of activity found in Step 1 ($8 per guest) and the fixed cost component found in Step 2 ($8,000), write the equation representing the costs' behavior. This is the equation for the line connecting the January and July data points on our graph.

$$y = \$8x + \$8,000$$

Where

$$y = \text{total monthly utilities cost}$$
$$x = \text{number of guests}$$

This is the equation used by the manager in the first half of the chapter to express the hotel's utility costs.

These three steps may seem familiar to you. If so, that's because you probably learned how to find the equation for a straight line ($y = mx + b$) in a high school math class. The high-low method follows the very same steps to find the equation for the straight line connecting the highest and lowest-volume data points. The only difference is in the nomenclature: cost equations use "v" to stand for the slope of the line (rather than "m") and "f" to stand for the *y*-intercept (rather than "b"). Otherwise, it's the exact same process you learned in your high school math class.

One major drawback of the high-low method is that it uses only two data points: January and July. Because we ignored every other month, the line might not be representative of those months. In our example, the high-low line is representative of the other data points, but in other situations, it may not be. Therefore, the better method to use is regression analysis, which is explained next.

Regression Analysis

5 Use regression analysis to analyze cost behavior

Regression analysis is a statistical procedure for determining the line and associated cost equation that best fit *all of the data points in the data set, not just the high-volume and low-volume data points*. In fact, some refer to regression analysis as "the line of best fit." Since the statistical analysis considers all of the data points when forming the line, it is usually more accurate than the high-low method. A statistic (called the R-square) generated by regression analysis also tells us *how well* the line fits the data points. Regression analysis is tedious to complete by hand but simple to do using Microsoft Excel (see the "Technology Makes It Simple" feature on page 329). Many graphing calculators also perform regression analysis.

Regression analysis using Microsoft Excel gives us the output shown in Exhibit 6-15. The output looks complicated, but for our purposes, we only need to consider the three highlighted pieces of information:

EXHIBIT 6-15 Output of Microsoft Excel Regression Analysis

	A	B	C	D	E	F	G	H	I
1	SUMMARY OUTPUT								
2									
3		*Regression Statistics*							
4	Multiple R		0.973273						
5	R Square		0.94726						
6	Adjusted R Square		0.941986						
7	Standard Error		8053.744						
8	Observations		12						
9									
10	ANOVA								
11			df	SS	MS	F	Significance F		
12	Regression		1	11650074512	1.17E + 10	179.6110363	1.02696E-07		
13	Residual		10	648627988.2	64862799				
14	Total		11	12298702500					
15									
16			Coefficients	Standard Error	t Stat	P-value	Lower 95%	Upper 95%	Lower 95.0%	Upper 95.0%
17	Intercept		14538.05	11898.3624	1.221853	0.249783701	−11973.15763	41049.25	−11973.16	41049.25
18	X Variable 1		7.849766	0.585720166	13.4019	1.02696E-07	6.5446997	9.154831	6.5447	9.154831

1. Intercept coefficient (this refers to the vertical intercept) = 14,538.05
2. X Variable 1 coefficient (this refers to the slope) = 7.85 (rounded)
3. The R-square value (the goodness-of-fit statistic) = 0.947 (rounded)

Let's look at each piece of information, starting with the highlighted information at the bottom of the output:

1. The Intercept coefficient is the vertical intercept of the mixed cost line. It's the fixed cost component of the mixed cost. Regression analysis tells us that the fixed component of the monthly utility bill is $14,538. Why is this different from the $8,000 fixed component we found using the high-low method? It's because regression analysis considers *every* data point, not just the high- and low-volume data points, when forming the best fitting line.

2. The "X Variable 1 coefficient" is the line's slope, or our variable cost per guest. Regression analysis tells us that the hotel spends an extra $7.85 on utilities for every guest it serves. This is slightly lower than the $8 per guest amount we found using the high-low method.

   Using the regression output, we can write the monthly utilities cost equation as follows:

   $$y = \$7.85x + \$14,538$$

   where

   y = total monthly utilities cost
   x = number of guests

3. Now, let's look at the R-square statistic highlighted near the top of Exhibit 6-15. The R-square statistic is often referred to as a "goodness-of-fit" statistic because it tells

> **Why is this important?**
>
> "Regression analysis is **fast** and **easy** to perform using Microsoft Excel. **Regression analysis** gives managers the most **representative** cost equations, allowing them to make the most **accurate** cost projections."

us how well the regression line fits the data points. The R-square can range in value from zero to one, as shown in Exhibit 6-16. If there were no relationship between the number of guests and the hotel's utility costs, the data points would be scattered randomly (rather than being in a linear pattern) and the R-square would be close to zero. If there were a *perfect* relationship between the number of guests and the hotel's utility cost, a *perfectly* straight line would run through *every* data point and the R-square would be 1.00. In our case, the R-square of 0.947 means that the regression line fits the data quite well (it's very close to 1.00). In other words, the data points *almost* fall in a straight line (as you can see in Exhibit 6-13).

EXHIBIT 6-16 Range of R-square Values

The R-square provides managers with very helpful information. The higher the R-square, the stronger the relationship between cost and volume. The stronger the relationship, the more confidence the manager would have in using the cost equation to predict costs at different volumes within the same relevant range.

As a rule of thumb:

- An R-square over 0.80 generally indicates that the cost equation is very reliable for predicting costs at other volumes within the relevant range.
- An R-square between 0.50 and 0.80 means that the manager should use the cost equation with caution since the equation will likely result in some estimation error.
- An R-square less than 0.50 means the equation should probably not be used. Rather, the manager should try modeling cost behavior using a different activity base (for example, room occupancy rate) because the current measure of volume is only weakly related to the costs.

Regression analysis can also help managers implement ABC. Recall from Chapter 4 that managers must choose a cost allocation base for every activity cost pool. The cost allocation base should be the primary cost driver of the costs in that pool. Management will use logic to come up with a short list of potential cost drivers for each activity cost pool. Then, management can run a regression analysis for each potential cost driver to see how strongly related it is to the activity costs in the pool. Managers compare the R-squares from each regression to see which one is highest. The regression with the highest R-square identifies the primary cost driver.

Adding a Regression Line, Regression Equation, and R-Square Value to a Scatterplot

Rather than obtaining the full regression output pictured in Exhibit 6-15 and selecting the necessary pieces of information from it, you can command Excel to add the regression equation, regression line, and R-square value directly to a scatterplot. You'll be amazed at how quickly and easily you can create a professional-quality graph using the instructions found in the "Technology Makes It Simple" feature on the next page.

Technology Makes It Simple — Excel 2016

Adding a Regression Line, Equation, and R-square to the Scatterplot

Rather than obtaining a full regression output, you can command Excel to display the regression line, the associated cost equation, and the R-square directly on the scatterplot. Just follow these simple instructions:

1. Start with the Excel scatterplot you created using the directions found on page 324.
2. Point the cursor at any data point on your scatterplot and *right* click on the mouse.
3. Choose "Add Trendline." You will see the regression line added to the chart and a "Format Trendline" dialog box will open.
4. Check the two boxes: "Display Equation on Chart" and "Display R-squared value on chart."
5. OPTIONAL: To force the regression line to stretch *back* to the *y*-axis fill in the "Forecast Backward" box with the *lowest x*-value (volume) in your data set. This number is easily found by hovering your cursor over the lowest volume data point on the chart.

Technology Makes It Simple — Excel 2016

Regression Analysis

1. If you created a scatterplot, you have already done this first step. In an Excel spreadsheet, type in your data as pictured in Exhibit 6-12. Put the volume data in one column and the associated cost data in the next column.
2. Click on the "Data" tab on the menu bar.
3. Next, click on "Data Analysis." If you don't see it on your toolbar, follow the directions for add-ins given below before continuing.
4. From the list of data analysis tools, select "Regression," then "OK."
5. Follow the two "Input" instructions on the screen:
   i. Highlight (or type in) the *y*-axis data range (this is the cost data) with your cursor.
   ii. Highlight (or type in) the *x*-axis data range (this is the volume data) with your cursor.
   iii. Click "OK."
6. That's all. Excel gives you the output shown in Exhibit 6-15.

DIRECTIONS FOR ADD-INs: It's easy and free to add the "Data Analysis Toolpak" if it's not already on your toolbar. You'll only need to add it once, and then it will always be on your toolbar. Simply follow these instructions:

1. Click on the "File" tab on the menu bar. Then click "Options" on the left-hand side of the screen.
2. Click "Add-Ins" on the left-hand side of the screen.
3. In the "Manage" box at the bottom of the screen, select "Excel Add-Ins" and click "GO."
4. In the "Add-Ins available" box, select the "Analysis ToolPak" check box and then click "OK." If asked, click "Yes" to install.
5. That's all. You should now see "Data Analysis" on your Excel toolbar.

Data Concerns

Cost equations are only as good as the data on which they are based. For example, if the hotel's utility bills are seasonal, management may want to develop separate cost equations for each season. For example, management might develop a winter utility bill cost equation using historical data from only the winter months and a summer utility bill using data from only the summer months. Inflation can also affect predictions. If inflation is running rampant, managers should adjust projected costs by the inflation rate. Even if the economy is experiencing low inflation rates, certain industries (such as health care and higher education) or raw material inputs (such as corn prices) may be experiencing large price changes. In our example, management would need to consider whether the rates charged by the utility companies for electricity and natural gas are expected to increase or decrease in the coming year.

Another cause for concern is outliers, or abnormal data points. Outliers can distort the results of the high-low method and regression analysis. Recall that the high-low method uses only two data points—the data points associated with the highest and lowest volumes of activity. If either of these points is an outlier, the resulting line and cost equation will be skewed. Because regression analysis uses all data points, any outlier in the data will affect the resulting line and cost equation, but to a lesser extent.

For example, let's say management's historical data set resulted in the scatterplot pictured in Exhibit 6-17. The low-volume data point looks like it might be an outlier. Notice how the high-low line is highly skewed as a result. However, the regression line remains fairly representative of the other data points, even though it is being pulled slightly toward the outlier. Remember to always investigate potential outliers to help determine whether or not to remove them from the data set before proceeding with regression or the high-low method.

EXHIBIT 6-17 Effect of Outlier on Cost Equations

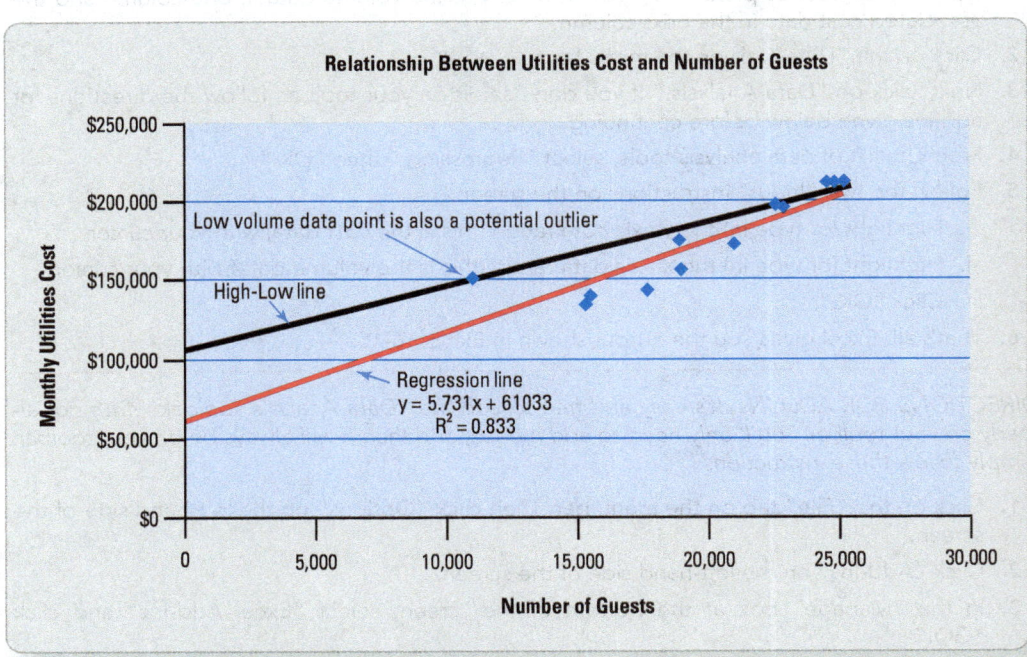

What Are the Roles of Variable Costing and the Contribution Margin Income Statement?

You have just learned about different cost behaviors. As you'll see in the coming chapters, almost all business decisions are influenced by cost behavior. In the following sections, we'll explain how the accounting system can communicate cost behavior information to managers so that they have it readily available for planning, decision-making, and performance evaluation purposes.

6 Describe variable costing and prepare a contribution margin income statement

Comparing Absorption Costing and Variable Costing

So far in this textbook, we have used a costing concept known as absorption costing. Why? Generally Accepted Accounting Principles (GAAP) requires absorption costing for external financial reporting and the Internal Revenue Service (IRS) requires it for tax preparation. Under **absorption costing**, all manufacturing-related costs, whether fixed or variable, are "absorbed" into the cost of the product. In other words, all direct materials, direct labor, and manufacturing overhead (MOH) costs are treated as product costs, as described in Chapter 2. We used absorption costing, also known as "traditional" or "full costing," when we illustrated job costing and process costing in Chapters 3, 4, and 5.

Under absorption costing, no distinction is made between manufacturing costs that rise and fall with production volume and manufacturing costs that remain fixed. As a review,

- variable manufacturing costs would include direct material, direct labor, and variable MOH costs such as the utilities used during the production process.
- fixed MOH costs would include property taxes and insurance on the plant, straight-line depreciation on the plant, lease payments on the production equipment and the portion of utilities that are not affected by changes in production volume.

Supporters of absorption costing argue that all of these costs—whether variable or fixed—are necessary for production to occur, so *all* of these costs should become part of the product cost.

Many accountants and managers do not agree, however. They argue that fixed manufacturing costs are related to the available production capacity and will be incurred *regardless* of the actual production volume that occurs during the period. Since these costs will be incurred regardless of volume, they should be treated as period costs and expensed immediately. This argument has led to the development and use of an alternative costing system known as **variable costing** (or **direct costing**) in which only *variable* manufacturing costs are treated as product costs. Since GAAP and the IRS require absorption costing for external reporting, variable costing may only be used for internal management purposes.

One benefit of variable costing is that it often leads to better decisions. By assigning only variable manufacturing costs to each unit of product, managers can easily see how much additional manufacturing cost will be incurred every time another unit is produced. In addition, the unit cost of the product will not be affected by the number of units produced during the period, as it is when fixed manufacturing costs are absorbed into the unit cost. As we'll discuss later, another benefit of variable costing is that operating income cannot be manipulated by manufacturing more product than is needed, as absorption costing can. Therefore, variable costing can lead to better inventory management.

To summarize, keep this important rule of thumb in mind:

> Managers often prefer variable costing because (1) it shows them the incremental cost of manufacturing each additional unit of product, and (2) operating income cannot be manipulated by changing inventory levels between periods.

Let's illustrate this concept using an example. Exhibit 6-18 provides the most recent annual data for ShredCo, a maker of electronic paper shredders.

EXHIBIT 6-18 ShredCo Data

Variable costs:	
Direct material cost per unit produced	$35
Direct labor cost per unit produced	$10
Variable MOH cost per unit produced	$5
Variable operating expenses per unit sold	$2
Fixed costs:	
Fixed MOH	$1,000,000
Fixed operating expenses	$300,000
Other information:	
Units produced	40,000 units
Sales price per unit	$100

Exhibit 6-19 shows the product cost of one unit under both absorption costing and variable costing. Notice that the only difference is the treatment of fixed MOH. Absorption costing includes fixed MOH ($25) in the product cost, whereas variable costing does not. The $75 product cost shown in Exhibit 6-19 will be used by the company to (1) record the value of inventory on the balance sheet and (2) record Cost of Goods Sold on the income statement when the inventory is eventually sold.

EXHIBIT 6-19 Comparing Inventoriable Product Costs

	A	B	C
1	Manufacturing Costs Per Unit	Absorption Costing	Variable Costing
2	Direct material cost per unit	$ 35	$ 35
3	Direct labor cost per unit	10	10
4	Variable MOH cost per unit	5	5
5	Fixed MOH cost per unit ($1,000,000 ÷ 40,000 units)	25	0
6	Total cost per unit	$ 75	$ 50
7			

Under variable costing, no fixed MOH is assigned to the product cost.

Why is this important?

"Variable costing **helps** manufacturers **identify** the **variable cost** of making each unit of a product. This information will be **critical** to making many business **decisions**, such as whether or not to outsource production."

Notice how variable costing shows managers exactly how much extra cost ($50) will be incurred every time a unit is made. This transparency is not the case with absorption costing, which can easily mislead managers. To illustrate, let's assume that the company decides to produce an extra 5,000 units with its existing capacity. Using variable costing, we see the additional production cost will really be $250,000 (5,000 units × $50). However, absorption costing could mislead the manager into believing that the extra cost would be $375,000 (5,000 × $75). The fallacy in this erroneous analysis stems from treating the $25 of fixed MOH in the product cost as if it were variable. In fact, the company will *not* incur an additional $25 of fixed cost with every unit produced. Rather, the company will incur $1 million of fixed cost *regardless* of the production volume, as long as the production volume stays within the company's relevant range (which in most cases is its existing production capacity). Variable costing tends be the better costing system for internal decision-making purposes because the reported unit cost is purely variable in nature.

Exhibit 6-20 illustrates period costs under both costing systems. Remember that these are often referred to as "operating expenses" in the income statement. Notice again that the only difference is the treatment of fixed MOH. Under absorption costing, *none* of the fixed MOH is expensed as a period cost. Under variable costing, *all* of the fixed MOH ($1 million) is expensed as a period cost.

EXHIBIT 6-20 Comparing Period Costs (Operating Expenses)

	A	B	C
1	Operating Expenses of the Period	Absorption Costing	Variable Costing
2	Variable operating expenses when 40,000 units are sold (40,000 × $2)	$ 80,000	$ 80,000
3	Fixed operating expenses	300,000	300,000
4	Fixed MOH	0	1,000,000
5	Total operating expenses (period costs)	$ 380,000	$ 1,380,000
6			

Under variable costing, fixed MOH is treated as a period cost.

Keep the following rule of thumb in mind:

The ONLY difference between absorption costing and variable costing is the treatment of fixed MOH, and the timing with which it is expensed:
- Under variable costing, fixed MOH is expensed immediately as a period cost (operating expense).
- Under absorption costing, fixed MOH becomes part of the product cost of each unit, which isn't expensed until the inventory is sold (as Cost of Goods Sold).

Try It!

Sony makes DVD players and uses both absorption and variable costing. Assume Sony incurred the following manufacturing costs in producing 10,000 DVD players last month:

Manufacturing Costs	Total Cost	Per Unit Cost
Direct materials	$ 70,000	$ 7.00
Direct labor	40,000	4.00
Variable MOH	90,000	9.00
Fixed MOH	120,000	12.00
Total	$320,000	$32.00

1. What is the product cost per unit, using absorption costing?
2. How will fixed MOH be expensed if absorption costing is used?
3. What is the product cost per unit, using variable costing?
4. How will fixed MOH be expensed if variable costing is used?

Please see page 380 for solutions.

The Contribution Margin Income Statement

Now that you know the difference between absorption costing and variable costing, let's see how the information is communicated to managers using a different income statement format.

Comparing Income Statement Formats

Let's start with the situation in which the company sells *exactly* all of the units it produced during the period. In our example, this means that the company sells all 40,000 units it produced during the year. This situation occurs most frequently with lean producers who use just-in-time (JIT) inventory systems. Exhibit 6-21 shows a traditional income statement, which is based on absorption costing. Notice how Cost of Goods Sold is calculated using the $75 product cost shown in Exhibit 6-19.

EXHIBIT 6-21 Traditional Income Statement Based on Absorption Costing

	A	B	C	D
1	ShredCo			
2	Traditional Income Statement (Absorption Costing)			
3	For the Year Ended December 31			
4				
5	Sales revenue (40,000 × $100)	$ 4,000,000		
6	Less: Cost of goods sold (40,000 × $75)	3,000,000		
7	Gross profit	$ 1,000,000		
8	Less: Operating expenses [$300,000 + (40,000 × $2)]	380,000		
9	Operating income	$ 620,000		
10				

In contrast, Exhibit 6-22 shows a **contribution margin income statement**, which is an income statement organized by cost behavior. When manufacturers use variable costing, they report income internally using a contribution margin income statement format.

EXHIBIT 6-22 Contribution Margin Income Statement Using Variable Costing

	A	B	C	D
1	ShredCo			
2	Contribution Margin Income Statement (Variable Costing)			
3	For the Year Ended December 31			
4				
5	Sales revenue (40,000 × $100)	$ 4,000,000		
6	Less variable expenses:			
7	Variable cost of goods sold (40,000 × $50)	2,000,000		
8	Variable operating expenses (40,000 × $2)	80,000		
9	Contribution margin	$ 1,920,000		
10	Less fixed expenses:			
11	Fixed MOH	1,000,000		
12	Fixed operating expenses	300,000		
13	Operating income	$ 620,000		
14				

Notice the following in Exhibit 6-22:

- The contribution margin income statement is organized by cost behavior.
- All variable costs are expensed *above* the contribution margin line. As a result, only the *variable* product cost ($50, from Exhibit 6-19) is used when calculating Variable Cost of Goods Sold.
- All fixed costs, including fixed MOH, are expensed *below* the contribution margin line.
- The **contribution margin** is equal to sales revenue minus variable expenses. It shows managers how much profit has been made on sales before considering fixed costs.
- The operating income ($620,000) is the *same* in both statements. For manufacturers, this equality will *only* occur when all of units produced during a period are also sold during that same period, resulting in no change in inventory levels.
- For service and merchandising companies, operating income will *always* be the same regardless of the income statement format used.

The contribution margin income statement may only be used for internal management purposes, never for external reporting. Managers like the contribution margin format because it allows them to quickly see which costs will change with fluctuations in volume and which costs will remain the same. For example, if sales volume increases 10%, managers would expect sales revenue and variable costs to increase by 10%. As a result, the contribution margin should also increase 10%. On the other hand, all fixed costs shown below the contribution margin will not change as a result of changes in volume.

> **Why is this important?**
> "The **contribution margin** income statement allows **managers** to **quickly** see which costs will **change** with **volume**, and which will remain **fixed**."

Service and Merchandising Companies

Since service and merchandising companies don't manufacture products, they don't have manufacturing overhead. Therefore, variable costing and absorption costing do not apply to them because these costing concepts deal with how to treat fixed manufacturing overhead. However, many service and merchandising companies like to use the contribution margin format of the income statement for internal management purposes. Why? Because the contribution margin income statement clearly communicates cost behavior information to managers who need this information for planning and decision-making purposes. Exhibit 6-23 shows the contribution margin income statement for the service firm introduced in Chapter 2. Notice once again how all variable expenses are deducted from revenue to arrive at the company's contribution margin. Next, all fixed expenses are subtracted from the contribution margin to arrive at operating income.

EXHIBIT 6-23 Contribution Margin Income Statement of a Service Company

	A	B	C	D
1	WSC Consulting			
2	Contribution Margin Income Statement			
3	For the Year Ended December 31			
4				
5	Sales revenue	$ 160,000		
6	Less: Variable expenses	2,500		
7	Contribution margin	$ 157,500		
8	Less: Fixed expenses	127,500		
9	Operating income	$ 30,000		
10				

Note: Recall that service firms only have operating expenses and no Cost of Goods Sold.

The contribution margin income statement format is essentially the same, regardless of whether the company is a service firm, a merchandiser, or a manufacturer. The main differences are as follows:

- Service firms have no Cost of Goods Sold, so all of their costs are *operating expenses* that are simply classified as either variable or fixed. If mixed, the company first estimates the variable and fixed portions based on the methods, such as regression analysis, discussed earlier in this chapter.

- Merchandising companies have Cost of Goods Sold, but because they purchase all of their inventory, rather than manufacture it, *all of a merchandiser's Cost of Goods Sold is considered variable*. An example is pictured in Exhibit 6-24.

- For service and merchandising companies, operating income will always be the same, regardless of whether the company uses a traditional income statement or a contribution margin income statement format.

EXHIBIT 6-24 Contribution Margin Income Statement for a Merchandising Company

	A	B	C	D
1	**Wholesome Foods**			
2	**Income Statement**			
3	**For the Year Ended December 31**			
4	(all figures shown in thousands of dollars)			
5				
6	Sales revenue	$ 150,000		
7	Less variable expenses:			
8	Cost of goods sold	106,500		
9	Variable operating expenses	3,000		
10	Contribution margin	$ 40,500		
11	Less: Fixed operating expenses	6,000		
12	Operating income	$ 34,500		
13				

Note: For a retailer, all of Cost of Goods Sold is considered variable.

Comparing Operating Income: Variable Versus Absorption Costing

For manufacturers, operating income will not always be the same between the two costing systems. In fact, it will *only* be the same if the manufacturer sells *exactly* what it produced during the period, as was the case in Exhibits 6-21 and 6-22. This scenario is typical of a lean producer. However, traditional manufacturers in a growing economy often produce extra safety stock, *increasing* their inventory levels to ensure against unexpected demand. On the other hand, in periods of economic recession (such as in the years 2008–2009) companies often *reduce* their inventory levels to decrease costs, build cash reserves, and adjust for lower sales demand.

We will discuss how inventory levels impact operating income, for both absorption and variable costing, under three possible scenarios:

1. Inventory levels remain constant
2. Inventory levels increase
3. Inventory levels decrease

As we discuss each scenario, keep in mind that in our example, absorption costing assigned $25 of fixed MOH to each unit of product produced by ShredCo (Exhibit 6-19).

Scenario 1: Inventory Levels Remain Constant

As shown in Exhibits 6-21, 6-22, and 6-25, when inventory levels remain constant, both absorption costing and variable costing result in the *same* operating income. This scenario usually occurs at lean manufacturers since they only produce enough inventory to fill new customer orders.

EXHIBIT 6-25 Inventory Levels Remain Constant

When inventory levels remain constant, *all* fixed MOH incurred during the period ($1,000,000) is expensed under both costing systems. Under variable costing, it is expensed as a period cost ($1,000,000), as shown in Exhibit 6-22. Under absorption costing, it is first absorbed into the product's cost ($25 of fixed MOH in the unit product cost) and then expensed as Cost of Goods Sold when the product is sold. As shown in Exhibit 6-21, when all product is sold in the same period as it is produced, exactly $1,000,000 (= 40,000 × $25) of fixed MOH is expensed as part of Cost of Goods Sold. As a result of expensing the same amount of fixed MOH ($1,000,000) under both costing systems, operating income will be the same regardless of which costing system is used.

Scenario 2: Inventory Levels Increase

As shown in Exhibit 6-26, when inventory levels increase, operating income will be *greater* under absorption costing than it is under variable costing. This scenario typically occurs at traditional manufacturers during times of economic growth.

EXHIBIT 6-26 Inventory Levels Increase

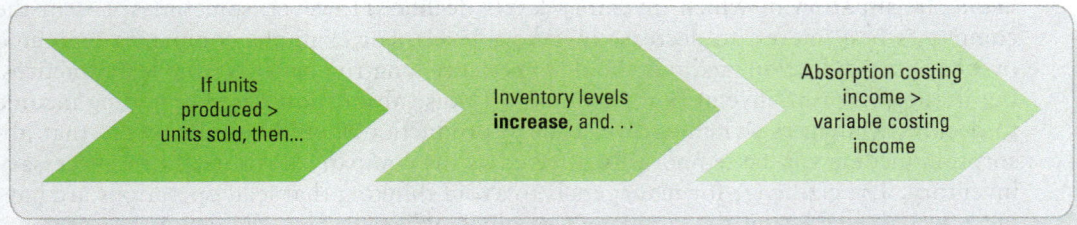

Recall that under variable costing, all fixed MOH incurred during the period ($1,000,000) is expensed as a period cost. However, under absorption costing when inventory levels increase, some of the fixed MOH remains "trapped" on the balance sheet as part of the cost of inventory. For example, let's say only 30,000 of the 40,000 units are sold, leaving 10,000 units still in ending inventory. As a result, $750,000 of fixed MOH is expensed as part of Cost of Goods Sold (30,000 units × $25) while $250,000 of fixed MOH (10,000 units × $25) remains in inventory. As a result, *more* fixed MOH cost is expensed under variable costing ($1,000,000) than under absorption costing ($750,000), leading to a higher operating income under absorption costing.

Thus, under absorption costing, managers can misuse their powers by continuing to build up unwarranted levels of inventory simply to increase operating income. The more inventory builds up, the more favorable operating income will be. Unfortunately, as we learned in Chapter 4, building unnecessary inventory is wasteful and should be avoided. Because of this drawback to absorption costing, many companies prefer to use variable costing to evaluate managers' performance. Since variable costing expenses all fixed MOH in the current period regardless of the amount of inventory produced, managers have no financial incentive to build unnecessary inventory.

Scenario 3: Inventory Levels Decrease

As shown in Exhibit 6-27, when inventory levels decrease, operating income will be *greater* under variable costing than it is under absorption costing. This scenario typically occurs at traditional manufacturers during times of economic recession. It also occurs when traditional manufacturers are in the process of switching to lean operations, which carry little to no inventory.

EXHIBIT 6-27 Inventory Levels Decrease

Recall that under variable costing, all fixed MOH incurred during the period ($1,000,000) is expensed as a period cost. However, under absorption costing, when inventory levels decrease all of the fixed MOH of the period is expensed as part of Cost of Goods Sold *plus* some of the fixed MOH from the previous period. For example, let's say that 45,000 units are sold, comprised of the 40,000 units produced in the current period and 5,000 units produced in the previous period. For the sake of simplicity, we'll assume the same unit costs were incurred in the previous period. As a result of selling 45,000 units this year, $1,125,000 of fixed MOH is expensed as Cost of Goods Sold (45,000 × $25). This figure consists of $1,000,000 from the current year (40,000 × $25) *plus* $125,000 from the previous year (5,000 × $25). As a result, *more* fixed MOH cost is expensed under absorption costing ($1,125,000) than under variable costing ($1,000,000), leading to a lower net income under absorption costing.

Managers who are evaluated based on absorption income have every incentive to *avoid* the situation in which inventory levels decline. However, sometimes it is in the company's best interest to decrease inventory levels. For example, companies switching over to lean production methods should experience long-run benefits from lean practices, but in the short run, inventory reductions will cause absorption-based operating income to decline. Managers switching over to lean production should be fully aware that absorption income will be temporarily affected as the company sheds itself of unnecessary inventory. The challenge for managers is to avoid thinking that lean operations are having a negative effect on the company's earnings, when, in fact, the temporary decrease in operating income is simply a result of the costing system. Again, variable costing is not affected by inventory fluctuations, making it the better costing system for evaluating performance.

Reconciling Operating Income Between the Two Costing Systems

As discussed, absorption costing is required by GAAP and the IRS, yet variable costing is preferred for internal decision-making and performance evaluation purposes. Thus, managers are often exposed to both sets of information. For manufacturers, the costing systems will yield different results for operating income when inventory levels increase or decline. Managers can easily reconcile the difference between the two income figures using the following formula:

> Difference in operating income = (Change in inventory level, in units) × (Fixed MOH per unit)

We'll illustrate the use of this formula next.

Reconciling Income When Inventory Levels Increase (Scenario 2)

Let's try this formula with the example in which 40,000 units are produced, yet only 30,000 are sold. Using the formula, we predict the difference in operating income will be:

> Difference in operating income = (Change in inventory level, in units) × (Fixed MOH per unit)
> $250,000 = 10,000 units × $ 25

Because the inventory level has *grown*, we would expect operating income under absorption costing to be *greater* than it is under variable costing by $250,000 (see Exhibit 6-26). Exhibit 6-28, which presents comparative income statements, verifies this prediction: Absorption costing income ($390,000) is *higher* than variable costing income ($140,000) by $250,000.

EXHIBIT 6-28 Comparing Income When Inventory Levels Increase

Panel A: Absorption Costing:

	A	B	C	D
1	ShredCo			
2	Traditional Income Statement (Absorption Costing)			
3	For the Year Ended December 31			
4				
5	Sales revenue (30,000 × $100)	$ 3,000,000		
6	Less: Cost of goods sold (30,000 × $75)	2,250,000		
7	Gross profit	$ 750,000		
8	Less: Operating expenses [$300,000 + (30,000 × $2)]	360,000		
9	Operating income	$ 390,000		
10				

Panel B: Variable Costing:

	A	B	C	D
1	ShredCo			
2	Contribution Margin Income Statement (Variable Costing)			
3	For the Year Ended December 31			
4				
5	Sales revenue (30,000 × $100)	$ 3,000,000		
6	Less variable expenses:			
7	Variable cost of goods sold (30,000 × $50)	1,500,000		
8	Variable operating expenses (30,000 × $2)	60,000		
9	Contribution margin	$ 1,440,000		
10	Less fixed expenses:			
11	Fixed MOH	1,000,000		
12	Fixed operating expenses	300,000		
13	Operating income	$ 140,000		
14				

Reconciling Income When Inventory Levels Decrease (Scenario 3)

Now let's briefly consider the situation in which inventory decreases rather than increases. Let's assume that 45,000 units are sold, comprised of 40,000 that were produced in the current period plus 5,000 units that were produced in the previous period. The formula used to reconcile income suggests that operating income under absorption costing will be *lower* than it is under variable costing (see Exhibit 6-27) by $125,000:

> Difference in operating income = (Change in inventory level, in units) × (Fixed MOH per unit)
> $125,000 = 5,000 units × $ 25

Exhibit 6-29 verifies the truth of this prediction. Operating income under absorption costing ($735,000) is $125,000 *lower* than operating income under variable costing ($860,000).

Key Points to Remember

You have just learned about variable costing and the contribution margin income statement. Some key points to remember are summarized in Exhibit 6-30.

EXHIBIT 6-29 Comparing Income When Inventory Levels Decrease

Panel A: Absorption Costing:

	A	B	C	D
1	ShredCo			
2	Traditional Income Statement (Absorption Costing)			
3	For the Year Ended December 31			
4				
5	Sales revenue (45,000 × $100)	$ 4,500,000		
6	Less: Cost of goods sold (45,000 × $75)	3,375,000		
7	Gross profit	$ 1,125,000		
8	Less: Operating expenses [$300,000 + (45,000 × $2)]	390,000		
9	Operating income	$ 735,000		
10				

Panel B: Variable Costing:

	A	B	C	D
1	ShredCo			
2	Contribution Margin Income Statement (Variable Costing)			
3	For the Year Ended December 31			
4				
5	Sales revenue (45,000 × $100)	$ 4,500,000		
6	Less variable expenses:			
7	Variable cost of goods sold (45,000 × $50)	2,250,000		
8	Variable operating expenses (45,000 × $2)	90,000		
9	Contribution margin	$ 2,160,000		
10	Less fixed expenses:			
11	Fixed MOH	1,000,000		
12	Fixed operating expenses	300,000		
13	Operating income	$ 860,000		
14				

EXHIBIT 6-30 Key Points about Variable Costing and the Contribution Margin Income Statement

Variable Costing

- Treats all fixed MOH costs as operating expenses in the period incurred, rather than treating fixed MOH as an inventoriable product cost
- Can only be used for internal management purposes; never for external financial reporting or tax purposes
- Is often better for decision making than absorption costing because it clearly shows managers the additional cost of making one more unit of product (the variable cost per unit)
- Is often better for performance evaluation than absorption costing because it gives managers no incentive to build unnecessary inventory
- Will result in a different operating income than absorption costing for manufacturers whose inventory levels *increase* or *decrease* from the previous period

The Contribution Margin Income Statement

- Is organized by cost behavior. First, all variable expenses are deducted from sales revenue to arrive at the company's contribution margin. Next, all fixed expenses are deducted from the contribution margin to arrive at operating income
- Is often more useful than a traditional income statement for planning and decision making because it clearly distinguishes the costs that will be affected by changes in volume (the variable costs) from the costs that will be unaffected (fixed costs)
- Can only be used for internal management purposes, and never for external financial reporting
- Will show the same operating income as a traditional income statement for (1) service firms, (2) merchandising companies, and (3) manufacturers *only* if their inventory levels remain stable
- For retailers, all of Cost of Goods Sold is considered variable

Decision Guidelines

Cost Behavior

As the manager of a local fitness club, Fitness-for-Life, you'll want to plan for operating costs at various levels of membership. Before you can make forecasts, you'll need to make some of the following decisions.

Decision	Guidelines
How can I separate the fixed and the variable components of a mixed cost?	• Managers typically use the high-low method or regression analysis. • The high-low method uses only two historical data points to form the cost equation and therefore may not be very indicative of the cost's true behavior. • Regression analysis uses every data point provided to determine the cost equation that best fits the data. It is simple to do with Excel but tedious to do by hand.
I've used the high-low method to formulate a cost equation. Can I tell how well the cost equation fits the data?	The only way to determine how well the high-low cost equation fits the data is by (1) plotting the data, (2) drawing a line through the data points associated with the highest and lowest volume, and (3) visually inspecting the resulting graph to see if the line is representative of the other plotted data points.
I've used regression analysis to formulate a cost equation. Can I tell how well the cost equation fits the data?	The R-square is a "goodness-of-fit" statistic that tells how well the regression analysis cost equation fits the data. The R-square ranges from 0 to 1, with 1 being a perfect fit. When the R-square is high, the cost equation should render fairly accurate predictions.
Do I need to be concerned about anything before using the high-low method or regression analysis?	Cost equations are only as good as the data on which they are based. Managers should plot the historical data to see if a relationship between cost and volume exists (if so, the data points will fall in a linear pattern). In addition, scatterplots help managers identify outliers. Managers should consider removing outliers before further analysis. Managers should also adjust cost equations for seasonal data, inflation, and price changes.
Can I present the club's financial statements in a manner that will help with planning and decision making?	Managers often use contribution margin income statements for internal planning and decision making. Contribution margin income statements organize costs by *behavior* (fixed versus variable) rather than by *function* (product versus period).
What's the difference between absorption and variable costing?	Fixed manufacturing costs are treated as: • product costs under absorption costing. • period costs under variable costing.
How are product costs calculated under absorption costing and variable costing?	**Absorption Costing** Direct materials + Direct labor + Variable MOH + Fixed MOH = Product cost **Variable Costing** Direct materials + Direct labor + Variable MOH = Product cost
Why is variable costing often used for internal management purposes?	• Variable costing and the contribution margin income statement help managers easily predict the cost of operating at different volumes within the relevant range. • Variable costing helps managers with decision making because it allows them to easily see the cost of making one more unit of product. • Variable costing does not give managers incentives to build up unnecessary inventory.

SUMMARY PROBLEM 2

As the new manager of a local fitness club, Fitness-for-Life, you have been studying the club's financial data. You would like to determine how the club's costs behave in order to make accurate predictions for next year. Here is information from the last six months:

Month	Club Membership (number of members)	Total Operating Costs	Average Operating Costs per Member
July	450	$ 8,900	$19.78
August	480	$ 9,800	$20.42
September	500	$10,100	$20.20
October	550	$10,150	$18.45
November	560	$10,500	$18.75
December	525	$10,200	$19.43

Requirements

1. By looking at the Total Operating Costs and the Average Operating Costs per Member, can you tell whether the club's operating costs are variable, fixed, or mixed? Explain your answer.
2. Use the high-low method to determine the club's monthly operating cost equation.
3. Using your answer from Requirement 2, predict total monthly operating costs if the club has 600 members.
4. Can you predict total monthly operating costs if the club has 3,000 members? Explain your answer.
5. Prepare the club's traditional income statement and its contribution margin income statement for the month of July. Assume that your cost equation from Requirement 2 accurately describes the club's cost behavior. The club charges members $30 per month for unlimited access to its facilities.
6. *Optional*: Perform regression analysis using Microsoft Excel. What is the monthly operating cost equation? What is the R-square? Why is the cost equation different from that in Requirement 2?

■ SOLUTIONS

Requirement 1

By looking at Total Operating Costs, we can see that the club's operating costs are not purely fixed; otherwise, total costs would remain constant. By looking at the Average Operating Costs per Member, we can see that the operating costs are not purely variable; otherwise, the "per-member" cost would remain constant. Therefore, the club's operating costs are mixed.

Requirement 2

Use the high-low method to determine the club's operating cost equation:

Step 1: The highest volume month is November, and the lowest volume month is July. Therefore, we use **only these two months** to determine the cost equation. The first step is to find the variable cost per unit of activity, which is the slope of the line connecting the November and July data points:

$$\frac{\text{Rise}}{\text{Run}} = \frac{\text{Change in } y}{\text{Change in } x} = \frac{y\,(\text{high}) - y\,(\text{low})}{x\,(\text{high}) - x\,(\text{low})} = \frac{(\$10{,}500 - \$8{,}900)}{(560 - 450 \text{ members})} = \$14.55 \text{ per member (rounded)}$$

Step 2: The second step is to find the fixed cost component (vertical intercept) by plugging in the slope and either July or November data to a mixed costs equation:

$$y = vx + f$$

Using November data:

$$\$10{,}500 = (\$14.55/\text{member} \times 560 \text{ guests}) + f$$

Solving for f:

$$f = \$2{,}352$$

Or we can use July data to reach the same conclusion:

$$\$8{,}900 = (\$14.55/\text{members} \times 450 \text{ guests}) + f$$

Solving for f:

$$f = \$2{,}352 \text{ (rounded)}$$

Step 3: Write the monthly operating cost equation:

$$y = \$14.55x + \$2{,}352$$

where,

$$x = \text{number of members}$$
$$y = \text{total monthly operating costs}$$

Requirement 3

Predict total monthly operating costs when volume reaches 600 members:

$$y = (\$14.55 \times 600) + \$2{,}352$$
$$y = \$11{,}082$$

Requirement 4

Our current data and cost equation are based on 450 to 560 members. If membership reaches 3,000, operating costs could behave much differently. That volume falls outside our current relevant range.

Requirement 5

The club had 450 members in July and total operating costs of $8,900. Thus, its traditional income statement is as follows:

	A	B	C	D
1	FITNESS-FOR-LIFE			
2	Income Statement			
3	For the Month Ended July 31			
4				
5	Club membership revenue (450 × $30)	$ 13,500		
6	Less: Operating expenses (given)	8,900		
7	Operating income	$ 4,600		
8				

To prepare the club's contribution margin income statement, we need to know how much of the total $8,900 operating costs is fixed and how much is variable. If the cost equation from Requirement 2 accurately reflects the club's cost behavior, fixed costs will be $2,352 and variable costs will be $6,548 (= $14.55 × 450). The contribution margin income statement would look like this:

	A	B	C	D
1	FITNESS-FOR-LIFE			
2	Contribution Margin Income Statement			
3	For the Month Ended July 31			
4				
5	Club membership revenue (450 × $30)	$ 13,500		
6	Less: Variable expenses (450 × $14.55)	6,548		
7	Contribution margin	6,952		
8	Less: Fixed expenses	2,352		
9	Operating income	$ 4,600		
10				

Requirement 6

Regression analysis using Microsoft Excel results in the following cost equation and R-square:

$$y = \$11.80x + \$3,912$$

where,

x = number of members
y = total monthly operating costs

R-square = 0.8007

The cost equation is different in Requirement 6 than Requirement 2 because the regression analysis cost equation uses all of the data points, not just the data from November and July. Therefore, it better represents all of the data. The high R-square means that the regression line fits the data well and that predictions based on this cost equation should be quite accurate.

SUMMARY PROBLEM 3

Kelley Industries makes high-performance swimwear for triathletes. Kelley's manufacturing costs for the production of 100,000 swimsuits were as follows:

	Total Manufacturing Cost for 100,000 units	Absorption Costing Per unit product cost	Variable Costing Per unit product cost
Direct Materials	$1,800,000		
Direct Labor	375,000		
Variable MOH	250,000		
Fixed MOH	300,000		
Total Cost	$2,725,000		

Requirements

1. Calculate the product cost per unit using (1) absorption costing and (2) variable costing.
2. If inventory increases by 4,000 units over the preceding period, by how much would operating income differ between the two costing methods? Explain.

▪ SOLUTIONS

Requirement 1

The unit product cost is found by dividing the each manufacturing cost by the number of units produced (100,000) during the period. Under absorption costing, all manufacturing costs are "absorbed" into the product cost. However, under variable costing, only the variable manufacturing costs (DM, DL, and variable MOH) are treated as product costs. Under variable costing, the fixed MOH ($300,000) is expensed as an operating expense of the period.

	Total Manufacturing Cost for 100,000 units	Absorption Costing Per-unit product cost	Variable Costing Per-unit product cost
Direct Materials	$1,800,000	$18.00	$18.00
Direct Labor	375,000	3.75	3.75
Variable MOH	250,000	2.50	2.50
Fixed MOH	300,000	3.00	
Total Cost	$2,725,000	$27.25	$24.25

Requirement 2

When inventory levels fluctuate, operating income will differ between variable costing or absorption costing. The difference can be found as follows:

> Difference in operating income = (Change in inventory level, in units) × (Fixed MOH per unit)
> $12,000 = 4,000 units × $3 per unit

When inventory levels rise, absorption costing will result in a higher operating income; in this case, by $12,000. The difference arises because under absorption costing, $3 of fixed MOH is "trapped" on the balance sheet with every unit still in inventory. However, under variable costing, all fixed MOH is expensed as a period cost. Hence, $12,000 more is expensed under variable costing than absorption costing, leading to a higher operating income under absorption costing.

END OF CHAPTER

Learning Objectives

- 1 Describe key characteristics and graphs of various cost behaviors
- 2 Use cost equations to express and predict costs
- 3 Use account analysis and scatterplots to analyze cost behavior
- 4 Use the high-low method to analyze cost behavior
- 5 Use regression analysis to analyze cost behavior
- 6 Describe variable costing and prepare a contribution margin income statement

Accounting Vocabulary

Absorption Costing. (p. 331) The costing method where products "absorb" both fixed and variable manufacturing costs.

Account Analysis. (p. 322) A method for determining cost behavior that is based on a manager's judgment in classifying each general ledger account as a variable, fixed, or mixed cost.

Committed Fixed Costs. (p. 311) Fixed costs that are locked in because of previous management decisions; management has little or no control over these costs in the short run.

Contribution Margin. (p. 334) Sales revenue minus variable expenses.

Contribution Margin Income Statement. (p. 334) Income statement that organizes costs by *behavior* (variable costs or fixed costs) rather than by *function*.

Cost Behavior. (p. 308) A behavior that describes how costs change as volume changes.

Cost Equation. (p. 309) A mathematical equation for a straight line that expresses how a cost behaves.

Curvilinear Costs. (p. 318) A cost behavior that is not linear (not a straight line).

Discretionary Fixed Costs. (p. 311) Fixed costs that are a result of annual management decisions; fixed costs that are controllable in the short run.

Fixed Costs. (p. 311) Costs that do not change in total despite wide changes in volume.

High-Low Method. (p. 324) A method for determining cost behavior that is based on two historical data points: the highest and lowest volume of activity.

Mixed Cost. (p. 314) Costs that change, but *not* in direct proportion to changes in volume. Mixed costs have both variable cost and fixed cost components.

Outliers. (p. 323) Abnormal data points; data points that do not fall in the same general pattern as the other data points.

Regression Analysis. (p. 326) A statistical procedure for determining the line that best fits the data by using *all of the historical data points, not just the high and low data points*.

Relevant Range. (p. 316) The band of volume where total fixed costs remain constant at a certain level and where the variable cost *per unit* remains constant at a certain level.

Scatterplot. (p. 322) A graph that plots historical cost and volume data.

Step Costs. (p. 317) A cost behavior that is fixed over a small range of activity and then jumps to a different fixed level with moderate changes in volume.

Variable Costs. (p. 308) Costs incurred for every unit of activity. As a result, total variable costs change in direct proportion to changes in volume.

Variable Costing. (p. 331) The costing method that assigns only *variable* manufacturing costs to products. All fixed manufacturing costs (fixed MOH) are expensed as period costs. Also known as *direct costing*.

MyAccountingLab Go to www.myaccountinglab.com for the following Quick Check, Short Exercises, Exercises, and Problems. They are available with immediate grading, explanations of correct and incorrect answers, and interactive media that acts as your own online tutor.

Quick Check

1. *(Learning Objective 1)* A graph of a variable cost starts at
   a. any point on the *y*-axis and is horizontal.
   b. any point on the *y*-axis and slopes upward.
   c. the origin and slopes upward.
   d. the origin and is horizontal.

2. *(Learning Objective 2)* Which of the following is true?
   a. Total fixed costs increase when volume increases.
   b. Total fixed costs decrease when volume increases.
   c. Fixed cost per unit increases when volume increases.
   d. Fixed cost per unit decreases when volume increases.

3. (Learning Objective 2) In the cost equation $y = vx + f$, the term "v" stands for
   a. total cost.
   b. variable cost per unit.
   c. fixed cost.
   d. total variable cost.

4. (Learning Objective 2) If $x = 35$, $v = \$100$, and $f = \$1,000$, then total costs equal
   a. $4,500.
   b. $1,100.
   c. $100.
   d. $3,500.

5. (Learning Objective 2) Which of the following is *false*?
   a. Step costs are fixed over small ranges of activity.
   b. Curvilinear costs can be approximated as mixed costs or broken into smaller relevant ranges for cost prediction purposes.
   c. Changes in the variable costs per unit often occur within a given relevant range.
   d. The concept of relevant range is applicable to both fixed and variable costs.

6. (Learning Objective 3) Which of the following is *false*?
   a. When performing account analysis, managers use their judgment to classify cost behavior.
   b. Scatterplots should be prepared to help identify outliers.
   c. When creating a scatterplot, volume should be plotted on the x-axis while cost should be plotted on the y-axis.
   d. Data points falling in a linear pattern suggest a weak relationship between cost and volume.

7. (Learning Objective 4) Which of the following is *false* about the high-low method?

   a. It yields an equation for a straight line connecting the high and low data points.
   b. Selection of the high and low data points should be based on cost, not volume.
   c. The slope found from the method represents the variable cost per unit.
   d. It is based on only two data points.

8. (Learning Objective 5) Which of the following is true about regression analysis?
   a. The resulting S-squared statistic shows how well the line fits the data points.
   b. It is based on two data points.
   c. It is sometimes referred to as the line of best fit.
   d. It is theoretically less sound than the high-low method.

9. (Learning Objective 6) Which of the following is true regarding variable costing?
   a. It treats variable MOH costs as period costs, rather than as product costs.
   b. It is allowed by GAAP for external reporting purposes.
   c. It treats fixed MOH costs as period costs, rather than as product costs.
   d. It is allowed by the IRS for tax preparation.

10. (Learning Objective 6) Which of the following is *false*?
    a. The operating income of manufacturers will always be the same, regardless of whether variable or absorption costing is used.
    b. The contribution margin is equal to sales revenue minus variable expenses.
    c. A contribution margin income statement is organized by cost behavior.
    d. Under absorption costing, the fluctuation of inventory levels will impact operating income, regardless of sales revenue.

Quick Check Answers

1. c 2. b 3. d 4. b 5. c 6. d 7. b 8. c 9. c 10. a

Short Exercises

S6-1 Identify cost behavior *(Learning Objectives 1 & 2)*

The following chart shows three different costs: Cost A, Cost B, and Cost C. For each cost, the chart shows the total cost and cost per unit at two different volumes within the same relevant range. Based on this information, identify each cost as fixed, variable, or mixed. Explain your answers.

	A	B	C	D	E	F
1		At 1,000 units			At 4,000 units	
2		Total Cost	Cost per Unit		Total Cost	Cost per Unit
3	Cost A	$ 75,000	$ 75.00		$ 75,000	$ 18.75
4	Cost B	$ 6,000	$ 6.00		$ 24,000	$ 6.00
5	Cost C	$ 32,000	$ 32.00		$ 68,000	$ 17.00
6						

S6-2 Identify cost behavior *(Learning Objectives 1 & 2)*

Many costs are associated with owning a car. Assuming that miles driven is the volume activity, classify each of the following costs associated with car ownership as mainly variable or fixed.

a. Purchase price of the car $25,000
b. Finance charges on car loan
c. Gas
d. Oil changes every 5,000 miles
e. Replacement tires
f. Insurance costs of $100 per month
g. License plate/registration of $200 per year
h. SiriusXM Radio subscription cost
i. Car washes (one per week)
j. Monthly parking fees for work lot
k. Traffic violation ticket

S6-3 Compute fixed costs per unit *(Learning Objective 2)*

Scott Equipment produces high-quality soccer balls. If the fixed cost per ball is $3 when the company produces 15,000 balls, what is the fixed cost per ball when it produces 22,500 balls? Assume that both volumes are in the same relevant range.

S6-4 Predict total mixed costs *(Learning Objective 2)*

Top Care Brushes produces a premium hair brush. Total manufacturing costs are $250,000 when 20,000 brushes are produced. Of this amount, total variable costs are $80,000. What are the total production costs when 25,000 hairbrushes are produced? Assume the same relevant range.

S6-5 Predict and graph total mixed costs *(Learning Objectives 1 & 2)*

Suppose Anytime Wireless offers an international calling plan that charges $8.00 per month plus $0.20 per minute for calls outside the United States.

1. Under this plan, what is your monthly international long-distance cost if you call Europe for
   a. 30 minutes?
   b. 60 minutes?
   c. 120 minutes?
2. Draw a graph illustrating your total cost under this plan. Label the axes and show your costs at 30, 60, and 120 minutes.

S6-6 Classify cost behavior *(Learning Objectives 1 & 2)*

The ReCycle is a bicycle built largely from recycled materials. Identify the following costs connected with the manufacture of the ReCycle bike as variable or fixed:

a. Rubber used in bike tires
b. Recycled aluminum used to make the bike frame
c. Lubricant used on clipless pedal springs
d. Quality inspector's salary
e. Depreciation on equipment used to machine the aluminum in the bike frame
f. Renewable cork used to make the saddle (the seat)
g. Patent on belt drive (used instead of a chain)

S6-7 Prepare and analyze a scatterplot *(Learning Objective 3)*

Montrose Oil and Lube is a car care center specializing in ten-minute oil changes. Montrose Oil and Lube has two service bays, which limits its capacity to 4,000 oil changes per month. The following information was collected over the past six months:

Month	Number of Oil Changes	Operating Expenses
January	3,200	$36,400
February	2,600	$31,900
March	2,800	$32,850
April	2,700	$32,500
May	3,600	$37,000
June	2,900	$33,700

1. Prepare a scatterplot graphing the volume of oil changes (x-axis) against the company's monthly operating expenses (y-axis). Graph by hand or use Excel.
2. How strong a relationship does there appear to be between the company's operating expenses and the number of oil changes performed each month? Explain. Do there appear to be any outliers in the data? Explain.
3. Based on the graph, do the company's operating costs appear to be fixed, variable, or mixed? Explain how you can tell.
4. Would you feel comfortable using this information to project operating costs for a volume of 3,800 oil changes per month? Explain.

S6-8 Use the high-low method *(Learning Objective 4)*

Refer to the Montrose Oil and Lube data in S6-7. Use the high-low method to determine the variable and fixed cost components of Montrose Oil and Lube's operating costs. Use this information to project the monthly operating costs for a month in which the company performs 3,400 oil changes.

S6-9 Use the high-low method *(Learning Objective 4)*

Brimfield Catering uses the high-low method to predict its total overhead costs. Past records show that total overhead cost was $25,600 when 860 hours were worked and $27,800 when 960 hours were worked. If Brimfield Catering has 885 hours scheduled for next month, what is the expected total overhead cost for next month?

S6-10 Predicting costs in a health-care setting *(Learning Objective 4)*

The Surgical Care Unit of Gold Care Health Group uses the high-low method to predict its total surgical unit supplies costs. It appears that nursing hours worked is a good predictor of surgical unit supplies costs in the unit. The supervisor for the unit has gone through the records for the past year and has found that June had the fewest nursing hours worked at 850 hours, while September had the most nursing hours worked at 1,325 hours. In June, total surgical unit supplies cost $40,000 and in September, total surgical unit supplies cost $49,975. If plans for the Surgical Care Unit call for 875 nursing hours to be worked next month, what is the expected surgical unit supplies cost for the month?

S6-11 Analyze a scatterplot *(Learning Objectives 3 & 4)*

The local Hyatt Place hotel collected seven months of data on the number of room-nights rented per month and the monthly utilities cost. The data were graphed, resulting in the following scatterplot:

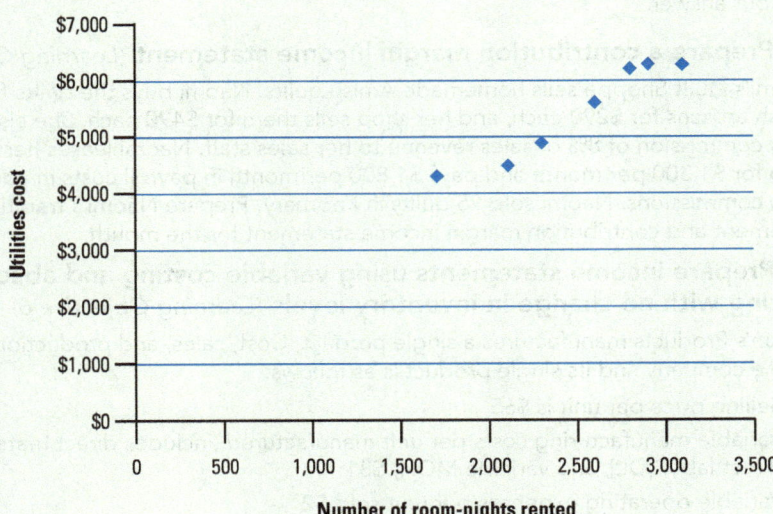

1. Based on this scatterplot, how strong a relationship does there appear to be between the number of room-nights rented per month and the monthly utilities cost?
2. Do there appear to be any outliers in the data? Explain.
3. Suppose management performs the high-low method using this data. Do you think the resulting cost equation would be very accurate? Explain.

S6-12 Theoretical comparison of high-low and regression analysis *(Learning Objectives 4 & 5)*

Refer to the Hyatt Place scatterplot in S6-11.

1. Would the high-low method or regression analysis result in a more accurate cost equation for the data pictured in the scatter plot? Explain.
2. A regression analysis of the data revealed an R-square figure of 0.939. Interpret this figure in light of the lowest and highest possible R-square values.
3. As a manager, would you be confident predicting utilities costs for other room-night volumes within the same relevant range?

S6-13 Write a cost equation given regression output *(Learning Objective 5)*

A legal firm wanted to determine the relationship between its monthly operating costs and a potential cost driver, professional hours. An excerpt from the output of a regression analysis performed using Excel showed the following information:

	A	B	C	D	E	F	G
1		**SUMMARY OUTPUT**					
2		*Regression Statistics*					
3	Multiple R		0.92				
4	R Square		0.84				
5	Adjusted R Square		0.81				
6	Standard Error		148.38				
7	Observations		12				
8	**ANOVA**						
9		df	SS	MS	F	Significance F	
10	Regression	1	573,116.90	573,116.90	26.03	0.00	
11	Residual	10	110,083.10	22,016.62			
12	Total	11	683,200.00				
13							
14			Standard			Lower	Upper
15		Coefficients	Error	t Stat	P-value	95%	95%
16	Intercept	1,263.34	806.85	1.57	0.18	−810.75	3,337.42
17	X Variable 1	0.26	0.05	5.10	0.00	0.13	0.39
18							

a. Given this output, write the legal firm's monthly cost equation.
b. Should management use this equation to predict monthly operating costs? Explain your answer.

S6-14 Prepare a contribution margin income statement *(Learning Objective 6)*

Naomi's Quilt Shoppe sells homemade Amish quilts. Naomi buys the quilts from local Amish artisans for $290 each, and her shop sells them for $490 each. She also pays a sales commission of 8% of sales revenue to her sales staff. Naomi leases her country-style shop for $1,300 per month and pays $1,800 per month in payroll costs in addition to the sales commissions. Naomi sold 95 quilts in February. Prepare Naomi's traditional income statement and contribution margin income statement for the month.

S6-15 Prepare income statements using variable costing and absorption costing with no change in inventory levels *(Learning Objective 6)*

Dalton's Products manufactures a single product. Cost, sales, and production information for the company and its single product is as follows:

- Selling price per unit is $65
- Variable manufacturing costs per unit manufactured (includes direct materials [DM], direct labor [DL], and variable MOH) $31
- Variable operating expenses per unit sold $2
- Fixed manufacturing overhead (MOH) in total for the year $208,000
- Fixed operating expenses in total for the year $89,000
- Units manufactured and sold for the year 13,000 units

Requirements

1. Prepare an income statement for the upcoming year using variable costing.
2. Prepare an income statement for the upcoming year using absorption costing.

S6-16 Prepare income statements using variable costing and absorption costing when inventory units increase *(Learning Objective 6)*

Gleason Manufacturing manufactures a single product. Cost, sales, and production information for the company and its single product is as follows:

- Sales price per unit $47
- Variable manufacturing costs per unit manufactured (DM, DL, and variable MOH) $23
- Variable operating expenses per unit sold $1
- Fixed manufacturing overhead (MOH) in total for the year $322,000
- Fixed operating expenses in total for the year $47,000
- Units manufactured during the year 23,000 units
- Units sold during the year 18,000 units

Requirements

1. Prepare an income statement for the upcoming year using variable costing.
2. Prepare an income statement for the upcoming year using absorption costing.
3. What causes the difference in income between the two methods?

S6-17 Identify cost behavior graph *(Learning Objectives 1 & 2)*

Following are a series of cost behavior graphs. The total cost is shown on the vertical (y) axis and the volume (activity) is shown on the horizontal (x) axis.

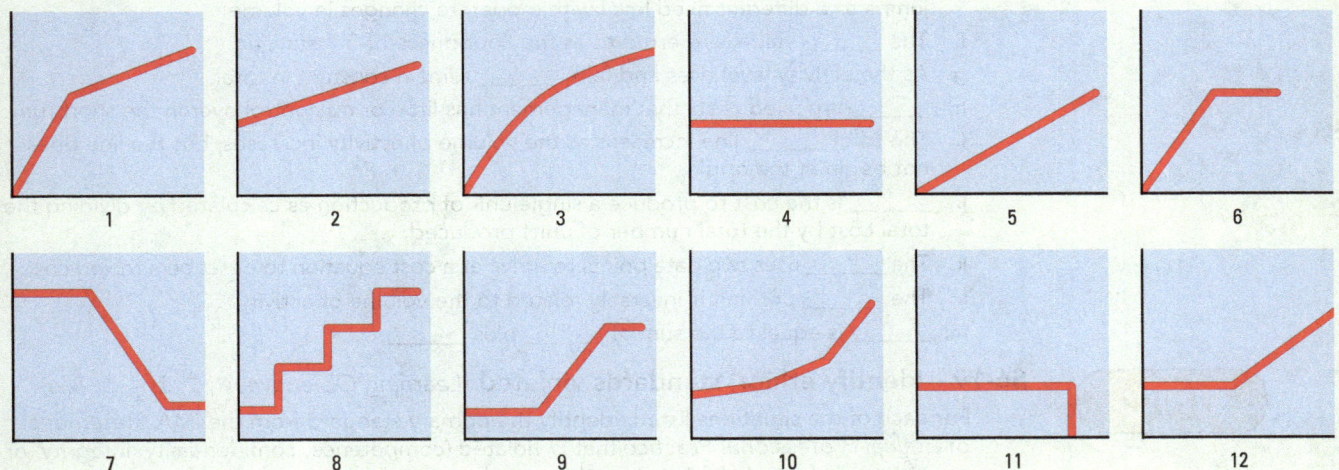

For each of the following situations, identify the graph that most closely represents the cost behavior pattern of the cost in that situation. Some graphs may be used more than once or not at all.

a. Monthly factory equipment depreciation, straight-line method is used
b. Monthly electric cost for a convenience store; $50 base monthly fee plus $.006 per kilowatt used
c. Total salary costs for a craft supplies store; managers are paid a salary, and the other workers are paid by the hour
d. Oil disposal fees for an automotive maintenance company. The oil disposal fee is based on two components: a $100 base fee plus a usage fee (to encourage reduction of waste):

Up to 10 barrels	$ 6 per barrel
11–25 barrels	$ 9 per barrel
More than 26 barrels	$13 per barrel

e. Monthly smartphone expense for a mobile grooming business; the phones are billed at a rate of $40 for unlimited voice, data, and text for each cell phone
f. Wood costs for a table manufacturer; the cost of direct materials per table is $52.00
g. Customer service representatives are paid $15.25 per hour
h. Monthly vehicle lease costs for a company that pays $295 month plus $0.25 per mile for any miles driven over 1,000 per month
i. Monthly gas bill for the restaurant's delivery vehicles; cost of gas is constant at $1.95 per gallon
j. Monthly copier costs; the lease is $110 per month with a fee of $0.02 per copy for any copies over 50,000 copies in that month

S6-18 Identify cost behavior terms *(Learning Objectives 1, 2, 3, 4, & 5)*

Complete the following statements with one of the terms listed here. You may use a term more than once, and some terms may not be used at all.

Account analysis	Average cost per unit	Committed fixed costs	Curvilinear cost(s)
Fixed cost(s)	High-low method	Mixed cost(s)	R-square
Regression analysis	Step cost(s)	Total cost(s)	Variable cost(s)

a. An s-shaped line would represent a _____.
b. The cost equation resulting from using _____ is described as the "line of best fit."
c. _____ is a method for determining cost behavior that is based on a manager's judgment.
d. The vertical intercept of the _____ line is zero.
e. _____ are a type of cost behavior that is fixed over a small range of activity and then jumps to a different fixed level with moderate changes in volume.
f. The _____ value is referred to as the "goodness-of-fit" statistic.
g. As the activity level rises and falls, _____ remain constant in total.
h. _____ are fixed costs that management has little or no control over in the short run.
i. The total _____ line increases as the volume of activity increases, but the line does not begin at the origin.
j. _____ is the cost to produce a single unit of production as calculated by dividing the total cost by the total number of units produced.
k. The _____ uses two data points to arrive at a cost equation to describe a mixed cost.
l. The _____ per unit is inversely related to the volume of activity.
m. _____ is equal to the sum of _____ plus _____.

ETHICS

S6-19 Identify ethical standards violated *(Learning Objectives 1, 2, 3, 4, 5, & 6)*

For each of the situations listed, identify the primary standard from the IMA *Statement of Ethical Professional Practice* that is violated (competence, confidentiality, integrity, or credibility). Refer to Exhibit 1-7 for the complete standard.

1. Audrey is an accountant for Simply Green Consulting. At a party, she overhears a man talking about an upcoming contract on which his company will be bidding. She listens closer and hears specific variable cost information that the man shares. She returns to work the next day and shares this competitor's cost information with her friend, who is working on preparing Simply Green Consulting's bid.
2. Morgan does not disclose on the financial statements that variable costing, rather than absorption costing, was used.
3. Atwood Mobile operates in a highly competitive environment. Cost information is highly confidential since most jobs are obtained through a bidding process based on variable costing, or in some cases absorption costing. Joshua Gilner is the manager of the Accounting Department of Atwood Mobile. He neglects to talk with his new hires about the confidentiality of data, nor is there a formal policy in place about nondisclosure.
4. The CEO of a small company visits a competitor's dumpster and takes several trash bags containing discarded papers and reports. The CEO directs Brandon to go through the competitor's trash to find any information about the competitor's costs for a contract coming up for bid. Brandon goes through the papers to find the information because he does not want to lose his job.

5. Tyler struggled through regression analysis in his college courses. Now his manager has asked him to run a regression analysis to create a model for predicting overhead costs. He runs the regression and creates the model. He gives his manager the cost equation for overhead costs, even though he does not really understand it or have any way of checking to see if he did it correctly. Tyler is hesitant to ask for help because he just started this job and he wants to look impressive.

EXERCISES Group A

E6-20A Forecast costs at different volumes *(Learning Objectives 1 & 2)*

Farnsworth Drycleaners has capacity to clean up to 7,500 garments per month.

Requirements

1. Complete the following schedule for the three volumes shown.

	4,500 Garments	6,000 Garments	7,500 Garments
Total variable costs		$4,200	
Total fixed costs			
Total operating costs			
Variable cost per garment			
Fixed cost per garment		$2.40	
Average cost per garment			

2. Why does the average cost per garment change?
3. Suppose the owner, Dustin Farnsworth, erroneously uses the average cost per unit *at full capacity* to predict total costs at a volume of 4,500 garments. Would he overestimate or underestimate his total costs? By how much?

E6-21A Prepare income statement in two formats *(Learning Objective 6)*

Refer to the Farnsworth Drycleaners in E6-20A. Assume that Farnsworth charges customers $10 per garment for dry cleaning. Prepare Farnsworth's *projected* income statement if 4,260 garments are cleaned in July. First, prepare the income statement using the traditional format; then prepare Farnsworth's contribution margin income statement.

E6-22A Use unit cost data to forecast total costs *(Learning Objective 2)*

Rollins Mailbox produces decorative mailboxes. The company's average cost per unit is $23.43 when it produces 1,400 mailboxes.

Requirements

1. What is the total cost of producing 1,400 mailboxes?
2. If $20,202 of the total costs is fixed, what is the variable cost of producing each mailbox?
3. Write Rollins Mailbox's cost equation.
4. If the plant manager uses the average cost per unit to predict total costs, what would the forecast be for 1,500 mailboxes?
5. If the plant manager uses the cost equation to predict total costs, what would the forecast be for 1,500 mailboxes?
6. What is the dollar difference between your answers to questions 4 and 5? Which approach to forecasting costs is appropriate? Why?

E6-23A Use a cost equation to forecast total costs *(Learning Objective 2)*

The Carrollton Buffet offers an all-you-can-eat buffet meal for $30 per person. The restaurant employs ten salaried employees. Rent for the building, employee salaries, and other fixed costs for the restaurant are $143,000 per month when the restaurant serves meals to up to 14,000 guests in that month. If the restaurant were to serve more than 14,000 guests in any given month, it would need to hire two additional servers and two additional kitchen staff for an additional fixed cost of $22,000 per month. The variable cost of food is $15 per guest.

Requirements

1. What is the restaurant's cost equation for estimating costs if the number of guests to be served is up to 14,000 guests per month?
2. If the restaurant were to serve 13,000 guests in May, what would be the:
   a. Estimated total cost? (Use the cost equation from Requirement 1.)
   b. Average cost per guest?
3. If the restaurant were to serve 11,000 guests in June, what would be the:
   a. Estimated total cost using the cost equation from Requirement 1?
   b. Estimated total cost using the average per guest cost from Requirement 2b?
   c. Why is there a difference in the two cost estimates?
4. What is the restaurant's cost equation for estimating costs if the number of guests to be served is more than 14,000 guests per month?
5. If the restaurant were to serve 15,000 guests in July, what would be the estimated total cost? (Use the cost equation from Requirement 4.)

E6-24A Sustainability and cost estimation *(Learning Objective 2)*

SUSTAINABILITY

Moonlight Entertainment is a provider of cable, Internet, and on-demand video services. Moonlight currently sends monthly bills to its customers via the postal service. Because of a concern for the environment and recent increases in postal rates, Moonlight management is considering offering an option to its customers for paperless billing. In addition to saving printing, paper, and postal costs, paperless billing will save energy and water (through reduced paper needs, reduced waste disposal, and reduced transportation needs.) Although Moonlight would like to switch to 100% paperless billing, many of its customers are not comfortable with paperless billing or may not have online access, so the paper billing option will remain regardless of whether Moonlight adopts a paperless billing system or not.

The cost of the paperless billing system would be $288,600 per quarter with no variable costs since the costs of the system are the salaries of the clerks and the cost of leasing the computer system. The paperless billing system being proposed would be able to handle up to 990,000 bills per quarter (more than 990,000 bills per quarter would require a different computer system and is outside the scope of the current situation at Moonlight).

The company has gathered its cost data for the past year by quarter for paper, toner cartridges, printer maintenance costs, and postage costs for its billing department. The cost data are as follows:

	Quarter 1	Quarter 2	Quarter 3	Quarter 4
Total paper, toner, printer maintenance, and postage costs	$689,400	$705,000	$810,000	$720,000
Total number of bills mailed	616,000	621,000	750,000	625,000

Requirements

1. Calculate the variable cost per bill mailed under the current paper-based billing system. Use the high-low method.
2. Assume that the company projects that it will have a total of 760,000 bills to mail in the upcoming quarter. If enough customers choose the paperless billing option so that 45% of the mailings can be converted to paperless, how much would the company save from the paperless billing system (be sure to consider the cost of the paperless billing system)?
3. What if only 40% of the mailings are converted to the paperless option (assume a total of 760,000 bills)? Should the company still offer the paperless billing system? Explain your rationale.

E6-25A Create a scatterplot *(Learning Objective 3)*

Melody Leigh, owner of Broadway Floral, operates a local chain of floral shops. Each shop has its own delivery van. Instead of charging a flat delivery fee, Leigh wants to set the delivery fee based on the distance driven to deliver the flowers. Leigh wants to separate the fixed and variable portions of her van operating costs so that she has a better idea of how delivery distance affects these costs. She has the following data from the past seven months:

Month	Miles Driven	Van Operating Costs
January	15,500	$5,390
February	17,400	$5,280
March	15,400	$4,960
April	16,300	$5,340
May	16,500	$5,450
June	15,200	$5,230
July	14,400	$4,680

Requirements

1. Prepare a scatterplot of Broadway Floral's volume (miles driven) and van operating costs.
2. Does the data appear to contain any outliers? Explain.
3. How strong a relationship is there between miles driven and van operating costs?

E6-26A Continuation of E6-25A: High-low method *(Learning Objective 4)*

Refer to Broadway Floral's data in E6-25A. Use the high-low method to determine Broadway Floral's cost equation for van operating costs. Use your results to predict van operating costs at a volume of 16,500 miles.

E6-27A Continuation of E6-25A: Regression analysis *(Learning Objective 5)*

Refer to the Broadway Floral data in E6-25A. Use Microsoft Excel to do the following:

Requirements

1. Run a regression analysis.
2. Determine the company's cost equation (use the output from the Excel regression).
3. Determine the R-square (use the output from the Excel regression). What does Broadway Floral's R-square indicate?
4. Predict van operating costs at a volume of 16,500 miles assuming the company would use the cost equation from the Excel regression regardless of its R-square. Should the company rely on this cost estimate? Why or why not?

E6-28A Regression analysis using Excel output *(Learning Objective 5)*

Assume that Broadway Floral does a regression analysis on the next year's data using Excel. The output generated by Excel is as follows:

	A	B	C	D	E	F	G
1		**SUMMARY OUTPUT**					
2		*Regression Statistics*					
3	Multiple R		0.69				
4	R Square		0.47				
5	Adjusted R Square		0.37				
6	Standard Error		218.13				
7	Observations		7				
8	**ANOVA**						
9		df	SS	MS	F	Significance F	
10	Regression	1	214,895.40	214,895.40	4.52	0.0869	
11	Residual	5	237,904.60	47,580.92			
12	Total	6	452,800.00				
13							
14			Standard			Lower	Upper
15		Coefficients	Error	t Stat	P-value	95%	95%
16	Intercept	2,163.80	1,426.35	1.52	0.19	−1,502.75	5,830.36
17	X Variable 1	0.19	0.09	2.13	0.09	−0.04	0.42
18							

Requirements

1. Determine the firm's cost equation (use the output from the Excel regression).
2. Determine the R-square (use the output from the Excel regression). What does Broadway Floral's R-square indicate?
3. Predict van operating costs at a volume of 16,000 miles assuming the company would use the cost equation from the Excel regression regardless of its R-square. Should the company rely on this cost estimate? Why or why not?

E6-29A Create a scatterplot for a hospital laboratory *(Learning Objective 3)*

The manager of the main laboratory facility at Elmhurst Health Center is interested in being able to predict the overhead costs each month for the lab. The manager believes that total overhead varies with the number of lab tests performed but that some costs remain the same each month regardless of the number of lab tests performed.

The lab manager collected the following data for the first seven months of the year:

Month	Number of Lab Tests Performed	Total Laboratory Overhead Costs
January	3,000	$21,900
February	2,850	$20,600
March	3,400	$28,900
April	3,700	$31,000
May	3,900	$28,000
June	1,900	$20,200
July	2,050	$14,000

Requirements

1. Prepare a scatterplot of the lab's volume (number of lab tests performed) and total laboratory overhead costs.
2. Does the data appear to contain any outliers? Explain.
3. How strong a relationship is there between the number of lab tests performed and laboratory overhead costs?

E6-30A Using the high-low method to predict overhead for a hospital laboratory *(Learning Objective 4)*

Refer to the laboratory overhead cost and activity data for Elmhurst Health Center in E6-29A. Use the high-low method to determine the laboratory's cost equation for total laboratory overhead. Use your results to predict total laboratory overhead if 3,100 lab tests are performed next month.

E6-31A Using regression analysis output to predict overhead for a hospital laboratory (Learning Objective 5)

Using the data provided in E6-29A, the laboratory manager performed a regression analysis to predict total laboratory overhead costs. The output generated by Excel is as follows:

	A	B	C	D	E	F	G
1		SUMMARY OUTPUT					
2		Regression Statistics					
3	Multiple R		0.878214				
4	R Square		0.77126				
5	Adjusted R Square		0.725512				
6	Standard Error		3156.338706				
7	Observations		7				
8	ANOVA						
9		df	SS	MS	F	Significance F	
10	Regression	1	167956201.28	167956201.28	16.858885	0.009301	
11	Residual	5	49812370.15	9962474.03			
12	Total	6	217768571.43				
13							
14			Standard			Lower	Upper
15		Coefficients	Error	t Stat	P-value	95%	95%
16	Intercept	3187.94	5092.169	0.626	0.559	−9901.898	16277.778
17	X Variable 1	6.84	1.666	4.106	0.009	2.558	11.123
18							

Requirements

1. Determine the lab's cost equation (use the output from the Excel regression).
2. Determine the R-square (use the output from the Excel regression).
3. Predict the total laboratory overhead for the month if 3,100 tests are performed.

E6-32A Performing a regression analysis to predict overhead for a hospital laboratory (Learning Objective 5)

The manager of the main laboratory facility at Elmhurst Health Center (from E6-29A) collects seven additional months of data after obtaining the regression results in E6-31A. The number of tests performed and the total monthly overhead costs for the lab follow:

Month	Number of Lab Tests Performed	Total Laboratory Overhead Costs
August	3,350	$23,500
September	3,700	$27,550
October	3,650	$24,500
November	3,450	$26,400
December	4,200	$28,500
January	2,500	$22,800
February	3,800	$25,350

Use Excel to do the following:

Requirements

1. Run a regression analysis using data for August through February.
2. Determine the lab's cost equation (use the output from the regression analysis you performed using Excel).
3. Determine the R-square using the Excel output you obtain. What does the lab's R-square indicate?
4. Predict the lab's total overhead costs for the month if 3,500 tests are performed.

E6-33A Predict operating costs using high-low method (Learning Objective 4)

Lakeview Apartments is an 800-unit apartment complex. When the apartments are 90% occupied, monthly operating costs total $220,040. When occupancy dips to 80%, monthly operating costs fall to $215,480. The owner of the apartment complex is worried because many of the apartment residents work at a nearby manufacturing plant that has just announced that it will close in three months. The apartment owner fears that occupancy of her apartments will drop to 55% if residents lose their jobs and move away. Assuming the same relevant range, what can the owner expect her operating costs to be if occupancy falls to 55%?

E6-34A Use the high-low method (Learning Objective 4)

Summerville Company, which uses the high-low method to analyze cost behavior, has determined that machine hours best predict the company's total utilities cost. The company's cost and machine hour usage data for the first six months of the year follow:

Month	Total Cost	Machine Hours
January	$3,420	1,090
February	$3,760	1,120
March	$3,532	1,080
April	$3,720	1,220
May	$4,800	1,330
June	$4,192	1,480

Requirements

Using the high-low method, answer the following questions:
1. What is the variable utilities cost per machine hour?
2. What is the fixed cost of utilities each month?
3. If Summerville Company uses 1,210 machine hours in a month, what will its total costs be?

E6-35A Compare absorption and variable costing (Learning Objective 6)

Royal Industries has one product. Information about the production and sales of that product for the past year follow.

Selling price per unit	$ 49.00
Direct material per unit	$ 18.00
Direct labor per unit	$ 6.00
Total annual manufacturing overhead	$ 221,000
Fixed portion of annual manufacturing overhead	$ 187,000
Variable operating expenses per unit sold	$ 3.00
Fixed operating expenses per year in total	$ 47,000
Units manufactured	17,000
Units sold	13,000

The company had no beginning inventory.

Requirements

1. Prepare two income statements for the year, one using absorption costing and one using variable costing. Use those statements to answer the following questions:
    a. What is the product cost per unit using absorption costing?
    b. What is the product cost per unit using variable costing?
    c. What is the ending inventory balance using absorption costing?
    d. What is the ending inventory balance using variable costing?
    e. What is cost of goods sold using absorption costing?
    f. What is cost of goods sold using variable costing?
    g. What is operating income using absorption costing?
    h. What is operating income using variable costing?

2. What is the underlying reason for the difference in operating income between the two costing methods?

E6-36A Prepare a contribution margin income statement *(Learning Objective 6)*

Five Macaws is a specialty pet gift shop selling exotic pet-related items online. The shop has no physical location. Results for last year are shown next:

	A	B	C	D
1	**Five Macaws**			
2	**Traditional Income Statement (Absorption Costing)**			
3	**For the Year Ended December 31**			
4				
5	Sales revenue		$ 990,000	
6	Less: Cost of goods sold		673,000	
7	Gross profit		$ 317,000	
8	Less operating expenses:			
9	Selling and marketing expenses	$ 65,500		
10	Website maintenance expenses	58,000		
11	Other operating expenses	17,600	141,100	
12	Operating income		$ 175,900	
13				

For internal planning and decision-making purposes, the owner of Five Macaws would like to translate the company's income statement into the contribution margin format. Since Five Macaws is online only, all of its cost of goods sold is variable. A large portion of the selling and marketing expenses consists of freight-out charges ($19,400), which were also variable. Only 20% of the remaining selling and marketing expenses and 25% of the website expenses were variable. Of the other operating expenses, 90% were fixed. Based on this information, prepare Five Macaws' contribution margin income statement for last year.

E6-37A Prepare a contribution margin income statement *(Learning Objective 6)*

Charleston Carriage Company offers guided horse-drawn carriage rides through historic Greenville, South Carolina. The carriage business is highly regulated by the city. Charleston Carriage Company has the following operating costs during April:

Monthly depreciation expense on carriages and stable	$2,900
Fee paid to the City of Greenville	10% of ticket revenue
Cost of souvenir set of postcards given to each passenger	$0.55/set of postcards
Brokerage fee paid to independent ticket brokers (60% of tickets are issued through these brokers; 40% are sold directly by the Charleston Carriage Company)	$1.40/ticket sold by broker
Monthly cost of leasing and boarding the horses	$48,000
Carriage drivers (tour guides) are paid on a per passenger basis	$3.90 per passenger
Monthly payroll costs of non-tour guide employees	$7,600
Marketing, website, telephone, and other monthly fixed costs	$7,350

During April (a month during peak season), Charleston Carriage Company had 13,400 passengers. Eighty percent of passengers were adults ($20 fare) while 20% were children ($12 fare).

Requirements

1. Prepare the company's contribution margin income statement for the month of April. Round all figures to the nearest dollar.
2. Assume that passenger volume increases by 19% in May. Which figures on the income statement would you expect to change, and by what percentage would they change? Which figures would remain the same as in April?

E6-38A Prepare income statements using variable costing and absorption costing with changing inventory levels *(Learning Objective 6)*

Hadlock Manufacturing manufactures a single product that it will sell for $68 per unit. The company is looking to project its operating income for its first two years of operations. Cost information for the single unit of its product is as follows:

- Direct material per unit produced $30
- Direct labor cost per unit produced $11
- Variable manufacturing overhead (MOH) per unit produced $5
- Variable operating expenses per unit sold $3
- Fixed manufacturing overhead (MOH for each year is $176,000, while fixed operating expenses for each year will be $86,000.

During its first year of operations, the company plans to manufacture 22,000 units and anticipates selling 16,000 of those units. During the second year of its operations, the company plans to manufacture 22,000 units and anticipates selling 24,000 units (it has units in beginning inventory for the second year from its first year of operations).

Requirements

1. Prepare an absorption costing income statement for the following:
    a. The first year of operations
    b. The second year of operations
2. Before you prepare the variable costing income statements for Hadlock, predict the company's operating income using variable costing for both its first year and its second year without preparing the variable costing income statements. *Hint:* Calculate the variable costing operating income for a given year by taking that year's absorption costing operating income and adding or subtracting the difference in operating income as calculated using the following formula:

Difference in operating income = (Change in inventory level in units × Fixed MOH per unit)

3. Prepare a variable costing income statement for each of the following years:
    a. The first year of operations
    b. The second year of operations

E6-39A Prepare a variable costing income statement given an absorption costing income statement *(Learning Objective 6)*

Bruno Industries manufactures and sells a single product. The controller has prepared the following income statement for the most recent year:

	A	B	C	D
1	**Bruno Industries**			
2	**Traditional Income Statement (Absorption Costing)**			
3	**For the Year Ended December 31**			
4				
5	Sales revenue	$ 406,000		
6	Less: Cost of goods sold	329,000		
7	Gross profit	$ 77,000		
8	Less: Operating expenses	73,000		
9	Operating income	$ 4,000		
10				

The company produced 8,000 units and sold 7,000 units during the year ending December 31. Fixed manufacturing overhead (MOH) for the year was $152,000, while fixed operating expenses were $62,000. The company had no beginning inventory.

Requirements

1. Will the company's operating income under variable costing be higher, lower, or the same as its operating income under absorption costing? Why?
2. Project the company's operating income under variable costing without preparing a variable costing income statement.
3. Prepare a variable costing income statement for the year.

E6-40A Absorption and variable costing income statements (Learning Objective 6)

The annual data that follow pertain to Aqua Goggles, a manufacturer of swimming goggles (the company had no beginning inventory):

Sales price	$ 45
Variable manufacturing expense per unit	$ 20
Sales commission expense per unit	$ 7
Fixed manufacturing overhead	$ 1,980,000
Fixed operating expenses	$ 250,000
Number of goggles produced	220,000
Number of goggles sold	198,000

Requirements

1. Prepare both conventional (absorption costing) and contribution margin (variable costing) income statements for Aqua Goggles for the year.
2. Which statement shows the higher operating income? Why?
3. The company marketing vice president believes a new sales promotion that costs $140,000 would increase sales to 220,000 goggles. Should the company go ahead with the promotion? Give your reason.

EXERCISES Group B

E6-41B Forecast costs at different volumes (Learning Objectives 1 & 2)

Whitman Drycleaners has the capacity to clean up to 6,000 garments per month.

Requirements

1. Complete the following schedule for the three volumes shown.

	3,000 Garments	4,500 Garments	6,000 Garments
Total variable costs		$3,375	
Total fixed costs			
Total operating costs			
Variable cost per garment			
Fixed cost per garment		$2.40	
Average cost per garment			

2. Why does the average cost per garment change?
3. The owner, Ellen Whitman, uses the average cost per unit *at full capacity* to predict total costs at a volume of 3,000 garments. Would she overestimate or underestimate total costs? By how much?

E6-42B Prepare income statement in two formats (Learning Objective 6)

Refer to the Whitman Drycleaners in E6-41B. Assume that Whitman charges customers $9 per garment for dry cleaning. Prepare Whitman's *projected* income statement if 4,220 garments are cleaned in March. First, prepare the income statement using the traditional format; then prepare Whitman's contribution margin income statement.

E6-43B Use unit cost data to forecast total costs *(Learning Objective 2)*

Melcher Mailboxes produces decorative mailboxes. The company's average cost per unit is $20.43 when it produces 1,000 mailboxes.

Requirements

1. What is the total cost of producing 1,000 mailboxes?
2. If $10,430 of the total costs are fixed, what is the variable cost of producing each mailbox?
3. Write Melcher Mailboxes' cost equation.
4. If the plant manager uses the average cost per unit to predict total costs, what would the forecast be for 1,700 mailboxes?
5. If the plant manager uses the cost equation to predict total costs, what would the forecast be for 1,700 mailboxes?
6. What is the dollar difference between your answers to Requirements 4 and 5? Which approach to forecasting costs is appropriate? Why?

E6-44B Use a cost equation to forecast total costs *(Learning Objective 2)*

The Minerva Buffet offers an all-you-can-eat buffet meal for $35 per person. The restaurant employs ten salaried employees. Rent for the building, employee salaries, and other fixed costs for the restaurant are $148,500 per month when the restaurant serves meals to up to 14,000 guests in that month. If the restaurant were to serve more than 14,000 guests in any given month, it would need to hire two additional servers and two additional kitchen staff for an additional fixed cost of $53,000 per month. The variable cost of food is $14 per guest.

Requirements

1. What is the restaurant's cost equation for estimating costs if the number of guests to be served is up to 14,000 guests per month?
2. If the restaurant were to serve 13,500 guests in May, what would be the:
   a. Estimated total cost? (Use the cost equation from Requirement 1.)
   b. Average cost per guest?
3. If the restaurant were to serve 11,700 guests in June, what would be the:
   a. Estimated total cost using the cost equation from Requirement 1)?
   b. Estimated total cost using the average per guest cost from Requirement 2b?
   c. Why is there a difference in the two cost estimates?
4. What is the restaurant's cost equation for estimating costs if the number of guests to be served is more than 14,000 guests per month?
5. If the restaurant were to serve 15,500 guests in July, what would be the estimated total cost? (Use the cost equation from Requirement 4.)

E6-45B Sustainability and cost estimation *(Learning Objective 2)*

SUSTAINABILITY

Skye Entertainment is a provider of cable, Internet, and on-demand video services. Skye currently sends monthly bills to its customers via the postal service. Because of a concern for the environment and recent increases in postal rates, Skye's management is considering offering an option to its customers for paperless billing. In addition to saving printing, paper, and postal costs, paperless billing will save energy and water (through reduced paper needs, reduced waste disposal, and reduced transportation needs). Although Skye would like to switch to 100% paperless billing, many of its customers are not comfortable with paperless billing or may not have online access, so the paper billing option will remain regardless of whether Skye adopts a paperless billing system or not.

The cost of the paperless billing system would be $81,800 per quarter with no variable costs since the costs of the system are the salaries of the clerks and the cost of leasing the computer system. The paperless billing system being proposed would be able to handle up to 1,000,000 bills per quarter (more than 1,000,000 bills per quarter would require a different computer system and is outside the scope of the current situation at Skye).

Skye has gathered its cost data for the past year by quarter for paper, toner cartridges, printer maintenance costs, and postage costs for its billing department. The cost data are as follows:

	Quarter 1	Quarter 2	Quarter 3	Quarter 4
Total paper, toner, printer maintenance, and postage costs	$592,500	$600,000	$750,000	$610,000
Total number of bills mailed	475,000	495,000	700,000	500,000

Requirements

1. Calculate the variable cost per bill mailed under the current paper-based billing system. Use the high-low method.
2. Assume that the company projects that it will have a total of 740,000 bills to mail in the upcoming quarter. If enough customers choose the paperless billing option so that 20% of the mailing can be converted to paperless, how much would the company save from the paperless billing system (be sure to consider the cost of the paperless billing system)?
3. What if only 10% of the mailings are converted to the paperless option (assume a total of 740,000 bills)? Should the company still offer the paperless billing system? Explain your rationale.

E6-46B Create a scatter plot *(Learning Objective 3)*

Tammy Lotta, owner of Fourth Street Floral, operates a local chain of floral shops. Each shop has its own delivery van. Instead of charging a flat delivery fee, Lotta wants to set the delivery fee based on the distance driven to deliver the flowers. Lotta wants to separate the fixed and variable portions of her van operating costs so that she has a better idea of how delivery distance affects these costs. She has the following data from the past seven months:

Month	Miles Driven	Van Operating Costs
January	15,800	$5,460
February	17,300	$5,680
March	14,600	$4,940
April	16,000	$5,310
May	17,100	$5,830
June	15,400	$5,420
July	14,100	$4,880

Requirements

1. Prepare a scatterplot of Fourth Street Floral's volume (miles driven) and van operating costs.
2. Do the data appear to contain any outliers? Explain.
3. How strong of a relationship is there between miles driven and van operating expenses?

E6-47B Continuation of E6-46B: High-low method *(Learning Objective 4)*

Refer to Lotta's Fourth Street Floral data in E6-46B. Use the high-low method to determine the company's cost equation for van operating costs. Use your results to predict van operating costs at a volume of 15,500 miles.

E6-48B Continuation of E6-46B: Regression analysis *(Learning Objective 5)*

Refer to the Fourth Street Floral data in E6-46B. Use Microsoft Excel to run a regression analysis, then do the following calculations:

Requirements

1. Determine the firm's cost equation (use the output from the Excel regression).
2. Determine the R-square (use the output from the Excel regression). What does Fourth Street Floral's R-square indicate?
3. Predict van operating costs at a volume of 15,500 miles assuming the company would use the cost equation from the Excel regression regardless of its R-square. Should the company rely on this cost estimate? Why or why not?

E6-49B Regression analysis using Excel output *(Learning Objective 5)*

Assume that Fourth Street Floral does a regression analysis on the next year's data using Excel. The output generated by Excel is as follows:

	A	B	C	D	E	F	G
1		**SUMMARY OUTPUT**					
2		*Regression Statistics*					
3	Multiple R		0.95				
4	R Square		0.90				
5	Adjusted R Square		0.87				
6	Standard Error		124.99				
7	Observations		7				
8	ANOVA						
9		df	SS	MS	F	Significance F	
10	Regression	1	668,089.58	668,089.58	42.77	0.0013	
11	Residual	5	78,110.42	15,622.08			
12	Total	6	746,200.00				
13							
14			Standard			Lower	Upper
15		Coefficients	Error	t Stat	P-value	95%	95%
16	Intercept	931.23	678.87	1.37	0.23	−813.87	2,676.33
17	X Variable 1	0.28	0.04	6.54	0.00	0.17	0.39
18							

Requiremets

1. Determine the firm's cost equation (use the output from the Excel regression).
2. Determine the R-square (use the output from the Excel regression). What does Fourth Street Floral R-square indicate?
3. Predict van operating costs at a volume of 15,000 miles assuming the company would use the cost equation from the Excel regression regardless of its R-square. Should the company rely on this cost estimate? Why or why not?

E6-50B Create a scatterplot for a hospital laboratory *(Learning Objective 3)*

The manager of the main laboratory facility at Rosedale Health Center is interested in being able to predict the overhead costs each month for the lab. The manager believes that total overhead varies with the number of lab tests performed but that some costs remain the same each month regardless of the number of lab tests performed.

The lab manager collected the following data for the first seven months of the year.

Month	Number of Lab Tests Performed	Total Laboratory Overhead Costs
January	3,250	$27,600
February	3,000	$24,800
March	3,750	$25,900
April	3,500	$23,500
May	4,200	$27,000
June	2,200	$18,800
July	3,400	$26,500

Requirements

1. Prepare a scatterplot of the lab's volume (number of lab tests performed) and total laboratory overhead costs.
2. Do the data appear to contain any outliers? Explain.
3. How strong of a relationship is there between the number of lab tests performed and laboratory overhead costs?

E6-51B Using the high-low method to predict overhead for a hospital laboratory *(Learning Objective 4)*

Refer to the laboratory overhead cost and activity data for Rosedale Health Center in E6-50B. Use the high-low method to determine the laboratory's cost equation for total laboratory overhead. Use your results to predict total laboratory overhead if 2,700 lab tests are performed next month.

E6-52B Using regression analysis output to predict overhead for a hospital laboratory (Learning Objective 5)

Using the data provided in E6-50B, the laboratory manager performed a regression analysis to predict total laboratory overhead costs. The output generated by Excel is as follows:

	A	B	C	D	E	F	G
1		SUMMARY OUTPUT					
2		Regression Statistics					
3	Multiple R		0.779237				
4	R Square		0.60721				
5	Adjusted R Square		0.528651				
6	Standard Error		2067.910396				
7	Observations		7				
8	ANOVA						
9		df	SS	MS	F	Significance F	
10	Regression	1	33053018.68	33053018.68	7.729434	0.038894	
11	Residual	5	21381267.03	4276253.406			
12	Total	6	54434285.71				
13							
14			Standard			Lower	Upper
15		Coefficients	Error	t Stat	P-value	95%	95%
16	Intercept	12412.72	4548.903	2.729	0.041	−719.391	24106.041
17	X Variable 1	3.74	1.346	2.780	0.039	0.282	7.204
18							

Requirements

1. Determine the lab's cost equation (use the output from the Excel regression).
2. Determine the R-square (use the output from the Excel regression).
3. Predict the total laboratory overhead for the month if 2,700 tests are performed.

E6-53B Performing a regression analysis to predict overhead for a hospital laboratory (Learning Objective 5)

The manager of the main laboratory facility at Rosedale Health Center (from E6-50B) collects seven additional months of data after obtaining the regression results in the prior period. The number of tests performed and the total monthly overhead costs for the lab follows:

Month	Number of Lab Tests Performed	Total Laboratory Overhead Costs
August	2,900	$24,250
September	3,200	$26,100
October	4,050	$30,200
November	4,200	$33,500
December	4,100	$31,400
January	2,650	$20,500
February	3,350	$27,750

Use Excel to perform the requirements.

Requirements

1. Run a regression analysis using data from August through February.
2. Determine the lab's cost equation (use the output from the regression analysis you perform using Excel).
3. Determine the R-square using the Excel output you obtain. What does the lab's R-square indicate?
4. Predict the lab's total overhead costs for the month if 2,800 tests are performed.

E6-54B Predict operating costs using high-low method *(Learning Objective 4)*

Creekside Apartments is a 900-unit apartment complex. When the apartments are 90% occupied, monthly operating costs total $223,360. When occupancy dips to 80%, monthly operating costs fall to $218,320. The owner of the apartment complex is worried because many of the apartment residents work at a nearby manufacturing plant that has just announced it will close in three months. The apartment owner fears that occupancy of her apartments will drop to 65% if residents lose their jobs and move away. Assuming the same relevant range, what should the owner expect operating costs to be if occupancy falls to 65%?

E6-55B Use the high-low method *(Learning Objective 4)*

Bates Company, which uses the high-low method to analyze cost behavior, has determined that machine hours best predict the company's total utilities cost. The company's cost and machine hour usage data for the first six months of the year follow:

Month	Total Cost	Machine Hours
January	$3,420	1,080
February	$3,760	1,160
March	$3,388	1,030
April	$3,780	1,230
May	$4,000	1,360
June	$4,076	1,460

Requirements

Using the high-low method, answer the following questions:

1. What is the variable utilities cost per machine hour?
2. What is the fixed cost of utilities each month?
3. If Bates Company uses 1,200 machine hours in a month, what will its total costs be?

E6-56B Compare absorption and variable costing *(Learning Objective 6)*

Chief Industries has one product. Information about the production and sales of that product for the past year follow.

Selling price per unit	$ 65.00
Direct material per unit	$ 20.00
Direct labor per unit	$ 8.00
Total annual manufacturing overhead	$ 288,000
Fixed portion of annual manufacturing overhead	$ 224,000
Variable operating expenses per unit sold	$ 1.00
Fixed operating expenses per year in total	$ 32,000
Units manufactured	16,000
Units sold	12,000

The company had no beginning inventory.

Requirements

1. Prepare two income statements for the year, one using absorption costing and one using variable costing. Use those statements to answer the following questions:
    a. What is the product cost per unit using absorption costing?
    b. What is the product cost per unit using variable costing?
    c. What is the ending inventory balance using absorption costing?
    d. What is the ending inventory balance using variable costing?
    e. What is cost of goods sold using absorption costing?
    f. What is cost of goods sold using variable costing?
    g. What is operating income using absorption costing?
    h. What is operating income using variable costing?
2. What is the underlying reason for the difference in operating income between the two costing methods?

E6-57B Prepare a contribution margin income statement *(Learning Objective 6)*

Three Turtles is a specialty pet gift shop selling exotic pet-related items online. The shop has no physical location. Results for last year are shown next:

	A	B	C	D
1		Three Turtles		
2		Traditional Income Statement (Absorption Costing)		
3		For the Year Ended December 31		
4				
5	Sales revenue		$ 990,000	
6	Less: Cost of goods sold		672,000	
7	Gross profit		$ 318,000	
8	Less operating expenses:			
9	Selling and marketing expenses	$ 62,000		
10	Website maintenance expenses	58,500		
11	Other operating expenses	17,000	137,500	
12	Operating income		$ 180,500	
13				

For internal planning and decision-making purposes, the owner of Three Turtles would like to translate the company's income statement into the contribution margin format. Since Three Turtles is online only, all of its cost of goods sold is variable. A large portion of the selling and marketing expenses consists of freight-out charges $19,000, which were also variable. Only 20% of the remaining selling and marketing expenses and 25% of the website expenses were variable. Of the other operating expenses, 90% were fixed.

Based on this information, prepare Three Turtles' contribution margin income statement for last year.

E6-58B Prepare a contribution margin income statement *(Learning Objective 6)*

Vintage Carriage Company offers guided horse-drawn carriage rides through historic Camden, South Carolina. The carriage business is highly regulated by the city. Vintage Carriage Company has the following operating costs during April:

Monthly depreciation expense on carriages and stable	$2,300
Fee paid to the City of Camden	10% of ticket revenue
Cost of souvenir set of postcards given to each passenger	$0.75/set of postcards
Brokerage fee paid to independent ticket brokers (60% of tickets are issued through these brokers; 40% are sold directly by the Vintage Carriage Company)	$1.50/ticket sold by broker
Monthly cost of leasing and boarding the horses	$49,000
Carriage drivers (tour guides) are paid on a per passenger basis	$3.90 per passenger
Monthly payroll costs of non-tour guide employees	$7,900
Marketing, website, telephone, and other monthly fixed costs	$7,200

During April (a month during peak season), Vintage Carriage Company had 13,500 passengers. Eighty percent of passengers were adults ($26 fare) while 20% were children ($18 fare).

Requirements

1. Prepare the company's contribution margin income statement for the month of April. Round all figures to the nearest dollar.
2. Assume that passenger volume increases by 18% in May. Which figures on the income statement would you expect to change, and by what percentage would they change? Which figures would remain the same as in April?

E6-59B Prepare income statements using variable costing and absorption costing with changing inventory levels *(Learning Objective 6)*

Squire Manufacturing manufactures a single product that it will sell for $77 per unit. The company is looking to project its operating income for its first two years of operations. Cost information for the single unit of its product is as follows:

- Direct material per unit produced $37
- Direct labor cost per unit produced $9
- Variable manufacturing overhead (MOH) per unit produced $4
- Variable operating expenses per unit sold $6

Fixed manufacturing overhead (MOH) for each year is $184,000, while fixed operating expenses for each year will be $80,000.

During its first year of operations, the company plans to manufacture 23,000 units and anticipates selling 21,000 of those units. During the second year of its operations, the company plans to manufacture 23,000 units and anticipates selling 24,000 units (it has units in beginning inventory for the second year from its first year of operations).

Requirements

1. Prepare an absorption costing income statement for:
   a. The first year of operations
   b. The second year of operations
2. Before you prepare the variable costing income statements for Squire, predict the company's operating income using variable costing for both its first year and its second year without preparing the variable costing income statements. *Hint*: Calculate the variable costing operating income for a given year by taking that year's absorption costing operating income and adding or subtracting the difference in operating income as calculated using the following formula:

   Difference in operating income = (Change in inventory level in units × Fixed MOH per unit)

3. Prepare a variable costing income statement for:
   a. The first year of operations
   b. The second year of operations

E6-60B Prepare a variable costing income statement given an absorption costing income statement *(Learning Objective 6)*

Rathke Industries manufactures and sells a single product. The controller has prepared the following income statement for the most recent year:

	A	B	C	D
1	Rathke Industries			
2	Traditional Income Statement (Absorption Costing)			
3	For the Year Ended December 31			
4				
5	Sales revenue	$ 595,000		
6	Less: Cost of goods sold	510,000		
7	Gross profit	$ 85,000		
8	Less: Operating expenses	65,000		
9	Operating income	$ 20,000		
10				

The company produced 14,000 units and sold 8,500 units during the year ending December 31. Fixed manufacturing overhead (MOH) for the year was $266,000, while fixed operating expenses were $58,000. The company had no beginning inventory.

Requirements

1. Will the company's operating income under variable costing be higher, lower, or the same as its operating income under absorption costing? Why?
2. Project the company's operating income under variable costing without preparing a variable costing income statement.
3. Prepare a variable costing income statement for the year.

E6-61B Absorption and variable costing income statements
(Learning Objective 6)

The annual data that follow pertain to Aquatic Optics, a manufacturer of swimming goggles (the company has no beginning inventory):

Sales price	$ 47
Variable manufacturing expense per unit	$ 16
Sales commission expense per unit	$ 5
Fixed manufacturing overhead	$2,000,000
Fixed operating expense	$ 260,000
Number of goggles produced	200,000
Number of goggles sold	192,000

Requirements
1. Prepare both conventional (absorption costing) and contribution margin (variable costing) income statements for Aquatic Optics for the year.
2. Which statement shows the higher operating income? Why?
3. The company's marketing vice president believes a new sales promotion that costs $155,000 would increase sales to 200,000 goggles. Should the company go ahead with the promotion? Give your reason.

PROBLEMS Group A

P6-62A Analyze cost behavior at a hospital using various cost estimation methods *(Learning Objectives 1, 2, 3, 4, & 5)*

Sandy Dawson is the Chief Operating Officer at Mercy Hospital in Atlanta, Georgia. She is analyzing the hospital's overhead costs but is not sure whether nursing hours or the number of patient days would be the best cost driver to use for predicting the hospital's overhead. She has gathered the following information for the last six months of the most recent year:

Month	Hospital Overhead Costs	Nursing Hours	Number of Patient Days	Overhead Cost per Nursing Hour	Overhead Cost per Patient Day
July	$483,000	24,500	3,790	$19.71	$127.44
August	$535,000	28,500	4,310	$18.77	$124.13
September	$411,000	19,500	4,230	$21.08	$ 97.16
October	$451,000	20,500	3,450	$22.00	$130.72
November	$576,000	32,000	5,710	$18.00	$100.88
December	$446,000	20,000	3,290	$22.30	$135.56

Requirements
1. Are the hospital's overhead costs fixed, variable, or mixed? Explain.
2. Graph the hospital's overhead costs against nursing hours. Use Excel or graph by hand.
3. Graph the hospital's overhead costs against the number of patient days. Use Excel or graph by hand.
4. Do the data appear to be sound, or do you see any potential data problems? Explain.
5. Use the high-low method to determine the hospital's cost equation using nursing hours as the cost driver. Predict total overhead costs if 25,500 nursing hours are predicted for the month.

6. Dawson runs a regression analysis using nursing hours as the cost driver to predict total hospital overhead costs. The Excel output from the regression analysis is as follows:

	A	B	C	D	E	F	G
1	SUMMARY OUTPUT – Nursing hours as cost driver						
2	Regression Statistics						
3	Multiple R		0.984685				
4	R Square		0.969605				
5	Adjusted R Square		0.962006				
6	Standard Error		11,992.70481				
7	Observations		6				
8	ANOVA						
9		df	SS	MS	F	Significance F	
10	Regression	1	18,352,033,459	18,352,033,459	127.599774	0.00035	
11	Residual	4	525,299,875	143,824,969			
12	Total	5	18,877,333,334				
13							
14			Standard			Lower	Upper
15		Coefficients	Error	t Stat	P-value	95%	95%
16	Intercept	199,609.79	25,618.85	7.792	0.001	128,480.456	270,739.118
17	X Variable 1	11.75	1.041	11.296	0.000	8.865	14.643
18							

If 25,500 nursing hours are predicted for the month, what is the total predicted hospital overhead?

7. Dawson then ran the regression analysis using number of patient days as the cost driver. The Excel output from the regression is shown here:

	A	B	C	D	E	F	G
1	SUMMARY OUTPUT – Using number of patient days as cost driver						
2	Regression Statistics						
3	Multiple R		0.750775				
4	R Square		0.563662				
5	Adjusted R Square		0.454578				
6	Standard Error		45,438.70968				
7	Observations		6				
8	ANOVA						
9		df	SS	MS	F	Significance F	
10	Regression	1	10,668,627,982	10,668,627,982	5.167216	0.08543	
11	Residual	4	8,258,705,351	2,064,676,338			
12	Total	5	18,927,333,333				
13							
14			Standard			Lower	Upper
15		Coefficients	Error	t Stat	P-value	95%	95%
16	Intercept	265,475.95	97,762.101	2.176	0.053	−5,955.158	536,907.056
17	X Variable 1	52.83	23.241	2.273	0.085	−11.697	117.359
18							

If 3,680 patient days are predicted for the month, what is the total predicted hospital overhead?

8. Which regression analysis (using nursing hours or using number of patient days as the cost driver) produces the best cost equation? Explain your answer.

P6-63A **Analyze cost behavior** *(Learning Objectives 1, 2, 3, & 4)*

Pursell Industries is in the process of analyzing its manufacturing overhead costs. Management is not sure if the number of units produced or number of direct labor (DL) hours is the best cost driver to use for predicting manufacturing overhead (MOH) costs. The following information is available:

	Manufacturing Overhead Costs	Direct Labor Hours	Units Produced	MOH Cost per DL Hour	MOH Cost per Unit Produced
July	$475,000	25,500	3,640	$18.63	$130.49
August	$518,000	28,000	4,350	$18.50	$119.08
September	$469,000	22,000	4,260	$21.32	$110.09
October	$460,000	22,800	3,420	$20.18	$134.50
November	$586,000	31,000	5,800	$18.90	$101.03
December	$450,000	22,200	3,280	$20.27	$137.20

Requirements

1. Are manufacturing overhead costs fixed, variable, or mixed? Explain.
2. Graph the company's manufacturing overhead costs against DL hours. Use Excel or graph by hand.
3. Graph the company's manufacturing overhead costs against units produced. Use Excel or graph by hand.
4. Do the data appear to be sound, or do you see any potential data problems? Explain.
5. Use the high-low method to determine the company's manufacturing overhead cost equation using DL hours as the cost driver. Assume that management believes all data to be accurate and wants to include all of it in the analysis.
6. Estimate manufacturing overhead costs if the company incurs 26,000 DL hours in January.

P6-64A   Prepare traditional and contribution margin income statements
(Learning Objective 6)

The Willowick Ice Cream Shoppe sold 8,700 servings of ice cream during June for $3 per serving. The shop purchases the ice cream in large tubs from the Deluxe Ice Cream Company. Each tub costs the shop $12 and has enough ice cream to fill 30 ice cream cones. The shop purchases the ice cream cones for $0.25 each from a local warehouse club. Located in an outdoor mall, the rent for the shop space is $1,600 per month. The shop expenses $200 a month for the depreciation of the shop's furniture and equipment. During June, the shop incurred an additional $2,600 of other operating expenses (75% of these were fixed costs).

Requirements

1. Prepare The Willowick Ice Cream Shoppe's June income statement using a traditional format.
2. Prepare The Willowick Ice Cream Shoppe's June income statement using a contribution margin format.

P6-65A   Determine financial statement components *(Learning Objective 6)*

Value Strings produces student-grade violins for beginning violin students. The company produced 2,500 violins in its first month of operations. At month end, 750 finished violins remained unsold. There was no inventory in work in process. Violins were sold for $122.50 each. Total costs from the month are as follows:

Direct materials used	$125,500
Direct labor	$ 50,000
Variable manufacturing overhead	$ 32,000
Fixed manufacturing overhead	$ 42,500
Variable selling and administrative expenses	$ 8,000
Fixed selling and administrative expenses	$ 12,100

The company prepares traditional (absorption costing) income statements for its bankers. Value Strings would also like to prepare contribution margin income statements for management use. Compute the following amounts that would be shown on these income statements:

1. Gross profit
2. Contribution margin
3. Total expenses shown **below** the **gross profit** line
4. Total expenses shown **below** the **contribution margin** line
5. Dollar value of ending inventory under absorption costing
6. Dollar value of ending inventory under variable costing
7. Which income statement will have a higher operating income? By how much? Explain.

P6-66A Absorption and variable costing income statements
(Learning Objective 6)

Mario's Foods produces frozen meals, which it sells for $8 each. The company uses the FIFO inventory costing method, and it computes a new monthly fixed manufacturing overhead rate based on the actual number of meals produced that month. All costs and production levels are exactly as planned. The following data are from the company's first two months in business:

	January	February
Sales	1,400 meals	1,800 meals
Production	2,000 meals	1,400 meals
Variable manufacturing expense per meal	$ 4	$ 4
Sales commission expense per meal	$ 2	$ 2
Total fixed manufacturing overhead	$ 700	$ 700
Total fixed marketing and administrative expenses	$ 500	$ 500

Requirements

1. Compute the product cost per meal produced under absorption costing and under variable costing. Do this first for January and then for February.
2. Prepare separate monthly income statements for January and for February, using the following:
   a. Absorption costing
   b. Variable costing
3. Is operating income higher under absorption costing or variable costing in January? In February? Explain the pattern of differences in operating income based on absorption costing versus variable costing.

PROBLEMS Group B

P6-67B Analyze cost behavior at a hospital using various cost estimation methods *(Learning Objectives 1, 2, 3, 4 & 5)*

Louis Becker is the Chief Operating Officer at Union Hospital in Newark, New Jersey. She is analyzing the hospital's overhead costs but is not sure whether nursing hours or the number of patient days would be the best cost driver to use for predicting the hospital's overhead. She has gathered the following information for the last six months of the most recent year:

Month	Hospital Overhead Costs	Nursing Hours	Number of Patient Days	Overhead Cost per Nursing Hour	Overhead Cost per Patient Day
July	$476,000	24,000	3,720	$19.83	$127.96
August	$512,000	26,000	4,320	$19.69	$118.52
September	$424,000	20,000	4,220	$21.20	$100.47
October	$448,000	22,500	3,470	$19.91	$129.11
November	$555,000	30,000	5,690	$18.50	$ 97.54
December	$431,000	22,000	3,210	$19.59	$134.27

Requirements

1. Are the hospital's overhead costs fixed, variable, or mixed? Explain.
2. Graph the hospital's overhead costs against nursing hours. Use Excel or graph by hand.
3. Graph the hospital's overhead costs against the number of patient days. Use Excel or graph by hand.
4. Do the data appear to be sound, or do you see any potential data problems? Explain.
5. Use the high-low method to determine the hospital's cost equation using nursing hours as the cost driver. Predict total overhead costs if 25,500 nursing hours are predicted for the month.
6. Becker runs a regression analysis using nursing hours as the cost driver to predict total hospital overhead costs. The Excel output from the regression analysis is as follows:

	A	B	C	D	E	F	G
1	SUMMARY OUTPUT– Nursing hours as cost driver						
2	Regression Statistics						
3	Multiple R		0.984895				
4	R Square		0.970018				
5	Adjusted R Square		0.962523				
6	Standard Error		9,883.836352				
7	Observations		6				
8	ANOVA						
9		df	SS	MS	F	Significance F	
10	Regression	1	12,642,572,449	12,642,572,449	129.414926	0.000341	
11	Residual	4	390,760,884	97,690,221			
12	Total	5	13,033,333,333				
13							
14			Standard			Lower	Upper
15		Coefficients	Error	t Stat	P-value	95%	95%
16	Intercept	131,004.69	30,448.454	4.303	0.013	46,466.228	215,543.149
17	X Variable 1	14.26	1.253	11.376	0.000	10.777	17.735
18							

If 25,500 nursing hours are predicted for the month, what is the total predicted hospital overhead?

7. Becker then ran the regression analysis using number of patient days as the cost driver. The Excel output from the regression is as follows:

	A	B	C	D	E	F	G
1	SUMMARY OUTPUT – Using number of patient days as cost driver						
2	Regression Statistics						
3	Multiple R		0.818166				
4	R Square		0.669396				
5	Adjusted R Square		0.586745				
6	Standard Error		32,820.99359				
7	Observations		6				
8	ANOVA						
9		df	SS	MS	F	Significance F	
10	Regression	1	8,724,462,852	8,724,462,852	8.099072	0.046589	
11	Residual	4	4,308,870,482	1,077,217,620			
12	Total	5	13,033,333,334				
13							
14			Standard			Lower	Upper
15		Coefficients	Error	t Stat	P-value	95%	95%
16	Intercept	280,775.96	69,320.327	4.05	0.015	88,311.882	473,240.047
17	X Variable 1	47.15	16.568	2.846	0.047	1.151	93.153
18							

If 3,680 patient days are predicted for the month, what is the total predicted hospital overhead?

8. Which regression analysis (using nursing hours or using number of patient days as the cost driver) produces the best cost equation? Explain your answer.

P6-68B Analyze cost behavior *(Learning Objectives 1, 2, 3, & 4)*

Watson Industries is in the process of analyzing its manufacturing overhead costs. Management is not sure if the number of units produced or the number of direct labor (DL) hours is the best cost driver to use for predicting manufacturing overhead (MOH) costs. The following information is available:

Month	Manufacturing Overhead Costs	Direct Labor Hours	Units Produced	MOH Cost per DL Hour	MOH Cost per Unit Produced
July	$485,000	25,000	3,800	$19.40	$127.63
August	$540,000	26,700	4,360	$20.22	$123.85
September	$420,000	20,000	4,210	$21.00	$ 99.76
October	$462,000	21,900	3,450	$21.10	$133.91
November	$579,000	32,000	5,600	$18.09	$103.39
December	$455,000	20,400	3,270	$22.30	$139.14

Requirements

1. Are manufacturing overhead costs fixed, variable, or mixed? Explain.
2. Graph the company's manufacturing overhead costs against DL hours.
3. Graph the company's manufacturing overhead costs against units produced.
4. Do the data appear to be sound, or do you see any potential data problems? Explain.
5. Use the high-low method to determine the company's manufacturing overhead cost equation using DL hours as the cost driver. Assume that management believes all the data to be accurate and wants to include all of it in the analysis.
6. Estimate manufacturing overhead costs if the company incurs 26,000 DL hours in January.

P6-69B Prepare traditional and contribution margin income statements *(Learning Objective 6)*

The Edgewater Ice Cream Shoppe sold 8,900 servings of ice cream during June for $4 per serving. The shop purchases the ice cream in large tubs from the Premium Ice Cream Company. Each tub costs the shop $15 and has enough ice cream to fill 30 ice cream cones. The shop purchases the ice cream cones for $0.10 each from a local warehouse club. Located in an outdoor mall, the rent for the shop space is $1,950 a month. The shop expenses $210 a month for the depreciation of the shop's furniture and equipment. During June, the shop incurred an additional $2,000 of other operating expenses (75% of these were fixed costs).

Requirements

1. Prepare The Edgewater Ice Cream Shoppe's June income statement using a traditional format.
2. Prepare The Edgewater Ice Cream Shoppe's June income statement using a contribution margin format.

P6-70B Determine financial statement components *(Learning Objective 6)*

World Strings produces student-grade violins for beginning violin students. The company produced 2,700 violins in its first month of operations. At month end, 800 finished violins remained unsold. There was no inventory in work in process. Violins were sold for $120.00 each. Total costs from the month are as follows:

Direct materials used	$120,300
Direct labor	$ 65,000
Variable manufacturing overhead	$ 28,000
Fixed manufacturing overhead	$ 64,800
Variable selling and administrative expenses	$ 10,000
Fixed selling and administrative expenses	$ 12,900

The company prepares traditional (absorption costing) income statements for its bankers. World Strings would also like to prepare contribution margin income statements for management use. Compute the following amounts that would be shown on these income statements:

1. Gross profit
2. Contribution margin
3. Total expenses shown **below** the **gross profit** line
4. Total expenses shown **below** the **contribution margin** line
5. Dollar value of ending inventory under absorption costing
6. Dollar value of ending inventory under variable costing
7. Which income statement will have a higher operating income? By how much? Explain.

P6-71B Absorption and variable costing income statements
(Learning Objective 6)

Murphy's Foods produces frozen meals, which it sells for $7 each. The company uses the FIFO inventory costing method, and it computes a new monthly fixed manufacturing overhead rate based on the actual number of meals produced that month. All costs and production levels are exactly as planned. The following data are from the company's first two months in business:

	January	February
Sales	1,400 meals	1,600 meals
Production	2,000 meals	1,400 meals
Variable manufacturing expense per meal	$ 5	$ 5
Sales commission expense per meal	$ 1	$ 1
Total fixed manufacturing overhead	$ 700	$ 700
Total fixed marketing and administrative expenses	$ 500	$ 500

Requirements

1. Compute the product cost per meal produced under absorption costing and under variable costing. Do this first for January and then for February.
2. Prepare separate monthly income statements for January and for February, using (a) absorption costing and (b) variable costing.
3. Is operating income higher under absorption costing or variable costing in January? In February? Explain the pattern of differences in operating income based on absorption costing versus variable costing.

Serial Case

C6-72 Calculate and compare cost estimates using high-low and regression methods *(Learning Objectives 4 & 5)*

This case is a continuation of the Caesars Entertainment Corporation serial case that began in Chapter 1. Refer to the introductory story in Chapter 1 (see page 43) for additional background. (The components of the Caesars serial case can be completed in any order.)

Caesar Entertainment Corporation's Form 10-K contains a variety of data in addition to financial statements. Below is a list that contains Caesars' food and beverage costs (adapted) taken from its Statements of Operations for the past 22 years. In addition, the number of hotel rooms and suites owned by Caesars at the end of each of those 22 years has been gathered from other information provided in the Form 10-Ks.

Caesars Entertainment Corporation Selected data from Form 10-K (adapted)

Year ended	Food and beverage costs	# of hotel rooms & suites
12/31/2014	$ 694,000,000	39,218
12/31/2013	$ 639,000,000	42,200
12/31/2012	$ 634,000,000	42,710
12/31/2011	$ 665,700,000	42,890
12/31/2010	$ 621,300,000	42,010
12/31/2009	$ 596,000,000	41,830
12/31/2008	$ 639,500,000	39,170
12/31/2007	$ 716,500,000	38,130
12/31/2006	$ 697,600,000	38,060
12/31/2005	$ 482,300,000	43,060
12/31/2004	$ 278,100,000	17,220
12/31/2003	$ 255,200,000	14,780
12/31/2002	$ 240,600,000	14,551
12/31/2001	$ 232,400,000	13,598
12/31/2000	$ 228,000,000	11,562
12/31/1999	$ 218,600,000	11,760
12/31/1998	$ 116,600,000	11,685
12/31/1997	$ 103,600,000	8,197
12/31/1996	$ 95,900,000	6,478
12/31/1995	$ 91,500,000	5,736
12/31/1994	$ 82,800,000	5,367
12/31/1993	$ 76,500,000	5,348

Requirements

1. Using the high-low method, find the following cost estimates:
   a. Variable food and beverage cost per hotel room/suite
   b. Fixed food and beverage cost per hotel room/suite
2. Perform a regression analysis using Excel. Use **# of hotel rooms & suites** as the X and the **Food and beverage costs** as the Y in your regression analysis.
   a. What is the estimated variable food and beverage cost per hotel room/suite?
   b. What is the estimated fixed food and beverage cost per hotel room/suite?
   c. In your opinion, is the number of hotel rooms and suites a good predictor of Caesars' food and beverage costs? Why or why not?

Compare the estimates of variable and fixed costs calculated using the high-low method to the estimates calculated using the regression method. Which method would most likely provide a better cost estimate? Explain.

CRITICAL THINKING
Discussion & Analysis

A6-73 Discussion Questions

1. Briefly describe an organization with which you are familiar. Describe a situation when a manager in that organization could use cost behavior information and how the manager could use the information.

2. How are fixed costs similar to step fixed costs? How are fixed costs different from step fixed costs? Give an example of a step fixed cost and describe why that cost is not considered to be a fixed cost.

3. Describe a specific situation when a scatter plot could be useful to a manager.

4. What is a mixed cost? Give an example of a mixed cost. Sketch a graph of this example.

5. Compare discretionary fixed costs to committed fixed costs. Think of an organization with which you are familiar. Give two examples of discretionary fixed costs and two examples of committed fixed costs which that organization may have. Explain why the costs you have chosen as examples fit within the definitions of "discretionary fixed costs" and "committed fixed costs."

6. Define the terms "independent variable" and "dependent variable," as used in regression analysis. Illustrate the concepts of independent variables and dependent variables by selecting a cost a company would want to predict and what activity it might use to predict that cost. Describe the independent variable and the dependent variable in that situation.

7. Define the term "relevant range." Why is it important to managers?

8. Describe the term "R-square." If a regression analysis for predicting manufacturing overhead using direct labor hours as the dependent variable has an R-square of 0.40, why might this be a problem? Given the low R-square value, describe the options a manager has for predicting manufacturing overhead costs. Which option do you think is the best option for the manager? Defend your answer.

9. Over the past year, a company's inventory has increased significantly. The company uses absorption costing for financial statements, but internally, the company uses variable costing for financial statements. Which set of financial statements will show the highest operating income? What specifically causes the difference between the two sets of financial statements?

10. A company has adopted a lean production philosophy and, as a result, has cut its inventory levels significantly. Describe the impact on the company's external financial statements as a result of this inventory reduction. Also describe the impact of the inventory reduction on the company's internal financial statements that are prepared using variable costing.

11. What costs might a business incur by not adopting paperless services? Is paperless only profitable to large businesses or is it applicable to small businesses? Explain what factors might be involved in changing over to paperless billing.

12. How might the principles of sustainability (such as increased efficiency) affect cost behavior overall? Think of an example of a sustainable change in process or material that could impact the cost equation for that cost (i.e., the total fixed cost versus the variable cost per unit). Describe this example in detail and what might happen to total fixed costs and per unit variable costs.

Application & Analysis
Mini Cases

A6-74 Cost Behavior in Real Companies
Choose a company with which you are familiar that manufactures a product or provides a service. In this activity, you will be making reasonable estimates of the costs and activities associated with this company; companies do not typically publish internal cost or process information.

Basic Discussion Questions
1. Describe the company you selected and the products or services it provides.
2. List ten costs that this company would incur. Include costs from a variety of departments within the company, including human resources, sales, accounting, production (if a manufacturer), service (if a service company), and others. Make sure that you have at least one cost from each of the following categories: fixed, variable, and mixed.
3. Classify each of the costs you listed as either fixed, variable, or mixed. Justify why you classified each cost as you did.
4. Describe a potential cost driver for each of the variable and mixed costs you listed. Explain why each cost driver would be appropriate for its associated cost.
5. Discuss how easy or difficult it was for you to decide whether each cost was fixed, variable, or mixed. Describe techniques a company could use to determine whether a cost is fixed, variable, or mixed.

ETHICS

A6-75 Ethics of building inventory *(Learning Objective 6)*
Fanfare Products, Inc., is a manufacturer of mobile devices. Kyle is the plant manager at Fanfare's Toledo, Ohio, plant. The Toledo plant manufactures a smartphone, the Zoom, which has sold well for the past six months. Kyle is being considered for promotion to manager of the entire West Coast division of Fanfare Products. Bethany is an accounting supervisor at Fanfare Products and is a good friend of Kyle's.

Kyle and Bethany are having lunch in the company cafeteria. There are about six weeks left in the current fiscal year. Kyle is concerned that his plant will be showing a loss rather than the healthy profit he had projected for the year. The reason for the shortfall is that demand has radically declined for the Zoom smartphone currently manufactured by Kyle's plant. New smartphones with more features have been brought to market by Fanfare's competitors. Engineers at Fanfare are currently working on an updated model of the Zoom, but it will not be ready for production in Kyle's plant for another five months. If Kyle's plant shows a loss this year, Kyle will not receive his performance bonus for the year. He also knows that his chance of promotion to the West Coast manager will be greatly reduced.

Bethany thinks about Kyle's situation. She then shares with him a strategy that he can use to help increase his profits. She explains that under absorption costing, the more units in ending inventory, the more costs can be deferred. Using her tablet, she makes up a quick example in Excel to show him how he can turn his situation around and show operating income for the year.

Bethany's first spreadsheet assumes that five units are produced and sold in this hypothetical situation:

	A	B	C	D
1		Scenario #1		
2		Traditional Income Statement (5 units produced and 5 units sold)		
3		For the year ended December 31		
4				
5	Sales revenue		$ 150	
6	Less: Cost of goods sold		115	
7	Gross profit		$ 35	
8	Less: Operating expenses		55	
9	Operating income (loss)		$ (20)	
10				

If five units are produced and sold, the hypothetical company would have a loss of $20. Now Bethany changes just one fact; instead of producing five units, the company in the example produces ten units. No other facts change—the company still sells just five units. Bethany shows Kyle the revised income statement under the increased production scenario:

	A	B	C	D
1		Scenario #2		
2	Traditional Income Statement (10 units produced and 5 units sold)			
3	For the year ended December 31			
4				
5	Sales revenue		$ 150	
6	Less: Cost of goods sold		65	
7	Gross profit		$ 85	
8	Less: Operating expenses		55	
9	Operating income (loss)		$ 30	
10				

Under this second scenario, the operating income would be $30, which is quite a bit higher than the original scenario. Bethany again emphasizes that the only fact that was different between the two scenarios is that production, and therefore ending inventory, increased in the second scenario.

Bethany then urges Kyle to put on a major production push in the last month of the year. If he does, he will be able to push his income up to near projected levels. With the higher income, he will receive his annual performance bonus. In addition, he feels that his chances of getting the West Coast manager position are excellent.

Requirements

1. Using the IMA *Statement of Ethical Professional Practice* (refer to Exhibit 1-7) as an ethical framework, answer the following questions:
   a. What is (are) the ethical issue(s) in this situation?
   b. What are Bethany's responsibilities as a management accountant?
   c. Has Bethany violated any part of the IMA *Statement of Ethical Professional Practice*? Support your answer.
2. What causes the shift from a loss to a profit in the hypothetical example?
3. What problems, if any, are caused by building inventories at year end?
4. What could Fanfare Products do to prevent future situations like the one described in this case?

A6-76 Cost behavior and Air Force One (Learning Objectives 1, 2, & 3)

REAL LIFE

The U.S. government estimated[4] that Air Force One costs the taxpayers $179,750 per hour. Air Force One is a custom-built Boeing 747 for the president's use while in office. (There are technically a few planes that are used as Air Force One; whichever one the president is on is called "Air Force One.") While the president is in office, the president is required by law to use Air Force One for all air travel.

The 747 used for Air Force One has 4,000 square feet of space inside on three levels. In addition to having a large office and a conference room, the plane also houses a medical suite and a doctor. The doctor is permanently assigned to Air Force One. The plane has two food preparation galleys that can feed 100 people at a time. There are also quarters on the plane for those people who travel with the president, including senior advisors, Secret Service, and the press. In addition, several cargo jets typically are used to carry extra provisions, people, and equipment.

The $179,750 cost per hour estimate includes fuel, maintenance, engineering support, repairs, food and lodging for the pilots and crew, and other costs. It also includes the cost of military staffing for the onboard communications equipment. The cost may also include the costs of flying extra aircraft and costs of advance scouting trips to the destination to make sure that everything goes as planned.

When Air Force One is used for official business, the taxpayers must pay for the traveling costs for the president's immediate family, Secret Service detail, and the White House staff who are traveling with the president.

When Air Force One is used for political purposes, the president's campaign fund is required to reimburse the government for the cost of food, lodging, and other related expenses. The campaign fund must also reimburse the government for the amount that is the equivalent of airfare that would have been paid if a commercial airline had been used.

[4]"Presidential Travel: Policy and Costs," Congressional Research Service, May 17, 2012, retrieved from www.fas.org/sgp/crs/misc/RS21835.pdf on January 3, 2016.

The same reimbursement policy is in effect for trips that are categorized as personal trips; the president must reimburse the government for the cost of food, lodging, comparable airfare, and other related expenses.

Questions

1. Is the $179,750 cost per hour a fixed, variable, or mixed cost? Explain.
2. Exact details about the cost composition of the Air Force One travel are kept secret to protect the president. Use your imagination, and the reading above, to make a list of the costs that you think might be included in $179,750 per hour cost estimate.
3. Categorize each cost in your list as fixed, variable, or mixed.
4. The number of trips taken by the president in any given year fluctuates and is dependent on the political climate, crises, economics, and the like. How useful do you think this cost per hour is?
5. What purpose(s) can the $179,750 cost per hour be used for? Are there any purposes for which that cost is not representative of the "true" cost?
6. Can you think of a better way to represent/communicate the cost of Air Force One?
7. Do you think the reimbursement policy is fair to the *president*? Why or why not?
8. Do you think the reimbursement policy is fair to the *taxpayers*? Why or why not?

Try It Solutions

page 313:

a. Total fixed costs do not react to wide changes in volume; therefore, total fixed costs will still be $100,000.
b. Fixed costs per unit decrease as volume increases. At the higher occupancy, the fixed cost per guest is as follows:

$$\$100,000 \div 16,000 \text{ guests} = \$6.25 \text{ per guest}$$

If only 2,000 guests stay during the month, the fixed cost per guest is much higher ($50).

page 315:

1. The monthly cost of belonging to the fitness club can be expressed as:

$$y = \$5x + \$30$$

where y = monthly cost of belonging to the club and,

x = number of instructor-led exercise classes attended.

2. If you attend five classes in a month, your total cost will be $55 [= ($5 × 5 classes) + $30].
3. If you attend 10 classes in a month, your total cost will be $80 [= ($5 × 10 classes) + $30]. The cost does not double when the number of classes attended doubles. The variable portion of the bill doubles from $25 to $50, but the fixed portion of the bill ($30) stays constant.

page 333:

1. $32.00. Absorption costing treats all manufacturing costs as inventoriable product costs, regardless of whether they are fixed or variable.
2. $12.00 of fixed MOH will be expensed as part of Cost of Goods Sold every time a unit is sold.
3. $20.00. Variable costing treats only variable manufacturing costs (direct materials, direct labor, and variable MOH) as inventoriable product costs. Fixed MOH is not included in the product cost.
4. $120,000 of fixed MOH will be expensed as a period cost (operating expense) of the month.

7

Cost-Volume-Profit Analysis

clivewa/Shutterstock

Source: http://corporate.art.com/aboutus/default.asp

Learning Objectives

- **1** Calculate the unit contribution margin and the contribution margin ratio
- **2** Use CVP analysis to find breakeven points and target profit volumes
- **3** Use CVP analysis to measure the impact of changing business conditions
- **4** Find breakeven and target profit volumes for multiproduct companies
- **5** Determine a firm's margin of safety, operating leverage, and most profitable cost structure

Art.com, Inc., is the world's largest online retailer of posters, prints, photography, and framed art. The company offers over 2 million different images and has generated sales from over 19 million customers in 150 different countries. Art.com has 25 localized websites that utilize each country's native language and currency and offers local e-mail support. It also offers free iPhone and iPad apps that allow customers to turn personal photos into professionally framed art as well as preview art by importing it into a photo of their own living space. Innovations such as these continue to drive the company's success.

Before launching Art.com in 1998, how did the company's founders determine the volume of art they would need to sell just to break even? How did they estimate the volume they would need to sell to achieve their target profit? And as the company continues to operate and expand into new markets, how do managers respond to fluctuating business conditions, such as changing fixed and variable costs and pricing pressures from competitors? Cost-volume-profit analysis helps managers answer these questions.

In the last chapter, we discussed cost behavior patterns and the methods managers use to determine how the company's costs behave. We showed how managers use the contribution margin income statement to separately display the firm's variable and fixed costs. In this chapter, we show how managers identify the volume of sales necessary to achieve breakeven or a target profit. We also look at how changes in costs, sales price, and volume affect the firm's profit. Finally, we discuss ways to identify the firm's risk level, including ways to gauge how easily a firm's profits can turn to losses if sales volume declines.

How Does Cost-Volume-Profit Analysis Help Managers?

Cost-volume-profit analysis, or CVP, is a powerful tool that helps managers make important business decisions. **Cost-volume-profit analysis** expresses the relationships among costs, volume, and the company's profit. Entrepreneurs and managers use CVP analysis to determine the sales volume that will be needed just to break even or to cover costs. They also use CVP to determine the sales volume that will be needed to earn a target profit, such as $100,000 per month. And because business conditions are always changing, CVP can help managers prepare for and respond to economic changes, such as increases in costs from suppliers.

Let's begin our discussion by looking at the data needed for CVP analysis.

Data and Assumptions Required for CVP Analysis

CVP analysis relies on the interdependency of five components, or pieces of information, shown in Exhibit 7-1.

EXHIBIT 7-1 Components of CVP Analysis

Let's examine this information in terms of a simple company example. Kay Martin, an entrepreneur, has just started a company to sell art posters through a website. Kay's software tabulates all customer orders each day and then automatically places the order to buy posters from a wholesaler. Kay buys only what she needs to fill the prior day's sales orders, so she carries no inventory. The posters cost $21 each, and Kay sells them for $35 each. Customers pay the shipping costs, so there are no other variable selling costs. Monthly fixed costs for website maintenance, software, and office rental total $7,000. Kay's relevant range extends from 0 to 2,000 posters a month. Beyond this volume, Kay will need to hire an employee and upgrade her website software to handle the increased volume. Additionally, the wholesaler will offer a volume discount if she purchases more than 2,000 posters a month.

Thus, we know the following information holds true within Kay's relevant range (0–2,000 posters per month):

- Sales price = $35 per poster
- Variable cost = $21 per poster
- Fixed costs = $7,000 per month

For CVP to be accurate, certain assumptions must be met. We'll itemize each of these assumptions, and check off whether Kay's business meets the assumptions.

1. **Sales price remains constant throughout the relevant range of volume, resulting in revenue that is linear.** In Kay's business, each poster generates $35 of sales revenue, with no volume discounts. Therefore, revenue could be graphed as a straight line beginning at the origin and sloping upward at a rate of $35 per poster sold. ✓

2. **Managers can classify each cost (or the components of mixed costs) as either variable or fixed. These costs are linear throughout the relevant range of volume.** In Kay's business, variable costs are $21 per poster, and fixed costs are $7,000 per month. These costs are expected to remain the same unless Kay's volume exceeds 2,000 posters per month. Thus, we could draw each of these costs as straight lines on a graph, just as we did in Chapter 6. ✓

3. **Inventory levels will not change.** Kay keeps no inventory. If she did, CVP analysis would still work as long as she did not allow her inventory levels to fluctuate very much from one period to the next. ✓

4. **The mix of products offered for sale remains constant.** <u>Sales mix</u> is the combination of products that make up total sales. For example, Art.com may sell 15% posters, 25% unframed photographs, and 60% framed prints. If profits differ across products, changes in sales mix will affect CVP analysis. Kay currently offers only one size of poster, so her sales mix is 100% posters. Later in this chapter text we will expand her product offerings to illustrate how sales mix impacts CVP analysis. ✓

Now that we know Kay's business meets these assumptions, we can proceed with confidence about the CVP results we will obtain. When assumptions are not met perfectly, managers should consider the results of CVP analysis to be approximations rather than exact figures.

The Unit Contribution Margin

The last chapter introduced the **contribution margin income statement**, which separates costs on the income statement by cost behavior rather than by function (product cost versus period cost). Many managers prefer the contribution margin income statement because it gives them the information for CVP analysis in a "ready-to-use" format. On these income statements, the contribution margin is the "dividing line"—all variable expenses go above the line, and all fixed expenses go below the line. The results of Kay's first month of operations is shown in Exhibit 7-2.

1 Calculate the unit contribution margin and the contribution margin ratio

EXHIBIT 7-2 Contribution Margin Income Statement

	A	B	C	D
1	**Kay Martin Posters**			
2	**Contribution Margin Income Statement**			
3	**Month Ended August 31**			
4				
5	Sales revenue (550 posters × $35 per poster)	$ 19,250		
6	Less: Variable expenses (550 posters × $21 per poster)	11,550		
7	Contribution margin	7,700		
8	Less: Fixed expenses	7,000		
9	Operating income	$ 700		
10				

Notice that the **contribution margin** is the excess of sales revenue over variable expenses. The contribution margin tells managers how much revenue is left—after paying variable expenses—to *contribute* toward the company's fixed expenses and operating income—hence the name contribution margin.

The contribution margin is stated as a *total* amount on the contribution margin income statement. However, managers often want to know the contribution margin on a *per unit* basis in order to get a better understanding of how profitable each unit is to the company's bottom line. A product's **contribution margin per unit**—or **unit contribution margin**—is the excess of the selling price per unit over the variable cost per unit. Kay's only variable cost is the price she pays for each poster ($21). However, some businesses pay a sales commission on each unit sold or have other variable costs, such as shipping costs, associated with each unit sold. *All variable costs, whether product costs or period costs, must be included when calculating the contribution margin per unit.* Kay's variable cost per unit is simply the price she pays for each poster. Therefore, her unit contribution margin is calculated as follows:

> **Why is this important?**
>
> "The **unit** contribution margin tells **managers** how much **profit** they make on **each unit** before considering **fixed** costs."

Sales price per poster....................................	$ 35
Less: Variable cost per poster......................	21
Contribution margin per poster....................	$ 14

The unit contribution margin is a very powerful piece of information for owners and managers to know. Kay now knows that every time she sells a poster, she will make $14 that can be used to pay for fixed expenses and generate a profit. In other words, her operating income will *improve* by $14 every time she sells another unit. For example, let's say Kay sells 551 posters rather than 550, as pictured in Exhibit 7-2. Her operating income would be $14 higher than before ($714 instead of $700). We can prove this as shown in Exhibit 7-3:

EXHIBIT 7-3 Operating Income Comparison When One More Poster Is Sold

	A	B	C	D
1	**Kay Martin Posters**			
2	**Contribution Margin Income Statement**			
3	**Month in which 551 posters are sold**		For comparison	
4		551 posters	550 posters	Difference
5	Sales revenue (551 posters × $35 per poster)	$ 19,285	$ 19,250	$ 35
6	Less: Variable expenses (551 posters × $21 per poster)	11,571	$ 11,550	$ 21
7	Contribution margin	7,714	$ 7,700	$ 14
8	Less: Fixed expenses	7,000	$ 7,000	$ -
9	Operating income	$ 714	$ 700	$ 14
10				
11	(Notice operating income is $14 higher when one more poster is sold.)			

Keep the following important rule of thumb in mind:

> Every time another unit is sold, the company's operating income will improve by the amount of the unit contribution margin ($14 in our example). This holds true whether the company is operating at a profit or at a loss. When companies offer more than one type of product, each product will have a unique unit contribution margin that shows how much profit each unit adds to the company's operating income. The higher the contribution margin per unit, the more profitable each unit is.

Managers often want to predict operating income at different sales volumes. Managers do not need to produce a full income statement to make these predictions. Rather, they can use the unit contribution margin to quickly forecast operating income at any volume within their relevant range. First, they multiply the unit contribution margin by the number of units they expect to sell in order to predict the total contribution margin from the sales. Then they simply subtract fixed costs. Let's verify using 551 posters as the volume:

Contribution margin (551 posters × $14 per poster)....................	$ 7,714
Less: Fixed expenses...	7,000
Operating income...	$ 714

Notice that this is exactly what we found above when we prepared a full income statement for a volume of 551 units. The unit contribution margin offers managers a quick shortcut to predicting operating income at different volumes of sales.

The Contribution Margin Ratio

In addition to computing the unit contribution margin, managers often compute the **contribution margin ratio**, which is the ratio of contribution margin to sales revenue. Kay can compute her contribution margin ratio at the unit level as follows:

$$\text{Contribution margin ratio} = \frac{\text{Contribution margin per unit}}{\text{Sales price per unit}} = \frac{\$14}{\$35} = 40\%$$

Kay can also compute the contribution margin ratio using any volume of sales. Let's use her current sales volume, pictured in Exhibit 7-2:

$$\text{Contribution margin ratio} = \frac{\text{Contribution margin}}{\text{Sales revenue}} = \frac{\$7,700}{\$19,250} = 40\%$$

The contribution margin ratio is the percentage of each sales dollar that is available for covering fixed expenses and generating a profit. As shown in Exhibit 7-4, each *$1.00* of sales revenue contributes $0.40 toward fixed expenses and profit, while the remaining $0.60 of each sales dollar is used to pay for variable costs.

EXHIBIT 7-4 Breakdown of $1 of Sales Revenue

Managers can also use the contribution margin ratio to quickly forecast operating income within their relevant range. For example, let's say Kay wants to know what her operating income would be if she generates $70,000 of sales revenue one month. To find the answer, Kay simply multiplies her forecasted sales revenue ($70,000) by the contribution margin ratio (40%) to arrive at the total contribution margin. Then she subtracts fixed expenses to arrive at her predicted operating income:

Contribution margin ($70,000 sales × 40%)....................	$28,000
Less: Fixed expenses...	7,000
Operating income..	$21,000

The reason this works goes back to the definition of the contribution ratio shown above. When we multiply the contribution margin ratio by expected sales revenue, the sales revenue terms cancel out, leaving the total contribution margin. Let's verify. If Kay has $70,000 of sales revenue, she has sold 2,000 posters ($70,000 ÷ $35 per poster). Her complete contribution margin income statement would be calculated as shown in Exhibit 7-5.

EXHIBIT 7-5 Operating Income for $70,000 of Sales Revenue

	A	B	C	D
1	**Kay Martin Posters**			
2	**Contribution Margin Income Statement**			
3	**For a month with $70,000 of Sales Revenue**			
4				
5	Sales revenue (2,000 posters × $35 per poster)	$ 70,000		
6	Less: Variable expenses (2,000 posters × $21 per poster)	42,000		
7	Contribution margin (2,000 posters × $14 per poster)	28,000		
8	Less: Fixed expenses	7,000		
9	Operating income	$ 21,000		
10				

The contribution margin per unit and the contribution margin ratio help managers quickly and easily predict income at different sales volumes. However, when predicting profits, managers must keep in mind the relevant range. Recall that Kay's relevant range extends to only 2,000 posters per month. At a higher volume of sales, her variable cost per unit may be lower than $21 (due to volume discounts from her suppliers), and her monthly fixed expenses may be higher than $7,000 (due to upgrading her system and hiring an employee to handle the extra sales volume). Thus, she won't be able to predict operating income at volumes greater than 2,000 posters per month without finding out more about how her costs will change.

We've seen how managers use the contribution margin to predict income; but managers use the contribution margin for other purposes too, such as motivating the sales force. Salespeople who know the contribution margin of each product can generate more profit for the company by emphasizing high-margin products. This is why many companies base sales commissions on the contribution margins produced by sales rather than on sales revenue alone.

In the next section, we'll see how managers use CVP analysis to determine the company's breakeven point.

▶ Try It!

Rachel runs her own hot dog stand on the U of A campus. The monthly cost of the cart rental and business permit is $300. Rachel spends $0.50 on each hot dog sold, including bun and condiments. She sells each hot dog for $2.00.

1. What is the contribution margin per unit?
2. What is the contribution margin ratio?
3. Predict operating income for a month in which Rachel sells 1,000 hot dogs.

Please see page 441 for solutions.

How Do Managers Find the Breakeven Point?

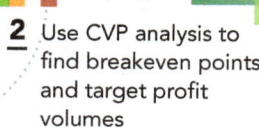

2 Use CVP analysis to find breakeven points and target profit volumes

A company's **breakeven point** is the sales level at which *operating income is zero*. In other words, at the breakeven point, total revenues equal total expenses. Sales below the breakeven point result in a loss; sales above the breakeven point provide a profit. Before Kay started her business, she wanted to figure out how many posters she would have to sell just to break even.

Cost-Volume-Profit Analysis

There are three ways to calculate the breakeven point. All three approaches are based on the income statement, so they all reach the same conclusion. The first two methods find breakeven in terms of sales *units*, whereas the last approach finds breakeven in terms of sales revenue (sales dollars).

1. The income statement approach
2. The shortcut approach using the *unit* contribution margin
3. The shortcut approach using the contribution margin *ratio*

Let's examine these three approaches in detail.

> **Why is this important?**
>
> "Businesses **don't** want to operate at a **loss**. CVP analysis helps **managers** determine how many units they need to sell **just** to **break even**."

The Income Statement Approach

The income statement approach starts with the contribution margin income statement and then breaks it down into smaller components:

SALES REVENUE − VARIABLE EXPENSES − FIXED EXPENSES = OPERATING INCOME

$$\left(\begin{array}{c}\text{Sales price}\\\text{per unit}\end{array} \times \text{Units sold}\right) - \left(\begin{array}{c}\text{Variable cost}\\\text{per unit}\end{array} \times \text{Units sold}\right) - \text{Fixed expenses} = \text{Operating income}$$

Let's use this approach to find Kay's breakeven point. Recall that Kay sells her posters for $35 each and that her variable cost is $21 per poster. Kay's fixed expenses total $7,000. At the breakeven point, operating income is zero. We use this information to solve the income statement equation for the number of posters Kay must sell to break even.

SALES REVENUE − VARIABLE EXPENSES − FIXED EXPENSES = OPERATING INCOME

$$\left(\begin{array}{c}\text{Sales price}\\\text{per unit}\end{array} \times \text{Units sold}\right) - \left(\begin{array}{c}\text{Variable cost}\\\text{per unit}\end{array} \times \text{Units sold}\right) - \text{Fixed expenses} = \text{Operating income}$$

($35 × Units sold) − ($21 × Units sold) − $7,000 = $ 0
($35 − $21) × Units sold − $7,000 = $ 0
$14 × Units sold = $7,000
Units sold = $7,000/$14
Sales in units = 500 posters

Kay must sell 500 posters to break even. Her breakeven point in sales revenue is $17,500 (500 posters × $35).

You can check this answer by creating a contribution margin income statement using a sales volume of 500 posters, as shown in Exhibit 7-6:

EXHIBIT 7-6 Contribution Margin Income Statement at Breakeven

	A	B	C	D
1	Kay Martin Posters			
2	Contribution Margin Income Statement			
3	For a month in which 500 posters are sold			
4				
5	Sales revenue (500 posters × $35 per poster)	$ 17,500		
6	Less: Variable expenses (500 posters × $21 per poster)	10,500		
7	Contribution margin (500 posters × $14 per poster)	7,000		
8	Less: Fixed expenses	7,000		
9	Operating income	$ 0		
10				

Notice that at breakeven a firm's fixed expenses ($7,000) equal its contribution margin ($7,000). In other words, the firm has generated *just* enough contribution margin to cover its fixed expenses but *not* enough to generate a profit.

The Shortcut Approach Using the Unit Contribution Margin

Many managers prefer to use a shortcut formula rather than the income statement approach. To develop the formula, we start with the contribution margin income statement and then rearrange some of its terms:

$$\underbrace{\text{SALES REVENUE} - \text{VARIABLE EXPENSES}}_{\text{Contribution margin}} - \text{FIXED EXPENSES} = \text{OPERATING INCOME}$$

Contribution margin − Fixed expenses = Operating income

Contribution margin = Fixed expenses + Operating income

(Contribution margin per unit × Units sold) = Fixed expenses + Operating income

As a final step, we divide both sides of the equation by the contribution margin per unit. Now we have the shortcut formula:

$$\text{Sales in units} = \frac{\text{Fixed expenses} + \text{Operating income}}{\text{Contribution margin per unit}}$$

Kay can use this shortcut approach to find her breakeven point in units. Kay's fixed expenses total $7,000, and her unit contribution margin is $14. At the breakeven point, operating income is zero. Thus, Kay's breakeven point in units is as follows:

$$\text{Sales in units} = \frac{\$7,000 + \$0}{\$14}$$
$$= 500 \text{ posters}$$

Why does this shortcut approach work? Recall that each poster provides $14 of contribution margin. To break even, Kay must generate enough contribution margin to cover $7,000 of fixed expenses. At the rate of $14 per poster, Kay must sell 500 posters ($7,000/$14) to cover her $7,000 of fixed expenses. Because the shortcut formula simply rearranges the income statement equation, the breakeven point is the same under both methods (500 posters). Keep the following important rule of thumb in mind:

> Since the breakeven point occurs when operating income is equal to zero, always use "zero" as the operating income in the formula to find the company's breakeven point.

The Shortcut Approach Using the Contribution Margin Ratio

It is easy to compute the breakeven point in *units* for a simple business like Kay's which has only one product. But what about companies that have thousands of products such as Art.com, The Home Depot, and Amazon.com? It doesn't make sense for these companies to determine the number of each product they need to sell to break even. Can you imagine a Home Depot manager describing breakeven as 100,000 wood screws, two million nails, 3,000 lawn mowers, 10,000 gallons of paint, and so forth? It simply doesn't make sense. Therefore, multiproduct companies usually compute breakeven in terms of *sales revenue* (dollars).

The formula to find the sales revenue needed to break even is derived in much the same way as the earlier formula. The only difference is that to find the answer in terms of sales revenue (*dollars*) we must divide the numerator by the contribution margin *ratio* rather than the contribution margin *per unit*:

$$\text{Sales in dollars} = \frac{\text{Fixed expenses} + \text{Operating income}}{\text{Contribution margin ratio}}$$

Recall that Kay's contribution margin ratio is 40%. At the breakeven point, operating income is $0, so Kay's breakeven point in sales revenue is as follows:

$$\text{Sales in dollars} = \frac{\$7{,}000 + \$0}{40\%}$$
$$= \$17{,}500$$

This is the same breakeven sales revenue we calculated in Exhibit 7-6 (500 posters × $35 sales price = $17,500).

Why does the contribution margin ratio formula work? Recall from Exhibit 7-4 that each dollar of Kay's sales contributes $0.40 to fixed expenses and profit. To break even, she must generate enough contribution margin at the rate of $0.40 per sales dollar to cover the $7,000 fixed expenses ($7,000 ÷ 0.40 = $17,500).

When determining which formula to use, keep the following rules of thumb in mind:

- To find breakeven in terms of *units*, divide fixed expenses by the contribution margin *per unit*.
- To find breakeven in terms of sales revenue (*dollars*), divide fixed expenses by the contribution margin ratio.

Try It!

Rachel runs her own hot dog stand on the U of A campus. The monthly cost of the cart rental and business permit is $300. Rachel's contribution margin per unit is $1.50 and her contribution margin ratio is 75%.

1. How many hot dogs does Rachel need to sell each month to break even?
2. How much sales revenue does Rachel need to generate each month to break even?

Please see page 441 for solutions.

How Do Managers Find the Volume Needed to Earn a Target Profit?

Entrepreneurs and managers don't want their businesses to just break even; they want to earn a profit, and they usually have specific profit goals in mind. For example, Kay doesn't want to just break even—she wants her business to be her sole source of income. She would like the business to earn $4,900 of profit each month. How many posters must Kay sell each month to reach her target profit?

> **Why is this important?**
> "**Companies** want to make a profit. **CVP** analysis helps **managers** determine **how many** units they need to sell to earn a **target** amount of **profit**."

How Much Must We Sell to Earn a Target Profit?

To find the number of units a company must sell to earn a target profit, we can use the same three approaches as we used earlier in the chapter for finding breakeven. The only difference from our prior analysis is that instead of determining the sales level needed for *zero profit* (breakeven), Kay now wants to know how many posters she must sell to earn a $4,900 profit. To find the answer, Kay uses the shortcut formula and simply inserts $4,900 as the target operating income:

$$\text{Sales in } units = \frac{\text{Fixed expenses} + \text{Operating income}}{\text{Contribution margin } per\ unit}$$

$$= \frac{\$7,000 + \$4,900}{\$14}$$

$$= \frac{\$11,900}{\$14}$$

$$= 850 \text{ posters}$$

This analysis shows that Kay must sell 850 posters each month to earn an operating income of $4,900 a month. Notice that this level of sales falls within Kay's current relevant range (0–2,000 posters per month), so the conclusion that she would earn $4,900 of income at this sales volume is valid. If the calculation resulted in a sales volume outside the current relevant range (greater than 2,000 units), we would need to reassess our cost assumptions.

Assume that Kay also wants to know how much sales revenue she'll need to generate each month to earn $4,900 of monthly profit. Because she already knows the number of units needed (850), she can easily translate this volume into sales revenue:

$$850 \text{ posters} \times \$35 \text{ sales price/poster} = \$29,750 \text{ sales revenue}$$

Kay could have also found the answer directly by using the shortcut formula based on the contribution margin *ratio*:

$$\text{Sales in } dollars = \frac{\text{Fixed expenses} + \text{Operating income}}{\text{Contribution margin } ratio}$$

$$= \frac{\$7,000 + \$4,900}{40\%}$$

$$= \frac{\$11,900}{40\%}$$

$$= \$29,750$$

Finally, Kay could have used the income statement approach to find the same answer:

SALES REVENUE	−	VARIABLE EXPENSES	−	FIXED EXPENSES	=	OPERATING INCOME
($35 × Units sold)	−	($21 × Units sold)	−	$7,000	=	$ 4,900
($35	−	$21) × Units sold	−	$7,000	=	$ 4,900
		$14 × Units sold			=	$11,900
				Units sold	=	$11,900/$14
				Units sold	=	850 posters

We can prove that our answers from any of the three approaches are correct by preparing Kay's income statement for a sales volume of 850 units, as shown in Exhibit 7-7:

EXHIBIT 7-7 Operating Income for a Volume of 850 Posters

	A	B	C	D
1	Kay Martin Posters			
2	Contribution Margin Income Statement			
3	For a month in which 850 posters are sold			
4				
5	Sales revenue (850 posters × $35 per poster)	$ 29,750		
6	Less: Variable expenses (850 posters × $21 per poster)	17,850		
7	Contribution margin (850 posters × $14 per poster)	11,900		
8	Less: Fixed expenses	7,000		
9	Operating income	$ 4,900		
10				

Keep the following important rule of thumb in mind:

> When finding the volume needed to earn a target profit, use the target profit as the operating income in the formulas.

Try It!

Rachel runs her own hot dog stand on the U of A campus. The monthly cost of the cart rental and business permit is $300. Rachel's contribution margin per unit is $1.50, and her contribution margin ratio is 75%.

1. How many hot dogs does Rachel need to sell each month to earn a target profit of $900 a month?
2. How much sales revenue does Rachel need to generate each month to earn a target profit of $900 per month?

Please see page 441 for solutions.

Graphing CVP Relationships

By graphing the CVP relationships for her business, Kay can see at a glance how changes in the levels of sales will affect profits. As in the last chapter, the volume of units (posters) is placed on the horizontal x-axis, while dollars is placed on the vertical y-axis. Then, she follows five steps to graph the CVP relations for her business, as illustrated in Exhibit 7-8. This graph also shows the linear nature of Kay's costs and revenues. Recall that CVP analysis assumes costs and revenues will be linear throughout the relevant range.

STEP 1: Choose a sales volume, such as 1,000 posters. Plot the point for total sales revenue at that volume: 1,000 posters × $35 per poster = sales of $35,000. Draw the *sales*

EXHIBIT 7-8 Cost-Volume-Profit Graph

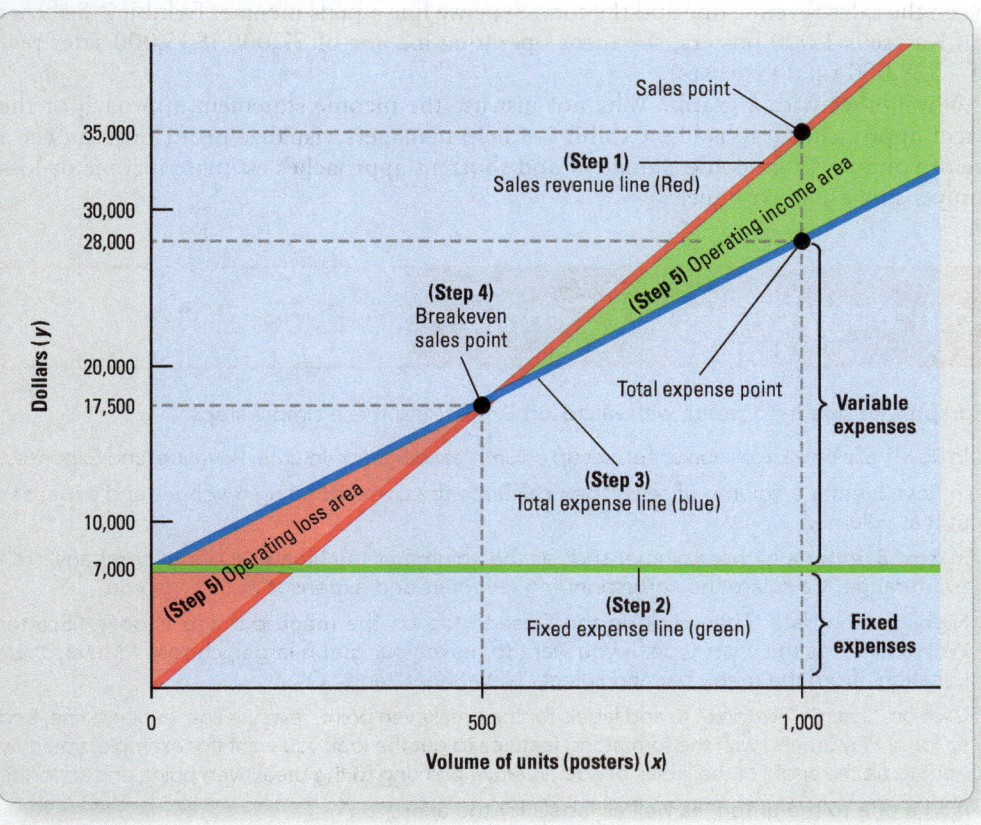

revenue line from the origin (0) through the $35,000 point. Why does the sales revenue line start at the origin? If Kay does not sell any posters, there is no sales revenue.

STEP 2: Draw the *fixed expense line*, a horizontal line that intersects the y-axis at $7,000. Recall that the fixed expense line is flat because fixed expenses are the same ($7,000) no matter how many posters Kay sells within her relevant range (up to 2,000 posters per month).

STEP 3: Draw the *total expense line*. Total expense is the sum of variable expense plus fixed expense. Thus, total expense is a *mixed* cost. So, the total expense line follows the form of the mixed cost line. Begin by computing variable expense at the chosen sales volume: 1,000 posters × $21 per poster = variable expense of $21,000. Add variable expense to fixed expense: $21,000 + $7,000 = $28,000. Plot the total expense point ($28,000) for 1,000 units. Then, draw a line through this point from the $7,000 fixed expense intercept on the dollars axis. This is the *total expense line*. Why does the total expense line start at the fixed expense line? If Kay sells no posters, she still incurs the $7,000 fixed cost for the website maintenance, software, and office rental, but she incurs no variable costs.

STEP 4: Identify the *breakeven point*. The breakeven point is the point where the sales revenue line intersects the total expense line. This is the point where sales revenue equals total expenses. Our previous analyses told us that Kay's breakeven point is 500 posters, or $17,500 in sales. The graph shows this information visually.

STEP 5: Mark the *operating income* and the *operating loss* areas on the graph. To the left of the breakeven point, the total expense line lies above the sales revenue line. Expenses exceed sales revenue, leading to an operating loss. If Kay sells only 300 posters, she incurs an operating loss. The amount of the loss is the vertical distance between the total expense line and the sales revenue line:

Sales revenue	−	Variable expenses	−	Fixed expenses	=	Operating income (Loss)
(300 × $35)	−	(300 × $21)	−	$7,000	=	$(2,800)

To the right of the breakeven point, the business earns a profit. The vertical distance between the sales revenue line and the total expense line equals income. Exhibit 7-8 shows that if Kay sells 1,000 posters, she earns operating income of $7,000 ($35,000 sales revenue − $28,000 total expenses).

Why bother with a graph? Why not just use the income statement approach or the shortcut approach? Graphs like Exhibit 7-8 help managers visualize profit or loss over a range of volume. The income statement and shortcut approaches estimate income or loss for only a single sales volume.

Technology Makes It Simple — Excel 2016

CVP graphs are simple to create with Microsoft Excel using these simple steps:

1. In Row 1 of a new Excel worksheet, set up column headings for Volume, Revenue, and Expenses.
2. In Row 2, enter a volume of zero. Then calculate the corresponding revenues and expenses at that volume.
3. In Row 3, enter a higher volume, such as the volume at the high end of the company's relevant range. Calculate the corresponding revenues and expenses at that volume.
4. Highlight the data. Then click on the "Insert" tab on the menu bar and choose "Scatter With a Line" as the chart type. If you want to make your graph larger, choose "Move Chart Location" from the menu bar and select "New Sheet" and "OK."
5. Click on "Insert" "Textbox" to add labels for the breakeven point, revenue line, expense line, and so forth. Play around with the formatting features to get the look you want (for example, you may want to tilt the angle of the labels or add an arrow pointing to the breakeven point, and so forth).
6. Add a title to the graph, as well as labels for the axes.

Decision Guidelines

CVP Analysis

Your friend wants to open her own ice cream parlor after college. She needs help making the following decisions:

Decision	Guidelines
How much will I earn on every ice cream cone I sell?	The unit contribution margin shows managers how much is earned on each unit sold after paying for variable *costs but before considering fixed expenses*. The unit contribution margin is the amount each unit earns that contributes toward fixed expenses and generating a profit. Each time a unit is sold, the company's operating income will improve by the amount of the unit contribution margin. It is computed as follows: Sales price per unit Less: Variable cost per unit Contribution margin per unit The contribution margin ratio shows managers how much contribution margin is earned on every $1 of sales. It is computed as follows: $$\text{Contribution margin ratio} = \frac{\text{Contribution margin}}{\text{Sales revenue}}$$
Can I quickly forecast my income without creating a full income statement?	The contribution margin concept allows managers to forecast income quickly at different sales volumes. First, find the total contribution margin (by multiplying the forecasted number of units by the unit contribution margin or by multiplying the forecasted sales revenue by the contribution margin ratio) and then subtract all fixed expenses.
How can I compute the *number of ice cream cones* I'll have to sell to break even or earn a target profit?	*Income Statement Approach:* SALES REVENUE − VARIABLE EXPENSES − FIXED EXPENSE = OPERATING INCOME $$\left(\begin{array}{c}\text{Sales price per unit}\\ \times \text{ Units sold}\end{array}\right) - \left(\begin{array}{c}\text{Variable cost per unit}\\ \times \text{ Units sold}\end{array}\right) - \text{Fixed expenses} = \text{Operating income}$$ *Shortcut Unit Contribution Margin Approach:* $$\text{Sales in } \textit{units} = \frac{\text{Fixed expenses} + \text{Operating income}}{\text{Contribution margin } \textit{per unit}}$$
How can I compute the *amount of sales revenue* (in dollars) I'll have to generate to break even or earn a target profit?	*Shortcut Contribution Margin Ratio Approach:* $$\text{Sales in } \textit{dollars} = \frac{\text{Fixed expenses} + \text{Operating income}}{\text{Contribution margin } \textit{ratio}}$$
What will my profits look like over a range of volumes?	CVP graphs show managers, at a glance, how different sales volumes will affect profits.

SUMMARY PROBLEM 1

Fleet Foot buys hiking socks for $6 a pair and sells them for $10. Management budgets monthly fixed expenses of $10,000 for sales volumes between 0 and 12,000 pairs.

Requirements

1. Use the income statement approach and the shortcut unit contribution margin approach to compute monthly breakeven sales in units.
2. Use the shortcut contribution margin ratio approach to compute the breakeven point in sales revenue (sales dollars).
3. Compute the monthly sales level (in units) required to earn a target operating income of $14,000. Use either the income statement approach or the shortcut contribution margin approach.
4. Prepare a graph of Fleet Foot's CVP relationships, similar to Exhibit 7-8. Draw the sales revenue line, the fixed expense line, and the total expense line. Label the axes, the breakeven point, the operating income area, and the operating loss area.

■ SOLUTIONS

Requirement 1
Income Statement Approach:

SALES REVENUE − VARIABLE EXPENSES − FIXED EXPENSES = OPERATING INCOME

$$\left(\text{Sales price per unit} \times \text{Units sold}\right) - \left(\text{Variable cost per unit} \times \text{Units sold}\right) - \text{Fixed expenses} = \text{Operating income}$$

($10 × Units sold) − ($6 × Units sold) − $10,000 = $0
($10 − $6) × Units sold = $10,000
$4 × Units sold = $10,000
Units sold = $10,000 ÷ $4
Breakeven sales in units = 2,500 units

Shortcut Unit Contribution Margin Approach:

$$\text{Sales in units} = \frac{\text{Fixed expenses} + \text{Operating income}}{\text{Contribution margin per unit}}$$

$$= \frac{\$10,000 + \$0}{(\$10 - \$6)}$$

$$= \frac{\$10,000}{\$4}$$

$$= 2,500 \text{ units}$$

Requirement 2

$$\text{Sales in dollars} = \frac{\text{Fixed expenses} + \text{Operating income}}{\text{Contribution margin ratio}}$$

$$= \frac{\$10,000 + \$0}{0.40^*}$$

$$= \$25,000$$

$$^*\text{Contribution margin ratio} = \frac{\text{Contribution margin per unit}}{\text{Sales price per unit}} = \frac{\$4}{\$10} = 0.40$$

Requirement 3
Income Statement Equation Approach:

SALES REVENUE	−	VARIABLE EXPENSES	− FIXED EXPENSES	= OPERATING INCOME
$\left(\begin{array}{c}\text{Sales price}\\\text{per unit}\end{array} \times \text{Units sold}\right)$	−	$\left(\begin{array}{c}\text{Variable cost}\\\text{per unit}\end{array} \times \text{Units sold}\right)$	− Fixed expenses	= Operating income
($10 × Units sold)	−	($6 × Units sold)	− $10,000	= $14,000
($10	−	$6) × Units sold		= $10,000 + $14,000
		$4 × Units sold		= $24,000
		Units sold		= $24,000 ÷ $4
		Units sold		= 6,000 units

Shortcut Unit Contribution Margin Approach:

$$\text{Sales in units} = \frac{\text{Fixed expenses} + \text{Operating income}}{\text{Contribution margin per unit}}$$

$$= \frac{\$10,000 + \$14,000}{(\$10 - \$6)}$$

$$= \frac{\$24,000}{\$4}$$

$$= 6,000 \text{ units}$$

Requirement 4

3 Use CVP analysis to measure the impact of changing business conditions

How Do Managers Use CVP to Make Decisions When Business Conditions Change?

In today's fast-changing business world, managers need to be prepared for increasing costs, pricing pressure from competitors, and other changing business conditions.

Managers use CVP analysis to conduct **sensitivity analysis**. Sensitivity analysis is a "what-if" technique that asks what results will be if actual prices or costs change or if an underlying assumption such as sales mix changes. For example, increased competition may force Kay to consider lowering her sales price. In addition, her suppliers may increase the cost of posters. How will these changes affect Kay's operating income, her breakeven point, and the volume needed to earn her target profit? How can CVP analysis help Kay respond to these changing business conditions? We'll tackle these issues next.

Changing the Sales Price and Volume

Let's assume that Kay has now been in business for several months and is typically selling 950 posters a month. Because of new competition, Kay is considering cutting her sales price from $35 to $31 per poster. If her variable expenses remain $21 per poster and her fixed expenses remain at $7,000, how many posters will she need to sell to break even? To answer this question, Kay calculates a new unit contribution margin using the new sales price:

New sales price per poster..................................	$ 31
Less: Variable cost per poster............................	21
New contribution margin per poster.................	$ 10

She then uses the new unit contribution margin to compute breakeven sales in units:

$$\text{Sales in units} = \frac{\text{Fixed expenses} + \text{Operating income}}{\text{Contribution margin per unit}}$$

$$= \frac{\$7{,}000 + \$0}{\$10}$$

$$= 700 \text{ posters}$$

With the original $35 sale price, Kay's breakeven point was 500 posters. If Kay lowers the sales price to $31 per poster, her breakeven point increases to 700 posters. The lower sales price means that each poster contributes *less* toward fixed expenses ($10 versus $14 before the price change), so Kay must sell 200 *more* posters to break even. Each dollar of sales revenue would contribute $0.32 ($10/$31) rather than $0.40 toward covering fixed expenses and generating a profit.

If Kay reduces her sales price to $31, how many posters must she sell to achieve her $4,900 monthly target profit? Kay again uses the new unit contribution margin to determine how many posters she will need to sell to reach her profit goals:

$$\text{Sales in units} = \frac{\$7{,}000 + \$4{,}900}{\$10}$$

$$= 1{,}190 \text{ posters}$$

> **Why is this important?**
>
> "**CVP analysis** helps managers prepare for and respond to **economic** changes, such as increasing costs and **pressure** to drop sales prices, so companies can remain **competitive** and **profitable**."

With the original sales price, Kay needed to sell only 850 posters per month to achieve her target operating income. If Kay cuts her sales price (and, therefore, her contribution margin), she must sell more posters to achieve her financial goals. Exhibit 7-9 shows the effect of changes in sales price on breakeven and target profit volumes.

EXHIBIT 7-9 The Effect of Changes in Sales Price on Breakeven and Target Profit Volumes

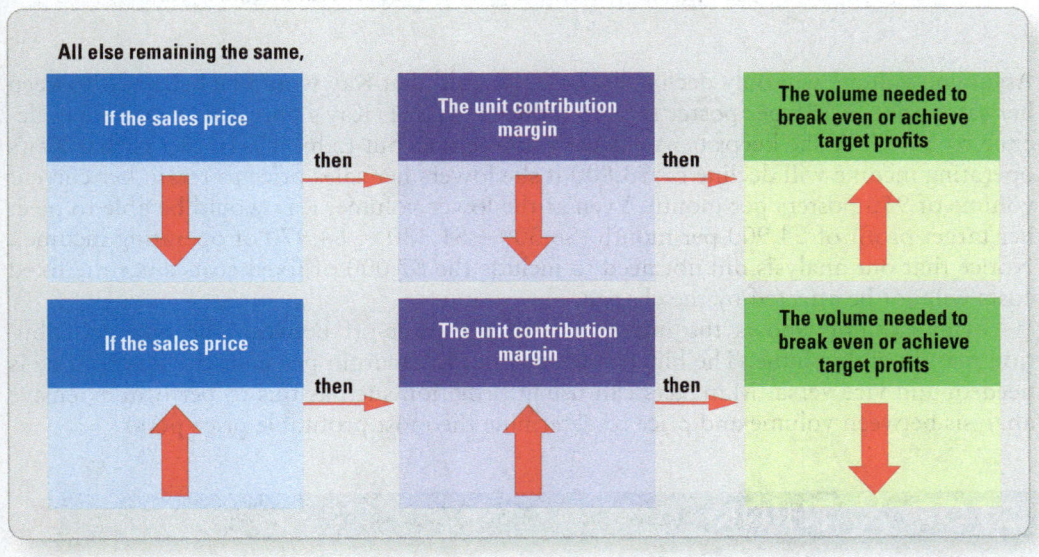

Let's also consider what will happen to Kay's operating income if she reduces the sales price from $35 per poster to $31 per poster. Exhibit 7-10 shows a "before and after" analysis of her operating income. Recall from our earlier discussion that Kay has now been in business several months and typically sells 950 posters a month. If Kay has to reduce her sales price to $31 per poster to retain her current volume of 950 posters per month, her operating income will go down by $3,800 a month from where it currently stands and she will no longer reach her target profit of $4,900 per month.

EXHIBIT 7-10 Before and After Analysis of Change in Sales Price

	A	B		C	D	F
1	**Kay Martin Posters**					
2	**Contribution Margin Income Statement**					
3	For a month in which 950 posters are sold	Before Changing Price		After Changing Price		Difference
4		Per Unit	Total	Per Unit	Total	
5	Sales revenue	$ 35	$ 33,250	$ 31	$ 29,450	$ (3,800)
6	Less: Variable expenses	21	19,950	21	19,950	0
7	Contribution margin	$ 14	$ 13,300	$ 10	$ 9,500	$ (3,800)
8	Less: Fixed expenses		7,000		7,000	0
9	Operating income		$ 6,300		$ 2,500	$ (3,800)
10						
11						

But what if Kay doesn't decrease her sales price? Let's say Kay has a loyal following of customers, and so she believes that sales volume will only decline by 10% if she leaves her sales price at $35 per poster rather than decreasing it to $31. How much will her operating income decline? Kay could create a full "before and after" income statement at the new volume, as we did in Exhibit 7-10, to find the answer. However, there is a quicker way. Kay can simply compute the *change* in operating income that would result from the decreased volume:

Contribution margin per unit given current sales price of $35	$ 14
Multiplied by expected decline in volume (10% × 950 posters)	×95
Expected decline in operating income if price is not reduced	$ 1,330

Assuming volume will only decline by 10%, we find that Kay would be better off to keep her sales price at $35 per poster than to reduce it to $31. Kay's operating income will decline by $1,330 if she keeps her sales price where it is, but Exhibit 7-10 shows that Kay's operating income will decline by $3,800 if she lowers her sales price to retain her current volume of 950 posters per month. Even at the lower volume, Kay would be able to meet her target profit of $4,900 per month ($6,300 − $1,330 = $4,970 of operating income). Notice that our analysis did not need to include the $7,000 of fixed costs since the fixed costs will not be affected by the change.

This example shows the importance of the trade-off between the unit contribution margin and volume. The higher the contribution margin per unit, the less volume is needed, and vice versa. Managers can use information such as this to perform extensive analysis between volume and price to determine the most profitable price point.

STOP & THINK

Kay believes she could dominate the e-commerce art poster business if she cut the sales price to $20. Is this a good idea?

Answer: No. The variable cost per poster is $21. If Kay sells posters for $20 each, she loses $1 on each poster. Kay will incur a loss if the sales price is less than the variable cost.

Changing Variable Costs

Let's assume that Kay does *not* lower her sales price. However, Kay's supplier raises the price for each poster to $24 (instead of the original $21). To remain competitive, Kay cannot pass this increase on to her customers, so she holds her sales price at the original $35 per poster. Her fixed costs remain $7,000. How many posters must she sell to break even after her supplier raises the price? Kay's new contribution margin per unit drops to $11 ($35 sales price per poster −$24 variable cost per poster). So, her new breakeven point is as follows:

$$\text{Sales in units} = \frac{\text{Fixed expenses} + \text{Operating income}}{\text{Contribution margin per unit}}$$

$$= \frac{\$7,000 + \$0}{\$11.00}$$

$$= 637 \text{ posters}$$

Kay will have to sell *more* units (637 versus 500 originally) just to break even. Keep the following rule of thumb in mind:

> Higher variable costs have the same effect as lower selling prices—they both reduce the product's unit contribution margin. As a result, more units need to be sold to break even or achieve target profits.

As shown in Exhibit 7-11, a *decrease* in variable costs would have just the opposite effect. Lower variable costs increase the contribution margin that each poster provides and, therefore, lowers the breakeven point.

EXHIBIT 7-11 The Effect of Changes in Variable Costs on Breakeven and Target Profit Volumes

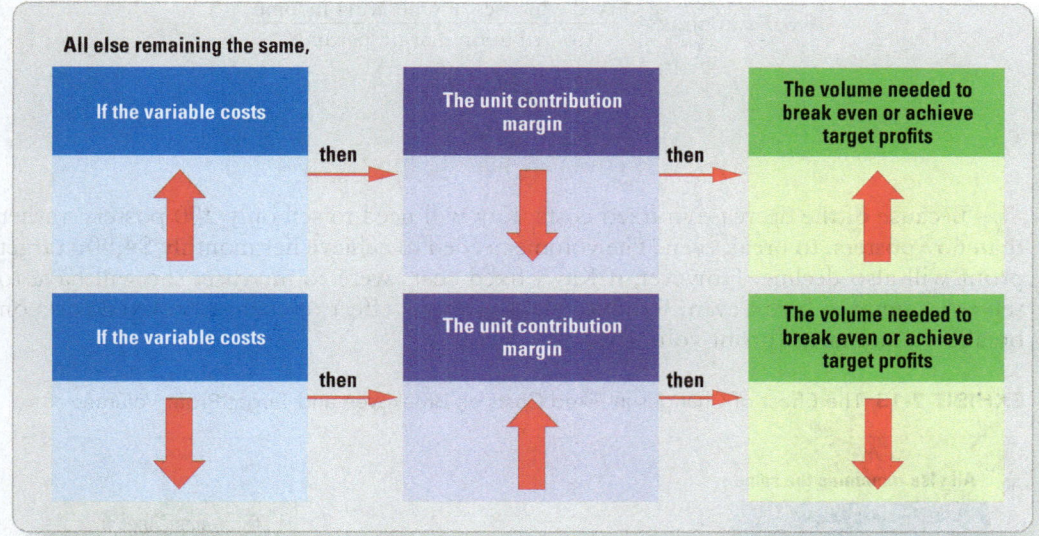

Let's also consider what will happen to Kay's operating income because of the increase in variable costs coupled with the 10% decline in volume from keeping her sales price at $35 per poster. Exhibit 7-12 shows a "before and after" analysis of Kay's operating income, starting with her original monthly income, then considering the decrease in sales volume due to competition, and finally considering the increase in variable costs from her suppliers.

EXHIBIT 7-12 Comparison of Operating Income as Volume Declines and Variable Costs Increase

	A	B		C		D	E		F
1	**Kay Martin Posters**								
2	**Contribution Margin Income Statement**	**Originally**		**10% lower volume:**			**10% lower volume**		
3	**Per month, under various scenarios**	**950 posters**		**855 posters**			**and higher variable costs**		
4		Per Unit	Total	Per Unit		Total	Per Unit		Total
5	Sales revenue	$ 35	$ 33,250	$ 35	$	29,925	$ 35	$	29,925
6	Less: Variable expenses	21	19,950	21		17,955	24		20,520
7	Contribution margin	$ 14	$ 13,300	$ 14	$	11,970	$ 11	$	9,405
8	Less: Fixed expenses		7,000			7,000			7,000
9	Operating income		$ 6,300		$	4,970		$	2,405
10									
11									

Exhibit 7-12 shows that competition, coupled with increased costs from her suppliers, would take a drastic toll on Kay's original operating income. Thus, Kay will need to consider new business tactics to offset these detrimental factors. Perhaps she could lower her fixed costs or generate more volume by selling additional types of products. We'll consider these options next.

Changing Fixed Costs

Having considered possible changes in sales price, volume, and variable costs, Kay has now turned her attention to fixed costs. Kay has decided she really doesn't need a storefront office at a retail strip mall because she doesn't have many walk-in customers. She could drastically decrease her monthly fixed costs from $7,000 to $3,190 by moving her office out of prime retail space to an industrial park.

How will this decrease in fixed costs affect Kay's breakeven point? *Changes in fixed costs do not affect the contribution margin.* Therefore, Kay's unit contribution margin is still $11 per poster given the increased cost from her supplier ($35 sales price − $24 variable cost). However, her breakeven point changes because her fixed costs change:

$$\text{Sales in units} = \frac{\text{Fixed expenses} + \text{Operating income}}{\text{Contribution margin per unit}}$$

$$= \frac{\$3{,}190 + \$0}{\$11.00}$$

$$= 290 \text{ posters}$$

Because of the decrease in fixed costs, Kay will need to sell only 290 posters, rather than 637 posters, to break even. The volume needed to achieve her monthly $4,900 target profit will also decline. However, if Kay's fixed costs were to *increase*, she will have to sell *more* units to break even. Exhibit 7-13 shows the effect of changes in fixed costs on breakeven and target profit volumes.

EXHIBIT 7-13 The Effect of Changes in Fixed Costs on Breakeven and Target Profit Volumes

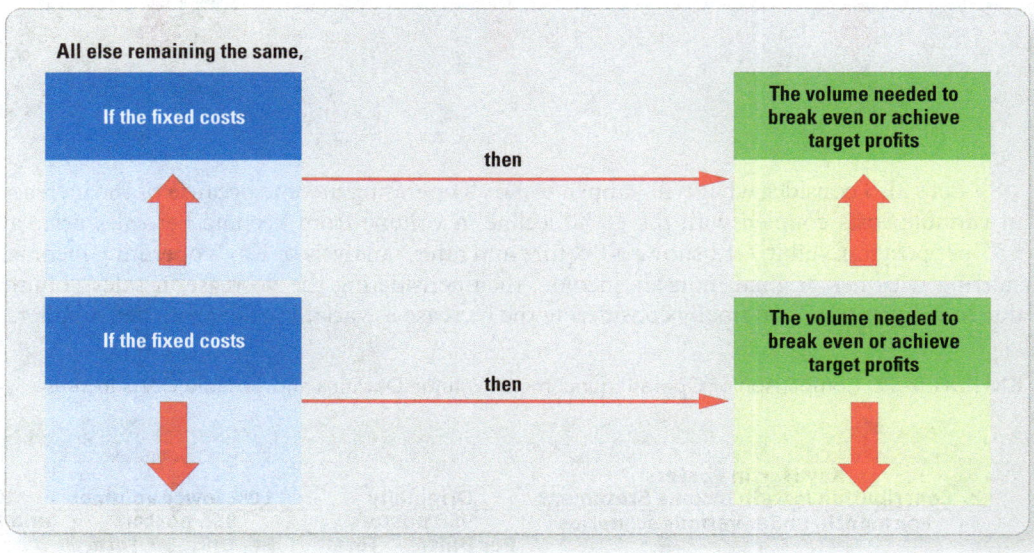

Finally, let's consider how the decreased fixed costs will affect Kay's operating income. Exhibit 7-14 shows that with the substantial decrease in fixed costs, Kay's operating income will almost be back to where it was before competition drove down her volume and suppliers increased their costs. Kay has successfully used CVP analysis to make decisions that will keep her business operating above her target operating income of $4,900 per month.

EXHIBIT 7-14 Before and After changes in Volume, Variable Costs, and Fixed Costs

	A	B		C	D
1	**Kay Martin Posters**			**10% lower volume (855)**	
2	**Contribution Margin Income Statement**	**Originally**		**higher variable costs**	
3	**Per month, under various scenarios**	**950 posters**		**and lower fixed costs**	
4		Per Unit	Total	Per Unit	Total
5	Sales revenue	$ 35	$ 33,250	$ 35	$ 29,925
6	Less: Variable expenses	21	19,950	24	20,520
7	Contribution margin	$ 14	$ 13,300	$ 11	$ 9,405
8	Less: Fixed expenses		7,000		3,190
9	Operating income		$ 6,300		$ 6,215
10					
11					

STOP & THINK

Kay has been considering advertising as a means to increase her sales volume. Kay could spend an extra $2,200 per month on website banner ads. How many *extra* posters would Kay have to sell *just to pay for the advertising?* (Use Kay's new contribution margin of $11 per poster.)

Answer: CVP is very useful for isolating and addressing individual business decisions. Instead of using *all* of Kay's fixed costs, we can isolate *just* the fixed costs relating to advertising ($2,200). This will allow us to figure out how many *extra* posters Kay would have to sell each month to break even on (or pay for) the advertising cost. Advertising is a fixed cost, so Kay's contribution margin remains $11 per poster.

$$\text{Sales in units} = \frac{\text{Fixed expenses} + \text{Operating income}}{\text{Contribution margin per unit}}$$

$$= \frac{\$2,200 + \$0}{\$11.00}$$

$$= 200 \text{ posters}$$

Kay must sell 200 *extra* posters each month just to pay for the cost of advertising. If she sells fewer than 200 extra posters, she'll increase her volume but lose money on the advertising. If she sells more than 200 extra posters, her plan will have worked—she'll increase her volume and her profit.

We have seen that changes in sales prices, variable costs, and fixed costs can have dramatic effects on the volume of product that companies must sell to achieve breakeven and target profits. Companies often turn to automation and overseas production to decrease variable labor costs, but this approach, in turn, increases their fixed costs and variable shipping costs. In recent years, many food producers have systematically reduced the size of their products to decrease the variable cost of direct materials. For example, ice cream, which in the past was primarily sold in half gallons, is now sold in smaller containers. Why make this change? Customers are less responsive, in terms of buying fewer units, to slightly smaller packages than they are to increases in prices. Thus, CVP analysis has shown that it is more profitable to decrease variable materials costs than to increase prices.

In the next section, we'll look at another tactic companies use to increase operating income: changing their sales mix to offer more products with higher contribution margins.

Sustainability and CVP

Sustainability initiatives can have a significant bearing on the cost information used in CVP analysis. For example, Coca-Cola, a recognized leader in corporate sustainability, has been working steadily to reduce the amount of packaging used for its products. The reduced use of plastic, aluminum, and cardboard translates into lower variable costs of production and distribution. Let's take a closer look at plastic beverage containers in particular.

According to the American Chemistry Council and the Association of Postconsumer Plastic Recyclers, most single-serving plastic beverage containers are made of PET (polyethylene teraphthalate), whereas larger beverage containers such as milk jugs are made from high-density polyethylene (HDPE). Both are petroleum-based products requiring the use of nonrenewable fossil fuels. Together, these two types of plastics comprise 96% of beverage containers sold in the United States. You can easily recognize these types of containers because they will be marked with either #1 (PET) or #2 (HDPE) inside of a recycling symbol. While the recycling rate for these plastics has continued to rise annually, only 31.8% of all plastic beverage containers are currently recycled. This means that nearly 6.5 billion pounds of plastic beverage containers are sent to landfills each year![1]

As part of its sustainability initiatives, Coca-Cola is making strides to reduce its use of PET. First, the company is "lightweighting" its packaging; that is, it is making the bottles thinner and lighter. Its goal is to reduce all packaging by 25% by 2020. Second, the company is increasing the amount of recycled PET and renewable materials used in its beverage containers. The company's current goal is to obtain 40% of its PET from recycled PET (rPET) or renewable materials by 2020.[2] The need for increased consumer recycling plays a key role in these plans. But even more impressive, in 2015 the company released its first PET bottle made from 100% plant-based materials, such as plant waste from sugar cane operations. Why is this important? Traditionally, PET has been produced from petroleum. By reducing the need for fossil fuels, the company has reduced its carbon footprint and helped to create more sustainable packaging solutions for the long term.[3] What does this have to do with accounting? As a result of using less plastic and higher recycled content, the variable cost of packaging each unit and shipping the lighter weight containers has decreased. One might therefore assume that Coca-Cola needs to sell fewer units of product to achieve its target profit. However, keep in mind that the company had to incur many fixed costs to research, develop, and design these new bottles. As the Coca-Cola example shows, sustainability initiatives often result in both cost savings *and* additional costs. These costs and cost savings may be fixed or variable. Managers use CVP analysis to determine how these initiatives will impact the volume needed to achieve the company's operating income goals.

See Exercises E7-27A and E7-48B

4 Find breakeven and target profit volumes for multiproduct companies

Changing the Mix of Products Offered for Sale

So far, we have assumed that Kay sold only one-size posters. What would happen if she offered different types of products? Companies that sell more than one product must consider their <u>sales mix</u> when performing CVP analysis. The sales mix is the combination of products that make up total sales. Think of the sales mix as the "basket of products" sold by the company. For example, a movie theater may sell 20 popcorns, 25 sodas, and 15 boxes of candy for every 75 movie tickets sold. The combination of all of these different product sales, including the movie tickets, makes up the theater's total "sales basket." All else being equal, a company earns more operating income by selling high-contribution margin products than by selling an equal number of low-contribution margin products.

The same CVP formulas that are used to perform CVP analysis for a company with a single product can be used for any company that sells more than one product. However, the formulas use the *weighted-average contribution margin* of all products rather than the contribution margin of a sole product. Each product's contribution margin is *weighted* by the relative number of units sold. As before, the company can find the breakeven or the target profit volume in terms of units or in terms of sales revenue. We'll consider each in turn.

Multiproduct Company: Finding Breakeven in Terms of Sales Units

Suppose Kay plans to sell two types of posters. In addition to her regular-size posters, Kay plans to sell large posters. *Let's assume that none of Kay's original costs have changed.* Exhibit 7-15 shows that each regular poster will continue to generate $14 of contribution margin, while each large poster will generate $30 of contribution margin. Kay is adding the large-poster line because it carries a higher unit contribution margin.

---

[1] https://plastics.americanchemistry.com/Education-Resources/Publications/2014-National-Post-Consumer-Plastics-Bottle-Recycling-Report.pdf
[2] http://www.cokecce.com/system/file_resources/278/03_Our_sustainability_plan.pdf
[3] http://www.environmentalleader.com/2015/06/04/coca-cola-produces-worlds-first-100-plant-based-pet-bottle/

EXHIBIT 7-15 Calculating the Weighted-Average Contribution Margin per Unit

	Regular Posters	Large Posters	Total in "basket"
1 Calculating Weighted-Average Contribution Margin per Unit			
2 Sales price per unit	$ 35	$ 70	
3 Less: Variable cost per unit	21	40	
4 Contribution margin per unit	$ 14	$ 30	
5 Multiply by: Sales mix (number of units in "basket")	5	3	8
6 Contribution margin	$ 70	$ 90	$ 160
7			
8 Weighted-average contibution margin per unit ($160/8 units)			$ 20
9			

For every five regular posters sold, Kay expects to sell three large posters. In other words, she expects 5/8 of the sales in her "sales basket" to be regular posters and 3/8 to be large posters. This is a 5:3 sales mix. Exhibit 7-15 shows how Kay finds the total contribution margin and total number of units in the "sales basket" and then divides the two to find the weighted-average contribution margin per unit in the basket.

Notice that none of Kay's products actually generates $20 of contribution margin. However, if the sales mix is five regular posters to every three large posters, as expected, it is *as if* the contribution margin is $20 per unit. Once Kay has computed the weighted-average contribution margin per unit, she uses it in the shortcut formula to determine the total number of posters that would need to be sold to break even:

$$\text{Sales in total units} = \frac{\text{Fixed expenses} + \text{Operating income}}{\text{Weighted-average contribution margin per unit}}$$

$$= \frac{\$7{,}000 + \$0}{\$20}$$

$$= 350 \text{ posters}$$

In total, Kay must sell 350 posters to break even. However, this is the case only if 5/8 of the sales basket is regular posters and 3/8 of the sales basket is large posters. As a final step, we need to separate the entire sales basket needed to break even back into the two types of products in the basket: regular posters and large posters. We do this by multiplying the total number of units needed to break even (350) by the proportion of each product in the sales basket.

Breakeven sales of regular posters (350 × 5/8).................... 218.75 regular posters
Breakeven sales of large posters (350 × 3/8)...................... 131.25 large posters

We can prove this breakeven point as follows:

Contribution margin:
    Regular posters (218.75 × $14).................. $ 3,063
    Large posters (131.25 × $30)..................... 3,937
Contribution margin .... $ 7,000
Less: Fixed expenses.. 7,000
Operating income.. $ 0

As is often the case in real situations, these computations don't yield round numbers. Because Kay cannot sell partial posters, she must sell 219 regular posters and 132 large posters to avoid a loss.

We just found Kay's *breakeven* point, but Kay can also use the same steps to calculate the number of units she must sell to achieve a target profit. The only difference, as before, is that she would use *target profit*, rather than *zero*, as the operating income in the shortcut formula.

Try It!

Rachel runs her own hot dog stand on the U of A campus. The monthly cost of the cart rental and business permit is $300. Rachel's contribution margin is $1.50 per hot dog sold. She has recently added individual servings of potato chips to her product offering. Each bag of potato chips has a contribution margin of $0.75 per bag. Rachel sells 5 bags of potato chips for every 10 hot dogs.

1. What is Rachel's weighted-average contribution margin per unit?
2. How many total units must Rachel sell in a month to earn a target monthly profit of $900?
3. Of the total units needed to earn $900 of profit, how many are hot dogs and how many are bags of potato chips?

Please see page 442 for solutions.

Multiproduct Company: Finding Breakeven in Terms of Sales Revenue

Companies that offer hundreds or thousands of products (such as Walmart and Amazon.com) will not want to find the breakeven point in terms of units. Rather, they'll want to know breakeven (or target profit volumes) in terms of sales revenue. To find this sales volume, the company needs to know, or estimate, its weighted-average contribution margin ratio so that managers can use the shortcut formula introduced in the first half of the chapter. If a company prepares a contribution margin income statement that includes all of its products, the weighted-average contribution margin ratio is easily calculated as the total contribution margin divided by total sales. The contribution margin is *already* weighted by the company's *actual* sales mix! The following "Stop and Think" illustrates how Walmart would use this approach to calculate breakeven.

STOP & THINK

How would Walmart calculate its weighted-average contribution margin ratio? How much sales revenue must Walmart earn just to break even?

Answer: First, Walmart calculates its weighted-average contribution margin ratio based on its contribution margin income statement, as shown below:[4]

	A	B	C	D
1	**Walmart** **Contribution Margin Income Statement (estimated)** **For the fiscal year ended January 31, 2016**	(in millions)		
2	Sales revenue	$ 482,130		
3	Less: Variable expenses	370,000		
4	Contribution margin	112,130		
5	Less: Fixed expenses	88,025		
6	Operating income	$ 24,105		
7				
8	Weighted-Average Contribution Margin Ratio ($112,130/$482,130)	23.26%		
9				

Next, Walmart uses the weighted-average contribution margin ratio in the shortcut formula to predict the breakeven point:

$$\text{Sales in dollars} = \frac{\text{Fixed expenses} + \text{Operating income}}{\text{Weighted-average contribution margin ratio}}$$

$$= \frac{\$88,025 \text{ million} + \$0}{23.26\%}$$

$$= \$378,440 \text{ million (rounded)}$$

Walmart must achieve sales revenue of nearly $380,000 million just to break even.

---

[4]Estimated for teaching purposes only, based on Walmart's 2015 annual report.

Unlike Walmart, Kay's business to this point has been limited to a sole product (regular posters), which had a 40% contribution margin ratio. Since Kay is only thinking about selling large posters and doesn't yet sell them, she doesn't currently have a contribution margin income statement that includes both sizes of posters. However, she can easily estimate the weighted-average contribution margin ratio based on the expected sales mix. Exhibit 7-16 shows how Kay would first calculate the total contribution margin and total sales revenue in the sales basket based on sales mix assumptions. Next, she would divide the total contribution margin in the basket by the total sales in the basket to estimate the weighted-average contribution margin ratio.

EXHIBIT 7-16 Estimating the Weighted-Average Contribution Margin Ratio

	A	B	C	D
1	Calculating Weighted-Average Contribution Margin Ratio	Regular Posters	Large Posters	Total in "basket"
2	Contribution margin per unit	$ 14	$ 30	
3	Multiply by: Sales mix (number of units in "basket")	5	3	
4	Contribution margin	$ 70	$ 90	$ 160
5				
6	Sales price per unit	$ 35	$ 70	
7	Multiply by: Sales mix (number of units in "basket")	5	3	
8	Sales revenue	$ 175	$ 210	$ 385
9				
10	Weighted-average contribution margin ratio ($160/$385)			41.56%
11				

Notice how Kay's weighted-average contribution margin ratio (41.56%) will be higher than it was when she sold only regular posters (40%). That's because she expects to sell some large posters that have a 42.9% contribution margin ratio ($30/$70) in addition to the regular-sized posters. Because her sales mix would be changing, she would have a different contribution margin ratio.

Once Kay has calculated her weighted-average contribution margin ratio, she can use the shortcut formula to estimate breakeven in terms of sales revenue:

$$\text{Sales in dollars} = \frac{\text{Fixed expenses} + \text{Operating income}}{\text{Weighted-average contribution margin ratio}}$$

$$= \frac{\$7,000 + \$0}{41.56\%}$$

$$= \$16,844 \text{ (rounded)}$$

Kay could also use the formula to find the total sales revenue she would need to meet her target monthly operating income of $4,900.

If Kay's actual sales mix is not five regular posters to three large posters, her actual operating income will differ from the predicted amount. The sales mix greatly influences the breakeven point. When companies offer more than one product, they do not have a unique breakeven point. Every sales mix assumption leads to a different breakeven point.

STOP & THINK

Suppose Kay plans to sell a total of 800 posters in the 5:3 sales mix (500 regular posters and 300 large posters). She actually does sell 800 posters—375 regular and 425 large. The sale prices per poster, variable costs per poster, and fixed expenses are exactly as predicted. Without doing any computations, is Kay's actual operating income greater than, less than, or equal to her expected income?

Answer: Kay's actual sales mix did not turn out to be the 5:3 mix she expected. She actually sold more of the higher-margin large posters than the lower-margin regular posters. This favorable change in the sales mix causes her to earn a higher operating income than she expected.

What Are Some Common Indicators of Risk?

A company's level of risk depends on many factors, including the general health of the economy and the specific industry in which the company operates. In addition, a firm's risk depends on its current volume of sales and the relative amount of fixed and variable costs that make up its total costs. Next, we discuss how a firm can gauge its level of risk, to some extent, by its margin of safety and its operating leverage.

Margin of Safety

5 Determine a firm's margin of safety, operating leverage, and most profitable cost structure

The **margin of safety** is the excess of actual or expected sales over the sales needed to break even. This is the "cushion," or drop in sales, the company can absorb without incurring a loss. The higher the margin of safety, the greater the cushion against loss and the less risky the business plan. Managers use the margin of safety to evaluate the risk of current operations as well as the risk of new plans.

Let's continue to assume that Kay has been in business for several months and that she generally sells 950 posters a month. Let's go back to Kay's original data (selling one-size posters with a sales price of $35 per poster, variable cost of $21 per poster, and fixed costs of $7,000 per month). Kay's breakeven point in our original data is 500 posters. Kay can express her margin of safety in units, as follows:

Margin of safety in units	=	Expected (or actual) sales in units	−	Breakeven sales in units
	=	950 posters	−	500 posters
	=	450 posters		

Kay can also express her margin of safety in sales revenue (sales dollars):

Margin of safety in dollars	=	Expected (or actual) sales in dollars	−	Breakeven sales in dollars
	=	(950 posters × $35)	−	(500 posters × $35)
	=	$33,250	−	$17,500
	=	$15,750		

Sales would have to drop by more than 450 posters, or $15,750 a month, before Kay incurs a loss. This is a fairly comfortable margin.

Managers can also compute the margin of safety as a percentage of sales. Simply divide the margin of safety by sales. We obtain the same percentage whether we use units or dollars.

In units:

$$\text{Margin of safety as a percentage} = \frac{\text{Margin of safety in units}}{\text{Expected (or actual) sales in units}}$$

$$= \frac{450 \text{ posters}}{950 \text{ posters}}$$

$$= 47.4\% \text{ (rounded)}$$

In dollars:

$$\text{Margin of safety as a percentage} = \frac{\text{Margin of safety in dollars}}{\text{Expected (or actual) sales in dollars}}$$

$$= \frac{\$15,750}{\$33,250}$$

$$= 47.4\% \text{ (rounded)}$$

The margin of safety percentage tells Kay that sales would have to drop by more than 47.4% before she would incur a loss. If sales fall by less than 47.4%, she would still earn a profit. If sales fall exactly 47.4%, she would break even. This ratio tells Kay that her business plan is not unduly risky.

Operating Leverage

A company's **operating leverage** refers to the relative amount of fixed and variable costs that make up its total costs. Most companies have both fixed and variable costs. However, companies with *high* operating leverage have *relatively more fixed costs* and relatively fewer variable costs. Companies with high operating leverage include golf courses, airlines, and hotels. Because they have fewer variable costs, their contribution margin ratio is relatively high. Recall from the last chapter that Embassy Suites' variable cost of servicing each guest is low, which means that the hotel has a high contribution margin ratio and high operating leverage.

What does high operating leverage have to do with risk? If sales volume decreases, the total contribution margin will drop significantly because each sales dollar contains a high percentage of contribution margin. Yet, the high fixed costs of running the company remain. Therefore, the operating income of these companies can easily turn from profit to loss if sales volume declines. For example, airlines were financially devastated after September 11, 2001, because the number of people flying suddenly dropped, creating large reductions in contribution margin. Yet, the airlines had to continue paying their high fixed costs. High operating leverage companies are at *more* risk because their income declines drastically when sales volume declines.

> **Why is this important?**
>
> "The margin of safety and **operating leverage** help managers understand their **risk** if **volume** decreases due to a recession, **competition**, or other **changes** in the **marketplace**."

What if the economy is growing and sales volume *increases*? High operating leverage companies will reap high rewards. Because high operating leverage companies have high contribution margin ratios, each additional dollar of sales will contribute more to the firm's operating income. Exhibit 7-17 summarizes these characteristics.

EXHIBIT 7-17 Characteristics of High Operating Leverage Firms

- High operating leverage companies have the following:
    - —*Higher* fixed costs and *lower* variable costs
    - —*Higher* contribution margin ratios
- For high operating leverage companies, changes in volume significantly affect operating income, so they face the following:
    - —*Higher* risk
    - —*Higher* potential for reward

    Examples include golf courses, hotels, rental car agencies, theme parks, airlines, cruise lines, etc.

In contrast, companies with low operating leverage have relatively *fewer* fixed costs and relatively *more* variable costs. As a result, they have much lower contribution margin ratios. For example, retailers incur significant levels of fixed costs, but more of every sales dollar is used to pay for the merchandise (a variable cost), so less ends up as contribution margin. If sales volume declines, these companies have relatively fewer fixed costs to cover, so they are at *less* risk of incurring a loss. If sales volume increases, their relatively small contribution margins ratios add to the bottom line, but in smaller increments. Therefore, they reap less reward than high operating leverage companies experiencing the same volume increases. *In other words, at low operating leverage companies, changes in sales volume do not have as much impact on operating income as they do at high operating leverage companies.* Exhibit 7-18 summarizes these characteristics.

EXHIBIT 7-18 Characteristics of Low Operating Leverage Firms

- Low operating leverage companies have the following:
  —*Higher* variable costs and *lower* fixed costs
  —*Lower* contribution margin ratios
- For low operating leverage companies, changes in volume do NOT have as significant an effect on operating income, so they face the following:
  —*Lower* risk
  —*Lower* potential for reward
Examples include merchandising companies and fast-food restaurants.

A company's **operating leverage factor** tells managers how responsive a company's operating income is to changes in volume. The greater the operating leverage factor, the greater the impact a change in sales volume has on operating income.

The operating leverage factor, *at a given level of sales*, is calculated as follows:

$$\text{Operating leverage factor} = \frac{\text{Contribution margin}}{\text{Operating income}}$$

Why do we say, "at a given level of sales"? A company's operating leverage factor will depend, to some extent, on the sales level used to calculate the contribution margin and operating income. Most companies compute the operating leverage factor at their current or expected volume of sales, which is what we'll do in our examples.

What does the operating leverage factor tell us? Keep the following rule of thumb in mind:

The operating leverage factor, at a given level of sales, indicates the percentage change in operating income that will occur from a 1% change in sales volume. In other words, it tells us how responsive a company's operating income is to changes in sales volume.

The *lowest* possible value for this factor is 1, which occurs only if the company has *no* fixed costs (an *extremely low* operating leverage company). *For a minute, let's assume that Kay has no fixed costs.* Given this scenario, her unit contribution margin ($14 per poster) contributes directly to profit because she has no fixed costs to cover. In addition, she has *no* risk. The worst she can do is break even, and that will occur only if she doesn't sell any posters. Let's continue to assume that she generally sells 950 posters a month, so this will be the level of sales at which we need to know the contribution margin and operating income:

Contribution margin (950 posters × $14 per poster)..................	$ 13,300
Less: Fixed expenses..	0
Operating income..	$ 13,300

Given this information, Kay's operating leverage factor is as follows:

$$\text{Operating leverage factor} = \frac{\$13,300}{\$13,300}$$
$$= 1$$

What does this tell us? A factor is a multiplier; therefore:

- If Kay's volume changes by 1%, her operating income will change by 1% (= 1% × a factor of 1).
- If Kay's volume changes by 15%, her operating income will change by 15% (= 15% × a factor of 1).

Let's now see what happens to income and operating leverage if we assume, as usual, that Kay's fixed expenses are $7,000.

Contribution margin (950 posters × $14 per poster)	$13,300
Less: Fixed expenses	7,000
Operating income	$ 6,300

Now that we have once again assumed that Kay's fixed expenses are $7,000, her operating leverage factor is as follows:

$$\text{Operating leverage factor} = \frac{\$13,300}{\$6,300}$$

$$= 2.11 \text{ (rounded)}$$

Notice that her operating leverage factor is *higher* (2.11 versus 1) when she has *more* fixed costs ($7,000 versus $0). Kay's operating leverage factor of 2.11 tells us how responsive her income is to changes in volume. Again, a factor is a multiplier; therefore:

- If Kay's volume changes by 1%, her operating income will change by 2.11% (= 1% × a factor of 2.11).
- If Kay's volume changes by 15%, her operating income will change by 31.65% (= 15% × a factor of 2.11).

Managers use the firm's operating leverage factor to determine how vulnerable their operating income is to changes in sales volume—both positive and negative.

Keep the following rule of thumb in mind:

> The larger the operating leverage factor is, the greater the impact a change in sales volume has on operating income. This is true for both increases and decreases in volume.

Therefore, companies with higher operating leverage factors are particularly vulnerable to changes in volume. In other words, they have *both* higher risk of incurring losses if volume declines *and* higher potential reward if volume increases. Hoping to capitalize on the reward side, many companies have intentionally increased their operating leverage by lowering their variable costs while at the same time increasing their fixed costs. This strategy works well during periods of economic growth but can be detrimental when sales volume declines.

Choosing a Cost Structure

Managers often have some control over how the company's costs are structured—as fixed, variable, or a combination of the two. For example, let's assume that in addition to selling posters online, Kay has decided to lease a small retail kiosk at the local mall. To keep things simple, let's assume Kay will only be selling her regular-size posters, which sell for $35 each. Let's also assume the mall leasing agent has given Kay the following two options for leasing the space:

- Option 1: Pay $300 per month plus 10% of the sales revenue generated at the kiosk.
- Option 2: Pay $1,000 per month.

Which option should Kay choose? The answer depends on how many posters Kay thinks she will sell from the kiosk each month. As we see above, Option 1 has fewer fixed costs and more variable costs than Option 2. Thus, Kay's operating leverage would be lower under Option 1 than under Option 2. As a result, Option 1 carries less financial risk if sales volume is low, but less financial reward if sales volume is high. But how high must sales volume be to make Option 2 the better choice?

To answer this question, Kay will need to figure out her **indifference point**, the point at which she would be indifferent between the two options because they both would result in the same total cost. Once Kay knows the indifference point, she can better judge which option is preferable. Let's see how this is done.

First, Kay calculates the variable and fixed costs associated with each option, as shown in Exhibit 7-19. Notice that Kay does not need to consider any of her other business expenses (such as the cost of the posters themselves or the website maintenance costs) because they will not differ between the two kiosk leasing options. In deciding which lease option to take, Kay only needs to consider those costs that are associated with the lease decision.

EXHIBIT 7-19 Costs Associated with Each Leasing Option

	Option 1	Option 2
Variable cost: 10% of sales revenue (= 10% × $35 per poster)............	$ 3.50 per poster	0
Fixed cost:	$ 300	$ 1,000

Next, Kay develops an equation in which she sets the cost of each leasing option equal to the other. She then fills in the appropriate information and solves for number of units:

$$\text{Costs under Option 1} = \text{Costs under Option 2}$$

$$\text{Variable Costs} + \text{Fixed Costs} = \text{Variable Costs} + \text{Fixed Costs}$$

$$(\text{\# Units} \times \text{Variable cost per unit}) + \text{Fixed Costs} = (\text{\# Units} \times \text{Variable cost per unit}) + \text{Fixed Costs}$$

$$(\text{\# Units} \times \$3.50) + \$300 = (\text{\# Units} \times \$0) + \$1,000$$

$$(\text{\# Units} \times \$3.50) = \$700$$

$$\text{\# Units} = 200$$

Based on this analysis, Kay will be *indifferent* between the two leasing options if she sells *exactly* 200 posters per month at the kiosk. At a volume of 200 units, she would pay $1,000 for the lease under Option 1 [(200 × $3.50) + $300 = $1,000] and $1,000 for the lease under Option 2. Both options would result in the same cost.

But what if sales volume is lower or higher than 200 posters per month? As shown in Exhibit 7-20, Kay will prefer the lower operating leverage alternative (Option 1) if she sells *fewer* than 200 posters a month at the kiosk. However, she will prefer the higher operating leverage alternative (Option 2) if she sells *more* than 200 posters a month at the kiosk. Her decision will be based on whether she expects sales volume at the kiosk to be lower, or higher, than the indifference point.

Cost-Volume-Profit Analysis

EXHIBIT 7-20 Using an Indifference Point to Choose the Most Profitable Cost Structure

We can verify the conclusion presented in Exhibit 7-20 by calculating the lease costs at *any* volume of sales. First, let's assume that Kay expects to sell 100 posters a month at the kiosk. The lease cost under each option is calculated as follows:

Lease cost under Option 1: $300 + [10% × (100 units × $35 sales price)] = $650

Lease cost under Option 2: $1,000

As expected, when the sales volume is *lower* than the indifference point, the lease cost is lower under Option 1 than under Option 2.

Next, let's assume Kay expects to sell 500 posters a month at the mall kiosk. The lease cost is calculated as follows:

Lease cost under Option 1: $300 + [10% × (500 units × $35 sales price)] = $2,050

Lease cost under Option 2: $1,000

As expected, when the sales volume is *higher* than the indifference point, the lease cost is lower under Option 2 than under Option 1.

The following rule of thumb summarizes the conclusions presented in Exhibit 7-20:

When faced with a choice between cost structures, choose the lower operating leverage option when sales volume is expected to be lower than the indifference point. Choose the higher operating leverage option when sales volume is expected to be higher than the indifference point.

Managers can use this rule of thumb whenever they are faced with choices about how to structure their costs.

Try It!

Rachel runs her own hot dog stand on the U of A campus. The monthly cost of the cart rental and business permit is currently $300, but she has been given the option of changing the arrangements to $100 plus $0.25 for every unit of product sold from her stand.

1. At what point in sales volume will Rachel be indifferent between the two options?
2. If Rachel typically sells 700 units a month, which option will she prefer?

Please see page 442 for solutions.

In this chapter, we have discussed how managers use the contribution margin and CVP analysis to predict profits, determine the volume needed to achieve breakeven or a target profit, and assess how changes in the business environment affect their profits. In the next chapter, we look at several types of short-term decisions managers must make. Cost behavior and the contribution margin will continue to play an important role in these decisions.

Decision Guidelines

CVP Analysis

Your friend opened an ice cream parlor. But now she's facing changing business conditions. She needs help making the following decisions:

Decision	Guidelines
The cost of ice cream is rising, yet my competitors have lowered their prices. How will these factors affect the sales volume I'll need to break even or achieve my target profit?	Increases in variable costs (such as ice cream) and decreases in sales prices both decrease the unit contribution margin and contribution margin ratio. You will have to sell more units in order to achieve breakeven or a target profit. You can use sensitivity analysis to better pinpoint the actual volume you'll need to sell.
Would it help if I could renegotiate my lease with the landlord?	Decreases in fixed costs do not affect the firm's contribution margin. However, a decrease in fixed costs means that the company will have to sell fewer units to achieve breakeven or a target profit. Increases in fixed costs have the opposite effect.
I've been thinking about selling other products in addition to ice cream. Will this affect the sales volume I'll need to earn my target profit?	Your contribution margin ratio will change as a result of changing your sales mix. A company earns more income by selling higher-margin products than by selling an equal number of lower-margin products. If you can shift sales toward higher contribution margin products, you will have to sell fewer units to reach your target profit.
If the economy takes a downturn, how much risk do I face of incurring a loss?	The margin of safety indicates how far sales volume can decline before you would incur a loss. It can be calculated in terms of units or sales dollars using the following formula. $$\text{Margin of safety} = \text{Expected (or actual) sales} - \text{Breakeven sales}$$ The margin of safety can also be calculated as a percentage, as follows: $$\text{Margin of safety as a percentage} = \frac{\text{Margin of safety}}{\text{Expected (or actual) sales}}$$
How can I tell whether a change in sales volume will have much of an impact on my operating income?	The operating leverage factor indicates the percentage change in operating income that will occur from a 1% change in volume. It tells you how sensitive your company's operating income is to changes in volume. At a given level of sales, the operating leverage factor is as follows: $$\text{Operating leverage factor} = \frac{\text{Contribution margin}}{\text{Operating income}}$$
What is the indifference point and how do I find it?	The indifference point is the volume of sales at which total costs under one cost structure would be the same as total costs under an alternative cost structure. The indifference point is found by setting the total costs of one option equal to the total costs of another option, and then solving for the volume that equates the two options.
If given a choice between alternative cost structures, how do I choose the most profitable one?	Choose the *lower* operating leverage option when sales volume is expected to be *lower* than the indifference point. Choose the *higher* operating leverage option when sales volume is expected to be *higher* than the indifference point.

SUMMARY PROBLEM 2

Recall from Summary Problem 1 that Fleet Foot buys hiking socks for $6 a pair and sells them for $10. Monthly fixed costs are $10,000 (for sales volumes between 0 and 12,000 pairs), resulting in a breakeven point of 2,500 units. Assume that Fleet Foot has been selling 8,000 pairs of socks per month.

Requirements

1. What is Fleet Foot's current margin of safety in units, in sales dollars, and as a percentage? Explain the results.
2. At this level of sales, what is Fleet Foot's operating leverage factor? If volume declines by 25% due to increasing competition, by what percentage will the company's operating income decline?
3. Competition has forced Fleet Foot to lower its sales price to $9 a pair. How will this affect Fleet's breakeven point?
4. To compensate for the lower sales price, Fleet Foot wants to expand its product line to include men's dress socks. Each pair will sell for $7.00 and cost $2.75 from the supplier. Fixed costs will not change. Fleet expects to sell four pairs of dress socks for every one pair of hiking socks (at its new $9 sales price). What is Fleet's weighted-average contribution margin per unit? Given the 4:1 sales mix, how many of each type of sock will it need to sell to break even?

▪ SOLUTIONS

Requirement 1

Margin of safety in units = Expected sales in units − Breakeven sales in units
 = 8,000 − 2,500
 = 5,500 units

Margin of safety in dollars = Expected sales in dollars − Breakeven sales in dollars
 = (8,000 × $10) − (2,500 × $10)
 = $55,000

Margin of safety as a percentage = $\dfrac{\text{Margin of safety in units}}{\text{Expected sales in units}}$

 = $\dfrac{5{,}500 \text{ pairs}}{8{,}000 \text{ pairs}}$

 = 68.75%

Fleet Foot's margin of safety is quite high. Sales have to fall by more than 5,500 units (or $55,000) before Fleet incurs a loss. Fleet will continue to earn a profit unless sales drop by more than 68.75%.

Requirement 2

At its current level of volume, Fleet's operating income is as follows:

Contribution margin (8,000 pairs × $4 per pair)...............	$ 32,000
Less: Fixed expenses...	10,000
Operating income...	$ 22,000

Fleet's operating leverage factor at this level of sales is computed as follows:

$$\text{Operating leverage factor} = \frac{\text{Contribution margin}}{\text{Operating income}}$$

$$= \frac{\$32,000}{\$22,000}$$

$$= 1.45 \text{ (rounded)}$$

If sales volume declines by 25%, operating income will decline by 36.25% (Fleet's operating leverage factor of 1.45 multiplied by 25%).

Requirement 3

If Fleet drops its sales price to $9 per pair, its contribution margin per pair declines to $3 (sales price of $9 − variable cost of $6). Each sale contributes less toward covering fixed costs. Fleet's new breakeven point *increases* to 3,334 pairs of socks ($10,000 fixed costs ÷ $3 unit contribution margin).

Requirement 4

	A	B	C	D
	Calculating Weighted-Average Contribution Margin per Unit	**Hiking Socks**	**Dress Socks**	**Total in "basket"**
1				
2	Sales price per unit	$ 9.00	$ 7.00	
3	Less: Variable cost per unit	6.00	2.75	
4	Contribution margin per unit	$ 3.00	$ 4.25	
5	Multiply by: Sales mix (number of units in "basket")	1	4	5
6	Contribution margin	$ 3.00	$ 17.00	$ 20.00
7				
8	Weighted-average contribution margin per unit ($20/5 units)			$ 4.00
9				

$$\text{Sales in total units} = \frac{\text{Fixed expenses} + \text{Operating income}}{\text{Weighted-average contribution margin per unit}}$$

$$= \frac{\$10,000 + \$0}{\$4}$$

$$= 2,500 \text{ pairs of socks}$$

Breakeven sales of dress socks (2,500 × 4/5)......................	2,000 pairs dress socks
Breakeven sales of hiking socks (2,500 × 1/5)....................	500 pairs hiking socks

By expanding its product line to include higher-margin dress socks, Fleet is able to decrease its breakeven point back to its original level (2,500 pairs). However, to achieve this breakeven point, Fleet must sell the planned ratio of four pairs of dress socks to every one pair of hiking socks.

END OF CHAPTER

Learning Objectives

- 1 Calculate the unit contribution margin and the contribution margin ratio
- 2 Use CVP analysis to find breakeven points and target profit volumes
- 3 Use CVP analysis to measure the impact of changing business conditions
- 4 Find breakeven and target profit volumes for multiproduct companies
- 5 Determine a firm's margin of safety, operating leverage, and most profitable cost structure

Accounting Vocabulary

Breakeven Point. (p. 386) The sales level at which operating income is zero: Total revenues = Total expenses.

Contribution Margin. (p. 383) Sales revenue minus variable expenses.

Contribution Margin Income Statement. (p. 383) An income statement that groups costs by behavior rather than function; it can be used only by internal management.

Contribution Margin Per Unit. (p. 384) The excess of the unit sales price over the variable cost per unit; also called unit contribution margin.

Contribution Margin Ratio. (p. 385) Ratio of contribution margin to sales revenue.

Cost-Volume-Profit (CVP) Analysis. (p. 382) Expresses the relationships among costs, volume, and profit or loss.

Indifference Point. (p. 410) The volume of sales at which a company would be indifferent between alternative cost structures because they would result in the same total cost.

Margin of Safety. (p. 406) Excess of expected sales over breakeven sales; the drop in sales a company can absorb without incurring an operating loss.

Operating Leverage. (p. 407) The relative amount of fixed and variable costs that make up a firm's total costs.

Operating Leverage Factor. (p. 408) At a given level of sales, the contribution margin divided by operating income; the operating leverage factor indicates the percentage change in operating income that will occur from a 1% change in sales volume.

Sales Mix. (p. 402) The combination of products that make up total sales.

Sensitivity Analysis. (p. 396) A "what-if" technique that asks what results will be if actual prices or costs change or if an underlying assumption changes.

Unit Contribution Margin. (p. 384) The excess of the unit sales price over the variable cost per unit: also called contribution margin per unit.

MyAccountingLab Go to http://myaccountinglab.com/ for the following Quick Check, Short Exercises, Exercises, and Problems. They are available with immediate grading, explanations of correct and incorrect answers, and interactive media that acts as your own online tutor.

Quick Check

1. (Learning Objective 1) The contribution margin is
   a. sales revenue minus fixed expenses.
   b. sales revenue minus cost of goods sold.
   c. sales revenue minus variable expenses.
   d. sales revenue minus operating expenses.

2. (Learning Objective 1) The contribution margin ratio is
   a. contribution margin divided by variable expenses.
   b. sales revenue divided by contribution margin.
   c. contribution margin divided by sales revenue.
   d. fixed expenses divided by variable expenses.

3. (Learning Objective 2) The formula to find the breakeven point or a target profit volume in terms of number of units that need to be sold is
   a. (Fixed expenses + Variable expenses) ÷ Sales revenue.
   b. (Fixed expenses + Operating income) ÷ Sales revenue.
   c. (Fixed expenses + Variable expenses) ÷ Contribution margin per unit.
   d. (Fixed expenses + Operating income) ÷ Contribution margin per unit.

4. (Learning Objective 2) On a CVP graph, the breakeven point is
   a. the intersection of the total revenue line and the fixed expense line.
   b. the intersection of the total revenue line and the total expense line.
   c. the area between the variable expense line and the fixed expense line.
   d. the area between the total revenue line and the total expense line.

5. (Learning Objective 3) All else being equal, if a company's variable expenses increase,
   a. its breakeven point will decrease.
   b. there will be no effect on the breakeven point.
   c. its contribution margin ratio will increase.
   d. its contribution margin ratio will decrease.

6. (Learning Objective 3) All else being equal, a decrease in a company's fixed expenses will:
   a. increase the sales needed to break even.
   b. increase the contribution margin.
   c. decrease the sales needed to break even.
   d. decrease the contribution margin.

7. (Learning Objective 4) Which of the following is true regarding a company that offers more than one product?
   a. Breakeven should be found using a simple average contribution margin.
   b. Breakeven should be found for each product individually.
   c. It has one unique breakeven point.
   d. The breakeven point is dependent on sales mix assumptions.

8. (Learning Objective 5) A company with a low operating leverage
   a. has relatively more risk than a company with high operating leverage.
   b. has relatively more variable costs than fixed costs.
   c. has relatively more fixed costs than variable costs.
   d. has an equal proportion of fixed and variable costs.

9. (Learning Objective 5) For a given level of sales, a company's operating leverage is defined as
   a. contribution margin ÷ operating income.
   b. sales revenue ÷ contribution margin.
   c. contribution margin ÷ sales.
   d. operating income ÷ contribution margin.

10. (Learning Objective 5) Which of the following is false regarding choosing between two cost structures:
    a. The indifference point is the point where total revenues equal total expenses.
    b. The indifference point is the point at which costs under two options are the same.
    c. Choose the higher operating leverage option when sales volume is expected to be higher than the indifference point.
    d. Choose the lower operating leverage option when sales volume is expected to be lower than the indifference point.

Quick Check Answers

1. c 2. c 3. d 4. b 5. d 6. c 7. d 8. b 9. a 10. a

Short Exercises

FunTime Cruiseline Data Set used for S7-1 through S7-10:

FunTime Cruiseline offers nightly dinner cruises departing from several cities on the eastern coast of the United States including Charleston, Baltimore, and Alexandria. Dinner cruise tickets sell for $50 per passenger. FunTime Cruiseline's variable cost of providing the dinner is $30 per passenger, and the fixed cost of operating the vessels (depreciation, salaries, docking fees, and other expenses) is $210,000 per month. The company's relevant range extends to 20,000 monthly passengers.

S7-1 Compute unit contribution margin and contribution margin ratio
(Learning Objective 1)

Use the information from the FunTime Cruiseline Data Set to compute the following:
a. What is the contribution margin per passenger?
b. What is the contribution margin ratio?
c. Use the unit contribution margin to project operating income if monthly sales total 17,000 passengers.
d. Use the contribution margin ratio to project operating income if monthly sales revenue totals $595,000.

S7-2 Project change in income *(Learning Objective 1)*

Use the information from the FunTime Cruiseline Data Set. If FunTime Cruiseline sells an additional 700 tickets, by what amount will its operating income increase (or operating loss decrease)?

S7-3 Find breakeven *(Learning Objective 2)*

Use the information from the FunTime Cruiseline Data Set to compute the number of dinner cruise tickets it must sell to breakeven and the sales dollars needed to breakeven.

S7-4 Find target profit volume *(Learning Objective 2)*

Use the information from the FunTime Cruiseline Data Set. If FunTime Cruiseline has a target operating income of $30,000 per month, how many dinner cruise tickets must the company sell?

S7-5 Changes in sales price and variable costs *(Learning Objective 3)*

Use the information from the FunTime Cruiseline Data Set.

1. Suppose FunTime Cruiseline cuts its dinner cruise ticket price from $50 to $45 to increase the number of passengers. Compute the new breakeven point in units and in sales dollars. Explain how changes in sales price generally affect the breakeven point.
2. Assume that FunTime Cruiseline does *not* cut the price. FunTime Cruiseline could reduce its variable costs by no longer serving an appetizer before dinner. Suppose this operating change reduces the variable expense from $30 to $20 per passenger. Compute the new breakeven point in units and in dollars. Explain how changes in variable costs generally affect the breakeven point.

S7-6 Changes in fixed costs *(Learning Objective 3)*

Use the information from the FunTime Cruiseline Data Set. Suppose FunTime Cruiseline embarks on a cost reduction drive and slashes fixed expenses from $210,000 per month to $150,000 per month.

1. Compute the new breakeven point in units and in sales dollars.
2. Is the breakeven point higher or lower than in S7-3? Explain how changes in fixed costs generally affect the breakeven point.

S7-7 Compute weighted-average contribution margin *(Learning Objective 4)*

Use the information from the FunTime Cruiseline Data Set. Suppose FunTime Cruiseline decides to offer two types of dinner cruises: regular cruises and executive cruises. The executive cruise includes complimentary cocktails and a five-course dinner on the upper deck. Assume that fixed expenses remain at $210,000 per month and that the following ticket prices and variable expenses apply:

	Regular Cruise	Executive Cruise
Sales price per ticket	$50	$100
Variable expense per passenger	$30	$ 40

Assuming that FunTime Cruiseline expects to sell four regular cruises for every executive cruise, compute the weighted-average contribution margin per unit. Is it higher or lower than a *simple* average contribution margin? (A simple average is calculated by adding both contribution margins per passenger together and dividing by two.) Why? Is it higher or lower than the regular cruise contribution margin calculated in S7-1? Why? Will this new sales mix cause FunTime Cruiseline's breakeven point to increase or decrease from what it was when it sold only regular cruises?

S7-8 Continuation of S7-7: Breakeven *(Learning Objective 4)*

Refer to your answer to S7-7.

a. Compute the total number of dinner cruises that FunTime Cruiseline must sell to breakeven.
b. Compute the number of regular cruises and executive cruises the company must sell to breakeven.

S7-9 Compute margin of safety *(Learning Objective 5)*

Use the information from the FunTime Cruiseline Data Set. If FunTime Cruiseline sells 12,000 dinner cruises, compute the margin of safety

a. in units (dinner cruise tickets).
b. in sales dollars.
c. as a percentage of sales.

S7-10 Compute and use operating leverage factor *(Learning Objective 5)*

Use the information from the FunTime Cruiseline Data Set.

a. Compute the operating leverage factor when FunTime Cruiseline sells 12,000 dinner cruises.
b. If volume increases by 6%, by what percentage will operating income increase?
c. If volume decreases by 2%, by what percentage will operating income decrease?

S7-11 Calculate breakeven and target profit sales volumes *(Learning Objective 2)*

Boswell's Beanery is a locally owned specialty food product company in Northeast Ohio that has been in existence for over 30 years. Its products include flavored coffees and teas, dips, dressings, sauces, and seasonings. The company attends a variety of craft and other shows throughout the year and sets up a booth at each show to sell its products. Free samples are offered to show attendees, and the Boswell's booth is always packed. Shows that Boswell's attends include the Yankee Peddler Festival in Canal Fulton, Ohio, the Great Big Home + Garden Show at the Cleveland I-X Center, and the Ohio Mart at Stan Hywet in Akron, Ohio. Boswell's also sells its products online via its website.

Each of the shows that Boswell's attends has a different booth rental fee. Booth rental fees can range from $350 to $5,000 for each show.

Assume that the booth rental fee at the Great Big Home + Garden Show is $4,200 for the ten-day show and that Boswell's has an average contribution margin ratio of 40% on its products.

Questions

1. How much in sales does Boswell's need to break even on the Great Big Home + Garden Show, assuming that the booth rental fee is the only fixed cost of the show?
2. The Great Big Home + Garden Show runs for ten days. How much, on average, must Boswell's sell each day of the show to break even?
3. Assume that 100,000 people visit the home and garden show each year spread evenly throughout the ten-day period. If 5% of the attendees purchase from Boswell's at the show, how much must each customer purchase from Boswell's for the company to break even on the booth rental fee?
4. Assume now that Boswell's wants to make a target profit of $4,000 for the Great Big Home + Garden Show. What sales volume will allow Boswell's to achieve this target profit?

S7-12 Interpret a CVP graph *(Learning Objective 2)*

Describe what each letter stands for in the CVP graph.

The breakeven point is at ___I___ units and at ___J___ dollars of sales.

S7-13 Calculate impact of a change in selling price and sales volume on operating income *(Learning Objective 3)*

Angel Rain Gear sells monogrammed umbrellas on Etsy. Angel Rain Gear is currently selling 2,000 umbrellas a month at a price of $25 per umbrella. The variable cost of each umbrella sold includes $10 to purchase the merchandise from suppliers and a $3 commission paid to Etsy. Fixed costs are $2,500 per month. The company is considering raising the selling price of each umbrella to $30, but believes the number of umbrellas sold would drop by 25% as a result of the price increase. Should Angel Rain Gear raise the selling price of its umbrellas?

S7-14 Calculate breakeven for a multiproduct company *(Learning Objectives 1, 2, & 4)*

Popped! is a specialty popcorn store. It offers two varieties of popcorn: plain and flavored. The flavors range from Caramel Popcorn to Dark Chocolate Drizzled Popcorn to White Cheddar Popcorn. The plain popcorn sells for $2 per box and costs $0.80 per box to make. The flavored popcorn sells for $4 per box and costs $2.50 per box to make. Popped! has fixed costs per month of $3,240. Popped! sells 1 box of plain popcorn for every 4 boxes of flavored popcorn. How many boxes of plain popcorn and how many boxes of flavored popcorn must Popped! sell each month to break even?

S7-15 Compute margin of safety *(Learning Objective 5)*

Vicki sells authentic Amish quilts on her website. Suppose Vicki expects to sell 1,000 quilts during the coming year. Her average sales price per quilt is $250, and her average cost per quilt is $150. Her fixed expenses total $50,000. Compute her margin of safety

a. in units (quilts).
b. in sales dollars.
c. as a percentage of expected sales.

S7-16 Compute and use operating leverage factor *(Learning Objective 5)*

Use the data from S7-15 to compute Vicki's operating leverage factor at an expected sales level of 1,000 quilts. If sales volume increases 20%, by what percentage will her operating income change? Prove your answer by calculating operating income at a sales volume of 1,000 and a sales volume of 1,200.

S7-17 Calculating total costs under two different scenarios *(Learning Objective 5)*

The Cupcake Factory plans to open a new retail store in Austin, Texas. The store will sell specialty cupcakes for $6 per cupcake (each cupcake has a variable cost of $3). The company is negotiating its lease for the new store. The landlord has offered two leasing options: 1) a lease of $2,000 per month; or 2) a monthly lease cost of $800 plus 5% of the company's monthly sales revenue.

Requirements

1. If the Cupcake Factory plans to sell 3,400 cupcakes a month, which lease option would cost less each month? Why?
2. If the company plans to sell 5,200 cupcakes a month, which lease option would be more attractive? Why?

S7-18 Identify ethical standards violated *(Learning Objectives 1, 2, 3, 4, & 5)* **ETHICS**

For each of the situations listed, identify the primary standard from the IMA Statement of Ethical Professional Practice that is violated (competence, confidentiality, integrity, or credibility). Refer to Exhibit 1-7 for the complete standard.

1. Paige is an accountant for Brookdale Natural Foods, a national grocery chain. Paige prepares internal reports with the breakeven volumes for each division listed. She does not explain (or provide disclosure) that the breakeven numbers listed are based on the sales mix from the past year, even though the sales mix is expected to change this year. If the sales mix during the current year were to change, breakeven volumes would be significantly impacted.
2. Joe and Alex work at the same company. Joe, the manager of a production department, buys lunch for Alex, who works in Accounting. Alex is preparing the monthly projections for the various production departments. Joe wants Alex to be

conservative in his estimates of variable costs, so that Joe is more likely to obtain funding for an upcoming project.

3. Lindsay works in Accounting at a chain of car dealerships. Her best friend, Kasey, is looking for a new car. Lindsay shares the actual dealer variable cost of the model with Kasey so that Kasey can negotiate a better deal.

4. Sierra provides reports to key decision makers based on CVP assumptions despite knowing that the decision makers are looking at situations that would be outside of the company's current relevant range.

5. Connor's company has signed him up for outside training on operating leverage and cost structures. Connor decides to skip the training, figuring that he already does his job well and does not need continuing education.

EXERCISES Group A

E7-19A Prepare contribution margin income statements *(Learning Objective 1)*

Jamison Travel uses the contribution margin income statement internally. Jamison's first-quarter results are as follows:

	A	B	C	D
1	Jamison Travel			
2	Contribution Margin Income Statement			
3	Three Months Ended March 31			
4				
5	Sales revenue	$ 525,000		
6	Less: Variable expenses	210,000		
7	Contribution margin	$ 315,000		
8	Less: Fixed expenses	172,200		
9	Operating income	$ 142,800		
10				

Jamison's relevant range is sales of between $120,000 and $630,000.

Requirements

1. Prepare contribution margin income statements at sales levels of $230,000 and $400,000. (*Hint*: Use the contribution margin ratio.)
2. Compute breakeven sales in dollars.

E7-20A Work backward to find missing information *(Learning Objectives 1 & 2)*

Colton Dry Cleaners has determined the following about its costs: Total variable expenses are $42,000, total fixed expenses are $30,000, and the sales revenue needed to break even is $50,000. Determine the company's current 1) sales revenue and 2) operating income. (*Hint*: First, find the contribution margin ratio; then prepare the contribution margin income statement.)

E7-21A Find breakeven and target profit volume *(Learning Objectives 1 & 2)*

Socks Unlimited produces sports socks. The company has fixed expenses of $85,000 and variable expenses of $1.20 per package. Each package sells for $2.00.

Requirements

1. Compute the contribution margin per package and the contribution margin ratio.
2. Find the breakeven point in units and in dollars.
3. Find the number of packages Socks Unlimited needs to sell to earn a $22,000 operating income.

E7-22A Continuation of E7-21A: Changing costs *(Learning Objective 3)*

Refer to Socks Unlimited in E7-21A. If the company can decrease its variable costs to $1.00 per package by increasing its fixed costs to $100,000, how many packages will it have to sell to generate $22,000 of operating income? Is this more or less than before? Why?

Cost-Volume-Profit Analysis 421

E7-23A Find breakeven and target profit volume *(Learning Objectives 1 & 2)*

Owner Yang Wong is considering franchising her Noodle Time restaurant concept. She believes people will pay $6.50 for a large bowl of noodles. Variable costs are $1.95 a bowl. Wong estimates monthly fixed costs for franchisees at $8,400.

Requirements

1. Find a franchisee's breakeven sales in dollars.
2. Is franchising a good idea for Wong if franchisees want a minimum monthly operating income of $7,000 and Wong believes that most locations could generate $26,000 in monthly sales?

E7-24A Continuation of E7-23A: Changing business conditions *(Learning Objective 3)*

Refer to Noodle Time in E7-23A. Wong did franchise her restaurant concept. Because of Noodle Time's success, Noodles 'n More has come on the scene as a competitor. To maintain its market share, Noodle Time will have to lower its sales price to $6.00 per bowl. At the same time, Noodle Time hopes to increase each restaurant's volume to 6,000 bowls per month by embarking on a marketing campaign. Each franchise will have to contribute $500 per month to cover the advertising costs. Prior to these changes, most locations were selling 5,500 bowls per month.

Requirements

1. What was the average restaurant's operating income before these changes?
2. Assuming that the price cut and advertising campaign are successful at increasing volume to the projected level, will the franchisees still earn their target profit of $7,000 per month? Show your calculations.

E7-25A Compute breakeven and project income *(Learning Objectives 1 & 2)*

Robert's Steel Parts produces parts for the automobile industry. The company has monthly fixed expenses of $720,000 and a contribution margin of 90% of revenues.

Requirements

1. Compute Robert's Steel Parts' monthly breakeven sales in dollars.
2. Use the contribution margin ratio to project operating income (or loss) if revenues are $540,000 and if they are $1,040,000.
3. Do the results in Requirement 2 make sense given the breakeven sales you computed in Requirement 1? Explain.

E7-26A Continuation of E7-25A: Changing business conditions *(Learning Objective 3)*

Refer to Robert's Steel Parts in E7-25A. Robert feels like he's in a giant squeeze play: The automotive manufacturers are demanding lower prices, and the steel producers have increased raw material costs. Robert's contribution margin has shrunk to 60% of revenues. The company's monthly operating income, prior to these pressures, was $216,000.

Requirements

1. To maintain this same level of profit, what sales volume (in sales revenue) must Robert now achieve?
2. Robert believes that his monthly sales revenue will go only as high as $1,040,000. He is thinking about moving operations overseas to cut fixed costs. If monthly sales are $1,040,000, by how much will he need to cut fixed costs to maintain his prior profit level of $216,000 per month?

E7-27A Sustainability and CVP concepts *(Learning Objective 3)* **SUSTAINABILITY**

Dunlap Garage Doors manufactures a premium garage door. Currently, the price and cost data associated with the premium garage door are as follows:

Average selling price per premium garage door	$ 2,200
Average variable manufacturing cost per door	$ 500
Average variable selling cost per door	$ 160
Total annual fixed costs	$308,000

Dunlap Garage Doors has undertaken several sustainability projects over the past few years. Management is currently evaluating whether to develop a comprehensive software control system for its manufacturing operations that would significantly reduce scrap and waste generated during the manufacturing process. If the company were to implement this software control system in its manufacturing operations, use of the software control system would result in an increase of $70,400 in its annual fixed costs, while the average variable manufacturing cost per door would drop by $220.

Requirements

1. What is the company's current breakeven in units and in dollars?
2. If the company expects to sell 260 premium garage doors in the upcoming year, and it does not develop the software control system, what is its expected operating income from premium garage doors?
3. If the software control system were to be developed and implemented, what would be the company's new breakeven point in units and in dollars?
4. If the company expects to sell 260 premium garage doors in the upcoming year, and it develops the software control system, what is its expected operating income from premium garage doors?
5. If the company expects to sell 260 premium garage doors in the upcoming year, do you think the company should implement the software control system? Why or why not? What factors should the company consider?

E7-28A Work backward to find new breakeven point *(Learning Objectives 2 & 3)*

Eduardo Industries is planning on purchasing a new piece of equipment that will increase the quality of its production. It hopes the increased quality will generate more sales. The company's contribution margin ratio is 40%, and its current breakeven point is $350,000 in sales revenue. If the company's fixed expenses increase by $35,000 due to the equipment, what will its new breakeven point be (in sales revenue)?

E7-29A Calculate contribution margin and breakeven *(Learning Objectives 1, 2 & 5)*

The Ohio State Fair is one of the largest state fairs in the United States. It draws nearly one million visitors over the twelve-day period each July and August. The fair is a non-profit organization. It is self-supporting and needs, at a minimum, to break even by generating revenues through various activities.

Among the sources of revenue for The Ohio State Fair are the revenues generated from the food vendors. A number of food vendors offer a wide variety of fair foods to attendees, including funnel cakes, gyros, cotton candy, milkshakes, and corn dogs.

Assume the following schedule of fees for food vendors at the Ohio State Fair:

- $10 per linear foot for ground service fees (front footage × depth)
- 15% of concessions (food sales)
- $50 per 12-day parking permit
- $290 for 100-amp electrical service
- $50 per 12-day fair admittance pass (one is included with basic rental agreement)

Star Concessions is a vendor at the fair. It has a food booth that requires 15 feet of front frontage and is 12 feet deep. Star Concessions expects to have sales averaging $4,000 per day for each of the 12 days of the fair. It has a total of four employees who will work the fair throughout the entire 12-day period. Star Concessions pays for each employee's fair admission and parking. Assume that the employee wages for the 12-day period are expected to total $9,560.

Requirements

1. Of the fees listed in the schedule, which fees are variable with respect to the number of customers at the booth? Which fees are fixed?
2. What is the projected total fee that Star Concessions will need to pay to The Ohio State Fair assuming it meets its expected sales level for each of the 12 days of the fair?
3. Assume that variable costs are 60% of sales revenue. (This 60% includes the 15% concession fee charged by The Ohio State Fair.) How much in total sales revenue is needed for Star Concessions to break even?
4. Calculate Star Concessions' margin of safety both in dollars and percentage.

Cost-Volume-Profit Analysis

E7-30A Find consequence of rising fixed costs *(Learning Objectives 1 & 3)*

Mary Walker sells homemade knit scarves for $25 each at local craft shows. Her contribution margin ratio is 60%. Currently, the craft show entrance fees cost Mary $1,500 per year. The craft shows are raising their entrance fees by 25% next year. How many *extra* scarves will Mary have to sell next year just to pay for rising entrance fee costs?

E7-31A Extension of E7-30A: Multiproduct firm *(Learning Objective 4)*

Curtis Walker admired his wife's success at selling scarves at local craft shows (E7-30A), so he decided to make two types of plant stands to sell at the shows. Curtis makes twig stands out of downed wood from his backyard and the yards of his neighbors, so his variable cost is minimal (wood screws, glue, and so forth). However, Curtis has to purchase wood to make his oak plant stands. His unit prices and costs are as follows:

	Twig Stands	Oak Stands
Sales price	$14.00	$40.00
Variable cost	$ 2.00	$18.00

The twig stands are more popular, so Curtis sells four twig stands for every one oak stand. Mary charges her husband $350 to share her booth at the craft shows (after all, she has paid the entrance fees). How many of each plant stand does Curtis need to sell to break even? Will this affect the number of scarves Mary needs to sell to break even? Explain.

E7-32A Find breakeven for a multiproduct firm *(Learning Objective 4)*

Funtime Quadcopters plans to sell a standard quadcopter (toy drone) for $55 and a deluxe quadcopter for $85. Funtime purchases the standard quadcopter for $45 and the deluxe quadcopter for $65. Management expects to sell two deluxe quadcopters for every three standard quadcopters. The company's monthly fixed expenses are $11,900. How many of each type of quadcopter must Funtime sell monthly to break even? To earn $7,700?

E7-33A Breakeven and an advertising decision at a multiproduct company *(Learning Objectives 3 & 4)*

Wellington Medical Supply is a retailer of home medical equipment. Last year, Wellington's sales revenues totaled $6,300,000. Total expenses were $2,200,000. Of this amount, approximately $1,260,000 were variable, while the remainder were fixed. Since Wellington's offers thousands of different products, its managers prefer to calculate the breakeven point in terms of sales dollars rather than units.

Requirements

1. What is Wellington's current operating income?
2. What is Wellington's contribution margin ratio?
3. What is the company's breakeven point in sales dollars? (*Hint*: The contribution margin ratio calculated in Requirement 2 is already weighted by the company's actual sales mix.)
4. Wellington's top management is deciding whether to embark on a $190,000 advertising campaign. The marketing firm has projected annual sales volume to increase by 10% as a result of this campaign. Assuming that the projections are correct, what effect would this advertising campaign have on the company's annual operating income?

E7-34A Compute margin of safety and operating leverage *(Learning Objective 5)*

Terry's Towing Service has a monthly target operating income of $30,000. *Variable expenses* are 40% of sales, and monthly fixed expenses are $7,500.

Requirements

1. Compute the monthly margin of safety in dollars if the shop achieves its income goal.
2. Express Terry's margin of safety as a percentage of target sales.
3. What is Terry's operating leverage factor at the target level of operating income?
4. Assume that the company reaches its target. By what percentage will the company's operating income fall if sales volume declines by 12%?

E7-35A Use operating leverage factor to find fixed costs *(Learning Objective 5)*

Mogadore Manufacturing had a 1.25 operating leverage factor when sales were $60,000. The company's contribution margin ratio was 25%. What were the company's fixed expenses?

E7-36A Calculating total costs under two different scenarios *(Learning Objective 5)*

The Golden Candle Company plans to open a new retail store in Lewiston, Maine. The store will sell specialty candles for an average of $15 each. The average variable costs per candle are as follows:

- Wax $4
- Other additives $2
- Base $1

The company is negotiating its lease for the new location. The landlord has offered two leasing options:

Option A) a lease of $2,400 per month; or

Option B) a monthly lease cost of $1,200 plus 20% of the company's monthly sales revenue.

The company expects to sell approximately 350 candles per month.

Requirements

1. Which lease option is more attractive for the company under its current sales expectations? Calculate the total lease cost under:
   - Option A
   - Option B
2. At what level of sales (in units) would the company be indifferent between the two lease options? Show your proof.
3. If the company's expected sales were 500 candles instead of the projection listed in the exercise, which lease options would be more favorable for the company? Why?

E7-37A Comprehensive CVP analysis *(Learning Objectives 1, 2, 3, 4, & 5)*

Marcus Allen is evaluating a business opportunity to sell premium car wax at vintage car shows. The wax is sold in 64-ounce tubs. Marcus can buy the premium wax at a wholesale cost of $29 per tub. He plans to sell the premium wax for $84 per tub. He estimates fixed costs such as travel costs, booth rental cost, and lodging to be $880 per car show.

Requirements

1. Determine the number of tubs Marcus must sell per show to break even.
2. Assume Marcus wants to earn a profit of $1,320 per show.
   a. Determine the sales volume in units necessary to earn the desired profit.
   b. Determine the sales volume in dollars necessary to earn the desired profit.
   c. Using the contribution margin format, prepare an income statement (condensed version) to confirm your answers to parts a and b.
3. Determine the margin of safety between the sales volume at the breakeven point and the sales volume required to earn the desired profit. Determine the margin of safety in both sales dollars, units, and as a percentage.

E7-38A Comprehensive CVP analysis *(Learning Objectives 1, 2, 3, 4, & 5)*

Ruby Company manufactures and sells a single product. The company's sales and expenses for last year follow:

	Total	Per Unit	%
Sales	$150,000	$30	?
Variable expenses	?	?	?
Contribution margin	?	?	?
Fixed expenses	13,500		
Operating income	$ 16,500		

Requirements

1. Fill in the missing numbers in the preceding table. Use the following questions to help fill in the missing numbers in the table:
   a. What is the total contribution margin?
   b. What is the total variable expense?
   c. How many units were sold?
   d. What is the per-unit variable expense?
   e. What is the per-unit contribution margin?
2. Answer the following questions about breakeven analysis:
   a. What is the breakeven point in units?
   b. What is the breakeven point in sales dollars?
3. Answer the following questions about target profit analysis and safety margin:
   a. How many units must the company sell in order to earn a profit of $48,000?
   b. Go back to the data given in the table. What is the current margin of safety in units?
   c. Again, go back to the data in the table. What is the margin of safety in sales dollars?
   d. Again, go back to the data in the table. What is the margin of safety in percentage?

E7-39A Comprehensive CVP analysis *(Learning Objectives 1, 2, 3, 4, & 5)*

Alpha Manufacturing manufactures 256GB SD cards (memory cards for mobile phones, digital cameras, and other devices). Price and cost data for a relevant range extending to 200,000 units per month are as follows:

Sales price per unit (current monthly sales volume is 130,000 units)	$ 20.00
Variable costs per unit:	
Direct materials	$ 6.70
Direct labor	$ 7.00
Variable manufacturing overhead	$ 2.00
Variable selling and administrative expenses	$ 1.80
Monthly fixed expenses:	
Fixed manufacturing overhead	$102,300
Fixed selling and administrative expenses	$187,800

Requirements

1. What is the company's contribution margin per unit? Contribution margin percentage? Total contribution margin?
2. What would the company's monthly operating income be if the company sold 160,000 units?
3. What would the company's monthly operating income be if the company had sales of $4,500,000?
4. What is the breakeven point in units? In sales dollars?
5. How many units would the company have to sell to earn a target monthly profit of $260,100?
6. Management is currently in contract negotiations with the labor union. If the negotiations fail, direct labor costs will increase by 10% and fixed costs will increase by $22,500 per month. If these costs increase, how many units will the company have to sell each month to break even?
7. Return to the original data for this question and the rest of the questions. What is the company's current operating leverage factor (round to two decimals)?
8. If sales volume increases by 7%, by what percentage will operating income increase?
9. What is the company's current margin of safety in sales dollars? What is its margin of safety as a percentage of sales?

10. Say the company adds a second size of SD card (512GB in addition to 256GB). A 512GB SD card will sell for $45 and have variable cost per unit of $28 per unit. The expected sales mix is six of the 256GB SD cards for every one of the 512GB SD cards. Given this sales mix, how many of each type of SD card will the company need to sell to reach its target monthly profit of $260,100? Is this volume higher or lower than previously needed (in Question 5) to achieve the same target profit? Why?

EXERCISES Group B

E7-40B Prepare contribution margin income statements *(Learning Objective 1)*

Hopper Travel uses the contribution margin income statement internally. Hopper's second-quarter results are as follows:

	A	B
1	Hopper Travel	
2	Contribution Margin Income Statement	
3	Three Months Ended June 30	
4		
5	Sales revenue	$ 500,000
6	Less: Variable expenses	120,000
7	Contribution margin	$ 380,000
8	Less: Fixed expenses	171,000
9	Operating income	$ 209,000

Hopper's relevant range is sales of between $100,000 and $640,000.

Requirements

1. Prepare contribution margin income statements at sales levels of $200,000 and $420,000. (*Hint:* Use the contribution margin ratio.)
2. Compute breakeven sales in dollars.

E7-41B Work backward to find missing information *(Learning Objectives 1 & 2)*

Douglas Dry Cleaners has determined the following about its costs: Total variable expenses are $30,000, total fixed expenses are $28,000, and the sales revenue needed to break even is $35,000. Determine the company's current 1) sales revenue and 2) operating income. (*Hint:* First, find the contribution margin ratio; then prepare the contribution margin income statement.)

E7-42B Find breakeven and target profit volume *(Learning Objectives 1 & 2)*

Socks Incorporated produces sports socks. The company has fixed expenses of $100,000 and variable expenses of $1.00 per package. Each package sells for $2.00.

Requirements

1. Compute the contribution margin per package and the contribution margin ratio.
2. Find the breakeven point in units and in dollars.
3. Find the number of packages that Socks Incorporated needs to sell to earn a $23,000 operating income.

E7-43B Continuation of E7-42B: Changing costs *(Learning Objective 3)*

Refer to Socks Incorporated in E7-42B. If Socks Incorporated can decrease its variable costs to $0.80 per package by increasing its fixed costs to $125,000, how many packages will it have to sell to generate $23,000 of operating income? Is this more or less than before? Why?

Cost-Volume-Profit Analysis

E7-44B Find breakeven and target profit volume *(Learning Objectives 1 & 2)*

Owner Yuning Zhu is considering franchising her Oodles of Noodles restaurant concept. She believes people will pay $7.00 for a large bowl of noodles. Variable costs are $2.45 a bowl. Zhu estimates monthly fixed costs for franchisees at $7,800.

Requirements

1. Find a franchisee's breakeven sales in dollars.
2. Is franchising a good idea for Zhu if franchisees want a minimum monthly operating income of $7,150 and Zhu believes most locations could generate $21,500 in monthly sales?

E7-45B Continuation of E7-44B: Changing business conditions *(Learning Objective 3)*

Refer to Oodles of Noodles in E7-44B. Since franchising Oodles of Noodles, the restaurant has not been very successful due to The Noodle Company coming on the scene as a competitor. To increase its market share, Oodles of Noodles will have to lower its sales price to $6.50 per bowl. At the same time, Oodles of Noodles hopes to increase each restaurant's volume to 5,000 bowls per month by embarking on a marketing campaign. Each franchise will have to contribute $400 per month to cover the advertising costs. Prior to these changes, most locations were selling 4,500 bowls per month.

Requirements

1. What was the average restaurant's operating income before these changes?
2. Assuming the price cut and advertising campaign are successful at increasing volume to the projected level, will the franchisees earn their target profit of $7,150 per month?

E7-46B Compute breakeven and project income *(Learning Objectives 1 & 2)*

Oleg's Steel Parts produces parts for the automobile industry. The company has monthly fixed expenses of $750,000 and a contribution margin of 75% of revenues.

Requirements

1. Compute Oleg's Steel Parts' monthly breakeven sales in dollars.
2. Project operating income (or loss) if revenues are $550,000 and if they are $1,050,000.
3. Do the results in Requirement 2 make sense given the breakeven sales you computed in Requirement 1? Explain.

E7-47B Continuation of E7-46B: Changing business conditions *(Learning Objective 3)*

Refer to Oleg's Steel Parts in E7-46B. Oleg feels like he's in a giant squeeze play: The automotive manufacturers are demanding lower prices, and the steel producers have increased raw material costs. Oleg's contribution margin has shrunk to 45% of revenues. Oleg's monthly operating income, prior to these pressures, was $37,500.

Requirements

1. To maintain this same level of profit, what sales volume (in sales revenue) must Oleg now achieve?
2. Oleg believes that his monthly sales revenue will only go as high as $1,050,000. He is thinking about moving operations overseas to cut fixed costs. If monthly sales are $1,050,000, by how much will he need to cut fixed costs to maintain his prior profit level of $37,500 per month?

E7-48B Sustainability and CVP *(Learning Objective 3)*   **SUSTAINABILITY**

Kirby Garage Doors manufactures a premium garage door. Currently, the price and cost data associated with the premium garage door are as follows:

Average selling price per premium garage door	$ 3,000
Average variable manufacturing cost per door	$ 540
Average variable selling cost per door	$ 210
Total annual fixed costs	$270,000

Kirby Garage Doors has undertaken several sustainability projects over the past few years. Management is currently evaluating whether to develop a comprehensive software control system for its manufacturing operations that would significantly reduce scrap and waste generated during the manufacturing process. If the company were to implement this software control system in its manufacturing operations, use of the software control system would result in an increase of $30,000 in its annual fixed costs, while the average variable manufacturing cost per door would drop by $150.

Requirements

1. What is the company's current breakeven in units and in dollars?
2. If the company expects to sell 330 premium garage doors in the upcoming year, and it does not develop the software control system, what is its expected operating income from premium garage doors?
3. If the software control system were to be developed and implemented, what would be the company's new breakeven point in units and in dollars?
4. If the company expects to sell 330 premium garage doors in the upcoming year, and it develops the software control system, what is its expected operating income from premium garage doors?
5. If the company expects to sell 330 premium garage doors in the upcoming year, do you think the company should implement the software control system? Why or why not? What factors should the company consider?

E7-49B   Work backward to find new breakeven point *(Learning Objectives 2 & 3)*

Brewer Industries is planning on purchasing a new piece of equipment that will increase the quality of its production. It hopes the increased quality will generate more sales. The company's contribution margin ratio is 40%, and its current breakeven point is $250,000 in sales revenue. If the company's fixed expenses increase by $30,000 due to the equipment, what will its new breakeven point be (in sales revenue)?

E7-50B   Calculate contribution margin and breakeven *(Learning Objectives 1, 2, & 5)*

The Ohio State Fair is one of the largest state fairs in the United States. It draws nearly one million visitors over the twelve-day period each July and August. The fair is a nonprofit organization. It is self-supporting and needs, at a minimum, to break even by generating revenues through various activities.

Among the sources of revenue for The Ohio State Fair are the revenues generated from the food vendors. A number of food vendors offer a wide variety of fair foods to attendees, including funnel cakes, gyros, cotton candy, milkshakes, and corn dogs.

Assume the following schedule of fees for food vendors at The Ohio State Fair:

- $20 per linear foot for ground service fees (front footage x depth)
- 20% of concessions (food sales)
- $60 per 12-day parking permit
- $450 for 100-amp electrical service
- $30 per 12-day fair admittance pass (one is included with basic rental agreement)

Crystal Concessions is a vendor at the fair. It has a food booth that requires 15 feet of front frontage and is 10 feet deep. Crystal Concessions expects to have sales averaging $4,000 per day for each of the 12 days of the fair. It has a total of four employees who will work the fair throughout the entire 12-day period. Crystal Concessions pays for each employee's fair admission and parking. Assume that the employee wages for the 12-day period are expected to total $7,800.

Requirements

1. Of the fees listed in the schedule, which fees are variable with respect to the number of customers at the booth? Which fees are fixed?
2. What is the projected total fee that Crystal Concessions will need to pay to The Ohio State Fair assuming it meets its expected sales level for each of the 12 days of the fair?
3. Assume that variable costs are 75% of sales revenue. (This 75% includes the 20% concession fee charged by The Ohio State Fair.) How much in total sales revenue is needed for Crystal Concessions to break even?
4. Calculate Crystal Concessions' margin of safety both in dollars and percentage.

Cost-Volume-Profit Analysis 429

E7-51B Find consequence of rising fixed costs *(Learning Objectives 1 & 3)*

Debbie DeLozier sells homemade knit scarves for $15 each at local craft shows. Her contribution margin ratio is 60%. Currently, the craft show entrance fees cost Debbie $900 per year. The craft shows are raising their entrance fees by 10% next year. How many *extra* scarves will Debbie have to sell next year just to pay for rising entrance fee costs?

E7-52B Extension of E7-51B: Multiproduct firm *(Learning Objective 4)*

Chris DeLozier admired his wife's success at selling scarves at local craft shows (E7-51B), so he decided to make two types of plant stands to sell at the shows. Chris makes twig stands out of downed wood from his backyard and the yards of his neighbors, so his variable cost is minimal (wood screws, glue, and so forth). However, Chris has to purchase wood to make his oak plant stands. His unit prices and costs are as follows.

	Twig Stands	Oak Stands
Sales price	$17.00	$42.00
Variable cost	$ 3.50	$11.00

The twig stands are more popular, so Chris sells four twig stands for every one oak stand. Debbie charges her husband $255 to share her booths at the craft shows (after all, she has paid the entrance fees). How many of each plant stand does Chris need to sell to break even? Will this affect the number of scarves Debbie needs to sell to breakeven? Explain.

E7-53B Find breakeven for a multiproduct firm *(Learning Objective 4)*

Toyz Quadcopters plans to sell a standard quadcopter (toy drone) for $45 and a deluxe quadcopter for $55. Toyz purchases the standard quadcopter for $25 and the deluxe quadcopter for $35. Management expects to sell two deluxe quadcopters for every three standard quadcopters. The company's monthly fixed expenses are $19,000. How many of each type of quadcopter must Toyz sell monthly to break even? To earn $13,000?

E7-54B Breakeven and an advertising decision at a multiproduct company
(Learning Objectives 3 & 4)

Bangor Medical Supplies is a retailer of home medical equipment. Last year, Bangor's sales revenues totaled $6,200,000. Total expenses were $2,500,000. Of this amount, approximately $1,612,000 were variable, while the remainder were fixed. Since Bangor offers thousands of different products, its managers prefer to calculate the breakeven point in terms of sales dollars, rather than units.

Requirements

1. What is Bangor's current operating income?
2. What is Bangor's contribution margin ratio?
3. What is the company breakeven point in sales dollars? (*Hint:* The contribution margin ratio calculated in Requirement 2 is already weighted by the company's actual sales mix.) What does it mean?
4. Top management is deciding whether to embark on a $190,000 advertising campaign. The marketing firm has projected annual sales volume to increase by 16% as a result of this campaign. Assuming that the projections are correct, what effect would this advertising campaign have on Bangor's annual operating income?

E7-55B Compute margin of safety and operating leverage *(Learning Objective 5)*

Shannon's Towing Service has a monthly target operating income of $15,000. *Variable expenses* are 70% of sales, and monthly fixed expenses are $12,000.

Requirements

1. Compute the monthly margin of safety in dollars if the shop achieves its income goal.
2. Express Shannon's margin of safety as a percentage of target sales.
3. What is Shannon's operating leverage factor at the target level of operating income?
4. Assume that the company reaches its target. By what percentage will the company's operating income fall if sales volume declines by 8%?

E7-56B Use operating leverage factor to find fixed costs (Learning Objective 5)

Benson Manufacturing had a 1.25 operating leverage factor when sales were $50,000. The company's contribution margin ratio was 20%. What were the company's fixed expenses?

E7-57B Calculating total costs under two different scenarios (Learning Objectives 5)

The Glow Factory plans to open a new retail store in Racine, Wisconsin. The store will sell specialty candles for an average of $25 each. The average variable costs per candle are as follows:

- Wax $8
- Other additives $3
- Base $2

The company is negotiating its lease for the new location. The landlord has offered two leasing options:

> Option A) a lease of $4,500 per month; or
> Option B) a monthly lease cost of $1,500 plus 20% of the company's monthly sales revenue.

The company expects to sell approximately 400 candles per month.

Requirements

1. Which lease option is more attractive for the company under its current sales expectations? Calculate the total lease cost under:
   a. Option A
   b. Option B
2. At what level of sales (in units) would the company be indifferent between the two lease options? Show your proof.
3. If the company's expected sales were 800 candles instead of the projection listed in the exercise, which lease option would be more favorable for the company? Why?

E7-58B Comprehensive CVP analysis (Learning Objectives 1, 2, 3, 4, & 5)

Jake Spahr is evaluating a business opportunity to sell premium car wax at vintage car shows. The wax is sold in 64-ounce tubs. Jake can buy the premium wax at a wholesale cost of $32 per tub. He plans to sell the premium wax for $62 per tub. He estimates fixed costs such as travel costs, booth rental cost, and lodging to be $600 per car show.

Requirements

1. Determine the number of tubs Jake must sell per show to break even.
2. Assume Jake wants to earn a profit of $900 per show.
   a. Determine the sales volume in units necessary to earn the desired profit.
   b. Determine the sales volume in dollars necessary to earn the desired profit.
   c. Using the contribution margin format, prepare an income statement (condensed version) to confirm your answers to parts a and b.
3. Determine the margin of safety between the sales volume at the breakeven point and the sales volume required to earn the desired profit. Determine the margin of safety in both sales dollars, units, and as a percentage.

E7-59B Comprehensive CVP analysis (Learning Objectives 1, 2, 3, 4, & 5)

Sunflower Company manufactures and sells a single product. The company's sales and expenses for last year follow:

	Total	Per Unit	%
Sales	$115,000	$50	?
Variable expenses	?	?	?
Contribution margin	?	?	?
Fixed expenses	11,500		
Operating income	$ 46,000		

Requirements

1. Fill in the missing numbers in the preceding table. Use the following questions to help fill in the missing numbers in the table:
   a. What is the total contribution margin?
   b. What is the total variable expense?
   c. How many units were sold?
   d. What is the per-unit variable expense?
   e. What is the per-unit contribution margin?
2. Answer the following questions about breakeven analysis:
   a. What is the breakeven point in units?
   b. What is the breakeven point in sales dollars?
3. Answer the following questions about target profit analysis and safety margin:
   a. How many units must the company sell in order to earn a profit of $58,000?
   b. Go back to the data given in the table. What is the current margin of safety in units?
   c. Again, go back to the data in the table. What is the margin of safety in sales dollars?
   d. Again, go back to the data in the table. What is the margin of safety in percentage?

E7-60B Comprehensive CVP analysis *(Learning Objectives 1, 2, 3, 4, & 5)*

Gamma Manufacturing manufactures 256GB SD cards (memory cards for mobile phones, digital cameras, and other devices). Price and cost data for a relevant range extending to 200,000 units per month are as follows:

Sales price per unit (current monthly sales volume is 100,000 units)	$ 25.00
Variable costs per unit:	
Direct materials	$ 7.50
Direct labor	$ 5.00
Variable manufacturing overhead	$ 3.30
Variable selling and administrative expenses	$ 2.20
Monthly fixed expenses:	
Fixed manufacturing overhead	$241,600
Fixed selling and administrative expenses	$357,600

Requirements

1. What is the company's contribution margin per unit? Contribution margin percentage? Total contribution margin?
2. What would the company's monthly operating income be if the company sold 130,000 units?
3. What would the company's monthly operating income be if the company had sales of $4,500,000?
4. What is the breakeven point in units? In sales dollars?
5. How many units would the company have to sell to earn a target monthly profit of $259,700?
6. Management is currently in contract negotiations with the labor union. If the negotiations fail, direct labor costs will increase by 10% and fixed costs will increase by $23,500 per month. If these costs increase, how many units will the company have to sell each month to break even?
7. Return to the original data for this question and the rest of the questions. What is the company's current operating leverage factor (round to two decimals)?
8. If sales volume increases by 7%, by what percentage will operating income increase?
9. What is the company's current margin of safety in sales dollars? What is its margin of safety as a percentage of sales?
10. Say the company adds a second size of SD card (512GB in addition to 256GB). A 512GB SD card will sell for $50 and have variable cost per unit of $28 per unit. The expected sales mix is four of the 256GB SD cards for every one of the 512GB SD cards. Given this sales mix, how many of each type of SD card will the company need to sell to reach its target monthly profit of $259,700? Is this volume higher or lower than previously needed (in Question 5) to achieve the same target profit? Why?

PROBLEMS Group A

P7-61A Find missing data in CVP relationships *(Learning Objectives 1 & 2)*

The budgets of four companies yield the following information:

	Company			
	Q	R	S	T
Target sales	$680,000	$445,000	$224,000	$
Variable expenses	170,000			270,000
Fixed expenses		$159,000	$ 93,000	
Operating income (loss)	$150,000	$	$	$133,000
Units sold		106,800	12,500	18,000
Contribution margin per unit	$ 6.25	$	$ 8.96	$ 35.00
Contribution margin ratio		0.60		

Requirements

1. Fill in the blanks for each company.
2. Compute breakeven, in sales dollars, for each company. Which company has the lowest breakeven point in sales dollars? What causes the low breakeven point?

P7-62A Find breakeven and target profit and prepare income statements *(Learning Objectives 1 & 2)*

A traveling production of *Wicked* performs each year. The average show sells 1,400 tickets at $55 a ticket. There are 125 shows each year. The show has a cast of 45, each earning an average of $310 per show. The cast is paid only after each show. The other variable expense is program printing costs of $8 per guest. Annual fixed expenses total $829,600.

Requirements

1. Compute revenue and variable expenses for each show.
2. Use the income statement equation approach to compute the number of shows needed annually to break even.
3. Use the shortcut unit contribution margin approach to compute the number of shows needed annually to earn a profit of $6,533,100. Is this goal realistic? Give your reason.
4. Prepare *Wicked*'s contribution margin income statement for 125 shows each year. Report only two categories of expenses: variable and fixed.

P7-63A Comprehensive CVP problem *(Learning Objectives 1, 2, & 5)*

Spirit Calendars imprints calendars with college names. The company has fixed expenses of $1,095,000 each month plus variable expenses of $4.00 per carton of calendars. Of the variable expenses, 73% is cost of goods sold, while the remaining 27% relates to variable operating expenses. The company sells each carton of calendars for $12.00.

Requirements

1. Compute the number of cartons of calendars that Spirit Calendars must sell each month to break even.
2. Compute the dollar amount of monthly sales that the company needs in order to earn $312,000 in operating income (round the contribution margin ratio to two decimal places).
3. Prepare the company's contribution margin income statement for June for sales of 450,000 cartons of calendars.
4. What is June's margin of safety (in dollars)? What is the operating leverage factor at this level of sales?
5. By what percentage will operating income change if July's sales volume is 10% higher? Prove your answer.

P7-64A Compute breakeven, prepare CVP graph, and respond to change
(Learning Objectives 1, 2, & 3)

DoubleTyme Investors is opening an office in Jeffersonville, Indiana. Fixed monthly expenses are office rent ($2,300), depreciation on office furniture ($300), utilities ($250), special telephone lines ($660), a subscription to an online brokerage service ($690), and the salary of a financial planner ($7,800). Variable expenses include payments to the financial planner (10% of revenue), advertising (5% of revenue), supplies and postage (2% of revenue), and usage fees for the telephone lines and computerized brokerage service (3% of revenue).

Requirements

1. Compute the investment firm's breakeven revenue in dollars. If the average trade leads to $500 in revenue for DoubleTyme, how many trades must it make to break even?
2. Compute dollar revenues needed to earn monthly operating income of $3,200.
3. Graph DoubleTyme's CVP relationships. Assume that an average trade leads to $500 in revenue for the firm. Show the breakeven point, sales revenue line, fixed expense line, total expense line, operating loss area, operating income area, and sales in units (trades) and dollars when monthly operating income of $3,200 is earned. The graph should range from 0 to 40 units (trades).
4. Assume that the average revenue that DoubleTyme Investors earns decreases to $375 per trade. How does this affect the breakeven point in number of trades?

P7-65A Calculate impact of various changes on operating income *(Learning Objectives 2 & 3)*

Casual Seating Company is currently selling 2,000 oversized bean bag chairs a month at a price of $85 per chair. The variable cost of each chair sold includes $60 to purchase the bean bag chairs from suppliers and a $4 sales commission. Fixed costs are $10,000 per month.

The company is considering making several operational changes and wants to know how the change will impact its operating income.

Requirements:

1. Prepare the company's current contribution margin income statement.
2. Calculate the change in operating income that would result from implementing each of the following independent strategy alternatives. Compare each alternative to the current operating income as you calculated in Requirement 1. Consider each alternative separately.
    a. **Alternative 1:** The company believes volume will increase by 15% if salespeople are paid a commission of 10% of the sales price rather than the current $4 per unit.
    b. **Alternative 2:** The company believes that spending an additional $5,000 on advertising would increase sales volume by 10%.
    c. **Alternative 3:** The company is considering raising the selling price to $100, but believes volume would drop by 25% as a result.
    d. **Alternative 4:** The company would like to source the product from domestic suppliers who charge $12 more for each unit. Management believes that the "Made in the USA" label would increase sales volume by 15% and would allow the company to increase the sales price by $5 per unit. In addition, the company would have to spend an additional $3,000 in marketing costs to get the word out to potential customers of this change.

P7-66A CVP analysis at a multiproduct firm *(Learning Objectives 4 & 5)*

The contribution margin income statement of Morgantown Coffee for October follows:

	A	B	C
1	**Morgantown Coffee**		
2	**Contribution Margin Income Statement**		
3	**Month Ended October 31**		
4			
5	Sales revenue		$ 95,000
6	Less variable expenses:		
7	Cost of goods sold	$ 33,500	
8	Marketing expense	12,000	
9	General and administrative expense	2,000	47,500
10	Contribution margin		$ 47,500
11	Less fixed expenses:		
12	Marketing expense	$ 19,125	
13	General and administrative expense	3,375	22,500
14	Operating income		$ 25,000
15			

Morgantown Coffee sells three small coffees for every large coffee. A small coffee sells for $2.00, with a variable expense of $1.00. A large coffee sells for $4.00, with a variable expense of $2.00.

Requirements

1. Determine the coffee shop's monthly breakeven point in the numbers of small coffees and large coffees. Prove your answer by preparing a summary contribution margin income statement at the breakeven level of sales. Show only two categories of expenses: variable and fixed.
2. Compute the coffee shop's margin of safety in dollars.
3. Use the coffee shop's operating leverage factor (using the October contribution margin income statement) to determine its new operating income if sales volume increases 13%. Prove your results using the contribution margin income statement format. Assume that sales mix remains unchanged.

PROBLEMS Group B

P7-67B Find missing data in CVP relationships *(Learning Objectives 1 & 2)*

The budgets of four companies yield the following information:

	Company			
	Q	R	S	T
Target sales	$757,500	$445,000	$162,500	$ _____
Variable expenses	242,400	_____	_____	360,000
Fixed expenses	_____	159,000	81,000	_____
Operating income (loss)	$175,100	$ _____	$ _____	$152,000
Units sold	_____	106,800	15,625	20,000
Contribution margin per unit	$ 6.06	$ _____	$ 8.32	$ 32.00
Contribution margin ratio	_____	0.60	_____	_____

Requirements

1. Fill in the blanks for each company.
2. Compute breakeven, in sales dollars, for each company. Which company has the lowest breakeven point in sales dollars? What causes the low breakeven point?

P7-68B Find breakeven and target profit and prepare income statements
(Learning Objectives 1 & 2)

A traveling production of *Grease* performs each year. The average show sells 1,400 tickets at $50 per ticket. There are 100 shows a year. The show has a cast of 40, each earning an average of $340 per show. The cast is paid only after each show. The other variable expense is program printing expenses of $8 per guest. Annual fixed expenses total $1,582,000.

Requirements

1. Compute revenue and variable expenses for each show.
2. Compute the number of shows needed annually to break even.
3. Compute the number of shows needed annually to earn a profit of $4,836,400. Is this goal realistic? Give your reason.
4. Prepare *Grease*'s contribution margin income statement for 100 shows each year. Report only two categories of expenses: variable and fixed.

P7-69B Comprehensive CVP problem *(Learning Objectives 1, 2, & 5)*

Whoosh Calendars imprints calendars with college names. The company has fixed expenses of $1,095,000 each month plus variable expenses of $6.50 per carton of calendars. Of the variable expenses, 68% is cost of goods sold, while the remaining 32% relates to variable operating expenses. The company sells each carton of calendars for $16.50.

Requirements

1. Compute the number of cartons of calendars that Whoosh Calendars must sell each month to break even.
2. Compute the dollar amount of monthly sales that the company needs in order to earn $308,000 in operating income (round the contribution margin ratio to two decimal places).
3. Prepare the company's contribution margin income statement for June for sales of 450,000 cartons of calendars.
4. What is June's margin of safety (in dollars)? What is the operating leverage factor at this level of sales?
5. By what percentage will operating income change if July's sales volume is 16% higher? Prove your answer.

P7-70B Compute breakeven, prepare CVP graph, and respond to change
(Learning Objectives 1, 2, & 3)

William Investors is opening an office in Boise, Idaho. Fixed monthly costs are office rent ($2,100), depreciation on office furniture ($260), utilities ($280), special telephone lines ($600), a subscription to an online brokerage service ($640), and the salary of a financial planner ($3,120). Variable expenses include payments to the financial planner (16% of revenue), advertising (7% of revenue), supplies and postage (3% of revenue), and usage fees for the telephone lines and computerized brokerage service (6% of revenue).

Requirements

1. Compute the investment firm's breakeven revenue in dollars. If the average trade leads to $500 in revenue for William Investors, how many trades must be made to break even?
2. Compute dollar revenues needed to earn monthly operating income of $3,500.
3. Graph William's CVP relationships. Assume that an average trade leads to $500 in revenue for William Investors. Show the breakeven point, sales revenue line, fixed expense line, total expense line, operating loss area, operating income area, and sales in units (trades) and dollars when monthly operating income of $3,500 is earned. The graph should range from 0 to 40 units (trades).
4. Assume that the average revenue William Investors earns decreases to $400 per trade. How does this affect the breakeven point in number of trades?

P7-71B Calculate impact of various changes on operating income (Learning Objectives 2 & 3)

Comfy Seating Company is currently selling 3,500 oversized bean bag chairs a month at a price of $100 per chair. The variable cost of each chair sold includes $60 to purchase the bean bag chairs from suppliers and a $4 sales commission. Fixed costs are $6,000 per month.

The company is considering making several operational changes and wants to know how the change will impact its operating income.

Requirements

1. Prepare the company's current contribution margin income statement.
2. Calculate the change in operating income that would result from implementing each of the following independent strategy alternatives. Compare each alternative to the current operating income as you calculated in Requirement 1. Consider each alternative separately.
   a. **Alternative 1:** The company believes volume will increase by 15% if salespeople are paid a commission of 10% of the sales price rather than the current $4 per unit.
   b. **Alternative 2:** The company believes that spending an additional $5,000 on advertising would increase sales volume by 10%.
   c. **Alternative 3:** The company is considering raising the selling price to $120, but believes volume would drop by 25% as a result.
   d. **Alternative 4:** The company would like to source the product from domestic suppliers who charge $12 more for each unit. Management believes that the "Made in the USA" label would increase sales volume by 15% and would allow the company to increase the sales price by $5 per unit. In addition, the company would have to spend an additional $3,000 in marketing costs to get the word out to potential customers of this change.

P7-72B CVP analysis at a multiproduct firm (Learning Objectives 4 & 5)

The contribution margin income statement of Liberty Coffee for July follows:

	A	B	C
1	Liberty Coffee		
2	Contribution Margin Income Statement		
3	Month Ended July 31		
4			
5	Sales revenue		$ 144,000
6	Less variable expenses:		
7	Cost of goods sold	$ 57,000	
8	Marketing expense	12,000	
9	General and administrative expense	3,000	72,000
10	Contribution margin		$ 72,000
11	Less fixed expenses:		
12	Marketing expense	$ 35,700	
13	General and administrative expense	6,300	42,000
14	Operating income		$ 30,000
15			

Liberty Coffee sells three small coffees for every large coffee. A small coffee sells for $3.00, with a variable expense of $1.50. A large coffee sells for $5.00, with a variable expense of $2.50.

Requirements

1. Determine the coffee shop's monthly breakeven point in the numbers of small coffees and large coffees. Prove your answer by preparing a summary contribution margin income statement at the breakeven level of sales. Show only two categories of expenses: variable and fixed.
2. Compute the coffee shop's margin of safety in dollars.
3. Use the coffee shop's operating leverage factor (using the July contribution margin income statement) to determine its new operating income if sales volume increases 12%. Prove your results using the contribution margin income statement format. Assume that sales mix remains unchanged.

Serial Case

C7-73 Calculate breakeven and margin of safety after hotel renovation
(Learning Objective 2)

This case is a continuation of the Caesars Entertainment Corporation serial case that began in Chapter 1. Refer to the introductory story in chapter 1 (see page 43) for additional background. (The components of the Caesars serial case can be completed in any order.)

Caesars Palace® Las Vegas made headlines when it undertook a $75 million renovation. In mid-September 2015, the hotel closed its then-named Roman Tower, which was last updated in 2001, and started a major renovation of the 567 rooms housed in that tower. On January 1, 2016, the newly renamed Julius Tower reopened, replacing the Roman Tower. In addition to renovating the existing rooms and suites in the former Roman Tower, 20 guest rooms were added to the Roman Tower. With the renovation completed, Caesars expects the Julius Tower room rate to average around $149 per night. This increase, a $25 or 20.2% increase, reflects, in part, the room improvements.

Assume that the annual fixed operating costs for the Julius Tower in Caesars Palace® Las Vegas will be $5,000,000. This amount represents an increase of $200,000 per year compared to pre-renovation. Also assume that the variable cost per hotel room night after the renovation is $27; before the renovation, the variable cost per room night was $20.

The average hotel occupancy rate, in 2014, for Caesars Entertainment Corporation was 91.2%, according to its 2014 Form 10-K. By comparison, the average hotel occupancy rate in Las Vegas overall, for that same time period, was 86.8%, according to Stastia.com.

Requirements

1. What cost types, associated with a hotel room in the Julius Tower, are variable with respect to hotel room occupancy? What cost types are fixed with respect to hotel room occupancy?
2. Before the renovation, how many hotel room nights were needed to break even in the original Roman Tower (now Julius Tower)? Using Caesars' occupancy rate, what was the margin of safety in units before the renovation? What is the margin of safety in units if the Las Vegas hotel occupancy rate is used instead of Caesars' occupancy rate?
3. After the renovation, how many hotel room nights are needed to break even in the Julius Tower? Using Caesars' occupancy rate, what is the margin of safety in units after the renovation? What is the margin of safety in units if the Las Vegas hotel occupancy rate is used instead of Caesars' occupancy rate? Which hotel occupancy rate estimate is more appropriate in this case? Why?

CRITICAL THINKING

Discussion & Analysis

A7-74 Discussion Questions

1. Define breakeven point. Why is the breakeven point important to managers?
2. Describe four different ways cost-volume-profit analysis could be useful to management.
3. The purchasing manager for Rockwell Hall Bags has been able to purchase the material for its signature handbags for $9 less per bag than in the prior year. Keeping everything else the same, what effect would this reduction in material cost have on the breakeven point for Rockwell Hall Bags? Now assume that the sales manager decides to reduce the selling price of each handbag by $9. What would the net effect of both of these changes be on the breakeven point in units for Rockwell Hall Bags?
4. Describe three ways that cost-volume-profit concepts could be used by a service organization.
5. "Breakeven analysis isn't very useful to a company because companies need to do more than break even to survive in the long run." Explain why you agree or disagree with this statement.
6. What conditions must be met for cost-volume-profit analysis to be accurate?
7. Why is it necessary to calculate a weighted-average contribution margin ratio for a multi-product company when calculating the breakeven point for that company? Why can't all of the products' contribution margin ratios just be added together and averaged?
8. Is the contribution margin ratio of a grocery store likely to be higher or lower than that of a plastics manufacturer? Explain the difference in cost structure between a grocery store and a plastics manufacturer. How does the cost structure difference impact operating risk?
9. Alston Jewelry had sales revenues last year of $2.4 million, while its breakeven point (in dollars) was $2.2 million. What was Alston Jewelry's margin of safety in dollars? What does the term *margin of safety* mean? What can you discern about Alston Jewelry from its margin of safety?
10. Rondell Pharmacy is considering switching to the use of robots to fill prescriptions that consist of oral solids or medications in pill form. The robots will assist the human pharmacists and will reduce the number of human pharmacy workers needed. This change is expected to reduce the number of prescription filling errors, to reduce the customer's wait time, and to reduce the total overall costs. How does the use of the robots affect Rondell Pharmacy's cost structure? Explain the impact of this switch to robotics on Rondell Pharmacy's operating risk.
11. Suppose a company can replace the packing material it currently uses with a biodegradable packing material. The company believes this move to biodegradable packing materials will be well received by the general public. However, the biodegradable packing materials are more expensive than the current packing materials, and the contribution margin ratios of the related products will drop. What are the arguments for the company to use the biodegradable packing materials? What are the arguments for the company to not use the biodegradable materials? What do you think the company should do?
12. How can CVP techniques be used in supporting a company's sustainability efforts? Conversely, how might CVP be a barrier to sustainability efforts?

Application & Analysis

Mini Cases

A7-75 CVP for a Product

Select one product that you could make yourself. Examples of possible products could be cookies, birdhouses, jewelry, or custom T-shirts. Assume that you have decided to start a small business producing and selling this product. You will be applying the concepts of cost-volume-profit analysis to this potential venture.

Basic Discussion Questions

1. Describe your product. What market are you targeting this product for? What price will you sell your product for? Make projections of your sales in units over each of the upcoming five years.

2. Make a detailed list of all the materials needed to make your product. Include quantities needed of each material. Also include the cost of the material on a per-unit basis.

3. Make a list of all of the equipment you will need to make your product. Estimate the cost of each piece of equipment that you will need.

4. Make a list of all other expenses that would be needed to create your product. Examples of other expenses would be rent, utilities, and insurance. Estimate the cost of each of these expenses per year.

5. Now classify all of the expenses you have listed as being either fixed or variable. For mixed expenses, separate the expense into the fixed component and the variable component.

6. Calculate how many units of your product you will need to sell to break even in each of the five years you have projected.

7. Calculate the margin of safety in units for each of the five years in your projection.

8. Now decide how much you would like to make in before-tax operating income (target profit) in each of the upcoming five years. Calculate how many units you would need to sell in each of the upcoming years to meet these target profit levels.

9. How realistic is your potential venture? Do you think you would be able to break even in each of the projected five years? How risky is your venture (use the margin of safety to help answer this question). Do you think your target profits are achievable?

Decision Cases

A7-76 CVP analysis by an intern with an ethical dilemma *(Learning Objective 2)* **ETHICS**

Horner Work Wear, Inc., supplies uniforms for a variety of businesses. Collin Hoffman is a new intern in the Accounting Department at Horner. To expand sales, the company is considering paying commissions to its sales force. The controller, John Wallace, asks Collin to complete an analysis assuming sales would increase 25% under the proposed sales commission plan. This analysis should include 1) the new breakeven sales figure and 2) the operating profit under the new sales commission plan.

Collin does his best to perform the analysis. He is not exactly sure what he is doing but he does not want to appear like he does not understand accounting. After he gets his preliminary analysis finished, he calls his friend, Meghan Peyton, who is an accounting analyst at Scrubs and More, a competing uniform supplier. He knows Meghan from a church group and figures he can trust her. He tells her he is working on a new project and asks her if they can meet for dinner later, where he can ask her advice.

At dinner, Collin confesses to Meghan that he really does not know if he did his analysis correctly. Meghan assures him that she has worked on similar things at her company. She asks him if they can go over the analysis together. He readily agrees because this is just the type of help he had hoped to get. He shows her the spreadsheet he has been working on; the two of them discuss each item on the analysis. Collin explains his reasoning behind each calculation and his data assumptions. Meghan tells him that his analysis is thorough and agrees that he has done it all correctly as far as she can tell.

Now confident in his work, Collin turns in the proposed sales commission plan analysis the following day. His report ends with a recommendation that the new sales commission plan be undertaken, since it will lead to a significant increase in operating income with only a small increase in breakeven sales. John Wallace glances through the report and is impressed with the appearance of the report; it looks professional and complete. Since John has a lot of other work tasks, he approves the new sales commission plan without any further analysis or investigation.

When he is booking some payroll entries the following week, Collin realizes that he made an error in the CVP analysis he did for the sales commission project. He failed to include the monthly salaries of the sales staff in his computations. Collin is in a panic. If he tells John Wallace of his mistake, Collin is afraid he will not be offered a full-time position upon completion of his internship. Collin decides to keep quiet and not let the controller know of his error. He reasons that it is unlikely that the difference between what he projected versus the actual expenses will be discovered since Horner does not create detailed monthly operating statements.

Requirements

1. Using the IMA Statement of Ethical Professional Practice as an ethical framework, answer the following questions:
    a. What is (are) the ethical issue(s) in this situation?
    b. What are Collin Hoffman's responsibilities as a management accountant?
    c. What are John Wallace's responsibilities as a management accountant?
    d. What are Meghan Peyton's responsibilities as a management accountant?
2. What would be the impact on breakeven sales from failing to include the fixed monthly salaries? Would the breakeven using the erroneous data be lower or higher than the correct breakeven (the breakeven calculation including the monthly salaries)? Do you think this error would be likely to influence the decision of whether to proceed with the new sales commission proposal?
3. Discuss the specific steps Collin should take to resolve the situation. Refer to the IMA Statement of Ethical Professional Practice in your response.

REAL LIFE

A7-77 **Impact of increases in direct materials on product breakeven** (Learning Objectives 1, 2 & 3)

Goose down is used in a wide variety of products, including jackets, bedding, and pillows. In recent years, the cost of down has been increasing. For example, in 2009, a pound of goose down sold for $10; in 2014 it sold for $50.[5] Lands' End, a retailer of clothing and bedding items, uses goose down in many of its products.

The cost of down has increased because of a few reasons. First of all, China is one of the major producers of down in the world. China's wealth has been increasing. As a result, more families are moving from farms to urban areas thereby reducing the number of families who are farming. In addition, dietary preferences around the world are changing to more meat and fish over geese and ducks, decreasing the potential revenue from raising geese.

On the demand side, the demand for down is increasing. The increasing popularity of down jackets from a fashion standpoint is driving most of the increase in demand for down. In prior decades, down was just used for specialized winter sports apparel for skiing and climbing. Now down is used in popular, general fashions.

Some companies are developing synthetic substitutes for down as they try to counteract the increasing costs of the down. In the meantime, companies such as Lands' End, North Face, and other garment manufacturers are raising the prices of their products to counteract the increasing cost of down.

Requirements

1. Is the cost of down a fixed cost or a variable cost for a jacket manufacturer such as Lands' End?
2. If the cost of down increases, what happens to the breakeven point for a down-filled jacket product line at Lands' End?
3. If down increases by a certain percentage, will the selling price of a down-filled jacket need to change by that same percentage to maintain the same profit margin? Explain.
4. Let's look at a hypothetical example now. Assume that a Lands' End down jacket selling for $150 contains one pound of goose down. The cost per pound of down was $10 in 2009 and $50 in 2014, respectively. Lands' End has $250,000 of fixed costs related to the down jacket line and its other variable manufacturing costs (other direct materials, direct labor, and manufacturing overhead) total $60 per jacket. Assume that Lands' End does not increase the selling price of the down jacket over the five-year period. Calculate the breakeven number of jackets both in (a) 2009; and (b) 2014.
5. Assume now the same set of facts as in Question 4 but that Lands' End raises the selling price of each jacket by $25 in 2017. How does the breakeven volume of jackets change in 2017? (Assume that the cost of goose down in 2017 is the same as in 2014.)

[5] Source: "Down is Becoming Too Expensive," *Outside*, March 8, 2014, retrieved from http://www.outsideonline.com/1921851/down-becoming-too-expensive on January 3, 2016.

Try It Solutions

page 386:

1.
Sales price per unit	$2.00
Less: Variable cost per unit	0.50
Contribution margin per unit	$1.50

2. Contribution margin ratio = $\dfrac{\text{Contribution margin per unit}}{\text{Sales price per unit}} = \dfrac{\$1.50}{\$2.00} = 75\%$

3.
Contribution margin (1,000 hot dogs × $1.50 per hot dog)	$1,500
Less: Fixed expenses	300
Operating income	$1,200

page 389:

1. Sales in units to breakeven = $\dfrac{\text{Fixed expenses} + \text{Operating income}}{\text{Contribution margin per unit}}$

   $= \dfrac{\$300 + 0}{\$1.50} = 200$ hot dogs

2. Sales in dollars to breakeven = $\dfrac{\text{Fixed expenses} + \text{Operating income}}{\text{Contribution margin ratio}}$

   $= \dfrac{\$300 + 0}{75\%} = \$400$ of sales revenue

page 391:

1. Sales in units = $\dfrac{\text{Fixed expenses} + \text{Operating income}}{\text{Contribution margin per unit}}$

   $= \dfrac{\$300 + \$900}{\$1.50} = 800$ hot dogs per month

2. Sales in dollars = $\dfrac{\text{Fixed expenses} + \text{Operating income}}{\text{Contribution margin ratio}}$

   $= \dfrac{\$300 + \$900}{75\%} = \$1,600$ of sales revenue

page 404:

1.

	A	B	C	D
1	**Calculating Weighted-Average Contribution Margin per Unit**	Hotdogs	Potato Chips	Total in "basket"
2	Contribution margin per unit	$ 1.50	$ 0.75	
3	Multiply by: Sales mix (number of units in "basket")	10	5	15
4	Contribution margin	$ 15.00	$ 3.75	$ 18.75
5				
6	Weighted-average contibution margin per unit ($18.75/15 units)			$ 1.25
7				

2. $$\text{Sales in units} = \frac{\text{Fixed expenses} + \text{Operating income}}{\text{Contribution margin per unit}} = \frac{\$300 + \$900}{\$1.25} = 960 \text{ total units}$$

3. Hot dogs (960 × 10/15 sales mix)..................... 640

   Potato chips (960 × 5/15 sales mix)................. 320
   Total units 960

page 411:

1.

Costs under current option	=	Costs under new option		
Variable Cost + Fixed Costs	=	Variable Costs	+	Fixed Costs
0 + $300	=	($0.25 × # Units)	+	$100
$200	=	($0.25 × # Units)		
# Units	=	800		

Rachel will be indifferent between the two options if she sells exactly 800 units from her stand each month.

2. Since Rachel's typical sales volume (700 units) is less than the indifference point (800 units), she will prefer the option with the lower operating leverage (more variable costs and fewer fixed costs). In this case, that means her costs will be lower if she takes advantage of the new arrangement ($100 per month plus $0.25 for every unit sold) rather than continuing to operate under the current arrangement ($300 per month). As a result of lower costs, her operating income will be higher.

8

Relevant Costs for Short-Term Decisions

PA Images/Alamy

Sources: Nike, Inc. 2015 10-K; www.Forbes.com/powerful-brands/#/tab:rank_page:2

Learning Objectives

- **1** Describe and identify information relevant to short-term business decisions
- **2** Describe and apply different approaches to pricing
- **3** Decide whether to accept a special order
- **4** Decide whether to discontinue a product, department, or store
- **5** Factor resource constraints into product mix decisions
- **6** Analyze outsourcing (make-or-buy) decisions
- **7** Decide whether to sell a product "as is" or process it further

NIKE, Inc., is the largest seller of athletic footwear and apparel in the world. Nike is also synonymous with outsourcing: it doesn't manufacture any of its own products. Rather, Nike leaves the actual production of its branded products to independent contractors who operate over 600 factories, most of which are overseas. By outsourcing production to others, Nike can concentrate on its core competencies—the things it is really good at—including designing, developing, marketing, and selling athletic footwear, apparel, and equipment. But outsourcing is not without risks: Nike must rely on others to follow its standards for quality and fulfill production orders on a timely basis. In addition, sourcing the product overseas opens the company to exchange rate fluctuations, trade tariffs, port strikes, and other global risks. The upside? Nike's business model has allowed the company to develop one of the most iconic and valuable brands in the world.

In Chapter 7, we saw how managers use cost behavior to determine the company's break-even point and to estimate the sales volume needed to achieve target profits. In this chapter, we'll see how managers use their knowledge of cost behavior to make six different business decisions, such as whether to outsource production to other companies. The decisions we'll discuss in this chapter usually pertain to shorter periods of time, so managers do not need to worry about the time value of money. In other words, they do not need to compute the present value of the revenues and expenses relating to the decision. In Chapter 12, we will discuss longer-term decisions (such as buying equipment and undertaking plant expansions) in which the time value of money becomes important. Before we look at the six business decisions in detail, let's consider managers' decision-making process and the information managers need to evaluate their options.

How Do Managers Make Decisions?

Exhibit 8-1 illustrates how managers decide among alternative courses of action. Management accountants participate in most aspects of the decision cycle, ranging from identifying possible courses of action to collecting and analyzing relevant information that helps guide managers' ultimate decision. Once the decision has been implemented, managerial accountants follow up on the decision, comparing actual results to expectations. If the company's goals are not being achieved as well as anticipated, the cycle will begin again with new, corrective action

EXHIBIT 8-1 How Managers Make Decisions

Relevant Information

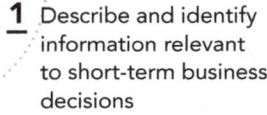

1 Describe and identify information relevant to short-term business decisions

When managers make decisions, they focus only on information that is *relevant* to the decisions. Exhibit 8-2 shows that <u>relevant information</u> has two characteristics:

1. It pertains to the *future*.
2. It *differs* among alternatives.

EXHIBIT 8-2 Relevant Information

Think of a recent decision you have made, such as your decision as to which college or university to attend. What influenced your decision? Some of the relevant financial information may have included the cost of tuition, the cost of room and board, and the financial aid package you were offered, including scholarships, work study, and loans. Some of the relevant nonfinancial information may have included the size of the school, the geographic location of the school, specific extracurricular activities of interest to you, or just the feeling you got from meeting people on campus.

Think about these factors for a moment and how they influenced your decision. When you compared colleges, you probably made a mental or written list about the things you liked better about one institution over another. In other words, you concentrated on those aspects that *differed* between institutions. For example, you may have thrown out some schools because the net cost was too high and you or your parents didn't want to pay that much for tuition in the *future*. Some schools may have been more prestigious than others, causing you to believe you would get better or higher-paying job offers in the *future*. And as for the nonfinancial factors, you probably envisioned what it would be like to attend the college in the *future*. In other words, you concentrated on information that *differed* between alternatives and that would affect your *future*. The same holds true for business decisions: managers focus on financial and nonfinancial information that *differs* among alternatives and that pertains to the *future*.

With the existence of big data and ERP systems, managers can easily become overwhelmed by the sheer magnitude of data that is available. Managers must use critical thinking skills (as outlined on page 18 in Chapter 1) to zero in on the larger business issue, the specific question that needs to be addressed, and the data that are *relevant* to answering the question. Managers need to clearly identify the assumptions being made, the "gray areas" that involve judgment, and the possible implications of the decision. Throughout this chapter, you'll see that we begin each decision with a set of assumptions, but then change one or more of the assumptions to see what impact it has on the resulting decision. Since no one has a crystal ball with which to see the future, the more assumptions that have been questioned and considered, the better prepared managers will be.

> ## Why is this important?
> "The accounting information used to make **business decisions** in this chapter focuses on one factor: **profitability**. However, in real life, managers should take a triple-bottom-line approach to decision making by considering the decision's impact on people and the environment."

Keys to Making Short-Term Special Decisions

Our approach to making short-term special decisions is called the *incremental analysis approach*. Instead of looking at the company's *entire* income statement under each decision alternative, we'll just look at how operating income would *change or differ* under each alternative. Using this approach, we'll leave out irrelevant information—the costs and revenues that won't differ between alternatives.

We'll consider six kinds of decisions in this chapter:

1. Pricing
2. Special orders
3. Discontinuing products, departments, or stores
4. Product mix when resources are constrained
5. Outsourcing (make or buy)
6. Selling as is or processing further

As you study these decisions, keep in mind the two keys to analyzing business decisions shown in Exhibit 8-3:

1. **Focus on relevant revenues, costs, and profits.** Most decisions boil down to a cost-benefit analysis. The important point is to identify and focus on only the *relevant* costs and benefits: those that will *differ* between alternatives and affect the *future*. Irrelevant information only clouds the picture and creates information overload.

2. **Use a contribution margin approach that separates variable costs from fixed costs.** Because fixed costs and variable costs behave differently, they must be analyzed separately. Traditional income statements based on absorption costing can mislead managers because they blend fixed and variable costs together. Contribution margin income statements, which isolate costs by behavior (variable or fixed), are much better suited for decision making.

Keep in mind that every business decision is unique. Just because a piece of information is relevant in one decision doesn't mean it will be relevant in the next. Each decision will need to be assessed individually to determine the relevant pieces of information. Also keep in mind that different costs are used for different purposes. For example, absorption-based costing is required by GAAP for external financial reporting purposes, yet variable costing is usually much better for decision-making purposes.

EXHIBIT 8-3 Two Keys to Making Short-Term Special Decisions

Decision Pitfalls to Avoid

Finally, there are a few common mistakes that managers sometimes make. We point out the pitfalls here so that you can train yourself to avoid them.

1. **Avoid including sunk costs in your analysis.** <u>Sunk costs</u> are costs that have been incurred in the past and cannot be changed regardless of which future action is taken. For example, a manager may have invested thousands of dollars in a computer

system that appeared to be a good investment at the time. However, with the passage of time and the speed of technological advances, using the old system may no longer be in the best interest of the organization, even if it is only one to two years old. Hindsight may even make the past decision appear foolish. When deciding whether or not to replace the system, the amount originally paid for the system is a sunk cost that should not be considered. Rather, only the *future* costs and benefits associated with continuing to use the old system versus investing in a new system should be considered.

2. **Avoid using unit costs unless they are purely variable in nature.** Recall from Chapter 6 that absorption costing includes both variable *and* fixed manufacturing costs. Variable production costs include direct material, direct labor, and variable overhead costs that will be incurred on every unit produced. On the other hand, fixed overhead cost will *not* be incurred on every unit produced but rather, will stay constant in total. Variable costing is usually better for decision-making purposes because it does not blend together the variable and fixed production costs. If you use unit costs in your analysis, make sure you first separate the fixed and variable components of the costs and then analyze the fixed cost in *total*, not on a per-unit basis.

Sustainability and Short-Term Business Decisions

For companies that embrace sustainability and the triple bottom line, almost every decision will be viewed through the lens of its impact on people and the planet, as well as profitability. For companies such as Nike that outsource key business functions, creating and maintaining sustainable practices throughout the company's supply chain can be challenging. While Nike's suppliers are contractually obligated to adhere to Nike's "Code of Conduct," which sets forth standards for equitable labor practices and environmentally sound manufacturing practices, the company's reputation could be harmed if the suppliers fail to comply. Here are just a few of the strides Nike has been making toward becoming more environmentally and socially sustainable:

- Nike is working with its contractors to create more environmentally sustainable production practices. The company's goal is to double its business, yet half its environmental impact. Since 2008, contract manufacturers have cut energy used per unit by 50%. The company aims to use 100% renewable energy by 2025. It is focused on using innovative materials and manufacturing techniques to decrease the amount of water used and carbon emitted from the manufacture of its products.

- Nike's goal by 2020 is to have zero waste from contractor factories sent to landfills. Product designers are working hard to create a cradle-to-cradle, closed-loop system where old shoes and manufacturing scraps are ground and reused in the production of new products, as well as courts, tracks, and other play surfaces. The ground recycled materials, aptly named "Nike Grind," are already incorporated into 71% of Nike's products.

- Since 2010, over 3 billion plastic bottles have been converted into recycled fibers for use in Nike's products, and approximately 30 million pairs of shoes have been recycled through the company's "reuse-a-shoe" program.

- Nike's contractors employ over one million factory workers. To make sure health, safety, and labor practices are carried out in accordance with Nike's Code of Conduct, the company employs over 150 people whose sole job is to monitor factories. Nike also works with third parties, such as the Fair Labor Association, to conduct independent monitoring. Each factory is scored on labor practices, in addition to traditional metrics such as cost, quality, and on-time delivery. Reports of noncompliance are investigated immediately, so that corrective action can be taken.

- The company is working toward forming a more diverse and inclusive workforce. Over 50% of company employees (noncontracted) are nonwhite and 41% of managers are women.
- Nike's goal is to invest at least 1.5% of annual pretax income in community impact initiatives. In 2015, Nike invested 1.9% of pretax income (approximately $80 million) in these initiatives. The company also promotes employee volunteerism and matches employee donations to nonprofits up to $10,000 per employee per year.

These are just a few of the ways Nike is embedding sustainability within the organization. You can find more information in Nike's FY14/15 Sustainable Business Report.

See Exercises E8-17A and E8-33B

Sources: Nike, Inc. 2015 10-K; Nike, Inc, FY14/15 Sustainable Business Report.

How Do Managers Make Pricing and Special Order Decisions?

2 Describe and apply different approaches to pricing

We'll start our discussion by looking at pricing decisions, which can be one of the most challenging decisions managers need to make. After that, we'll move on to special order decisions.

Regular Pricing Decisions

There is no way around it: pricing is a messy business. In your economics course, you learned that the price of a product is the point at which the supply curve and the demand curve intersect. But, in practice, what does this mean? Generally speaking, the higher the price, the lower the demand, while the lower the price, the higher the demand. To maximize its profits, a company needs to consider the *profit* that will be made at the various price points, not just the sales price alone. And as you know from earlier chapters, the profit made on a product is determined not only by its sales price, but also by its cost. In other words, cost is an important factor in determining profitability and pricing.

Exhibit 8-4 shows that managers start with three basic questions when setting regular prices for their products or services.

EXHIBIT 8-4 Regular Pricing Considerations

- What is our target profit?
- How much are customers willing to pay?
- Are we a price-taker or a price-setter for this product?

The answers to these questions are often complex and ever-changing. Let's consider each in turn.

First, managers must consider their target profit. Stockholders expect the company to achieve certain profits. Economic conditions, historical company earnings, industry risk, competition, and new business developments all affect the level of profit that stockholders expect. Stockholders usually tie their profit expectations to the amount of assets invested in the company. For example, stockholders may expect a 10% annual return on their investment. A company's stock price tends to decline if the company does not meet target profits, so managers must keep costs low while generating enough revenue to meet those targets.

Second, managers need to consider the price customers are willing to pay. The amount customers will pay depends on the competition, the product's uniqueness, whether the product is branded, the effectiveness of marketing campaigns, general economic conditions, and so forth. Focus groups and test markets are often used to help determine the price customers are willing to pay.

Third, managers must consider whether they are price-takers or price-setters. To address the third pricing question, imagine a continuum with price-takers at one end and price-setters at the other end. A company's products and services fall somewhere along this continuum, shown in Exhibit 8-5. Companies are price-takers when they have little or no control over the prices of their products or services. This occurs when their products and services are *not* unique, not branded, or when competition is heavy. Examples include food commodities (milk and corn), natural resources (oil and lumber), and generic consumer products and services (paper towels, dry cleaning, and banking).

EXHIBIT 8-5 Price-Takers Versus Price-Setters

Companies are price-setters when they have more control over pricing—in other words, they can "set" prices to some extent. Companies are price-setters when their products are unique, such as original art and jewelry, specially manufactured machinery, and custom-made furniture. Companies are also price-setters when there is little competition. For example, a gas station out in the middle of nowhere can charge any price it wants because there are no other gas stations around. Finally, companies also are price-setters if they have successfully branded their products, as Nike has.

Obviously, managers would rather be price-setters than price-takers. To gain more control over pricing, companies try to differentiate their products. They want to make their products unique in terms of features, service, or quality—or at least make you *think* their product is unique or somehow better even if it isn't. How do they do this? Primarily through advertising and branding. Consider Nike's tennis shoes, Starbucks's coffee, Apple's tablets, Kleenex's tissues, Tylenol's acetaminophen, Capital One's credit cards, Shell's gas—the list goes on and on. Are these products really better than or significantly different from their lower-priced competitors? If these companies can make you think so, they've gained more control over their pricing because you are willing to pay *more* for their products or services. The downside? These companies must charge higher prices or sell more units just to cover their marketing costs.

A company's approach to pricing depends on whether its product or service is on the price-taking or price-setting side of the spectrum. Price-setters emphasize a cost-plus pricing approach; price-takers emphasize a target costing approach. Keep in mind that many products fall somewhere along the continuum. Therefore, managers tend to use both approaches to some extent.

Why is this important?

"Both **branding** and product **differentiation** give managers more control over pricing. Without such features, a **company** must often settle for selling its **product** at the same price as its competitors."

Our pricing decision rule is as follows:

Cost-Plus Pricing

When a company is more of a price setter, such as Nike or Apple, it emphasizes a cost-plus approach to pricing. **Cost-plus pricing** starts with the product's total costs and *adds* a desired profit to determine a cost-plus price.

> Total cost
> Plus: Desired profit
> Cost-plus price

This information may seem familiar to you, and indeed it should. We talked about cost-plus pricing in Chapter 3 when we discussed how managers use job costing information to bid for custom jobs: They start with an estimate of the job's cost and then add a markup to arrive at the bid price. What we will do in this chapter is very similar, though we are going to consider an entire company rather than just one particular custom job.

For our example, let's consider Garnier Fructis, maker of branded shampoo.[1] Exhibit 8-6 contains information about the company:

EXHIBIT 8-6 Garnier's Data for the Year

Variable costs:		
Variable manufacturing costs (DM, DL, Variable MOH) per unit ....$1.20 per unit	}	$ 1.50 per unit
Variable operating expenses (sales commission and freight out) per unit ....$0.30 per unit		
Fixed costs:		
Fixed manufacturing overhead $2,000,000	}	$ 3,250,000
Fixed operating expenses $1,250,000		
Other information:		
Units needed		2,500,000
Plant capacity (units that could be produced with the existing capacity)		2,600,000
Total assets		$ 10,000,000
Desired return on assets		10%
Absorption cost per unit [= $1.20 variable mfg + ($2,000,000 fixed MOH ÷ 2,500,000)]		$ 2.00

Since Garnier is a branded product, the company will emphasize a cost-plus approach to pricing. In pricing decisions, *all costs are relevant* because the company must

---

[1] All references to Garnier Fructis in this hypothetical example were created by the author solely for academic purposes and are not intended, in any way, to represent the actual business practices of, or costs incurred by, Garnier.

cover all costs along the value chain before it can generate a profit. In other words, the price needs to be high enough to cover operating expenses (R&D, design, marketing, distribution, and customer service) as well as manufacturing costs. As stated in our keys to decision making, we'll separate the variable costs and fixed costs in our analysis. Exhibit 8-7 shows how Garnier would calculate its cost-plus price:

EXHIBIT 8-7 Cost-Plus Pricing Analysis

	A	B
1	**Cost -Plus Pricing Analysis**	**Total**
2	Variable manufacturing costs ($1.20 × 2,500,000 units)	$ 3,000,000
3	Variable operating expenses ($ 0.30 × 2,500,000 units)	750,000
4	Fixed manufacturing costs	2,000,000
5	Fixed operating expenses	1,250,000
6	Total costs across the value chain	$ 7,000,000
7	Plus: Desired profit (10% × $10 million of assets)	1,000,000
8	Sales revenue desired for 2,500,000 units	$ 8,000,000
9	Divided by: Number of units	2,500,000
10	Cost-plus price per unit	$ 3.20
11		

Notice how we first found the total costs for the needed volume and then added the desired profit, just as the "cost-plus" name implies. By doing so, we arrived at the total desired amount of sales revenue. Finally, we divided by the number of units needed to arrive at the cost-plus price per unit ($3.20).

Will the company stop there? No. The next thing it will do is figure out if customers are willing to pay that much for the product. The company will use focus groups and test marketing to find out whether the cost-plus price is too high, or even possibly too low, and then it will adjust accordingly. Notice also how volume played a big role in this decision. If Garnier can produce and sell a higher volume of product, the cost-plus price will be lower. Why? Because the fixed costs will be spread over more units. Thus, management may want to test out a range of volume assumptions in its analyses.

STOP & THINK

Based on the information in Exhibit 8-7, the product cost used for inventory valuation and Cost of Goods Sold is $2.00 per unit. Why can't management simply add the 10% desired return on assets to this figure to arrive at the cost-plus price?

Answer: The absorption cost per unit only includes production costs, not operating expenses. In pricing decisions, companies must consider *all* of their costs. In addition, the absorption cost per unit includes fixed manufacturing overhead. If volume were projected to be different than 2.5 million units, the absorption cost per unit would be different than $2.00.

Target Costing

When a company is a price-taker, it has no control over the price. It must simply use the same price as its competitors or people won't buy the product. In other words, price is a "given." The only thing the company can do to ensure an adequate amount of profit is control its own costs. Companies that have little control over pricing emphasize a target costing approach. As shown below, **target costing** starts with the market price of the product (the price customers are willing to pay) and subtracts the company's desired profit to determine the product's target total cost—the *total* cost to develop, design, produce, market, deliver, and service the product:

Revenue at market price
Less: Desired profit
Target total cost

As you can see, target costing is the *opposite* of cost-plus pricing. If the company's actual total costs are higher than the target total cost, managers must find ways to reduce costs so that they can meet profit goals. Managers often use activity-based costing (ABC) and lean thinking (as discussed in Chapter 4) to find ways to eliminate waste and reduce costs.

Let's look at an example of target costing. Assume that Garnier's shampoo is a *non-branded commodity* and that the current market price for similar shampoo is $3.00 per unit. Exhibit 8-8 calculates the target total cost and then compares it to the current total costs for the 2,500,000 units the company needs each year:

EXHIBIT 8-8 Target Costing Analysis

	A	B
1	**Target Costing Analysis**	**Total**
2	Revenue at market price (2,500,000 units × $3.00 sales price)	$ 7,500,000
3	Less: Desired profit (10% × $10 million of assets)	1,000,000
4	Target total cost	$ 6,500,000
5		
6	Versus: Current total costs (from Exhibit 8-7)	$ 7,000,000
7	Total cost reduction needed to achieve target profit	$ (500,000)
8		

As shown in Exhibit 8-8, Garnier's total costs are $500,000 higher than the target total cost. Therefore, the company needs to find ways to reduce total costs by $500,000 if it is to meet its profit goal. So, what are Garnier's options?

- Reduce fixed costs.
- Reduce the variable costs per unit.
- Try other strategies, such as branding, product differentiation, or adding more products to the company's product mix.
- Accept a lower profit.

Let's look at some of these options. Garnier may first try to reduce fixed manufacturing costs and fixed operating expenses. As we discussed in Chapter 6, committed fixed costs are virtually impossible to change in the short run. Therefore, the company would start by considering whether any discretionary fixed costs could be reduced or eliminated. While R&D and marketing are discretionary, cutting them may be detrimental to the company in the long run, so the managers need to carefully consider the long-term impact of cutting fixed costs.

Let's assume that Garnier has identified $100,000 of fixed cost savings. Since the company needs to reduce costs by a total of $500,000 in order to reach its profit goal, managers must now consider how to reduce the variable costs associated with each unit made and sold. Exhibit 8-9 shows that with the $100,000 reduction in fixed costs, the most Garnier can spend on each unit is $1.34 in order to meet its profit goal. The company will need to shave $0.16 off of the cost of every unit produced and sold.

EXHIBIT 8-9 Calculating Target Unit Variable Cost

	A	B
1	**Target Variable Cost per Unit**	**Total**
2	Target total cost from Exhibit 8-8	$ 6,500,000
3	Less: Fixed costs ($3,250,000 - $100,000 savings)	3,150,000
4	Target total variable cost	$ 3,350,000
5	Divided by: Number of units	2,500,000
6	Target variable cost per unit	$ 1.34
7		
8	Versus: Current variable cost per unit from Exhibit 8-6	$ 1.50
9	Cost reduction needed per unit to achieve desired profit	$ (0.16)
10		

How can managers achieve variable cost saving? Perhaps the company could renegotiate raw materials costs with its suppliers, change the packaging materials used, or restructure the way it awards sales commissions. Notice how managers need to think about *variable operating expenses*, as well as *variable manufacturing costs*. Many companies are reducing the actual size of their products to save money on direct materials. In other words, Garnier could sell slightly smaller bottles of shampoo. Smaller products also mean that more units can be shipped in the same cargo space, thereby saving on the variable cost of distributing each unit. Companies have found that consumers are less sensitive to reductions in the size of products than they are to increases in prices. Thus, trimming the contents of a product is often one strategy used to meet target variable costs.

Finally, the company can attempt different strategies that may actually include *increasing*, rather than decreasing, costs. For example, the company may need to increase marketing costs to boost volume or brand its product. It may need to spend *more* on research and development (R&D) to differentiate its product through innovation. Cost-volume-profit (CVP) analysis, as you learned in Chapter 7, can help companies determine whether these actions will be profitable. As you can see, managers don't have an easy task when the current total cost exceeds the target total cost. Sometimes, companies just can't compete given the current market price. If that's the case, they may have no other choice than to exit the market.

Special Order Decisions

A special order occurs when a customer requests a one-time order at a *reduced* sales price. Often, these special orders are for large quantities. Before agreeing to the special order, management must consider the questions shown in Exhibit 8-10.

3 Decide whether to accept a special order

EXHIBIT 8-10 Special Order Considerations

- Do we have excess capacity available to fill this order?

- Will the reduced sales price be high enough to cover the *incremental* costs of filling the order (the variable costs of filling the order and any additional fixed costs)?

- Will the special order affect regular sales in the long run?

First, managers must consider available capacity. If the company is already making as many units as possible and selling them all at its *regular* sales price, it wouldn't make sense to fill a special order at a *reduced* sales price. Therefore, excess capacity is almost a necessity for accepting a special order. This is true for companies that provide services as well as for manufacturers and merchandisers.

Second, managers need to consider whether the special reduced sales price is high enough to cover the *incremental* costs of filling the order. The special price *must* exceed the variable costs of filling the order. In other words, the special order must provide a positive contribution margin. In addition, the company must consider fixed costs. If the company has excess capacity, the existing fixed costs probably won't be affected by producing more units or delivering more service. However, in some cases, management may need to hire a consultant, pay an attorney for drawing up a contract, or incur some other fixed cost to fill the special order. If so, management will need to consider whether the special sales price is high enough to generate a positive contribution margin *and* cover the additional fixed costs.

Finally, managers need to consider whether the special order will affect regular sales in the long run. Will regular customers find out about the special order and demand a lower price? Will the special order customer come back *again and again*, asking for the same reduced price? Will the special order price start a price war with competitors? Managers must consider these questions before making their final decision. Managers may decide that any profit from the special sales order is not worth these risks.

Special Order Example

Let's assume that Garnier has successfully branded its product and is able to sell its name brand shampoo at the cost-plus price of $3.20 per bottle, as shown in Exhibit 8-7. Assume Aldi, a merchandiser that sells only generic products, has approached Garnier with an offer to buy 20,000 bottles of shampoo for $1.60 per bottle, which is half of Garnier's normal sales price. Also assume the following facts about the special order:

- Aldi wants the shampoo packaged under its own private label. The bottles used for the private-label shampoo will be slightly smaller, allowing Garnier to save $0.15 per unit on the direct material cost.
- Aldi will pay the shipping costs.
- No sales commission will be paid on this order since Aldi approached Garnier without sales people involved.
- Garnier will have to pay $2,000 in legal fees to draw up the contract.

Let's consider the issues raised in Exhibit 8-10.

First, let's find out if Garnier has excess capacity with which to produce this special order. According to Exhibit 8-6, Garnier has capacity to produce 2,600,000 units per period, but its current production and sales are only 2,500,000 per period. Thus, the company could make 100,000 more units per period with its current production capacity that would otherwise be left unused.

Second, let's consider the incremental costs of filling the order. Let's look at variable costs first. From Exhibit 8-6 we see that the variable cost to manufacture each unit is $1.20. However, Garnier will save $0.15 per bottle on direct materials. So the variable manufacturing cost associated with the order will be $1.05 per unit ($1.20 − $0.15). The variable operating expenses of $0.30 per unit (sales commission and freight out) won't be incurred on this order, so they aren't relevant to the decision.

Now let's look at fixed costs. Since Garnier has excess capacity, its *existing* fixed costs won't be affected by producing 20,000 more units. However, the company will incur an *extra* $2,000 of fixed costs to have an attorney draw up the sales contract.

Exhibit 8-11 completes the analysis by comparing the sales revenue that would be generated by the order with the incremental costs of filling the order.

EXHIBIT 8-11 Incremental Analysis of Special Sales Order

	A	B	C
1	Incremental Analysis for Special Order Decision	Per Unit	Total Order (20,000 units)
2	Revenue from special order	$ 1.60	$ 32,000
3	Less Variable expenses associated with the order:		
4	Variable manufacturing costs (DM, DL, Variable MOH)*	1.05	21,000
5	Contribution margin	$ 0.55	$ 11,000
6	Less additional fixed expenses associated with the order		2,000
7	Increase in operating income from the special order		$ 9,000
8			

*Normal variable cost of $1.20 per bottle less $0.15 savings per bottle on direct materials.

This analysis shows that Garnier could earn an extra $9,000 of operating income by accepting this special order.

Now let's consider the final issue raised in Exhibit 8-10: Will the special order affect regular sales in the long run? Since the product will be packaged under Aldi's private label, consumers won't know it is the same as Garnier's shampoo, but they may decide they like it just as much. As a result, Garnier may cannibalize sales of its own brand-name product. However, the fact that Garnier is only selling 20,000 units under the private label versus the 2.5 million units of its own label makes this risk fairly small. Plus, loyal brand-users probably won't try shampoo sold under other labels. Thus, Garnier will most likely decide to accept this order.

Notice that our analysis follows the two keys to making short-term special business decisions discussed earlier: (1) focus on relevant data (revenues and costs that *will differ* if Garnier accepts the special order) and (2) use a contribution margin approach that separates variable costs from fixed costs.

To summarize, for special sales orders, the decision rule is as follows:

Pitfall to Avoid on Special Order Decisions

One of the most common mistakes managers make when analyzing special orders is to base their decision on the unit product cost that uses absorption costing. Recall from Chapter 6 that under absorption costing, all manufacturing costs, including fixed MOH, are "absorbed" into the unit cost of the product. Absorption costing was used as the product cost when we studied job costing and process costing in Chapters 3, 4, and 5 because it is required by Generally Accepted Accounting Principles (GAAP) for external financial reporting purposes. Using the figures found in Exhibit 8-6, we see that the product cost of each bottle of shampoo, using absorption costing, is $2.00:

Product Cost at Current Production Level	Absorption Unit Cost
Variable manufacturing costs (DM, DL, Variable MOH) per unit	$1.20
Fixed manufacturing costs (Fixed MOH of $2,000,000 ÷ 2,500,000 units)	0.80
Cost per unit using absorption costing	$2.00

The $2.00 unit cost, which GAAP mandates for inventory and cost of goods sold valuation, is *not* a good basis for making a special order decision. Why? Because it is a mixed cost, which includes both fixed and variable components. If a manager simply compared the special order sales price of $1.60 per unit to the absorption cost of $2.00 per unit, the manager would incorrectly assume that the special order would result in a loss of $0.40 per unit, or $8,000 in total (20,000 units × $0.40) before even factoring in the extra $2,000 of attorney's fees. Even considering the $0.15 per unit direct materials cost savings, absorption costing is the wrong place to start. Since there is excess capacity in the plant, the reality of the situation is that fixed MOH will remain $2,000,000 in total, regardless of whether Garnier accepts the special order. Producing 20,000 more units will *not* increase total fixed costs by $0.80 per unit. The incremental cost incurred to make each additional bottle of shampoo is the variable cost per unit, not the absorption cost per unit. Keep the following important rule of thumb in mind:

> Never compare the special order sales price with the absorption cost per unit or your analysis will be flawed. Rather, use the contribution margin approach.

Try It!

Assume that a Campbell's soup plant is running at 90% of its monthly capacity. Campbell's has just received a special order to produce 40,000 cases of chicken noodle soup for a national supermarket. The supermarket will sell the soup under its own private brand label. The soup will be the same in all respects, except for the label, which will cost Campbell's an extra $5,000 in total to design. The supermarket has offered to pay only $19.00 per case, which is well under Campbell's normal sales price.

Costs at the current production level (450,000 cases) are as follows:

	Total Cost	Cost per Case (450,000 cases)
Direct Materials	$4,500,000	$10.00
Direct Labor	1,350,000	3.00
Variable MOH	900,000	2.00
Fixed MOH	2,700,000	6.00
Total	$9,450,000	$21.00

1. Is there enough excess capacity to fill this order?
2. Will Campbell's operating income increase or decrease if it accepts this special order? By how much?

Please see page 506 for solutions.

Decision Guidelines

Relevant Information for Business Decisions

Nike makes pricing and special order decisions. Even though it sells mass-produced tennis shoes and sports clothing, Nike has successfully branded its products with advertising. Nike's managers consider both quantitative and qualitative factors as they make pricing decisions. Here are key guidelines that Nike's managers follow in making their decisions.

Decision	Guidelines
What information is relevant to a short-term special business decision?	Relevant information has two characteristics: 1. It pertains to the *future*. 2. It *differs* between alternatives.
What are two key guidelines in making short-term special business decisions?	1. Focus on *relevant* data. 2. Use a *contribution margin* approach that separates variable costs from fixed costs.
What are two pitfalls to avoid in making business decisions?	1. Avoid including sunk costs. 2. Avoid using the absorption cost per unit since it includes both fixed and variable components.
How does a company's commitment to sustainability affect decision making?	Companies that are committed to sustainability will judge every decision through the lens of the triple bottom line, assessing the impact of the decision not only on company profit, but also on its consequences for people and the planet.
What should Nike consider in setting its regular product prices?	Nike considers the following: 1. The profit stockholders expect 2. The price customers are willing to pay 3. Whether it is a price-setter or a price-taker
Which approach should Nike take to pricing?	Nike has differentiated its products through advertising and branding. Thus, Nike tends to be a price-setter. Nike's managers can emphasize a cost-plus approach to pricing.
Which approach should discount shoe stores such as Payless ShoeSource take to pricing?	Payless ShoeSource sells generic shoes (no-name brands) at low prices. Payless is a price-taker, so managers use a target-costing approach to pricing.
Should Nike accept a large special order from a customer at a price that is lower than the normal sales price?	If the revenue from the order exceeds the incremental variable and fixed costs of filling the order, then accepting the order will increase operating income.

SUMMARY PROBLEM 1

Linger Industries makes tennis balls. Linger's only plant can produce up to 2.5 million cans of balls per year. Current production is two million cans. Annual manufacturing, selling, and administrative fixed costs total $700,000. The variable cost of making and selling each can of balls is $1. Stockholders expect a 12% annual return on the company's $3 million of assets.

Requirements

1. What is Linger Industries' current total cost of making and selling two million cans of tennis balls? What is the total cost *per unit* of making and selling each can of balls?
2. Assume that Linger Industries is a price-taker and the current market price is $1.45 per can of balls (this is the price at which manufacturers sell to retailers). What is the *target* total cost of producing and selling two million cans of balls? Given Linger Industries' current total costs, will the company reach stockholders' profit goals?
3. Continuing with Requirement 2, if Linger Industries cannot reduce its fixed costs, what is the target variable cost per can of balls?
4. Suppose Linger Industries could spend an extra $100,000 on advertising to differentiate its product so that it could be more of a price-setter. Assuming the original volume and costs plus the $100,000 of new advertising costs, what cost-plus price will Linger Industries want to charge for a can of balls?
5. Nike has just asked Linger Industries to supply 400,000 cans of balls at a special order price of $1.20 per can. Nike wants Linger Industries to package the balls under the Nike label (Linger will imprint the Nike logo on each ball and can). As a result, Linger Industries will have to spend $10,000 to change the packaging machinery. Assuming the original volume and costs, should Linger Industries accept this special order? Assume that Linger will incur variable selling costs as well as variable manufacturing costs related to this order.

▪ SOLUTIONS

Requirement 1
The current total cost and cost per unit are calculated as follows:

Fixed costs	$ 700,000
Plus: Total variable costs (2 million cans × $1 per unit)	2,000,000
Current total costs	$2,700,000
Divided by number of units	÷ 2,000,000
Total cost per can	$ 1.35

Requirement 2
The target total cost is as follows:

Revenue at market price (2,000,000 cans × $1.45 price)	$2,900,000
Less: Desired profit (12% × $3,000,000 of assets)	(360,000)
Target total cost	$2,540,000

Linger Industries' *current* total costs ($2,700,000 from Requirement 1) are $160,000 higher than the *target* total costs ($2,540,000). If Linger Industries can't cut costs, it won't be able to meet stockholders' profit expectations.

Requirement 3

Assuming that Linger Industries cannot reduce its fixed costs, the target variable cost per can is as follows:

Target total cost (from Requirement 2)	$ 2,540,000
Less: Fixed costs	(700,000)
Target total variable costs	$ 1,840,000
Divided by number of units	÷ 2,000,000
Target variable cost per unit	$ 0.92

Since Linger Industries cannot reduce its fixed costs, it needs to reduce variable costs by $0.08 per can ($1.00 − $0.92) to meet its profit goals. This would require an 8% cost reduction in variable costs, which may not be possible.

Requirement 4

If Linger Industries can differentiate its tennis balls, it will gain more control over pricing. The company's new cost-plus price would be as follows:

Current total costs (from Requirement 1)	$ 2,700,000
Plus: Additional cost of advertising	100,000
Plus: Desired profit (from Requirement 2)	360,000
Target revenue	$ 3,160,000
Divided by number of units	÷ 2,000,000
Cost-plus price per unit	$ 1.58

Linger Industries must study the market to determine whether retailers would pay $1.58 per can of balls.

Requirement 5

First, Linger determines that it has enough extra capacity (500,000 cans) to fill this special order (400,000). Next, Linger compares the revenue from the special order with the extra costs that will be incurred to fill the order. Linger will incur $1.00 of variable costs on each can of balls, plus the additional fixed cost of $10,000 for changing the labeling machine. Notice that Linger shouldn't compare the special order price ($1.20) with the total cost of making and selling each can ($1.35) because the unit cost contains both a fixed and variable component. The correct analysis is as follows:

Revenue from special order (400,000 × $1.20 per unit)	$ 480,000
Less: Variable cost of special order (400,000 × $1.00)	(400,000)
Contribution margin from special order	$ 80,000
Less: Additional fixed costs of special order	(10,000)
Operating income provided by special order	$ 70,000

The decision to accept the special order would increase operating income by $70,000. However, Linger Industries also needs to consider whether its regular customers will find out about the special price and demand lower prices, too. If Linger had simply compared the special order price of $1.20 to the total unit cost of making and selling each can ($1.35), it would have rejected the special order and missed out on the opportunity to make an additional $70,000 of profit.

How Do Managers Make Other Special Business Decisions?

4 Decide whether to discontinue a product, department, or store

In this part of the chapter, we'll consider four more business decisions:

- Whether to discontinue a product, department, or store
- How to factor constrained resources into product mix decisions
- Whether to make a product or outsource it (buy it)
- Whether to sell a product as is or process it further

Decisions to Discontinue Products, Departments, or Stores

Managers often must decide whether to discontinue products, departments, stores, or territories that are not as profitable as desired. For example, American Eagle and Sports Authority closed hundreds of retail locations in 2016. Kroger grocery stores eliminated obsolete movie rental departments and have replaced them with prepared meals, bulk foods, and larger produce departments. And every day, companies are deciding whether to eliminate older product lines and replace them with new product lines. How do managers make these decisions? Exhibit 8-12 shows some questions managers must consider when deciding whether to discontinue a product line, department, or retail store location.

EXHIBIT 8-12 Considerations for Discontinuing Products, Departments, or Stores

- Does the product provide a positive contribution margin?
- Are there any fixed costs that can be avoided if we discontinue the product?
- Will discontinuing the product affect sales of the company's other products?
- What could we do with the freed capacity?

In the first half of the chapter, we assumed that Garnier Fructis only made shampoo. Now, let's assume the company has other product lines, including hair styling products and skin moisturizers. Exhibit 8-13 illustrates Garnier's product line income statement in the contribution margin format. As you can see, a **product line income statement** shows the operating income of each product line, as well as the operating income for the company as a whole.

EXHIBIT 8-13 Product Line Income Statement

	Garnier Fructis			
	Product Line Contribution Margin Income Statement			
	For the Year Ended December 31			
		Product lines		
	Shampoo	Styling Products	Skin Moisturizers	Company Total
Sales revenue	$ 8,000,000	$ 1,500,000	$ 500,000	$ 10,000,000
Less variable expenses:				
Variable manufacturing costs	3,000,000	450,000	$ 250,000	$ 3,700,000
Variable operating expenses	750,000	150,000	125,500	1,025,500
Contribution margin	$ 4,250,000	$ 900,000	$ 124,500	$ 5,274,500
Less fixed expenses:				
Fixed manufacturing costs	1,600,000	300,000	100,000	2,000,000
Fixed operating expenses	1,000,000	187,500	62,500	1,250,000
Operating income	$ 1,650,000	$ 412,500	$ (38,000)	$ 2,024,500

In this exhibit, notice that the fixed costs, in total, are the same as what was shown in Exhibit 8-6. What differs is that the fixed costs have now been allocated among the various product lines. In our example, management has allocated fixed costs to each product line based on the percentage of revenue generated by the line. This is a common allocation system. It is also much like a tax: The higher the revenue, the higher the fixed cost allocation. For example, since 80% of the sales revenue is generated from shampoo sales, 80% of the fixed costs are allocated to the shampoo product line. Similarly, 15% of the fixed costs are allocated to styling products, and 5% are allocated to skin moisturizers. Keep in mind that management could have chosen another allocation system, which would have resulted in a different allocation of fixed costs.

Further, notice that the moisturizer product line appears to be unprofitable. Currently, the moisturizers have an operating loss of $38,000 per period. Without this loss, management erroneously believes the company's operating income could be $38,000 higher each period. Therefore, management is considering whether to discontinue the product line. Let's now consider how management should approach this decision.

Consider the Product's Contribution Margin and Avoidable Fixed Costs

In making this decision, management should consider the questions raised in Exhibit 8-12. The first question addresses the product line's contribution margin: is it positive or negative? Exhibit 8-13 shows that the moisturizers provide $124,500 of contribution margin. This positive contribution margin means the product line is generating enough revenue to cover its own variable costs, as well as provide another $124,500 that can be used to cover some of the company's fixed costs. Had the contribution margin been negative, management would either need to raise the price of the product or reduce variable costs. Management would rarely keep a product line with a negative contribution margin unless the product had a companion product whose sales would decline as a result. We'll discuss this possibility later.

The second question addresses fixed costs. *The important question is this: can any fixed costs be eliminated if the product line is discontinued?* Any fixed costs that can be eliminated as a result of discontinuing the product are known as **avoidable fixed costs**. These costs are relevant to the decision because they will be incurred *only* if the product line is retained. If the product line is discontinued, these costs will go away. In other words, avoidable fixed costs *differ* between alternatives.

On the other hand, **unavoidable fixed costs** are those fixed costs that will continue to be incurred even if the product line is discontinued. Unavoidable fixed costs are irrelevant to the decision because they will be incurred regardless of whether the product line is kept or discontinued. Exhibit 8-14 shows the company's fixed costs in more detail. Notice that total fixed costs ($2,000,000 of manufacturing costs and $1,250,000 of fixed operating expenses) are the same as shown in Exhibit 8-13. Managers will assess each fixed cost to determine how much, if any, is avoidable.

Exhibit 8-14 shows that management has identified $32,000 of fixed manufacturing costs and $45,000 of fixed operating expenses that can be eliminated if the moisturizers are discontinued. The avoidable fixed costs consist of a cancelable lease on equipment used to manufacture the moisturizers, advertisements for the moisturizers, and salaried employees who work solely on the moisturizer product line. Most of the fixed costs, such as property taxes, insurance, and depreciation, are unavoidable: they will continue even if the moisturizers are discontinued.

EXHIBIT 8-14 Analysis of the Company's Fixed Costs

	A	B	C
1	**Analysis of Fixed Expenses**	**Total Cost**	**Avoidable**
2	*Fixed manufacturing (Fixed MOH):*		
3	Property taxes	$ 180,000	$ -
4	Insurance	50,000	-
5	Depreciation on plant and production equipment	1,300,000	-
6	Fixed portion of utilities	70,000	-
7	Salaries of indirect labor (supervisors, janitors, etc.)	350,000	20,000
8	Equipment lease	50,000	12,000
9	Total fixed manufacturing costs	$ 2,000,000	$ 32,000
10			
11	*Fixed operating expenses (selling and administrative):*		
12	Building lease	$ 170,000	$ -
13	Telephone, internet, utilities	80,000	-
14	Depreciation on sales vehicles and office equipment	200,000	-
15	Advertisements	250,000	15,000
16	Sales and administrative salaries	550,000	30,000
17	Total fixed operating expenses	$ 1,250,000	$ 45,000
18			

With this information in hand, management can now determine whether or not to discontinue the moisturizers. Exhibit 8-15 presents management's analysis of the decision. In this analysis, managers compare the contribution margin provided by the moisturizers with the fixed costs that could be avoided if the moisturizers were discontinued.

EXHIBIT 8-15 Incremental Analysis for Discontinuing a Product Line

	A	B
1	**Incremental Analysis for Discontinuation Decision**	**Total**
2	Contribution margin lost if moisturizers are discontinued (Exhibit 8-13)	$ 124,500
3	Less fixed cost savings if moisturizers are discontinued (Exhibit 8-14):	
4	Avoidable fixed manufacturing costs	32,000
5	Avoidable fixed operating expenses	45,000
6	Operating income lost if moisturizers are discontinued	$ 47,500
7		

This analysis shows that the company's operating income would actually *decrease* by $47,500 if the moisturizers were discontinued. Therefore, the moisturizers should not be discontinued *unless* the company can use the capacity for some other product that would provide a higher profit.

Other Considerations

As noted in Exhibit 8-12, management must consider at least two other issues when making the decision to discontinue a product line, department, or store. First, will discontinuing the product line affect sales of the company's other products? As mentioned previously, some products have companion products whose sales would be hurt through discontinuing a particular product. For example, if customers always buy one bottle of shampoo every time they buy a bottle of skin moisturizer, then sales of shampoo might decline as a result of discontinuing the moisturizers. The potential loss in contribution margin on the shampoo would need to be factored into the decision. Since shampoo and styling products are not really companion products of skin moisturizers, we probably don't need to worry about the effect of discontinuing moisturizers on the sales of Garnier's other products. However, you can imagine that if the company sold shampoo and conditioner with the same fragrance, discontinuing one would affect sales of the other.

This is also true of store departments. Can you imagine a grocery store discontinuing its produce department? Sales of every other department in the store would decline as a result of shoppers' inability to purchase fruits and vegetables at the store. On the other hand, sometimes discontinuing a product, such as one particular laptop model, can increase the sales of the other company products (other laptop models). The same holds true for retail stores. For example, assume two Starbucks stores are located close to each other. If one store is closed, then sales at the other location might increase as a result.

The second question concerns freed capacity. If a product line, department, or store is discontinued, management needs to consider what it would do with the newly freed capacity. Could managers make a more profitable product or lease out the capacity to another company? For example, Kroger and other food stores used to have movie rental departments. With the advent of streaming services, such as Netflix, these departments no longer were as profitable as they were in the past. Therefore, Kroger discontinued them and replaced the retail space with larger produce departments, prepared foods, and other more profitable products. Management must consider which alternative use of the freed capacity will be most profitable. Finally, management should consider what to do with any newly freed labor capacity. To exercise corporate responsibility, management should do all it can to retrain employees for other areas of its operations rather than laying off employees.

The key to deciding whether to discontinue products, departments, or stores is to compare the lost contribution margin against the fixed costs that can be saved and to consider what could be done with the freed capacity. The decision rule is as follows:

Try It!

Assume Kroger's grocery store is deciding whether to eliminate the salad bar section of its stores. The product line income statement shows the following quarterly data for the salad bar operations:

- Sales revenue = $750,000
- Fixed costs = $100,000
- Variable costs = $600,000

1. Only $20,000 of fixed costs can be eliminated if the salad bar is eliminated. The remaining $80,000 of fixed costs are unavoidable. What will happen to Kroger's operating income if it discontinues the salad bars and does nothing with the freed capacity?
2. Management is thinking about replacing the salad bar section of the stores with a specialty olive bar, which is projected to bring in $200,000 of contribution margin each quarter while incurring no additional fixed costs. What will happen to Kroger's operating income if it replaces the salad bars with olive bars?

Please see page 506 for solutions.

Pitfall to Avoid on Discontinuation Decisions

One of the most common mistakes managers make when analyzing whether or not to discontinue a product is to base the decision on a product line income statement that contains an allocation of common fixed expenses. **Common fixed expenses** are those expenses that *cannot* be traced directly to a product line. For example, in Exhibits 8-13 and 8-14, we see that fixed MOH costs such as property taxes, insurance, and depreciation are all common production costs that have been allocated between the product lines. While appropriate for product costing purposes, the allocation of common fixed costs is not appropriate for making product discontinuation decisions. Nor is the allocation of common fixed operating expenses, such as the building lease, utilities, Internet, or depreciation of office equipment.

As shown in Exhibit 8-13, the allocation of common fixed costs suggests that the company's overall operating income would *increase* by $38,000 if the company stopped making the moisturizers. However, based on the correct analysis in Exhibit 8-15, we know the company's operating income would actually *decline* by $47,500 if the moisturizers were discontinued. Using the product line income statement with allocated common costs would have led managers to the wrong conclusion.

Since income statements with allocated common costs can potentially mislead managers, some companies prepare **segment margin income statements**, which contain *no* allocation of common fixed costs. Segment margin income statements look very similar to Exhibit 8-13, except for two differences:

1. Only direct fixed costs that can be traced to specific product lines are deducted from the product line's contribution margin. The resulting operating income or loss for each individual product line is known as a **segment margin**.
2. All common fixed costs are shown under the company "total" column but are not allocated among product lines.

We discuss and illustrate segment margin income statement in more detail in Chapter 10. Although segment margin income statements eliminate the issue surrounding the allocation of common fixed costs, they still do not completely address the question of how much operating income would be gained or lost if a product line was discontinued. Why? Because, not all direct fixed costs are avoidable. For example, Garnier may have a long-term lease on a piece of production equipment used only to make moisturizers. As a result, the lease cost is a direct cost of the moisturizer line and would be factored into the moisturizers' segment margin. However, if the lease is noncancellable, its cost cannot be avoided by discontinuing the product line. Thus, the company still needs to perform the analysis shown in Exhibit 8-15 to correctly determine the effect of discontinuing a segment on the company's operating income.

Product Mix Decisions When Resources Are Constrained

5 Factor resource constraints into product mix decisions

In Chapter 7, we learned that a product's contribution margin per unit shows the profit made on each unit *before* considering fixed costs. The higher the contribution margin per unit, the more profit is added to the company's bottom line with each sale. As a result, you might think that companies should always emphasize the products that have the highest contribution margin per unit. Sometimes this strategy is correct, but as you'll see in this section, when companies face a constraint, that strategy can actually lead to lower profit. Let's see why this is the case.

Often companies have **constraints** that restrict the amount of product they can manufacture or the amount of product they can sell. For a manufacturer, the production constraint is often the number of available machine hours. For a merchandiser, such as Walmart, the primary constraint is cubic feet of display space. To determine which products to emphasize producing or displaying, managers facing constraints should consider the questions shown in Exhibit 8-16.

EXHIBIT 8-16 Product Mix Considerations

- What constraint(s) stops us from making (or displaying) all of the units we can sell?
- Which products offer the highest contribution margin per unit of the constraint?
- Would emphasizing one product over another affect fixed costs or sales of other products?

For our example, we'll consider Union Bay, a manufacturer of shirts and jeans. As shown in Exhibit 8-17, Union Bay's shirts have a higher contribution margin per unit than the company's jeans:

EXHIBIT 8-17 Contribution Margin Data

	Per Unit	
	Shirts	Jeans
Sale price	$ 30	$ 60
Less: Variable expenses	(12)	(48)
Contribution margin	$ 18	$ 12
Contribution margin ratio:		
Shirts: $18 ÷ $30	60%	
Jeans: $12 ÷ $60		20%

Each time a shirt is sold, the company's operating income increases by $18, whereas every time a pair of jeans is sold, the company's operating income increases by $12. Therefore, managers might assume they should emphasize selling shirts rather than jeans. However, an important piece of information is missing—the time it takes to make each product.

Let's say the company uses the same machines to produce both jeans and shirts. Furthermore, the machines have only 2,000 hours of capacity per period. In this case, machine hours is a production constraint. Note that this is a short-term decision because in the long run, Union Bay could expand its production facilities. Let's also assume that Union Bay can produce either 20 pairs of jeans *or* 10 shirts per machine hour. The company will incur the same fixed costs either way, so fixed costs are irrelevant. Assuming Union Bay can sell all of the product it produces, which product should Union Bay emphasize?

To maximize profits when fixed costs are irrelevant, follow this decision rule:

Because *machine hours* is the constraint, Union Bay needs to figure out which product has the *highest contribution margin per machine hour*. As shown in Exhibit 8-18, the company will multiply the contribution margin per unit by the number of units made per machine hour, to find the *contribution margin per machine hour*.

EXHIBIT 8-18 Calculating the Contribution Margin per Unit of Constraint

	A	B	C
1	Product Mix Analysis When Demand Is Unlimited	Shirts	Jeans
2	Contribution margin per unit	$ 18	$ 12
3	Multiply by: Number of units produced per machine hour	10	20
4	Contribution margin per machine hour	$ 180	$ 240
5	Multiply by: Available capacity (number of machine hours)	2,000	2,000
6	Total contribution margin at full capacity	$ 360,000	$ 480,000
7			

This analysis shows that jeans have a higher contribution margin *per machine hour* ($240) than shirts ($180). Therefore, Union Bay will earn more profit by producing jeans. Why? Because even though jeans have a lower contribution margin *per unit*, Union Bay can make twice as many jeans as shirts with the available machine hours. Exhibit 8-18 also proves that Union Bay would have a higher total profit by making and selling only jeans. Multiplying the contribution margin per machine hour by the available number of machine hours (2,000), we see that Union Bay can earn $480,000 of contribution margin by producing jeans but only $360,000 by producing shirts.

To maximize profit, Union Bay should make 40,000 jeans (2,000 machine hours × 20 jeans per hour) and zero shirts. Why zero shirts? Because for every machine hour spent making shirts, Union Bay would *give up* $60 of contribution margin ($240 per hour for jeans versus $180 per hour for shirts).

Other Considerations

We've looked at the first two questions in Exhibit 8-16, so now let's tackle the final question: Would emphasizing one product over another affect fixed costs or sales of other products?

We made a couple of assumptions about Union Bay: (1) Fixed costs wouldn't be affected by whether jeans or shirts were produced, and (2) Union Bay's sales of other products, if any, wouldn't be hurt by this decision. Let's challenge each of these assumptions.

First, let's consider fixed costs. Fixed costs become relevant if they differ between product mix alternatives. For example, what if Union Bay had a month-to-month lease on a zipper machine used only for making jeans? If Union Bay made only shirts, and no jeans, it could *avoid* the lease cost, thereby decreasing fixed costs. However, if Union Bay makes even one pair of jeans, the company will need to lease the machine. In this case, the fixed cost associated with the zipper machine becomes relevant because it differs between alternative product mixes (shirts only *versus* jeans and shirts).

STOP & THINK

If Union Bay only makes shirts and no jeans, it can cancel its monthly zipper machine lease. As a result, the company would save $20,000 of fixed costs each month. Assuming unlimited demand for its products, should Union Bay only make shirts?

Answer: Compare the profitability of the products as follows:

	A	B	C
1	**Product Mix Analysis When Fixed Costs Are Relevant**	**Shirts**	**Jeans**
2	Total contribution margin at full capacity (Exhibit 8-18)	$ 360,000	$ 480,000
3	Less: Avoidable fixed costs	0	20,000
4	Net benefit from the product at full capacity	$ 360,000	$ 460,000
5			

Even taking into consideration the cancellable zipper machine lease, we find that producing jeans is still more profitable than producing shirts.

Second, let's consider product mix on sales of other products. Could making only jeans (and not shirts) hurt sales of the company's other products? As discussed earlier in the chapter, companies must always consider companion products, that is, products that customers typically purchase together. For example, consumers who purchase spaghetti sauce will probably also purchase spaghetti noodles. In the case of Union Bay, if ties and jackets are specifically designed and produced to coordinate with Union Bay shirts, the sales of these companion products will decline as a result of no longer producing shirts.

Changing Assumptions: Product Mix When Demand Is Limited

In our Union Bay example, we assumed that the company could sell as many jeans and shirts as it could produce with the available machine capacity. Let's change that assumption. Assume that as a result of competition, demand for Union Bay's jeans is limited to 30,000 pairs per period. Because demand is no longer unlimited, Union Bay should make only as many jeans as it can sell and use the remaining machine hours to produce shirts. Let's see how this change in sales demand affects optimal production levels and profitability.

If Union Bay makes only 30,000 jeans, it will use only 1,500 machine hours (30,000 jeans ÷ 20 jeans per machine hour). That leaves 500 machine hours available for making shirts. Exhibit 8-19 shows Union Bay's contribution margin under the revised product mix:

EXHIBIT 8-19 Product Mix Under Limited Demand

	A	B	C	D
1	Product Mix Analysis When Demand Is Limited	Shirts	Jeans	Total
2	Contribution margin per machine hour (from Exhibit 8-18)	$ 180	$ 240	
3	Multiply by: Number of machine hours devoted to product	500	1,500	2,000
4	Total contribution margin at full capacity	$ 90,000	$ 360,000	$ 450,000
5				

NOTE: 30,000 jeans divided by 20 jeans per hour = 1,500 machine hours devoted to jeans. This leaves 500 available machine hours for making shirts.

Because of the change in product mix, Union Bay's total contribution margin will fall from $480,000 (as shown in Exhibit 8-18) to $450,000, a $30,000 decline. Union Bay had to give up $60 of contribution margin per machine hour ($240 − $180) on the 500 hours it spent producing shirts rather than jeans. However, Union Bay had no choice—the company would have incurred an *actual loss* from producing jeans that it could not sell.

Pitfalls to Avoid in Constraint Decisions

When finding the contribution margin *per unit of constraint*, managers must carefully consider the mathematical operation they use. Managers always start with the contribution margin per unit, and then either *multiply* or *divide*, to arrive at the contribution margin *per unit of constraint*. In our example, an hour is the unit of constraint. The correct mathematical operation depends on whether (1) a number of units are produced per hour (such as 20 units per hour) or (2) a number of hours is needed per unit (such as 5 hours per unit). Using the correct operational sign will result in finding the contribution margin per hour:

- CM/Unit × Units/Hour = CM/Hour
- CM/Unit ÷ Hours/Unit = CM/Hour

The same logic holds true for any constraint. Always check your math to make sure you used the correct operational sign.

Outsourcing Decisions (Make or Buy)

Outsourcing decisions are sometimes called "make-or-buy" decisions because managers must decide whether to make a product or service in-house or buy it from another company. Sometimes people confuse the term *outsourcing* with the term *offshoring*.

6 Analyze outsourcing (make-or-buy) decisions

- **Outsourcing** refers to contracting an outside company to produce a product or perform a service. Outsourced work could be done domestically or overseas.
- **Offshoring** refers to having work performed overseas. Companies offshore work by either (1) operating their own manufacturing plants and call centers overseas or (2) outsourcing the overseas work to another company. Thus, offshored work is not necessarily outsourced work.

Outsourcing is not new. For years, companies have outsourced specialized services such as marketing, payroll processing, and legal work to firms that have expertise in those areas. More and more, brand-name companies are outsourcing the production of their products so that they can concentrate on their core competencies of marketing and product development. In fact, so much production is outsourced that contract manufacturing has become an entire industry. **Contract manufacturers,** such as those that Nike uses, are manufacturers that only make products for other companies, not for themselves. By using contract manufacturers, companies can avoid the risks associated with building manufacturing infrastructure. As we discussed in Chapter 7, companies with relatively more fixed costs have a riskier cost structure.

In deciding what to do, managers should consider the questions outlined in Exhibit 8-20.

EXHIBIT 8-20 Outsourcing Considerations

- How do our variable costs per unit compare to the outsourcing cost per unit?
- Are any fixed costs avoidable if we outsource?
- What could we do with the freed capacity?
- What volume do we need?

First, managers need to consider the variable cost of producing their own products (or services) with the variable costs charged by the outside company. The next two questions are similar to the questions managers consider when deciding to discontinue a product: Can any fixed costs be avoided, and what could we do with the freed capacity? Why are these questions so similar to what we considered with the discontinuation decision? Because in essence, outsourcing involves discontinuing an activity (such as production, marketing, payroll processing, and so forth) but paying another company to perform it.

Outsourcing Example

Assume that Sony is deciding whether to continue making its own earbuds or to outsource production to Shenzhen Electronics, a contract manufacturer specializing in consumer electronics. Let's assume Sony's cost to produce 2 million earbuds each period is as shown in Exhibit 8-21:[2]

EXHIBIT 8-21 Production Costs and Volume

	A	B	C
1	**Comparison of Variable and Absorption Costs**	**Variable Cost per Unit**	**Total Cost (2 million units)**
2	Direct materials	$ 4.00	$ 8,000,000
3	Direct labor	0.50	1,000,000
4	Variable MOH	1.50	3,000,000
5	Total variable manufacturing cost	$ 6.00	$ 12,000,000
6	Plus: Fixed MOH		4,000,000
7	Total manufacturing cost		$ 16,000,000
8	Divide by: Number of units		2,000,000
9	Total cost per unit (absorption costing)		$ 8.00
10			

Let's further assume that Shenzhen Electronics is willing to provide earbuds to Sony for $7.00 each. Should Sony make the earbuds or should it buy them from Shenzhen? The $7.00 price is less than the full absorption cost per unit ($8.00) but greater than Sony's variable cost per unit ($6.00).

---

[2] The hypothetical cost information was created solely for academic purposes and is not intended, in any way, to represent the actual costs incurred by Sony or the price that would be charged by Shenzhen Electronics.

Let's see how the questions addressed in Exhibit 8-20 apply to our example:

- **Variable costs:** The variable cost of producing each earbud ($6.00) is less than the outsourcing cost ($7.00). Based on variable costs alone, Sony should manufacture the earbuds in-house. However, managers must still consider fixed costs.
- **Fixed costs:** Let's assume that Sony could save $500,000 of fixed costs each period by outsourcing. Most of the savings would be the result of cancellable leases on specialized machinery used for making the earbuds. However, most of the fixed manufacturing costs, such as property taxes, relate to plant capacity and will continue to exist even if the company stops making earbuds.
- **Use of freed capacity:** We'll start by assuming that Sony has no other use for the production capacity, so it will remain idle. We will change this assumption later.

Given this information, what should Sony do? Exhibit 8-22 compares the two alternatives.

> **Why is this important?**
> "Almost any **business activity** can be **outsourced** (for example, manufacturing, marketing, and payroll). **Companies** often choose to retain only their **core competencies**—things they are *really* good at doing—and **outsource** just about everything else to companies that can do it *better* or more cost-effectively for them."

EXHIBIT 8-22 Incremental Analysis for Outsourcing Decisions

	A	B	C	D
1	Incremental Analysis Outsourcing Decision	Make Earbuds	Outsource Earbuds	Difference
2	Variable Costs:			
3	If make: $6.00 × 2 million units If outsource: $7.00 × 2 million units	$ 12,000,000	$ 14,000,000	$ 2,000,000
4	Plus: Fixed costs	4,000,000	3,500,000	(500,000)
5	Total cost of producing 2,000,000 units	$ 16,000,000	$ 17,500,000	$ 1,500,000
6				

This analysis shows that Sony should continue to make the earbuds. Why is this the case? As shown in the last column of Exhibit 8-22, the company would spend $2,000,000 more in variable costs to outsource the earbuds but would only save $500,000 in fixed costs. The net result is a $1,500,000 increase in total costs if the company outsources production.

Rather than looking at the *total* costs under both scenarios, another way to look at this decision is to simply focus on the "Difference" column shown in Exhibit 8-22. The cost-benefit analysis in Exhibit 8-23 shows this alternative approach:

EXHIBIT 8-23 Alternative Incremental Analysis

	A	B
1	Alternative Cost-Benefit Analysis	
2	Outsourcing Decision	
3	Variable cost per unit to outsource	$ 7.00
4	Less: Variable cost per unit to manufacture	6.00
5	Incremental variable cost per unit to outsource	$ 1.00
6	Multiply by: Number of units needed	2,000,000
7	Incremental variable cost to outsource	$ 2,000,000
8	Less: Fixed costs savings from outsourcing	500,000
9	Net extra cost to outsource	$ 1,500,000
10		

Notice how the analysis in both Exhibit 8-22 and Exhibit 8-23 is affected by volume, which we've currently assumed to be 2 million earbuds per period. If Sony needs fewer than 500,000 earbuds each period, then the decision to continue making the earbuds would be reversed and Sony would outsource the production. Why is this the case? Sony will pay $1 more in variable costs per unit to outsource production but can only save $500,000 in fixed costs by outsourcing. At higher volumes, the extra variable costs outweigh the cost savings; but at lower volumes (less than 500,000 units), the fixed cost savings are greater than the extra variable costs to outsource. As this example shows, volume is a key driver in the decision of whether or not to outsource

Notice how Exhibits 8-22 and 8-23 use our two keys for decision making: (1) focus on relevant data (costs that differ between alternatives), and (2) use a contribution margin approach that separates variable costs from fixed costs. Our decision rule for outsourcing is as follows:

Determining an Acceptable Outsourcing Price

In Chapter 7, we used the concept of an indifference point to help managers decide how to structure costs. We can use the same concept here to determine the maximum price Sony would be willing to pay to have another manufacturer make the earbuds. By knowing up front how much it would be willing to pay, the company can proactively seek bids from multiple contract manufacturers.

Exhibit 8-24 shows how to calculate the indifference point. The exhibit begins by equating the costs of making the earbuds with the costs of outsourcing the earbuds. Next, all of the information from Exhibit 8-22 is inserted into the equations, with the exception of the variable cost per unit under the outsourcing alternative. The variable cost of outsourcing each unit is the cost we wish to solve for.

EXHIBIT 8-24 Using an Indifference Point to Find an Acceptable Outsourcing Price

Costs of making earbuds	=	Costs of outsourcing earbuds
Variable Costs + Fixed Costs	=	Variable Costs + Fixed Costs
(2,000,000 units × $6) + $4,000,000	=	(2,000,000 units × Variable cost per unit) + $3,500,000
$16,000,000	=	(2,000,000 × Variable cost per unit) + $3,500,000
$12,500,000	=	(2,000,000 × Variable cost per unit)
Variable cost per unit	=	$6.25

This analysis shows that, all else being equal, Sony would be *indifferent* between making and outsourcing 2 million earbuds if the outsourcing price was exactly $6.25 a unit. Therefore, the most Sony would be willing to pay for this volume of earbuds would be $6.25 a unit.

Notice, again, that this analysis is dependent on production volume. For example, if Sony needs 3 million units, the most it would be willing to pay would be $6.17 per unit. Why the difference? By producing more units, Sony's fixed costs are being utilized more efficiently, driving down the average cost of making each unit. As Sony's own unit cost falls, so will the price it is willing to pay some other company to make the earbuds. The opposite is also true: the fewer units Sony needs, the more it will be willing to pay another company to make the earbuds.

Alternative Use of Freed Capacity

Now let's change one of our original assumptions. Instead of assuming that the production capacity will remain idle, let's assume that Sony could lease it out to another company for $2.5 million per period. In this case, Sony must consider its **opportunity cost**, which is the benefit foregone by choosing a particular course of action. If Sony continues to make its own earbuds, it will be losing out on the opportunity to earn lease income of $2.5 million per period.

Exhibit 8-25 incorporates this information into our analysis by showing lease income as additional income that *could be made* if the company outsources production. Thus, we show the lease income in the "Outsource Earbuds" column. This income offsets some of the cost associated with outsourcing. Alternatively, we could show the $2.5 million as an *additional* cost (an opportunity cost) in the "Make Earbuds" column.

EXHIBIT 8-25 Incremental Analysis Incorporating Next Best Use of Freed Capacity

	A	B	C	D
1	Incremental Analysis Outsourcing Decision	Make Earbuds	Outsource Earbuds	Difference
2	Variable Costs:			
3	If make: $6.00 × 2 million units If outsource: $7.00 × 2 million units	$ 12,000,000	$ 14,000,000	$ 2,000,000
4	Plus: Fixed costs	4,000,000	3,500,000	(500,000)
5	Total cost of producing 2,000,000 units	$ 16,000,000	$ 17,500,000	$ 1,500,000
6	Less: Lease income if outsource	0	2,500,000	2,500,000
7	Net cost	$ 16,000,000	$ 15,000,000	$ (1,000,000)
8				

This analysis shows that Sony will benefit by $1,000,000 each period by outsourcing production of the earbuds. This result holds regardless of whether we treat the $2.5 million lease as income in the "Outsource Earbuds" column or as an opportunity cost in the "Make Earbuds" column. Again, notice that a different production volume could potentially result in a different outcome.

Pitfall to Avoid on Outsourcing Decisions

One of the most common mistakes managers make when analyzing whether or not to outsource is to compare the absorption cost per unit ($8 in our example in Exhibit 8-21) with the outsourcing cost per unit ($7.00 in our example). Always remember that absorption costing includes fixed manufacturing costs. These costs are not *incurred* on a per-unit basis, but rather are incurred as a total, fixed amount. As we just saw in our example, some, but not all, of the fixed costs may also be avoided by outsourcing. Thus, to avoid this decision pitfall, don't ever use the absorption cost per unit; rather, compare the variable cost of producing in-house with the variable cost of outsourcing, and then factor in the relevant fixed costs.

Potential Benefits and Drawbacks of Outsourcing

Outsourcing has many benefits; otherwise so many companies wouldn't do it. As mentioned earlier, outsourcing allows companies to concentrate on their core competencies as well as take advantage of other companies' expertise and best practices. When volume is low or fluctuates greatly, outsourcing can reduce the risks associated with investing in capacity infrastructure (plant, equipment, and personnel). And, as highlighted in our analyses, outsourcing can be a lower cost alternative.

However, outsourcing is not without drawbacks. When a company outsources, it gives up control, including control over quality and production scheduling. It must rely on the supplier to provide the product or service at an agreed-upon level of quality, at agreed-upon delivery dates. Often, one or more employees are needed just to manage and oversee the relationship with the supplier. As we saw in the sustainability feature, Nike has over 150 people in house who monitor its contract manufacturers. The cost of employing any such additional personnel should also be considered when comparing the cost of outsourcing with the cost of producing in-house.

In addition, for those companies embracing the triple bottom line, outsourcing and offshoring have additional drawbacks. Why? Because, unfortunately, outsourcing often results in laying off employees. Moreover, offshored contract work is not subject to the same regulated labor practices and working conditions found in the United States. When companies offshore work, they need to make sure laborers are treated fairly and work in a safe environment. That's why Nike has a Code of Conduct for all of its contract manufacturers. While overseas labor is often cheap and readily available, the exploitation of any people, in any country, is not an acceptable business practice.

▶ Try It!

Rossignol makes downhill ski equipment. Assume that Atomic has offered to produce ski poles for Rossignol for $18 per pair. Rossignol needs 100,000 pairs of poles per period. Rossignol can only avoid $125,000 of fixed costs if it outsources; the remaining fixed costs are unavoidable. Rossignol currently has the following costs at a production level of 100,000 pairs of poles:

Manufacturing Costs	Total Cost	Cost per pair (100,000 pairs)
Direct Materials	$ 750,000	$ 7.50
Direct Labor	80,000	0.80
Variable MOH	520,000	5.20
Fixed MOH	650,000	6.50
Total	$2,000,000	$20.00

1. Should Rossignol outsource ski pole production if the next best use of the freed capacity is to leave it idle? What effect will outsourcing have on Rossignol operating income?
2. If the freed capacity could be used to produce ski boots that would provide $500,000 of operating income, should Rossignol outsource ski pole production?

Please see page 506 for solutions.

Decisions to Sell As Is or Process Further

7 Decide whether to sell a product "as is" or process it further

At what point in processing should a company sell its product? Many companies, especially those in the food processing and natural resource industries, face this business decision. Companies in these industries process a raw material (milk, corn, crude oil, lumber, and so forth) to a point before it is saleable. For example, Kraft pasteurizes raw milk before it is saleable. Kraft must then decide whether it should sell the pasteurized milk "as is" or process it further into other dairy products (reduced-fat milk, butter, sour cream, cottage cheese, yogurt, blocks of cheese, shredded cheese, and so forth). Managers consider the questions shown in Exhibit 8-26 when deciding whether to sell as is or process further.

EXHIBIT 8-26 Sell As Is or Process Further Considerations

- How much revenue will we receive if we sell the product as is?
- How much revenue will we receive if we sell the product *after* processing it further?
- How much extra will it cost to process the product further?

Let's consider Bertolli, the manufacturer of Italian food products. Suppose Bertolli spends $100,000 to process raw olives into 50,000 quarts of plain virgin olive oil. Should

Bertolli sell the olive oil as is, or should it spend more to process the olive oil into gourmet dipping oils, such as a Basil and Garlic Infused Dipping Oil? In making the decision, Bertolli's managers consider the following relevant information:[3]

- Bertolli could sell the plain olive oil for $5 per quart, for a total of $250,000 (50,000 × $5).
- Bertolli could sell the gourmet dipping oil for $7 per quart, for a total of $350,000 (50,000 × $7).
- Bertolli would have to spend $0.75 per quart, or $37,500 (50,000 × $0.75), to further process the plain olive oil into the gourmet dipping oil. This cost would include the extra direct materials required (such as basil, garlic, and the incremental cost of premium glass containers) as well as the extra conversion costs incurred (the cost of any *additional* machinery and labor that the company would need to purchase in order to complete the extra processing).

By examining the incremental analysis shown in Exhibit 8-27, Bertolli's managers can see that they can increase operating income by $62,500 by further processing the plain olive oil into the gourmet dipping oil. The extra $100,000 of revenue greatly exceeds the incremental $37,500 of cost incurred to further process the olive oil.

Notice that Bertolli's managers do *not* consider the $100,000 originally spent on processing the olives into olive oil. Why? It is a sunk cost. Recall from our previous discussion that a sunk cost is a past cost that cannot be changed regardless of which future action the company takes. Bertolli has incurred $100,000 regardless of whether it sells the olive oil as is or processes it further into gourmet dipping oils. Therefore, the cost is *not* relevant to the decision.

> **Why is this important?**
>
> "Some companies are able to sell their products at **different points** of completion. For example, some furniture **manufacturers** sell flat-packed bookshelves, TV stands, and home office furniture that the consumer must **finish assembling**. A **cost-benefit analysis** helps managers choose the most **profitable point** at which to sell the company's products."

EXHIBIT 8-27 Incremental Analysis for Sell As Is or Process Further Decision

	A	B	C	D
1	**Incremental Analysis** **Sell or Process Further Decision**	**Sell As Is**	**Process Further**	**Difference**
2	Revenues:			
3	If sell as is: $5.00 × 50,000 quarts If process further: $7.00 × 50,000 quarts	$ 250,000	$ 350,000	$ 100,000
4	Less: Extra cost of processing further	0	37,500	37,500
5	Net benefit to operating income	$ 250,000	$ 312,500	$ 62,500
6				

Thus, the decision rule is as follows:

---

[3] All references to Bertolli in this hypothetical example were created by the author solely for academic purposes and are not intended, in any way, to represent the actual business practices of, or costs incurred by, Bertolli.

Decision Guidelines

Short-Term Special Business Decisions

Nike's managers have faced many business decisions in building one of the most recognizable brands in the world. Here are some of the guidelines they have used to make profitable decisions.

Decision	Guidelines
Should we discontinue any segment of our operations (for example, a particular product line or retail store location)?	If the segment is generating a positive contribution margin it is helping to cover the company's fixed costs. However, some costs might be avoided by discontinuing the segment. Compare the contribution margin from the segment to the fixed cost savings to determine which course of action is most profitable. In addition, consider what would be done with the freed capacity and whether the discontinuation of the segment would have any effect (positive or negative) on sales in the company's remaining segments.
What decision pitfalls should be avoided when we decide whether or not to discontinue a segment?	Avoid including any allocation of common fixed costs in the analysis. These costs will not be avoided if the segment is discontinued; therefore, they are irrelevant to the decision.
Which products should we emphasize if we have a short-term production constraint, such as limited machine hours used to produce various products?	When there is a production constraint, managers should emphasize the products that have the highest contribution margin per the constraint, rather than the products that have the highest contribution margin per unit. In addition, managers need to consider the possible effect of emphasizing one product over another on the sale of companion products (such as coordinating sportswear).
What are some of the benefits and drawbacks of outsourcing?	Potential benefits: allows companies to focus on core competencies and purchase the expertise and best practices of other companies; lower costs; decreased risk of investing in too much plant capacity; flexibility. Potential drawbacks: less control over quality, delivery timing, labor practices, and working conditions which could impact a company's reputation. In addition, offshored work may be subject to import tariffs, shipping disruptions, and exchange rate fluctuations.
What financial considerations should we make when deciding whether to outsource any aspect of our operations?	Managers should compare the in-house variable cost per unit to the outsourcing cost per unit. In addition, they should consider whether any fixed costs could be avoided by outsourcing. Finally, they should consider what they would do with the freed capacity.
How should we determine the maximum price we are willing to pay for outsourcing?	Solve for the indifference point by setting the cost to make equal to the cost to outsource. The indifference point will be the maximum price you would pay.
How should we decide whether to sell our product "as is" or process it further?	Compare the incremental revenue gained from processing further to the extra cost to process further. If the incremental revenue exceeds the incremental cost, then process further.

SUMMARY PROBLEM 2

Requirements

1. Aziz produces Standard and Deluxe sunglasses:

	Per Pair	
	Standard	Deluxe
Sale price	$20	$30
Variable expenses	16	21

The company has 15,000 machine hours available. In one machine hour, Aziz can produce 70 pairs of the Standard model or 30 pairs of the Deluxe model. Assuming machine hours is a constraint, which model should Aziz emphasize?

2. SmartSocks incurs the following costs for 20,000 pairs of its high-tech hiking socks:

Direct materials	$ 20,000
Direct labor	80,000
Variable manufacturing overhead	40,000
Fixed manufacturing overhead	80,000
Total manufacturing cost	$220,000
Cost per pair ($220,000 ÷ 20,000)	$ 11

Another manufacturer has offered to sell SmartSocks similar socks for $10 a pair, a total purchase cost of $200,000. If SmartSocks outsources *and* leaves its plant idle, it can save $50,000 of fixed overhead cost. Or the company can use the released facilities to make other products that will contribute $70,000 to profits. In this case, the company will not be able to avoid any fixed costs. Identify and analyze the alternatives. What is the best course of action?

3. A local home improvement warehouse store shows the following product line income statement for the month. All common fixed costs are allocated to departments based on percentage of sales revenue generated by the department.

	A	B	C	D	E
1		Paint	Lumber	Lighting	Store Total
2	Sales	$ 500,000	$ 400,000	$ 100,000	$ 1,000,000
3	Less: Variable Costs	300,000	160,000	50,000	510,000
4	Contribution margin	200,000	240,000	50,000	490,000
5	Less: Direct Fixed Costs	50,000	40,000	35,000	125,000
6	Less: Common Fixed Costs	100,000	80,000	20,000	200,000
7	Operating Income (Loss)	$ 50,000	$ 120,000	($5,000)	$ 165,000
8					

Assuming $30,000 of the Lighting Department's direct fixed costs are avoidable, should the store managers discontinue the Lighting Department? The space currently occupied by the Lighting Department would be replaced with a Hardware Department that is expected to have sales of $200,000, variable costs of $80,000 and new direct fixed costs of $30,000.

SOLUTIONS

Requirement 1

	A	B	C
1	Product Mix Decision	Standard	Deluxe
2	Sales price per unit	$ 20	$ 30
3	Less: Variable cost per unit	16	21
4	Contribution margin per unit	$ 4	$ 9
5	Multiply by: Number of units produced per machine hour	70	30
6	Contribution margin per machine hour	$ 280	$ 270
7	Multiply by: Available capacity (number of machine hours)	15,000	15,000
8	Total contribution margin at full capacity	$ 4,200,000	$ 4,050,000
9			

Decision: Emphasize the Standard model because it has the higher contribution margin per unit of the constraint—machine hours—resulting in a higher contribution margin for the company.

Requirement 2

	A	B	C	D
1	Incremental Analysis Outsourcing Decision	Make Socks	Outsource and Leave Idle	Outsource and Make Other Products
2	Variable Costs:			
3	If make: DM, DL, Variable MOH If outsource: $10 × 20,000 units	$ 140,000	$ 200,000	$ 200,000
4	Plus: Fixed costs	80,000	30,000	80,000
5	Total cost of producing 2,000,000 units	$ 220,000	$ 230,000	$ 280,000
6	Less: Profit from other products	0	0	70,000
7	Net cost	$ 220,000	$ 230,000	$ 210,000
8				

Decision: SmartSocks should outsource the socks from the outside supplier and use the released facilities to make other products.

Requirement 3

	A	B	C
1	Incremental Analysis of Discontinuation Decision		Total
2	Contribution margin lost if Lighting is discontinued		$ 50,000
3	Less: Fixed costs savings if Lighting is discontinued		30,000
4	Income lost if Lighting is discontinued		$ 20,000
5			
6	Contribution margin from Hardware Department ($200,000–$80,000)	$ 120,000	
7	Less: Direct fixed costs	30,000	
8	Segment margin provided by the Hardware Department		$ 90,000
9	Net benefit of discontinuing the Lighting Department and replacing with a Hardware Department		$ 70,000
10			

Decision: Managers should discontinue the Lighting Department and replace it with a Hardware Department.

END OF CHAPTER

Learning Objectives

- 1 Describe and identify information relevant to short-term business decisions
- 2 Describe and apply different approaches to pricing
- 3 Decide whether to accept a special order
- 4 Decide whether to discontinue a product, department, or store
- 5 Factor resource constraints into product mix decisions
- 6 Analyze outsourcing (make-or-buy) decisions
- 7 Decide whether to sell a product "as is" or process it further

Accounting Vocabulary

Avoidable Fixed Costs. (461) Fixed costs that can be eliminated as a result of taking a particular course of action.

Common Fixed Expenses. (463) Expenses that cannot be traced to a particular product line.

Constraint. (464) A factor that restricts the production or sale of a product.

Contract Manufacturers. (468) Manufacturers that make products for other companies, not for themselves.

Cost-Plus Pricing. (450) An approach to pricing used by price-setters; cost-plus pricing begins with the product's total costs and adds the company's desired profit to determine a cost-plus price.

Offshoring. (467) Having work performed overseas. Offshored work can be performed either by the company itself or by outsourcing the work to another company.

Opportunity Cost. (471) The benefit forgone by choosing a particular alternative course of action.

Outsourcing. (467) Contracting an outside company to produce a product or perform a service. Outsourced work can be done domestically or overseas.

Product Line Income Statement. (460) An income statement that shows the operating income of each product line, as well as the company as a whole.

Relevant Information. (444) Expected *future* data that *differ* among alternatives.

Segment Margin. (464) The income resulting from subtracting only the direct fixed costs of a product line from its contribution margin. The segment margin contains no allocation of common fixed costs.

Segment Margin Income Statement. (464) A product line income statement that contains no allocation of common fixed costs. Only direct fixed costs that can be traced to specific product lines are subtracted from the product line's contribution margin. All common fixed costs remain unallocated and are shown only under the company total.

Sunk Cost. (446) A past cost that cannot be changed regardless of which future action is taken.

Target Costing. (451) An approach to pricing used by price-takers; target costing begins with the revenue at market price and subtracts the company's desired profit to arrive at the target total cost.

Unavoidable Fixed Costs. (461) Fixed costs that will continue to be incurred even if a particular course of action is taken.

MyAccountingLab — Go to http://myaccountinglab.com/ for the following Quick Check, Short Exercises, Exercises, and Problems. They are available with immediate grading, explanations of correct and incorrect answers, and interactive media that acts as your own online tutor.

Quick Check

1. (Learning Objective 1) Which of the following is *false*?
   a. Relevant information is always financial in nature.
   b. Relevant information always regards the future.
   c. Sunk costs are never relevant to a decision.
   d. Relevant information always differs among alternatives.

2. (Learning Objective 1) Keys to making short-term decisions include which of the following?
   a. Using a contribution margin approach that separates variable costs from fixed costs
   b. Focusing on relevant revenues, costs, and profits
   c. Both of the above
   d. None of the above

477

3. *(Learning Objective 2)* Which is true of price-setters?
   a. Their pricing approach emphasizes cost-plus pricing.
   b. Their pricing approach emphasizes target costing.
   c. Their products lack uniqueness.
   d. They are in highly competitive markets.

4. *(Learning Objective 3)* Which of the following should be considered for special order decisions?
   a. Whether the special order will affect regular sales in the long run
   b. Whether the special price will be high enough to cover incremental costs of filling the order
   c. Whether excess capacity exists
   d. All of the listed choices should be considered in special order decisions.

5. *(Learning Objective 2)* The formula for arriving at target cost is which of the following?
   a. Cost minus actual profit
   b. Revenue minus variable cost
   c. Revenue minus desired profit
   d. Revenue minus actual profit

6. *(Learning Objective 4)* Which of the following is *not* relevant when deciding whether or not to discontinue a product?
   a. Unavoidable fixed costs related to the product
   b. Avoidable fixed costs related to the product
   c. The product's contribution margin
   d. The effect of discontinuation on the sales of the company's other products.

7. *(Learning Objective 4)* A segment margin is the
   a. segment's contribution margin minus all fixed costs.
   b. segment's contribution margin minus allocated fixed costs.
   c. same as the segment's contribution margin.
   d. segment's contribution margin minus direct fixed costs.

8. *(Learning Objective 5)* When resources are constrained, which of the following should be used to guide product mix decisions?
   a. The products' gross margin per unit of constraint
   b. The products' contribution margin per unit of constraint
   c. The products' contribution margin
   d. The products' gross margin

9. *(Learning Objective 6)* Which of the following is *false*?
   a. Outsourcing decisions should take into consideration the intended use of freed capacity.
   b. Outsourcing refers to having work performed overseas.
   c. Outsourcing decisions are often referred to as "make-or-buy" decisions.
   d. Contract manufacturers are manufacturers that make products for other companies.

10. *(Learning Objective 7)* In making "sell as is" decisions, companies should consider all of the following EXCEPT for:
    a. Incremental costs that would be incurred by processing further.
    b. Costs incurred up to the "sell as is" decision point.
    c. Incremental revenues that would be earned by processing further.
    d. All of the above should be considered.

Quick Check Answers

1. a 2. c 3. a 4. d 5. c 6. a 7. d 8. b 9. b 10. b

Short Exercises

S8-1 Determine relevance of information *(Learning Objective 1)*

You are trying to decide whether to trade in your laser printer for a more recent model. Your usage pattern will remain unchanged, but the old and new printers use different toner cartridges. Are the following items relevant or irrelevant to your decision?
   a. The trade-in value of the old printer
   b. Paper costs
   c. The difference between the cost of toner cartridges
   d. The price of the new printer
   e. The price you paid for the old printer

S8-2 Determine pricing approach and target price (Learning Objective 2)

Winter Sports Inc. operates a Rocky Mountain ski resort. The company is planning its lift ticket pricing for the coming ski season. Investors would like to earn a 15% return on the company's $100 million of assets. The company incurs primarily fixed costs to groom the runs and operate the lifts. Winter Sports projects fixed costs to be $33,750,000 for the ski season. The resort serves 750,000 skiers and snowboarders each season. Variable costs are $10 per guest. Currently, the resort has such a favorable reputation among skiers and snowboarders that it has some control over the lift ticket prices.

1. Would Winter Sports emphasize target costing or cost-plus pricing. Why?
2. If other resorts in the area charge $65 per day, what price should Winter Sports charge?

S8-3 Use target costing to analyze data (Learning Objective 2)

See the Winter Sports Inc. data from S8-2. Assume that Winter Sports' reputation has diminished and other resorts in the vicinity are charging only $65 per lift ticket. Winter Sports has become a price-taker and won't be able to charge more than its competitors. At the market price, Winter Sports' managers believe they will still serve 750,000 skiers and snowboarders each season.

1. If Winter Sports can't reduce its costs, what profit will it earn? State your answer in dollars and as a percent of assets. Will investors be happy with the profit level? Show your analysis.
2. Assume that Winter Sports has found ways to cut its fixed costs to $30 million. What is its new target variable cost per skier/snowboarder? Assume investors want to earn a 15% return on assets. Compare this to the current variable cost per skier/snowboarder. Comment on your results.

S8-4 Analyze special order decision (Learning Objective 3)

Orr Products manufactures t-shirts. It has the following costs when its production level is 100,000 units (t-shirts):

	Total costs for 100,000 units
Direct materials	$ 320,000
Direct labor	40,000
Variable manufacturing overhead	85,000
Fixed manufacturing overhead	120,000
Total manufacturing costs	$ 565,000

The company's relevant range extends to 115,000 units. Orr has received a special order for 10,000 t-shirts at a special price of $50,000 for the entire order. The special order t-shirt would use a fabric that is less expensive than the standard fabric used by Orr, which would allow Orr to save $0.50 per t-shirt in direct materials when manufacturing this special order. Orr has the excess capacity to manufacture this special order. Its total fixed costs will not be impacted by the special order. What will happen to Orr's operating income if it accepts this special order?

S8-5 Special order decision (Learning Objective 3)

Shilling Manufacturing produces and sells oil filters for $3.25 each. A retailer has offered to purchase 20,000 oil filters for $1.55 per filter. Of the total manufacturing cost per filter of $2.10, $1.30 is the variable manufacturing cost per filter. For this special order, Shilling would have to buy a special stamping machine that costs $8,000 to mark the customer's logo on the special order oil filters. The machine would be scrapped when the special order is complete. This special order would use manufacturing capacity that would otherwise be idle. No variable nonmanufacturing costs would be incurred by the special order. Regular sales would not be affected by the special order.

Would you recommend that Shilling accept the special order under these conditions?

S8-6 Decide whether to discontinue a department *(Learning Objective 4)*

Devine Fashion in Chicago operates three departments: Men's, Women's, and Accessories. Devine Fashion allocates all fixed expenses (unavoidable building depreciation and utilities) based on each department's square footage. Departmental operating income data for the third quarter of the current year are as follows:

	A	B	C	D	E
1		Devine Fashions			
2		Product Line Contribution Margin Income Statement			
3		For the Year			
4					
5		Product lines			
6		Men's	Women's	Accessories	Company Total
7	Sales revenue	$ 105,000	$ 52,000	$ 101,000	$ 258,000
8	Less: Variable expenses	58,000	28,000	90,000	176,000
9	Contribution margin	$ 47,000	$ 24,000	$ 11,000	$ 82,000
10	Less: Fixed expenses	25,000	22,000	26,000	73,000
11	Operating income	$ 22,000	$ 2,000	$ (15,000)	$ 9,000
12					

The store will remain in the same building regardless of whether any of the departments are discontinued. Should Devine Fashion discontinue any of the departments? Give your reason.

S8-7 Discontinue a department: Revised information *(Learning Objective 4)*

Consider Devine Fashion from S8-6. Assume that the fixed expenses assigned to each department include only direct fixed costs of the department (rather than unavoidable fixed costs as given in S8-6):

- Salary of the department's manager
- Cost of advertising directly related to that department

If Devine Fashion discontinues a department, it will not incur these fixed expenses. Under these circumstances, should Devine Fashion discontinue any of the departments? Give your reason.

S8-8 Replace a department *(Learning Objective 4)*

Consider Devine Fashion from S8-6. Assume once again that all fixed costs are unavoidable. If the company discontinues one of the current departments, it plans to replace the discontinued department with a Shoe Department. The company expects the Shoe Department to produce $84,000 in sales and have $47,000 of variable costs. Because the shoe business would be new to Devine Fashion, the company would have to incur an additional $7,100 of fixed costs (advertising, new shoe display racks, and other fixed costs) per quarter related to the department. What should the company do now?

S8-9 Product mix decision: Unlimited demand *(Learning Objective 5)*

Storage Solutions produces plastic storage bins for household storage needs. The company makes two sizes of bins: Large (50 gallon) and Regular (35 gallon). Demand for the product is so high that the company can sell as many of each size as it can produce. The same machinery is used to produce both sizes. The machinery is available for only 3,000 hours per period. The company can produce 10 Large bins every hour compared to 15 Regular bins in the same amount of time. Fixed expenses amount to $110,000 per period. Sales prices and variable costs are as follows:

	Regular	Large
Sales price per unit	$8.10	$10.50
Variable cost per unit	$3.50	$ 4.20

1. Which product should Storage Solutions emphasize? Why?
2. To maximize profits, how many of each size bin should the company produce?
3. Given this product mix, what will the company's operating income be?

Relevant Costs for Short-Term Decisions **481**

S8-10 Product mix decision: Limited demand *(Learning Objective 5)*

Consider Storage Solutions from S8-9. Assume that demand for Regular bins is limited to 36,000 units and demand for Large bins is limited to 25,000 units.

1. How many of each size bin should the company make now?
2. Given this product mix, what will be the company's operating income?
3. Explain why the operating income is less than it was when the company was producing its optimal product mix.

S8-11 Outsourcing production decision *(Learning Objectives 1 & 6)*

Suppose a Luca's Garden restaurant is considering whether to (1) bake bread for its restaurant in-house or (2) buy the bread from a local bakery. The chef estimates that variable costs of making each loaf include $0.54 of ingredients, $0.20 of variable overhead (electricity to run the oven), and $0.71 of direct labor for kneading and forming the loaves. Allocating fixed overhead (depreciation on the kitchen equipment and building) based on direct labor assigns $1.04 of fixed overhead per loaf. None of the fixed costs are avoidable. The local bakery would charge Luca's Garden $1.72 per loaf.

1. What is the absorption cost of making a loaf of bread in-house? What is the variable cost per loaf?
2. Should Luca's Garden bake the bread in-house or buy from the local bakery? Why?
3. In addition to the financial analysis, what else should Luca's Garden consider when making this decision?

S8-12 Relevant information for outsourcing delivery function *(Learning Objectives 1 & 6)*

Myer Food in Bowling Green, Kentucky, manufactures and markets snack foods. Mila Giles manages the company's fleet of 220 delivery trucks. Giles has been charged with "reengineering" the fleet-management function. She has an important decision to make.

- Should she continue to manage the fleet in-house with the five employees reporting to her? To do so, she will have to acquire new fleet-management software to streamline Myer Food's fleet-management process.
- Should she outsource the fleet-management function to Fleet Management Services, a company that specializes in managing fleets of trucks for other companies? Fleet Management Services would take over the maintenance, repair, and scheduling of Myer Food's fleet (but Myer Food would retain ownership). This alternative would require Giles to lay off her five employees. However, her own job would be secure, as she would be Myer Food's liaison with Fleet Management Services.

Assume that Giles' records show the following data concerning Myer Food's fleet:

Book value of Myer Food's trucks, with an estimated five-year life	$ 3,800,000
Annual leasing fee for new fleet-management software	$ 9,000
Annual maintenance of trucks	$ 166,000
Fleet Supervisor Giles' annual salary	$ 65,000
Total annual salaries of Myer Food's five other fleet-management employees	$ 160,000

Suppose that Fleet Management Services offers to manage Myer Food's fleet for an annual fee of $280,000.

Which alternative will maximize Myer Food's short-term operating income?

S8-13 Scrap or process further decision *(Learning Objective 7)*

Mast Truck Accessories has an inventory of 485 obsolete remote entry keys that are carried in inventory at a manufacturing cost of $75,175. Production Supervisor Carla Lewis must decide to do one of the following:

- Process the inventory further at a cost of $30,000, with the expectation of selling it for $31,000.
- Scrap the inventory for a sales price of $4,000.

What should Lewis do? Present figures to support your decision.

S8-14 Determine most profitable final product *(Learning Objective 7)*

CocoaJoy processes cocoa beans into cocoa powder at a processing cost of $10,100 per batch. CocoaJoy can sell the cocoa powder as is, or it can process the cocoa powder further into chocolate syrup or boxed assorted chocolates. Once processed, each batch of cocoa beans would result in the following sales revenue:

Cocoa powder...	$ 15,000
Chocolate syrup	$101,000
Boxed assorted chocolates	$196,000

The cost of transforming the cocoa powder into chocolate syrup would be $67,000. Likewise, the company would incur $175,000 to transform the cocoa powder into boxed assorted chocolates. The company president has decided to make boxed assorted chocolates owing to its high sales value and to the fact that the $10,100 cost of processing cocoa beans "eats up" most of the cocoa powder profits. Has the president made the right or wrong decision? Explain your answer.

ETHICS

S8-15 Identify ethical standards violated *(Learning Objectives 1, 2, 3, 4, 5, 6, & 7)*

For each of the situations listed, identify the primary standard from the IMA *Statement of Ethical Professional Practice* that is violated (competence, confidentiality, integrity, or credibility). Refer to Exhibit 1-7 for the complete standard.

1. Seth is the controller for a small manufacturer. He mentions to a close friend that his company is going to start offshoring production to decrease labor costs.
2. Tiffany is a management accountant at a large electronics firm. She is instructed to prepare an analysis of the performance of an underperforming company division. Since Tiffany is afraid that many employees could lose their jobs if that division appears to be underperforming, Tiffany underestimates the amount of expenses generated by that division. Tiffany hopes that the division is not discontinued.
3. Adam Advertising Agency is looking at whether to continue to do its own payroll in-house or to outsource it to a payroll firm (a classic "make-or-buy" decision). Rosa, an accountant at Adam, does not tell management that the payroll firm bidding on the work is owned and managed by her mother.
4. Danthea, a CPA and a CMA, makes a YouTube video bragging about loopholes she has found to avoid taxes. These loopholes are questionable at best.
5. Brendan does not know how to categorize fixed costs as unavoidable or avoidable, so he guesses on the categorization of each fixed cost.

EXERCISES Group A

E8-16A Determine relevant and irrelevant information *(Learning Objective 1)*

O'Connor Frozen Foods purchased new computer-controlled production machinery last year from Advanced Enterprise. The equipment was purchased for $4.1 million and was paid for with cash. A representative from Advanced Enterprise recently contacted O'Connor management because Advanced Enterprise has an even more efficient piece of machinery available. The new design would double the production output of the equipment purchased last year but would cost O'Connor another $5.0 million. The old machinery was installed by an engineering firm; the same firm would be required to install the new machinery. Fixed selling costs would not change if the new machinery were to be purchased, but the variable selling cost per unit would decrease. Raw material costs (i.e., food ingredients) would remain the same with either machine. The new machinery would be purchased by signing a note payable at the bank, and interest would be paid monthly on the note payable. Maintenance costs on the new machine would be the same as the maintenance costs on the machinery purchased last year. Advanced Enterprise is offering a trade-in on the machinery purchased last year against the purchase price of the new machinery.

For each of the following costs, indicate whether or not each of the costs described would be relevant to O'Connor Frozen Foods' decision about whether to purchase the new machinery or not.

Item	Relevant	Not Relevant
a. Book value of old machine..		
b. Added profits from the increase in production resulting from the new machine ..		
c. Interest expense on new machine...		
d. Trade-in value of old machine..		
e. Maintenance cost of new machine...		
f. Variable selling costs...		
g. Installation cost of old machine		
h. Fixed selling costs		
i. Sales tax paid on old machine		
j. Cost of the new machine		
k. Installation cost of new machine		
l. Cost of the old machine...		
m. Accumulated depreciation on old machine		
n. Maintenance costs of old machine		
o. Cost per pound of food to be processed by the machinery		

E8-17A Sustainability and short-term decision making *(Learning Objective 1)*

Over the past several years, decommissioned U.S. warships have been turned into artificial reefs in the ocean by towing them out to sea and sinking them. The thinking was that sinking the ship would conveniently dispose of it while providing an artificial reef environment for aquatic life. In reality, some of the sunken ships have released toxins into the ocean and have been costly to decontaminate. Now the U.S. government is taking bids to instead dismantle and recycle ships that have recently been decommissioned (but have not been sunk yet.)

Assume that a recently decommissioned aircraft carrier, the USS *Stingray*, is estimated to contain approximately 40 tons of recyclable materials able to be sold for approximately $41.5 million. The low bid for dismantling and transporting the ship materials to appropriate facilities is $43.1 million. Recycling and dismantling the ship would create about 500 jobs for about a year in the Rust Belt. This geographic area has been experiencing record-high unemployment rates in recent years.

1. Is it more financially advantageous to sink the ship (assume that it costs approximately $0.7 million to tow a ship out to sea and sink it) or to dismantle and recycle it? Show your calculations.
2. From a sustainability standpoint, what should be done with the decommissioned aircraft carrier? List some of the qualitative factors that should enter into this analysis.
3. As a taxpayer, which action would you prefer (sink or recycle)? Defend your answer.

E8-18A Analyze special order decision *(Learning Objective 3)*

Jamison Paints makes and sells paint to home improvement stores. Jamison's only plant can produce up to 12 million cans of paint per year. Current annual production is 10 million cans. Fixed manufacturing, selling, and administrative costs total $15 million per year. The variable cost of making and selling each can of paint is $6.00. Stockholders expect a 15% annual return on the company's $40 million of assets.

Requirements

1. What is Jamison's current total cost of making and selling 10 million cans of paint? What is the current cost per can of paint?
2. Assume that Jamison is a price-taker and that the current wholesale market price is $8.00 per can of paint. What is the target total of cost in producing and selling 10 million cans of paint? Given Jamison's current total costs, will the company reach stockholders' profit goals?

3. Continuing with Requirement 2, let's say that Jamison has found ways to reduce its total fixed costs by $300,000. What is the target variable cost per can of paint?
4. Suppose Jamison plans to spend an additional $2 million on advertising to differentiate its product in order to increase sales volume to 10.5 million cans and become more of a price-setter. Assume that Jamison did reduce its total fixed costs by $300,000 as stated in Requirement 3 but could not find ways to save on its variable costs. What is the cost-plus price for a can of paint under these conditions?

E8-19A Pricing decisions given two scenarios *(Learning Objective 2)*

Dominic Builders builds 1,500-square-foot starter tract homes in the fast-growing suburbs of Atlanta. Land and labor are cheap, and competition among developers is fierce. The homes are "cookie-cutter," with any upgrades added by the buyer after the sale. Dominic Builders' costs per developed sublot are as follows:

Land	$ 52,000
Construction	$122,000
Landscaping	$ 6,000
Variable marketing costs	$ 3,000

Dominic Builders would like to earn a profit of 14% of the variable cost of each home sale. Similar homes offered by competing builders sell for $202,000 each.

Requirements

1. Which approach to pricing should Dominic Builders emphasize? Why?
2. Will Dominic Builders be able to achieve its target profit levels? Show your computations.
3. Bathrooms and kitchens are typically the most important selling features of a home. Dominic Builders could differentiate the homes by upgrading bathrooms and kitchens. The upgrades would cost $20,000 per home but would enable the company to increase the selling prices by $35,000 per home (in general, kitchen and bathroom upgrades typically add at least 150% of their cost to the value of any home). If Dominic Builders upgrades, what will the new cost-plus price per home be? Should the company differentiate its product in this manner? Show your analysis.

E8-20A Analyze special order decision *(Learning Objective 3)*

Perreth Industries has an annual plant capacity of 70,000 units; current production is 55,000 units per year. At the current production volume, the variable cost per unit is $30.00 and the fixed cost per unit is $4.10. The normal selling price of Perreth's product is $45.00 per unit. Perreth has been asked by Rummell Company to fill a special order for 10,000 units of the product at a special sales price of $25.00 per unit. Rummell is located in a foreign country where Perreth does not currently operate. Rummell will market the units in its country under its own brand name, so the special order is not expected to have any effect on Perreth's regular sales.

Requirements

1. How would accepting the special order impact Perreth's operating income? Should Perreth accept the special order?
2. How would your analysis change if the special order sales price were to be $40.00 per unit and Perreth would have to pay an attorney a fee of $15,000 to make sure it is complying with export laws and regulations relating to the special order?

E8-21A Special order decisions given two scenarios
(Learning Objective 3)

Suppose the Baseball Hall of Fame in Cooperstown, New York, has approached Collectibles & More with a special order. The Hall of Fame wants to purchase 53,000 baseball card packs for a special promotional campaign and offers $0.32 per pack, a total of $16,960. Collectibles & More's total production cost is $0.52 per pack, as follows:

Variable costs:	
Direct materials	$0.11
Direct labor	0.06
Variable overhead	0.10
Fixed overhead	0.25
Total cost	$0.52

Collectibles & More has enough excess capacity to handle the special order.

Requirements

1. Prepare an incremental analysis to determine whether Collectibles & More should accept the special sales order assuming fixed costs would not be affected by the special order.
2. Now assume that the Hall of Fame wants special hologram baseball cards. Collectibles & More must spend $5,100 to develop this hologram, which will be useless after the special order is completed. Should Collectibles & More accept the special order under these circumstances? Show your analysis.

E8-22A Special order decision and considerations *(Learning Objective 3)*

Jasper McKnight Sunglasses sell for about $150 per pair. Suppose the company incurs the following average costs per pair:

Direct materials	$40
Direct labor	12
Variable manufacturing overhead	8
Variable marketing expenses	3
Fixed manufacturing overhead	25*
Total costs	$88

*$2,100,000 total fixed manufacturing overhead/84,000 pairs of sunglasses

Jasper McKnight has enough idle capacity to accept a one-time-only special order from Arizona Glasses for 17,000 pairs of sunglasses at $63 per pair. Jasper McKnight will not incur any variable marketing expenses for the order.

Requirements

1. How would accepting the order affect Jasper McKnight's operating income? In addition to the special order's effect on profits, what other (longer-term qualitative) factors should Jasper McKnight's managers consider in deciding whether to accept the order?
2. Jasper McKnight's marketing manager, Nick Ferritto, argues against accepting the special order because the offer price of $63 is less than Jasper McKnight's $88 cost to make the sunglasses. Ferritto asks you, as one of Jasper McKnight's staff accountants, to explain whether his analysis is correct.

E8-23A Decide whether to discontinue a product line (Learning Objective 4)

Top managers of Vermont Flooring are alarmed by their operating losses. They are considering dropping the laminate flooring product line. Company accountants have prepared the following analysis to help make this decision:

	A	B	C	D
1	Vermont Flooring			
2	Product Line Contribution Margin Income Statement			
3	For the Year			
4				
5		Product lines		
6		Wood flooring	Laminate flooring	Company Total
7	Sales revenue	$ 306,000	$ 128,000	$ 434,000
8	Less: Variable expenses	156,000	82,000	238,000
9	Contribution margin	$ 150,000	$ 46,000	$ 196,000
10	Less fixed expenses:			
11	Manufacturing	75,000	55,000	130,000
12	Marketing and administrative	51,000	19,000	70,000
13	Operating income (loss)	$ 24,000	$ (28,000)	$ (4,000)
14				

Total fixed costs will not change if the company stops selling laminate flooring.

Requirements

1. Prepare an incremental analysis to show whether Vermont Flooring should discontinue the laminate flooring product line. Will discontinuing laminate flooring add $28,000 to operating income? Explain.
2. Assume that the company can avoid $32,000 of fixed expenses by discontinuing the laminate flooring product line (these costs are direct fixed costs of the laminate flooring product line). Prepare an incremental analysis to show whether the company should stop selling laminate flooring.
3. Now, assume that all of the fixed costs assigned to laminate flooring are direct fixed costs and can be avoided if the company stops selling laminate flooring. However, marketing has concluded that wood flooring sales would be adversely affected by discontinuing the laminate flooring line (retailers want to buy both from the same supplier). Wood flooring production and sales would decline 10%. What should the company do?

E8-24A Discontinuing a product line (Learning Objective 4)

Suppose Smithers Company is considering discontinuing its organic dried fruit product line. Assume that during the past year, the organic dried fruit's product line income statement showed the following:

	A	B	C	D
1	Sales revenue	$ 5,200,000		
2	Less: Cost of goods sold	6,500,000		
3	Gross profit	$ (1,300,000)		
4	Less: Operating expenses	1,500,000		
5	Operating income (loss)	$ (2,800,000)		
6				

Fixed manufacturing overhead costs account for 40% of the cost of goods, while only 30% of the operating expenses are fixed. Since the organic dried fruit line is just one of the company's fruit operations, only $750,000 of direct fixed costs (the majority of which is advertising) will be eliminated if the product line is discontinued. The remainder of the fixed costs will still be incurred by the company. If the company decides to discontinue the product line, what will happen to the company's operating income? Should Smithers Company discontinue the organic dried fruit product line?

E8-25A Identify constraint, then determine product mix *(Learning Objective 5)*

TreadFast produces two types of exercise treadmills: Regular and Deluxe. The exercise craze and related demand is such that TreadFast could use all of its available machine hours producing either model. The two models are processed through the same production department.

	A	B	C
1		Per Unit	
2		Deluxe	Regular
3	Sales price	$ 1,000	$ 540
4	Less expenses:		
5	Direct materials	340	80
6	Direct labor	82	194
7	Variable manufacturing overhead	152	76
8	Fixed manufacturing overhead*	80	40
9	Variable operating expenses	125	59
10	Total expenses	$ 779	$ 449
11	Operating income	$ 221	$ 91
12			

*Allocated on the basis of machine hours.

What product mix will maximize operating income? (*Hint:* Use the allocation of fixed manufacturing overhead to determine the proportion of machine hours used by each product.)

E8-26A Determine product mix for retailer—two stocking scenarios *(Learning Objective 5)*

Each morning, Larry Imery stocks the drink case at Larry's Beach Hut in Charlotte, North Carolina. Larry's Beach Hut has 110 linear feet of refrigerated display space for cold drinks. Each linear foot can hold either five 12-ounce cans or three 20-ounce plastic or glass bottles. The beverage stands sells three types of cold drinks:

1. Cola in 12-oz. cans for $1.40 per can
2. Bottled water in 20-oz. plastic bottles for $1.75 per bottle
3. Orange juice in 20-oz. glass bottles for $2.10 per bottle

Larry's Beach Hut pays its suppliers the following:

1. $0.20 per 12-oz. can of cola
2. $0.45 per 20-oz. bottle of water
3. $0.75 per 20-oz. bottle of orange juice

Larry's Beach Hut's monthly fixed expenses include the following:

Hut rental	$ 345
Refrigerator rental	65
Larry's salary	1,750
Total fixed expenses	$2,160

The beverage stand can sell all drinks stocked in the display case each morning.

Requirements

1. What is the constraining factor at Larry's Beach Hut? What should Larry stock to maximize profits? What is the maximum contribution margin he could generate from refrigerated drinks each day?
2. To provide variety to customers, suppose Larry refuses to devote more than 60 linear feet and no less than 20 linear feet to any individual product. Under this condition, how many linear feet of each drink should be stocked? How many units of each product will be available for sale each day?
3. Assuming the product mix calculated in Requirement 2, what contribution margin will be generated from refrigerated drinks each day?

E8-27A Analyze outsourcing decision *(Learning Objective 6)*

Shaw Enterprises manufactures one of the components used to assemble its main company product. Specialty Products, Inc., has offered to make the component at a cost of $12.80 per unit. Shaw Enterprises' current cost is $14.75 per unit of the component, based on the 100,000 components that Shaw Enterprises currently produces. This current cost per unit is based on the following calculations:

Direct material per unit	$ 5.00
Direct labor per unit	6.00
Variable manufacturing overhead per unit	1.75
Fixed manufacturing overhead per unit	2.00
Total manufacturing costs per unit	$ 14.75

None of Shaw Enterprises' fixed costs will be eliminated if the component is outsourced. However, the freed capacity could be used to build a new product. This new product would be expected to generate $30,000 of contribution margin per year.

Requirements

1. If Shaw Enterprises outsources the manufacturing of the component, will operating income increase or decrease? By how much?
2. What is the maximum price per unit Shaw Enterprises would be willing to pay if it outsources the component?

E8-28A Make-or-buy product component *(Learning Objective 6)*

InteliSystems manufactures an optical switch that it uses in its final product. InteliSystems incurred the following manufacturing costs when it produced 70,000 units last year:

	A	B	C	D
1	Direct materials	$ 560,000		
2	Direct labor	105,000		
3	Variable MOH	70,000		
4	Fixed MOH	455,000		
5	Total manufacturing cost for 70,000 units	$ 1,190,000		
6				

InteliSystems does not yet know how many switches it will need this year; however, another company has offered to sell InteliSystems the switch for $8.50 per unit. If InteliSystems buys the switch from the outside supplier, the manufacturing facilities that will be idle cannot be used for any other purpose; yet none of the fixed costs are avoidable.

Requirements

1. Given the same cost structure, should InteliSystems make or buy the switch? Show your analysis.
2. Now, assume that InteliSystems can avoid $105,000 of fixed costs a year by outsourcing production. In addition, because sales are increasing, InteliSystems needs 75,000 switches a year rather than 70,000 switches. What should the company do now?
3. Given the last scenario, what is the most InteliSystems would be willing to pay to outsource the switches?

Relevant Costs for Short-Term Decisions   489

E8-29A Make-or-buy decision with alternative use of facilities *(Learning Objective 6)*

Refer to E8-28A. InteliSystems needs 79,000 optical switches next year (assume same relevant range). By outsourcing them, InteliSystems can use its idle facilities to manufacture another product that will contribute $140,000 to operating income, but none of the fixed costs will be avoidable. Should InteliSystems make or buy the switches? Show your analysis.

E8-30A Determine maximum outsourcing price *(Learning Objective 6)*

Hamilton Containers manufactures a variety of boxes used for packaging. Sales of its Model A20 box have increased significantly to a total of 430,000 A20 boxes. Hamilton has enough existing production capacity to make all of the boxes it needs. The variable cost of making each A20 box is $0.80. By outsourcing the manufacture of these A20 boxes, Hamilton can reduce its current fixed costs by $103,200. There is no alternative use for the factory space freed up through outsourcing, so it will just remain idle.

What is the maximum Hamilton will pay per Model A20 box to outsource production of this box?

E8-31A Sell as is or process further *(Learning Objective 7)*

Werner Natural Dairy processes organic milk into plain yogurt. Werner sells plain yogurt to hospitals, nursing homes, and restaurants in bulk, one-gallon containers. Each batch, processed at a cost of $850, yields 540 gallons of plain yogurt. The company sells the one-gallon tubs for $8.00 each and spends $0.16 for each plastic tub. Werner has recently begun to reconsider its strategy. Management wonders if it would be more profitable to sell individual-sized portions of fruited organic yogurt at local food stores. Werner could further process each batch of plain yogurt into 11,520 individual portions (3/4 cup each) of fruited yogurt. A recent market analysis indicates that demand for the product exists. Werner would sell each individual portion for $0.56. Packaging would cost $0.07 per portion, and fruit would cost $0.10 per portion. Fixed costs would not change. Should Werner continue to sell only the gallon-sized plain yogurt (sell as is) or convert the plain yogurt into individual-sized portions of fruited yogurt (process further)? Why?

EXERCISES Group B

E8-32B Determine relevant and irrelevant information *(Learning Objective 1)*

Nicholson Produce is considering whether it should replace a veggie burger patty shaper machine. The new machine will produce 25% more veggie burger patties than the old machine in the same amount of time. (This machine is the bottleneck of the veggie burger patty process for Nicholson's.) The purchase of the new machine will cause fixed selling costs to increase, but per-unit variable selling costs will not be affected. The new machine will require installation by a specialty engineering firm. If the new machine is purchased, the old machine can be sold to an overseas food processing company. The old machine requires frequent (quarterly) repairs and maintenance to keep it running. The new machine will require maintenance only once per year. The new machine will be paid for by signing a note payable with the bank that will cover the cost of the machine and its installation. Nicholson will have to pay interest monthly on the note payable for the new machine. The note payable that was used to purchase the old machine was fully paid off two years ago.

For each of the following costs, indicate whether or not each of the costs described would be relevant to Nicholson Produce's decision about whether to purchase the new machine or to keep the old machine.

490 CHAPTER 8

Item	Relevant	Not Relevant
a. Cost per pound of vegetables		
b. Maintenance cost of new machine		
c. Variable selling costs		
d. Book value of old machine		
e. Interest expense on new machine		
f. Installation cost of old machine		
g. Interest expense on old machine		
h. Cost of new machine		
i. Sales value of old machine		
j. Repairs and maintenance costs of old machine		
k. Fixed selling costs		
l. Cost of old machine		
m. Accumulated depreciation on old machine		
n. Added profits from increase in production resulting from new machine		
o. Installation costs of new machine		

SUSTAINABILITY

E8-33B Sustainability and short-term decision making *(Learning Objective 1)*

Over the past several years, decommissioned U.S. warships have been turned into artificial reefs in the ocean by towing them out to sea and sinking them. The thinking was that sinking the ship would conveniently dispose of it while providing an artificial reef environment for aquatic life. In reality, some of the sunken ships have released toxins into the ocean and have been costly to decontaminate. Now the U.S. government is taking bids to instead dismantle and recycle ships that have recently been decommissioned (but have not been sunk yet).

Assume that a recently decommissioned aircraft carrier, the USS *Searay*, is estimated to contain approximately 40 tons of recyclable materials able to be sold for approximately $42.5 million. The low bid for dismantling and transporting the ship materials to appropriate facilities is $43.6 million. Recycling and dismantling the ship would create about 500 jobs for about a year in the Rust Belt. This geographic area has been experiencing record-high unemployment rates in recent years.

Requirements

1. Is it more financially advantageous to sink the ship (assume that it costs approximately $0.2 million to tow a ship out to sea and sink it) or to dismantle and recycle it? Show your calculations.
2. From a sustainability standpoint, what should be done with the decommissioned aircraft carrier? List some of the qualitative factors that should enter into this analysis.
3. As a taxpayer, which action would you prefer (sink or recycle)? Defend your answer.

E8-34B Analyze special order decision *(Learning Objective 3)*

Patterson Paints makes and sells paint to home improvement stores. Patterson's only plant can produce up to 13 million cans of paint per year. Current annual production is 10 million cans. Fixed manufacturing, selling, and administrative costs total $20 million per year. The variable cost of making and selling each can of paint is $5.50. Stockholders expect a 20% annual return on the company's $42 million of assets.

Requirements

1. What is Patterson's current total cost of making and selling 10 million cans of paint? What is the current cost per can of paint?
2. Assume that Patterson is a price-taker and that the current wholesale market price is $8.00 per can of paint. What is the target total of cost in producing and selling 10 million cans of paint? Given Patterson's current total costs, will the company reach stockholders' profit goals?
3. Continuing with Requirement 2, let's say that Patterson has found ways to reduce its total fixed costs by $500,000. What is the target variable cost per can of paint?

4. Suppose Patterson plans to spend an additional $4.5 million on advertising to differentiate its product in order to increase sales volume to 12 million cans and become more of a price-setter. Assume that Patterson did reduce its total fixed costs by $500,000 as stated in Requirement 3 but could not find ways to save on its variable costs. What is the cost-plus price for a can of paint under these conditions?

E8-35B Pricing decisions given two scenarios (Learning Objective 2)

Gunter Builders builds 1,500-square-foot starter tract homes in the fast-growing suburbs of Denver. Land and labor are cheap, and competition among developers is fierce. The homes are "cookie-cutter," with any upgrades added by the buyer after the sale. Gunter Builders' costs per developed sublot are as follows:

Land..	$ 50,000
Construction..	$120,000
Landscaping	$ 9,000
Variable marketing costs	$ 3,000

Gunter Builders would like to earn a profit of 14% of the variable cost of each home sale. Similar homes offered by competing builders sell for $203,000 each.

Requirements

1. Which approach to pricing should Gunter Builders emphasize? Why?
2. Will Gunter Builders be able to achieve its target profit levels? Show your computations.
3. Bathrooms and kitchens are typically the most important selling features of a home. Gunter Builders could differentiate the homes by upgrading bathrooms and kitchens. The upgrades would cost $14,000 per home but would enable Gunter Builders to increase the selling prices by $24,500 per home (in general, kitchen and bathroom upgrades typically add at least 150% of their cost to the value of any home). If Gunter Builders upgrades, what will the new cost-plus price per home be? Should the company differentiate its product in this manner? Show your analysis.

E8-36B Analyze special order decision (Learning Objective 3)

Windham Industries has an annual plant capacity of 80,000 units; current production is 65,000 units per year. At the current production volume, the variable cost per unit is $40.00, and the fixed cost per unit is $4.50. The normal selling price of Windham's product is $60.00 per unit. Windham has been asked by Ramone Company to fill a special order for 8,000 units of the product at a special sales price of $38.00 per unit. Ramone is located in a foreign country where Windham does not currently operate. Ramone will market the units in its country under its own brand name, so the special order is not expected to have any effect on Windham's regular sales.

Requirements

1. How would accepting the special order impact Windham's operating income? Should Windham accept the special order?
2. How would your analysis change if the special order sales price were to be $50.00 per unit and Windham would have to pay an attorney a fee of $35,000 to make sure it is complying with export laws and regulations relating to the special order?

E8-37B Special order decisions given two scenarios (Learning Objective 3)

Suppose the Baseball Hall of Fame in Cooperstown, New York, has approached International Cards with a special order. The Hall of Fame wishes to purchase 56,000 baseball card packs for a special promotional campaign and offers $0.43 per pack, a total of $24,080. International Cards' total production cost is $0.63 per pack, as follows:

Variable costs:	
Direct materials...	$0.13
Direct labor...	0.08
Variable overhead..	0.12
Fixed overhead	0.30
Total cost	$0.63

International Cards has enough excess capacity to handle the special order.

Requirements

1. Prepare an incremental analysis to determine whether International Cards should accept the special sales order assuming fixed costs would not be affected by the special order.
2. Now assume that the Hall of Fame wants special hologram baseball cards. International Cards will spend $5,000 to develop this hologram, which will be useless after the special order is completed. Should International Cards accept the special order under these circumstances? Show your analysis.

E8-38B Special order decision and considerations *(Learning Objective 3)*

Gentry Miller Sunglasses sell for $150 per pair. Suppose the company incurs the following average costs per pair:

Direct materials	$43
Direct labor	13
Variable manufacturing overhead	9
Variable marketing expenses	3
Fixed manufacturing overhead	16*
Total costs	$84

*$2,100,000 total fixed manufacturing overhead / 131,250 pairs of sunglasses

Gentry Miller has enough idle capacity to accept a one-time-only special order from Oregon Opticians for 21,000 pairs of sunglasses at $74 per pair. Gentry Miller will not incur any variable marketing expenses for the order.

Requirements

1. How would accepting the order affect Gentry Miller's operating income? In addition to the special order's effect on profits, what other (longer-term, qualitative) factors should the company's managers consider in deciding whether to accept the order?
2. Gentry Miller's marketing manager argues against accepting the special order because the offer price of $74 is less than the $84 cost to make the sunglasses. The marketing manager asks you, as one of Gentry Miller's staff accountants, to explain whether this analysis is correct.

E8-39B Decide whether to discontinue a product line *(Learning Objective 4)*

Top managers of Maine Flooring are alarmed by their operating losses. They are considering discontinuing the laminate flooring product line. Company accountants have prepared the following analysis to help make this decision:

	A	B	C	D
1	Maine Flooring			
2	Product Line Contribution Margin Income Statement			
3	For the Year Ended December 31			
4				
5		Product lines		
6		Wood flooring	Laminate flooring	Company Total
7	Sales revenue	$ 303,000	$ 120,000	$ 423,000
8	Less: Variable expenses	154,000	80,000	234,000
9	Contribution margin	$ 149,000	$ 40,000	$ 189,000
10	Less fixed expenses:			
11	Manufacturing	78,000	49,000	127,000
12	Marketing and administrative	52,000	15,000	67,000
13	Operating income (loss)	$ 19,000	$ (24,000)	$ (5,000)
14				

Total fixed costs will not change if the company stops selling laminate flooring.

Requirements

1. Prepare an incremental analysis to show whether Maine Flooring should discontinue the laminate flooring product line. Will discontinuing the laminate flooring add $24,000 to operating income? Explain.

2. Assume that the company can avoid $27,000 of fixed expenses by discontinuing the laminate flooring product line (these costs are direct fixed costs of the laminate flooring product line). Prepare an incremental analysis to show whether the company should stop selling laminate flooring.

3. Now, assume that all of the fixed costs assigned to laminate flooring are direct fixed costs and can be avoided if the company stops selling laminate flooring. However, marketing has concluded that wood flooring sales would be adversely affected by discontinuing the laminate flooring line (retailers want to buy both from the same supplier). Wood flooring production and sales would decline 10%. What should the company do?

E8-40B Discontinuing a product line (Learning Objective 4)

Suppose Eagle Products is considering discontinuing its soy cereal product line. Assume that during the past year, the soy cereal product line income statement showed the following:

	A	B	C	D
1	Sales revenue	$ 5,250,000		
2	Less: Cost of goods sold	6,250,000		
3	Gross profit	$ (1,000,000)		
4	Less: Operating expenses	1,550,000		
5	Operating income (loss)	$ (2,550,000)		
6				

Fixed manufacturing overhead costs account for 40% of the cost of goods, while only 30% of the operating expenses are fixed. Since the soy cereal line is just one of the company's breakfast cereals, only $725,000 of direct fixed costs (the majority of which is advertising) will be eliminated if the product line is discontinued. The remainder of the fixed costs will still be incurred by the company. If the company decides to discontinue the product line, what will happen to the company's operating income? Should Eagle Products discontinue the soy cereal product line?

E8-41B Identify constraint, then determine product mix (Learning Objective 5)

ExcerTreads produces two types of exercise treadmills: Regular and Deluxe. The exercise craze and related demand is such that ExcerTreads could use all of its available machine hours producing either model. The two models are processed through the same production department.

	A	B	C	D
1			Per Unit	
2		Deluxe	Regular	
3	Sales price	$ 1,020	$ 580	
4	Less expenses:			
5	Direct materials	320	110	
6	Direct labor	88	186	
7	Variable manufacturing overhead	168	84	
8	Fixed manufacturing overhead*	80	40	
9	Variable operating expenses	113	69	
10	Total expenses	$ 769	$ 489	
11	Operating income	$ 251	$ 91	
12				

*Allocated on the basis of machine hours.

What product mix will maximize operating income? (*Hint*: Use the allocation of fixed manufacturing overhead to determine the proportion of machine hours used by each product.)

E8-42B Determine product mix for retailer—two stocking scenarios (Learning Objective 5)

Each morning, Max Rouse stocks the drink case at Max's Beach Hut in Daytona Beach, Florida. Max's Beach Hut has 120 linear feet of refrigerated display space for cold drinks. Each linear foot can hold either five 12-ounce cans or four 20-ounce plastic or glass bottles.

The beverage stand sells three types of cold drinks:

1. Diet cola in 12-oz. cans for $1.60 per can
2. Bottled water in 20-oz. plastic bottles for $1.80 per bottle
3. Grape juice in 20-oz. glass bottles for $2.25 per bottle

Max's Beach Hut pays its suppliers the following:

1. $0.15 per 12-oz. can of diet cola
2. $0.30 per 20-oz. bottle of water
3. $0.70 per 20-oz. bottle of grape juice

Max's Beach Hut's monthly fixed expenses include the following:

Hut rental	$ 360
Refrigerator rental	75
Max's salary	1,750
Total fixed expenses	$2,185

The beverage stand can sell all the drinks stocked in the display case each morning.

Requirements

1. What is the constraining factor at Max's Beach Hut? What should Max stock to maximize profits? What is the maximum contribution margin he could generate from refrigerated drinks each day?
2. To provide variety to customers, suppose Max refuses to devote more than 75 linear feet and no less than 15 linear feet to any individual product. Under this condition, how many linear feet of each drink should be stocked? How many units of each product will be available for sale each day?
3. Assuming the product mix calculated in Requirement 2, what contribution margin will be generated from refrigerated drinks each day?

E8-43B Analyze outsourcing decision (Learning Objective 6)

McCall Enterprises manufactures one of the components used to assemble its main company product. Specialty Products, Inc., has offered to make the component at a cost of $14.10 per unit. McCall Enterprises' current cost is $17.00 per unit of the component, based on the 100,000 components that McCall Enterprises currently produces. This current cost per unit is based on the following calculations:

Direct material per unit	$ 5.50
Direct labor per unit	6.50
Variable manufacturing overhead per unit	2.00
Fixed manufacturing overhead per unit	3.00
Total manufacturing costs per unit	$ 17.00

None of McCall Enterprises' fixed costs will be eliminated if the component is outsourced. However, the freed capacity could be used to build a new product. This new product would be expected to generate $30,000 of contribution margin per year.

Requirements

1. If McCall Enterprises outsources the manufacturing of the component, will operating income increase or decrease? By how much?
2. What is the maximum price per unit McCall Enterprises would be willing to pay if it outsources the component?

E8-44B Make-or-buy product component *(Learning Objective 6)*

TechSystems manufactures an optical switch that it uses in its final product. TechSystems incurred the following manufacturing costs when it produced 71,000 units last year:

	A	B
1	Direct materials	$ 781,000
2	Direct labor	142,000
3	Variable MOH	213,000
4	Fixed MOH	390,500
5	Total manufacturing cost for 71,000 units	$ 1,526,500

TechSystems does not yet know how many switches it will need this year; however, another company has offered to sell TechSystems the switch for $18.50 per unit. If TechSystems buys the switch from the outside supplier, the manufacturing facilities that will be idle cannot be used for any other purpose, yet none of the fixed costs are avoidable.

Requirements

1. Given the same cost structure, should TechSystems make or buy the switch? Show your analysis.
2. Now, assume that TechSystems can avoid $95,000 of fixed costs a year by outsourcing production. In addition, because sales are increasing, TechSystems needs 76,000 switches a year rather than 71,000. What should TechSystems do now?
3. Given the last scenario, what is the most TechSystems would be willing to pay to outsource the switches?

E8-45B Make-or-buy decision with alternative use of facilities *(Learning Objective 6)*

Refer to E8-44B. TechSystems needs 78,000 optical switches next year (assume same relevant range). By outsourcing them, TechSystems can use its idle facilities to manufacture another product that will contribute $220,000 to operating income, but none of the fixed costs will be avoidable. Should TechSystems make or buy the switches? Show your analysis.

E8-46B Determine maximum outsourcing price *(Learning Objective 6)*

Henderson Containers manufactures a variety of boxes used for packaging. Sales of its Model A20 box have increased significantly to a total of 400,000 A20 boxes. Henderson has enough existing production capacity to make all of the boxes it needs. The variable cost of making each A20 box is $0.74. By outsourcing the manufacture of these A20 boxes, Henderson can reduce its current fixed costs by $72,000. There is no alternative use for the factory space freed up through outsourcing, so it will just remain idle.

What is the maximum Henderson will pay per Model A20 box to outsource production of this box?

E8-47B Sell as is or process further *(Learning Objective 7)*

OrganicPlus processes organic milk into plain yogurt. OrganicPlus sells plain yogurt to hospitals, nursing homes, and restaurants in bulk, one-gallon containers. Each batch, processed at a cost of $830, yields 750 gallons of plain yogurt. OrganicPlus sells the one-gallon tubs for $6.00 each and spends $0.10 for each plastic tub. Management has recently begun to reconsider its strategy. OrganicPlus wonders if it would be more profitable to sell individual-sized portions of fruited organic yogurt at local food stores. OrganicPlus could further process each batch of plain yogurt into 16,000 individual portions (3/4 cup each) of fruited yogurt. A recent market analysis indicates that demand for the product exists. OrganicPlus would sell each individual portion for $0.40. Packaging would cost $0.07 per portion, and fruit would cost $0.12 per portion. Fixed costs would not change. Should OrganicPlus continue to sell only the gallon-sized plain yogurt (sell as is) or convert the plain yogurt into individual-sized portions of fruited yogurt (process further)? Why?

PROBLEMS Group A

P8-48A Pricing of nursery plants *(Learning Objective 2)*

Flora Gardening operates a commercial plant nursery where it propagates plants for garden centers throughout the region. Flora Gardening has $5.25 million in assets. Its yearly fixed costs are $668,500, and the variable costs for the potting soil, container, label, seedling, and labor for each gallon-sized plant total $1.20. Flora Gardening's volume is currently 490,000 units. Competitors offer the same quality plants to garden centers for $3.70 each. Garden centers then mark them up to sell to the public for $9 to $11, depending on the type of plant.

Requirements

1. Flora Gardening owners want to earn a 12% return on the company's assets. What is Flora Gardening's target full cost?
2. Given Flora Gardening's current costs, will its owners be able to achieve their target profit? Show your analysis.
3. Assume that Flora Gardening has identified ways to cut its variable costs to $1.05 per unit. What is its new target fixed cost? Will this decrease in variable costs allow the company to achieve its target profit? Show your analysis.
4. Flora Gardening started an aggressive advertising campaign strategy to differentiate its plants from those grown by other nurseries. Flora Gardening doesn't expect volume to be affected, but it hopes to gain more control over pricing. If Flora Gardening has to spend $53,900 this year to advertise and its variable costs continue to be $1.05 per unit, what will its cost-plus price be? Do you think Flora Gardening will be able to sell its plants to garden centers at the cost-plus price? Why or why not?

P8-49A Special order decision and considerations *(Learning Objective 3)*

Coastal Safety manufactures flotation vests in Miami, Florida. Coastal Safety's contribution margin income statement for the most recent month contains the following data:

	A	B	C	D
1	Coastal Safety			
2	Contribution Margin Income Statement (Variable Costing)			
3	For Sales Volume of 32,000 Units			
4				
5		Per unit		
6	Sales revenue	$ 480,000		
7	Less variable expenses:			
8	Variable manufacturing costs (DM, DL, Variable MOH)	160,000		
9	Variable operating expenses (selling and administrative)	112,000		
10	Contribution margin	$ 208,000		
11	Less fixed expenses:			
12	Fixed manufacturing overhead	$ 126,000		
13	Fixed operating expenses (selling and administrative)	91,000		
14	Operating income (loss)	$ (9,000)		
15				

Suppose Dazzle Cruiselines wants to buy 4,600 vests from Coastal Safety. Acceptance of the order will not require any variable selling and administrative expenses. The special order will not affect fixed expenses. The Coastal Safety plant has enough unused capacity to manufacture the additional vests. Dazzle Cruiselines has offered $7 per vest, which is below the normal sale price of $15.

Requirements

1. Prepare an incremental analysis to determine whether Coastal Safety should accept this special sales order.
2. Identify long-term factors that Coastal Safety should consider in deciding whether to accept the special sales order.

P8-50A Prepare and use contribution margin statements for discontinuing a line decision *(Learning Objective 4)*

Members of the board of directors of Security Alliance have received the following operating income data for the year just ended:

	Security Alliance Product Line Contribution Margin Income Statement For the Year			
		Product lines		
		Industrial Systems	Household Systems	Company Total
Sales revenue		$ 310,000	$ 380,000	$ 690,000
Less cost of goods sold:				
Variable		32,000	46,000	78,000
Fixed		280,000	66,000	346,000
Gross profit		$ (2,000)	$ 268,000	$ 266,000
Less marketing and administrative expenses:				
Variable		63,000	69,000	132,000
Fixed		37,000	23,000	60,000
Operating income (loss)		$ (102,000)	$ 176,000	$ 74,000

Members of the board are surprised that the industrial systems product line is losing money. They commission a study to determine whether the company should discontinue the line. Company accountants estimate that discontinuing the industrial systems line will decrease fixed cost of goods sold by $80,000 and decrease fixed marketing and administrative expenses by $11,000.

Requirements

1. Prepare an incremental analysis to show whether Security Alliance should discontinue the industrial systems product line.
2. Prepare contribution margin income statements to show Security Alliance's total operating income under the two alternatives: (a) with the industrial systems line and (b) without the line. Compare the *difference* between the two alternatives' income numbers to your answer to Requirement 1. What have you learned from this comparison?

P8-51A Product mix decision under constraint *(Learning Objective 5)*

Agee Products, located in Peoria, Arizona, produces two lines of electric toothbrushes: Deluxe and Standard. Because Agee can sell all of the toothbrushes it produces, the owners are expanding the plant. They are deciding which product line to emphasize.

To make this decision, they assemble the following data:

	Per Unit	
	Deluxe Toothbrush	Standard Toothbrush
Sales price	$90	$46
Variable expenses	17	19
Contribution margin	$73	$27
Contribution margin ratio	81.1%	58.7%

After expansion, the factory will have a production capacity of 4,700 machine hours per month. The plant can manufacture either 56 Standard electric toothbrushes or 28 Deluxe electric toothbrushes per machine hour.

Requirements

1. Identify the constraining factor for Agee Products.
2. Prepare an analysis to show which product line to emphasize.

P8-52A Outsourcing decision given alternative use of capacity
(Learning Objective 6)

Mountain Sports manufactures snowboards. Its cost of making 1,850 bindings is as follows:

Direct materials	$ 18,500
Direct labor	2,900
Variable manufacturing overhead	1,285
Fixed manufacturing overhead	7,100
Total manufacturing costs	$ 29,785
Cost per pair ($29,785 ÷ 1,850)	$ 16.10

Suppose an outside supplier will sell bindings to Mountain Sports for $14 each. Mountain Sports will pay $1.00 per unit to transport the bindings to its manufacturing plant, where it will add its own logo at a cost of $0.70 per binding.

Requirements

1. Mountain Sports' accountants predict that purchasing the bindings from the outside supplier will enable the company to avoid $2,000 of fixed overhead. Prepare an analysis to show whether the company should make or buy the bindings.
2. The facilities freed by purchasing bindings from the outside supplier can be used to manufacture another product that will contribute $2,800 to profit. Total fixed costs will be the same as if Mountain Sports had produced the bindings. Show which alternative makes the best use of Mountain Sports facilities: (a) make bindings, (b) buy bindings and leave facilities idle, or (c) buy bindings and make another product.

P8-53A Sell as is or process further decisions *(Learning Objective 7)*

Noble Chemical has spent $240,000 to refine 71,000 gallons of acetone, which can be sold for $2.30 a gallon. Alternatively, Noble Chemical can process the acetone further. This processing will yield a total of 59,000 gallons of lacquer thinner that can be sold for $3.20 a gallon. The additional processing will cost $0.85 per gallon of lacquer thinner. To sell the lacquer thinner, Noble Chemical must pay shipping of $0.24 a gallon and administrative expenses of $0.12 a gallon on the thinner.

Requirements

1. Identify the sunk cost. Is the sunk cost relevant to Noble's decision? Why or why not?
2. Should Noble sell the acetone as is or process it into lacquer thinner? Show the expected net revenue difference between the two alternatives.

PROBLEMS Group B

P8-54B Pricing of nursery plants *(Learning Objective 2)*

Plants Galore operates a commercial plant nursery where it propagates plants for garden centers throughout the region. Plants Galore has $5.8 million in assets. Its yearly fixed costs are $742,000, and the variable costs for the potting soil, container, label, seedling, and labor for each gallon-sized plant total $1.55. Plants Galore's volume is currently 575,000 units. Competitors offer the same quality plants to garden centers for $3.80 each. Garden centers then mark them up to sell to the public for $8 to $10, depending on the type of plant.

Requirements

1. Plants Galore's owners want to earn a 11% return on the company's assets. What is Plants Galore's target full cost?
2. Given Plants Galore's current costs, will its owners be able to achieve their target profit? Show your analysis.
3. Assume that Plants Galore has identified ways to cut its variable costs to $1.40 per unit. What is its new target fixed cost? Will this decrease in variable costs allow the company to achieve its target profit? Show your analysis.
4. Plants Galore started an aggressive advertising campaign strategy to differentiate its plants from those grown by other nurseries. Plants Galore doesn't expect volume to be affected, but it hopes to gain more control over pricing. If Plants Galore has to spend $57,500 this year to advertise and its variable costs continue to be $1.40 per unit, what will its cost-plus price be? Do you think Plants Galore will be able to sell its plants to garden centers at the cost-plus price? Why or why not?

P8-55B Special order decision and considerations *(Learning Objective 3)*

Summer Fun manufactures flotation vests in Philadelphia, Pennsylvania. Summer Fun's contribution margin income statement for the most recent month contains the following data:

	A	B	C	D
1	Summer Fun			
2	Contribution Margin Income Statement (Variable Costing)			
3	For Sales Volume of 33,000 Units			
4				
5		Total		
6	Sales revenue	$ 462,000		
7	Less variable expenses:			
8	Variable manufacturing costs (DM, DL, Variable MOH)	99,000		
9	Variable operating expenses (selling and administrative)	111,000		
10	Contribution margin	$ 252,000		
11	Less fixed expenses:			
12	Fixed manufacturing overhead	122,000		
13	Fixed operating expenses (selling and administrative)	93,000		
14	Operating income (loss)	$ 37,000		
15				

Suppose Sparkle Cruiselines wishes to buy 4,600 vests from Summer Fun. Acceptance of the order will not require any variable selling and administrative expenses. The special order will not affect fixed expenses. The Summer Fun plant has enough unused capacity to manufacture the additional vests. Sparkle Cruiselines has offered $6 per vest, which is below the normal sale price of $14.

Requirements

1. Prepare an incremental analysis to determine whether Summer Fun should accept this special sales order.
2. Identify long-term factors that Summer Fun should consider in deciding whether to accept the special sales order.

P8-56B Prepare and use contribution margin statements for discontinuing a line decision (Learning Objective 4)

Members of the board of directors of Security First have received the following operating income data for the year just ended:

	Product Line Contribution Margin Income Statement For the Year			
		Product lines		
		Industrial Systems	Household Systems	Company Total
Sales revenue		$ 350,000	$ 380,000	$ 730,000
Less cost of goods sold:				
Variable		40,000	40,000	80,000
Fixed		270,000	69,000	339,000
Gross profit		$ 40,000	$ 271,000	$ 311,000
Less marketing and administrative expenses:				
Variable		64,000	70,000	134,000
Fixed		38,000	20,000	58,000
Operating income (loss)		$ (62,000)	$ 181,000	$ 119,000

Members of the board are surprised that the industrial systems product line is losing money. They commission a study to determine whether the company should discontinue the line. Company accountants estimate that discontinuing the industrial systems line will decrease fixed cost of goods sold by $77,000 and decrease fixed marketing and administrative expenses by $11,000.

Requirements

1. Prepare an incremental analysis to show whether Security First should discontinue the industrial systems product line.
2. Prepare contribution margin income statements to show Security First's total operating income under the two alternatives: (a) with the industrial systems line and (b) without the line. Compare the *difference* between the two alternatives' income numbers to your answer to Requirement 1. What have you learned from this comparison?

P8-57B Product mix decision under constraint (Learning Objective 5)

Brann Products, located in Ann Arbor, Michigan, produces two lines of electric toothbrushes: Deluxe and Standard. Because Brann can sell all the toothbrushes it can produce, the owners are expanding the plant. They are deciding which product line to emphasize. To make this decision, they assemble the following data:

	Per Unit	
	Deluxe Toothbrush	Regular Toothbrush
Sales price	$90	$52
Variable expenses	17	18
Contribution margin	$73	$34
Contribution margin ratio	81.1%	65.4%

After expansion, the factory will have a production capacity of 4,000 machine hours per month. The plant can manufacture either 65 Standard electric toothbrushes or 25 Deluxe electric toothbrushes per machine hour.

Requirements

1. Identify the constraining factor for Brann Products.
2. Prepare an analysis to show which product line to emphasize.

P8-58B Outsourcing decision given alternative use of capacity
(Learning Objective 6)

Snowy Mountain manufactures snowboards. Its cost of making 19,000 bindings is as follows:

Direct materials	$ 22,000
Direct labor	81,000
Variable manufacturing overhead	44,000
Fixed manufacturing overhead	81,000
Total manufacturing costs	$228,000
Cost per pair ($228,000 / 19,000)	$ 12.00

Suppose an outside supplier will sell bindings to Snowy Mountain for $15 each. Snowy Mountain would pay $2.00 per unit to transport the bindings to its manufacturing plant, where it would add its own logo at a cost $0.50 of per binding.

Requirements

1. Snowy Mountain's accountants predict that purchasing the bindings from an outside supplier will enable the company to avoid $1,900 of fixed overhead. Prepare an analysis to show whether the company should make or buy the bindings.
2. The facilities freed by purchasing bindings from the outside supplier can be used to manufacture another product that will contribute $3,100 to profit. Total fixed costs will be the same as if Snowy Mountain had produced the bindings. Show which alternative makes the best use of Snowy Mountain's facilities: (a) make bindings, (b) buy bindings and leave facilities idle, or (c) buy bindings and make another product.

P8-59B Sell as is or process further decisions *(Learning Objective 7)*

Lacerna Chemical has spent $245,000 to refine 70,000 gallons of acetone, which can be sold for $1.90 a gallon. Alternatively, Lacerna Chemical can process the acetone further. This processing will yield a total of 65,000 gallons of lacquer thinner that can be sold for $3.30 a gallon. The additional processing will cost $0.65 per gallon of lacquer thinner. To sell the lacquer thinner, Lacerna Chemical must pay shipping of $0.22 a gallon and administrative expenses of $0.13 a gallon on the thinner.

Requirements

1. Identify the sunk cost. Is the sunk cost relevant to Lacerna's decision? Why or why not?
2. Should Lacerna sell the acetone as is or process it into lacquer thinner? Show the expected net revenue difference between the two alternatives.

Serial Case

C8-60 Decide whether to discontinue a department *(Learning Objective 4)*

This case is a continuation of the Caesars Entertainment Corporation serial case that began in Chapter 1. Refer to the introductory story in Chapter 1 (see page 43) for additional background. (The components of the Caesars serial case can be completed in any order.)

What follows are the income statements for Caesars Entertainment Corporation for the three years ending December 31, 2012 through 2014.

Caesars Entertainment Corporation
Consolidated Statements of Operations (Condensed and adapted)
In millions, except per share date

	Years ended December 31,		
	2014	2013	2012
Revenues			
Casino revenue	$ 5,418	$ 5,529	$ 5,916
Food and beverage revenue	1,522	1,451	1,438
Rooms revenue	1,207	1,167	1,147
Other revenues	369	73	(315)
Net revenues	$ 8,516	$ 8,220	$ 8,186
Operating Expenses			
Direct casino expenses	$ 3,253	$ 3,112	$ 3,368
Direct food and beverage expenses	694	639	634
Direct rooms expenses	315	296	289
Miscellaneous expenses	4,706	6,199	3,761
Total operating expenses	$ 8,968	$ 10,246	$ 8,052
Income/(loss) from operations	$ (452)	$ 2,026	$ 134

Requirements:

Note: To answer these questions, calculate a segment margin for each of the departments. For the purpose of this case only, calculate segment margin as revenues less direct expenses. (We are modifying the concept of segment margin slightly here, given the information that is publicly available. We are essentially assuming that the direct expenses are the variable expenses.)

Using the statements of operations (income statements) given, answer the following questions.

1. Calculate the segment margin for the three departments: Casinos, Food and Beverage, and Rooms.
2. Given the segment margins that you calculated, should Caesars discontinue any of the three departments? Why or why not?
3. What expenses are likely to be included in "Miscellaneous expenses"? Should these expenses be allocated to the three departments if Caesars is evaluating whether it should discontinue any departments? Why or why not?

CRITICAL THINKING

Discussion & Analysis

A8-61 Discussion Questions

1. A beverage company is considering whether to discontinue its line of grape soda. What factors will affect the company's decision? What is a qualitative factor? Which of the factors you listed are qualitative?

2. What factors would be relevant to a restaurant that is considering whether to make its own dinner rolls or to purchase dinner rolls from a local bakery?

3. How would outsourcing change a company's cost structure? How might this change in cost structure help or harm a company's competitive position?

4. What is an opportunity cost? List possible opportunity costs associated with a make-or-buy decision.

5. What undesirable result can arise from allocating common fixed costs to product lines?

6. Why could a manager be justified in ignoring fixed costs when making a decision about a special order? When would fixed costs be relevant when making a decision about a special order?

7. What is the difference between segment margin and contribution margin? When would each be used?

8. Do joint costs affect a sell as is or process further decision? Why or why not?

9. How can "make-or-buy" concepts be applied to decisions at a service organization? What types of make-or-buy decisions might a service organization face?

10. Oscar Company builds outdoor furniture using a variety of woods and plastics. What is a constraint? List at least four possible constraints at Oscar Company.

11. Do an Internet search on the terms *carbon offset* and *carbon footprint*. What is a carbon footprint? What is a carbon offset? Why would carbon offsets be of interest to a company? What are some companies that offer (sell) carbon offsets?

12. A computer manufacturer is considering outsourcing its technical support call center to India. Its current technical support call center is located in Dellroy, Ohio. The current call center is one of the top employers in Dellroy and employs about 10% of the townspeople in Dellroy. The town has experienced high unemployment rates in the past two decades, and often the call employees are the sole breadwinners in their households. If the technical support call center were to be moved to India, the company would be able to pay about 50% less per hour than it currently pays in Dellroy, Ohio. From a triple-bottom-line perspective (people, planet, and profit), what factors are relevant to the company's decision to outsource its technical support call center? Be sure to discuss both quantitative and qualitative factors.

Application & Analysis

Mini Cases

A8-62 Outsourcing Decision at a Real Company

Go to the *New York Times* website (www.nytimes.com/) or to *USA Today* (www.usatoday.com/) and search for the term *outsource*. Find an article about a company making a decision to outsource a part of its business operations.

Basic Discussion Questions

1. Describe the company that is making the decision to outsource. What area of the business is the company looking to outsource, or did it already outsource?

2. Why did the company decide to outsource (or is considering outsourcing)?

3. List the revenues and costs that might be impacted by this outsourcing decision. The article will not list many, if any, of these revenues and costs; you should make reasonable

guesses about what revenues and/or costs would be associated with the business operation being outsourced.

4. List the qualitative factors that could influence the company's decision of whether or not to outsource this business operation. Again, you need to make reasonable guesses about the qualitative factors that might influence the company's decision to outsource or not to outsource.

ETHICS

A8-63 Ethics and outsourcing *(Learning Objectives 1, 2, 3, 4, 5, 6, & 7)*

Mrs. Yoder is a large family-style restaurant chain located throughout the Midwest in Amish communities. Currently, Mrs. Yoder makes its own biscuits. Customers love these biscuits; they are light, fluffy, and incredibly delicious.

People are not eating out at restaurants as much as they did before the recession hit in 2007. Like many other restaurants, Mrs. Yoder is under increasing pressure to control its costs to help to counteract the lower number of diners. As part of its efforts to remain cost competitive, Mrs. Yoder is analyzing whether it should continue to make its own biscuits or to outsource part of the biscuit-making process by purchasing ready-made dough from a national supplier.

Sean Murray works as a management accountant at the Mrs. Yoder restaurant group. Sean is asked by the controller to analyze whether the biscuits should continue to be made in-house from scratch or if the company should purchase ready-made dough from a national supplier.

Sean's mother-in-law, Blair Barker, is a salesperson for a national food manufacturer. Sean decides to get a bid from her before contacting any other suppliers. Blair has been struggling financially since the illness and subsequent death of Sean's father-in-law last year and could use the sales commissions generated by this order. Sean emails Blair and asks her for a bid price for the ready-made dough. Blair sends him a price of $33.20 per case (a case of dough makes 12 dozen biscuits).

Sean analyzes the cost of making the biscuits in-house. He arrives at the following schedule of cost for the dough to make 12 dozen biscuits:

	A	B	C	D
1	Cost item	Cost per 12 dozen biscuits		
2	Flour	$ 9.00		
3	Baking soda	0.12		
4	Baking powder	0.38		
5	Salt	0.24		
6	Unsalted butter	13.50		
7	Buttermilk	6.00		
8	Bakery labor	2.75		
9	Fixed manufacturing overhead*	2.24		
10	Cost per 12 dozen biscuits in-house	$ 34.23		
11				

*Allocated on basis of bakery labor hours

Sean's analysis shows that the restaurant should purchase the ready-made dough from the national supplier because the ready-made dough is less expensive than making the dough in-house. However, Sean has deliberately included all of the fixed costs in the cost calculation of making the biscuits in-house. Part of those fixed costs is unavoidable, but he does not distinguish between avoidable and unavoidable fixed costs in his analysis. The unavoidable portion of the fixed cost allocated to 12 dozen biscuits is $1.24.

Sean submits his analysis to the controller. In his report, Sean recommends that Mrs. Yoder choose Blair's firm to supply the dough for its biscuits. Sean chooses to say nothing about his relationship to Blair, figuring no one will know since his mother-in-law has a different last name than he does.

The controller accepts Sean's analysis, and Mrs. Yoder enters into a contract with Blair's firm for the ready-made dough.

Requirements

1. Using the IMA *Statement of Ethical Professional Practice* as an ethical framework (refer to Exhibit 1-7), answer the following questions:
   a. What is(are) the ethical issue(s) in this situation?
   b. What are Sean's responsibilities as a management accountant?
2. When making the decision to outsource the dough, what other factors should be considered?

A8-64 Starbucks food waste: Sell now or process further?
(Learning Objectives 1 & 6)

With nearly 18,000 stores in 60 countries, Starbucks serves a lot of coffee and pastries each day, and it also generates a lot of waste, including day-old pastries and coffee grounds. Starbucks continually wrestles with how to best handle this food waste.

A researcher in Hong Kong is developing a fungus that converts Starbucks food waste into useful chemicals through a process called biorefining. Basically, the Starbucks food and coffee waste products are blended with a special type of fungus that breaks the food's complex carbohydrates down into simple sugars. These sugars then go into a fermenter, where they are exposed to bacteria that break the sugar down into succinic acid. Succinic acid is a colorless, odorless substance that is frequently used in the production of medicines, foods, bioplastics, and laundry detergents.

Assuming that the biorefining process turns out to be technologically feasible, Starbucks will have another option for its food waste products. Let's assume that Starbucks has the following options for handling its food and coffee waste:

Day-old pastries disposal options
a. Discard in trash.
b. Donate the day-old pastries to local homeless shelters and other charitable organizations.
c. Sell the day-old pastries in its retail stores for 50% off.
d. Process the day-old pastries into succinic acid and sell the succinic acid to manufacturers or labs.

Coffee grounds disposal options
a. Discard in trash.
b. Give coffee grounds to customers through a program called Grounds for Your Garden. Plants such as roses, azaleas, and evergreens can be fertilized with coffee grounds.
c. Sell coffee grounds to commercial composters.
d. Process the food waste into succinic acid and sell the succinic acid to manufacturers or labs.

Starbucks has a goal of zero waste at its retail stores, so it is continually assessing its waste-disposal options. Coupled with its zero-waste goal, though, is its profit motive. Starbucks is a for-profit corporation and must balance its sustainability initiatives with the right economic choices for its shareholders.

Questions

1. For each of the disposal options for <u>day-old pastries</u>, answer the following questions:
   a. What revenue (if any) would be generated by this option?
   b. What cost reductions could Starbucks realize from this option?
   c. What costs would Starbucks incur for this option?
   d. What qualitative factors would Starbucks need to consider before choosing this option?
   e. What are the advantages associated with this option? What are the disadvantages associated with this option?
2. For each of the disposal options for <u>coffee grounds</u>, answer the following questions:
   a. What revenue (if any) would be generated by this option?
   b. What cost reductions could Starbucks realize from this option?
   c. What costs would Starbucks incur for this option?
   d. What qualitative factors would Starbucks need to consider before choosing this option?
   e. What are the advantages associated with this option? What are the disadvantages associated with this option?
3. For both day-old pastries and coffee grounds, are there any options that are particularly attractive in your viewpoint? Are there any options that would not be acceptable in your viewpoint? Justify your response.

Try It Solutions

page 456:

1. Yes, there is enough capacity to fill this special order. If the plant is producing 450,000 cases a month, yet only operating at 90% of capacity, it must have a capacity level of 500,000 cases per month (= 450,000 ÷ 90%). This means the plant has excess capacity of 50,000 cases per month, which is enough to fill the special order of 40,000 cases without increasing the current level of fixed costs ($2,700,000). Thus, the current level of fixed costs is irrelevant to the decision. Campbell's will *not* incur an additional $6.00 of fixed MOH for every case produced in this order.

2. Take a contribution margin approach to determining whether the special order is profitable:

	A	B	C
1	Incremental Analysis for Special Order Decision	Per Unit	Total Order (40,000 units)
2	Revenue from special order	$ 19.00	$ 760,000
3	Less: Variable expenses associated with the order (DM, DL, Variable MOH)	15.00	600,000
4	Contribution margin	$ 4.00	$ 160,000
5	Less: Additional fixed expenses associated with the order		5,000
6	Increase in operating income from the special order		$ 155,000
7			

page 463:

1. Analyze the revenues and costs that would be lost if the salad bar operation is discontinued:

	A	B	C
1	Incremental Analysis for Discontinuation Decision	Total	
2	Sales revenue from salad bars	$ 750,000	
3	Less: Variable expenses related to salad bars	600,000	
4	Contribution margin lost if salad bars are discontinued	$ 150,000	
5	Less: Fixed cost savings if salad bars are discontinued	20,000	
6	Operating income lost if salad bars are discontinued	$ 130,000	
7			
8			
9	If Salad Bars Are Replaced with Olive Bars	Total	
10	Contribution margin provided by olive bar	$ 200,000	
11	Less: Operating income lost if salad bars are discontinued	130,000	
12	Increase in operating income from replacing salad bars with olive bars	$ 70,000	
13			

page 472:

1. As shown below, the total cost of outsourcing the ski poles and leaving the freed capacity idle is $325,000 greater than the cost to produce the poles in-house. Rossignol should not outsource production because its operating income would decline by $325,000.

2. However, Rossignol's income would increase by $175,000 if it outsourced production and used the freed capacity to make ski boots.

	A	B	C	D
1	Incremental Analysis Outsourcing Decision	Make Ski Poles	Outsource Ski Poles	Difference
2	Variable Costs:			
3	If make: $13.50 × 100,000 units / If outsource: $18.00 × 100,000 units	$ 1,350,000	$ 1,800,000	$ 450,000
4	Plus: Fixed costs	650,000	525,000	(125,000)
5	Total cost of producing 100,000 units	$ 2,000,000	$ 2,325,000	$ 325,000
6	Less: Income from ski boots if outsource	0	500,000	500,000
7	Net cost	$ 2,000,000	$ 1,825,000	$ (175,000)
8				

9

Keith Homan/Alamy

Sources: Campbell Soup Company, 2015 Annual Report

The Master Budget

Learning Objectives

- **1** Describe how and why managers use budgets
- **2** Prepare the operating budgets
- **3** Prepare the financial budgets
- **4** Prepare budgets for a merchandiser

Campbell Soup Company, which has been in business for over 145 years, has had to remake itself continually as the demographic, economic, and cultural fabric of society has changed over time. The present is no different. The food industry is facing enormous demographic shifts, as consumers opt for fresher, healthier, and more organic foods and the millennial generation launches into one of the primary food-buying demographic groups. To not only cope with these changes, but also capitalize on them as business opportunities, Campbell redefined its purpose statement ("Real Food that Matters for Life Moments") and implemented new strategies. Some of these initiatives include developing new, healthier, and organic product lines, focusing more attention on digital marketing to reach the younger generation, making the company's food supply chain more transparent to consumers, increasing the company's presence in developing markets, and finally, becoming leaner and more cost-efficient. These strategies require that detailed plans be put in place. The company's managers express these plans, in financial terms, through budgets.

Budgeting is perhaps the most widely used management accounting tool employed by companies, organizations, and governments throughout the world. Even individuals, such as you and me, can benefit from creating a personal budget that shows how we plan to use our resources and to make sure our spending does not get out of control. For example, if your goal is to buy a car directly after college or a house five years after college, then you need to plan for these expenditures. Your budget should include saving enough money each year to accumulate the down payments you'll need. By carefully planning how you'll spend and save your resources, you'll have a better chance of reaching your goals.

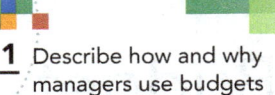

1 Describe how and why managers use budgets

How and Why Do Managers Use Budgets?

As you'll see throughout this chapter, management uses budgeting to express its plans and to assess how well it's reaching its goals. In this section, we'll take a closer look at how budgets are used and developed, the benefits of budgeting, and the particular budgets that are prepared as part of the company's master budget.

How Are Budgets Used?

All companies and organizations use budgets for the same reasons you would in your personal life—to plan for the future and control the revenues and expenses related to those plans. Exhibit 9-1 shows how managers use budgets in fulfilling their major responsibilities of planning, directing, and controlling operations. Budgeting is an ongoing cycle: Company strategies lead to detailed plans, which in turn lead to actions. Results are then compared to the budget to provide managers with feedback. This feedback allows managers to take corrective actions and, if necessary, revise strategies, which starts the cycle over.

EXHIBIT 9-1 Managers Use Budgets to Plan and Control Business Activities

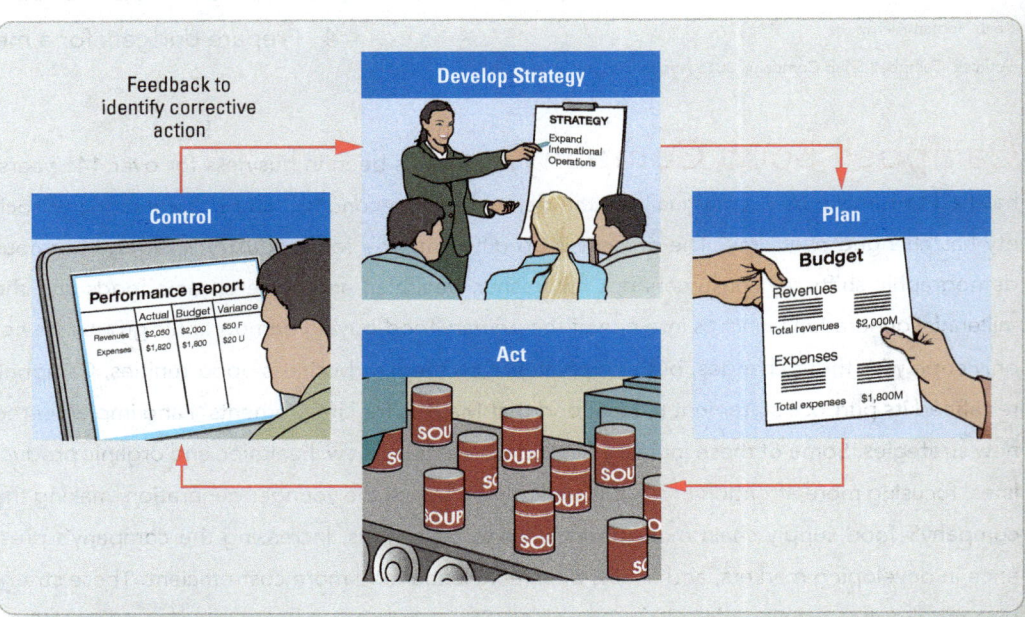

How Are Budgets Developed?

A company's budgeting process begins with its overall mission, or purpose statement, as illustrated in the chapter-opening story. Management then devises long-term strategic goals that will help the company fulfill its mission. **Strategic planning** involves setting long-term goals that may extend 5 to 10 years into the future. Long-term, loosely detailed budgets are often created to reflect expectations for these long-term goals.

Once the goals are set, management designs key strategies for attaining them. These strategies, such as Campbell's decision to launch an organic soup line and put more resources into digital marketing, are then put into place through the use of shorter-term budgets for an entire fiscal year. However, even a yearly budget is not detailed enough to guide many management decisions. For example, Campbell's soup production managers must know what month of the year they expect to receive and start using new production equipment. They must also decide how much of each raw material (organic vegetables, chicken, and so forth) to purchase each month to meet production requirements for both new and existing products. In turn, this will affect monthly cash needs. Therefore, companies usually prepare a budget for every month of the fiscal year.

Many companies set aside time during the last two quarters of the fiscal year to create their budget for the entire upcoming fiscal year. Other companies prepare rolling, or continuous budgets. A **rolling budget** is a budget that is continuously updated so that the next 12 months of operations are always budgeted. For example, as soon as January is over, the next January is added to the budget. The benefit of a rolling budget is that managers always have a budget for the next 12 months.

Who Is Involved in the Budgeting Process?

Rather than using a "top-down" approach in which top management determines the budget, most companies use some degree of participative budgeting. As the term implies, **participative budgeting** involves the participation of many levels of management. Participative budgeting is beneficial for the following reasons:

- Lower-level managers are closer to the action and should have a more detailed knowledge for creating realistic budgets.
- Managers are more likely to accept, and be motivated by, budgets they helped to create.

Participative budgeting also has disadvantages:

- The budget process can become much more complex and time consuming as more people participate in the process.
- Managers may intentionally build **slack** into the budget for their areas of operation by overbudgeting expenses or underbudgeting revenue. Why would they do this? They would do so for three possible reasons: (1) because of uncertainty about the future, (2) to make their performance look better when actual results are compared against budgeted amounts at the end of the period, and (3) to have the resources they need in the event of mandatory budget cuts.

Even with participative budgeting, someone must still have the "final say" on the budget. Often, companies use a **budget committee** to review the submitted budgets, remove unwarranted slack, and revise and approve the final budget. The budget committee frequently includes upper management, such as the CEO and CFO, as well as managers from every area of the value chain (such as research and development, marketing, and distribution). By using a cross-functional budget committee, the final budget is more likely to reflect a comprehensive view of the organization and be accepted by managers than if the budget were prepared by one person or department for the entire organization. The budget committee is often supported by full-time staff personnel devoted to updating and analyzing the budgets.

What Is the Starting Point for Developing the Budgets?

Many companies use the prior year's budgeted figures, or actual results, as the *starting point* for creating the budget for the coming year. Of course, those figures will then be modified to reflect

- new products, customers, or geographical areas;
- changes in the marketplace caused by competitors;
- changes in labor contracts, raw materials, and fuel costs;
- general inflation; and
- any new strategies.

This approach to budgeting may cause year-after-year increases that, after time, grow out of control. To prevent perpetual increases in budgeted expenses, many companies intermittently use zero-based budgeting. When a company implements **zero-based budgeting**, all managers begin with a budget of zero and must justify *every dollar* they put in the budget. This budgeting approach is very time consuming and labor intensive. Therefore, companies only use it from time to time in order to keep their expenses in check. For example, in 2015, as part of its quest to become leaner and more cost-efficient, Campbell's Soup Company announced plans to use zero-based budgeting to slash $200 million from its annual budget.[1]

What Are the Benefits of Budgeting?

Exhibit 9-2 summarizes three key benefits of budgeting. Budgeting forces managers to plan, promotes coordination and communication, and provides a benchmark for motivating employees and evaluating actual performance.

EXHIBIT 9-2 Benefits of Budgeting

Planning

Business managers are extremely busy directing the day-to-day operations of the company. The budgeting process forces managers to spend time planning for the future, rather than only concerning themselves with daily operations. The sooner companies develop a plan and have time to act on the plan, the more likely they will achieve their goals.

Coordination and Communication

The budget coordinates a company's activities. It forces managers to consider relations among operations across the entire value chain. For example, Campbell's decision to develop new product lines will first affect the research and development (R&D) function. Once new products are developed, however, the design and production teams will need to focus on how and where the products will be mass-produced. The marketing team will need to develop attractive labeling and create a successful advertising campaign. The distribution team may need to alter its current distribution system to accommodate the new products. And customer service will need to be ready to handle any complaints or warranty issues. All areas of the value chain are ultimately affected by management's plans. The budget process helps to communicate and coordinate the effects of the plan.

Benchmarking

Budgets provide a benchmark that motivates employees and helps managers evaluate performance. The budget provides a target that most managers will try to achieve, especially if they participated in the budgeting process and the budget has been set at a realistic level. Budgets should be achievable with effort. Budgets that are too "tight" (too hard to achieve) or too "loose" (too easy to achieve) do not provide managers with much motivation.

---

[1] http://www.wsj.com/articles/campbell-soup-to-unveil-cost-cutting-plan-1424268625

Think about exams for a moment. Some professors have a reputation for giving "impossible" exams, while others may be known for giving "easy" exams. In either of these cases, students are rarely motivated to put much effort into learning the material because they feel they won't be rewarded for their additional efforts. However, if students feel that a professor's exam can be achieved with effort, they will be more likely to devote themselves to learning the material. In other words, the perceived "fairness" of the exam affects how well the exam motivates students to study. Likewise, if a budget is perceived to be "fair," employees are likely to be motivated by it.

Budgets also provide a benchmark for evaluating performance. At the end of the period, companies use performance reports, such as the one pictured in Exhibit 9-3, to compare "actual" revenues and expenses against "budgeted" revenues and expenses. The **variance**, or difference between actual and budgeted figures, is used to evaluate how well the manager controlled operations and to determine whether the plan needs to be revised. The use of budgets for performance evaluation will be discussed in more detail in Chapters 10 and 11. In this chapter, we focus primarily on the use of budgets for planning purposes.

EXHIBIT 9-3 Summary Performance Report

	A	B	C	D
1	Summary Performance Report	Actual	Budget	Variance |Actual − Budget|
2	Sales revenue	$ 478,000	$ 450,000	$ 28,000
3	Less: Variable expenses	336,000	320,000	16,000
4	Contribution margin	$ 142,000	$ 130,000	$ 12,000
5	Less: Fixed expenses	23,000	25,000	2,000
6	Operating income	$ 119,000	$ 105,000	$ 14,000
7				

What Is the Master Budget?

The **master budget** is the comprehensive planning document for the entire organization. It consists of all the supporting budgets needed to create the company's budgeted financial statements. Exhibit 9-4 shows all the components of the master budget for a manufacturer as well as the order in which they are usually prepared. The master budgets of service and merchandising firms are less complex and are discussed in the final section of the chapter.

The **operating budgets** are the budgets needed to run the daily operations of the company. The operating budgets culminate in a budgeted income statement. As Exhibit 9-4 shows, the starting point of the operating budgets is the sales budget because it affects most other components of the master budget. After estimating sales, manufacturers prepare the production budget, which determines how many units need to be produced. Once production volume is established, managers prepare individual budgets for the direct materials, direct labor, and manufacturing overhead that will be needed to meet production. Next, managers prepare the operating expenses budget. After all of these budgets are prepared, management will be able to prepare the budgeted income statement.

As you'll see throughout the chapter, cost behavior will be an important factor in developing many of the operating budgets. Total fixed costs will not change as volume changes within the relevant range. However, total variable costs will fluctuate as volume fluctuates.

The **financial budgets** include the capital expenditures budget and the cash budgets. The financial budgets culminate in a budgeted balance sheet. The capital expenditures budget shows the company's plan for purchasing property, plant, and equipment. The cash budget forecasts the cash that will be available to run the company's operations and determines whether the company will have extra funds to invest or whether the company will need to borrow cash. Finally, the budgeted balance sheet forecasts the company's position at the end of the budget period.

EXHIBIT 9-4 Master Budget for a Manufacturing Company

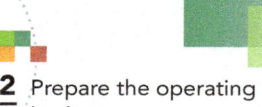 Prepare the operating budgets

How Are the Operating Budgets Prepared?

We will be following the budget process for Tucson Tortilla, a fairly small, independently owned manufacturer of tortilla chips. The company sells its product, by the case, to restaurants, grocery stores, and convenience stores. To keep our example simple, we will just show the budgets for the first three months of the fiscal year, rather than all 12 months. Since many companies prepare quarterly budgets (budgets that cover a three-month period), we'll also show the quarterly figures on each budget. For every budget, we'll walk through the calculations for the month of January. Then we'll show how the same pattern is used to create budgets for the months of February and March.

Sales Budget

The sales budget is the starting place for budgeting. Managers multiply the expected number of unit sales by the expected sales price per unit to arrive at the expected total sales revenue.

For example, Tucson Tortilla expects to sell 30,000 cases of tortilla chips in January, at a sales price of $20 per case, so the estimated sales revenue for January is as follows:

$$30{,}000 \text{ cases} \times \$20 \text{ per case} = \$600{,}000$$

Tucson Tortilla's sales budget for the first three months of the year is shown in Exhibit 9-5. As you can see, the monthly sales volume is expected to fluctuate. January sales are expected to be higher than February sales due to the extraordinary number of chips purchased for Super Bowl parties. Also, since more tortillas chips are sold when the weather warms up, the company expects sales to begin their seasonal upward climb beginning in March.

As shown in the lower portion of Exhibit 9-5, managers may also choose to indicate the type of sale that will be made. Tucson Tortilla expects 20% of its sales to be cash (COD) sales. Companies often use <u>COD</u> ("collect on delivery"[2]) collection terms if the customer is new, has a poor credit rating, or has not paid on time in the past. Tucson Tortilla will still sell to these customers but will demand payment immediately when the inventory is delivered.

> **Why is this important?**
> "The **sales budget** is the **basis** for every other budget. If sales are not forecasted as **accurately** as possible, all other budgets will be **off target**."

EXHIBIT 9-5 Sales Budget

	A	B	C	D	E
1		\multicolumn{4}{c}{Tucson Tortilla}
2		Sales Budget			
3		For the Quarter Ended March 31			
4		Month			
5		January	February	March	1st Quarter
6	Unit sales (cases)	30,000	20,000	25,000	75,000
7	Multiply by: Sales price per case	$ 20	$ 20	$ 20	$ 20
8	Total sales revenue	$ 600,000	$ 400,000	$ 500,000	$ 1,500,000
9					
10	**Type of sale:**				
11	Cash sales (20%)	$ 120,000	$ 80,000	$ 100,000	$ 300,000
12	Credit sales (80%)	480,000	320,000	400,000	1,200,000
13	Total sales revenue	$ 600,000	$ 400,000	$ 500,000	$ 1,500,000
14					

The remaining 80% of sales will be made on credit. Tucson Tortilla's credit terms are "net 30," meaning the customer has up to 30 days to pay for its purchases. Having this information available on the sales budget will help managers prepare the cash collections budget later.

Production Budget

Once managers have estimated how many units they expect to sell, they can figure out how many units they need to produce. Most manufacturers maintain some ending finished goods inventory, or <u>safety stock</u>, which is inventory kept on hand in case demand is higher than predicted, or the problems in the factory slow production (such as machine breakdown, employees out sick, and so forth). As a result, managers need to factor in the desired level of ending inventory when deciding how much inventory to produce. They do so as follows:

Let's walk through this calculation step by step:

- First, managers figure out how many total units they need. To do this, they add the number of units they plan to sell to the number of units they want on hand at the end

---

[2] In the past, COD meant "cash on delivery." However, as other forms of payment (such as checks, credit cards, and debit cards) have become more common, the word "cash" has been replaced with the word "collect" to incorporate these additional types of payments.

of the month. Let's assume Tucson Tortilla wants to maintain an ending inventory equal to 10% of the next month's expected sales (20,000 cases in February). Thus, the total number of cases needed in January is as follows:

> 30,000 cases for January sales + (10% × 20,000) = 32,000 total cases needed

- Next, managers calculate the amount of inventory they expect to have on hand at the beginning of the month. Since Tucson Tortilla desires ending inventory to be 10% of the next month's sales, managers expect to have 10% of January's sales on hand on December 31, which becomes the beginning balance on January 1:

> 10% × 30,000 cases = 3,000 cases in beginning inventory on January 1

- Finally, by subtracting what the company already has in stock at the beginning of the month from the total units needed, the company is able to calculate how many units to produce:

> 32,000 cases needed − 3,000 cases in beginning inventory = 29,000 cases to produce

Exhibit 9-6 shows Tucson Tortilla's production budget for the first three months of the year. As the red arrows show, the ending inventory from one month (January 31) always becomes the beginning inventory for the next month (February 1).

EXHIBIT 9-6 Production Budget

	January	February	March	1st Quarter
Tucson Tortilla				
Production Budget				
For the Quarter Ended March 31				
Unit sales (cases)	30,000	20,000	25,000	75,000
Plus: Desired ending inventory	2,000	2,500	3,200	3,200
Total needed	32,000	22,500	28,200	78,200
Less: Beginning inventory	3,000	2,000	2,500	3,000
Number of units to produce	29,000	20,500	25,700	75,200

NOTE: Management wants to maintain an ending inventory equal to 10% of the next month's projected sales. Projected April sales are 32,000 units. The quarter begins January 1 and ends March 31.

Now that the company knows how many units it plans to produce every month, it can figure out the amount of direct materials, direct labor, and manufacturing overhead that will be needed. As shown in the following sections, the company will create separate budgets for each of these three manufacturing costs: direct materials, direct labor, and manufacturing overhead. Each budget will be driven by the number of units to be *produced* each month.

▶ Try It!

Assume Tucson Tortilla's sales budget shows projected sales of 32,000 cases in April and 40,000 cases in May. The company's manager would like to maintain ending safety stock equal to 10% of the next month's projected sales. How many units should be produced in April?

Please see page 582 for solutions.

Direct Materials Budget

The format of the direct materials budget is quite similar to the production budget:

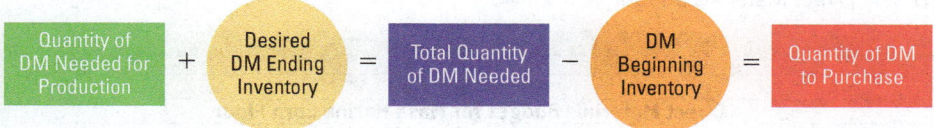

Let's walk through the process using January as an example:

- First, the company figures out the quantity of direct materials (DM) needed for production. Let's assume Tucson Tortilla's only direct material is masa harina, the special corn flour used to make tortilla chips. Each case of tortilla chips requires 5 pounds of this corn flour. Therefore, the quantity of direct materials needed for January production is as follows:

> 29,000 cases to be produced × 5 pounds per case = 145,000 pounds

- Next, the company adds in the desired ending inventory of direct materials. Some amount of direct materials safety stock is usually needed in case suppliers do not deliver all of the direct materials needed on time. Let's assume that Tucson Tortilla wants to maintain an ending inventory of direct materials equal to 10% of the materials needed for next month's production (102,500 required in February, as shown in Exhibit 9-7):

> 145,000 pounds + (10% × 102,500) = 155,250 total pounds needed

- Next, managers determine the direct materials inventory they expect to have on hand at the beginning of the month. Tucson Tortilla expects to have 10% of the materials needed for January's production in stock on December 31, which becomes the opening balance on January 1:

> 10% × 145,000 pounds = 14,500 pounds in beginning inventory

- Next, by subtracting what the company already has in stock at the beginning of the month from the total quantity needed, the company is able to calculate the quantity of direct materials it needs to purchase:

> 155,250 pounds needed − 14,500 pounds in beginning inventory = 140,750 pounds to purchase

- Finally, the company calculates the expected cost of purchasing those direct materials. Let's say Tucson Tortilla can buy the masa harina corn flour in bulk for $1.50 per pound.

> 140,750 pounds × $1.50 = $211,125

Exhibit 9-7 shows Tucson Tortilla's direct materials budget for the first three months of the year.

EXHIBIT 9-7 Direct Materials Budget

	A	B	C	D	E
1		\multicolumn{4}{c}{Tucson Tortilla}			
2		\multicolumn{4}{c}{Direct Materials Budget for Masa Harina Corn Flour}			
3		\multicolumn{4}{c}{For the Quarter Ended March 31}			
4		\multicolumn{3}{c}{Month}			1st Quarter
5		January	February	March	1st Quarter
6	Units (cases) to be produced (from production budget)	29,000	20,500	25,700	75,200
7	Multiply by: Quantity (pounds) of DM needed per unit	5	5	5	5
8	Quantity (pounds) needed for production	145,000	102,500	128,500	376,000
9	Plus: Desired ending inventory of DM	10,250	12,850	16,150	16,150
10	Total quantity (pounds) needed	155,250	115,350	144,650	392,150
11	Less: Beginning inventory of DM	14,500	10,250	12,850	14,500
12	Quantity (pounds) to purchase	140,750	105,100	131,800	377,650
13	Multiply by: Cost per pound	$ 1.50	$ 1.50	$ 1.50	$ 1.50
14	Total cost of DM purchases	$ 211,125	$ 157,650	$ 197,700	$ 566,475

NOTE: Management wants to maintain an ending inventory equal to 10% of the next month's production needs. Assume 161,500 pounds are needed for production in April.

Direct Labor Budget

The direct labor (DL) budget is determined as follows:

Tucson Tortilla's factory is fairly automated, so very little direct labor is required. Let's assume that each case requires only 0.05 of an hour. Direct laborers are paid $22 per hour. Thus, the direct labor cost for January is projected to be as follows:

29,000 cases × 0.05 hours per case = 1,450 hours required × $22 per hour = $31,900

The direct labor budget for the first three months of the year is shown in Exhibit 9-8.

EXHIBIT 9-8 Direct Labor Budget

	A	B	C	D	E
1		\multicolumn{4}{c}{Tucson Tortilla}			
2		\multicolumn{4}{c}{Direct Labor Budget}			
3		\multicolumn{4}{c}{For the Quarter Ended March 31}			
4		\multicolumn{3}{c}{Month}			1st Quarter
5		January	February	March	1st Quarter
6	Units (cases) to be produced (from production budget)	29,000	20,500	25,700	75,200
7	Multiply by: Direct labor hours per unit	0.05	0.05	0.05	0.05
8	Total hours required	1,450	1,025	1,285	3,760
9	Multiply by: Direct labor cost per hour	$ 22	$ 22	$ 22	$ 22
10	Total direct labor cost	$ 31,900	$ 22,550	$ 28,270	$ 82,720

Manufacturing Overhead Budget

The manufacturing overhead budget is highly dependent on cost behavior. Some overhead costs, such as indirect materials, are variable. For example, Tucson Tortilla considers the oil used for frying the tortilla chips to be an indirect material. Since a portion of the oil is absorbed into the chips, the amount of oil required increases as production volume increases. Thus, the cost is variable. The company also considers salt and cellophane packaging to be variable indirect materials. Tucson Tortilla expects to spend $1.25 on indirect materials for each case of tortilla chips produced, so January's budget for indirect materials is as follows:

$$29{,}000 \text{ cases} \times \$1.25 = \$36{,}250 \text{ of indirect materials}$$

Costs such as utilities and indirect labor are mixed costs. Mixed costs are usually separated into their variable and fixed components using one of the cost behavior estimation methods already discussed in Chapter 6. Based on engineering and cost studies, Tucson Tortilla has determined that each case of chips requires $0.75 of variable indirect labor and $0.50 of variable utility costs as a result of running the production machinery. These variable costs are budgeted as follows for January:

$$29{,}000 \text{ cases} \times \$0.75 = \$21{,}750 \text{ of variable indirect labor}$$
$$29{,}000 \text{ cases} \times \$0.50 = \$14{,}500 \text{ of variable factory utilities}$$

Finally, many manufacturing overhead costs are fixed. Tucson Tortilla's fixed costs include depreciation, insurance, and property taxes on the factory. The company also incurs some fixed indirect labor (salaried production engineers who oversee the daily manufacturing operation) and a fixed amount of utilities just to keep the lights, heat, or air conditioning on in the plant, regardless of the production volume.

Exhibit 9-9 shows that the manufacturing overhead budget usually has separate sections for variable and fixed overhead costs, so that managers can easily see which costs will change as production volume changes.

EXHIBIT 9-9 Manufacturing Overhead Budget

	Tucson Tortilla			
	Manufacturing Overhead Budget			
	For the Quarter Ended March 31			
		Month		
	January	February	March	1st Quarter
Cases to be produced (from production budget)	29,000	20,500	25,700	75,200
Variable MOH Costs:				
Indirect materials ($1.25 per case)	$ 36,250	$ 25,625	$ 32,125	$ 94,000
Indirect labor—variable portion ($0.75 per case)	21,750	15,375	19,275	56,400
Utilities—variable portion ($0.50 per case)	14,500	10,250	12,850	37,600
Total variable MOH	$ 72,500	$ 51,250	$ 64,250	$ 188,000
Fixed MOH Costs:				
Depreciation on factory and production equipment	$ 10,000	$ 10,000	$ 10,000	$ 30,000
Insurance and property taxes on the factory	3,000	3,000	3,000	9,000
Indirect labor—fixed portion	15,000	15,000	15,000	45,000
Utilities—fixed portion	2,000	2,000	2,000	6,000
Total fixed MOH	$ 30,000	$ 30,000	$ 30,000	$ 90,000
Total manufacturing overhead	$ 102,500	$ 81,250	$ 94,250	$ 278,000

Now that we have completed budgets for each of the three manufacturing costs (direct materials, direct labor, and manufacturing overhead), we turn our attention to operating expenses.

Operating Expenses Budget

Recall that all costs incurred in every area of the value chain, except production, must be expensed as operating expenses in the period in which they are incurred. Thus, all research and development, design, marketing, distribution, and customer service costs will be shown on the operating expenses budget.

Some operating expenses are variable, based on how many units will be *sold* (not produced). For example, to motivate its sales force to generate sales, Tucson Tortilla pays its sales representatives a $1.50 sales commission for every case they sell.

> 30,000 sales units × $1.50 = $45,000 sales commission expense in January

The company also incurs $2.00 of shipping costs on every case sold.

> 30,000 sales units × $2.00 = $60,000 shipping expense in January

Finally, the company knows that not all of the sales made on credit will eventually be collected. Based on experience, Tucson Tortilla expects monthly bad debt expense to be 1% of its credit sales. Since January credit sales are expected to be $480,000 (from Sales Budget, Exhibit 9-5), the company's bad debt expense for January is as follows:

> $480,000 of credit sales in January × 1% = $4,800 bad debt expense for January

Other operating expenses are fixed: They will stay the same each month even though sales volume fluctuates. For example, Tucson Tortilla's fixed operating expenses include salaries of office workers, office rent, depreciation on office equipment and sales vehicles, advertising, and telephone and Internet service.

As shown in Exhibit 9-10, operating expenses are usually shown according to their cost behavior.

EXHIBIT 9-10 Operating Expenses Budget

	A	B	C	D	E
1		\multicolumn{4}{c}{Tucson Tortilla}			
2		Operating Expenses Budget			
3		For the Quarter Ended March 31			
4			Month		
5		January	February	March	1st Quarter
6	Number of cases to be sold (from sales budget)	30,000	20,000	25,000	75,000
7	**Variable Operating Expenses:**				
8	Sales commissions expense ($1.50 per case sold)	$ 45,000	$ 30,000	$ 37,500	$ 112,500
9	Shipping expense ($2.00 per case sold)	60,000	40,000	50,000	150,000
10	Bad debt expense (1% of credit sales)	4,800	3,200	4,000	12,000
11	Total variable operating expenses	$ 109,800	$ 73,200	$ 91,500	$ 274,500
12					
13	**Fixed Operating Expenses:**				
14	Salaries	$ 20,000	$ 20,000	$ 20,000	$ 60,000
15	Office rent	4,000	4,000	4,000	12,000
16	Depreciation	6,000	6,000	6,000	18,000
17	Advertising	2,000	2,000	2,000	6,000
18	Telephone and internet	1,000	1,000	1,000	3,000
19	Total fixed operating expenses	$ 33,000	$ 33,000	$ 33,000	$ 99,000
20					
21	Total operating expenses	$ 142,800	$ 106,200	$ 124,500	$ 373,500
22					

Budgeted Income Statement

A budgeted income statement looks just like a regular income statement, except for the fact that it uses budgeted data. A company may prepare a budget in contribution margin format for internal use or in traditional format for both internal and external use. For example, often, a company will need to supply its lending institution with budgeted financial statements. Thus, we present the traditional format here. Recall the traditional format for an income statement:

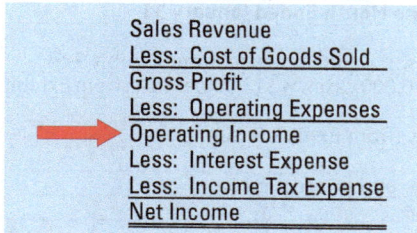

This text book has focused on a company's operating income rather than net income. However, a complete income statement would include any interest expense (and/or interest income) as well as a provision for income taxes. These additional costs are subtracted from operating income to arrive at net income.

We have already computed the budgeted sales revenue and operating expenses on separate budgets. But we still need to calculate the Cost of Goods Sold before we can prepare the income statement.

Tucson Tortilla computes its Cost of Goods Sold as follows:

This will be relatively simple for Tucson Tortilla since the company produces only one product.

The cost of manufacturing each case of tortilla chips is shown in Exhibit 9-11. Almost all of the information shown has already been presented and used to prepare the budgets for direct materials, direct labor, and manufacturing overhead. The only new piece of information is the total production volume for the year, budgeted to be 400,000 cases.

EXHIBIT 9-11 Budgeted Cost of Goods Sold per Unit

	A	B	C
1	**Budgeted Manufacturing Costs**		**Cost per Case**
2	Direct materials (5 pounds per case × $1.50 per pound)		$ 7.50
3	Direct labor (0.05 hours per case × $22 per hour)		1.10
4	Variable MOH:		
5	Indirect materials ($1.25 per case)	$ 1.25	
6	Indirect labor ($0.75 per case)	0.75	
7	Variable utilities ($.50 per case)	0.50	
8	Total variable MOH per case		2.50
9	Fixed MOH ($30,000 per month × 12 months)	$ 360,000	
10	Divided by: Budgeted production volume (cases)	400,000	
11	Total fixed MOH per case		0.90
12	Cost per case (absorption costing)		$ 12.00
13			

NOTE: Information taken from the DM, DL, and MOH budgets in Exhibits 9-7 through 9-9.

Exhibit 9-12 shows the company's budgeted income statement for January. Interest expense is budgeted to be zero since the company has no outstanding debt. The income tax expense is budgeted to be 35% of income before taxes. The company will prepare budgeted income statements for each month and quarter, as well as for the entire year.

EXHIBIT 9-12 Budgeted Income Statement

	A	B
1	Tucson Tortilla	
2	Budgeted Income Statement	
3	For the Month Ended January 31	
4		
5	Sales revenue (30,000 cases × $20 per case, from Exhibit 9-5)	$ 600,000
6	Less: Cost of goods sold (30,000 cases × $12.00 per case, from Exhibit 9-11)	360,000
7	Gross profit	240,000
8	Less: Operating expenses (from Exhibit 9-10)	142,800
9	Operating income	$ 97,200
10	Less: Interest expense (or add interest income)	0
11	Less: Income tax expense	34,020
12	Net income	$ 63,180
13		

NOTE: The corporate income tax rate for most companies is currently 35% of income before tax. Thus, the budgeted income tax is $34,020 (= $97,200 × 35%).

> **Why is this important?**
>
> "The **budgeted income statement** helps managers know in advance whether their plans will result in an **acceptable** level of **income**. If not, **management** will need to consider how it can cut expenses or increase **sales revenues**."

We have now completed the operating budgets for Tucson Tortilla. In the second half of the chapter, we'll prepare Tucson Tortilla's financial budgets.

Decision Guidelines

The Master Budget

Let's consider some of the decisions Campbell Soup Company made as it set up its budgeting process.

Decision	Guidelines
What should be the driving force behind the budgeting process?	The company's long-term goals and strategies drive the budgeting of the company's resources.
What are budgets used for?	Managers use budgets to help them fulfill their primary responsibilities: planning, directing, and controlling operations. Managers use feedback from the budgeting process to take corrective actions and, if necessary, revise strategies.
Who should be involved in the budgeting process?	Budgets tend to be more realistic and more motivational if lower-level managers, as well as upper-level managers, are allowed to participate in the budgeting process. The budgeting process tends to encompass a more comprehensive view when managers from all areas of the value chain participate in the process and serve on the budget committee.
What period of time should the budgets cover?	Long-term, strategic planning often results in forecasts of revenues and expenses 5 to 10 years into the future. Monthly and yearly budgets provide much more detailed information to aid management's shorter-term decisions.
How tough should the budget be to achieve?	Budgets are more useful for motivating employees and evaluating performance if they can be achieved with effort. Budgets that are too tight (too hard to achieve) or too loose (too easy to achieve) are not as beneficial.
What benefits should a company expect to obtain from developing a budget?	Benefits include the following: • Planning • Coordination and communication • Benchmarking (used for both motivation and performance evaluation)
What budgets should be included in a manufacturer's master budget?	The *operating budgets* include all budgets necessary to create a budgeted income statement. For a manufacturer, this includes the following: • Sales budget • Production budget • Direct materials budget • Direct labor budget • Manufacturing overhead budget • Operating expenses budget • Budgeted income statement The *financial budgets* include the capital expenditures budget, the cash budgets, and the budgeted balance sheet.

SUMMARY PROBLEM 1

Pillows Unlimited makes decorative throw pillows for home use. The company sells the pillows to home décor retailers for $14 per pillow. Each pillow requires 1.25 yards of fabric, which the company obtains at a cost of $6 per yard. The company would like to maintain an ending stock of fabric equal to 10% of the next month's production requirements. The company would also like to maintain an ending stock of finished pillows equal to 20% of the next month's sales. Sales (in units) are projected to be as follows for the first three months of the year:

January	100,000
February	110,000
March	115,000

Requirements

Prepare the following budgets for the first three months of the year, as well as a summary budget for the quarter:

1. Prepare the sales budget, including a separate section that details the type of sales made. For this section, assume that 10% of the company's pillows are cash sales, while the remaining 90% are sold on credit terms.

2. Prepare the production budget. Assume that the company anticipates selling 120,000 units in April.

3. Prepare the direct materials budget. Assume the company needs 150,000 yards of fabric for production in April.

■ SOLUTIONS

Requirement 1

	A	B	C	D	E
1		\multicolumn{4}{c}{Pillows Unlimited}
2		\multicolumn{4}{c}{Sales Budget}
3		\multicolumn{4}{c}{For the Quarter Ended March 31}
4		\multicolumn{3}{c}{Month}	
5		January	February	March	1st Quarter
6	Unit sales	100,000	110,000	115,000	325,000
7	Multiply by: Unit selling price	$ 14	$ 14	$ 14	$ 14
8	Total sales revenue	$ 1,400,000	$ 1,540,000	$ 1,610,000	$ 4,550,000
9					
10	**Type of sale:**				
11	Cash sales (10%)	$ 140,000	$ 154,000	$ 161,000	$ 455,000
12	Credit sales (90%)	1,260,000	1,386,000	1,449,000	4,095,000
13	Total sales revenue	$ 1,400,000	$ 1,540,000	$ 1,610,000	$ 4,550,000
14					

Requirement 2

	A	B	C	D	E
1		\multicolumn{4}{c}{Pillows Unlimited}			
2		\multicolumn{4}{c}{Production Budget}			
3		\multicolumn{4}{c}{For the Quarter Ended March 31}			
4		\multicolumn{3}{c}{Month}			
5		January	February	March	1st Quarter
6	Unit sales	100,000	110,000	115,000	325,000
7	Plus: Desired ending inventory	22,000	23,000	24,000	24,000
8	Total needed	122,000	133,000	139,000	349,000
9	Less: Beginning inventory	20,000	22,000	23,000	20,000
10	Number of units to produce	102,000	111,000	116,000	329,000

NOTE: January 1 inventory balance (20,000) is the same as the December 31 balance, which is calculated as 20% of the projected units sales in January (100,000). March desired ending inventory (24,000) is 20% of April's projected units sales (120,000).

Requirement 3

	A	B	C	D	E
1		\multicolumn{4}{c}{Pillows Unlimited}			
2		\multicolumn{4}{c}{Direct Materials Budget}			
3		\multicolumn{4}{c}{For the Quarter Ended March 31}			
4		\multicolumn{3}{c}{Month}			
5		January	February	March	1st Quarter
6	Units to be produced (from production budget)	102,000	111,000	116,000	329,000
7	Multiply by: Quantity (yards) of DM needed per unit	1.25	1.25	1.25	1.25
8	Quantity (yards) needed for production	127,500	138,750	145,000	411,250
9	Plus: Desired ending inventory of DM	13,875	14,500	15,000	15,000
10	Total quantity (yards) needed	141,375	153,250	160,000	426,250
11	Less: Beginning inventory of DM	12,750	13,875	14,500	12,750
12	Quantity (yards) to purchase	128,625	139,375	145,500	413,500
13	Multiply by: Cost per yard	$ 6.00	$ 6.00	$ 6.00	$ 6.00
14	Total cost of DM purchases	$ 771,750	$ 836,250	$ 873,000	$2,481,000

NOTE: January 1 inventory balance (12,750) is the same as the December 31 balance, which is calculated as 10% of the quantity (yards) needed for production in January (127,500). March desired ending inventory of DM (15,000) is 10% of April's projected quantity needed for production (150,000).

How Are the Financial Budgets Prepared?

3 Prepare the financial budgets

In the first half of the chapter, we prepared Tucson Tortilla's operating budgets, culminating with the company's budgeted income statement. In this part of the chapter, we turn our attention to Tucson Tortilla's financial budgets. Managers typically prepare a capital expenditures budget as well as three separate cash budgets:

1. Cash collections (or receipts) budget
2. Cash payments (or disbursements) budget
3. Combined cash budget, complete with financing arrangements

Finally, managers prepare the budgeted balance sheet. Each of these budgets is illustrated next.

Capital Expenditures Budget

The capital expenditures budget shows the company's intentions to invest in new property, plant, or equipment (capital investments). When planned capital investments are significant, this budget must be developed early in the process because the additional investments may affect depreciation expense, interest expense (if funds are borrowed to pay for the investments), or dividend payments (if stock is issued to pay for the investments). Chapter 12 contains a detailed discussion of the capital budgeting process, including the techniques managers use in deciding whether to make additional capital investments.

Exhibit 9-13 shows Tucson Tortilla's capital expenditures budget for the first three months of the year. Tucson Tortilla expects to invest in new computers, printers, delivery vans, and production equipment in January. The depreciation expense shown in the operating expenses budget and the depreciation shown in the MOH budget reflect these anticipated investments. No other capital investments are planned in the first quarter of the year.

EXHIBIT 9-13 Capital Expenditures Budget

	A	B	C	D	E
1		Tucson Tortilla			
2		Capital Expenditures Budget			
3		For the Quarter Ended March 31			
4		Month			
5		January	February	March	1st Quarter
6	Computers and printers	$ 15,000	0	0	15,000
7	Delivery vans	35,000	0	0	35,000
8	Production equipment	75,000	0	0	75,000
9	Total new capital investments	$ 125,000	0	0	$ 125,000
10					

Cash Collections Budget

The cash collections budget is all about timing: *When* does Tucson Tortilla expect to receive cash from its sales? Of course, Tucson Tortilla will receive cash immediately on its cash (COD) sales. From the Sales Budget (Exhibit 9-5), we see that the company expects the following cash sales in January:

$$\text{Cash (COD) sales} = \$120{,}000$$

However, most of the company's sales are made on credit. Recall that Tucson Tortilla's credit terms are "net 30 days," meaning customers have 30 days to pay. Therefore, most customers will wait nearly 30 days (a full month) before paying. However, some companies may be experiencing cash flow difficulties and may not be able to pay Tucson Tortilla on time. As a result, Tucson Tortilla doesn't expect to receive payment on all of its credit sales the month after the sale.

Based on collection history, Tucson Tortilla expects 85% of its credit sales to be collected in the month after sale, and 14% to be collected two months after the sale. Tucson Tortilla expects that 1% of credit sales will never be collected and therefore has recognized a 1% bad debt expense in its operating expenses budget. Furthermore, assume that December credit sales were $500,000 and November credit sales were $480,000.

> Anticipated January Collections of Credit Sales:
> 85% × $500,000 (December credit sales) = $425,000
> 14% × $480,000 (November credit sales) = $ 67,200

Exhibit 9-14 shows Tucson Tortilla's expected cash collections for the first three months of the year.

EXHIBIT 9-14 Cash Collections Budget

	January	February	March	1st Quarter
Tucson Tortilla				
Cash Collections Budget				
For the Quarter Ended March 31				
Cash sales in current month (from sales budget)	$ 120,000	$ 80,000	$ 100,000	$ 300,000
Collection on credit sales:				
85% of credit sales made one month ago	425,000	408,000	272,000	1,105,000
14% of credit sales made two months ago	67,200	70,000	67,200	204,400
Total cash collections	$ 612,200	$ 558,000	$ 439,200	$1,609,400

NOTE: Cash and credit sales are shown in Sales Budget (Exhibit 9-5).
January:
$425,000 = 85% of December credit sales ($500,000)
$67,200 = 14% of November credit sales ($480,000)
February:
$408,000 = 85% of January credit sales ($480,000)
$70,000 = 14% of December credit sales ($500,000)
March:
$272,000 = 85% of February credit sales ($320,000)
$67,200 = 14% of January credit sales ($480,000)

Try It!

Assume Georgio's has the following budgeted sales for the quarter:

	January	February	March
COD sales	$ 10,000	$ 20,000	$ 15,000
Credit sales	100,000	110,000	120,000
Total sales	$110,000	$130,000	$135,000

Determine Georgio's budget for March cash collections assuming credit sales are collected as follows: 90% is collected the month after sale, 8% is collected two months after the month of sale, and 2% is never collected.

Please see page 582 for solutions.

Cash Payments Budget

The cash payments budget is also about timing: *When* will Tucson Tortilla pay for its direct materials purchases, direct labor costs, manufacturing overhead costs, operating expenses, capital expenditures, and income taxes? Let's tackle each cost, one at a time.

DIRECT MATERIALS PURCHASES Tucson Tortilla has been given "net 30 days" payment terms from its suppliers of the corn flour used to make the tortilla chips. Therefore, Tucson

Tortilla waits a month before it pays for the direct materials purchases shown in the Direct Materials Budget (Exhibit 9-7). So, the company will pay for its December purchases (projected to be $231,845) in January, its January purchases of $211,125 (Exhibit 9-7) in February, its February purchases of $157,650 (Exhibit 9-7) in March, and so forth:

	A	B	C	D	E
1	**Calculating Cash Payments for Direct Materials Purchases**		Month		
2		January	February	March	1st Quarter
3	Total cost of DM purchases (from Exhibit 9-7)	$ 211,125	$ 157,650	$ 197,700	$ 566,475
4					
5	Cash payments for DM purchases **(paid one month after purchase)**	231,845	$ 211,125	$ 157,650	$ 600,620
6					

NOTE: December DM purchases are expected to be $231,845.

DIRECT LABOR Tucson Tortilla's factory employees are paid twice a month for the work they perform during the month. Therefore, January's direct labor cost of $31,900 (Exhibit 9-8) will be paid in January, and likewise, for each month.

	A	B	C	D	E
1			Month		
2	**Calculating Cash Payments for Direct Labor**	January	February	March	1st Quarter
3	Total cost of direct labor (from Exhibit 9-8)	$ 31,900	$ 22,550	$ 28,270	$ 82,720
4					
5	Cash payments for direct labor **(paid the same month)**	$ 31,900	$ 22,550	$ 28,270	$ 82,720
6					

MANUFACTURING OVERHEAD Tucson Tortilla must consider when it pays for its manufacturing overhead costs. Let's assume that the company pays for all manufacturing overhead costs except for depreciation, insurance, and property taxes in the month in which they are incurred. Depreciation is a noncash expense, so it never appears on the cash payments budget. Insurance and property taxes are typically paid on a semiannual basis. While Tucson Tortilla budgets a cost of $3,000 per month for factory insurance and property tax, it doesn't actually pay these costs on a monthly basis. Rather, Tucson Tortilla prepays its insurance and property tax twice a year, in January and July. The amount of these semiannual payments is calculated as shown:

$3,000 monthly cost × 12 months = $36,000 ÷ 2 = $18,000 payments in January and July

So, the cash payments for manufacturing overhead costs are expected to be as follows:

	A	B	C	D	E
1	**Calculating Cash Payments for Manufacturing Overhead**		Month		
2		January	February	March	1st Quarter
3	Total manufacturing overhead (from Exhibit 9-9)	$ 102,500	$ 81,250	$ 94,250	$ 278,000
4	Less: Depreciation **(not a cash expense)**	10,000	10,000	10,000	30,000
5	Less: Property tax and insurance **(paid twice a year, not monthly)**	3,000	3,000	3,000	9,000
6	Plus: Semiannual **payments** for property taxes and insurance	18,000	0	0	18,000
7	Cash payments for manufacturing overhead	$ 107,500	$ 68,250	$ 81,250	$ 257,000
8					

OPERATING EXPENSES Let's assume that the company pays for all operating expenses, except depreciation and bad debt expense, in the month in which they are incurred. Both depreciation and bad debt expense are noncash expenses, so they never appear on the cash payments budget. Bad debt expense simply recognizes the sales revenue that will never be collected. Therefore, these noncash expenses need to be deducted from the total operating expenses to arrive at cash payments for operating expenses:

	A	B	C	D	E
1	**Calculating Cash Payments for**		Month		
2	**Operating Expenses**	January	February	March	1st Quarter
3	Total operating expenses (from Exhibit 9-10)	$ 142,800	$ 106,200	$ 124,500	$ 373,500
4	Less: Depreciation (*not a cash expense*)	6,000	6,000	6,000	18,000
5	Less: Bad debt expense (*not a cash expense*)	4,800	3,200	4,000	12,000
6	Cash Payments for operating expenses	$ 132,000	$ 97,000	$ 114,500	$ 343,500

CAPITAL EXPENDITURES The timing of these cash payments has already been scheduled on the capital expenditures budget in Exhibit 9-13. Furthermore, let's assume the capital expenditures are paid for when they are purchased.

INCOME TAXES Corporations must make quarterly income tax payments for their estimated income tax liability. For corporations like Tucson Tortilla which have a December 31 fiscal year-end, the first income tax payment is not due until April 15. The remaining payments are due June 15, September 15, and December 15. As a result, Tucson Tortilla will not show any income tax payments in the first quarter of the year.

DIVIDENDS Like many corporations, Tucson Tortilla pays dividends to its shareholders on a quarterly basis. Tucson Tortilla plans to pay $25,000 in cash dividends in January for the company's earnings in the fourth quarter of the previous year.

Finally, we pull all of these cash payments together onto a single budget, as shown in Exhibit 9-15.

EXHIBIT 9-15 Cash Payments Budget

	A	B	C	D	E
1		**Tucson Tortilla**			
2		**Cash Payments Budget**			
3		**For the Quarter Ended March 31**			
4			Month		
5		January	February	March	1st Quarter
6	Cash payments for direct materials purchases	$ 231,845	$ 211,125	$ 157,650	$ 600,620
7	Cash payments for direct labor	31,900	22,550	28,270	82,720
8	Cash payments for manufacturing overhead	107,500	68,250	81,250	257,000
9	Cash payments for operating expenses	132,000	97,000	114,500	343,500
10	Cash payments for capital investments	125,000	0	0	125,000
11	Cash payments for income taxes	0	0	0	0
12	Cash payments for dividends	25,000	0	0	25,000
13	Total cash payments	$ 653,245	$ 398,925	$ 381,670	$ 1,433,840

Combined Cash Budget

The combined cash budget simply merges the budgeted cash collections and cash payments to forecast the company's ending cash position. Exhibit 9-16 shows the following:

- Budgeted cash collections for the month are added to the beginning cash balance to determine the total cash available.
- Budgeted cash payments are then subtracted to determine the ending cash balance before financing.
- Based on the ending cash balance before financing, the company knows whether it needs to borrow money or whether it has excess funds with which to repay debt or invest.

By looking at Exhibit 9-16, we see that Tucson Tortilla expects to begin the month with $36,100 of cash. However, by the end of the month, it will be short of cash. Therefore, the company's managers must plan for how they will handle this shortage. One strategy would be to delay the purchase of equipment planned for January. Another strategy would be to borrow money. Let's say Tucson Tortilla has prearranged a line of credit that carries an interest rate of prime plus 1%. A <u>line of credit</u> is a lending arrangement from a bank in which a company is allowed to borrow money as needed, up to a specified maximum amount, yet only pay interest on the portion that is actually borrowed until it is repaid.

EXHIBIT 9-16 Combined Cash Budget

	A	B	C	D	E
1		Tucson Tortilla			
2		Combined Cash Budget			
3		For the Quarter Ended March 31			
4		Month			
5		January	February	March	1st Quarter
6	Beginning cash balance	$ 36,100	$ 15,055	$ 153,980	$ 36,100
7	Plus: Cash collections (Exhibit 9-14)	612,200	558,000	439,200	1,609,400
8	Total cash available	648,300	573,055	593,180	1,645,500
9	Less: Cash payments (Exhibit 9-15)	653,245	398,925	381,670	1,433,840
10	Ending cash balance before financing	$ (4,945)	$ 174,130	$ 211,510	$ 211,660
11	Financing:				
12	Plus: New borrowings	20,000	0	0	20,000
13	Less: Debt repayments	0	20,000	0	20,000
14	Less: Interest payments	0	150	0	150
15	Ending cash balance	$ 15,055	$ 153,980	$ 211,510	$ 211,510
16					

The line of credit will enable Tucson Tortilla to borrow funds to meet its short-term cash deficiencies. Let's say that Tucson Tortilla wants to maintain an ending cash balance of at least $15,000. By borrowing $20,000 on its line of credit at the end of January, the company will have slightly more ($15,055) than its minimum desired balance.

The cash budget also shows that Tucson Tortilla will be able to repay this borrowing, along with the accrued interest, in February. Assuming Tucson Tortilla borrows the $20,000 for a full month at an interest rate of 9%, February's interest payment would be calculated as follows:

$$\$20{,}000 \text{ loan} \times 1/12 \text{ of the year} \times 9\% \text{ interest rate} = \$150$$

> **Why is this important?**
>
> "The combined **cash budget** lets managers know in **advance** when they will be short on cash and will need to **borrow** money, or when they may have **extra funds** to invest."

Exhibit 9-16 also shows that Tucson Tortilla expects to have a fairly substantial cash balance at the end of both February and March. The company's managers use the cash budgets to determine when this cash will be needed and to decide how to invest it accordingly. Since the first quarterly income tax payment is due April 15, management will want to invest most of this excess cash in a safe, short-term investment, such as a money market fund or short-term certificate of deposit. The company will also need cash in April to pay shareholders a quarterly dividend. Any cash not needed in the short run can be invested in longer-term investments. Managers exercising good cash management should have a plan in place for both cash deficiencies and cash excesses.

Budgeted Balance Sheet

Exhibit 9-17 shows Tucson Tortilla's budgeted balance sheet as of January 31. The company will prepare a budgeted balance sheet for each month of the year.

EXHIBIT 9-17 Budgeted Balance Sheet

	A	B
1	Tucson Tortilla	
2	Budgeted Balance Sheet	
3	January 31	
4	**Assets:**	
5	Cash, from cash budget	$ 15,055
6	Accounts receivable, net of allowance[A]	549,450
7	Raw materials inventory, from DM budget (10,250 pounds × $1.50 per pound)	15,375
8	Finished goods inventory, from production budget (2,000 cases × $12.00 per case)	24,000
9	Prepaid property taxes and insurance[B]	15,000
10	Total current assets	618,880
11	Property, plant, and equipment,[C] net of $1,920,000 of accumulated depreciation[D]	4,430,000
12	Total assets	$ 5,048,880
13		
14	**Liabilities and Stockholders' Equity:**	
15	Accounts payable[E]	$ 211,125
16	Income tax liability, from Income Statement Budget	34,020
17	Other current liabilities (line of credit, from combined cash budget)	20,000
18	Total current liabilities	265,145
19	Stockholders' equity[F]	4,783,735
20	Total liabilities and stockholders' equity	$ 5,048,880
21		

NOTE: Calculations for amounts itemized below.

[A] **Accounts Receivable, Net of Allowance**

January credit sales (from sales budget, Exhibit 9-5)	$480,000
15% of December's credit sales ($500,000) yet to be collected	75,000
Accounts receivable, January 31	$555,000
Less: Allowance for uncollectible accounts (assume $750 balance prior to additional $4,800 bad debt expense, Exhibit 9-10)	(5,550)
Accounts receivable, net of allowance for uncollectible accounts	$549,450

[B] **Prepaid Property Tax and Insurance**

Semiannual payment made in January (cash payments for MOH, p. 526)	$18,000
Less: January cost (MOH budget, Exhibit 9-9)	3,000
Prepaid property tax and insurance, January 31	$15,000

[C] **Property, Plant, and Equipment**

December 31 balance (assumed)	$6,225,000
Plus: January's investment in new equipment (capital expenditures budget, Exhibit 9-13)	125,000
Property, plant, and equipment, January 31	$6,350,000

[D] **Accumulated Depreciation**

December 31 balance (assumed)	$1,904,000
Plus: January's depreciation from manufacturing overhead budget, Exhibit 9-9	10,000
Plus: January's depreciation from operating expenses budget, Exhibit 9-10	6,000
Accumulated depreciation, January 31	$1,920,000

E Accounts Payable	
January's DM purchases to be paid in February (p. 526 and Exhibit 9-15)	211,125
Accounts payable, January 31	$211,125

F Stockholders' Equity	
December 31 balance of common stock and retained earnings (assumed)	$4,720,555
Plus: January's net income (budgeted income statement, Exhibit 9-12)	63,180
Stockholders' equity, January 31	$4,783,735

Sensitivity Analysis and Flexible Budgeting

The master budget models the company's *planned* activities. Managers try to use the best estimates possible when creating budgets. However, managers do not have a crystal ball for making predictions. Some of the key assumptions (such as sales volume) used to create the budgets may turn out to be different than originally predicted. How do managers prepare themselves for potentially different scenarios? They use sensitivity analysis and flexible budgeting.

As shown in Exhibit 9-18, **sensitivity analysis** is a *what-if* technique that asks *what* a result will be *if* a predicted amount is not achieved or *if* an underlying assumption changes. For example, *what if* shipping costs increase due to increases in gasoline prices? *What if* the cost of the corn flour increases or union workers negotiate a wage increase? *What if* sales are 15% cash and 85% credit, rather than 20% cash and 80% credit? How will any or all of these changes in key assumptions affect Tucson Tortilla's budgeted income and budgeted cash position?

EXHIBIT 9-18 Sensitivity Analysis

In addition to these "what-if" scenarios, management is particularly concerned with sales projections. Why? Because the sales budget is the driving force behind most of the other budgets. If the budgeted sales figures change, then most other budgets will also change. To address this concern, managers often prepare **flexible budgets**, which are budgets prepared for different volumes of activity. We'll discuss flexible budgets in Chapter 10, where we show how flexible budgets are often used to evaluate performance at the end of the period.

Sensitivity analysis and flexible budgeting are fairly easy to perform using Excel or special budgeting software. Managers simply change one or more of the underlying assumptions in the budgets, such as sales volume, and the software automatically computes a complete set of revised budgets based on the changes.

Armed with a better understanding of how changes in key assumptions will affect the company's bottom line and cash position, today's managers can be prepared to lead the company when business conditions change.

> ### Technology Makes it Simple — Excel 2016
>
> Sensitivity analysis is relatively easy to perform using spreadsheet software such as Microsoft Excel. We'll use the Direct Materials Budget pictured in Exhibit 9-7 as an example. Once the worksheet is set up, it can be used over and over for unlimited changes in assumptions. While we illustrate just one budget here, in real life, companies tie all of the individual budgets together such that if an assumption changes in one budget, the effect automatically ripples through the entire master budget. For example, a change of a key assumption in the sales budget would have an impact on almost every other budget in the master budget.
>
> 1. In a new spreadsheet, list the key factors that impact the budget (for example, units produced (Cell A19), pounds of materials needed per unit (Cell A20), cost per pound (Cell A21), desired level of ending inventory (Cell A22), and so forth).
> 2. Next, input the key assumptions corresponding to each of these factors (for example 29,000 units (Cell B19), 5 pounds needed per unit (Cell B20), material cost of $1.50 per pound (Cell B21), desired ending inventory equal to 10% of next month's quantity needed (Cell B22), and so forth).
> 3. Set up the Direct Materials Budget, as pictured in Exhibit 9-7. However, do not input any actual numbers. Rather, input cell references and formulas *for each cell*. For example:
>   a. Cell B6 should reference the cell containing the number of units to be produced (=B19) and Cell B7 should reference the cell containing the assumption for pounds needed per unit (= B20).
>   b. Cell B8 should have a formula multiplying units produced by pounds per unit (= B6*B7).
>   c. Cell E6 should add cells B6, C6, and D6 (= B6 + C6 + D6).
> 4. Once you have formulated the entire budget in this manner, change one of the assumptions and notice how the effect ripples through the budget. The first time you use it, you may want to double check the figures by hand to make sure you correctly formulated the cells. Once you are sure the cell references and formulas are correct, you can use the spreadsheet for an unlimited amount of sensitivity analyses.

How Do the Budgets for Service and Merchandising Companies Differ?

Earlier in this chapter, we presented the master budget for a manufacturing company. The components of the master budget for a manufacturing company were summarized in Exhibit 9-4. The master budgets for service companies and merchandising companies are somewhat less complex and will be described next.

4 Prepare budgets for a merchandiser

Service Companies

Recall that service companies have no merchandise inventory. Therefore, their operating budgets only include the sales budget, the operating expenses budget, and the budgeted income statement, as shown in Exhibit 9-19 on the next page. Notice that the financial budgets are the same as those a manufacturer would prepare.

Merchandising Companies

Since merchandising companies purchase ready-made products, they do not need to prepare the production, direct materials, direct labor, or manufacturing overhead budgets. Replacing these budgets is a combined **cost of goods sold, inventory, and purchases budget**, as shown in Exhibit 9-20 on the next page.

EXHIBIT 9-19 Master Budget for a Service Company

EXHIBIT 9-20 Master Budget for a Merchandising Company

The cost of goods sold, inventory, and purchases budget follows the same general format as the manufacturer's production budget except that it is calculated at cost (in dollars) rather than in units:[3]

Cost of Goods Sold	(the inventory we plan to sell during the month, at cost)
Plus: Desired Ending Inventory	(the amount of inventory we want on hand at month's end)
Total Inventory Needed	(the total amount of inventory needed)
Less: Beginning Inventory	(the amount of inventory we have on hand)
Inventory to Purchase	(the amount of inventory we need to purchase)

[3] A merchandiser could first prepare this budget in units and then convert it to dollars. However, merchandisers usually have hundreds or thousands of products for sale, so it is often simpler to state it directly in dollars.

Notice that the format of the budget is easy to remember because it follows the name of the budget: We start with *Cost of Goods Sold*, then consider *inventory* levels, and finally arrive at the amount of inventory to *purchase*. Let's try an example:

Let's say one Circle J convenience store expects sales of $500,000 in January, $520,000 in February, $530,000 in March, and $550,000 in April. Let's also assume that management sets its prices to achieve an overall 40% gross profit. As a result, Cost of Goods Sold is 60% of the sales revenue (100% − 40%). Finally, management wishes to have ending inventory equal to 10% of the next month's Cost of Goods Sold. Exhibit 9-21 shows Circle J's cost of goods sold, inventory, and purchases budget for the first three months of the year. Keep in mind that all figures (other than Sales Revenue) are shown at cost.

EXHIBIT 9-21 Merchandiser's Cost of Goods Sold, Inventory, and Purchases Budget

	A	B	C	D	E
1		\multicolumn{4}{c}{Circle J Convenience Stores}	
2		\multicolumn{4}{c}{Cost of Goods Sold, Inventory, and Purchases Budget}	
3		\multicolumn{4}{c}{For the Quarter Ended March 31}	
4		\multicolumn{3}{c}{Month}	
5		January	February	March	1st Quarter
6	Budgeted sales revenue	$ 500,000	$ 520,000	$ 530,000	$ 1,550,000
7					
8	Cost of goods sold	$ 300,000	$ 312,000	$ 318,000	$ 930,000
9	Plus: Desired ending inventory	31,200	31,800	33,000	33,000
10	Total inventory required	331,200	343,800	351,000	963,000
11	Less: Beginning inventory	30,000	31,200	31,800	30,000
12	Amount of inventory to purchase	$ 301,200	$ 312,600	$ 319,200	$ 933,000
13					

NOTE: Management would like to maintain an ending inventory equal to 10% of the next month's Cost of Goods Sold. The January 1 balance ($30,000) is the same as the December 31 balance, which is 10% of January's Cost of Goods Sold ($300,000). Also, assume April sales are projected to be $550,000, so April's Cost of Goods Sold is $330,000 (= 60% × $550,000).

Figures from this budget are then used as follows:

- *Cost of Goods Sold* is used in preparing the budgeted income statement.
- *Ending Inventory* is used in preparing the budgeted balance sheet.
- *Purchases of Inventory* is used in preparing the cash payments budget.

Impact of Credit and Debit Card Sales on Budgeting

Consumers often use credit and debit cards to pay for online and in-store purchases at retailers, gas stations, and restaurants. In fact, over 26.2 billion transactions totaling roughly $4 trillion were made by credit cards in 2014.[4] What implications do these payment methods have for the merchants who accept "plastic" in place of cash or checks?

- Credit card companies (Visa, MasterCard, American Express, and Discover) and their issuing banks charge the merchant a transaction fee for each purchase made using plastic. The fee, officially known in business as "interchange," is usually a fixed amount per transaction *plus* a percentage of the amount charged. For example, the typical transaction fee for each credit card sale is between $0.05 and $0.20, *plus* 1–3% of the amount charged.[5] The actual fee will depend on the credit card brand, the merchant's industry, and whether or not the card is present (for example, online sales). Reward cards, such as those tied to frequent flyer miles, typically charge higher fees.
- In exchange for the fee, the credit card company and its issuing bank pays the merchant the entire amount of the purchase *less* the transaction fee. A deposit is made to the merchant's bank account within a few days of the sale.

---

[4] http://www.creditcards.com/credit-card-news/credit-card-market-share-statistics-1264.php
[5] https://www.mastercard.us/en-us/about-mastercard/what-we-do/interchange.html and https://usa.visa.com/dam/VCOM/download/merchants/Visa-USA-Interchange-Reimbursement-Fees-2015-April-18.pdf

Debit card transaction fees are usually lower than credit card transaction fees. Why?

1. Since debit card purchases require an associated personal identification number (PIN), the risk of fraud is lower than it is with a credit card. Thus, the issuing credit card company will have lower costs associated with stolen and fraudulently used cards.
2. Debit card sales are paid to the merchant using money that is in the customer's bank account, rather than money that is in essence loaned to the customer by the credit card company. Since the cash used for the deposit is not subject to credit risk, it is made with "cheaper" funds.
3. Beginning October 1, 2011, the Federal Reserve set a cap on the debit card transaction fees that banks can charge merchants. The new limit is as follows:

> Limit on *debit* card fees = $0.22 per transaction + 0.05% of the amount of the transaction

Notice that the amount charged on the value of the transaction (0.0005) is substantially less than it is for a typical credit card transaction.[6]

Although credit and debit card transaction fees are costly to merchants, the acceptance of plastic payment methods also has benefits:

- Merchants would lose potential sales if they did not allow customers to pay with credit and debit cards. For example, Aldi, the low-cost grocery store with over 1,500 stores in the United States, only started accepting credit cards in 2016. Previously, the merchant only accepted debit cards because of the lower transaction fees. However, as part of Aldi's aggressive plan for growth in the U.S., management decided that they could attract more shoppers, and shoppers from a different socio-economic class, if they accepted credit cards in addition to debit cards.[7]
- The acceptance of credit and debit cards decreases the costs associated with bounced checks, misappropriation of cash, and the activities associated with preparing and transporting cash deposits (sometimes via armored vehicle collection services).
- Merchants receive the cash quickly, which may improve their cash flow.

Let's try an example:

Say a customer purchases some clothes at Urban Outfitters for $75 and uses a MasterCard to pay for the purchase. Let's also assume that MasterCard charges Urban Outfitters a transaction fee equal to $0.15 + 2% of the amount charged. The transaction fee on this sale would be:

> Transaction Fee = $0.15 + (2% × Amount Charged)
> $1.65 = $0.15 + (2% × $75)

Within a few days, MasterCard would deposit the following amount in Urban Outfitters' bank account:

> Cash Deposited = Amount Charged on Credit Card − Transaction Fee
> $73.35 = $75.00 − $1.65

---

[6] www.federalreserve.gov/newsevents/press/bcreg/20110629a.htm. Banks with less than $10 billion in assets are exempt from the new cap. In addition, if a bank does not have fraud prevention policies and procedures in place, the cap is $0.21 per transaction rather than $0.22 per transaction.

[7] http://www.cnbc.com/2016/03/02/no-frills-supermarket-aldi-to-accept-credit-cards.html

The anticipation of this credit card sale would be shown in the budgets as follows:

- The $75 sale would be shown in the sales budget, *in the month of sale*.
- The $1.65 transaction fee would be shown in the operating expenses budget, *in the month of sale*.
- The $73.35 would be shown as a cash receipt on the cash collections budget, *in the month of collection* (which is typically within one to seven days of the actual sale).

When preparing the master budget, merchants need to consider:

- The percentage of sales that will be made using debit cards and credit cards,
- The different transaction fees charged for debit and credit card transactions, and
- The length of time between the sale and the deposit.

Retail Credit Cards

Many retailers, such as Macy's and Old Navy, issue their own credit cards in addition to accepting credit cards such as Visa and MasterCard. When a customer uses a store-based credit card, no transaction fee is incurred. However, the risk of collection falls back on the merchant, rather than on a third-party credit card company. The merchant must wait for the customer to make payments on the credit card bill. The cash collection may occur over several months, several years, or never. The cash collections budget will take into account the aging of these receivables. Likewise, the operating expenses budget will need to take into consideration possible bad debts. Finally, the company will need to budget for interest income assessed on unpaid balances and any fees charged to the customer for late payments.

Exhibit 9-22 compares third-party credit cards with retail credit cards.

EXHIBIT 9-22 Comparison of Credit Cards

Third-Party Credit Cards (e.g., Visa and MasterCard)*
- Merchant accepts "plastic payment" in the form of a third-party credit card (e.g., Visa).
- Credit card issuer (e.g., Visa) pays merchant amount of purchase, less a transaction fee.
- Credit card issuer (e.g., Visa) assumes collection risk.
- Consumer owes credit card issuer amount of purchase, plus interest on any outstanding unpaid balance from earlier periods.

Retail Credit Cards (e.g., Macy's):
- Merchant accepts "plastic payment" in the form of the merchant's own retail card.
- No third-party transaction fee is involved.
- Merchant assumes collection risk.
- Consumer owes issuing merchant amount of purchase, plus interest on any outstanding unpaid balance from earlier periods.

*The actual issuers of third-party credit cards are member banks of Visa and MasterCard's network, such as JP Morgan Chase, Capital One, and Citigroup. These member banks process the payments and receive the transaction fees. They also pay additional fees to Visa and MasterCard. Thus, Exhibit 9-22 is a simplification of the actual business relationships surrounding credit cards, but serves as a useful illustration for how "plastic" payments affect merchant budgeting.

Sustainability and Budgeting

Campbell Soup Company is a recognized leader in corporate responsibility. The company has been listed on the Dow Jones Sustainability Index for the last seven consecutive years and has ranked in the Top 10 Best Corporate Citizens (large company category) by Corporate Responsibility Magazine for the fourth consecutive year.[8] How does the company do it? Managers at Campbell set long-term sustainability targets and benchmark actual yearly performance against those targets. Each of these targets requires actions that will impact the company's annual budgets. For example, the company has set long-term environmental goals for 2020 that include:[9]

- Cutting water use and greenhouse gases emissions per pound of ingredient by 20% and cutting fertilizer per pound of ingredient by 10%
- Recycling 95% of waste generated
- Reducing packaging material by 100 million pounds and delivering 100% of packaging from sustainable materials
- Reducing energy use by 35% and sourcing 40% of energy used from renewable or alternative energy sources

The adoption of these long-term goals will affect most, if not all, of the company's shorter-term budgets. For example, the reduction of water, energy, and packaging materials at the plants will affect the MOH and direct materials budget, while the recycling of waste will create some additional income. The goal of cutting greenhouse gas emissions will impact the company's capital expenditure budget, as the company invests in new technologies such as the biogas digester being used by one of the company's plants in Ohio. These plans will, in turn, affect the cash budgets.

In addition to environmental goals, the company also has social impact goals, which will be reflected in the company's budgets. These goals include:

- Increasing the nutritional value of its products
- Reducing childhood obesity and hunger
- Promoting volunteerism

These plans also play out in the company's manufacturing budgets (production of healthier products) and operating expense budgets (funding social wellness programs). While this chapter has focused on the use of budgets for planning purposes, recall that budgets also serve as benchmarks for judging performance. Each year, Campbell publishes its Corporate Social Responsibility scorecard to show how well it is achieving its environmental and social impact goals. For example, in 2014, the company had an 86% worldwide recycling rate, decreased packaging by 89 million pounds, reduced water use and greenhouse gas emissions, and gave over $70 million to charitable causes.

By using budgets for both planning and performance evaluation, Campbell is making strides in becoming the type of sustainable company envisioned by management.

See Exercises E9-17A and E9-37B

---

[8] http://www.campbellsoupcompany.com/pressrelease/campbell-named-to-the-dow-jones-sustainability-indices-for-seventh-consecutive-year/
[9] 2014 Corporate Social Responsibility Report

Decision Guidelines

The Master Budget

Let's consider some decisions managers need to make with respect to budgeting.

Decision	Guidelines
What is the key to preparing the cash collections and cash payments budgets?	The key to preparing the cash budgets is *timing*. *When* will cash be received, and *when* will cash be paid? The timing of cash collections and cash payments often differs from the period in which the related revenues and expenses are recognized on the income statement.
What can be done to prepare for possible changes in key, underlying budget assumptions?	Management uses sensitivity analysis to understand how changes in key, underlying assumptions might affect the company's financial results. This awareness helps managers cope with changing business conditions when they occur.
How does sustainability impact budgeting?	Companies that are planning on adopting any sustainable practice will want to capture those plans in their budgets. Any or all of the budgets could be impacted by plans to adopt sustainable practices.
How does the master budget of a service company differ from that of a manufacturer?	Service companies have no inventory to make or sell, thus their operating budgets are less complex. The operating budgets include the: • Sales budget • Operating expenses budget • Budgeted income statement
How does the master budget of a merchandising company differ from that of a manufacturer?	Merchandising companies buy their inventory, rather than make it. In place of the production budget, they use a "cost of goods sold, inventory, and purchases" budget. This budget follows the same basic format as the production budget. The amounts on the budget are calculated at cost, rather than in units. The operating budgets include the: • Sales budget • Cost of goods sold, inventory, and purchases budget • Operating expenses budget • Budgeted income statement
How does the acceptance of debit and credit card payments affect a merchant's budgets?	Merchants must budget for the transaction fees charged by the credit card companies and their issuing banks. The transaction fee needs to be shown on the operating expenses budget. The amount of credit and debit card sales, net of the transaction fee, will be shown on the cash collections budget.
How are credit and debit card transaction fees calculated?	The transaction fee is typically a set dollar amount per transaction, plus a percentage of the amount of sale charged on a credit or debit card. For example: $$\text{Transaction Fee} = \$0.25 + (2\% \times \text{Amount Charged})$$
How does the acceptance of debit and credit cards affect the cash collection budget?	The amount of cash shown on the cash collections budget will be the net amount deposited: $$\text{Cash Deposited} = \text{Amount Charged on Credit Card} - \text{Transaction Fee}$$

SUMMARY PROBLEM 2

The following information was taken from the Pillows Unlimited sales budget, found in Summary Problem 1 on page 523:

	A	B	C	D	E
1		Pillows Unlimited			
2		Sales Budget: Type of Sale			
3		For the Quarter Ended March 31			
4		Month			
5		January	February	March	1st Quarter
6	**Type of sale:**				
7	Cash sales (10%)	$ 140,000	$ 154,000	$ 161,000	$ 455,000
8	Credit sales (90%)	1,260,000	1,386,000	1,449,000	4,095,000
9	Total sales revenue	$ 1,400,000	$ 1,540,000	$ 1,610,000	$ 4,550,000
10					

The company's collection history indicates that 75% of credit sales is collected in the month after the sale, 15% is collected two months after the sale, 8% is collected three months after the sale, and the remaining 2% is never collected.

Assume the following additional information was gathered about the types of sales made in the fourth quarter (October through December) of the previous year:

	A	B	C	D	E
1		Pillows Unlimited			
2		Sales Budget: Type of Sale			
3		For the Quarter Ended December 31			
4		Month			
5		October	November	December	4th Quarter
6	**Type of sale:**				
7	Cash sales (10%)	$ 142,800	$ 151,200	$ 137,200	$ 431,200
8	Credit sales (90%)	1,285,200	1,360,800	1,234,800	3,880,800
9	Total sales revenue	$ 1,428,000	$ 1,512,000	$ 1,372,000	$ 4,312,000
10					

The following information was taken from the Pillows Unlimited direct materials budget, found in Summary Problem 1 on page 523:

	A	B	C	D	E
1		Pillows Unlimited			
2		Excerpt from Direct Materials Budget			
3		For the Quarter Ended March 31			
4		Month			
5		January	February	March	1st Quarter
6	Total cost of DM purchases	$ 771,750	$ 836,250	$ 873,000	$ 2,481,000
7					

Assume that the total cost of direct materials purchases in December was $725,000. The company pays 40% of its direct materials purchases in the month of purchase and pays the remaining 60% in the month after purchase.

Requirements

1. Prepare the cash collections budget for January, February, and March, as well as a summary for the first quarter.
2. Prepare the cash payments budget for direct materials purchases for the months of January, February, and March, as well as a summary for the quarter.

SOLUTIONS

Requirement 1

	A	B	C	D	E
1		Pillows Unlimited			
2		Cash Collections Budget			
3		For the Quarter Ended March 31			
4		Month			
5		January	February	March	1st Quarter
6	Cash sales in current month	$ 140,000	$ 154,000	$ 161,000	$ 455,000
7	Collection on credit sales:				
8	75% of credit sales made one month ago	926,100	945,000	1,039,500	2,910,600
9	15% of credit sales made two months ago	204,120	185,220	189,000	578,340
10	8% of credit sales made three months ago	102,816	108,864	98,784	310,464
11	Total cash collections	$ 1,373,036	$ 1,393,084	$ 1,488,284	$ 4,254,404
12					

NOTE: Cash and credit sales are shown on the sales budget

January:
$926,100 = 75% of December credit sales ($1,234,800)
$204,120 = 15% of November credit sales ($1,360,800)
$102,816 = 8% of October credit sales ($1,285,200)

February:
$945,000 = 75% of January credit sales ($1,260,000)
$185,220 = 15% of December credit sales ($1,234,800)
$108,864 = 8% of November credit sales ($1,360,800)

March:
$1,039,500 = 75% of February credit sales ($1,386,000)
$189,000 = 15% of January credit sales ($1,260,000)
$98,784 = 8% of December credit sales ($1,234,800)

Requirement 2

	A	B	C	D	E
1		Pillows Unlimited			
2		Cash Payments Budget			
3		For the Quarter Ended March 31			
4		Month			
5		January	February	March	1st Quarter
6	40% of current month DM purchases	$ 308,700	$ 334,500	$ 349,200	$ 992,400
7	60% of last month's DM purchases	435,000	463,050	501,750	1,399,800
8	Total cash payments	$ 743,700	$ 797,550	$ 850,950	$ 2,392,200
9					

NOTE: Payments calculated as follows:

January:
$308,700 = 40% of January DM purchases ($771,750)
$435,000 = 60% of December DM purchases ($725,000)

February:
$334,500 = 40% of February DM purchases ($836,250)
$463,050 = 60% of January DM purchases ($771,750)

March:
$349,200 = 40% of March DM purchases ($873,000)
$501,750 = 60% of February DM purchases ($836,250)

END OF CHAPTER

Learning Objectives

1. Describe how and why managers use budgets
2. Prepare the operating budgets
3. Prepare the financial budgets
4. Prepare budgets for a merchandiser

Accounting Vocabulary

Budget Committee. (p. 509) A committee comprised of upper management as well as cross-functional managers that reviews, revises, and approves the final budget.

COD. (p. 513) Collect on Delivery, or Cash on Delivery. A sales term indicating that the inventory must be paid for at the time of delivery.

Cost of Goods Sold, Inventory, and Purchases Budget. (p. 531) A merchandiser's budget that computes the cost of goods sold, the amount of desired ending inventory, and amount of merchandise to be purchased.

Financial Budgets. (p. 511) The financial budgets include the capital expenditures budget and the cash budget. It culminates in a budgeted balance sheet.

Flexible Budgets. (p. 530) Budgets prepared for different volumes of activity.

Line of Credit. (p. 528) A lending arrangement from a bank in which a company is allowed to borrow money as needed, up to a specified maximum amount, yet only pay interest on the portion that is actually borrowed until it is repaid.

Master Budget. (p. 511) The comprehensive planning document for the entire organization. The master budget includes the operating budgets and the financial budgets.

Operating Budgets. (p. 511) The budgets needed to run the daily operations of the company. The operating budgets culminate in a budgeted income statement.

Participative Budgeting. (p. 509) Budgeting that involves the participation of many levels of management.

Rolling Budget. (p. 509) A budget that is continuously updated so that the next 12 months of operations are always budgeted; also known as a *continuous budget*.

Safety Stock. (p. 513) Extra inventory kept on hand in case demand is higher than expected or problems in the factory slow production.

Sensitivity Analysis. (p. 530) A *what-if* technique that asks what a result will be if a predicted amount is not achieved or if an underlying assumption changes.

Slack. (p. 509) Intentionally overstating budgeted expenses or understating budgeted revenues in order to cope with uncertainty, make performance appear better, or make room for potential budget cuts.

Strategic Planning. (p. 508) Setting long-term goals that may extend 5 to 10 years into the future.

Variance. (p. 511) The difference between actual and budgeted figures (revenues and expenses).

Zero-Based Budgeting. (p. 510) A budgeting approach in which managers begin with a budget of zero and must justify every dollar put into the budget.

MyAccountingLab Go to http://myaccountinglab.com/ for the following Quick Check, Short Exercises, Exercises, and Problems. They are available with immediate grading, explanations of correct and incorrect answers, and interactive media that acts as your own online tutor.

Quick Check

1. *(Learning Objective 1)* Which term describes the situation in which a manager intentionally overbudgets expenses or underbudgets revenue?
    a. Participative budgeting
    b. Budgetary slack
    c. Strategic planning
    d. Benchmarking

2. *(Learning Objective 1)* Benefits of budgeting include
    a. benchmarking.
    b. planning.
    c. coordination and communication.
    d. all of the above.

3. *(Learning Objective 1)* The comprehensive planning document for the entire organization is called the _____ budget.
   a. financial
   b. cash
   c. master
   d. operating

4. *(Learning Objective 2)* Which of the following budgets must be prepared first, as it serves as a basis for most other budgets?
   a. Production budget
   b. Operating expenses budget
   c. Cash budget
   d. Sales budget

5. *(Learning Objective 2)* The operating budgets culminate in the budgeted
   a. statement of owners' equity.
   b. balance sheet.
   c. income statement.
   d. statement of cash flows.

6. *(Learning Objective 3)* Which of the following are noncash expenses that will always result in differences between the budgeted operating expenses for a given period and the budgeted cash payments for the same period?
   a. Depreciation expense and bad debt expense
   b. Advertising expense and bad debt expense
   c. Depreciation expense and rent expense
   d. Advertising expense and rent expense

7. *(Learning Objective 3)* Which budget reflects the company's plans to invest in new property, plant, and equipment?
   a. Direct materials budget
   b. Operating expenses budget
   c. Cash collections budget
   d. Capital expenditures budget

8. *(Learning Objective 4)* Which of the following budgets is unique to merchandising companies?
   a. Direct materials budget
   b. Operating expenses budget
   c. Production budget
   d. Cost of Goods Sold, Inventory, and Purchases budget

9. *(Learning Objective 4)* Which of the following is true?
   a. Only debit card transaction fees are limited by law.
   b. Only credit card transaction fees are limited by law.
   c. Both credit card and debit card transaction fees are limited by law.
   d. Neither credit card nor debit card transaction fees are limited by law.

10. *(Learning Objective 4)* Which of the following is true for merchants who accept payments made by Visa, MasterCard, and other forms of "plastic"?
    a. Transaction fees are generally a fixed amount per month.
    b. Credit card fees are usually lower than debit card fees.
    c. Transaction fees should be budgeted for in the operating expenses budget.
    d. Retail cards (such as Target and Kohl's charge cards) have similar transaction fees to those issued by Visa and MasterCard.

Quick Check Answers

1. b 2. d 3. c 4. d 5. c 6. a 7. d 8. d 9. a 10. c

Short Exercises

S9-1 Order of preparation and components of master budget *(Learning Objective 1)*

Identify the order in which a manufacturer would prepare the following budgets. Also note whether each budget is an operating budget or a financial budget.

a. Budgeted income statement
b. Production budget
c. Combined cash budget
d. Budgeted balance sheet
e. Direct materials budget
f. Cash payments budget
g. Sales budget

S9-2 Explain why companies use zero-based budgeting *(Learning Objective 1)*

Unilever is a multinational consumer goods company headquartered in Rotterdam, Netherlands, and London, United Kingdom. Some of its major brands in the United States include Dove, Hellman's, Lipton, and Ben & Jerry's. The company is organized into four main divisions: Foods, Refreshment (beverages and ice cream), Home Care, and Personal Care.

Despite reporting better than expected results for 2015, the Unilever CEO, Paul Polman, warned that the company expected tougher market conditions in 2016. Speaking in mid-January 2016, Polman pointed to the volatility in the stock market in January 2016 as evidence of the tougher market conditions.

Polman stated that Unilever would be rolling out a zero-based budgeting initiative across the entire company. This initiative was expected to save approximately €1 billion (about $1.09 billion in US dollars) per year by 2018. Unilever was seeking steady improvement in its gross profit.

Requirements

1. What is zero-based budgeting?
2. What is gross profit?
3. How would zero-based budgeting help Unilever increase its gross profit?
4. How would zero-based budgeting impact Unilever's cash flows?
5. What benefits does zero-based budgeting potentially hold for Unilever? What disadvantages?
6. Put yourself in the position of a brand manager for Unilever. Imagine that your brand has been performing well over the past three years. How would you feel about the zero-based budgeting initiative? How could this impact your work performance?

S9-3 Understanding key terms and definitions *(Learning Objectives 1 & 2)*

Listed next are several terms. Complete each of the following statements with one of these terms. You may use a term more than once, and some terms may not be used at all.

Budget committees	Financial budgets	Master budget	Operating budgets
Participative budgeting	Production budget	Rolling budget	Safety stock
Slack	Strategic planning	Variance	Zero-based budgeting

a. _____ is extra inventory of finished goods that is kept on hand in case demand is higher than predicted or problems in the factory slow production.

b. Managers will sometimes build _____ into their budgets to protect themselves against unanticipated expenses or lower revenues.

c. The sales budget and production budget are examples of _____.

d. The _____ is used to forecast how many units should be made to meet the sales projections.

e. _____ is a budgeting process that begins with departmental managers and flows up through middle management to top management.

f. _____ is a budget that is continuously updated by adding months to the end of the budgeting period.

g. The _____ is the difference between actual and budgeted figures and is used to evaluate how well the manager controlled operations during the period.

h. _____ is the comprehensive planning document for the entire organization.

i. When an organization builds its budgets from the ground up, it is using _____.

j. These budgets, _____, project both the collection and payment of cash and forecast the company's budgeted balance sheet.

k. _____ is the process of setting long-term goals that may extend several years into the future.

l. _____ are often used by companies to review submitted budgets, make revisions as needed, and approve the final budgets.

S9-4 Sales Budget *(Learning Objective 2)*

Jefferson Sports Medicine, Inc., offers two types of physical exams for students: the basic physical and the extended physical. The charge for the basic physical is $60, while the charge for the extended physical is $135. Jefferson expects to perform 220 basic physicals and 190 extended physicals in July, 235 basic and 200 extended in August, and 105 basic and 110 extended in September. Prepare the sales budget for the service revenue expected from the physical exams performed for the second quarter (July through September), with a column for each month and for the quarter in total.

S9-5 Production budget *(Learning Objective 2)*

Nichols Cycles manufactures chainless bicycles. On March 31, Nichols Cycles had 100 bikes in inventory. The company has a policy that the ending inventory in any month must be 10% of the following month's expected sales. Nichols Cycles expects to sell the following number of bikes in each of the next four months:

April..	1,000 bikes
May..	1,170 bikes
June...	1,360 bikes
July..	1,250 bikes

Prepare a production budget for the second quarter, with a column for each month and for the quarter.

S9-6 Direct materials budget *(Learning Objective 2)*

Breadmaster produces organic bread that is sold by the loaf. Each loaf requires 1/2 of a pound of flour. The bakery pays $2.00 per pound of the organic flour used in its loaves. The bakery expects to produce the following number of loaves in each of the upcoming four months:

July..	1,540 loaves
August...	1,820 loaves
September...	1,660 loaves
October...	1,460 loaves

The bakery has a policy that it will have 20% of the following month's flour needs on hand at the end of each month. At the end of June, there were 154 pounds of flour on hand. Prepare the direct materials budget for the third quarter, with a column for each month and for the quarter.

S9-7 Direct labor budget *(Learning Objective 2)*

The Production Department of Whistler Manufacturing has prepared the following schedule of units to be produced over the first quarter of the upcoming year:

	January	February	March
Units to be produced...	560	630	860

Each unit requires 6.0 hours of direct labor. Direct labor workers are paid an average of $19 per hour. How much direct labor will be budgeted in January, February, March, and for the quarter in total?

S9-8 Manufacturing overhead budget *(Learning Objective 2)*

Monocle Corporation is preparing its manufacturing overhead budget. The direct labor budget for the upcoming quarter is as follows:

	April	May	June
Budgeted direct labor hours...................................	490	730	600

The company's variable manufacturing overhead rate is $1.70 per direct labor hour, and the company's fixed manufacturing overhead is $3,800 per month. How much manufacturing overhead will be budgeted for April? For May? For June? For the quarter in total?

S9-9 Operating expenses budget *(Learning Objective 2)*

Wellfleet Corporation is preparing its operating expenses budget. The budgeted unit sales for the upcoming quarter are as follows:

	July	August	September
Budgeted unit sales	1,220	1,480	1,740

The company's variable operating expenses are $3.00 per unit. Fixed monthly operating expenses include $5,700 for salaries, $3,800 for office rent, and $2,900 for depreciation. How much operating expenses will be budgeted for July? For August? For September? For the quarter in total?

S9-10 Budgeted income statement *(Learning Objective 2)*

Oregon Weights Company manufactures a specialty precision scale. For January, the company expects to sell 1,500 scales at an average price of $2,320 per unit. The average manufacturing cost of each unit sold is $1,420. Variable operating expenses for the company will be $1.40 per unit sold and fixed operating expenses are expected to be $7,600 for the month. Monthly interest expense is $3,300. The company has a tax rate of 40% of income before taxes. Prepare Oregon Weights Company's budgeted income statement for January.

S9-11 Cash collections budget *(Learning Objective 3)*

Kessler Service anticipates the following sales revenue over a five-month period:

	November	December	January	February	March
Sales revenue	$16,500	$11,200	$15,200	$13,200	$14,400

The company's sales are 30% cash and 70% credit. Its collection history indicates that credit sales are collected as follows:

25% in the month of the sale
50% in the month after the sale
20% two months after the sale
5% are never collected

How much cash will be collected in January? In February? In March? For the quarter in total?

S9-12 Cash payments budget *(Learning Objective 3)*

Finley Corporation is preparing its cash payments budget for next month. The following information pertains to the cash payments:

a. Finley Corporation pays for 50% of its direct materials purchases in the month of purchase and the remainder the following month. Last month's direct material purchases were $78,000, while the company anticipates $88,000 of direct material purchases next month.

b. Direct labor for the upcoming month is budgeted to be $35,000 and will be paid at the end of the upcoming month.

c. Manufacturing overhead is estimated to be 150% of direct labor cost each month and is paid in the month in which it is incurred. This monthly estimate includes $10,000 of depreciation on the plant and equipment.

d. Monthly operating expenses for next month are expected to be $49,000, which includes $2,700 of depreciation on office equipment and $1,700 of bad debt expense. These monthly operating expenses are paid during the month in which they are incurred.

e. Finley Corporation will be making an estimated tax payment of $8,600 next month.

How much cash will be paid out next month?

S9-13 Cash budget *(Learning Objective 3)*

SaveCo Services, Inc., has $8,600 cash on hand on May 1. The company requires a minimum cash balance of $7,500. May cash collections are $548,480. Total cash payments for May are $563,420. Prepare a cash budget for May. How much cash, if any, will SaveCo need to borrow by the end of May?

S9-14 Estimate credit card fees *(Learning Objective 4)*

The local grocery store expects that customers will use credit cards to pay for a total of 90,000 sales transactions during the month of April. These transactions are expected to amount to $1,000,000 in total sales revenue. The credit card issuers charge the store a transaction fee equal to $0.45 per transaction plus 1.5% of the amount charged. When budgeting for operating expenses in April, how much should the store expect to incur for credit card transaction fees?

S9-15 Cost of goods sold, inventory, and purchases budget *(Learning Objective 4)*

Quinn Company sells mobile phones worldwide. The company expects to sell 4,600 mobile phones for $160 each in January and 4,000 mobile phones for $190 each in February. All sales are cash only. Quinn expects cost of goods sold to average 50% of sales revenue. The company also expects to sell 4,200 mobile phones in March for $240 each. Quinn's target ending inventory is $15,000 plus 60% of the next month's cost of goods sold.

1. Prepare the sales budget for January and February.
2. Prepare the company's cost of goods sold, inventory, and purchases budget for January and February.

S9-16 Identify ethical standards violated *(Learning Objectives 1, 2, 3, & 4)*

ETHICS

For each of the situations listed, identify the primary standard from the IMA *Statement of Ethical Professional Practice* that is violated (competence, confidentiality, objectivity, or credibility). Refer to Exhibit 1-7 for the complete standard.

1. Ryan, an accountant for Black Hat Company, builds some slack into the budget for the Human Resources (HR) Department so that the targets are easier to achieve. Ryan is dating the manager of the HR Department.
2. Daniel knows that the laws concerning credit and debit card fees have changed in the past year but does not know what the changes are specifically. He does not investigate before preparing the cash budget.
3. When out with friends, Maureen complains loudly about the budgeting process at her company. She feels the budgeting process is overly precise. She illustrates her point with specific numbers from the budget.
4. Mackenzie is the controller for Shady Hollow Parks. When she prepares the budgets for the upcoming year for upper management, she realizes that her department has higher costs than any other department. She aggregates the numbers with some other departments so that it is not obvious that her department is overspending.
5. Carly is caught on video as she brags about illegally downloading software that she feels is overpriced. The video is uploaded to YouTube.

EXERCISES Group A

E9-17A Budgeting and sustainability *(Learning Objectives 1 & 2)*

SUSTAINABILITY

Riley Beverages manufactures its own soda pop bottles. The bottles are made from polyethylene terephthalate (PET), a lightweight yet strong plastic. Riley uses as much PET recycled resin pellets in its bottles as it can, both because using recycled PET helps Riley to meet its sustainability goals and because recycled PET is less expensive than virgin PET.

Riley is continuing to search for ways to reduce its costs and its impact on the environment. PET plastic is melted and blown over soda bottle molds to produce the bottles. One idea Riley's engineers have suggested is to retrofit the soda bottle molds and change the plastic formulation slightly so that 25% less PET plastic is used for each bottle. The average kilograms of PET per soda bottle before any redesign is 0.004 kg. The cost of retrofitting the soda bottle molds will result in a one-time charge of $22,112, while the plastic reformulation will cause the average cost per kilogram of PET plastic to change from $3.00 to $3.30.

Riley's management is analyzing whether the change to the bottle molds to reduce PET plastic usage should be made. Management expects the following number of soda bottles to be used in the upcoming year:

	Quarter 1	Quarter 2	Quarter 3	Quarter 4
Number of soda pop bottles to be produced	2,000,000	2,600,000	2,300,000	3,100,000

For the upcoming year, management expects the beginning inventory of PET to be 800 kilograms, while ending inventory is expected to be 1,760 kilograms. During the first three quarters of the year, management wants to keep the ending inventory of PET at the end of each quarter equal to 10% of the following quarter's PET needs.

Requirements

1. Using the original data (before any redesign of soda bottles), prepare a direct materials budget to calculate the cost of PET purchases in each quarter for the upcoming year and for the year in total.
2. Assume that the company retrofits the soda bottle molds and changes the plastic formulation slightly so that less PET plastic is used in each bottle. Now prepare a direct materials budget to calculate the cost of PET purchases in each quarter for the upcoming year and for the year in total for this possible scenario.
3. Compare the cost of PET plastic for Requirement 1 (original data) and for Requirement 2 (making change to using less PET). What is the direct material cost savings from making the change to using less PET? Compare the total of those savings to the cost of retrofitting the soda bottle molds. Should the company make the change? Explain your rationale.

E9-18A Sales budget for a retail organization *(Learning Objective 2)*

Johnston Bookstore is the bookstore on campus for students and faculty. The bookstore shows the following sales projections in units by quarter for the upcoming year:

Quarter	Books	School Supplies	Apparel	Miscellaneous
1st	1,570	200	580	690
2nd	800	190	330	540
3rd	1,790	240	880	890
4th	670	180	540	440

The average price of an item in each of the departments is as follows:

	Average sales price per unit
Books	$85
School supplies	$18
Apparel	$29
Miscellaneous	$ 6

Requirement

Prepare a sales budget for the upcoming year by quarter for the Johnston Bookstore, with sales categorized by the four product groupings (books, school supplies, apparel, and miscellaneous).

E9-19A Service revenue budget for a not-for-profit organization *(Learning Objective 2)*

Spring Garden Preschool operates a not-for-profit morning preschool. Each family pays a nonrefundable registration fee of $120 per child per school year. Monthly tuition for the eight-month school year varies depending on the number of days per week that the child attends preschool. The monthly tuition is $125 for the two-day program, $150 for the three-day program, $165 for the four-day program, and $180 for the five-day program. The following enrollment has been projected for the coming year:

Two-day program	78 children
Three-day program	44 children
Four-day program	56 children
Five-day program	20 children

In addition to the morning preschool, Spring Garden Preschool offers a Lunch Bunch program where kids have the option of staying an extra hour for lunch and playtime. The preschool charges an additional $2 per child for every Lunch Bunch attended. Historically, half of the children stay for Lunch Bunch an average of 15 times a month.

Requirement
Calculate Spring Garden Preschool's budgeted revenue for the school year.

E9-20A Production budget *(Learning Objective 2)*
Hoffman Foods produces specialty soup sold in jars. The projected sales in dollars and jars for each quarter of the upcoming year are as follows:

	Total sales revenue	Number of jars sold
1st quarter	$181,000	152,500
2nd quarter	$219,000	181,500
3rd quarter	$255,000	213,000
4th quarter	$199,000	160,500

Hoffman anticipates selling 223,000 jars with total sales revenue of $260,000 in the first quarter of the year *following* the year given in the preceding table. Hoffman has a policy that the ending inventory of jars must be 30% of the following quarter's sales. Prepare a production budget for the year that shows the number of jars to be produced each quarter and for the year in total.

E9-21A Direct materials budget *(Learning Objective 2)*
Sacco Industries manufactures a popular interactive stuffed animal for children that requires three computer chips inside each toy. The company pays $2 for each computer chip. To help to guard against stockouts of the computer chip, Sacco Industries has a policy stating that the ending inventory of computer chips should be at least 25% of the following month's production needs. The production schedule for the first four months of the year is as follows:

	Stuffed animals to be produced
January	5,600
February	4,800
March	4,200
April	4,000

Requirement
Prepare a direct materials budget for the first quarter that shows both the number of computer chips needed and the dollar amount of the purchases in the budget.

E9-22A Production and direct materials budgets *(Learning Objective 2)*
Osborne Manufacturing produces self-watering planters for use in upscale retail establishments. Sales projections for the first five months of the upcoming year show the estimated unit sales of the planters each month to be as follows:

	Number of planters to be sold
January	3,400
February	3,800
March	3,300
April	4,900
May	4,600

Inventory at the start of the year was 850 planters. The desired inventory of planters at the end of each month in the upcoming year should be equal to 25% of the following month's budgeted sales. Each planter requires three pounds of polypropylene (a type of plastic). The company wants to have 20% of the polypropylene required for next month's production on hand at the end of each month. The polypropylene costs $0.20 per pound.

Requirements

1. Prepare a production budget for each month in the first quarter of the year, including production in units for each month and for the quarter.
2. Prepare a direct materials budget for the polypropylene for each month in the first quarter of the year, including the pounds of polypropylene required and the total cost of the polypropylene to be purchased.

E9-23A Direct labor budget *(Learning Objective 2)*

Dominion Industries manufactures three models of a product in a single plant with two departments: Cutting and Assembly. The company has estimated costs for each of the three product models: the Economy, the Standard, and the Premium models. The company is currently analyzing direct labor hour requirements for the upcoming year.

	Cutting	Assembly
Estimated hours per unit:		
Economy	1.2	2.8
Standard	1.3	2.2
Premium	1.4	2.1
Direct labor hour rate	$10	$12

Budgeted unit production for each of the products is as follows:

	Number of units to be produced
Product model:	
Economy	510
Standard	700
Premium	860

Requirement

Prepare a direct labor budget for the upcoming year that shows the budgeted direct labor costs for each department and for the company as a whole.

E9-24A Manufacturing overhead budget *(Learning Objective 2)*

The Stenback Company is in the process of preparing its manufacturing overhead budget for the upcoming year. Sales are projected to be 48,000 units. Information about the various manufacturing overhead costs follows:

	Variable rate per unit	Total fixed costs
Indirect materials	$0.90	
Supplies	$0.70	
Indirect labor	$0.40	$64,000
Plant utilities	$0.10	$34,000
Repairs and maintenance	$0.50	$10,000
Depreciation on plant and equipment		$45,000
Insurance on plant and equipment		$20,000
Plant supervision		$68,000

Requirement

Prepare the manufacturing overhead budget for the Stenback Company for the upcoming year.

E9-25A Operating expenses budget and an income statement (Learning Objective 2)

Evansville Preschool operates a not-for-profit morning preschool that operates eight months of the year. The preschool has 190 kids enrolled in its various programs. The preschool's primary expense is payroll. Teachers are paid a flat salary each of the eight months as follows:

Teachers of two-day program..	$ 428 per month
Teachers of three-day program..	$ 657 per month
Teachers of four-day program..	$ 856 per month
Teachers of five-day program..	$1,075 per month
Preschool director's salary...	$1,500 per month

Evansville Preschool has 9 two-day program teachers, 4 three-day program teachers, 5 four-day program teachers, and 4 five-day program teachers. The preschool also has a director.

In addition to the salary expense, the preschool must pay federal payroll taxes (FICA taxes) in the amount of 7.65% of salary expense. The preschool leases its facilities from a local church, paying $4,050 every month it operates. Fixed operating expenses (telephone, Internet access, bookkeeping services, and so forth) amount to $890 per month over the nine-month school year. Variable monthly expenses (over the eight-month school year) for art supplies and other miscellaneous supplies are $13 per child. Revenue for the entire nine-month school year from tuition, registration fees, and the lunch program is projected to be $241,300.

Requirements

1. Prepare Evansville Preschool's monthly operating expenses budget. Round all amounts to the nearest dollar.
2. Using your answer from Requirement 1, create Start Evansville Preschool's budgeted income statement for the entire eight-month school year. You may group all operating expenses together.
3. Start Evansville is a not-for-profit preschool. What might the preschool do with its projected income for the year?

E9-26A Budgeted income statement (Learning Objective 2)

Delta Labs performs a specialty lab test for local companies for $45 per test. For the upcoming quarter, Delta Labs is projecting the following sales:

	January	February	March
Number of lab tests	5,600	4,900	5,700

The budgeted cost of performing each test is $21. Operating expenses are projected to be $59,000 in January, $57,000 in February, and $58,000 in March. Delta Labs is subject to a corporate tax rate of 30%.

Requirement

Prepare a budgeted income statement for the first quarter, with a column for each month and for the quarter.

E9-27A Budgeted income statement (Learning Objective 2)

Suffield Motors is a chain of car dealerships. Sales in the fourth quarter of last year were $4,400,000. Suppose management projects that its current year's quarterly sales will increase by 7% in quarter 1, by another 2% in quarter 2, by another 4% in quarter 3, and by another 3% in quarter 4. Management expects cost of goods sold to be 40% of revenues every quarter, while operating expenses should be 35% of revenues during each of the first two quarters, 25% of revenues during the third quarter, and 20% during the fourth quarter.

Requirement

Prepare a budgeted income statement for each of the four quarters and for the entire year.

E9-28A Cash collections budget *(Learning Objective 3)*

Holiday Corporation has found that 60% of its sales in any given month are credit sales, while the remainder are cash sales. Of the credit sales, Holiday Corporation has experienced the following collection pattern:

25% received in the month of the sale
50% received in the month after the sale
16% received two months after the sale
9% of the credit sales are never received

November sales for last year were $90,000, while December sales were $115,000. Projected sales for the next three months are as follows:

January sales	$145,000
February sales	$125,000
March sales	$180,000

Requirement
Prepare a cash collections budget for the first quarter, with a column for each month and for the quarter.

E9-29A Cash payments budget *(Learning Objective 3)*

The Robbins Company is preparing its cash payments budget. The following items relate to cash payments the company anticipates making during the second quarter of the upcoming year.

a. The company pays for 45% of its direct materials purchases in the month of purchase and the remainder the following month. The company's direct material purchases for March through June are anticipated to be as follows:

March	April	May	June
$118,000	$132,000	$122,000	$147,000

b. Direct labor is paid in the month in which it is incurred. Direct labor for each month of the second quarter is budgeted as follows:

April	May	June
$60,000	$70,000	$85,000

c. Manufacturing overhead is estimated to be 140% of direct labor cost each month. This monthly estimate includes $36,000 of depreciation on the plant and equipment. All manufacturing overhead (excluding depreciation) is paid in the month in which it is incurred.

d. Monthly operating expenses for March through June are projected to be as follows:

March	April	May	June
$74,000	$87,000	$84,000	$92,000

Monthly operating expenses are paid in the month after they are incurred. Monthly operating expenses include $8,000 for monthly depreciation on administrative offices and equipment, and $2,800 for bad debt expense.

e. The company plans to pay $7,000 (cash) for a new server in May.

f. The company must make an estimated tax payment of $14,000 on June 15.

Requirement
Prepare a cash payments budget for April, May, and June and for the quarter.

E9-30A Combined cash budget *(Learning Objective 3)*

Bentfield Health Center provides a variety of medical services. The company is preparing its cash budget for the upcoming third quarter. The following transactions are expected to occur:

a. Cash collections from services in July, August, and September are projected to be $91,000, $151,000, and $124,000, respectively.
b. Cash payments for the upcoming third quarter are projected to be $142,000 in July, $103,000 in August, and $133,000 in September.
c. The cash balance as of the first day of the third quarter is projected to be $31,000.
d. The health center has a policy that it must maintain a minimum cash balance of $25,000. The health center has a line of credit with the local bank that allows it to borrow funds in months that it would not otherwise have its minimum balance. If the company has more than its minimum balance at the end of any given month, it uses the excess funds to pay off any outstanding line of credit balance. Each month, Bentfield Health Center pays interest on the prior month's line of credit ending balance. The actual interest rate that the health center will pay floats since it is tied to the prime rate. However, the interest rate paid during the budget period is expected to be 2% of the prior month's line of credit ending balance (if the company did not have an outstanding balance at the end of the prior month, then the health center does not have to pay any interest). All line of credit borrowings are taken or paid off on the first day of the month. As of the first day of the third quarter, Bentfield Health Center did not have a balance on its line of credit.

Requirement
Prepare a combined cash budget for Bentfield Health Center for the third quarter, with a column for each month and for the quarter total.

E9-31A Sales and cash collections budgets *(Learning Objectives 2 & 3)*

Augustine Reeds, a manufacturer of saxophone, oboe, and clarinet reeds, has projected sales to be $904,000 in October, $964,000 in November, $1,045,000 in December, and $936,000 in January. Augustine's sales are 20% cash and 80% credit. The company's collection history indicates that credit sales are collected as follows:

30% in the month of the sale
60% in the month after the sale
8% two months after the sale
2% are never collected

Requirements
1. Prepare a sales budget for all four months, showing the breakdown between cash and credit sales.
2. Prepare a cash collections budget for December and January. Round all answers up to the nearest dollar.

E9-32A Budgeted balance sheet *(Learning Objective 3)*

Use the following information to prepare a budgeted balance sheet for Luda Corporation at March 31. Show computations for the cash and stockholders' equity amounts.

a. March 31 inventory balance, $18,265
b. March payments for inventory, $4,600
c. March payments of accounts payable and accrued liabilities, $8,700
d. March 31 accounts payable balance, $1,700
e. February 28 furniture and fixtures balance, $34,600; accumulated depreciation balance, $29,860
f. February 28 stockholders' equity, $30,000
g. March depreciation expense, $400
h. Cost of goods sold, 40% of sales
i. Other March expenses, including income tax, total $9,000; paid in cash

j. February 28 cash balance, $11,600
k. March budgeted sales, $12,300
l. March 31 accounts receivable balance, one-fourth of March sales
m. March cash receipts, $14,700

E9-33A Incomplete cash budget *(Learning Objective 3)*

You recently began a job as an accounting intern at Rockwall Adventures. Your first task was to help prepare the cash budget for February and March. Unfortunately, the computer with the budget file crashed, and you did not have a backup or even a hard copy. You ran a program to salvage bits of data from the budget file. After entering the following data in the budget, you may have just enough information to reconstruct the budget.

Rockwall Adventures eliminates any cash deficiency by borrowing the exact amount needed from State Street Bank, where the current interest rate is 6%. Rockwall Adventures pays interest on its outstanding debt at the end of each month. The company also repays all borrowed amounts at the end of the month as cash becomes available.

Requirement
Complete the following cash budget:

	A	B	C
1	Rockwall Adventures		
2	Combined Cash Budget		
3	February and March		
4		February	March
5	Beginning cash balance	$ 16,900	$?
6	Plus: Cash collections	?	80,000
7	Plus: Cash from sale of plant assets	0	2,000
8	Total cash available	$ 107,300	$?
9	Less: Cash payments (purchase inventory)	$?	$ 41,400
10	Less: Cash payments (operating expenses)	47,700	?
11	Total cash payments	$ 98,400	$?
12	(1) Ending cash balance before financing	$?	$ 25,100
13	Minimum cash balance desired	21,000	21,000
14	Cash excess (deficiency)	$?	$?
15	Financing:		
16	Plus: New borrowings	$?	$?
17	Less: Debt repayments	?	?
18	Less: Interest payments	?	?
19	(2) Total effects of financing	$?	$?
20	Ending cash balance (1) + (2)	$?	$?
21			

E9-34A Credit and debit card fees calculation and analysis *(Learning Objective 4)*

The Red Lantern, a local Thai restaurant, expects sales to be $500,000 in January. Its average customer restaurant bill is $40. Only 20% of the restaurant bills are paid with cash; 70% are paid with credit cards and 10% with debit cards. The transaction fees charged by the credit and debit card issuers are as follows:

Credit cards: $0.50 per transaction + 2% of the amount charged

Debit cards: $0.22 per transaction + 1% of the amount charged

Requirements

1. How much of the total sales revenue is expected to be paid in cash?
2. How many customer transactions does the company expect in January?
3. How much of the total sales revenue is expected to be paid with credit cards?
4. How many customer transactions will be paid for by customers using credit cards?
5. When budgeting for January's operating expenses, how much should the restaurant expect to incur in credit card transaction fees?
6. How much of the total sales revenue is expected to be paid with debit cards?
7. How many customer transactions will be paid for by customers using debit cards?
8. When budgeting for January's operating expenses, how much should the restaurant expect to incur in debit card transaction fees?

9. How much money will be deposited in the restaurant's bank account during the month of January related to credit and debit card sales? Assume the credit and debit card issuers deposit the funds on the same day the transactions occur at the restaurant (there is no processing delay).
10. What is the total amount of money that the restaurant expects to deposit in its bank account during the month of January from cash, credit card, and debit card sales? Again assume the credit and debit card issuers deposit the funds on the same day that the transaction occurs.

E9-35A **Cost of goods sold, inventory, and purchases budget** *(Learning Objectives 3 & 4)*

Kent Corner Shoppe is a local convenience store with the following information:
- October sales were $250,000.
- Sales are projected to go up by 12% in November and another 30% in December and then return to the October level in January.
- 20% of sales are made in cash, while the remaining 80% are paid by credit or debit cards. The credit card companies and banks (debit card issuers) charge a 2% transaction fee and deposit the net amount (sales price less the transaction fee) in the store's bank account daily.
- Kent Corner Shoppe's gross profit is 25% of its sales revenue.
- For the next several months, the store wants to maintain an ending merchandise inventory equal to $15,000 + 15% of the next month's cost of goods sold. The September 30 inventory was $43,125.
- Expected monthly operating expenses include:
  o Wages of store workers are $9,200 per month
  o Utilities expense of $1,000 in November and $1,500 in December
  o Property tax expense of $2,000 per month
  o Property and liability insurance expense of $500 per month
  o Depreciation expense of $6,500 per month
  o Transactions fees, as stated above, are 2% of credit and debit card sales

Prepare the following budgets for November and December:
1. Sales budget
2. Cost of goods sold, inventory and purchases budget
3. Operating expense budget
4. Budgeted income statement

E9-36A **Cost of goods sold, inventory, and purchases budget** *(Learning Objective 4)*

Ace Electronics sells tablets. Its sales budget for the nine months ended September 30 follows:

Ace Electronics
Sales Budget
For the Nine Months Ended September 30

	Quarter Ended			
	Mar 31	Jun 30	Sep 30	Nine-Month Total
Cash sales, 40%.............	$ 50,000	$ 70,000	$ 60,000	$180,000
Credit sales, 60%............	75,000	105,000	90,000	270,000
Total sales, 100%.............	$125,000	$175,000	$150,000	$450,000

In the past, cost of goods sold has been 70% of total sales. The director of marketing and the financial vice president agree that each quarter's ending inventory should not be below $20,000 plus 15% of cost of goods sold for the following quarter. The marketing director expects sales of $225,000 during the fourth quarter. The January 1 inventory was $33,125.

Requirement

Prepare a cost of goods sold, inventory, and purchases budget for each of the first three quarters of the year. Compute cost of goods sold for the entire nine-month period.

EXERCISES Group B

E9-37B Budgeting and sustainability *(Learning Objectives 1 and 2)*

SUSTAINABILITY

Jerico Beverages manufactures its own soda pop bottles. The bottles are made from polyethylene terephthalate (PET), a lightweight yet strong plastic. The company uses as much PET recycled resin pellets in its bottles as it can, both because using recycled PET helps Jerico to meet its sustainability goals and because recycled PET is less expensive than virgin PET.

Jerico is continuing to search for ways to reduce its costs and its impact on the environment. PET plastic is melted and blown over soda bottle molds to produce the bottles. One idea Jerico's engineers have suggested is to retrofit the soda bottle molds and change the plastic formulation slightly so that 25% less PET plastic is used for each bottle. The average kilograms of PET per soda bottle before any redesign is 0.008 kg. The cost of retrofitting the soda bottle molds will result in a one-time charge of $21,470, while the plastic reformulation will cause the average cost per kilogram of PET plastic to change from $2.00 to $2.30.

Jerico's management is analyzing whether the change to the bottle molds to reduce PET plastic usage should be made. Management expects the following number of soda bottles to be used in the upcoming year:

	Quarter 1	Quarter 2	Quarter 3	Quarter 4
Number of soda pop bottles to be produced..................	2,300,000	2,500,000	2,700,000	2,400,000

For the upcoming year, management expects the beginning inventory of PET to be 3,680 kilograms, while ending inventory is expected to be 4,380 kilograms. During the first three quarters of the year, management wants to keep the ending inventory of PET at the end of each quarter equal to 20% of the following quarter's PET needs.

Requirements

1. Using the original date (before any redesign of soda bottles), prepare a direct materials budget to calculate the cost of PET purchases in each quarter for the upcoming year and for the year in total.
2. Assume that the company retrofits the soda bottle molds and changes the plastic formulation slightly so that less PET plastic is used in each bottle. Now prepare a direct materials budget to calculate the cost of PET purchases in each quarter for the upcoming year and for the year in total for this possible scenario.
3. Compare the cost of PET plastic for Requirement 1 (original data) and for Requirement 2 (making the change to using less PET). What is the direct material cost saving from making the change to using less PET? Compare the total of those savings to the cost of retrofitting the soda bottle molds. Should the company make the change? Explain your rationale.

E9-38B Sales budget for a retail organization *(Learning Objective 2)*

Hartford Bookstore is the bookstore on campus for students and faculty. The bookstore shows the following sales projections in units by quarter for the upcoming year:

Quarter	Books	School Supplies	Apparel	Miscellaneous
1st................	1,570	250	560	690
2nd...............	860	110	370	590
3rd................	1,750	280	800	870
4th................	660	160	590	410

The average price of an item in each of the departments is as follows:

	Average sales price per unit
Books...	$89
School supplies	$18
Apparel...	$22
Miscellaneous..	$ 3

Requirement

Prepare a sales budget for the upcoming year by quarter for the Hartford Bookstore, with sales categorized by the four product groupings (books, school supplies, apparel, and miscellaneous).

E9-39B Service revenue budget for a not-for-profit organization (Learning Objective 2)

Danville Preschool operates a not-for-profit morning preschool. Each family pays a non-refundable registration fee of $105 per child per school year. Monthly tuition for the eight-month school year varies depending on the number of days per week that the child attends preschool. The monthly tuition is $140 for the two-day program, $160 for the three-day program, $185 for the four-day program, and $200 for the five-day program. The following enrollment has been projected for the coming year:

Two-day program	82 children
Three-day program	50 children
Four-day program	52 children
Five-day program	18 children

In addition to the morning preschool, Danville Preschool offers a Lunch Bunch program where kids have the option of staying an extra hour for lunch and playtime. The preschool charges an additional $2 per child for every Lunch Bunch attended. Historically, half of the children stay for Lunch Bunch an average of 10 times a month.

Requirement
Calculate Danville Preschool's budgeted revenue for the school year.

E9-40B Production budget (Learning Objective 2)

Gable Foods produces specialty soup sold in jars. The projected sales in dollars and jars for each quarter of the upcoming year are as follows:

	Total sales revenue	Number of jars sold
1st quarter	$186,000	152,500
2nd quarter	$216,000	182,500
3rd quarter	$255,000	214,000
4th quarter	$190,000	165,000

Gable anticipates selling 222,000 jars, with total sales revenue of $261,000 in the first quarter of the year following the year given in the preceding table. The company has a policy that the ending inventory of jars must be 25% of the following quarter's sales. Prepare a production budget for the year that shows the number of jars to be produced each quarter and for the year in total.

E9-41B Direct materials budget (Learning Objective 2)

Moe Industries manufactures a popular interactive stuffed animal for children that requires four computer chips inside each toy. The company pays $3 for each computer chip. To help to guard against stockouts of the computer chip, Moe Industries has a policy stating that the ending inventory of computer chips should be at least 30% of the following month's production needs. The production schedule for the first four months of the year is as follows:

	Stuffed animals to be produced
January	5,200
February	4,800
March	4,100
April	4,700

Requirement
Prepare a direct materials budget for the first quarter that shows both the number of computer chips needed and the dollar amount of the purchases in the budget.

E9-42B Production and direct materials budgets *(Learning Objective 2)*

Edsel Manufacturing produces self-watering planters for use in upscale retail establishments. Sales projections for the first five months of the upcoming year show the estimated unit sales of the planters each month to be as follows:

	Number of planters to be sold
January	3,500
February	3,400
March	3,600
April	4,000
May	4,200

Inventory at the start of the year was 350 planters. The desired inventory of planters at the end of each month in the upcoming year should be equal to 10% of the following month's budgeted sales. Each planter requires two pounds of polypropylene (a type of plastic). The company wants to have 20% of the polypropylene required for next month's production on hand at the end of each month. The polypropylene costs $0.25 per pound.

Requirements

1. Prepare a production budget for each month in the first quarter of the year, including production in units for each month and for the quarter.
2. Prepare a direct materials budget for the polypropylene for each month in the first quarter of the year, including the pounds of polypropylene required and the total cost of the polypropylene to be purchased.

E9-43B Direct labor budget *(Learning Objective 2)*

George Industries manufactures three models of a product in a single plant with two departments: Cutting and Assembly. The company has estimated costs for each of the three product models: the Standard, the Deluxe, and the Premium models.

The company is currently analyzing direct labor hour requirements for the upcoming year.

	Cutting	Assembly
Estimated hours per unit:		
Standard	1.5	2.5
Deluxe	1.8	2.9
Premium	1.9	2.0
Direct labor hour rate	$8	$10

Budgeted unit production for each of the products is as follows:

	Number of units to be produced
Product model:	
Standard	520
Deluxe	730
Premium	890

Requirement

Prepare a direct labor budget for the upcoming year that shows the budgeted direct labor costs for each department and for the company as a whole.

E9-44B Manufacturing overhead budget *(Learning Objective 2)*

The Grant Company is in the process of preparing its manufacturing overhead budget for the upcoming year. Sales are projected to be 49,000 units. Information about the various manufacturing overhead costs follows:

	Variable rate per unit	Total fixed costs
Indirect materials	$1.30	
Supplies	$1.00	
Indirect labor	$0.80	$66,000
Plant utilities	$0.30	$34,000
Repairs and maintenance	$0.30	$13,000
Depreciation on plant and equipment		$41,000
Insurance on plant and equipment		$29,000
Plant supervision		$65,000

Requirement
Prepare the manufacturing overhead budget for the Grant Company for the upcoming year.

E9-45B Operating expenses budget and an income statement *(Learning Objective 2)*

Maple Ridge Preschool operates a not-for-profit morning preschool that operates eight months of the year. The preschool has 165 kids enrolled in its various programs. The preschool's primary expense is payroll. Teachers are paid a flat salary each of the nine months as follows:

Salary data	
Teachers of two-day program	$ 440 per month
Teachers of three-day program	$ 663 per month
Teachers of four-day program	$ 860 per month
Teachers of five-day program	$1,060 per month
Preschool director's salary	$1,450 per month

Maple Ridge Preschool has 8 two-day program teachers, 4 three-day program teachers, 5 four-day program teachers, and 3 five-day program teachers. The preschool also has a director.

In addition to the salary expense, Maple Ridge Preschool must pay federal payroll taxes (FICA taxes) in the amount of 7.65% of salary expense. The preschool leases its facilities from a local church, paying $4,060 per month. Fixed operating expenses (telephone, Internet access, bookkeeping services, and so forth) amount to $920 per month over the eight-month school year. Variable monthly expenses (over the eight-month school year) for art supplies and other miscellaneous supplies are $10 per child. Revenue for the entire nine-month school year from tuition, registration fees, and the lunch program is projected to be $230,600.

Requirements
1. Prepare Maple Ridge Preschool's monthly operating expenses budget. Round all amounts to the nearest dollar.
2. Using your answer from Requirement 1, create Maple Ridge Preschool's budgeted income statement for the entire nine-month school year. You may group all operating expenses together.
3. Maple Ridge Preschool is a not-for-profit preschool. What might the preschool do with its projected income for the year?

E9-46B Budgeted income statement *(Learning Objective 2)*

Barrett Labs performs a specialty lab test for local companies for $52 per test. For the upcoming quarter, Barrett Labs is projecting the following sales:

	January	February	March
Number of tests	5,400	4,500	5,500

The budgeted cost of performing each test is $25. Operating expenses are projected to be $61,000 in January, $54,000 in February, and $64,000 in March. Barrett Labs is subject to a corporate tax rate of 30%.

Requirement

Prepare a budgeted income statement for the first quarter, with a column for each month and for the quarter in total.

E9-47B Budgeted income statement *(Learning Objective 2)*

City Motors is a chain of car dealerships. Sales in the fourth quarter of last year were $4,000,000. Suppose its management projects that its current year's quarterly sales will increase by 3% in quarter 1, by another 7% in quarter 2, by another 6% in quarter 3, and by another 5% in quarter 4. Management expects cost of goods sold to be 55% of revenues every quarter, while operating expenses should be 20% of revenues during each of the first two quarters, 35% of revenues during the third quarter, and 25% during the fourth quarter.

Requirement

Prepare a budgeted income statement for each of the four quarters and for the entire year.

E9-48B Cash collections budget *(Learning Objective 3)*

Raber Corporation has found that 60% of its sales in any given month are credit sales, while the remainder are cash sales. Of the credit sales, the company has experienced the following collection pattern:

25% received in the month of the sale
50% received in the month after the sale
18% received two months after the sale
7% of the credit sales are never received

November sales for last year were $85,000, while December sales were $120,000. Projected sales for the next three months are as follows:

January sales	$170,000
February sales	$125,000
March sales	$185,000

Requirement

Prepare a cash collections budget for the first quarter, with a column for each month and for the quarter.

E9-49B Cash payments budget *(Learning Objective 3)*

DeWitt Corporation is preparing its cash payments budget. The following items relate to cash payments the company anticipates making during the second quarter of the upcoming year.

a. DeWitt Corporation pays for 55% of its direct materials purchases in the month of purchase and the remainder the following month. The company's direct material purchases for March through June are anticipated to be as follows:

March	April	May	June
$112,000	$137,000	$121,000	$146,000

b. Direct labor is paid in the month in which it is incurred. Direct labor for each month of the second quarter is budgeted as follows:

April	May	June
$58,000	$68,000	$83,000

c. Manufacturing overhead is estimated to be 160% of direct labor cost each month. This monthly estimate includes $34,000 of depreciation on the plant and equipment. All manufacturing overhead (excluding depreciation) is paid in the month in which it is incurred.
d. Monthly operating expenses for March through June are projected to be as follows:

March	April	May	June
$75,000	$86,000	$84,000	$97,000

Monthly operating expenses are paid in the month after they are incurred. Monthly operating expenses include $12,000 for monthly depreciation on administrative offices and equipment, and $3,400 for bad debt expense.

e. DeWitt Corporation plans to pay $6,000 (cash) for a new server in May.
f. DeWitt Corporation must make an estimated tax payment of $14,000 on June 15.

Requirement
Prepare a cash payments budget for April, May, and June and for the quarter.

E9-50B Combined cash budget *(Learning Objective 3)*

Corrigan Health Center provides a variety of medical services. The company is preparing its cash budget for the upcoming third quarter. The following transactions are expected to occur:

a. Cash collections from services in July, August, and September are projected to be $99,000, $156,000, and $120,000, respectively.
b. Cash payments for the upcoming third quarter are projected to be $145,000 in July, $101,000 in August, and $137,000 in September.
c. The cash balance as of the first day of the third quarter is projected to be $31,000.
d. Corrigan Health Center has a policy that it must maintain a minimum cash balance of $24,000. The company has a line of credit with the local bank that allows it to borrow funds in months that it would not otherwise have the minimum balance. If the company has more than the minimum balance at the end of any given month, it uses the excess funds to pay off any outstanding line of credit balance. Each month, Corrigan Health Center pays interest on the prior month's line of credit ending balance. The actual interest rate that the health center will pay floats since it is tied to the prime rate. However, the interest rate paid during the budget period is expected to be 2% of the prior month's line of credit ending balance (if it did not have an outstanding balance at the end of the prior month, then the company does not have to pay any interest). All line of credit borrowings are taken or paid off on the first day of the month. As of the first day of the third quarter, Corrigan Health Center did not have a balance on its line of credit.

Requirement
Prepare a combined cash budget for Corrigan Health Center for the third quarter, with a column for each month and for the quarter total.

E9-51B Sales and cash collections budgets *(Learning Objectives 2 & 3)*

Alexander Reeds, a manufacturer of saxophone, oboe, and clarinet reeds, has projected sales to be $904,000 in October, $960,000 in November, $1,060,000 in December, and $930,000 in January. Alexander's sales are 30% cash and 70% on credit. The company's collection history indicates that credit sales are collected as follows:

20% in the month of the sale
65% in the month after the sale
10% two months after the sale
5% are never collected

Requirements
1. Prepare a sales budget for all four months, showing the breakdown between cash and credit sales.
2. Prepare a cash collection budget for December and January. Round all answers up to the nearest dollar.

E9-52B Budgeted balance sheet *(Learning Objective 3)*

Use the following information to prepare a budgeted balance sheet for Boswell Corporation at March 31. Show computations for the cash and owners' equity amounts.

a. March 31 inventory balance, $16,375
b. March payments for inventory, $4,500
c. March payments of accounts payable and accrued liabilities, $8,200
d. March 31 accounts payable balance, $1,900
e. February 28 furniture and fixtures balance, $34,300; accumulated depreciation balance, $29,850
f. February 28 owners' equity, $31,000
g. March depreciation expense, $800
h. Cost of goods sold, 70% of sales
i. Other March expenses, including income tax, total $9,000; paid in cash
j. February 28 cash balance, $11,200
k. March budgeted sales, $12,500
l. March 31 accounts receivable balance, one-fourth of March sales
m. March cash receipts, $14,200

E9-53B Incomplete cash budget *(Learning Objective 3)*

You recently began a job as an accounting intern at Whitewater Adventures. Your first task was to help prepare the cash budget for February and March. Unfortunately, the computer with the budget file crashed, and you did not have a backup or even a hard copy. You ran a program to salvage bits of data from the budget file. After entering the following data in the budget, you may have just enough information to reconstruct the budget.

Whitewater Adventures eliminates any cash deficiency by borrowing the exact amount needed from State Street Bank, where the current interest rate is 7%. Whitewater Adventures pays interest on its outstanding debt at the end of each month. The company also repays all borrowed amounts at the end of the month, as cash becomes available.

Requirement
Complete the following cash budget:

	A	B	C
1	Whitewater Adventures		
2	Combined Cash Budget		
3	February and March		
4		February	March
5	Beginning cash balance	$ 16,800	$?
6	Plus: Cash collections	?	80,200
7	Plus: Cash from sale of plant assets	0	2,400
8	Total cash available	$ 106,800	$?
9	Less: Cash payments (purchase inventory)	$?	$ 41,200
10	Less: Cash payments (operating expenses)	47,600	?
11	Total cash payments	$ 98,500	$?
12	(1) Ending cash balance before financing	$?	$ 23,300
13	Minimum cash balance desired	20,000	20,000
14	Cash excess (deficiency)	$?	$?
15	Financing:		
16	Plus: New borrowings	$?	$?
17	Less: Debt repayments	?	?
18	Less: Interest payments	?	?
19	(2) Total effects of financing	$?	$?
20	Ending cash balance (1) + (2)	$?	$?
21			

E9-54B Credit and debit card fees calculation and analysis *(Learning Objective 4)*

The Blue Lamp, a local Italian restaurant, expects sales to be $400,000 in January. Its average customer restaurant bill is $50. Only 15% of the restaurant bills are paid with cash; 75% are paid with credit cards, and 10% with debit cards. The transaction fees charged by the credit and debit card issuers are as follows:

Credit cards: $0.50 per transaction + 2% of the amount charged
Debit cards: $0.20 per transaction + 1% of the amount charged

Requirements

1. How much of the total sales revenue is expected to be paid in cash?
2. How many customer transactions does the company expect in January?
3. How much of the total sales revenue is expected to be paid with credit cards?
4. How many customer transactions will be paid for by customers using credit cards?
5. When budgeting for January's operating expenses, how much should the restaurant expect to incur in credit card transaction fees?
6. How much of the total sales revenue is expected to be paid with debit cards?
7. How many customer transactions will be paid for by customers using debit cards?
8. When budgeting for January's operating expenses, how much should the restaurant expect to incur in debit card transaction fees?
9. How much money will be deposited in the restaurant's bank account during the month of January related to credit and debit card sales? Assume the credit and debit card issuers deposit the funds on the same day the transactions occur at the restaurant (there is no processing delay).
10. What is the total amount of money that the restaurant expects to deposit in its bank account during the month of January from cash, credit card, and debit card sales? Again assume the credit and debit card issuers deposit the funds on the same day that the transaction occurs.

E9-55B Cost of goods sold, inventory, and purchases budget *(Learning Objectives 3 & 4)*

Case Corner Shoppe is a local convenience store with the following information:

- October sales were $200,000.
- Sales are projected to go up by 20% in November and another 10% in December and then return to the October level in January.
- 25% of sales are made in cash, while the remaining 75% are paid by credit or debit cards. The credit card companies and banks (debit card issuers) charge a 2% transaction fee and deposit the net amount (sales price less the transaction fee) in the store's bank account daily.
- Case Corner Shoppe's gross profit is 40% of its sales revenue.
- For the next several months, the store wants to maintain an ending merchandise inventory equal to $5,000 + 15% of the next month's cost of goods sold. The September 30 inventory was $23,000.
- Expected monthly operating expenses include:
    - Wages of store workers are $8,700 per month
    - Utilities expense of $1,600 in November and $2,200 in December
    - Property tax expense of $2,000 per month
    - Property and liability insurance expense of $1,000 per month
    - Depreciation expense of $6,500 per month
    - Transaction fees, as stated above, are 2% of credit and debit card sales

Requirements

Prepare the following budgets for November and December:
1. Sales budget
2. Cost of goods sold, inventory, and purchases budget
3. Operating expense budget
4. Budgeted income statement

E9-56B Cost of goods sold, inventory, and purchases budget *(Learning Objective 4)*

Scott Electronics sells tablets. Its sales budget for the nine months ended September 30 follows:

Scott Electronics
Sales Budget
For the Nine Months Ended September 30

	Quarter			Nine-Month Total
	Mar 31	Jun 30	Sep 30	
Cash sales, 40%	$ 50,000	$ 70,000	$ 60,000	$ 180,000
Credit sales, 60%	75,000	105,000	90,000	270,000
Total sales, revenue	$ 125,000	$ 175,000	$ 150,000	$ 450,000

In the past, cost of goods sold has been 70% of total sales. The director of marketing and the financial vice president agree that each quarter's ending inventory should not be below $10,000 plus 15% of cost of goods sold for the following quarter. The marketing director expects sales of $245,000 during the fourth quarter. The January 1 inventory was $23,125.

Requirement

Prepare a cost of goods sold, inventory, and purchases budget for each of the first three quarters of the year. Compute cost of goods sold for the entire nine-month period.

PROBLEMS Group A

P9-57A Comprehensive budgeting problem *(Learning Objectives 2 & 3)*

Martin Manufacturing is preparing its master budget for the first quarter of the upcoming year. The following data pertain to Martin Manufacturing's operations:

Current Assets as of December 31 (prior year):	
Cash	$ 4,500
Accounts receivable, net	$ 47,000
Inventory	$ 15,700
Property, plant, and equipment, net	$120,000
Accounts payable	$ 42,400
Capital stock	$124,000
Retained earnings	$ 23,100

a. Actual sales in December were $70,000. Selling price per unit is projected to remain stable at $10 per unit throughout the budget period. Sales for the first five months of the upcoming year are budgeted to be as follows:

January	$ 80,000
February	$ 92,000
March	$ 99,000
April	$ 97,000
May	$ 85,000

b. Sales are 30% cash and 70% credit. All credit sales are collected in the month following the sale.

c. Martin Manufacturing has a policy stating that each month's ending inventory of finished goods should be 25% of the following month's sales (in units).
d. Of each month's direct materials purchases, 20% are paid for in the month of purchase, while the remainder is paid for in the month following purchase. Two pounds of direct material is needed per unit at $2 per pound. Ending inventory of direct materials should be 10% of next month's production needs.
e. Most of the labor at the manufacturing facility is indirect, but there is some direct labor incurred. The direct labor hours per unit is 0.01. The direct labor rate per hour is $12 per hour. All direct labor is paid for in the month in which the work is performed. The direct labor total cost for each of the upcoming three months is as follows:

January	$ 996
February	$1,125
March	$1,182

f. Monthly manufacturing overhead costs are $5,000 for factory rent, $3,000 for other fixed manufacturing expenses, and $1.20 per unit for variable manufacturing overhead. No depreciation is included in these figures. All expenses are paid in the month in which they are incurred.
g. Computer equipment for the administrative offices will be purchased in the upcoming quarter. In January, Martin Manufacturing will purchase equipment for $5,000 (cash), while February's cash expenditures will be $12,000 and March's cash expenditures will be $16,000.
h. Operating expenses are budgeted to be $1.00 per unit sold plus fixed operating expenses of $1,000 per month. All operating expenses are paid in the month in which they are incurred. No depreciation is included in these figures.
i. Depreciation on the building and equipment for the general and administrative offices is budgeted to be $4,600 for the entire quarter, which includes depreciation on new acquisitions.
j. Martin Manufacturing has a policy that the ending cash balance in each month must be at least $4,000. It has a line of credit with a local bank. The company can borrow in increments of $1,000 at the beginning of each month, up to a total outstanding loan balance of $150,000. The interest rate on these loans is 1% per month simple interest (not compounded). The company would pay down on the line of credit balance in increments of $1,000 if it has excess funds at the end of the quarter. The company would also pay the accumulated interest at the end of the quarter on the funds borrowed during the quarter.
k. The company's income tax rate is projected to be 30% of operating income less interest expense. The company pays $10,000 cash at the end of February in estimated taxes.

Requirements

1. Prepare a schedule of cash collections for January, February, and March, and for the quarter in total. Use the following format:

	A	B	C	D	E
1		Cash Collections Budget			
2		For the Quarter Ended March 31			
3		Month			
4		January	February	March	Quarter
5	Cash sales				
6	Credit sales				
7	Total cash collections				
8					

2. Prepare a production budget, using the following format:

	A	B	C	D	E
1		Production Budget			
2		For the Quarter Ended March 31			
3		Month			
4		January	February	March	Quarter
5	Unit sales*				
6	Plus: Desired ending inventory				
7	Total needed				
8	Less: Beginning inventory				
9	Number of units to produce				
10					

*Hint: Unit sales = Sales in dollars/Selling price per unit

3. Prepare a direct materials budget, using the following format:

	A	B	C	D	E
1		Direct Materials Budget			
2		For the Quarter Ended March 31			
3		Month			
4		January	February	March	Quarter
5	Units to be produced (from Production Budget)				
6	Multiply by: Quantity (pounds) of DM needed per unit				
7	Quantity (pounds) needed for production				
8	Plus: Desired ending inventory of DM				
9	Total quantity (pounds) needed				
10	Less: Beginning inventory of DM				
11	Quantity (pounds) to purchase				
12	Multiply by: Cost per pound				
13	Total cost of DM purchases				
14					

4. Prepare a cash payments budget for the direct material purchases from Requirement 3, using the following format. (Use the accounts payable balance at December 31 of prior year for the prior month payment in January.)

	A	B	C	D	E
1		Cash Payments for Direct Materials Budget			
2		For the Quarter Ended March 31			
3		Month			
4		January	February	March	Quarter
5	20% of current month DM purchases				
6	80% of prior month DM purchases				
7	Total cash payments				
8					

5. Prepare a cash payments budget for direct labor, using the following format:

	A	B	C	D	E
1		Cash Payments for Direct Labor Budget			
2		For the Quarter Ended March 31			
3		Month			
4		January	February	March	Quarter
5	Total cost of direct labor				
6					

6. Prepare a cash payments budget for manufacturing overhead costs, using the following format:

	A	B	C	D	E
1		Cash Payments for Manufacturing Overhead Budget			
2		For the Quarter Ended March 31			
3		Month			
4		January	February	March	Quarter
5	Variable manufacturing overhead costs				
6	Rent (fixed)				
7	Other fixed MOH				
8	Cash payments for manufacturing overhead				
9					

7. Prepare a cash payments budget for operating expenses, using the following format:

	A	B	C	D	E
1		Cash Payments for Operating Expenses Budget			
2		For the Quarter Ended March 31			
3		Month			
4		January	February	March	Quarter
5	Variable operating expenses				
6	Fixed operating expenses				
7	Cash payments for operating expenses				
8					

8. Prepare a combined cash budget, using the following format:

	A	B	C	D	E
1		Combined Cash Budget			
2		For the Quarter Ended March 31			
3		Month			
4		January	February	March	Quarter
5	Beginning cash balance				
6	Plus: Cash collections				
7	Total cash available				
8	Less cash payments:				
9	Direct material purchases				
10	Direct labor				
11	Manufacturing overhead costs				
12	Operating expenses				
13	Tax payment				
14	Equipment purchases				
15	Total cash payments				
16	Ending cash balance before financing				
17	Financing:				
18	Plus: New borrowings				
19	Less: Debt repayments				
20	Less: Interest payments				
21	Ending cash balance				
22					

9. Calculate the budgeted manufacturing cost per unit, using the following format (assume that fixed manufacturing overhead is budgeted to be $0.80 per unit for the year):

	A	B	C	D
1	Budgeted Manufacturing Cost per Unit			
2				
3	Direct materials cost per unit			
4	Direct labor cost per unit			
5	Variable manufacturing overhead costs per unit			
6	Fixed manufacturing overhead costs per unit			
7	Budgeted cost of manufacturing one unit			
8				

10. Prepare a budgeted income statement for the quarter ending March 31, using the following format:

	A	B	C	D
1	Budgeted Income Statement			
2	For the Quarter Ended March 31			
3				
4	Sales revenue			
5	Less: Cost of goods sold*			
6	Gross profit			
7	Less: Operating expenses			
8	Less: Depreciation expense			
9	Operating income			
10	Less: Interest expense			
11	Less: Income tax expense			
12	Net income			
13				

*Hint: Cost of goods sold = Budgeted cost of manufacturing one unit × Number of units sold

P9-58A Cash budgets under two alternatives (Learning Objectives 2 & 3)

Each autumn, as a hobby, Hannah Olson weaves cotton placemats to sell at a local craft shop. The mats sell for $30 per set of four mats. The shop charges a 20% commission and remits the net proceeds to Olson at the end of December. Olson has woven and sold 26 sets in each of the last two years. She has enough cotton in inventory to make another 26 sets. She paid $8 per set for the cotton. Olson uses a four-harness loom that she purchased for cash exactly two years ago. It is depreciated at the rate of $5 per month. The accounts payable relate to the cotton inventory and are payable by September 30.

Olson is considering buying an eight-harness loom so that she can weave more intricate patterns in linen. The new loom costs $1,000; it would be depreciated at $20 per month. Her bank has agreed to lend her $1,000 at 18% interest, with $200 principal plus accrued interest payable each December 31. Olson believes she can weave 16 linen placemat sets in time for the Christmas rush if she does not weave any cotton mats. She predicts that each linen set will sell for $65. Linen costs $20 per set. Olson's supplier will sell her linen on credit, payable December 31.

Olson plans to keep her old loom whether or not she buys the new loom. The balance sheet for her weaving business at August 31 is as follows:

	A	B	C	D
1	Hannah Olson, Weaver			
2	Balance Sheet			
3	August 31			
4	Assets:			
5	Current assets:			
6	Cash	$ 65		
7	Inventory of cotton	208		
8	Total current assets	$ 273		
9	Property, plant, and equipment:			
10	Loom	$ 250		
11	Accumulated depreciation	(120)		
12	Total property, plant, and equipment	$ 130		
13	Total assets	$ 403		
14				
15	Liabilities and Stockholders' Equity:			
16	Accounts payable	$ 88		
17	Stockholders' equity	315		
18	Total liabilities and stockholders' equity	$ 403		
19				

Requirements

1. Prepare a combined cash budget for the four months ending December 31, for two alternatives: weaving the placemats in cotton using the existing loom and weaving the placemats in linen using the new loom. For each alternative, prepare a budgeted income statement for the four months ending December 31 and a budgeted balance sheet at December 31.
2. On the basis of financial considerations only, what should Olson do? Give your reason.
3. What nonfinancial factors might Olson consider in her decision?

P9-59A Comprehensive summary problem *(Learning Objectives 2 & 3)*

Birdfeeders Unlimited makes backyard birdfeeders. The company sells the birdfeeders to home improvement stores for $15 per birdfeeder. Each birdfeeder requires 1.5 board feet of wood, which the company obtains at a cost of $4 per board foot. The company would like to maintain an ending stock of wood equal to 10% of the next month's production requirements. The company would also like to maintain an ending stock of finished birdfeeders equal to 20% of the next month's sales.

Sales data for the company is as follows:

	Units
October actual sales (prior year)	92,000
November actual sales (prior year)	85,000
December actual sales (prior year)	78,000
January projected sales	80,000
February projected sales	90,000
March projected sales	95,000
April projected sales	105,000

In any given month, 20% of the total sales are cash sales, while the remainder are credit sales.

The company's collection history indicates that 80% of credit sales is collected in the month after the sale, 10% is collected two months after the sale, 6% is collected three months after the sale, and the remaining 4% is never collected.

Assume that the total cost of direct materials purchases in December was $550,000. The company pays 45% of its direct materials purchases in the month of purchase and pays the remaining 55% in the month after purchase.

Requirements

Prepare the following budgets for the first three months of the year, as well as a summary budget for the quarter:

1. Prepare the sales budget, including a separate section that details the type of sales made (cash versus credit).
2. Prepare the production budget.
3. Prepare the direct materials purchases budget. Assume the company needs 120,000 board feet of wood for production in April.
4. Prepare the cash collections budget for January, February, and March, as well as a summary for the first quarter.
5. Prepare the cash payments budget for direct materials purchases for the months of January, February, and March, as well as a summary for the first quarter.

P9-60A Budgeted income statement *(Learning Objective 2)*

The budget committee of Hilton Fashions, an upscale women's clothing retailer, has assembled the following data. As the business manager, you must prepare the budgeted income statements for May and June.

a. Sales in April were $50,000. You forecast that monthly sales will increase 8% in May and an additional 4% in June.

b. Hilton Fashions maintains inventory of $11,000 plus 20% of sales revenues budgeted for the following month. Monthly purchases average 50% of sales revenues in that same month. Actual inventory on April 30 is $21,800. Sales budgeted for July are $55,000.

c. Monthly salaries amount to $3,000. Sales commissions equal 5% of sales for that month. Combine salaries and commissions into a single figure.

d. Other monthly expenses are as follows:

Rent expense	$3,200, paid as incurred
Depreciation expense	$ 500
Insurance expense	$ 300, expiration of prepaid amount
Income tax	20% of operating income

Requirement
Prepare Hilton Fashions' budgeted income statements for May and June. Show cost of goods sold computations.

P9-61A Cash budgets *(Learning Objective 3)*

Eli's Restaurant Supply is preparing its cash budgets for the first two months of the upcoming year. Here is the information about the company's upcoming cash receipts and cash disbursements:

a. Sales are 65% cash and 35% credit. Credit sales are collected 20% in the month of sale and the remainder in the month after sale. Actual sales in December were $54,000. Schedules of budgeted sales for the two months of the upcoming year are as follows:

	Budgeted Sales Revenue
January	$62,000
February	$70,000

b. Actual purchases of direct materials in December were $24,500. The company's purchases of direct materials in January are budgeted to be $24,000 and $26,000 in February. All purchases are paid 40% in the month of purchase and 60% the following month.

c. Salaries and sales commissions are also paid half in the month earned and half the next month. Actual salaries were $8,000 in December. Budgeted salaries in January are $9,000 and February budgeted salaries are $10,500. Sales commissions each month are 8% of that month's sales.

d. Rent expense is $3,500 per month.

e. Depreciation is $2,100 per month.

f. Estimated income tax payments are made at the end of January. The estimated tax payment is projected to be $12,500.

g. The cash balance at the end of the prior year was $22,000.

Requirements

1. Prepare schedules of (a) budgeted cash collections, (b) budgeted cash payments for purchases, and (c) budgeted cash payments for operating expenses. Show totals for each month and totals for January and February combined.
2. Prepare a combined cash budget similar to exhibits in the chapter. If no financing activity takes place, what is the budgeted cash balance on February 28?

P9-62A Combined cash budget and a budgeted balance sheet *(Learning Objective 3)*

Hugo Medical Supply has applied for a loan. Pacific Commerce Bank has requested a budgeted balance sheet as of April 30 and a combined cash budget for April. As Hugo Medical Supply's controller, you have assembled the following information:

a. March 31 equipment balance, $52,600; accumulated depreciation, $41,300
b. April capital expenditures of $42,400 budgeted for cash purchase of equipment
c. April depreciation expense, $700
d. Cost of goods sold, 60% of sales
e. Other April operating expenses, including income tax, total $14,200, 35% of which will be paid in cash and the remainder accrued at April 30

f. March 31 owners' equity, $92,600
g. March 31 cash balance, $40,300
h. April budgeted sales, $90,000, 70% of which is for cash. Of the remaining 30%, half will be collected in April and half in May.
i. April cash collections on March sales, $29,100
j. April cash payments of March 31 liabilities incurred for March purchases of inventory, $17,300
k. March 31 inventory balance, $29,200
l. April purchases of inventory, $10,700 for cash and $36,300 on credit. Half of the credit purchases will be paid in April and half in May.

Requirements

1. Prepare the budgeted balance sheet for Hugo Medical Supply at April 30. Show separate computations for cash, inventory, and owners' equity balances.
2. Prepare the combined cash budget for April.
3. Suppose Hugo Medical Supply has become aware of more efficient (and more expensive) equipment than it budgeted for purchase in April. What is the total amount of cash available for equipment purchases in April, before financing, if the minimum desired ending cash balance is $14,000? (For this requirement, disregard the $42,400 initially budgeted for equipment purchases.)
4. Before granting a loan to Hugo Medical Supply, Pacific Commerce Bank asks for a sensitivity analysis assuming that April sales are only $60,000 rather than the $90,000 originally budgeted. (While the cost of goods sold will change, assume that purchases, depreciation, and the other operating expenses will remain the same as in the earlier requirements.)
    a. Prepare a revised budgeted balance sheet for Hugo Medical Supply, showing separate computations for cash, inventory, and owners' equity balances.
    b. Suppose Hugo Medical Supply has a minimum desired cash balance of $25,000. Will the company need to borrow cash in April?

P9-63A **Cost of goods sold, inventory, and purchases budget** (Learning Objective 4)

College Logos buys logo-imprinted merchandise and then sells it to university bookstores. Sales are expected to be $2,003,000 in September, $2,230,000 in October, $2,376,000 in November, and $2,520,000 in December. College Logos sets its prices to earn an average 30% gross profit on sales revenue. The company does not want inventory to fall below $435,000 plus 15% of the next month's cost of goods sold.

Requirement
Prepare a cost of goods sold, inventory, and purchases budget for the months of October and November.

P9-64A **Prepare comprehensive budgets for a retailer** (Learning Objectives 2, 3, & 4)

Dollar Dime Store is a local discount store with the following information:

- October sales are projected to be $350,000.
- Sales are projected to increase by 15% in November and another 20% in December and then return to the October level in January.
- 30% of sales are made in cash while the remaining 70% are paid by credit or debit card. The credit card companies and banks (debit card issuers) charge a 2% transaction fee and deposit the net amount (sales price less the transaction fee) in the store's bank account daily. The store does not accept checks. Because of the payment mechanisms, there is no risk of nonpayment or bad-debts.
    o The store's gross profit is 25% of sales revenue.
    o For the next several months, the store wants to maintain an ending inventory equal to $10,000 plus 20% of the next month's cost of goods sold. All purchases for merchandise are made on account and paid in the month following the purchase. The September 30 inventory is expected to be $62,500.
- Expected monthly operating expenses and details about payments include the following.
    o Wages of store workers should be $8,000 per month and are paid on the last day of each month.

- o Utilities expense is expected to be $1,200 per month in September, October, and November.
- o Utilities expense is expected to be $2,000 per month during the colder months of December, January, and February.
- o All utility bills are paid the month after incurred.
- o Property tax is $24,000 per year and is paid semiannually each December and June.
- o Property and liability insurance is $12,000 per year and is paid semiannually each January and July.
- o Depreciation expense is $144,000 per year; the straight-line method is used.
- o Transa ction fees, as stated earlier, are 2% of credit and debit card sales.
- Cash dividends of $275,000 are to be paid in December.
- Assume the cash balance on October 31 is $20,000. The company wants to maintain a cash balance of at least $20,000 at the end of every month.
- The company has arranged a line of credit with a local bank at a 5% interest rate. There is no outstanding debt as of October 31.

Requirements

Prepare the following budgets for November and December:
1. Sales budget
2. Cost of goods sold, inventory, and purchases budget
3. Operating expense budget
4. Budgeted income statement
5. Cash collections budget
6. Cash payments budget
7. Combined cash budget

PROBLEMS Group B

P9-65B Comprehensive budgeting problem *(Learning Objectives 2 & 3)*

Conrad Manufacturing is preparing its master budget for the first quarter of the upcoming year. The following data pertain to Conrad Manufacturing's operations:

Current assets as of December 31 (prior year):	
Cash	$ 4,460
Accounts receivable, net	$ 49,000
Inventory	$ 15,600
Property, plant, and equipment, net	$121,500
Accounts payable	$ 43,000
Capital stock	$127,000
Retained earnings	$ 22,800

a. Actual sales in December were $76,000. Selling price per unit is projected to remain stable at $9 per unit throughout the budget period. Sales for the first five months of the upcoming year are budgeted to be as follows:

January	$80,100
February	$89,100
March	$82,800
April	$85,500
May	$77,400

b. Sales are 30% cash and 70% credit. All credit sales are collected in the month following the sale.

c. Conrad Manufacturing has a policy stating that each month's ending inventory of finished goods should be 10% of the following month's sales (in units).
d. Of each month's direct materials purchases, 20% are paid for in the month of purchase, while the remainder is paid for in the month following purchase. Two pounds of direct material is needed per unit at $1.50 per pound. Ending inventory of direct materials should be 20% of next month's production needs.
e. Most of the labor at the manufacturing facility is indirect, but there is some direct labor incurred. The direct labor hours per unit is 0.03. The direct labor rate per hour is $13 per hour. All direct labor is paid for in the month in which the work is performed. The direct labor total cost for each of the upcoming three months is as follows:

January	$3,510
February	$3,834
March	$3,600

f. Monthly manufacturing overhead costs are $6,500 for factory rent, $2,900 for other fixed manufacturing expenses, and $1.40 per unit for variable manufacturing overhead. No depreciation is included in these figures. All expenses are paid in the month in which they are incurred.
g. Computer equipment for the administrative offices will be purchased in the upcoming quarter. In January, the company will purchase equipment for $5,800 (cash), while February's cash expenditure will be $11,600 and March's cash expenditure will be $15,800.
h. Operating expenses are budgeted to be $1.20 per unit sold plus fixed operating expenses of $1,400 per month. All operating expenses are paid in the month in which they are incurred. No depreciation is included in these figures.
i. Depreciation on the building and equipment for the general and administrative offices is budgeted to be $4,900 for the entire quarter, which includes depreciation on new acquisitions.
j. Conrad Manufacturing has a policy that the ending cash balance in each month must be at least $4,400. The company has a line of credit with a local bank. It can borrow in increments of $1,000 at the beginning of each month, up to a total outstanding loan balance of $160,000. The interest rate on these loans is 1% per month simple interest (not compounded). The company would pay down on the line of credit balance in increments of $1,000 if it has excess funds at the end of the quarter. The company would also pay the accumulated interest at the end of the quarter on the funds borrowed during the quarter.
k. The company's income tax rate is projected to be 30% of operating income less interest expense. The company pays $10,800 cash at the end of February in estimated taxes.

Requirements

1. Prepare a schedule of cash collections for January, February, and March, and for the quarter in total.

	A	B	C	D	E
1		Cash Collections Budget			
2		For the Quarter Ended March 31			
3		Month			
4		January	February	March	Quarter
5	Cash sales				
6	Credit sales				
7	Total cash collections				
8					

2. Prepare a production budget.

	A	B	C	D	E
1		\multicolumn{4}{c}{Production Budget}
2		\multicolumn{4}{c}{For the Quarter Ended March 31}
3		\multicolumn{3}{c}{Month}	
4		January	February	March	Quarter
5	Unit sales*				
6	Plus: Desired ending inventory				
7	Total needed				
8	Less: Beginning inventory				
9	Number of units to produce				
10					

*Hint: Unit sales = Sales in dollars/Selling price per unit

3. Prepare a direct materials budget.

	A	B	C	D	E
1		\multicolumn{4}{c}{Direct Materials Budget}
2		\multicolumn{4}{c}{For the Quarter Ended March 31}
3		\multicolumn{3}{c}{Month}	
4		January	February	March	Quarter
5	Units to be produced (from Production Budget)				
6	Multiply by: Quantity (pounds) of DM needed per unit				
7	Quantity (pounds) needed for production				
8	Plus: Desired ending inventory of DM				
9	Total quantity (pounds) needed				
10	Less: Beginning inventory of DM				
11	Quantity (pounds) to purchase				
12	Multiply by: Cost per pound				
13	Total cost of DM purchases				
14					

4. Prepare a cash payments budget for the direct material purchases from Requirement 3, using the following format. (Use the accounts payable balance at December 31 of prior year for the prior month payment in January.)

	A	B	C	D	E
1		\multicolumn{4}{c}{Cash Payments for Direct Materials Budget}
2		\multicolumn{4}{c}{For the Quarter Ended March 31}
3		\multicolumn{3}{c}{Month}	
4		January	February	March	Quarter
5	20% of current month DM purchases				
6	80% of prior month DM purchases				
7	Total cash payments				
8					

5. Prepare a cash payments budget for direct labor, using the following format:

	A	B	C	D	E
1		\multicolumn{4}{c}{Cash Payments for Direct Labor Budget}
2		\multicolumn{4}{c}{For the Quarter Ended March 31}
3		\multicolumn{3}{c}{Month}	
4		January	February	March	Quarter
5	Total cost of direct labor				
6					

6. Prepare a cash payments budget for manufacturing overhead costs.

	A	B	C	D	E
1		Cash Payments for Manufacturing Overhead Budget			
2		For the Quarter Ended March 31			
3		Month			
4		January	February	March	Quarter
5	Variable manufacturing overhead costs				
6	Rent (fixed)				
7	Other fixed MOH				
8	Cash payments for manufacturing overhead				
9					

7. Prepare a cash payments budget for operating expenses.

	A	B	C	D	E
1		Cash Payments for Operating Expenses Budget			
2		For the Quarter Ended March 31			
3		Month			
4		January	February	March	Quarter
5	Variable operating expenses				
6	Fixed operating expenses				
7	Cash payments for operating expenses				
8					

8. Prepare a combined cash budget.

	A	B	C	D	E
1		Combined Cash Budget			
2		For the Quarter Ended March 31			
3		Month			
4		January	February	March	Quarter
5	Beginning cash balance				
6	Plus: Cash collections				
7	Total cash available				
8	Less cash payments:				
9	Direct material purchases				
10	Direct labor				
11	Manufacturing overhead costs				
12	Operating expenses				
13	Tax payment				
14	Equipment purchases				
15	Total cash payments				
16	Ending cash balance before financing				
17	Financing:				
18	Plus: New borrowings				
19	Less: Debt repayments				
20	Less: Interest payments				
21	Ending cash balance				
22					

9. Calculate the budgeted manufacturing cost per unit (assume that fixed manufacturing overhead is budgeted to be $0.70 per unit for the year).

	A	B	C	D
1	**Budgeted Manufacturing Cost per Unit**			
2				
3	Direct materials cost per unit			
4	Direct labor cost per unit			
5	Variable manufacturing overhead costs per unit			
6	Fixed manufacturing overhead costs per unit			
7	Budgeted cost of manufacturing one unit			
8				

10. Prepare a budgeted income statement for the quarter ending March 31.

	A	B	C	D
1	**Budgeted Income Statement**			
2	**For the Quarter Ended March 31**			
3				
4	Sales revenue			
5	Less: Cost of goods sold*			
6	Gross profit			
7	Less: Operating expenses			
8	Less: Depreciation expense			
9	Operating income			
10	Less: Interest expense			
11	Less: Income tax expense			
12	Net income			
13				

*Hint: Cost of goods sold = Budgeted cost of manufacturing one unit × Number of units sold

P9-66B Cash budgets under two alternatives *(Learning Objectives 2 & 3)*

Each autumn, as a hobby, Joann Denton weaves cotton placemats to sell at a local craft shop. The mats sell for $20 per set of four mats. The shop charges a 15% commission and remits the net proceeds to Denton at the end of December. Denton has woven and sold 22 sets in each of the last two years. She has enough cotton in inventory to make another 22 sets. She paid $8 per set for the cotton. Denton uses a four-harness loom that she purchased for cash exactly two years ago. It is depreciated at the rate of $12 per month. The accounts payable relate to the cotton inventory and are payable by September 30.

Denton is considering buying an eight-harness loom so that she can weave more intricate patterns in linen. The new loom costs $1,000; it would be depreciated at $20 per month. Her bank has agreed to lend her $1,000 at 9% interest, with $200 principal plus accrued interest payable each December 31. Denton believes she can weave 10 linen place mat sets in time for the Christmas rush if she does not weave any cotton mats. She predicts that each linen set will sell for $40. Linen costs $5 per set. Denton's supplier will sell her linen on credit, payable December 31.

Denton plans to keep her old loom whether or not she buys the new loom. The balance sheet for her weaving business at August 31 is as follows:

	A	B	C	D
1	**Joann Denton, Weaver**			
2	**Balance Sheet**			
3	**August 31**			
4	**Assets:**			
5	Current assets:			
6	Cash	$ 70		
7	Inventory of cotton	176		
8	Total current assets	$ 246		
9	Property, plant, and equipment:			
10	Loom	$ 600		
11	Accumulated depreciation	(288)		
12	Total property, plant, and equipment	$ 312		
13	Total assets	$ 558		
14				
15	**Liabilities and Stockholders' Equity:**			
16	Accounts payable	$ 94		
17	Stockholders' equity	464		
18	Total liabilities and stockholders' equity	$ 558		
19				

Requirements

1. Prepare a combined cash budget for the four months ending December 31, for two alternatives: weaving the placemats in cotton using the existing loom and weaving the placemats in linen using the new loom. For each alternative, prepare a budgeted income statement for the four months ending December 31 and a budgeted balance sheet at December 31.
2. On the basis of financial considerations only, what should Denton do? Give your reason.
3. What nonfinancial factors might Denton consider in her decision?

P9-67B Comprehensive summary problem *(Learning Objectives 2 & 3)*

Birdhouses Inc. makes backyard birdhouses. The company sells the birdhouses to home improvement stores for $20 per birdfeeder. Each birdhouse requires 2.0 board feet of wood, which the company obtains at a cost of $5 per board foot. The company would like to maintain an ending stock of wood equal to 15% of the next month's production requirements. The company would also like to maintain an ending stock of finished birdfeeders equal to 10% of the next month's sales.

Sales data for the company is as follows:

	Units
October actual sales (prior year)	72,000
November actual sales (prior year)	84,000
December actual sales (prior year)	91,000
January projected sales	95,000
February projected sales	105,000
March projected sales	110,000
April projected sales	125,000

In any given month, 25% of the total sales are cash sales, while the remainder are credit sales.

The company's collection history indicates that 75% of credit sales is collected in the month after the sale, 15% is collected two months after the sale, 8% is collected three months after the sale, and the remaining 2% is never collected.

Assume that the total cost of direct materials purchases in December was $1,001,000. The company pays 60% of its direct materials purchases in the month of purchase and pays the remaining 40% in the month after purchase.

Requirements

1. Prepare the following budgets for the first three months of the year, as well as a summary budget for the quarter.
2. Prepare the sales budget, including a separate section that details the type of sales made (cash versus credit).
3. Prepare the production budget.
4. Prepare the direct materials purchases budget. Assume the company needs 242,000 board feet of wood for production in April.
5. Prepare the cash collections budget for January, February, and March, as well as a summary for the first quarter.
6. Prepare the cash payments budget for direct materials purchases for the months of January, February, and March, as well as a summary for the first quarter.

P9-68B Budgeted income statement *(Learning Objective 2)*

The budget committee of Chelsey Fashions, an upscale women's clothing retailer, has assembled the following data. As the business manager, you must prepare the budgeted income statements for May and June.

a. Sales in April were $35,000. You forecast that monthly sales will increase 10% in May and an additional 2% in June.

b. The company maintains inventory of $9,000 plus 10% of the sales revenue budgeted for the following month. Monthly purchases average 50% of sales revenue in that same month. Actual inventory on April 30 is $12,850. Sales budgeted for July are $45,000.

c. Monthly salaries amount to $3,000. Sales commissions equal 10% of sales for that month. Combine salaries and commissions into a single figure.

d. Other monthly expenses are as follows:

Rent expense	$2,800, paid as incurred
Depreciation expense	$ 700
Insurance expense	$ 400, expiration of prepaid amount
Income tax	20% of operating income

Requirement

Prepare Chelsey Fashions' budgeted income statements for May and June. Show cost of goods sold computations.

P9-69B Cash budgets *(Learning Objective 3)*

Ivan's Restaurant Supply is preparing its cash budgets for the first two months of the upcoming year. Here is the information about the company's upcoming cash receipts and cash disbursements:

a. Sales are 70% cash and 30% credit. Credit sales are collected 10% in the month of sale and the remainder in the month after sale. Actual sales in December were $54,000. Schedules of budgeted sales for the two months of the upcoming year are as follows:

	Budgeted sales revenue
January	$60,000
February	$68,000

b. Actual purchases of materials in December were $23,000. The company's purchases of direct materials in January are budgeted to be $20,500 and $26,000 in February. All purchases are paid 40% in the month of purchase and 60% the following month.

c. Salaries and sales commissions are also paid half in the month earned and half the next month. Actual salaries were $7,000 in December. Budgeted salaries in January are $8,000, and February budgeted salaries are $9,500. Sales commissions each month are 15% of that month's sales.

d. Rent expense is $2,900 per month.

e. Depreciation is $2,200 per month.
f. Estimated income tax payments are made at the end of January. The estimated tax payment is projected to be $13,000.
g. The cash balance at the end of the prior year was $24,000.

Requirements

1. Prepare schedules of (a) budgeted cash collections, (b) budgeted cash payments for purchases, and (c) budgeted cash payments for operating expenses. Show totals for each month and totals for January and February combined.
2. Prepare a combined cash budget. If no financing activity takes place, what is the budgeted cash balance on February 28?

P9-70B Combined cash budget and a budgeted balance sheet *(Learning Objective 3)*

Fairview Medical Supply has applied for a loan. First American Bank has requested a budgeted balance sheet at April 30 and a combined cash budget for April. As Fairview Medical Supply's controller, you have assembled the following information:

a. March 31 equipment balance, $52,700; accumulated depreciation, $41,100
b. April capital expenditures of $42,700 budgeted for cash purchase of equipment
c. April depreciation expense, $500
d. Cost of goods sold, 60% of sales
e. Other April operating expenses, including income tax, total $13,400, 30% of which will be paid in cash and the remainder accrued at April 30
f. March 31 owners' equity, $93,600
g. March 31 cash balance, $40,100
h. April budgeted sales, $91,000, 70% of which is for cash. Of the remaining 30%, half will be collected in April and half in May.
i. April cash collections on March sales, $29,200
j. April cash payments of March 31 liabilities incurred for March purchases of inventory, $17,100
k. March 31 inventory balance, $29,800
l. April purchases of inventory, $10,100 for cash and $36,800 on credit. Half of the credit purchases will be paid in April and half in May

Requirements

1. Prepare the budgeted balance sheet for Fairview Medical Supply at April 30. Show separate computations for cash, inventory, and stockholders' equity balances.
2. Prepare the combined cash budget for April.
3. Suppose Fairview Medical Supply has become aware of more efficient (and more expensive) equipment than it budgeted for purchase in April. What is the total amount of cash available for equipment purchases in April, before financing, if the minimum desired ending cash balance is $19,000? (For this requirement, disregard the $42,700 initially budgeted for equipment purchases.)
4. Before granting a loan to Fairview Medical Supply, First American Bank asks for a sensitivity analysis assuming that April sales are only $60,667 rather than the $91,000 originally budgeted. (While the cost of goods sold will change, assume that purchases, depreciation, and the other operating expenses will remain the same as in the earlier requirements.)
   a. Prepare a revised budgeted balance sheet for the company, showing separate computations for cash, inventory, and stockholders' equity balances.
   b. Suppose Fairview Medical Supply has a minimum desired cash balance of $20,000. Will the company need to borrow cash in April?

P9-71B Cost of goods sold, inventory, and purchases budget *(Learning Objective 4)*

Carlton Logos buys logo-imprinted merchandise and then sells it to university bookstores. Sales are expected to be $2,007,000 in September, $2,200,000 in October, $2,377,000 in November, and $2,500,000 in December. Carlton Logos sets its prices to earn an average 40% gross profit on sales revenue. The company does not want inventory to fall below $415,000 plus 20% of the next month's cost of goods sold.

Requirement

Prepare a cost of goods sold, inventory, and purchases budget for the months of October and November.

P9-72B Prepare comprehensive budgets for a retailer *(Learning Objectives 2, 3, & 4)*

Dollar Discount Store is a local discount store with the following information:
- October sales are projected to be $300,000.
- Sales are projected to increase by 10% in November and another 20% in December and then return to the October level in January.
- 25% of sales are made in cash, while the remaining 75% are paid by credit or debit cards. The credit card companies and banks (debit card issuers) charge a 2% transaction fee and deposit the net amount (sales price less the transaction fee) in the store's bank account daily. The store does not accept checks. Because of the payment mechanisms, there is no risk of nonpayment or bad-debts.
- The store's gross profit is 25% of its sales revenue.
- For the next several months, the store wants to maintain an ending merchandise inventory equal to $5,000 + 20% of the next month's cost of good sold. All purchases for merchandise are made on account and paid in the month *following* the purchase. The September 30 inventory is expected to be $50,000.
- Expected monthly operating expenses and details about payments include the following.
  o Wages of store workers should be $9,000 per month and are paid on the last day of each month.
  o Utilities expense is expected to be $1,200 per month in September, October, and November.
  o Utilities expense is expected to be $2,000 per month during the colder months of December, January, and February.
  o All utility bills are paid the month after incurred.
  o Property tax is $24,000 per year and is paid semiannually each December and June.
  o Property and liability insurance is $12,000 per year and is paid semiannually each January and July.
  o Depreciation expense is $144,000 per year; the straight-line method is used.
  o Transaction fees, as stated earlier, are 2% of credit and debit card sales.
- Cash dividends of $225,000 are to be paid in December.
- Assume the cash balance on October 31 is $10,000. The company wants to maintain a cash balance of at least $10,000 at the end of every month.
- The company has arranged a line of credit with a local bank at a 5% interest rate. There is no outstanding debt as of October 31.

Requirements

Prepare the following budgets for November and December:
1. Sales budget
2. Cost of goods sold, inventory, and purchases budget
3. Operating expense budget
4. Budgeted income statement
5. Cash collections budget
6. Cash payments budget
7. Combined cash budget

Serial Case

C9-73 Prepare a budget for newly renovated hotel *(Learning Objective 2)*

This case is a continuation of the Caesars Entertainment Corporation serial case that began in Chapter 1. Refer to the introductory story in Chapter 1 (see page 43) for additional background. (The components of the Caesars serial case can be completed in any order.)

Caesars Palace® Las Vegas will use budgets to make its financial plans. Let's assume that Caesars prepares budgets for each of its hotel towers, including the new Julius Tower. Here is a list of budgeting assumptions[10] for the Julius Tower for 2016:

Data table for Julius Tower budget assumptions	
Number of hotel rooms in the Julius Tower	587
Average occupancy rate for Caesars Entertainment Corporation	91.2%
Average hotel room rate per night	$ 149
Total budgeted fixed costs for the Julius Tower	$ 2,390,000
Variable cost per Julius Tower room night	$ 27

Requirements

1. How many Julius Tower hotel room nights should be budgeted to be booked in 2016? (Remember that 2016 is a leap year and, therefore, has an extra calendar day or 366 days.)
2. What would be the budgeted net revenue from the Julius Tower hotel rooms in 2016?
3. What would be the budgeted variable costs for the Julius Tower hotel in 2016?
4. Prepare a budget for 2016 for the Julius Tower using the assumptions provided above and the numbers you have calculated. Does it appear that the Julius Tower will be generating a healthy amount of income for Caesars Palace® Las Vegas? Explain.

---

[10] All Julius Tower assumptions are hypothetical and simply provided for educational use only.

CRITICAL THINKING

Discussion & Analysis

A9-74 Discussion Questions

1. "The sales budget is the most important budget." Do you agree or disagree? Explain your answer.
2. List at least four reasons why a company would use budgeting.
3. Describe the difference between an operating budget and a capital expenditures budget.
4. Describe the process for developing a budget.
5. Compare and contrast "participative budgeting" with "top-down" budgeting.
6. What is a budget committee? What is the budget committee's role in the budgeting process?
7. What are operating budgets? List at least four operating budgets.
8. What are financial budgets? List at least three financial budgets.
9. Managers may build slack into their budgets so that their target numbers are easier to attain. What might be some drawbacks to building slack into the budgets?
10. How does the master budget for a service company differ from a master budget for a manufacturing company? Which (if any) operating budgets differ and how, specifically, do they differ? Which (if any) financial budgets differ and how, specifically, do they differ?
11. Give an example of a sustainable practice that would affect a company's budget. How might this sustainable practice, if adopted, impact the company's budget in both the short-term and in the long-term?
12. Why might a company want to state environmental goals for increased sustainability in its budgets? Explain.

Application & Analysis

Mini Cases

A9-75 Budgeting for a Single Product

In this activity, you will be creating budgets for a single product for each of the months in an upcoming quarter. Select a product that you could purchase in large quantities (at a Sam's Club or other warehouse retail chain) and repackage into smaller quantities to offer for sale at a sidewalk café, a sporting event, a flea market, or other similar venue. Investigate the price and quantity at which this product is available at the warehouse. Choose a selling price for the smaller (repackaged) package. Make reasonable assumptions about how many of the smaller units you can sell in each of the next four months (you will need the fourth month's sales in units for the operating budgets).

Basic Discussion Questions

1. Describe your product. What is your cost of this product? What size (quantity) will you purchase? At what price will you sell your repackaged product? Make projections of your sales in units in each of the upcoming three months.
2. Estimate how many hours you will spend in each of the upcoming three months doing the purchasing, repackaging, and selling. Select a reasonable wage rate for yourself. What will your total labor costs be in each of the upcoming three months?
3. Prepare a sales budget for each of the upcoming three months.
4. Prepare the direct material budgets for the upcoming three months, assuming that you need to keep 10% of the direct materials needed for next month's sales on hand at the end of each month (this requirement is why you needed to estimate unit sales for four months).
5. Prepare a direct labor budget (for your labor) for each of the upcoming three months.

6. Think about any other expenses you are likely to have (i.e., booth rental at a flea market or a vendor license). Prepare the operating expenses budget for each of the upcoming three months.

7. Prepare a budgeted income statement that reflects the budgets you prepared, including the sales budget, direct materials budget, direct labor budget, and the operating expenses budget. This budgeted income statement should include one column for each of the three months in the quarter, and it should also include a total column that represents the totals of the three months. What is your projected profit by month and for the quarter?

A9-76 Ethics and budgetary slack (Learning Objectives 1, 2, 3, & 4)

Gutierrez Company, a publicly held corporation, operates a regional chain of large drugstores. Each drugstore is operated by a general manager and a controller. The general manager is responsible for the day-to-day operations of the store, while the controller is responsible for the budget and other financial tasks. The general manager, Tracie Kappan, has been at Gutierrez Company for several years. Employee turnover is high at Gutierrez Company, just as it is in the retail industry in general. Kappan just hired a new controller, Min Yang.

Yang was asked to prepare the master budget. Each retail location prepares its master budget once a year and then submits that budget to company headquarters for approval. Once approved by headquarters, the master budget is used to evaluate the store's performance. These performance evaluations directly affect the managers' bonuses and whether additional company funds are invested in that location.

When Yang was almost done preparing the budget, Kappan instructed him to increase the amounts budgeted for labor and supplies by 20%. When asked why, Kappan responded that this budgetary cushion gives store management flexibility in running the store. For example, because company headquarters tightly controls operating funds and capital improvement funds, any extra money budgeted for labor and supplies can be used to replace store furnishings or to pay bonuses to help to retain good employees. She explains that the chance of getting extra funds from company headquarters is not good; this "cushion" is usually the only opportunity to replace store décor or to pay bonuses to key employees. Kappan also needs extra funds occasionally to make "under the table" payments to employees as incentives to work extra hours or to keep them from leaving for a higher-paying job.

Yang feels conflicted. He is eager to please Kappan, and he is wondering what he should do in this situation.

Requirements

1. Using the IMA *Statement of Ethical Professional Practice* as an ethical framework, answer the following questions:
   a. What are the ethical issue(s) in this situation?
   b. What are Yang's responsibilities as a management accountant?
2. Would your answer differ if Gutierrez Company were instead owned by one individual instead of being publicly held? Why or why not?
3. Would anyone be harmed if slack were to be built into the budget? Why or why not?
4. Discuss the specific steps Yang should take in this situation. Refer to the IMA *Statement of Ethical Professional Practice* in your response.

A9-77 Budgeting issues at the movies (Learning Objectives 1, 2, 3, & 4)

Movies are expensive to produce and market. According to IMDb, the most expensive film on record is *Pirates of the Caribbean: On Stranger Tides*, with a total budget of $378.5 million.[11] This movie and its budget were widely publicized prior to the premiere of the film, and moviegoers were eager to see the results of this massive movie budget.

Like other large projects, movies have budgets. Potential financiers look at the budget, the script, and other factors to decide whether to invest in the movie. Several categories of costs will be in a movie's budget, including:

- Story rights
- Screenplay
- Producers and directors
- Cast

[11] Source: https://en.wikipedia.org/wiki/List_of_most_expensive_films, accessed January 7, 2016

- Production costs
- Special effects
- Music

The typical film budget you read about in the press includes only expenses. The movie budgets released to the general public do not include estimated box office receipts or other revenue streams. In addition, movie budgets do not usually include marketing costs, which can be another 50% or more of the film's publicized budget.

Producers and directors will frequently release budget figures for upcoming movies, and these budget figures will be reported in several news outlets. However, *Los Angeles Times* writer Patrick Goldstein states that "everyone" lies about their movie budgets.[12] For example, it was reported initially that *The Avengers*, a Marvel Studios film, had an overall budget of $170 million. Another source indicated that the budget for *The Avengers* was $260 million. Which one of these figures was the "correct" budget figure? No one outside of the management of the movie really knows.

Requirements

1. Budgeting for a movie can be challenging. Frequently, budget items change as the movie production progresses. If budgeting for a movie is difficult, why prepare a movie budget?
2. What reasons can a movie director have for misrepresenting the overall budget for a particular movie? Is misrepresenting a movie budget unethical? Do you think misrepresenting a movie's total budgeted expenditures to the public harms anyone? Why or why not?
3. "If a Hollywood movie's box office number exceeds its production budget, then that movie makes a profit." From reading the information given in the case, do you agree with this statement? Why or why not?
4. Sometimes actors, directors, and producers are asked to take a lower salary up front and instead receive a percentage of the film's overall gross profits (from box office receipts, DVD sales, and similar revenue streams). Why might the film company propose this arrangement? Why might the actors, directors, and producers accept this arrangement? Would this type of arrangement (lower salary up front with a percentage of the film's gross profits later) make the budgeting process easier or more challenging? Why?

Try It Solutions

page 514:

The company should produce 32,800 cases, calculated as follows:

Unit sales for April	32,000
Plus: Desired ending inventory (10% of May sales of 40,000)	4,000
Total units needed	36,000
Less: Beginning inventory (March ending inventory = 10% of April sales of 32,000)	3,200
Units to produce	32,800

page 525:

$122,000, calculated as follows:

	March Budgeted Collections
COD sales in March	$ 15,000
Credit sales from February ($110,000 × 90%)	99,000
Credit sales from January ($100,000 × 8%)	8,000
Total cash collections	$122,000

[12] http://cigsandredvines.blogspot.com/2010/03/everyone-lies-about-their-budget-la.html

10

Performance Evaluation

Rachel Youdelman/Pearson Education, Inc.

Sources: http://www.pepsico.com/Brands/BrandExplorer#top-global-brands

Learning Objectives

- **1** Understand decentralization and describe different types of responsibility centers
- **2** Develop performance reports
- **3** Calculate ROI, sales margin, and capital turnover
- **4** Describe strategies and mechanisms for determining a transfer price
- **5** Prepare and evaluate flexible budget performance reports
- **6** Describe the balanced scorecard and identify KPIs for each perspective

PepsiCo, which turned 50 years old in 2015, sells products in over 200 countries around the world. PepsiCo's top 22 brands each generate over $1 billion in annual sales. In addition to its well-known beverages, including Pepsi, Mountain Dew, Gatorade, and Tropicana, the company also owns all of the Frito-Lay snack brands, such as Ruffles, Doritos, and Cheetos. Pepsi also owns all of the Quaker Oat brands, such as Life and Cap'n Crunch cereals. How does such a large and diverse company coordinate, control, and evaluate such a vast array of operations? First, the company is segmented into separate operating divisions based on geographic location (for example, North America, Europe and Sub-Saharan Africa, and Latin America). In some geographic areas it is further segmented into different product types (Beverages, Quaker products, and Frito-Lay products). Second, a manager is assigned responsibility for each segment and for each operating function (production, sales, etc.) within each segment. PepsiCo's vision, "*Performance with a Purpose*," integrates sustainability and the triple bottom line into the company's business strategy. As a result, each segment is evaluated in terms not only of its financial performance, but also its impact on society and the environment.

In Chapter 9, we saw how businesses such as Campbell Soup Company and Tucson Tortilla set strategic goals and then develop planning budgets to help reach those goals. In this chapter, we'll see how companies use budgets and other tools, such as the balanced scorecard, to evaluate performance and control operations.

How Does Decentralization Affect Performance Evaluation?

1 Understand decentralization and describe different types of responsibility centers

In a small company, such as Tucson Tortilla (discussed in Chapter 9), the owner or top manager often makes all planning and operating decisions. Small companies can use *centralized* decision making because of the smaller scope of their operations. However, when a company grows, it is impossible for a single person to manage the entire organization's operations. Therefore, most companies, like PepsiCo, decentralize as they grow.

Companies that <u>decentralize</u> split their operations into different operating segments. Top management delegates decision-making responsibility to the segment managers and determines the type of decentralization that best suits the company's strategy. For example, decentralization may be based on

- geographic area
- product line
- distribution channel (such as retail sales versus online sales)
- customer base
- business function

PepsiCo decentralizes its company by brand in North America (Frito-Lay, Quaker Foods, Pepsi Beverages) and by geographic area in other parts of the world (Latin America; Europe and Sub-Saharan Africa; Asia, Middle East, and North Africa).

Advantages and Disadvantages of Decentralization

Before we look at specific types of business segments, let's consider some of the advantages and disadvantages of decentralization.

Advantages

Most growing companies decentralize out of necessity. However, decentralization provides many potential benefits.

FREES TOP MANAGEMENT'S TIME By delegating responsibility for daily operations to segment managers, top management can concentrate on long-term strategic planning and higher-level decisions that affect the entire company.

ENCOURAGES USE OF EXPERT KNOWLEDGE Decentralization allows top management to hire the expertise each business segment needs to excel in its specific operations. Specialized knowledge often helps segment managers make better decisions than the top company managers could make.

IMPROVES CUSTOMER AND SUPPLIER RELATIONS Segment managers focus on just one segment of the company, allowing them to maintain close contact with important customers and suppliers. Thus, decentralization often leads to improved customer and supplier relations, which can result in quicker customer response times.

PROVIDES TRAINING Decentralization also provides segment managers with training and experience necessary to become effective top managers. Companies often groom their lower-level managers to move up through the company, taking on additional responsibility and gaining more knowledge of the company with each step.

IMPROVES MOTIVATION AND RETENTION Empowering segment managers to make decisions increases managers' motivation and job satisfaction, which often improves job performance and retention.

Disadvantages

The many advantages of decentralization usually outweigh the disadvantages. However, decentralization can cause potential problems, including the following.

POTENTIAL DUPLICATION OF COSTS Decentralization may cause a company to duplicate certain costs or assets. For example, several business segments could maintain their own payroll and human resource departments. Companies can often avoid such duplications by providing centralized services. For example, Marriott segments its hotels by property type (limited service, full-service, international), yet each hotel property shares one centralized reservations website platform.

POTENTIAL PROBLEMS ACHIEVING GOAL CONGRUENCE <u>Goal congruence</u> occurs when the goals of the segment managers align with the goals of top management. Decentralized companies often struggle to achieve goal congruence. Segment managers may not fully understand the big picture, or the ultimate goals that upper management is trying to achieve. They may make decisions that are good for their segment but may be detrimental to another segment of the company or the company as a whole. For example, to control costs, one division may decide to offshore production to an overseas factory with poor working conditions. However, top management may embrace, promote, and market social responsibility and the use of fair labor practices. If so, the division is not acting in accordance with top management's goals.

Performance Evaluation Systems

Once a company decentralizes operations, top management is no longer involved in running the day-to-day operations of the segments. Performance evaluation systems provide upper management with the feedback it needs to maintain control over the entire organization, even though it has delegated responsibility and decision-making authority to segment managers. To be effective, performance evaluation systems should

- clearly communicate expectations,
- provide benchmarks that promote goal congruence and coordination between segments, and
- motivate segment managers (possibly through paying bonus incentives to managers who achieve performance targets).

Responsibility accounting, discussed next, is an integral part of most companies' performance evaluation systems.

What Is Responsibility Accounting?

A <u>responsibility center</u> is part of an organization whose manager is accountable for planning and controlling certain activities. Lower-level managers are often responsible for budgeting and controlling costs of a single value chain function. For example, at PepsiCo, one manager is responsible for planning and controlling the *production* of Frito-Lay products at a single plant, while another is responsible for planning and controlling the *distribution* of the product to customers. Lower-level managers report to higher-level managers, who have broader responsibilities. For example, managers in charge of production and distribution report to senior managers responsible for profits earned by an entire product line.

<u>Responsibility accounting</u> is a system for evaluating the performance of each responsibility center and its manager. Responsibility accounting performance reports compare plans (budgets) with actual results for each center. Superiors then evaluate how well each manager controlled the operations for which he or she was responsible.

Types of Responsibility Centers

Exhibit 10-1 illustrates four types of responsibility centers, as described briefly in the following paragraphs.

EXHIBIT 10-1 Four Types of Responsibility Centers

Cost Center

In a <u>cost center</u>, managers are accountable for costs only. Manufacturing operations, such as the Frito-Lay plant in Casa Grande, Arizona, are cost centers. The plant manager controls costs by using lean thinking to eliminate waste. The plant is near net-zero waste and uses solar energy for much of its power. The plant manager is *not* responsible for generating revenues because he or she is not involved in selling the product. The plant manager is evaluated on his or her ability to control *costs* by comparing actual costs to budgeted costs.

Revenue Center

In a <u>revenue center</u>, managers are accountable primarily for revenues. Many times, revenue centers are sales territories, such as geographic areas within the country. Revenue center performance reports compare actual revenues to budgeted revenues.

Profit Center

In a <u>profit center</u>, managers are accountable for both revenues and costs, and therefore profits. For example, at PepsiCo, a manager may be responsible for the entire line of brand products, such as Mountain Dew or Aquafina. This manager is accountable for increasing sales revenue *and* controlling costs to achieve profit goals for the entire brand or product line. Superiors evaluate the manager's performance by comparing actual revenues, expenses, and profits to the budget.

Investment Center

In an <u>investment center</u>, managers are responsible for (1) generating revenues, (2) controlling costs, and (3) efficiently managing the division's assets. Investment centers are generally large divisions of a corporation. For example, PepsiCo has six divisions:

- Frito-Lay North America
- Quaker Foods North America

- North America Beverages
- Latin America
- Europe Sub-Saharan Africa
- Asia, Middle East, and North Africa

Investment centers are treated almost as if they were standalone companies. Division managers generally have broad responsibility, including deciding how to use assets. As a result, managers are held responsible for generating as much profit as they can with those assets.

Organization Chart

Exhibit 10-2 shows a partial organization chart for a company such as PepsiCo.

- At the top level, the CEO oversees each of the divisions (*investment centers*).
- The manager of each division oversees all of the product lines (*profit centers*) in that division. For example, the VP of North America Beverages is responsible for the profitable operation of Pepsi, Gatorade, Tropicana, Mountain Dew, Aquafina, and the company's other North America beverage brands.[1]
- The manager of each product line is responsible for evaluating lower-level managers of *cost centers* (such as manufacturing plants) and *revenue centers* (such as sales territories).

EXHIBIT 10-2 Partial Organization Chart

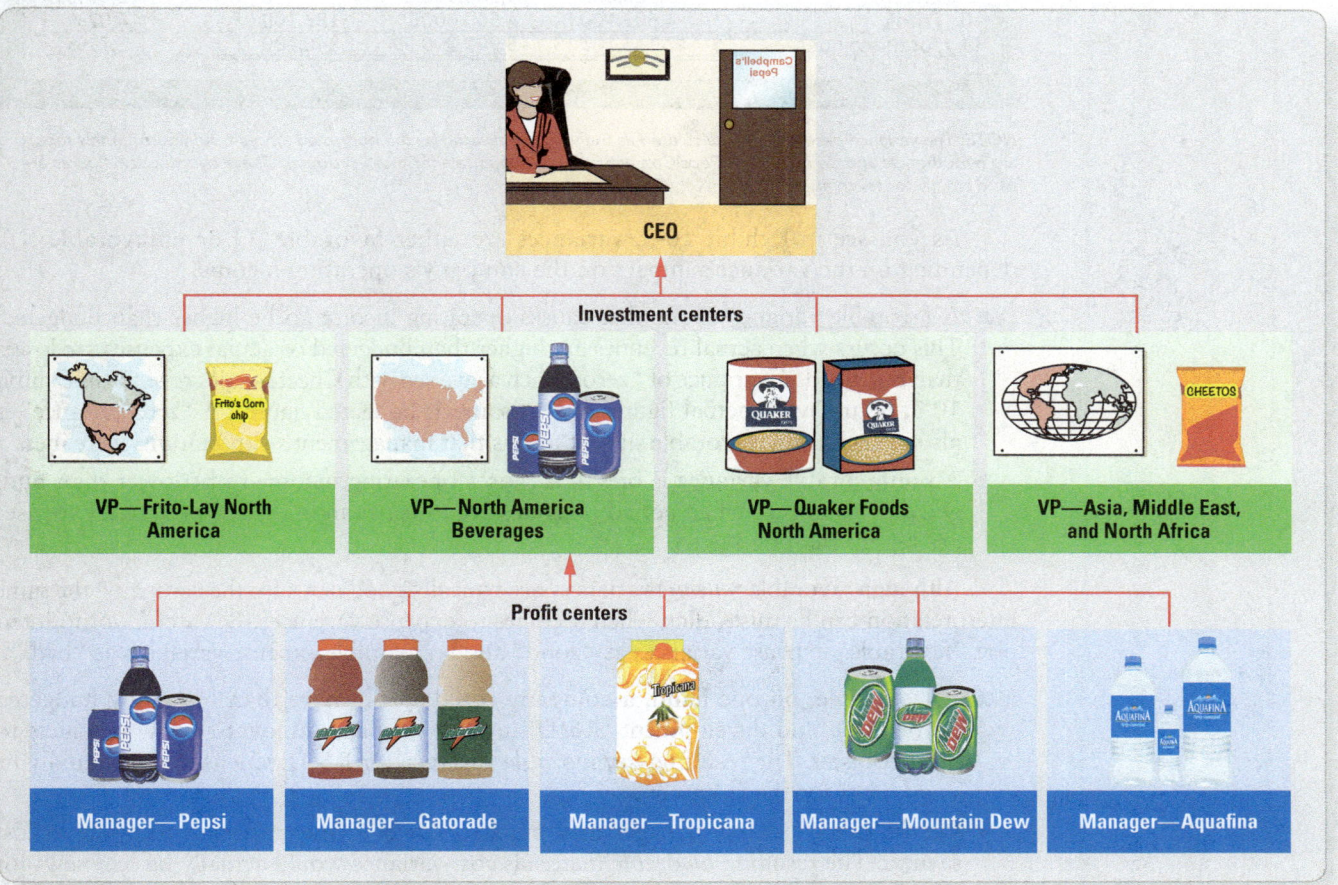

[1] For the sake of simplicity, we only illustrate four of the six divisions.

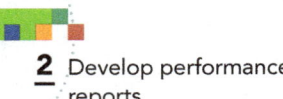

2 Develop performance reports

Responsibility Center Performance Reports

As introduced in Chapter 9, a **performance report** compares actual revenues and actual expenses against budgeted figures. The difference between actual figures and budgeted figures is known as a **variance**. The specific figures included on each performance report will depend on the type of responsibility center being evaluated. For example,

- the performance reports of cost centers will only include *costs* incurred within the center
- the performance reports of revenue centers will only include the *revenues* generated by the center

Exhibit 10-3 illustrates a partial performance report for a hypothetical revenue center—the hypothetical Midwest Sales Region of Frito-Lay products. Since the manager is only responsible for generating sales revenue, only revenues are included in the report.

EXHIBIT 10-3 Partial Performance Report for a Revenue Center

	A	B	C	D	E	F	G
1		Midwest Sales Region					
2		Monthly Performance Report					
3		For the Month Ended March 31					
4	Product	Actual Sales	Budgeted Sales	Variance		Variance Percentage	
5	Sun Chips	$ 2,367,200	$ 2,400,000	$ 32,800	U	1.37%	U
6	Doritos	15,896,000	15,000,000	896,000	F	5.97%	F
7	Lay's	9,325,500	9,000,000	325,500	F	3.62%	F
8	Tostitos	1,374,300	1,500,000	125,700	U	8.38%	U
9	Cheetos	13,500,000	13,500,000	0	F	0.00%	F
10	Fritos	4,683,100	4,500,000	183,100	F	4.07%	F
11	Total revenues	$ 47,146,100	$ 45,900,000	$ 1,246,100	F	2.71%	F
12							

NOTE: The variance percentage is calculated as the variance divided by the budgeted amount. All figures in this report are hypothetical and do not reflect PepsiCo's actual sales or budgets for these products. These hypothetical figures are used strictly for teaching purposes.

As you see in Exhibit 10-3, variances are either favorable (F) or unfavorable (U), depending on the variance's impact on the company's operating income.

- A **favorable variance** is one that causes operating income to be higher than budgeted. This occurs when actual revenues are higher than budgeted or actual expenses are lower than budgeted. A variance of "zero," such as we see with Cheetos sales revenue in Exhibit 10-3, occurs when actual figures are the same as budgeted figures. A "zero variance" is also interpreted as favorable since it means that management's expectations were met.
- An **unfavorable variance** is one that causes operating income to be lower than budgeted. This occurs when actual revenues are lower than budgeted or actual expenses are higher than budgeted.

Although favorable *revenue* variances are typically good news for the company, the same interpretation can be misleading when it comes to expense variances. Be careful *not* to interpret "favorable" expense variances as "good" and unfavorable expense variances as "bad."

- For example, on one hand, a company could spend more than originally budgeted on research and development (R&D) in order to bring innovative new products to market faster. The resulting *unfavorable* variance for R&D expenses may actually be *good* news for the company.
- On the other hand, a manager may purchase lower-quality materials to generate cost savings. The resulting *favorable* materials cost variance would actually be *bad* news for the company, since it would most likely result in reducing the quality of the end product.

Most companies' accounting software will use positive and negative numbers to indicate whether a variance is favorable or unfavorable. The direction of the sign (positive or negative) will depend on whether the variance is calculated as budget minus actual or as actual minus budget. Practice varies in this regard, especially when it comes to expense variances. To avoid any confusion over the direction of the sign, we use the U and F notation along with the absolute value of the variance. Just remember that when you are working with real companies, you will rarely see the U or F notation on the performance reports. Rather, you will see positive and negative variances that you will need to interpret using the definitions just presented.

Managers use a technique called **management by exception** when analyzing performance reports. Management by exception means that managers will only investigate budget variances that are relatively large. Let's use a personal example to illustrate this concept. Consider your monthly cell phone bill. You probably have an expectation of how large your monthly cell phone bill will be. If the actual bill is close to your expectation, you'll just pay the bill without giving it too much additional thought. However, if the actual bill is much higher or much lower than you expected, you probably will look at the detailed charges for calls, texts, and data usage to determine why the bill was so much different than what you expected.

> **Why is this important?**
>
> "Variances are always **favorable** or **unfavorable**, depending on whether they increase or decrease operating income. **Computer** software usually indicates the **directional** impact of the variance using **positive** and **negative numbers**, rather than a U or F notation."

Managers do the same thing. If the actual costs or revenues are close to budget, they assume operations are in control. However, if the variance between budget and actual is relatively large, they'll investigate the cause of the variance. Managers often have a decision rule for variance investigation that is expressed as a percentage, dollar amount, or a combination of the two. For example, the manager of the Midwest Sales Region may decide to investigate only those variances that are greater than 5% *and* $150,000. Exhibit 10-3 shows that the variance for both Doritos and Tostitos exceeds 5%. However, of the two, only the Doritos variance exceeds $150,000. Therefore, the manager would only investigate the Doritos variance.

Segment Margin

The performance reports of profit and investment centers include both revenues and expenses. Performance reports are often presented in the contribution margin format rather than the traditional income statement format. These reports often include a line called "segment margin." A **segment margin** is the operating income generated by a profit or investment center *before* subtracting common fixed costs that have been allocated to the center. Exhibit 10-4 illustrates a hypothetical performance report for Tropicana products.

EXHIBIT 10-4 Performance Report Highlighting the Profit Center's Segment Margin

	A	B	C	D	E	F	G
1			Tropicana Products				
2		Segment Margin Performance Report for the Fiscal Year Ended December 31					
3		(all figures in millions of dollars)					
4		Actual		Budgeted	Variance		Variance %
5	Sales revenue	$	4,314	$ 4,300	$ 14	F	0.3% F
6	Less variable expenses:						
7	Variable cost of goods sold		1,728	1,720	8	U	0.5% U
8	Variable operating expenses		508	515	7	F	1.4% F
9	Contribution Margin		2,078	2,065	13	F	0.6% F
10	Less direct fixed expenses:						
11	Fixed manufacturing overhead		1,228	1,215	13	U	1.1% U
12	Fixed operating expenses		405	415	10	F	2.4% F
13	Segment Margin		445	435	10	F	2.3% F
14	Less: Common fixed expenses allocated to the profit center		36	35	1	U	2.9% U
15	Operating income	$	409	$ 400	$ 9	F	2.3% F
16							

NOTE: All figures in this report are hypothetical and do not reflect the actual or budgeted sales and expense data for Tropicana products. These hypothetical figures are used strictly for teaching purposes.

As you look at Exhibit 10-4, notice that fixed expenses are separated into two categories:

- **Direct fixed expenses**, which include those fixed expenses that can be traced to the profit center. An example might include advertisements for Tropicana orange juice.
- **Common fixed expenses**, which include those fixed expenses that *cannot* be traced to the profit center. Rather, these are fixed expenses incurred by the overarching investment center (North America Beverages) that have been allocated among the different profit centers in the division. For example, these allocated costs may include the division's cost of providing a common computer information system, human resources department, payroll department, and legal department. By sharing these services, the different product lines avoid duplication of the costs and assets that would otherwise need to be maintained by the individual profit centers.

Since the manager of the profit center has little to no control over the allocation of the common fixed expenses, he or she should not be held responsible for them.[2] Therefore, the manager is typically held responsible for the center's segment margin, not its operating income.

Organization-wide Performance Reports

Exhibit 10-5 illustrates how the performance reports for each level of management shown in Exhibit 10-2 flow *up* to the top of the company. Notice the following in the exhibit:

- The operating income from each profit center, such as Tropicana products (at the bottom of the exhibit), flows into the performance report for an investment center (in the middle of the exhibit).
- Likewise, the operating income from each investment center, such as North America Beverages, flows into the performance report for the entire company (at the top of the exhibit).
- Costs incurred by corporate headquarters (shown in the top of the exhibit) are treated as a cost center and are typically not allocated to any of the divisions.
- In addition to those performance reports pictured, performance reports related to the cost and revenue centers under each profit center would exist and flow up to the profit centers.

Responsibility accounting assigns managers responsibility for their segment's performance. But superiors should not misuse the system to erroneously find fault or place blame. Some variances are controllable, while others are not.

For example, managers have no control over the general economic conditions of the country that may reduce sales. Nor do they have control over droughts, floods, and frosts that increase the cost of the agricultural materials in their products. Likewise, they have little or no control over the cost of electricity and gas used to power plants and deliver products. Managers need to carefully consider the causes of large variances so that they can focus on improving those that are controllable, while developing strategies for minimizing the risk associated with uncontrollable variances.

Evaluation of Investment Centers

3 Calculate ROI, sales margin, and capital turnover

As discussed above, investment centers are typically large divisions of a company. The duties of an investment center manager are similar to those of a CEO of an entire company. Investment center managers are responsible for *both* generating profit *and* making the best use of the investment center's assets. For example, an investment center manager has the authority to decide how much inventory to hold, what types of investments to make, how aggressively to collect accounts receivable and whether to open new stores or close old ones. In this section, we'll look at the two performance measures most commonly used

---

[2] The various methods used to allocate centralized service expenses and other common fixed expenses are covered in more advanced cost accounting textbooks.

EXHIBIT 10-5 Organization-wide Performance Reports

PepsiCo
Performance Report for the Fiscal Year Ended 2015
(all figures in millions of dollars)

Division Operating Income	Actual	Budgeted	Variance		Variance %	
Frito-Lay North America	$ 4,304	$ 4,100	$ 204	F	5.0%	F
Quaker Foods North America	560	550	10	F	1.8%	F
Latin Americas Foods	(206)	50	256	U	512.0%	U
North America Beverages	2,785	2,770	15	F	0.5%	F
Europe Sub-Saharan Africa	1,081	1,100	19	U	1.7%	U
Asia, Middle East and North Africa	941	930	11	F	1.2%	F
Corporate, unallocated	(1,112)	(1,300)	188	F	14.5%	F
Total operating income	$ 8,353	$ 8,200	$ 153	F	1.9%	F

North America Beverages
Performance Report for the Fiscal Year Ended 2015
(all figures in millions of dollars)

Product Line Operating Income	Actual	Budgeted	Variance		Variance %	
Pepsi	$ 804	$ 800	$ 4	F	0.5%	F
Mountain Dew	434	440	6	U	1.4%	U
Gatorade	614	605	9	F	1.5%	F
Aquafina	331	325	6	F	1.8%	F
Tropicana	409	400	9	F	2.3%	F
Sierra Mist	62	75	13	U	17.3%	U
Other beverages	131	125	6	F	4.8%	F
Total division operating income	$ 2,785	$ 2,770	$ 15	F	0.5%	F

Tropicana
Performance Report for the Fiscal Year Ended 2015
(all figures in millions of dollars)

	Actual	Budgeted	Variance		Variance %	
Sales revenue	$ 4,314	$ 4,300	$ 14	F	0.3%	F
Less: Variable expenses	2,236	2,235	1	U	0.0%	U
Contribution margin	2,078	2,065	13	F	0.6%	F
Less: Direct fixed expenses	1,633	1,630	3	U	0.2%	U
Segment margin	445	435	10	F	2.3%	F
Less: Allocated common expenses	36	35	1	U	2.9%	U
Operating income	$ 409	$ 400	$ 9	F	2.3%	F

NOTE: All figures in this exhibit, except for the actual operating income of each division for 2015 are hypothetical and used strictly for teaching purposes.

to assess the performance of investment centers: (1) return on investment and (2) residual income. To do this, we'll first need some financial data.

Exhibit 10-6 shows actual 2015 data for two of PepsiCo's divisions.[3] Statement of Financial Accounting Standards Number 131 (SFAS 131) requires publicly traded companies to disclose this type of segment information in the footnotes to their financial statements.[4]

---

[3] PepsiCo Inc. 2015 10(K).

[4] SFAS 131, "Disclosures about Segments of an Enterprise and Related Information," June 1997, Financial Accounting Standards Board, Norwalk, CT.

EXHIBIT 10-6 Division Information for PepsiCo Inc.

2015 Division Data (All figures are in millions of dollars)	Operating Income	Assets	Sales Revenue
PepsiCo Americas Beverages ("Beverage")	$2,785	$28,128	$20,618
Frito-Lay North America ("Snack")	$4,304	$5,375	$14,782

Exhibit 10-6 shows that the Frito-Lay North America division (henceforth referred to as the Snack division) is providing more profit to the company than is PepsiCo Americas Beverages division (henceforth referred to as the Beverage division). However, a simple comparison between the operating income of each division is misleading because it does not consider the size of each division. To adequately evaluate an investment center's financial performance, top managers assess each division's operating income *in relationship to its assets*. This relationship is typically evaluated by calculating the division's return on investment or residual income.

Return on Investment (ROI)

Return on investment (ROI) measures the amount of income an investment center earns relative to the size of its assets. Companies typically define ROI as follows:

$$\text{ROI} = \frac{\text{Operating income}}{\text{Total assets}}$$

Let's calculate the ROI for both the Snack division and the Beverage division, using the income and assets of each division found in Exhibit 10-6:

$$\text{Beverage Division ROI} = \frac{\$2{,}785}{\$28{,}128} = 9.9\% \text{ (rounded)}$$

$$\text{Snack Division ROI} = \frac{\$4{,}304}{\$5{,}375} = 80.1\% \text{ (rounded)}$$

The resulting ROI indicates that the Snack division is generating much more income for every dollar of its assets than is the Beverage division:

- The Beverage division earns nearly $0.10 on every $1.00 of assets.
- The Snack division earns just over $0.80 on every $1.00 of assets.

If you had $1,000 to invest, would you rather invest it in the Beverage division or the Snack division? Management would much rather have a 80% return on its investment than a 10% return. When top management decides how to invest excess funds, they often consider each division's ROI. A division with a higher ROI is more likely to receive extra funds because it has a track record of providing a higher return with the investment. However, perhaps management feels that operations could be improved in a weaker division by investing in new technology, plants, and equipment. Thus, the division with a weaker ROI may also receive an infusion of capital.

In addition to comparing ROI across divisions, management also compares a division's ROI across time to determine whether the division is becoming more or less profitable. For example, Exhibit 10-7 shows the actual ROI of the two divisions over the past five years.

> **Why is this important?**
>
> "**ROI** is one of the most commonly used **performance** metrics. It allows management to view profitability in **relation** to the size of the **investment**. Just like with your own personal investments, the **higher** the return, the **better**."

EXHIBIT 10-7 Actual Division ROI over Time (rounded)

ROI (rounded)	2015	2014	2013	2012	2011
Beverage	10%	8%	9%	10%	11%
Snack	80%	76%	73%	68%	67%

The ROI of the Snack division has been trending upward over the last five years, showing just how profitable this division is to PepsiCo. However, the Beverage division's ROI has been relatively constant over the past five years. As with variances, management will investigate significant changes in ROI.

In addition to benchmarking ROI over time, management often benchmarks divisional ROI with other companies in the same industry to determine how each division is performing compared to its competitors. For example, PepsiCo may benchmark its ROI against that of the Coca-Cola Company.

Sales Margin and Capital Turnover

To determine what is driving a division's ROI, management often restates the ROI equation in its expanded form:

$$\text{ROI} = \frac{\text{Operating income}}{\text{Sales}} \times \frac{\text{Sales}}{\text{Total assets}} = \frac{\text{Operating income}}{\text{Total assets}}$$

Notice that sales, or sales revenue, is incorporated in the denominator of the first term and in the numerator of the second term. When the two terms are multiplied together, sales revenue cancels out, leaving the original ROI formula.

Why do managers rewrite the ROI formula this way? Because it helps them better understand how they can improve their ROI. The first term in the expanded equation is the **sales margin**, which focuses on profitability by showing how much operating income the division earns on every $1 of sales revenue. Sales margin is defined as:

$$\text{Sales margin} = \frac{\text{Operating income}}{\text{Sales}}$$

Let's calculate each division's sales margin using the information in Exhibit 10-6:

$$\text{Beverage Division Sales Margin} = \frac{\$2{,}785}{\$20{,}618} = 13.5\% \text{ (rounded)}$$

$$\text{Snack Division Sales Margin} = \frac{\$4{,}304}{\$14{,}782} = 29.1\% \text{ (rounded)}$$

The Beverage division is earning nearly $0.14 on every $1.00 of sales revenue, whereas the Snack division is earning about $0.29 on every $1.00 of sales revenue. Overall, the products in the Snack division are twice as profitable as the products in the Beverage division. To improve this statistic, the division manager needs to focus on cutting costs so that more operating income can be earned for every dollar of sales revenue. However, they'll need to be careful in cutting costs, so as not to jeopardize the long-term success of the division.

Next, let's consider each division's **capital turnover**, which focuses on how efficiently the division uses its assets to generate sales revenue. Capital turnover is defined as:

$$\text{Capital turnover} = \frac{\text{Sales}}{\text{Total assets}}$$

Let's calculate each division's capital turnover using the information from Exhibit 10-6:

$$\text{Beverage Division Capital Turnover} = \frac{\$20{,}618}{\$28{,}128} = 0.73 \text{ (rounded)}$$

$$\text{Snack Division Capital Turnover} = \frac{\$14{,}782}{\$5{,}375} = 2.75 \text{ (rounded)}$$

The Beverage division has a capital turnover of 0.73, which means the division generates $0.73 of sales revenue with every $1 of assets. The Snack division generates $2.75 of sales revenue with every $1.00 of assets. The Snack division uses its assets more efficiently in generating sales than does the Beverage division. To improve this statistic, the Beverage division manager should try to reduce or eliminate nonproductive assets—for example, by collecting accounts receivables more aggressively or decreasing inventory levels.

As the following table shows, the Snack division's ROI is higher than that of the Beverage division because (1) the division is earning more profit on every dollar of sales *and* (2) the division is generating more sales revenue with every dollar of assets:

	Sales Margin	×	Capital Turnover	= ROI
Beverage	13.5%	×	0.73	= 9.9% (rounded)
Snack	29.1%	×	2.75	= 80.1% (rounded)

Residual Income (RI)

Rather than using ROI to evaluate the performance of their investment centers, many companies use the concept of residual income. Similar to ROI, the residual income calculation is based on both the division's operating income and its assets, thereby measuring the division's profitability with respect to the size of its assets. However, the residual income calculation incorporates one more important piece of information: management's target rate of return. The target rate of return is the minimum acceptable rate of return that top management expects a division to earn with its assets. Management's target rate of return is based on many factors. Some of these factors include:

- the risk level of the division's business
- interest rates
- investors' expectations
- return being earned by other divisions
- general economic conditions

As these factors change over time, management's target rate of return will also change.

Residual income (RI) determines whether the division has created any excess (or residual) income above and beyond management's expectations. Residual income is calculated as follows:

$$\text{RI} = \text{Operating income} - \text{Minimum acceptable income}$$

The minimum acceptable income is defined as top management's target rate of return multiplied by the division's total assets. Thus,

$$\text{RI} = \text{Operating income} - (\text{Target rate of return} \times \text{Total assets})$$

Notice in this equation that the RI compares the division's actual operating income with the minimum operating income that top management expects *given the size of the division's assets*. A positive RI means that the division's operating income exceeds top management's target rate of return. A negative RI means the division is not meeting the target rate of return.

Let's calculate the residual income for the Beverage division, assuming a 25% target rate of return.[5] Recall that all PepsiCo data were stated in millions.

$$\text{Beverage RI} = \$2{,}785 - (25\% \times \$28{,}128) = (\$4{,}247) \text{ million}$$

The Beverage division's RI is negative. This means that the division did not use its assets as effectively as top management expected, and it was therefore unable to achieve the minimum ROI of 25%. Recall that the Beverage division's ROI was approximately 10%.

Let's also calculate the RI for the Snack division:

$$\text{Snack division RI} = \$4{,}304 - (25\% \times \$5{,}375) = \$2{,}960 \text{ million}$$

The positive RI indicates that the Snack division exceeded top management's 25% target return expectations. The RI calculation also confirms what we learned about the Snack division's ROI. Recall that the Snack division's ROI was about 80%, which is higher than the targeted minimum of 25%.

Exhibit 10-8 summarizes the performance measures we have just discussed.

EXHIBIT 10-8 Summary of Investment Center Performance Measures

Performance Measure	Formula
ROI	$\text{ROI} = \dfrac{\text{Operating income}}{\text{Total assets}}$
Sales Margin	$\text{Sales margin} = \dfrac{\text{Operating income}}{\text{Sales}}$
Capital Turnover	$\text{Capital turnover} = \dfrac{\text{Sales}}{\text{Total assets}}$
Residual Income	$\text{RI} = \text{Operating income} - (\text{Target rate of return} \times \text{Total assets})$

Goal Congruence

Since the ROI calculation already shows managers whether or not the division has reached the target rate of return, why do some companies prefer using residual income rather than ROI? The answer is that residual income often leads to better goal congruence. For example, say a manager is considering investing in a new $100,000 piece of equipment that would provide $30,000 of annual income. Upper management would want the divisions to invest in this equipment because its return (30%) exceeds the target rate (25%). But what will the division managers do?

- If evaluated based on residual income, division managers will invest in the equipment because it will increase the division's residual income by $5,000 [= $30,000 − (25% × $100,000)].
- If evaluated based on ROI, the division manager's decision may depend on its current ROI. If the division's current ROI is *less than* 30%, the manager has an incentive to invest in the equipment in order to *increase* the division's overall ROI. However,

---

[5] Management's actual target rate of return is unknown; 25% is used simply for illustrative purposes.

if the division's current ROI is *greater than* 30%, investing in the equipment would *decrease* the division's ROI. In this case, the manager would probably *not* invest in the equipment.

Thus, residual income enhances goal congruence, whereas ROI may or may not.

Quaker Foods North America is another one of PepsiCo's divisions. The division had assets of $966 million, operating income of $695 million, and sales revenue of $2,636 million.
1. Compute Quaker's ROI, sales margin, and capital turnover.
2. Compute Quaker's residual income, assuming the minimum acceptable rate of return is 25%.

Please see page 652 for solutions.

Measurement Issues

The ROI and RI calculations appear to be very straightforward; however, management must come to some decisions before these calculations can be made. Most of these decisions involve how to measure the assets used in the ROI and RI calculations.

- **Which balance sheet date should we use?** Because total assets will differ between the beginning of the period and the end of the period, companies must choose a particular point in time for measuring assets. In the PepsiCo example, we chose to use total assets at the *end* of the year. Some companies use the average of the beginning of the year and the end of the year.

- **Should we include all assets?** Management must also decide if it wants to include *all* assets in the total asset figure. Many companies with retail locations are continually buying land on which to build future retail outlets. Until those stores are built and opened, the land (including any construction in progress) is a nonproductive asset, which is not generating any operating income. Including nonproductive assets in the total asset figure will drive down ROI and RI. Therefore, some firms do not include nonproductive assets in these calculations.

- **Should we use the gross book value or net book value of the assets?** The **gross book value** is the historical cost of the assets. The **net book value** is the historical cost of the assets *less* accumulated depreciation. Using the net book value of assets has a definite drawback. Because of depreciation, the net book value of assets continues to decrease over time until the assets are fully depreciated. As a result, ROI and RI get *larger over time simply because of depreciation* rather than from actual improvements in operations.

    In general, calculating ROI based on the net book value of assets gives managers an incentive to continue using old, outdated equipment because the net book value of the asset keeps decreasing. However, top management may want the division to invest in new technology to create operational efficiency. The long-term effects of using outdated equipment may be devastating as competitors use new technology to produce cheaper products and sell at lower prices. Thus, to create goal congruence, some companies prefer calculating ROI based on the gross book value of assets or even based on the assets' current replacement cost, rather than the assets' net book value.

- **Should we make other adjustments to income or assets?** Some companies use a modified residual income calculation referred to as economic value added (EVA®). To arrive at EVA, managers make several adjustments to the way income and assets are measured in the residual income formula. For example, research and development expenses are often added back to income (not viewed as expenses), while total assets are usually reduced by the company's current liabilities. EVA calculations are covered in more advanced accounting and finance textbooks.

Limitations of Financial Performance Evaluation

One serious drawback of financial performance measures is their short-term focus. Companies usually prepare performance reports and calculate ROI and RI using a time frame of one year or less. Given the short time frame, division managers have an incentive to take actions that will lead to an immediate increase in these measures, even if such actions may not be in the company's long-term interest (such as cutting back on R&D or advertising).

Many potentially positive actions, however, may take longer than one year to generate income at the targeted level. Many product life cycles start slow, even incurring losses in the early stages, before generating profit. If managers are evaluated on short-term financial performance only, they may be hesitant to introduce new products that may take time to generate acceptable profits.

As a potential remedy, management can measure financial performance using a longer time horizon, such as three to five years. Extending the time frame gives segment managers the incentive to think long term rather than short term and make decisions that will positively impact the company over the next several years.

As discussed earlier in this book, many companies are incorporating the triple bottom line (people, planet, and profit) into their performance evaluation systems. The second half of this chapter describes how the inclusion of nonfinancial performance metrics, including environmental metrics, can give managers a more balanced view of the company's performance.

What Is Transfer Pricing?

In large, diversified companies, one division will often buy products or components from another division rather than from an outside supplier. For example, one division of General Electric may purchase some of the parts it needs to produce wind turbines from another division that makes those parts. The price charged for the internal sale of product between two different divisions of the same company is known as the **transfer price**.

The transfer price becomes sales revenue for the selling division and a cost for the buying division. Therefore, the operating income, ROI, sales margin, and residual income of each division will be affected by the transfer price that is used. Setting a fair transfer price is often difficult since each division will want to maximize its own profits. The selling division will want the price to be as high as possible, while the buying division will want the price to be as low as possible.

4 Describe strategies and mechanisms for determining a transfer price

In selecting the transfer price, management's ultimate goal should be to optimize the company's *overall* profitability by encouraging a transfer to take place *only* if the company would benefit by the exchange. This benefit is usually a result of cost savings. For example, if excess capacity exists, the incremental cost of manufacturing additional product for an internal sale is the variable cost of production. Furthermore, the selling division can often avoid certain marketing or distribution costs on internal sales. **Vertical integration**, the practice of purchasing other companies within one's supply chain, is predicated on the notion that a company's profits can be maximized by owning one's supplier.

Strategies and Mechanisms for Determining a Transfer Price

The following strategies are often used to determine the transfer price.

1. **Market price:** If an outside market for the product exists, the market price is often viewed as the fairest price to use. The selling division will obtain the sales revenue it would have received on an outside sale, and the buying division will pay what it would have paid for product from an outside supplier. If the selling division can save on marketing or distribution costs, the market price could be reduced by all or a portion of the cost savings in arriving at the transfer price.

2. **Negotiated price:** Division managers negotiate until they reach agreement on a transfer price. The negotiated transfer price will usually be somewhere between the variable cost and the market price. The *lowest* acceptable price to the selling division will be the variable cost of producing and selling the product. Any lower price would result in a negative contribution margin to the selling division. The *highest* acceptable price to the buying division will be the market price. Any higher price would result in additional cost to the buying division. The disadvantage of this method is that negotiation takes time and effort, and may cause friction between company managers.

3. **Cost:** If no outside market for the product exists, then some definition of cost is often used to set the transfer price. As noted, variable cost would be the lowest fair price to use if excess capacity exists, whereas full absorption cost (including fixed manufacturing overhead) is also often viewed as a reasonable price. Additionally, a profit markup can be added to either definition of cost to arrive at a fair transfer price. The disadvantage of this method is that the selling division has no incentive to control costs since it will be reimbursed by the buying division for the costs it incurs.

These strategies are summarized in Exhibit 10-9.

> **Why is this important?**
>
> "Each division's **profits** will be affected by the **transfer price** that is used. The **selling division** will want the price to be as **high** as possible, whereas the **buying division** will want it to be as **low** as possible."

EXHIBIT 10-9 Strategies for Determining Transfer Price

	Advantages	Disadvantages	Considerations
Market Price	Usually viewed as fair by both parties.	Can only be used if an outside market exists.	The market price could be reduced by any cost savings occurring from the internal sale (e.g., marketing costs).
Negotiated Price	Allows division managers to act autonomously rather than being dictated a transfer price by top management.	Takes time and effort. May lead to friction (or better understanding) between division managers.	Negotiated transfer price will generally fall in the range between: • Variable cost (low end) • Market price (high end)
Cost -or- Cost Plus a Markup	Useful if a market price is not available.	Selling division has no incentive to control costs. A "fair" markup may be difficult to determine.	Several definitions of cost could be used, ranging from variable cost to full absorption cost.

Let's try an example. Assume a division of GE produces a component used in the assembly of wind turbines. The division's manufacturing costs and variable selling expenses related to the component are as follows:

	Cost per Unit
Direct materials	$500
Direct labor	75
Variable manufacturing overhead	100
Fixed manufacturing overhead (at current production level)	150
Variable selling expenses (only incurred on sales to outside customers)	80

A different division of GE is just beginning to get into the turbine assembly business and is interested in purchasing the component in-house rather than buying it from an outside supplier. The production division has sufficient excess capacity with which to make the extra components. Because of competition, the market price for this component is $1,000 regardless of whether the component is produced by GE or another company.

1. **What is the highest, and possibly fairest, acceptable transfer price?** The highest acceptable transfer price is the market price of $1,000. Many would say that this is also the fairest price because the selling division would receive, and the buying division would pay, what it normally would on the open market for the component.

2. **Assuming the transfer price is negotiated between the divisions, what would be the lowest acceptable transfer price?** Because there is excess capacity, fixed costs would not increase as a result of the additional production volume; therefore, fixed costs become irrelevant. The lowest acceptable price would be the variable costs incurred by the selling division for making the component and selling it in-house. The variable manufacturing costs (direct materials, direct labor, and variable manufacturing overhead) add up to $675. In this particular case, the $80 of variable selling expense would *not* be considered because it is only incurred on sales to outside customers. Thus, the lowest acceptable transfer price would be $675. A transfer price lower than $675 would result in a negative contribution margin, which would result in a loss to the selling division. If the $80 of variable selling expense would be incurred regardless of whether the sale was made in-house or to an outside customer, then the lowest acceptable transfer price would be $755 (= $675 + $80).

3. **If GE's policy requires all in-house transfers to occur at full absorption cost plus 10%, what transfer price would be used?** Assume that the increased production level needed to fill the transfer would result in fixed manufacturing overhead (MOH) decreasing by $25 per unit. The full absorption cost includes all manufacturing costs (direct materials, direct labor, variable MOH, and fixed MOH). After ramping up production to fill this in-house order, the fixed MOH per unit would be $125 (= $150 − $25). Thus, the full absorption cost would be $800 (= $500 + $75 + $100 + $125). The transfer price would be $880, which is 10% over the full absorption cost [= $800 + (10% × $800)].

Global Considerations

In addition to these strategies for setting the transfer price, management should consider the following factors if the divisions operate in different areas of the globe:

- Do the divisions operate under different taxing authorities such that income tax rates are higher for one division than the other?
- Would the amount paid for customs and duties be impacted by the transfer price?

If either of these situations exists, then management will want to carefully craft the transfer price to avoid as much income tax, customs, and duties as legally possible.

Keep in mind that internal sales should be encouraged only if the company, overall, would profit by the exchange taking place. This additional profit is usually the result of cost savings that occur from producing the product internally rather than buying it on the open market. Any transfer price selected is simply a mechanism for dividing this additional profit between the selling and the buying divisions.

Decision Guidelines

Performance Evaluation

Let's consider some issues regarding performance evaluation.

Decision	Guidelines
How do companies decentralize?	Managers determine the type of segmentation that best suits the company's strategy. Companies often decentralize by geographic area, product line, distribution channel, customer base, or business function.
What should managers be held responsible for?	**Cost center:** Manager is responsible for costs. **Revenue center:** Manager is responsible for revenues. **Profit center:** Manager is responsible for both revenues and costs and, therefore, profits. **Investment center:** Manager is responsible for revenues, costs, and the efficient use of the assets invested in the division.
How should upper management evaluate the performance of the responsibility centers and their managers?	Actual performance should be compared with the budget. Using management by exception, any large variances should be investigated, with an emphasis on uncovering information rather than placing blame.
How are variances interpreted?	Favorable (F) variances increase income from what was budgeted, while Unfavorable (U) variances decrease income. Favorable cost variances are not necessarily "good," and unfavorable cost variances are not necessarily "bad."
What is a segment margin?	A segment margin is the operating income achieved by the segment *before* subtracting any common fixed costs that have been allocated to the segment.
What additional measures are used to evaluate investment centers?	ROI and residual income—both performance measures evaluate the division in terms of how profitable the division is relative to the size of its assets.
How is ROI calculated?	$$\text{ROI} = \frac{\text{Operating income}}{\text{Total assets}}$$ ROI can also be calculated as: $$\text{Sales margin} \times \text{Capital turnover}$$
How is sales margin calculated?	$$\text{Sales margin} = \frac{\text{Operating income}}{\text{Sales}}$$ The sales margin tells managers how much operating income is earned on every \$1 of sales revenue.
How is capital turnover calculated?	$$\text{Capital turnover} = \frac{\text{Sales}}{\text{Total assets}}$$ The capital turnover tells managers how much sales revenue is generated for every \$1 of assets invested in the division.
How is residual income calculated?	$$\text{RI} = \text{Operating income} - (\text{Target rate of return} \times \text{Total assets})$$ If residual income is positive, it means the division has earned income in excess of upper management's target rate of return. If it is negative, then the division has not met management's expectations.
What is a transfer price, and how is it determined?	A transfer price is the price charged between divisions for the internal sale of a product. The transfer price is often based on the following: • Market price of product • Negotiated price (usually between variable cost and market price) • Cost (variable or absorption) or cost plus a markup

SUMMARY PROBLEM 1

The following table contains actual segment data for two of PepsiCo's geographic divisions: (1) Europe and Sub-Saharan Africa (ESSA) and (2) Asia, Middle East, and North Africa (AMENA).

2015 Data (All figures are in millions of dollars)	Operating Income	Assets	Sales Revenue
Europe, Sub-Saharan Africa (ESSA)	$1,081	$12,225	$10,510
Asia, Middle East, North Africa (AMENA)	$941	$5,901	$6,375

Requirements

1. Compute each division's ROI.
2. Compute each division's sales margin.
3. Compute each division's capital turnover.
4. Comment on the results of the preceding calculations.
5. Compute each division's residual income, assuming upper management desires a 25% minimum rate of return.
6. How does the ROI of these two divisions compare to that of the two divisions, Beverages and Snacks, discussed in the chapter?

■ SOLUTIONS

1. ROI

$$\text{ESSA ROI} = \frac{\$1,081}{\$12,225} = 8.8\% \text{ (rounded)}$$

$$\text{AMENA ROI} = \frac{\$941}{\$5,901} = 15.9\% \text{ (rounded)}$$

2. Sales Margin

$$\text{ESSA sales margin} = \frac{\$1,081}{\$10,510} = 10.3\% \text{ (rounded)}$$

$$\text{AMENA sales margin} = \frac{\$941}{\$6,375} = 14.8\% \text{ (rounded)}$$

3. Capital Turnover

$$\text{ESSA capital turnover} = \frac{\$10,510}{\$12,225} = 0.86 \text{ (rounded)}$$

$$\text{AMENA capital turnover} = \frac{\$6,375}{\$5,901} = 1.08 \text{ (rounded)}$$

4. ESSA has a lower ROI (8.8%) than does AMENA (15.9%). The reason for AMENA's stronger performance lies both in its ability to generate more operating income on every dollar of sales, as shown by the sales margin (14.8% versus 10.3%), and its ability to generate more sales with its assets, as shown by the capital turnover rate (1.08 versus 0.86). To increase ROI, ESSA needs to concentrate on becoming more efficient with its assets in order to increase its capital turnover. At the same time, it needs to carefully cut costs, potentially through employing lean thinking, in order to increase its sales margin.

5. Residual Income

$$\text{ESSA Residual income} = \$1{,}081 - (25\% \times \$12{,}225) = (\$1{,}975) \text{ million (rounded)}$$

$$\text{AMENA Residual income} = \$941 - (25\% \times \$5{,}901) = (\$534) \text{ million (rounded)}$$

Assuming management's minimum acceptable rate of return is 25%, the negative residual income means that neither division is generating income at an acceptable level.

6. The ROI provided by ESSA (8.8%) and the ROI provided by AMENA (15.9%) are in the same range as the ROI provided by the Beverage division (9.9%) but are significantly lower than the ROI provided by the Snack division (80.1%).

How Do Managers Use Flexible Budgets to Evaluate Performance?

In the first part of this chapter, we looked at performance reports that compared actual costs with the original planning budget. There is nothing wrong with comparing actual results against the master planning budget, as we did in Exhibits 10-3, 10-4, and 10-5; many companies do so. However, managers can often gain better insights by comparing actual results against a **flexible budget**, which is a budget prepared for a different level of volume than the one originally anticipated.

To illustrate this concept, let's return to Tucson Tortilla, the company we used in Chapter 9 to illustrate budgeting. Exhibit 10-10 shows a performance report that compares actual results against the master planning budget for the month of January. The master budget figures are drawn from the sales budget (Exhibit 9-5), operating expenses budget (Exhibit 9-10), and the budgeted cost of goods sold (Exhibits 9-11 and 9-12), while the actual results were gathered from the company's general ledger. As discussed earlier in the chapter, performance reports are often shown in contribution margin format rather than in the traditional income statement format, although either format is acceptable.

5 Prepare and evaluate flexible budget performance reports

EXHIBIT 10-10 Master Budget Performance Report

	Actual	Master Budget	Master Budget Variance		Master Budget Variance %	
Tucson Tortilla						
Master Budget Performance Report						
For the Month Ended January 31						
Sales volume (number of cases sold)	32,370	30,000	2,370	F	7.9%	F
Sales revenue ($20 per case)	$ 653,874	$ 600,000	$ 53,874	F	9.0%	F
Less variable expenses:						
Cost of goods sold ($12.00 per case sold)	391,540	360,000	31,540	U	8.8%	U
Sales commission ($1.50 per case sold)	49,860	45,000	4,860	U	10.8%	U
Shipping expense ($2.00 per case sold)	62,180	60,000	2,180	U	3.6%	U
Bad debt expense (1% of credit sales)	6,270	4,800	1,470	U	30.6%	U
Contribution margin	$ 144,024	$ 130,200	$ 13,824	F	10.6%	F
Less fixed expenses:						
Salaries	23,000	20,000	3,000	U	15.0%	U
Office rent	4,000	4,000	0	F	0.0%	F
Depreciation	6,000	6,000	0	F	0.0%	F
Advertising	3,100	2,000	1,100	U	55.0%	U
Telephone and internet	980	1,000	20	F	2.0%	F
Operating income	$ 106,944	$ 97,200	$ 9,744	F	10.0%	F

NOTE: The company expects 80% of sales will be made on credit terms. Cost of Goods Sold is treated as a variable cost here for the sake of simplicity. All individual manufacturing cost variances are discussed in Chapter 11.

The difference between the actual revenues and expenses and the master planning budget is known as a **master budget variance**. This variance is really the result of an "apples-to-oranges" comparison. Why is this the case? Notice how the comparison is made between actual results for the *actual volume* of cases sold (32,370 cases) and the budgeted revenues and costs for the *planning volume* (30,000). Of course, we would expect the actual revenues and variable expenses to be higher than budgeted simply because sales volume was 7.9% higher than budgeted. However, we wouldn't expect fixed costs to change as long as the actual volume was still within the company's current relevant range. But notice that actual fixed expenses were 0% to 55% higher than expected. Management will want to understand why these variances occurred.

To provide more of an "apples-to-apples" comparison, many companies compare actual results to a flexible budget prepared *for the actual sales volume achieved* (32,370 cases).

This flexible budget will be used strictly for evaluating performance. Notice the distinction between the purposes of the two budgets:

- The original master budget for 30,000 cases was used for *planning purposes at the beginning of the period.*
- The new flexible budget for 32,370 cases will be used for *performance evaluation purposes at the end of the period.*

In essence, the flexible budget is the budget managers *would have* prepared at the beginning of the period if they had a crystal ball telling them the correct volume (32,370 cases rather than 30,000 cases). The flexible budget allows managers to compare actual revenues and expenses with what they would have expected given the actual sales volume. By creating a flexible budget, managers will be able to determine the portion of the master budget variance that is due to unanticipated changes in *volume* and the portion of the master budget variance that is due to factors *other than volume*.

Creating a Flexible Budget Performance Report

To create a flexible budget like the one shown in Exhibit 10-11, managers simply use the actual sales volume (32,370 cases) and the original budget assumptions (shown in parentheses on each line). For example, the flexible budget shown in bold font in Exhibit 10-11 includes the following calculations:

- Sales Revenue: 32,370 cases × $20 per case = $647,400
- Cost of Goods Sold: 32,370 cases × $12 per case = $388,440
- Sales Commission: 32,370 cases × $1.50 per case = $48,555
- Shipping Expense: 32,370 cases × $2.00 per case = $64,740
- Bad Debt Expense: $647,400 of flexible budget sales revenue × 80% credit sales × 1% = $5,179
- Fixed Operating Expense: the same as originally budgeted, assuming the actual volume falls within the company's current relevant range for fixed costs.

> **Why is this important?**
>
> "A **flexible** budget performance report allows management to make an **"apples-to-apples"** comparison between what **actually** happened and what would have been **budgeted** if management would have known, in advance, the **actual** sales **volume** for the period."

EXHIBIT 10-11 Flexible Budget Performance Report

Tucson Tortilla
Flexible Budget Performance Report
For the Month Ended January 31

	Actual	Flexible Budget Variance	Flexible Budget	Volume Variance	Master Budget
Sales volume (number of cases sold)	32,370		32,370		30,000
Sales revenue ($20 per case)	$ 653,874		$ 647,400		$ 600,000
Less variable expenses:					
Cost of goods sold ($12.00 per case sold)	391,540		388,440		360,000
Sales commission ($1.50 per case sold)	49,860		48,555		45,000
Shipping expense ($2.00 per case sold)	62,180		64,740		60,000
Bad debt expense (1% of credit sales)	6,270		5,179		4,800
Contribution margin	$ 144,024		$ 140,486		$ 130,200
Less fixed expenses:					
Salaries	23,000		20,000		20,000
Office rent	4,000		4,000		4,000
Depreciation	6,000		6,000		6,000
Advertising	3,100		2,000		2,000
Telephone and internet	980		1,000		1,000
Operating income	$ 106,944		$ 107,486		$ 97,200

NOTE: The company expects 80% of sales will be made on credit terms. Cost of Goods Sold is treated as a variable cost here for the sake of simplicity. All individual manufacturing cost variances are discussed in Chapter 11.

Notice how this performance report includes the same actual costs (on the left) and master budget figures (on the right) shown in Exhibit 10-10. The flexible budget is placed in the middle column of the performance report. Two columns flank the middle column: Flexible Budget Variance and Volume Variance.

Keep the following important rule of thumb in mind:

> The flexible budget shows what revenues and expenses should have been, given the actual sales volume. It is created using the original budget assumptions for variable costs per unit and fixed costs, but calculated using the *actual sales volume* rather than the planning sales volume.

Try It!

Sam operates his own summer lawn-mowing business using a truck and equipment used solely for business purposes. Sam budgets $10 per job for variable expenses (gas for his truck and equipment) and $500 per month for fixed expenses (insurance and lease payments). Sam expected to have 100 mowing jobs during the month of June but actually had 125.

How much should be reflected in the flexible budget for (1) variable expenses, (2) fixed expenses, and (3) total operating expenses?

Please see page 652 for solutions.

Volume Variance

The **volume variance** is the difference between the master budget and the flexible budget. Recall that the only difference between these two budgets is the *volume* of units on which they are based. They both use the *same* budget assumptions but a different volume. The master planning budget is based on 30,000 cases. The flexible budget is based on 32,370 cases. The volume variance arises *only* because the volume of cases actually sold differs from the volume originally anticipated in the master budget, hence the name *volume variance*. The volume variances are shown in blue ink in Exhibit 10-12.

EXHIBIT 10-12 Volume Variances

	Actual	Flexible Budget Variance	Flexible Budget	Volume Variance		Master Budget
Tucson Tortilla						
Flexible Budget Performance Report						
For the Month Ended January 31						
Sales volume (number of cases sold)	32,370		32,370	2,370	F	30,000
Sales revenue ($20 per case)	$ 653,874		$ 647,400	47,400	F	$ 600,000
Less variable expenses:						
Cost of goods sold ($12.00 per case sold)	391,540		388,440	28,440	U	360,000
Sales commission ($1.50 per case sold)	49,860		48,555	3,555	U	45,000
Shipping expense ($2.00 per case sold)	62,180		64,740	4,740	U	60,000
Bad debt expense (1% of credit sales)	6,270		5,179	379	U	4,800
Contribution margin	$ 144,024		$ 140,486	$ 10,286	F	$ 130,200
Less fixed expenses:						
Salaries	23,000		20,000	0	F	20,000
Office rent	4,000		4,000	0	F	4,000
Depreciation	6,000		6,000	0	F	6,000
Advertising	3,100		2,000	0	F	2,000
Telephone and internet	980		1,000	0	F	1,000
Operating income	$ 106,944		$ 107,486	$ 10,286	F	$ 97,200

NOTE: For determining whether the volume variance is favorable or unfavorable, keep in mind that the master budget was the original goal. Therefore, the flexible budget is evaluated against the master budget goal.

The volume variance represents the portion of the master budget variance in Exhibit 10-10 that management would expect considering that 2,370 more cases were sold than originally anticipated. For example, because of the increase in sales volume, the volume variance shows that

- sales revenue *should have been* $47,400 higher than originally budgeted, Cost of Goods Sold *should have been* $28,440 higher than originally budgeted (and so forth with the other variable expenses),
- Fixed expenses *should have had zero variance*, and
- operating income *should have been* $10,286 higher than originally budgeted.

However, the master budget variance in Exhibit 10-10 revealed that

- sales revenue was *actually* $53,874 higher than budgeted, rather than $47,400 higher,
- Cost of Goods Sold was *actually* $31,540 higher than budgeted, rather than $28,440 higher (and so forth with the other variable expenses),
- some of the fixed costs were *actually* higher than budgeted, and
- operating income was *actually* $9,744 higher than budgeted rather than $10,286 higher.

So, why were actual revenues and expenses still higher than they should have been, even considering the increase in number of cases sold? The answers can be found in the flexible budget variance.

Flexible Budget Variance

The **flexible budget variance** is the difference between the flexible budget and actual results. The flexible budget variances are shown in dark orange ink in Exhibit 10-13.

EXHIBIT 10-13 Flexible Budget Variances and Volume Variances

	A	B	C	D	E	F	G	H
1				Tucson Tortilla				
2				Flexible Budget Performance Report				
3				For the Month Ended January 31				
4								
5		Actual	Flexible Budget Variance		Flexible Budget	Volume Variance		Master Budget
6	Sales volume (number of cases sold)	32,370			32,370	2,370	F	30,000
7								
8	Sales revenue ($20 per case)	$ 653,874	$ 6,474	F	$ 647,400	47,400	F	$ 600,000
9	Less variable expenses:							
10	Cost of goods sold ($12.00 per case sold)	391,540	3,100	U	388,440	28,440	U	360,000
11	Sales commission ($1.50 per case sold)	49,860	1,305	U	48,555	3,555	U	45,000
12	Shipping expense ($2.00 per case sold)	62,180	2,560	F	64,740	4,740	U	60,000
13	Bad debt expense (1% of credit sales)	6,270	1,091	U	5,179	379	U	4,800
14	Contribution margin	$ 144,024	$ 3,538	F	$ 140,486	10,286	F	$ 130,200
15	Less fixed expenses:							
16	Salaries	23,000	3,000	U	20,000	0	F	20,000
17	Office rent	4,000	0	F	4,000	0	F	4,000
18	Depreciation	6,000	0	F	6,000	0	F	6,000
19	Advertising	3,100	1,100	U	2,000	0	F	2,000
20	Telephone and internet	980	20	F	1,000	0	F	1,000
21	Operating income	$ 106,944	$ 542	U	$ 107,486	10,286	F	$ 97,200
22								

Because all variances related to volume have already been accounted for through the volume variance, the flexible budget variance highlights *causes other than volume*. For example:

- The $6,474 F variance for sales revenue means that the cases were sold at an average price *higher* than $20 per case.
- The $3,100 U variance for Cost of Goods Sold means that the cases cost more to make than $12.00 per case (we'll delve into this deeper in Chapter 11).

- The $1,305 U variance for commission expense means that the commissions were paid at a rate *higher* than $1.50 per case.
- The $2,560 F variance for shipping expense means that the shipping costs were *lower* than $2.00 per case.
- The $1,091 U variance for bad debt expense means that either more than 80% of sales were made on credit or bad debts were expensed at a rate greater than 1%.
- The fixed costs variances mean that factors other than volume caused some fixed costs to be different from what was originally planned.

Underlying Causes of the Variances

Now that we have prepared a flexible budget performance report, it's easy to see how the master budget variance in Exhibit 10-10 can be viewed as a combination of two separate variances, (1) the volume variance and (2) the flexible budget variance. For example we can see how the $9,744 F master budget variance for operating income shown in Exhibit 10-10 was the result not only of higher volume, but also of other factors. In fact, Exhibit 10-13 shows that the higher volume should have resulted in $10,286 of additional operating income, but other factors increased a number of Tucson Tortilla's costs, preventing the company from realizing the full effect of the increased volume.

Exhibit 10-14 shows that the master budget variance can be a combination of *favorable* variances (as in Panel A), a combination of *unfavorable* variances (as in Panel B), or a combination of one favorable variance *and* one unfavorable variance (as in Panel C).

EXHIBIT 10-14 Master Budget Variance

For example, in Panel C we see that the variances for Shipping Expenses consist of a *favorable* flexible budget variance ($2,560 F) and an *unfavorable* volume variance ($4,740 U). Together, these two variances *net* to an unfavorable master budget variance of $2,180 U. This example illustrates why it's important to separate the overall master budget variance into its two components. Only by separating the variances would a manager know that the shipping expenses were actually lower per case than anticipated but higher overall due to the volume of cases shipped.

Investigating Causes for the Variances

As discussed in the first half of the chapter, managers will use *management by exception* to determine which variances to investigate. Upper management will rely on the managers of each responsibility center to provide answers to their inquiries. At other times, upper management knows the reasons for the variances, yet needs the performance report to understand how their operational decisions affected the company's finances.

For example, let's assume that upper management decided to modify its sales strategy from the original plan found in the master budget. In an attempt to increase sales, upper management decided to

- spend more on advertising,
- increase the salaries of the sales staff,
- pay a higher sales commission per case, and
- ease credit terms so that more customers qualified for credit, rather than COD terms.

The unfavorable *flexible budget variances* for advertising, salaries, commissions, and bad debt expense shown in Exhibit 10-13 reflect these operational changes. However, the variances for sales revenue shown in Exhibit 10-13 also show the positive effect of these changes: the additional sales revenue was more than enough to offset the increased costs. Not only was extra sales volume generated, but sales were also made at a higher price per case than budgeted (as shown by the favorable flexible budget variance for sales revenue). Finally, as a result of the increased volume, management was able to negotiate a lower shipping cost per case, resulting in a favorable flexible budget variance for shipping. All in all, operating income was higher than originally planned, so management's strategy paid off.

Manufacturing Cost Variances

Manufacturing cost variances receive a great deal of attention from management. The flexible budget variance is often separated into more detailed variances to better illuminate why the variance occurred. For example, was the flexible budget variance for Cost of Goods Sold due to the direct materials, direct labor, or manufacturing overhead that went into making these products? Perhaps it was due to a combination of all three. Furthermore, did the variance result from using more of these manufacturing inputs than originally anticipated (for example, more direct labor hours) or because the price of the inputs changed (for example, a higher average wage rate for factory employees)? Chapter 11 is devoted to explaining how managers dig deeply into the manufacturing cost variances to better understand why they occur.

▶ Try It!

Sam operates his own summer lawn-mowing company using a truck and equipment dedicated solely to business operations. Complete the flexible budget performance report below to answer the following questions:

1. What is the volume variance for total operating expenses? Favorable or unfavorable?
2. What is the flexible budget variance for total operating expenses? Favorable or unfavorable?
3. What is the master budget variance for total operating expenses? Favorable or unfavorable?

	A	B	C D	E	F	G	H
1	**Sam's Mowing Business** **Flexible Budget Performance Report for June**	**Actual**	**Flexible Budget Variance**	**Flexible Budget**	**Volume Variance**		**Master Budget**
2	Sales volume (number of mowing jobs)	125		125			100
3							
4	Operating expenses:						
5	Variable operating expenses ($10 per job)	$ 1,370		$ 1,250			$ 1,000
6	Fixed operating expenses ($500 per month)	475		500			500
7	Total operating expenses	$ 1,845		$ 1,750			$ 1,500
8							

Please see page 652 for solutions.

How Do Companies Incorporate Nonfinancial Performance Measurement?

In the past, performance evaluation systems revolved almost entirely around *financial* performance. On the one hand, this focus makes sense because one of the primary goals of any company, even those companies that adhere to the notion of a triple bottom line (profit, people, and planet), is to generate profit for its owners. On the other hand, *current* financial performance tends to reveal the results of *past* decisions and actions rather than indicate *future* performance of the company. As a result, financial performance measures are known as <u>lag indicators</u>. Management also needs <u>lead indicators</u>, which are performance measures that predict future performance.

6 Describe the balanced scorecard and identify KPIs for each perspective

> **Why is this important?**
> "Rather than **focusing** strictly on financial performance, the **balanced scorecard** includes **operational** performance measures that give managers a **holistic** view of the company's **performance**."

The Balanced Scorecard

In the early 1990s, Robert Kaplan and David Norton introduced the <u>balanced scorecard</u>.[6] The balanced scorecard recognizes that management must consider *both* financial performance measures *and* operational performance measures when judging the performance of a company and its segments. These measures should be linked with the company's goals and its strategy for achieving those goals. The balanced scorecard represents a major shift in corporate performance measurement: Financial indicators are no longer the sole measure of performance; they are now only *one* measure among a broader set of performance measures. Keeping score of operational performance measures *and* traditional financial performance measures gives management a "balanced," comprehensive view of the organization.

The Four Perspectives of the Balanced Scorecard

The balanced scorecard views the company from four different perspectives, each of which evaluates a specific aspect of organizational performance:

1. Financial perspective
2. Customer perspective
3. Internal business perspective
4. Learning and growth perspective

Exhibit 10-15 on the next page illustrates how the company's strategy affects, and, in turn, is affected by all four perspectives. In addition, it shows the cause-and-effect relationship linking the four perspectives. Take a moment to look at it now.

Companies that adopt the balanced scorecard develop specific objectives they want to achieve within each of the four perspectives. These objectives are critical to the company's overall success. As shown in Exhibit 10-16, companies use <u>key performance indicators (KPIs)</u>, which are summary performance metrics, to assess how well they are achieving their goals. For example, the company could use "*average customer satisfaction rating*" as a KPI to measure the company's ability to please customers. "*Number of warranty claims*" could be used to measure the company's ability to produce quality products.

KPIs are continually measured and are reported on a <u>performance scorecard</u> or performance dashboard, a report that allows managers to visually monitor and focus on managing the company's key activities and strategies as well as business risks. Performance dashboards are often updated in real time, using data from the company's ERP

---

[6] Robert Kaplan and David Norton, "The Balanced Scorecard—Measures That Drive Performance," *Harvard Business Review on Measuring Corporate Performance*, Boston, 1991, pp. 123–145; and Robert Kaplan and David Norton, *Translating Strategy into Action: The Balanced Scorecard*, Boston, Harvard Business School Press, 1996.

EXHIBIT 10-15 The Four Perspectives of the Balanced Scorecard

EXHIBIT 10-16 Linking Company Goals to Key Performance Indicators

system.[7] Short-term and long-term targets for each KPI should also be displayed on the dashboard or scorecard so that managers can determine whether the company is improving and moving toward each objective, or whether new strategies need to be developed. To focus attention on the most critical elements to success and to prevent information overload, management should use only a few KPIs for each balanced scorecard perspective.

Let's now consider each of the perspectives and how they are linked together. We'll also present some of the more commonly used KPIs.

---

[7] http://www.forbes.com/sites/davelavinsky/2013/09/06/executive-dashboards-what-they-are-why-every-business-needs-one/#658ffc657568

Financial Perspective

The financial perspective helps managers answer the question, *"How do we look to shareholders?"* Shareholders are primarily concerned with the company's profitability. As shown in Exhibit 10-17, managers must continually attempt to increase profits through the following:

1. **increasing revenue:** introducing new products, gaining new customers, expanding into new markets
2. **controlling costs:** seeking to minimize costs without jeopardizing quality or long-run success, eliminating costs associated with wasteful activities
3. **increasing productivity:** using existing assets as efficiently as possible

> **Common KPIs:** *sales revenue growth, sales margin, gross margin percentage, capital turnover, ROI, residual income, earnings per share*

EXHIBIT 10-17 Financial Perspective

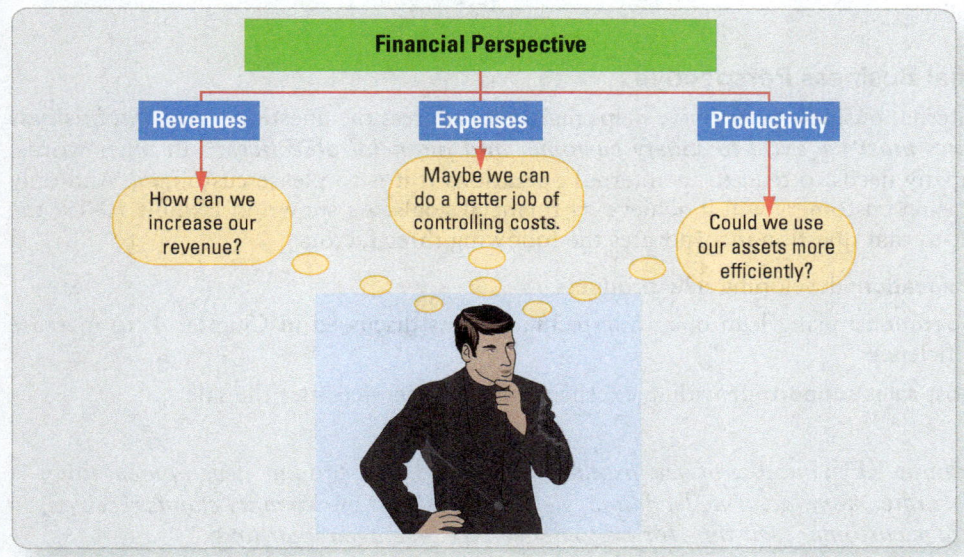

Customer Perspective

The customer perspective helps managers evaluate the question, *"How do customers see us?"* Customer satisfaction is a top priority for long-term success. If customers aren't happy, they won't come back. Therefore, customer satisfaction is critical for the company to achieve its financial goals.

As shown in Exhibit 10-18, customers are typically concerned with four product or service attributes:

1. **price:** the lower, the better
2. **quality:** the higher, the better
3. **sales service:** the importance of knowledgeable and helpful salespeople
4. **delivery time:** the shorter, the better

> **Common KPIs:** *average customer satisfaction rating, percentage of market share, increase in the number of customers, number of repeat customers, rate of on-time deliveries.*

EXHIBIT 10-18 Customer Perspective

Internal Business Perspective

The internal business perspective helps managers address the question, *"At what business processes must we excel to satisfy customer and financial objectives?"* In other words, a company needs to tend to its internal operations if it is to please customers. And only by pleasing customers will it achieve its financial goals. As shown in Exhibit 10-19, the answer to that question incorporates the following three factors:

1. **innovation:** developing new products
2. **operations:** using lean operating techniques, as discussed in Chapter 4, to increase efficiency
3. **post-sales support:** providing excellent customer service after the sale

> **Common KPIs:** *number of new products developed, new product development time, defect rate, manufacturing lead time, yield rate, number of warranty claims received, average customer wait time for customer service, average repair time*

EXHIBIT 10-19 Internal Business Perspective

Learning and Growth Perspective

The learning and growth perspective helps managers assess the question, *"Can we continue to improve and create value?"* Much of a company's success boils down to its people. A company cannot be successful in the other perspectives (financial, customer, internal operations) if it does not have the right people in the right positions, a solid and ethical leadership team, and the information systems that employees need. Therefore, the learning and growth perspective lays the foundation needed for success in the other perspectives. As shown in Exhibit 10-20, the learning and growth perspective focuses on the following three factors:

1. **employee capabilities:** critical and creative thinkers, skilled, knowledgeable, and motivated
2. **information system capabilities:** a system that provides timely and accurate data
3. **the company's "climate for action":** the corporate culture supports communication, teamwork, change, and employee growth

> **Common KPIs:** *hours of employee training, employee satisfaction, employee turnover, percentage of processes with real-time feedback, percentage of employees with access to real-time data, number of employee suggestions implemented, percentage of employees involved in problem solving teams, employee rating of communication and corporate culture*

EXHIBIT 10-20 Learning and Growth Perspective

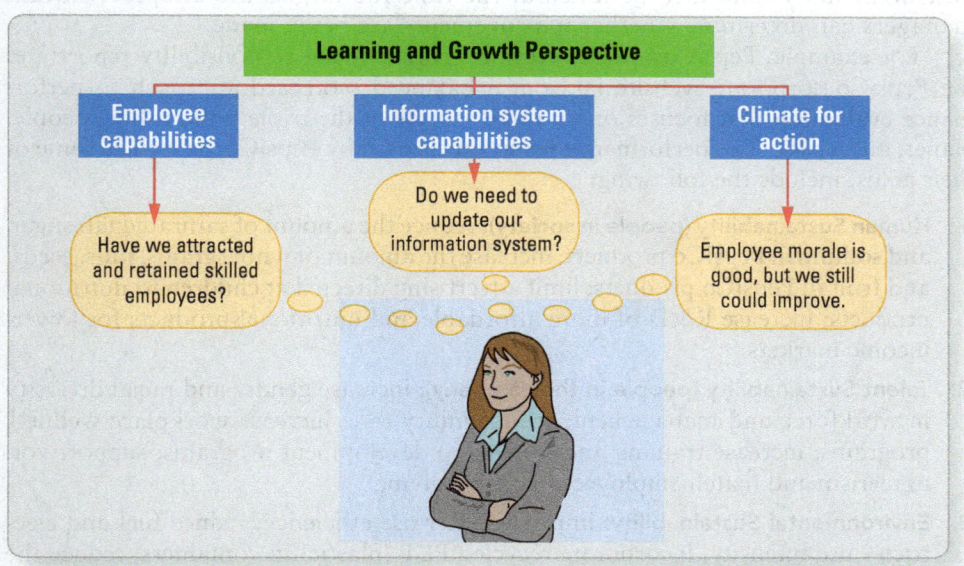

In summary, the balanced scorecard focuses on measuring those aspects of a company's operations that are critical to its success. By focusing on more than just financial metrics, it gives management a broader and more holistic view of the company's performance.

Sustainability and Performance Evaluation

Companies that embrace sustainability, like PepsiCo, incorporate sustainability-related KPIs in their performance evaluation system. Some companies will integrate sustainability-related KPIs into the four traditional balanced scorecard perspectives while others will include separate sustainability, community, or corporate responsibility sections.

For example, KPIs that fit into the four traditional perspectives might include the following:

- Financial perspective: *water cost, recycling revenues, waste-disposal costs*
- Customer perspective: *number of green products, percentage of products reclaimed after use*
- Internal Business perspective: *energy consumption, water consumption, greenhouse gas emissions*
- Learning and Growth perspective: *number of functions with environmental responsibilities, management attention to environmental issues*

Alternatively, companies may choose to add a "Sustainability" or "Community" perspective to their balanced scorecards. For example a community perspective might include the following KPIs:

- Community perspective: *percentage of profit donated to local schools and organizations, percentage of materials sourced locally, product safety ratings, number of hours devoted to local volunteering*

KPIs relating to sustainability and social responsibility should be objective and measurable, with both short-term and long-term targets specified. Baseline measurements should also be taken at the time the targets are adopted, so that managers can determine whether improvements are being made.

For example, PepsiCo's most recent corporate social responsibility report and the PepsiCo corporate website laid out a balanced scorecard approach to performance evaluation that focuses on all three aspects of the triple bottom line: people, planet, and profit. The performance perspectives used by PepsiCo, as well as some of their goals, include the following:

1. **Human Sustainability (people in society):** reduce the amount of saturated fat, sugar, and sodium in PepsiCo products; increase the amount of whole grains, nuts, seeds, and fruit in PepsiCo products; limit advertising directed at children to nutritional products; increase R&D of more affordable and nutritional products for lower-income markets

2. **Talent Sustainability (people in the company):** increase gender and racial diversity in workforce and management; reduce injury rate; increase workplace wellness programs; increase training and leadership development programs; support volunteerism and match employee charitable giving

3. **Environmental Sustainability:** improve water-use efficiency; reduce fuel and electricity use intensity, incorporate recycled PET (plastic) in containers; reduce the amount of material in packaging; reduce waste to landfill; reduce supply-chain greenhouse gas emissions; promote beverage container recycling programs; increase use of sustainable agricultural practices

4. **Financial Performance:** grow international revenues; increase operating profit; improve brand equity scores; increase market share; deliver high shareholder returns

5. **Responsible and Sustainable Sourcing:** increase use of minority- and women-owned vendors; increase use of suppliers that participate in the carbon disclosure project program

6. **Community and Philanthropy:** increase the gross dollar amount and percentage of operating income contributed through the Pepsi Foundation.

PepsiCo reports the KPIs used to evaluate these goals on its corporate website.

See Exercises E10-29A and E10-42B

Decision Guidelines

Performance Evaluation and the Balanced Scorecard

Decision	Guidelines
How can flexible budgets aid in performance evaluation?	There is nothing wrong with comparing actual results against the master planning budget. However, managers usually gain additional insights by comparing actual results against a flexible budget, which is a budget prepared for the actual volume achieved, rather than the volume originally used for planning purposes.
What is the master budget variance?	The master budget variance is the difference between the actual results and the master planning budget. This variance can be decomposed into two separate variances: (1) a volume variance and (2) a flexible budget variance, by first creating a flexible budget.
How is a flexible budget prepared?	A flexible budget is prepared by multiplying the budgeted revenue per unit and the budgeted variable cost per unit by the actual volume achieved. Since total fixed costs are not affected by changes in volume, they are the same on the flexible budget as they were on the original master budget. The flexible budget presents the revenues and expenses that management would have expected, given the actual volume achieved.
What is the volume variance?	The volume variance is the difference between the master planning budget and the flexible budget. It represents the portion of the master budget variance that was caused by actual volume being different than originally budgeted.
What is the flexible budget variance?	The flexible budget variance is the difference between actual costs and the flexible budget. It represents the portion of the master budget variance that was caused by factors *other than* volume differences.
Should the performance evaluation system include lag or lead measures?	Better performance evaluation systems include *both* lag and lead measures. Lag measures reveal the results of past actions, while lead measures predict future performance.
What are the four balanced scorecard perspectives?	1. Financial perspective 2. Customer perspective 3. Internal business perspective 4. Learning and growth perspective
How do companies include sustainability-related KPIs in their balanced scorecards?	Companies either include sustainability-related KPIs within each of the four perspectives, or they add separate perspectives for sustainability and/or corporate responsibility.

SUMMARY PROBLEM 2

Requirements

1. Each of the following describes a key performance indicator. Determine which of the balanced scorecard perspectives is being addressed (financial, customer, internal business, or learning and growth).
    a. Employee turnover
    b. Earnings per share
    c. Percentage of on-time deliveries
    d. Revenue growth rate
    e. Percentage of defects discovered during manufacturing
    f. Number of warranties claimed
    g. New product development time
    h. Number of repeat customers
    i. Number of employee suggestions implemented

2. Read the following company initiatives and determine which of the balanced scorecard perspectives is being addressed (financial, customer, internal business, or learning and growth).
    a. Purchasing efficient production equipment
    b. Providing employee training
    c. Updating retail store lighting to improve customer experience
    d. Paying quarterly dividends
    e. Updating the company's information system

■ SOLUTIONS

Requirement 1
a. Learning and growth
b. Financial
c. Customer
d. Financial
e. Internal business
f. Internal business
g. Internal business
h. Customer
i. Learning and growth

Requirement 2
a. Internal business
b. Learning and growth
c. Customer
d. Financial
e. Learning and growth

END OF CHAPTER

Learning Objectives

- 1 Understand decentralization and describe different types of responsibility centers
- 2 Develop performance reports
- 3 Calculate ROI, sales margin, and capital turnover
- 4 Describe strategies and mechanisms for determining a transfer price
- 5 Prepare and evaluate flexible budget performance reports
- 6 Describe the balanced scorecard and identify KPIs for each perspective

Accounting Vocabulary

Balanced Scorecard. (p. 609) A performance evaluation system that integrates financial and operational performance measures along four perspectives: financial, customer, internal business, and learning and growth.

Capital Turnover. (p. 593) Sales revenue divided by total assets. The capital turnover shows how much sales revenue is generated with every $1.00 of assets.

Common Fixed Expenses. (p. 590) Fixed expenses that *cannot* be traced to the segment.

Cost Center. (p. 586) A responsibility center in which managers are responsible for controlling costs.

Decentralize. (p. 584) A process where companies split their operations into different operating segments.

Direct Fixed Expenses. (p. 590) Fixed expenses that can be traced to the segment.

Favorable Variance. (p. 588) A variance that causes operating income to be higher than budgeted.

Flexible Budget. (p. 603) A summarized budget prepared for different levels of volume.

Flexible Budget Variance. (p. 606) The difference between the flexible budget and actual results. The flexible budget variances are due to *something other than volume*.

Goal Congruence. (p. 585) When the goals of the segment managers align with the goals of top management.

Gross Book Value. (p. 596) Historical cost of assets.

Investment Center. (p. 586) A responsibility center in which managers are responsible for generating revenues, controlling costs, and efficiently managing the division's assets.

Key Performance Indicators (KPIs). (p. 609) Summary performance metrics used to assess how well a company is achieving its goals.

Lag Indicators. (p. 609) Performance indicators that reveal the results of past actions and decisions.

Lead Indicators. (p. 609) Performance measures that predict future performance.

Management by Exception. (p. 589) A management technique in which managers only investigate budget variances that are relatively large.

Master Budget Variance. (p. 603) The difference between actual results and the master budget.

Net Book Value. (p. 596) Historical cost of assets less accumulated depreciation.

Performance Reports. (p. 588) Reports that compare actual results against budgeted figures.

Performance Scorecard or Performance Dashboard. (p. 609) A report displaying the measurement of KPIs, as well as their short-term and long-term targets.

Profit Center. (p. 586) A responsibility center in which managers are responsible for both revenues and costs, and therefore profits.

Residual Income. (p. 594) Operating income minus the minimum acceptable operating income given the size of the division's assets.

Responsibility Accounting. (p. 585) A system for evaluating the performance of each responsibility center and its manager.

Responsibility Center. (p. 585) A part of an organization whose manager is accountable for planning and controlling certain activities.

Return on Investment (ROI). (p. 592) Operating income divided by total assets. The ROI measures the profitability of a division relative to the size of its assets.

Revenue Center. (p. 586) A responsibility center in which managers are responsible for generating revenue.

Sales Margin. (p. 593) Operating income divided by sales revenue. The sales margin shows how much income is generated for every $1.00 of sales.

Segment Margin. (p. 589) The operating income generated by a profit or investment center *before* subtracting the common fixed costs that have been allocated to the center.

Transfer Price. (p. 597) The price charged for the internal sale of product between two different divisions of the same company.

Unfavorable Variance. (p. 588) A variance that causes operating income to be lower than budgeted.

Variance. (p. 588) The difference between actual figures and budgeted figures.

Vertical Integration. (p. 597) The acquisition of companies within one's supply chain.

Volume Variance. (p. 605) The difference between the master budget and the flexible budget. The volume variance arises *only* because the actual sales volume differs from the volume originally anticipated in the master budget.

Quick Check

1. *(Learning Objective 1)* Companies often decentralize their operations by
   a. product line.
   b. customer base.
   c. geographic area.
   d. all of the above.

2. *(Learning Objective 1)* Which of the following is *not* an advantage of decentralization?
   a. Improved customer relations
   b. Use of expert knowledge
   c. Frees top management's time
   d. Achieving goal congruence

3. *(Learning Objective 1)* In terms of responsibility centers, a large corporate division would be considered a(n)
   a. cost center.
   b. revenue center.
   c. profit center.
   d. investment center.

4. *(Learning Objective 2)* Which of the following is true?
   a. Favorable variances should always be interpreted as "good news" for the company.
   b. Management by exception means that managers investigate all unfavorable variances but not all favorable variances.
   c. Favorable variances are variances that cause operating income to be higher than budgeted.
   d. Unfavorable variances should always be interpreted as "bad news" for the company.

5. *(Learning Objective 2)* A segment margin is the operating income generated by subtracting
   a. only direct fixed expenses from a segment's contribution margin.
   b. only common fixed expenses from a segment's contribution margin.
   c. all expenses from a segment's sales revenue.
   d. all fixed expenses from a segment's contribution margin.

6. *(Learning Objective 3)* Return on investment (ROI) can be restated as which of the following?
   a. Sales margin ÷ capital turnover
   b. Sales margin × capital turnover
   c. Residual income ÷ sales margin
   d. Residual income × sales margin

7. *(Learning Objective 4)* Which of the following is *not* a valid strategy for determining a transfer price?
   a. Using a negotiated price
   b. Using some definition of cost
   c. Using the price set by GAAP
   d. Using the market price

8. *(Learning Objective 5)* Which of the following is *false*?
   a. The volume variance is due to causes other than volume.
   b. The difference between actual results and the master budget is called the master budget variance.
   c. The master budget variance can be split into two components: a volume variance and a flexible budget variance.
   d. The flexible budget is prepared using the actual volume achieved during the period.

9. *(Learning Objective 6)* "Number of new products developed" would be a key performance indicator (KPI) for which of the four balanced scorecard perspectives?
   a. Customer
   b. Internal business
   c. Financial
   d. Learning and growth

10. *(Learning Objective 6)* "Hours of employee training" would be a key performance indicator (KPI) for which of the four balanced scorecard perspectives?
    a. Customer
    b. Internal business
    c. Financial
    d. Learning and growth

Quick Check Answers

1. d 2. d 3. d 4. c 5. a 6. b 7. c 8. a 9. b 10. d

Short Exercises

S10-1 Identify and understand responsibility centers *(Learning Objective 1)*

Fill in the blanks with the word or phrase that best completes each sentence. Not all words and phrases are used, and some may be used more than once.

cost center	investment center	lower
revenue center	responsibility center	higher
profit center	the same	

a. The Foodservice Sales Territory Manager in charge of General Mills' Greater Baltimore/Washington, D.C., sales territory oversees a(n) _____.
b. The payroll department of Target Corporation, a retailer, is a(n) _____. _____ is any segment of the business whose manager is accountable for specific activities.
c. The Bakery Department of Whole Foods Market, Inc., would be considered to be a(n) _____.
d. The Procter & Gamble Company headquarters, located in Cincinnati, Ohio, would be a(n) _____.
e. The Floral Department at the Middletown, Maryland, Safeway grocery store would be considered to be a(n) _____.
f. Toyota Motor North America, a division of Toyota Motor Corporation, is a(n) _____.
g. The production line at the Honda plant in Lincoln, Alabama, where Honda Pilot sport utility vehicles are manufactured, is considered to be a(n) _____.
h. The Boise, Idaho, location of the Olive Garden chain restaurant would be a(n) _____.
i. Managers of cost and revenue centers are at _____ levels of the organization than are managers of investment centers.

S10-2 Identify types of responsibility centers *(Learning Objective 1)*

Identify each responsibility center as a cost center, a revenue center, a profit center, or an investment center.

a. Baskin-Robbins is a subsidiary of Dunkin' Brands; Dunkin' Brands owns and operates nearly 2,500 ice cream specialty stores in the United States.
b. The Legal Department of the Progressive Group of Insurance Companies prepares its budget and subsequent performance report on the basis of its expected expenses for the year.
c. The online division of David's Bridal, Inc., reports both revenues and expenses.
d. Time Warner Inc.'s investor relations website provides operating and financial information to investors and other interested parties.
e. The manager of the Speedway convenience store located on Verona Road in Madison, Wisconsin, is evaluated based on the store's revenues and expenses.
f. A charter airline records revenues and expenses for each airplane each month. Each airplane's performance report shows its income, including its revenues and expenses.
g. The manager of the southeastern sales territory is evaluated based on a comparison of current period sales against budgeted sales.
h. The Bakery Department of a Kroger grocery store reports income for the current year.

S10-3 Identify centralized and decentralized organizations (Learning Objective 1)

The following table lists a series of descriptions of decentralized organizations or centralized organizations. For each description, indicate whether that scenario is more typical of a decentralized organization or a centralized organization.

Characteristic	Decentralized (D) or Centralized (C)
a. Summit Corporation now has a single payroll department, a single human resource department, and a single administrative headquarters since the corporation "flattened" its organization structure.	
b. Crafty Times is a small, independent craft shop and is managed by its owner.	
c. The Terracotta Company, Inc., is managed by its owner, who oversees production, sales, engineering, and the other administrative functions.	
d. Cheshire Furniture, Inc., is divided into several operating units.	
e. Duffy Holdings wants its managers to be able to respond quickly to changes in local market demand so that the managers have the authority to make decisions about product offerings and pricing.	
f. Palm Springs Resorts and Hotels, Inc., wants to empower its managers to make decisions so that the managers' motivation is increased and retention of managers increases.	
g. Tanner Corporation has formal training programs for lower-level managers and has a policy that it promotes from within the company whenever possible.	

S10-4 Classify types of subunits (Learning Objective 1)

Each of the following managers has been given certain decision-making authority. Classify each manager according to the type of responsibility center he or she manages.

a. Managers of various corporate-owned Grand Hyatt locations
b. Manager of the complimentary breakfast buffet at the Hyatt Place in Richmond, Virginia
c. Manager (CEO) of the Hyatt Hotels Corporation
d. Manager of the Housekeeping Department for the Columbus Hyatt Regency Hotel
e. Manager of the Hyatt Place corporate division
f. Manager of Hyatt Hotel's central reservation office

S10-5 Calculate performance report variances (Learning Objective 2)

The following is a partial performance report for a revenue center for the Southwest Division of Hosta Restaurants.

	Hosta Restaurants			
	Sales Revenue—Southwest Division			
	For the Month Ended June 30			

Product	Actual Sales	Budgeted Sales	Variance	Variance Percentage
Food	$ 144,300	$ 148,000	?	?
Dessert	16,100	17,500	?	?
Bar	52,250	55,000	?	?
Catering	39,480	42,000	?	?

Fill in the missing amounts. Indicate whether each variance is favorable (F) or unfavorable (U).

S10-6 Calculate ROI, capital turnover, and sales margin *(Learning Objectives 3)*

Irvin Chemical Corporation has three divisions. Following is division information from the most recent year.

Division Information for Irvin Chemical
For the Year Ending December 31

(All information is in millions of dollars)	Operating Income	Assets	Sales Revenue
Functional Ingredients	$6,188	$13,000	$22,100
Consumer Markets	$1,290	$10,750	$21,500
Performance Materials	$4,375	$14,000	$17,500

For each of the three divisions, calculate sales margin, capital turnover, and return on investment (ROI).

Epic Sports Data Set used for S10-7 through S10-9:

Epic Sports Company makes snowboards, downhill skis, cross-country skis, skateboards, surfboards, and in-line skates. The company has found it beneficial to split operations into two divisions based on the climate required for the sport: Snow Sports and Non-Snow Sports. The following divisional information is available for the past year:

	Sales	Operating Income	Total Assets	Current Liabilities
Snow Sports	$5,800,000	$1,044,000	$4,500,000	$450,000
Non-Snow Sports	$8,800,000	$1,584,000	$6,400,000	$700,000

Epic's management has specified a target 16% rate of return.

S10-7 Calculate ROI *(Learning Objective 3)*

Refer to Epic Sports Data Set.

1. Calculate each division's ROI.
2. Top management has extra funds to invest. Which division will most likely receive those funds? Why?
3. Can you explain why one division's ROI is higher? How could management gain more insight?

S10-8 Compute sales margin and capital margin turnover *(Learning Objective 3)*

Refer to the Epic Sports Data Set.

1. Compute each division's sales margin. Interpret your results.
2. Compute each division's capital turnover (round to two decimal places). Interpret your results.
3. Use your answers to Question 2 along with your answers to Question 1 to recalculate ROI using the expanded formula. Do your answers agree with your ROI calculations in S10-7?

S10-9 Compute residual income *(Learning Objective 3)*

Refer to the Epic Sports Data Set. Compute each division's residual income. Interpret your results. Are your results consistent with each division's ROI?

S10-10 Analyze transfer price scenario *(Learning Objective 4)*

Dyson, the vacuum cleaner manufacturer, made a large investment in a battery technology firm, Sakti3. Sakti3 is a Michigan-based start-up that is working on a solid-state battery. These solid-state batteries would last approximately twice as long as current lithium-ion batteries. Solid-state batteries also do not use liquid electrolyte, the lithium-ion substance that can cause fires. The solid-state battery technology has not yet been perfected, but Dyson has made the gamble that it will be able to use these batteries in its products (including hand-held vacuums) within the next few years. Dyson plans to build a large battery factory for Sakti3 to produce these solid-state batteries. In addition to batteries for its hand-held vacuums, the factory will manufacture batteries for a wide variety of household products and for electric vehicles. When it moves into producing batteries for electric cars, Sakti3 will be competing with companies such as Tesla Motors, Panasonic, and LG Chem.

Requirements

1. Between Dyson and Sakti3, which is the selling division and which is the buying division with respect to solid-state batteries and transfer pricing?
2. Assume that the battery factory has been built in Michigan and is producing a variety of batteries that can be used both in Dyson's hand-held vacuums and in other companies' vacuums. List as many costs as you can imagine that might be incurred by the factory in the production of the batteries.
3. If Dyson uses "cost" as the basis for the internal transfer price for the Sakti3 batteries to be used in its hand-held vacuums, what costs (from the list in the preceding question) do you think should be included in the transfer price? Explain.

S10-11 Determine transfer price range *(Learning Objective 4)*

Dexter Manufacturing makes a variety of products, including lawn mowers. Dexter's Lawn Mower Division can use a component, K32, manufactured by Dexter's Electrical Division. The market price for K32 is $17 per unit. The variable cost per unit for K32 in the Electrical Division is $8, while the absorption cost per unit is $13. The divisions at Dexter use a negotiated price strategy to set transfer prices between divisions. The Electrical Division has excess capacity.

What is the lowest acceptable transfer price to the Electrical Division? What is the highest acceptable transfer price that the Lawn Mower Division would pay? Explain your answer.

S10-12 Interpret a performance report *(Learning Objective 5)*

The following is a partially completed performance report for Sunshine Pools.

	A	B	C	D	E	F	G	H
1				Sunshine Pools				
2			Flexible Budget Performance Report: Sales and Operating Expenses					
3				For the Year Ended April 30				
4								
5		Actual	Flexible Budget Variance		Flexible Budget	Volume Variance		Master Budget
6	Sales volume (number of pools installed)	5	?		?	?		4
7								
8	Sales revenue	$ 102,000	?		$ 108,000	?		$ 86,400
9	Operating expenses:							
10	Variable expenses	$ 50,000	?		$ 52,000	?		$ 41,600
11	Fixed expenses	24,000	?		28,100	?		28,100
12	Total operating expenses	$?	?		?	?		$?
13								

1. How many pools did Sunshine Pools originally think it would install in April?
2. How many pools did Sunshine Pools actually install in April?
3. How many pools is the flexible budget based on? Why?
4. What was the budgeted sales price per pool?
5. What was the budgeted variable cost per pool?
6. Define the flexible budget variance. What causes it?
7. Define the volume variance. What causes it?
8. Fill in the missing numbers in the performance report.

Performance Evaluation

S10-13 Complete a master budget performance report (Learning Objective 5)

The following table contains a hypothetical partial master budget performance report for New England Fudge Company. Fill in the missing amounts. Be sure to indicate whether variances are favorable (F) or unfavorable (U).

	A	B	C	D	E	F	G	H
1				New England Fudge Company				
2			Flexible Budget Performance Report: Sales and Operating Expenses					
3				For the Year Ended December 31				
4								
5		Actual	Flexible Budget Variance		Flexible Budget	Volume Variance		Master Budget
6	Sales volume (number of cases sold)	13,200			13,200			12,000
7								
8	Sales revenue ($26 per case)	$ 338,200			$ 343,200			$ 312,000
9	Less variable expenses:							
10	Sales expense ($2 per case sold)	$ 24,500			$ 26,400			$ 24,000
11	Shipping expense ($5 per case sold)	65,500			66,000			60,000
12	Contribution margin	248,200			250,800			228,000
13	Less fixed expenses:							
14	Salaries	12,200			10,800			10,800
15	Office rent	3,500			3,500			3,500
16	Operating income	$ 232,500			$ 236,500			$ 213,700
17								

S10-14 Classify KPIs by balanced scorecard perspective (Learning Objective 6)

Classify each of the following key performance indicators according to the balanced scorecard perspective it addresses. Choose from financial perspective, customer perspective, internal business perspective, or learning and growth perspective.

a. Employee satisfaction ratings
b. Return on Investment (ROI)
c. Gross margin growth
d. Number of information system upgrades completed
e. New product development time
f. Number of customer complaints
g. Number of new patents
h. Percentage of products with online help manuals
i. Customer satisfaction survey ratings
j. Downtime (the amount of time service is not available)
k. Percentage of orders filled each week
l. Employee turnover rate

S10-15 Use vocabulary terms (Learning Objectives 1, 2, 3, 4, 5, & 6)

Complete the following statements with one of the terms listed here. You may use a term more than once. Some terms may not be used at all.

Capital turnover	Direct fixed expenses	Flexible budget variance
Key performance indicators (KPIs)	Profit center	Sales margin
Common fixed expenses	Favorable variance	Goal congruence
Management by exception	Return on investment (ROI)	Unfavorable variance
Cost center	Flexible budget	Investment center
Master budget variance	Revenue center	Volume variance

a. Fixed expenses that can be traced to the segment are called _____.
b. _____ shows how much income is generated for every $1.00 of sales.
c. _____ are included on balanced scorecards and help managers assess how well the company's objectives are being met.

d. The difference between actual results and the master budget is called the _____.
e. When the goals of the segment managers in a company are the same, then _____ is achieved.
f. The local branch office of a national bank is considered to be a(n) _____.
g. Fixed expenses that cannot be traced to the segment are called _____.
h. A(n) _____ is a budget prepared for a different volume level than that which was originally anticipated.
i. The difference between the flexible budget and actual results is called the _____.
j. _____ measures the profitability of a division relative to the size of its assets.
k. If budgeted salary expense is higher than the actual salary expense, then a(n) _____ will result.
l. A(n) _____ manager is responsible for generating revenue.
m. The _____ arises only because the actual volume sold differs from the volume originally anticipated in the master budget.
n. _____ shows how much sales revenue is generated with every $1.00 of assets.
o. If budgeted sales revenue is greater than the actual sales revenue, then a(n) _____ will result.
p. _____ is a management technique in which managers only investigate budget variances that are relatively large.
q. The legal department of a manufacturer is considered to be a(n) _____.
r. The headquarters for an international consulting firm is considered to be a(n) _____.

ETHICS

S10-16   Identify ethical standards violated *(Learning Objectives 1, 2, 3, 4, 5, & 6)*

For each of the situations listed, identify the primary standard from the IMA *Statement of Ethical Professional Practice* that is violated (competence, confidentiality, integrity, or credibility). Refer to Exhibit 1-7 for the complete standard.

1. In casual conversation with friends on a Friday night, Peter talks about how transfer prices are set at the company where he is an accountant. As part of that conversation, he shares the variable costs of the company's main product.
2. Jake, the controller who oversees transfer policies at Nealy Industries, does not inform management that his sister is the principal partner in a consulting firm that is bidding on work at Nealy Industries.
3. In the year-end report to the board of directors, Connor, the controller, prepares the performance report. The board will base the annual bonuses on this report. Connor designs the report so that the favorable Key Performance Indicators (KPIs) are displayed prominently, while the KPIs that are unfavorable are either not included, or are buried deep in the later pages of the report so that they are unlikely to be seen.
4. Each month, Kate, a corporate controller, prepares segment reports for all of the divisions of her company. In these reports, she includes every general ledger account. As a result, the report for each division is several pages long and no one except Kate and her staff can interpret the reports.
5. In the past six years since he graduated with an accounting degree, Phil has not attended any continuing education seminars. A major part of Phil's job involves preparing performance reports. He has figured that he knows enough to do his job since he has not forgotten any relevant information from his college degree program.

EXERCISES Group A

E10-17A Identify type of responsibility center *(Learning Objective 1)*

Each of the following situations describes an organizational unit. Identify which type of responsibility center each underlined item is (cost, revenue, profit, or investment center).

Organization
a. <u>Sherwin-Williams Store #1933</u> is located in Copley, Ohio. The store sells paints, wallpapers, and supplies to do-it-yourself customers and to professional wall covering installers.
b. The <u>Accounting Research and Compliance Department</u> at FirstEnergy is responsible for researching how new accounting pronouncements and rules will impact FirstEnergy's financial statements.
c. The <u>Southwestern Sales Region</u> of McDermott Foods is responsible for selling the various product lines of McDermott.
d. The <u>Taxation Department</u> at Verizon Communications, Inc., is responsible for preparing the federal, state, and local income and franchise tax returns for the corporation.
e. The <u>Roseville Chipotle restaurant</u> in Minnesota, is owned by its parent Chipotle Mexican Grill, Inc. The Roseville Chipotle, like other Chipotle restaurants, serves burritos, fajitas, and tacos and competes in the "fast-casual" dining category.
f. <u>Trek Bicycle Corporation</u> manufactures and distributes bicycles and cycling products under the Trek, Gary Fisher, Bontrager, and Klein brand names.
g. <u>The Hershey Company</u> is one of the oldest chocolate companies in the United States. Its product lines include the Mauna Loa Macadamia Nuts, Dagoba Organic Chocolates, and Joseph Schmidt Confections.
h. The <u>Human Resources Department</u> is responsible for recruiting and training for the Kohl's Corporation.
i. The <u>reservation office</u> for BlueSky Airlines, Inc., is responsible for both online sales and counter sales.
j. The <u>Disney Store</u> at Spring Hill Mall in West Dundee, Illinois, is owned by The Walt Disney Company.
k. H & R Block Tax Services, H & R Block Bank, and McGladrey are all divisions of their parent corporation, <u>H & R Block</u>.

E10-18A Complete and analyze a performance report *(Learning Objective 2)*

One subunit of Bacall Sports Manufacturing Company had the following financial results last month:

	Actual	Budgeted	Variance*	Variance Percentage*
Bacall Sports Manufacturing Company—Water Sports Subunit				
Monthly Performance Report				
For the Month				
Direct materials	$ 16,095	$ 15,000		
Direct labor	15,240	16,000		
Indirect labor	29,200	25,000		
Utilities	16,395	15,000		
Depreciation	24,000	24,000		
Repairs and maintenance	6,285	7,500		
Total	107,215	102,500		

*Be sure to indicate whether each variance is favorable (F) or unfavorable (U).

Requirements

1. Complete the performance evaluation report for this subunit (round to four decimals).
2. Based on the data presented, what type of responsibility center is the subunit?
3. Which items should be investigated if part of the management's decision criteria is to investigate all variances exceeding $2,500 or 12.5%?
4. Should only unfavorable variances be investigated? Explain.

E10-19A Prepare a segment margin performance report *(Learning Objective 2)*

Drizzdale Industries has gathered the following information about the actual sales revenues and expenses for its pharmaceuticals segment for the most recent year.

Sales	$ 866,320
Variable Cost of Goods Sold	$ 143,325
Variable Operating Expenses	$ 162,162
Direct Fixed Manufacturing Overhead	$ 96,300
Direct Fixed Operating Expenses	$ 17,280
Common Fixed Expenses	$ 14,140

Budgeted data for the same time period for the pharmaceutical segment are as follows (all data are in millions):

Budgeted sales in units	9,100
Budgeted average selling price per unit	$ 85
Variable Cost of Goods Sold per unit	$ 15
Variable Operating Expenses per unit	$ 18
Direct Fixed Manufacturing Overhead (in total)	$ 90,000
Direct Fixed Operating Expenses (in total)	$ 16,000
Common Fixed Expenses Allocated to the Pharmaceutical Segment	$ 14,000

Prepare a segment margin performance report for the pharmaceutical segment. In this report, be sure to include lines for the contribution margin, the segment margin, and operating income. Calculate a variance and a variance percentage for each line in the report. Round to the nearest hundredth for the variance percentages (for example, if your answer is 16.2384%, round it to 16.24%).

E10-20A Compute and interpret the expanded ROI equation *(Learning Objective 3)*

Rogers, a national manufacturer of lawn-mowing and snow-blowing equipment, segments its business according to customer type: Professional and Residential. Assume the following divisional information was available for the past year (in thousands of dollars):

	Sales	Operating Income	Total Assets
Residential	$ 850,000	$ 68,000	$200,000
Professional	$1,095,000	$153,300	$365,000

Assume that management has a 25% target rate of return for each division.

Requirements

Round all of your answers to four decimal places.
1. Calculate each division's ROI.
2. Calculate each division's sales margin. Interpret your results.
3. Calculate each division's capital turnover. Interpret your results.
4. Use the expanded ROI formula to confirm your results from Requirement 1. What can you conclude?
5. Calculate each division's residual income (RI). Interpret your results.

E10-21A Relationship between ROI and residual income (Learning Objective 3)

Data on three unrelated companies are given in the following table.

	Georgeville, Inc.	Bayside Company	Blue Hat Industries
Sales	$117,000	?	$520,000
Operating income	$ 35,100	$164,000	?
Total assets	$ 90,000	?	?
Sales margin	?	20%	8%
Capital turnover	?	4.10	?
Return on investment (ROI)	?	?	20%
Target rate of return	9%	21%	?
Residual income (RI)	?	?	$ 4,160

Requirement
Fill in the missing information in the preceding table.

E10-22A Compute ROI and residual income (Learning Objective 3)

Results from Elite Corporation's most recent year of operations are presented in the following table.

Operating income	$ 9,000
Total assets	$15,000
Current liabilities	$ 3,600
Sales	$36,000
Target rate of return	14%

Requirements
1. Calculate the sales margin, capital turnover, and return on investment (ROI).
2. Calculate the residual income (RI).

E10-23A Comparison of ROI and residual income (Learning Objective 3)

Montgomery Ceramics, a division of Watson Corporation, has an operating income of $77,000 and total assets of $440,000. The required rate of return for the company is 14%. The company is evaluating whether it should use return on investment (ROI) or residual income (RI) as a measurement of performance for its division managers.

The manager of Montgomery Ceramics has the opportunity to undertake a new project that will require an investment of $110,000. This investment would earn $13,200 for the company.

Requirements
1. What is the original return on investment (ROI) for Montgomery Ceramics (before making any additional investment)?
2. What would the ROI be for Montgomery Ceramics if this investment opportunity were undertaken? Would the manager of the Montgomery Ceramics division want to make this investment if she were evaluated based on ROI? Why or why not?
3. What is the ROI of the investment opportunity? Would the investment be desirable from the standpoint of Watson Corporation? Why or why not?
4. What would the residual income (RI) be for Montgomery Ceramics if this investment opportunity were to be undertaken? Would the manager of the Montgomery Ceramics division want to make this investment if she were evaluated based on RI? Why or why not?
5. What is the RI of the investment opportunity? Would the investment be desirable from the standpoint of Watson Corporation? Why or why not?
6. Which performance measurement method, ROI or RI, promotes goal congruence? Why?

E10-24A Determine transfer price range *(Learning Objective 4)*

Graham Motors manufactures specialty tractors. It has two divisions: a Tractor Division and a Tire Division. The Tractor Division can use the tires produced by the Tire Division. The market price per tire is $45.

The Tire Division has the following costs per tire:

Direct material cost per tire $22
Conversion costs per tire $5

Fixed manufacturing overhead cost for the year is expected to total $120,000. The Tire Division expects to manufacture 40,000 tires this year. The fixed manufacturing overhead per tire is $3 ($120,000 divided by 40,000 tires).

Requirements

1. Assume that the Tire Division has excess capacity, meaning that it can produce tires for the Tractor Division without giving up any of its current tire sales to outsiders. If Graham Motors has a negotiated transfer price policy, what is the lowest acceptable transfer price? What is the highest acceptable transfer price?
2. If Graham Motors has a cost-plus transfer price policy of full absorption cost plus 30%, what would the transfer price be?
3. If the Tire Division is currently producing at capacity (meaning that it is selling every single tire it has the capacity to produce), what would likely be the fairest transfer price strategy to use? What would be the transfer price in this case?

E10-25A Comprehensive flexible budget problem *(Learning Objectives 2 & 5)*

The Happy Balloon Company produces party balloons that are sold in multi-pack cases. To follow is the company's performance report in contribution margin format for August:

	A	B	C	D	E
1		The Happy Balloon Company			
2		Actual vs. Budget Performance Report			
3		For the Month Ended August 31			
4					Master
5		Actual	Master Budget		Budget Variance
6					
7	**Sales volume (number of cases sold)**	60,000	55,000		
8	Sales revenue	$ 185,000	$ 165,000		
9	Less: Variable expenses	99,500	88,000		
10	Contribution margin	$ 85,500	$ 77,000		
11	Less: Fixed expenses	69,000	68,000		
12	Operating income	$ 16,500	$ 9,000		
13					

Requirements

1. What is the budgeted sales price per unit?
2. What is the budgeted variable expense per unit?
3. What is the budgeted fixed cost for the period?
4. Compute the master budget variances. Be sure to indicate each variance as favorable (F) or unfavorable (U).
5. Management would like to determine the portion of the master budget variance that is (a) due to volume being different than originally anticipated and (b) due to some other unexpected cause. Prepare a flexible budget performance report to address these questions, using the actual sales volume of 60,000 units and the budgeted sales volume of 55,000 units. Use the original budget assumptions for sales price, variable cost per unit, and fixed costs, assuming the relevant range stretches from 50,000 to 75,000 units.
6. Using the flexible budget performance report you prepared for Requirement 5, answer the following questions:
   a. How much of the master budget variance (calculated in Requirement 4) for operating income is due to volume being higher than expected?
   b. How much of the master budget variance for variable expenses is due to some cause other than volume?
   c. What could account for the flexible budget variance for sales revenue?
   d. What is the volume variance for fixed expenses? Why is it this amount?

Performance Evaluation

E10-26A Prepare a flexible budget performance report *(Learning Objective 5)*

Main Street Muffins sells its muffins to restaurants and coffee houses for an average selling price of $26 per case. The following information relates to the budget for Main Street Muffins for this year (all figures are annual totals unless otherwise noted):

Budgeted sales in cases	9,100 cases
Packaging cost per case	$ 1
Shipping expense per case	$ 2
Sales commission expense	5% of sales price
Salaries expense	$6,500
Office rent	$3,900
Depreciation	$2,500
Insurance expense	$1,800
Office supplies expense	$ 900

During the year, Main Street Muffins actually sold 9,500 cases, resulting in total sales revenue of $255,200. Actual expenses (in total) from this year are as follows:

Packaging cost	$ 10,600
Shipping expense	$ 19,500
Sales commission expense	$ 12,760
Salaries expense	$ 7,300
Office rent	$ 3,900
Depreciation	$ 2,500
Insurance expense	$ 1,600
Office supplies expense	$ 1,600

Requirement

Construct a flexible budget performance report for Main Street Muffins for the year. Be sure to indicate whether each variance is favorable (F) or unfavorable (U).

E10-27A Work backward to find missing values *(Learning Objective 5)*

Newton Industries has a relevant range extending to 31,800 units each month. The following performance report provides information about Newton's budget and actual performance for April:

	Actual	Flexible Budget Variance		Flexible Budget	Volume Variance		Master Budget
Output units	28,000			?			31,800
Sales revenue	$ 251,000	$ 6,000	F	?	?		?
Less: Variable expenses	201,500	?		?	?	$	198,750
Contribution margin	?	?		?	?		?
Less: Fixed expenses	15,000	?		?	?		24,000
Operating income	?	?		?	?		?

Requirement

Fill in all missing numbers in the table. Be sure to label any variances as favorable or unfavorable.

E10-28A Construct a balanced scorecard (Learning Objective 6)

Dakota Corporation is preparing its balanced scorecard for the past quarter. The balanced scorecard contains four perspectives: financial, customer, internal business process, and learning and growth. Through its strategic management planning process, Dakota Corporation has selected two specific objectives for each of the four perspectives; these specific objectives are listed in the following table.

Specific Objective
1. Increase sales of core product line.
2. Improve production efficiency.
3. Increase number of employees with access to customer relationship database.
4. Increase number of customers.
5. Improve post-sales service.
6. Increase customer retention.
7. Increase Return on Investment (ROI).
8. Improve employee morale.

Dakota Corporation has collected key performance indicators (KPIs) to measure progress toward achieving its specific objectives. The following table contains the KPIs and corresponding data that Dakota Corporation has collected for the past quarter.

	A	B	C
1	KPI	Goal	Actual
2	Percentage of employees with access to customer relationship database	78%	80%
3	Average repair time (number of days)	1.3	1
4	Sales revenue growth—core product line	$2,150,000	$2,050,000
5	Employee satisfaction survey (1-5, with 1 as most satisfied)	1.5	1.1
6	ROI	20%	24%
7	Number of repeat customers	100,000	104,000
8	Number of units produced per hour	7.2	7.3
9	Number of customers	135,000	120,000
10			

Requirement

Prepare a balanced scorecard report for Dakota Corporation, using the following format.

Dakota Corporation
Balanced Scorecard Report
For Quarter Ended December 31

Perspective	Objective	KPI	Goal	Actual	Goal Achieved? (✓ if met)
Financial					
Customer					
Internal Business Process					
Learning and Growth					

For each of the specific objectives listed, place that objective under the appropriate perspective heading in the report. Select a KPI from the list of KPIs that would be appropriate to measure progress toward each objective. (There are two specific objectives for each perspective and one KPI for each of the specific objectives.) In the last column in the balanced scorecard report, place a check mark if the associated KPI goal has been achieved.

Performance Evaluation

E10-29A Sustainability and the balanced scorecard *(Learning Objective 6)*

Classify each of the following sustainability key performance indicators (KPIs) according to the balanced scorecard perspective it addresses. Choose from the following five perspectives:

- Financial perspective
- Customer perspective
- Internal business perspective
- Learning and growth perspective
- Community perspective

SUSTAINABILITY

KPI

a. Number of employees on sustainability teams
b. Number of green products
c. Cubic meters of natural gas used for heating facilities
d. Revenue from recycling packaging materials
e. Customer survey rating company's green reputation
f. Percentage of products reclaimed after customer use
g. Number of employee hours devoted to local volunteering
h. Number of functions with environmental responsibilities
i. Total liters of water used
j. Volume of Global Greenhouse Gas (GHG) emissions
k. Number of sustainability training hours
l. Total megawatt hours of electricity purchased
m. Percent of bottles and cans sold recovered through company-supported recovery programs
n. Indirect greenhouse gas emissions from electricity purchased and consumed
o. Percentage of profit donated to local schools
p. Waste-disposal costs
q. Charitable contributions as a percent of income
r. Cost of water used

EXERCISES Group B

E10-30B Identify type of responsibility center *(Learning Objective 1)*

Each of the following situations describes an organizational unit. Identify which type of responsibility center each underlined item is (cost, revenue, profit, or investment center).

Organization
a. The <u>3M Company</u> manufactures and distributes products under the Post-it, Scotch, Nexcare, and Thinsulate brand names.
b. <u>The J.M. Smucker Company Store and Café</u> is located in Orrville, Ohio. The store sells a variety of company products, while the café offers items made with ingredients from the Smucker's brands.
c. The Fairmont Chicago, The Fairmont Royal York in Toronto, and The Fairmont Orchid in Hawaii are all hotels owned by their parent corporation, <u>Fairmont Hotels & Resorts</u>.
d. The <u>Dairy Group Account team</u> of the Dean Foods Company is responsible for sales and servicing for the SUPERVALU, Target, and Costco accounts.
e. The <u>Goodyear Tire & Rubber Company</u> is one of the oldest tire companies in the world. Its geographic regions include North America, Europe, Africa, South America, Asia, and Australia.
f. In addition to other accounting duties, the <u>Financial Reporting and Control & Analysis Department</u> at Progressive Insurance is responsible for performing a monthly analysis of general ledger accounts and fluctuations as a control mechanism.
g. The <u>reservation office</u> for CharterNow Airlines, Inc., is responsible for both website sales and counter sales.
h. The <u>Information System Department</u> is responsible for designing, installing, and servicing the information systems throughout Kohl's Corporation.
i. The <u>JCPenney store</u> in the Oakpark Shopping Center in Kansas City is owned by the JCPenney Company, Inc.
j. The <u>Human Resources Department</u> at American Greetings is responsible for hiring and training new associates.
k. The <u>Barnes & Noble bookstore</u> in Asheville, North Carolina, is owned by its parent, Barnes & Noble, Inc.

E10-31B Complete and analyze a performance report *(Learning Objective 2)*

One subunit of Contest Sports Manufacturing Company had the following financial results last month:

	A	B	C	D	E	F	G
1		Contest Sports Manufacturing Company—Water Sports Subunit					
2		Monthly Performance Report					
3		For the Month					
4							
5		Actual	Budgeted	Variance*		Variance Percentage*	
6	Direct materials	$ 12,930	$ 12,000				
7	Direct labor	13,265	14,000				
8	Indirect labor	23,380	20,000				
9	Utilities	16,455	15,000				
10	Depreciation	30,250	30,250				
11	Repairs and maintenance	4,205	5,000				
12	Total	$ 100,485	$ 96,250				
13							

*Be sure to indicate whether each variance is favorable (F) or unfavorable (U).

Requirements

1. Complete the performance evaluation report for this subunit (round to four decimals).
2. Based on the data presented, what type of responsibility center is this subunit?
3. Which items should be investigated if part of management's decision criteria is to investigate all variances exceeding $2,900 or 13%?
4. Should only unfavorable variances be investigated? Explain.

E10-32B Prepare a segment margin performance report *(Learning Objective 2)*

Campbell Industries has gathered the following information about the actual sales revenues and expenses for its pharmaceuticals segment for the most recent year (all data is in millions).

Sales	$824,320
Variable Cost of Goods Sold	$185,840
Variable Operating Expenses	$229,632
Direct Fixed Manufacturing Overhead	$102,600
Direct Fixed Operating Expenses	$ 16,960
Common Fixed Expenses	$ 17,340

Budgeted data for the same time period for the pharmaceutical segment are as follows (all data are in millions):

Budgeted sales in units	9,200
Budgeted average selling price per unit	$ 80
Variable Cost of Goods Sold per unit	$ 20
Variable Operating Expenses per unit	$ 26
Direct Fixed Manufacturing Overhead (in total)	$ 95,000
Direct Fixed Operating Expenses (in total)	$ 16,000
Common Fixed Expenses Allocated to the Pharmaceutical Segment	$ 17,000

Prepare a segment margin performance report for the pharmaceutical segment. In this report, be sure to include lines for the contribution margin, the segment margin, and operating income. Calculate a variance and a variance percentage for each line in the report. Round to the nearest hundredth for the variance percentages (for example, if your answer is 16.2384%, round it to 16.24%).

E10-33B Compute and interpret the expanded ROI equation
(Learning Objective 3)

Zeldas, a national manufacturer of lawn-mowing and snow-blowing equipment, segments its business according to customer type: Professional and Residential. Assume that the following divisional information was available for the past year (in thousands of dollars):

	Sales	Operating Income	Total Assets
Residential	$ 635,500	$ 63,550	$205,000
Professional	$1,031,250	$165,000	$375,000

Management has a 25% target rate of return for each division.

Requirements

1. Calculate each division's ROI. Round all of your answers to four decimal places.
2. Calculate each division's sales margin. Interpret your results.
3. Calculate each division's capital turnover. Interpret your results.
4. Use the expanded ROI formula to confirm your results from Requirement 1. What can you conclude?
5. Calculate each division's residual income (RI). Interpret your results.

E10-34B Relationship between ROI and residual income *(Learning Objective 3)*

Data on three unrelated companies are given in the following table.

	Columbus, Inc.	Kemp Company	Sargent Industries
Sales	$105,000	?	$525,000
Operating income	$ 37,800	$110,600	?
Total assets	$ 84,000	?	?
Sales margin	?	14%	15%
Capital turnover	?	4.00	?
Return on investment (ROI)	?	?	42%
Target rate of return	12%	21%	?
Residual income	?	?	$ 41,250

Requirement

Fill in the missing information.

E10-35B Compute ROI and residual income *(Learning Objective 3)*

Results from Supreme Corporation's most recent year of operations are presented in the following table:

Operating income	$ 8,060
Total assets	$15,500
Current liabilities	$ 4,300
Sales	$31,000
Target rate of return	16%

Requirements

1. Calculate the sales margin, capital turnover, and return on investment (ROI).
2. Calculate the residual income (RI).

E10-36B Comparison of ROI and residual income *(Learning Objective 3)*

Jackson Ceramics, a division of Dunlap Corporation, has an operating income of $82,000 and total assets of $410,000. The required rate of return for the company is 10%. The company is evaluating whether it should use return on investment (ROI) or residual income (RI) as a measurement of performance for its division managers.

The manager of Jackson Ceramics has the opportunity to undertake a new project that will require an investment of $164,000. This investment would earn $21,320 for the company.

Requirements

1. What is the original return on investment (ROI) for Jackson Ceramics (before making any additional investment)?
2. What would the ROI be for Jackson Ceramics if this investment opportunity were undertaken? Would the manager of the Jackson Ceramics division want to make this investment if she were evaluated based on ROI? Why or why not?
3. What is the ROI of the investment opportunity? Would the investment be desirable from the standpoint of Dunlap Corporation? Why or why not?
4. What would the residual income (RI) be for Jackson Ceramics if this investment opportunity were to be undertaken? Would the manager of the Jackson Ceramics division want to make this investment if she were evaluated based on RI? Why or why not?
5. What is the RI of the investment opportunity? Would the investment be desirable from the standpoint of Dunlap Corporation? Why or why not?
6. Which performance measurement method, ROI or RI, promotes goal congruence? Why?

E10-37B Determine transfer price range *(Learning Objective 4)*

Howard Motors manufactures specialty tractors. It has two divisions: a Tractor Division and a Tire Division. The Tractor Division can use the tires produced by the Tire Division. The market price per tire is $70.

The Tire Division has the following costs per tire:

Direct material cost per tire $29
Conversion costs per tire $4

Fixed manufacturing overhead cost for the year is expected to total $120,000. The Tire Division expects to manufacture 60,000 tires this year. The fixed manufacturing overhead per tire is $2 ($120,000 divided by 60,000 tires).

Requirements

1. Assume that the Tire Division has excess capacity, meaning that it can produce tires for the Tractor Division without giving up any of its current tire sales to outsiders. If Howard Motors has a negotiated transfer price policy, what is the lowest acceptable transfer price? What is the highest acceptable transfer price?
2. If Howard Motors has a cost-plus transfer price policy of full absorption cost plus 20%, what would the transfer price be?
3. If the Tire Division is currently producing at capacity (meaning that it is selling every single tire it has the capacity to produce), what would likely be the fairest transfer price strategy to use? What would be the transfer price in this case?

E10-38B Comprehensive flexible budget problem *(Learning Objectives 2 & 5)*

The Celebration Balloon Company produces party balloons that are sold in multi-pack cases. To follow is the company's performance report in contribution margin format for August:

	A	B	C	D	E
1	The Celebration Balloon Company				
2	Actual vs. Budget Performance Report				
3	For the Month Ended August 31				
4					Master Budget Variance
5		Actual	Master Budget		
6	Sales volume (number of cases sold)	70,000	62,000		
7	Sales revenue	$ 295,000	$ 248,000		
8	Less: Variable expenses	175,000	148,800		
9	Contribution margin	$ 120,000	$ 99,200		
10	Less: Fixed expenses	72,000	70,000		
11	Operating income	$ 48,000	$ 29,200		
12					

Requirements

1. What is the budgeted sales price per unit?
2. What is the budgeted variable expense per unit?
3. What is the budgeted fixed cost for the period?
4. Compute the master budget variances. Be sure to indicate each variance as favorable (F) or unfavorable (U).
5. Management would like to determine the portion of the master budget variance that is (a) due to volume being different than originally anticipated, and (b) due to some other unexpected cause. Prepare a flexible budget performance report to address these questions, using the actual sales volume of 70,000 units and the budgeted sales volume of 62,000 units. Use the original budget assumptions for sales price, variable cost per unit, and fixed costs, assuming the relevant range stretches from 50,000 to 75,000 units.
6. Using the flexible budget performance report you prepared for Requirement 5, answer the following questions:
   a. How much of the master budget variance (calculated in Requirement 4) for operating income is due to volume being higher than expected?
   b. How much of the master budget variance for variable expenses is due to some cause other than volume?
   c. What could account for the flexible budget variance for sales revenue?
   d. What is the volume variance for fixed expenses? Why is it this amount?

E10-39B Prepare a flexible budget performance report *(Learning Objective 5)*

Stone Canyon Muffins sells its muffins to restaurants and coffee houses for an average selling price of $27 per case. The following information relates to the budget for Stone Canyon Muffins for this year (all figures are annual totals unless otherwise noted):

Budgeted sales in cases	9,300 cases
Packaging cost per case	$ 4.00
Shipping expense per case	$ 2.00
Sales commission expense	1% of sales price
Salaries expense	$7,000
Office rent	$3,800
Depreciation	$2,600
Insurance expense	$2,500
Office supplies expense	$ 600

During the year, Stone Canyon Muffins actually sold 9,500 cases, resulting in total sales revenue of $264,100. Actual expenses (in total) from this year are as follows:

Packaging cost	$ 39,300
Shipping expense	$ 21,800
Sales commission expense	$ 2,641
Salaries expense	$ 8,500
Office rent	$ 3,800
Depreciation	$ 2,600
Insurance expense	$ 2,300
Office supplies expense	$ 1,300

Requirement

Construct a flexible budget performance report for Stone Canyon Muffins for the year. Be sure to indicate whether each variance is favorable (F) or unfavorable (U).

E10-40B Work backward to find missing values *(Learning Objective 5)*

Randall Corporation has a relevant range extending to 31,500 units each month. The following performance report provides information about Randall's budget and actual performance for November.

	A	B	C	D	E	F	G	H
1			Randall Industries					
2		Flexible Budget Performance Report: Sales and Operating Expenses						
3		For the Month Ended November 30						
4								
5		Actual	Flexible Budget Variance		Flexible Budget	Volume Variance		Master Budget
6	Output units	29,000			?			31,500
7								
8	Sales revenue	$ 246,500	$ 5,800	F	?	?		?
9	Less: Variable expenses	202,000	?		?	?	$	195,300
10	Contribution margin	?	?		?	?		?
11	Less: Fixed expenses	19,500	?		?	?		25,000
12	Operating income	?	?		?	?		?
13								

Requirement

Fill in all missing numbers in the table. Be sure to label any variances as favorable or unfavorable.

E10-41B Construct a balanced scorecard *(Learning Objective 6)*

Royal Corporation is preparing its balanced scorecard for the past quarter. The balanced scorecard contains four perspectives: financial, customer, internal business process, and learning and growth. Through its strategic management planning process, Royal Corporation has selected two specific objectives for each of the four perspectives; these specific objectives are listed in the following table.

Specific Objective
1. Increase Return on Investment (ROI).
2. Develop new core products.
3. Improve employee product knowledge.
4. Increase customer retention.
5. Improve production efficiency.
6. Increase market share.
7. Increase sales of core product line.
8. Improve employee job satisfaction.

Royal Corporation has collected key performance indicators (KPIs) to measure progress toward achieving its specific objectives. The following table contains the KPIs and corresponding data that Royal Corporation has collected for the past quarter.

	A	B	C
1	KPI	Goal	Actual
2	Hours of employee training provided	2,375	2,425
3	Number of units produced per hour	6.9	7.2
4	ROI	19%	26%
5	Employee turnover rate (number of employees leaving company/total number of employees)	6%	9%
6	Sales revenue growth—core product line	$ 2,100,000	$ 2,150,000
7	Market share percentage	17%	20%
8	Number of new core products	14	21
9	Number of repeat customers	101,000	100,000
10			

Requirement

Prepare a balanced scorecard report for Royal Corporation, using the following format.

Royal Corporation
Balanced Scorecard Report
For Quarter Ended December 31

Perspective	Objective	KPI	Goal	Actual	Goal Achieved? (✓ if met)
Financial					
Customer					
Internal Business Process					
Learning and Growth					

For each of the specific objectives listed, place that objective under the appropriate perspective heading in the report. Select a KPI from the list of KPIs that would be appropriate to measure progress toward each objective. (There are two specific objectives for each perspective and one KPI for each of the specific objectives.) In the last column in the balanced scorecard report, place a check mark if the associated KPI goal has been achieved.

E10-42B Sustainability and the balanced scorecard (Learning Objective 6)

SUSTAINABILITY

Classify each of the following sustainability key performance indicators (KPIs) according to the balanced scorecard perspective it addresses. Choose from the following five perspectives:
- Financial perspective
- Customer perspective
- Internal business perspective
- Learning and growth perspective
- Community perspective

KPI

a. Number of employee hours devoted to volunteering at Habitat for Humanity
b. Packaging use ratio, defined as grams of materials used per liter of product produced
c. Percent of bottles and cans sold recovered through company-supported recovery programs
d. Revenue from recycling packaging materials
e. Percentage of products sourced locally
f. Percent of plants in compliance with internal waste-water treatment standards
g. Number of sustainability training hours

h. Waste-disposal costs
i. Number of employees on sustainability teams
j. Percentage of recycled content in products
k. Cost of water used
l. Percentage of products reclaimed after customer use
m. Total megajoules of energy used
n. Number of green products
o. Customer survey rating company's green reputation
p. Product safety ratings
q. Number of functions with environmental responsibilities
r. Direct greenhouse gas emissions

PROBLEMS Group A

P10-43A Prepare a budget with different volumes for planning *(Learning Objective 5)*

Outrageous Bubbles, Inc., produces multicolored bubble solution used for weddings and other events. The company's master budget income statement for March follows. It is based on expected sales volume of 55,000 bubble kits.

OUTRAGEOUS BUBBLES, INC.
Master Budget Income Statement
Month Ended March 31

Sales revenue	$170,500
Variable expenses:	
Cost of goods sold	$ 68,750
Sales commissions	13,750
Utility expense	5,500
Fixed expenses:	
Salary expense	30,000
Depreciation expense	20,000
Rent expense	15,000
Utility expense	7,000
Total expenses	$160,000
Operating income	$ 10,500

Outrageous Bubbles' plant capacity is 62,500 kits. If actual volume exceeds 62,500 kits, the company must expand the plant. In that case, salaries will increase by 10%, depreciation by 15%, and rent by $4,000. Fixed utilities will be unchanged by any volume increase.

Requirements

1. Prepare flexible budget income statements for the company, showing output levels of 55,000, 60,000, and 65,000 kits.
2. Graph the behavior of the company's total costs. Use total costs on the y-axis and volume (in thousands of bubble kits) on the x-axis.
3. Why might Outrageous Bubbles' managers want to see the graph you prepared in Requirement 2 as well as the columnar format analysis in Requirement 1? What is the disadvantage of the graphic approach?

P10-44A Prepare and interpret a performance report *(Learning Objective 2)*

Refer to the Outrageous Bubbles data in P10-43A. The company sold 60,000 bubble kits during March, and its actual operating income was as follows:

OUTRAGEOUS BUBBLES, INC.
Income Statement
Month Ended March 31

Sales revenue	$194,000
Variable expenses:	
Cost of goods sold	$ 75,500
Sales commissions	16,500
Utility expense	6,000
Fixed expenses:	
Salary expense	32,200
Depreciation expense	20,000
Rent expense	14,550
Utility expense	7,000
Total expenses	$171,750
Operating income	$ 22,250

Requirements

1. Prepare an income statement performance report for March.
2. What accounts for most of the difference between actual operating income and master budget operating income?
3. What is Outrageous Bubbles' master budget variance for operating income? Explain why the income statement performance report provides Outrageous Bubbles' managers with more useful information than the simple master budget variance. What insights can Outrageous Bubbles' managers draw from this performance report?

P10-45A Evaluate divisional performance *(Learning Objective 3)*

NYC Paints is a national paint manufacturer and retailer. The company is segmented into five divisions: Paint Stores (branded retail location), Consumer (paint sold through stores such as Sears, Home Depot, and Lowe's), Automotive (sales to auto manufacturers), International, and Administration. The following is selected hypothetical divisional information for the company's two largest divisions: Paint Stores and Consumer (in thousands of dollars).

	Sales	Operating Income	Total Assets
Paint Stores	$3,950,000	$553,000	$1,975,000
Consumer	$1,100,000	$176,000	$2,000,000

Assume that management has specified a 21% target rate of return.

Requirements

Round all calculations to two decimal places.

1. Calculate each division's ROI.
2. Calculate each division's sales margin. Interpret your results.
3. Calculate each division's capital turnover. Interpret your results.
4. Use the expanded ROI formula to confirm your results from Requirement 1. Interpret your results.
5. Calculate each division's RI. Interpret your results and offer recommendations for any divisions with negative RI.
6. Total asset data were provided in this problem. If you were to gather this information from an annual report, how would you measure total assets? Describe your measurement choices and some of the pros and cons of those choices.

7. Describe some of the factors that management considers when setting its minimum target rate of return.
8. Explain why some firms prefer to use RI rather than ROI for performance measurement.
9. Explain why budget versus actual performance reports are insufficient for evaluating the performance of investment centers.

P10-46A Collect and analyze division data from an annual report *(Learning Objective 3)*

Jubilee Company segments its company into four distinct divisions. The net revenues, operating profit, and total assets for these divisions are disclosed in the footnotes to Jubilee Company's consolidated financial statements and the following presented information:

Notes to Consolidated Financial Statements

Note 1-Basis of Presentation and Our Divisions:

We manufacture, market, and sell a variety of products through our divisions, including furniture and fixtures for the home, office, stores, and health-care facilities. The accounting policies are the same for each division, as indicated in Note 2.

	Net Revenue			Operating Profit		
	2017	2016	2015	2017	2016	2015
Home furnishings	$10,750	$9,650	$9,250	$2,795	$2,520	$1,970
Office furniture	9,500	8,600	8,300	1,995	1,815	1,755
Store displays	12,100	10,900	10,400	1,210	1,070	1,010
Health-care furnishings	2,000	1,850	1,750	660	635	615
Total division	$34,350	$31,000	$29,700	$6,660	$6,040	$5,350
Corporate				(290)	(250)	(205)
Total	$34,350	$31,000	$29,700	$6,370	$5,790	$5,145

Corporate includes the costs of our corporate headquarters, centrally managed initiatives, and certain gains and losses that cannot be accurately allocated to specific divisions, such as derivative gains and losses.

	Amortization of Intangible Assets			Depreciation and Other Amortization		
	2017	2016	2015	2017	2016	2015
Home furnishings	$18	$13	$13	$415	$405	$410
Office furniture	78	73	73	285	265	260
Store displays	76	71	69	475	420	380
Health-care furnishings			5	35	40	37
Total division	$172	$157	$160	$1,210	$1,130	$1,087
Corporate				35	40	39
Total	$172	$157	$160	$1,245	$1,170	$1,126

	Total Assets			Capital Spending		
	2017	2016	2015	2017	2016	2015
Home furnishings	$5,000	$3,750	$3,250	$505	$515	$475
Office furniture	7,600	7,000	6,800	520	350	295
Store displays	11,000	9,800	9,400	865	695	560
Health-care furnishings	1,000	800	750	25	25	30
Total division	$24,600	$21,350	$20,200	$1,915	$1,585	$1,360
Corporate	1,710	5,270	3,470	190	195	80
Total	$26,310	$26,620	$23,670	$2,105	$1,780	$1,440

Corporate assets consist of cash, short-term investments, and property, plant, and equipment. The corporate property, plant, and equipment include the headquarters building, equipment within, and the surrounding property.

Requirements

1. What are Jubilee Company's four business divisions? Make a table listing each division, along with its net revenues, operating profit, and total assets in 2017.
2. Use the data you collected in Requirement 1 to calculate each division's sales margin in 2017. Interpret your results.
3. Use the data you collected in Requirement 1 to calculate each division's capital turnover in 2017. Interpret your results.
4. Use the data you collected in Requirement 1 to calculate each division's ROI in 2017. Interpret your results.
5. Can you calculate RI using the data presented? Why or why not?

P10-47A Determine transfer price at a manufacturer under various scenarios
(Learning Objective 4)

Assume the Small Components Division of Martin Manufacturing produces a video card used in the assembly of a variety of electronic products. The division's manufacturing costs and variable selling expenses related to the video card are as follows:

	Cost per unit
Direct materials	$12.00
Direct labor	$ 9.00
Variable manufacturing overhead	$ 7.00
Fixed manufacturing overhead (at current production level)	$ 6.00
Variable selling expenses	$ 7.00

The Computer Division of Martin Manufacturing can use the video card produced by the Small Components Division and is interested in purchasing the video card in-house rather than buying it from an outside supplier. The Small Components Division has sufficient excess capacity with which to make the extra video cards. Because of competition, the market price for this video card is $30 regardless of whether the video card is produced by Martin Manufacturing or another company.

Requirements

1. What is the highest acceptable transfer price for the divisions?
2. Assuming the transfer price is negotiated between the divisions of the company, what would be the lowest acceptable transfer price? Assume variable selling expenses pertain to outside sales only.
3. Which transfer price would the manager of the Small Components Division prefer? Which transfer price would the manager of the Computer Division prefer?
4. If the company's policy requires that all in-house transfers must be priced at full absorption cost plus 9%, what transfer price would be used? Assume that the increased production level needed to fill the transfer would result in fixed manufacturing overhead decreasing by $2.00 per unit. *(Round your answer to the nearest cent.)*
5. If the company's policy requires that all in-house transfers must be priced at total manufacturing variable cost plus 18%, what transfer price would be used? Assume that the company does not consider fixed manufacturing overhead in setting its internal transfer price in this scenario. *(Round your answer to the nearest cent.)*
6. Assume now that the company does incur the variable selling expenses on internal transfers. If the company policy is to set transfer prices at 107% of the sum of the full absorption cost and the variable selling expenses, what transfer price would be set? Assume that the fixed manufacturing overhead would drop by $2.00 per unit as a result of the increased production resulting from the internal transfers. *(Round your answer to the nearest cent.)*

P10-48A Evaluate subunit performance (Learning Objectives 2 & 6)

One subunit of Carlton Sports Company had the following financial results last month:

	A	B	C	D	E	F	G
1		Carlton Sports Manufacturing Company—Team Sports Subunit					
2		Monthly Performance Report					
3		For the Month					
4							
5		Actual	Budgeted	Variance*		Variance Percentage*	
6	Sales	$ 546,000	$ 500,000				
7	Less: Variable expenses	388,500	375,000				
8	Contribution margin	$ 157,500	$ 125,000				
9	Less: Direct fixed expenses	52,050	50,000				
10	Segment margin	$ 105,450	$ 75,000				
11	Less: Common fixed expenses	38,500	25,000				
12	Operating income	$ 66,950	$ 50,000				
13							

*Be sure to indicate whether each variance is favorable (F) or unfavorable (U).

Requirements

1. Complete the performance evaluation report for this subunit (round to three decimal places).
2. Based on the data presented, what type of responsibility center is this subunit?
3. Which items should be investigated if part of the management's decision criteria is to investigate all variances equal to or exceeding $13,500 and exceeding 16% (both criteria must be met)?
4. Should only unfavorable variances be investigated? Explain.
5. Is it possible that the variances are due to a higher-than-expected sales volume? Explain.
6. Do you think management will place equal weight on each of the $13,500 variances? Explain.
7. Which balanced scorecard perspective is being addressed through this performance report? In your opinion, is this performance report a lead or lag indicator? Explain.
8. Give one key performance indicator for the other three balanced scorecard perspectives. Indicate which perspective is being addressed by the indicator you list. Are they lead or lag indicators? Explain.

PROBLEMS Group B

P10-49B Prepare a budget with different volumes for planning (Learning Objective 5)

Popping Bubbles produces multicolored bubble solution used for weddings and other events.

Popping Bubbles' plant capacity is 72,500 kits. If actual volume exceeds 72,500 kits, the company must expand the plant. In that case, salaries will increase by 10%, depreciation by 15%, and rent by $7,000. Fixed utilities will be unchanged by any volume increase.

The company's master budget income statement for October follows. It is based on expected sales volume of 65,000 bubble kits.

POPPING BUBBLES, INC.
Master Budget Income Statement
Month Ended October 31

Sales revenue	$188,500
Variable expenses:	
Cost of goods sold	78,000
Sales commissions	13,000
Utility expense	13,000
Fixed expenses:	
Salary expense	33,000
Depreciation expense	18,000
Rent expense	11,000
Utility expense	5,000
Total expenses	$171,000
Operating income	$ 17,500

Requirements

1. Prepare flexible budget income statements for the company, showing output levels of 65,000, 70,000, and 75,000 kits.
2. Graph the behavior of the company's total costs. Use total costs on the y-axis and volume (in thousands of bubble kits) on the x-axis.
3. Why might Popping Bubbles' managers want to see the graph you prepared in Requirement 2 as well as the columnar format analysis in Requirement 1? What is the disadvantage of the graphic approach?

P10-50B **Prepare and interpret a performance report** *(Learning Objective 2)*

Refer to the Popping Bubbles' data in P10-49B. The company sold 70,000 bubble kits during March and its actual operating income was as follows:

POPPING BUBBLES, INC.
Master Budget Income Statement
Month Ended October 31

Sales revenue	$211,000
Variable expenses:	
Cost of goods sold	$ 84,500
Sales commissions	15,500
Utility expense	14,000
Fixed expenses:	
Salary expense	35,100
Depreciation expense	18,000
Rent expense	10,550
Utility expense	5,000
Total expenses	$182,650
Operating income	$ 28,350

Requirements

1. Prepare an income statement performance report for October.
2. What accounts for most of the difference between actual operating income and master budget operating income?
3. What is Popping Bubbles' master budget variance for operating income? Explain why the income statement performance report provides Popping Bubbles' managers with more useful information than the simple master budget variance. What insights can Popping Bubbles' managers draw from this performance report?

P10-51B **Evaluate divisional performance** *(Learning Objective 3)*

Sacramento Paints is a national paint manufacturer and retailer. The company is segmented into five divisions: Paint Stores (branded retail locations), Consumer (paint sold through stores like Sears, Home Depot, and Lowe's), Automotive (sales to auto manufacturers), International, and Administration. The following is selected hypothetical divisional information for its two largest divisions: Paint Stores and Consumer (in thousands of dollars).

	Sales	Operating Income	Total Assets
Paint Stores	$3,880,000	$465,600	$1,552,000
Consumer	$1,300,000	$221,000	$2,600,000

Assume that management has specified a 21% target rate of return.

Requirements

Round all calculations to four decimal places.

1. Calculate each division's ROI.
2. Calculate each division's sales margin. Interpret your results.
3. Calculate each division's capital turnover. Interpret your results.
4. Use the expanded ROI formula to confirm your results from Requirement 1. Interpret your results.
5. Calculate each division's RI. Interpret your results and offer recommendations for any division with negative RI.
6. Total asset data were provided in this problem. If you were to gather this information from an annual report, how would you measure total assets? Describe your measurement choices and some of the pros and cons of those choices.
7. Describe some of the factors that management considers when setting its minimum target rate of return.
8. Explain why some firms prefer to use RI rather than ROI for performance measurement.
9. Explain why budget versus actual performance reports are insufficient for evaluating the performance of investment centers.

P10-52B **Collect and analyze division data from an annual report** *(Learning Objective 3)*

BOGO Company segments its company into four distinctive divisions. The net revenues, operating profit, and total assets for these divisions are disclosed in the footnotes to BOGO Company's consolidated financial statements and presented here.

	Net Revenue			Operating Profit		
	2017	2016	2015	2017	2016	2015
Home furnishings	$9,500	$8,400	$8,000	$2,565	$2,290	$1,740
Office furniture	8,500	7,600	7,300	1,615	1,435	1,375
Store displays	12,500	11,300	10,800	1,500	1,360	1,300
Health-care furnishings	1,500	1,350	1,250	480	455	435
Total division	$32,000	$28,650	$27,350	$6,160	$5,540	$4,850
Corporate				(340)	(300)	(255)
Total	$32,000	$28,650	$27,350	$5,820	$5,240	$4,595

Corporate includes the costs of our corporate headquarters, centrally managed initiatives, and certain gains and losses that cannot be accurately allocated to specific divisions, such as derivative gains and losses.

	Amortization of Intangible Assets			Depreciation and Other Amortization		
	2017	2016	2015	2017	2016	2015
Home furnishings	$ 16	$ 11	$ 11	$ 430	$ 420	$ 425
Office furniture	76	71	71	290	270	265
Store displays	78	73	71	495	440	400
Health-care furnishings			6	35	40	37
Total division	$170	$155	$159	$1,250	$1,170	$1,127
Corporate				20	25	24
Total	$170	$155	$159	$1,270	$1,195	$1,151

	Total Assets			Capital Spending		
	2017	2016	2015	2017	2016	2015
Home furnishings	$ 7,600	$ 6,350	$ 5,850	$ 495	$ 505	$ 465
Office furniture	5,000	4,400	4,200	475	305	250
Store displays	15,625	14,425	14,025	820	650	515
Health-care furnishings	750	550	500	35	35	40
Total division	$28,975	$25,725	$24,575	$1,825	$1,495	$1,270
Corporate	1,760	5,320	3,520	205	210	95
Total	$30,735	$31,045	$28,095	$2,030	$1,705	$1,365

Corporate assets consist of cash, short-term investments, and property, plant, and equipment. The corporate property, plant, and equipment include the headquarters building, equipment within, and the surrounding property.

Requirements

1. What are BOGO Company's four business divisions? Make a table listing each division, along with its net revenues, operating profit, and total assets in 2017.
2. Use the data you collected in Requirement 1 to calculate each division's sales margin in 2017. Interpret your results.
3. Use the data you collected in Requirement 1 to calculate each division's capital turnover in 2017. Interpret your results.
4. Use the data you collected in Requirement 1 to calculate each division's ROI in 2017. Interpret your results.
5. Can you calculate RI using the data presented? Why or why not?

P10-53B **Determine transfer price at a manufacturer under various scenarios**
(Learning Objective 4)

Assume the Small Components Division of Lang Manufacturing produces a video card used in the assembly of a variety of electronic products. The division's manufacturing costs and variable selling expenses related to the video card are as follows:

	Cost per unit
Direct materials	$ 14.00
Direct labor	$ 4.00
Variable manufacturing overhead	$ 8.00
Fixed manufacturing overhead (at current production level)	$ 9.00
Variable selling expenses	$ 10.00

The Computer Division of Lang Manufacturing can use the video card produced by the Small Components Division and is interested in purchasing the video card in-house rather than buying it from an outside supplier. The Small Components Division has sufficient excess capacity with which to make the extra video cards. Because of competition, the market price for this video card is $30 regardless of whether the video card is produced by Lang Manufacturing or another company.

Requirements

1. What is the highest acceptable transfer price for the divisions?
2. Assuming the transfer price is negotiated between the divisions of the company, what would be the lowest acceptable transfer price? Assume variable selling expenses pertain to outside sales only.
3. Which transfer price would the manager of the Small Components Division prefer? Which transfer price would the manager of the Computer Division prefer?
4. If the company's policy requires that all in-house transfers must be priced at full absorption cost plus 14%, what transfer price would be used? Assume that the increased production level needed to fill the transfer would result in fixed manufacturing overhead decreasing by $3.00 per unit. *(Round your answer to the nearest cent.)*
5. If the company's policy requires that all in-house transfers must be priced at total manufacturing variable cost plus 18%, what transfer price would be used? Assume that the company does not consider fixed manufacturing overhead in setting its internal transfer price in this scenario. *(Round your answer to the nearest cent.)*
6. Assume now that the company does incur the variable selling expenses on internal transfers. If the company policy is to set transfer prices at 102% of the sum of the full absorption cost and the variable selling expenses, what would the transfer price be set at? Assume that the fixed manufacturing overhead would drop by $3.00 per unit as a result of the increased production resulting from the internal transfers. *(Round your answer to the nearest cent.)*

P10-54B Evaluate subunit performance *(Learning Objectives 2 & 6)*

One subunit of Carolina Sports Company had the following financial results last month:

	Actual	Budgeted	Variance*	Variance Percentage*
Carolina Sports Manufacturing Company—Water Sports Subunit				
Monthly Performance Report				
For the Month				
Sales	$ 486,000	$ 450,000		
Less: Variable expenses	260,000	250,000		
Contribution margin	$ 226,000	$ 200,000		
Less: Direct fixed expenses	52,000	50,000		
Segment margin	$ 174,000	$ 150,000		
Less: Common fixed expenses	35,000	25,000		
Operating income	$ 139,000	$ 125,000		

*Be sure to indicate whether each variance is favorable (F) or unfavorable (U).

Requirements

1. Complete the performance evaluation report for the subunit (round to three decimal places).
2. Based on the data presented, what type of responsibility center is this subunit?
3. Which items should be investigated if part of management's decision criteria is to investigate all variances equal to or exceeding $10,000 and exceeding 14% (both criteria must be met)?
4. Should only unfavorable variances be investigated? Explain.
5. Is it possible that the variances are due to a higher-than-expected sales volume? Explain.
6. Do you think management will place equal weight on each of the $10,000 variances? Explain.

7. Which balanced scorecard perspective is being addressed through this performance report? In your opinion, is this performance report a lead or lag indicator? Explain.
8. List one key performance indicator for the other three balanced scorecard perspectives. Indicate which perspective is being addressed by the indicators you list. Are they lead or lag indicators? Explain.

Serial Case

C10-55 Analyze segment reporting at a hotel *(Learning Objective 1)*

This case is a continuation of the Caesars Entertainment Corporation serial case that began in Chapter 1. Refer to the introductory story in Chapter 1 (see page 43) for additional background. (The components of the Caesars serial case can be completed in any order.)

Caesars Entertainment Corporation reports several types of revenues in its Form 10-K, including Casino, Food and Beverage, Rooms, and Other.

Questions

1. Would Caesars Palace® Las Vegas be likely to use these categories (as listed in the Form 10-K for Caesars Entertainment Corporation) as its segments in its internal reporting? If not, what segments make sense for Caesars Palace® Las Vegas to use in making decisions and evaluating performance for its performance?
2. Give an example of each of the following responsibility centers as related to Caesars Palace® Las Vegas:
   a. Cost center
   b. Revenue center
   c. Profit center
   d. Investment center
3. What performance measure(s) can be used to evaluate each of the responsibility center examples you just listed for Caesars Palace® Las Vegas?

CRITICAL THINKING

Discussion & Analysis

A10-56 Discussion Questions

1. Describe at least four advantages of decentralization. Also describe at least two disadvantages of decentralization.

2. Compare and contrast a cost center, a revenue center, a profit center, and an investment center. List a specific example of each type of responsibility center. How is the performance of managers evaluated in each type of responsibility center?

3. Explain the potential problem that could arise from using ROI as the incentive measure for managers. What are some specific actions a company might take to resolve this potential problem?

4. Describe at least two specific actions that a company could take to improve its ROI.

5. Define residual income. How is it calculated? Describe the major weakness of residual income.

6. Compare and contrast a master budget and a flexible budget.

7. Describe two ways managers can use flexible budgets.

8. Define key performance indicator (KPI). What is the relationship between KPIs and a company's objectives? Select a company of any size with which you are familiar. List at least four examples of specific objectives that a company might have and one potential KPI for each of those specific objectives.

9. List and describe the four perspectives found on a balanced scorecard. For each perspective, list at least two examples of KPIs that might be used to measure performance on that perspective.

10. Contrast lag indicators with lead indicators. Provide an example of each type of indicator.

11. Some companies integrate sustainability measures into the traditional four perspectives in their balanced scorecards. Other companies create a new perspective (or two) for sustainability. Which method do you think would result in better supporting sustainability efforts throughout the organization? Explain your viewpoint.

12. Find an annual report for a publicly held company (go to the company's website and look for "Investor Relations" or a similar link). How many sustainability initiatives can you find in the annual report? What internal balanced scorecard measures do you think they might use to measure progress on each sustainability initiative? (You will have to use your imagination, since typically most balanced scorecard measures are not publicly disclosed.)

Application & Analysis

Mini Cases

A10-57 Segmented Financial Information

Select a company you are interested in and obtain its annual reports by going to the company's website. Download the annual report for the most recent year. (On many companies' websites, you will need to visit the Investor Relations section to obtain the company's financial statements.) You may also collect the information from the company's Form 10-K, which can be found at http://sec.gov/idea/searchidea/companysearch_idea.html.

Basic Discussion Questions

1. Locate the company's annual report as outlined previously. Find the company's segment information; it should be in the "Notes to Consolidated Financial Statements" or another, similarly named section. Look for the word "Segment" in a heading; that is usually the section you need.

2. List the segments as reported in the annual report. Make a table listing each operating segment, its revenues, income, and assets.

3. Use the data you collected in Requirement 2 to calculate each segment's sales margin. Interpret your results.
4. Use the data you collected in Requirement 2 to calculate each segment's capital turnover. Interpret your results.
5. Use the data you collected in Requirement 2 to calculate each segment's ROI. Interpret your results.
6. Can you calculate RI using the data presented? Why or why not?
7. The rules for how segments should be presented in the annual report are governed by external financial accounting rules. The information you gathered for the previous requirements would be used by investors and other external stakeholders in their analysis of the company and its stock. Internally, the company most likely has many segments. Based on what you know about the company and its products or services, list at least five potential segments that the company might use for internal reporting. Explain why this way of segmenting the company for internal reporting could be useful to managers.

Decision Cases

A10-58 Collect and analyze divisional data *(Learning Objective 3)*

The Ford Motor Company operates two segments (Ford refers to its segments as "sectors"). Using the company's website, locate sector information for 2015 in the company's 2015 annual report. (*Hint:* Look under Investor Relations.) Most of the information will be in the Financial Statements and related Notes to the Consolidated Financial Statements (found in the Form 10-K).

REAL LIFE

Requirements

1. What are Ford's reported sectors in its Balance Sheet and Income Statement? Gather data about each segment's net sales, operating income, and identifiable assets.
2. Calculate the ROI for each segment.
3. Which segment has the highest ROI? Explain why.
4. If you were on the top management team and could allocate extra funds to only one division, which division would you choose? Why?

A10-59 Ethics and performance evaluation *(Learning Objective 2)*

Costello Company has several divisions. The controller, Sarah James, prepares monthly segment reports for each division. Each division manager is evaluated annually, based largely on the segment margin for the manager's division. The segment margin for the division determines whether the manager receives a bonus, the amount of any bonus, and whether the division will even continue to be operated. Since operating losses reflect common fixed costs being allocated to a division, company management allows a division to show an operating loss in one or more years. However, the division is likely to be closed if its segment margin is negative for three consecutive years since management feels that the division is then a drain on the overall company's profits.

ETHICS

The past few years have been tough years for the Small Engines division. The economy has caused sales to shrink. In addition, the production manager, Daniel Whalen, has had some personal problems and has not been focused on work. Whalen thinks his personal issues are behind him now, and he is looking forward to better results in future years—as long as his division is not discontinued due to its poor operating results in the past few years. Here is an excerpt from the segment report for the Small Engines division for the past three years:

Costello Company—Small Engines Division
Segment Margin Performance Report
For the Fiscal Years Ending December 31
(all figures in thousands of dollars)

Product	2016	2015	2014
Sales revenue	$6,098	$6,501	$6,652
Less: Variable expenses			
Variable cost of goods sold	4,728	5,319	5,412
Variable operating expenses	693	517	564
Contribution margin	$ 677	$ 665	$ 676
Less: Direct fixed expenses			
Fixed manufacturing overhead	652	621	639
Fixed operating expenses	79	57	54
Segment margin	$ (54)	$ (13)	$ (17)
Less: Common fixed expenses	30	72	41
Operating income (loss)	$ (84)	$ (85)	$ (58)

James, the controller, is in a relationship with Whalen, the division manager of Small Engines. She wants to do whatever she can to help him with his work situation; she knows he is a good person and works hard. Once she sees the segment margin report for the Small Engines division, she realizes that there is a strong possibility that the Small Engines division will be closed due to segment margin losses over the past three years. She analyzes the preliminary segment margin performance report and realizes that there is an easy way that she could help. She could move some of the direct fixed expenses listed on the Small Engine segment report into the common fixed expenses allocated to the Small Engine division. She reasons that the overall operating income for the Small Engine division will remain the same and it really isn't hurting anyone to do this. In fact, she actually feels that she is helping the company and its employees. By the simple act of shifting some of the direct fixed costs to the common fixed expenses, she will be saving people's jobs by preventing the division from being closed.

There is very little chance of this shift between fixed expense categories being caught because the segment reports are hard to understand. No one in the company outside of the Accounting Department understands what is included in "Direct fixed expenses" versus "Common fixed costs." James has used a convoluted allocation system for years, and company management has given up on understanding it and just accepts the monthly reports. Company management figures that overall the company does well, so the hard-to-understand accounting reports are just a necessary evil.

Requirements:

1. Using the IMA *Statement of Ethical Professional Practice* as an ethical framework (see Exhibit 1-7), answer the following questions:
   a. What is (are) the ethical issue(s) in this situation?
   b. What are James' responsibilities as a management accountant?
2. Do you agree with James' reasoning that no one would get hurt by her actions? Why or why not?
3. Do you agree with James' assessment that she is actually helping the company and that this justifies her actions?

A10-60 Analyzing segment margins reports *(Learning Objective 3)*

The Procter & Gamble Company (P&G), a global consumer goods company, was one of the top 25 manufacturers in the United States based on 2015 revenues.[8] Its products include Bounty paper towels, Head & Shoulders shampoo, Tide laundry detergent, Gillette razors, and Pampers disposable diapers. In its annual report and Form 10-K, P&G lists five segments:

- Beauty, hair, and personal care
- Grooming
- Health care
- Fabric care and home care
- Baby, feminine, and family care

Obtain P&G's Form 10-K for 2015 by entering the phrase "Procter & Gamble investor relations form 10-K" in a search engine such as Google. Once on P&G's investor relations' web page, click on the link for annual reports and click through to find the 2015 Form 10-K. Once in the Form 10-K, go to Note 12, Segment Information. It should be found under Item 8, Financial Statements and Supplementary Data.

Questions

1. For each of the five segments, write a brief description of what products and services are included in each segment by using the information in the Segment Information section in the Form 10-K.

2. Within Note 12, locate the table that contains Global Segment Results. You will use this table to find Net earnings (loss) and Net sales for each year (2013–2015) and segment. For each of the five segments of P&G, calculate a profitability ratio for each year by using the following formula:

    Net earnings (loss) ÷ Net sales

3. For each of the segments for the years 2013 through 2015, answer the following questions:
    a. Did net sales increase, decrease, or remain about the same?
    b. Did earnings (loss) increase, decrease, or remain about the same?
    c. Did the profitability ratio (as calculated in question 2) increase, decrease, or remain about the same?

4. Of the five segments, which two segments appear to be the strongest based on the limited information you can find in the Form 10-K, Item 8, Financial Statements, and Supplementary Data? Support your answer.

5. Of the five segments, which segment appears to be the weakest based on the limited information you have located in the Form 10-K, Item 8, Financial Statements, and Supplementary Data? Support your answer.

---

[8] Source: https://en.wikipedia.org/wiki/List_of_largest_manufacturing_companies_by_revenue, retrieved January 14, 2016.

Try It Solutions

page 596:

1. ROI = Operating income/Total assets = $695/$966 = 71.9%
   Sales margin = Operating income/Sales revenue = $695/$2,636 = 26.4%
   Capital turnover = Sales revenue/Total assets = $2,636/$966 = 2.73

2. Residual income = Operating income − (Target rate of return × Total assets) =
   $695 million − (25% × $966 million) = $453.5 million

page 605:

The flexible budget is prepared using the original master budget assumptions for the *actual* volume achieved (125 jobs) rather than the volume originally anticipated (100 jobs). Therefore, the flexible budget should reflect the following expenses:

1. $1,250 of variable expenses (= 125 jobs × $10 per job)
2. $500 of fixed expenses
3. $1,750 for total operating expenses (= $1,250 + $500)

page 608:

	A	B	C	D	E	F	G	H
1	Sam's Lawn Mowing Business Flexible Budget Performance Report for June	Actual	Flexible Budget Variance		Flexible Budget	Volume Variance		Master Budget
2	Sales volume (number of mowing jobs)	125	0	F	125	25	F	100
3								
4	Operating expenses:							
5	Variable operating expenses ($10 per job)	$ 1,370	$ 120	U	$ 1,250	$ 250	U	$ 1,000
6	Fixed operating expenses ($500 per month)	475	25	F	500	0	F	500
7	Total operating expenses	$ 1,845	$ 95	U	$ 1,750	$ 250	U	$ 1,500
8								

1. The volume variance is the difference between the operating expenses in the flexible budget and what was budgeted for operating expenses in the master budget: $250 (= $1,750 − $1,500). Because the expenses in the flexible budget are higher than in the master budget, the variance is unfavorable.

2. The flexible budget variance is the difference between actual operating expenses and what was budgeted for expenses in the flexible budget: $95 (= $1,845 − $1,750). Because actual expenses are higher than budgeted, the variance is unfavorable.

3. The master budget variance is the difference between the actual operating expenses and what was budgeted for operating expenses in the master budget: $345 (= $1,845 − $1,500). Because actual expenses are higher than budgeted, the variance is unfavorable. It is also the total combination of the volume variance ($250 U) and flexible budget variance ($95 U).

11

Standard Costs and Variances

Sources: Apple 2015 10-K
http://www.zdnet.com/article/apple-watch-costs-under-85-to-make/

Learning Objectives

- **1** Explain how and why standard costs are developed
- **2** Compute and evaluate direct materials variances
- **3** Compute and evaluate direct labor variances
- **4** Explain the advantages and disadvantages of using standard costs and variances
- **5** Compute and evaluate variable overhead variances
- **6** Compute and evaluate fixed overhead variances
- **7** (Appendix) Record standard costing journal entries

Apple Inc. is well known for its innovative products such as the iPhone, iPad, and Apple Watch. But how much does it cost Apple to manufacture these products? Although Apple never releases its actual unit costs for each product, a market intelligence company by the name of IHS Technology has performed "tear-down" research to determine the cost of the direct materials in each product. For example, IHS estimates that the cost of direct materials in a 38 mm Apple Watch Sport includes $20.50 for the LG Display, $10.20 for the processor, $7.20 for the memory, $0.80 for the battery, $9.00 for the charger and spare wristband, and so forth. The total estimated cost of direct materials for an Apple Watch Sport is $83.70, purportedly giving the Apple Watch the lowest direct material cost compared to retail price ($300–$350) of any Apple product. What IHS Technology did was very similar to what many manufacturers do: They estimate how much it should cost, in terms of direct materials, direct labor, and manufacturing overhead, to produce their products. These estimates, known as standard costs, are used as performance benchmarks. They are also used by companies to prepare budgets, such as Apple's direct materials budget for the 169 million iPhones, 68 million iPads, and undisclosed number of Apple Watches sold during fiscal 2015.

In Chapter 9 we described how managers of Tucson Tortilla planned for the coming year by preparing a master budget. In Chapter 10, we saw how its managers could evaluate performance by comparing actual to budgeted revenues and costs. To gain a better understanding of the master budget variance, managers created a flexible budget to separate the master budget variance into two components: (1) a volume variance and (2) a flexible budget variance. In this chapter, we'll see how Tucson Tortilla's managers can deepen their analysis by further separating the flexible budget variance into two additional variances. To do this, we'll first need to discuss standard costs.

What Are Standard Costs?

1 Explain how and why standard costs are developed

Think of a <u>standard cost</u> as the budgeted cost for a single unit of product. For Tucson Tortilla, a single unit of product is one case of tortilla chips. A company that produces many different products will develop a standard cost for each different product. For example, Colgate-Palmolive will develop a standard cost for each type of toothpaste, soap, and laundry detergent it produces. Even service companies develop standard costs. For example, many hospitals develop standard costs for routine procedures, such as tonsillectomies. The standard cost becomes the benchmark for evaluating actual costs.

For example, let's say the standard cost of producing one case of tortilla chips is $12.00, yet the company actually incurred $12.10 to produce each case during July. The company's managers will want to know why the difference, or variance, of $0.10 per case occurred. Although $0.10 per case may not seem like much, it really is a lot when you consider that the company produces thousands of cases per month. High-volume companies like Coca-Cola, which sells 1.9 billion servings of product *each day*,[1] are eager to control every penny of cost associated with each unit of product. In highly competitive markets, the company will not be able to pass along cost increases to consumers in the form of price increases. That means that the company's profit margin will shrink with every additional penny of cost incurred. Managers' ability to understand the reasons behind cost variances is a critical factor in controlling future costs.

In our example, why did Tucson Tortilla spend more than anticipated? Perhaps the price of flour increased. Or perhaps more labor was needed than originally expected. Or extraordinarily hot weather could have driven up the cost of air conditioning used in manufacturing facility. As you can see, the variance in cost could have been due to direct materials, direct labor, manufacturing overhead, or any combination of the three. Managers will be able to understand the reasons for this unfavorable variance only by investigating further.

Types of Standards

When managers develop standard costs (often simply referred to as <u>standards</u>), they must first determine what type of standard they want to create. <u>Ideal standards</u> are standards based on perfect or ideal conditions. These types of standards, which are also known as <u>perfection standards</u>, do not allow for any poor-quality raw materials, waste in the production process, machine breakdown, or other inefficiencies. This type of standard is best suited for companies that strive for perfection, such as those that implement lean production systems described in Chapter 4.[2]

Rather than using ideal standards, many companies use <u>practical (or attainable) standards</u> that are based on currently attainable conditions. Practical standards include allowances for *normal* amounts of waste and inefficiency. Many managers believe that practical standards make the best cost benchmarks and provide the most employee motivation since they can be attained with a reasonable amount of effort.

> ■ **Why is this important?**
>
> "Managers use **standard costs** as a **benchmark** against which to **evaluate** actual costs. If actual costs are **substantially different** than standard costs, **managers** will want to know why so that they have a basis for **improving operations**."

[1] The Coca-Cola Company 2015 10-K.

[2] In fact, many lean producers do not advocate the use of standards at all. Since one of the primary goals of lean production is continuous improvement, advocates argue that no standard is ideal enough. Improvements can always be made.

Information Used to Develop and Update Standards

Managers draw on many sources of information when setting standards. They consider the amount of material and labor used on each unit produced in the *past*. They also consider the *current* cost of inputs, such as negotiated labor rates and raw materials prices. Finally, they estimate how *future* changes in the economy or in the manufacturing process might affect the standards being developed. Engineering studies help determine the amount of time and quantity of material that *should be* needed to produce each unit.

In order to serve as realistic benchmarks, standards, once developed, need to be kept up to date. Standards should be reviewed at least once a year, and they should be adjusted whenever a long-term change in costs or inputs is anticipated. For example, standards should be adjusted when:

- a new labor contract is negotiated with union workers,
- a non-temporary change in raw material costs occurs, or
- a part of the production process is reengineered.

Using outdated standards defeats the entire purpose of using standards in the first place.

Computing Standard Costs

Manufacturers typically prepare standard costs for the direct material, direct labor, and manufacturing overhead required for each unit of product. With respect to manufacturing overhead (MOH), some manufacturers only set standards for the variable MOH per unit since the fixed MOH per unit will fluctuate with changes in volume. Many companies also prepare standards for operating expenses. For simplicity, we'll limit our discussion to the three manufacturing costs. We will also assume that Tucson Tortilla has decided to develop practical, rather than ideal, standards.

Standard Cost of Direct Materials

In Chapter 9, we learned that Tucson Tortilla's only direct material (DM) is *masa harina* corn flour. Engineering studies show that each case of chips requires five pounds of flour, including allowances for normal amounts of spoilage and waste. The company can purchase the flour, including freight-in and purchase discounts, for $1.50 per pound. Therefore, the standard DM cost per case of tortilla chips is calculated as follows:

Standard Quantity of DM	×	Standard Price of DM	=	Standard Cost of DM per Case
5 lbs	×	$1.50/pound	=	$7.50

This calculation reveals that Tucson Tortilla expects to spend $7.50 on the direct materials for each case of tortilla chips produced.

Standard Cost of Direct Labor

Companies compute the standard cost of direct labor (DL) in a similar fashion. In Chapter 9, we learned that each case of tortilla chips requires only 0.05 hours of direct labor. This time requirement includes allowances for cleanup, breaks, and so forth since employees are paid for that time as well as actual work time. Furthermore, direct laborers are paid $22 per hour, including payroll taxes and employee benefits. Therefore, the standard DL cost per case of tortilla chips is:

Standard Quantity of DL	×	Standard Price of DL	=	Standard Cost of DL per Case
0.05 DL hours	×	$22.00/DL hour	=	$1.10

Since the production process is fairly automated, the company only anticipates spending $1.10 of direct labor on each case.

Standard Cost of Manufacturing Overhead

Since most of Tucson Tortilla's production process is automated, the company allocates its manufacturing overhead (MOH) using machine hours (MH) as its allocation base. Engineering studies indicate that each case of chips requires 0.10 machine hours to produce. In Chapter 9, we learned that the company expects to produce 400,000 cases of chips during the year. Therefore, the total allocation base is 40,000 machine hours.

Rather than using one predetermined overhead rate as discussed in Chapter 3, some manufacturers split their manufacturing overhead into two rates: a fixed MOH rate and a variable MOH rate. Let's see how this is done.

At a volume of 400,000 cases, Tucson Tortilla expects total variable overhead to be $1,000,000. Using this information, Tucson Tortilla calculates its predetermined *variable* MOH rate as follows:

Total estimated variable MOH ÷ Total estimated amount of the allocation base = Variable MOH rate
$1,000,000 ÷ 40,000 machine hours = $25/machine hour

Using the variable MOH rate, Tucson Tortilla can compute the standard cost of variable manufacturing overhead per case as follows:

Standard Quantity of MH × Variable MOH rate = Standard Variable MOH per Case
0.10 machine hours × $25/machine hour = $2.50

In Chapter 9, we learned that the company expects to incur $30,000 of fixed overhead each month, resulting in a total of $360,000 for the year. Therefore, the fixed MOH rate can be calculated as follows:

Total estimated fixed MOH ÷ Total estimated amount of the allocation base = Fixed MOH rate
$360,000 ÷ 40,000 machine hours = $9/machine hour

The standard cost of *fixed* manufacturing overhead *per case* is calculated as follows:

Standard Quantity of MH × Fixed MOH rate = Standard Fixed MOH per Case
0.10 machine hours × $9/machine hour = $0.90

Standard Cost of One Unit

Exhibit 11-1 shows how Tucson Tortilla adds together the standard cost of direct materials, direct labor, and manufacturing overhead to determine the standard cost of producing one case of tortilla chips.

EXHIBIT 11-1 Standard Cost of Producing One Unit of Product

Manufacturing Cost	Standard Quantity (SQ)		Standard Price (SP)		Standard Cost per Case
Direct Materials	5.00 pounds	×	$ 1.50 per pound	=	$ 7.50
Direct Labor	0.05 DL hours	×	$ 22.00 per DL hour	=	1.10
Variable MOH	0.10 machine hours	×	$ 25.00 per machine hour	=	2.50
Fixed MOH	0.10 machine hours	×	$ 9.00 per machine hour	=	0.90
Total					$ 12.00

The $12-per-case figure shown in Exhibit 11-1 may look familiar to you. Indeed, it is the same budgeted unit cost that we used in Chapter 9 when we calculated Cost of Goods Sold for the budgeted Income Statement (Exhibit 9-12) used for planning purposes. We also used the $12-per-case standard cost when we calculated Cost of Goods Sold for the flexible budget used for performance evaluation purposes (Exhibit 10-10). Although we presented the budgeting chapter prior to this chapter, most companies develop standard costs *first* and *then* use that information to help develop their budgets. Standard costs ease the budgeting process by providing a basis for calculating many figures in the master budget.

Sustainability and Standards

Many companies are reengineering their products, packaging, and production processes to save environmental resources and money. For example, Apple's packaging on the iPhone 6s is 20% lighter and takes up 34% less volume than its predecessor. It also consists of 60% recycled fiber. The company also found that by focusing on the aluminum used in its iPhone enclosure, it could significantly reduce greenhouse gases. So the iPhone was reengineered to reintegrate more scrap aluminum from the production process. Whereas toxic materials, such as mercury, lead, and arsenic were once commonplace in consumer electronics and their manufacturing processes, these substances have been removed from all Apple products over the course of the last 10 years and substituted with other materials. Sustainability initiatives such as these require managers to rethink their direct materials quantity and price standards, as fewer materials and different types of materials are used.

Reengineering the production process may also result in changes to manufacturing overhead standards. For example, Apple just conducted 13 energy audits in its supplier plants in China, Taiwan, and Japan that resulted in identifying over $32 million in annual cost savings. The company is in the process of building solar arrays and investing in other clean energy projects in Asia that will reduce carbon emissions at manufacturing plants by the equivalent of taking 6 million cars off the road each year. Initiatives such as these will require management to amend existing manufacturing overhead standards.

Operating cost standards, such as the standard cost of distributing each product, will also change as the lighter products and smaller containers reduce trucking costs. The standard cost of selling each unit may also be affected by sustainability initiatives. For example 97% of all Apple retail stores and 100% of Apple data centers are now powered by 100% renewable energy. Companies may also find themselves creating standards for the amount of waste that leaves the production process in the form of air pollution, waste-to-landfill refuse, and waste water. Apple has the goal of zero-waste-to-landfill at all iPhone and Apple Watch final assembly plants by 2017, as well as all of its retail stores. It also measures corporate water use per employee and has been able to reduce that figure by 25% since 2013.

Finally, companies can create standards for operational measures that focus on the entire life cycle of the product, all the way from cradle to grave. Apple measures the environmental impact of consumer use and disposal of its products. As a result, Apple has reduced the amount of energy required to power its products by 64% from what it was less than 10 years ago, and through its "take-back" program, Apple collects and diverts products that consumers no long want. In 2015 alone, Apple recovered over 90 million pounds of e-waste. To recycle e-waste more efficiently, the company has developed a line of robots that can disassemble and sort the parts for an iPhone in only 11 seconds! The parts are sold as valuable commodities that decrease the need for mining and extraction of precious natural resources.

See Exercises E11-25A and E11-41B

Source: Apple Environmental Responsibility Report, 2016 Progress Report, covering fiscal 2015.

Try It!

Hannah owns a fruit smoothie shop at the local mall. Each smoothie requires ¼ pound of mixed berries, which are expected to cost $4 per pound during the summer months. Shop employees are paid $10 per hour. Variable overhead consists of utilities and supplies. The variable overhead rate is $0.05 per minute of DL time. Each smoothie should require 3 minutes of DL time.

1. What is the standard cost of direct materials for each smoothie?
2. What is the standard cost of direct labor for each smoothie?
3. What is the standard cost of variable overhead for each smoothie?

Please see page 709 for solutions.

How Do Managers Use Standard Costs to Compute DM and DL Variances?

We just showed how managers develop standard costs. Managers use standards at the beginning of the period to help with the budgeting planning process. Managers also use standards at the end of the period to evaluate performance and help control future costs. Let's see how this is done.

Using Standard Costs to Develop the Flexible Budget

As we saw in the last chapter, managers often compare actual costs against a flexible budget, rather than directly against the planning budget. Recall that the flexible budget reflects the total cost that *should have been incurred, given the actual volume achieved*. In the last chapter, we created and evaluated the flexible budget performance report for the actual volume *sold* during the month of January. In this chapter, we are going to drill down farther into the company's operations, by evaluating the costs incurred to *produce* Tucson Tortilla's product.

For example, let's assume that Tucson Tortilla actually produced 31,000 cases of chips during the month of January, even though the company originally planned to produce 29,000 cases (Exhibit 9-6). Exhibit 11-2 shows the flexible budget for variable production costs. To generate the flexible budget, managers multiplied the standard costs per unit by the *actual number of units produced*. Notice the mixture of favorable and unfavorable flexible budget variances. We'll refer back to this exhibit quite often as we explore the reasons for these variances in the next sections.

EXHIBIT 11-2 Comparing Variable Production Costs with the Flexible Budget

	A	B	C	D	E	F
1	Flexible Budget Performance Report for Variable Production Costs	Standard Cost per Case	Actual Cost for 31,000 cases	Flexible Budget for 31,000 Cases	Flexible Budget Variance	
2	Direct materials	$ 7.50	$ 224,000	$ 232,500	$ 8,500	F
3	Direct labor	$ 1.10	$ 34,875	$ 34,100	$ 775	U
4	Variable MOH	$ 2.50	$ 85,200	$ 77,500	$ 7,700	U
5						

2 Compute and evaluate direct materials variances

Direct Materials Variances

From Exhibit 11-2 we know that Tucson Tortilla spent $8,500 less on direct materials (DM) than standards indicated would be spent to make 31,000 cases. Was this because the company *paid* less for the material than expected, *used* less material than expected, or a combination of the two?

When the amount of materials purchased is the same as the amount used (our example here), we can split the flexible budget variance for direct materials into two separate variances: a price variance and a quantity variance, as shown in Exhibit 11-3.

EXHIBIT 11-3 Splitting the Direct Material Flexible Budget Variance into Two Components

The way we do this is illustrated in Exhibit 11-4. In this model, notice that the company's actual costs are on the top-left side and are stated as Actual Quantity (AQ) × Actual Price (AP). The company's flexible budget is shown on the top-right side and is stated as the standard cost allowed *for the actual volume of output*. It is computed as the Standard Quantity Allowed (SQA) for the actual output × Standard Price (SP). As shown in the bottom box of the exhibit, the difference between the two outside terms is the total direct materials flexible budget variance, which we have shortened to "Total DM Variance" for the sake of simplicity.

EXHIBIT 11-4 Direct Materials Variances if DM Purchased Equals DM Used

Next, we insert a middle term in the top row of the exhibit. The middle term is a mixture of the two outside terms and is defined as Actual Quantity (AQ) × Standard Price (SP). This middle term will help us separate the total flexible budget variance into two components: a price variance and a quantity variance.

The <u>direct materials price variance</u> tells managers how much of the total variance is due to paying a higher or lower price than expected for the direct materials it purchased. The <u>direct materials quantity variance</u> tells managers how much of the total variance is due to using a larger or smaller quantity of direct materials than expected. The formulas for these variances are shown in the middle row of Exhibit 11-4.

Let's see how this works for Tucson Tortilla. First, we'll need the following information:

Actual data for January:	
Number of cases produced.....................	31,000 cases
Direct materials purchased....................	160,000 pounds at $1.40 per pound
Direct materials used............................	160,000 pounds

Next, we'll insert our company-specific data into the basic model, as shown in Exhibit 11-5. Notice how the "Actual Cost" of $224,000 is the same as what we showed in Exhibit 11-2. Also, the "Standard Cost Allowed" of $232,500 and the total favorable direct materials variance of $8,500 are the same as the figures shown in Exhibit 11-2.

EXHIBIT 11-5 Tucson Tortilla's Direct Materials Variances

The calculations in Exhibit 11-5 show us that the total direct materials variance of $8,500 is in fact the result of two causes: (1) a favorable price variance of $16,000 and (2) an unfavorable quantity variance of $7,500. The two variances net together to equal the total favorable direct materials flexible budget variance of $8,500.

In the next sections, we'll explain these variances in more detail and show how formulas can be used as an alternative to creating the diagrams illustrated in Exhibits 11-4 and 11-5.

Direct Materials Price Variance

The direct materials price variance tells managers how much of the overall variance is due to paying a higher or lower price than expected for the quantity of materials it *purchased*. As you can see in Exhibit 11-4, the price variance is computed by comparing the company's actual costs on the left side of the model with the middle term in the model. The lavender boxes in the middle row show that we can simplify the calculations by factoring out the actual quantity (AQ) purchased from both terms in the model as follows:

$$\text{DM price variance} = (AQ \times AP) - (AQ \times SP)$$
$$= AQ\,(AP - SP)$$

The simplified equation should make sense: it simply calculates the price differential between what was paid for the direct material input (pounds of corn flour, in our case) and the price anticipated by the standards. The price differential is then multiplied by the quantity of direct materials *purchased*.

Since the amount of materials purchased may be different from the amount of materials used, we will henceforth use the notation AQP to denote the "Actual Quantity Purchased" and AQU to denote the "Actual Quantity Used." In our current example, Tucson Tortilla both purchased and used the same amount of direct materials during January. However, this more specific notation will help us later when we encounter a situation in which the amount of material *purchased* differs from the amount of material *used*.

Let's use the simplified equation to calculate Tucson Tortilla's DM price variance:

$$\begin{aligned}
\text{DM price variance} &= \text{Actual Quantity Purchased} \times (\text{Actual Price} - \text{Standard Price}) \\
&= \text{AQP} \times (\text{AP} - \text{SP}) \\
&= 160{,}000 \text{ lbs} \times (\$1.40 - \$1.50) \\
&= 160{,}000 \text{ lbs} \times (\$0.10) \\
&= \$16{,}000 \text{ F}
\end{aligned}$$

From this analysis we see that Tucson Tortilla spent $0.10 *less* than anticipated per pound. Since the company purchased 160,000 pounds of flour, it ended up spending $16,000 less than standards anticipated. This is a favorable variance because the cost per pound is *less* than expected.

Direct Materials Quantity Variance

Unlike the price variance, which is based on the amount of materials *purchased*, the direct materials quantity variance is based on the amount of materials *used* during the period. It tells managers how much of the total direct materials variance is due to *using* more or less materials than anticipated by the standards. As you can see in Exhibit 11-4, the quantity variance is computed by comparing the company's standard cost allowed for the actual volume of output with the middle term in the model. Again, we can algebraically simplify these calculations into the equation shown next.

$$\begin{aligned}
\text{DM quantity variance} &= \text{Standard Price} \times (\text{Actual Quantity Used} - \text{Standard Quantity Allowed}) \\
&= \text{SP} \times (\text{AQU} - \text{SQA}) \\
&= \$1.50 \times [160{,}000 \text{ lbs} - (31{,}000 \text{ cases} \times 5 \text{ lbs/case})] \\
&= \$1.50 \times (160{,}000 \text{ lbs} - 155{,}000 \text{ lbs}) \\
&= \$1.50 \times 5{,}000 \text{ lbs} \\
&= \$7{,}500 \text{ U}
\end{aligned}$$

Note the following:

1. Since this variance addresses the efficiency with which materials were used, the calculation involves the quantity of direct materials *used* during the period (AQU), *not* the quantity *purchased* (AQP).
2. To calculate the standard quantity of materials allowed (SQA), we start with the number of units actually produced (31,000 cases) and then multiply it by the standard quantity of material allowed per unit (5 lb per case). The result (155,000 lb) tells us how much direct material the company expected to use given the actual volume of output.

From this analysis, we see that the company used 5,000 more pounds of corn flour during the period than standards indicated should be used. At a standard price of $1.50 per pound, the excess use of flour cost the company an unanticipated $7,500. This variance is unfavorable because the company used more direct materials than it should have.

Evaluating Direct Materials Variances

Exhibit 11-6 shows us that the favorable total direct materials flexible budget variance of $8,500 resulted from

1. purchasing the corn flour at a better-than-expected price, resulting in a savings of $16,000, and
2. using more corn flour than expected, resulting in an additional cost of $7,500.

EXHIBIT 11-6 Summary of Direct Materials Variances

Management will want to know why both of these variances occurred. The best source of information about the price variance is the purchasing supervisor. The supervisor should know why the company was able to purchase the materials at a better-than-expected price. Perhaps alternative suppliers entered the market. Or a bumper crop of corn pushed down corn flour prices at all suppliers. On the other hand, perhaps the company was able to make use of faster payment terms and as a result was able to obtain the flour at a greater discount. Maybe the purchasing agent bought lower-grade corn flour. Many possibilities exist.

Note that while the variance is referred to as "favorable," the result may not necessarily be a "good" thing. For example, if the company bought lower-grade corn flour, did it have a detrimental impact on the taste of the tortilla chips? Or did it cause additional waste or spoilage that might account for the unfavorable quantity variance?

Management will learn more about the quantity variance by talking with the production supervisor. The production supervisor is in the best position to know why extra corn flour was used. Was something wrong with the corn flour when it arrived (torn bags, inadequate moisture content, and so forth)? Did an accident occur in transporting the corn flour from the raw material storage area to the production area? Was a batch of chips ruined by adding too much salt? Again, many possibilities exist.

Management will want to uncover the root cause of each variance to determine whether or not the extra cost was controllable. For example, if the corn flour was in poor condition when it arrived, Tucson Tortilla may be able to receive a credit from its supplier or the transportation company that trucked in the flour. Additionally, Tucson Tortilla may want to search for a new supplier. If the cause was a human error in the factory, precautionary measures might be developed that would prevent such errors in the future.

Computing DM Variances when the Quantity of DM Purchased Differs from the Quantity of DM Used

In the example just illustrated, we assumed that the quantity of direct materials purchased was the same as the quantity of direct materials used. This is often the case with lean producers since they buy inventory "just in time" to use it in production. However, traditional manufacturers often buy extra safety stock to ensure they have enough raw materials on hand to meet production if sales demand exceeds the forecast. Recall that we took safety stock into consideration in Chapter 9 when we budgeted the amount of direct materials to purchase (see Exhibit 9-7). As a result, manufacturers often buy slightly more than they immediately need. If raw materials inventory has grown too large, however, companies will intentionally buy less than the amount required for production in order to shrink their inventory. In either case, the quantity of direct materials purchased may differ from the quantity of direct materials used.

When this occurs, managers still compute the price and quantity variances but keep the following important points in mind:

1. The DM price variance will be based on the quantity of DM *purchased* (AQP).
2. The DM quantity variance will be based on the quantity of DM *used* (AQU).
3. The DM price and quantity variances will no longer sum (or net) to the total flexible budget variance.

Let's try an example. Assume that the following activity took place in February:

Actual data for February:	
Number of cases produced...............................	20,000 cases
Direct materials purchased.............................	105,000 pounds at $1.45 per pound
Direct materials used......................................	98,000 pounds

We can compute the DM price and quantity variances using the same formulas developed in the preceding section.

The price variance is based on the actual quantity *purchased* (AQP):

$$\begin{aligned}\text{DM price variance} &= \text{AQP} \times (\text{AP} - \text{SP}) \\ &= 105{,}000 \text{ lbs} \times (\$1.45 - \$1.50) \\ &= 105{,}000 \text{ lbs} \times (\$0.05) \\ &= \$5{,}250 \text{ F}\end{aligned}$$

By purchasing 105,000 pounds of corn flour at a price that was $0.05 less than standard, the company saved $5,250.

The quantity variance is based on the actual quantity of materials *used* (AQU):

$$\begin{aligned}\text{DM quantity variance} &= \text{SP} \times (\text{AQU} - \text{SQA}) \\ &= \$1.50 \times [98{,}000 \text{ lbs} - (20{,}000 \text{ cases} \times 5 \text{ lbs/case})] \\ &= \$1.50 \times (98{,}000 \text{ lbs} - 100{,}000 \text{ lbs}) \\ &= \$1.50 \times (2{,}000 \text{ lbs}) \\ &= \$3{,}000 \text{ F}\end{aligned}$$

This analysis reveals that the company used 2,000 fewer pounds of corn flour than standards projected, resulting in a cost savings of $3,000.

Try It!

Hannah owns a fruit smoothie shop at the local mall. Each smoothie requires ¼ pound of mixed berries, which are expected to cost $4 per pound during the summer months. During the month of June, Hannah purchased and used 1,300 pounds of mixed berries at a cost of $3.75 per pound. Hannah's shop sold 5,000 smoothies during the month.

1. Calculate the DM price variance. Is the variance favorable or unfavorable?
2. Calculate the DM quantity variance (also known as a DM efficiency variance). Is the variance favorable or unfavorable?
3. Calculate the total DM variance. Is the variance favorable or unfavorable?

Please see page 709 for solutions.

3 Compute and evaluate direct labor variances

Direct Labor Variances

From Exhibit 11-2 we know that Tucson Tortilla only spent $775 more than anticipated on direct labor. Because this is such a small variance, some managers might not consider investigating it. However, it's possible that the total variance is made up of large but offsetting individual variances, similar to what we saw with the direct materials variances. By splitting the total direct labor variance into two separate variances, a rate variance and an efficiency variance, we can find out whether the company *paid a higher wage rate* to the factory workers than expected, *used* more time in making the chips than expected, or some combination of these two factors.

Let's assume the following information about Tucson Tortilla's January operations:

Actual data for January:	
Number of cases produced...............	31,000 cases
Direct labor hours............................	1,500 hours
Direct labor cost...............................	$34,875 (resulting in an average wage rate of $23.25/hr*)

* $34,875/1,500 hours = $23.25/hr

Exhibit 11-7 shows that the general model for direct labor (DL) variances is almost identical to the model used for direct materials variances. The only real difference is in the names of the variances. For example, instead of a DM *price* variance, we have a DL *rate* variance. The **direct labor rate variance** tells managers how much of the total direct labor variance is due to paying a higher or lower hourly wage rate than anticipated.

Likewise, instead of the DM *quantity* variance, we have a DL *efficiency* variance. The quantity of time used in production tells management how efficiently employees were working. Therefore, the **direct labor efficiency variance** tells managers how much of the total labor variance is due to using a greater or lesser amount of time than anticipated.

While the terminology for DL variances is slightly different than it was for DM variances, the calculations are essentially the same.

EXHIBIT 11-7 Calculation of Tucson Tortilla's Direct Labor Variances

Although the total direct labor variance is small ($775), Exhibit 11-7 shows us the importance of digging down deeper: the total variance is made up of (1) an unfavorable rate variance of $1,875 and (2) an offsetting favorable efficiency variance of $1,100. In the next sections, we'll go over these variances in more detail.

Direct Labor Rate Variance

As shown in Exhibit 11-7, the direct labor rate variance is computed on the left side of the model by comparing the company's actual costs with the middle term in the model. Alternatively, we can algebraically simplify the equation, just like we did for the direct materials variances. The resulting simplified equation is as follows:

$$\begin{aligned} \text{DL rate variance} &= \text{Actual Hours} \times (\text{Actual Rate} - \text{Standard Rate}) \\ &= \text{AH} \times (\text{AR} - \text{SR}) \\ &= 1{,}500 \text{ hrs} \times (\$23.25 - \$22.00) \\ &= 1{,}500 \text{ hrs} \times \$1.25 \\ &= \$1{,}875 \text{ U} \end{aligned}$$

This analysis shows management the overall dollar impact of paying an average wage rate that was higher than anticipated. The human resources supervisor and the production supervisor should be able to explain why this happened. Several possibilities exist. For example, perhaps some lower paid employees were sick or on vacation, and higher paid employees filled in during their absence. Perhaps a wage premium was offered to workers during January to keep morale up during this peak production month. Even though the variance was "unfavorable," neither of these possible explanations suggests poor management. Rather, they simply explain why the average wage rate paid was higher than expected, resulting in an unanticipated additional cost of $1,875.

Direct Labor Efficiency Variance

As you can see in Exhibit 11-7, the efficiency variance is computed on the right side of the model by comparing the company's standard cost allowed with the middle term in the model. Again, we can algebraically simplify these calculations as follows:

$$\begin{aligned} \text{DL efficiency variance} &= \text{Standard Rate} \times (\text{Actual Hours} - \text{Standard Hours Allowed}) \\ &= \text{SR} \times (\text{AH} - \text{SHA}) \\ &= \$22.00 \times [1{,}500 \text{ hrs} - (31{,}000 \text{ cases} \times 0.05 \text{ hrs/case})] \\ &= \$22.00 \times (1{,}500 \text{ hrs} - 1{,}550 \text{ hrs}) \\ &= \$22.00 \times (50 \text{ hrs}) \\ &= \$1{,}100 \text{ F} \end{aligned}$$

Notice that to calculate the standard hours of time allowed (SHA), we start with the actual number of units produced (31,000 cases) and multiply it by the standard amount of time allowed per unit (0.05 hours per case). The result (1,550 hours) tells us how many hours of direct labor the company expected to use given the actual volume of output.

From this analysis, we see that the company used 50 fewer hours of direct labor than standards indicated would be used. At a standard labor rate of $22.00 per hour, the efficient use of time saved the company an unanticipated $1,100. This variance is favorable, because workers used *less* time than anticipated.

Although this variance is fairly small, management may still want to investigate. The production supervisor would be in the best position to explain the favorable variance. Perhaps by using higher-skilled, higher-paid individuals, the work was performed at a faster speed. By searching out the root cause, management may gain a better understanding of how the efficiency occurred and whether similar efficiencies might be replicated in the future or in other areas of operations. Exhibit 11-8 summarizes Tucson Tortilla's direct labor variances for January.

EXHIBIT 11-8 Summary of Direct Labor Variances

Summary of Direct Materials and Direct Labor Variances

Exhibit 11-9 summarizes the formulas for the direct materials and direct labor variances, as well as the party responsible for best explaining why the variance occurred.

EXHIBIT 11-9 Summary of DM and DL Variance Formulas

Variance	Formula	Inquire with...
Direct Materials Price Variance	= Actual Quantity Purchased × (Actual Price − Standard Price) = AQP × (AP − SP)	Purchasing Supervisor
Direct Materials Quantity Variance	= Standard Price × (Actual Quantity Used − Standard Quantity Allowed) = SP × (AQU − SQA)	Production Supervisor
Direct Labor Rate Variance	= Actual Hours × (Actual Rate − Standard Rate) = AH × (AR − SR)	Human Resources and Production Supervisors
Direct Labor Efficiency Variance	= Standard Rate × (Actual Hours − Standard Hours Allowed) = SR × (AH − SHA)	Production Supervisor

4 Explain the advantages and disadvantages of using standard costs and variances

Advantages and Disadvantages of Using Standard Costs and Variances

The practice of using standard costs and variances was developed in the early twentieth century, during the advent and growth of mass manufacturing. Although many manufacturers continue to use standard costs and variances, others do not. Management must weigh the costs against the benefits to decide whether they want to use standard costs and perform detailed variance analysis. Even if management uncovers variances, they will want to use management by exception to determine which variances are significant enough to warrant investigation.

Advantages

- **Cost benchmarks:** One of the greatest advantages of using standard costs is having a benchmark by which to judge actual costs. However, this benchmark is valid only if the standards are kept up to date.
- **Usefulness in budgeting:** Standards are often used as the basis for many components in the master budget, such as the direct materials, direct labor, and manufacturing overhead budgets.

- **Motivation:** The use of practical, or attainable, standards should increase employee motivation because it gives employees a reasonable goal to achieve.
- **Standard costing systems simplify bookkeeping:** Many manufacturers use standards as the backbone to their standard costing system. In a standard costing system, all manufacturing costs entering Work in Process Inventory are recorded at standard cost rather than actual cost. Variances between actual costs and standard costs are immediately captured in variance accounts in the general ledger. This type of costing system is described in the appendix to this chapter.

Disadvantages

Despite the prevalence of standard costing over the past century, many contemporary manufacturers are moving away from the use of standards. Here are some of the reasons:

- **Outdated or inaccurate standards:** As mentioned previously, standard costs can quickly become outdated or inaccurate as the cost of inputs or the production process changes. Standards should be reviewed and updated at least yearly. They should also be updated whenever a change in process or input costs is considered to be nontemporary. Keeping standards up to date is costly.
- **Lack of timeliness:** In the past, variances were often computed once a month. In today's fast-paced world, such information is often too old to be useful. As a result, some companies are moving toward the daily calculation of variances.
- **Focus on operational performance measures and visual management:** Because of the need for timely data, many lean producers are placing greater emphasis on operational performance measures that are collected daily, or even hourly, and visually displayed where front-line workers can immediately see performance levels. They find such visual reminders much more effective for motivating front-line employees than relying on price and efficiency variances.
- **Lean thinking:** As discussed in Chapter 4, lean companies strive for continual improvement. That means that current standards are not "good enough." Rather than focusing on whether or not production has met current standards, lean producers focus on finding new ways to decrease waste, increase efficiency, and increase quality. They concentrate on looking forward rather than looking at the past.
- **Increase in automation and decrease in direct labor:** Most manufacturers have shifted toward automated production processes. For many manufacturers, direct labor is no longer a primary component of production or a driver of overhead costs. In addition, for companies that pay employees a salary rather than an hourly wage rate, direct labor is a fixed cost, rather than a variable cost. Finally, at lean companies, employees tend to be multiskilled and cross-trained to perform a number of duties rather than a single, repetitive task. These front-line workers are held in high esteem by management and are considered to be part of a team effort rather than a labor force to be controlled. To these companies, direct labor standards are no longer relevant or helpful.
- **Unintended behavioral consequences:** Use of traditional standards can cause unintended behavioral consequences. For example, to obtain a favorable price variance, the purchasing supervisor may buy larger quantities of raw materials than needed. Likewise, a production manager may overproduce to obtain a favorable fixed overhead volume variance (discussed in the second half of the chapter). However, as we learned in Chapter 4, holding or producing excess quantities of inventories is wasteful and costly, and should be avoided.

Decision Guidelines

Standard Costs and Variances

Let's consider some decisions management must make with regard to standard costs and variances.

Decision	Guidelines
What is a standard cost and how can it be used?	A standard cost is a budget for a single unit of product. Standards costs are used as performance benchmarks against which to evaluate actual costs. Standards costs are also used for developing the direct materials, direct labor, and manufacturing overhead budgets.
Should we use ideal (perfection) standards or practical (attainable) standards?	Since ideal standards are only achievable under flawless conditions, they are best suited for lean producers that strive for perfection. Practical standards, which are attainable with effort, are typically used by traditional manufacturers that want to use motivational, yet realistic, benchmarks.
What information is used to develop standards?	Companies use a combination of historical, current, and projected data to develop standards. Managers often use engineering time and motion studies to determine the quantity of time and materials needed to produce each unit.
How often should standard costs be updated?	Standard costs should be reviewed at least once a year and updated whenever a non-temporary change in costs, inputs, or processes occurs.
How is the direct materials price variance computed?	= Actual Quantity Purchased × (Actual Price − Standard Price) = AQP × (AP − SP)
How is the direct materials quantity variance computed?	= Standard Price × (Actual Quantity Used − Standard Quantity Allowed) = SP × (AQU − SQA)
How is the direct labor rate variance computed?	= Actual Hours × (Actual Rate − Standard Rate) = AH × (AR − SR)
How is the direct labor efficiency variance computed?	= Standard Rate × (Actual Hours − Standard Hours Allowed) = SR × (AH − SHA)
Who is usually in the best position to explain why the variances occurred?	DM price variance: Purchasing Supervisor DM quantity variance: Production Supervisor DL rate variance: Production and Human Resources Supervisors DL efficiency variance: Production Supervisor

SUMMARY PROBLEM 1

Memoirs, Inc., produces several different styles and sizes of picture frames. The collage frame consists of 12 interconnected matted picture slots, each surrounded by a wood frame. Engineering studies indicate that each collage frame will require the following direct materials and direct labor:

Materials and Labor:	Quantity of Input	Price of Input
Wood trim for frame borders	18 feet	$ 0.35 per foot
Mattes for individual pictures	12 mattes	$ 0.05 per matte
Sheet glass top	4 square feet	$ 4.00 per square foot
Pressboard frame backing	4 square feet	$ 0.25 per square foot
Direct Labor	0.25 hours	$16 per hour

The following activity regarding direct labor and wood trim occurred during March:

Number of frames produced	25,000 frames
Wood trim purchased	450,000 feet at $0.37 per foot
Wood trim used	455,000 feet
Direct labor hours	6,500 hours
Direct labor cost	$100,750 (resulting in an average wage rate of $15.50/hr*)

* $100,750/6,500 hours = $15.50/hr

Requirements

1. Calculate the standard direct materials cost and standard direct labor cost for each collage frame.
2. Calculate the wood trim direct materials price and quantity variances for the month of March.
3. Calculate the direct labor rate and efficiency variances for the month of March.

▪ SOLUTIONS

Requirement 1

The standard cost of direct materials and direct labor is calculated by multiplying the standard quantity of input needed for each collage frame by the standard price of the input:

Materials and Labor:	Quantity of Input (a)	Price of Input (b)	Standard Cost (a × b)
Wood trim for frame borders	18 feet	$ 0.35 per foot	$ 6.30
Mattes for individual pictures	12 mattes	$ 0.05 per matte	0.60
Sheet glass top	4 square feet	$ 4.00 per square foot	16.00
Pressboard frame backing	4 square feet	$ 0.25 per square foot	1.00
Direct material cost per unit			$23.90
Direct Labor	0.25 hours	$16 per hour	$ 4.00

Requirement 2
The direct materials price variance is based on the quantity of materials (wood trim) *purchased*:

$$\text{DM price variance} = \text{AQP} \times (\text{AP} - \text{SP})$$
$$= 450{,}000 \text{ ft} \times (\$0.37 - \$0.35)$$
$$= 450{,}000 \text{ ft} \times \$0.02$$
$$= \$9{,}000 \text{ U}$$

The company spent $0.02 per foot more than anticipated on the 450,000 feet of wood trim that it purchased, resulting in an unfavorable price variance of $9,000.

The direct materials quantity variance is based on the quantity of materials (wood trim) *used*:

$$\text{DM quantity variance} = \text{SP} \times (\text{AQU} - \text{SQA})$$
$$= \$0.35 \times [455{,}000 \text{ ft} - (25{,}000 \text{ frames} \times 18 \text{ ft/frame})]$$
$$= \$0.35 \times (455{,}000 \text{ ft} - 450{,}000 \text{ ft})$$
$$= \$0.35 \times 5{,}000 \text{ ft}$$
$$= \$1{,}750 \text{ U}$$

This analysis reveals that using 5,000 more feet of wood trim than anticipated resulted in an unanticipated additional cost of $1,750.

Requirement 3
The direct labor rate variance is computed as follows:

$$\text{DL rate variance} = \text{AH} \times (\text{AR} - \text{SR})$$
$$= 6{,}500 \text{ hrs} \times (\$15.50 - \$16.00)$$
$$= 6{,}500 \text{ hrs} \times (\$0.50)$$
$$= \$3{,}250 \text{ F}$$

The company spent $0.50 less per hour than anticipated, resulting in a $3,250 F variance over the 6,500 hours that were worked.

The direct labor efficiency variance is calculated as follows:

$$\text{DL efficiency variance} = \text{SR} \times (\text{AH} - \text{SHA})$$
$$= \$16.00 \times [6{,}500 - (25{,}000 \text{ frames} \times 0.25 \text{ hrs/frame})]$$
$$= \$16.00 \times (6{,}500 - 6{,}250 \text{ hrs})$$
$$= \$16.00 \times 250 \text{ hrs}$$
$$= \$4{,}000 \text{ U}$$

At a standard labor rate of $16.00 per hour, the extra use of direct labor hours cost the company an unanticipated $4,000.

How Do Managers Use Standard Costs to Compute MOH Variances?

In the first half of the chapter we learned how Tucson Tortilla developed standard costs and then used those standards to evaluate its direct materials and direct labor costs. In this half of the chapter, we'll look at the four manufacturing overhead (MOH) variances that are typically computed: two related to variable MOH costs and two related to fixed MOH costs.

Variable Manufacturing Overhead Variances

From Exhibit 11-2, we learned that Tucson Tortilla had an unfavorable variable overhead flexible budget variance of $7,700. But why did this unexpected additional cost occur?

Manufacturers usually split the total variable MOH variance into rate and efficiency variances, just as they do for direct labor. Exhibit 11-10 (on the next page) shows that the general model for calculating variable MOH rate and efficiency variances is almost identical to the model used for direct labor rate and efficiency variances. The only real difference in the calculations is the rate that is used: we use the *variable manufacturing overhead rate*, not the direct labor wage rate. And since Tucson Tortilla allocates its overhead using machine hours, the hours refer to machine hours rather than direct labor hours.[3] Here is the information from January's operations:

5 Compute and evaluate variable overhead variances

Data for January	
Number of cases produced	31,000 cases
Standard variable MOH rate	$25 per machine hour
Standard hours required per case	0.10 machine hours
Actual machine hours	3,000 machine hours
Actual variable MOH costs	$85,200 (resulting in an *actual* variable MOH rate of $28.40 per machine hour)*

*$85,200/3,000 hours = $28.40/machine hour

Variable Overhead Rate Variance

As shown in Exhibit 11-10, the **variable overhead rate variance** is the difference between the actual variable MOH costs incurred during the period ($85,200) and the amount of variable MOH costs expected ($75,000) considering the actual machine (mch) hours used. It tells managers whether more or less was spent on variable overhead than expected given the actual machine hours run. As a result, the variable overhead rate variance is also sometimes called the **variable overhead spending variance**. The variance formula can be algebraically simplified into the following formula:

> Variable MOH rate variance = Actual Hours × (Actual Rate − Standard Rate)
> = AH × (AR − SR)
> = 3,000 mch hrs × ($28.40 − $25.00)
> = 3,000 mch hrs × ($3.40)
> = $10,200 U

The interpretation of this variance is not quite as straightforward as the interpretation of the direct labor rate variance. First, variable MOH is made up of a number of different costs, including indirect materials, indirect labor, and other variable overhead costs

---

[3] Many companies allocate manufacturing overhead using direct labor hours rather than machine hours. For these companies, the hours used in calculating the manufacturing overhead variances will be *identical* to the hours used in calculating the direct labor variances.

EXHIBIT 11-10 Calculation of Variable Overhead Variances

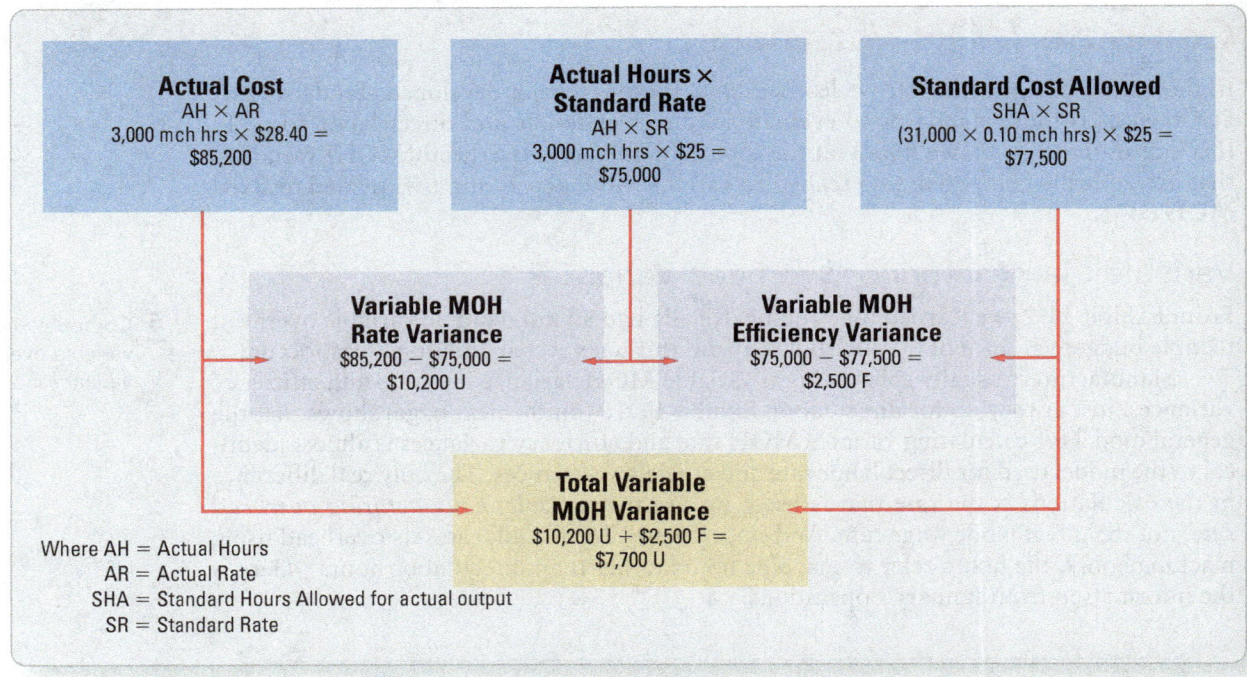

such as the variable portion of the utility bill. One particular cost (for example, indirect materials) could be higher than expected, yet another cost (for example, indirect labor) could be less than expected. As a result, the variance could be due to more than one input.

Second, we don't know if the variance is due to *using* more of the input than expected (for example, using more indirect materials than expected) or because the input *cost more* than expected from the suppliers. On average, management expected variable overhead to cost $25 per machine hour. However, we see that the actual rate ($28.40 per machine hour) turned out to be quite a bit higher. The production supervisor and purchasing manager are usually in the best position to help management understand why this variance occurred.

Variable Overhead Efficiency Variance

As shown in Exhibit 11-10, the <u>variable overhead efficiency variance</u> is the difference between the actual machine hours run and the standard machine hours allowed for the actual production volume, calculated at the standard variable MOH rate. Again, it can be algebraically simplified into the following formula:

Variable MOH efficiency variance = Standard Rate × (Actual Hours − Standard Hours Allowed)
= SR × (AH − SHA)
= $25 × [3,000 mch hrs − (31,000 cases × 0.10 mch hrs/case)]
= $25 × (3,000 mch hrs − 3,100 mch hrs)
= $25 × (100 mch hrs)
= $2,500 F

The efficiency variance does not tell management anything with regard to how efficiently variable manufacturing overhead was used. Rather, it is directly tied to the efficiency with which the machine hours were used. It tells managers how much of the total variable MOH variance is due to using more or fewer machine hours than anticipated for the actual volume of output. The production supervisor would be in the best position to explain why this variance occurred.

Fixed Manufacturing Overhead Variances

The calculation and interpretation of the fixed overhead variances are much different than the variances we have discussed thus far. Why? Because all of the manufacturing costs we have analyzed thus far have been *variable* costs. However, fixed overhead is expected to remain constant, regardless of volume fluctuations.

As shown in Chapter 9 (Exhibit 9-9), Tucson Tortilla expects to incur $30,000 of fixed overhead each month. Fixed overhead costs such as straight-line depreciation on the plant, property insurance, property tax, and the monthly salaries of indirect laborers should not vary month to month as production levels fluctuate to meet demand. However, let's assume that the company actually incurred $31,025 of fixed overhead.

6 Compute and evaluate fixed overhead variances

Fixed Overhead Budget Variance

The <u>fixed overhead budget variance</u> measures the difference between the actual fixed overhead costs incurred and the budgeted fixed overhead costs. This variance is sometimes referred to as the <u>fixed overhead spending variance</u> because it specifically looks at whether the company spent more or less than anticipated on fixed overhead costs. As shown in Exhibit 11-11, the calculation of this variance is straightforward. The difference between Tucson Tortilla's actual fixed overhead costs ($31,025) and its budgeted fixed overhead costs ($30,000) results in an unfavorable fixed overhead budget variance of $1,025. The variance is unfavorable if actual fixed overhead costs are more than budgeted and favorable if actual costs are lower than budgeted.

EXHIBIT 11-11 Calculation of Fixed Overhead Variances

The best way to uncover the cause of the fixed overhead budget variance is to compare each fixed overhead cost component against the budgeted amount. Perhaps indirect laborers received a raise that was not foreseen when the budget was prepared. Perhaps the insurance company increased its premiums or the city increased property taxes. Although the variance is labeled "unfavorable," the reason for the variance may not be a bad thing. Nor may it be controllable. For example, let's say the unfavorable variance was caused by a raise in salary given to certain indirect laborers in the plant. The raise may result in a boost to employee morale, leading to better productivity. If the unfavorable variance was caused by an increase in city property taxes, management may have little recourse. If, however, the variance was caused by an increase in insurance premiums, management may decide to shop around for a different insurance carrier. As these potential explanations indicate, the variance could be due to a number of different factors.

Fixed Overhead Volume Variance

As shown in Exhibit 11-11, the **fixed overhead volume variance** is the difference between the budgeted fixed overhead cost and the *standard fixed overhead cost* allocated to production.[4] The standard cost is calculated the same way we calculated earlier standard costs: we start with the actual volume produced (31,000 cases) and then multiply it by the standard hours allowed per case (0.10 machine hrs) to get the standard hours allowed. Finally, we multiply the standard hours allowed by the fixed MOH rate ($9/machine hour) to get the standard fixed overhead cost allocated to production:

Standard Fixed Overhead Cost Allocated to Production = (Standard Hours Allowed × Standard Rate)
= (31,000 cases × 0.10 mch hrs/case) × $9/mch hr
= 3,100 mch hrs × $9/mch hr
= $27,900

Now that we have calculated the standard fixed overhead allocated to production, we can compute the fixed overhead volume variance as follows:

Fixed Overhead Volume Variance = Budgeted Fixed Overhead Cost − Standard Fixed Overhead Cost Allocated to Production
= $30,000 − $27,900
= $2,100 U

The fixed overhead volume variance results from two causes:

1. Treating fixed overhead costs *as if* they were variable in order to allocate the costs to individuals units of product; and
2. Incorrectly estimating the level of activity when calculating the predetermined fixed MOH rate.

For example, Tucson Tortilla calculated its predetermined fixed MOH rate ($9/machine hour) based on an estimated yearly production volume of 400,000 cases. Recall from Chapter 6 that fixed costs per unit of activity vary inversely with changes in volume. Had the production estimate been higher than 400,000 cases, the predetermined fixed overhead rate would have been lower than $9 per machine hour. If, however, the production estimate had been lower than 400,000 cases, the fixed overhead rate would have been higher than $9 per machine hour. Since production volume (31,000 cases) was not the same as anticipated (33,333 cases per month on average = 400,000 cases per year/12 months), we expect a difference between what was budgeted for fixed overhead and the amount of fixed overhead allocated to production.

In essence, the fixed overhead volume variance measures the utilization of the fixed capacity costs. If volume is higher than originally anticipated, the variance will be favorable because more units were produced with the same amount of fixed resources. In essence, the company used those fixed resources more efficiently. In this situation, the standard fixed overhead cost allocated to production is *greater* than the amount budgeted. In other words, the company *overallocated* fixed overhead to production, as shown in Exhibit 11-12.

EXHIBIT 11-12 Favorable Fixed Overhead Volume Variance

---

[4] In Chapter 3 we learned about a *normal* costing system in which manufacturing overhead is allocated to production using a predetermined MOH rate multiplied by the actual quantity of the allocation base used (such as actual machine hours used by the job). In a *standard* costing system, companies allocate manufacturing overhead to production differently: they multiply the predetermined manufacturing overhead rate by the *standard quantity of the allocation base allowed* rather than by the *actual quantity of the allocation base used*.

In contrast, if production volume is lower than anticipated, the variance is denoted as unfavorable due to the fact that fixed costs were not used to produce as many units as anticipated. Since the number of units produced (31,000 cases) was less than anticipated (33,333 on average per month), production capacity was used less efficiently than anticipated, leading to an unfavorable volume variance. In this situation, the standard fixed overhead cost allocated to production is less than the amount budgeted. In other words, the company *underallocated* fixed overhead, as shown in Exhibit 11-13.

EXHIBIT 11-13 Unfavorable Fixed Overhead Volume Variance

Keep the following rule of thumb in mind:

> When production volume is *higher* than anticipated, the fixed overhead volume variance will be *favorable*. When it is *lower* than anticipated, the fixed overhead volume variance will be *unfavorable*.

Extreme caution should be used when interpreting the volume variance. Again, favorable does not equate with "good," nor does unfavorable equate with "bad." For companies striving to create lean production environments, production levels will naturally fall as the company sheds itself of excess inventory, leading to an unfavorable volume variance. Has a "bad" decision been made? Absolutely not. The lean producer will generally be much more efficient in the long run than its traditional counterpart. The challenge during the transition phase will be for management to determine how to best use the newly freed capacity, and not be misled by the resulting temporary unfavorable volume variances that may occur.

Try It!

Hannah owns a fruit smoothie shop at the local mall. The budgeted monthly fixed overhead costs consist of the store lease payment ($1,000), advertising ($250), equipment depreciation ($125), and store Wi-Fi ($80). Actual fixed overhead expenses for June were $1,600. When calculating the fixed overhead rate, Hannah anticipated selling 4,800 smoothies during each summer month. She actually sold 5,000 in June.

1. What is the fixed overhead budget variance for the month of June? Is the variance favorable or unfavorable?
2. Will Hannah's fixed overhead volume variance for the month of June be favorable or unfavorable? Explain.

Please see page 709 for solutions.

Standard Costing Systems

As we have just seen, many manufacturers calculate standard costs and perform variance analysis outside of their general ledger accounting system. However, other companies integrate standards directly into their general ledger accounting. This method of accounting, called standard costing, is discussed in the appendix to this chapter.

Decision Guidelines

Standard Costs and Variances

Let's consider some of management's decisions related to overhead variances.

Decision	Guidelines
Should we calculate and interpret all manufacturing overhead variances the same way?	Variable overhead costs are expected to change in total as production volume changes. However, fixed overhead costs should stay constant within a relevant range of production. Therefore, management will want to analyze variable and fixed MOH variances separately.
What variable overhead variances should we compute?	• The variable overhead rate (or spending) variance tells managers if they spent more or less than anticipated on variable MOH costs considering the actual hours of work used. • The variable overhead efficiency variance tells managers nothing about the efficiency with which variable overhead costs were used. Rather, it is tied directly to the efficiency with which machine hours or labor hours were used.
How is the variable overhead *rate* (or *spending*) variance computed?	= Actual Hours × (Actual Rate − Standard Rate) = AH × (AR − SR)
How is the variable overhead *efficiency* variance computed?	= Standard Rate × (Actual Hours − Standard Hours Allowed) = SR × (AH − SHA)
What fixed overhead variances should we compute?	• The fixed overhead budget (or spending) variance tells managers if they spent more or less than anticipated on fixed overhead costs. • The fixed overhead volume variance tells managers if too much or too little fixed overhead was allocated to production due to the actual volume of production being different than the volume used to calculate the predetermined fixed MOH rate.
How is the fixed overhead *budget* variance computed?	= Actual fixed overhead − Budgeted fixed overhead
How is the fixed overhead *volume* variance computed?	= Budgeted fixed overhead − Standard fixed overhead cost allocated to production = Budgeted fixed overhead − (SHA × SR)
How should management uncover the root causes of the overhead variances?	Management will want to compare the actual cost of individual MOH components (such as indirect labor, utilities, property taxes) against the budgeted costs for those same components. The purchasing and production supervisors are usually in the best position to offer insights as to why the variances occurred.
How should the fixed overhead volume variance be interpreted?	• A favorable variance means that more units were produced than originally anticipated, leading to an overallocation of fixed MOH. • An unfavorable variance means that fewer units were produced than originally anticipated, leading to an underallocation of fixed MOH.

SUMMARY PROBLEM 2

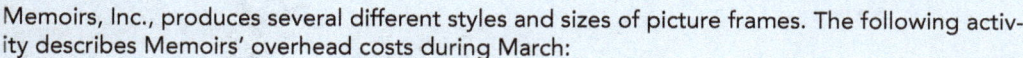

Memoirs, Inc., produces several different styles and sizes of picture frames. The following activity describes Memoirs' overhead costs during March:

Number of frames produced	25,000 frames
Predetermined variable MOH rate	$ 6.00 per DL hour
Predetermined fixed MOH rate	$ 12.00 per DL hour
Budgeted fixed manufacturing overhead	$70,000
Actual direct labor hours	6,500 hours
Actual variable manufacturing overhead	$40,625, resulting in an actual rate of $6.25* per DL hour
Actual fixed manufacturing overhead	$68,000
Standard direct labor allowed per unit	0.25 hours per frame

*$40,625/6,500 hours

Requirements

1. Calculate the variable overhead rate and efficiency variances for the month of March.
2. Calculate the fixed overhead budget and volume variances for the month of March.
3. Calculate the total fixed overhead variance for the month of March.

SOLUTIONS

Requirement 1

Variable MOH rate variance = Actual Hours × (Actual Rate − Standard Rate)
= AH × (AR − SR)
= 6,500 hrs × ($6.25 − $6.00)
= 6,500 hrs × ($0.25)
= $1,625 U

Variable MOH efficiency variance = Standard Rate × (Actual Hours − Standard Hours Allowed)
= SR × (AH − SHA)
= $6.00 × [6,500 − (25,000 frames × 0.25 hrs/frame)]
= $6.00 × (6,500 − 6,250 hrs)
= $6.00 × 250 hrs
= $1,500 U

Requirements 2 & 3

The fixed overhead variances are calculated as follows:

- The budget variance is favorable since less was spent on fixed overhead than budgeted.
- The volume variance is favorable since more was allocated to production than was budgeted. This means that more units were produced than budgeted.
- As a result of the two favorable variances, the total fixed overhead variance is also favorable.

Appendix 11A

Standard Costing

Many companies integrate standard costs directly into their general ledger accounting by recording inventory-related costs at standard cost rather than at actual cost. This method of accounting is called **standard costing** or **standard cost accounting**. Standard costing not only saves on bookkeeping costs but also isolates price and quantity variances as soon as they occur. The variances will be clearly displayed for management on a standard costing income statement, which we will show you in Exhibit 11-14. Before we go through the journal entries, keep the following key points in mind:

1. Each type of variance discussed has its own general ledger account. A debit balance means that the variance is unfavorable since it decreases income (just like an expense). A credit balance means that the variance is favorable since it increases income (just like a revenue).

2. Just as in job costing, the manufacturing costs flow through the inventory accounts in the following order: raw materials → work in process → finished goods → cost of goods sold. The difference is that *standard costs* rather than actual costs are used to record the manufacturing costs entered into the inventory accounts.

3. At the end of the period, the variance accounts are closed to Cost of Goods Sold to correct for the fact that the standard costs recorded in the accounts were different from actual costs. Assuming that most inventory worked on during the period has been sold, any error from using standard costs rather than actual costs is contained in Cost of Goods Sold. Closing the variance accounts to Cost of Goods Sold corrects the Cost of Goods Sold balance and zeros out the temporary variance accounts.

7 Record standard costing journal entries

Journal Entries

We use Tucson Tortilla's January transactions, just as we did in the chapter, to demonstrate standard costing.

1. **Recording Raw Materials Purchases**—Tucson Tortilla debits Raw Materials Inventory for the *actual quantity* of corn flour purchased (160,000 pounds) recorded at the *standard price* ($1.50 per pound). It credits Accounts Payable for the *actual quantity* of corn flour purchased (160,000 pounds) recorded at the *actual price* ($1.40 per pound) because this is the amount owed to Tucson Tortilla's suppliers. The difference is the direct materials *price* variance.

	Raw Materials Inventory (160,000 × $1.50)	240,000	
	Accounts Payable (160,000 × $1.40)		224,000
	DM Price Variance		16,000
	(to record purchase of raw materials)		

The favorable price variance is the same as that shown in Exhibit 11-5. Since it is favorable, it has a credit balance, which increases Tucson Tortilla's January profits.

2. **Recording Use of Direct Materials**—When Tucson Tortilla *uses* direct materials, it debits Work in Process Inventory at the *standard price* ($1.50) × *standard quantity* of direct materials that should have been used (31,000 cases × 5 lb per case = 155,000 pounds). *This maintains Work in Process Inventory at a purely standard cost.* Raw Materials Inventory is credited for the *actual quantity* of materials used in production (160,000 pounds) recorded at the *standard price* ($1.50) since this is the price at which the materials were entered into Raw Materials Inventory in the previous journal entry. The difference is the direct materials *quantity* variance. The direct

materials quantity variance is recorded when Tucson Tortilla records the *use* of direct materials:

	Work in Process Inventory (155,000 × $1.50)	232,500	
	DM Quantity Variance	7,500	
	Raw Materials Inventory (160,000 × $1.50)		240,000
	(to record use of direct materials)		

The unfavorable quantity price variance is the same as that shown in Exhibit 11-5. Since it is unfavorable, it has a debit balance, which decreases Tucson Tortilla's January profits.

3. **Recording Direct Labor Costs**—Since Work in Process Inventory is maintained at standard cost, Tucson Tortilla debits Work in Process Inventory for the *standard rate* for direct labor ($22 per hour) × *standard hours* of direct labor that should have been worked (31,000 cases × 0.05 hours per case = 1,550 hours). Tucson Tortilla credits Wages Payable for the *actual* hours worked at the *actual* wage rate since this is the amount owed to employees. At the same time, Tucson Tortilla records the direct labor rate and efficiency variances calculated in Exhibit 11-7. The *unfavorable* DL Rate Variance is recorded as a *debit*, while the *favorable* DL Efficiency Variance is recorded as a *credit*.

	Work in Process Inventory (1,550 hrs × $22)	34,100	
	DL Rate Variance (Exhibit 11-7)	1,875	
	DL Efficiency Variance (Exhibit 11-7)		1,100
	Wages Payable (1,500 hrs × $23.25)		34,875
	(to record use of direct labor)		

4. **Recording Actual Manufacturing Overhead Costs**—Tucson Tortilla records manufacturing overhead costs as usual, debiting the variable and fixed manufacturing overhead accounts and crediting various accounts. The actual costs can be found in Exhibits 11-10 and 11-11:

	Variable Manufacturing Overhead (Exhibit 11-10)	85,200	
	Fixed Manufacturing Overhead (Exhibit 11-11)	31,025	
	Various Accounts		116,225
	(to record actual overhead costs incurred)		

5. **Allocating Overhead**—In standard costing, the overhead allocated to Work in Process Inventory is computed using the standard overhead rates ($25/machine hour for variable overhead and $9/machine hour for fixed overhead) × standard quantity of the allocation base allowed for the actual output (31,000 cases × 0.10 MH per case = 3,100 MH). As usual, the Variable and Fixed Manufacturing Overhead accounts are credited when allocating overhead:

	Work in Process Inventory	105,400	
	Variable Manufacturing Overhead (3,100 MH × $25/MH)		77,500
	Fixed Manufacturing Overhead (3,100 MH × $9/MH)		27,900
	(to allocate overhead costs to Work in Process inventory)		

This journal entry corresponds with our calculations in Exhibits 11-10 and 11-11.

6. **Recording the Completion**—So far, Work in Process Inventory has been debited with $372,000 of manufacturing cost ($232,500 of direct materials + $34,100 of direct labor + $105,400 of MOH). Does this make sense? According to Exhibit 11-1, the standard cost of manufacturing one case is $12.00. If we take the $372,000 of cost and divide it by 31,000 cases, we get $12.00 per case. This is how it should be—through the standard costing journal entries, Tucson Tortilla has successfully recorded each case at its standard cost of $12. In addition, it has captured all of the variances in separate variance accounts on the general ledger. As the units are completed, the standard cost of each case is transferred out of Work in Process Inventory and into Finished Goods Inventory:

	Finished Goods Inventory (31,000 × $12.00)		372,000	
	Work in Process Inventory (31,000 × $12.00)			372,000
	(to record completion of the 31,000 cases)			

7. **Recording the Sale and Release of Inventory**—Let's assume that 32,370 cases were sold on account in January at an average price of $20.20 per case. The following journal entry would reflect the sale:

	Accounts Receivable (32,370 × $20.20)		653,874	
	Sales Revenue (32,370 × $20.20)			653,874
	(to record the sale of 32,370 cases)			

Under a perpetual inventory system, Tucson Tortilla must also release inventory for the cases it has sold. Since all cases produced during the year were recorded at standard cost ($12.00 each), they must be removed from Finished Goods Inventory and be entered into Cost of Goods Sold at the same standard cost:

	Cost of Goods Sold (32,370 × $12.00)		388,440	
	Finished Goods Inventory (32,370 × $12.00)			388,440
	(to record cost of goods sold for the 32,370 cases)			

8. **Closing Manufacturing Overhead**—Tucson Tortilla must close its temporary MOH accounts. Rather than closing them directly to Cost of Goods Sold, as we did in Chapter 3, in a standard costing system the accounts are closed to variance accounts. The company closes the Variable Manufacturing Overhead account to the variable MOH variances shown in Exhibit 11-10:

	Variable Overhead Rate Variance		10,200	
	Variable Overhead Efficiency Variance			2,500
	Variable Manufacturing Overhead			7,700
	(to close the Variable MOH account)			

Likewise, it closes the Fixed Manufacturing Overhead account to the fixed MOH variances shown in Exhibit 11-11:

	Fixed Overhead Budget Variance	1,025	
	Fixed Overhead Volume Variance	2,100	
	Fixed Manufacturing Overhead		3,125
	(to close the Fixed MOH account)		

These two journal entries zero out the two manufacturing overhead accounts.

Standard Costing Income Statement

Exhibit 11-14 shows a standard costing income statement that highlights the variances for Tucson Tortilla's management. It shows Cost of Goods Sold, first at standard cost and then at actual cost. Although the overall effect of the cost variances was minimal ($3,100 U), the report clearly shows management the size and direction of each variance. Managers will use management by exception to determine which variances, if any, they wish to investigate.

EXHIBIT 11-14 Standard Costing Income Statement

	A	B	C	D	E	F
1		Tucson Tortilla				
2		Standard Cost Income Statement				
3		For the Month Ended January 31				
4						
5	Sales revenue (32,370 × $20.20)				$	653,874
6	Less: Cost of goods sold, *at standard cost (32,370 × $12)*			$ 388,440		
7	Plus/(less) manufacturing cost variances:					
8	DM price variance	$	(16,000)	F		
9	DM quantity variance		7,500	U		
10	DL rate variance		1,875	U		
11	DL efficiency variance		(1,100)	F		
12	Variable MOH rate variance		10,200	U		
13	Variable MOH efficiency variance		(2,500)	F		
14	Fixed MOH budget variance		1,025	U		
15	Fixed MOH volume variance		2,100	U		
16	Total manufacturing cost variances				3,100 U	
17	**Cost of goods sold, at actual cost**					391,540
18	Gross Profit					262,334
19	Less: Operating expenses					155,390
20	Operating income					$ 106,944
21						

As a final step at the end of the period, all of the cost variance accounts are closed to zero-out their balances. Why? For two reasons: (1) The financial statements prepared for *external* users never show variances (variances are only for internal management's use) and (2) the general ledger must be corrected for the fact that standard costs, rather than actual costs, were used to record manufacturing costs. Since all of the cases produced were sold, the error in costing currently exists in the Cost of Goods Sold account. Although we do not show the journal entry to close the variance accounts here, all favorable variance accounts would be debited, while all unfavorable variance accounts would be credited. The net unfavorable amount of the variances of $3,100 would be debited to Cost of Goods Sold to increase the balance in this account to its correct amount.

END OF CHAPTER

Learning Objectives

- 1 Explain how and why standard costs are developed
- 2 Compute and evaluate direct materials variances
- 3 Compute and evaluate direct labor variances
- 4 Explain the advantages and disadvantages of using standard costs and variances
- 5 Compute and evaluate variable overhead variances
- 6 Compute and evaluate fixed overhead variances
- 7 (Appendix) Record standard costing journal entries

Accounting Vocabulary

Attainable Standards. (p. 654) Standards based on currently attainable conditions that include allowances for normal amounts of waste and inefficiency. Also known as practical standards.

Direct Labor Efficiency Variance. (p. 664) This variance tells managers how much of the total labor variance is due to using a greater or lesser amount of time than anticipated. It is calculated as follows: SR × (AH – SHA).

Direct Labor Rate Variance. (p. 664) This variance tells managers how much of the total labor variance is due to paying a higher or lower hourly wage rate than anticipated. It is calculated as follows: AH × (AR – SR).

Direct Materials Price Variance. (p. 659) This variance tells managers how much of the total direct materials variance is due to paying a higher or lower price than expected for the direct materials it purchased. It is calculated as follows: AQP × (AP – SP).

Direct Materials Quantity Variance. (p. 659) This variance tells managers how much of the total direct materials variance is due to using a larger or smaller quantity of direct materials than expected. It is calculated as follows: SP × (AQU – SQA).

Fixed Overhead Budget Variance. (p. 673) This variance measures the difference between the actual fixed overhead costs incurred and the budgeted fixed overhead costs. This variance is sometimes referred to as the fixed overhead spending variance because it specifically looks at whether the company spent more or less than anticipated on fixed overhead costs.

Fixed Overhead Spending Variance. (p. 673) Another name for the Fixed Overhead Budget Variance. This variance measures the difference between the actual fixed overhead costs incurred and the budgeted fixed overhead costs.

Fixed Overhead Volume Variance. (p. 674) This variance is the difference between the budgeted fixed overhead cost and the *standard fixed overhead cost* allocated to production. In essence, the fixed overhead volume variance measures the utilization of the fixed capacity costs. If volume is higher than originally anticipated, the variance will be favorable. If volume is lower than originally anticipated, the variance will be unfavorable.

Ideal Standards. (p. 654) Standards based on perfect or ideal conditions that do not allow for any waste in the production process, machine breakdown, or other inefficiencies. Also known as perfection standards.

Perfection Standards. (p. 654) Standards based on perfect or ideal conditions that do not allow for any waste in the production process, machine breakdown, or other inefficiencies. Also known as ideal standards.

Practical Standards. (p. 654) Standards based on currently attainable conditions that include allowances for normal amounts of waste and inefficiency. Also known as attainable standards.

Standard Cost. (p. 654) The budgeted cost for a single unit of product. Also simply referred to as standards.

Standard Cost Accounting. (p. 679) Another common name for standard costing.

Standard Costing. (p. 679) Also known as standard cost accounting. A method of accounting in which product costs are entered into the general ledger inventory accounts at standard cost rather than actual cost. The variances are captured in their own general ledger accounts and displayed on a standard costing income statement prior to being closed out at the end of the period.

Standards. (p. 654) Another common name for standard costs.

Variable Overhead Efficiency Variance. (p. 672) This variance tells managers how much of the total variable MOH variance is due to using more or fewer hours of the allocation base (usually machine hours or DL hours) than anticipated for the actual volume of output. It is calculated as follows: SR × (AH – SHA).

Variable Overhead Rate Variance. (p. 671) Also called the variable overhead spending variance. This variance tells managers whether more or less was spent on variable overhead than they expected would be spent for the hours worked. It is calculated as follows: AH × (AR – SR).

Variable Overhead Spending Variance. (p. 671) Another common name for variable overhead rate variance.

Quick Check

1. **(Learning Objective 1)** Which of the following is true?
    a. Ideal standards are based on currently attainable conditions.
    b. Practical standards are based on ideal conditions.
    c. A standard cost is the budgeted cost for one unit.
    d. Standards should never be updated.

2. **(Learning Objective 2)** The direct material price variance can be defined as which of the following?
    a. Standard quantity allowed × (Actual price − Standard price)
    b. Actual quantity purchased × (Actual price − Standard price)
    c. Standard price × (Actual quantity used − Standard quantity allowed)
    d. Actual price × (Actual quantity used − Standard quantity allowed)

3. **(Learning Objective 2)** The direct material quantity variance can be defined as which of the following?
    a. Actual price × (Actual quantity used − Standard quantity allowed)
    b. Standard quantity allowed × (Actual price − Standard price)
    c. Standard price × (Actual quantity used − Standard quantity allowed)
    d. Actual quantity purchased × (Actual price − Standard price)

4. **(Learning Objective 3)** The direct labor rate variance can be defined as which of the following?
    a. Actual hours × (Actual rate − Standard rate)
    b. Actual rate × (Actual hours − Standard hours allowed)
    c. Standard hours allowed × (Actual rate − Standard rate)
    d. Standard rate × (Actual hours − Standard hours allowed)

5. **(Learning Objective 3)** The direct labor efficiency variance can be defined as which of the following?
    a. Standard hours allowed × (Actual rate − Standard rate)
    b. Standard rate × (Actual hours − Standard hours allowed)
    c. Actual hours × (Actual rate − Standard rate)
    d. Actual rate × (Actual hours − Standard hours allowed)

6. **(Learning Objective 4)** Which of the following is **not** an advantage of using standard costs?
    a. Standards can cause unintended behavioral consequences.
    b. Standards are useful for budgeting.
    c. Standards serve as cost benchmarks.
    d. Standards can simplify bookkeeping.

7. **(Learning Objective 5)** The variable overhead rate variance can be defined as which of the following?
    a. Standard hours allowed × (Actual rate − Standard rate)
    b. Standard rate × (Actual hours − Standard hours allowed)
    c. Actual rate × (Actual hours − Standard hours allowed)
    d. Actual hours × (Actual rate − Standard rate)

8. **(Learning Objective 6)** Which of the following is **not** true about the fixed overhead budget variance?
    a. It is the difference between actual fixed overhead and budgeted fixed overhead.
    b. It is the difference between the budgeted fixed overhead and the standard fixed overhead allocated to production.
    c. It can be either favorable or unfavorable.
    d. It is sometimes referred to as the fixed overhead spending variance.

9. **(Learning Objective 6)** Which of the following is **not** true about the fixed overhead volume variance?
    a. It is partially the result of treating fixed overhead costs as if they were variable for allocating the costs to individual units of production.
    b. If production volume is lower than originally anticipated, then fixed overhead cost would be underallocated.
    c. It is partially the result of incorrectly estimating the level of activity when calculating the predetermined fixed manufacturing overhead rate.
    d. If production volume is greater than originally anticipated, the variance will be unfavorable.

10. **(Learning Objective 7—Appendix)** Which of the following is **not** true about standard costing systems?
    a. A standard cost income statement shows cost of goods sold at standard, along with all of the variances needed to adjust cost of goods sold back to actual.
    b. Each type of variance has its own general ledger account.
    c. At the end of the period, the variances are closed to the Sales Revenue account.
    d. Standard costs are used to record the manufacturing costs entered into the inventory accounts.

Quick Check Answers

1. c 2. b 3. c 4. a 5. b 6. a 7. d 8. b 9. d 10. c

Short Exercises

S11-1 Compute the standard cost of direct materials (Learning Objective 1)

Swirl Confections is known for its rich dark chocolate fudge. Swirl sells its fudge to local retailers. A "unit" of fudge is a 10-pound batch. The standard quantities of ingredients for a batch include 5 cups of sugar, 21 ounces of chocolate chips, 17 ounces of butter, and 28 ounces of evaporated milk. The standard costs for each of the ingredients are as follows: $0.21 per cup of sugar, $0.10 per ounce of chocolate chips, $0.07 per ounce of butter, and $0.09 per ounce of evaporated milk. Calculate the standard direct material cost per batch of fudge.

S11-2 Compute the standard cost of direct labor (Learning Objective 1)

Swirl Confections produces fudge in 10-pound batches. Each batch takes 0.25 hours of direct labor, which includes allowances for breaks, cleanup, and other downtime. Swirl pays its direct labor workers an average of $20.50 per hour. Calculate the standard direct labor cost per batch of fudge.

S11-3 Explain a direct material variance (Learning Objective 2)

A Cadbury Creme Egg is an egg-shaped chocolate candy that weighs about 35 grams, or a little more than 1.2 ounces. It is filled with a white fondant and a smaller amount of yellow fondant, meant to mimic an actual egg. (Fondant is a type of sugar syrup.) In the United States, Cadbury Creme Eggs are marketed and distributed by The Hershey Company. The Creme Eggs are produced by Cadbury Adams in Canada and by Cadbury UK in the United Kingdom. In the UK factory, 1.5 million Creme Eggs are manufactured per day. Creme Eggs are sold every year from New Year's Day until Easter.

In 2015, Cadbury changed its formula for the eggs by replacing its Cadbury Dairy Milk chocolate with "standard cocoa mix chocolate." The standard chocolate is a less expensive ingredient than the Cadbury Dairy Milk chocolate. The company assured customers that the taste of the Creme Eggs would not change.

Consumers reacted negatively to the recipe change. Sales of Cadbury Creme Eggs have fallen by more than $14 million since the chocolate substitution; this drop has been speculated to have been caused by the change in the recipe.

Assuming that Cadbury uses standard costing in its manufacturing operations, what variance would have been impacted by the decrease in the cost of the chocolate used in the Cadbury eggs? Would this variance have been favorable or unfavorable? What position or department within Cadbury would have been responsible for that variance?

S11-4 Calculate direct material variances when the quantity purchased equals the quantity used (Learning Objective 2)

Streetsboro Ceramics produces large planters to be used in urban landscaping projects. A special earth clay is used to make the planters. The standard quantity of clay used for each planter is 24 pounds. The company uses a standard cost of $1.96 per pound of clay. Streetsboro produced 3,500 planters in May. In that month, 87,500 pounds of clay were purchased and used at the total cost of $168,000.

Requirements

1. Calculate the direct material price variance.
2. Calculate the direct material quantity variance.

S11-5 Calculate direct material variances when the quantity purchased differs from the quantity used (Learning Objective 2)

Mitchell Products manufactures faux boulders to be used in various landscaping applications. A special resin is used to make the boulders. The standard quantity of resin used for each boulder is 2 pounds. Mitchell Products uses a standard cost of $1.80 per pound for the resin. The company produced 11,000 boulders in June. In that month, 21,750 pounds of resin were purchased at a total cost of $43,500. A total of 21,500 pounds were used in producing the boulders in June.

Requirements

1. Calculate the direct material price variance.
2. Calculate the direct material quantity variance.

S11-6 Calculate direct labor variances *(Learning Objective 3)*

Edelman Oil performs oil changes. The standard wage rate for oil change technicians is $17 per hour. By analyzing its past records of time spent on oil changes, the company has developed a standard of 18 minutes (or 0.30 hours) per oil change.

In July, 1,600 oil changes were performed at Edelman Oil. Oil change technicians worked a total of 310 direct labor hours at an average rate of $24 per hour.

Requirements

1. Calculate the direct labor rate variance.
2. Calculate the direct labor efficiency variance.

S11-7 Identify advantages and disadvantages of standard costs and variance analysis *(Learning Objective 4)*

In the following list, identify whether the situation would indicate that a company should use standard costs and variance analysis or if the company should move away from standard costs and variance analysis.

Situation	Use standard costs	Move away from standard costs
1. Would like to simplify the bookkeeping process		
2. Would like to use operational performance measures and visual management cues		
3. Would like to facilitate the budgeting process		
4. There has been an increase in automation in the manufacturing process and a corresponding decrease in direct labor		
5. Will be implementing lean practices throughout the organization		
6. Need timely reports about production results		
7. Would like to increase employee motivation levels		
8. Want benchmarks by which to judge actual costs		

S11-8 Calculate variable overhead variances *(Learning Objective 5)*

Shepard Industries produced 4,000 tables last month. The standard variable manufacturing overhead (MOH) rate used by the company is $24 per machine hour. Each table requires 0.3 machine hours. Actual machine hours used last month were 1,170, and the actual variable MOH rate last month was $22.00.

Requirements

1. Calculate the variable overhead rate variance.
2. Calculate the variable overhead efficiency variance.

S11-9 Calculate fixed overhead variances *(Learning Objective 6)*

Boxer Manufacturing produces luxury dog houses. Each dog house requires 4.0 hours of machine time for its elaborate trim and finishing. For the current year, Boxer calculated its predetermined fixed manufacturing overhead (MOH) rate to be $26 per machine hour. The company budgets its fixed MOH to be $202,000 per month. Last month, Boxer produced 2,000 dog houses and incurred $198,400 (actual) of fixed MOH.

Requirements

1. Calculate the fixed overhead budget variance.
2. Calculate the fixed overhead volume variance.

S11-10 Calculate and interpret fixed overhead variances (Learning Objective 6)

Calvin Industries produces high-end flutes for professional musicians across the globe. Actual fixed manufacturing overhead for the year was $1,250,000, while the budgeted fixed manufacturing overhead was $1,270,000. Using a standard costing system, the company allocated $1,200,000 of overhead to production.

Requirements

1. Calculate the total fixed overhead variance. What does this tell managers?
2. Determine the fixed overhead budget variance. What does this tell managers?
3. Determine the fixed overhead volume variance. What does this tell managers?

S11-11 Calculate overhead rates (Learning Objectives 5 & 6)

The Spartan Restaurant Group supplies its franchise restaurants with many pre/manufactured ingredients (such as bags of frozen French fries), while other ingredients (such as lettuce and tomatoes) are sourced locally. Assume that the manufacturing plant processing the fries anticipated incurring a total of $4,212,000 of manufacturing overhead during the year. Of this amount, $1,170,000 is fixed. Manufacturing overhead is allocated based on machine hours. The plant anticipates running the machines 234,000 hours next year.

Requirements

1. Compute the standard variable overhead rate.
2. Compute the standard fixed manufacturing overhead rate.

S11-12 Calculate and interpret overhead variances (Learning Objective 6)

Assume that the Janis Corporation's manufacturing facility actually incurred $2,980,000 of manufacturing overhead for the year. Total fixed manufacturing overhead was budgeted at $3,010,000. Using a standard costing system, the company allocated $2,941,000 of fixed manufacturing overhead to production.

Requirements

1. Calculate the total fixed manufacturing overhead variance. What does this tell managers?
2. Determine the fixed overhead budget variance. What does this tell managers?
3. Determine the fixed overhead volume variance. What does this tell managers?
4. Doublecheck: Do the two variances (computed in Requirements 2 and 3) sum to the total overhead variance computed in Requirement 1?

S11-13 Record costing transactions (Learning Objective 7)

During the week, the Spartan Restaurant Group's French fry manufacturing facility purchased 10,200 pounds of potatoes at a price of $1.06 per pound. The standard price per pound is $1.02. During the week, 9,150 pounds of potatoes were used. The standard quantity of potatoes that should have been used for the actual volume of output was 9,000 pounds.

Requirements

1. Record the following transactions using a standard cost accounting system:
   a. The purchase of potatoes
   b. The use of potatoes
2. Are the variances favorable or unfavorable? Explain.

S11-14 Record standard costing transactions (Learning Objective 7)

During the week, the Spartan Restaurant Group's French fry manufacturing facility incurred 1,500 hours of direct labor. Direct laborers were paid $12.20 per hour. The standard hourly labor rate is $11.80. Standards indicate that for the volume of output actually achieved, the factory should have used 2,200 hours.

Requirements

1. Record the labor transactions using a standard cost accounting system.
2. Are the variances favorable or unfavorable? Explain.

ETHICS

S11-15 Identify ethical standards violated *(Learning Objectives 1, 2, 3, 4, 5, & 6)*

For each of the situations listed, identify the primary standard from the *IMA Statement of Ethical Professional Practice* that is violated (competence, confidentiality, integrity, or credibility). Refer to Exhibit 1-7 for the complete standard.

1. Hayden is the chief accountant at Appleville Industries. Each month, he prepares variance reports that are given to all department managers. The variance reports are frequently late and usually contain a few errors.
2. Bradley has just started to work at Willis Lake Supply. In his first week, he is asked to fill in for a senior accountant who is out of the office for six weeks on maternity leave. He is asked to prepare the standard costing journal entries. Bradley does not know how to do this work, but he decides to guess because he does not want to appear stupid by asking for help.
3. When Amelia prepares variance reports, only favorable variances are listed. Unfavorable variances are provided only if someone specifically asks.
4. Melissa, an accountant at Youngstown Industries, and Brendan, an accountant at Goodtown Manufacturing, exchanged cost and other production data so that they would have benchmarks to use for their company reports.
5. Liam accepts an all-expenses-paid trip to Honolulu, Hawaii, from a major supplier.

S11-16 Vocabulary *(Learning Objectives 1, 2, 3, 4, 5, & 6)*

Match the term on the left with the definition on the right.

Term	Definition
1. Direct labor rate variance	a. Measures the difference between the actual fixed MOH costs incurred and the budgeted fixed MOH costs
2. Fixed overhead budget variance	b. Tells managers how much of the total variance is due to using a greater or lesser amount of time being worked than anticipated
3. Standard cost	c. Tells managers how much of the total variance is due to paying a different price than expected for direct materials
4. Variable overhead efficiency variance	d. Tells managers how much of the total variable MOH variance is due to using more or less hours of the allocation base than anticipated for the actual volume of output
5. Direct materials quantity variance	e. Measures the difference between the budgeted fixed MOH costs and the standard allocated fixed MOH costs
6. Direct labor efficiency variance	f. Tells managers how much of the total variance is due to paying a different hourly wage rate than anticipated
7. Variable overhead rate variance	g. Also known as attainable standards
8. Practical standards	h. Also called the variable overhead spending variance
9. Ideal standards	i. Tells managers how much of the total variance is due to using a different quantity of direct materials than expected
10. Direct materials price variance	j. Standards based on conditions that do not allow for any waste in the production process
11. Fixed overhead volume variance	k. The budgeted cost for a single unit of product

EXERCISES Group A

E11-17A Calculate standard cost and gross profit per unit *(Learning Objective 1)*

Bent Tree Coffee purchases green coffee beans from various suppliers and then roasts the coffee beans in its roasting facility. The roasted beans are sold in 20-pound cases to grocery stores and restaurants for $75 per case. Each case of roasted coffee beans requires 20 pounds of unroasted green coffee beans. The company can purchase the green coffee beans, including freight-in and purchase discounts, for $2.00 per pound. Each case of roasted coffee beans requires 0.10 hours of direct labor in the production process. Direct laborers are paid $23 per hour, which includes payroll taxes and employee benefits. The company uses machine hours to allocate its manufacturing overhead. Each case of roasted coffee beans requires 0.20 machine hours to produce. The company expects to produce 500,000 cases of roasted coffee beans in the upcoming year. At this production volume, the company expects total variable manufacturing overhead to be $3,000,000 for the year. The company also expects to incur $50,000 of fixed manufacturing overhead per month, or $600,000 for the year.

Requirements

1. What is the standard cost of producing one 20-pound case of roasted coffee beans?
2. What is the standard gross profit per 20-pound case of roasted coffee beans?
3. How often should the company reassess standard quantities and standard prices for inputs?

E11-18A Calculate standard cost per unit *(Learning Objective 1)*

Grow Right Products is a manufacturer of large flower pots for urban settings. The company has these standards:

Direct materials (resin)	9.6 pounds per pot at a cost of $4.55 per pound
Direct labor	1.0 hour at a cost of $15.80 per hour
Standard variable manufacturing overhead rate	$3.40 per direct labor hour
Predetermined fixed manufacturing overhead rate	$6.00 per direct labor hour

Grow Right allocates variable and fixed manufacturing overhead to production based on standard direct labor hours.

Requirements

1. Compute the standard cost of each of the following inputs per pot: direct materials, direct labor, variable manufacturing overhead, and fixed manufacturing overhead.
2. Determine the standard cost of one flower pot.

E11-19A Calculate and explain direct material variances *(Learning Objective 2)*

World Class Rings produces class rings. Its best-selling model has a direct materials standard of 16 grams of a special alloy per ring. This special alloy has a standard cost of $63.30 per gram. In the past month, the company purchased 16,800 grams of this alloy at a total cost of $1,061,760. A total of 16,300 grams were used last month to produce 1,000 rings.

Requirements

1. What is the actual cost per gram of the special alloy that World Class Rings purchased last month?
2. What is the direct material price variance?
3. What is the direct material quantity variance?
4. How might the direct material price variance for the company last month be causing the direct material quantity variance?

E11-20A Calculate missing direct material variables (Learning Objective 2)

Last month, Talley Corporation purchased and used the same quantity of material in producing its product, speed bumps for traffic control. Complete the following table.

Direct materials information	Medium speed bump	Large speed bump
Standard pounds per unit	15	?
Standard price per pound	$ 1.00	$ 1.80
Actual quantity purchased and used per unit	?	16
Actual price paid for material per pound	$ 1.80	$ 2.10
Direct materials price variance	$1,120 U	$ 1,920 U
Direct materials quantity variance	$ 100 F	?
Total direct material variance	?	$ 480 U
Number of units produced	100	400

E11-21A Calculate and explain direct labor variances (Learning Objective 3)

Malbasa Tax Services prepares tax returns for senior citizens. The standard in terms of (direct labor) time spent on each return is 4 hours. The direct labor standard wage rate at the firm is $16.50 per hour. Last month, 3,570 direct labor hours were used to prepare 900 tax returns. Total wages were $66,045.

Requirements

1. What is the actual (direct labor) wage rate per hour paid last month?
2. What is the direct labor rate variance?
3. What is the direct labor efficiency variance?
4. How might the direct labor rate variance for the firm last month be causing the direct labor efficiency variance?

E11-22A Calculate and interpret direct material and direct labor variances (Learning Objectives 2 & 3)

The Windam Restaurant Group manufactures the bags of frozen French fries used at its franchised restaurants. Last week, Windam purchased and used 98,000 pounds of potatoes at a price of $0.85 per pound. During the week, 2,100 direct labor hours were incurred in the plant at a rate of $12.45 per hour. The standard price per pound of potatoes is $1.00, and the standard direct labor rate is $12.15 per hour. Standards indicate that for the number of bags of frozen fries produced, the factory should have used 95,000 pounds of potatoes and 2,000 hours of direct labor.

Requirements

1. Determine the direct material price and quantity variances. Be sure to label each variance as favorable or unfavorable.
2. Think of a plausible explanation for the variances found in Requirement 1.
3. Determine the direct labor rate and efficiency variances. Be sure to label each variance as favorable or unfavorable.
4. Could the explanation for the labor variances be tied to the material variances? Explain.

E11-23A Calculate the material and labor variances (Learning Objectives 2 & 3)

Boat Guard, which used a standard cost accounting system, manufactured 210,000 boat fenders during the year, using 1,780,000 feet of extruded vinyl purchased at $1.30 per foot. Production required 4,900 direct labor hours that cost $13.00 per hour. The materials standard was 8 feet of vinyl per fender at a standard cost of $1.40 per foot. The labor standard was 0.024 direct labor hour per fender at a standard cost of $12.00 per hour.

Requirements

1. Compute the price and quantity variances for direct materials. Compute the rate and efficiency variances for direct labor.
2. Does the pattern of variances suggest that the company's managers have been making trade-offs? Explain.

E11-24A Record materials and labor transactions *(Learning Objective 7)*

Refer to the data in E11-23A.

Requirements

1. Make the journal entries to record the purchase and use of direct materials.
2. Make the journal entries to record the direct labor.

E11-25A Calculate the standard cost of a product before and after proposed sustainability effort changes *(Learning Objectives 1 & 4)*

SUSTAINABILITY

Melford Containers currently uses a recycled plastic to make bottles for the food industry.

Current bottle production information:

The cost and time standards per batch of 10,000 bottles are as follows:

Plastic 240 kilograms at $4.00 per kg
Direct labor 2.0 hours at $20.00 per hour

The variable manufacturing overhead rate is based on total estimated variable manufacturing overhead of $400,000 and estimated total DLH of 10,000. Melford allocates its variable manufacturing overhead based on direct labor hours (DLH).

Proposed changes to bottle design and production process:

The container division manager is considering having both the bottle redesigned and the bottle production process reengineered so that the plastic usage would drop by 30% overall due both to generating less scrap in the manufacturing process and using less plastic in each bottle. In addition to decreasing the amount of plastic used in producing the bottles, the additional following benefits would be realized:

a. Direct labor hours would be reduced by 20% because less scrap would be handled in the production process.

b. Total estimated variable manufacturing overhead would be reduced by 10% because less scrap would need to be hauled away, less electricity would be used in the production process, and less inventory would need to be stocked.

Requirements

1. Calculate the standard cost per batch of 10,000 bottles using the current data (before the company makes any changes). Include direct materials, direct labor, and variable manufacturing overhead in the standard cost per unit.
2. Calculate the standard cost per batch of 10,000 bottles if the company makes the changes to the bottle design and production process so that less plastic is used. Include direct materials, direct labor, and variable manufacturing overhead in the standard cost per unit.
3. Calculate the cost savings per batch by comparing the standard cost per batch under each scenario (current versus proposed change). Assume that the total cost to implement the changes would be $106,400. How many batches of bottles would need to be produced after the changes to have the cost savings total equal the cost to make these changes?
4. What other benefits might arise from making this change to using less plastic in the manufacture of the bottles? Are there any risks? What would you recommend the company do?

E11-26A Recognize advantages and disadvantages of standard cost and variance analysis in various situations *(Learning Objective 4)*

The following scenarios describe situations currently facing companies. For each scenario, indicate whether or not a standard costing system would be beneficial in that situation and explain why or why not. Each scenario is independent of the other scenarios.

a. As the company grows, the bookkeeping for actual direct material purchases, actual payroll costs, and actual manufacturing overhead is becoming increasingly complex; the number of transactions to be recorded has significantly increased. Much time is being spent by both managers and accountants in the company recording all of the actual transaction data.

b. Lean practices are being implemented throughout the organization at all levels and in all departments. One of the goals of the lean movement is to eliminate inventories if at all possible. Another goal is to strive for continuous improvement in both the time spent in the manufacturing process and the amount of materials used in the product.

c. The company has started using several real-time operating performance metrics to manage operations. Examples of metrics being used include manufacturing lead time in days, manufacturing volume by day, downtime in hours, material cost by day, and several other measures. These performance metrics are available to management in a dashboard that is updated hourly.

d. Management wants to design an incentive system that would pay out monthly incentives to factory workers if certain cost and time standards are achieved (or beaten). The goal of this program would be to increase employee motivation levels.

e. An exercise equipment manufacturer has recently installed a robotic manufacturing system. This robotic system will be used for most of the welding, painting, assembly, and testing processes in its facility. The workers who used to do these tasks (welding, painting, assembly, and testing) will be retrained and will instead oversee various production lines rather than working directly on the products.

f. The company has recently begun manufacturing a new type of computer chip. The company has very little experience with this type of product or the manufacturing process used for manufacturing the chips. Managers want to be able to have cost benchmarks so that they can judge whether the actual costs are reasonable for this product.

g. A rare and expensive chemical is used in the production of the company's main product. The cost of this material fluctuates wildly on a day-to-day basis, depending on market conditions. In addition, company engineers are continually working to redesign the product to use less of this material. Small incremental decreases in the material usage are being achieved on an ongoing basis.

E11-27A Compute and interpret overhead variances *(Learning Objectives 5 & 6)*

Aloha Foods processes bags of organic frozen fruits sold at specialty grocery stores. The company allocates manufacturing overhead based on direct labor hours. Aloha has budgeted fixed manufacturing overhead for the year to be $626,000. The predetermined fixed manufacturing overhead rate is $16.20 per direct labor hour, while the standard variable manufacturing overhead rate is $0.70 per direct labor hour. The direct labor standard for each case is one-quarter (0.25) of an hour.

The company actually processed 158,000 cases of frozen organic fruits during each year and incurred $682,460 of manufacturing overhead. Of this amount, $636,000 was fixed. The company also incurred a total of 40,400 direct labor hours.

Requirements

1. How much variable overhead would have been allocated to production? How much fixed overhead would have been allocated to production?
2. Compute the variable MOH rate variance and the variable MOH efficiency variance. What do these variances tell managers?
3. Compute the fixed MOH budget variance and the fixed overhead volume variance. What do these variances tell managers?

Data Set for E11-28A through E11-32A

Country Designs is a manufacturer of large flower pots for urban settings. The company has these standards:

Direct materials (resin)	13 pounds per pot at a cost of $4.00 per pound
Direct labor	4.0 hours at a cost of $17.00 per hour
Standard variable manufacturing overhead rate	$7.00 per direct labor hour
Budgeted fixed manufacturing overhead	$50,000
Standard fixed MOH rate	$10.00 per direct labor hour (DLH)

Country Designs allocated fixed manufacturing overhead to production based on standard direct labor hours. Last month, the company reported the following actual results for the production of 1,300 flower pots:

Direct materials	Purchased 18,510 pounds at a cost of $4.50 per pound; used 17,810 pounds to produce 1,300 pots
Direct labor	Worked 4.5 hours per flower pot (5,850 total DLH) at a cost of $16.00 per hour
Actual variable manufacturing overhead	$7.20 per direct labor hour for total actual variable manufacturing overhead of $42,120
Actual fixed manufacturing overhead	$49,500
Standard fixed manufacturing overhead allocated based on actual production	$52,000

E11-28A Calculate and interpret direct material variances *(Learning Objective 2)*

Refer to the Country Designs data set.

Requirements

1. Compute the direct material price variance and the direct material quantity variance.
2. Who is *generally* responsible for each variance?
3. Interpret the variances.

E11-29A Calculate and interpret direct labor variances *(Learning Objective 3)*

Refer to the Country Designs data set.

Requirements

1. Compute the direct labor rate variance and the direct labor efficiency variance.
2. What is the total variance for direct labor?
3. Who is *generally* responsible for each variance?
4. Interpret the variances.

E11-30A Calculate and interpret overhead variances *(Learning Objectives 5 & 6)*

Refer to the Country Designs data set.

Requirements

1. Compute the variable manufacturing overhead variances. What do each of these variances tell management?
2. Compute the fixed manufacturing overhead variances. What do each of these variances tell management?

E11-31A Make journal entries in a standard costing system *(Learning Objective 7)*

Refer to the Country Designs data set. Assume the company uses a standard cost accounting system.

Requirements

1. Record Country Designs' direct material and direct labor journal entries.
2. Record Country Designs' journal entries for manufacturing overhead, including the entry that records the overhead variances and closes the Variable and Fixed Manufacturing Overhead accounts.
3. Record the journal entries for the completion and sale of the 1,300 flower pots, assuming Country Designs sold (on account) all of the flower pots at a sales price of $500 each. (There were no beginning or ending inventories.)

E11-32A Prepare a standard cost income statement *(Learning Objective 7)*

Refer to the Country Designs data set. Prepare a standard cost income statement for the company's management. Assume that sales were $650,000 and actual marketing and administrative expenses were $78,000.

EXERCISES Group B

E11-33B Calculate standard cost and gross profit per unit *(Learning Objective 1)*

Crooked River Coffee purchases green coffee beans from various suppliers and then roasts the coffee beans in its roasting facility. The roasted beans are sold in 25-pound cases to grocery stores and restaurants for $70 per case. Each case of roasted coffee beans requires 25 pounds of unroasted green coffee beans. The company can purchase the green coffee beans, including freight-in and purchase discounts, for $1.50 per pound. Each case of roasted coffee beans requires 0.10 hours of direct labor in the production process. Direct laborers are paid $24 per hour, which includes payroll taxes and employee benefits. The company uses machine hours as to allocate its manufacturing overhead. Each case of roasted coffee beans requires 0.30 machine hours to produce. The company expects to produce 250,000 cases of roasted coffee beans in the upcoming year. At this production volume, the company expects total variable manufacturing overhead to be $1,500,000 for the year. The company also expects to incur $18,750 of fixed manufacturing overhead per month, or $225,000 for the year.

Requirements

1. What is the standard cost of producing one 25-pound case of roasted coffee beans?
2. What is the standard gross profit per 25-pound case of roasted coffee beans?
3. How often should the company reassess standard quantities and standard prices for inputs?

E11-34B Calculate the standard cost per unit *(Learning Objective 1)*

City Grow Products is a manufacturer of large flower pots for urban settings. The company has these standards:

Direct materials (resin)	9.2 pounds per pot at a cost of $4.55 per pound
Direct labor	1.6 hours at a cost of $16.60 per hour
Standard variable manufacturing overhead	$3.60 per direct labor hour
Predetermined fixed manufacturing overhead rate	$6.50 per direct labor hour

City Grow allocates variable and fixed manufacturing overhead to production based on standard direct labor hours.

Requirements

1. Compute the standard cost of each of the following inputs per pot: direct materials, direct labor, variable manufacturing overhead, and fixed manufacturing overhead.
2. Determine the standard cost of one flower pot.

E11-35B Calculate and explain direct material variances (Learning Objective 2)

Star Class Rings produces class rings. Its best-selling model has a direct material standard of 8 grams of a special alloy per ring. This special alloy has a standard cost of $64.50 per gram. In the past month, the company purchased 9,000 grams of this alloy at a total cost of $577,800. A total of 8,600 grams were used last month to produce 1,000 rings.

Requirements

1. What is the actual cost per gram of the special alloy that Star Class Rings purchased last month?
2. What is the direct material price variance?
3. What is the direct material quantity variance?
4. How might the direct material price variance for the company last month be causing the direct material quantity variance?

E11-36B Calculate missing direct material variables (Learning Objective 2)

Last month, Bugsby Corporation purchased and used the same quantity of material in producing its speed bumps, a traffic control product. Complete the following table:

	Medium speed bump	Large speed bump
Standard pounds per unit	15	?
Standard price per pound	$ 3.50	$3.90
Actual quantity purchased and used per unit	?	16
Actual price paid for material	$ 4.10	$ 4.70
Direct materials price variance	$ 2,520 U	$ 7,680 U
Direct materials quantity variance	$ 1,050 F	?
Total direct material variance	?	$ 5,340 U
Number of units produced	300	600

E11-37B Calculate and explain direct labor variances (Learning Objective 3)

Russell Tax Services prepares tax returns for senior citizens. The standard in terms of (direct labor) time spent on each return is 3.0 hours. The direct labor standard wage rate at the firm is $16.50 per hour. Last month, 1,470 direct labor hours were used to prepare 500 tax returns. Total wages were $26,460.

Requirements

1. What is the actual (direct labor) wage rate per hour paid last month?
2. What is the direct labor rate variance?
3. What is the direct labor efficiency variance?
4. How might the direct labor rate variance for the firm last month be causing the direct labor efficiency variance?

E11-38B Calculate and interpret direct material and direct labor variances (Learning Objectives 2 & 3)

The Rosenbaum Restaurant Group manufactures the bags of frozen French fries used at its franchised restaurants. Last week, Rosenbaum purchased and used 98,000 pounds of potatoes at a price of $0.70 per pound. During the week, 1,700 direct labor hours were incurred in the plant at a rate of $12.20 per hour. The standard price per pound of potatoes is $0.85, and the standard direct labor rate is $11.95 per hour. Standards indicate that for the number of bags of frozen fries produced, the factory should have used 94,000 pounds of potatoes and 1,400 hours of direct labor.

Requirements

1. Determine the direct material price and quantity variances. Be sure to label each variance as favorable or unfavorable.
2. Think of a plausible explanation for the variances found in Requirement 1.
3. Determine the direct labor rate and efficiency variances. Be sure to label each variance as favorable or unfavorable.
4. Could the explanation for the labor variances be tied to the material variances? Explain.

E11-39B Complete and analyze a performance report *(Learning Objectives 2 & 3)*

Dock Guard, which uses a standard cost accounting system, manufactured 230,000 boat fenders during the year, using 1,660,000 feet of extruded vinyl purchased at $1.20 per foot. Production required 4,400 direct labor hours that cost $15.50 per hour. The materials standard was 7 feet of vinyl per fender at a standard cost of $1.25 per foot. The labor standard was 0.027 direct labor hour per fender at a standard cost of $15.00 per hour.

Requirements

1. Compute the price and quantity variances for direct materials. Compute the rate and efficiency variances for direct labor.
2. Does the pattern of variances suggest that the company's managers have been making trade-offs? Explain.

E11-40B Record materials and labor transactions *(Learning Objective 7)*

Refer to the data in E11-39B.

Requirements

1. Make journal entries to record the purchase and use of direct materials.
2. Make journal entries to record the direct labor.

E11-41B Calculate the standard cost of a product before and after proposed sustainability effort changes *(Learning Objectives 1 & 4)*

SUSTAINABILITY

Warner Containers currently uses a recycled plastic to make bottles for the food industry.

Current bottle production information:

The cost and time standards per batch of 10,000 bottles are as follows:

Plastic 300 kilograms at $5.00 per kg
Direct labor 2.0 hours at $20.00 per hour

The variable manufacturing overhead rate is based on total estimated variable manufacturing overhead of $600,000 and estimated total DLH of 10,000. The company allocates its variable manufacturing overhead based on direct labor hours.

Proposed changes to bottle design and production process:

The container division manager is considering having both the bottle redesigned and the bottle production process reengineered so that the plastic usage would drop by 25% overall due both to generating less scrap in the manufacturing process and using less plastic in each bottle. In addition to decreasing the amount of plastic used in producing the bottles, the additional following benefits would be realized:

a. Direct labor hours would be reduced by 20% because less scrap would be handled in the production process.
b. Total estimated variable manufacturing overhead would be reduced by 5% because less scrap would need to be hauled away, less electricity would be used in the production process, and less inventory would need to be stocked.

Requirements

1. Calculate the standard cost per batch of 10,000 bottles using the current data (before the company makes any changes). Include direct materials, direct labor, and variable manufacturing overhead in the standard cost per unit.
2. Calculate the standard cost per batch of 10,000 bottles if the company makes the changes to the bottle design and production process so that less plastic is used. Include direct materials, direct labor, and variable manufacturing overhead in the standard cost per unit.
3. Calculate the cost savings per batch by comparing the standard cost per batch under each scenario (current versus proposed change). Assume that the total cost to implement the changes would be $175,050. How many batches of bottles would need to be produced after the change to have the cost savings total equal the cost to make the changes?
4. What other benefits might arise from making this change to using less plastic in the manufacture of the bottles? Are there any risks? What would you recommend the company do?

E11-42B Recognize advantages and disadvantages of standard cost and variance analysis in various situations *(Learning Objective 4)*

The following scenarios describe situations currently facing companies. For each scenario, indicate whether or not a standard costing system would be beneficial in that situation and explain why or why not. Each scenario is independent of the other scenarios.

a. Management wants to design an incentive system that would pay out monthly incentives to factory workers if certain cost and time standards are achieved (or beaten). The goal of this program would be to increase employee motivation levels.

b. The company has recently begun manufacturing a new type of computer chip. The company has very little experience with this type of product or with the manufacturing process used for manufacturing the chips. Managers want to be able to have cost benchmarks so that they can judge whether the actual costs are reasonable for this product.

c. An exercise equipment manufacturer has recently installed a robotic manufacturing system. This robotic system will be used for most of the welding, painting, assembly, and testing processes in its facility. The workers who used to do these tasks (welding, painting, assembly, and testing) will be retrained and will instead oversee various production lines rather than working directly on the products.

d. Lean practices are being implemented throughout the organization at all levels and in all departments. One of the goals of the lean movement is to eliminate inventories if at all possible. Another goal is to strive for continuous improvement in both the time spent in the manufacturing process and the amount of materials used in the product.

e. The company has started using several real-time operating performance metrics to manage operations. Examples of metrics being used include manufacturing lead time in days, manufacturing volume by day, downtime in hours, material cost by day, and several other measures. These performance metrics are available to management in a dashboard that is updated hourly.

f. As the company grows, the bookkeeping for actual direct material purchases, actual payroll costs, and actual manufacturing overhead is becoming increasingly complex; the number of transactions to be recorded has significantly increased. Much time is being spent by both managers and accountants in the company recording all of the actual transaction data.

g. A rare and expensive chemical is used in the production of the company's main product. The cost of this material fluctuates wildly on a day-to-day basis, depending on market conditions. In addition, company engineers are continually working to redesign the product to use less of this material. Small incremental decreases in the material usage are being achieved on an ongoing basis.

E11-43B Calculate and interpret overhead variances *(Learning Objectives 5 & 6)*

Wright Foods processes bags of organic frozen vegetables sold at specialty grocery stores. Wright allocates manufacturing overhead based on direct labor hours. The company has budgeted fixed manufacturing for the year to be $626,000. The predetermined fixed manufacturing overhead rate is $16.60 per direct labor hour, while the standard variable manufacturing overhead rate is $0.85 per direct labor hour. The direct labor standards for each case is one-quarter (0.25) of an hour.

The company actually processed 160,000 cases of frozen organic vegetables during the year and incurred $681,200 of manufacturing overhead. Of this amount, $632,000 was fixed. The company also incurred a total of 41,000 direct labor hours.

Requirements

1. How much variable overhead would have been allocated to production? How much fixed overhead would have been allocated to production?
2. Compute the variable MOH rate variance and the variable MOH efficiency variance. What do these variances tell managers?
3. Compute the fixed MOH budget variance and the fixed overhead volume variance. What do these variances tell managers?

Data Set for E11-44B through E11-48B

Elegant Designs is a manufacturer of large flower pots for urban settings. The company has these standards:

Direct materials (resin)	10 pounds per pot at a cost of $3.00 per pound
Direct labor	5.0 hours at a cost of $19.00 per hour
Standard variable manufacturing overhead rate	$3.00 per direct labor hour
Budgeted fixed manufacturing overhead	$94,000
Standard fixed MOH rate	$12.00 per direct labor hour (DLH)

Elegant Designs allocates fixed manufacturing overhead to production based on standard direct labor hours. Last month, Elegant Designs reported the following actual results for the production of 1,600 flower pots:

Direct materials	Purchased 17,820 pounds at a cost of $3.50 per pound; used 17,120 pounds to produce 1,600 pots
Direct labor	Worked 5.5 hours per unit (8,800 total DLH) at a cost of $18.00 per hour
Actual variable manufacturing overhead	$3.20 per direct labor hour for total actual variable manufacturing overhead of $28,160
Actual fixed manufacturing overhead.....................	$93,500
Standard fixed manufacturing overhead allocated based on actual production	$96,000

E11-44B Calculate and interpret direct materials variances *(Learning Objective 2)*

Refer to the Elegant Designs data set.

Requirements

1. Compute the direct material price variance and the direct material quantity variance.
2. Who is generally responsible for each variance?
3. Interpret the variances.

E11-45B Calculate and interpret direct labor variances *(Learning Objective 3)*

Refer to the Elegant Designs data set.

Requirements

1. Compute the direct labor rate variance and the direct labor efficiency variance.
2. What is the total variance for direct labor?
3. Who is generally responsible for each variance?
4. Interpret the variances.

E11-46B Calculate and interpret overhead variances *(Learning Objectives 5 & 6)*

Refer to the Elegant Designs data set. Calculate and interpret overhead variances.

Requirements

1. Compute the variable manufacturing overhead variances. What do each of these variances tell management?
2. Compute the fixed manufacturing overhead variances. What do each of these variances tell management?

E11-47B Make journal entries in a standard costing system *(Learning Objective 7)*

Refer to the Elegant Designs data set. Assume the company uses a standard cost accounting system.

Requirements

1. Record Elegant Designs' direct materials and direct labor journal entries.
2. Record Elegant Designs' journal entries for manufacturing overhead, including the entry that records the overhead variances and closes the Variable and Fixed Manufacturing Overhead accounts.
3. Record the journal entries for the completion and sale of the 1,600 flower pots, assuming Elegant Designs sold (on account) all of the flower pots at a sales price of $530 each (there were no beginning or ending inventories).

E11-48B Prepare a standard cost income statement *(Learning Objective 7)*

Refer to the Elegant Designs data set. Prepare a standard cost income statement for the company's management. Assume that sales were $848,000 and actual marketing and administrative expenses were $76,500.

PROBLEMS Group A

P11-49A Calculate and explain direct material and direct labor variances
(Learning Objectives 1, 2, & 3)

Dazzle Fabrics manufactures a specialty monogrammed blanket. The following are the cost standards for this blanket:

Direct materials (fabric).........................	2.0 yards per blanket at $7.00 per yard
Direct labor	0.5 direct labor hours per blanket at $19.00 per hour

Actual results from last month's production of 2,400 blankets are as follows:

Actual cost of 6,240 yards of direct material (fabric) purchased	$ 40,560
Actual yards of direct material (fabric) used	5,540
Actual wages for 1,350 direct labor hours worked..	$ 24,840

Requirements

1. What is the standard direct material cost for one blanket?
2. What is the actual cost per yard of fabric purchased?
3. Calculate the direct material price and quantity variances.
4. What is the standard direct labor cost for one blanket?
5. What is the actual direct labor cost per hour?
6. Calculate the direct labor rate and efficiency variances.
7. Analyze each variance and speculate as to what may have caused that variance.
8. Look at all four variances together (the big picture). How might they all be related? What variance is very likely to have caused the other variances?

P11-50A Comprehensive standards and variances problem (Learning Objectives 1, 2, 3, 5, & 6)

Conrad Awning manufactures awnings and uses a standard cost system. The company allocates overhead based on the number of direct labor hours. The following are the company's cost and standards data:

Standards:

Direct materials 24.0 yards per awning at $11.00 per yard
Direct labor 2.0 hours per awning at $12.00 per hour
Variable MOH standard rate $7.00 per direct labor hour
Predetermined fixed MOH standard rate $8.00 per direct labor hour
Total budgeted fixed MOH cost $21,700

Actual cost and operating data from the most recent month are as follows:

Purchased 38,400 yards at a total cost of $399,360
Used 34,900 yards in producing 1,500 awnings
Actual direct labor cost of $34,727 for a total of 2,870 hours
Actual variable MOH $20,377
Actual fixed MOH $26,200

All manufacturing overhead is allocated on the basis of direct labor hours.

Requirements

1. Calculate the standard cost of one awning.
2. Calculate the following variances:
   a. The direct material variances.
   b. The direct labor variances.
   c. The variable manufacturing overhead variances.
   d. The fixed manufacturing overhead variances.
3. Explain what each of the variances you calculated means and give at least one possible explanation for each of those variances. Are any of the variances likely to be interrelated?

P11-51A Comprehensive standards and variances problem
(Learning Objectives 1, 2, 3, 4, 5, & 6)

Seacrest Manufacturing produces ceramic teapots. Seacrest allocates overhead based on the number of direct labor hours. The company is looking into using a standard cost system and has developed the following standards (one "unit" is a batch of 100 teapots):

Standards:

Direct material 30 pounds per batch at $3.00 per pound
Direct labor 2.0 hours per batch at $12.00 per hour
Variable MOH standard rate $2.00 per direct labor hour
Predetermined fixed MOH standard rate $7.00 per direct labor hour
Total budgeted fixed MOH cost $1,670

Actual cost and operating data from the most recent month are as follows:

Purchased 3,040 pounds at a cost of $2.90 per pound
Used 3,000 pounds in producing 80 batches
Actual direct labor cost of $2,142 at an average direct labor cost per hour of $12.60
Actual variable MOH $442
Actual fixed MOH $2,270

All manufacturing overhead is allocated on the basis of direct labor hours.

Requirements

1. Calculate the standard cost of one batch.
2. Calculate the following variances:
   a. The direct material variances.
   b. The direct labor variances.
   c. The variable manufacturing overhead variances.
   d. The fixed manufacturing overhead.
3. Have the company's managers done a good job or a poor job controlling materials, labor, and overhead costs? Why or why not?
4. Describe how the company's managers can benefit from the standard costing system. Do you think the company should continue with the standard cost system?

P11-52A Work backward through labor variances *(Learning Objective 3)*

Woodsy Music manufactures harmonicas. Woodsy uses standard costs to judge performance. Recently, a clerk mistakenly threw away some of the records, and only partial data for September exist. Woodsy knows that the total direct labor variance for the month was $320 F and that the standard labor rate was $12 per hour. A recent pay cut caused a favorable labor rate variance of $0.70 per hour. The standard direct labor hours for actual September outputs were 5,300.

Requirements

1. Find the actual number of direct labor hours worked during September. First, find the actual direct labor rate her hour. Then, determine the actual number of direct labor hours worked by setting up the computation of the total direct labor variance as given.
2. Compute the direct labor rate and efficiency variances. Do these variances suggest that the manager may have made trade-offs? Explain.

P11-53A Determine all variances and make journal entries
(Learning Objectives 2, 3, 5, 6, & 7)

Pizarro Clothing manufactures embroidered jackets. The company uses a standard cost system to control manufacturing costs. The following data represent the standard unit cost of a jacket:

Direct materials (3.0 sq. ft × $4.00 per sq. ft).................................		$ 12.00
Direct labor (2.0 hours × $9.60 per hour)...		19.20
Manufacturing overhead:		
Variable (2.0 hours × $0.66 per hour)	$1.32	
Fixed (2.0 hours × $2.30 per hour)	4.60	$ 5.92
Total standard cost per jacket..		$ 37.12

Fixed overhead in total was budgeted to be $62,900 for each month.

Actual data for November of the current year include the following:

a. Actual production was 13,300 jackets.
b. Actual direct material used was 2.70 square feet per jacket at an actual cost of $4.20 per square foot.
c. Actual direct labor usage of 24,400 hours for a total cost of $241,560.
d. Actual fixed overhead cost was $56,902, while actual variable overhead cost was $20,740.

Requirements

1. Compute the price and quantity variances for direct materials.
2. Compute the rate and efficiency variances for direct labor.
3. Compute the rate and efficiency variances for variable overhead.
4. Compute the fixed overhead budget variance and the fixed overhead volume variance.
5. Company management intentionally purchased superior materials for November production. How did this decision affect the other cost variances? Overall, was the decision wise? Explain.
6. Journalize the usage of direct materials and the assignment of direct labor, including the related variances.

PROBLEMS Group B

P11-54B Calculate and explain direct material and direct labor variances
(Learning Objectives 1, 2, & 3)

Athena Fabrics manufactures a specialty monogrammed blanket. The following are the cost and labor standards for this blanket:

Direct material (fabric): 2.0 yards per blanket at $7.50 per yard
Direct labor: 0.5 direct labor hours per blanket at $16.00 per hour

Actual results from last month's production of 1,900 blankets are as follows:

Actual cost of 4,940 yards of direct material (fabric) purchased: $35,074
Actual yards of direct material (fabric) used: 4,490
Actual wages for 1,090 direct labor hours worked: $16,568

Requirements

1. What is the standard direct material cost for one blanket?
2. What is the actual cost per yard of fabric purchased?
3. Calculate the direct material price and quantity variances.
4. What is the standard direct labor cost for one blanket?
5. What is the actual direct labor cost per hour?
6. Calculate the direct labor rate and efficiency variances.
7. Analyze each variance and speculate as to what may have caused that variance.
8. Look at all four variances together (the big picture). How might they all be related? What variance is very likely to have caused the other variances?

P11-55B Comprehensive standards and variances problem
(Learning Objectives 1, 2, 3, 5, & 6)

Nautical Awning manufactures awnings and uses a standard cost system. Nautical allocates overhead based on the number of direct labor hours. The following are the company's cost and standards data:

Direct material 18.0 yards per awning at $10.00 per yard
Direct labor 2.0 hours per awning at $13.00 per hour
Variable MOH standard rate $5.00 per direct labor hour
Predetermined fixed MOH standard rate $10.00 per direct labor hour
Total budgeted fixed MOH cost $34,000

Actual cost and operating data from the most recent month follows:

Purchased 35,460 yards at a total cost of $333,324
Used 31,300 yards in producing 1,800 awnings
Actual direct labor cost of $45,457 for a total of 3,470 hours
Actual variable MOH cost $19,085
Actual fixed MOH cost $39,500

All manufacturing overhead is allocated on the basis of direct labor hours.

Requirements

1. Calculate the standard cost of one awning.
2. Calculate the following variances:
   a. The direct material variances.
   b. The direct labor variances.
   c. The variable manufacturing overhead variances.
   d. The fixed manufacturing overhead variances.

3. Explain what each of the variances you calculated means and give at least one possible explanation for each of those variances. Are any of the variances likely to be interrelated?

P11-56B Comprehensive standards and variances problem
(Learning Objectives 1, 2, 3, 4, 5, & 6)

Dolson Manufacturing produces ceramic teapots. Dolson allocates overhead based on the number of direct labor hours. The company is looking into using a standard cost system and has developed the following standards (one "unit" is a batch of 100 teapots).

Standards:
Direct material 70 pounds per batch at $4.00 per pound
Direct labor 3.0 hours per batch at $19.00 per hour
Variable MOH standard rate $3.00 per direct labor hour
Predetermined fixed MOH standard rate $6.00 per direct labor hour
Total budgeted fixed MOH cost $1,560

Actual cost and operating data from the most recent month follows:
Purchased 5,670 pounds at a cost of $3.90 per pound
Used 5,000 pounds in producing 70 batches
Actual direct labor cost of $4,554 at an average direct labor cost per hour of $19.80
Actual variable MOH cost $736
Actual fixed MOH cost $1,660

All manufacturing overhead is allocated on the basis of direct labor hours.

Requirements
1. Calculate the standard cost of one batch.
2. Calculate the following variances:
   a. The direct material variances.
   b. The direct labor variances.
   c. The variable manufacturing overhead variances.
   d. The fixed manufacturing overhead variances.
3. Have the company's managers done a good job or a poor job controlling materials, labor, and overhead costs? Why or why not?
4. Describe how the company's managers can benefit from the standard costing system. Do you think the company should continue with the standard cost system?

P11-57B Work backward through labor variances *(Learning Objective 3)*

Folklore Music manufactures harmonicas. Folklore uses standard costs to judge performance. Recently, a clerk mistakenly threw away some of the records, and only partial data for July exist. Folklore knows that the total direct labor variance for the month was $350 F and that the standard labor rate was $11 per hour. A recent pay cut caused a favorable labor rate variance of $0.40 per hour. The standard direct labor hours for actual July outputs were 5,910.

Requirements
1. Find the actual number of direct labor hours worked during July. First, find the actual direct labor rate per hour. Then, determine the actual number of direct labor hours worked by setting up the computation of the total direct labor variance as given.
2. Compute the direct labor rate and efficiency variances. Do these variances suggest that the manager may have made trade-offs? Explain.

P11-58B Determine all variances and make journal entries
(Learning Objectives 2, 3, 5, 6, & 7)

Figaro Company manufactures embroidered jackets. The company uses a standard cost system to control manufacturing costs. The following data represent the standard unit cost of a jacket:

Direct materials (3.0 sq. ft. × $3.95 per sq. ft).................		$11.85
Direct labor (2.0 hours × $9.20 per hour)........................		18.40
Manufacturing overhead:		
Variable (2.0 hours × $0.60 per hour).........................	$1.20	
Fixed (2.0 hours × $2.30 per hour)..............................	4.60	5.80
Total standard cost per jacket...		$36.05

Fixed overhead in total was budgeted to be $63,600 for each month.

Actual data for November of the current year include the following:

a. Actual production was 13,800 jackets.
b. Actual direct materials usage was 2.50 square feet per jacket at an actual cost of $4.10 per square foot.
c. Actual direct labor usage of 25,400 hours for a total cost of $238,760.
d. Actual fixed overhead cost was $59,202, while actual variable overhead cost was $19,050.

Requirements

1. Compute the price and quantity variances for direct materials.
2. Compute the rate and efficiency variances for direct labor.
3. Compute the rate and efficiency variances for variable overhead.
4. Compute the fixed overhead budget variance and the fixed overhead volume variance.
5. Company management intentionally purchased superior materials for November production. How did this decision affect the other cost variances? Overall, was the decision wise? Explain.
6. Journalize the usage of direct materials and the assignment of direct labor, including the related variances.

Serial Case

C11-59 Calculate labor variances in a hotel *(Learning Objective 3)*

This case is a continuation of the Caesars Entertainment Corporation serial case that began in Chapter 1. Refer to the introductory story in Chapter 1 (see page 43) for additional background. (The components of the Caesars serial case can be completed in any order.) Housekeeping is a significant cost in running a hotel; housekeeping includes daily cleaning of occupied guest rooms and guest bathrooms. Before the late 2015 renovation, the Roman Tower, formerly known as the Julius Tower, had 567 rooms. What follows is a table of selected hypothetical data regarding 2015 housekeeping costs in the Roman Tower:

Data table for Roman Tower housekeeping usage[5]	
STANDARD DATA - Roman Tower 2015	
Standard hours per hotel room cleaning	0.25
Total standard housekeeping hours in 2015—Roman Tower	36,399.25
Standard average housekeeper wage rate per hour	$ 14.50
Budgeted number of rooms to be cleaned in 2015	147,375
ACTUAL DATA - Roman Tower 2015	
Actual hours per hotel room cleaning	0.30
Total actual housekeeping hours in 2015—Roman Tower	43,679.10
Actual average housekeeper wage rate per hour	$ 13.50
Actual number of rooms cleaned in 2015	145,597

Requirements

1. Calculate the Labor Rate Variance (LRV) for the Roman Tower housekeeping in 2015.
   Hint: LRV = Actual Hours × (Actual Rate − Standard Rate). Answer the following questions about the LRV:
   a. Is the LRV favorable or unfavorable? How do you know?
   b. What are some possible reasons for this labor rate variance?
2. Calculate the Labor Efficiency Variance (LEV) for the Roman Tower housekeeping in 2015. *Hint:* LEV = Standard Rate × (Actual Hours − Standard Hours). Answer the following questions about the LEV:
   a. Is the LEV favorable or unfavorable? How do you know?
   b. What are some possible reasons for this labor efficiency variance?

---

[5]All of these Roman Tower housekeeping assumptions are hypothetical and provided for educational use only.

CRITICAL THINKING

Discussion & Analysis

A11-60 Discussion Questions

1. Suppose a company is implementing lean accounting throughout the organization. Why might standard costing *not* be beneficial for that company?

2. What advantages might a company experience if it adopts ideal standards for its direct material standards and direct labor standards? What advantages are there to using practical standards? As an employee, which would you prefer and why? Does your answer change if you are the manager in charge of production? Why or why not?

3. Select a product with which you are familiar. Describe what type of standards (direct material and direct labor) might be in effect for that product wherever it is produced. For each of these standards, discuss how those standards may become outdated. How frequently would you think the company would need to evaluate each of the standards?

4. Service organizations also use standards. Describe what types of standards might be in effect at each of the following types of organizations:
   - Hospitals
   - Law firms
   - Accounting firms
   - Auto repair shops
   - Fast-food restaurants

5. What does the direct materials price variance measure? Who is generally responsible for the direct materials price variance? Describe two situations that could result in a favorable materials price variance. Describe two situations that could result in an unfavorable materials price variance.

6. What does the direct materials quantity variance measure? Who is generally responsible for the direct materials quantity variance? Describe two situations that could result in a favorable direct materials quantity variance. Describe two situations that could result in an unfavorable direct materials quantity variance.

7. What does the direct labor rate variance measure? Who is generally responsible for the direct labor rate variance? Describe two situations that could result in a favorable labor rate variance. Describe two situations that could result in an unfavorable direct labor rate variance.

8. What does the direct labor efficiency variance measure? Who is generally responsible for the direct labor efficiency variance? Describe two situations that could result in a favorable direct labor efficiency variance. Describe two situations that could result in an unfavorable direct labor efficiency variance.

9. Describe at least four ways a company could use standard costing and variance analysis.

10. What are the two variable manufacturing overhead variances? What does each measure? Who within the organization would be responsible for each of these variances?

11. Suppose a company that makes and sells spaghetti sauce in plastic jars makes a change to its bottle that allows it to use significantly less plastic in each bottle. Describe at least four ways this change could help the company and its sustainability efforts.

12. Think of a company that manufactures a product. What type of standards do you think that company might have regarding its sustainability efforts? Do you think sustainability standards would be beneficial for the company? Why or why not?

Application & Analysis
Mini Cases

A11-61 Analyzing Variances and Potential Causes

Go to YouTube.com and search for clips from the show *Unwrapped* on Food Network or *How It's Made* on the Discovery Channel. Watch a clip for a product you find interesting. Companies are not likely to disclose everything about their production process and other trade secrets. When you answer the following questions, you may have to make reasonable assumptions or guesses about the manufacturing process, materials, and labor.

Basic Discussion Questions

1. Describe the product that is being produced. Briefly outline the production process.
2. What direct materials are used to make this product? In general, what has happened to the cost of these materials over the past year? To find information about the price of materials, you might try one of these sources (or a combination of these sources):
   a. Go to the *New York Times* website (http://nytimes.com/) or to *USA Today* (http://www.usatoday.com/) and search for each of the materials.
   b. Find the company's annual report on its website and read its discussion about its cost of production.
3. Given what you have discovered about the cost of materials for this product, were the price variances for each material likely to be favorable or unfavorable (answer separately for each individual material)?
4. In general, what has probably occurred to the cost of direct labor for this company? Again, to find clues about its labor costs, you might try one of the options listed in question 2. If you cannot find anything specific about this company, then discuss what has happened to the cost of labor in general over the past year.
5. Given what you have discovered about the cost of labor, was the labor rate variance likely to be favorable or unfavorable?
6. It is unlikely that the company has released information about its quantity (efficiency) variances. In general, though, what could cause this company's material quantity variances to be favorable? What could cause these material quantity variances to be unfavorable?
7. In general, what could cause this company's labor efficiency variances to be favorable? What could cause these labor efficiency variances to be unfavorable?

A11-62 Evaluate standard setting approaches
(Learning Objectives 1, 2, 3, 4, 5, & 6)

Pella is one of the world's largest manufacturers of wood windows and doors. In 1992, Pella entered the national retail market with its ProLine windows and doors, manufactured in Carroll, Iowa. Since then, Pella has introduced many new product lines with manufacturing facilities in several states.

Suppose Pella has been using a standard cost system that bases price and quantity standards on Pella's historical long-run average performance. Assume Pella should use some basis other than historical performance for setting standards.

Requirements

1. List the types of variances you recommend that Pella compute (for example, direct materials price variance for glass). For each variance, what specific standards would Pella need to develop? In addition to cost standards, do you recommend that Pella develop any nonfinancial standards? Explain.
2. There are many approaches to setting standards other than simply using long-run average historical prices and quantities.
   a. List three alternative approaches that Pella could use to set standards and explain how Pella could implement each alternative.
   b. Evaluate each alternative method of setting standards, including the pros and cons of each method.
   c. Write a memo to Pella's controller detailing your recommendations. First, should Pella retain its historical data-based standard cost approach? If not, which alternative approach should it adopt?

ETHICS

A11-63 Ethics involved with choice of cost driver
(Learning Objectives 1, 2, 3, 4, 5, 6, & 7)

The Green Gnome Company manufactures lawn and garden concrete and resin statues. It uses a standard costing system for its products. Managers and production personnel are paid bonuses based on attainment of material, labor, and overhead standards. The standards are recommended by a committee that is composed of engineers, production staff, and accountants. The accounting manager, however, has the final say on what the standards will be for each upcoming year.

Four years ago, the senior management at Green Gnome adopted a "zero-defects" strategy throughout the organization. As part of the zero-defects strategy, the company has been using ideal standards. Senior management has pointed out that it does not want to build waste into the standards by using practical standards. The adoption of ideal standards has been somewhat problematic at Green Gnome, and there has been a lot of resistance from employees to the ideal standards.

Greg Hanes is the accounting manager at Green Gnome and is currently evaluating the material, labor, and overhead standards for the upcoming year. The standards committee has already met and made its recommendations. The standards are, as dictated by senior management, extremely tight and allow for zero waste, breakdowns, or downtime.

The plant manager, Sheryl Radison, comes to Greg and asks him to loosen the standards for the upcoming year. The plant manager is upset that the standards are set at a 100% efficiency rate (zero defects). Sheryl points out that everyone's bonus is on the line if the standards are not met. Some jobs may also be lost if standards are not met. Sheryl feels that the standards are unattainable and are not fair to employees. Sheryl even indicates that Greg's job might possibly be on the line if another year goes by without standards being achieved.

Greg gets together with a close friend, Paula Brown, and discusses the matter at length with her. He tells her he feels guilty if the production staff does not get bonuses because of the way that the standards are set. He is also worried about his own job over the long run; it is in his best interests to have a good relationship with the plant manager. The economy is bad, and he does not know how long it would take to get a new job. Greg shows Paula the ideal standards recommended by the committee and then shows her the adjustments that he thinks he could make to help make the standards achievable. Paula agrees that the standards should be adjusted.

Requirements

1. Using the IMA *Statement of Ethical Professional Practice* as an ethical framework, answer the following questions:
    a. What is (are) the ethical issue(s) in this situation?
    b. What are Greg Hanes's responsibilities as a management accountant?
2. Should Greg adjust the standards to a more achievable level in this situation? Support your answer.
3. Describe another way that Greg could handle this situation that would not violate the IMA *Statement of Ethical Professional Practice*.

REAL LIFE

A11-64 Impact of manufacturing process changes on variances
(Learning Objectives 1, 2, 3, 4, 5, & 6)

The luxury-goods manufacturer, Louis Vuitton, has several factories in the United States, France, and Spain that produce its bags and accessories. Part of the Louis Vuitton brand appeal to consumers is its exclusivity; its bags and accessories are not mass-marketed. Rather than growing the brand and losing the appeal of its exclusivity, Vuitton has been working to improve the efficiency of the manufacturing processes at its factories. During a ten-year period, Vuitton implemented the following changes at some of its locations:[6]

> **Reorganization:** Workers were reorganized into teams of about 10 arranged in U-shaped clusters. This reorganization freed up 10% more floor space and allowed Vuitton to hire 300 new people without adding another factory.
> **Robots:** Robots were installed at Vuitton's shoe factory in Italy. Prior to the robot installation, workers walked back and forth from the shelves to their workstations. The robots now retrieve the foot molds around which a shoe is made, resulting in significant time savings.
> **Software:** Software was developed to help leather cutters identify the flaws in the leather being used to manufacture bags. The software determines where to place the pattern pieces for the dozens of pieces of leather in a bag, drastically reducing the amount of leather waste.

[6] C. Passariello, "At Vuitton, Growth in Small Batches," *Wall Street Journal*, June 27, 2011.

Questions

1. Before the company makes any changes to its standards, it must consider the impact of the manufacturing process changes on its variances. Indicate the impact of the changed process on each variance as *favorable*, *unfavorable*, or *unchanged/unknown*.

	Direct material price variance	Direct material quantity variance	Direct labor rate variance	Direct labor efficiency variance	Variable MOH rate variance	Variable MOH efficiency variance	Fixed overhead budget variance	Fixed overhead volume variance
Reorganization								
Robots								
Software								

2. For each of the improvement projects listed in the case, describe which standards would need to be adjusted for future variance analysis.

Try It Solutions

page 658:

1. Standard cost of direct materials

    = Standard quantity of DM × Standard price of DM
    = 0.25 lb × $4.00/lb
    = $1.00

2. Standard cost of direct labor

    = Standard quantity of DL × Standard price of DL
    = 3 minutes × ($10 per hour ÷ 60 minutes per hour)
    = $0.50

3. Standard cost of variable overhead

    = Standard quantity of DL minutes × Variable overhead rate
    = 3 minutes × $0.05 per minute
    = $0.15

page 663:

1. DM price variance

    = Actual Quantity Purchased × (Actual Price − Standard Price)
    = AQP × (AP − SP)
    = 1,300 lb × ($3.75/lb − $4.00/lb)
    = $325 F

    The price variance is favorable since the berries cost less per pound than anticipated.

2. DM quantity variance

    = Standard Price × (Actual Quantity Used − Standard Quantity Allowed)
    = SP × (AQU − SQA)
    = $4.00/lb × [1,300 lb − (5,000 smoothies × 0.25 lb/smoothie)]
    = $4.00/lb × (1,300 lb − 1,250 lb)
    = $200 U

    The quantity variance is unfavorable since the business used more berries than anticipated.

3. The total DM variance is $125 F. The total DM variance is the difference between the actual DM cost of $4,875 (= 1,300 lb × $3.75/lb) and the flexible budget for DM of $5,000 [5,000 smoothies × standard DM cost per smoothie of $1.00 (= 0.25 lb × $4.00 per pound)]. Since the company both purchased and used the same quantity of DM, it is also the combination of the DM price variance ($325 F) and the DM quantity variance ($200 U). The lower-than-expected price of berries more than offset the additional quantity the shop used, thus resulting in an overall favorable variance.

page 675:

1. The fixed overhead budget variance is $145 U. It is the difference between what was budgeted for fixed overhead ($1,455) and what was actually incurred ($1,600). The variance is unfavorable since actual fixed overhead was higher than budgeted.

2. Since Hannah's actual store volume was higher than anticipated, the fixed overhead volume variance will be favorable. By producing at a higher volume, Hannah was able to use the store's fixed overhead costs more efficiently.

12

Capital Investment Decisions and the Time Value of Money

Learning Objectives

- **1** Describe the importance of capital investments and the capital budgeting process
- **2** Use the payback and accounting rate of return methods to make capital investment decisions
- **3** Use the time value of money to compute the present and future values of single lump sums and annuities
- **4** Use discounted cash flow models to make capital investment decisions
- **5** Compare and contrast the four capital budgeting methods

Wendy M. Tietz

Sources: Cedarpoint.com; Cedar Fair, L.P. 2015 10(K) filing, http://www.toledoblade.com/Retail/2015/09/10/Cedar-Point-plans-r 241-foot-tall-ride.html; http://coaster-nation.com/2015-golden-ticke award-winners-announced/

Cedar Fair Entertainment

Company is a leading operator of amusement parks in the United States and Canada, entertaining over 24 million guests each year. The company's flagship park, Cedar Point, in Sandusky, Ohio, is known as the "Roller Coaster Capital of the World." The park has a world-record-breaking collection of 18 roller coasters, as well as an abundance of non-coaster rides and attractions. The newest roller coaster, "Valravn," which opened in 2016, is set to break 10 world records, including the tallest, fastest, and longest dive roller coaster in the world. Valravn cost about $25 million to build. Historical evidence has shown management that park attendance, revenues, profits, and spending per guest are driven by their ability to invest in new attractions. Thus, the company routinely spends well over $100 million a year in capital improvements at all of its amusement parks, continually adding new attractions that will draw people to the parks. The results of management's strategy are clear: Cedar Point has been voted the "Best Amusement Park in the World" for 16 consecutive years by *Amusement Today*'s international survey.

As the chapter-opening story shows, companies must continually evaluate whether they need to invest in new property, buildings, equipment, or projects in order to remain competitive or increase their revenue stream. Companies also initiate capital improvements in order to save on existing costs. For example, many companies are investing in highly efficient heating, ventilation, and air-conditioning (HVAC) systems to save millions of dollars on annual energy costs while at the same time reducing the use of fossil fuels. Management must carefully consider whether the additional revenues or cost savings will be worth the high price of these new capital investments. In this chapter, we'll see how companies such as Cedar Fair use net present value, payback period, and other capital investment analysis techniques to assess possible new investments.

What Is Capital Budgeting?

The process of making capital investment decisions is often referred to as **capital budgeting**. Companies make capital investments when they acquire *capital assets*—assets used for long periods of time. Capital investments include investments in new equipment, new plants, new vehicles, and new information technology. In addition to affecting operations for many years, capital investments usually require large sums of money. Cedar Point's decision to spend $25 million on the Valravn roller coaster will tie up resources for years to come.

1 Describe the importance of capital investments and the capital budgeting process

Capital investment decisions affect all types of businesses as they try to become more efficient by automating production and implementing new technologies. For example, within the last 10 years, self-service checkout machines at grocery stores and self-service check-in kiosks at airports have become commonplace. These devices end up decreasing the company's labor costs by shifting the burden of labor to the end consumer. Businesses are always striving to cut costs, improve customer response time, decrease waste, and improve quality by implementing the latest technologies. These new technologies cost money up front but end up saving businesses cash in the long run. How do managers decide whether these expansions in plant, technology, and equipment will be good investments? They use capital budgeting analysis.

Four Popular Methods of Capital Budgeting Analysis

In this chapter, we discuss four common methods of analyzing potential capital investments:

1. Payback period
2. Accounting rate of return (ARR)
3. Net present value (NPV)
4. Internal rate of return (IRR)

> **Why is this important?**
> "Each of these **four methods** help managers **decide** whether it would be wise to **invest** large sums of money in **new technologies**, buildings, or equipment."

The first two methods, payback period and accounting rate of return, work well for capital investments that have a relatively short lifespan, such as computer equipment and software. They also work well as screening devices to quickly weed out less desirable investments from those that show more promise. The payback period provides management with valuable information on how fast the cash invested in the asset will be recouped. The accounting rate of return indicates the profitability of the investment with respect to its impact on operating income. Despite the insights provided by the payback period and ARR, these two methods are inadequate if the capital investments have a longer lifespan. Why? Because these methods do not consider the time value of money. The last two methods, net present value and internal rate of return, factor in the time value of money, so they are more appropriate for longer-term capital investments such as Cedar Fair's new roller coasters and rides. Management often uses a combination of methods to make final capital investment decisions.

Focus on Cash Flows

Generally Accepted Accounting Principles (GAAP) is based on accrual accounting, but capital budgeting focuses on cash flows. The desirability of a capital asset depends on its ability to generate *net cash inflows*—that is, inflows in excess of outflows—over the asset's useful life. Recall that operating income based on accrual accounting contains noncash expenses such as depreciation expense and bad debt expense. The capital investment's *net cash inflows*, therefore, will differ from the operating income generated from the asset. Of the four capital budgeting methods covered in this chapter, only the accounting rate of return method uses accrual-based accounting income. The other three methods use the investment's projected *net cash inflows*.

What do the projected net cash inflows include? Cash *inflows* include future cash revenue generated from the investment, any future savings in ongoing cash operating costs resulting from the investment, and any future residual value of the asset. To determine the investment's *net* cash inflows, the inflows are *netted* against the investment's future cash *outflows*, such as the investment's ongoing cash operating costs and refurbishment, repairs, and maintenance costs. The initial investment itself is also a significant cash outflow. However, in our calculations, *we refer to the amount of the initial investment separately from all other cash flows related to the investment.*

While the capital budgeting methods discussed in this chapter seem procedurally cut and dry, remember that they are based on estimates and assumptions about cash flows in an uncertain future. These predictions must consider many unknown factors, such as changing consumer preferences, competition, resource costs, general economic conditions, and government regulations. The further into the future the decision extends, the more likely actual results will differ from predictions. In general, decisions that rely on long-term estimates are riskier than those that rely on short-term estimates. Much of capital investment analysis revolves around estimating future cash flows as accurately as possible. The "answers" given by the four methods will only be as good as the assumptions used in predicting future cash flows.

Capital Budgeting Process

As shown in Exhibit 12-1, the first step in the capital budgeting process is to identify potential capital investments—for example, new technology and equipment that may make the company more efficient, competitive, and profitable. Employees, consultants, and outside sales vendors often submit capital investment proposals to management. The second step is to estimate the investments' future net cash inflows. In other words, managers must make realistic estimates about future costs, revenues, and savings that are expected to occur as a result of making the capital investment. As discussed previously, this step can be very challenging. However, managers must make the best estimates possible given the information that is currently available.

The third step is to analyze the investments using one or more of the four methods listed earlier in the chapter. Sometimes the analysis involves a two-stage process. In the first stage, managers screen the investments using one or both of the methods that do *not* incorporate the time value of money: payback period or accounting rate of return. These simple methods quickly weed out undesirable investments. Potential investments that "pass the initial test" go on to a second stage of analysis. In the second stage, managers further analyze the potential investments using the net present value or internal rate of return method. Because these methods consider the time value of money, they provide more accurate information about the potential investment's profitability. Since each method evaluates the potential investment from a different angle, some companies use all four methods to get the most complete picture they can about the investment.

Because of limited resources, most companies cannot immediately invest in every capital project that appears promising. Therefore, the fourth step of the budgeting process, pictured in Exhibit 12-1, is to engage in **capital rationing**. Capital rationing means the company must choose among alternative investments due to limited funds. Managers often rank the order in which they will pursue investments, based on which investments are deemed most important, have the shortest payback period, or are expected to yield the highest return. The list of potential investments is constantly revisited as consumer tastes, newer technologies, competition, and general economic forces continually change.

EXHIBIT 12-1 Capital Budgeting Process

As a final step in the capital budgeting process, most companies perform **post-audits** in which they compare the investment's actual net cash inflows with the net cash inflows that were originally estimated. Post-audits help companies determine whether the investments are going as planned and deserve continued support or whether new strategies need to be developed to improve the profitability of underperforming assets. Managers also use feedback from post-audits to better estimate net cash inflows for future projects. If managers expect routine post-audits, they will more likely submit realistic estimates with their capital investment proposals.

Sustainability and Capital Investments

Investments in environmentally friendly technology often require large capital outlays that are assessed using capital investment analysis. In recent years, companies have focused a great deal of attention on the amount and type of energy used in their corporate and retail buildings, manufacturing plants, and delivery fleets. Investments in renewable energy have risen dramatically in recent years, especially with respect to wind and solar energy projects, which have become much more financially attractive as a result of the decreasing cost of wind turbines and photovoltaic technology. For example, Intel, Johnson & Johnson, and Toyota use solar energy panels on their manufacturing rooftops, and Staples and UPS are investing in hybrid delivery fleets. Technological strides in energy-monitoring sensors and HVAC (heating, ventilation, and air conditioning) systems have also enabled companies to become more energy efficient.

Regulation is impacting capital investments, too. For example, beginning in 2017 all new construction in San Francisco will be required to have rooftop solar systems. At the historic 2015 Paris Climate Conference (COP 21), 195 countries agreed to take action that will limit global warming to less than 2 degrees Celsius. As a result, additional investment in clean energy is expected in future years. Companies need to be aware of grants and tax breaks that governmental agencies sometimes offer for investing in green technology. Government-sponsored incentives should be treated as reductions in the initial cost of the investment or as periodic cost savings, depending on how the incentive is structured and when it is received. When analyzing more sustainable capital investments, companies should factor in future cost savings produced from having fewer lawsuits, regulatory fines, and cleanup costs as a result of investing in green technology.

One of the largest movements toward sustainability in built environments can be traced to the LEED certification process, which began in 2000. **LEED**, which stands for Leadership in Energy and Environmental Design, is a certification system developed by the U.S. Green Building Council as a means of promoting sustainable practices in the building and construction industry. The LEED certification process is meant to serve as a guide for the design, construction, operation, and maintenance of built environments. Some companies, such as Starbucks, are committed to seeking LEED certification on all of their new retail locations. Many university campuses have made similar commitments. Organizations seeking LEED certification for their building projects assess the following six factors:

1. Location and Transportation
2. Sustainable Sites
3. Water Efficiency
4. Energy and Atmosphere
5. Materials and Resources
6. Indoor Environmental Quality

LEED projects can be certified at the basic (certified), silver, gold, or platinum level, depending on the number of points earned over all of the categories. For example, Toyota's new $1 billion North American headquarters that will open in 2017 is seeking the highest "Platinum" level of LEED certification. Over 80,000 buildings have been certified to date, and another 1 million are currently in process. Why do companies care about LEED certification? Besides being better for the planet and the people who work in the buildings, LEED-certified buildings typically have lower operating costs, which often result in higher returns on the investment. Additionally, LEED-certified buildings have a competitive advantage over noncertified buildings. As a result, LEED-certified buildings often attract more potential buyers and command higher lease prices. You can learn more about LEED certification at USGB.org.

See Exercises E12-23A and E12-42B

Sources: usgbc.org; http://newsroom.unfccc.int/unfccc-newsroom/finale-cop21; www.environmentalleader.com/2016/05/03/hybrid-electric-delivery-trucks-extend-ups-fleet-range-improve-fuel-economy/; www.environmentalleader.com/2016/06/07/toyotas-new-hq-targets-leed-platinum-houses-7-7mw-solar-system/; www.environmentalleader.com/2011/07/06/staples-coke-ge-among-newest-clean-fleets-partners/; www.starbucks.com/responsibility/environment/leed-certified-stores; www.environmentalleader.com/2016/06/08/breeam-green-building-rating-system-arrives-in-us/

How Do Managers Calculate the Payback Period and Accounting Rate of Return?

2 Use the payback and accounting rate of return methods to make capital investment decisions

Payback Period

Payback period is the length of time it takes to recover, in net cash inflows, the cost of the capital outlay. The payback period measures how quickly managers expect to recover their investment dollars. The shorter the payback period, the more attractive the asset, *all else being equal*. Why? The quicker an investment pays itself back, the less the inherent risk that the investment will become unprofitable. The method used to compute the payback period depends on whether net cash inflows are expected to be equal each year or whether they will vary each year. To illustrate, we'll discuss three capital investments being considered by Tierra Firma, a company that makes and sells camping equipment. For the sake of simplicity, let's assume that each of the following potential investments is expected to cost $240,000:

- An updated energy-efficient HVAC system for the company's corporate offices. (*Estimated six-year useful life with no residual value; equal annual net cash energy savings of $60,000*)
- Investment in hardware and software to develop a business-to-business (B2B) portal that will allow the company to reduce the cost of purchasing components throughout its supply chain. (*Estimated three-year useful life with no residual value; equal annual net cash savings of $80,000*)
- New production equipment designed to reduce waste, time, manual labor, and energy consumption (*Estimated six-year useful life with $30,000 residual value; unequal yearly net cash savings as pictured later in Exhibit 12-3*)

> **Why is this important?**
> "Companies want to **recover their cash** as quickly as possible. The **payback period** tells managers **how long** it will take before the investment is **recouped**."

Payback Period with Equal Annual Net Cash Inflows

When net cash inflows are equal each year, managers compute the payback period as follows:

$$\text{Payback period} = \frac{\text{Initial investment}}{\text{Expected annual net cash inflow}}$$

Since the new HVAC system will cost $240,000 and is expected to generate equal annual net cash inflows of $60,000, we compute the payback period as follows:

$$\text{Payback period for HVAC system} = \frac{\$240,000}{\$60,000} = 4 \text{ years}$$

The left side of Exhibit 12-2 verifies that Tierra Firma expects to recoup the $240,000 investment in the HVAC system by the end of Year 4, when the accumulated net cash inflows total $240,000.

EXHIBIT 12-2 Payback Period—Equal Annual Net Cash Inflows

Year	Payback Analysis for HVAC Initial Investment: $240,000		Year	Payback Analysis for B2B portal Initial Investment: $240,000	
	Annual Net Cash Inflow	Accumulated Net Cash Inflow		Annual Net Cash Inflow	Accumulated Net Cash Inflow
1	$ 60,000	$ 60,000	1	$ 80,000	$ 80,000
2	$ 60,000	120,000	2	$ 80,000	160,000
3	$ 60,000	180,000	3	$ 80,000	240,000
4	$ 60,000	240,000			
5	$ 60,000	300,000			
6	$ 60,000	360,000			

Likewise, Tierra Firma can compute the payback period of the B2B portal using the same formula. Recall that the B2B portal will cost $240,000 and result in equal annual cash inflows of $80,000:

$$\text{Payback period for B2B portal} = \frac{\$240,000}{\$80,000} = 3 \text{ years}$$

The right side of Exhibit 12-2 verifies that Tierra Firma will recoup the $240,000 investment for the B2B portal by the end of Year 3, when the accumulated net cash inflows total $240,000.

Payback Period with Unequal Net Cash Inflows

The payback formula only works when net cash inflows are the same each period. When periodic cash flows are expected to be unequal, managers must accumulate net cash inflows until the amount of the investment is recovered. Recall that Tierra Firma is also considering investing in new production equipment that has (1) *unequal* net cash inflows during its six-year life and (2) a $30,000 residual value at the end of its life. The production equipment is expected to generate net cash inflows of $100,000 in Year 1, $80,000 in Year 2, $50,000 each year in Years 3–5, $30,000 in Year 6, and $30,000 when it is sold at the end of its life. Exhibit 12-3 shows the payback schedule for these unequal annual net cash inflows.

EXHIBIT 12-3 Payback Period—Unequal Annual Net Cash Inflows

	A	B	C
1	**Payback Analysis for Production Equipment**		
	Unequal Net Cash Inflows		
2	Initial Investment: **$240,000**		
3	Year	Annual Net Cash Inflow	Accumulated Net Cash Inflow
4	1	$ 100,000	$ 100,000
5	2	80,000	180,000
6	3	50,000	230,000
7	4	50,000	280,000
8	5	50,000	330,000
9	6	30,000	360,000
10	Residual value	30,000	390,000

Payback period is between 3 and 4 years. After 3 years, there is still $10,000 to recoup before payback of $240,000 is reached.

By the end of Year 3, the company has recovered $230,000 of the $240,000 initially invested and is only $10,000 short of payback. Because the expected net cash inflow in Year 4 is $50,000, by the end of Year 4, the company will have recovered *more* than the initial investment. Therefore, the payback period is somewhere between three and four years. Assuming that the cash flow occurs evenly throughout the fourth year, the payback period is calculated as follows:

$$\text{Payback Period} = 3 \text{ years} + \frac{\$10,000 \text{ (amount needed to complete recovery in Year 4)}}{\$50,000 \text{ (projected net cash inflow in Year 4)}}$$

$$= 3.2 \text{ years}$$

Criticism of the Payback Period Method

A major criticism of the payback method is that it focuses only on time, not on profitability. The payback period considers only those cash flows that occur *during* the payback period. This method ignores any cash flows that occur *after* that period, including any residual value. For example, Exhibit 12-2 shows that the HVAC system will continue to generate net cash inflows for two years after its payback period. These additional net cash inflows amount to $120,000 ($60,000 × 2 years), yet the payback method ignores this extra cash. A similar situation occurs with the production equipment. As shown in Exhibit 12-3, the production equipment will provide an additional $150,000 of net cash inflows, including residual value, after its payback period of 3.2 years. In contrast, the B2B portal's useful life, as shown in Exhibit 12-2, is the *same* as its payback period (three years). Since no additional cash flows occur after the payback period, the B2B portal will merely cover its cost and provide no profit. Because this is the case, the company has little or no reason to invest in the B2B portal, even though its payback period is the shortest of all three investments.

Exhibit 12-4 compares the payback period of the three investments. As the exhibit illustrates, the payback method does not consider the asset's profitability. *The method only tells management how quickly it will recover its cash.* Even though the B2B portal has the shortest payback period, both the HVAC system and the production equipment are better investments because they provide profit. The key point is that the investment with the shortest payback period is best *only when all other factors are the same*. Therefore, managers usually use the payback method as a screening device to "weed out" investments that will take too long to recoup. They rarely use payback period as the sole method for deciding whether to invest in the asset.

EXHIBIT 12-4 Comparing Payback Periods Between Investments

When using the payback period method, managers are guided by the following decision rule:

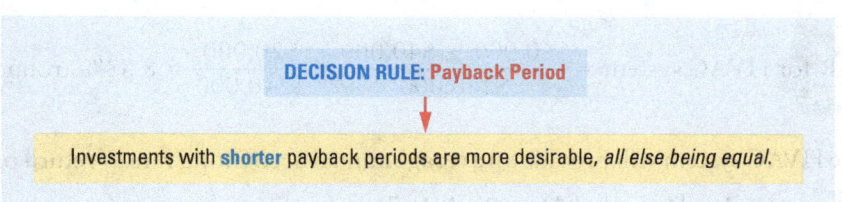

Try It!

The Bruce Company is considering investing in a wind turbine to generate its own power. Any unused power will be sold back to the local utility company. Between cost savings and new revenues, the company expects to generate net cash inflows of $750,000 per year from the turbine. The turbine would cost $4 million and is expected to have a 20-year useful life, with no residual value. Calculate the payback period.

Please see page 777 for solutions.

Accounting Rate of Return (ARR)

Companies are in business to earn profits. One measure of profitability is the **accounting rate of return (ARR)** on an asset:[1]

$$\text{Accounting rate of return} = \frac{\text{Average annual operating income from asset}}{\text{Initial investment}}$$

---

[1] Some managers prefer to use the average investment, rather than the initial investment, as the denominator. For simplicity, we will use the initial amount of the investment.

The ARR focuses on the *operating income, not the net cash inflow*, that an asset generates. The ARR measures the average annual rate of return over the asset's life. Operating income is based on *accrual accounting*. Therefore, any noncash expenses such as depreciation expense must be subtracted from the asset's net cash inflows to arrive at its operating income. Assuming that depreciation expense is the only noncash expense relating to the investment, we can rewrite the ARR formula as follows:

$$\text{ARR} = \frac{\text{Average annual net cash inflow} - \text{Annual depreciation expense}}{\text{Initial investment}}$$

Exhibit 12-5 reviews how to calculate annual depreciation expense using the straight-line method.

EXHIBIT 12-5 Review of Straight-Line Depreciation Expense Calculation

$$\text{Annual straight-line depreciation expense} = \frac{\text{Initial cost of asset} - \text{Residual value}}{\text{Useful life of asset (in years)}}$$

Investments with Equal Annual Net Cash Inflows

Recall that the HVAC system, which costs $240,000, has equal annual net cash inflows of $60,000, a six-year useful life, and no residual value.

First, we must find the HVAC system's annual depreciation expense:

$$\text{Annual depreciation expense} = \frac{\$240,000 - 0}{6 \text{ years}} = \$40,000$$

Now, we can complete the ARR formula:

$$\text{ARR for HVAC system} = \frac{\$60,000 - \$40,000}{\$240,000} = \frac{\$20,000}{\$240,000} = 8.33\% \text{ (rounded)}$$

The HVAC system will provide an average annual accounting rate of return of 8.33%.

Investments with Unequal Net Cash Inflows

Now, consider the company's potential investment in new production equipment. Recall that the new production equipment would also cost $240,000 but it had unequal net cash inflows during its life (as pictured in Exhibit 12-3) and a $30,000 residual value at the end of its life. Since the yearly net cash inflows vary in size, we need to first calculate the equipment's *average* annual net cash inflows:[2]

Total net cash inflows *during* operating life of asset (does not include the residual value at the end of life)[2] from Exhibit 12-3	$360,000
Divide by: Asset's operating life (in years)	÷ 6 years
Average annual net cash inflow from asset	$ 60,000

Now, let's calculate the asset's annual depreciation expense:

$$\text{Annual depreciation expense} = \frac{\$240,000 - \$30,000}{6 \text{ years}} = \$35,000$$

---

[2] The residual value is not included in the net cash inflows *during* the asset's operating life because we are trying to find the asset's average *annual operating* income. We assume that the asset will be sold for its expected residual value ($30,000) at the *end* of its life, resulting in no additional accounting gain or loss.

Notice how the expected residual value drives down the annual depreciation expense. Now that we have calculated the terms for the numerator, we can complete the ARR calculation as follows:

$$\text{ARR for production equipment} = \frac{\$60{,}000 - \$35{,}000}{\$240{,}000} = \frac{\$25{,}000}{\$240{,}000} = 10.42\% \text{ (rounded)}$$

Companies usually have a minimum required accounting rate of return for new investments. If Tierra Firma required an ARR of at least 10%, its managers would not approve the HVAC investment but would approve the production equipment investment. The decision rule is as follows:

Try It!

The Bruce Company is considering investing in a wind turbine to generate its own power. Any unused power will be sold back to the local utility company. Between cost savings and new revenues, the company expects to generate $750,000 per year in net cash inflows from the turbine. The turbine would cost $4 million and is expected to have a 20-year useful life with no residual value. Calculate the accounting rate of return (ARR).

Please see page 777 for solutions.

In summary, the payback period focuses on the time it takes for a company to recoup its cash investment. However, it ignores all cash flows occurring after the payback period, including any residual value. As a result, the payback period does not consider the profitability of the project.

On the other hand, the ARR measures the profitability of the asset over its entire life. The ARR is the only method that focuses on accrual-based accounting income rather than net cash inflows. Since investors tend to focus on accounting earnings, it is important for managers to understand what impact an investment will have on the company's operating income.

The payback period and ARR methods are simple and quick to compute, so managers often use them to screen out undesirable investments and to gain a more complete picture of the investment's desirability. However, both methods ignore the time value of money. In the next sections, we will review the theory behind the time value of money and then apply it to capital investments using the NPV and IRR methods.

Decision Guidelines

Capital Budgeting

Amazon.com started as a virtual retailer. It held no inventory. Instead, it bought books and CDs only as needed to fill customer orders. As the company grew, its managers decided to invest in their own warehouse facilities. Why? Owning warehouse facilities allows Amazon.com to save money by buying in bulk. Also, shipping all items in the customer's order in one package from one location saves shipping costs. Here are some of the guidelines Amazon.com's managers used as they made the major capital budgeting decision to invest in building warehouses.

Decision	Guidelines
Why is this decision important?	Capital budgeting decisions typically require large investments and affect operations for years to come.
What method shows us how soon we will recoup our cash investment?	The payback method shows how quickly managers will recoup their investment. The method highlights investments that are too risky due to long payback periods. However, it doesn't reveal any information about the investment's profitability.
Does any method consider the impact of the investment on accrual-based accounting income?	The accounting rate of return is the only capital budgeting method that shows how the investment will affect accrual-based accounting income, which is important to financial statement users. All other methods of capital investment analysis focus on the investment's net cash inflows.
How do we compute the payback period if cash flows are *equal*?	$$\text{Payback period} = \frac{\text{Initial investment}}{\text{Expected annual net cash inflow}}$$
How do we compute the payback period if cash flows are *unequal*?	Accumulate net cash inflows until the amount invested is recovered.
How do we compute the ARR?	$$\text{Accounting rate of return} = \frac{\text{Average annual operating income from asset}}{\text{Initial investment}}$$ We can also write this formula as follows: $$\text{ARR} = \frac{\text{Average annual net cash inflow} - \text{Annual depreciation expense}}{\text{Initial investment}}$$

SUMMARY PROBLEM 1

Sonoma is considering investing in solar paneling for the roof of its large distribution facility. The investment will cost $9 million and have a six-year useful life and no residual value. Because of rising utility costs, the company expects the yearly utility savings to increase over time, as follows:

Year 1	$1,000,000
Year 2	$1,500,000
Year 3	$2,000,000
Year 4	$2,500,000
Year 5	$3,500,000
Year 6	$4,500,000

The company uses the payback period and ARR to screen potential investments. Company policy requires a payback period of less than five years and an ARR of at least 10%. Any potential investments that do not meet these criteria will be removed from further consideration.

1. Calculate the payback period of the solar panels.
2. Calculate the ARR of the solar panels.
3. Should Sonoma turn down the solar panel investment or consider it further?

▪ SOLUTIONS

1. Since the net cash flows are uneven, Sonoma cannot use the simple payback formula. Rather, Sonoma must add up the accumulated net cash inflows until payback is reached, as follows:

	A	B	C	D	E
1	Payback Analysis for Solar Panels				
2	Unequal Net Cash Inflows				
3	Initial Investment: $9 million				
4					
5	Year	Annual Net Cash Inflow	Accumulated Net Cash Inflow		
6	1	$ 1,000,000	$ 1,000,000		
7	2	1,500,000	2,500,000		
8	3	2,000,000	4,500,000		
9	4	2,500,000	7,000,000		
10	5	3,500,000	10,500,000		
11	6	4,500,000	15,000,000		
12					

Payback occurs between four and five years. After four years, $2 million is left to be recouped before payback is reached. Since the company expects $3.5 million of savings in Year 5, we can further estimate the payback period as follows:

$$\text{Payback} = 4 \text{ years} + \frac{\$2 \text{ million}}{\$3.5 \text{ million}} = 4.57 \text{ years}$$

2. The ARR formula is as follows:

$$ARR = \frac{\text{Average annual net cash inflow} - \text{Annual depreciation expense}}{\text{Initial investment}}$$

To use this formula, we first need to find the *average* annual net cash inflows of the solar panels. We find the average by taking the total expected cash inflows during the six-year life of the asset ($15 million) and dividing it by six years:

Total net cash inflows during six-year life..............................	$15,000,000
Divide by: Useful life..	÷ 6 years
Average annual net cash inflow...	$ 2,500,000

Next, find annual depreciation expense:

$$\text{Annual depreciation} = \$9 \text{ million} \div 6 \text{ years} = \$1,500,000$$

Finally, use these figures in the ARR formula:

$$ARR = \frac{\$2,500,000 - \$1,500,000}{\$9,000,000} = 11.11\%$$

3. The payback period is less than five years and the ARR is greater than 10%. Therefore, the company should further consider the solar panel proposal.

How Do Managers Compute the Time Value of Money?

A dollar received today is worth more than a dollar to be received in the future. Why? Because you can invest today's dollar and earn extra income with it. The fact that invested money earns income over time is called the **time value of money**. Because of the time value of money, cash flows received sooner in time are worth more than cash flows received later in time. In other words, the timing of the cash flows received from a capital investment is important. The NPV and IRR methods of analyzing capital investments take the time value of money into consideration. This section reviews time value of money concepts to make sure you have a firm foundation for discussing these two methods.

3 Use the time value of money to compute the present and future values of single lump sums and annuities

Factors Affecting the Time Value of Money

The time value of money depends on several key factors:

1. The principal amount (p)
2. The number of periods (n)
3. The interest rate (i)

The principal (p) refers to the amount of the investment or borrowing. Because this chapter deals with capital investments, we'll primarily discuss the principal in terms of investments. However, the same concepts apply to borrowings (which you probably discussed in your financial accounting course when you studied bonds payable). We state the principal as either a single lump sum or an annuity. For example, if you want to save money for a new car after college, you may decide to invest a single lump sum of $10,000 in a certificate of deposit (CD). However, you may not currently have $10,000 to invest. Instead, you may invest funds as an annuity, depositing $2,000 at the end of each year in a bank savings account. An **annuity** is a stream of *equal installments* made at *equal time intervals*. An *ordinary annuity* is an annuity in which the installments occur at the *end* of each period. Throughout this chapter, all references to annuities will be treated as ordinary annuities because they are best suited to capital budgeting cash flow assumptions.[3]

> **Why is this important?**
> "The **time value of money** is a critical factor in many management **decisions**. In addition to its use in capital investment analysis, it's also used for **personal financial planning** (such as retirement planning), **business valuation** (for purchasing businesses), and **financing decisions** (borrowing and lending)."

The number of periods (n) is the length of time from the beginning of the investment until termination. All else being equal, the shorter the investment period, the lower the total amount of interest earned. If you withdraw your savings after four years rather than five years, you will earn less interest. If you begin to save for retirement at age 22 rather than age 45, you will earn more interest before you retire. In this chapter, the number of periods is stated in years.[4]

The interest rate (i) is the annual percentage earned on the investment. **Simple interest** means that interest is calculated *only* on the principal amount. **Compound interest** means that interest is calculated on the principal *and* on all interest earned to date. *Compound interest assumes that all interest earned will remain invested at the same interest rate, not withdrawn and spent.* Exhibit 12-6 compares simple interest (6%) on a five-year, $10,000 CD with interest compounded yearly. As you can see, the amount of compound interest earned each year grows as the base on which it is calculated (principal plus cumulative interest to date) grows. Over the life of this particular investment, the total amount of compound interest is about 13% more than the total amount of simple interest. Most investments yield compound interest, so we assume compound interest rather than simple interest for the rest of this chapter.

---

[3] In contrast to an *ordinary annuity*, an *annuity due* is an annuity in which the installments occur at the *beginning* of each period.

[4] The number of periods can also be stated in days, months, or quarters. If so, the interest rate needs to be adjusted to reflect the number of time periods in the year.

EXHIBIT 12-6 Simple Versus Compound Interest for a Principal Amount of $10,000 at 6% over Five Years

	A	B	C	D	E	F	G	H	I
1		**Simple Interest Calculation**					**Compound Interest Calculation**		
2	Year	Principal	Interest rate	Interest		Year	Principal*	Interest rate	Interest
3	1	$ 10,000	6%	600		1	$ 10,000	6%	$ 600
4	2	$ 10,000	6%	600		2	$ 10,600	6%	$ 636
5	3	$ 10,000	6%	600		3	$ 11,236	6%	$ 674
6	4	$ 10,000	6%	600		4	$ 11,910	6%	$ 715
7	5	$ 10,000	6%	600		5	$ 12,625	6%	$ 758
8				$ 3,000					$ 3,383
9									
10									

*NOTE: For compound interest calculations, the principal is the original amount ($10,000) plus the cumulative interest earned to date. For example, the principal amount in Year 2 ($10,600) is the original $10,000 plus the $600 of interest earned during Year 1. The principal amount in Year 3 ($11,236) is the original principal ($10,000) plus the interest earned in Year 1 and Year 2 ($600 + $636).

Fortunately, time value calculations involving compound interest do not have to be as tedious as those shown in Exhibit 12-6. Rather, they can be easily performed using Excel financial functions, a business calculator, or formulas and tables. Using these tools simplifies the calculations. In the next sections, we will discuss how to use these tools to perform time value of money calculations.

Future Values and Present Values: Points Along the Time Continuum

Consider the time line in Exhibit 12-7. The future value or present value of an investment simply refers to the value of an investment at different points in time.

EXHIBIT 12-7 Present Value and Future Value Along the Time Continuum

We can calculate the future value or the present value of any investment by knowing (or assuming) information about the three factors listed earlier: (1) the principal amount, (2) the number of periods, and (3) the interest rate. For example, in Exhibit 12-6, we calculated the interest that would be earned on (1) a $10,000 principal (2) invested for five years (3) at 6% interest. The future value of the investment is its worth at the end of the five-year time frame—the original principal *plus* the interest earned. In our example, the future value of the investment is as follows:

> Future value = Principal + Interest earned
> = $10,000 + $3,383
> = $13,383

If we invest $10,000 *today*, its *present value* is simply the $10,000 principal amount. So, another way of stating the future value is as follows:

> Future value = Present value + Interest earned

We can rearrange the equation as follows:

> Present value = Future value − Interest earned
> $10,000 = $13,383 − $3,383

The only difference between present value and future value is the amount of interest that is earned in the intervening time span.

Future Value and Present Value Factors

Calculating each period's compound interest, as we did in Exhibit 12-6, and then adding it to the present value to determine the future value (or subtracting it from the future value to determine the present value) is tedious. Fortunately, mathematical formulas simplify future value and present value calculations. Mathematical formulas have been developed that specify future values and present values for unlimited combinations of interest rates (i) and time periods (n). Separate formulas exist for single lump-sum investments and annuities.

The formulas have been calculated using various interest rates and time periods. The results are displayed in tables. The formulas and resulting tables are shown in Appendix 12A at the end of this chapter:

1. Present Value of $1 (Table A, p. 743)—*used for lump-sum amounts*
2. Present Value of Annuity of $1 (Table B, p. 744)—*used for annuities*
3. Future Value of $1 (Table C, p. 745)—*used for lump-sum amounts*
4. Future Value of Annuity of $1 (Table D, p. 746)—*used for annuities*

Take a moment to look at these tables because we are going to use them throughout the rest of the chapter. Note that the columns are interest rates (i) and the rows are periods (n).

The data in each table, known as future value factors (FV factors) and present value factors (PV factors), are for an amount of $1. To find the future value or present value of an amount other than $1, you simply multiply the factor found in the table by the actual amount of the lump sum or annuity.

Rather than using these tables, you may wish to use Microsoft Excel or a business calculator that has been programmed with time value of money functions. These technology applications make time value of money computations much easier because you do not need to find the correct PV and FV factors in the tables. Rather, you simply enter the principal amount, interest rate, and number of time periods in the electronic device and instruct the technology to solve for the present or future value for you.

> **Why is this important?**
>
> "The **easiest** way to find **present values** (PV) and **future values** (FV) is to use the PV and FV functions in **Excel**. The 'Technology Makes it Simple' **features** will show you how."

Throughout the remainder of this chapter, we will be displaying technology features that provide you with easy instruction on how to perform time value of money, NPV, and IRR calculations using Excel. In addition, Appendix 12B illustrates the exact Excel keystrokes to use to solve every chapter example. Appendix 12C also illustrates how to solve every chapter example using a TI-83 or TI-84 graphing calculator.

As you will see, using a programmed calculator or Excel results in slightly different answers than those presented in the text when using the tables. The differences are due to the fact that the PV and FV factors found in the tables have been rounded to three digits. Finally, all end-of-chapter homework material in MyAccountingLab has been solved using the tables, Excel, and programmed calculators so that you will have the exact solution for the method you choose to use.

Calculating Future Values of Single Sums and Annuities Using FV Factors

Let's go back to our $10,000 lump-sum investment. If we want to know the future value of the investment five years from now at an interest rate of 6%, we determine the FV factor from the table labeled Future Value of $1 (Appendix 12A, Table C). We use this table for lump-sum amounts. We look down the 6% column and across the five periods row and find that the future value factor is 1.338. We finish our calculations as follows:

$$\begin{aligned} \text{Future value} &= \text{Principal amount} \times (\text{FV factor for } i = 6\%, n = 5) \\ &= \$10,000 \times (1.338) \\ &= \$13,380 \end{aligned}$$

This figure agrees with our earlier calculation of the investment's future value ($13,383) in Exhibit 12-6. (The difference of $3 is due to two facts: (1) the tables round the FV and PV factors to three decimal places, and (2) we rounded our earlier yearly interest calculations in Exhibit 12-6 to the nearest dollar.)

Let's also consider our alternative investment strategy: investing $2,000 at the end of each year for five years. The procedure for calculating the future value of an annuity is similar to calculating the future value of a lump-sum amount. This time, we use the Future Value of Annuity of $1 table (Appendix 12A, Table D). Assuming 6% interest, we once again look down the 6% column. Because we will be making five annual installments, we look across the row marked 5 periods. The Annuity FV factor is 5.637. We finish the calculation as follows:

$$\begin{aligned} \text{Future value} &= \text{Amount of each cash installment} \times (\text{Annuity FV factor for } i = 6\%, n = 5) \\ &= \$2,000 \times (5.637) \\ &= \$11,274 \end{aligned}$$

This is considerably less than the future value ($13,380) of the lump sum of $10,000 even though we invested $10,000 out of pocket either way.

STOP & THINK

Explain why the future value of the annuity is less than the future value of the lump sum even though you are investing a total of $10,000 in both situations.

Answer: Even though you invested $10,000 out of pocket in both situations, the timing of the investment significantly affects the amount of interest earned. The $10,000 lump sum invested immediately earns interest for the full five years. However, the annuity doesn't begin earning interest until Year 2 (because the first installment isn't made until the *end* of Year 1). In addition, the amount invested begins at $2,000 and doesn't reach a full $10,000 until the end of Year 5. Therefore, the base on which the interest is earned is smaller than the lump-sum investment for the entire five-year period.

Technology Makes It Simple Excel 2016

Future Value Computations

1. In an Excel spreadsheet click on **Formulas**.
2. Click on **Financial**.
3. Choose **FV** from the dropdown list. The following will appear as a dialog box:

   Rate
   Nper
   Pmt
   Pv
   Type

4. Fill in the interest **Rate**, in decimal format (for example, 14% would be input as .14).
5. Fill in the number of periods (for example, five years would be input as 5 in the space by **Nper**).
6. If the amount is an annuity, fill in the yearly installment as a negative number in the space by **Pmt**.
7. If the amount is a lump sum, fill in the lump sum as a negative number in the space by **Pv**.
8. Leave the space by **Type** blank.
9. The future value is shown under the dialog box.

Note: Appendix 12B illustrates each chapter example using these basic Excel instructions.

Calculating Present Values of Single Sums and Annuities Using PV Factors

The process for calculating present values—often called discounting cash flows—is similar to the process for calculating future values. The difference is the point in time at which you are assessing the investment's worth. Rather than determining its value at a future date, you are determining its value at an earlier point in time (today). For our example, let's assume that you've just won the lottery after purchasing one $5 lottery ticket. The state offers you three payout options for your after-tax prize money:

Option #1: $1,000,000 now
Option #2: $150,000 at the end of each year for the next 10 years
Option #3: $2,000,000 10 years from now

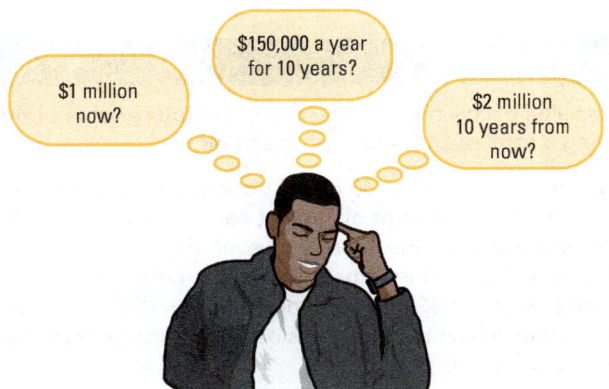

Which alternative should you take? You might be tempted to wait 10 years to "double" your winnings. You may be tempted to take the money now and spend it. However, let's assume that you plan to prudently invest all money received—no matter when you receive it—so that you have financial flexibility in the future (for example, for buying a house, retiring early, and taking vacations). How can you choose among the three payment alternatives when the *total amount* of each option varies ($1,000,000 versus $1,500,000 versus $2,000,000) and the *timing* of the cash flows varies (now versus some each year versus later)? Comparing these three options is like comparing apples to oranges—we just can't do it—unless we find some common basis for comparison. Our common basis for comparison will be the prize money's worth at a certain point in time—namely, today. In other words, if we convert each payment option to its *present value*, we can compare apples to apples.

We already know the principal amount and timing of each payment option, so the only assumption we'll have to make is the interest rate. The interest rate will vary depending on the amount of risk you are willing to take with your investment. Riskier investments (such as stock investments) command higher interest rates; safer investments (such as FDIC-insured bank deposits) yield lower interest rates. Let's assume that after investigating possible investment alternatives, you choose an investment contract with an 8% annual return.

We already know that the present value of Option #1 is $1,000,000. Let's convert the other two payment options to their present values so that we can compare them. We'll need to use the Present Value of Annuity of $1 table (Appendix 12A, Table B) to convert payment Option #2 (since it's an annuity) and the Present Value of $1 table (Appendix 12A, Table A) to convert payment Option #3 (because it's a single lump sum). To obtain the PV factors, we look down the 8% column and across the 10 period row. Then, we finish the calculations as follows:

Option #1

Present value = $1,000,000

Option #2

Present value = Amount of each cash installment × (Annuity PV factor for $i = 8\%$, $n = 10$)
Present value = $150,000 × (6.710)
Present value = $1,006,500

Option #3

Present value = Principal amount × (PV factor for $i = 8\%$, $n = 10$)
Present value = $2,000,000 × (0.463)
Present value = $926,000

Exhibit 12-8 shows that we have converted each payout option to a common basis—its worth today—so we can make a valid comparison of the options. Based on this comparison, we should choose Option #2 because its worth, in today's dollars, is the highest of the three options.

EXHIBIT 12-8 Comparing Present Values of Lottery Payout Options at $i = 8\%$

STOP & THINK

Suppose you decide to invest your lottery winnings very conservatively. You decide to invest in a risk-free investment that earns only 3%. Would you still choose payout Option #2? Explain your decision.

Answer: Using a 3% interest rate, we find that the present values of the payout options are as follows:

Payment Options	Present Value of Lottery Payout (Present value calculation, $i = 3\%$, $n = 10$)
Option #1.............................	$1,000,000
	(already stated at its present value)
Option #2.............................	$1,279,500
	(= $150,000 × 8.530)
Option #3.............................	$1,488,000
	(= $2,000,000 × 0.744)

When the lottery payout is invested at 3% rather than 8%, the present values change. Option #3 is now the best alternative because its present value is the highest. Present values and future values are extremely sensitive to changes in interest rate assumptions, especially when the investment period is relatively long.

Now that we have studied time value of money concepts, we will discuss the two capital budgeting methods that incorporate the time value of money: net present value (NPV) and internal rate of return (IRR).

Technology Makes It Simple — Excel 2016

Present Value Computations

1. In an Excel spreadsheet click on **Formulas**.
2. Click on **Financial**.
3. Choose **PV** from the dropdown list. The following will appear as a dialog box:

   Rate

   Nper

   Pmt

   FV

   Type

4. Fill in the interest **Rate**, in decimal format (for example, 14% would be input as .14).
5. Fill in the number of periods (for example, five years would be input as 5).
6. If the amount is an annuity, fill in the yearly installment as a negative number in the space by **Pmt**.
7. If the amount is a lump sum, fill in the lump sum as a negative number in the space by **FV**.
8. Leave the space by **Type** blank.
9. The present value is shown under the dialog box.

Note: Appendix 12B illustrates each chapter example using these basic Excel instructions.

How Do Managers Calculate the Net Present Value and Internal Rate of Return?

4 Use discounted cash flow models to make capital investment decisions

Neither the payback period nor the ARR incorporates the time value of money. *Discounted cash flow methods*—the NPV and the IRR—overcome this weakness. These methods incorporate compound interest by assuming that companies will reinvest future cash flows when they are received. Most companies use discounted cash flow methods to help make capital investment decisions.

The NPV and IRR methods rely on present value calculations to compare the cost of the initial investment with the expected net cash inflows that will result from making the investment. Recall that an investment's *net cash inflows* include all *future* cash flows related to the investment, such as future increased revenues and cost savings netted against the investment's future cash operating costs. Because the cash outflow for the investment occurs *now* but the net cash inflows from the investment occur in the *future*, companies can make valid "apple-to-apple" comparisons only when they convert the cash flows to the *same point in time*—namely, the present. Companies use the present value rather than the future value to make the comparison because the investment's initial cost is already stated at its present value.[5] As shown in Exhibit 12-9, a favorable investment is one in which the present value of the investment's net cash inflows exceeds the initial cost of the investment.

Why is this important?

"The **NPV method** lets managers make an **'apples-to-apples' comparison** between the **cash flows** they will receive in the **future** from the investment and the **price** they must **currently pay** to 'purchase' those future cash flows (the cost of the initial **investment**)."

---

[5] If the investment is to be purchased through lease payments, rather than a current cash outlay, we would still use the current cash price of the investment as its initial cost. If no current cash price is available, we would discount the future lease payments back to their present value to estimate the investment's current cash price.

EXHIBIT 12-9 Comparing the Present Value of an Investment's Net Cash Inflows Against the Cost of the Initial Investment

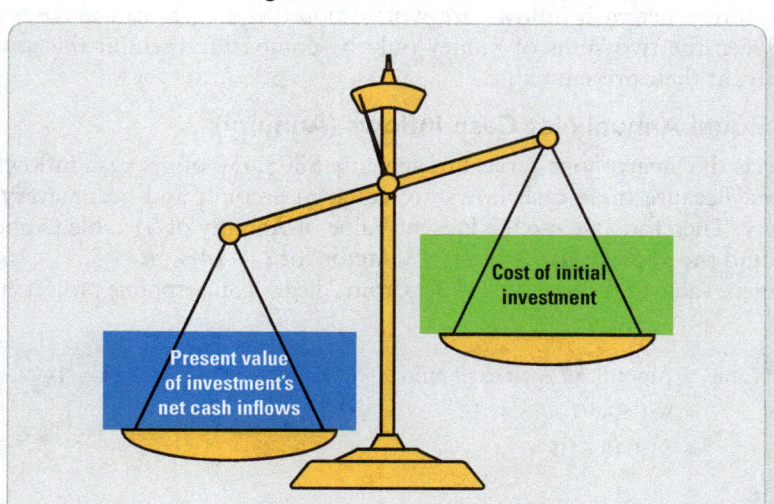

Net Present Value (NPV)

To illustrate how these discounted cash flow methods work, we'll consider two investments currently under consideration by Allegra. Allegra is a contract manufacturer that is considering producing smartphones and Bluetooth speakers for potential name-brand customers. The products require different specialized manufacturing equipment. To keep things simple, let's say that each piece of equipment costs $1 million, has a five-year expected life, and zero residual value. From now on, we'll refer to these potential investments as the Smartphone project and the Speaker project: The two potential investments have different patterns of predicted net cash inflows:

	Annual Net Cash Inflows	
Year	Smartphones	Speakers
1	$ 305,450	$ 500,000
2	305,450	350,000
3	305,450	300,000
4	305,450	250,000
5	305,450	40,000
Total	$1,527,250	$1,440,000

As you can see from the data, the Smartphone project is expected to generate more net cash inflows in total, but the Speaker project is expected to bring cash in sooner. To decide how attractive each investment is, we find its **net present value (NPV)**. The NPV is the *difference* between the present value of the investment's net cash inflows and the cost of the initial investment. We *discount* the net cash inflows to their present value—just as we did in the lottery example—using Allegra's minimum desired rate of return. This rate is called the **discount rate** because it is the interest rate used for the present value calculations. It's also called the **required rate of return** or **hurdle rate** because the investment must meet or exceed this rate to be acceptable. The discount rate depends on the riskiness of investments. The higher the risk, the higher the discount rate. Allegra's discount rate for these investments is 14%.

We compare the present value of the net cash inflows to the cost of the initial investment to decide which projects meet or exceed management's minimum desired rate of return. In other words, management is deciding whether the $1 million is worth more (because the company would have to give it up now to invest in the project) or whether the project's future net cash inflows are worth more. Managers can make a valid comparison between the two sums of money only by comparing them at the *same* point in time—namely, at their present value.

NPV with Equal Annual Net Cash Inflows (Annuity)

Allegra expects the Smartphone project to generate $305,450 of net cash inflows each year for five years. Because these cash flows are equal in amount and occur every year, they are an annuity. Therefore, we use the Present Value of Annuity of $1 table (Appendix 12A, Table B) to find the appropriate Annuity PV factor for $i = 14\%$, $n = 5$.

The present value of the net cash inflows from Allegra's Smartphone project is as follows:

$$\text{Present value} = \text{Amount of each cash inflow} \times (\text{Annuity PV factor for } i = 14\%, n = 5)$$
$$= \$305,450 \times (3.433)$$
$$= \$1,048,610$$

Next, we subtract the investment's initial cost ($1 million) from the present value of the net cash inflows ($1,048,610). The difference of $48,610 is the net present value (NPV), as shown in Exhibit 12-10.

EXHIBIT 12-10 NPV of Equal Net Cash Inflows—Smartphone Project

	A	B	C	D	E	F
1	**NPV Calculation for *Equal* Annual Net Cash Inflows**	**Annuity PV Factor** ($i = 14\%$)		**Annual Net Cash Inflow**		**Present Value**
2	Present value of annuity, $n = 5$	3.433	× $	305,450	= $	1,048,610
3	Less: Initial investment					1,000,000
4	Net present value (NPV)				$	48,610
5						

NOTE: Arithmetic signs are only shown for illustrative teaching purposes. They are not typically displayed in spreadsheets.

A *positive* NPV means that the investment earns *more* than the required rate of return. A *negative* NPV means that the investment fails to earn the required rate of return. This leads to the following decision rule:

In Allegra's case, the Smartphone project is an attractive investment. The $48,610 positive NPV means that the Smartphone project earns *more than* Allegra's 14% target rate of return. In other words, management would prefer to give up $1 million today to receive the Smartphone project's future net cash inflows. Why? Because those future net cash inflows are worth more than $1 million in today's dollars (they are worth $1,048,610).

Another way managers can use present value analysis is to start the capital budgeting process by computing the total present value of the net cash inflows from the project to determine the *maximum* the company can invest in the project and still earn the target rate of return. For Allegra, the present value of the net cash inflows is $1,048,610. This means that Allegra can invest a maximum of $1,048,610 and still earn the 14% target rate of return. Because Allegra's managers believe they can undertake the project for $1 million, the project is an attractive investment.

Try It!

The Bruce Company is considering investing in a wind turbine to generate its own power. Any unused power will be sold back to the local utility company. Between cost savings and new revenues, the company expects to generate $750,000 per year in net cash inflows from the turbine. The turbine would cost $4 million and is expected to have a 20-year useful life with no residual value. Calculate the NPV assuming the company uses a 12% hurdle rate.

Please see page 778 for solutions.

NPV with Unequal Annual Net Cash Inflows

In contrast to the Smartphone project, the net cash inflows of the Speaker project are unequal—$500,000 in Year 1, $350,000 in Year 2, and so forth. Because these amounts vary by year, Allegra's managers *cannot* use the annuity table to compute the present value of the Speaker project. They must compute the present value of each individual year's net cash inflows *separately, as separate lump sums received in different years,* using the Present Value of $1 table (Appendix 12A, Table A).

Exhibit 12-11 shows that the $500,000 net cash inflow received in Year 1 is discounted using a PV factor of $i = 14\%$, $n = 1$, while the $350,000 net cash inflow received in Year 2 is discounted using a PV factor of $i = 14\%$, $n = 2$, and so forth. After separately discounting each of the five years' net cash inflows, we find that the *total* present value of the Speaker project's net cash inflows is $1,078,910. Finally, we subtract the investment's cost ($1 million) to arrive at the Speaker project's NPV: $78,910.

EXHIBIT 12-11 NPV with Unequal Net Cash Inflows—Speaker Project

	A	B	C	D	E	F
1	NPV Calculation for *Unequal* Net Cash Inflows	PV Factor ($i = 14\%$)		Net Cash Inflow		Present Value
2	Present value of net cash inflows:					
3	Year 1 ($n = 1$)	0.877	× $	500,000	= $	438,500
4	Year 2 ($n = 2$)	0.769	×	350,000	=	269,150
5	Year 3 ($n = 3$)	0.675	×	300,000	=	202,500
6	Year 4 ($n = 4$)	0.592	×	250,000	=	148,000
7	Year 5 ($n = 5$)	0.519	×	40,000	=	20,760
8	Total present value of net cash inflows				$	1,078,910
9	Less: Initial investment					1,000,000
10	Net present value (NPV)				$	78,910
11						

Because the NPV is positive, Allegra expects the Speaker project to earn more than the 14% target rate of return, making this an attractive investment.

Capital Rationing and the Profitability Index

Exhibits 12-10 and 12-11 show that both the Smartphone and Speaker projects have positive NPVs. Therefore, both are attractive investments. Because resources are limited, companies are not always able to invest in all capital assets that meet their investment criteria. For example, Allegra may not have the funds to pursue both the Speaker and Smartphone projects at this time. In this case, the Speaker project is more profitable because

> **Why is this important?**
>
> "The profitability index allows managers to **compare** potential investments of **different sizes** so that they can choose the **most profitable** investment."

it yields a higher NPV. The Speaker project should earn an additional $78,910 beyond the 14% required rate of return, while the Smartphone project returns an additional $48,610.

This example illustrates an important point. The Smartphone project promises more *total* net cash inflows. But the *timing* of the Speaker cash flows—loaded near the beginning of the project—gives the Speaker investment a higher NPV. The Speaker project is more attractive because of the time value of money. Its dollars, which are received sooner, are worth more now than the more distant dollars of the Smartphone project. In addition, the payback period for the Speaker project is 2.5 years, whereas the payback period for the Smartphone project is 3.27 years. Considering both methods, the Speaker project seems like the more prudent investment.

Comparing the NPV of the Smartphone and Speaker projects is valid *only* because both projects require the same initial cost—$1 million. In contrast, Exhibit 12-12 summarizes three capital investment options that Raycor, a sporting goods manufacturer, faces. Each capital project requires a different initial investment. All three projects are attractive because each yields a positive NPV. Assuming that Raycor can invest in only one project at this time, which one should it choose? Project B yields the highest NPV, but it also requires a larger initial investment than the alternatives.

EXHIBIT 12-12 Raycor's Capital Investment Options

	A	B	C	D
1	Comparing NPVs	Project A	Project B	Project C
2	Present value of net cash inflows	$ 150,000	$ 238,000	$ 182,000
3	Less: Initial investment	125,000	200,000	150,000
4	Net present value (NPV)	$ 25,000	$ 38,000	$ 32,000
5				

To choose among the projects, Raycor computes the **profitability index** (also known as the **present value index**). The profitability index is computed as follows:

> Profitability index = Present value of net cash inflows ÷ Initial investment

The profitability index computes the number of dollars returned for every dollar invested, *with all calculations performed in present value dollars*. It allows us to compare alternative investments in present value terms, like the NPV method, but it also considers differences in the investments' initial cost. Let's compute the profitability index for all three alternatives.

Present value of net cash inflows	÷	Initial investment	=	Profitability index
Project A: $150,000	÷	$125,000	=	1.20
Project B: $238,000	÷	$200,000	=	1.19
Project C: $182,000	÷	$150,000	=	1.21

The profitability index shows that Project C is the best of the three alternatives because it returns $1.21 in present value dollars for every $1.00 invested. Projects A and B return slightly less.

Let's also compute the profitability index for Allegra's Smartphone and Speaker projects:

Present value of net cash inflows	÷	Initial investment	=	Profitability index
Smartphones: $1,048,610	÷	$1,000,000	=	1.049
Speakers: $1,078,910	÷	$1,000,000	=	1.079

The profitability index confirms our prior conclusion that the Speaker project is more profitable than the Smartphone project. The Speaker project returns $1.079 (in present value dollars) for every $1.00 invested. This return is beyond the 14% return already used to discount the cash flows. We did not need the profitability index to determine that the Speaker project was preferable because both projects required the same investment ($1 million).

NPV of a Project with Residual Value

Many assets yield cash inflows at the end of their useful lives because they have residual value. Companies discount an investment's residual value to its present value when determining the *total* present value of the project's net cash inflows. The residual value is discounted as a single lump sum—not an annuity—because it will be received only once, when the asset is sold.

Suppose Allegra expects the Smartphone project equipment to be worth $100,000 at the end of its five-year life. This represents an additional *lump-sum* future cash inflow from the Smartphone project. To determine the Smartphone project's NPV, we discount the residual value ($100,000) using the Present Value of $1 table ($i = 14\%$, $n = 5$) (see Appendix 12A, Table A). We then *add* its present value ($51,900) to the present value of the Smartphone project's other net cash inflows ($1,048,610), as shown in Exhibit 12-13:

EXHIBIT 12-13 NPV of a Project with Residual Value

	A	B	C	D	E	F
1	NPV Calculation Including Residual Value	PV Factor (i = 14%)		Net Cash Inflow		Present Value
2	Present value of annuity, n = 5	3.433	× $	305,450	= $	1,048,610
3	Plus: Present value of residual value, end of Year 5	0.519	×	100,000	=	51,900
4	Total present value					$ 1,100,510
5	Less: Initial investment					1,000,000
6	Net present value (NPV)					$ 100,510
7						

Because of the expected residual value, the Smartphone project is now more attractive than the Speaker project because its NPV ($100,510) is higher than the Speaker project ($78,910) and both projects require the same investment ($1 million).

Technology Makes It Simple — Excel 2016

Net Present Value (NPV) Calculations

1. In an Excel spreadsheet, type in the future cash flows expected from the investment. Begin with the cash flow expected in Year 1. In the next cell, type in the cash flow expected in Year 2. Continue in the same fashion until all future cash flows are shown in separate cells, in the order in which they are expected to be received.
2. Click on **Formulas**.
3. Click on **Financial**.
4. Choose **NPV** from the drop down list. The following will appear as a dialog box:

    Rate

    Value 1

5. Fill in the interest **Rate**, in decimal format (for example, 14% would be input as .14).
6. Next to **Value 1**, highlight the array of cells containing the cash flow data from Step 1.
7. The **"Formula result"** will appear at the bottom of the dialog box. The result is the present value of the future cash flows.
8. Finally, subtract the initial cost of the investment to obtain the NPV.

Note: Appendix 12B illustrates each chapter example using these basic Excel instructions.

Sensitivity Analysis

Capital budgeting decisions affect cash flows far into the future. Allegra's managers might want to know whether their decision would be affected by any of their major assumptions. For example, consider the following:

- Changing the discount rate from 14% to 12% or to 16%
- Changing the net cash inflows by 10%
- Changing an expected residual value

Managers can use Excel or programmed calculators to quickly perform sensitivity analysis.

Internal Rate of Return (IRR)

The NPV method only tells management whether the investment exceeds the hurdle rate. Since both the Smartphone player and Speaker projects yield positive NPVs, we know they provide *more* than a 14% rate of return. But what exact rate of return would these investments provide? The IRR method answers that question.

The **internal rate of return (IRR)** is the rate of return, based on discounted cash flows, that a company can expect to earn by investing in the project. *It is the interest rate that makes the NPV of the investment equal to zero*:

$$NPV = 0$$

Let's look at this concept in another light by inserting the definition of NPV:

$$\text{Present value of the investment's net cash inflows} - \text{Initial investment} = 0$$

Or if we rearrange the equation:

$$\text{Initial investment} = \text{Present value of the investment's net cash inflows}$$

> **Why is this important?**
>
> "In the past, finding an investment's **IRR** was time consuming and difficult. However, using **Excel** now makes it **fast** and **easy**."

In other words, the IRR is the *interest rate* that makes the cost of the investment equal to the present value of the investment's net cash inflows. The higher the IRR, the more desirable the project. Like the profitability index, the IRR can be used in the capital rationing process.

IRR computations are very easy to perform using Excel or programmed calculators. (See the "Technology Makes It Simple" feature at the end of this section.) However, IRR computations are much more cumbersome to perform using the tables.

IRR with Equal Annual Net Cash Inflows (Annuity)

When the investment is an annuity, we can develop a formula that will tell us the Annuity PV factor associated with the investment's IRR. We start with the equation given previously and then substitute in as follows:

Initial investment = Present value of the investment's net cash inflows

Initial investment = Amount of each equal net cash inflow × Annuity PV factor ($i = ?, n =$ given)

Finally, we rearrange the equation to obtain the following formula:

$$\frac{\text{Initial investment}}{\text{Amount of each equal net cash inflow}} = \text{Annuity PV factor } (i = ?, n = \text{given})$$

Let's use this formula to find the Annuity PV factor associated with Allegra's Smartphone project. Recall that the project would cost $1 million and result in five equal yearly cash inflows of $305,450:

$$\frac{\$1,000,000}{\$305,450} = \text{Annuity PV factor } (i = ?, n = 5)$$

$$3.274 = \text{Annuity PV factor } (i = ?, n = 5)$$

Next, we find the interest rate that corresponds to this Annuity PV factor. Turn to the Present Value of Annuity of $1 table (Appendix 12A, Table B). Scan the row corresponding to the project's expected life—five years, in our example. Choose the column(s) with the number closest to the Annuity PV factor you calculated using the formula. The 3.274 annuity factor is in the 16% column.

Therefore, the IRR of the Smartphone project is 16%.

Allegra expects the project to earn an internal rate of return of 16% over its life. Exhibit 12-14 confirms this result: Using a 16% discount rate, the project's NPV is zero. In other words, 16% is the discount rate that makes the cost of the initial investment equal to the present value of the investment's net cash inflows.

EXHIBIT 12-14 IRR of the Smartphone Project

	A	B	C	D	E	F
1	NPV Calculation for *Equal* Annual Net Cash Inflows	Annuity PV Factor (i = 16%)		Annual Net Cash Inflow		Present Value (rounded)
2	Present value of annuity, n = 5	3.274	× $	305,450	= $	1,000,000
3	Less: Initial investment					1,000,000
4	Net present value (NPV)				$	0
5						

To decide whether the project is acceptable, compare the IRR with the minimum desired rate of return. The decision rule is as follows:

Recall that Allegra's hurdle rate is 14%. Because the Smartphone project's IRR (16%) is higher than the hurdle rate (14%), Allegra would find the project to be an attractive investment.

In the Smartphone project, the exact Annuity PV factor (3.274) appears in the Present Value of an Annuity of $1 table (Appendix 12A, Table B). Many times, the exact factor will not appear in the table. For example, let's find the IRR of Tierra Firma's proposed HVAC system. Recall that the HVAC system would cost $240,000 and result in annual net cash inflows of $60,000 over its six-year life. We find its Annuity PV factor using the formula given previously:

$$\frac{\text{Initial investment}}{\text{Amount of each equal net cash inflow}} = \text{Annuity PV factor } (i = ?, n = \text{given})$$

$$\frac{\$240{,}000}{\$60{,}000} = \text{Annuity PV factor } (i = ?, n = 6)$$

$$4.00 = \text{Annuity PV factor } (i = ?, n = 6)$$

Now, look in the Present Value of Annuity of $1 table in the row marked 6 periods (Appendix 12A, Table B). You will not see 4.00 under any column. The closest two factors are 3.889 (at 14%) and 4.111 (at 12%).

Thus, the HVAC's IRR is somewhere between 12% and 14%.

Using Excel's IRR function, we would find the exact IRR is 12.98%. If Tierra Firma had a 14% hurdle rate, it would *not* invest in the HVAC system because its IRR is less than 14%.

▶ Try It!

The Bruce Company is considering investing in a wind turbine to generate its own power. Any unused power will be sold back to the local utility company. Between cost savings and new revenues, the company expects to generate $750,000 per year in net cash inflows from the turbine. The turbine would cost $4 million and is expected to have a 20-year useful life with no residual value. Calculate the internal rate of return (IRR).

Please see page 778 for solutions.

IRR with Unequal Annual Net Cash Inflows

Because the Speaker project has unequal cash inflows, Allegra cannot use the Present Value of Annuity of $1 table to find the asset's IRR. Rather, Allegra must use a trial-and-error procedure to determine the discount rate that makes the project's NPV equal to zero. Recall from Exhibit 12-11 that the Speaker's NPV using a 14% discount rate is $78,910. Since the NPV is *positive*, the IRR must be *higher* than 14%. Allegra performs the trial-and-error process using *higher* discount rates until it finds the rate that brings the net present value of the Speaker project to *zero*. Exhibit 12-15 shows that at 16%, the Speaker has an NPV of $40,390; therefore, the IRR must be higher than 16%. At 18%, the NPV is $3,980, which is very close to zero. Thus, the IRR must be slightly higher than 18%. If we use Excel's IRR function rather than the trial-and-error procedure, we would find that the IRR is 18.23%. The IRR is higher than Allegra's 14% hurdle rate, so the Speaker project is attractive.

EXHIBIT 12-15 Finding the Speaker's IRR Through Trial and Error

	A	B	C	D	E	F	G	H	I	J	K	L
1		\multicolumn{5}{c}{Calculations using 16% interest rate}			\multicolumn{4}{c}{Calculations using 18% interest rate}	
2	NPV Calculation for *Unequal* Net Cash Inflows	PV Factor (i = 16%)		Net Cash Inflow		Present Value at 16%		PV Factor (i = 18%)		Net Cash Inflow		Present Value at 18%
3	Present value of net cash inflows:											
4	Year 1 (n = 1)	0.862	× $	500,000	= $	431,000		0.847	× $	500,000	= $	423,5
5	Year 2 (n = 2)	0.743	×	350,000	=	260,050		0.718	×	350,000	=	251,3
6	Year 3 (n = 3)	0.641	×	300,000	=	192,300		0.609	×	300,000	=	182,7
7	Year 4 (n = 4)	0.552	×	250,000	=	138,000		0.516	×	250,000	=	129,0
8	Year 5 (n = 5)	0.476	×	40,000	=	19,040		0.437	×	40,000	=	17,4
9	Total present value of net cash inflows					$ 1,040,390						$ 1,003,9
10	Less: Initial investment					1,000,000						1,000,0
11	Net present value (NPV)					$ 40,390						$ 3,9
12												

> **Technology Makes It Simple — Excel 2016**
>
> ### Internal Rate of Return (IRR) Calculations
>
> 1. In an Excel spreadsheet, first type in the initial investment as a negative number—for example, –1000000 for a $1 million investment. In the next cell, type in the cash flow expected in Year 1. In the following cell, type in the cash flow expected in Year 2. Continue in the same fashion until all future cash flows are shown in separate cells, in the order in which they are expected to be received.
> 2. Click on **Formulas**.
> 3. Click on **Financial**.
> 4. Choose **IRR** from the dropdown list. The following will appear as a dialog box: **Values**
> 5. Next to **Values**, highlight the array of cells containing the data from Step 1.
> 6. The **"Formula result"** will appear at the bottom of the dialog box. The result is the Internal Rate of Return (IRR).
>
> *Note:* Appendix 12B illustrates each chapter example using these basic Excel instructions.

How Do the Capital Budgeting Methods Compare?

We have discussed four capital budgeting methods commonly used by companies to make capital investment decisions—two that ignore the time value of money (payback period and ARR) and two that incorporate the time value of money (NPV and IRR). Exhibit 12-16 summarizes the similarities and differences between the two methods that ignore the time value of money.

5 Compare and contrast the four capital budgeting methods

EXHIBIT 12-16 Capital Budgeting Methods That *Ignore* the Time Value of Money

Payback Period	ARR
• Simple to compute	• The only method that focuses on the accrual-based operating income from the investment, rather than cash flows
• Focuses on the time it takes to recover the company's cash investment	
• Ignores any cash flows occurring after the payback period, including any residual value	• Shows the impact of the investment on operating income, which is important to financial statement users
• Highlights risks of investments with longer cash recovery periods	• Measures the average profitability of the asset over its entire life
• Ignores the time value of money	• Ignores the time value of money

Exhibit 12-17 considers the similarities and differences between the two methods that incorporate the time value of money.

EXHIBIT 12-17 Capital Budgeting Methods That *Incorporate* the Time Value of Money

NPV	IRR
• Incorporates the time value of money and the asset's net cash inflows over its entire life	• Incorporates the time value of money and the asset's net cash inflows over its entire life
• Indicates whether the asset will earn the company's minimum required rate of return	• Computes the project's unique rate of return
• Shows the excess or deficiency of the asset's present value of net cash inflows over the cost of the initial investment	• No additional steps needed for capital rationing decisions when assets require different initial investments
• The profitability index should be computed for capital rationing decisions when the assets require different initial investments	

Keep in mind that managers often use more than one method to gain different perspectives on the risks and returns of potential capital investments.

STOP & THINK

A pharmaceutical company is considering two research projects that require the same initial investment. Project A has an NPV of $232,000 and a 3-year payback period. Project B has an NPV of $237,000 and a payback period of 4.5 years. Which project would you choose?

Answer: Many managers would choose Project A even though it has a slightly lower NPV. Why? The NPV is only $5,000 lower, yet the payback period is significantly shorter. The uncertainty of receiving operating cash flows increases with each passing year. Managers often forgo small differences in expected cash inflows to decrease the risk of investments.

Decision Guidelines

Capital Budgeting

Here are more of the guidelines Amazon.com's managers used as they made the major capital budgeting decision to invest in building warehouses.

Decision	Guidelines
Which capital budgeting methods are best?	No one method is best. Each method provides a different perspective on the investment decision.
Why do the NPV and IRR models calculate the present value of an investment's net cash flows?	Because an investment's cash inflows occur in the future, yet the cash outlay for the investment occurs now, all of the cash flows must be converted to a common point in time. These methods use the *present* value as the common point in time.
How do we know if investing in warehouse facilities will be worthwhile?	Investment in warehouse facilities may be worthwhile if the NPV is positive or the IRR exceeds the required rate of return.
How do we compute the net present value (NPV) if the investment has equal annual cash inflows?	Compute the present value of the investment's net cash inflows using the Present Value of an Annuity of $1 table and then subtract the investment's cost. Alternatively, use the NPV function in Excel (see Appendix 12B for instructions).
How do we compute the net present value (NPV) if the investment has unequal annual cash inflows?	Compute the present value of each year's net cash inflows using the Present Value of $1 (lump sum) table, sum the present value of the inflows, and then subtract the investment's cost. Alternatively, use the NPV function in Excel (see Appendix 12B for instructions).
How do we compare potential investments that have differing initial costs?	Use the profitability index, which is computed as $$\text{Profitability index} = \text{Present value of net cash inflows} \div \text{Initial investment}$$
How do we compute the internal rate of return (IRR) if the investment has equal annual cash inflows?	Find the interest rate that yields the following Annuity PV factor: $$\text{Annuity PV factor} = \frac{\text{Initial investment}}{\text{Amount of each equal net cash inflow}}$$
How do we compute the internal rate of return (IRR) if the investment has unequal annual cash inflows?	Use trial and error. Alternatively, use the IRR function in Excel (see Appendix 12B for instructions).

SUMMARY PROBLEM 2

Sonoma is considering investing in solar paneling for the roof of its large distribution facility. The investment will cost $9 million and have a six-year useful life and no residual value. Because of rising utility costs, the company expects the yearly utility savings to increase over time, as follows:

Year 1	$1,000,000
Year 2	$1,500,000
Year 3	$2,000,000
Year 4	$2,500,000
Year 5	$3,500,000
Year 6	$4,500,000

The solar panels have already passed the payback period and ARR screening (see Summary Problem 1 on pages 721–722).

1. Compute the NPV of the solar panels, given the company's 12% hurdle rate.
2. Estimate the IRR of the solar panels or use Excel to find the exact IRR.
3. Should Sonoma invest in the solar paneling? Why or why not?

SOLUTIONS

1. The NPV of the solar panels is found by subtracting the initial cost of the solar panels ($9 million) from the present value of the future cash flows as follows:

	A	B	C	D	E	F
1	NPV Calculation for *Unequal* Net Cash Inflows	PV Factor (*i* = 12%)		Net Cash Inflow		Present Value
2	Present value of net cash inflows:					
3	Year 1 (*n* = 1)	0.893	× $	1,000,000	= $	893,000
4	Year 2 (*n* = 2)	0.797	×	1,500,000	=	1,195,500
5	Year 3 (*n* = 3)	0.712	×	2,000,000	=	1,424,000
6	Year 4 (*n* = 4)	0.636	×	2,500,000	=	1,590,000
7	Year 5 (*n* = 5)	0.567	×	3,500,000	=	1,984,500
8	Year 6 (*n* = 6)	0.507	×	4,500,000	=	2,281,500
9	Total present value of net cash inflows				$	9,368,500
10	Less: Initial investment					9,000,000
11	Net present value (NPV)				$	368,500
12						

Alternatively, the NPV can be found using the NPV function in Excel. First, click on "Formulas," then "Financial," then "NPV." Next, input the hurdle rate (12%) and highlight the array of yearly cash flows to find their present value. Finally, subtract the $9 million initial investment. Note that the NPV will be slightly different ($366,838) from that shown above ($368,500) because the PV factors in the table are rounded to three decimal points.

2. Since the NPV is positive when a hurdle rate of 12% is used, the IRR must be higher than 12%. If we calculate the NPV using a hurdle rate of 14%, the NPV is negative, meaning the IRR is less than 14%. Thus, the IRR is somewhere between 12% and 14%. Alternatively, the IRR can be found using the IRR function in Excel. First, click on "Formulas," then "Financial," then "IRR." Next, highlight the array of numbers that first contains the initial investment as a negative cash flow (−9,000,000) and then contains the yearly cash flows shown above. The IRR is displayed as 13.126%.

3. The solar panel proposal meets all of the company's capital investment criteria. It has a payback of less than five years, an ARR greater than 10%, and an IRR of over 12%. Therefore, the solar panels appear to be a good capital investment from both a financial and environmental standpoint.

Appendix 12A

Present Value Tables and Future Value Tables

Table A Present Value of $1

Present Value of $1

Periods	1%	2%	3%	4%	5%	6%	8%	10%	12%	14%	16%	18%	20%
1	0.990	0.980	0.971	0.962	0.952	0.943	0.926	0.909	0.893	0.877	0.862	0.847	0.833
2	0.980	0.961	0.943	0.925	0.907	0.890	0.857	0.826	0.797	0.769	0.743	0.718	0.694
3	0.971	0.942	0.915	0.889	0.864	0.840	0.794	0.751	0.712	0.675	0.641	0.609	0.579
4	0.961	0.924	0.888	0.855	0.823	0.792	0.735	0.683	0.636	0.592	0.552	0.516	0.482
5	0.951	0.906	0.863	0.822	0.784	0.747	0.681	0.621	0.567	0.519	0.476	0.437	0.402
6	0.942	0.888	0.837	0.790	0.746	0.705	0.630	0.564	0.507	0.456	0.410	0.370	0.335
7	0.933	0.871	0.813	0.760	0.711	0.665	0.583	0.513	0.452	0.400	0.354	0.314	0.279
8	0.923	0.853	0.789	0.731	0.677	0.627	0.540	0.467	0.404	0.351	0.305	0.266	0.233
9	0.914	0.837	0.766	0.703	0.645	0.592	0.500	0.424	0.361	0.308	0.263	0.225	0.194
10	0.905	0.820	0.744	0.676	0.614	0.558	0.463	0.386	0.322	0.270	0.227	0.191	0.162
11	0.896	0.804	0.722	0.650	0.585	0.527	0.429	0.350	0.287	0.237	0.195	0.162	0.135
12	0.887	0.788	0.701	0.625	0.557	0.497	0.397	0.319	0.257	0.208	0.168	0.137	0.112
13	0.879	0.773	0.681	0.601	0.530	0.469	0.368	0.290	0.229	0.182	0.145	0.116	0.093
14	0.870	0.758	0.661	0.577	0.505	0.442	0.340	0.263	0.205	0.160	0.125	0.099	0.078
15	0.861	0.743	0.642	0.555	0.481	0.417	0.315	0.239	0.183	0.140	0.108	0.084	0.065
20	0.820	0.673	0.554	0.456	0.377	0.312	0.215	0.149	0.104	0.073	0.051	0.037	0.026
25	0.780	0.610	0.478	0.375	0.295	0.233	0.146	0.092	0.059	0.038	0.024	0.016	0.010
30	0.742	0.552	0.412	0.308	0.231	0.174	0.099	0.057	0.033	0.020	0.012	0.007	0.004
40	0.672	0.453	0.307	0.208	0.142	0.097	0.046	0.022	0.011	0.005	0.003	0.001	0.001

The factors in the table were generated using the following formula:

$$\text{Present value of } \$1 = \frac{1}{(1+i)^n}$$

where:
i = annual interest rate
n = number of periods

Table B Present Value of Annuity of $1

Present Value of Annuity of $1

Periods	1%	2%	3%	4%	5%	6%	8%	10%	12%	14%	16%	18%	20%
1	0.990	0.980	0.971	0.962	0.952	0.943	0.926	0.909	0.893	0.877	0.862	0.847	0.833
2	1.970	1.942	1.913	1.886	1.859	1.833	1.783	1.736	1.690	1.647	1.605	1.566	1.528
3	2.941	2.884	2.829	2.775	2.723	2.673	2.577	2.487	2.402	2.322	2.246	2.174	2.106
4	3.902	3.808	3.717	3.630	3.546	3.465	3.312	3.170	3.037	2.914	2.798	2.690	2.589
5	4.853	4.713	4.580	4.452	4.329	4.212	3.993	3.791	3.605	3.433	3.274	3.127	2.991
6	5.795	5.601	5.417	5.242	5.076	4.917	4.623	4.355	4.111	3.889	3.685	3.498	3.326
7	6.728	6.472	6.230	6.002	5.786	5.582	5.206	4.868	4.564	4.288	4.039	3.812	3.605
8	7.652	7.325	7.020	6.733	6.463	6.210	5.747	5.335	4.968	4.639	4.344	4.078	3.837
9	8.566	8.162	7.786	7.435	7.108	6.802	6.247	5.759	5.328	4.946	4.607	4.303	4.031
10	9.471	8.983	8.530	8.111	7.722	7.360	6.710	6.145	5.650	5.216	4.833	4.494	4.192
11	10.368	9.787	9.253	8.760	8.306	7.887	7.139	6.495	5.938	5.453	5.029	4.656	4.327
12	11.255	10.575	9.954	9.385	8.863	8.384	7.536	6.814	6.194	5.660	5.197	4.793	4.439
13	12.134	11.348	10.635	9.986	9.394	8.853	7.904	7.103	6.424	5.842	5.342	4.910	4.533
14	13.004	12.106	11.296	10.563	9.899	9.295	8.244	7.367	6.628	6.002	5.468	5.008	4.611
15	13.865	12.849	11.938	11.118	10.380	9.712	8.559	7.606	6.811	6.142	5.575	5.092	4.675
20	18.046	16.351	14.877	13.590	12.462	11.470	9.818	8.514	7.469	6.623	5.929	5.353	4.870
25	22.023	19.523	17.413	15.622	14.094	12.783	10.675	9.077	7.843	6.873	6.097	5.467	4.948
30	25.808	22.396	19.600	17.292	15.372	13.765	11.258	9.427	8.055	7.003	6.177	5.517	4.979
40	32.835	27.355	23.115	19.793	17.159	15.046	11.925	9.779	8.244	7.105	6.234	5.548	4.997

The factors in the table were generated using the following formula:

$$\text{Present value of annuity of \$1} = \frac{1}{i}\left[1 - \frac{1}{(1+i)^n}\right]$$

where:
i = annual interest rate
n = number of periods

Table C Future Value of $1

Future Value of $1

Periods	1%	2%	3%	4%	5%	6%	8%	10%	12%	14%	16%	18%	20%
1	1.010	1.020	1.030	1.040	1.050	1.060	1.080	1.100	1.120	1.140	1.160	1.180	1.200
2	1.020	1.040	1.061	1.082	1.103	1.124	1.166	1.210	1.254	1.300	1.346	1.392	1.440
3	1.030	1.061	1.093	1.125	1.158	1.191	1.260	1.331	1.405	1.482	1.561	1.643	1.728
4	1.041	1.082	1.126	1.170	1.216	1.262	1.360	1.464	1.574	1.689	1.811	1.939	2.074
5	1.051	1.104	1.159	1.217	1.276	1.338	1.469	1.611	1.762	1.925	2.100	2.288	2.488
6	1.062	1.126	1.194	1.265	1.340	1.419	1.587	1.772	1.974	2.195	2.436	2.700	2.986
7	1.072	1.149	1.230	1.316	1.407	1.504	1.714	1.949	2.211	2.502	2.826	3.185	3.583
8	1.083	1.172	1.267	1.369	1.477	1.594	1.851	2.144	2.476	2.853	3.278	3.759	4.300
9	1.094	1.195	1.305	1.423	1.551	1.689	1.999	2.358	2.773	3.252	3.803	4.435	5.160
10	1.105	1.219	1.344	1.480	1.629	1.791	2.159	2.594	3.106	3.707	4.411	5.234	6.192
11	1.116	1.243	1.384	1.539	1.710	1.898	2.332	2.853	3.479	4.226	5.117	6.176	7.430
12	1.127	1.268	1.426	1.601	1.796	2.012	2.518	3.138	3.896	4.818	5.936	7.288	8.916
13	1.138	1.294	1.469	1.665	1.886	2.133	2.720	3.452	4.363	5.492	6.886	8.599	10.699
14	1.149	1.319	1.513	1.732	1.980	2.261	2.937	3.797	4.887	6.261	7.988	10.147	12.839
15	1.161	1.346	1.558	1.801	2.079	2.397	3.172	4.177	5.474	7.138	9.266	11.974	15.407
20	1.220	1.486	1.806	2.191	2.653	3.207	4.661	6.728	9.646	13.743	19.461	27.393	38.338
25	1.282	1.641	2.094	2.666	3.386	4.292	6.848	10.835	17.000	26.462	40.874	62.669	95.396
30	1.348	1.811	2.427	3.243	4.322	5.743	10.063	17.449	29.960	50.950	85.850	143.371	237.376
40	1.489	2.208	3.262	4.801	7.040	10.286	21.725	45.259	93.051	188.884	378.721	750.378	1,469.772

The factors in the table were generated using the following formula:

Future value of $1 = (1 + i)^n$

where:
    i = annual interest rate
    n = number of periods

Table D Future Value of Annuity of $1

Future Value of Annuity of $1

Periods	1%	2%	3%	4%	5%	6%	8%	10%	12%	14%	16%	18%	20%
1	1.000	1.000	1.000	1.000	1.000	1.000	1.000	1.000	1.000	1.000	1.000	1.000	1.000
2	2.010	2.020	2.030	2.040	2.050	2.060	2.080	2.100	2.120	2.140	2.160	2.180	2.200
3	3.030	3.060	3.091	3.122	3.153	3.184	3.246	3.310	3.374	3.440	3.506	3.572	3.640
4	4.060	4.122	4.184	4.246	4.310	4.375	4.506	4.641	4.779	4.921	5.066	5.215	5.368
5	5.101	5.204	5.309	5.416	5.526	5.637	5.867	6.105	6.353	6.610	6.877	7.154	7.442
6	6.152	6.308	6.468	6.633	6.802	6.975	7.336	7.716	8.115	8.536	8.977	9.442	9.930
7	7.214	7.434	7.662	7.898	8.142	8.394	8.923	9.487	10.089	10.730	11.414	12.142	12.916
8	8.286	8.583	8.892	9.214	9.549	9.897	10.637	11.436	12.300	13.233	14.240	15.327	16.499
9	9.369	9.755	10.159	10.583	11.027	11.491	12.488	13.579	14.776	16.085	17.519	19.086	20.799
10	10.462	10.950	11.464	12.006	12.578	13.181	14.487	15.937	17.549	19.337	21.321	23.521	25.959
11	11.567	12.169	12.808	13.486	14.207	14.972	16.645	18.531	20.655	23.045	25.733	28.755	32.150
12	12.683	13.412	14.192	15.026	15.917	16.870	18.977	21.384	24.133	27.271	30.850	34.931	39.581
13	13.809	14.680	15.618	16.627	17.713	18.882	21.495	24.523	28.029	32.089	36.786	42.219	48.497
14	14.947	15.974	17.086	18.292	19.599	21.015	24.215	27.975	32.393	37.581	43.672	50.818	59.196
15	16.097	17.293	18.599	20.024	21.579	23.276	27.152	31.772	37.280	43.842	51.660	60.965	72.035
20	22.019	24.297	26.870	29.778	33.066	36.786	45.762	57.275	72.052	91.025	115.380	146.628	186.688
25	28.243	32.030	36.459	41.646	47.727	54.865	73.106	98.347	133.334	181.871	249.214	342.603	471.981
30	34.785	40.568	47.575	56.085	66.439	79.058	113.283	164.494	241.333	356.787	530.312	790.948	1,181.882
40	48.886	60.402	75.401	95.026	120.800	154.762	259.057	442.593	767.091	1,342.025	2,360.757	4,163.213	7,343.858

The factors in the table were generated using the following formula:

$$\text{Future value of annuity of } \$1 = \frac{(1 + i)^n - 1}{i}$$

where:
i = annual interest rate
n = number of periods

Appendix 12B

Solutions to Chapter Examples Using Microsoft Excel

Technology Makes It Simple — Excel 2016

Future Value Examples from Chapter

Example 1: Future Value of a Lump Sum

Let's use our lump-sum investment example from page 726 of the text. Assume that you invest $10,000 for five years at an interest rate of 6%. Use the following procedure to find its future value five years from now:

1. In an Excel spreadsheet, click on **Formulas**.
2. Click on **Financial**.
3. Choose **FV** from the dropdown list. The following will appear as a dialog box. Fill in the variables as follows:

    Rate = **.06**

    Nper = **5**

    Pmt = (leave blank since this is used for annuities)

    PV = **−10000** (the negative sign indicates that the amount is a cash outflow, not inflow)

    Type = (leave blank)
4. The future value now appears under the dialog box as = **$13,382.26** (rounded).

Example 2: Future Value of an Annuity

Let's use the annuity investment example from page 726 of the text. Assume that you invest $2,000 at the end of each year for five years. The investment earns 6% interest. Use the following procedures to find the investment's future value five years from now.

1. In an Excel spreadsheet, click on **Formulas**.
2. Click on **Financial**.
3. Choose **FV** from the dropdown list. The following will appear as a dialog box. Fill in the variables as follows:

    Rate = **.06**

    Nper = **5**

    Pmt = **−2000** (the negative sign indicates that the amount is a cash outflow, not inflow)

    PV = (leave blank because this is used for lump-sum amounts)

    Type = (leave blank)
4. The future value now appears under the dialog box as = **$11,274.19** (rounded).

Present Value Examples from Chapter

Example 1: Present Value of an Annuity—Lottery Option #2

Let's use the lottery payout Option #2 from pages 727–728 of the text for our example. Option #2 was to receive $150,000 at the end of each year for the next 10 years. The interest rate was assumed to be 8%. Use the following procedures to find the present value of the payout option:

1. In an Excel spreadsheet, click on **Formulas**.
2. Click on **Financial**.
3. Choose **PV** from the dropdown list. The following will appear as a dialog box. Fill in the variables as follows:

    Rate = **.08**

    Nper = **10**

    Pmt = **–150000**

    Fv = (leave blank since this is used for lump sums)

    Type = (leave blank)

4. The present value answer now appears under the dialog box as = **$1,006,512.21** (rounded).

Example 2: Present Value of a Lump Sum—Lottery Option #3

Let's use the lottery payout Option #3 from pages 727–728 of the text for our example. Option #3 was to receive $2 million 10 years from now. The interest rate was assumed to be 8%. Use the following procedures to find the present value of the payout option:

1. In an Excel spreadsheet, click on **Formulas**.
2. Click on **Financial**.
3. Choose **PV** from the dropdown list. The following will appear as a dialog box. Fill in the variables as follows:

    Rate = **.08**

    Nper = **10**

    Pmt = (leave blank since this is used for annuities)

    FV = **–2000000**

    Type = (leave blank)

4. The present value answer now appears under the dialog box as = **$926,386.98** (rounded).

NPV Examples from Chapter

Example 1: NPV of Allegra's Smartphone Project—An Annuity

Recall from page 731 of the text that the Smartphone project required an investment of $1 million and was expected to generate equal net cash inflows of $305,450 each year for five years. The company's discount rate was 14%.

1. In an Excel spreadsheet, type in the future cash flows expected from the investment in the order in which they are expected to be received. Your spreadsheet should show five consecutive cells as follows: 305450, 305450, 305450, 305450, 305450.
2. Click on **Formulas**.
3. Click on **Financial**.

4. Choose **NPV** from the dropdown list. The following will appear as a dialog box. Fill in the variables as follows:

    Rate = .14

    Value 1 = (Highlight array of cells containing the cash flow data from Step 1)

5. The present value of the cash flows appears at the bottom of the dialog box as = 1,048,634.58.

6. Finally, subtract the initial cost of the investment ($1 million) to obtain the NPV = **$48,634.58**.

Example 2: NPV of Allegra's Speaker Project—Unequal Cash Flows

Recall from page 733 of the text that the Speaker project required an investment of $1 million and was expected to generate the unequal periodic cash inflows shown in Exhibit 12-11. The company's discount rate was 14%.

1. In an Excel spreadsheet, type in the future cash flows expected from the investment in the order in which they are expected to be received. Your spreadsheet should show five consecutive cells with the following values in them: 500000, 350000, 300000, 250000, 40000.

2. Click on **Formulas**.

3. Click on **Financial**.

4. Choose **NPV** from the dropdown list. The following will appear as a dialog box. Fill in the variables as follows:

    Rate = .14

    Value 1 = (Highlight array of cells containing the cash flow data from Step 1)

5. The present value of the cash flows appears at the bottom of the dialog box as = 1,079,196.40 (rounded).

6. Finally, subtract the initial cost of the investment ($1 million) to obtain the NPV = **$79,196.40** (rounded).

Example 3: NPV of an Investment with a Residual Value

If an investment has a residual value, simply add the residual value as an additional cash inflow in the year in which it is to be received. For example, assume as we did in Exhibit 12-13 on page 735 that the Smartphone project equipment will be worth $100,000 at the end of its five-year life. This represents an additional expected cash inflow to the company in Year 5. The company's discount rate was 14%.

1. In an Excel spreadsheet, type in the future cash flows expected from the investment in the order in which they are expected to be received. Your spreadsheet should show five consecutive cells with the following values in them: 305450, 305450, 305450, 305450, 405450

2. Click on **Formulas**.

3. Click on **Financial**.

4. Choose **NPV** from the dropdown list. The following will appear as a dialog box. Fill in the variables as follows:

    Rate = .14

    Value 1 = (Highlight array of cells containing the cash flow data from Step 1)

5. The present value of the cash flows appears at the bottom of the dialog box as = 1,100,571.45 (rounded).

6. Finally, subtract the initial cost of the investment ($1 million) to obtain the NPV = **$100,571.45** (rounded).

IRR Examples from Chapter

Example 1: IRR of Allegra's Smartphone Project—An Annuity

Recall from page 737 that the Smartphone project required an investment of $1 million and was expected to generate equal net cash inflows of $305,450 each year for five years.

1. In an Excel spreadsheet, first type in the initial investment as a negative number and then type in the future cash flows expected from the investment in the order in which they are expected to be received. Your spreadsheet should show the following consecutive cells: **–1000000, 305450, 305450, 305450, 305450, 305450.**
2. Click on **Formulas**.
3. Click on **Financial**.
4. Choose **IRR** from the dropdown list. The following will appear as a dialog box. Fill in the variables as follows:

    Values = (Highlight array of cells containing the data from Step 1)
5. The IRR appears at the bottom of the dialog box as = **16.01% (rounded)**.

Example 2: IRR of Allegra's Speaker Project—Unequal Cash Flows

Recall from page 733 that the Speaker project required an investment of $1 million and was expected to generate the unequal periodic cash inflows shown in Exhibit 12-11.

1. In an Excel spreadsheet, first type in the initial investment as a negative number and then type in the future cash flows expected from the investment in the order in which they are expected to be received. Your spreadsheet should show the following consecutive cells: **–1000000, 500000, 350000, 300000, 250000, 40000.**
2. Click on **Formulas**.
3. Click on **Financial**.
4. Choose **IRR** from the dropdown list. The following will appear as a dialog box. Fill in the variables as follows:

    Values = (Highlight array of cells containing the data from Step 1)
5. The IRR appears at the bottom of the dialog box as = **18.23% (rounded)**.

Example 3: IRR of an Investment with a Residual Value

If an investment has a residual value, simply add the residual value as an additional cash inflow in the year in which it is to be received. For example, assume as we did in Exhibit 12-13 on page 735 that the Smartphone project equipment will be worth $100,000 at the end of its five-year life. This represents an additional expected cash inflow to the company in Year 5.

1. In an Excel spreadsheet, type in the future cash flows expected from the investment in the order in which they are expected to be received. Your spreadsheet should show six consecutive cells with the following values in them: **–1000000, 305450, 305450, 305450, 305450, 405450.**
2. Click on **Formulas**.
3. Click on **Financial**.
4. Choose **IRR** from the dropdown list. The following will appear as a dialog box. Fill in the variables as follows:

    Values = (Highlight array of cells containing the data from Step 1)
5. The IRR appears at the bottom of the dialog box as = **17.95% (rounded)**.

Appendix 12C

Using a TI-83, TI-83 Plus, TI-84, or TI-84 Plus Calculator to Perform Time Value of Money Calculations

Technology Makes It Simple

Time Value of Money Calculations

Using a TI-83, TI-83 Plus, TI-84, or TI-84 Plus Calculator to Perform Time Value of Money Calculations

Steps to perform basic present value and future value calculations:

1. On the TI-83 Plus or TI-84 Plus: Press [APPS] *to show the applications menu.*
   On the TI-83 or TI-84: Press [2nd] [X^{-1}] [ENTER] *to show the applications menu.*
2. Choose **Finance** *to see the finance applications menu.*
3. Choose **TVM solver** *to obtain the list of time value of money (TVM) variables:*

   N = *number of periods (years)*

   I% = *interest rate per year* (**do not convert percentage to a decimal**)

   PV = *present value*

   PMT = *amount of each annuity installment*

   FV = *future value*

   P/Y = *number of compounding periods per year* (**leave setting at 1**)

   C/Y = *number of coupons per year* (**leave setting at 1**)

   PMT: **End** or Begin *(leave setting on* **End** *to denote an ordinary annuity)*

4. **Enter the known variables** and **set all unknown variables to zero** (except P/Y and C/Y, which need to be left set at 1).
5. To compute the unknown variable, scroll to the line for the variable you want to solve and then press [ALPHA] [ENTER].
6. The answer will now appear on the calculator.
7. Press [2nd] [QUIT] *to exit the TVM solver when you are finished.* **If you would like to do more TVM calculations, you do not need to exit. Simply repeat Steps 4 and 5 using the new data.**

Comments:

  i. The order in which you input the variables does not matter.
  ii. The answer will be shown as a negative number unless you input the original cash flow data as a negative number. **Use the [(-)] key to enter a negative number, not the minus key; otherwise you will get an error message.** The calculator follows a cash flow sign convention that assumes that all positive figures are cash inflows and all negative figures are cash outflows.
  iii. The answers you get will vary slightly from those found using the PV and FV tables in Appendix 12A. Why? Because the PV and FV factors in the tables have been rounded to three digits.

Example 1: Future Value of a Lump Sum

Let's use our lump-sum investment example from the text. Assume that you invest $10,000 for five years at an interest rate of 6%. Use the following procedure to find its future value five years from now:

1. On the TI-83 Plus or TI-84 Plus: Press [APPS] *to show the applications menu.*

   On the TI-83 or TI-84: Press [2nd] [X⁻¹] [ENTER] *to show the applications menu.*
2. Choose **Finance** *to see the finance applications menu.*
3. Choose **TVM solver** *to obtain the list of time value of money (TVM) variables.*
4. Fill in the variables as follows:

   N = **5**

   I% = **6**

   PV = **−10000** *(Be sure to use the negative number (−) key, not the minus sign.)*

   PMT = **0**

   FV = **0**

   P/Y = **1**

   C/Y = **1**

   PMT: **End** or Begin
5. To compute the unknown future value, scroll down to **FV** and press [ALPHA] [ENTER].
6. The answer will now appear as **FV** = **13,382.26** (rounded).

If you forgot to enter the $10,000 principal as a negative number (in Step 4), the FV will be displayed as a negative number.

Example 2: Future Value of an Annuity

Let's use the annuity investment example from the text. Assume that you invest $2,000 at the end of each year for five years. The investment earns 6% interest. Use the following procedure to find the investment's future value five years from now:

1. On the TI-83 Plus or TI-84 Plus: Press [APPS] *to show the applications menu.*

   On the TI-83 or TI-84: Press [2nd] [X⁻¹] [ENTER] *to show the applications menu.*
2. Choose **Finance** *to see the finance applications menu.*
3. Choose **TVM solver** *to obtain the list of time value of money (TVM) variables.*
4. Fill in the variables as follows:

   N = **5**

   I% = **6**

   PV = **0**

   PMT = **−2000** *(Be sure to use the negative number (−) key, not the minus sign.)*

   FV = **0**

   P/Y = **1**

   C/Y = **1**

   PMT: **End** or Begin
5. To compute the unknown future value, scroll down to **FV** and press [ALPHA] [ENTER].
6. The answer will now appear as **FV** = **11,274.19 (rounded)**.

If you forgot to enter the $2,000 annuity as a negative number (in Step 4), the FV will be displayed as a negative number.

Example 3: Present Value of an Annuity—Lottery Option #2

Let's use the lottery payout Option #2 from the text for our example. Option #2 was to receive $150,000 at the end of each year for the next 10 years. The interest rate was assumed to be 8%. Use the following procedure to find the present value of this payout option:

1. On the TI-83 Plus or TI-84 Plus: Press [APPS] *to show the applications menu.*

   On the TI-83 or TI-84: Press [2nd] [X⁻¹] [ENTER] *to show the applications menu.*
2. Choose **Finance** *to see the finance applications menu.*

3. Choose **TVM solver** *to obtain the list of time value of money (TVM) variables.*
4. Fill in the variables as follows:

    N = **10**

    I% = **8**

    PV = **0**

    PMT = **–150000** *(Be sure to use the negative number (–) key, not the minus sign.)*

    FV = **0**

    P/Y = **1**

    C/Y = **1**

    PMT: **End** or Begin

5. To compute the unknown present value, scroll down to **PV** and press [ALPHA] [ENTER].
6. The answer will now appear as **PV = 1,006,512.21** (rounded).

Had we not entered the annuity as a negative figure, the present value would have been shown as a negative number.

Example 4: Present Value of a Lump Sum—Lottery Option #3

Let's use the lottery payout Option #3 from the text as our example. Option #3 was to receive $2 million 10 years from now. The interest rate was assumed to be 8%. Use the following procedure to find the present value of this payout option:

1. On the TI-83 Plus or TI-84 Plus: Press [APPS] *to show the applications menu.*

    On the TI-83 or TI-84: Press [2nd] [X⁻¹] [ENTER] *to show the applications menu.*
2. Choose **Finance** *to see the finance applications menu.*
3. Choose **TVM solver** *to obtain the list of time value of money (TVM) variables.*
4. Fill in the variables as follows:

    N = **10**

    I% = **8**

    PV = **0**

    PMT = **0**

    FV = **–2000000** *(Be sure to use the negative number (-) key, not the minus sign.)*

    P/Y = **1**

    C/Y = **1**

5. PMT: **End** or Begin
6. To compute the unknown present value, scroll down to **PV** and press [ALPHA] [ENTER].
7. The answer will now appear as **PV = 926,386.98** (rounded).

Had we not entered the $2 million future cash flow as a negative, the present value would have been shown as a negative number.

Technology Makes It Simple

NPV Calculations

Using a TI-83, TI-83 Plus, TI-84, or TI-84 Plus calculator to perform NPV calculations

Steps to performing NPV calculations:

If you are currently in the TVM solver mode, exit by pressing [2nd] [Quit].

1. On the TI-83 Plus or TI-84 Plus: Press [APPS] *to show the applications menu.*

    On the TI-83 or TI-84: Press [2nd] [X⁻¹] [ENTER] *to show the applications menu.*
2. Choose **Finance** *to see the finance applications menu.*

3. Choose **npv** *to obtain the NPV prompt:* **npv(**.
4. Fill in the following information, being careful to use the correct symbols: **npv (hurdle rate, initial investment*, {cash flow in Year 1, cash flow in Year 2, etc.})**
5. To compute the NPV, press [ENTER].
6. The answer will now appear on the calculator.
7. To exit the worksheet, press [CLEAR]. Alternatively, if you would like to change any of the assumptions for sensitivity analysis, you may press [2nd] [ENTER] to recall the formula, edit any of the values, and then recompute the new NPV by pressing [ENTER].

Note: If you would like to find just the present value (not the NPV) of a stream of unequal cash flows, use a zero (0) for the initial investment.

Example 1: NPV of Allegra's Smartphone Project—An Annuity

Recall that the Smartphone project required an investment of $1 million and was expected to generate equal net cash inflows of $305,450 each year for five years. The company's discount, or hurdle rate, was 14%.

1. On the TI-83 Plus or TI-84 Plus: Press [APPS] *to show the applications menu.*

    On the TI-83 or TI-84: Press [2nd] [X⁻¹] [ENTER] *to show the applications menu.*
2. Choose **Finance** *to see the finance applications menu.*
3. Choose **npv** *to obtain the NPV prompt:* **npv(**.
4. Fill in the following information, paying close attention to using the correct symbols:

    npv (14, –1000000, {305450, 305450, 305450, 305450, 305450}) *(Be sure to use the negative number (–) key, not the minus sign.)*
5. To compute the NPV, press [ENTER].
6. The answer will now appear on the calculator: **48,634.58** (rounded).
7. [CLEAR] the worksheet or recall it [2nd] [ENTER] for sensitivity analysis.

Example 2: NPV of Allegra's Speaker Project—Unequal Cash Flows

Recall that the Speaker project required an investment of $1 million and was expected to generate the unequal periodic cash inflows shown in Exhibit 12-11. The company's discount rate was 14%.

1. On the TI-83 Plus or TI-84 Plus: Press [APPS] *to show the applications menu.*

    On the TI-83 or TI-84: Press [2nd] [X⁻¹] [ENTER] *to show the applications menu.*
2. Choose **Finance** *to see the finance applications menu.*
3. Choose **npv** *to obtain the NPV prompt:* **npv(**.
4. Fill in the following information, paying close attention to using the correct symbols:

    npv (14, –1000000, {500000, 350000, 300000, 250000, 40000}) *(Be sure to use the negative number (–) key, not the minus sign.)*
5. To compute the NPV, press [ENTER].
6. The answer will now appear on the calculator: **79,196.40** (rounded).
7. [CLEAR] the worksheet or recall it [2nd] [ENTER] for sensitivity analysis.

Example 3: Investment with a Residual Value

If an investment has a residual value, simply add the residual value as an additional cash inflow in the year in which it is to be received. For example, assume as we did in Exhibit 12-13 that the Smartphone project equipment will be worth $100,000 at the end of its five-year life. This represents an additional expected cash inflow to the company in Year 5, so we'll show the cash inflow in Year 5 to be $405,450 (= $305,450 + $100,000). The company's discount rate was 14%.

1. On the TI-83 Plus or TI-84 Plus: Press [APPS] *to show the applications menu.*

    On the TI-83 or TI-84: Press [2nd] [X⁻¹] [ENTER] *to show the applications menu.*
2. Choose **Finance** *to see the finance applications menu.*

---

*The initial investment must be entered as a negative number.

3. Choose **npv** to obtain the NPV prompt: **npv(**.
4. Fill in the following information, paying close attention to using the correct symbols:

   npv (14, −1000000, {305450, 305450, 305450, 305450, 405450}) *(Be sure to use the negative number (−) key, not the minus sign.)*
5. To compute the NPV, press [ENTER].
6. The answer will now appear on the calculator: **100,571.45** (rounded).
7. [CLEAR] the worksheet or recall it [2nd] [ENTER] for sensitivity analysis.

Technology Makes It Simple

IRR Calculations

Using a TI-83, TI-83 Plus, TI-84, or TI-84 Plus calculator to perform IRR calculations

The procedure for finding the IRR is virtually identical to the procedure used to find the NPV. The only differences are that we choose IRR rather than NPV from the Finance menu and we don't insert a given hurdle rate.

Steps to performing IRR calculations:

If you are currently in the TVM solver mode, exit by pressing [2nd] [Quit].

1. On the TI-83 Plus or TI-84 Plus: Press [APPS] *to show the applications menu.*

   On the TI-83 or TI-84: Press [2nd] [X^{-1}] [ENTER] *to show the applications menu.*
2. Choose **Finance** *to see the finance applications menu.*
3. Choose **irr** *to obtain the IRR prompt:* **irr(**.
4. Fill in the following information, paying close attention to using the correct symbols: **irr (initial investment*, {cash flow in Year 1, cash flow in Year 2, etc.})**
5. To compute the IRR press [ENTER].
6. The answer will now appear on the calculator.
7. To exit the worksheet, press [CLEAR]. Alternatively, if you would like to change any of the assumptions for sensitivity analysis, you may press [2nd] [ENTER] to recall the formula, edit any of the values, and then recompute the new IRR by pressing [ENTER].

Example 1: IRR of Allegra's Smartphone Project—An Annuity

Recall that the Smartphone project required an investment of $1 million and was expected to generate equal net cash inflows of $305,450 each year for five years. Use the following procedure to find the investment's IRR:

1. On the TI-83 Plus or TI-84 Plus: Press [APPS] *to show the applications menu.*

   On the TI-83 or TI-84: Press [2nd] [X^{-1}] [ENTER] *to show the applications menu.*
2. Choose **Finance** *to see the finance applications menu.*
3. Choose **irr** *to obtain the IRR prompt:* **irr(**.
4. Fill in the following information, paying close attention to using the correct symbols:

   irr (−1000000, {305450, 305450, 305450, 305450, 305450}) *(Be sure to use the negative number (−) key, not the minus sign.)*
5. To compute the IRR, press [ENTER].
6. The answer will now appear on the calculator: **16.01** (rounded).
7. [CLEAR] the worksheet or recall it [2nd] [ENTER] for sensitivity analysis.

---

*The initial investment must be entered as a negative number.

Example 2: IRR of Allegra's Speaker Project—Unequal Cash Flows

Recall that the Speaker project required an investment of $1 million and was expected to generate the unequal periodic cash inflows shown in Exhibit 12-11. Use the following procedures to find the investment's IRR:

1. On the TI-83 Plus or TI-84 Plus: Press [APPS] *to show the applications menu.*

   On the TI-83 or TI-84: Press [2nd] [X^{-1}] [ENTER] *to show the applications menu.*
2. Choose **Finance** *to see the finance applications menu.*
3. Choose **irr** *to obtain the IRR prompt:* **irr(.**
4. Fill in the following information, paying close attention to using the correct symbols:

   irr (−1000000, {500000, 350000, 300000, 250000, 40000}) *(Be sure to use the negative number (−) key, not the minus sign.)*
5. To compute the IRR, press [ENTER].
6. The answer will now appear on the calculator: **18.23** (rounded).
7. [CLEAR] the worksheet or recall it [2nd] [ENTER] for sensitivity analysis.

Example 3: Investment with a Residual Value

If an investment has a residual value, simply add the residual value as an additional cash inflow in the year in which it is to be received. For example, assume as we did in Exhibit 12-13 that the Smartphone project equipment will be worth $100,000 at the end of its five-year life. This represents an additional expected cash inflow to the company in Year 5, so we'll show the cash inflow in Year 5 to be $405,450 (= $305,450 + $100,000).

1. On the TI-83 Plus or TI-84 Plus: Press [APPS] *to show the applications menu.*

   On the TI-83 or TI-84: Press [2nd] [X^{-1}] [ENTER] *to show the applications menu.*
2. Choose **Finance** *to see the finance applications menu.*
3. Choose **irr** *to obtain the IRR prompt:* **irr(.**
4. Fill in the following information, paying close attention to using the correct symbols:

   irr (−1000000, {305450, 305450, 305450, 305450, 405450}) *(Be sure to use the negative number (−) key, not the minus sign.)*
5. To compute the IRR, press [ENTER].
6. The answer will now appear on the calculator: **17.95** (rounded).
7. [CLEAR] the worksheet or recall it [2nd] [ENTER] for sensitivity analysis.

END OF CHAPTER

Learning Objectives

- 1 Describe the importance of capital investments and the capital budgeting process
- 2 Use the payback and accounting rate of return methods to make capital investment decisions
- 3 Use the time value of money to compute the present and future values of single lump sums and annuities
- 4 Use discounted cash flow models to make capital investment decisions
- 5 Compare and contrast the four capital budgeting methods

Accounting Vocabulary

Accounting Rate of Return (ARR). (p. 717) A measure of profitability computed by dividing the average annual operating income from an asset by the initial investment in the asset.

Annuity. (p. 723) A stream of equal installments made at equal time intervals.

Capital Budgeting. (p. 711) The process of making capital investment decisions. Companies make capital investments when they acquire *capital assets*—assets used for a long period of time.

Capital Rationing. (p. 712) Choosing among alternative capital investments due to limited funds.

Compound Interest. (p. 723) Interest computed on the principal *and* all interest earned to date.

Discount Rate. (p. 731) Management's minimum desired rate of return on an investment; also called the hurdle rate and required rate of return.

Hurdle Rate. (p. 731) Management's minimum desired rate of return on an investment; also called the discount rate and required rate of return.

Internal Rate of Return (IRR). (p. 736) The rate of return (based on discounted cash flows) that a company can expect to earn by investing in a capital asset. The interest rate that makes the NPV of the investment equal to zero.

LEED. (p. 714) LEED, which stands for Leadership in Energy and Environmental Design, is a certification system developed by the U.S. Green Building Council as a way of promoting and evaluating environmentally friendly construction projects.

Net Present Value (NPV). (p. 731) The *difference* between the present value of the investment's net cash inflows and the investment's cost.

Payback Period. (p. 714) The length of time it takes to recover, in net cash inflows, the cost of a capital outlay.

Post-Audits. (p. 713) Comparing a capital investment's actual net cash inflows to its projected net cash inflows.

Present Value Index. (p. 734) An index that computes the number of dollars returned for every dollar invested, *with all calculations performed in present value dollars*. It is computed as present value of net cash inflows divided by investment; also called profitability index.

Profitability Index. (p. 734) An index that computes the number of dollars returned for every dollar invested, *with all calculations performed in present value dollars*. Computed as present value of net cash inflows divided by investment; also called present value index.

Required Rate of Return. (p. 731) Management's minimum desired rate of return on an investment; also called the discount rate and hurdle rate.

Simple Interest. (p. 723) Interest computed *only* on the principal amount.

Time Value of Money. (p. 723) The fact that money can be invested to earn income over time.

Quick Check

1. *(Learning Objective 1)* Which of the following methods of analyzing capital investments factors in the time value of money?
    a. Payback period
    b. Accounting rate of return
    c. Internal rate of return
    d. All of the above methods factor in the time value of money.

2. *(Learning Objective 2)* After identifying potential capital investments, the next step in the capital budgeting process is which of the following?
    a. Performing post-audits of the capital investments
    b. Engaging in capital rationing
    c. Analyzing potential investments through at least one of the four methods
    d. Estimating the future net cash inflows of the investments

3. *(Learning Objective 2)* Which of the following is *false* with regard to the payback period?
    a. All else being equal, a shorter payback period is more desirable than a longer payback period.
    b. It is computed as follows, regardless of whether cash flows are equal or unequal: Initial investment ÷ Expected annual net cash inflow.
    c. The payback period is the length of time it takes to recover the initial cost of the capital investment.
    d. The payback period gives no indication of the investment's profitability.

4. *(Learning Objective 2)* Which of the following methods focuses on the operating income an asset generates rather than the net cash inflows it generates?
    a. Payback period
    b. Accounting rate of return
    c. Internal rate of return
    d. Net present value

5. *(Learning Objective 2)* In order to convert the *average annual net cash inflow* from the asset back to the *average annual operating income* from the asset, one must
    a. add annual depreciation expense.
    b. subtract annual depreciation expense.
    c. multiply by annual depreciation expense.
    d. divide by annual depreciation expense.

6. *(Learning Objective 3)* The time value of money depends on which of the following factors?
    a. Principal amount
    b. Interest rate
    c. Number of periods
    d. All of the above

7. *(Learning Objective 4)* The internal rate of return is which of the following?
    a. The internal management's minimum required rate of return
    b. The accounting rate of return minus 1%
    c. The interest rate that makes the NPV of an investment equal to zero
    d. The amount of time it takes to recoup the initial investment

8. *(Learning Objective 4)* An investment's NPV is calculated as which of the following?
    a. The present value of the net cash inflows from the investment minus the investment's initial investment
    b. The investment's initial investment minus the present value of the investment
    c. The future value of the investment minus the investment's initial investment
    d. The investment's initial investment minus the future value of the investment

9. *(Learning Objective 4)* When potential capital investments of different size are compared, management should choose the one with the
    a. highest NPV.
    b. lowest IRR.
    c. lowest NPV.
    d. highest profitability index.

10. *(Learning Objective 5)* Which of the following methods calculates the investment's unique rate of return?
    a. Internal rate of return
    b. Payback period
    c. Net present value
    d. Accounting rate of return

Quick Check Answers

1. c 2. d 3. b 4. b 5. b 6. d 7. c 8. a 9. d 10. a

Short Exercises

S12-1 Order the capital budgeting process *(Learning Objective 1)*

Place the following activities in order from first to last to illustrate the capital budgeting process:
a. Make investments
b. Use feedback to reassess investments already made
c. Identify potential capital investments
d. Screen/analyze investments using one or more of the methods discussed
e. Budget capital investments
f. Project investments' cash flows
g. Perform post-audits

Playmore Products Data Set used for S12-2 through S12-5:

Playmore Products is considering producing toy action figures and sandbox toys. The products require different specialized machines, each costing $1 million. Each machine has a five-year life and zero residual value. The two products have different patterns of predicted net cash inflows:

Year	Annual Net Cash Inflows	
	Toy action figure project	Sandbox toy project
1	$ 312,500	$ 518,000
2	312,500	380,000
3	312,500	340,000
4	312,500	240,000
5	312,500	50,000
Total	$1,562,500	$1,528,000

Playmore will consider making capital investments only if the payback period of the project is less than 3.5 years and the ARR exceeds 8%.

S12-2 Compute payback period—equal cash inflows *(Learning Objective 2)*

Refer to the Playmore Products Data Set. Calculate the toy action figure project's payback period. If the toy action figure project had a residual value of $175,000, would the payback period change? Explain and recalculate if necessary. Does this investment pass Playmore's payback period screening rule?

S12-3 Compute payback period—unequal cash inflows *(Learning Objective 2)*

Refer to the Playmore Products Data Set. Calculate the sandbox toy project's payback period. If the sandbox toy project had a residual value of $175,000, would the payback period change? Explain and recalculate if necessary. Does this investment pass Playmore's payback period screening rule?

S12-4 Compute ARR—equal cash inflows *(Learning Objective 2)*

Refer to the Playmore Products Data Set. Calculate the toy action figure project's ARR. If the toy action figure project had a residual value of $175,000, would the ARR change? Explain and recalculate if necessary. Does this investment pass Playmore's ARR screening rule?

S12-5 Compute ARR—unequal cash inflows *(Learning Objective 2)*

Refer to the Playmore Products Data Set. Calculate the sandbox toy project's ARR. If the sandbox toy project had a residual value of $175,000, would the ARR change? Explain and recalculate if necessary. Does this investment pass Playmore's ARR screening rule?

S12-6 Find the present values of future cash flows *(Learning Objective 3)*

Your grandmother would like to share some of her fortune with you. She offers to give you money under one of the following scenarios (you get to choose):
1. $8,750 a year at the end of each of the next seven years
2. $48,750 (lump sum) now
3. $99,350 (lump sum) seven years from now

Calculate the present value of each scenario using a 6% interest rate. Which scenario yields the highest present value? Would your preference change if you used a 12% interest rate?

S12-7 Show how timing affects future values *(Learning Objective 3)*

Assume that you make the following investments:
a. You invest a lump sum of $7,550 for three years at 12% interest. What is the investment's value at the end of three years?
b. In a different account earning 12% interest, you invest $2,517 at the end of each year for three years. What is the investment's value at the end of three years?
c. What general rule of thumb explains the difference in the investments' future values?

S12-8 Compare payout options at their future values *(Learning Objective 3)*

Listed below are three lottery payout options.

  Option 1: $940,000 now
  Option 2: $148,000 at the end of each year for the next ten years
  Option 3: $1,850,000 ten years from now

Rather than compare the payout options at their present values (as is done in the chapter), compare the payout options at their future value ten years from now.
a. Using an 8% interest rate, what is the future value of each payout option?
b. Rank your preference of payout options.
c. Does computing the future value rather than the present value of the options change your preference of payout options? Explain.

S12-9 Relationship between the PV tables *(Learning Objective 3)*

Use the Present Value of $1 table (Appendix 12A, Table A) to determine the present value of $1 received one year from now. Assume a 10% interest rate. Use the same table to find the present value of $1 received two years from now. Continue this process for a total of five years.
a. What is the *total* present value of the cash flows received over the five-year period?
b. Could you characterize this stream of cash flows as an annuity? Why or why not?
c. Use the Present Value of Annuity of $1 table (Appendix 12A, Table B) to determine the present value of the same stream of cash flows. Compare your results to your answer in Part A.
d. Explain your findings.

S12-10 Compute NPV—equal net cash inflows *(Learning Objective 4)*

Woodsy Music is considering investing $625,000 in private lesson studios that will have no residual value. The studios are expected to result in annual net cash inflows of $90,000 per year for the next nine years. Assuming that Woodsy Music uses an 8% hurdle rate, what is the net present value (NPV) of the studio investment? Is this a favorable investment?

S12-11 Compute IRR—equal net cash inflows *(Learning Objective 4)*

Refer to Woodsy Music in S12-10. What is the approximate internal rate of return (IRR) of the studio investment?

S12-12 Compute NPV—unequal net cash inflows *(Learning Objective 4)*

The local supermarket is considering investing in self-checkout kiosks for its customers. The self-checkout kiosks will cost $45,500 and have no residual value. Management expects the equipment to result in net cash savings over three years as customers grow accustomed to using the new technology: $14,000 the first year; $21,000 the second year; $27,000 the third year. Assuming a 14% discount rate, what is the NPV of the kiosk investment? Is this a favorable investment? Why or why not?

S12-13 Compute IRR—unequal net cash inflows *(Learning Objective 4)*

Refer to the supermarket in S12-12. What is the approximate internal rate of return (IRR) of the kiosk investment?

S12-14 Compare the capital budgeting methods *(Learning Objective 5)*

Fill in each statement with the appropriate capital budgeting method: payback period, ARR, NPV, or IRR.

a. _____ ignores salvage value after the payback period.
b. _____ uses discounted cash flows to determine the asset's unique rate of return.
c. _____ highlights risky investments.
d. In capital rationing decisions, the profitability index must be computed to compare investments requiring different initial investments when the _____ method is used.
e. _____ and _____ incorporate the time value of money.
f. _____ focuses on time, not profitability.
g. _____ uses accrual accounting income.
h. _____ measures profitability but ignores the time value of money.
i. _____ finds the discount rate that brings the investment's NPV to zero.

S12-15 Identify capital investments *(Learning Objective 1)*

Which of the following purchases would be considered capital investments?

a. The upgrade of the customer service fleet to new fuel-efficient vehicles has a cost of $400,000.
b. The cost of raw materials for the year is estimated at $570,000.
c. All of the computers at the help desk are being upgraded at a cost of $202,000.
d. The total cost of the management succession program for the coming year is projected to be $330,000.
e. The cost to retrofit one of a company's closed retail outlets into a customer service center is projected to be $250,000.
f. The cost of workers' compensation insurance for the coming year is projected to be $430,000.
g. To support the launch of the new product line, staff training costs are $175,000.
h. The cost to purchase a new retail commerce system for the company's website is $1,785,000.
i. The replacement of the engine on one of the company's aircraft is $240,000 (this will not increase the useful life of the plane).
j. The delivered, installed cost of a new production line is $720,000.

S12-16 Identify ethical standards violated *(Learning Objectives 1, 2, 3, 4, & 5)*

ETHICS

For each of the situations listed, identify the primary standard from the IMA *Statement of Ethical Professional Practice* that is violated (competence, confidentiality, integrity, or credibility). Refer to Exhibit 1-7 for the complete standard.

a. Luciana accepts a kickback payment from a contractor to make sure that the contactor's bid is accepted.
b. Ben is a staff accountant. He has recently been moved into a position where he will be working on capital budgeting proposals. Ben does not know how to make an NPV calculation, but he does not take the steps to acquire the skills. He figures he can use ARR and payback for investment analysis instead.
c. Dania does not include an estimate of maintenance costs associated with a new computer system. She knows that her department needs the computer system. If the maintenance costs were included in the estimate, the computer system purchase might not be approved.
d. Gordon is anxious to impress his date, Laura. Laura works in Purchasing, while Gordon works in Accounting. When they start talking about people they work with, Gordon shares salary information about each person.
e. Emmanuel's company is in negotiations to purchase one of its suppliers. Emmanuel, a management accountant, does not disclose that his mother is a major stockholder of the supplier.

EXERCISES Group A

E12-17A Compute payback period—equal cash inflows (Learning Objective 2)

Root Products is considering acquiring a manufacturing plant. The purchase price is $900,000. The owners believe the plant will generate net cash inflows of $300,000 annually. It will have to be replaced in eight years. To be profitable, the investment's payback period must occur before the investment's replacement date. Use the payback method to determine whether Root Products should purchase this plant.

E12-18A Compute payback period and analyze changes (Learning Objective 2)

The Cleveland Foodbank is a nonprofit organization that receives donations of food and distributes this food to appropriate charitable organizations. Many times, large quantities of food need to be shrinkwrapped to secure the items for shipping to the charitable organizations. The VP of Operations at the Cleveland Foodbank recently performed a time study of the time that its warehouse personnel spend waiting for the shrinkwrap machine to become available. He used this wait time data and the following assumptions to determine the financial benefit of buying a second shrinkwrap machine.

- Cost of new shrinkwrap machine plus installation = $24,000
- Average wait time per warehouse picker per day = 60 minutes
- Number of warehouse pickers = 7
- Hourly wage of warehouse personnel = $12.00
- Foodbank is open 5 days a week, 52 weeks a year, except for 10 holidays
- Expected useful life of machine = 15 years
- Expected salvage value = $2,000

Requirements

1. What is the expected net cash inflow per year from purchasing a second shrinkwrap machine (i.e., how much cost could be saved each year by eliminating the wait time)?
2. What is the payback period of the second shrinkwrap machine? Round your answer to the nearest two decimal places.
3. What would the expected net cash inflow per year be if the hourly wage rate used for this analysis was increased by 25% to reflect the cost of employee benefits?
4. What is the payback period of the second shrinkwrap machine when the increased wage rate is used to calculate the expected net cash inflow per year? Round your answer to the nearest two decimal places.
5. Did the payback period using the increased hourly wage rate increase or decrease as compared to the original payback period using the hourly rate without any benefits included? Explain.

E12-19A Compute payback period—unequal cash inflows (Learning Objective 2)

Robinson Hardware is adding a new product line that will require an investment of $1,550,000. Managers estimate that this investment will have a 10-year life and generate net cash inflows of $330,000 the first year, $275,000 the second year, and $250,000 each year thereafter for eight years. The investment has no residual value. Compute the payback period.

E12-20A ARR with unequal cash inflows (Learning Objective 2)

Refer to the Robinson Hardware information in E12–19A. Compute the ARR for the investment.

E12-21A Compute and compare ARR (Learning Objective 2)

Star Golf Products is considering whether to upgrade its equipment. Managers are considering two options. Equipment manufactured by Heatherwood Inc. costs $900,000 and will last six years and have no residual value. The Heatherwood equipment will generate annual operating income of $153,000. Equipment manufactured by Riverland Limited costs $1,350,000 and will remain useful for seven years. It promises annual operating income of $249,750, and its expected residual value is $100,000.

Which equipment offers the higher ARR?

E12-22A Compare retirement savings plans (Learning Objective 3)

Assume that you want to retire early at age 52. You plan to save using one of the following two strategies: (1) save $2,700 a year in an IRA beginning when you are 27 and ending when you are 52 (25 years) or (2) wait until you are 37 to start saving and then save $4,500 per year for the next 15 years. Assume that you will earn the historic stock market average of 10% per year.

Requirements

1. How much out-of-pocket cash will you invest under the two options?
2. How much savings will you have accumulated at age 52 under the two options?
3. Explain the results.
4. If you let the savings continue to grow for 10 more years (with no further out-of-pocket investments), under each scenario, what will the investment be worth when you are age 62?

E12-23A Calculate the payback and NPV for a sustainable energy project (Learning Objectives 1 & 3)

SUSTAINABILITY

Grant Industries is evaluating whether to invest in solar panels to provide some of the electrical needs of its main office building in Buffalo, New York. The solar panel project would cost $600,000 and would provide cost savings in its utility bills of $50,000 per year. It is anticipated that the solar panels would have a life of 20 years and would have no residual value.

Requirements

1. Calculate the payback period in years of the solar panel project.
2. If the company uses a discount rate of 12%, what is the net present value of this project?
3. If the company has a rule that no projects will be undertaken that have a payback period of more than five years, would this investment be accepted? If not, what arguments could the energy manager make to try to obtain approval for the solar panel project?
4. What would you do if you were in charge of approving capital investment proposals?

E12-24A Fund future cash flows (Learning Objective 3)

Samantha wants to take the next four years off work to travel around the world. She estimates her annual cash needs at $30,000 (if she needs more, she'll work odd jobs). Samantha believes she can invest her savings at 8% until she depletes her funds.

Requirements

1. How much money does Samantha need now to fund her travels?
2. After checking with a number of banks, Samantha learns she'll be able to invest her funds only at 6%. How much does she need now to fund her travels?

E12-25A Choosing a lottery payout option (Learning Objective 3)

Congratulations! You've won a state lotto! The state lottery offers you the following (after-tax) payout options:

Option #1: $14,500,000 six years from now
Option #2: $2,200,000 at the end of each year for the next six years
Option #3: $12,500,000 four years from now

Requirement

Assuming that you can earn 6% on your funds, which option would you prefer?

E12-26A Solve various time value of money scenarios (Learning Objective 3)

1. Suppose you invest a sum of $4,000 in an interest-bearing account at the rate of 10% per year. What will the investment be worth six years from now?
2. How much would you need to invest now to be able to withdraw $6,000 at the end of every year for the next 20 years? Assume a 12% interest rate.

3. Assume that you want to have $160,000 saved seven years from now. If you can invest your funds at a 6% interest rate, how much do you currently need to invest?
4. Your aunt Eugenia plans to give you $2,000 at the end of every year for the next 10 years. If you invest each of her yearly gifts at a 12% interest rate, how much will they be worth at the end of the 10-year period?
5. Suppose you want to buy a small cabin in the mountains four years from now. You estimate that the property will cost $51,000 at that time. How much money do you need to invest each year in an interest-bearing account earning 6% per year to accumulate the purchase price?

E12-27A Calculate NPV—equal annual cash inflows *(Learning Objective 4)*

Use the NPV method to determine whether Vargas Products should invest in the following projects:

- *Project A* costs $280,000 and offers eight annual net cash inflows of $56,000. Vargas Products requires an annual return of 16% on projects like A.
- *Project B* costs $380,000 and offers nine annual net cash inflows of $74,000. Vargas Products demands an annual return of 12% on investments of this nature.

Requirement
What is the NPV of each project? What is the maximum acceptable price to pay for each project?

E12-28A Calculate IRR—equal cash inflows *(Learning Objective 4)*

Refer to Vargas Products in E12-27A. Compute the IRR of each project and use this information to identify the better investment.

E12-29A Calculate NPV—unequal cash flows *(Learning Objective 4)*

Walker Industries is deciding whether to automate one phase of its production process. The manufacturing equipment has a six-year life and will cost $905,000. Projected net cash inflows are as follows:

Year 1	$262,000
Year 2	$255,000
Year 3	$224,000
Year 4	$210,000
Year 5	$204,000
Year 6	$173,000

Requirements
1. Compute this project's NPV using Walker Industries' 14% hurdle rate. Should the company invest in the equipment? Why or why not?
2. Walker Industries could refurbish the equipment at the end of six years for $105,000. The refurbished equipment could be used one more year, providing $72,000 of net cash inflows in Year 7. In addition, the refurbished equipment would have a $55,000 residual value at the end of Year 7. Should Walker Industries invest in the equipment and refurbish it after six years? Why or why not? (*Hint:* In addition to your answer to Requirement 1, discount the additional cash outflow and inflows back to the present value.)

E12-30A Compute IRR—unequal cash flows *(Learning Objective 4)*

Brooklyn Tables is considering an equipment investment that will cost $960,000. Projected net cash inflows over the equipment's three-year life are as follows: Year 1: $484,000; Year 2: $388,000; and Year 3: $286,000. Brooklyn Tables wants to know the equipment's IRR.

Requirement
Use trial and error to find the IRR within a 2% range. (*Hint:* Use Brooklyn Tables' hurdle rate of 8% to begin the trial-and-error process.)

Optional: Use a business calculator or spreadsheet to compute the exact IRR.

E12-31A Capital rationing decision (Learning Objective 4)

Stanton Manufacturing is considering three capital investment proposals. At this time, the company has funds available to pursue only one of the three investments.

	Equipment A	Equipment B	Equipment C
Present value of net cash inflows	$1,710,000	$1,950,000	$2,180,000
Investment	(1,425,000)	(1,875,000)	(1,744,000)
NPV	$ 285,000	$ 75,000	$ 436,000

Requirement
Which investment should Stanton Manufacturing pursue at this time? Why?

Wolf Valley Expansion Data Set used for E12-32A through E12-33A:

Assume that Wolf Valley's managers developed the following estimates concerning a planned expansion to its Brook Park Lodge (all numbers assumed):

Number of additional skiers per day	125
Average number of days per year that weather conditions allow skiing at Wolf Valley	160
Useful life of expansion (in years)	8
Average cash spent by each skier per day	$ 240
Average variable cost of serving each skier per day	$ 142
Cost of expansion	$8,000,000
Discount rate	12%

Assume that Wolf Valley uses the straight-line depreciation method and expects the lodge expansion to have a residual value of $1,000,000 at the end of its eight-year life.

E12-32A Compute payback and ARR with residual value (Learning Objective 2)

Consider how Wolf Valley, a popular ski resort, could use capital budgeting to decide whether the $8 million Brook Park Lodge expansion would be a good investment.

Requirements
1. Compute the average annual net cash inflow from the expansion.
2. Compute the average annual operating income from the expansion.
3. Compute the payback period.
4. Compute the ARR.

E12-33A Calculate NPV with and without residual value (Learning Objective 4)

Refer to the Wolf Valley Data Set in E12-32A.

Requirements
1. What is the project's NPV? Is the investment attractive? Why or why not?
2. Assume that the expansion has no residual value. What is the project's NPV? Is the investment still attractive? Why or why not?

E12-34A Compute payback period and discuss qualitative factors (Learning Objectives 2 and 5)

A variety of robots were featured at the 2016 National Restaurant Show that could be used for a variety of tasks in restaurants. These robots were introduced at the same time that an ongoing debate ensued in the United States about the merits of a national minimum wage of $15 per hour for every worker. A former McDonald's USA CEO, Ed Rensi, said that purchasing a $35,000 robotic arm would be cheaper than paying fast-food workers $15 per hour for food preparation tasks like bagging French fries.

To test the former CEO's assertion using a hypothetical example, make the following assumptions:

a. For the cost of the hourly workers, use a total wage rate of $18 per hour to reflect payroll taxes (the hourly wage rate used here is higher than $15 since payroll taxes can add 15% or more to the hourly wage rate).

b. Assume that freight and installation for the robot's initial placement in a McDonald's restaurant will be a one-time cost of $5,000.

c. The robot will require annual maintenance service. Assume an annual service contract is required that costs 10% of the original robot cost including the original freight/installation.

d. Assume that the robot will replace 10 employee hours per day, 360 days per year (the robot will not, at least initially, be as versatile as a person and cannot fully eliminate all food prep workers at this point).

e. Electricity and supplies consumed by the robot will be assumed to be $1,500 per year.

Requirements

1. What would the payback period be on a McDonald's robot used for food preparation? (Round to the nearest two decimal places.)
2. What qualitative factors would McDonald's need to consider when deciding whether to purchase robots to replace some of its food preparation workers?
3. Given the payback period, would net present value (NPV) or internal rate of return (IRR) be likely to be useful tools for analyzing this decision? Support your response.

E12-35A Comparing capital budgeting methods *(Learning Objective 5)*

The following table contains information about four projects in which Andrews Corporation has the opportunity to invest. This information is based on estimates that different managers have prepared about their potential project.

Project	Investment Required	Net Present Value	Life of Project	Internal Rate of Return	Profitability Index	Payback Period in Years	Accounting Rate of Return
A	$ 205,000	$ 61,770	5	24%	1.30	2.77	17%
B	$ 420,000	$ 19,032	6	22%	1.05	3.18	15%
C	$1,010,000	$214,075	3	19%	1.21	2.13	11%
D	$1,540,000	$ 2,796	4	12%	1.00	3.03	21%

Requirements

1. Rank the four projects in order of preference by using the
   a. net present value.
   b. project profitability index.
   c. internal rate of return.
   d. payback period.
   e. accounting rate of return.
2. Which method(s) do you think is best for evaluating capital investment projects in general? Why?

EXERCISES Group B

E12-36B Compute payback period—equal cash inflows *(Learning Objective 2)*

Langor Products is considering acquiring a manufacturing plant. The purchase price is $2,400,000. The owners believe the plant will generate net cash inflows of $300,000 annually. It will have to be replaced in nine years. To be profitable, the investment's payback period must occur before the investment's replacement date. Use the payback method to determine whether Langor should purchase this plant.

E12-37B Compute payback period and analyze changes *(Learning Objective 2)*

The Cleveland Foodbank is a nonprofit organization that receives donations of food and distributes this food to appropriate charitable organizations. Many times, large quantities of food need to be shrinkwrapped to secure the items for shipping to the charitable organizations. The VP of Operations at the Cleveland Foodbank recently performed a time study of the time that its warehouse personnel spend waiting for the shrinkwrap machine to become available. He used this wait time data and the following assumptions to determine the financial benefit of buying a second shrinkwrap machine.

- Cost of new shrinkwrap machine plus installation = $25,000
- Average wait time per warehouse picker per day = 60 minutes
- Number of warehouse pickers = 7
- Hourly wage of warehouse personnel = $14.00
- Foodbank is open 5 days a week, 52 weeks a year, except for 10 holidays
- Expected useful life of machine = 15 years
- Expected salvage value = $1,000

Requirements

1. What is the expected net cash inflow per year from purchasing a second shrinkwrap machine (i.e., how much cost could be saved each year by eliminating the wait time)?
2. What is the payback period of the second shrinkwrap machine? Round your answer to the nearest two decimal places.
3. What would the expected net cash inflow per year be if the hourly wage rate used for this analysis was increased by 20% to reflect the cost of employee benefits?
4. What is the payback period of the second shrinkwrap machine when the increased wage rate is used to calculate the expected net cash inflow per year? Round your answer to the nearest two decimal places.
5. Did the payback period using the increased hourly wage rate increase or decrease as compared to the original payback period using the hourly rate without any benefits included? Explain.

E12-38B Compute payback period—unequal cash inflows *(Learning Objective 2)*

Archer Hardware is adding a new product line that will require an investment of $1,460,000. Managers estimate that this investment will have a 10-year life and generate net cash inflows of $335,000 the first year, $285,000 the second year, and $240,000 each year thereafter for eight years. The investment has no residual value. Compute the payback period.

E12-39B ARR with unequal cash inflows *(Learning Objective 2)*

Refer to the Archer Hardware information in E12-38B. Compute the ARR for the investment.

E12-40B Compute and compare ARR *(Learning Objective 2)*

Atlanta Tennis Products is considering whether to upgrade its manufacturing equipment. Managers are considering two options. Equipment manufactured by Kunshier Inc. costs $1,200,000 and will last for four years with no residual value. The Kunshier equipment will generate annual operating income of $198,000. Equipment manufactured by Preston Limited costs $1,100,000 and will remain useful for five years. It promises annual operating income of $236,500, and its expected residual value is $100,000. Which equipment offers the higher ARR?

E12-41B Compare retirement savings plans *(Learning Objective 3)*

Assume you want to retire early at age 53. You plan to save using one of the following two strategies: (1) save $3,600 a year in an IRA beginning when you are 28 and ending when you are 53 (25 years) or (2) wait until you are 41 to start saving and then save $7,500 per year for the next 12 years. Assume you will earn the historic stock market average of 12% per year.

Requirements

1. How much out-of-pocket cash will you invest under the two options?
2. How much savings will you have accumulated at age 53 under the two options?
3. Explain the results.
4. If you were to let the savings continue to grow for nine more years (with no further out-of-pocket investments), under each scenario, what will the investments be worth when you are age 62?

E12-42B **Calculate the payback and NPV for a sustainable energy project** *(Learning Objectives 1 & 3)*

SUSTAINABILITY

Herschel Industries is evaluating whether to invest in solar panels to provide some of the electrical needs of its main building in Innsbrook, Virginia. The solar panel project would cost $550,000 and would provide cost savings in its utility bills of $80,000 per year. It is anticipated that the solar panels would have a life of 15 years and would have no residual value.

Requirements

1. Calculate the payback period in years of the solar panel project.
2. If the company uses a discount rate of 10%, what is the net present value of this project?
3. If the company has a rule that no projects will be undertaken that would have a payback period of more than five years, would this investment be accepted? If not, what arguments could the energy manager make to try to obtain approval for the solar panel project?
4. What would you do if you were in charge of approving capital investment proposals?

E12-43B **Fund future cash flows** *(Learning Objective 3)*

Hazel wants to take the next six years off work to travel around the world. She estimates her annual cash needs at $35,000 (if she needs more, she'll work odd jobs). Hazel believes she can invest her savings at 6% until she depletes her funds.

Requirements

1. How much money does Hazel need now to fund her travels?
2. After checking with a number of banks, Hazel learns she'll only be able to invest her funds at 4%. How much does she need now to fund her travels?

E12-44B **Choosing a lottery payout option** *(Learning Objective 3)*

Congratulations! You've won a state lotto! The state lottery offers you the following (after-tax) payout options:

Option #1: $12,000,000 six years from now
Option #2: $2,200,000 at the end of each year for the next five years
Option #3: $10,500,000 four years from now

Requirement

Assuming that you can earn 10% on your funds, which option would you prefer?

E12-45B **Solve various time value of money scenarios** *(Learning Objective 3)*

Solve these various time value of money scenarios.

1. Suppose you invest a sum of $3,000 in an interest-bearing account at the rate of 10% per year. What will the investment be worth six years from now?
2. How much would you need to invest now to be able to withdraw $6,000 at the end of every year for the next 20 years? Assume a 12% interest rate.
3. Assume that you want to have $135,000 saved seven years from now. If you can invest your funds at an 8% interest rate, how much do you currently need to invest?
4. Your aunt Gracen plans to give you $3,500 at the end of every year for the next ten years. If you invest each of her yearly gifts at a 12% interest rate, how much will they be worth at the end of the ten-year period?

5. Suppose you would like to buy a small cabin in the mountains four years from now. You estimate that the property will cost $53,000 at that time. How much money would you need to invest each year in an interest-bearing account at the rate of 8% per year in order to accumulate the purchase price?

E12-46B   Calculate NPV—equal annual cash inflows *(Learning Objective 4)*

Use the NPV method to determine whether McKnight Products should invest in the following projects:

- *Project A* costs $265,000 and offers seven annual net cash inflows of $65,000. McKnight Products requires an annual return of 16% on projects like A.
- *Project B* costs $385,000 and offers nine annual net cash inflows of $72,000. McKnight Products demands an annual return of 12% on investments of this nature.

Requirement

What is the NPV of each project? What is the maximum acceptable price to pay for each project?

E12-47B   Calculate IRR—equal cash inflows *(Learning Objective 4)*

Refer to McKnight Products in E12-46B. Compute the IRR of each project and use this information to identify the better investment.

E12-48B   Calculate NPV—unequal cash flows *(Learning Objective 4)*

Fielding Industries is deciding whether to automate one phase of its production process. The manufacturing equipment has a six-year life and will cost $910,000.

Projected net cash inflows are as follows:	
Year 1	$264,000
Year 2	$252,000
Year 3	$222,000
Year 4	$210,000
Year 5	$203,000
Year 6	$173,000

Requirements

1. Compute this project's NPV using Fielding Industries' 16% hurdle rate. Should the company invest in the equipment? Why or why not?
2. Fielding Industries could refurbish the equipment at the end of six years for $102,000. The refurbished equipment could be used for one more year, providing $74,000 of net cash inflows in Year 7. Additionally, the refurbished equipment would have a $50,000 residual value at the end of Year 7. Should the company invest in the equipment and refurbish it after six years? Why or why not? (*Hint:* In addition to your answer to Requirement 1, discount the additional cash outflows and inflows back to the present value.)

E12-49B   Compute IRR—unequal cash flows *(Learning Objective 4)*

Newark Tables is considering an equipment investment that will cost $955,000. Projected net cash inflows over the equipment's three-year life are as follows: Year 1: $492,000; Year 2: $394,000; and Year 3: $286,000. Newark Tables wants to know the equipment's IRR.

Requirement

Use trial and error to find the IRR within a 2% range. (*Hint:* Use Newark Tables' hurdle rate of 10% to begin the trial-and-error process.)

Optional: Use a business calculator or spreadsheet to compute the exact IRR.

E12-50B Capital rationing decision (Learning Objective 4)

Luton Manufacturing is considering three capital investment proposals. At this time, Luton only has funds available to pursue one of the three investments.

	Equipment A	Equipment B	Equipment C
Present value of net cash inflows	$1,700,000	$1,970,000	$2,220,000
Investment	(1,360,000)	(1,588,710)	(2,000,000)
NPV	$ 340,000	$ 381,290	$ 220,000

Requirement

Which investment should Luton pursue at this time? Why?

Soar Mountain Data Set used for E12-51B–E12-52B.

Assume that Soar Mountain's managers developed the following estimates concerning a planned expansion of its State Park Lodge (all numbers assumed):

Number of additional skiers per day	118
Average number of days per year that weather conditions allow skiing at Soar Mountain	164
Useful life of expansion (in years)	10
Average cash spent by each skier per day	$ 238
Average variable cost of serving each skier per day	$ 134
Cost of expansion	$9,500,000
Discount rate	12%

Assume that Soar Mountain uses the straight-line depreciation method and expects the lodge expansion to have a residual value of $700,000 at the end of its 10-year life.

E12-51B Compute payback and ARR with residual value (Learning Objective 2)

Consider how Soar Mountain, a popular ski resort, could use capital budgeting to decide whether the $9.5 million State Park Lodge expansion would be a good investment.

Requirements

1. Compute the average annual net cash inflow from the expansion.
2. Compute the average annual operating income from the expansion.
3. Compute the payback period.
4. Compute the ARR.

E12-52B Calculate NPV with and without residual value (Learning Objective 4)

Refer to the Soar Mountain Data Set in E12-51B.

Requirements

1. What is the project's NPV? Is the investment attractive? Why or why not?
2. *Assume the expansion has no residual value.* What is the project's NPV? Is the investment still attractive? Why or why not?

E12-53B Compute payback period and discuss qualitative factors (Learning Objectives 2 and 5)

A variety of robots were featured at the 2016 National Restaurant Show that could be used for a variety of tasks in restaurants. These robots were introduced at the same time that an ongoing debate ensued in the United States about the merits of a national minimum wage of $15 per hour for every worker. A former McDonald's USA CEO, Ed Rensi, said that purchasing a $35,000 robotic arm would be cheaper than paying fast-food workers $15 per hour for food preparation tasks like bagging French fries.

Capital Investment Decisions and the Time Value of Money

To test the former CEO's assertion using a hypothetical example, make the following assumptions:

a. For the cost of the hourly workers, use a total wage rate of $17.50 per hour to reflect payroll taxes (the hourly wage rate used here is higher than $15 since payroll taxes can add 15% or more to the hourly wage rate).

b. Assume that freight and installation for the robot's initial placement in a McDonald's restaurant will be a one-time cost of $5,500.

c. The robot will require annual maintenance service. Assume an annual service contract is required that costs 12% of the original robot cost including the original freight/installation.

d. Assume that the robot will replace 10 employee hours per day, 360 days per year (the robot will not, at least initially, be as versatile as a person and cannot fully eliminate all food prep workers at this point).

e. Electricity and supplies consumed by the robot will be assumed to be $2,000 per year.

Requirements

1. What would the payback period be on a McDonald's robot used for food preparation? (Round to the nearest two decimal places.)
2. What qualitative factors would McDonald's need to consider when deciding whether to purchase robots to replace some of its food preparation workers?
3. Given the payback period, would net present value (NPV) or internal rate of return (IRR) be likely to be useful tools for analyzing this decision? Support your response.

E12-54B **Comparing capital budgeting methods** *(Learning Objective 5)*

The following table contains information about four projects in which Orion Corporation has the opportunity to invest. This information is based on estimates that different managers have prepared about the company's potential project.

Project	Investment Required	Net Present Value	Life of Project	Internal Rate of Return	Profitability Index	Payback Period in Years	Accounting Rate of Return
A	$ 220,000	$ 61,190	5	23%	1.28	2.82	20%
B	$ 410,000	$ 37,744	6	22%	1.09	3.20	14%
C	$1,030,000	$191,498	3	18%	1.19	2.17	13%
D	$1,545,000	$ 52,680	4	12%	1.03	3.07	24%

Requirements

1. Rank the four projects in order of preference by using the
   a. net present value.
   b. project profitability index.
   c. internal rate of return.
   d. payback period.
   e. accounting rate of return.
2. Which method(s) do you think is best for evaluating capital investment projects in general? Why?

PROBLEMS Group A

P12-55A **Solve various time value of money scenarios** *(Learning Objectives 3 & 4)*

1. Irving just hit the jackpot in Las Vegas and won $35,000! If he invests it now at a 10% interest rate, how much will it be worth in fifteen years?
2. Trent would like to have $3,500,000 saved by the time he retires in 30 years. How much does he need to invest now at a 14% interest rate to fund his retirement goal?
3. Assume that Ramona accumulates savings of $1.5 million by the time she retires. If she invests this savings at 12%, how much money will she be able to withdraw at the end of each year for twenty years?
4. Jessica plans to invest $4,000 at the end of each year for the next seven years. Assuming a 10% interest rate, what will her investment be worth seven years from now?

5. Assuming a 6% interest rate, how much would Katie have to invest now to be able to withdraw $13,000 at the end of each year for the next nine years?
6. Victor is considering a capital investment that costs $510,000 and will provide the following net cash inflows:

Year	Net Cash Inflow
1	$304,000
2	$206,000
3	$108,000

Using a hurdle rate of 12%, find the NPV of the investment.
7. What is the IRR of the capital investment described in Question 6?

P12-56A **Retirement planning in two stages** *(Learning Objective 3)*

You are planning for a very early retirement. You would like to retire at age 40 and have enough money saved to be able to draw $205,000 per year for the next 30 years (based on family history, you think you'll live to age 70). You plan to save for retirement by making 10 equal annual installments (from age 30 to age 40) into a fairly risky investment fund that you expect will earn 10% per year. You will leave the money in this fund until it is completely depleted when you are 70 years old. To make your plan work, answer the following questions:

1. How much money must you accumulate by retirement? (*Hint:* Find the present value of the $205,000 withdrawals.)
2. How does this amount compare to the total amount you will draw out of the investment during retirement? How can these numbers be so different?
3. How much must you pay into the investment each year for the first ten years? (*Hint:* Your answer from Requirement 1 becomes the future value of this annuity.)
4. How does the total out-of-pocket savings compare to the investment's value at the end of the ten10-year savings period and the withdrawals you will make during retirement?

P12-57A **Evaluate an investment using all four methods** *(Learning Objectives 2 & 4)*

Blue Water World is considering purchasing a water park in Columbus, Ohio, for $2,050,000. The new facility will generate annual net cash inflows of $515,000 for eight years. Engineers estimate that the facility will remain useful for eight years and have no residual value. The company uses straight-line depreciation. Its owners want payback in less than five years and an ARR of 12% or more. Management uses a 14% hurdle rate on investments of this nature.

Requirements

1. Compute the payback period, the ARR, the NPV, and the approximate IRR of this investment. (If you use the tables to compute the IRR, answer with the closest interest rate shown in the tables.)
2. Recommend whether the company should invest in this project.

P12-58A **Compare investments with different cash flows and residual values** *(Learning Objectives 2 & 4)*

Scribbles Inc. operates a chain of coffee shops. The company is considering two possible expansion plans. Plan A would open eight smaller shops at a cost of $8,440,000. Expected annual net cash inflows are $1,400,000 with zero residual value at the end of ten years. Under Plan B, Scribbles would open three larger shops at a cost of $8,340,000. This plan is expected to generate net cash inflows of $1,200,000 per year for ten years, the estimated life of the properties. Estimated residual value is $1,075,000. Scribbles uses straight-line depreciation and requires an annual return of 8%.

Requirements

1. Compute the payback period, the ARR, and the NPV of these two plans. What are the strengths and weaknesses of these capital budgeting models?
2. Which expansion plan should Scribbles choose? Why?
3. Estimate Plan A's IRR. How does the IRR compare with the company's required rate of return?

PROBLEMS Group B

P12-59B Solve various time value of money scenarios *(Learning Objectives 3 & 4)*

1. Charlie just hit the jackpot in Las Vegas and won $30,000! If he invests it now, at a 14% interest rate, how much will it be worth fifteen years from now?
2. Roderick would like to have $3,000,000 saved by the time he retires in 40 years. How much does he need to invest now at a 10% interest rate to fund his retirement goal?
3. Assume that Penny accumulates savings of $2 million by the time she retires. If she invests this savings at 12%, how much money will she be able to withdraw at the end of each year for fifteen years?
4. Hannah plans to invest $3,000 at the end of each year for the next eight years. Assuming a 14% interest rate, what will her investment be worth eight years from now?
5. Assuming a 6% interest rate, how much would Rachel have to invest now to be able to withdraw $12,000 at the end of every year for the next nine years?
6. Darren is considering a capital investment that costs $500,000 and will provide the following net cash inflows:

Year	Net Cash Inflow
1	$308,000
2	$205,000
3	$102,000

Using a hurdle rate of 12%, find the NPV of the investment.

7. What is the IRR of the capital investment described in Question 6?

P12-60B Retirement planning in two stages *(Learning Objective 3)*

You are planning for an early retirement. You would like to retire at age 40 and have enough money saved to be able to draw $225,000 per year for the next 40 years (based on family history, you think you'll live to age 80). You plan to save by making 20 equal annual installments (from age 20 to age 40) into a fairly risky investment fund that you expect will earn 12% per year. You will leave the money in this fund until it is completely depleted when you are 80 years old.

To make your plan work, answer the following:

1. How much money must you accumulate by retirement? (*Hint:* Find the present value of the $225,000 withdrawals.)
2. How does this amount compare to the total amount you will draw out of the investment during retirement? How can these numbers be so different?
3. How much must you pay into the investment each year for the first twenty years? (*Hint:* Your answer from Requirement 1 becomes the future value of this annuity.)
4. How does the total out-of-pocket savings compare to the investment's value at the end of the twenty-year savings period and the withdrawals you will make during retirement?

P12-61B Evaluate an investment using all four methods *(Learning Objectives 2 & 4)*

Lazy River World is considering purchasing a water park in Chattanooga, Tennessee, for $1,950,000. The new facility will generate annual net cash inflows of $505,000 for eight years. Engineers estimate that the facility will remain useful for eight years and have no residual value. The company uses straight-line depreciation. Its owners want payback in less than five years and an ARR of 10% or more. Management uses a 14% hurdle rate on investments of this nature.

Requirements

1. Compute the payback period, the ARR, the NPV, and the approximate IRR of this investment.
2. Recommend whether the company should invest in this project.

P12-62B Compare investments with different cash flows and residual values
(Learning Objectives 2 & 4)

Tree City Inc. operates a chain of coffee shops. The company is considering two possible expansion plans. Plan A would involve opening eight smaller shops at a cost of $8,940,000. Expected annual net cash inflows are $1,600,000, with zero residual value at the end of ten years. Under Plan B, Tree City would open three larger shops at a cost of $8,540,000. This plan is expected to generate net cash inflows of $1,400,000 per year for ten years, the estimated life of the properties. Estimated residual value for Plan B is $1,075,000. Tree City uses straight-line depreciation and requires an annual return of 8%.

Requirements

1. Compute the payback period, the ARR, and the NPV of these two plans. What are the strengths and weaknesses of these capital budgeting models?
2. Which expansion plan should Tree City choose? Why?
3. Estimate Plan A's IRR. How does the IRR compare with the company's required rate of return?

Serial Case

C12-63 Calculate payback period and NPV after hotel renovation *(Learning Objective 2)*

This case is a continuation of the Caesars Entertainment Corporation serial case that began in Chapter 1. Refer to the introductory story in Chapter 1 (see page 43) for additional background. (The components of the Caesars serial case can be completed in any order.)

Caesars Palace® Las Vegas made headlines when it undertook a $75 million renovation. In mid-September 2015, the hotel closed its then-named Roman Tower, which was last updated in 2001, and started a major renovation of the 567 rooms housed in that tower. On January 1, 2016, the newly renamed Julius Tower reopened, replacing the Roman Tower. In addition to renovating the existing rooms and suites in the former Roman Tower, 20 guest rooms were added to the Roman Tower.

Assume that the annual fixed operating costs for the Julius Tower will be $2,390,000 and that the variable cost per hotel room night after the renovation is $27. Also assume that maintenance costs in the seventh year, after the renovation, will be $17,000,000; maintenance costs, twelve years after the renovation, are estimated at $25,000,000. The towers in Caesars Palace® Las Vegas are generally renovated once every fifteen years. Assume the renovated tower's room rate is $149 per night, and 91.2% occupancy is expected on average.

Questions

1. In number of years, what is the payback period of the renovation? Ignore the maintenance costs in the seventh and twelfth years for the purpose of the payback calculation.
2. What is the net present value (NPV) of this investment? Assume an interest rate of 10%.
3. What qualitative factors did Caesars's management likely consider when making the decision to renovate the hotel?

CRITICAL THINKING

Discussion & Analysis

A12-64 Discussion Questions

1. Describe the capital budgeting process in your own words.

2. Define *capital investment*. List at least three examples of capital investments other than the examples provided in the chapter.

3. "As the required rate of return increases, the net present value of a project also increases." Explain why you agree or disagree with this statement.

4. Summarize the net present value method for evaluating a capital investment opportunity. Describe the circumstances that create a positive net present value. Describe the circumstances that may cause the net present value of a project to be negative. Describe the advantages and disadvantages of the net present value method.

5. Net cash inflows and net cash outflows are used in the net present value method and in the internal rate of return method. Explain why accounting net income is not used instead of cash flows.

6. Suppose you are a manager and you have three potential capital investment projects from which to choose. Funds are limited, so you can only choose one of the three projects. Describe at least three methods you can use to select the one project in which to invest.

7. The net present value method assumes that future cash inflows are immediately reinvested at the required rate of return, while the internal rate of return method assumes that future cash inflows are immediately invested at the internal rate of return rate. Which assumption is better? Explain your answer.

8. The decision rule for NPV analysis states that the project with the highest NPV should be selected. Describe at least two situations when the project with the highest NPV may not necessarily be the best project to select.

9. List and describe the advantages and disadvantages of the internal rate of return method.

10. List and describe the advantages and disadvantages of the payback method.

11. Oftentimes, investments in sustainability projects do not meet traditional investment selection criteria. Suppose you are a manager and have prepared a proposal to install solar panels to provide lighting for the office. The payback period for the project is longer than the company's required payback period, and the project's net present value is slightly negative. What arguments could you offer to the capital budgeting committee for accepting the solar energy project in spite of it not meeting the capital selection criteria?

12. Think of a company with which you are familiar. What are some examples of possible sustainable investments that the company may be able to undertake? How might the company management justify these possible investments?

Application & Analysis

Mini Cases

A12-65 Evaluating the Purchase of an Asset with Various Capital Budgeting Methods

In this activity, you will be evaluating whether you should purchase a hybrid car or its gasoline-engine counterpart. Select two car models that are similar, with one being a hybrid model and one being the nonhybrid model. (For example, the Honda Civic is available as a hybrid or a gasoline-engine model.) Assume that you plan to keep your car for ten years and that at the end of the ten years, the resale value of both models will be negligible.

Basic Discussion Questions

1. Research the cost of each model (include taxes and title costs). Also, obtain an estimate of the miles-per-gallon fuel efficiency of each model.

2. Estimate the number of miles you drive each year. Also estimate the cost of a gallon of fuel.

3. Given your previous estimates from 1 and 2, estimate the total fuel cost of driving the hybrid model for one year. Also estimate the total fuel cost of driving the nonhybrid model for one year. Calculate the fuel cost savings offered by the hybrid model over the nonhybrid model.

4. Calculate the NPV of the hybrid model, using the annual fuel savings as the annual cash inflow for the 10 years you would own the car. Assume a required rate of return of 10%.

5. Compare the NPV of the hybrid model with the cost of the gasoline-engine model. Which model has the lowest cost (the lowest NPV)? From a purely financial standpoint, does the hybrid model make sense?

6. Now look at the payback period of the hybrid model. Use the difference between the cost of the hybrid model and the gasoline-engine model as the investment. Use the annual fuel savings as the expected annual net cash inflow. Ignoring the time value of money, how long does it take for the additional cost of the hybrid model to pay for itself through fuel savings?

7. What qualitative factors might affect your decision about which model to purchase?

ETHICS

A12-66   Ethics involved with capital budgeting proposal (Learning Objectives 1, 2, 3, 4, & 5)

Carlson Products, Inc., is a manufacturer of a variety of construction products, including insulation, pipe, and gypsum. The company has been experiencing steady growth over the past few decades and is moderately profitable.

The board of directors at Carlson has developed criteria that all capital budgeting projects undertaken at Carlson must meet in order to be approved:

1. The project's net present value (NPV) must be positive. The company uses a hurdle rate of 10% when calculating NPV.

2. The project's payback period must be less than four years.

3. The project's accounting rate of return (ARR) must be greater than 8%.

Samantha Pace is a division manager at Carlson. She is developing a proposal to install solar panels at the company's Flagstaff, Arizona, manufacturing facility. The solar panels, requiring an investment of $1.25 million, will significantly reduce the company's carbon footprint. The project will help the company to save approximately 25% of its current energy costs at that facility. Samantha is excited about this project, both for its dollar savings and for its sustainability impact. She finalizes the calculations for the capital budgeting criteria for the solar panel proposal and is delighted to see that her proposed project meets all of the company's capital budgeting criteria. She sends the proposal to Peter Nichols, the controller for Carlson. Peter is responsible for approving all proposed capital budgeting projects that require less than a $2 million investment. Carlson's board of directors must approve all capital budgeting projects that require more than a $2 million investment.

Peter reviews the solar panel proposal. He thinks it is a promising project and feels that the company should undertake this project and other sustainability projects so that the company can reduce its environmental impact.

As he double checks the calculations in Samantha's proposal, he discovers that she has made a few mistakes. Instead of using a hurdle rate of 10%, she actually used a hurdle rate of 6%. She also did not include the impact of the annual depreciation expense for the solar panels in the calculation of ARR. If Peter makes the corrections, the solar panel project will fail the NPV criteria and the ARR criteria.

Peter is conflicted over what to do. He knows that no one is likely to discover Samantha's errors in the capital budgeting proposal if he approves it; the errors are not obvious. He really wants to approve the project, since he believes strongly that these types of initiatives are the direction in which Carlson Products needs to head in order to remain competitive in the future. He also can rationalize that the impact of the errors is minimal and that the project does not fail the capital budgeting criteria by a significant margin. On the other hand, he knows that the board of directors of Carlson has been rigid in its application of the capital budgeting criteria in the projects it has reviewed.

Requirements

1. Using the IMA *Statement of Ethical Professional Practice* as an ethical framework, answer the following questions:
   a. What is(are) the ethical issue(s) in this situation?
   b. What are Peter's responsibilities as a management accountant? Should he approve the solar panel project? Why or why not?
2. Are there any better alternative courses of action that Peter might take to resolve this conflict than to simply approve or reject the proposal? Support your answer.

A12-67 Capital budgeting qualitative factors *(Learning Objectives 1, 2, 3, 4, & 5)*

REAL LIFE

For years, it has been cheaper to manufacture many products overseas (China and other countries) than in the United States. Labor is still less expensive overseas than in the United States, but the cost difference has been decreasing.

General Electric (GE) has brought back its refrigerator production to the United States from overseas and has announced plans to produce a new top load washer in the United States as well.

In recent years, Google's Motorola announced that it would be assembling its Moto X smartphone in Fort Worth, Texas, making it the first smartphone assembled in the United States. Lenovo also recently opened a new ThinkPad manufacturing facility in North Carolina.

For these companies, it is likely that the capital budgeting proposals for the U.S. manufacturing sites did not meet the companies' standard capital budgeting criteria. Yet the companies are still opting to manufacture some products in the United States, where it is, for the time being, more expensive than other locations.

Questions

1. What qualitative factors would likely have been considered when GE, Google, and Lenovo made their decisions to invest in U.S. manufacturing facilities? In other words, why would GE, Google, and Lenovo decide to manufacture products in the United States when all of these companies have well-established facilities and supply chains in China?
2. What challenges will these companies likely face in manufacturing products in U.S. plants?
3. What stakeholders are impacted, either positively or negatively, by the decision to manufacture in the United States? How are these stakeholders impacted?
4. What ethical issues potentially arise from not producing in the lowest cost location?

Try It Solutions

page 717:

Since the net cash inflows are expected to be equal each year, payback is calculated as follows:

$$\text{Payback period} = \frac{\text{Initial investment}}{\text{Expected annual net cash inflow}} = \frac{\$4,000,000}{\$750,000} = 5.33 \text{ years}$$

page 719:

ARR is calculated as follows:

$$\text{ARR} = \frac{\text{Average annual net cash inflow} - \text{Annual depreciation expense}}{\text{Initial investment}}$$

The ARR focuses on the operating income generated from the investment, not the net cash inflow from the investment. Thus, to use this formula, we need to find the annual depreciation expense, which will be used to reconcile net cash inflows back to operating income:

$$\text{Annual depreciation} = \frac{\$4 \text{ million}}{20 \text{ years}} = \$200,000$$

Now we calculate ARR as follows:

$$\text{ARR} = \frac{\$750{,}000 - \$200{,}000}{\$4{,}000{,}000} = 13.75\%$$

page 733:

The NPV is the difference between the present value of the wind turbine's future net cash flows ($750,000 per year for 20 years) and the cost of the initial investment ($4 million). It can be found using the Annuity PV factor for $i = 12\%$, $n = 20$, as follows:

	A	B	C	D	E	F
1	NPV Calculation for *Equal* Annual Net Cash Inflows	Annuity PV Factor ($i = 12\%$)		Annual Net Cash Inflow		Present Value
2	Present value of annuity, $n = 20$	7.469	× $	750,000	= $	5,601,750
3	Less: Initial investment					4,000,000
4	Net present value (NPV)				$	1,601,750
5						

Alternatively, one can use the NPV function in Excel to arrive at an NPV of $1,602,083.

The positive NPV indicates that the wind turbine will earn more than the company's 12% hurdle rate. Therefore, it is a favorable investment.

page 738:

The easiest way to calculate the IRR is by using the IRR function in Excel, which results in an IRR of 18.07%.

Alternatively, one can look for the Annuity PV factor for $n = 20$ that is closest to the following:

$$\frac{\text{Initial investment}}{\text{Amount of each equal net cash inflow}} = \frac{\$4{,}000{,}000}{\$750{,}000} = 5.33$$

The Annuity PV factor at $n = 20$ that is closest to 5.33 occurs when $i = 18\%$. At 18%, the Annuity PV factor is 5.353. Thus, the IRR of the wind turbine is close to 18%.

13

Statement of Cash Flows

Marie C. Fields/Shutterstock

Sources: www.nerdwallet.com/blog/credit-card-data/average-credit-card-debt-household/

Learning Objectives

1. Classify cash flows as operating, investing, or financing activities
2. Prepare the statement of cash flows using the indirect method
3. Prepare the statement of cash flows using the direct method

In the past 35 years, the United States has seen the proliferation of credit card debt. From 1980 to 2015, the average household credit card debt grew from $518 to $15,762. In 2015, the total national consumer credit card debt stood at $733 billion, making it the fourth-largest class of debt, behind mortgages, student loans, and automobile loans. Why do people use credit cards? Some people use credit cards simply as a matter of convenience, so they don't have to carry cash or personal checks. Others use credit cards to earn rewards, such as free airplane miles. But many people use credit cards because they do not have enough funds to pay for the things they need or want. In other words, the cash they generate from their salary or wages is not high enough to cover their expenses (such as food, clothing, housing, and entertainment) and to make necessary debt payments (such as monthly car and student loan payments). In the end, credit card debt is incurred because cash inflows are not high enough to cover cash outflows.

Just as cash flows are important to personal finances, they are equally important to a company's finances. To better understand the financial health of a company, we must understand how the company generates cash, and how the cash is being used. That's exactly the kind of information that is presented in the statement of cash flows.

As the opening story shows, good cash management is critical to individuals and companies alike. Managers use cash budgets, as discussed in Chapter 9, to plan for their cash needs. But investors and creditors, who want to understand how the company is generating and using cash, do not have access to internal cash budgets. Rather, they must rely on the company's financial statements to provide them with information on whether the company's cash increased or decreased over the course of the year, and the reasons for the change. In this chapter, we'll discuss how the statement of cash flows presents investors, creditors, and managers with important information on how a company generated and used cash over a given period of time.

What Is the Statement of Cash Flows?

Companies prepare four basic financial statements:

1. Income statement
2. Balance sheet
3. Statement of stockholders' equity
4. Statement of cash flows[1]

You are already familiar with the first three statements from your financial accounting course. These statements do not present much information about the company's cash. For example, the balance sheet gives a "snapshot" of the company's ending cash balance, but it does not report whether cash increased or decreased during the period or why. The **statement of cash flows** is an important and necessary statement because it shows the overall increase or decrease in cash during the period, as well as *how* the company *generated* and *used* cash during the period. Exhibit 13-1 shows the basic format of a statement of cash flows.

EXHIBIT 13-1 Basic Format of the Statement of Cash Flows

	A	B
1	SportsTime, Inc.	
2	Statement of Cash Flows	
3	For the year ended December 31, 2017	
4		
5	Cash provided (or used) by **operating** activities (*itemized list*)	$ XXX
6	Cash provided (or used) by **investing** activities (*itemized list*)	XX
7	Cash provided (or used) by **financing** activities (*itemized list*)	XX
8	Net increase (or decrease) in cash	XXX
9	Cash, beginning of the year	XX
10	Cash, end of the year	$ XXX
11		

Why is this important?

"The statement of cash flows shows how the company **generated** and **used cash** during the year, enabling **managers, investors, and creditors** to predict whether the company can meet its cash **obligations** in the future."

Why is cash so important? It is important because anyone involved with the company has certain expectations regarding the company's cash:

- Employees expect payment of their salaries and wages.
- Suppliers expect payment for their products and services.
- Creditors expect to be repaid loans and interest payments.
- Investors expect dividends.
- Governmental taxing authorities expect payment of income taxes, payroll taxes, and property taxes.

The statement of cash flows helps all of these stakeholders evaluate how the company has generated and used cash in the past, which in turn helps them predict whether the company will

---

[1] Statement of Accounting Standards No. 95 governs cash flow reporting. The standard was produced by the Financial Accounting Standards Board in 1987.

be able to meet its cash obligations in the future. It also helps managers understand if the company is generating sufficient cash from its day-to-day operating activities to enable investments in new equipment, new stores, or new businesses. If insufficient cash is being generated from the day-to-day operations of the company to fund these investments, then the company may need to cut back on expenses or planned investments, or consider raising more capital through selling stocks or taking out loans.

Typically, the statement of cash flows defines "cash" as all cash and cash equivalents. Cash generally includes petty cash, checking, and savings accounts. **Cash equivalents** include very safe, highly liquid assets that are readily convertible into cash, such as money market funds, certificates of deposit that mature in less than three months, and U.S. Treasury bills. Throughout this chapter, any references to cash will include cash and cash equivalents.

Three Types of Activities That Generate and Use Cash

As Exhibit 13-1 illustrates, the statement of cash flows classifies all business transactions into three different types of activities. These activities are presented on the statement of cash flows in the following order:

1. Operating activities
2. Investing activities
3. Financing activities

1 Classify cash flows as operating, investing, or financing activities

Let's take a look at the kind of transactions that would fall under each category.

Operating Activities

Operating activities primarily consist of the day-to-day profit-making activities of the company. These activities include such transactions as making or buying inventory, selling inventory, selling services, paying employees, and advertising. These activities typically affect current asset accounts such as inventory and accounts receivable, as well as current liability accounts such as salaries payable and accounts payable. Operating activities also include *any other activity that affects net income* (not just operating income). Therefore, this category also includes receiving interest income and paying interest expense, receiving dividend income, and paying for income tax expense. Keep the following rule of thumb in mind when deciding if an activity should be classified as an operating activity:[2]

> **Why is this important?**
> "**Financial statement** readers want to know how much of the company's cash was generated from **day-to-day** company **operations** versus how much was raised by **selling investments** or company stock, or by **borrowing money**. A company that doesn't raise sufficient **cash** from operations won't be able to **survive** in the long run."

> Transactions that affect net income, current assets, and current liabilities are classified as operating activities on the statement of cash flows.

Investing Activities

Investing activities include transactions that involve buying or selling long-term assets. These activities include buying or selling property, plant, or equipment; buying or selling stock in other companies (if the stock is meant to be held for the long term); or loaning money to other companies with the goal of earning interest income from the loan. Keep the following rule of thumb in mind when deciding if an activity should be classified as an investing activity:

> Transactions that affect long-term assets are classified as investing activities on the statement of cash flows.

---

[2] Because the entire statement of cash flows, including cash flows from operating, investing, and financing activities, is needed to explain the change in the company's cash account during the year, the change in the cash account is the only current asset account excluded from this rule of thumb.

Financing Activities

Financing activities include transactions that either generate capital for the company or pay it back. These activities include selling company stock, issuing long-term debt (such as notes or bonds), buying back company stock (also known as treasury stock), paying dividends to stockholders, and repaying the principal amount on loans. Keep the following rule of thumb in mind when deciding whether an activity should be classified as a financing activity:

> Transactions that affect long-term liabilities and stockholders' equity are classified as financing activities on the statement of cash flows.

Exhibit 13-2 presents a list of common sources and uses of cash and shows how they are classified on the statement of cash flows. We have italicized those items that you may have difficulty remembering because they are not completely intuitive.

EXHIBIT 13-2 Classification of Activities on the Statement of Cash Flows

Operating Activities
(Cash flows related to the primary, day-to-day profit-making activities of the company; these activities affect net income, current assets, and current liabilities)

- Cash received from sale of services or merchandise
- *Cash received from interest income*
- *Cash received from dividend income*
- Cash paid to purchase inventory
- Cash paid for selling, general, and administrative expenses
- *Cash paid for interest expense*
- Cash paid for income taxes

Non-cash adjustments to net income (indirect method):
- Depreciation and amortization expense
- Gain or loss on sale of property, plant, or equipment

Investing Activities
(Cash flows related to buying and selling investments; these activities affect long-term assets)

- Cash received from sale of property, plant, or equipment
- Cash received from collection of long-term loans
- Cash received from sale of long-term equity (stock) investments
- Cash paid to purchase property, plant, or equipment
- Cash paid for purchasing long-term equity (stock) investments

Financing Activities
(Cash flows related to generating and repaying capital; these activities affect long-term liabilities and stockholders' equity accounts)

- Cash received from issuing long-term debt (such as notes and bonds)
- Cash received from issuing stock
- Cash received from using a line of credit
- Cash used to pay back long-term debt
- *Cash used to pay dividends*
- Cash used to buy back company stock (treasury stock)

For example, consider the following:

- Even though interest income and dividend income are earned from investments, they are both classified as cash flows from operating activities because they *affect (increase) net income*.
- Interest expense occurs because the company has borrowed money, so you might think this is a financing activity. However, it is classified as an operating activity because it *affects (decreases) net income*.
- Certain revenues and expenses (such as depreciation) affect net income, yet do not generate or use cash. Under the indirect method, they are used in the operating section of the statement of cash flows to reconcile accrual basis net income back to the cash basis.
- The *payment* of dividends is a distribution of the company's equity (not an expense on the income statement); therefore, it is classified as a financing activity.

Noncash Investing and Financing Activities

Sometimes companies have significant investing or financing activities that do not involve cash. For example, a company may purchase property, plant, or equipment by issuing common stock to the seller, rather than paying cash. Liabilities, such as bonds or notes payable, may be extinguished by converting them to common stock.

Any significant noncash investing or financing activity must be disclosed in a supplementary schedule to the statement of cash flows or in a footnote to the financial statements. Why? Because these activities will affect *future* cash flows, such as the future payment of dividends and interest. Since financial statement readers use the statement of cash flows to make predictions about future cash flows, they need to be made aware of any noncash investing or financing transactions that took place during the year.

Try It!

Classify each of the following transactions as an operating, investing, or financing activity.
1. Selling inventory
2. Issuing stock
3. Paying dividends
4. Paying employee salaries
5. Buying a new fleet of vehicles with cash

Please see page 837 for solutions.

Two Methods of Presenting Operating Activities

The operating activities section of the statement of cash flows may be presented using either the direct or indirect method. These different methods only affect the *format* of the presentation. Both methods result in the *same* dollar figure for the net cash provided by operating activities. Keep in mind that these methods only affect the operating activities section and have no bearing on the investing or financing sections of the statement.

Direct Method

The **direct method** lists the receipt and payment of cash for specific operating activities. For example, the operating activities would list line items such as the following:

- Cash receipts from customers
- Cash payments for inventory
- Cash payments for salaries and wages
- Cash payments for insurance

In essence, the direct method lists many of the same items shown on the income statement but calculates them on a cash rather than an accrual basis. The **accrual basis of accounting** requires that revenues are recorded when they are earned (when the sale takes place) rather than when cash is received on the sale. Likewise, expenses are recorded when they are incurred, rather than when they are paid. These timing differences give rise to current assets such as accounts receivable and current liabilities such as wages payable. Thus, accrual-based net income almost always differs from the cash basis.

Indirect Method

The **indirect method** begins with the company's net income, which is prepared on an accrual basis and then reconciles it back to the cash basis through a series of adjustments. This method reconciles net income to the cash basis by adjusting for (1) noncash revenues (such as gains on the sale of property, plant, and equipment) or noncash expenses (such as depreciation or amortization), and (2) changes in the current asset and current liability accounts. For example, an increase in accounts receivable indicates that more sales were made than were collected. Therefore, an adjustment would be made to net income to reflect this increase in accounts receivable.

Which Method Is Most Commonly Used?

Recent surveys show that over 99% of companies currently use the indirect method.[3] Why? Because it is easier and, therefore, less costly to prepare. Furthermore, if a company chooses to use the direct method, it must also provide a supplementary schedule reconciling net income to the cash basis. In essence, a company that chooses to use the direct method must also perform the indirect method for a supplementary disclosure.

Currently, the Financial Accounting Standards Board (FASB) and International Accounting Standards Board (IASB) *encourage* companies to use the direct method. However, the boards have jointly proposed that companies be *required* to use the direct method in the future.[4] The outcome of this proposal is uncertain at this time. The second half of the chapter will illustrate both the indirect and direct methods.

Sustainability and the Statement of Cash Flows

You've just learned that *all* business transactions must be classified into one of three different types of activities for the statement of cash flows. A company's sustainability initiatives will also fall into the same three categories. Some examples are listed next.

Operating Activities—affect net income, current assets, and current liabilities

- Expenses related to researching and developing sustainable products and packaging
- Income generated from selling scrap and recyclable materials
- Income and expenses related to producing, marketing, and distributing new "green" products

Investing Activities—affect long-term assets

- Investments in solar paneling or wind turbines
- Investments in environmentally friendly production equipment
- Investments in LEED certified buildings

See Exercises E13-21A and E13-31B

---

[3] American Institute of Certified Public Accountants, *Accounting Trends and Techniques: 2010*, New York, NY, 2010.

[4] Financial Accounting Standards Board, *Financial Accounting Series Discussion Paper Number 1630-100: Preliminary Views on Financial Statement Presentation*, Norwalk, CT, October 16, 2008, Paragraph 3.70–3.83.

Financing Activities—affect long-term liabilities and owners' equity
- Stocks issued to raise capital for projects involving biofuel production
- Bonds issued to raise capital for investing in a fleet of hybrid delivery vehicles

Sustainability initiatives, such as those listed above, are not itemized separately in the statement of cash flows. Rather, they are presented in combination with other similar activities. For example, all capital investments, whether or not environmentally friendly, are presented as "investments in plant and equipment." However, to provide more detailed information to both internal and external users, companies may disclose cash flows related to significant sustainability initiatives on their corporate websites or in Corporate Social Responsibility (CSR) reports. These disclosures help investors and other stakeholders understand how the company is positioning itself to address social and environmental issues that impact the company's operations, and therefore profitability and cash position, in the future.

Decision Guidelines

Statement of Cash Flows

The following guidelines present some decisions that need to be made before preparing the statement of cash flows.

Decision	Guidelines
What financial statements should my company prepare?	A set of financial statements includes the (1) income statement, (2) balance sheet, (3) statement of stockholders' equity, and (4) statement of cash flows.
How should my company define "cash" for the statement of cash flows?	The statement of cash flows usually explains changes in both cash and cash equivalents. Cash and cash equivalents include petty cash, checking and savings account deposits, money markets, short-term certificates of deposit, and U.S. Treasury bills.
What types of cash flows should be presented on the statement of cash flows?	All cash flows must be classified into one of the following three categories: 1. Cash flows from operating activities 2. Cash flows from investing activities 3. Cash flows from financing activities
How can I tell if a cash transaction should be classified as an operating activity?	Cash flows from operating activities include the day-to-day profit-making activities of the firm. These activities include any transactions that affect net income (including interest income and expense, and dividend income), current assets, or current liabilities.
How can I tell if a cash transaction should be classified as an investing activity?	Cash flows from investing activities include all transactions that affect long-term assets.
How can I tell if a cash transaction should be classified as a financing activity?	Cash flows from financing activities include transactions that generate capital for the company or pay it back. These transactions affect long-term liabilities and stockholders' equity.
My company purchased a piece of land in exchange for company stock. Since the transaction didn't affect cash, do we include it on the statement of cash flows?	Even though the transaction didn't affect cash this year, it needs to be disclosed because it will affect *future* cash flows. All significant noncash investing or financing transactions need to be disclosed either in a supplementary schedule to the statement of cash flows or in a footnote to the financial statements.
Should my company use the direct or indirect method for presenting the cash flows from operating activities?	Either method is currently acceptable. However, if you use the direct method, you must also present a supplementary schedule that is the same as the information presented using the indirect method. As a result, the vast majority of companies use the indirect method.

SUMMARY PROBLEM 1

Classify each of the following transactions as an operating, investing, or financing activity; or a noncash investing and financing activity.

1. Payment of salaries
2. Purchase of land with cash
3. Issuance of stock
4. Repayment of long-term notes
5. Payment of rent
6. Collection of sales revenue
7. Conversion of bonds payable to common stock
8. Loss on the sale of equipment
9. Purchase of another company's stock (to be held for more than one year)
10. Purchase of merchandise inventory
11. Proceeds from the sale of a building
12. Payment of dividends
13. Collection of interest income
14. Purchase of treasury stock (company buys back its own stock)
15. Payment of interest on long-term debt

▪ SOLUTION

Transaction	Type of Activity
1. Payment of salaries	Operating
2. Purchase of land with cash	Investing
3. Issuance of stock	Financing
4. Repayment of long-term notes	Financing
5. Payment of rent	Operating
6. Collection of sales revenue	Operating
7. Conversion of bonds payable to common stock	Noncash Investing and Financing; must be disclosed, even though it doesn't use cash
8. Loss on the sale of equipment	Operating
9. Purchase of another company's stock (to be held for more than one year)	Investing
10. Purchase of merchandise inventory	Operating
11. Proceeds from the sale of a building	Investing
12. Payment of dividends	Financing
13. Collection of interest income	Operating
14. Purchase of treasury stock (company buys back its own stock)	Financing
15. Payment of interest on long-term debt	Operating

How Is the Statement of Cash Flows Prepared Using the Indirect Method?

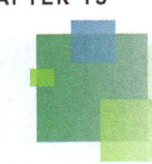

2 Prepare the statement of cash flows using the indirect method

In this section, we'll use the indirect method to prepare the statement of cash flows for SportsTime, Inc., a regional retailer of sporting goods equipment.

Information Needed to Prepare the Statement of Cash Flows

In order to prepare the statement of cash flows, the following company information is needed:

1. Income statement for the current year
2. **Comparative balance sheets** (balance sheets for the end of the current year and prior year)
3. Miscellaneous additional information relating to investing and financing transactions

Exhibit 13-3 presents SportsTime's income statement, and Exhibit 13-4 presents the company's comparative balance sheets. Additional information about the company's investing and financing transactions will be presented as needed throughout the remainder of this chapter.

> ### ■ Why is this important?
> "**Most companies** currently use the **indirect method**, so understanding how it is prepared and **interpreted** is crucial. This method highlights the **differences** between accrual based net income and the **cash basis**."

EXHIBIT 13-3 Income Statement

	A	B	C
1	SportsTime, Inc.		
2	Income Statement		
3	For the Year Ended December 31, 2017		
4			
5	Sales revenues		$ 9,500,000
6	Less: Cost of goods sold		7,125,000
7	Gross profit		2,375,000
8	Less operating expenses:		
9	Salaries and wages expense	$ 580,000	
10	Insurance expense	25,000	
11	Depreciation expense	142,000	
12	Other operating expenses	230,000	
13	Total operating expenses		977,000
14	Operating income		$ 1,398,000
15	Plus other income and less other expenses:		
16	Interest expense	60,000	
17	Gain on sale of PP&E	1,000	
18	Total other income and expenses		59,000
19	Income before income taxes		1,339,000
20	Less: Income tax expense		401,700
21	Net income		$ 937,300
22			

Preparing the Cash Flows from Operating Activities

The indirect method requires that we begin the operating activities section with the company's accrual-based net income, which is found on the income statement. Then, we make all adjustments needed to convert, or reconcile, net income back to a cash basis. These adjustments will include the following:

- Noncash expenses and revenues (found on the income statement)
- Changes in the current asset accounts (found on the comparative balance sheets)
- Changes in the current liability accounts (found on the comparative balance sheets)

EXHIBIT 13-4 Comparative Balance Sheets

SportsTime, Inc.
Comparative Balance Sheets
December 31, 2017 and 2016

Assets	2017	2016	Increase (Decrease)
Current assets:			
Cash	$ 203,500	$ 125,000	78,500
Accounts receivable	365,000	330,000	35,000
Inventory	632,000	657,000	(25,000)
Prepaid insurance	20,000	15,000	5,000
Total current assets	1,220,500	1,127,000	
Property, plant, and equipment	3,415,000	2,900,000	515,000
Less: Accumulated depreciation	(499,000)	(380,000)	119,000
Investments	285,000	185,000	100,000
Total assets	$ 4,421,500	$ 3,832,000	
Liabilities			
Current liabilities:			
Accounts payable	$ 245,000	$ 285,000	(40,000)
Wages payable	57,000	48,500	8,500
Interest payable	3,000	8,000	(5,000)
Income taxes payable	146,700	120,000	26,700
Other accrued expenses payable	15,500	28,500	(13,000)
Total current liabilities	467,200	490,000	
Long-term liabilities	550,000	750,000	(200,000)
Total liabilities	1,017,200	1,240,000	
Stockholders' equity			
Common stock	1,100,000	1,100,000	0
Retained earnings	2,304,300	1,492,000	812,300
Total stockholders' equity	3,404,300	2,592,000	
Total liabilities and equity	$ 4,421,500	$ 3,832,000	

Noncash Expenses

Depreciation expense is perhaps the most common noncash expense found on the income statement. Depreciation is simply the systematic write-off of the cost of plant and equipment over time. No cash actually trades hands when depreciation expense is recorded. Since depreciation expense reduced net income by $142,000 (Exhibit 13-3), but didn't use cash, we must *add it back* to net income to convert net income back to the cash basis. Therefore, we begin our statement of cash flows by adding back depreciation expense, as shown (in blue) in Exhibit 13-5.

We would also add back any amortization of intangible assets or depletion of natural resources for the same reason. SportsTime's income statement does not show any amortization or depletion expense, so these adjustments are not needed.

Noncash Revenues

The income statement in Exhibit 13-3 shows a $1,000 gain on the sale of property, plant, and equipment (PP&E). A gain on the sale arises when the equipment is sold for *more* than its net book value. The **net book value** is the original cost of the equipment less its accumulated depreciation. Let's assume that SportsTime sold some old display shelves and dressing room chairs for $3,000. Company records indicate that this equipment originally

EXHIBIT 13-5 Adjusting Net Income for Depreciation Expense

	A	B	C
1	SportsTime, Inc.		
2	Statement of Cash Flows—Operating Activities Section (Indirect Method)		
3	For the Year Ended December 31, 2017		
4			
5	**Operating Activities:**		
6	Net income		$ 937,300
7	Adjustments to reconcile net income to cash basis:		
8	Depreciation expense	$ 142,000	
9			

cost $25,000 and that at the time of sale, accumulated depreciation on this equipment totaled $23,000. The gain on sale would have been calculated as follows:

Sale price of equipment		$3,000
Original cost of the equipment	$25,000	
Less: Accumulated depreciation	23,000	
Net book value of equipment		2,000
Gain on sale		$1,000

The actual cash received on the sale, $3,000, will be reported as a source of cash in the investing section of the statement of cash flows. But the $1,000 gain, which increased accrual-based net income, does not actually represent cash received. Therefore, the $1,000 gain must be *deducted* from net income to convert it back to the cash basis. Exhibit 13-6 incorporates this gain (in blue) on our developing statement of cash flows.

EXHIBIT 13-6 Adjusting Net Income for Gain on Sale

	A	B	C
1	SportsTime, Inc.		
2	Statement of Cash Flows—Operating Activities Section (Indirect Method)		
3	For the Year Ended December 31, 2017		
4			
5	**Operating Activities:**		
6	Net income		$ 937,300
7	Adjustments to reconcile net income to cash basis:		
8	Depreciation expense	$ 142,000	
9	Gain on sale of equipment	(1,000)	
10			

Conversely, a loss on the sale of equipment would have occurred if the equipment was sold for *less* than the equipment's net book value. Since a loss doesn't represent a pay-out of cash (in fact, cash is received for the sale) we would *add back the loss* to net income to convert it back to the cash basis.

Changes in Current Asset Accounts

The next step in preparing the statement of cash flows is to adjust net income for any changes in current asset accounts. The comparative balance sheets in Exhibit 13-4 shows that the balance in all current asset accounts changed over the year. Remember, the entire statement of cash flows is attempting to explain the change in the cash account. So, we will need to analyze the changes to all current asset accounts *except* for cash.

Let's first look at those accounts that had *increases* over the course of the year: accounts receivable and prepaid insurance.

ACCOUNTS RECEIVABLE Exhibit 13-4 shows a $35,000 increase in accounts receivable. An *increase* in accounts receivable indicates that *more* sales were made than were collected. To reconcile net income back to the cash basis, we need to subtract any sales that were not yet collected in cash. To do so, we *subtract* the $35,000 *increase* in accounts receivable from net income.

PREPAID INSURANCE Exhibit 13-4 shows a $5,000 increase in prepaid insurance. An *increase* in prepaid insurance indicates that the company *paid more* for insurance than was recorded as insurance expense. To reconcile net income to the cash basis, we need to subtract *more* than was expensed. To do so, we *subtract* the $5,000 *increase* in prepaid insurance from net income.

Exhibit 13-7 illustrates the general rule for reconciling net income to cash basis for *increases* in any current asset accounts.

EXHIBIT 13-7 General Rule for Increases in Current Asset Accounts

Now let's look at an example of a current asset account that decreased over the course of the year.

INVENTORY Exhibit 13-4 shows a $25,000 *decrease* in inventory. The *decrease* in inventory indicates that the company sold more merchandise inventory than it purchased. Its inventory level shrunk. So the Cost of Goods Sold expensed on the income statement is greater than the cash paid to purchase the merchandise from the company's suppliers. To reconcile net income back to the cash basis, we need to subtract *less* than the amount expensed. To do so, we *add back* the $25,000 *decrease* in inventory to net income.

Exhibit 13-8 illustrates the general rule for reconciling net income to cash basis for *decreases* in any current asset accounts.

EXHIBIT 13-8 General Rule for Decreases in Current Asset Accounts

The general rule of thumb for current asset accounts is as follows:

> If a current asset account *increases*, then *subtract* the change from net income.
> If a current asset account *decreases*, then *add* the change to net income.

Notice that for changes in current assets, we reconcile net income back to the cash basis by adjusting in the *opposite* direction. The adjustments for changes in current asset accounts are pictured in blue in Exhibit 13-9.

EXHIBIT 13-9 Adjusting Net Income for Changes in Current Asset Accounts

	A	B	C
1	SportsTime, Inc.		
2	Statement of Cash Flows—Operating Activities Section (Indirect Method)		
3	For the Year Ended December 31, 2017		
4			
5	**Operating Activities:**		
6	Net income		$ 937,300
7	Adjustments to reconcile net income to cash basis:		
8	Depreciation expense	$ 142,000	
9	Gain on sale of equipment	(1,000)	
10	Increase in accounts receivable	(35,000)	
11	Decrease in inventory	25,000	
12	Increase in prepaid insurance	(5,000)	
13			

Changes in Current Liability Accounts

Now let's take a look at one current liability account that decreased over the course of the year (interest payable) and another that increased (wages payable).

INTEREST PAYABLE Exhibit 13-4 shows a $5,000 *decrease* in interest payable. A *decrease* in interest payable indicates that the company paid out more than it expensed for interest expense during the year. Therefore, to reconcile net income to the cash basis, we need to subtract *more* than was expensed. To do so, we subtract the $5,000 decrease in interest payable from net income.

Exhibit 13-10 shows the general rule for reconciling net income to cash basis for any *decreases* in current liability accounts.

EXHIBIT 13-10 General Rule for Decreases in Current Liability Accounts

WAGES PAYABLE Exhibit 13-4 shows a $8,500 *increase* in wages payable. An *increase* in wages payable indicates that more wage expense was incurred than was paid. To reconcile net income to the cash basis, we need to subtract *less* than was expensed. Therefore, we need to add back the $8,500 increase in wages payable to net income.

Exhibit 13-11 illustrates the general rule for reconciling net income to cash basis for *increases* in any current liability account.

EXHIBIT 13-11 General Rule for Increases in Current Liability Accounts

The general rule of thumb for current liability accounts is as follows:

If a current liability account *increases*, then *add* the change to net income.
If a current liability account *decreases*, then *subtract* the change from net income.

Notice that for changes in current liabilities, we reconcile net income back to the cash basis by adjusting in the *same* direction. The adjustments for changes in current liability accounts are pictured in blue in Exhibit 13-12.

EXHIBIT 13-12 Cash Flows from Operating Activities (Indirect Method)

	A	B	C
1	SportsTime, Inc.		
2	Statement of Cash Flows—Operating Activities Section (Indirect Method)		
3	For the Year Ended December 31, 2017		
4			
5	**Operating Activities:**		
6	Net income		$ 937,300
7	Adjustments to reconcile net income to cash basis:		
8	Depreciation expense	$ 142,000	
9	Gain on sale of equipment	(1,000)	
10	Increase in accounts receivable	(35,000)	
11	Decrease in inventory	25,000	
12	Increase in prepaid insurance	(5,000)	
13	Decrease in accounts payable	(40,000)	
14	Increase in wages payable	8,500	
15	Decrease in interest payable	(5,000)	
16	Increase in income taxes payable	26,700	
17	Decrease in other accrued expenses payable	(13,000)	
18	Total reconciling adjustments		103,200
19	Net cash provided by operating activities		1,040,500
20			

Interpreting Cash Flows from Operating Activities

Exhibit 13-12 shows the completed operating activities section of the statement of cash flows. As you can see, the day-to-day profit-making activities of the company have generated over $1 million in cash during the year. That's a positive sign—a company that is not providing cash from operating activities can't survive in the long run. It also shows that cash was drained by allowing accounts receivable to increase and by paying down many of the company's current liabilities (such as accounts payable, interest payable, and other accrued expenses). Finally, this reconciliation shows that net cash provided by operations was $103,200 higher than net income, once again showing that accrual-based net income differs from the cash basis.

> ### Try It!
>
> Assume you are in charge of preparing the operating activities section of the statement of cash flows using the indirect method. In order to reconcile the company's net income back to the cash basis, would you (1) add or (2) subtract each of the following?
>
> 1. An increase in accounts receivable
> 2. Depreciation expense
> 3. A decrease in accounts payable
> 4. A gain on the sale of equipment
> 5. A decrease in prepaid insurance
> 6. An increase in wages payable

Please see page 837 for solutions.

Preparing the Cash Flows from Investing Activities

Recall that transactions affecting long-term asset accounts are classified as investing activities. So the first step in preparing the investing section is to determine whether any changes occurred in the long-term assets accounts during the year. The comparative balance sheets presented in Exhibit 13-4 show changes in three long-term asset accounts:

1. Property, Plant, and Equipment—increase of $515,000
2. Accumulated Depreciation (a contra asset to Property, Plant, and Equipment)—increase of $119,000
3. Investments—increase of $100,000

After noting these changes, we would need to delve into the company's records (such as the general journal) to find more information about these investing activities. The following additional information was found:

> a. Equipment originally costing $25,000 was sold for $3,000. The equipment had accumulated depreciation of $23,000, resulting in a gain of $1,000.
> b. The company purchased $100,000 of stock in XYZ company.
>   No stock investments were sold during the year.

Now let's see how we use this information to sort out investment activities that took place during the year.

Property, Plant, and Equipment

By analyzing the change in this account, we can figure out how much cash the company paid for new property, plant, and equipment (PP&E) during the year:

Beginning balance, PP&E (from Exhibit 13-4)	$2,900,000
Plus: Purchases of PP&E	?
Less: Original cost of equipment sold (from the additional information given)	(25,000)
Ending balance, PP&E (from Exhibit 13-4)	$3,415,000

We can illustrate this relationship in the form of an equation and then solve for the unknown amount:

> Beginning PP&E + Purchases of PP&E − PPE sold = Ending PP&E
> $2,900,000 + ??? − $25,000 = $3,415,000

We can rearrange the equation as follows:

> Purchases of PP&E = $3,415,000 + $25,000 − $2,900,000

Solving the equation yields the following:

> Purchases of PP&E = $540,000

On the statement of cash flows, we will show that $540,000 was used to purchase new property, plant, and equipment. Additionally, the sale of the old equipment for $3,000 will be shown as a *receipt* of cash. Notice that the statement of cash flows doesn't just show the net change in the Property, Plant, and Equipment account. Rather, the company needs to show the purchase and sale of plant assets separately.

Accumulated Depreciation

This account is reconciled as follows:

Beginning balance, Accumulated depreciation (Exhibit 13-4)	$380,000
Plus: Depreciation expense (Exhibit 13-3)	142,000
Less: Accumulated depreciation on sold equipment (from the additional information given)	(23,000)
Ending balance, Accumulated depreciation (Exhibit 13-4)	$499,000

We already accounted for the depreciation expense as an adjustment to net income in the operating activities section of the statement of cash flows. Likewise, the accumulated depreciation on the sold equipment was taken into account in calculating the gain on sale. This, too, became an adjustment to net income in the operating activities section. Because we have completely reconciled the change in this account and have already made the necessary adjustments, no other adjustments are needed.

Investments

Changes in long-term investments are analyzed as follows:

Beginning balance, Investments (Exhibit 13-4)	$185,000
Plus: Purchases of stock investments (from the additional information given)	?
Less: Sale of stock investments	?
Ending balance, Investments (Exhibit 13-4)	$285,000

According to the additional information given, SportsTime purchased $100,000 of new stock investments during the year and did not sell any. Therefore, the investment account is completely reconciled as follows:

> Beginning investments + Purchases of investments − Investments sold = Ending investments
> $185,000 + $100,000 − $0 = $285,000

Any purchase or sale of long-term investments needs to be listed *separately* on the statement of cash flows. Keep in mind that if the company had sold some investments for an amount that differed from the original purchase price, a gain or loss would have resulted. This gain or loss would be shown as an adjustment to net income in the operating section of the statement, much like a gain or loss on the sale of property, plant, or equipment.

Now that we have analyzed the changes in each long-term asset account, we can prepare the investing section of the statement of cash flows. Exhibit 13-13 shows that the company used much of the cash it generated from operations ($1,040,500, from Exhibit 13-12) to pay for new investments in property, plant, and equipment ($540,000) and new stock investments ($100,000).

EXHIBIT 13-13 Investing Activities Section of the Statement of Cash Flows

	A	B	C
1	SportsTime, Inc.		
2	Statement of Cash Flows—Investing Activities Section		
3	For the Year Ended December 31, 2017		
4			
5	Investing Activities:		
6	Cash used to purchase property, plant, and equipment	$ (540,000)	
7	Proceeds from the sale of equipment	3,000	
8	Cash used to purchase investments in stock	(100,000)	
9	Net cash used by investing activities		(637,000)
10			

Preparing the Cash Flows from Financing Activities

Financing activities include transactions that either generate capital for the company or pay it back. Financing activities affect long-term liabilities and owners' equity accounts. The comparative balance sheets shown in Exhibit 13-4 show changes in the company's long-term liabilities, common stock, and retained earnings accounts. We'll have to analyze the changes in each of these accounts to determine the cash provided and used by financing activities. We'll also need the following information obtained from company records.

a. $100,000 of new bonds were issued during the year.
b. $300,000 of bonds were repaid during the year.
c. The board of directors declared cash dividends of $125,000 during the year.

Long-Term Liabilities

Any change in long-term liabilities can be explained either by new borrowings (issuance of notes or bonds payable) or by the repayment of principal on existing debt:

Beginning balance, Long-term liabilities (Exhibit 13-4)	$750,000
Plus: Cash proceeds from new bond issuance	?
Less: Repayment of principal on existing debt	?
End balance, Long-term liabilities (Exhibit 13-4)	$550,000

The additional information provided reconciles this account as follows:

Beginning long-term liabilities + Bond issuance − Repayments of principal = Ending long-term liabilities
$750,000 + $100,000 − $300,000 = $550,000

We'll need to show the issuance and repayments separately on the statement of cash flows.

Common Stock

There was no change in the common stock account on the balance sheet (Exhibit 13-4); therefore, we can conclude that no transactions involving common stock took place during the year.

Retained Earnings

Retained earnings represents the cumulative earnings of a company, less distributions to the company's owners. We analyze the retained earnings account as follows:

Beginning balance, Retained earnings (Exhibit 13-4)	$1,492,000
Plus: Net income (Exhibit 13-3)	937,300
Less: Dividends declared during the year (from the additional information given)	(125,000)
Ending balance, Retained earnings (Exhibit 13-4)	$2,304,300

Since there was no dividends payable shown on the balance sheet, we can conclude that all dividends declared during the year ($125,000) were also paid out to stockholders. Remember, dividends are a distribution of capital back to the owners, not an expense on the income statement. Therefore, the dividends paid will be shown as a use of cash in the financing section of the statement of cash flows.

Exhibit 13-14 shows the completed statement of cash flows for SportsTime, prepared using the indirect method. The information provided in the financing section shows that the company used $300,000 for paying down long-term debt but obtained $100,000 of new debt (perhaps at a lower interest rate). The company used an additional $125,000 to pay dividends to its owners.

EXHIBIT 13-14 Statement of Cash Flows (Indirect Method)

	A	B	C
1	SportsTime, Inc.		
2	Statement of Cash Flows (Indirect Method)		
3	For the Year Ended December 31, 2017		
4			
5	**Operating Activities:**		
6	Net income		$ 937,300
7	Adjustments to reconcile net income to cash basis:		
8	Depreciation expense	$ 142,000	
9	Gain on sale of equipment	(1,000)	
10	Increase in accounts receivable	(35,000)	
11	Decrease in inventory	25,000	
12	Increase in prepaid insurance	(5,000)	
13	Decrease in accounts payable	(40,000)	
14	Increase in wages payable	8,500	
15	Decrease in interest payable	(5,000)	
16	Increase in income taxes payable	26,700	
17	Decrease in other accrued expenses payable	(13,000)	
18	Total reconciling adjustments		103,200
19	Net cash provided by operating activities		1,040,500
20			
21	**Investing Activities:**		
22	Cash used to purchase property, plant, and equipment	$ (540,000)	
23	Proceeds from the sale of equipment	3,000	
24	Cash used to purchase investments in stock	(100,000)	
25	Net cash used by investing activities		(637,000)
26			
27	**Financing Activities:**		
28	Proceeds from bond issuance	$ 100,000	
29	Repayment of long-term debt	(300,000)	
30	Cash payments for dividends	(125,000)	
31	Net cash used by financing activities		(325,000)
32	Net increase in cash		78,500
33	Cash, beginning of the year		125,000
34	Cash, end of the year		$ 203,500
35			

Interpreting the Statement of Cash Flows

The statement of cash flows shown in Exhibit 13-14 presents a detailed explanation of how SportsTime generated and used cash during the year. In summary, we see that a little over $1 million in cash was generated by the company's day-to-day operating activities. Roughly 61% of this cash was used to purchase new, long-term investments, and 31% was used to decrease company debt and pay dividends. The remaining 8% was added to the company's cash balance, leaving cash $78,500 higher than it was at the beginning of the year.

Free Cash Flow

Many potential investors calculate the company's free cash flow using the information provided on the statement of cash flows. **Free cash flow** represents the amount of excess cash a business generates after taking into consideration the capital expenditures necessary to maintain its business. This cash can then be used for expansion, to pay dividends, to pay down debt, or for any other business purpose (which is why it is called "free"). Essentially, it is the cash generated from the company's core business that is "left over" after paying bills and making capital expenditures. Free cash flow is calculated as follows:

$$\text{Free cash flow} = \text{Net cash provided by operating activities} - \text{Capital expenditures}$$

Using the information provided in Exhibit 13-14, we can calculate SportsTime's free cash flow as follows:

$$= \$1,040,500 - \$540,000$$
$$= \$500,500$$

The presence of free cash flow means that SportsTime has the ability to expand, produce new products, pay dividends, buy back treasury stock, or reduce its debt. Potential investors place high value on a company's ability to generate free cash flow and often use it as a means of valuing stock.

Recap: Steps to Preparing the Statement of Cash Flows Using the Indirect Method

Exhibit 13-15 summarizes the steps used to create a statement of cash flows using the indirect method.

EXHIBIT 13-15 Steps for Using the Indirect Method

Step 1. Begin the operating section with the company's net income and add back any noncash expenses (such as depreciation or losses on the sale of property, plant, and equipment) and subtract any noncash revenues (such as gains on the sale of property, plant, or equipment). This information is found on the company's income statement.

Step 2. Adjust net income for all changes in current asset and current liability accounts (other than the Cash account) that are found on the company's comparative balance sheet:
- **Add back** decreases in current asset accounts and increases in current liability accounts.
- **Subtract** increases in current asset accounts and decreases in current liability accounts.

Step 3. Prepare the investing section by analyzing the changes in all long-term asset accounts found on the company's comparative balance sheet. Separately list all cash transactions that took place during the year affecting these accounts (such as buying and selling property). Any gains or losses on sales, depreciation, or amortization of these assets has already been accounted for in the operating section.

Step 4. Prepare the financing section by analyzing the changes in all long-term liability and equity accounts found on the company's comparative balance sheet. Separately list all cash transactions that took place during the year affecting these accounts (such as issuing new debt or paying down existing debt, selling stock, buying treasury stock, or paying dividends).

Step 5. Present a subtotal of the amount of cash provided or used by each of the three types of activities (operating, investing, and financing). Use the subtotals to find the overall increase or decrease in cash during the year. Then add the increase to (or subtract the decrease from) the company's beginning cash balance to arrive at the ending cash balance shown on the company's balance sheet.

How Is the Statement of Cash Flows Prepared Using the Direct Method?

In this section, we'll prepare the statement of cash flows using the direct method. Keep in mind that the choice of method (indirect versus direct) only affects the operating activities section of the statement of cash flows. The investing and financing sections are the same regardless of the method used.

3 Prepare the statement of cash flows using the direct method

Overview

The direct method lists the receipt and payment of cash for specific operating activities. For example, the operating activities would list such line items as follows:

- Cash receipts from customers
- Cash payments (to suppliers) for purchase of inventory
- Cash payments (to employees) for salaries and wages

In essence, the direct method lists many of the same items shown on the income statement but calculates them on a cash rather than an accrual basis. Exhibit 13-16 shows SportsTime's statement of cash flows using the direct method. Notice the reference numbers (1–7) provided in the operating activities section the schedule. These reference numbers are only provided for the sake of instruction and are never included on an actual statement of cash flows. In the following section, we'll show the supporting calculations for each referenced line item on the statement.

> **Why is this important?**
>
> "In the **future**, the **FASB** and **IASB** may require companies to use the **direct method**. This method shows, in a straightforward manner, what the company **received and paid cash** for during the year."

EXHIBIT 13-16 Statement of Cash Flows (Direct Method)

	A	B	C	D
1		SportsTime, Inc.		
2		Statement of Cash Flows (Direct Method)		
3		For the Year Ended December 31, 2017		
4				
5	**Operating Activities:**	Ref.*		
6	Cash receipts from customers	(1)	$ 9,465,000	
7	Cash payments for inventory	(2)	(7,140,000)	
8	Cash payments for insurance	(3)	(30,000)	
9	Cash payments for salaries and wages	(4)	(571,500)	
10	Cash payments for interest expense	(5)	(65,000)	
11	Cash payments for income taxes	(6)	(375,000)	
12	Cash payments for other operating expenses	(7)	(243,000)	
13	Net cash provided by operating activities			1,040,500
14				
15	**Investing Activities:**			
16	Cash used to purchase property, plant, and equipment		$ (540,000)	
17	Proceeds from the sale of equipment		3,000	
18	Cash used to purchase investments in stock		(100,000)	
19	Net cash used by investing activities			(637,000)
20				
21	**Financing Activities:**			
22	Proceeds from bond issuance		$ 100,000	
23	Repayment of long-term debt		(300,000)	
24	Cash payments for dividends		(125,000)	
25	Net cash used by financing activities			(325,000)
26	Net increase in cash			78,500
27	Cash, beginning of the year			125,000
28	Cash, end of the year			$ 203,500
29				

*NOTE: The reference numbers are provided for the sake of instruction only and are never actually shown on the statement of cash flows.

Notice that the net cash provided by operating activities ($1,040,500) is the *same* as we found using the indirect method (shown in Exhibit 13-14).

Determining Cash Payments and Receipts

The best way to make sure you've captured all cash transactions from operating activities is to analyze *every* current asset and current liability account shown on the balance sheet (Exhibit 13-4) and incorporate related information from the income statement (Exhibit 13-3) as necessary. Let's start with current assets.

(1) Cash Receipts from Customers

To determine the amount of cash received from customers we must analyze accounts receivable. Accounts receivable increases when sales are made and decreases when cash is collected:

Beginning balance, Accounts receivable (Exhibit 13-4)	$ 330,000
Plus: Sales revenue (Exhibit 13-3)	9,500,000
Less: Cash collections of accounts receivable	?
Ending balance, Accounts receivable (Exhibit 13-4)	$ 365,000

Solving for the unknown, we determine that cash collections of sales must be $9,465,000.

(2) Cash Payments for Inventory

The next current asset account on the balance sheet is inventory. We'll use this account, along with accounts payable (current liability), to figure out how much cash was used to purchase inventory. First, let's think about what affects the inventory account: The account increases for the purchase of inventory and decreases for the cost of goods sold. Therefore, we can establish the following relationship:

Beginning balance, Inventory (Exhibit 13-4)	$ 657,000
Plus: Purchases of inventory	?
Less: Cost of goods sold (Exhibit 13-3)	(7,125,000)
Ending balance, Inventory (Exhibit 13-4)	$ 632,000

Solving for the unknown, we determine that purchases of inventory must have been $7,100,000.

However, did the company pay for all of these purchases during the year? We'll only know by investigating the changes in accounts payable (we assume SportsTime uses accounts payable only for inventory purchases):

Beginning balance, Accounts payable (Exhibit 13-4)	$ 285,000
Plus: Purchases of inventory	7,100,000
Less: Cash payments for inventory	(?)
Ending balance, Accounts payable (Exhibit 13-4)	$ 245,000

Solving for the unknown, we determine that payments for inventory must have been $7,140,000.

(3) Cash Payments for Insurance

The next current asset on the balance sheet is prepaid insurance. This account will increase for purchases of insurance and decrease as a result of recording insurance expense:

Beginning balance, Prepaid insurance (Exhibit 13-4)	$ 15,000
Plus: Payments for insurance	?
Less: Insurance expense (Exhibit 13-3)	(25,000)
Ending balance, Prepaid insurance (Exhibit 13-4)	$ 20,000

Solving for the unknown, we determine that payments for insurance must have been $30,000.

Now that we've analyzed all of the current asset accounts found on the company's balance sheet, we turn our attention to the current liability accounts shown in Exhibit 13-4. The first current liability shown is accounts payable. We've already analyzed that account when calculating the amount of inventory purchased. The remaining current liability accounts include wages payable, interest payable, income taxes payable, and other accrued expenses payable. We'll examine each of these next.

(4) Cash Payments for Salaries and Wages

Wages payable increases when we record salaries and wages expense and decreases when the company pays its employees:

Beginning balance, Wages payable (Exhibit 13-4)	$ 48,500
Plus: Salaries and wages expense (Exhibit 13-3)	580,000
Less: Payments for salaries and wages	(?)
Ending balance, Wages payable (Exhibit 13-4)	$ 57,000

Solving for the unknown, we determine that payments for salaries and wages must have been $571,500.

(5) Cash Payments for Interest Expense

Interest payable increases when we record interest expense and decreases when the company pays interest:

Beginning balance, Interest payable (Exhibit 13-4)	$ 8,000
Plus: Interest expense (Exhibit 13-3)	60,000
Less: Payments for interest	(?)
Ending balance, Interest payable (Exhibit 13-4)	$ 3,000

Solving for the unknown, we determine that payments for interest expense must have been $65,000.

(6) Cash Payments for Income Taxes

Income taxes payable increases when we record income tax expense and decreases when the company pays income taxes:

Beginning balance, Income taxes payable (Exhibit 13-4)	$120,000
Plus: Income tax expense (Exhibit 13-3)	401,700
Less: Payments for income taxes	(?)
Ending balance, Income taxes payable (Exhibit 13-4)	$146,700

Solving for the unknown, we determine that payments for income taxes must have been $375,000.

(7) Cash Payments for Other Operating Expenses

SportsTime's income statement lists many of their operating expenses separately: salaries and wages expense, insurance expense, and depreciation expense. It then lumps together its remaining operating expenses, as shown in Exhibit 13-3. "Other operating expenses" would include such expenses as rent, utilities, telephone and Internet, and supplies. Sports-Time records liabilities for these expenses as "other accrued expenses payable":

Beginning balance, Other accrued expenses payable (Exhibit 13-4)	$ 28,500
Plus: Other operating expenses (Exhibit 13-3)	230,000
Less: Payments for other operating expenses	(?)
Ending balance, Other accrued expenses payable (Exhibit 13-4)	$ 15,500

Solving for the unknown, we determine that payments for other operating expenses must have been $243,000.

Cash Flows from Operating Activities

By analyzing each current asset and current liability account, we have figured out the actual cash receipts and cash payments made for each operating activity during the year. After listing each transaction separately (Exhibit 13-16), we see that the net cash flow from operating activities totals $1,040,500, just as it did using the indirect method.

Comparing the Direct and Indirect Methods

As you can see, the direct method requires much more analysis than the indirect method. As a result, most companies currently use the indirect method. However, the FASB and IASB have jointly recommended that companies use the direct method because it shows cash receipts and cash payments in a much more straightforward manner. Nonetheless, both methods result in the same *net* amount of cash provided by operating activities (for SportsTime, $1,040,500).

Decision Guidelines

Statement of Cash Flows

Companies have a choice of using the indirect method or direct method. The following decision guidelines provide general guidance for preparing the statement of cash flows using either method.

Decision	Guidelines
What kind of information is needed in order to prepare the statement of cash flows?	The following information is needed: 1. Income statement for the year 2. Balance sheets for the current and prior year (comparative balance sheets) 3. Additional information about investing and financing activities that occurred during the year
If my company uses the indirect method, what adjustments should be shown when reconciling net income to the cash basis?	1. All noncash expenses are **added back** to net income. 2. All noncash revenues are **deducted** from net income. 3. All changes in current asset and current liability accounts will either be added or deducted from net income (as indicated below).
To reconcile net income to the cash basis, do we add or subtract changes in current asset accounts? (indirect method)	• If a current asset account **increases**, then **subtract** the change from net income. • If a current asset account **decreases**, then **add** the change to net income.
To reconcile net income to the cash basis, do we add or subtract changes in current liability accounts? (indirect method)	• If a current liability account **increases**, then **add** the change to net income. • If a current liability account **decreases**, then **subtract** the change from net income.
What process should be used to prepare the investing section of the statement of cash flows?	You will need to analyze the change in every long-term asset account found on the balance sheet. Purchases and sales of investments need to be disclosed separately on the statement of cash flows. (You can't just show the net change in each account.)
What process should be used to prepare the financing section of the statement of cash flows?	You will need to analyze the change in every long-term liability and owners' equity account found on the balance sheet to determine the financing transactions that took place during the year.
My company has decided to use the direct method. What process should be used to prepare the operating section of the statement of cash flows?	Each current asset and current liability account will need to be analyzed to determine the cash transactions underlying the change in the account. These transactions typically include the following: • Receipts from customers • Payments for inventory • Payments for salaries and wages • Payments for other operating expenses (listed separately, or grouped together, depending on the presentation of expenses in the income statement)

SUMMARY PROBLEM 2

Urban Togs is a regional retailer of trend-setting clothing that is made with socially and environmentally friendly practices. The company's income statement and comparative balance sheets are presented below. In addition, the following information was gathered from the company's records:

a. No new debt was issued during the year.
b. Dividends of $200,000 were declared by the board of directors.
c. Equipment with an original cost of $20,000 was sold for $9,000. The equipment had accumulated depreciation of $15,000 at the time of sale.

Requirement

Prepare the company's statement of cash flows using the indirect method.

	A	B	C
1	Urban Togs		
2	Income Statement		
3	For the Year Ended December 31, 2017		
4			
5	Sales revenues		$ 4,750,000
6	Less: Cost of goods sold		3,562,500
7	Gross profit		1,187,500
8	Less operating expenses:		
9	Salaries and wages expense	$ 340,000	
10	Insurance expense	10,000	
11	Depreciation expense	75,000	
12	Other operating expenses	125,000	
13	Total operating expenses		550,000
14	Operating income		$ 637,500
15	Plus other income and less other expenses:		
16	Interest expense	8,000	
17	Gain on sale of PP&E	4,000	
18	Total other income and expenses		4,000
19	Income before income taxes		633,500
20	Less: Income tax expense		190,050
21	Net income		$ 443,450
22			

	Urban Togs Comparative Balance Sheets December 31, 2017 and 2016		
Assets	2017	2016	Increase (Decrease)
Current assets:			
Cash	$ 187,000	$ 85,000	102,000
Accounts receivable	37,000	57,000	(20,000)
Inventory	337,500	350,000	(12,500)
Prepaid insurance	5,000	3,000	2,000
Total current assets	566,500	495,000	
Property, plant, and equipment	1,860,000	1,660,000	200,000
Less: Accumulated depreciation	(310,000)	(250,000)	60,000
Investments	50,000	50,000	0
Total assets	$ 2,166,500	$ 1,955,000	
Liabilities			
Current liabilities:			
Accounts payable	$ 65,000	$ 85,000	(20,000)
Wages payable	29,000	25,000	4,000
Interest payable	2,000	8,000	(6,000)
Income taxes payable	100,050	85,000	15,050
Other accrued expenses payable	13,000	18,000	(5,000)
Total current liabilities	209,050	221,000	
Long-term liabilities	80,000	100,000	(20,000)
Total liabilities	289,050	321,000	
Stockholders' equity			
Common stock	850,000	850,000	0
Retained earnings	1,027,450	784,000	243,450
Total stockholders' equity	1,877,450	1,634,000	
Total liabilities and equity	$ 2,166,500	$ 1,955,000	

▪ SOLUTION

The following steps are taken to prepare the statement of cash flows using the indirect method:

1. We begin the operating section with the company's net income, and we add back any noncash expenses (depreciation) and then subtract any noncash revenues (gains on the sale of property, plant, or equipment).

2. We then adjust net income for all changes in current asset and current liability accounts (other than the cash account):

   • We *add* decreases in current asset accounts and increases in current liability accounts.

   • We *subtract* increases in current asset accounts and decreases in current liability accounts.

3. To prepare the investing section, we analyze the changes in all long-term asset accounts. We separately list all cash transactions that took place during the year (for example, buying and selling property, plant, and equipment or long-term investments). Any gains, losses, depreciation, or amortization of these assets have already been accounted for in the operating section.

4. To prepare the financing section, we analyze the changes in all long-term liability and equity accounts. We separately list all cash transactions that took place during the year (for example, issuing new debt or paying down existing debt, selling stock, buying treasury stock, or paying dividends).

	A	B	C
1	Urban Togs		
2	Statement of Cash Flows (Indirect Method)		
3	For the Year Ended December 31, 2017		
4			
5	**Operating Activities:**		
6	Net income		$ 443,450
7	Adjustments to reconcile net income to cash basis:		
8	Depreciation expense	$ 75,000	
9	Gain on sale of equipment	(4,000)	
10	Decrease in accounts receivable	20,000	
11	Decrease in inventory	12,500	
12	Increase in prepaid insurance	(2,000)	
13	Decrease in accounts payable	(20,000)	
14	Increase in wages payable	4,000	
15	Decrease in interest payable	(6,000)	
16	Increase in income taxes payable	15,050	
17	Decrease in other accrued expenses payable	(5,000)	
18	Total reconciling adjustments		89,550
19	Net cash provided by operating activities		533,000
20			
21	**Investing Activities:**		
22	Cash used to purchase property, plant, and equipment	$ (220,000)	
23	Proceeds from the sale of equipment	9,000	
24	Net cash used by investing activities		(211,000)
25			
26	**Financing Activities:**		
27	Repayment of long-term debt	$ (20,000)	
28	Cash payments for dividends	(200,000)	
29	Net cash used by financing activities		(220,000)
30	Net increase in cash		102,000
31	Cash, beginning of the year		85,000
32	Cash, end of the year		$ 187,000
33			

Analysis of Investing and Financing Activities:
Property, Plant, and Equipment:

Beginning balance, PP&E	$1,660,000
Plus: Purchases of PP&E	?
Less: Original cost of equipment sold (given)	(20,000)
Ending balance, PP&E	$1,860,000

Solving for the unknown, the company must have purchases of $220,000 of property, plant, and equipment. This will be shown as an investing activity.

Accumulated Depreciation:

Beginning balance, Accumulated depreciation...	$250,000
Plus: Depreciation expense...	75,000
Less: Accumulated depreciation on sold equipment (given)............................	(15,000)
Ending balance, Accumulated depreciation	$310,000

The depreciation expense will be shown as an operating activity.

Gain on Sale of Equipment:

Sale price of equipment (given)...		$9,000
Original cost of the equipment...	$20,000	
Less: Accumulated depreciation	15,000	
Net book value of equipment...		5,000
Gain on sale		$4,000

The $4,000 gain on sale will be shown as an adjustment to net income in the operating section, while the $9,000 cash received will be shown as an investing activity.

Long-Term Liabilities:

Beginning balance, Long-term liabilities..	$100,000
Plus: Cash proceeds from new bond issuance (given)	0
Less: Repayment of principal on existing debt...	?
End balance, Long-term liabilities	$ 80,000

Solving for the unknown, the company must have repaid $20,000 of principal on the existing long-term debt. This will be shown as a financing activity.

Retained Earnings:

Beginning balance, Retained earnings..	$ 784,000
Plus: Net income	443,450
Less: Dividends declared during the year (given)	(200,000)
Ending balance, Retained earnings..	$1,027,450

The payment of dividends will be shown as a financing activity.

END OF CHAPTER

Learning Objectives

- 1 Classify cash flows as operating, investing, or financing activities
- 2 Prepare the statement of cash flows using the indirect method
- 3 Prepare the statement of cash flows using the direct method

Accounting Vocabulary

Accrual Basis of Accounting. (p. 784) Revenues are recorded when they are earned (when the sale takes place) rather than when cash is received on the sale. Likewise, expenses are recorded when they are incurred rather than when they are paid.

Cash Equivalents. (p. 781) Very safe, highly liquid assets that are readily convertible into cash, such as money market funds, certificates of deposit that mature in less than three months, and U.S. treasury bills.

Comparative Balance Sheets. (p. 788) A comparison of the balance sheets from the end of two fiscal periods, usually highlighting the changes in each account.

Direct Method. (p. 783) A method of presenting cash flows from operating activities that separately lists the receipt and payment of cash for specific operating activities.

Financing Activities. (p. 782) Activities that either generate capital for the company or pay it back, such as issuing stock or long-term debt, paying dividends, and repaying principal amounts on loans; this includes all activities that affect long-term liabilities and owners' equity.

Free Cash Flow. (p. 798) The amount of excess cash a business generates after taking into consideration the capital expenditures necessary to maintain its business. It is calculated as net cash flow from operating activities minus capital expenditures.

Indirect Method. (p. 784) A method of presenting the cash flows from operating activities that begins with the company's net income, which is prepared on an accrual basis, and then reconciles it back to the cash basis through a series of adjustments.

Investing Activities. (p. 781) Activities that involve buying or selling long-term assets, such as buying or selling property, plant, or equipment; buying or selling stock in other companies (if the stock is meant to be held for the long term); or loaning money to other companies with the goal of earning interest income from the loan.

Net Book Value. (p. 789) The original cost of plant or equipment less its accumulated depreciation.

Operating Activities. (p. 781) The day-to-day profit-making activities of the company, such as making or buying inventory, selling inventory, selling services, paying employees, advertising, and so forth; this also includes *any other activity that affects net income* (not just operating income), current assets, or current liabilities.

Statement of Cash Flows. (p. 780) One of the four basic financial statements; the statement shows the overall increase or decrease in cash during the period as well as how the company generated and used cash during the period.

Quick Check

1. *(Learning Objective 1)* Which of the following is **not** one of the activities found on the statement of cash flows?
   a. Administrative activities
   b. Financing activities
   c. Investing activities
   d. Operating activities

2. *(Learning Objective 1)* Transactions that affect long-term liabilities and stockholders' equity are classified as which of the following?
   a. Administrative activities
   b. Financing activities
   c. Investing activities
   d. Operating activities

3. *(Learning Objective 1)* Transactions that affect long-term assets are classified as which of the following?
   a. Operating activities
   b. Investing activities
   c. Administrative activities
   d. Financing activities

4. *(Learning Objective 1)* Transactions that affect net income, current assets, and current liabilities are classified as which of the following?
   a. Investing activities
   b. Financing activities
   c. Administrative activities
   d. Operating activities

5. *(Learning Objective 1)* Interest and dividend income are both classified as
   a. financing activities.
   b. administrative activities.
   c. operating activities.
   d. investing activities.

6. *(Learning Objective 1)* The payment of dividends is classified as a(n)
   a. administrative activity.
   b. investing activity.
   c. operating activity.
   d. financing activity.

7. *(Learning Objective 1)* Which method of preparing the statement of cash flows is most commonly used in the United States, even though FASB and IASB encourage the use of the other method?
   a. Accrual
   b. Direct
   c. Indirect
   d. Standard

8. *(Learning Objective 2)* If using the indirect method, which of the following statements is correct?
   a. An increase in a current asset account should be subtracted from net income.
   b. An increase in a current liability account should be subtracted from net income.
   c. A decrease in a current liability account should be added to net income.
   d. None of the items listed is correct if using the indirect method.

9. *(Learning Objective 3)* The difference between the two methods of presenting the statement of cash flows is only found in the section reporting
   a. financing activities.
   b. administrative activities.
   c. operating activities.
   d. investing activities.

10. *(Learning Objective 3)* Which one of the following lines would be found on the statement of cash flows for a company using the direct method?
    a. Increase in prepaid insurance
    b. Gain on sale of property, plant, and equipment
    c. Depreciation expense
    d. Cash receipts from customers

Quick Check Answers

1. a 2. b 3. b 4. d 5. c 6. d 7. c 8. a 9. c 10. d

Short Exercises

S13-1 Classifying cash flows *(Learning Objective 1)*

Breakneck Creek Corporation is preparing its statement of cash flows (indirect method) for the past year. Listed below are items used in preparing the company's statement of cash flows. Specify how each item would be treated on Breakneck Creek Corporation's statement of cash flows by using the following abbreviations:

1. Operating activity—addition to net income (O+)
2. Operating activity—subtraction from net income (O–)
3. Financing activity (F)
4. Investing activity (I)
5. Activity that is not on the statement of cash flows (NA)

a. Decrease in inventory	____	h. Depreciation expense	____
b. Increase in accounts receivable	____	i. Retained earnings	____
c. Repayment of long-term loan	____	j. Increase in prepaid insurance expense	____
d. Loss on sale of building	____	k. Gain on sale of land	____
e. Payment of dividends to stockholders	____	l. Sale of common stock	____
f. Increase in accounts payable	____	m. Sale of equipment no longer being used	____
g. Net income	____	n. Decrease in accrued taxes payable	____

S13-2 Preparing the operating cash flows section (indirect method)
(Learning Objective 2)

Majestic Corporation began the year with accounts receivable, inventory, and prepaid expenses totaling $67,000. At the end of the year, Majestic had a total of $77,000 for these current assets. At the beginning of the year, it owed current liabilities of $42,000, and at year-end, current liabilities totaled $39,000.

Net income for the year was $80,000. Included in net income was a $6,000 gain on the sale of land and depreciation expense of $7,000.

Show how Majestic should report cash flows from operating activities for the year. The company uses the indirect method.

S13-3 Identifying activities for the statement of cash flows—indirect method
(Learning Objectives 1 & 2)

Identify each of Knox Industries' transactions listed below as operating (O), investing (I), financing (F), noncash investing and financing (NIF), or a transaction that is not reported on the statement of cash flows (NA). Also indicate whether the transaction increases (+) or decreases (−) cash. The indirect method is used for operating activities.

a. Issuance of common stock for cash	____	i. Cash sale of land (no gain or loss)	____
b. Purchase of new forklift with cash	____	j. Sale of long-term investment (no gain or loss)	____
c. Purchase of equipment by issuing note payable	____	k. Increase in salaries payable	____
d. Depreciation of building	____	l. Amortization of patent	____
e. Decrease in raw materials inventory	____	m. Purchase building with cash	____
f. Payment of cash dividend	____	n. Decrease in accrued taxes payable	____
g. Increase in prepaid rent expense	____	o. Gain on sale of equipment	____
h. Purchase of treasury stock	____	p. Repayment of long-term debt	____

S13-4 Classify cash flows as operating, investing, or financing
(Learning Objectives 1 & 2)

For each of the following situations, identify whether the activity is an operating, investing, or financing activity and compute the cash provided or used by the activity. The indirect method is used.

Activity	Operating (O) Investing (I) Financing (F)	Amount of Cash Flow	Increase (+) Decrease (−)

a. A building with a cost of $188,000 and accumulated depreciation of $44,000 was sold for a $17,000 gain.

b. Net income for last year was $117,000. The accumulated depreciation balance increased by $20,000. There were no changes in noncash current assets or liabilities. There were also no sales of plant assets.

c. Net income was $23,000 for the year. Accounts receivable increased by $8,000, and accounts payable increased by $1,000. There were no other changes in the noncash current assets and current liabilities. There was no depreciation for the year.

d. Bonds payable with a face value of $60,000 were retired with a cash payment for their face value. New bonds were issued later in the year for $37,000.

e. Bonds payable were retired for their face value of $65,000 (cash paid). Cash dividends of $11,000 were also paid. A new long-term note payable was signed for cash proceeds of $25,000.

f. A plant asset with a cost of $66,000 and accumulated depreciation of $15,000 was sold for a $12,000 loss.

g. Current assets (not including cash) increased by $1,000, and current liabilities decreased by $10,000. There was no depreciation. Net income was $55,000 for the year.

h. Common stock was issued for $260,000 cash. Dividends of $25,000 were paid in cash.

i. Noncash current assets decreased by $6,000, and current liabilities decreased by $15,000. Depreciation was $14,000 for the year, while net income was $53,000.

S13-5 Calculate investing cash flows *(Learning Objectives 1, 2, & 3)*

McCabe Company reported the following financial statements for 2016 and 2017:

	A	B	C
1	McCabe Company		
2	Income Statement		
3	For the Year Ended December 31, 2017		
4			
5	Sales revenues		$ 4,810,000
6	Less: Cost of goods sold		2,890,000
7	Gross profit		1,920,000
8	Less operating expenses:		
9	Salaries and wages expense	$ 370,000	
10	Insurance expense	14,000	
11	Depreciation expense	71,000	
12	Other operating expenses	127,000	
13	Total operating expenses		582,000
14	Operating income		$ 1,338,000
15	Plus other income and less other expenses:		
16	Interest expense	6,100	
17	Other income and expenses	0	
18	Total other income and expenses		6,100
19	Income before income taxes		1,331,900
20	Less: Income tax expense		403,700
21	Net income		$ 928,200
22			

McCabe Company
Comparative Balance Sheets
December 31, 2017 and 2016

Assets	2017	2016
Current assets:		
Cash	$ 585,000	$ 468,000
Accounts receivable	78,000	14,000
Inventory	990,000	240,000
Prepaid insurance	4,500	4,500
Total current assets	$ 1,657,500	$ 726,500
Property, plant, and equipment	$ 1,250,000	$ 1,130,000
Less: Accumulated depreciation	(277,000)	(206,000)
Investments	46,000	68,000
Total assets	$ 2,676,500	$ 1,718,500
Liabilities		
Current liabilities:		
Accounts payable	$ 24,000	$ 47,000
Wages payable	14,000	15,000
Interest payable	2,200	5,600
Income taxes payable	276,000	35,000
Other accrued expenses payable	28,000	15,000
Total current liabilities	$ 344,200	$ 117,600
Long-term liabilities	69,000	85,000
Total liabilities	$ 413,200	$ 202,600
Stockholders' equity		
Common stock	$ 723,000	$ 773,000
Retained earnings	1,540,300	742,900
Total stockholders' equity	$ 2,263,300	$ 1,515,900
Total liabilities and equity	$ 2,676,500	$ 1,718,500

Compute the following investing cash flows:

a. Purchases of plant assets (all were for cash). There were no sales of plant assets.

b. Proceeds from the sale of investments. There were no purchases of investments.

S13-6 Calculate financing cash flows *(Learning Objectives 2 & 3)*

Use the data given in S13-5 for the McCabe Company to compute the following financing cash flows:

a. New borrowing or payment of long-term notes payable. McCabe Company had only one long-term note payable transaction during the year (this long-term note payable is the only long-term liability that the company has).

b. Issuance of common stock or retirement of common stock. The company had only one common stock transaction during the year.

c. Payment of cash dividends (same as dividends declared).

S13-7 Classify cash flows as operating, investing, or financing
(Learning Objectives 1, 2, & 3)

The items in the following table may or may not appear in a statement of cash flows.

	Operating (O) Investing (I) Financing (F)	Direct (D) Indirect (I) Both (B)	Increase (+) Decrease (−)
1. Issuance of stock			
2. Principal payments on long-term notes payable			
3. Depreciation expense			
4. Increase in accounts receivable			
5. Cash received from customers			
6. Purchase of plant assets with cash			
7. Decrease in payroll taxes payable			
8. Cash paid to suppliers			
9. Dividends paid			
10. Increase in salaries payable			
11. Cash paid for taxes			
12. Purchase of treasury stock			

For each of the items in the table, indicate the following:
1. Would the item appear on the statement of cash flows under operating activities (O), investing activities (I), or financing activities (F)?
2. Would the item appear on the statement of cash flows using the direct method (D), indirect method (I), or both (B)?
3. Would the item result in an increase (+) or a decrease (−) when computing cash flow?

S13-8 Prepare statement of cash flows (indirect method) *(Learning Objective 2)*

Daniel Corporation uses the indirect method to prepare its statement of cash flows. Data related to cash activities for last year are as follows:

Net income	$ 92,900
Dividends paid (cash)	$ 50,800
Depreciation expense	$ 11,000
Net decrease in current assets	$ 21,000
Issued new long-term notes payable for cash	$ 51,800
Paid cash for building	$275,000
Net decrease in current liabilities	$ 5,600
Sold long-term investment for cash	$100,000

Answer the following questions:
1. What was the net cash flow from operating activities for the year?
2. What was the cash flow from (or used for) investing activities for the year?
3. What was the cash flow from (or used for) financing activities for the year?
4. What was the net change in cash for the year?
5. If the beginning balance of cash for the year was $154,000, what was the balance of cash at the end of the year?

S13-9 Calculate increase or decrease in current assets and liabilities
(Learning Objective 2)

A recent statement of cash flows for Oleg Company reported the following information:

	A	B	C
1	Net income		$ 452,800
2	Adjustments to reconcile net income to cash basis:		
3	Depreciation expense	$ 64,000	
4	Accounts receivable	(29,000)	
5	Inventory	16,200	
6	Other current assets	(8,600)	
7	Accounts payable	(17,000)	
8	Other current liabilities	195,000	
9	Total reconciling adjustments		220,600
10	Net cash provided by operating activities		$ 673,400
11			

Based on the information presented in the statement of cash flows for Oleg Company, determine whether the following accounts increased or decreased during the period: Accounts Receivable, Inventory, Other Current Assets, Accounts Payable, and Other Current Liabilities.

S13-10 Prepare statement of cash flows (direct method) *(Learning Objective 3)*

Commander Corporation uses the direct method to prepare its statement of cash flows. Data related to cash activities for last year appear next.

Paid for equipment	$17,000	Paid for interest	$ 4,700
Paid to suppliers	$39,000	Paid for utilities	$20,000
Paid for insurance	$ 9,800	Paid dividends	$ 7,400
Depreciation expense	$ 3,300	Received from customers	$51,000
Paid for advertising	$ 7,300	Paid for taxes	$ 5,600
Received from sale of land	$20,000	Received from issuing long-term note payable	$26,000
Received from sale of plant assets	$ 6,700	Paid to employees	$16,000

Answer the following questions:

1. What was the net cash flow from operating activities for the year?
2. What was the net cash flow from investing activities for the year?
3. What was the net cash flow from financing activities for the year?
4. What was the net change in cash for the year?
5. If the beginning balance of cash for the year was $342,000, what was the balance of cash at the end of the year?

S13-11 Identify ethical standards violated *(Learning Objectives 1, 2, & 3)*

For each of the situations listed, identify the primary standard from the IMA *Statement of Ethical Professional Practice* that is violated (competence, confidentiality, integrity, or credibility). Refer to Exhibit 1-7 for the complete standard.

a. Chrissy uses the indirect method to prepare the statement of cash flows, even though her company has adopted International Financial Reporting Standards. She is unfamiliar with the steps required to produce a statement using the direct method.

b. Layne is an accountant at Black Squirrel Radio Group, Inc. She has helped to prepare the financial statements. She knows that the internal controls over cash are weak, but she does not speak up because she feels that it is not her job.

c. The statement of cash flows has never been Erik's strength; he struggled with it in school. This year, Erik cannot get the statement of cash flows to balance, so he decides to hide the amount that the statement is off by adding that difference to one of the items in the operating section.

d. Mark does not disclose to upper management that his sister is a partner in the accounting firm that the company is hiring for the audit.

e. Quinn is an accountant at Murphy & Swanson, Inc. Quinn confides to a close friend that he is concerned about the future of Murphy & Swanson. Quinn explains that operating cash flows are negative; this information is on the not-yet-released financial statements.

EXERCISES Group A

E13-12A Prepare operating cash flows section (indirect method)
(Learning Objective 2)

The comparative balance sheet for Coastal Travel Services, Inc., for December 31, 2017 and 2016, is as follows:

	A	B	C
1	**Coastal Travel Services, Inc.**		
2	**Comparative Balance Sheets**		
3	**December 31, 2017 and 2016**		
4	Assets	2017	2016
5	Current assets:		
6	Cash	$ 44,000	$ 17,000
7	Accounts receivable	80,000	85,000
8	Inventory	61,000	20,000
9	Prepaid insurance	8,000	16,000
10	Total current assets	$ 193,000	$ 138,000
11			
12	Land	$ 108,000	$ 121,000
13	Equipment	80,000	58,000
14	Less: Accumulated depreciation	(16,000)	(11,000)
15	Total assets	$ 365,000	$ 306,000
16			
17	Liabilities		
18	Current liabilities:		
19	Accounts payable	$ 30,000	$ 36,000
20	Wages payable	35,000	27,000
21	Interest payable	16,000	15,000
22	Income taxes payable	11,000	8,000
23	Total current liabilities	$ 92,000	$ 86,000
24			
25	Notes payable (long term)	100,000	91,000
26	Total liabilities	$ 192,000	$ 177,000
27			
28	Stockholders' equity		
29	Common stock	$ 136,000	$ 116,000
30	Retained earnings	37,000	13,000
31	Total stockholders' equity	$ 173,000	$ 129,000
32			
33	Total liabilities and equity	$ 365,000	$ 306,000
34			

The following information is taken from the records of Coastal Travel Services, Inc.:

a. Land was sold for $9,200.
b. Equipment was purchased for cash.
c. There were no disposals of equipment during the year.
d. The common stock was issued for cash.
e. Net income for 2017 was $32,000.
f. Cash dividends paid during the year were $8,000.

Coastal Travel Services, Inc., uses the indirect method for preparing the statement of cash flows. Prepare the operating section of the statement of cash flows for 2017.

E13-13A Prepare statement of cash flows (indirect method)
(Learning Objective 2)

Using the data given in E13-12A, prepare the statement of cash flows (indirect method) for Coastal Travel Services, Inc., for 2017.

E13-14A Calculate cash flows from operating, investing, and financing activities (direct method) *(Learning Objectives 2 & 3)*

Compute the following cash flows for Clear Media Services Company for the past year, assuming the company uses the direct method:

1. The beginning balance of Retained Earnings was $138,000, while the end of the year balance of Retained Earnings was $180,000. Net income for the year was $60,000. No dividends payable were on the balance sheet. How much was paid in cash dividends during the year?
2. The beginning and ending balances of the Common Stock account were $215,000 and $270,000, respectively. Where would the increase in Common Stock appear on the statement of cash flows?
3. The beginning and ending balances of the Treasury Stock account were $53,000 and $80,000, respectively. Where would the increase in Treasury Stock appear on the statement of cash flows?
4. The Property, Plant, & Equipment (net) increased by $13,000 during the year to have a balance of $155,000 at the end of the year. Depreciation for the year was $17,000. Acquisitions of new plant assets paid for with cash during the year totaled $41,000. Plant assets were sold at a loss of $2,000.
   a. What were the cash proceeds from the sale of plant assets?
   b. What amount would be reported on the investing section of the statement of cash flows? Would it be a source of cash or a use of cash?
   c. What amount, if any, would be reported on the operating section of the statement of cash flows?

E13-15A Calculate operating cash flows (indirect method)
(Learning Objective 2)

Ericson Corporation has the following activities for the past year:

Net income.....................................	$?	Cost of goods sold...........................	$ 49,000
Payment of dividends......................	$ 6,000	Other operating expenses................	$ 14,000
Proceeds from issuance of stock......	$ 73,000	Depreciation expense......................	$ 20,000
Purchase of treasury stock...............	$ 13,000	Purchase of equipment with cash.....	$ 26,000
Sales revenue...................................	$124,000	Proceeds from sale of land...............	$ 19,000
Payment of long-term note payable..	$ 13,000	Increase in current assets other than cash........	$ 6,000
Decrease in current liabilities............	$ 9,000		

Requirement

Prepare the operating activities section of Ericson Corporation's statement of cash flows for the year ended December 31, using the indirect method for operating cash flows.

E13-16A Prepare statement of cash flows (indirect method)
(Learning Objective 2)

Using the data given in E13-15A, prepare statement of cash flows for Ericson Corporation for the year. Ericson Corporation uses the indirect method for operating activities.

E13-17A Prepare statement of cash flows (indirect method)
(Learning Objective 2)

Innovations Corporation is preparing its statement of cash flows for the past year. The company has gathered the following information about the past year just ended on December 31.

Retire bond payable (long-term)	$ 17,000	Decrease in accounts receivable	$ 8,000
Paid dividends in cash	$ 30,000	Increase in salaries payable	$ 9,000
Decrease in inventory	$ 10,000	Depreciation expense	$16,000
Decrease in accounts payable	$ 11,000	Increase in prepaid insurance	$ 200
Sold land (investment)	$ 18,000	Decrease in other short-term liabilities	$ 2,000
Increase in interest payable	$ 700	Increase in taxes payable	$ 4,000
Cash balance, beginning of year	$ 90,000	Purchase of new computer system with cash	$17,000
Net income	$ 91,000		

Requirement
Prepare a statement of cash flows for the past year using the indirect method.

E13-18A Compute operating cash flows using direct method
(Learning Objective 3)

Middleton Spas provides the following data for the year just ended on December 31.

Payment of long-term note payable	$ 4,000	Payments to employees	$ 64,000
Depreciation expense	$ 4,400	Proceeds from sale of land	$ 40,500
Purchase of equipment with cash	$ 9,500	Payment of dividends	$ 11,000
Purchase of treasury stock	$ 12,500	Payments to suppliers	$ 65,000
Gain on sale of land	$ 1,000	Increase in salaries payable	$ 12,000
Cost of goods sold	$108,000	Payment of income tax	$ 9,500
Proceeds from issuance of common stock	$ 12,500	Collections from customers	$153,000
Beginning balance, cash	$ 15,000	Sales revenue	$167,000

Requirement
Prepare the operating activities section of Middleton Spas' statement of cash flows for the year just ended, using the direct method for operating cash flows.

E13-19A Prepare statement of cash flows (direct method)
(Learning Objective 3)

Using the data from E13-18A, prepare the statement of cash flows using the direct method.

E13-20A Prepare statement of cash flows (direct method)
(Learning Objective 3)

Shadi Interiors began the year with cash of $55,000. During the year, Shadi Interiors earned service revenue of $404,000. Cash collections for the year were $400,000. Expenses for the year were $365,000, with $350,000 of that total paid in cash. The company also used cash to purchase equipment for $70,000 and to pay a cash dividend to stockholders of $25,000. During the year, the company also borrowed $44,000 cash by issuing a long-term note payable.

Requirement
Prepare the company's statement of cash flows using the direct method.

E13-21A Classify sustainable activities' effect on cash flows
(Learning Objectives 1, 2, & 3)

SUSTAINABILITY

The Plastic Lumber Company, Inc., (PLC) is a manufacturer that takes in post-consumer plastics (i.e., empty milk jugs) and recycles those plastics into a "plastic lumber" that can be used to build furniture, decking, and a variety of other items. Because Plastic Lumber has a strong focus on sustainability, the company managers try, whenever possible, to use recycled materials and to invest in sustainable projects.

Last year, the company engaged in several sustainable practices that have an impact on its cash flows. For each of the transactions listed below, indicate whether the transaction would have affected the operating, investing, or financing cash flows of the company. Additionally, indicate whether each transaction would have increased (+) or decreased (−) cash.

Transactions:

1. New production equipment that is 60% more energy efficient than the old equipment was purchased for cash.
2. When the plastic wood is cut into lengths needed to build park benches, the end pieces cut off are scrap. PLC sold this cutting scrap to another recycler.
3. Engineers at PLC performed research into a new process that injects tiny air bubbles into the plastic to reduce the usage of raw materials (plastics) and to reduce the weight of the finished products.
4. Throughout the year, PLC participated in several trade shows that featured green products for use by parks and recreation facilities. For each trade show, PLC incurred cash expenses for transportation, registration, meals and lodging, and booth setup.
5. A Toyota Prius hybrid automobile was purchased for use by the CEO of PLC. PLC paid cash.
6. PLC issues long-term bonds during the year to help finance growth.
7. PLC became a minority partner in a solar-panel electricity generation project by investing $1 million in cash in the project.
8. A fleet of plug-in electric cars was purchased for sales staff. PLC paid cash.
9. A wind-turbine was built to power part of PLC's operations. PLC paid cash.
10. PLC installed a "living roof" on its manufacturing facility. This roof is made mostly from sedum runoff and doubles the expected life of the roof over that of a conventional roof. The plants also reduce heating and cooling needs by providing an extra layer of insulation. Additionally, the plants absorb carbon dioxide to help reduce greenhouse gases. The living roof was paid for with cash.

EXERCISES Group B

E13-22B Prepare operating cash flows section (indirect method)
(Learning Objective 2)

The comparative balance sheet for Seaway Travel Services, Inc., for December 31, 2017 and 2016, is as follows:

		2017	2016
	Seaway Travel Services, Inc.		
	Comparative Balance Sheets		
	December 31, 2017 and 2016		
	Assets		
	Current assets:		
	Cash	$ 45,000	$ 12,000
	Accounts receivable	75,000	81,000
	Inventory	59,000	19,000
	Prepaid insurance	14,000	17,000
	Total current assets	$ 193,000	$ 129,000
	Land	$ 101,000	$ 117,000
	Equipment	76,000	56,000
	Less: Accumulated depreciation	(19,000)	(14,000)
	Total assets	$ 351,000	$ 288,000
	Liabilities		
	Current liabilities:		
	Accounts payable	$ 25,000	$ 32,000
	Wages payable	32,000	21,000
	Interest payable	14,000	12,000
	Income taxes payable	12,000	10,000
	Total current liabilities	$ 83,000	$ 75,000
	Notes payable (long term)	98,000	88,000
	Total liabilities	$ 181,000	$ 163,000
	Stockholders' equity		
	Common stock	$ 125,000	$ 115,000
	Retained earnings	45,000	10,000
	Total stockholders' equity	$ 170,000	$ 125,000
	Total liabilities and equity	$ 351,000	$ 288,000

The following information is taken from the records of Seaway Travel Services, Inc.:

a. Land was sold for $13,000.
b. Equipment was purchased for cash.
c. There were no disposals of equipment during the year.
d. The common stock was issued for cash.
e. Net income for 2017 was $40,000.
f. Cash dividends paid during the year were $5,000.

Seaway Travel Services, Inc., uses the indirect method for preparing the statement of cash flows. Prepare the operating section of the statement of cash flows for 2017.

E13-23B Prepare statement of cash flows (indirect method) *(Learning Objective 2)*

Using the data given in E13-22B, prepare the statement of cash flows (indirect method) for Seaway Travel Services, Inc., for 2017.

E13-24B Calculate cash flows from operating, investing, and financing activities (direct method) *(Learning Objectives 2 & 3)*

Compute the following cash flows for High Seas Nautical Company for the past year, assuming the company uses the direct method:

1. The beginning balance of Retained Earning was $137,000, while the end of the year balance of Retained Earnings was $175,000. Net income for the year was $61,000. No dividends payable were on the balance sheet. How much was paid in cash dividends during the year?

2. The beginning and ending balances of the Common Stock account were $212,000 and $274,000, respectively. Where would the increase in Common Stock appear on the statement of cash flows?
3. The beginning and ending balances of the Treasury Stock account were $57,000 and $75,000, respectively. Where would the increase in Treasury Stock appear on the statement of cash flows?
4. Property, Plant, and Equipment (net) increased by $11,000 during the year to have a balance of $152,000 at the end of the year. Depreciation for the year was $17,000. Acquisitions of new plant assets paid for with cash during the year totaled $37,000. Plant assets were sold at a loss of $3,000.
   a. What were the cash proceeds from the sale of plant assets?
   b. What amount would be reported on the investing section of the statement of cash flows? Would it be a source of cash or a use of cash?
   c. What amount would be reported on the operating section of the statement of cash flows? How would it be presented?

E13-25B Calculate operating cash flows (indirect method) *(Learning Objective 2)*

Thompson Corporation has the following activities for the past year:

Net income..	$?	Cost of goods sold............................	$53,000
Payment of dividends.........................	$ 8,000	Other operating expenses.................	$13,000
Proceeds from issuance of stock........	$ 79,000	Depreciation expense.......................	$22,000
Purchase of treasury stock.................	$ 16,000	Purchase of equipment with cash.....	$28,000
Sales revenue.....................................	$118,000	Proceeds from sale of land...............	$23,000
Payment of long-term note payable...	$ 11,000	Increase in current assets other than cash........	$ 7,000
Decrease in current liabilities..............	$ 6,000		

Requirement

Prepare the operating activities section of Thompson Corporation's statement of cash flows for the year ended December 31, using the indirect method for operating cash flows.

E13-26B Prepare statement of cash flows (indirect method)
(Learning Objective 2)

Using the data given in E13-25B, prepare the statement of cash flows for Thompson Corporation for the year. The company uses the indirect method for operating activities.

E13-27B Prepare statement of cash flows (indirect method)
(Learning Objective 2)

The Dragon Corporation is preparing its statement of cash flows for the past year just ended on December 31. The controller has gathered the following information about the past year.

Retire bond payable (long-term)........	$12,000	Decrease in accounts receivable........	$ 8,000
Paid dividends in cash........................	$33,000	Increase in salaries payable...............	$ 6,000
Decrease in inventory.........................	$10,000	Depreciation expense........................	$14,000
Decrease in accounts payable............	$12,000	Increase in prepaid insurance............	$ 700
Sold land (investment)........................	$23,000	Decrease in other short-term liabilities..	$ 1,000
Increase in interest payable...............	$ 400	Increase in taxes payable...................	$ 2,000
Cash balance, beginning of year........	$91,000	Purchase of new computer system with cash....	$ 9,000
Net income...	$89,000		

Requirement

Prepare a statement of cash flows for the past year using the indirect method.

E13-28B Compute operating cash flows using the direct method
(Learning Objective 3)

Comfort Spas provides the following data for the year just ended December 31.

Payment of long-term note payable	$ 4,500	Payments to employees	$ 63,000
Depreciation expense	$ 4,800	Proceeds from sale of land	$ 41,000
Purchase of equipment with cash	$ 7,500	Payment of dividends	$ 14,000
Purchase of treasury stock	$ 11,500	Payments to suppliers	$ 62,000
Gain on sale of land	$ 1,100	Increase in salaries payable	$ 13,000
Cost of goods sold	$113,000	Payment of income tax	$ 9,000
Proceeds from issuance of common stock	$ 14,500	Collections from customers	$151,000
Beginning balance, cash	$ 14,500	Sales revenue	$169,000

Requirement
Prepare the operating activities section of Comfort Spas' statement of cash flows for the year ended December 31 using the direct method for operating cash flows.

E13-29B Prepare statement of cash flows (direct method) *(Learning Objective 3)*
Using the data for E13-28B, prepare the statement of cash flows using the direct method.

E13-30B Prepare statement of cash flows (direct method) *(Learning Objective 3)*
Shabnam Interiors began the year with cash of $55,000. During the year, Shabnam Interiors earned service revenue of $406,000. Cash collections for the year were $405,000. Expenses for the year were $375,000, with $360,000 of that total paid in cash. The company also used cash to purchase equipment for $85,000 and to pay a cash dividend to stockholders of $24,000. During the year, the company borrowed $58,000 cash by issuing a long-term note payable.

Requirement
Prepare the company's statement of cash flows using the direct method.

E13-31B Classify sustainable activities' effect on cash flows
(Learning Objectives 1, 2, & 3)

SUSTAINABILITY

The Plastic Lumber Company, Inc. (PLC) is a manufacturer that takes in post-consumer plastics (i.e., empty milk jugs) and recycles those plastics into a "plastic lumber" that can be used to build furniture, decking, and a variety of other items. Because Plastic Lumber has a strong focus on sustainability, the company managers try, whenever possible, to use recycled materials and to invest in sustainable projects.

Last year, the company engaged in several sustainable practices that have an impact on its cash flows. For each of the transactions listed below, indicate whether the transaction would have affected the operating, investing, or financing cash flows of the company. Additionally, indicate whether each transaction would have increased (+) or decreased (−) cash.

Transactions:
1. PLC became a minority partner in a wind-turbine project by investing $2 million in cash in the project.
2. A new delivery truck that uses biofuel was purchased for cash.
3. PLC built a new building for its manufacturing facility. The new building is LEED certified and was paid for with cash.
4. PLC sold plastic scrap generated by its manufacturing process.
5. Engineers and scientists at PLC performed research into whether another kind of post-consumer plastic not currently used in its plastics extrusion process could be used.
6. Throughout the year, PLC participated in several trade shows that featured green products for use by parks and recreation facilities. For each trade show, PLC incurred cash expenses for transportation, registration, meals and lodging, and booth setup.

7. Solar panels were installed on PLC's administrative offices to supply part of the electricity needed for its operations. PLC paid cash.
8. Six Toyota Prius Hybrid automobiles were purchased for the use of the sales staff. PLC paid cash.
9. PLC issued common stock during the year to help finance growth.
10. New production equipment that is 75% more energy efficient than the old equipment was purchased for cash.

PROBLEMS Group A

P13-32A Prepare statement of cash flows (indirect method)
(Learning Objective 2)

Prepare a statement of cash flows using the indirect method. The income statement for 2017 and the balance sheets for 2017 and 2016 are presented for Harding Industries, Inc.

A	B	C
Harding Industries, Inc.		
Income Statement		
For the Year Ended December 31, 2017		
Sales revenues		$ 956,000
Less: Cost of goods sold		381,000
Gross profit		$ 575,000
Less operating expenses:		
Salaries and wages expense	$ 190,000	
Insurance expense	10,500	
Depreciation expense	52,000	
Other operating expenses	84,000	
Total operating expenses		336,500
Operating income		$ 238,500
Plus other income and less other expenses:		
Interest expense	$ 5,800	
Gain on sale of PP&E	4,000	
Total other income and expenses		1,800
Income before income taxes		$ 236,700
Less: Income tax expense		71,010
Net income		$ 165,690

	A	B	C
1	**Harding Industries, Inc.**		
2	**Comparative Balance Sheets**		
3	**December 31, 2017 and 2016**		
4	Assets	2017	2016
5	Current assets:		
6	Cash	$ 474,000	$ 286,000
7	Accounts receivable	71,000	125,000
8	Inventory	329,000	216,000
9	Prepaid insurance	8,500	5,500
10	Total current assets	$ 882,500	$ 632,500
11			
12	Property, plant, and equipment	$ 625,000	$ 595,000
13	Less: Accumulated depreciation	(152,000)	(110,000)
14	Investments	87,000	75,000
15	Total assets	$ 1,442,500	$ 1,192,500
16			
17	Liabilities		
18	Current liabilities:		
19	Accounts payable (inventory purchases)	$ 59,000	$ 32,000
20	Wages payable	16,300	17,300
21	Interest payable	1,500	700
22	Income taxes payable	62,010	13,000
23	Other accrued expenses payable	6,500	3,200
24	Total current liabilities	$ 145,310	$ 66,200
25			
26	Long-term liabilities	68,000	26,000
27	Total liabilities	$ 213,310	$ 92,200
28			
29	Stockholders' equity		
30	Common stock	$ 602,000	$ 602,000
31	Retained earnings	627,190	498,300
32	Total stockholders' equity	$ 1,229,190	$ 1,100,300
33			
34	Total liabilities and equity	$ 1,442,500	$ 1,192,500
35			

Additional information follows:

a. Sold plant asset for $4,300. The original cost of this plant asset was $10,300 and it had $10,000 of accumulated depreciation associated with it.
b. Paid $6,500 on the bonds payable; issued $48,500 of new bonds payable.
c. Declared and paid cash dividends of $36,800.
d. Purchased new investment for $12,000. Paid cash.
e. Purchased new equipment for $40,300. Paid cash.

Requirement

Prepare a statement of cash flows for Harding Industries, Inc., for the year ended December 31, 2017, using the indirect method.

P13-33A Prepare statement of cash flows (indirect method)
(Learning Objectives 1 & 2)

The 2017 and 2016 balance sheets of Rabb Corporation follow. The 2017 income statement is also provided. Rabb had no noncash investing and financing transactions during 2017. During the year, the company sold equipment for $15,100, which had originally cost $13,500 and had a book value of $10,500. The company did not issue any notes payable during the year but did issue common stock for $31,000. The company purchased plant assets and long-term investments with cash.

Rabb Corporation
Income Statement
For the Year Ended December 31, 2017

Sales revenues		$ 347,000
Less: Cost of goods sold		76,000
Gross profit		$ 271,000
Less operating expenses:		
Salaries and wages expense	$ 24,500	
Depreciation expense	5,900	
Other operating expenses	13,000	
Total operating expenses		$ 43,400
Operating income		$ 227,600
Plus other income and less other expenses:		
Interest expense	$ 9,900	
Gain on sale of PP&E	4,600	
Total other income and expenses		5,300
Income before income taxes		$ 222,300
Less: Income tax expense		37,000
Net income		$ 185,300

Rabb Corporation
Comparative Balance Sheets
December 31, 2017 and 2016

Assets	2017	2016
Current assets:		
Cash	$ 51,500	$ 20,500
Accounts receivable	32,300	29,100
Inventory	86,500	93,000
Prepaid insurance	3,300	2,600
Total current assets	$ 173,600	$ 145,200
Property, plant, and equipment	152,000	138,000
Less: Accumulated depreciation	(30,300)	(27,400)
Investments	117,000	0
Total assets	$ 412,300	$ 255,800
Liabilities		
Current liabilities:		
Accounts payable	$ 33,900	$ 36,500
Wages payable	2,900	7,300
Interest payable	2,100	0
Income taxes payable	5,400	0
Other accrued expenses payable	18,500	22,500
Total current liabilities	$ 62,800	$ 66,300
Long-term liabilities	76,000	110,000
Total liabilities	$ 138,800	$ 176,300
Stockholders' equity		
Common stock	102,000	71,000
Retained earnings	171,500	8,500
Total stockholders' equity	$ 273,500	$ 79,500
Total liabilities and equity	$ 412,300	$ 255,800

Requirements

1. Prepare the statement of cash flows for Rabb Corporation for 2017 using the indirect method.
2. Evaluate the company's cash flows for the year. Discuss each of the categories of cash flows in your response.

P13-34A Prepare a statement of cash flows (direct method)
(Learning Objectives 1 & 3)

Williams Digital Services, Inc., has provided the following data from the company's records for the year just ended December 31:

a. Collection of interest	$ 5,200
b. Cash sales	$252,500
c. Credit sales	$673,500
d. Proceeds from sale of long-term investment	$ 12,300
e. Gain on sale of investment	$ 2,100
f. Payments to suppliers	$570,000
g. Cash payments to purchase plant assets	$ 52,400
h. Depreciation expense	$ 63,200
i. Salaries expense	$ 77,100
j. Payment of short-term note payable by issuing common stock	$ 71,700
k. Cost of goods sold	$567,000
l. Proceeds from issuance of long-term note payable	$ 24,900
m. Income tax expense and payment	$ 38,000
n. Proceeds from issuance of common stock	$ 21,500
o. Receipt of cash dividends	$ 6,600
p. Interest revenue	$ 6,100
q. Payment of cash dividends	$ 28,200
r. Collections of accounts receivable	$572,000
s. Amortization expense	$ 3,700
t. Payments on long-term notes payable	$ 44,500
u. Interest expense and payments	$ 12,400
v. Purchase of equipment by issuing common stock to seller	$ 17,900
w. Payment of salaries	$ 74,400
x. Proceeds from sale of plant assets	$ 24,700
y. Loss on sale of plant assets	$ 3,800
z. Cash and cash equivalents balance, beginning of year	$ 25,500

Requirements

1. Prepare the statement of cash flows for Williams Digital Services, Inc., using the direct method for cash flows from operations. Note that you will need to calculate the ending balance of cash and cash equivalents. Include a schedule of noncash investing and financing activities.
2. Evaluate Williams' cash flows for the year. Discuss each of the categories of cash flows in your response.

P13-35A Prepare statements of cash flows (indirect and direct method)
(Learning Objectives 1, 2, & 3)

Marshall Sign Company, Inc., has the following comparative balance sheet as of March 31, 2017.

Marshall Sign Company, Inc.
Comparative Balance Sheets
March 31, 2017 and 2016

Assets	2017	2016	Increase (Decrease)
Current assets:			
Cash	$ 55,900	$ 14,200	41,700
Accounts receivable	51,600	53,200	(1,600)
Inventory	65,100	60,100	5,000
Prepaid insurance	4,100	5,500	(1,400)
Total current assets	$ 176,700	$ 133,000	
Land	35,500	97,500	(62,000)
Equipment, net	71,600	70,300	1,300
Investments	10,100	6,900	3,200
Total assets	$ 293,900	$ 307,700	
Liabilities			
Current liabilities:			
Accounts payable	$ 4,700	$ 3,500	1,200
Note payable, short-term	43,200	48,000	(4,800)
Income tax payable	13,900	15,600	(1,700)
Salary payable	9,400	12,200	(2,800)
Interest payable	8,400	7,400	1,000
Accrued liabilities	1,900	3,300	(1,400)
Total current liabilities	$ 81,500	$ 90,000	
Long-term liabilities	49,000	93,400	(44,400)
Total liabilities	$ 130,500	$ 183,400	
Stockholders' equity			
Common stock	69,000	61,600	7,400
Retained earnings	94,400	62,700	31,700
Total stockholders' equity	$ 163,400	$ 124,300	
Total liabilities and equity	$ 293,900	$ 307,700	

Selected transaction data for the year ended March 31, 2017, include the following:

a. Net income .... $ 77,100
b. Paid long-term note payable with cash .... $ 59,500
c. Cash payments to employees .... $ 41,800
d. Loss on sale of land .... $ 9,900
e. Acquired equipment by issuing long-term note payable .... $ 15,100
f. Cash payments to suppliers $145,700
g. Cash paid for interest .... $ 3,200
h. Depreciation expense on equipment .... $ 13,800
i. Paid short-term note payable by issuing common stock .... $ 4,800
j. Paid cash dividends .... $ 45,400
k. Received cash for issuance of common stock .... $ 2,600
l. Cash received from customers $296,100
m. Cash paid for income taxes .... $ 12,200
n. Sold land for cash .... $ 52,100
o. Interest received (in cash) .... $ 1,900
p. Purchased long-term investment for cash .... $ 3,200

Requirements

1. Prepare the statement of cash flows for Marshall Sign Company, Inc., for the year ended March 31, 2017, using the indirect method for operating cash flows. Include a schedule of noncash investing and financing activities. All of the current accounts, except short-term notes payable, result from operating transactions.
2. Also prepare a schedule of cash flows from operations using the *direct* method.

PROBLEMS Group B

P13-36B Prepare statement of cash flows (indirect method)
(Learning Objective 2)

Prepare the statement of cash flows using the indirect method. The income statement for 2017 and the balance sheets for 2017 and 2016 are presented for Hall Industries.

	A	B	C
1	Hall Industries, Inc.		
2	Income Statement		
3	For the Year Ended December 31, 2017		
4			
5	Sales revenues		$ 953,000
6	Less: Cost of goods sold		377,000
7	Gross profit		$ 576,000
8	Less operating expenses:		
9	Salaries and wages expense	$ 187,000	
10	Insurance expense	12,000	
11	Depreciation expense	46,700	
12	Other operating expenses	84,000	
13	Total operating expenses		329,700
14	Operating income		$ 246,300
15	Plus other income and less other expenses:		
16	Interest expense	5,400	
17	Gain on sale of PP&E	3,500	
18	Total other income and expenses		1,900
19	Income before income taxes		$ 244,400
20	Less: Income tax expense		73,320
21	Net income		$ 171,080
22			

	A	B	C
1	**Hall Industries, Inc.**		
2	**Comparative Balance Sheets**		
3	**December 31, 2017 and 2016**		
4	**Assets**	**2017**	**2016**
5	Current assets:		
6	Cash	$ 477,000	$ 291,000
7	Accounts receivable	71,000	122,000
8	Inventory	334,000	213,000
9	Prepaid insurance	6,500	5,000
10	Total current assets	$ 888,500	$ 631,000
11			
12	Property, plant, and equipment	600,000	590,000
13	Less: Accumulated depreciation	(150,000)	(113,000)
14	Investments	91,000	78,000
15	Total assets	$ 1,429,500	$ 1,186,000
16			
17	**Liabilities**		
18	Current liabilities:		
19	Accounts payable (inventory purchases)	$ 54,000	$ 40,000
20	Wages payable	16,100	17,800
21	Interest payable	1,800	500
22	Income taxes payable	64,320	10,500
23	Other accrued expenses payable	6,100	3,000
24	Total current liabilities	$ 142,320	$ 71,800
25			
26	Long-term liabilities	60,000	25,000
27	Total liabilities	$ 202,320	$ 96,800
28			
29	**Stockholders' equity**		
30	Common stock	601,000	601,000
31	Retained earnings	626,180	488,200
32	Total stockholders' equity	$ 1,227,180	$ 1,089,200
33			
34	Total liabilities and equity	$ 1,429,500	$ 1,186,000
35			

Additional information follows:

a. Sold plant asset for $4,200. The original cost of this plant asset was $10,400 and it had $9,700 of accumulated depreciation associated with it.
b. Paid $4,500 on the bonds payable; issued $39,500 of new bonds payable.
c. Declared and paid cash dividends of $33,100.
d. Purchased new investment for $13,000. Paid cash.
e. Purchased new equipment for $20,400. Paid cash.

Requirement

Prepare a statement of cash flows for Hall Industries, Inc., for the year ended December 31, 2017, using the indirect method.

P13-37B Prepare statement of cash flows (indirect method)
(Learning Objectives 1 & 2)

The 2017 and 2016 balance sheets of Gibson Corporation follow. The 2017 income statement is also provided. Gibson had no noncash investing and financing transactions during 2017. During the year, the company sold equipment for $15,200, which had originally cost $12,800 and had a book value of $11,300. The company did not issue any notes payable during the year but did issue common stock for $31,000. The company purchased plant assets and long-term investments with cash.

Gibson Corporation
Income Statement
For the Year Ended December 31, 2017

Sales revenues		$ 344,000
Less: Cost of goods sold		77,000
Gross profit		$ 267,000
Less operating expenses:		
Salaries and wages expense	$ 25,000	
Depreciation expense	4,700	
Other operating expenses	13,000	
Total operating expenses		42,700
Operating income		$ 224,300
Plus other income and less other expenses:		
Interest expense	9,300	
Gain on sale of PP&E	3,900	
Total other income and expenses		5,400
Income before income taxes		$ 218,900
Less: Income tax expense		36,500
Net income		$ 182,400

Gibson Corporation
Comparative Balance Sheets
December 31, 2017 and 2016

Assets	2017	2016
Current assets:		
Cash	$ 48,500	$ 20,500
Accounts receivable	32,300	29,900
Inventory	86,500	93,000
Prepaid insurance	3,000	2,500
Total current assets	$ 170,300	$ 145,900
Property, plant, and equipment	151,000	134,000
Less: Accumulated depreciation	(30,600)	(27,400)
Investments	110,000	0
Total assets	$ 400,700	$ 252,500
Liabilities		
Current liabilities:		
Accounts payable	$ 33,400	$ 36,700
Wages payable	2,700	7,600
Interest payable	2,800	0
Income taxes payable	5,500	0
Other accrued expenses payable	18,700	22,600
Total current liabilities	$ 63,100	$ 66,900
Long-term liabilities	76,000	112,000
Total liabilities	$ 139,100	$ 178,900
Stockholders' equity		
Common stock	102,000	71,000
Retained earnings	159,600	2,600
Total stockholders' equity	$ 261,600	$ 73,600
Total liabilities and equity	$ 400,700	$ 252,500

Requirements

1. Prepare the statement of cash flows for Gibson Corporation for 2017 using the indirect method.
2. Evaluate the company's cash flows for the year. Discuss each of the categories of cash flows in your response.

P13-38B Prepare a statement of cash flows (direct method)
(Learning Objectives 1 & 3)

Huggins Digital Services, Inc., has provided the following data from the company's records for the year just ended December 31:

a. Collection of interest	$ 5,700
b. Cash sales	$251,000
c. Credit sales	$677,500
d. Proceeds from sale of long-term investment	$ 12,400
e. Gain on sale of investment	$ 2,900
f. Payments to suppliers	$572,500
g. Cash payments to purchase plant assets	$ 52,500
h. Depreciation expense	$ 63,700
i. Salaries expense	$ 77,200
j. Payment of short-term note payable by issuing common stock	$ 71,800
k. Cost of goods sold	$565,500
l. Proceeds from issuance of long-term note payable	$ 24,900
m. Income tax expense and payment	$ 38,400
n. Proceeds from issuance of common stock	$ 22,000
o. Cash receipt of dividend revenue	$ 6,800
p. Interest revenue	$ 5,800
q. Payment of cash dividends	$ 28,100
r. Collections of accounts receivable	$572,000
s. Amortization expense	$ 3,300
t. Payments on long-term notes payable	$ 43,500
u. Interest expense and payments	$ 12,900
v. Purchase of equipment by issuing common stock to seller	$ 17,200
w. Payment of salaries	$ 74,200
x. Proceeds from sale of plant assets	$ 24,400
y. Loss on sale of plant assets	$ 3,500
z. Cash and cash equivalents balance, beginning of year	$ 25,100

Requirements

1. Prepare the statement of cash flows for Huggins Digital Services, Inc., using the direct method for cash flows from operations. Note that you will need to calculate the ending balance of cash and cash equivalents. Include a schedule of noncash investing and financing activities.
2. Evaluate the company's cash flows for the year. Discuss each of the categories of cash flows in your response.

P13-39B Prepare statements of cash flows (indirect and direct method)
(Learning Objectives 1, 2, & 3)

Graphic Company, Inc., has the following comparative balance sheet as of March 31, 2017.

Graphic Company, Inc.
Comparative Balance Sheets
March 31, 2017 and 2016

Assets	2017	2016	Increase (Decrease)
Current assets:			
Cash	$ 55,400	$ 14,900	40,500
Accounts receivable	51,600	53,300	(1,700)
Inventory	64,900	59,800	5,100
Prepaid insurance	4,100	5,300	(1,200)
Total current assets	$ 176,000	$ 133,300	
Land	34,000	95,500	(61,500)
Equipment, net	71,500	70,400	1,100
Investments	9,800	6,900	2,900
Total assets	$ 291,300	$ 306,100	
Liabilities			
Current liabilities:			
Accounts payable	$ 4,900	$ 3,500	1,400
Note payable, short-term	43,200	48,500	(5,300)
Income tax payable	13,800	15,100	(1,300)
Salary payable	9,400	12,400	(3,000)
Interest payable	8,200	7,000	1,200
Accrued liabilities	2,600	3,700	(1,100)
Total current liabilities	$ 82,100	$ 90,200	
Long-term liabilities	48,300	93,700	(45,400)
Total liabilities	$ 130,400	$ 183,900	
Stockholders' equity			
Common stock	69,400	61,900	7,500
Retained earnings	91,500	60,300	31,200
Total stockholders' equity	$ 160,900	$ 122,200	
Total liabilities and equity	$ 291,300	$ 306,100	

Selected transaction data for the year ended March 31, 2017, include the following:

a. Net income, $76,800
b. Paid long-term note payable with cash, $59,600
c. Cash payments to employees, $42,700
d. Loss on sale of land, $9,200
e. Acquired equipment by issuing long-term note payable, $14,200
f. Cash payments to suppliers, $145,600
g. Cash paid for interest, $3,000
h. Depreciation expense on equipment, $13,100
i. Paid short-term note payable by issuing common stock, $5,300
j. Paid cash dividends, $45,600
k. Received cash for issuance of common stock, $2,200
l. Cash received from customers, $295,200
m. Cash paid for income taxes, $11,600
n. Sold land for cash, $52,300
o. Interest received (in cash), $1,800
p. Purchased long-term investment for cash, $2,900

Requirements

1. Prepare the statement of cash flows for Graphic Company, Inc., for the year ended March 31, 2017, using the indirect method for operating cash flows. Include a schedule of noncash investing and financing activities. All of the current accounts except short-term notes payable result from operating transactions.
2. Also prepare a schedule of cash flows from operations using the *direct* method.

Serial Case

C13-40 Analyze a statement of cash flows *(Learning Objective 1)*

This case is a continuation of the Caesars Entertainment Corporation serial case that began in Chapter 1. Refer to the introductory story in Chapter 1 (see page 43) for additional background. (The components of the Caesars serial case can be completed in any order.)

Following are the consolidated statements of cash flows for Caesars Entertainment Corporation for the years ended December 31, 2012 through 2014.[5]

Caesars Entertainment Corporation
Consolidated Statements of Cash Flows (condensed and adapted)
in millions

	Year Ended December 31,		
	2014	2013	2012
Cash flows from operating activities			
Net loss	$ (2,866)	$ (2,940)	$ (1,503)
Adjustments to reconcile cash flows	2,131	2,841	1,536
Cash flows from operating activities	(735)	(99)	33
Cash flows from investing activities			
Acquisitions of property and equipment	(998)	(726)	(507)
Other investing activities	309	791	(718)
Cash flows from investing activities	(689)	65	(1,225)
Cash flows from financing activities			
Proceeds from inssuance of long-term debt	4,436	6,039	4,162
Repayments of long-term debt	(2,833)	(6,605)	(2,661)
Other financing activities	(89)	1,217	(28)
Cash flows from financing activities	1,514	651	1,473
Net cash flows from operating, investing, and financing	90	617	281
Other adjustments to cash	(55)	396	586
Net increase (decrease) in cash and cash equivalents	35	1,013	867
Cash and cash equivalents, beginning of period	2,771	1,758	891
Cash and cash equivalents, end of period	$ 2,806	$ 2,771	$ 1,758

Questions

1. Looking at the statements of cash flows above, which activity has generated the most cash for Caesars?
2. Now switch to thinking about Caesars's renovation of its hotel tower in Caesars Palace® Las Vegas. How would the renovation expenditures be reported in the statement of cash flows?
3. After completion, how should the interest, on the renovation cost, be reported on the statement of cash flows?

---

[5]All statements have been condensed and adapted for educational purposes.

CRITICAL THINKING

Discussion & Analysis

A13-41 Discussion Questions

1. How do managers use the statement of cash flows?
2. Describe at least four needs for cash within a business.
3. Define an "operating activity." List two examples of an operating activity on the statement of cash flows that would *increase* cash. List two examples of an operating activity that would *decrease* cash.
4. Define an "investing activity." List two examples of an investing activity on the statement of cash flows that would *increase* cash. List two examples of an investing activity that would *decrease* cash.
5. Define a "financing activity." List two examples of a financing activity on the statement of cash flows that would *increase* cash. List two examples of a financing activity that would *decrease* cash.
6. Define a "noncash investing or financing" activity. Describe an activity that would need to be disclosed as a noncash investing or financing activity.
7. Describe the difference between the direct and the indirect methods of preparing the operating section of the statement of cash flows.
8. Describe the process for reconciling net income to the cash basis. What items are added to net income? What items are subtracted from net income?
9. When preparing a statement of cash flows using the indirect method, what information is needed? What documents or statements would be used?
10. Summarize the process for preparing the operating section of the statement of cash flows when using the direct method.
11. Provide an example of an operating cash inflow that could result from sustainability activities. Also provide an example of an operating cash outflow that would support sustainability.
12. Think of a company with which you are familiar. Describe an investing activity related to a company's sustainability efforts that would be classified as a use of cash on a company's statement of cash flows. Describe a financing activity related to a company's sustainability efforts that would be classified as a use of cash on a company's statement of cash flows.

Application & Analysis
Mini Cases

A13-42 Cash Flow Statements from Companies in the Same Industry

Select an industry in which you are interested and select two companies within that industry. Obtain their annual reports by going to each company's website and downloading the report for the most recent year. (On many company websites, you will need to visit the Investor Relations section or other similarly named link to obtain the company's financial statements.)

Basic Discussion Questions

For each of the companies you selected, answer the following:

1. Which method is used to calculate the cash provided or used by operations?
2. What items increased cash provided by operations?
3. What items decreased cash provided by operations?
4. Overall, was cash increased or decreased by operating activities?

5. Did investing activities in total increase cash or decrease cash during the year? What were the major uses or sources of cash related to investing?

6. Did financing activities in total increase cash or decrease cash during the year? What were the major uses or sources of cash related to financing?

7. What items (if any) are disclosed as significant noncash financing or investing activities? Now that you have looked at each company's cash flow statements individually, compare the two companies. What can you tell about each company from its statement of cash flows? Can you tell if one company is stronger than the other from their statements of cash flows? What clues do you have?

ETHICS

A13-43 Ethics involved with statement of cash flows preparation
(Learning Objectives 1, 2, & 3)

The Green Giraffe Restaurant Group has 21 restaurants scattered across the midwestern portion of the United States. Green Giraffe is not publicly held but is owned by a small group of investors.

For years, the company has used the indirect method in preparing its statement of cash flows. Recently, it has come to the attention of a few of the investors that the statement of cash flows might be easier to understand and use if it were prepared using the direct method. At the quarterly meeting of the investors, they decide that the statement of cash flows for the Green Giraffe Restaurant Group should be prepared using the direct method.

Christopher Wargo is the controller for the Green Giraffe Restaurant Group. He graduated from college several years ago. He vaguely recalls learning about the direct method for preparing the statement of cash flows in college but has never used the method. Wargo is rather resentful that the investors are dictating accounting policy; he feels that the financial reporting that is currently done is adequate. Besides, even if the company reports using the direct method, a supplemental schedule of the indirect method will still need to be prepared. This change just seems to create extra work for Wargo.

Wargo decides he'll just do his best in preparing the statement using the direct method. He looks online and finds the Wikipedia page for the statement of cash flows and uses that model to prepare the statement. The company's information system is not set up to collect data for the direct method at this time. The data can be obtained, but it will take several days. Wargo decides to just estimate the numbers that he's missing rather than spend the time to get the correct numbers. He feels it is unlikely that the auditors will find these few numbers that he has plugged; after all, the totals will be correct. This shortcut he is taking will save him hours of work.

Requirements

1. Using the IMA *Statement of Ethical Professional Practice* as an ethical framework, answer the following questions:
    a. What is(are) the ethical issue(s) in this situation?
    b. What are Wargo's responsibilities as a management accountant?

2. Discuss what Wargo should do in this situation. Refer to the IMA *Statement of Ethical Professional Practice* in your response.

A13-44 Analyzing statements of cash flows (Learning Objectives 1, 2, & 3)

Sears Holding Corporation (SHLD) announced in April 2016 that it would be closing 68 Kmart and 10 Sears stores during the second half of 2016. The stores it is closing have not been profitable for Sears, and it is looking to improve profitability with the closures.

Similarly, Wal-Mart Stores, Inc. (WMT) announced in January 2016 that it would be closing 269 stores worldwide. Again, this move is an effort to increase profitability for Wal-Mart.

Sears' fiscal year-end is the Saturday closest to January 31. Following are its statement of cash flows for the most recent three years.

Sears Holding Corporation
Statements of Cash Flows
(in millions)

	Year Ended		
	Jan. 30, 2016	Jan. 31, 2015	Feb. 1, 2014
Operating activities:			
Net income (loss)	$(1,128)	$(1,810)	$(1,116)
Adjustments to convert to cash basis	(1,039)	423	7
Net cash used by operations	(2,167)	(1,387)	(1,109)
Investing activities:			
Sales of property and investments	2,730	424	995
Purchases of PP&E	(211)	(270)	(329)
Other investing activities	-	173	(2)
Net cash provided by investing	2,519	327	664
Financing activities:			
Proceeds from issuance of debt	-	1,025	994
Repayments of debt	(1,405)	(80)	(83)
Other increases (decreases) in debt	1,091	(1,117)	238
Dividends paid for Sears Canada	(50)	(27)	(14)
Other financing activities	-	484	(233)
Net cash provided (used) by financing	(364)	285	902
Effect of exchange rates	-	(3)	(38)
Net change in cash	(12)	(778)	419
Cash, beginning of year	250	1,028	609
Cash, end of year	$238	$250	$1,028

Wal-Mart's fiscal year-end is January 31. To follow are its statements of cash flows for the most recent three years.

Wal-Mart Stores, Inc.
Statements of Cash Flows
(in millions)

	Fiscal Years Ended		
	Jan. 31, 2016	Jan. 31, 2015	Jan. 31, 2014
Operating activities:			
Net income (loss)	$15,080	$17,099	$16,695
Adjustments to convert to cash basis	12,309	11,465	6,562
Net cash provided by operations	27,389	28,564	23,257
Investing activities:			
Purchases of PP&E	(11,477)	(12,174)	(13,115)
Proceeds from disposal of PP&E	635	570	727
Proceeds from disposal of some ops	246	671	-
Other investing activities	(79)	(192)	(138)
Net cash used by investing	(10,675)	(11,125)	(12,526)
Financing activities:			
Net change in borrowings	1,235	(6,288)	911
Proceeds from issuance of debt	39	5,174	7,072
Repayments of long-term debt	(4,432)	(3,904)	(4,968)
Dividends paid	(6,294)	(6,185)	(6,139)
Purchase of company stock	(4,112)	(1,015)	(6,683)
Other financing activities	(2,558)	(2,853)	(982)
Net cash provided (used) by financing	(16,122)	(15,071)	(10,789)
Effect of exchange rates	(1,022)	(514)	(442)
Net change in cash	(430)	1,854	(500)
Cash, beginning of year	9,135	7,281	7,781
Cash, end of year	$8,705	$9,135	$7,281

Requirements

1. Using its statements of cash flows, answer the following questions about Sears:
   a. Is Sears generating cash from its operations?
   b. Describe what investing activities Sears has been involved in over the past three years. Are investing activities an overall source or use of funds for Sears?
   c. What financing activities has Sears been undertaking in the past three years? Has it been paying dividends to its common stockholders? (Note: Sears Canada is a holding that does not represent Sears common stockholders.)
   d. How will the closure of the Kmart and Sears stores impact the 2016 statement of cash flows?
2. Using its statements of cash flows, answer the following questions about Wal-Mart:
   a. Is Wal-Mart generating cash from its operations?
   b. Describe what investing activities Wal-Mart has been involved in over the past three years. Are investing activities an overall source or use of funds for Wal-Mart?
   c. What financing activities has Wal-Mart been undertaking in the past three years? Has it been paying dividends to its common stockholders?
   d. How will the closure of the Wal-Mart stores impact the 2016 statement of cash flows?
3. Judging from the statements of cash flows, which company, Sears or Wal-Mart, is healthier?
4. Why do you think Sears and Wal-Mart would have fiscal year-ends around January 31 rather than using a calendar year-end of December 31?

A13-45 Use cash flow data to evaluate potential investments
(Learning Objectives 1 & 2)

Your company has some excess cash and would like to invest it in the stock of another company. You investigate several different stocks and are trying to decide which stock would be the best investment for your company. One factor you investigate is each company's cash flow. The summaries of the cash flow statements for your three top stock choices follow:

(000s omitted)	Dalton Corp.	Meredith Enterprises	Thornton, Inc.
Net cash provided by (used for) operating activities	$(20,000)	$ 28,100	$ 16,000
Cash provided by (used for) investing activities:			
Cash used to purchase plant or equipment		$(12,100)	$(25,000)
Proceeds from the sale of equipment	$8,000		
Cash used to purchase investments in stock		(5,000)	
Net cash provided by (used for) investing activities	8,000	(17,100)	$(25,000)
Cash provided by (used for) financing activities:			
Proceeds from bond issuance	23,500	4,000	5,000
Repayment of long-term debt	(1,000)	(2,000)	
Cash proceeds from issuance of stock			12,000
Cash payments for dividends	(2,500)	(5,000)	
Net cash provided by (used for) financing activities	20,000	(3,000)	17,000
Net increase in cash	$ 8,000	$ 8,000	$ 8,000

Although you will look at many other criteria in your stock purchase recommendation, what can you tell about each of the three companies listed? Based solely on cash flow, which stock appears to be better?

Try It Solutions

page 783:

1. Operating
2. Financing
3. Financing
4. Operating
5. Investing

page 794:

1. Subtract increases in current asset accounts.
2. Add back depreciation expense since it is a noncash expense.
3. Subtract decreases in current liability accounts.
4. Subtract gain made on a sale since it represents noncash revenue.
5. Add decreases in current asset accounts.
6. Add increases in current liability accounts.

14

Financial Statement Analysis

Kurt Brady/Alamy

Sources: https://corporate.target.com/corporate-responsibility; https://corporate.target article/2014/04/bullseye-love-history-of-target-logo; https://corporate.target.com/abou awards-recognition; https://nrf.com/2015/top100-table

Learning Objectives

- **1** Perform a horizontal analysis of financial statements
- **2** Perform a vertical analysis of financial statements
- **3** Prepare and use common-size financial statements
- **4** Compute the standard financial ratios

With over $73 billion in annual sales, Target Corporation is currently the sixth-largest retailer in the United States. Its trademark symbol, the bull's-eye, is recognized by 96% of people surveyed. Target has a reputation for being one of the largest supporters of corporate social responsibility. Ever since 1962, Target has committed 5% of its yearly income to support local communities. In addition, Target is committed to integrating environmental sustainability throughout its business operations. As a result of these corporate practices, *Fortune* magazine has ranked Target Corporation as one of "America's Most Admired Companies," and *Corporate Responsibility* magazine has ranked Target as one of the 100 Best Corporate Citizens.

All of these accolades might lead one to believe that Target must be highly profitable. Indeed, Target has earned yearly net income from continuing operations since before the turn of the twenty-first century. But net income alone does not tell the whole story. Has revenue grown steadily, or have there been large fluctuations—ups and downs—over the course of recent years? How big was each year's profit in relation to sales? For every dollar sold, how much of it ended up as gross profit, and how much of it was eaten up by operating expenses? What kind of return has the company been providing to shareholders? And how quickly has Target been able to sell its highly seasonable and fashion-trended merchandise? Financial statement analysis can help us answer these questions.

In this chapter, we'll examine several analytical tools that are frequently used to judge the financial performance of a company as a whole. To illustrate, we'll apply these tools to Supermart, a regional retailer of general merchandise that is similar to, but much smaller than Target. Then we will apply these analytical tools directly to Target Corporation's financial statements in the mid-chapter and end-of-chapter summary problems.

What Are the Most Common Methods of Analysis?

There are three ways to analyze financial statements:

- **Horizontal analysis** provides a year-to-year comparison of a company's performance in different periods.
- **Vertical analysis** provides a means of evaluating the relative size of each line item in the financial statements. It also allows us to compare companies of different size.
- **Ratio analysis** provides a means of evaluating the relationships between key components of the financial statements.

We'll explain the first two methods in this half of the chapter and then devote the second half of the chapter to ratio analysis.

To use these tools, we must begin with the company's financial statements. Exhibit 14-1 presents Supermart's income statement for the last two years, while Exhibit 14-2 presents the company's balance sheet for the last two years.

> **Why is this important?**
> "Evaluating the **performance** of a company is difficult without some type of **benchmark** for **comparison**. Therefore, managers typically benchmark **financial performance** over time, against other companies, or against **industry averages**."

EXHIBIT 14-1 Supermart Income Statement

	A	B	C
1		Supermart	
2		Income Statement	
3		For the Years Ended December 31, 2017 and 2016	
4		(amounts in thousands)	
5		2017	2016
6	Sales revenues	$ 858,000	$ 803,000
7	Less: Cost of goods sold	513,000	509,000
8	Gross profit	$ 345,000	$ 294,000
9	Less: Operating expenses	244,000	237,000
10	Operating income	$ 101,000	$ 57,000
11	Less: Interest expense	20,000	14,000
12	Income before income taxes	$ 81,000	$ 43,000
13	Less: Income tax expense	33,000	17,000
14	Net income	$ 48,000	$ 26,000
15			

What Is Horizontal Analysis?

1 Perform a horizontal analysis of financial statements

Managers, investors, and creditors are interested in knowing whether a company's revenues, expenses, assets, and liabilities are increasing or decreasing over time, and to what extent. To address this issue, financial statement users perform <u>horizontal analysis</u>, which is the comparison of financial statement line items between accounting periods. The change in each line item between periods is stated as a dollar amount and also as a percentage. The comparison can be made between months, quarters, or years. In our example, we'll be comparing years (2017 versus 2016). For each line item in the financial statements, we compare the balances between periods as follows:

STEP 1: To find the dollar amount of the change, subtract the line item's balance in the earlier period from its balance in the later period.

STEP 2: To find the percentage change, divide the dollar amount of change by the balance in the earlier period. The earlier period is often referred to as the base year.

EXHIBIT 14-2 Supermart Balance Sheet

	A	B	C
1	Supermart		
2	Balance Sheets		
3	December 31, 2017 and 2016		
4		(amounts in thousands)	
5		2017	2016
6	**Assets**		
7	Current assets:		
8	Cash	$ 29,000	$ 32,000
9	Accounts receivable	114,000	85,000
10	Inventory	113,000	111,000
11	Other current assets	6,000	8,000
12	Total current assets	$ 262,000	$ 236,000
13	Property, plant, and equipment, net	507,000	399,000
14	Other noncurrent assets	18,000	9,000
15	Total assets	$ 787,000	$ 644,000
16			
17	**Liabilities**		
18	Current liabilities:		
19	Accounts payable	$ 73,000	$ 68,000
20	Notes payable	42,000	27,000
21	Accrued liabilities	27,000	31,000
22	Total current liabilities	$ 142,000	$ 126,000
23	Long-term liabilities	289,000	198,000
24	Total liabilities	$ 431,000	$ 324,000
25			
26	**Stockholders' equity**		
27	Common stock, no par	$ 186,000	$ 186,000
28	Retained earnings	170,000	134,000
29	Total stockholders' equity	$ 356,000	$ 320,000
30			
31	Total liabilities and equity	$ 787,000	$ 644,000
32			

Let's illustrate with Supermart's sales revenue, shown in Exhibit 14-1:

STEP 1: Compute the dollar amount of change in sales revenue from 2016 to 2017:

$$\begin{array}{ccc} 2017 & 2016 & \text{Increase} \\ \$858,000 - \$803,000 & = & \$55,000 \end{array}$$

STEP 2: Divide the dollar amount of change by the balance in the base year (2016):

$$\text{Percentage change} = \frac{\text{Dollar amount of change}}{\text{Base-year amount}}$$

$$= \frac{\$55,000}{\$803,000} = 0.068 \text{ (rounded)} = 6.8\%$$

We now see that Supermart's sales revenue increased by $55,000, or 6.8%, over the previous year.

Horizontal Analysis of the Income Statement

Exhibit 14-3 shows a complete horizontal analysis of Supermart's income statement.

EXHIBIT 14-3 Supermart Comparative Income Statement—Horizontal Analysis

	Supermart Comparative Income Statement For the Years Ended December 31, 2017 and 2016			
	(amounts in thousands)		Increase/(Decrease)	
	2017	2016	Change	Percentage
Sales revenues	$ 858,000	$ 803,000	$ 55,000	6.8%
Less: Cost of goods sold	513,000	509,000	4,000	0.8%
Gross profit	$ 345,000	$ 294,000	$ 51,000	17.3%
Less: Operating expenses	244,000	237,000	7,000	3.0%
Operating income	$ 101,000	$ 57,000	$ 44,000	77.2%
Less: Interest expense	20,000	14,000	6,000	42.9%
Income before income taxes	$ 81,000	$ 43,000	$ 38,000	88.4%
Less: Income tax expense	33,000	17,000	16,000	94.1%
Net income	$ 48,000	$ 26,000	$ 22,000	84.6%

The horizontal analysis shows that sales increased by almost 7%, yet the cost of goods sold increased by less than 1%. Supermart was either able to raise its prices, find cheaper suppliers, or sell products with higher margins. As a result, gross profit was about 17% higher than that of the previous year. Supermart was also able to hold its operating expenses to a 3% increase. These factors all contributed to increasing operating income by 77% over the previous year! Interest expense increased by almost 43% as a result of more debt (as shown in the company's comparative balance sheet in Exhibit 14-2), possibly combined with a higher interest rate. Finally, as a result of the increased income, income taxes also increased substantially. The end result was almost an 85% increase in net income over the previous year.

Horizontal Analysis of the Balance Sheet

Exhibit 14-4 shows a complete horizontal analysis of Supermart's balance sheet.

The horizontal analysis shows that Supermart's accounts receivable grew substantially over the year (34%), while its cash decreased about 9%. The company may have relaxed its credit terms to generate more sales. The company also has taken on more short- and long-term debt, which may have been used to finance the significant additions to property, plant, and equipment and the increase in noncurrent assets that occurred during the year.

Trend Percentages

Trend percentages are a form of horizontal analysis that indicate the direction a business is taking over a longer period of time, such as 3, 5, or 10 years. For example, in Exhibit 14-3, we saw that Supermart's net income increased a whopping 85% over the previous year. Has income always been increasing at such a significant rate? Or was that an isolated growth spurt limited to a one-year period? Investors typically like to see smooth growth trends over time rather than large, sporadic fluctuations in sales and net income.

Trend percentages are computed by first selecting a base year. The base-year amounts are set equal to 100%. The amount of each line item in the following years is expressed as a percentage of the base-year amount as follows:

$$\text{Trend \%} = \frac{\text{Line item balance (\$) in any year}}{\text{Line item balance (\$) in base year}} \times 100$$

EXHIBIT 14-4 Comparative Balance Sheet—Horizontal Analysis

	A	B	C	D	E
1		Supermart			
2		Comparative Balance Statement			
3		December 31, 2017 and 2016			
4					
5		(amounts in thousands)		Increase/(Decrease)	
6	**Assets**	2017	2016	Change	Percentage
7	Current assets:				
8	Cash	$ 29,000	$ 32,000	$ (3,000)	−9.4%
9	Accounts receivable	114,000	85,000	29,000	34.1%
10	Inventory	113,000	111,000	2,000	1.8%
11	Other current assets	6,000	8,000	(2,000)	−25.0%
12	Total current assets	$ 262,000	$ 236,000	$ 26,000	11.0%
13	Property, plant, and equipment, net	507,000	399,000	108,000	27.1%
14	Other noncurrent assets	18,000	9,000	9,000	100.0%
15	Total assets	$ 787,000	$ 644,000	$ 143,000	22.2%
16					
17	**Liabilities**				
18	Current liabilities:				
19	Accounts payable	$ 73,000	$ 68,000	$ 5,000	7.4%
20	Notes payable	42,000	27,000	15,000	55.6%
21	Accrued liabilities	27,000	31,000	(4,000)	−12.9%
22	Total current liabilities	$ 142,000	$ 126,000	$ 16,000	12.7%
23	Long-term liabilities	289,000	198,000	91,000	46.0%
24	Total liabilities	$ 431,000	$ 324,000	$ 107,000	33.0%
25					
26	**Stockholders' equity**				
27	Common stock, no par	$ 186,000	$ 186,000	0	0.0%
28	Retained earnings	170,000	134,000	36,000	26.9%
29	Total stockholders' equity	$ 356,000	$ 320,000	36,000	11.3%
30					
31	Total liabilities and equity	$ 787,000	$ 644,000	$ 143,000	22.2%
32					

Supermart's sales revenue and trend percentages from 2012 to 2017 are pictured in Exhibit 14-5. We selected 2012 as the base year, so that year's percentage is set equal to 100. For example, to find the trend percentage for 2017, we performed the following calculation: $858,000 ÷ $600,000 = 1.43 × 100 = 143%.

EXHIBIT 14-5 Supermart's Sales Trend

	A	B	C	D	E	F	G
1	Supermart Trend Data	2017	2016	2015	2014	2013	Base Year 2012
2	Sales revenue	$ 858,000	$ 803,000	$ 690,000	$ 648,000	$ 618,000	$ 600,000
3	Trend percentage	143%	134%	115%	108%	103%	100%
4							

From the percentages, we see that sales increased at a fairly slow, even rate in the earlier years (2012–2015). However, the rate of increase picked up in the later years (2016 and 2017). Supermart is obviously experiencing growth, either in existing store sales, or by adding new retail locations. Trend data are often pictured using line graphs. In fact, publicly traded companies show the trend of their stock returns in the 10-K filings required by the Securities and Exchange Commission (SEC). Exhibit 14-6 shows Supermart's sales trend. As you can see, sales have increased every year, but the rate of increase has been larger in recent years (as shown by the steeper incline of the line from 2015 to 2017).

You can perform a trend analysis on any item you consider important. Trend analysis is widely used to predict future financial figures.

EXHIBIT 14-6 Line Graph of Sales Trend

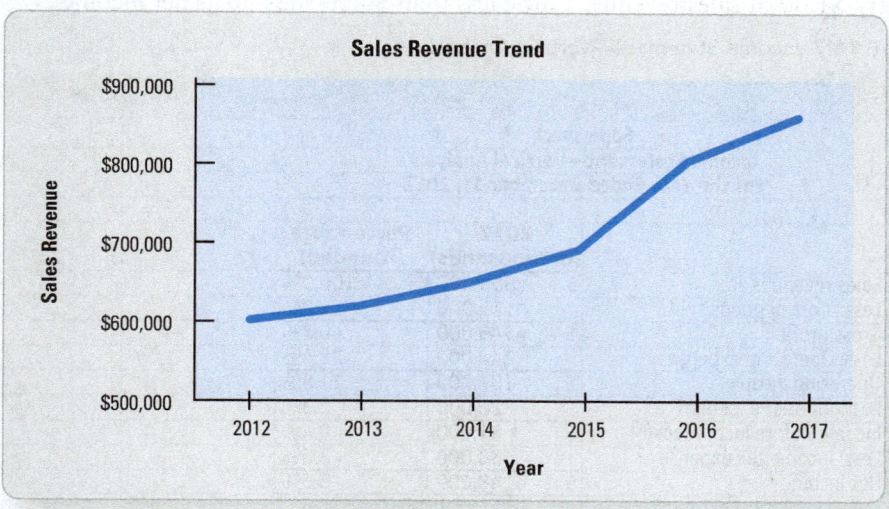

Try It!

Starbucks Corporation's net revenues from 2011 to 2015 were as follows (in millions of dollars):*

- $19,162.7 (2015)
- $16,447.8 (2014)
- $14,866.8 (2013)
- $13,299.5 (2012)
- $11,700.4 (2011)

Calculate trend percentages for the five-year period using 2011 as the base year.

Source: Starbucks Corporation 2015 10-K and 2012 10-K.
Please see page 893 for solutions.

What Is Vertical Analysis?

Horizontal analysis shows how different financial statement line items change over time. However, additional analysis is needed to understand the composition of the financial statements, in terms of the relative size of each line item as a proportion of the company's total sales or total assets.

Vertical analysis shows the relative size of each financial statement line item as a percentage of a total amount, or base figure. The base figure is set at 100%. When performing vertical analysis of an income statement, sales revenue is usually considered the base figure (100%).

2 Perform a vertical analysis of financial statements

$$\text{Vertical analysis \% for income statement} = \frac{\text{Each income statement line item}}{\text{Sales revenue}}$$

Exhibit 14-7 shows the vertical analysis of Supermart's 2017 income statement. The vertical analysis shows that Supermart's gross profit is 40% of sales revenue. Operating expenses use up 28% of each dollar sold, while income taxes and interest use up another 6%.

As a result of all of these expenses, only 5.6% of every sales dollar ends up as net income (for every $1.00 of sales revenue, a little less than $0.06 ends up as net income).

EXHIBIT 14-7 Income Statement—Vertical Analysis

	A	B	C	D	E
1		Supermart			
2		Income Statement—Vertical Analysis			
3		For the Year Ended December 31, 2017			
4					
5			2017 (in thousands)	Percentage (rounded)	
6	Sales revenues	$	858,000	100.0%	
7	Less: Cost of goods sold		513,000	59.8%	
8	Gross profit	$	345,000	40.2%	
9	Less: Operating expenses		244,000	28.4%	
10	Operating income	$	101,000	11.8%	
11	Less: Interest expense		20,000	2.3%	
12	Income before income taxes	$	81,000	9.4%	
13	Less: Income tax expense		33,000	3.8%	
14	Net income	$	48,000	5.6%	
15					

When performing vertical analysis of a balance sheet, total assets is usually considered the base (100%).

$$\text{Vertical analysis \% for balance sheet} = \frac{\text{Each balance sheet line item}}{\text{Total assets}}$$

Exhibit 14-8 shows the vertical analysis of Supermart's 2017 balance sheet. The base amount (100%) is total assets.

EXHIBIT 14-8 Balance Sheet—Vertical Analysis

	A	B	C	D
1		Supermart		
2		Balance Sheet—Vertical Analysis		
3		December 31, 2017		
4				
5		2017 (in thousands)	Percentage (rounded)	
6	Assets			
7	Current assets:			
8	Cash	$ 29,000	3.7%	
9	Accounts receivable	114,000	14.5%	
10	Inventory	113,000	14.4%	
11	Other current assets	6,000	0.8%	
12	Total current assets	$ 262,000	33.3%	
13	Property, plant, and equipment, net	507,000	64.4%	
14	Other noncurrent assets	18,000	2.3%	
15	Total assets	$ 787,000	100.0%	
16				
17	Liabilities			
18	Current liabilities:			
19	Accounts payable	$ 73,000	9.3%	
20	Notes payable	42,000	5.3%	
21	Accrued liabilities	27,000	3.4%	
22	Total current liabilities	$ 142,000	18.0%	
23	Long-term liabilities	289,000	36.7%	
24	Total liabilities	$ 431,000	54.8%	
25				
26	Stockholders' equity			
27	Common stock, no par	$ 186,000	23.6%	
28	Retained earnings	170,000	21.6%	
29	Total stockholders' equity	$ 356,000	45.2%	
30				
31	Total liabilities and equity	$ 787,000	100.0%	
32				

The vertical analysis of Supermart's balance sheet reveals that most of the company's assets (64%) consist of property, plant, and equipment. Inventory and receivables together make up about 29% of the company's assets. While the company is in the business of selling merchandise and therefore needs a fair amount of inventory, the receivables balance may be higher than desirable. Current liabilities are only 18% of total assets, but long-term debt is double that amount. Finally, stockholders' equity makes up a significant portion of total assets (45%).

How Do We Compare One Company with Another?

Horizontal analysis and vertical analysis provide a great deal of useful data about a company. However, many times we want to **benchmark**, or compare, a company against either (1) its competitor or (2) industry averages.

3 Prepare and use common-size financial statements

To compare Supermart to another company, we can use a common-size statement. A **common-size statement** reports only percentages—the same percentages that appear in a vertical analysis. By using only the percentages rather than gross dollar amounts, we are able to compare companies that vary in terms of size. For example, in Exhibit 14-9 we use common-size income statements to compare Supermart, a smaller regional retailer, to Target, a large national retailer.

EXHIBIT 14-9 Common-Size Income Statements

	A	B	C
1	Supermart and Target		
2	Common Size Income Statements		
3			
4		Supermart	Target*
5	Sales revenues	100.0%	100.0%
6	Less: Cost of goods sold	59.8%	70.5%
7	Gross profit	40.2%	29.5%
8	Less: Operating expenses	28.4%	22.0%
9	Operating income	11.8%	7.5%
10	Less: Interest expense	2.3%	0.8%
11	Income before income taxes	9.4%	6.7%
12	Less: Income tax expense	3.8%	2.2%
13	Net income	5.6%	4.5%
14			

*NOTE: Adapted from Target's 2015 income statement. Only income from continuing operations is included.

Exhibit 14-9 shows that Supermart is actually more profitable, on each dollar of sales revenue (5.6%), than Target (4.5%). Supermart's gross profit (40.2%) is about 11 percentage points higher than Target's (29.5%), but its operating expenses use up more of each sales dollar (28.4%) than do Target's operating expenses (22.0%). Likewise, Supermart's income taxes and interest expense also use up a slightly larger percentage of sales revenue.

Using Microsoft Excel

While horizontal and vertical analyses are tedious to perform by hand, spreadsheet software, such as Microsoft Excel, takes the grunt work out of the analyses, allowing managers to focus on interpreting the data. Each of the exhibits in this chapter was constructed using Microsoft Excel, allowing you to easily duplicate them yourself. In an Excel worksheet, simply type in the company's financial statements, as pictured in Exhibits 14-1 and 14-2, and then instruct the software to perform the calculations described earlier in the chapter. Finally, in order to obtain a trend graph, like that pictured in Exhibit 14-6, simply highlight the Sales Revenue data shown in Exhibit 14-5, and then click on "Insert," "Line Graph." Excel is also useful for calculating the ratios described in the second half of the chapter.

Decision Guidelines

Horizontal and Vertical Analyses

In order to make well-informed financial decisions, investors, creditors, and managers need to determine how well the company is performing. The following guidelines help these decision makers judge the financial performance of a company.

Decision	Guidelines
What methods are generally used to evaluate a company's performance?	• Horizontal analysis • Vertical analysis • Ratio analysis
How is horizontal analysis performed?	Horizontal analysis is a two-step process: 1. To find the dollar amount of the change, subtract the line item's balance in the earlier period from its balance in the later period. 2. To find the percentage change, divide the dollar amount of change by the balance in the earlier period. The earlier period is often referred to as the base year.
How does trend analysis differ from horizontal analysis?	Horizontal analysis performed over a longer period of time (3–10 years) is usually called trend analysis. When performing trend analysis, a base year is chosen and set to 100%. All years after the base year are calculated as a percentage of the base year. $$\text{Trend \%} = \frac{\text{Line item balance (\$) in any year}}{\text{Line item balance (\$) in base year}} \times 100$$
What line item on the income statement is used as the base amount (100%) for vertical analysis?	Net sales revenue is generally used as the base amount (100%) for vertical analysis of the income statement. $$\text{Vertical analysis \% for income statement} = \frac{\text{Each income statement line item}}{\text{Sales revenue}}$$
What line item on the balance sheet is used as the base amount (100%) for vertical analysis?	Total assets are generally used as the base amount (100%) for vertical analysis of the balance sheet. $$\text{Vertical analysis \% for balance sheet} = \frac{\text{Each balance sheet line item}}{\text{Total assets}}$$
How can I compare two companies that differ in size?	Common-size income statements and balance sheets are generally used to compare companies that differ in size. Common-size financial statements present side-by-side vertical analyses percentages of different companies.

SUMMARY PROBLEM 1

Target Corporation's annual sales and net income data for the years 2009–2015 as well as the company's 2015 and 2014 comparative income statements (adapted) are presented below.[1]

	A	B	C	D	E	F	G	H
1	(in millions)	2015	2014	2013	2012	2011	2010	2009
2	Sales revenue	$ 73,785	$ 72,618	$ 71,279	$ 73,301	$ 69,865	$ 67,390	$ 65,357
3	Net income	$ 3,321	$ 2,449	$ 2,694	$ 2,999	$ 2,929	$ 2,920	$ 2,488
4								

	A	B	C	D	E
1		Target Corporation			
2		Income Statements (Adapted)			
3		For the Fiscal Years 2015 and 2014			
4		(amounts in millions)			
5		2015	2014		
6	Sales revenues	$ 73,785	$ 72,618		
7	Less: Cost of goods sold	51,997	51,278		
8	Gross profit	21,788	21,340		
9	Less: Operating expenses	16,258	16,805		
10	Operating income	5,530	4,535		
11	Less: Interest expense	607	882		
12	Income before income taxes	4,923	3,653		
13	Less: Income tax expense	1,602	1,204		
14	Net income	$ 3,321	$ 2,449		
15					

Requirements

1. Perform a trend analysis of sales revenues and net income for the years 2009–2015, using 2009 as the base year. Comment on the results.
2. Perform a horizontal analysis of the income statements for the years 2014–2015 and comment on the results.
3. Perform a vertical analysis of the income statements for the years 2014–2015 and comment on the results.

▪ SOLUTIONS

Requirement 1

	A	B	C	D	E	F	G	H
1	(in millions)	2015	2014	2013	2012	2011	2010	2009
2	Sales revenue	$ 73,785	$ 72,618	$ 71,279	$ 73,301	$ 69,865	$ 67,390	$ 65,357
3	Trend percentage	113%	111%	109%	112%	107%	103%	100%
4								
5	Net income	$ 3,321	$ 2,449	$ 2,694	$ 2,999	$ 2,929	$ 2,920	$ 2,488
6	Trend percentage	133%	98%	108%	121%	118%	117%	100%
7								

[1] Adapted from Target's income statements: 2015 fiscal year ended January 30, 2016, and 2014 fiscal year ended January 31, 2015. Net income shown is from continuing operations and does not include gains and losses from discontinued operations.

Sales revenue is currently 113% of the base-year amount. Revenue has gradually increased over time, with a slight dip in 2013. Net income is currently 133% of what it was in 2009. However, the increase has not been gradual, like it was with sales revenue, except in 2010–2012. The years 2013–2015 showed significant fluctuations in net income that do not correspond directly with the increase in sales. Thus, factors other than sales must have had a significant influence on net income during the most recent years.

Requirement 2

	A	B	C	D	E
1		Target Corporation			
2		Horizontal Analysis of Comparative Income Statements (Adapted)			
3		For the Fiscal Years 2015 and 2014			
4					
5		(amounts in millions)		Increase/(Decrease)	
6		2015	2014	Change	Percentage
7	Sales revenues	$ 73,785	$ 72,618	$ 1,167	1.6%
8	Less: Cost of goods sold	51,997	51,278	719	1.4%
9	Gross profit	21,788	21,340	448	2.1%
10	Less: Operating expenses	16,258	16,805	(547)	-3.3%
11	Operating income	5,530	4,535	995	21.9%
12	Less: Interest expense	607	882	(275)	-31.2%
13	Income before income taxes	4,923	3,653	1,270	34.8%
14	Less: Income tax expense	1,602	1,204	398	33.1%
15	Net income	$ 3,321	$ 2,449	$ 872	35.6%
16					

Sales revenue increased at a slightly higher rate than Cost of Goods Sold, leading to a 2.1% increase in Gross Profit. Target was able to reduce its operating costs by 3.3% and its interest expense by 31.2%, leading to a 35.6% increase in net income.

Requirement 3

	A	B	C	D	E
1		Target Corporation			
2		Income Statements (Adapted)			
3		For the Fiscal Years 2015 and 2014			
4					
5		2015		2014	
6		Amount (in millions)	Percent (rounded)	Amount (in millions)	Percent (rounded)
7	Sales revenues	$ 73,785	100.0%	$ 72,618	100.0%
8	Less: Cost of goods sold	51,997	70.5%	51,278	70.6%
9	Gross profit	21,788	29.5%	21,340	29.4%
10	Less: Operating expenses	16,258	22.0%	16,805	23.1%
11	Operating income	5,530	7.5%	4,535	6.2%
12	Less: Interest expense	607	0.8%	882	1.2%
13	Income before income taxes	4,923	6.7%	3,653	5.0%
14	Less: Income tax expense	1,602	2.2%	1,204	1.7%
15	Net income	$ 3,321	4.5%	$ 2,449	3.4%
16					

In 2015, the vertical analysis shows that Target's gross profit is about 29% of sales, whereas operating expenses use up 22% of the company's sales. In 2015, interest expense and income taxes, combined, use up another 3% of sales revenue. As a result, in 2015, net income is approximately 4.5% of sales revenue. This means that for every dollar of sales revenue generated by the company, only about four cents ends up as net income. The 2014 vertical analysis shows fairly similar percentages, aside from slightly different percentages (about 0.5%–1% different) for operating expenses, interest expense, and income taxes.

What Are Some of the Most Common Financial Ratios?

In this half of the chapter, we'll discuss many different financial ratios that managers, investors, and creditors use when analyzing a company's financial statements. After illustrating how to compute these ratios using Supermart's data, we'll compare them to the ratios of three department store retailers that are in the same industry peer group according to each of the companies' 10-K filings. The three retailers include: Walmart (which is the largest retailer in the world), Macy's, and Kohl's. In the end-of-chapter Summary Problem, you'll get the chance to calculate these ratios for Target Corp, which is also in the same industry peer group. Most of the information needed for these ratios can be found in the company's financial statements (refer to Supermart's income statement and balance sheet in Exhibits 14-1 and 14-2, respectively). A few of the ratios require the knowledge of the company's closing market price, which can be found online or in the *Wall Street Journal*. Other ratios require knowledge of the number of shares outstanding. This information can be obtained in the company's 10-K filing.

The ratios we'll discuss in this chapter may be classified as follows:

1. Measuring ability to pay current liabilities
2. Measuring ability to sell inventory and collect receivables
3. Measuring ability to pay long-term debt
4. Measuring profitability
5. Analyzing stock investments

4 Compute the standard financial ratios

Measuring Ability to Pay Current Liabilities

Working capital is defined as follows:

$$\text{Working capital} = \text{Current assets} - \text{Current liabilities}$$

Working capital measures the ability to meet short-term obligations with current assets. Supermart's 2017 working capital is calculated as follows:

$$\$262,000 - \$142,000 = \$120,000$$

This shows that Supermart has ample current assets to meet its current obligations. Rather than measuring working capital alone, managers often measure the company's ability to meet current obligations by calculating two common ratios: the *current ratio* and the *acid-test*, or *quick, ratio*.

Current Ratio

The most widely used ratio is the **current ratio**, which is current assets divided by current liabilities. The current ratio measures the ability to pay current liabilities with current assets.

Supermart's current ratio at December 31, 2017 and 2016 is calculated as follows:[2]

> **Why is this important?**
>
> "Managers use different **financial ratios** to evaluate a company's performance, depending on the underlying **need**. For example, if a manager wants to know how **quickly inventory** is selling, he or she will calculate inventory **turnover**. If a manager wants to know how easily the **company** will be able to meet its current **obligations**, he or she will calculate the current ratio or the **acid-test ratio**."

	Formula	Supermart's Current Ratio	
		2017	2016
Current ratio =	$\dfrac{\text{Current assets}}{\text{Current liabilities}}$	$\dfrac{\$262,000}{\$142,000} = 1.85$	$\dfrac{\$236,000}{\$126,000} = 1.87$

[2]The solutions to all ratio calculations in this chapter have been rounded.

What is an acceptable current ratio? The answer depends on the industry, though a current ratio in the range of 1.5 to 2.0 is generally considered fairly strong. Of the three retailers we are comparing, Kohl's has the strongest current ratio, showing that it has the ability to pay off short-term obligations with short-term assets with relative ease:[3]

Company	Current Ratio
Walmart	0.93
Macy's	1.34
Kohl's	1.87

Acid-Test Ratio

The **acid-test ratio**, or **quick ratio**, tells us whether the entity could pay all of its current liabilities if they came due *immediately*. That is, could the company pass this *acid test*?

To compute the acid-test ratio, we add cash, short-term investments, and net current receivables (accounts and notes receivable, net of allowances) and divide this sum by current liabilities. Inventory and prepaid expenses are *not* included in the acid test because they are the least liquid current assets. Supermart's acid-test ratios for 2017 and 2016 follow:

	Supermart's Acid-Test Ratio	
Formula	2017	2016
Acid-test ratio = $\dfrac{\text{Cash + Short-term investments + Net current receivables}}{\text{Current liabilities}}$	$\dfrac{\$29{,}000 + \$0 + \$114{,}000}{\$142{,}000} = 1.01$	$\dfrac{\$32{,}000 + \$0 + \$85{,}000}{\$126{,}000} = 0.93$

An acid-test ratio of 0.90 to 1.00 is acceptable in most industries. We do not present comparative statistics for Walmart, Macy's, and Kohl's, since their balance sheets do not identify short-term investments separately.

Measuring Ability to Sell Inventory and Collect Receivables

The ability to sell inventory and collect receivables is fundamental to business. In this section, we discuss three ratios that measure the company's ability to sell inventory and collect receivables.

Inventory Turnover

Inventory turnover measures the number of times a company sells its average level of inventory during a year. A high rate of turnover indicates ease in selling inventory; a low rate indicates difficulty. A value of "6" means that the company sold its average level of inventory six times—every two months—during the year.

To compute inventory turnover, we divide cost of goods sold by the average inventory for the period. We use the cost of goods sold—not sales—because both cost of goods sold and inventory are stated *at cost*. Sales at *retail prices* are not comparable with inventory *at cost*.

Supermart's inventory turnover for 2017 is as follows:

Formula	Supermart's 2017 Inventory Turnover
Inventory turnover = $\dfrac{\text{Cost of goods sold}}{\text{Average inventory}}$	$\dfrac{\$513{,}000}{(\$111{,}000 + \$113{,}000)/2} = 4.6$

---

[3] All information given for Walmart Stores, Inc., Macy's Inc., and Kohl's Corporation was calculated using the companies' financial statements reported for fiscal year 2015 (fiscal year ended January 30, 2016), as found in each company's SEC 10-K filing.

Notice that average inventory is calculated by adding the beginning inventory ($111,000) and ending inventory ($113,000) for the period, and then dividing by two.

Inventory turnover varies widely with the nature of the business. Because of product innovation, some industries (for example, high-technology industries) must turn their inventory very quickly to avoid inventory obsolescence. However, in other industries, the risk of obsolescence is not so great.

Of the three retailers we are comparing, Walmart has the strongest inventory turnover by far, selling its average inventory over 8 times a year:

Company	Inventory Turnover
Walmart	8.06
Macy's	3.02
Kohl's	3.12

Accounts Receivable Turnover

Accounts receivable turnover measures the ability to collect cash from credit customers. This means that the higher the ratio, the faster the cash collections. But a receivable turnover that's too high may indicate that credit is too tight, causing the loss of sales to good customers.

For illustrative purposes, we'll assume that all of Supermart's sales were made on account. The accounts receivable turnover is computed by dividing net credit sales by average net accounts receivable. Supermart's accounts receivable turnover ratio for 2017 is computed as follows:

Formula	Supermart's 2017 Accounts Receivable Turnover
Accounts receivable turnover = $\dfrac{\text{Net credit sales}}{\text{Average net accounts receivable}}$	$\dfrac{\$858,000}{(\$85,000 + \$114,000)/2} = 8.6$

We don't show comparative statistics for Walmart, Macy's, or Kohl's because we don't know the percentage of sales made on account (most customers at these stores pay with cash, debit, or third-party credit cards, such as Visa and Mastercard).

Days' Sales in Receivables

The **days' sales in receivables** ratio also measures the ability to collect receivables. Days' sales in receivables tell us how many days' sales remain in Accounts Receivable. To compute the ratio, we can follow a logical two-step process:

1. Divide net sales by 365 days to figure average sales for one day.
2. Divide this average day's sales amount into average net accounts receivable.

This two-step process is illustrated using Supermart's 2017 data as follows:

Formula	Supermart's 2017 Days' Sales in Accounts Receivable
Days' sales in *average* Accounts receivable:	
1. One day's sales = $\dfrac{\text{Net sales}}{365 \text{ days}}$	$\dfrac{\$858,000}{365 \text{ days}} = \$2,351$
2. Days' sales in average accounts receivable = $\dfrac{\text{Average net accounts receivable}}{\text{One day's sales}}$	$\dfrac{(\$85,000 + \$114,000)/2}{\$2,351} = 42 \text{ days}$

Supermart's ratio tells us that 42 average days' sales remain in accounts receivable and need to be collected. Let's assume that, like many companies, Supermart gives its customers 30 days to pay. Supermart's ratio shows that, on average, customers are taking longer—about 42 days—to pay. This could be a result of general economic conditions (such as a recession), or Supermart's particular customer base. In either event, Supermart may need to increase its efforts to collect receivables more quickly if it expects to be paid within 30 days of sale.

> ### Try It!
>
> Select 2015 financial data for Starbucks Corporation is as follows (in millions of dollars):*
> - Current assets $4,352.7
> - Inventory $1,306.4 (end of fiscal 2015) and $1,090.9 (end of fiscal 2014)
> - Current liabilities $3,653.5
> - Cost of goods sold $7,787.5
>
> 1. Calculate the current ratio.
> 2. Calculate inventory turnover.

Source: Starbucks Corporation 2015 10-K.
Please see page 893 for solutions.

Measuring Ability to Pay Long-Term Debt

The ratios discussed so far yield insight into current assets and current liabilities. They help us measure ability to sell inventory, collect receivables, and pay current liabilities. Most businesses also have long-term debt. Two key indicators of a business's ability to pay long-term liabilities are the *debt ratio* and the *times-interest-earned ratio*.

Debt Ratio

The relationship between total liabilities and total assets—called the **debt ratio**—shows the proportion of assets financed with debt. When the debt ratio is 1, all of the assets are financed with debt. A debt ratio of 0.50 means that debt finances half the assets; the owners of the business have financed the other half. The higher the debt ratio, the higher the company's financial risk. The debt ratios for Supermart at the end of 2017 and 2016 follow:

		Supermart's Debt Ratio	
Formula		2017	2016
Debt ratio = Total liabilities / Total assets		$431,000 / $787,000 = 0.55	$324,000 / $644,000 = 0.50

Supermart's debt ratio increased slightly in 2017. Of the three retailers we are comparing, Walmart has the lowest debt ratio, indicating that only 58% of its assets are financed with debt:

Company	Debt Ratio
Walmart	0.58
Macy's	0.79
Kohl's	0.60

Times-Interest-Earned Ratio

The debt ratio says nothing about ability to pay interest expense. Analysts use the **times-interest-earned ratio** to relate operating income to interest expense. This ratio is also called the **interest-coverage ratio**. It measures the number of times operating income can cover interest expense. A high interest-coverage ratio indicates ease in paying interest expense; a low ratio suggests difficulty.

To compute this ratio, we divide operating income by interest expense. Calculation of Supermart's times-interest-earned ratio follows:

Formula		Supermart's Times-Interest-Earned Ratio	
		2017	2016
Times-interest-earned ratio =	$\dfrac{\text{Income from operations}}{\text{Interest expense}}$	$\dfrac{\$101,000}{\$20,000}$ = 5.05	$\dfrac{\$57,000}{\$14,000}$ = 4.07

The company's times-interest-earned ratio shows that in 2017, the company could pay its interest about five times over with the amount of operating income it earned. Therefore, Supermart should have little trouble paying the interest expense it owes to creditors. Of the three retailers we are comparing, Walmart has the strongest times interest earned ratio, indicating that it could pay off its interest expense nine times over with income from operations. In other words, it should have no trouble meeting its interest obligations:

Company	Times-Interest-Earned Ratio
Walmart	9.46
Macy's	5.62
Kohl's	4.75

Measuring Profitability

The fundamental goal of business is to earn a profit. Ratios that measure profitability are often reported in the business press. We examine six profitability measures.

Gross Profit Percentage

Recall from earlier chapters that gross profit (also called gross margin) is found by subtracting Cost of Goods Sold from Sales Revenue. For merchandising companies, this measure of profitability is key because it tells managers and investors how much profit has been made from just marking up the sales price over the cost of the merchandise. In other words, it reflects pricing decisions as well as control over purchasing and manufacturing costs. The **gross profit percentage** tells managers the fraction of each sales dollar that is gross profit, or markup over the cost of the merchandise. This profit can then be used to pay for operating expenses, interest, and income taxes. The ratio is calculated as follows:

Formula		Supermart's Gross Profit %	
		2017	2016
Gross profit percentage =	$\dfrac{\text{Gross profit}}{\text{Net sales}}$	$\dfrac{\$345,000}{\$858,000}$ = 40.2%	$\dfrac{\$294,000}{\$803,000}$ = 36.6%

The gross profit percentage is part of vertical analysis, but since this percentage is so important to merchandising companies, it is worth repeating here. The gross profit percentage will vary, depending on the company. Higher end merchandising companies will have higher gross margin percentages, whereas discount retailers will have lower gross margin percentages. For example, of the three companies we are comparing, you can see that Walmart's gross profit percentage is lower than Macy's and Kohl's:

Company	Gross Profit Percentage
Walmart	25.1%
Macy's	39.1%
Kohl's	36.1%

Operating Income Percentage

Throughout this text we have focused on operating income rather than net income because the income a company earns from its primary operations is vitally important to managers. Recall that operating income differs from net income in that it does not include interest income or interest expense (a financing decision) or income taxes. In other words, it is the profit from the company's primary business before paying interest to creditors or income taxes to the government. Thus, the **operating income percentage** shows the percentage of each sales dollar that becomes income from the company's primary business operations before interest and income taxes. The ratio is calculated as follows:

Formula	Supermart's Operating Income %	
	2017	2016
Operating income percentage = $\dfrac{\text{Operating income}}{\text{Net sales}}$	$\dfrac{\$101,000}{\$858,000} = 11.8\%$	$\dfrac{\$57,000}{\$803,000} = 7.1\%$

The operating income percentage reflects not only pricing decisions but also the efficiency with which management has controlled operating expenses. Of the three companies we are comparing, Kohl's has the highest operating income percentage:

Company	Operating Income Percentage
Walmart	5.0%
Macy's	7.5%
Kohl's	8.1%

Rate of Return on Net Sales

In business, the term *return* is used broadly as a measure of profitability. Consider a ratio called the **rate of return on net sales**, or simply **return on sales**. This ratio shows the percentage of each sales dollar earned as net income. Supermart's rate of return on sales follows:

Formula	Supermart's Rate of Return on Sales	
	2017	2016
Rate of return on sales = $\dfrac{\text{Net income}}{\text{Net sales}}$	$\dfrac{\$48,000}{\$858,000} = 5.6\%$	$\dfrac{\$26,000}{\$803,000} = 3.2\%$

Companies strive for a high rate of return on sales. The higher the rate of return, the more sales dollars end up as profit. Supermart experienced a significant increase in its return on sales in the last year. Return on sales varies greatly depending on the industry. General merchandise retailers typically have a very low return on sales. All three of the retailers we are comparing have fairly similar ratios (in the 3–4% range), although Macy's is slightly stronger than the others:

Company	Rate of Return on Sales
Walmart	3.05%
Macy's	3.95%
Kohl's	3.50%

Rate of Return on Total Assets

The **rate of return on total assets**, or simply **return on assets**, measures success in using assets to earn a profit. Two groups finance a company's assets:

1. Creditors have loaned money to the company, and they earn interest.
2. Shareholders have invested in stock, and their return is net income.

The sum of interest expense and net income is the return to the two groups that have financed the company's assets. The higher the return, the better. Computation of the return-on-assets ratio for Supermart follows:

Formula	Supermart's 2017 Rate of Return on Total Assets
Rate of return on assets = $\dfrac{\text{Net income} + \text{Interest expense}}{\text{Average total assets}}$	$\dfrac{\$48{,}000 + \$20{,}000}{(\$644{,}000 + \$787{,}000)/2} = 9.5\%$

Of the three retailers we are comparing, Walmart has the strongest return on assets, although the other two companies are not very much lower:

Company	Rate of Return on Assets
Walmart	8.56%
Macy's	6.84%
Kohl's	7.16%

Rate of Return on Common Stockholders' Equity

A popular measure of profitability is **rate of return on common stockholders' equity**, often shortened to **return on equity**. This ratio shows the relationship between net income and common stockholders' equity—how much income is earned for each $1 invested by the common shareholders.

To compute this ratio, we subtract preferred dividends from net income to get net income available to the common stockholders. Then, we divide net income available to common stockholders by average common equity during the year. Common equity is total stockholders' equity minus preferred equity. The 2017 rate of return on common stockholders' equity for Supermart follows:

Formula	Supermart's 2017 Rate of Return on Common Stockholders' Equity
Rate of return on common stockholders' equity = $\dfrac{\text{Net income} - \text{Preferred dividends}}{\text{Average common stockholders' equity}}$	$\dfrac{\$48{,}000 - \$0}{(\$320{,}000 + \$356{,}000)/2} = 14.2\%$

Supermart's return on equity (14.2%) is higher than its return on assets (9.5%). This difference results from borrowing at one rate—for example, 8%—and investing the money to earn a higher rate, such as the firm's 14.2% return on equity.

This practice is called **trading on the equity**, or using **leverage**. It is directly related to the debt ratio. The higher the debt ratio reaches, the higher the leverage. Companies that finance operations with debt are said to *leverage* their positions.

During good times, leverage increases profitability. But leverage can have a negative impact on profitability. Therefore, leverage is a double-edged sword, increasing profits during good times but compounding losses during bad times. Of the three retailers we are comparing, Macy's has the strongest return on equity:

Company	Rate of Return on Common Stockholders' Equity
Walmart	18.15%
Macy's	22.23%
Kohl's	11.72%

Earnings per Share of Common Stock

Earnings per share of common stock, or simply **earnings per share (EPS)**, is perhaps the most widely quoted of all financial statistics. EPS is the only ratio that must appear on the face of the income statement. EPS is the amount of net income earned for each share of the company's outstanding *common* stock. Recall the following:

$$\text{Outstanding stock} = \text{Issued stock} - \text{Treasury stock}$$

Earnings per share is computed by dividing net income available to common stockholders by the number of common shares outstanding during the year. Preferred dividends are subtracted from net income because the preferred stockholders have priority.

Let's assume Supermart has no preferred stock outstanding, no preferred dividends, and ten million shares of common stock outstanding throughout 2016 and 2017. Since all of Supermart's financial data has rounded off three zeros (stated in thousands of dollars in Exhibits 14-1 and 14-2), we'll also need to round off three zeros from the number of shares outstanding, leaving 10,000 shares for the calculation. Given this information, we calculate the company's EPS as follows:

	Formula	Supermart's Earnings per Share	
		2017	2016
Earnings per share of common stock =	$\dfrac{\text{Net income} - \text{Preferred dividends}}{\text{Number of shares of common stock outstanding}}$	$\dfrac{\$48{,}000 - \$0}{10{,}000} = \$4.80$	$\dfrac{\$26{,}000 - \$0}{10{,}000} = \$2.60$

Supermart's EPS increased significantly. Most companies strive to increase EPS each year, but general economic conditions, such as a recession, can prevent companies from doing so. Of the three retailers we are comparing, Walmart has the strongest EPS:

Company	Earnings Per Share
Walmart	$ 4.58
Macy's	$ 3.26
Kohl's	$ 3.48

Analyzing Stock Investments

Investors purchase stock to earn a return on their investment. This return consists of two parts: (1) gains (or losses) from selling the stock at a price above (or below) the purchase price and (2) dividends. The ratios we examine in this section help analysts evaluate stock investments.

Price/Earnings Ratio

The <u>price/earnings ratio</u> is the ratio of the market price of a share of common stock to the company's earnings per share. It shows the market price of $1 of earnings. This ratio, abbreviated P/E, appears in the stock listings of the *Wall Street Journal*. The daily closing price of all publicly traded stocks can also be found online or in the *Wall Street Journal*.

Assume the market price of Supermart's common stock was $60 at the end of 2017 and $35 at the end of 2016. Supermart's P/E ratio is calculated as follows:

Formula	Supermart's Price/Earnings Ratio	
	2017	2016
P/E ratio = $\dfrac{\text{Market price per share of common stock}}{\text{Earnings per share}}$	$\dfrac{\$60.00}{\$4.80} = 12.5$	$\dfrac{\$35.00}{\$2.60} = 13.5$

Supermart's P/E ratio of 12.5 means that the company's stock is selling at 12.5 times earnings. The P/E ratios of the three retailers we are comparing are all very strong, but Walmart's is highest:

Company	Price/Earnings Ratio
Walmart	14.49
Macy's	12.40
Kohl's	14.30

Dividend Yield

<u>Dividend yield</u> is the ratio of dividends per share to the stock's market price per share. This ratio measures the percentage of a stock's market value that is returned annually as dividends. *Preferred* stockholders, who invest primarily to receive dividends, pay special attention to dividend yield.

Supermart paid annual cash dividends of $1.20 per share of common stock in 2017 and $1.00 in 2016, and market prices of the company's common stock were $60 in 2017 and $35 in 2016. The firm's dividend yield on common stock follows:

Formula	Supermart's Dividend Yield on Common Stock	
	2017	2016
Dividend yield on common stock* = $\dfrac{\text{Dividend per share of common stock}}{\text{Market price per share of common stock}}$	$\dfrac{\$1.20}{\$60.00} = 2.0\%$	$\dfrac{\$1.00}{\$35.00} = 2.9\%$

*Dividend yields may also be calculated for preferred stock.

An investor who buys Supermart common stock for $60 can expect to receive 2% of the investment annually in the form of cash dividends.

The dividends paid by companies vary substantially. Of the three retailers we are comparing, Kohl's has the strongest dividend yield:

Company	Dividend Yield
Walmart	2.95%
Macy's	3.44%
Kohl's	3.62%

Book Value per Share of Common Stock

Book value per share of common stock is common equity divided by the number of common shares outstanding. Common equity equals total stockholders' equity less preferred equity. Supermart has no preferred stock outstanding. Its book-value-per-share-of-common-stock ratios are calculated as follows:

		Supermart's Book Value per Share of Common Stock	
	Formula	2017	2016
Book value per share of common stock =	Total stockholders' equity − Preferred equity / Number of shares of common stock outstanding	($356,000 − $0) / 10,000 = $35.60	($320,000 − $0) / 10,000 = $32.00

Many experts argue that book value is not useful for investment analysis. It bears no relationship to market value and provides little information beyond stockholders' equity reported on the balance sheet. But some investors base their investment decisions on book value. For example, some investors rank stocks on the basis of the ratio of market price to book value. To these investors, the lower the ratio, the more attractive the stock, as this implies that the stock might be undervalued.

Red Flags in Financial Statement Analysis

Analysts look for *red flags* that may signal financial trouble. Recent accounting scandals highlight the importance of these red flags. The following conditions may reveal that the company is too risky:

- **Movement of Sales, Inventory, and Receivables.** Sales, receivables, and inventory generally move together. Increased sales lead to higher receivables and require more inventory to meet demand. Strange movements among sales, inventory, and receivables make the financial statements look suspect.
- **Earnings Problems.** Has net income decreased significantly for several years in a row? Has income turned into a loss? Most companies cannot survive years of consecutive losses.
- **Decreased Cash Flow.** Cash flow validates net income. Is net cash flow from operations consistently lower than net income? If so, the company is in trouble. Are the sales of plant assets a major source of cash? If so, the company may face a cash shortage.
- **Too Much Debt.** How does the company's debt ratio compare to that of major competitors? If the debt ratio is too high, the company may be unable to pay its debts.
- **Inability to Collect Receivables.** Are days' sales in receivables growing faster than those of competitors? A cash shortage may be looming.
- **Buildup of Inventories.** Is inventory turnover too slow? If so, the company may be unable to sell goods, or it may be overstating inventory.

Sustainability and Financial Statement Analysis

Financial statement analysis only evaluates the financial viability of a company using short-term data from the last few years of operations. Even a 5- to 10-year trend analysis will not adequately predict the long-term sustainability of a company. Thus, financial statement analysis, by itself, is insufficient for stakeholders who desire a more comprehensive view of an organization. Increasingly, investors are using a triple-bottom-line approach to evaluating a company's performance, not only focusing on historical financial ratios and trends, but also requesting information about the company's environmental and social practices.

For example, as of April 2016, over 1,500 institutional investors with over $62 trillion of assets under management had signed on to the Principles of Responsible Investing (PRI) backed by the United Nations (UN). In short, these principles state that investors will include environmental, social, and governance information when making investment decisions. Information about these factors can be found in some of the following documents:

- *Securities and Exchange Commission (SEC) 10-K filings of publicly traded companies.* SEC rules dictate that publicly traded companies disclose any material information that would be necessary to prevent misleading financial statement readers. With respect to the environment, companies must disclose any aspects of their business operations, including pending lawsuits and risk factors, which are deemed to be material. Examples include the cost of complying with environmental laws and regulations, potential monetary damages from health and environmental litigation, and risks associated with the scarcity of water and raw materials needed for operations. Additionally, any material risks specific to the company as a result of global warming must also be disclosed.

- *Corporate Social Responsibility (CSR) reports and company websites.* The vast majority of large companies now issue CSR reports. (In the United States, over 80% of companies on the S&P 500 issue CSR reports, whereas, internationally, over 95% of the Global 500 companies issue CSR reports.) These reports typically discuss the company's initiatives, goals, and performance with respect to environmental and social impact. Chapter 15 discusses the format and content of these reports in more detail. Unlike 10-K reports, the information contained in CSR reports is not always audited. However, the Big Four accounting firms are the leaders in providing assurance services for CSR data.

In the future, information relating to the triple bottom line may be found in what is known as an *integrated report*. Integrated reporting, or <IR>, is a concept in its infancy that is currently being piloted by a number of large, global companies. The idea behind <IR> is to provide "one-stop shopping" whereby both material financial and nonfinancial information is contained in one report so that stakeholders can obtain a holistic, balanced view of the organization.

▶ See Exercises E14-22A and E14-33B

Sources: https://unpri.org/about; Securities and Exchange Commission (SEC) 17 CFR Parts 211, 231, and 241 (Release Nos. 33-9106, 34-61469, and FR-82), Commission Guidance Regarding Disclosure Related to Climate Change; www.ga-institute.com/news-and-events/media-coverage.html; www.ey.com/US/en/Services/Specialty-Services/Climate-Change-and-Sustainability-Services/Value-of-sustainability-reporting

Decision Guidelines

Using Ratios in Financial Statement Analysis

How can investors, creditors, and managers measure a company's ability to pay bills, sell inventory, collect receivables, pay long-term debt, and so forth? How can they evaluate stock investments? The decision guidelines summarize the ratios that help to answer these questions.

Ratio	Computation	Information Provided
Measuring ability to pay current liabilities:		
1. Current ratio	$\dfrac{\text{Current assets}}{\text{Current liabilities}}$	Measures ability to pay current liabilities with current assets
2. Acid-test (quick) ratio	$\dfrac{\text{Cash} + \text{Short-term investments} + \text{Net current receivables}}{\text{Current liabilities}}$	Shows ability to pay all current liabilities if they come due immediately
Measuring ability to sell inventory and collect receivables:		
3. Inventory turnover	$\dfrac{\text{Cost of goods sold}}{\text{Average inventory}}$	Indicates salability of inventory—the number of times a company sells its average inventory during a year
4. Accounts receivable turnover	$\dfrac{\text{Net credit sales}}{\text{Average net accounts receivable}}$	Measures ability to collect cash from credit customers
5. Days' sales in receivables	$\dfrac{\text{Average net accounts receivable}}{\text{One day's sales}}$	Shows how many days' sales remain in Accounts Receivable—how many days it takes to collect the average level of receivables
Measuring ability to pay long-term debt:		
6. Debt ratio	$\dfrac{\text{Total liabilities}}{\text{Total assets}}$	Indicates percentage of assets financed with debt
7. Times-interest-earned ratio	$\dfrac{\text{Income from operations}}{\text{Interest expense}}$	Measures the number of times operating income can cover interest expense

Ratio	Computation	Information Provided
Measuring profitability:		
8. Gross profit percentage	$\dfrac{\text{Gross profit}}{\text{Net sales}}$	Shows the percentage of each sales dollar that becomes gross profit, or markup over the cost of merchandise.
9. Operating income percentage	$\dfrac{\text{Operating income}}{\text{Net sales}}$	Shows the percentage of each sales dollar that becomes income from the company's primary business operations before interest and income taxes.
10. Rate of return on net sales	$\dfrac{\text{Net income}}{\text{Net sales}}$	Shows the percentage of each sales dollar earned as net income
11. Rate of return on total assets	$\dfrac{\text{Net income} + \text{Interest expense}}{\text{Average total assets}}$	Measures how profitably a company uses its assets
12. Rate of return on common stockholders' equity	$\dfrac{\text{Net income} - \text{Preferred dividends}}{\text{Average common stockholders' equity}}$	Gauges how much income is earned for each dollar invested by common shareholders
13. Earnings per share of common stock	$\dfrac{\text{Net income} - \text{Preferred dividends}}{\text{Number of shares of common stock outstanding}}$	Gives the amount of net income earned for each share of the company's common stock
Analyzing stock as an investment:		
14. Price/earnings ratio	$\dfrac{\text{Market price per share of common stock}}{\text{Earnings per share}}$	Indicates the market price of $1 of earnings
15. Dividend yield	$\dfrac{\text{Annual dividend per share of common (or preferred) stock}}{\text{Market price per share of common (or preferred) stock}}$	Shows the percentage of a stock's market value returned as dividends to stockholders each year
16. Book value per share of common stock	$\dfrac{\text{Total stockholders' equity} - \text{Preferred equity}}{\text{Number of shares of common stock outstanding}}$	Indicates the recorded accounting amount for each share of common stock outstanding

SUMMARY PROBLEM 2

Target Corporation's income statement was presented in Summary Problem 1. The company's balance sheets (adapted) at the end of fiscal years 2015 and 2014 are presented below.[4]

	Target Corporation Balance Sheets (Adapted) End of Fiscal Year		
		(amounts in millions)	
		2015	2014
	Assets		
	Current assets:		
	Cash, cash equivalents, and short term investments	$ 4,046	$ 2,210
	Inventory	8,601	8,282
	Other current assets	1,483	3,132
	Total current assets	14,130	13,624
	Property, plant, and equipment, net	25,217	25,952
	Other noncurrent assets	915	1,596
	Total assets	$ 40,262	$ 41,172
	Liabilities		
	Current liabilities:		
	Accounts payable	$ 7,418	$ 7,759
	Other current liabilities	5,204	3,977
	Total current liabilities	12,622	11,736
	Long-term liabilities	14,683	15,439
	Total liabilities	27,305	27,175
	Stockholders' equity		
	Common stock, and additional paid in capital	5,398	4,952
	Retained earnings	7,559	9,045
	Total stockholders' equity	12,957	13,997
	Total liabilities and stockholders' equity	$ 40,262	$ 41,172

NOTE: Target's 2015 and 2014 fiscal years ended January 30, 2016 and January 31, 2015, respectively.

Other company information follows:
- The company has few receivables since customers pay with cash, debit, or credit cards. Target's credit card operations were sold in 2013. Therefore, receivables are reported as part of other current assets.
- There were 627.7 million common shares issued and outstanding at the end of fiscal year 2015. Target had no preferred stock issued or outstanding.
- Cash dividends of $2.20 per share were declared during fiscal year 2015.
- The closing market price per share was $72.42 on January 30, 2016 (the end of fiscal year 2015).[4]

Requirement 1

Calculate the following ratios for fiscal year 2015:

1. Current ratio
2. Acid-test ratio
3. Inventory turnover

---

[4]http://finance.yahoo.com

4. Debt ratio
5. Times-interest-earned ratio
6. Rate of return on net sales
7. Rate of return on total assets
8. Rate of return on common stockholders' equity
9. Earnings per share of common stock
10. Price/earnings ratio
11. Dividend yield
12. Book value per share of common stock

SOLUTIONS

Requirement 1

$$1)\ \text{Current ratio} = \frac{\text{Current assets}}{\text{Current liabilities}}$$

$$= \frac{\$14{,}130}{\$12{,}622} = 1.12$$

$$2)\ \text{Acid-test ratio} = \frac{\text{Cash + ST investments + Net current receivables}}{\text{Current liabilities}}$$

$$= \frac{\$4{,}046 + 0 + \$0}{\$12{,}622} = 0.32$$

$$3)\ \text{Inventory turnover} = \frac{\text{Cost of goods sold}}{\text{Average inventory}}$$

$$= \frac{\$51{,}997}{(\$8{,}282 + \$8{,}601)/2} = 6.16$$

$$4)\ \text{Debt ratio} = \frac{\text{Total liabilities}}{\text{Total assets}}$$

$$= \frac{\$27{,}305}{\$40{,}262} = 0.68$$

$$5)\ \text{Times-interest-earned ratio} = \frac{\text{Income from operations}}{\text{Interest expense}}$$

$$= \frac{\$5{,}530}{\$607} = 9.11$$

6) Rate of return on net sales = $\dfrac{\text{Net income}}{\text{Sales revenue}}$

$= \dfrac{\$3,321}{\$73,785} = 4.50\%$

7) Rate of return on total assets = $\dfrac{\text{Net income} + \text{Interest expense}}{\text{Average total assets}}$

$= \dfrac{\$3,321 + \$607}{(\$41,172 + \$40,262)/2} = 9.65\%$

8) Rate of return on common stockholders' equity = $\dfrac{\text{Net income} - \text{Preferred dividends}}{\text{Average common stockholder's equity}}$

$= \dfrac{\$3,321 - \$0}{(\$12,957 + 13,997)/2} = 24.64\%$

9) Earnings per share of common stock = $\dfrac{\text{Net income} - \text{Preferred dividends}}{\text{Number of shares of common stock outstanding}}$

$= \dfrac{\$3,321}{627.7} = \$5.29$

10) Price/earnings ratio = $\dfrac{\text{Market price per share of common stock}}{\text{Earnings per share}}$

$= \dfrac{\$72.42}{\$5.29} = 13.69$

11) Dividend yield = $\dfrac{\text{Dividend per share of common stock}}{\text{Market price per share of common stock}}$

$= \dfrac{\$2.20}{\$72.42} = 3.04\%$

12) Book value per share of common stock = $\dfrac{\text{Total stockholders' equity} - \text{Preferred equity}}{\text{Number of shares of common stock outstanding}}$

$= \dfrac{\$12,957 - 0}{627.7} = \$20.64$

END OF CHAPTER

Learning Objectives

1. Perform a horizontal analysis of financial statements
2. Perform a vertical analysis of financial statements
3. Prepare and use common-size financial statements
4. Compute the standard financial ratios

Accounting Vocabulary

Accounts Receivable Turnover. (p. 851) Measures a company's ability to collect cash from credit customers. To compute accounts receivable turnover, divide net credit sales by average net accounts receivable.

Acid-Test Ratio. (p. 850) Ratio of the sum of cash plus short-term investments plus net current receivables to total current liabilities. It tells whether the entity can pay all of its current liabilities if they come due immediately; also called the *quick ratio*.

Benchmarking. (p. 845) The practice of comparing a company with other companies or industry averages.

Book Value per Share of Common Stock. (p. 858) Common stockholders' equity divided by the number of shares of common stock outstanding. It is the recorded amount for each share of common stock outstanding.

Common-Size Statement. (p. 845) A financial statement that reports only percentages (no dollar amounts).

Current Ratio. (p. 849) Current assets divided by current liabilities. It measures the ability to pay current liabilities with current assets.

Days' Sales in Receivables. (p. 851) Ratio of average net accounts receivable to one day's sales. It indicates how many days' sales remain in Accounts Receivable awaiting collection.

Debt Ratio. (p. 852) Ratio of total liabilities to total assets. It shows the proportion of a company's assets that is financed with debt.

Dividend Yield. (p. 857) Ratio of dividends per share of stock to the stock's market price per share. It tells the percentage of a stock's market value that the company returns to stockholders annually as dividends.

Earnings per Share (EPS). (p. 856) Amount of a company's net income for each share of its outstanding common stock.

Gross Profit Percentage. (p. 853) The fraction of each dollar of sales revenue that is gross profit, or markup over the cost of the merchandise.

Horizontal Analysis. (p. 839) The comparison of financial statement line items between accounting periods. Changes are shown in gross dollar amounts and as percentages.

Interest-Coverage Ratio. (p. 853) Ratio of income from operations to interest expense. It measures the number of times that operating income can cover interest expense; also called the *times-interest-earned ratio*.

Inventory Turnover. (p. 850) Ratio of cost of goods sold to average inventory. It indicates how rapidly inventory is sold.

Leverage. (p. 856) Earning more income on borrowed money than the related interest expense, thereby increasing the earnings for the owners of the business; also called *trading on equity*.

Operating Income Percentage. (p. 854) The percentage of each sales dollar that becomes income from the company's primary business operations before considering interest and income taxes.

Price/Earnings (P/E) Ratio. (p. 857) Ratio of the market price of a share of common stock to the company's earnings per share. It measures the value that the stock market places on $1 of a company's earnings.

Quick Ratio. (p. 850) Ratio of the sum of cash plus short-term investments plus net current receivables to total current liabilities. It tells whether the entity can pay all its current liabilities if they come due immediately; also called the *acid-test ratio*.

Rate of Return on Common Stockholders' Equity. (p. 855) Net income minus preferred dividends divided by average common stockholders' equity. It is a measure of profitability; also called *return on equity*.

Rate of Return on Net Sales. (p. 854) Ratio of net income to net sales. It is a measure of profitability; also called *return on sales*.

Rate of Return on Total Assets. (p. 855) Net income plus interest expense divided by average total assets. This ratio measures a company's success in using its assets to earn income for the people who finance the business; also called *return on assets*.

Ratio Analysis. (p. 839) Evaluating the relationships between two or more key components of the financial statements.

Return on Assets. (p. 855) Net income plus interest expense, divided by average total assets. This ratio measures a company's success in using its assets to earn income for the people who finance the business; also called *rate of return on total assets*.

Return on Equity. (p. 855) Net income minus preferred dividends, divided by average common stockholders' equity. It is a measure of profitability; also called *rate of return on common stockholders' equity*.

Return on Sales. (p. 854) Ratio of net income to net sales. It is a measure of profitability; also called *rate of return on net sales*.

Times-Interest-Earned Ratio. (p. 853) Ratio of income from operations to interest expense. It measures the number of times operating income can cover interest expense; also called the *interest-coverage ratio*.

Trading on Equity. (p. 856) Earning more income on borrowed money than the related interest expense, thereby increasing the earnings for the owners of the business; also called *leverage*.

Trend Percentages. (p. 841) A form of horizontal analysis over a longer span of time in which percentages are computed by selecting a base year as 100% and expressing amounts for the following years as a percentage of the base amount.

Vertical Analysis. (p. 839) Analysis that shows the relative size of each financial statement line item as a percentage of a base figure. The base figure is usually total sales (for the income statement) or total assets (for the balance sheet).

Working Capital. (p. 849) Current assets minus current liabilities; measures a business's ability to meet its short-term obligations with its current assets.

MyAccountingLab Go to http://myaccountinglab.com/ for the following Quick Check, Short Exercises, Exercises, and Problems. They are available with immediate grading, explanations of correct and incorrect answers, and interactive media that acts as your own online tutor.

Quick Check

1. *(Learning Objective 1)* Which of the following provides a year-to-year comparison of a company's performance in two different years?
   a. Horizontal analysis
   b. Vertical analysis
   c. Ratio analysis
   d. Time study analysis

2. *(Learning Objective 1)* A trend study compares financial performance against
   a. the previous year.
   b. a selected base year.
   c. other companies within the industry.
   d. the company's first year of operations.

3. *(Learning Objective 2)* When performing vertical analysis, each line item on the income statement is computed as a percentage of which of the following?
   a. Net income
   b. Operating expenses
   c. Sales revenue
   d. Cost of goods sold

4. *(Learning Objective 2)* When performing vertical analysis, each line item on the balance sheet is computed as a percentage of which of the following?
   a. Total cash flows
   b. Total stockholders' equity
   c. Total assets
   d. Total liabilities

5. *(Learning Objective 3)* Which of the following is used to compare one company against another or against an industry average, using percentages as a comparison mechanism?
   a. Percentage statement
   b. Horizontal statement
   c. Comparison statement
   d. Common-size statement

6. *(Learning Objective 4)* Working capital is defined as
   a. current assets minus current liabilities.
   b. current liabilities minus current assets.
   c. current liabilities plus current assets.
   d. cash minus current liabilities.

7. *(Learning Objective 4)* Which of the following ratios measures a company's ability to pay current liabilities?
   a. Inventory turnover
   b. Debt ratio
   c. Dividend yield
   d. Acid-test, or quick, ratio

8. *(Learning Objective 4)* Which of the following ratios is used to measure profitability?
   a. Current ratio
   b. Rate of return on net sales
   c. Times interest earned
   d. Days' sales in receivables

9. *(Learning Objective 4) Leverage* refers to how companies finance their operations with
   a. issued stock.
   b. treasury stock.
   c. inventory.
   d. debt.

10. *(Learning Objective 4)* Which of the following is generally undesirable?
    a. Increase in times-interest-earned ratio
    b. Decrease in days' sales in receivables
    c. Decrease in inventory turnover
    d. Decrease in debt ratio

Quick Check Answers

1. a 2. b 3. c 4. c 5. d 6. a 7. d 8. b 9. d 10. c

Short Exercises

S14-1 Horizontal analysis of revenue and cost of sales *(Learning Objective 1)*

Parkins Corporation reported the following on its comparative income statement:

(in millions)	2017	2016	2015
Revenue	$13,390	$12,875	$12,500
Cost of sales	$ 6,550	$ 5,750	$ 5,000

Perform a horizontal analysis of revenues and gross profit—both in dollar amounts and in percentages—for 2017 and 2016.

S14-2 Find trend percentages *(Learning Objective 1)*

Bradley Group reported the following revenues and net income amounts:

(in millions)	2017	2016	2015	2014
Revenue	$8,670	$7,990	$7,565	$8,500
Net income	$ 636	$ 594	$ 570	$ 600

a. Show Bradley Group's trend percentages for revenues and net income. Use 2014 as the base year and round to the nearest percent.
b. Which measure increased faster during 2015–2017?

S14-3 Vertical analysis of assets *(Learning Objective 2)*

McCormick Optical Company reported the following amounts on its balance sheet at December 31:

Cash and receivables	$ 49,980
Inventory	43,470
Property, plant, and equipment, net	116,550
Total assets	$210,000

Perform a vertical analysis of McCormick Optical Company's assets at year end.

S14-4 Prepare common-size income statements *(Learning Objective 3)*

Compare Martinez and Rojo by converting their income statements to common size.

	Martinez	Rojo
Net sales	$10,900	$19,536
Cost of goods sold	6,660	14,203
Other expense	3,564	4,356
Net income	$ 676	$ 977

Which company earns more net income? Which company's net income is a higher percentage of its net sales?

S14-5 Analyze common-size income statements *(Learning Objectives 1, 2, & 3)*

Pandora Internet Radio by Pandora Media is a streaming music service. Its free advertising-supported radio service was first launched in 2005. Pandora users streamed 20.03 billion hours of Internet radio during 2014. In December 2014, there were 81.5 million active users of Pandora, making it the largest streaming music service currently. Pandora has a database of over 1,000,000 songs from over 125,000 artists.

Pandora offers its streaming music through two services:

1. Free Service: This option allows the listener access to the music by including advertisements.
2. Pandora One: This option is a paid subscription model without any advertisements; it also allows users to have more daily skips and longer listening times.

While Pandora currently has plenty of cash from its investors, it has yet to generate a profit since its inception. Pandora is facing increasing competition from sources such as Apple Music (approximately 6.5 million subscribers in 2015), Spotify (approximately 20 million paid subscribers in 2015), and other streaming services. In addition, Pandora's costs in some areas are increasing.

When Pandora released its earnings for the third quarter of 2015, earnings were less than expected by investors and Pandora's stock price fell sharply. Following are excerpts from Pandora's statement of operations, both in dollars and in common-size formats. (These excerpts are condensed for educational use only.)

	Three months ended September 30, 2014	Three months ended September 30, 2015	Nine months ended September 30, 2014	Nine months ended September 30, 2015
Pandora Media, Inc.				
Excerpt from Condensed Consolidated Statements of Operations - in DOLLARS				
(in thousands, except per share amounts) - UNAUDITED				
Revenues				
Advertising	$ 194,293	$ 254,656	$ 512,251	$ 664,316
Subscription and other	45,300	56,906	140,551	163,570
Total revenue	239,593	311,562	652,802	827,886
Cost of revenue				
Cost of revenue - Content acquisition costs	111,315	211,272	331,051	467,429
Cost of revenue - Other	15,453	21,414	44,421	57,690
Total cost of revenue	126,768	232,686	375,472	525,119
Gross profit	112,825	78,876	277,330	302,767
Operating expenses				
Product development	13,381	21,849	38,288	56,466
Sales and marketing	72,320	107,286	200,416	285,595
General and administrative	29,143	35,603	81,369	111,169
Total operating expenses	114,844	164,738	320,073	453,230
Loss from operations	$ (2,019)	$ (85,862)	$ (42,743)	$ (150,463)

Source: Pandora Media, Inc., 3rd Quarter 2015, Financial Results

	Three months ended September 30, 2014	Three months ended September 30, 2015	Nine months ended September 30, 2014	Nine months ended September 30, 2015
Pandora Media, Inc.				
Excerpt from Condensed Consolidated Statements of Operations - COMMON-SIZE				
(in thousands, except per share amounts) - UNAUDITED				
Revenues				
Advertising	81%	82%	78%	80%
Subscription and other	19%	18%	22%	20%
Total revenue	100%	100%	100%	100%
Cost of revenue				
Cost of revenue - Content acquisition costs	46%	68%	51%	56%
Cost of revenue - Other	6%	7%	7%	7%
Total cost of revenue	53%	75%	58%	63%
Gross profit	47%	25%	42%	37%
Operating expenses				
Product development	6%	7%	6%	7%
Sales and marketing	30%	34%	31%	34%
General and administrative	12%	11%	12%	13%
Total operating expenses	48%	53%	49%	55%
Loss from operations	-1%	-28%	-7%	-18%

Source: Pandora Media, Inc., 3rd Quarter 2015, Financial Results

Requirements

1. Using the statement of operations excerpt *in dollars*, what can you say about how Pandora is doing in the third quarter of 2015 compared to the third quarter of 2014? What can you say about how Pandora is doing for the nine months ended September 30, 2015 compared to September 30, 2014? Can you tell if the rate of increase is greater for revenues or expenses from 2014 to 2015? Why or why not?
2. Using the statement of operations excerpt *in dollars* again, why is the loss from operations larger in 2015 than in 2014?
3. Using the *common-size* statement of operations excerpt, what can you say about how Pandora is doing in the third quarter of 2015 compared to the third quarter of 2014? What can you say about how Pandora is doing for the nine months ended September 30, 2015 compared to September 30, 2014? Is the rate of increase greater for revenues or expenses from 2014 to 2015?
4. Using the *common-size* statement of operations excerpt again, why is the loss from operations larger in 2015 than in 2014? Also, what can you say about the mix of advertising revenue versus subscription revenue?
5. Which statement (dollars versus common-size) is more useful for analyzing the financial performance of Pandora in this case? Explain.

Cartwright's Data Set used for S14-6 through S14-10:

Cartwright's, a home-improvement store chain, reported these summarized figures:

	A	B
1	Cartwright's	
2	Income Statement	
3	For the Year Ended December 31, 2017	
4		
5		**2017**
6	Sales revenues	$ 34,988,900
7	Less: Cost of goods sold	21,766,030
8	Gross profit	$ 13,222,870
9	Less: Operating expenses	5,088,250
10	Operating income	$ 8,134,620
11	Less: Interest expense	217,800
12	Income before income taxes	$ 7,916,820
13	Less: Income tax expense	1,925,750
14	Net income	$ 5,991,070
15		

	A	B	C
1	Cartwright's		
2	Balance Sheets		
3	December 31, 2017 and 2016		
4			
5		2017	2016
6	**Assets**		
7	Current assets:		
8	Cash	$ 1,200,000	$ 810,000
9	Short-term investments	203,200	260,000
10	Accounts receivable	100,800	378,500
11	Inventory	4,676,000	4,190,000
12	Other current assets	508,000	409,500
13	Total current assets	$ 6,688,000	$ 6,048,000
14	Other noncurrent assets	11,437,000	11,620,000
15	Total assets	$ 18,125,000	$ 17,668,000
16			
17	**Liabilities**		
18	Current liabilities:		
19	Accounts payable	$ 3,400,000	$ 2,750,000
20	Notes payable	890,000	655,000
21	Accrued liabilities	110,000	195,000
22	Total current liabilities	$ 4,400,000	$ 3,600,000
23	Long-term liabilities	4,300,000	4,216,000
24	Total liabilities	$ 8,700,000	$ 7,816,000
25			
26	**Stockholders' equity**		
27	Common stock, no par	$ 2,502,000	$ 2,000,000
28	Retained earnings	6,923,000	7,852,000
29	Total stockholders' equity	$ 9,425,000	$ 9,852,000
30			
31	Total liabilities and equity	$ 18,125,000	$ 17,668,000
32			

S14-6   Find current ratio *(Learning Objective 4)*

Refer to the Cartwright's Data Set.

a. Compute Cartwright's current ratio at December 31, 2017 and 2016.

b. Did Cartwright's current ratio improve, deteriorate, or hold steady during 2017?

S14-7   Analyze inventory and receivables *(Learning Objective 4)*

Use the Cartwright's Data Set to compute the following:

a. The rate of inventory turnover for 2017.

b. Days' sales in average receivables during 2017. Assume all sales are on credit.

S14-8   Compute and interpret debt ratio *(Learning Objective 4)*

Refer to the Cartwright's Data Set.

a. Compute the debt ratio at December 31, 2017.

b. Is Cartwright's ability to pay its liabilities strong or weak? Explain your reasoning.

S14-9   Compute profitability ratios *(Learning Objective 4)*

Use the Cartwright's Data Set to compute these profitability measures for 2017:

a. Gross profit percentage

b. Operating income percentage

c. Rate of return on net sales

d. Rate of return on total assets

e. Rate of return on common stockholders' equity

Are these rates of return strong or weak?

S14-10 Determine earnings per share (Learning Objective 4)

Use the Cartwright's Data Set when making the following calculations:

a. Compute earnings per share (EPS) for Cartwright's. The number of shares outstanding was 720,000.

b. Compute Cartwright's price/earnings ratio. The price of a share of Cartwright's is $62.50.

S14-11 Identify ethical standards violated (Learning Objectives 1, 2, 3, & 4)

ETHICS

For each of the situations listed, identify the primary standard from the IMA *Statement of Ethical Professional Practice* that is violated (competence, confidentiality, integrity, or credibility). Refer to Exhibit 1-6 for the complete standard.

1. Ben has not participated in any continuing education activities since he graduated five years ago because life has just been too busy. He is unprepared for the company to implement the new revenue recognition standards.

2. Tim, the corporate controller, prepares a report for the board of directors that summarizes the year. Tim, wanting to look good, only includes the favorable ratios and favorable events in this report.

3. Colton talks about the financial woes of the company he works for when he is out with a group of friends. He shares that the company will not be able to meet the ratios specified in the loan covenants.

4. Jordan prepares the financial statements, but the internal control system weaknesses are not disclosed.

5. Sarah, an accountant working in the Accounts Payable Department, writes a company check to herself for $1,500 to temporarily borrow money to pay her apartment rent; she plans on paying the money back after her next paycheck.

EXERCISES Group A

E14-12A Trend analysis of working capital (Learning Objective 1)

Compute the dollar amount of change and the percentage of change in Gambol News Group's working capital each year during 2016 and 2017. Is this trend favorable or unfavorable?

	2017	2016	2015
Total current assets	$275,640	$254,000	$214,500
Total current liabilities	$195,000	$182,000	$152,000

E14-13A Horizontal analysis (Learning Objective 1)

Prepare a horizontal analysis of the following comparative income statement of The Ruby Group.

	A	B	C
1	The Ruby Group		
2	Income Statement		
3	For the Years Ended December 31, 2017 and 2016		
4		(amounts in thousands)	
5		2017	2016
6	Sales revenues	$ 458,800	$ 400,000
7	Less: Cost of goods sold	209,820	195,000
8	Gross profit	$ 248,980	$ 205,000
9	Less: Operating expenses	95,670	90,000
10	Operating income	$ 153,310	$ 115,000
11	Less: Interest expense	4,250	3,125
12	Income before income taxes	$ 149,060	$ 111,875
13	Less: Income tax expense	16,420	11,875
14	Net income	$ 132,640	$ 100,000
15			

Why did net income increase by a higher percentage than net sales revenue during 2017?

E14-14A Compute trend percentages *(Learning Objective 1)*

Compute trend percentages for Elsie Snyder Realtors' net revenue and net income for the following five-year period, using 2013 as the base year.

(in thousands)	2017	2016	2015	2014	2013
Net revenue	$1,254	$1,026	$988	$893	$950
Net income	$ 174	$ 162	$114	$102	$120

Which grew faster during the period, net revenue or net income?

E14-15A Perform vertical analysis *(Learning Objective 2)*

Riley Designs has requested that you perform a vertical analysis of its balance sheet.

	A	B
1	Riley Designs, Inc.	
2	Balance Sheet	
3	As of December 31	
4		
5		For the year (in thousands)
6	**Assets**	
7	Total current assets	$ 43,605
8	Property, plant, and equipment, net	204,915
9	Other noncurrent assets	36,480
10	Total assets	$ 285,000
11		
12	**Liabilities**	
13	Total current liabilities	$ 52,440
14	Long-term liabilities	108,870
15	Total liabilities	$ 161,310
16		
17	**Stockholders' equity**	
18	Total stockholders' equity	123,690
19		
20	Total liabilities and equity	$ 285,000
21		

E14-16A Prepare a common-size income statement *(Learning Objective 3)*

Prepare a comparative common-size income statement for Jubilee Corporation. To an investor, how does 2017 compare with 2016? Explain your reasoning.

	A	B	C
1	Jubilee Corporation		
2	Income Statement		
3	For the Years Ended December 31, 2017 and 2016		
4		(amounts in thousands)	
5		2017	2016
6	Sales revenues	$ 494,208	$ 429,000
7	Less: Cost of goods sold	172,640	160,000
8	Gross profit	$ 321,568	$ 269,000
9	Less: Operating expenses	143,370	135,000
10	Operating income	$ 178,198	$ 134,000
11	Less: Interest expense	7,500	6,000
12	Income before income taxes	$ 170,698	$ 128,000
13	Less: Income tax expense	33,990	24,000
14	Net income	$ 136,708	$ 104,000
15			

E14-17A Calculate ratios *(Learning Objective 4)*

Kelleher Crafts has provided the following data:

	A	B	C
1	**Balance sheet item:**	**Current year**	**Preceding year**
2	Cash	$ 16,000	$ 21,000
3	Short-term investments	$ 14,730	$ 25,500
4	Net receivables	$ 50,000	$ 76,140
5	Inventory	$ 74,000	$ 73,000
6	Prepaid expenses	$ 17,260	$ 9,500
7	Total current assets	$ 171,990	$ 205,140
8	Total current liabilities	$ 117,000	$ 88,000
9			
10	**Income statement:**		
11	Net credit sales	$ 434,350	
12	Cost of goods sold	$ 323,400	
13			

Requirement

Compute the following ratios for the current year for Kelleher Crafts:

a. Current ratio
b. Acid-test ratio
c. Inventory turnover
d. Days' sales in average receivables (assume all sales are on credit)

E14-18A More ratio analysis *(Learning Objective 4)*

McKay Frames has asked you to determine whether the company's ability to pay current liabilities and total liabilities improved or deteriorated during 2017. To answer that question, compute these ratios for 2017 and 2016, using the following data:

	A	B	C
1		**2017**	**2016**
2	Cash	$ 59,500	$ 49,500
3	Short-term investments	$ 28,500	$ 0
4	Net receivables	$ 137,150	$ 127,300
5	Inventory	$ 250,800	$ 284,960
6	Total assets	$ 555,000	$ 486,000
7	Total current liabilities	$ 285,000	$ 208,000
8	Long-term notes payable	$ 48,000	$ 30,140
9	Income from operations	$ 164,350	$ 169,260
10	Interest expense	$ 47,500	$ 42,000
11			

a. Current ratio
b. Acid-test ratio
c. Debt ratio
d. Times-interest-earned ratio

E14-19A Compute profitability ratios *(Learning Objective 4)*

Compute six ratios that measure Spenser Corporation's ability to earn profits. The company's comparative income statement follows. The data for 2015 are given as needed.

	A	B	C
1	Spenser Corporation		
2	Income Statement		
3	For the Years Ended December 31, 2017 and 2016		
4	(amounts in thousands)		
5		2017	2016	2015
6	Sales revenues	$ 211,400	$ 182,910	
7	Less: Cost of goods sold	105,000	96,000	
8	Gross profit	$ 106,400	$ 86,910	
9	Less: Operating expenses	53,000	46,000	
10	Operating income	$ 53,400	$ 40,910	
11	Less: Interest expense	5,385	6,459	
12	Income before income taxes	$ 48,015	$ 34,451	
13	Less: Income tax expense	22,647	16,160	
14	Net income	$ 25,368	$ 18,291	
15				
16	Additional data:			
17	Total assets	$ 207,000	$ 195,000	$ 180,000
18	Common stockholders' equity	$ 101,000	$ 92,000	$ 61,110
19	Preferred dividends	$ 2,980	$ 2,980	$ 0
20	Common shares outstanding during the year	27,985	27,985	26,000
21				

Did the company's operating performance improve or deteriorate during 2017?

E14-20A Compute stock ratios *(Learning Objective 4)*

Evaluate the common stock of McKnight State Bank as an investment. Specifically, use the three stock ratios to determine whether the common stock has increased or decreased in attractiveness during the past year.

	Current year	Last year
Net income	$ 80,400	$ 47,200
Dividends—common	$ 21,580	$ 21,580
Dividends—preferred	$ 14,000	$ 14,000
Total stockholders' equity at year end (includes 83,000 shares of common stock)	$809,300	$639,150
Preferred stock, 6%	$220,000	$220,000
Market price per share of common	$ 20.00	$ 8.00

E14-21A Calculate ratios *(Learning Objective 4)*

Freedom Corporation reported these figures:

Freedom Corporation Balance Sheets December 31, 2017 and 2016 (amounts in thousands)			Freedom Corporation Income Statement For the Year Ended December 31, 2017 (amounts in thousands)	
	2017	2016		2017
Assets			Sales revenues	$ 15,330
Current assets:			Less: Cost of goods sold	5,120
Cash	$ 3,720	$ 2,600	Gross profit	$ 10,210
Accounts receivable	3,000	2,460	Less: Operating expenses	3,010
Inventory	1,900	1,300	Operating income	$ 7,200
Other current assets	2,300	1,990	Less: Interest expense	300
Total current assets	$ 10,920	$ 8,350	Income before income taxes	$ 6,900
Other assets	20,000	18,000	Less: Income tax expense	4,550
Total assets	$ 30,920	$ 26,350	Net income	$ 2,350
Liabilities				
Total current liabilities	$ 12,000	$ 10,500		
Long-term liabilities	7,920	8,050		
Total liabilities	$ 19,920	$ 18,550		
Stockholders' equity				
Total common stockholders' equity	11,000	7,800		
Total liabilities and equity	$ 30,920	$ 26,350		

Freedom Corporation has 2,500,000 shares of common stock outstanding. Its stock has traded recently at $32.90 per share. You would like to gain a better understanding of Freedom Corporation's financial position. Assume all sales are on credit. Calculate the following ratios for 2017 and interpret the results:

a. Inventory turnover
b. Days' sales in receivables
c. Acid-test ratio
d. Times-interest-earned
e. Gross profit percentage
f. Operating income percentage
g. Return on stockholders' equity
h. Earnings per share
i. Price/earnings ratio

E14-22A Classify company sustainability measurements into triple-bottom-line components *(Learning Objective 4)*

SUSTAINABILITY

In its 2014/2015 Sustainable Business Report and its annual report, NIKE, Inc., describes several sustainability goals and commitments it has made. In the following list, categorize each goal (or measurement) as to whether it is oriented toward the *people*, *planet*, or *profit* component of the triple bottom line.

	Goal or Commitment	People, Profit, or Planet?
a.	Use only renewable energy by the end of fiscal year 2025	
b.	Grow revenues to $50 billion by the end of fiscal year 2020	
c.	Reduce water usage in textile dyeing by 20% by 2020	
d.	Inspire majority of employees to engage in their communities with time, expertise, and money	
e.	Increase employee volunteer hours in their communities	
f.	Calculate sustainability performance scores for over 80% of all NIKE products by 2020	
g.	Continue to shift worker responsibilities from low-skilled machinery work to a more enriched job, including collaboration, problem solving, and communications	
h.	Increase the number of women in leadership positions	
i.	Reduce carbon emissions per unit of apparel and footwear by 10% as compared to 2015	
j.	Increase return on invested capital for shareholders	
k.	Reduce waste generated by 5% per unit in distribution centers by 2020	
l.	Invest a minimum of 1.5% of pre-tax income in community programs	

EXERCISES Group B

E14-23B Trend analysis of working capital (Learning Objective 1)

Compute the dollar amount of change and the percentage of change in Crocker News Group's working capital each year during 2016 and 2017. Is this trend favorable or unfavorable?

	2017	2016	2015
Total current assets...	$358,290	$323,500	$291,500
Total current liabilities	$189,000	$175,000	$154,000

E14-24B Horizontal analysis (Learning Objective 1)

Prepare a horizontal analysis of the following comparative income statement of The Slate Group.

	A	B	C
1	The Slate Group		
2	Income Statement		
3	For the Years Ended December 31, 2017 and 2016		
4		(amounts in thousands)	
5		2017	2016
6	Sales revenues	$ 460,000	$ 400,000
7	Less: Cost of goods sold	216,200	200,000
8	Gross profit	$ 243,800	$ 200,000
9	Less: Operating expenses	105,800	100,000
10	Operating income	$ 138,000	$ 100,000
11	Less: Interest expense	9,000	6,000
12	Income before income taxes	$ 129,000	$ 94,000
13	Less: Income tax expense	18,600	14,000
14	Net income	$ 110,400	$ 80,000
15			

Why did net income increase by a higher percentage than net sales revenue during 2017?

E14-25B Compute trend percentages *(Learning Objective 1)*

Compute trend percentages for Barb Sayre Realtors' net revenue and net income for the following five-year period, using 2013 as the base year.

(in thousands)	2017	2016	2015	2014	2013
Net revenue	$1,397	$1,265	$1,177	$1,034	$1,100
Net income	$ 217	$ 196	$ 133	$ 126	$ 140

Which grew faster during the period, net revenue or net income?

E14-26B Perform vertical analysis *(Learning Objective 2)*

Carolina Designs has requested that you perform a vertical analysis of its balance sheet.

	A	B
1	Carolina Designs, Inc.	
2	Balance Sheet	
3	As of December 31	
4		
5		For the year (in thousands)
6	Assets	
7	Total current assets	$ 41,720
8	Property, plant, and equipment, net	202,720
9	Other noncurrent assets	35,560
10	Total assets	$ 280,000
11		
12	Liabilities	
13	Total current liabilities	$ 52,920
14	Long-term liabilities	106,400
15	Total liabilities	$ 159,320
16		
17	Stockholders' equity	
18	Total stockholders' equity	120,680
19		
20	Total liabilities and equity	$ 280,000
21		

E14-27B Prepare common-size income statement *(Learning Objective 3)*

Prepare a comparative common-size income statement for Wolf Corporation. To an investor, how does 2017 compare with 2016? Explain your reasoning.

	A	B	C
1	Wolf Corporation		
2	Income Statement		
3	For the Years Ended December 31, 2017 and 2016		
4		(amounts in thousands)	
5		2017	2016
6	Sales revenues	$ 458,800	$ 400,000
7	Less: Cost of goods sold	209,820	195,000
8	Gross profit	$ 248,980	$ 205,000
9	Less: Operating expenses	95,670	90,000
10	Operating income	$ 153,310	$ 115,000
11	Less: Interest expense	4,250	3,125
12	Income before income taxes	$ 149,060	$ 111,875
13	Less: Income tax expense	16,420	11,875
14	Net income	$ 132,640	$ 100,000
15			

E14-28B Calculate ratios *(Learning Objective 4)*

Ponderosa Crafts has provided the following data:

	A	B	C
1	**Balance sheet item:**	**Current year**	**Preceding year**
2	Cash	$ 16,500	$ 23,500
3	Short-term investments	$ 10,750	$ 24,000
4	Net receivables	$ 49,000	$ 77,360
5	Inventory	$ 81,000	$ 78,500
6	Prepaid expenses	$ 21,500	$ 8,000
7	Total current assets	$ 178,750	$ 211,360
8	Total current liabilities	$ 125,000	$ 86,000
9			
10	**Income statement:**		
11	Net credit sales	$ 427,050	
12	Cost of goods sold	$ 319,000	
13			

Requirement

Compute the following ratios for the current year for Ponderosa Crafts:

a. Current ratio
b. Acid-test ratio
c. Inventory turnover
d. Days' sales in average receivables (assume all sales are on credit)

E14-29B More ratio analysis *(Learning Objective 4)*

Bricker Frames has asked you to determine whether the company's ability to pay current liabilities and total liabilities improved or deteriorated during 2017. To answer this question, compute these ratios for 2017 and 2016, using the following data:

	A	B	C
1		**2017**	**2016**
2	Cash	$ 61,500	$ 47,000
3	Short-term investments	$ 26,000	$ 0
4	Net receivables	$ 126,560	$ 118,240
5	Inventory	$ 236,300	$ 271,320
6	Total assets	$ 564,000	$ 492,000
7	Total current liabilities	$ 278,000	$ 204,000
8	Long-term notes payable	$ 20,920	$ 46,920
9	Income from operations	$ 166,110	$ 159,580
10	Interest expense	$ 49,000	$ 39,500
11			

a. Current ratio
b. Acid-test ratio
c. Debt ratio
d. Times-interest-earned ratio

E14-30B Compute profitability ratios *(Learning Objective 4)*

Compute six ratios that measure Tomloff Corporation's ability to earn profits. The company's comparative income statement follows. The data for 2015 are given as needed.

	A	B	C
1	Tomloff Corporation		
2	Income Statement		
3	For the Years Ended December 31, 2017 and 2016		
4	(amounts in thousands)		
5		2017	2016	2015
6	Sales revenues	$ 178,120	$ 167,725	
7	Less: Cost of goods sold	94,000	88,000	
8	Gross profit	$ 84,120	$ 79,725	
9	Less: Operating expenses	43,000	35,000	
10	Operating income	$ 41,120	$ 44,725	
11	Less: Interest expense	7,360	8,100	
12	Income before income taxes	$ 33,760	$ 36,625	
13	Less: Income tax expense	11,495	23,207	
14	Net income	$ 22,265	$ 13,418	
15				
16	Additional data:			
17	Total assets	$ 203,000	$ 192,000	$ 179,000
18	Common stockholders' equity	$ 110,050	$ 86,000	$ 77,000
19	Preferred dividends	$ 2,660	$ 2,660	0
20	Common shares outstanding during the year	26,140	26,140	24,000
21				

Did the company's operating performance improve or deteriorate during 2017?

E14-31B Compute stock ratios *(Learning Objective 4)*

Evaluate the common stock of Mumford State Bank as an investment. Specifically, use the three stock ratios to determine whether the common stock has increased or decreased in attractiveness during the past year.

	Current year	Last year
Net income	$ 68,250	$ 57,500
Dividends—common	$ 22,575	$ 22,575
Dividends—preferred	$ 14,500	$ 14,500
Total stockholders' equity at year-end (includes 86,000 shares of common stock)	$ 852,800	$ 642,100
Preferred stock (6%)	$ 225,000	$ 225,000
Market price per share of common stock	$ 18.80	$ 12.50

E14-32B Calculate ratios *(Learning Objective 4)*

Thornton Corporation reported these figures:

	A	B	C	D	E	F
1	**Thornton Corporation**				**Thornton Corporation**	
2	**Balance Sheets**				**Income Statement**	
3	**December 31, 2017 and 2016**				**For the Year Ended December 31, 2017**	
4	*(amounts in thousands)*				*(amounts in thousands)*	
5		2017	2016			2017
6	**Assets**				Sales revenues	$ 13,140
7	Current assets:				Less: Cost of goods sold	1,980
8	Cash	$ 5,700	$ 2,700		Gross profit	$ 11,160
9	Accounts receivable	2,100	1,860		Less: Operating expenses	660
10	Inventory	1,000	800		Operating income	$ 10,500
11	Other current assets	3,950	2,640		Less: Interest expense	500
12	Total current assets	$ 12,750	$ 8,000		Income before income taxes	$ 10,000
13	Other assets	23,500	20,000		Less: Income tax expense	7,000
14	Total assets	$ 36,250	$ 28,000		Net income	$ 3,000
15						
16	**Liabilities**					
17	Total current liabilities	$ 15,000	$ 12,500			
18	Long-term liabilities	6,250	5,500			
19	Total liabilities	$ 21,250	$ 18,000			
20						
21	**Stockholders' equity**					
22	Total common stockholders' equity	15,000	10,000			
23						
24	Total liabilities and equity	$ 36,250	$ 28,000			
25						

Thornton Corporation has 3,125,000 shares of common stock outstanding. Its stock has traded recently at $31.20 per share. You would like to gain a better understanding of Thornton Corporation's financial position. Assume all sales are on credit. Calculate the following ratios for 2017 and interpret the results:

a. Inventory turnover
b. Days' sales in receivables
c. Acid-test ratio
d. Times-interest-earned
e. Gross profit percentage
f. Operating income percentage
g. Return on stockholders' equity
h. Earnings per share
i. Price/earnings ratio

E14-33B **Classify company sustainability measurements into triple-bottom-line components** *(Learning Objective 4)*

In its 2014/2015 Sustainable Business Report and its annual report, NIKE, Inc., describes several sustainability goals and commitments it has made. In the following list, categorize each goal (or measurement) as to whether it is oriented toward the *people*, *planet*, or *profit* component of the triple bottom line.

Goal or Commitment	People, Profit, or Planet?
a. Provide access to early active lifestyle programs for kids ages 7 to 12	
b. Increase use of more sustainable materials in apparel and footwear by 2010	
c. Return 100% of wastewater cleaner than required by law by 2020	
d. Eliminate excessive overtime violations in contract factories	
e. Increase diluted earnings per share	
f. Achieve goal of zero discharge of hazardous chemicals throughout all supply chains	
g. Strive for a diverse workforce	
h. Eliminate landfill and incinerator waste from footwear manufacturing by 2020	
i. Increase availability of training to all employees	
j. Reduce waste generated by 5% per unit in finished goods manufacturing by 2020	
k. Reduce the average environmental footprint (impact) of each NIKE product by 10% by 2020	
l. Grow revenues to $50 billion by the end of fiscal year 2020	

PROBLEMS Group A

P14-34A Prepare trend analysis *(Learning Objectives 1 & 4)*

Net sales revenue, net income, and common stockholders' equity for Vallen Optical Corporation, a manufacturer of contact lenses, follow for a four-year period.

(in thousands)	2017	2016	2015	2014
Net sales revenue	$7,437	$7,035	$6,499	$6,700
Net income	$ 700	$ 476	$ 420	$ 560
Ending common stockholders' equity	$5,525	$3,225	$5,275	$3,125

Requirements

1. Compute trend percentages for each item for 2014 through 2017. Use 2014 as the base year.
2. Compute the rate of return on common stockholders' equity for 2015 through 2017.

P14-35A Comprehensive analysis *(Learning Objectives 2, 3, & 4)*

Block Department Stores' chief executive officer (CEO) has asked you to compare the company's profit performance and financial position with the average for the industry. The CEO has given you the company's income statement and balance sheet, as well as the industry average data for retailers.

Block Department Stores, Inc.
Income Statement Compared with Industry Average
For the Year Ended December 31

(amounts in thousands)

	Block	Industry Average
Sales revenues	$ 782,000	100.0%
Less: Cost of goods sold	526,286	65.7%
Gross profit	$ 255,714	34.3%
Less: Operating expenses	164,220	19.5%
Operating income	$ 91,494	14.8%
Less: Interest expense	1,173	0.5%
Income before income taxes	$ 90,321	14.3%
Less: Income tax expense	5,083	0.3%
Net income	$ 85,238	14.0%

Block Department Stores, Inc.
Balance Sheet Compared with Industry Average
As of December 31
(amounts in thousands)

	Block	Industry Average
Assets		
Current assets	$ 312,340	70.9%
Fixed assets, net	117,760	23.7%
Intangible assets, net	5,980	0.7%
Other assets	23,920	4.7%
Total assets	$ 460,000	100.0%
Liabilities		
Current liabilities	$ 213,440	48.3%
Long-term liabilities	104,880	16.7%
Total liabilities	$ 318,320	65.0%
Stockholders' equity		
Total common stockholders' equity	$ 141,680	35.0%
Total liabilities and equity	$ 460,000	100.0%

Requirements

1. Prepare a common-size income statement and balance sheet for Block Department Stores. The first column of each statement should present Block Department Stores' common-size statement, while the second column should present the industry averages.
2. For the profitability analysis, compute Block Department Stores' (a) ratio of gross profit to sales, (b) ratio of operating income to sales, and (c) ratio of net income to sales. Compare these figures with the industry averages. Is Block Department Stores' profit performance better or worse than the industry average?
3. For the analysis of financial position, compute Block Department Stores' (a) ratio of current assets to total assets and (b) ratio of stockholders' equity to total assets. Compare these ratios with the industry averages. Is Block Department Stores' financial position better or worse than the industry averages?

P14-36A Effect of transactions on ratios (Learning Objective 4)

Financial statement data of *Pacific Traveler* magazine include the following items (dollars in thousands):

Cash	$ 24,500
Accounts receivable, net	$ 83,000
Inventories	$180,500
Total assets	$660,000
Short-term notes payable	$ 49,500
Accounts payable	$106,000
Accrued liabilities	$ 44,500
Long-term liabilities	$182,800
Net income	$ 63,180
Common shares outstanding	54,000

Requirements

1. Compute *Pacific Traveler's* current ratio, debt ratio, and earnings per share. Round all ratios to two decimal places.
2. Compute the three ratios after evaluating the effect of each transaction that follows. Consider each transaction *separately*.
   a. Purchased inventory on account, $75,000
   b. Borrowed $264,000 on a long-term note payable
   c. Issued 6,750 shares of common stock, receiving cash of $210,000
   d. Received cash on account, $20,500

P14-37A Ratio analysis over two years (Learning Objective 4)

Comparative financial statement data of Tennyson, Inc., follow:

Tennyson, Inc. Comparative Income Statements For the Years Ended December 31, 2017 and 2016		
	(amounts in thousands)	
	2017	2016
Sales revenues	$ 445,910	$ 425,080
Less: Cost of goods sold	236,000	224,000
Gross profit	$ 209,910	$ 201,080
Less: Operating expenses	132,000	128,000
Operating income	$ 77,910	$ 73,080
Less: Interest expense	10,600	11,600
Income before income taxes	$ 67,310	$ 61,480
Less: Income tax expense	18,860	19,630
Net income	$ 48,450	$ 41,850

	A	B	C	D
1	Tennyson, Inc.			
2	Comparative Balance Sheets			
3	December 31, 2017 and 2016			
4	(amounts in thousands)			
5		2017	2016	2015*
6	Assets			
7	Current assets:			
8	Cash	$ 98,000	$ 99,000	
9	Accounts receivable	118,500	114,500	$ 103,500
10	Inventory	132,000	163,000	$ 157,000
11	Prepaid expenses	13,500	8,500	
12	Total current assets	$ 362,000	$ 385,000	
13	Property, plant, and equipment, net	205,000	174,000	
14	Total assets	$ 567,000	$ 559,000	
15				
16	Liabilities			
17	Current liabilities	$ 200,000	$ 220,000	
18	Long-term liabilities	139,000	157,000	
19	Total liabilities	$ 339,000	$ 377,000	
20				
21	Stockholders' equity			
22	Preferred stock, 7%	$ 95,000	$ 95,000	
23	Total common stockholders' equity	133,000	87,000	$ 133,000
24	Total stockholders' equity	$ 228,000	$ 182,000	
25				
26	Total liabilities and equity	$ 567,000	$ 559,000	
27				

*Selected 2015 amounts

1. Market price of Tennyson's common stock: $43.51 at December 31, 2017, and $31.36 at December 31, 2016
2. Common shares outstanding: 11,000,000 during 2017 and 11,000,000 during 2016
3. All sales are credit sales

Requirements

1. Compute the following ratios for 2017 and 2016:
    a. Current ratio
    b. Times-interest-earned ratio
    c. Inventory turnover
    d. Operating income percentage
    e. Return on common stockholders' equity
    f. Earnings per share of common stock
    g Price/earnings ratio
2. Decide (a) whether Tennyson's ability to pay debts and to sell inventory improved or deteriorated during 2017 and (b) whether the investment attractiveness of its common stock appears to have increased or decreased.

P14-38A Make an investment decision (Learning Objective 4)

Assume that you are purchasing an investment and have decided to invest in a company in the smartphone business. You have narrowed the choice to Best Digital Electronics or Zone Network Electronics and have assembled the following data.

Selected income statement data for the current year follows:

	Best Digital	Zone Network
Net sales (all on credit)	$467,200	$ 569,400
Cost of goods sold	$203,000	$ 242,000
Interest expense	—	$ 19,500
Net income	$ 72,800	$ 95,400

Selected balance sheet data at the *beginning* of the current year follow:

	Best Digital	Zone Network
Current receivables, net	$ 45,060	$ 53,780
Inventories	$ 73,000	$ 73,000
Total assets	$262,000	$ 274,000
Common stock:		
$1 par (13,000 shares)	$ 13,000	
$1 par (18,000 shares)		$ 18,000

Selected balance sheet and market-price data at the *end* of the current year follow:

	Best Digital	Zone Network
Current assets:		
Cash	$ 27,000	$ 18,000
Short-term investments	$ 38,520	$ 15,400
Current receivables, net	$ 37,500	$ 44,500
Inventories	$ 72,000	$ 103,000
Prepaid expenses	$ 4,980	$ 6,100
Total current assets	$180,000	$ 187,000
Total assets	$300,000	$ 325,000
Total current liabilities	$102,000	$ 95,000
Total liabilities	$102,000	$ 143,000
Common stock:		
$1 par (13,000 shares)	$ 13,000	
$1 par (18,000 shares)		$ 18,000
Total stockholders' equity	$198,000	$ 182,000
Market price per share of common stock	$ 98.00	$ 100.70

Your strategy is to invest in companies that have low price/earnings ratios but appear to be in good shape financially. Assume that you have analyzed all other factors and that your decision depends on the results of ratio analysis.

Requirement

Compute the following ratios for both companies for the current year and decide which company's stock better fits your investment strategy. Assume all sales are on credit.

a. Acid-test ratio
b. Inventory turnover
c. Days' sales in average receivables
d. Debt ratio
e. Gross profit percentage
f. Earnings per share of common stock
g. Price/earnings ratio

PROBLEMS Group B

P14-39B Prepare trend analysis *(Learning Objectives 1 & 4)*

Net sales revenue, net income, and common stockholders' equity for Connor Vision Corporation, a manufacturer of contact lenses, follow for a four-year period.

(in thousands)	2017	2016	2015	2014
Net sales revenue	$7,809	$7,261	$6,439	$6,850
Net income	$ 738	$ 498	$ 468	$ 600
Ending common stockholders' equity	$5,600	$3,400	$4,600	$3,200

Requirements

1. Compute trend percentages for each item for 2014 through 2017. Use 2014 as the base year.
2. Compute the rate of return on common stockholders' equity for 2015 through 2017.

P14-40B Comprehensive analysis *(Learning Objectives 2, 3, & 4)*

Ambrose Department Stores' chief executive officer (CEO) has asked you to compare the company's profit performance and financial position with the average for the industry. The CEO has given you the company's income statement and balance sheet, as well as the industry average data for retailers.

	A	B	C
1	Ambrose Department Stores, Inc.		
2	Income Statement Compared with Industry Average		
3	For the Year Ended December 31		
4		*(amounts in thousands)*	
5		Ambrose	Industry Average
6	Sales revenues	$ 784,000	100.0%
7	Less: Cost of goods sold	527,632	65.9%
8	Gross profit	$ 256,368	34.1%
9	Less: Operating expenses	163,856	19.4%
10	Operating income	$ 92,512	14.7%
11	Less: Interest expense	784	0.4%
12	Income before income taxes	$ 91,728	14.3%
13	Less: Income tax expense	7,056	0.4%
14	Net income	$ 84,672	13.9%
15			

	A	B	C
1	Ambrose Department Stores, Inc.		
2	Balance Sheet Compared with Industry Average		
3	As of December 31		
4	*(amounts in thousands)*		
5		Ambrose	Industry Average
6	Assets		
7	Current assets	$ 324,000	70.8%
8	Fixed assets, net	122,880	23.8%
9	Intangible assets, net	9,120	0.8%
10	Other assets	24,000	4.6%
11	Total assets	$ 480,000	100.0%
12			
13	Liabilities		
14	Current liabilities	$ 224,640	48.1%
15	Long-term liabilities	105,600	16.5%
16	Total liabilities	$ 330,240	64.6%
17			
18	Stockholders' equity		
19	Total common stockholders' equity	$ 149,760	35.4%
20			
21	Total liabilities and equity	$ 480,000	100.0%
22			

Requirements

1. Prepare a common-size income statement and balance sheet for Ambrose Department Stores. The first column of each statement should present Ambrose Department Stores' common-size statement, while the second column should present the industry averages.
2. For the profitability analysis, compute Ambrose Department Stores' (a) ratio of gross profit to sales, (b) ratio of operating income to sales, and (c) ratio of net income to sales. Compare these figures with the industry averages. Is Ambrose Department Stores' profit performance better or worse than the average for the industry?
3. For the analysis of financial position, compute Ambrose Department Stores' (a) ratios of current assets to total assets and (b) ratio of stockholders' equity to total assets. Compare these ratios with the industry averages. Is Ambrose Department Stores' financial position better or worse than the industry averages?

P14-41B Effect of transactions on ratios *(Learning Objective 4)*

Financial statement data of *Backroad Travel* magazine include the following information (dollars in thousands):

Cash	$ 25,000
Accounts receivable, net	$ 83,500
Inventories	$169,500
Total assets	$680,000
Short-term notes payable	$ 51,500
Accounts payable	$105,000
Accrued liabilities	$ 43,500
Long-term liabilities	$208,000
Net income	$ 74,520
Common shares outstanding	46,000

Requirements

1. Compute *Backroad Travel*'s current ratio, debt ratio, and earnings per share. Round all ratios to two decimal places.
2. Compute the three ratios after evaluating the effect of each transaction that follows. Consider each transaction *separately*.
   a. Purchased inventory on account, $60,000
   b. Borrowed $170,000 on a long-term note payable
   c. Issued 5,750 shares of common stock, receiving cash of $136,000
   d. Received cash on account, $22,000

P14-42B Ratio analysis over two years *(Learning Objective 4)*

Comparative financial statement data of Hollingsworth, Inc., follow:

	A	B	C
1	Hollingsworth, Inc.		
2	Comparative Income Statements		
3	For the Years Ended December 31, 2017 and 2016		
4		(amounts in thousands)	
5		2017	2016
6	Sales revenues	$ 449,990	$ 441,010
7	Less: Cost of goods sold	234,000	226,000
8	Gross profit	$ 215,990	$ 215,010
9	Less: Operating expenses	140,000	135,000
10	Operating income	$ 75,990	$ 80,010
11	Less: Interest expense	10,200	12,600
12	Income before income taxes	$ 65,790	$ 67,410
13	Less: Income tax expense	6,690	20,310
14	Net income	$ 59,100	$ 47,100
15			

Hollingsworth, Inc.
Comparative Balance Sheets
December 31, 2017 and 2016
(amounts in thousands)

	2017	2016	2015*
Assets			
Current assets:			
Cash	$ 97,000	$ 98,000	
Accounts receivable	123,500	158,500	$ 120,000
Inventory	133,000	127,000	$ 155,500
Prepaid expenses	10,500	7,500	
Total current assets	$ 364,000	$ 391,000	
Property, plant, and equipment, net	206,000	177,000	
Total assets	$ 570,000	$ 568,000	
Liabilities			
Current liabilities	$ 208,000	$ 230,000	
Long-term liabilities	138,000	118,000	
Total liabilities	$ 346,000	$ 348,000	
Stockholders' equity			
Preferred stock, 7%	$ 90,000	$ 90,000	
Total common stockholders' equity	134,000	130,000	$ 110,000
Total stockholders' equity	$ 224,000	$ 220,000	
Total liabilities and equity	$ 570,000	$ 568,000	

*Selected 2015 amounts

1. Market price of Hollingsworth's common stock: $50.60 at December 31, 2017, and $33.49 at December 31, 2016
2. Common shares outstanding: 12,000,000 during 2017 and 12,000,000 during 2016
3. All sales are credit sales

Requirements

1. Compute the following ratios for 2017 and 2016:
   a. Current ratio
   b. Times-interest-earned ratio
   c. Inventory turnover
   d. Operating income percentage
   e. Return on common stockholders' equity
   f. Earnings per share of common stock
   g. Price/earnings ratio
2. Decide (a) whether Hollingsworth's ability to pay debts and to sell inventory improved or deteriorated during 2017 and (b) whether the investment attractiveness of its common stock appears to have increased or decreased.

P14-43B Make an investment decision *(Learning Objective 4)*

Assume that you are purchasing an investment and have decided to invest in a company in the smartphone business. You have narrowed the choice to Digital Plus Electronics or Speed Network Electronics and have assembled the following data.

Selected income statement data for the current year follow:

	Digital Plus	Speed Network
Net sales (all on credit)	$401,500	$554,800
Cost of goods sold	$209,000	$231,000
Interest expense	—	$ 16,500
Net income	$ 49,000	$ 63,000

Selected balance sheet data at the *beginning* of the current year follow:

	Digital Plus	Speed Network
Current receivables, net	$ 34,300	$ 53,480
Inventories	$ 86,000	$ 77,000
Total assets	$258,000	$276,000
Common stock:		
$1 par (10,000 shares)	$ 10,000	
$1 par (14,000 shares)		$ 14,000

Selected balance sheet and market-price data at the *end* of the current year follow:

	Digital Plus	Speed Network
Current assets:		
Cash	$ 30,500	$ 22,000
Short-term investments	52,220	21,200
Current receivables, net	35,000	40,000
Inventories	66,000	98,000
Prepaid expenses	2,280	6,800
Total current assets	$186,000	$188,000
Total assets	$436,000	$434,375
Total current liabilities	$109,000	$104,000
Total liabilities	$109,000	$139,000
Common stock:		
$1 par (10,000 shares)	$ 10,000	
$1 par (14,000 shares)		$ 14,000
Total stockholders' equity	$327,000	$295,375
Market price per share of common stock	$ 73.50	$ 81.90

Your strategy is to invest in companies that have low price/earnings ratios but appear to be in good shape financially. Assume that you have analyzed all other factors and that your decision depends on the results of ratio analysis.

Requirement

Compute the following ratios for both companies for the current year and decide which company's stock better fits your investment strategy. Assume all sales are on credit.

a. Acid-test ratio
b. Inventory turnover
c. Days' sales in average receivables
d. Debt ratio
e. Gross profit percentage
f. Earnings per share of common stock
g. Price/earnings ratio

Serial Case

C14-44 Analyze various financial statement ratios *(Learning Objective 1)*

This case is a continuation of the Caesars Entertainment Corporation serial case that began in Chapter 1. Refer to the introductory story in Chapter 1 (see page 43) for additional background. (The components of the Caesars serial case can be completed in any order.)

The statements of operations (income statements) and balance sheets for Caesars Entertainment Corporation[5] follow.

[5]All statements have been condensed and adapted for educational purposes.

Caesars Entertainment Corporation
Consolidated Statements of Operations (condensed and adapted)
In millions, except per share data

	Years Ended December 31,		
	2014	2013	2012
Net revenues	$ 8,516	$ 8,220	$ 8,186
Operating expenses	8,968	10,246	8,052
Income (loss) from operations	(452)	(2,026)	134
Interest expense	(2,670)	(2,252)	(2,100)
Other gains (losses)	(95)	28	162
Loss from continuing operations before taxes	(3,217)	(4,250)	(1,804)
Income tax benefit	543	1,517	701
Loss from continuing operations, net of taxes	(2,674)	(2,733)	(1,103)
Other items	(109)	(215)	(405)
Net loss	$ (2,783)	$ (2,948)	$ (1,508)

Caesars Entertainment Corporation
Consolidated Balance Sheets (condensed and adapted)
In millions

	As of December 31,	
	2014	2013
Assets		
Current Assets		
Cash and cash equivalents	$ 2,806	$ 2,771
Restricted cash	76	88
Receivables, net	518	620
Prepayments and other current assets	230	246
Inventories	43	45
Total current assets	3,673	3,770
Property and equipment, net	13,456	13,238
Goodwill and other intangible assets	5,516	6,551
Other long-term assets	890	1,130
Total assets	$ 23,535	$ 24,689
Liabilities and stockholders' equity		
Current liabilities		
Accounts payable	$ 349	$ 443
Accrued expenses	1,199	1,212
Interest payable	736	390
Other current liabilities	15,996	486
Total current liabilities	18,280	2,531
Long-term debt	7,434	20,918
Other long-term liabilities	2,563	3,144
Total liabilities	28,277	26,593
Stockholders' equity (deficit)		
Common stock	1	1
Treasury stock	(19)	(16)
Additional paid-in capital	8,140	7,231
Retained earnings (accumulated deficit)	(13,104)	(10,321)
Other stockholders' equity items	240	1,201
Total stockholders' equity (deficit)	(4,742)	(1,904)
Total liabilities and stockholders' equity	$ 23,535	$ 24,689

Requirements

1. Calculate Caesars's net working capital for 2014 and 2013. What does the net working capital figure mean? Did Caesars's net working capital improve from 2013 to 2014? Explain.
2. Calculate Caesars's current ratio for 2014 and 2013.
3. Calculate accounts receivable turnover for 2014. Assume all net revenue is from credit sales. Next, calculate days' sales outstanding. What does this number mean?
4. Calculate the times-interest-earned ratio for 2014. What does this ratio mean?

CRITICAL THINKING

Discussion & Analysis

A14-45 Discussion & Questions

1. Describe horizontal analysis. Describe vertical analysis. What is each technique used for? How are the two methods similar? How are they different?
2. How is the current ratio calculated? What is it used to measure? How is it interpreted?
3. Assume a company has a current ratio of 2.0. List two examples of transactions that could cause the current ratio to increase. Also list two examples of transactions that could cause the current ratio to decrease.
4. What does the accounts receivable turnover measure? What does a relatively high accounts receivable turnover indicate about a company?
5. Describe the set of circumstances that could result in net income increasing while return on investment (ROI) decreases.
6. Suppose a company has a relatively high inventory turnover. What does the high inventory turnover indicate about the company's short-term liquidity?
7. Describe at least four financial conditions that may signal financial trouble.
8. Describe at least two reasons that a company's ratios might not be comparable over time.
9. Compare and contrast the current ratio and the quick ratio.
10. Describe why book value per share of common stock may not be useful for investment analysis.
11. Find a recent annual report for a publicly held company in which you are interested. Summarize what sustainability information is provided in that annual report. Based on the sustainability information provided in the annual report, what measurements do you think the company might use to track its sustainability efforts? (You can use your imagination here; the actual sustainability measures are unlikely to be in the annual report.)
12. There are three components in the triple bottom line; *people*, *planet*, and *profit*. Which component do you think is most important? Why?

Application & Analysis

Mini Cases

A14-46 Calculating Ratios for Companies Within the Same Industry

Select an industry you are interested in and select three companies within that industry. Obtain their annual reports by going to each company's website and downloading the report for the most recent year. (On many companies' websites, you will need to visit the Investor Relations section to obtain the company's financial statements.) You may also collect the information from the company's Form 10-K, which can be found by searching online for "SEC Edgar database" and then using that site to locate the Form 10-K of interest to you.

Basic Discussion Questions

For each of the three companies you selected, answer the following:

1. Calculate two ratios that measure the ability to pay current liabilities.
2. Calculate at least two ratios that measure the ability to sell inventory and collect receivables.
3. Calculate at least two ratios that measure the ability to pay long-term debt.
4. Calculate at least two ratios that measure profitability.
5. Calculate at least two ratios that help to analyze the stock as an investment.

Now that you have crunched the numbers, interpret the ratios. What can you tell about each company and its financial position? Is one company clearly better than the others in terms of its financial position, or are all three companies similar to each other?

A14-47 Ethics of financial statement analysis *(Learning Objectives 1, 2, 3, & 4)*

Fitness Mania is a small technology start-up company that specializes in personal fitness mobile apps. The three founders have been working hard on the company for the past two years since they founded Fitness Mania.

The owners of Fitness Mania want to expand its business lines to include personal fitness trackers. To get into the manufacture and sale of personal fitness trackers, Fitness Mania will need to raise approximately $5 million from additional investors.

Fitness Mania's CEO is making a presentation to a group of potential investors who are interested in funding the new fitness tracker project. This presentation could make or break Fitness Mania, so it is a high-stakes presentation. The CEO knows that, while several of Fitness Mania's ratios are strong, it is still struggling a bit financially. Some of Fitness Mania's ratios would raise red flags to potential investors.

The controller of Fitness Mania is Tom Black. Tom likes working for the start-up company, and he strongly believes in Fitness Mania's mission, which is to improve fitness while making it fun. Fitness Mania's products are potentially life changing for the people who use them to get more fit.

Fitness Mania's CEO asks Tom to prepare a report for the investors that emphasizes the strong ratios while burying the weaker ratios deep in the report.

Tom prepares a report that emphasizes the strong ratios. The weaker ratios are buried deep within the report. Tom has included a lot of extra data in the report to help to camouflage those weaker ratios. Tom also went one step further in the report preparation: He changed a few of the weaker ratios to make them appear stronger.

Tom rationalizes his actions by thinking that the revised report contributes to a greater good. The customers who use their fitness software products are likely to become healthier and have longer lives. He thinks that a few adjustments to the report are relatively minor when compared to the benefits that would be reaped by Fitness Mania's new product offerings if the potential investors do decide to invest in Fitness Mania.

Requirements

Using the IMA *Statement of Ethical Professional Practice* (Exhibit 1-7) as an ethical framework, answer the following questions:

a. What is (are) the ethical issue(s) in this situation?
b. What are Tom's responsibilities as a management accountant?

A14-48 Using financial statement ratios to analyze Coca-Cola and PepsiCo *(Learning Objectives 1, 2, 3, & 4)*

The Coca-Cola Company and PepsiCo, Inc., are fierce competitors in the beverage and snack markets. A perennial question among consumers is "Coke or Pepsi"? In this case, we will be looking at the financial positions of both companies to answer the question of which company is in a stronger financial position, Coke or Pepsi.

Following is a table of various financial data and ratios for both Coca-Cola and PepsiCo. The data are arranged in alphabetic order.

	A	B	C	D	E	F	G	H
1		\multicolumn{3}{c}{The Coca-Cola Company}		\multicolumn{3}{c}{PepsiCo, Inc.}
2		Selected Financial Data				Selected Financial Data		
3		For years ended December 31				For years ended December 26, 27, and 28, respectively		
4								
5		2015	2014	2013		2015	2014	2013
6	Acid-test ratio	0.58	0.56	0.62		0.68	0.48	0.54
7	Current ratio	1.24	1.02	1.13		1.31	1.14	1.24
8	Debt ratio	0.71	0.67	0.63		0.83	0.75	0.69
9	Earnings per share	$ 1.69	$ 1.62	$ 1.94		$ 3.71	$ 4.31	$ 4.37
10	Inventory turnover	5.83	5.61	5.63		9.68	9.43	8.94
11	Net income ($ in millions)	$ 7,351	$ 7,098	$ 8,584		$ 5,452	$ 6,513	$ 6,740
12	Rate of return on sales	16.60%	15.43%	18.32%		8.65%	9.77%	10.15%
13	Receivables turnover	10.54	9.85	9.73		9.64	9.80	9.49
14	Return on assets	9.01%	8.33%	10.27%		9.16%	10.03%	10.06%
15	Operating income percentage	19.70%	21.11%	21.83%		13.25%	14.37%	14.61%
16	Revenues ($ in millions)	$ 44,294	$ 45,998	$ 46,854		$ 63,056	$ 66,683	$ 66,415
17	Times-interest-earned ratio	10.20	20.10	22.09		8.61	10.54	10.65
18	Working capital ($ in millions)	$ 6,465	$ 612	$ 3,493		$ 5,453	$ 2,571	$ 4,364
19								

Requirements

1. Rearrange the data and ratios into a report format that groups similar data and ratios together, to make it easier to analyze the data.
2. Using the given financial data for The Coca-Cola Company, discuss the company's:
   a. Ability to pay current liabilities;
   b. Ability to sell inventory and collect receivables;
   c. Ability to pay long-term debt; and
   d. Profitability.
3. Using the given financial data for PepsiCo, Inc., discuss the company's:
   a. Ability to pay current liabilities;
   b. Ability to sell inventory and collect receivables;
   c. Ability to pay long-term debt; and
   d. Profitability.
4. Now compare Coca-Cola's financial position to PepsiCo's financial position. How do the two companies compare in the following areas?
   a. Ability to pay current liabilities
   b. Ability to sell inventory and collect receivables
   c. Ability to pay long-term debt
   d. Profitability
5. What conclusions can you draw from your analysis of the two companies? Which company do you think is in a stronger financial position?

Team Project

A14-49 Comparison of common-size financials *(Learning Objective 3)*

Select a company and obtain its financial statements. Convert the income statement and the balance sheet to common size and compare the company you selected to the industry average. Discuss how the company you selected measures up to the industry averages and form an opinion as to whether this company is above average, average, or below average. Use Google to find resources for identifying industry averages and common-size statements by industry. Clearly identify your sources and discuss why the source(s) you have used are likely to be reliable sources.

Try It Solutions

page 843:

Trend percentages are calculated by dividing each year's revenue by the base year's revenue, which in this case is $11,700.4. The trend percentages for 2011–2015 are as follows:

	A	B	C	D	E	F
1	Starbucks Trend Data	2015	2014	2013	2012	Base Year 2011
2	Sales revenue	$ 19,162.7	$ 16,447.8	$ 14,866.8	$ 13,299.5	$ 11,700.4
3	Trend percentage	164%	141%	127%	114%	100%
4						

page 852:

1. The current ratio is calculated as follows: $\dfrac{\text{Current assets}}{\text{Current liabilities}} = \dfrac{\$4{,}352.7}{\$3{,}653.5} = 1.19$

2. Inventory turnover is calculated as follows:

$\dfrac{\text{Cost of goods sold}}{\text{Average inventory}} = \dfrac{\$7{,}787.5}{(\$1{,}306.4 + \$1{,}090.9)/2} = 6.50$

15 Sustainability

Markus Mainka/Alamy

Sources: 2015 Southwest Airlines One Report; Southwest Airlines Co. 2015 10-K filing.

Learning Objectives

- **1** Describe sustainability and how it can create business value
- **2** Describe sustainability reporting and the GRI framework
- **3** Describe EMA systems and their uses and challenges

Southwest Airlines is renowned for having a positive corporate culture that embraces employees as the heart of its operations. Unlike other major airlines, after 9/11 and the economic crisis of 2008, Southwest refused to lay off employees. The result? Southwest has been listed for 22 consecutive years on Forbes's list of the "World's Most Admired Companies." It has also made Forbes's "Best Employer" list and *Corporate Responsibility* magazine's "Best Corporate Citizens" list. How does Southwest do it? The company embraces the triple bottom line: people, planet, and profit. Not only does Southwest treat its employees well, returning over $620 million to employees in 2015 as part of its profit sharing plan, but it also treats customers well by offering two free checked bags, no change fees, and frequent flyer points that can be used to book any flight at any time. From an environmental perspective, Southwest has been able to increase its jet fuel efficiency by 29% since 2005 and the company has increased recycling efforts, not only with in-flight and corporate waste, but even with its used airplane seats and billboards. As a result, Southwest earned the 2015 "Airports Going Green Award" from the Chicago Department of Aviation. How have all of these measures affected the company's profitability? Southwest has had 43 consecutive years of profit, which is unheard of in the airline industry, especially during the turbulent periods following 9/11 and the latest economic crisis.

In this chapter, we'll explore why sustainability has become such a driving force in business. We'll also look at how sustainability reporting and environmental management accounting (EMA) can help support an organization's journey toward sustainability. Finally, we'll consider some of the challenges associated with setting up and using EMA systems.

What Is Sustainability, and How Does It Create Business Value?

The dictionary definition of **sustainability** refers to the ability of a system to maintain its own viability, endure without giving way, or use resources so they are not depleted or permanently damaged.[1] In other words, it's the ability of a system, including our economic system, to operate in such a manner that it is able to continue indefinitely. With respect to business, the most widely used definition of sustainability traces its roots to a report developed by the United Nations (UN) in 1987 in which sustainable development was defined as "development that meets the needs of the present generation without compromising the ability of future generations to meet their own needs."[2] As shown in Exhibit 15-1, the report identified three factors relating to sustainability: environmental, social, and economic. The UN's 2030 Agenda for Sustainable Development, which was ratified in 2015, continues to reaffirm the importance of each of these factors on a global scale.[3]

1 Describe sustainability and how it can create business value

EXHIBIT 15-1 Three Interrelated Factors of Sustainability

As a result of the UN report, forward-thinking businesses, such as Southwest Airlines, adhere to the notion of a triple bottom line. The **triple bottom line** is a concept that views a company's performance not only in terms of its ability to generate economic profits for its owners, as has traditionally been the case, but also in terms of its impact on people and the planet. A company will only be viable, or sustainable, in the long run if all three of these factors are considered when making business decisions. For example, a company will not be able to survive in the long run if the natural resources it relies on (e.g., air, water, soil, minerals, plants, fuel supplies, etc.) or people it relies on (e.g., suppliers, customers, employees, communities) are in jeopardy. The world is a system connected by space and time. Air pollution in North America, for example, affects air quality in Europe and the melting of polar ice caps (space connections). Choices we make about

---

[1] www.merriam-webster.com; http://dictionary.reference.com
[2] Brundtland Report, World Commission on Environment and Development (WCED), 1987, www.un-documents.net/our-common-future.pdf
[3] https://sustainabledevelopment.un.org/post2015/transformingourworld

our energy sources today will impact future generations (time connections). Because of these connections, companies that do not incorporate sustainability into their core business values put their own long-term success at risk, as well as the long-term survival of the planet's inhabitants.

Historical Overview

The Industrial Revolution, which began roughly 200 years ago, is based on what is sometimes referred to as a linear "take–make–waste" system in which companies "take" natural resources (lumber, minerals, water, fossil fuels), "make" them into products, and then sell the products to consumers or commercial enterprises that eventually dispose of the products and packaging as "waste."[4] Since the end of World War II, the U.S. economy has developed a consumer mindset that has focused on using (consuming) and throwing away products for the sake of convenience, rather than conserving resources for future generations. In essence, we have become a disposable society. However, because of the limited supply of natural resources, including potable water, tillable soil, and fossil-based fuels, we have realized that the current linear economic system is not sustainable in the long run. As a result, the last 30 years have seen an increased interest in creating more sustainable business models. This interest has escalated dramatically in the last 10 years. Whereas the business community often fought pressures to become more environmentally friendly from **non-governmental organizations (NGOs)**, such as Greenpeace and the Sierra Club, in the latter part of the last century, businesses now are finding ways to partner with these same organizations to develop better, more sustainable business practices.

December 2015 was a watershed moment for the world as 196 countries gathered and negotiated the Paris Agreement at the 2015 United Nations Climate Change Conference (COP21). The essence of the agreement, which is legally binding, is to limit global warming to less than 2 degrees Celsius above pre-industrial levels. A total of 175 countries signed the agreement on Earth Day, 2016. This agreement is a major stepping stone in international efforts to limit global warming. It sends a strong signal to businesses and the capital markets to invest in a technology and business models that have low greenhouse gas emissions (such as carbon dioxide and methane). No doubt, further environmental regulations will follow as a result of this agreement.[5]

The new, forward-thinking business model of the twenty-first century takes cues from the creative ways in which natural ecological systems create zero waste. In nature, the output and death of one organism or process become the input to life of another. Nothing becomes waste, and the system continues indefinitely. It is a *circular*, rather than *linear*, system. Likewise, businesses are now beginning to adopt operating strategies that will conserve natural resources and eliminate waste, through reducing inputs and reusing, repurposing, and recycling outputs. Business executives are now beginning to take a "systems thinking" approach. Rather than concerning themselves with only **internal costs** (those costs that are incurred and paid for by the organization and recorded in their GAAP-based accounting records), managers and accountants are now considering the **external costs** borne by society as a result of the company's operations and the products and services it sells. For example, greenhouse gas emissions caused by distribution trucks and landfill sites are external costs borne by society that impact the health and wellness of the planet and its inhabitants. To decrease harmful emissions, many distributors are now switching to hybrid and natural gas vehicles, while many landfills are capturing the methane and using it to generate power.

Both internal and external costs can be illuminated through the use of life-cycle assessment. As shown in Exhibit 15-2, **life-cycle assessment, or LCA**, involves studying the

---

[4] Paul Hawken, *The Ecology of Commerce*, 1993, New York: HarperCollins.
[5] www.un.org/sustainabledevelopment/blog/2015/12/the-paris-agreement-faqs

environmental and social impact of each product or service over the course of its *entire life*, from "cradle to grave" (all the way from sourcing to disposal). One of the ultimate goals of LCA is to replace the current cradle-to-grave system with a circular cradle-to-cradle system, such that the company's end product and packaging never go to waste, but are fully used (such as ice cream packaged in an ice cream cone) or become input to another product (such as Nike's creation of fitness apparel from recycled plastic beverage containers). LCA illuminates both internal and external costs, so that companies have a more complete set of information from which to generate cost-effective solutions to environmental and social concerns.

EXHIBIT 15-2 LCA: Assessing Product Impact from Cradle-to-Grave

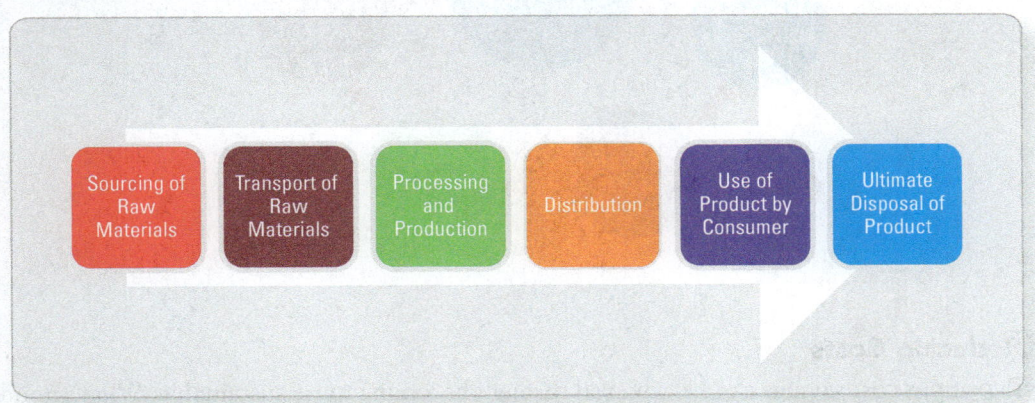

Business is now at a tipping point. The twentieth-century business model that often gravitated toward the exploitation of nature and people in pursuit of profit is changing into a life-sustaining business model. Because of their global reach and economic power, large corporations are recognizing that they are often in a better position to bring about positive world change than are many national governments and nonprofit agencies. As a result, businesses are beginning to embed sustainability into their core business functions, rather than simply tacking on isolated and temporary solutions to environmental and social issues brought to their attention by activists. Rather than taking a defensive stance as many companies did during the twentieth century, businesses are going on the offensive by making sustainability a driving force in every aspect of the value chain.

The Business Case for Sustainability

Businesses are continuing to evolve: they are now realizing they can act as positive agents of change while at the same time upholding their fiduciary responsibility to stockholders. In fact, in a recent survey, CEOs indicated that sustainability has become a more strategic and integral part of their business operations.[6] The outdated tension between profit creation and social responsibility is evaporating, as corporations recognize the business opportunity and value created through embedding sustainability throughout their core business functions. They are beginning to realize that sustainability and profitability are not at odds but often go hand in hand. In other words, sustainability simply makes good business sense. In this section, we explore some of the most compelling business reasons for adopting sustainable business practices, as illustrated in Exhibit 15-3.

---

[6] www.mckinsey.com/business-functions/sustainability-and-resource-productivity/our-insights/sustainabilitys-strategic-worth-mckinsey-global-survey-results

EXHIBIT 15-3 Business Reasons for Adopting Sustainable Practices

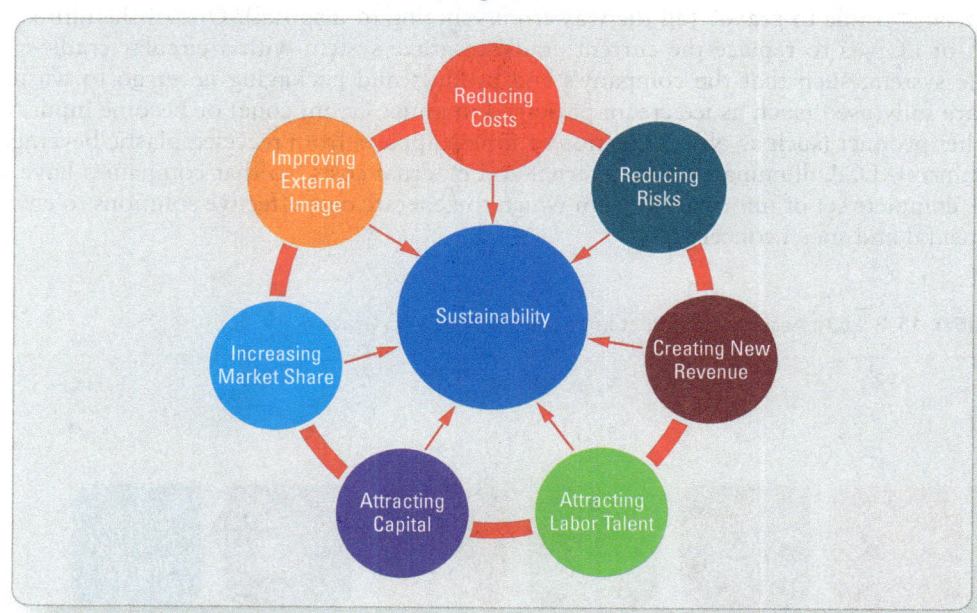

Reducing Costs

Enormous cost savings can be achieved through becoming more sustainable. What's good for the environment can also be good for the bottom line. Most of these savings come through the reduction of waste, such as the waste of materials, packaging, and energy. In fact, a relatively new term, **eco-efficiency**,[7] has been coined to signify the economic savings that can be achieved by producing goods and services with fewer ecological resources. A few examples are as follows:

- Companies are evaluating the energy intensity of their buildings. Many companies are changing out their old incandescent light bulbs to energy-efficient LED (light-emitting diode) or CFL (compact fluorescent lamp) lighting, which often results in a payback of energy cost savings in less than one year. In addition, these types of bulbs have a longer life, thus requiring lower labor cost to change them when they burn out. For example, the Clark County School District (Las Vegas) replaced the lighting in 152 of its buildings. This energy efficiency initiative alone saved the District over $2.25 million in just one year.[8] Likewise, the city of Las Vegas installed new LED streetlights that are saving the city over $2 million per year.[9] New, energy-efficient HVAC systems (heating, ventilating, and air conditioning) are likewise providing companies with enormous savings. The environmental savings are clear: less fossil fuel is used, fewer greenhouse gasses are emitted, and less material is needed to produce replacement bulbs.

- Companies with large fleets, such as UPS, Walmart, and Staples, are investing in hybrid vehicles as a means of reducing their fuel needs. They are also reassessing their route logistics to decrease the number of miles traveled per unit of product delivered. These measures not only conserve fossil fuels and prevent air pollution but also save money. For example, between 2005 and 2015, Walmart *doubled* its fleet efficiency (cases shipped per gallon of fuel), sparing the planet of 650,000 metric tons of CO_2 per year and saving the company nearly $1 *billion* in 2015 alone.[10]

---

[7] This term was coined by the World Business Council for Sustainable Development in its 1992 publication, "Changing Course."
[8] www.environmentalleader.com/2013/10/30/las-vegas-school-district-saves-12500-per-day-from-lighting-retrofit
[9] www.environmentalleader.com/2013/09/12/led-street-lights-save-las-vegas-2-million-per-year
[10] http://news.walmart.com/news-archive/2015/11/17/walmart-marks-fulfillment-of-key-global-responsibility-commitments

- Companies are performing **waste audits**, in which they study the stream of waste coming from their operations (solid waste, water discharge, chemicals, etc.) to identify waste that can be avoided and alternative uses for the remaining waste. By reducing the amount of waste sent to landfills, companies are able to avoid the tipping fees charged by waste collection companies. For example, in 2016, Unilever announced that it has now achieved "zero waste to landfill" at all 240 of its factories worldwide, plus 400 other facilities, such as offices and distribution centers. According to Unilever, its waste diversion efforts have saved the company over $225 million.[11]

- Companies are assessing the amount of materials and packaging used with their products. For example, by making its products thinner and lighter, Apple has been able to significantly reduce its carbon emissions while at the same time making the products more desirable to consumers. Even the smallest changes in packaging can have monumental effects. For example, one pizza producer saved over $600,000 in one year just from shaving 1/8" × 1/8" × 1/32" off of each pizza box. The savings resulted from a reduction in materials used for each pizza box (the equivalent of 3,000 trees) *and* the ability to ship 6,848 more pizzas in each truckload (saving on gasoline).[12] In another example, IKEA saved over 1.2 million euros in a single year just from figuring out a way to reduce the amount of packaging needed for one of its sofas.[13] Companies are now considering packaging, as much as manufacturing, when designing their products.

- Companies are also assessing the waste that occurs simply from the way they've always operated their businesses. For example, hotels used to change sheets and towels every day. Now, most hotels are moving toward changing sheets and towels every two or three days, instead of once a day, unless requested otherwise by the customer. This measure saves the cost of maid time (labor) as well as the cost of laundering (water, energy, detergent) while also benefiting the environment. Since implementing its Travel with Purpose strategy, Hilton says it has reduced energy use by 14.5%, carbon output by 20.9%, waste output by 27.6%, and water use by 14.1%, compared to 2009 levels. In the process, Hilton's worldwide environmental management is credited with saving the company over $550 million.[14]

These are just a few examples of how companies are reducing their environmental impact while at the same time reducing costs. For more examples, you may wish to sign up for a free daily e-mail at Environmentalleader.com. The daily e-mail provides current news on the sustainability initiatives of well-known businesses so that you can see more examples of how businesses are reducing their environmental impact while at the same time improving their bottom line.

Generating New Revenue Streams

Sustainable product innovation can provide companies with new revenue streams. Some entrepreneurial businesses begin with a mission of providing only sustainable products. For example, Method gained market share by providing consumers with biodegradable household cleaners and soaps. Clif Bar is now a leading maker of organic energy and nutrition foods, and Terracycle makes all of its products out of recycled materials. Existing companies can also benefit from developing more sustainable products. For example, Procter & Gamble used LCA to determine that the majority of energy consumed in the life cycle of its laundry detergent was the result of consumers washing their clothes in hot water. As a result, the company developed Tide Coldwater®, which is effective as a laundering agent in cold water.

> **Why is this important?**
> "In order to **grow** the company, **managers** must listen to what their **customers**, stockholders, employees, and creditors want. Increasingly, these stakeholders want **more sustainable** operations."

---

[11] www.triplepundit.com/2015/02/unilever-zero-waste-program-saves-225-million-creating-jobs
[12] www.chainalytics.com/ikea-save-millions-packaging-optimization/
[13] www.wsj.com/articles/ikea-cant-stop-obsessing-about-its-packaging-1434533401
[14] www.environmentalleader.com/2016/01/07/hilton-cuts-carbon-output-20-9-saves-550m/

Recycling and repurposing can also provide companies with new revenue streams. After performing waste audits, companies seek alternative uses for the materials in their waste streams. By finding commercial alternatives to sending waste to landfills, companies are often able to reap significant recycling revenues. Unilever found innovative uses for the materials formerly in its waste stream. For example, the scraps left over from cutting tea bags out of fabric rolls are now sold to another company that uses the material for making pet beds. Rather than paying for these materials to be sent to landfills, as was done in the past, Unilever is now earning revenues from selling the materials.

Sustainability can also provide a competitive advantage for companies that become first movers. For example, Toyota was the first company to develop and market an affordable hybrid vehicle. As a result, the Toyota Prius still dominates the hybrid vehicle market even though most major car manufacturers are offering hybrid alternatives.

Finally, with the new Paris Agreement in place, companies will be looking for new products and services that will help them achieve their low-emission goals. Over 87% of companies of all sizes have made public commitments to decrease emissions and increase energy efficiency.[15] The demand for low-emission technology will spur product and service innovations.

Increasing Market Share

Consumers, supply-chain customers, and special interest groups are also putting pressure on companies to become more socially and environmentally sustainable. Consumers are increasingly selecting products not only on the basis of price and quality, but also on the basis of environmental and social impact. For example, many consumers now demand environmentally sensitive packaging, such as recyclable containers or packaging made from post-consumer-use materials. Companies, such as GE, Unilever, and Target, are capitalizing on this market trend. Each of these companies generates over $1 billion a year in sales from sustainable products. In 2014, over 50% of Unilever's market growth came from its Sustainable Living Brands.[16] In other words, sustainable products are driving sales and market share.

Many companies are now practicing **supply-chain assessment**, whereby purchasing decisions are influenced by how well suppliers manage the social and environmental impact of their operations. Companies can, and do, refuse to purchase materials from suppliers that do not adhere to their environmental and social justice standards. As a result, companies that don't adopt sustainable practices are likely to lose business, while those that embed sustainability through their entire organization are likely to gain market share.

Improving External Image

Community members and special interest groups can also place pressure on businesses by boycotting or picketing companies with poor environmental and social practices. A company's external image can either hurt or improve sales. For example, in 2004, Walmart started a "green" campaign, along with significant changes to its operations, because of bad publicity over its environmental impact. Because of Walmart's sheer size, even one small move by the company has enormous effects on the environment. Likewise, The Home Depot intensified its journey to sustainability after protestors headlined the company's lumber procurement practices. Even Apple has received bad press due to the labor conditions at overseas factories in the company's supply chain. Thus, companies need to carefully scrutinize not only their own internal operations, but all of the companies in their supply chain. Social responsibility is now a determining factor in shaping a company's image.

Reducing Compliance and Litigation Risks

In many cases, companies must become more sustainable to assure regulatory compliance. If they do not comply with environmental regulations, they will face substantial fines, thus compromising their profitability. In the United States, the Environmental Protection Agency (EPA), which began operations in 1970, is the regulatory agency charged with writing, implementing, and enforcing environmental laws passed by Congress. These regulations pertain to air quality, water quality, land issues, chemicals, hazardous substances, and so forth.

Smith/MCT/Newscom

[15] www.environmentalleader.com/2016/07/07/tide-of-global-climate-agreements-produces-a-wave-of-products-and-services
[16] www.environmentalleader.com/2016/01/07/how-unilever-ge-ikea-turn-a-profit-from-sustainability

European countries, in general, have even more stringent environmental laws and regulations. For example, in the United Kingdom, the Climate Change Act (2008) commits the UK to an 80% reduction in carbon emissions by 2050. Because many U.S. companies have foreign operations, they need to be aware of the environmental regulations in each geographic location in which they operate.

Rather than simply adhering to current regulations, companies need to anticipate more stringent regulations in the future. The Paris Agreement mentioned earlier in the chapter makes future regulation all the more likely. Rather than just complying with current regulations, companies may benefit from getting ahead of the game. For example, DuPont foresaw the eventual regulation of chlorofluorocarbons (CFCs), which are potent greenhouse gases. DuPont was able to gain substantial market share by developing CFC alternatives and phasing out its CFC production far ahead of its competitors that simply struggled to meet regulatory requirements.[17]

Regulatory fines and environmental litigation can be extremely costly. For example, in 2016 Volkswagen agreed to a $15.3 billion settlement as a result of rigging the environmental tests of its diesel vehicles to hide the fact that they were emitting more pollutants than allowed under California regulations. The agreement "should send a very clear message that when you break the laws designed to protect public health in this country, there are serious consequences," stated EPA Administrator Gina McCarthy.[18] Another notable environmental fine relates to the BP *Deepwater Horizon* oil spill of 2010. In 2015, BP reached a $20.8 billion litigation settlement with the U.S. Department of Justice. In addition, BP paid out billions in operations response and cleanup costs, claims to individuals and businesses, and other proposed litigation settlements. BP estimates the total cost for the disaster at $54.6 billion.[19]

Attracting and Retaining Labor Talent

In a recent survey of CFOs, "improving employee morale and hiring" was listed as one of the top five reasons for becoming more sustainable.[20] Companies are finding that they are better able to recruit top talent and retain employees longer when the organization is more sustainable. Because hiring and training new employees is costly, organizations save money by retaining good employees longer. Currently, the average employee tenure is less than five years.[21] Thus, preventing turnover can result in cost savings.

Companies are also realizing "soft" benefits from providing more sustainable work environments. These benefits include higher productivity, less absenteeism, more employee engagement, and lower health-care costs. For example, KeyBank has redesigned the physical layout of its headquarters such that all of the cubicles are positioned near the exterior windows of the building in order to provide employees with natural light. Higher-level managers have their offices in the interior of the building but have glass walls to allow the natural light to penetrate. This is the opposite of traditional office configurations in which the higher-level executives receive outer offices that block the natural light from getting to the interior cubicles. KeyBank employees also have the option of using treadmill workstations and mobile workstations that are not pre-assigned to specific personnel. Another example comes from Intel. Intel provides employees in its Chandler, Arizona, operations with free, healthy fresh fruit all day long and access to a free onsite fitness facility. Initiatives such as these help boost employee health and wellness, as well as employee morale.

Costco, a large national retailer, provides another good example. Bucking the trend of most retailers to pay minimum wage, Costco's starting wage rate for employees is more than $3 per hour greater than minimum wage. Most employees also received health-care benefits. The company believes their policy is more profitable in the long run because it decreases turnover and maximizes employee productivity and loyalty. Costco is supporting a move in Congress to increase the national minimum wage rate.[22]

[17] Chris Laszlo, *Sustainable Value: How the World's Leading Companies Are Doing Well by Doing Good*, 2008, Stanford University Press.
[18] www.bloomberg.com/news/articles/2016-06-28/volkswagen-to-pay-14-7-billion-to-settle-u-s-emissions-claims
[19] http://money.cnn.com/2015/10/06/news/companies/deepwater-horizon-bp-settlement
[20] www.fuqua.duke.edu/news_events/news-releases/cfo-survey-2013-q2/#.UffCPYHD_IU
[21] http://bls.gov/news.release/pdf/tenure.pdf
[22] The Plain Dealer, March 7, 2013. "Costco pays more than norm, backs higher minimum wage."

Attracting Capital

Many institutional and retail investors (individual investors) are taking sustainability into account when making investment decisions. The growth of socially responsible investment indices, such as the Dow Jones Sustainability Index (DJSI), NASDAQ OMX CRD Global Sustainability Index, and FTSE4Good Index, has put increasing pressure on corporations to pay attention to sustainability.

As of 2016, over 1,500 institutional investors with over $62 trillion of assets under management had become signatories of the UN-backed **Principles for Responsible Investment (PRI)**. In short, these six principles include a commitment of signatories to incorporate environmental, social, and governance issues into investment analysis and decision making as part of their fiduciary responsibility to act in the long-term interests of their beneficiaries.[23] Furthermore, a 2015 survey conducted by the CFA Institute revealed that 73% of investors (portfolio managers and research analysts) take ESG (Environmental, Social, and Governance) information into account when making investment decisions.[24]

Principles for Responsible Investment (PRI)

In addition to investors, lenders are increasingly taking sustainability into account when making credit decisions. Companies that do not adhere to sustainable practices may be at greater risk of defaulting on future loan payments. Why? Because they may be subject to future liabilities related to their detrimental impact on society and the environment.

In this section, we have shown why adopting sustainable practices makes good business sense. In the next section, we describe how sustainability reporting is used to move companies in a more sustainable direction.

What Is Sustainability Reporting?

2 Describe sustainability reporting and the GRI framework

Sustainability reporting is best viewed as a *process* that helps companies set goals, measure performance, and manage change as they move toward an economic model that produces long-term economic profit as well as environmental care and social responsibility.[25] A **sustainability report** is the primary document used for communicating a company's performance on all three pillars of the triple bottom line: economic, environmental, and social. Sustainability reports are often referred to as *Corporate Social Responsibility (CSR) reports* or *Environmental, Social, and Governance (ESG) reports*.

Current State of Sustainability Reporting

The vast majority of large companies now issue CSR reports. Over 80% of companies on the S&P 500 issued CSR reports in 2015, whereas in 2011, only 20% did.[26] Internationally, 92% of the Global 250 companies (the largest 250 companies in the world) now issue CSR reports.[27] As a result, large corporations that do not issue CSR reports are now in the minority.

Although sustainability reporting is still a voluntary practice in the United States, some countries (such as France, Denmark, Norway, Indonesia, and South Africa) and some stock exchanges (such as those in Brazil, Malaysia, and Singapore) require certain sustainability disclosures. In the United States, the NASDAQ urges listed companies to report on issues such as greenhouse gas emissions, water use, and gender equality—or to explain why they don't.[28] In late 2015, the World Federation of Exchanges (the trade association representing 64 public stock exchanges around the globe, whose 44,000 listed companies represent 75% of the world's GDP) issued guidance and recommendations about sustainability-related key performance indicators (KPIs) that could be reported to

---

[23] http://unpri.org
[24] Environment, Social, and Governance (ESG) Survey, CFA Institute, June 2015.
[25] Global Reporting Initiative, G4 Reporting Guidelines, Reporting Principles, and Standard Disclosures, http://globalreporting.org
[26] www.ga-institute.com/nc/issue-master-system/news-details/article/flash-report-eighty-one-percent-81-of-the-sp-500-index-companies-published-corporate-sustainabi.html
[27] Currents of change: The KPMG Survey of Corporate Responsibility Reporting 2015.
[28] http://www.sustainability-reports.com/titel-1150/

investors to ensure more efficient and transparent capital markets.[29] While these guidelines are not binding, they do send a clear signal that sustainability disclosures are important to the capital markets.

The Securities and Exchange Commission (SEC) requires publicly traded companies to disclose any material information that would be necessary to prevent misleading the readers of financial statements. With respect to the environment, companies must disclose any aspects of their business operations, pending lawsuits, and risk factors that are deemed to be material. Examples include the cost of complying with environmental laws and regulations, potential monetary damages from health and environmental litigation, and risks associated with the scarcity of water and raw materials needed for operations. Additionally, any material risks specific to the company as a result of global warming must also be disclosed.

Finally, while not required, there is a growing trend for companies to include some CSR information in their annual reports, as well as issue standalone reports. Of the largest 100 companies in 45 different countries (4,500 companies in all), 56% include some CSR information in their annual reports, while 73% issue standalone sustainability reports.[30]

Reasons for Sustainability Reporting

Sustainability reporting is a costly process, so why do firms do it? They must believe the benefits exceed the cost. As outlined earlier in the chapter, economic profit often goes hand in hand with a business's journey toward sustainability. Sustainability reporting serves several business-enhancing purposes:

1. Sustainability reporting is used as an internal change management tool. A familiar phrase in business is, "You can't manage what you don't measure." A similar adage is, "What gets measured gets managed . . . and what gets managed, gets done." Thus, measurement is a key driver of organizational change. Companies need baseline measurements to assess where they currently stand on social and environmental performance before they are able to set realistic goals and develop strategies and initiatives to move toward those goals.

   At its core, management accounting seeks to measure, collect, analyze, and report data that are relevant to managers as they plan, direct, and control company operations. Viewed in this light, sustainability reporting is simply an expansion of the cost and revenue data traditionally used in the management process. Sustainability reporting simply adds a layer of quantifiable nonfinancial data to the decision-making process.

2. Companies use their CSR reports as a means of disclosing their social and environmental impact information to

   - consumers,
   - companies in their supply chain,
   - investors and creditors,
   - stock exchanges and organizations that identify and rank the most sustainable companies in a wide variety of industries, and
   - other stakeholders, such as NGOs, local communities, and employees.

Framework for Sustainability Reporting

The **Global Reporting Initiative (GRI)**, a nonprofit organization founded in 1997, has developed the leading framework used for sustainability reporting by companies worldwide. The GRI's mission is to make sustainability reporting standard practice by providing

---

[29] World Federation of Exchanges ESG Recommendation Guidance and Metrics, October 2015.
[30] Currents of change: The KPMG Survey of Corporate Responsibility Reporting 2015.

guidance and support to organizations.[31] The GRI has continued to refine and update its reporting guidelines based on the experiences and needs of CSR preparers and users. The latest guidelines, G4, were released in May 2013.

While use of the GRI framework is not mandatory for sustainability reporting, over 24,000 CSR reports have been issued that reference the GRI framework.[32]

Development of the G4 Guidelines

The G4 Guidelines are the outcome of a multi-stakeholder process that included experts, businesses, and civil labor organizations from all over the world. Public opinion was also gathered during a public comment period. The G4 Guidelines were developed so that they could be used universally by organizations of any size in any region of the world. A consortium of large businesses, such as GE, Goldman Sachs, and Alcoa, as well as all of the **Big Four** accounting firms (Deloitte, EY, KPMG, and PricewaterhouseCoopers), provided financial support for the project and expertise on its technical features. Since the root business of the Big Four firms is auditing, the consortium's inclusion of the Big Four lends credibility to the verifiability of the metrics (KPIs) included in the reporting guidelines.

Summary of the G4 Guidelines

The heart of the G4 Guidelines focuses on the concepts of materiality and the triple bottom line: Organizations should report on those environmental, social, and economic aspects of their business that are *material* to their stakeholders. **Materiality** is loosely defined as those aspects that "reflect the organization's significant economic, environmental and social impact; or substantively influence the assessments and decisions of stakeholders."[33] As a result, one of the first steps in preparing a CSR report is to identify and engage stakeholders, including stockholders, creditors, suppliers, employees, community members, and NGOs, in a meaningful ongoing conversation to identify material aspects of the organization's operations.

Organizations and their stakeholders use the framework shown in Exhibit 15-4 to identify the aspects of the triple bottom line that are material to their organization. Note the following in Exhibit 15-4:

- The G4 framework is organized around the three "categories" of the triple bottom line: economic, environmental, and social. In addition, the social category contains four subcategories: (1) labor practices and decent work, (2) human rights, (3) society, and (4) product responsibility.

- Within each category, the framework identifies several "aspects" of business that might be material to the organization.

- Each "aspect" can be measured and reported on using one or more "indicators." Metrics such as these are often referred to as KPIs (key performance indicators). The number of indicators for each aspect is listed in parentheses in Exhibit 15-4. A detailed description of each indicator can be found in the G4 Guidelines at globalreporting.org.

Let's look at an example from Exhibit 15-4. "Water" is the third aspect listed in the "Environmental" category. In applying the G4 guidelines, a company and its stakeholders would need to decide how significant water is to the company's operations. If water is considered to be material, then the company should disclose information about its use of water in its CSR report. To do this, the company would measure and report on the three indicators listed for water in the G4 Guidelines: (1) total water withdrawn by source (such as groundwater, surface water, municipal water), (2) water sources significantly affected by withdrawal (such as size of water source and its importance to indigenous peoples), and (3) percentage and total volume of water recycled and reused.

---

[31] www.globalreporting.org
[32] http://database.globalreporting.org/
[33] Global Reporting Initiative, G4 Reporting Guidelines, Reporting Principles and Standard Disclosures, http://globalreporting.org

EXHIBIT 15-4 Aspects (and Number of Indicators) Within Each G4 Category

Economic Category:
- Economic Performance (4 indicators)
- Market presence (2)
- Indirect economic impacts (2)
- Procurement practices (1)

Environmental Category:
- Materials (2 indicators)
- Energy (5)
- Water (3)
- Biodiversity (4)
- Emissions (7)
- Effluents and waste (5)
- Products and services (2)
- Compliance (1)
- Transport (1)
- Overall (1)
- Supplier environmental assessment (2)
- Environmental grievance mechanism (1)

Social Category:

Subcategory: Labor Practices and Decent Work
- Employment (3 indicators)
- Labor/management relations (1)
- Occupational health and safety (4)
- Training and education (3)
- Diversity and equal opportunity (1)
- Equal remuneration for women and men (1)
- Supplier assessment for labor practices (2)
- Labor practices grievance mechanisms (1)

Subcategory: Human Rights
- Investment (2)
- Non-discrimination (1)
- Freedom of association and collective bargaining (1)
- Child labor (1)
- Forced or compulsory labor (1)
- Security practices (1)
- Indigenous rights (1)
- Assessment (1)
- Supplier human rights assessment (2)
- Human rights grievance mechanism (1)

Subcategory: Society
- Local communities (2)
- Anti-corruption (3)
- Public policy (1)
- Anti-competitive behavior (1)
- Compliance (1)
- Supplier assessment for impacts on society (2)
- Grievance mechanisms for impacts on society (1)

Subcategory: Product Responsibility
- Customer health and safety (2)
- Product and service labeling (3)
- Marketing communications (2)
- Customer privacy (1)
- Compliance (1)

Let's apply this information to a real-life example. Intel's manufacture of semiconductors is a very water-intensive process. Intel would not be able to survive as a company without access to billions of gallons of water per year. Thus, the company would not be viable, nor could it be profitable, without access to this natural resource. Thus, water is a material aspect of Intel's business. Likewise, water is a main ingredient in Coca-Cola's beverages, so Coca-Cola also considers water to be a material aspect of its business. On the other hand, water is not material to a financial institution, such as KeyBank, that uses very little water. As a result of focusing on material aspects of individual businesses, the GRI framework is customizable to every type of organization.

Since water is a material environmental aspect of Intel's business, Intel's CSR report discloses information on several water indicators: total water withdrawn, the source and geographic location of water supplies, the amount of water lost to evaporation, the amount of water conserved, and the amount of water discharged. Because water is so critical to Intel's business, the company has performed and disclosed a complete water footprint analysis. (You may wish to look at this information on page 86 of Intel's 2015 CSR report.)

Organizations have a choice as to whether they wish to issue a **core report** or a **comprehensive report**. The reports differ as to how many indicators are included:

- Core report—*at least one* indicator related to each identified material aspect must be disclosed.
- Comprehensive report—*all indicators* related to each identified material aspect must be disclosed.

As noted, Intel has reported on all three indicators relating to water.

In addition to the specific disclosures just discussed, all CSR reports that reference the G4 Guidelines must also contain general disclosures regarding the following:

- Strategy and analysis (vision and strategy for managing triple bottom line impacts)
- Organizational profile (summary of the company's location, size, products, and brands)
- Identified material aspects and boundaries (process for determining materiality; the portion of the company included in the report, that is, the whole company or only certain segments)
- Stakeholder engagement (identification and selection of stakeholders, and frequency of engagement)
- Report profile (reporting period and content index)
- Governance (governance structure and composition)
- Ethics and integrity (mechanisms for seeking advice and reporting concerns about unethical or unlawful behavior)

This section of the text only provides a brief overview of the G4 Guidelines. A complete description of the G4 Guidelines and reporting process is available at globalreporting.org.

Assurance of Data in CSR Reports

CSR reports gain more credibility if they are verified by external parties, much like financial statements become more credible when they are audited by independent CPAs. Whereas the SEC requires that publicly traded companies have their financial statements audited annually, no such requirement exists for CSR reports. Nonetheless, two-thirds of the Global 250 companies have invested in assurance services on at least some aspects of their CSR reports.[34] **Assurance** is a term used to denote an independent party's external validation of management's assertions. The Big Four accounting firms are the leading assurance service providers for CSR reports.[35] The Big Four firms hire many experts in other fields, such as engineers, to aid accountants in their assurance service practices. If you would like to see an example of an assurance report, the Independent Accountants' Review Report can be found on page 80 of Intel's 2015 CSR report. The report lists the indicators that were assured, as well as the criteria used for assurance. You'll note that the GRI G4 guidelines are referenced in the report.

Sustainability Accounting Standards Board (SASB)

The GRI is not the only organization working on sustainability reporting. The Sustainability Accounting Standards Board (SASB) is an independent non-profit whose mission is to develop and disseminate sustainability accounting standards that help public corporations disclose material, decision-useful information to investors.[36]

---

[34] Currents of change: The KPMG Survey of Corporate Responsibility Reporting 2015.
[35] http://research.verdantix.com/index.cfm/papers/Press.Details/press_id/105/verdantix-global-survey-finds-the-big-four-accounting-firms-continue-to-dominate-the-sustainability-brands-landscape
[36] SASB.org

Whereas the GRI provides companies with complete freedom in determining the aspects of sustainability that are material to their organization, SASB is trying to standardize reporting to make it more comparable between companies within the same industry. In March 2016, the SASB released the culmination of a four-year project in which it issued *provisional* standards for all 79 SIC (Standard Industrial Classification) industries. For each industry, SASB has devised a list of sustainability topics that are material to the industry, a list of metrics to be reported for each topic, and protocols for how to collect and measure the metrics. Thus, as stated in its mission, SASB is attempting to standardize the sustainability information that would be provided by publicly traded companies in any given industry. You can go on the website (SASB.org), put in a stock ticker symbol for any publicly traded company, and find the provisional sustainability topics, metrics, and protocols applicable to that company.

For example, let's look at Southwest Airlines. SASB lists four main sustainability-related topics that should be reported for airlines:

1. Environmental footprint of fuel use
2. Labor relations
3. Competitive behavior (since only four airlines account for 75% of the market)
4. Accidents and safety management

SASB lists metrics and protocols for each of these topics. For example, fuel use has several metrics, including Scope 1 emissions (direct emissions from the company's own operations), management's short-term and long-term strategy for managing emissions, total fuel used, and percentage of renewable fuel used. Keep in mind that these provisional standards were just released in 2016 and are still under comment and review. They are not yet mandatory.

Note that the GRI Framework and SASB are not at odds but rather, are complementary. Both have the common goal of advancing sustainability reporting. Whereas the GRI attempts to provide guidance to all companies in disclosing sustainability information that is relevant to a multitude of stakeholders, SASB more specifically wishes to create mandatory, industry-specific disclosures for companies that are publicly traded on U.S. stock exchanges and targets investors as the audience for this information.[37]

You can keep up with recent developments at SASB.org.

Try It!

Classify each of the following GRI aspects according to GRI category: economic, environmental, or social. If it is social, further classify it according to its subcategory. Use Exhibit 15-4 as a guide.

1. Customer health and safety
2. Child labor
3. Emissions
4. Market presence
5. Equal remuneration for women and men
6. Energy
7. Anti-corruption
8. Procurement practices

Please see page 944 for solutions.

---

[37] www.sasb.org/approach/key-relationships

3 Describe EMA systems and their uses and challenges

What Is Environmental Management Accounting (EMA)?

In the last section, we described sustainability reporting and CSR reports. In this section, we describe the information needed for sustainability reporting. We also describe some of the uses of this information, as well as the challenges in collecting it.

EMA Systems

Environmental management accounting (EMA) is a system used for the identification, collection, analysis, and use of information needed for internal decision making and external reporting. EMA collects two types of information: monetary and physical.

Monetary Information

Monetary information is the type of information traditionally used in accounting systems. Although presented in monetary terms, the categories of costs are quite different from what has traditionally been collected and reported by financial and management accounting systems. For example, the monetary information reported in an EMA system may include:[38]

1. **Materials costs of product outputs:** These costs include the purchase costs of natural resources that are converted into products. An example would be the purchase cost of lumber for the manufacture of picnic tables. This category is similar to direct materials, since these materials become part of the final product.
2. **Materials costs of non-product outputs:** These costs include the costs of water and energy that become nonproduct output, such as air emissions and waste. An example would be the cost of water used as a coolant in a plant's manufacturing system.
3. **Waste and emission control costs:** These costs include the costs for handling, treating, and disposing of all forms of waste and emissions, including solid waste, hazardous waste, wastewater, and air emissions. An example would be the cost associated with treatment and disposal of hazardous by-products at a chemical production facility.
4. **Prevention costs:** These costs are incurred to prevent environmental costs. An example would be the costs of monitoring water output for contaminants.
5. **Research and development (R&D) costs:** These costs include the costs of R&D projects related to environmental issues. An example would be the costs of running a laboratory aimed at developing biodegradable products.
6. **Intangible costs:** These costs include the costs of future liabilities, future regulations, productivity, company image, and stakeholder relations. An example would be the cost of a future lawsuit filed for an infringement of environmental regulations.

Physical Information

Physical information has not traditionally been part of managerial accounting systems, but it is a vital part of EMA systems. Examples of physical information include the following:

1. Quantity of air emissions
2. Tons of solid waste generated
3. Gallons of wastewater generated
4. Pounds of packaging recycled
5. Total amount of water consumed

By collecting and measuring physical information, such as tons of waste sent to landfills, EMA systems provide managers with a clearer view of the company's physical impact on the environment. The adage "You can't manage what you don't measure" applies. If a company doesn't measure physical impact information, management has little chance of trying to reduce it.

[38] International Federation of Accountants (IFAC), 2005, *International Guidance Document of EMA*, New York: IFAC.

Materials Flow Accounting

To track their environmental inputs and outputs, organizations can use **materials flow accounting (MFA)**. As shown in Exhibit 15-5, MFA involves tracking all of the physical inputs (materials, energy, water, and so forth) and reconciling them with the output generated (including product units, wastewater generated, air emissions, packaging, and by-products). The goal is to track where everything is going; once it is visible, steps can be taken to reduce usage or to increase efficiencies. Essentially, MFA calculates the amount of waste and emissions from a manufacturing system by tracing materials (including energy) to the finished product. Identifying the processes that lead to waste and emissions can highlight opportunities for improvement.

EXHIBIT 15-5 Materials Flow Accounting: Equating Inputs with the Company's Outputs

ISO 14000

How do companies gain the knowledge and expertise necessary to develop and implement EMA systems? The International Organization for Standardization (ISO) has developed the ISO 14000 series of standards, which address various aspects of EMA systems. The ISO 14000 series has more than 22 standards and guidelines pertaining to environmental sustainability. In the words of the ISO, the standards provide a "practical toolbox" that help organizations implement environmental management systems. Some of these tools include LCA, greenhouse gas accounting, materials flow accounting, eco-efficiency assessment, environmental product labeling, and others.[39]

Uses of Environmental Management Accounting Information

The information contained in and produced by an organization's EMA system is designed to help support managers' primary responsibilities: planning, directing, controlling, and decision making. Specific operational and decision-making situations where management accountants can support sustainability efforts include compliance, strategy development, systems and information flow, costing, investment appraisal, performance management, and external reporting. We'll discuss each of these areas next.

Compliance

Companies are confronted with many environmental laws and regulations that can impact their operations. An EMA system gathers the information necessary to ensure that the organization complies with these laws and regulations. Management accountants also use this information to help managers understand the potential financial implications of pending environmental legislation and of past practices that may have caused environmental damage.

---

[39] International Standards Organization, "ISO 14000—Environmental Management," 2009, www.iso.org/iso/home/standards/management-standards/iso14000.htm

For example, **Extended Producer Responsibility (EPR) laws** require manufacturers in certain industries to "take back" a large percentage of their products at the end of the products' life in order to reduce the amount of waste ending up in landfills and the environment. EPR laws are gaining traction, especially in the electronics industry due to the volume of e-waste produced each year. However, they are also beginning to surface in other industries. For example, Rhode Island recently passed an EPR law related to mattresses. The EMA system would help gather the physical information required by these laws as well as provide managers with the costs of both compliance and noncompliance. The financial ramifications should drive product engineers to develop ways of recycling, repurposing, or reusing product components.

Strategy Development

In order to succeed in the long term, organizations need to integrate sustainability into their business strategy. Management accountants can use the information from the EMA system to help identify the environmental impact of a potential strategic decision, identify opportunities to make more efficient use of resources, and take advantage of the organization's strengths. Additionally, they can help to assess the potential costs of *not* undertaking particular environmental initiatives.

Systems and Information Flow

Management accountants can help to assess the need for new information systems. They can also help to implement new systems and suggest system modifications as the organization's information needs change. New environmental laws, new products, new processes, and new technologies all create demand for new or updated information systems.

> **Why is this important?**
> "Management **accountants** are increasingly called upon to incorporate **environmental impact** information in the **analyses** they **provide** to management."

Costing

Management accountants can help to make environmental costs more visible. Methods can be improved for allocating environmental costs (such as waste removal, water, and energy costs) to specific products, activities, or departments. Management accountants can also help to identify and estimate potential future environmental costs that should be recognized as potential liabilities in current periods.

Investment Appraisal

Management accountants can help to ensure that environmental and social costs and savings are included in capital investment analysis. Investment appraisals should include traditionally ignored factors, such as enhanced reputation, improved employee morale, and reduction of litigation and compliance risk. An analytical tool known as **Social Return on Investment (SROI)** can be used to explain social and environmental value in monetary terms. SROI works similarly to ROI calculations, but it includes estimates of the social and environmental costs and savings. Inclusion of this information can dramatically affect the results of traditional ROI calculations. LCA, described earlier, can also provide companies with the financial rationale for making new investments, such as exemplified by Procter & Gamble's investment in developing a cool-water detergent.

Performance Management

As discussed earlier, sustainability reporting is most often used as an internal change management tool, whereby performance is measured across a variety of environmental and social metrics, goals are set, and progress toward the goals is measured. Thus, performance management is at the heart of sustainability reporting.

Many companies are now beginning to disclose their carbon and water footprints. A **carbon footprint** is a measure of the total emissions of carbon dioxide and other greenhouse gases (GHGs), often expressed for simplicity as tons of equivalent carbon dioxide. It can be calculated for individual products, individual processes, or the organization as a whole. Once the carbon footprint has been measured, managers can work toward reducing it. Additionally, the **Carbon Disclosure Project**, a nonprofit organization, collects carbon footprint information from the world's largest companies each year and disseminates that information to institutional investors and other stakeholders.

Some companies, such as Timberland and Disney, are investing in reforestation projects to offset their carbon footprints in an effort to become more carbon neutral. Other companies provide customers with the opportunity to purchase carbon offsets. For example, United Airlines has partnered with Sustainable Travel International to provide a carbon offset program for its customers. At United's website, travelers have the option to calculate the carbon emissions associated with their travel and then purchase enough carbon offsets to make their travel carbon neutral. The carbon offsets are typically invested in reforestation and renewable energy projects.[40]

Similarly, a **water footprint** is the total volume of water use associated with the processes and products of a business. Some companies, such as Coca-Cola and Intel, measure their water footprint, thus enabling production engineers to consider means for reducing the footprint.

External Reporting

As discussed earlier, EMA systems provide the information used for the sustainability reporting process. Thus, EMA systems collect the information that is necessary for companies to produce CSR reports.

Challenges to Implementing EMA Systems

There are several challenges inherent in implementing and using an EMA system within an organization. Communication issues, hidden costs, aggregated accounting information, the historical orientation of accounting, and the newness of environmental management accounting are all potentially challenging areas.

Communication Issues

For an EMA system to work effectively, many different employees within the organization need to communicate and work together. For example, members of the environmental staff possess knowledge about environmental issues impacting the organization. Technical and production engineers have experience with the flow of materials, energy, and water throughout the company operations. Management accountants have expertise in accounting, cost assignment, and regulatory reporting. In reality, all areas of the value chain will need to coordinate efforts if sustainability is to be embedded within the fabric of the organization. Communication and coordination can sometimes be challenging, yet it is necessary in order to provide the information needed to strategically manage the organization's journey toward sustainability.

Hidden Costs

In a traditional accounting system, many indirect costs are assigned to overhead because they are difficult to trace directly to a product or process. As a result, many environmental costs may get buried in the overhead account. Making environmental costs visible is a vital step in managing environmental costs.

Aggregated Accounting Information

Depending on the sophistication of the company's information system, accounting data are often aggregated into a limited number of accounts. For example, some companies still post material purchases into one "Purchases" account. Such a basic system does not allow management to identify the specific types and quantities of materials purchased (for example, hazardous and nonhazardous), the cost per unit for the material, or the product for which it was purchased. If this specific information is tracked on the production floor, it is often not connected to the general ledger accounting data. In a similar vein, labor costs are often simply recorded as payroll expense or part of manufacturing overhead, rather than specifying whether the labor was related to product output, waste management, or environmental damage prevention. For an EMA system to be effective, accounting information will need to be tagged with multiple identifiers to serve various information needs.

[40] http://united.com

Historical Orientation of Accounting

Financial accounting systems focus on providing the historical, transaction-based cost information needed for preparing financial statements in accordance with Generally Accepted Accounting Principles (GAAP). However, for an EMA system to be effective in helping management make good decisions, it will need to include a more open-minded and forward-looking definition of cost. For example, an EMA system might include an estimate of the cost of lost sales resulting from poor environmental performance. Or it might include an estimate of the cost of losing access to markets with environment-related product restrictions. It might also include an estimate of costs externalized to society. Both accountants and management will need to expand their view of what constitutes a "cost" as they develop EMA systems for their companies.

Undeveloped Field

Environmental management accounting is a relatively new, undeveloped field. Tools for providing environmental management accounting information are being developed and refined constantly as the field evolves. Organizations are still working to discover what information they need and how it can be reported in an accurate, timely, verifiable, and relevant manner.

> **Why is this important?**
>
> "In order to provide managers with relevant **environmental information**, accountants will need to rethink their **traditional views** on what constitutes a **'cost'** and expand their costing systems to provide more **detailed information**."

Future of Environmental Management Accounting

This chapter has briefly summarized the state of environmental management accounting as it exists today. There are a number of valid business reasons for organizations to commit to sustainability reporting and producing CSR reports. Organizations can use EMA, utilizing both monetary and physical information, to support these efforts. The field of environmental management accounting is relatively new and so can be challenging to implement. However, advances are being made every day.

Sustainability is a growing concern worldwide. Management accountants have a critical responsibility and opportunity to assist their organizations in supporting sustainability through the use of environmental management accounting information that is accurate, timely, and relevant.

Decision Guidelines

Decision	Guidelines
What three performance factors should be considered if a company wishes to become more sustainable?	The three pillars of sustainability are economic, environmental, and social performance. Together, these three factors are known as the triple bottom line.
Why can't companies continue to operate under the linear "take–make–waste" economic model?	Because of the earth's limited resources, the old economic model is not viable in the long run.
Why should a company use life-cycle assessment (LCA) to evaluate its products and services?	LCA helps companies assess the social and environmental impacts of its products and services all the way from cradle to grave. Thus, it helps uncover previously hidden external costs, as well as traditionally captured internal costs. By understanding the full costs of the product, companies can work toward reducing negative impacts and increasing positive impacts.
How does sustainability increase business value?	Sustainable practices help companies: 1. Reduce costs 2. Generate new revenue streams 3. Increase market share 4. Improve external image 5. Reduce risks 6. Attract labor talent 7. Attract capital
What is sustainability reporting, and why should companies adopt it?	Sustainability reporting is a process used by companies to set goals, measure performance, and manage change as they move toward a more sustainable economic model. Sustainability reporting is used as an internal management change tool, as well as a basis for preparing CSR reports.
How prevalent are CSR reports, and who uses them?	The majority of large domestic and international companies prepare CSR reports, thus putting peer pressure on those who currently do not issue reports. CSR reports are used as a way of communicating sustainability performance to a wide variety of external stakeholders.
Is there a common framework used by all CSR reports?	The Global Reporting Initiative (GRI) has developed the most widely used framework. The G4 Guidelines are the most recent version of the framework.
How is the framework organized?	The framework is organized around the three categories of the triple bottom line: economic, environmental, and social. Companies report on those aspects of each category that are material to their operations.
What types of information should an environmental management accounting (EMA) system collect and analyze?	EMA systems focus on both monetary and physical information. Materials flow accounting (MFA) is often used to track all physical inputs and reconcile them with all of the company's outputs, including waste and emissions.
How is EMA information used?	EMA information is used to support management in planning, directing, and controlling operations. EMA information assists managers in determining how to best integrate sustainable practices throughout the organization. EMA also generates the information needed for external reporting purposes.
What challenges does management face in implementing EMA systems?	EMA systems provide much more detail than traditional accounting systems and will require effective communication throughout the organization. The existing accounting system will need to be revamped, replaced, or supplemented to provide management with the environmental information it needs. Accountants will need to rethink the traditional definitions of "cost" and expand traditional cost categories as they develop EMA systems.

CHAPTER 15 END OF CHAPTER

Learning Objectives

- 1 Describe sustainability and how it can create business value
- 2 Describe sustainability reporting and the GRI framework
- 3 Describe EMA systems and their uses and challenges

Accounting Vocabulary

Assurance. (p. 906) An independent party's external validation of management's assertions.

Big Four. (p. 904) The largest four accounting firms in the world: Deloitte, EY, KPMG, and PriceWaterhouseCoopers.

Carbon Disclosure Project. (p. 910) A nonprofit organization that collects and disseminates carbon footprint information.

Carbon Footprint. (p. 910) A measure of the total emissions of carbon dioxide and other greenhouse gases (GHGs), often expressed for simplicity as tons of equivalent carbon dioxide.

Comprehensive Report. (p. 906) A GRI-referenced report in which *all indicators* related to each identified material aspect are disclosed.

Core Report. (p. 906) A GRI-referenced report in which *at least one* indicator related to each identified material aspect is disclosed.

Eco-Efficiency. (p. 898) Achieving economic savings by producing goods and services with fewer ecological resources.

Environmental Management Accounting (EMA). (p. 908) A system used for the identification, collection, analysis, and use of two types of information for internal decision making—monetary and physical information.

Extended Producer Responsibility (EPR) laws. (p. 910) Laws that require product manufacturers to "take back" a large percentage of the products they manufacture at the end of the product's life in order to reduce the amount of waste ending up in landfills and the environment.

External Costs. (p. 896) Costs borne by society as a result of a company's operations and the products and services it sells.

Global Reporting Initiative (GRI). (p. 903) A nonprofit organization whose mission is to make sustainability reporting standard practice by providing guidance and support to organizations. The developer of the G4 Guidelines.

Internal Costs. (p. 896) Costs that are incurred and paid for by the organization and recorded in GAAP-based accounting records.

Life-Cycle Assessment (LCA). (p. 896) Studying the environmental and social impacts of a product or service over its entire life, from "cradle to grave."

Materiality. (p. 904) An important concept in CSR reporting defined as those aspects of a business that reflect the organization's significant economic, environmental, and social impacts, or substantively influence the assessments and decisions of stakeholders.

Materials Flow Accounting (MFA). (p. 909) An accounting system in which all physical inputs to an organization's operations are reconciled with output generated. The goal is to track where all physical inputs are going.

Monetary Information. (p. 908) The type of information traditionally used in accounting systems.

Non-Governmental Organizations (NGOs). (p. 896) Not-for-profit organizations that serve the public interest, such as Greenpeace and Sierra Club.

Physical Information. (p. 908) A vital part of environmental management accounting systems. Examples include: quantity of air emissions, tons of solid waste generated, gallons of wastewater generated, pounds of packaging recycled, and total amount of water consumed.

Principles for Responsible Investment (PRI). (p. 902) Six principles of investing, including a commitment to incorporate environmental, social, and governance issues into investment analysis and decision making.

Social Return on Investment (SROI). (p. 910) An analytical tool that is used to explain social and environmental value in monetary terms.

Supply-Chain Assessment. (p. 900) Making purchase decisions based partially on how well suppliers manage the social and environmental impact of their operations.

Sustainability. (p. 895) The ability of a system to endure without giving way or to use resources so that they are not depleted or permanently damaged. In business, sustainability is also defined as the ability to meet the needs of the present without compromising the ability of future generations to meet their own needs.

Sustainability Report. (p. 902) The primary document used for communicating a company's performance on all three pillars of the triple bottom line: economic, environmental, and social. Also known as a Corporate Social Responsibility (CSR) report.

Sustainability Reporting. (p. 902) A process that helps companies set goals, measure performance, and manage change as they move toward an economic model that produces long-term economic profit as well as environmental care and social responsibility.

Triple Bottom Line. (p. 895) Evaluating a company's performance not only by its ability to generate economic profits, but also by its impact on people and the planet.

Waste Audits. (p. 899) Studying the stream of waste coming from company operations (solid waste, water discharge, chemicals, etc.) to determine waste that can be avoided and alternative uses for the remaining waste.

Water Footprint. (p. 911) The total volume of water use associated with the processes and products of a business.

Quick Check

1. *(Learning Objective 1)* Which of the following is *not* one of the three factors related to sustainability?
   a. Ecologic
   b. Social
   c. Environment
   d. Economic

2. *(Learning Objective 1)* Which of the following items would be considered an *external* cost?
   a. Monthly trash hauling fee
   b. Annual audit by public accounting firm
   c. Impact of oil spill on aquatic life
   d. Salary cost of sustainability officer

3. *(Learning Objective 1)* LCA stands for which of the following?
   a. Life costs aggregated
   b. Lower cost always
   c. Lowest-cost audit
   d. Life-cycle assessment

4. *(Learning Objective 1)* Which of the following would *not* be a reason to adopt sustainable business practices?
   a. Improving external image
   b. Reducing costs
   c. Increasing compliance risks
   d. Producing new revenue streams

5. *(Learning Objective 2)* What is the current status of sustainability reporting in the United States?
   a. The SEC requires that publicly traded companies disclose any material information to prevent misleading the readers of financial statements.
   b. Sustainability reporting using the GRI G4 reporting guidelines is required for all companies doing business in the United States, regardless of size.
   c. All companies listed on the New York Stock Exchange (NYSE) must issue sustainability reports using the NYSE's sustainability reporting guidelines.
   d. Sustainability reporting using the GRI G4 reporting guidelines is required for all publicly traded companies.

6. *(Learning Objective 2)* Which of the following would be a reason for a company to undertake sustainability reporting?
   a. The sustainability report can communicate the company's social and environmental impact to consumers, investors, and other stakeholders.
   b. Sustainability reporting can be an internal change management tool.
   c. Neither a nor b is a reason for sustainability reporting.
   d. Both a and b are reasons for sustainability reporting.

7. *(Learning Objective 2)* Which of the following aspects would *not* be included in the environmental category of the GRI G4 reporting guidelines?
   a. Emissions
   b. Transport
   c. Training and education
   d. Energy

8. *(Learning Objective 2)* Which of the following aspects would *not* be included in the economic category of the GRI G4 reporting guidelines?
   a. Indirect economic impacts
   b. Market presence
   c. Procurement practices
   d. Equal remuneration for women and men

9. *(Learning Objective 2)* Which of the following aspects would *not* be included in the social category of the GRI G4 reporting guidelines?
   a. Child labor
   b. Environmental grievance mechanism
   c. Anti-corruption
   d. Labor/management relations

10. *(Learning Objective 3)* Which of the following is *not* a challenge to implementing and using an environmental management accounting system?
    a. Communication issues
    b. Hidden costs
    c. Historical orientation of accounting
    d. All of the above items are challenges.

Quick Check Answers

1. a 2. c 3. d 4. c 5. a 6. d 7. c 8. d 9. b 10. d

Short Exercises

S15-1 Identifying reasons to pursue sustainability *(Learning Objective 1)*

Listed below are several reasons an organization might pursue sustainability initiatives. Classify each reason as either: *reducing costs, creating new revenue streams, reducing risks, increasing and retaining market share,* or *attracting capital*.

a. Jiangsu Redbud Dyeing Technology in China, a supplier to Walmart, had to go green as a condition of continuing to be part of Walmart's supply chain.
b. The architectural firm of Perkins + Will recently retrofitted its 25-year-old office building to the LEED platinum level, achieving the highest score ever for a LEED platinum building in North America.
c. The cleaning product company Method produces a dish and hand soap made with plastic trash recovered from the Pacific Ocean.
d. Johnson & Johnson (J & J) experienced a significant increase in the number of non-compliance notices it received in a recent year. As a result, J & J has increased sustainability training throughout the company and has increased management attention on sustainability processes.
e. Air France-KLM strives to keep its top spot in the Travel & Leisure sector in the Dow Jones Sustainability Index (DJSI); many institutional investors will only invest in companies listed on the DJSI.

S15-2 Identify aspects within each G4 category on a GRI report *(Learning Objective 2)*

For each of the following items, identify whether the item would be classified under the *Economic, Environmental,* or *Social* G4 category on a GRI report.

a. Emissions
b. Supplier assessment for impacts on society
c. Customer privacy
d. Diversity and equal opportunity
e. Product and service labeling
f. Supplier human rights assessment
g. Economic performance
h. Materials
i. Effluents and waste
j. Training and education
k. Indirect economic impacts
l. Customer health and safety
m. Market presence
n. Anti-competitive behavior
o. Forced or compulsory labor
p. Employment
q. Energy

S15-3 Identify aspects within each G4 Social subcategory on a GRI report *(Learning Objective 2)*

For each of the following items, identify whether the item would be classified under the *Labor Practices and Decent Work, Human Rights, Society,* or *Product Responsibility* subcategory of the Social G4 category on a GRI report.

a. Employment
b. Supplier human rights assessment
c. Customer health and safety
d. Forced or compulsory labor
e. Equal remuneration for women and men
f. Training and education

g. Indigenous rights
h. Marketing communications
i. Diversity and equal opportunity
j. Customer privacy
k. Product and service labeling
l. Supplier assessment for impacts on society
m. Local communities
n. Anti-competitive behavior

S15-4 Classifying sustainability costs *(Learning Objective 3)*

As discussed in the chapter, there are at least six categories of costs (monetary information) associated with sustainability efforts. In the table to follow, identify the proper sustainability cost category for each of the costs listed.

Cost	Sustainability cost category
Cost of installing scrubbers to control air pollution at an electricity-generation plant	
Cost to the company's image and goodwill resulting from a large chemical spill	
Cost of water used to cool extruded products in a manufacturing plant	
Cost of canvas used in producing tote bags	
Cost of air-monitoring equipment to ensure that scrubbers are functioning properly (scrubbers are air-pollution control equipment)	

S15-5 Distinguish between monetary and physical information *(Learning Objective 3)*

For each of the following examples of information, specify whether it would be included in an environmental management accounting system as monetary information (M), physical information (P), or not included in the environmental management accounting system (NA).

1. Gallons of toxic waste generated
2. Pounds of cardboard recycled
3. Tons of scrap metal recycled
4. Wages of workers to comply with new EPA standards
5. Cost of the CEO's salary
6. Gallons of lubricants used in machinery
7. Cost of wages for quality control inspector
8. Cost of materials used in lab to neutralize toxins
9. Total kilowatt-hours of electricity used
10. Cost of wages for plant manager
11. Cost of electricity used to power manufacturing facilities
12. Cost of sulfur used in erasers
13. Cost of shipping raw materials between company plants
14. Costs of running a laboratory to develop alternative energy sources
15. Cost of upgrading factory equipment to reduce emissions

S15-6 Identify implementation challenges *(Learning Objective 3)*

Implementing an environmental management accounting (EMA) system can have several challenges. Following are several implementation scenarios. For each scenario, identify which type of implementation challenge it represents (a. communication issue; b. hidden cost; c. aggregated accounting information; d. historical orientation of accounting; or e. newness of EMA).

1. Company accountants can find little guidance on how to develop a sound environmental management accounting system.
2. The water usage costs are included in the overhead account.

3. The cost of future lost sales resulting from the poor publicity generated by a large chemical spill are not included in the results of operations provided to management, even though the lost sales are significant.
4. The costs of handling hazardous materials are included with the material handling costs for all materials.
5. The production staff does not interact or share information with the accounting staff.

S15-7 Define key sustainability terms *(Learning Objectives 1, 2, & 3)*

Complete the following statements with one of the terms listed. You may use a term more than once. Some terms may not be used at all.

Assurance	Global Reporting Initiative (GRI)	Materials flow accounting	Sustainability
Eco-efficiency	Internal cost	Non-governmental organizations (NGOs)	Sustainability Accounting Standards Board (SASB)
External cost	Life-cycle assessment	Social return on investment	Sustainability report

a. The G4 guidelines were developed by the _____, a nonprofit organization whose mission is to help to standardize sustainability reporting practices.
b. The impact of the *Deepwater Horizon* (BP) oil spill on ecosystems in and around the Gulf of Mexico is an example of a(n) _____.
c. The _____ is developing a sustainability disclosure reporting framework.
d. _____ is often defined as the ability to meet the needs of the present generation without compromising the ability of future generations to meet their own needs.
e. When NIKE is able to achieve cost savings by producing its shoes with fewer resources, it is practicing _____.
f. When a company studies the environmental and social impact of one of its products over the product's entire life, it is performing a(n) _____.
g. A Corporate Social Responsibility (CSR) report is also known as a(n) _____.
h. The cost of cleaning up the *Deepwater Horizon* oil spill to be paid by BP is a(n) _____.
i. When the Big Four accounting firm of Deloitte validated UPS's sustainability report, Deloitte was providing _____.
j. _____ is an analytical tool that is used to explain social and environmental value in monetary terms.
k. Doctors Without Borders and the American Society for the Prevention of Cruelty to Animals (ASPCA) are both examples of _____.
l. The goal of _____ is to track where all physical inputs are going in an organization's operations.

ETHICS

S15-8 Identify ethical standards violated *(Learning Objectives 1, 2, & 3)*

For each of the situations listed, identify the primary standard from the IMA Statement of Ethical Professional Practice that is violated (competence, confidentiality, integrity, or credibility). Refer to Exhibit 1-7 for the complete standard.

1. Chris is asked to prepare the GRI report for the year, but he has not attended GRI training. He decides to muddle his way through the report.
2. George is frustrated because he feels that his company is not moving fast enough to adopt sustainable practices and GRI reporting. He talks to a reporter about some potential environmental fines the company might receive, thinking that if the company is embarrassed publicly, it will move faster on sustainability initiatives.
3. Kayleigh does not disclose that her brother is the president of the consulting firm her organization is hiring for some GRI reporting work.
4. Cynthia is a staff accountant at Briar Industries. Since Briar's GRI report is not audited, Cynthia omits a few numbers that, if published, would cause Briar to look less environmentally friendly. Cynthia figures that she is not likely to get caught and the report is not required.
5. Marcia skipped attending her company's training on GRI reporting because, even though she was required to go, attendance would not be taken.

EXERCISES Group A

E15-9A Identify impact of sustainability efforts *(Learning Objective 1)*

Sustainability involves more than just the impact of actions on the environment. The triple bottom line recognizes that a company has to measure its impact on people, planet, and profit for its long-term economic and social viability. To follow are examples of green initiatives recently undertaken at Procter and Gamble (P&G). For each example, indicate whether the impact of this initiative would be primarily economic, environmental, or social.

a. Partnered with UNICEF to provide vaccinations to women and children at risk for maternal and neonatal tetanus
b. Partnered with Feeding America to help fight hunger
c. Adopted long-term goals of integrating 100% renewable or recycled materials into product lines and packaging
d. Aided 60 countries and saved thousands of lives by developing and providing PUR water filtration packets via the Children's Safe Drinking Water (CSDW) Program
e. Provided disaster relief to Haiti, donating PUR packets and various hygiene products
f. Planned to create products and packaging in such a way that consumer waste goes to recycling, compost, or waste-to-energy rather than landfills
g. Shareholder's equity decreased in the most recent year
h. Worked to improve and preserve the quality of water within regions and communities where operations take place to avoid contributing to water scarcity
i. Within the past year, decreased the amount of company printed pages by 11 million through combined efforts with Xerox
j. Saw total shareholder return increased in the past fiscal year
k. Moved toward 100% renewable energy to power plants to completely eliminate petroleum-based CO_2 emissions
l. Planned to eliminate manufacturing waste that is currently sent to landfills
m. Funded NGO efforts to educate children in India through Project Shiksha

E15-10A Sustainability and the value chain *(Learning Objective 1)*

Each of the following scenarios describes a sustainability-related cost item for organizations in recent years. For each scenario, identify which function of the value chain that cost would represent (R&D, design, purchasing/producing, marketing, distributing, or customer service). *Note: The companies and products used in this exercise are real companies with a strong sustainable practices commitment.*

a. The Target Corporation, a retailing company, offers a line of garments that have been treated for stain management. However, such treatments usually include a chemical (PFOA) that has been found to be potentially harmful to humans, so Target only purchases from manufacturers that offer PFOA-free alternatives. The cost of the garments treated with the PFOA-alternatives would fall into which function in the value chain?
b. Patagonia, a clothing manufacturer, launched a program called the Common Threads Initiative. In an effort to prevent clothing from going to landfills, the company collects used and damaged garments from consumers. These textiles are then salvaged and recycled as new products. The costs involved in running this program to take back used garments would fall into which function in the value chain?
c. To help offset carbon emissions, U-Haul, a moving truck rental company, gives its consumers an option to donate $1 to $5 at the time of a transaction. Just two years after its launch, $1,000,000 was raised and 133,000 trees were planted with the proceeds. The cost of these carbon offsets purchased for the vehicles rented by U-Haul would fall into which function in the value chain?

d. Bert's Bees, a manufacturer of products such as lip balm, has developed a new soap label called TerraSkin™ Wraps that is "treeless" and "bleach-free" (it is a paper-label alternative). The cost of researching the proper process and combinations of components for this new label would fall into which function in the value chain?

e. The Kellogg Company, known for its breakfast cereals, has successfully switched the majority of its packaging over to 100% recycled materials, 35% of which is consumer-recycled. According to the company's analysis, the impact of this achievement can be found in the decreased overall carbon footprint left by the company, as well as increased recyclability of this packaging. The cost of designing the life cycle of Kellogg's packaging would fall into which function in the value chain?

f. General Mills produces a variety of different foods. The company recognizes the importance of encouraging good nutrition among the youth of America and has launched a special initiative to ensure that its marketing strategies promote healthy lifestyles. It avoids targeting children under 12 with advertisements for foods that are high in sugar. The cost of these marketing campaigns would fall into which function in the value chain?

E15-11A Sustainability and job costing *(Learning Objective 1)*

Lowell Plastics manufactures custom park furniture and signage from recycled plastics (primarily shredded milk jugs). Many of the company's customers are municipalities that are required by law to purchase goods that meet certain recycled-content guidelines. (Recycled content can include post-consumer waste materials, pre-consumer waste materials, and recovered materials.) As a result, Lowell Plastics includes two types of direct material charges in its job cost for each job: (1) virgin materials (non-recycled) and (2) recycled-content materials. Lowell Plastics also keeps track of the pounds of each type of direct material, so that the final recycled-content percentage for the job can be reported to the customer. The company also reports on the percentage of recycled content to total plastic used each month on its own internal reporting system to help to encourage managers to use recycled content whenever possible.

Lowell Plastics uses a predetermined manufacturing overhead rate of $9 per direct labor hour. Here is a summary of the materials and labor used on a recent job for Norton County:

Description	Quantity	Cost
Virgin materials	50 pounds	$ 4.30 per pound
Recycled-content materials	50 pounds	$ 2.60 per pound
Direct labor	12 hours	$ 13.00 per hour

Requirements

1. Calculate the total cost of the Norton County job.
2. Calculate the percentage of recycled-content materials used in the Norton County job (using pounds). If items purchased by Norton County are required by county charter to contain at least 60% recycled content, does this job meet that requirement?

E15-12A Sustainability and activity-based costing *(Learning Objective 1)*

Shaffer Industries manufactures a variety of custom widgets. The company has traditionally used a plantwide manufacturing overhead rate based on machine hours to allocate manufacturing overhead to its products. The company estimates that it will incur $1,080,000 in total manufacturing overhead costs in the upcoming year and will use 9,000 machine hours.

Up to this point, hazardous waste-disposal fees have been absorbed into the plantwide manufacturing overhead rate and allocated to all products as part of the manufacturing overhead process. Recently, the company has been experiencing significantly increased waste-disposal fees for hazardous waste generated by certain products, and, as a result, profit margins on all products have been negatively impacted. Company management wants to implement an activity-based costing system so that managers know the cost of each product, including its hazardous waste-disposal costs.

Expected usage and costs for manufacturing overhead activities for the upcoming year are as follows:

Description of cost pool	Estimated cost	Cost driver	Estimated activity for the year
Machine maintenance costs	$ 450,000	Number of machine hours	9,000
Engineering change orders	$ 70,000	Number of change orders	1,000
Hazardous waste disposal	$ 560,000	Pounds of hazardous material generated	2,000
Total overhead cost	$ 1,080,000		

During the year, Job 356 is started and completed. Usage data for this job are as follows:

290 pounds of direct material at $70 per pound
50 direct labor hours used at $25 per labor hour
140 machine hours used
11 change orders
80 pounds of hazardous waste generated

Requirements

1. Calculate the cost of Job 356 using the traditional plantwide manufacturing overhead rate based on machine hours.
2. Calculate the cost of Job 356 using activity-based costing.
3. If you were a manager, which cost estimate would provide you more useful information? How might you use this information?

E15-13A Sustainability and process costing (Learning Objective 1)

Sorrento Industries manufactures plastic bottles for the food industry. On average, Sorrento pays $71 per ton for its plastics. Sorrento's waste-disposal company has increased its waste-disposal charge to $56 per ton for solid and inert waste. Sorrento generates a total of 500 tons of waste per month.

The company's managers have been evaluating the production processes for areas to cut waste. In the process of making plastic bottles, a certain amount of machine "drool" occurs. Machine drool is the excess plastic that "drips" off the machine between molds. In the past, Sorrento has discarded the machine drool. In an average month, 170 tons of machine drool are generated.

Management has arrived at three possible courses of action for the machine drool issue:

1. Do nothing and pay the increased waste-disposal charge.
2. Sell the machine drool waste to a local recycler for $13 per ton.
3. Reengineer the production process at an annual cost of $45,000. This change in the production process would reduce the amount of machine drool generated by 60% each month. The remaining machine drool would then be sold to a local recycler for $13 per ton.

Requirements

1. What is the annual cost of the machine drool currently? Include both the original plastics cost and the waste-disposal cost.
2. How much would the company save per year (net) if the machine drool were to be sold to the local recycler?
3. How much would the company save per year (net) if the production process were to be reengineered?
4. What do you think the company should do? Explain your rationale.

E15-14A Sustainability and cost behavior *(Learning Objective 1)*

Lunar Entertainment is a provider of cable, Internet, and on-demand video services. Lunar currently sends monthly bills to its customers via the postal service. Because of a concern for the environment and recent increases in postal rates, Lunar management is considering offering an option to its customers for paperless billing. In addition to saving printing, paper, and postal costs, paperless billing will save energy and water (through reduced paper needs, waste disposal, and transportation needs). While Lunar would like to switch to 100% paperless billing, many of its customers are not comfortable with paperless billing or may not have online access, so the paper billing option will remain regardless of whether or not Lunar adopts a paperless billing system.

The cost of the paperless billing system would be $48,800 per quarter with no variable costs since the costs of the system are the salaries of the clerks and the cost of leasing the computer system. The paperless billing system being proposed would be able to handle up to 900,000 bills per quarter (more than 900,000 bills per quarter would require a different computer system and is outside the scope of the current situation at Lunar).

Lunar has gathered its cost data for the past year by quarter for paper, toner cartridges, printer maintenance costs, and postage costs for the billing department. The cost data are as follows:

	Quarter 1	Quarter 2	Quarter 3	Quarter 4
Total paper, toner, printer maintenance, and postage costs	$689,400	$705,000	$810,000	$720,000
Total number of bills mailed	616,000	621,000	750,000	625,000

Requirements

1. Calculate the variable cost per bill mailed under the current paper-based billing system. Use the high-low method.
2. Assume that the company projects that it will have a total of 640,000 bills to mail in the upcoming quarter. If enough customers choose the paperless billing option so that 15% of the mailings can be converted to paperless, how much would the company save from the paperless billing system (be sure to consider the cost of the paperless billing system)?
3. What if only 5% of the mailings are converted to the paperless option (assume a total of 640,000 bills)? Should the company still offer the paperless billing system? Explain your rationale.

E15-15A Sustainability and CVP concepts *(Learning Objective 1)*

Krugman Garage Doors manufactures a premium garage door. Currently, the price and cost data associated with the premium garage door are as follows:

Average selling price per premium garage door...	$ 1,000
Average variable manufacturing cost per door	$ 500
Average variable selling cost per door	$ 100
Total annual fixed costs	$ 200,000

Krugman Garage Doors has undertaken several sustainability projects over the past few years. Management is currently evaluating whether to develop a comprehensive software control system for its manufacturing operations that would significantly reduce scrap and waste generated during the manufacturing process. If the company were to implement this software control system in its manufacturing operations, use of the software control system would result in an increase of $50,000 in its annual fixed costs while the average variable manufacturing cost per door would drop by $100.

Requirements

1. What is the company's current breakeven point in units and in dollars?
2. If the company expects to sell 590 premium garage doors in the upcoming year, and it does not develop the software control system, what is its expected operating income from premium garage doors?
3. If the software control system were to be developed and implemented, what would be the company's new breakeven point in units and in dollars?
4. If the company expects to sell 590 premium garage doors in the upcoming year, and it develops the software control system, what is its expected operating income from premium garage doors?
5. If the company expects to sell 590 premium garage doors in the upcoming year, do you think the company should implement the software control system? Why or why not? What factors should the company consider?

E15-16A Sustainability and short-term decision making *(Learning Objective 1)*

Over the past several years, decommissioned U.S. warships have been turned into artificial reefs in the ocean by towing them out to sea and sinking them. The thinking was that sinking the ship would conveniently dispose of it while providing an artificial reef environment for aquatic life. In reality, some of the sunken ships have released toxins into the ocean and have been costly to decontaminate. Now the U.S. government is taking bids to instead dismantle and recycle ships that have recently been decommissioned (but have not been sunk yet).

Assume that a recently decommissioned aircraft, the USS *Freedom*, is estimated to contain approximately 40 tons of recyclable materials able to be sold for approximately $33.9 million. The low bid for dismantling and transporting the ship materials to appropriate facilities is $35.7 million. Recycling and dismantling the ship would create about 500 jobs for about a year in the Rust Belt. This geographic area has been experiencing record-high unemployment rates in recent years.

Requirements

1. Is it more financially advantageous to sink the ship (assume that it costs approximately $0.9 million to tow a ship out to sea and sink it) or to dismantle and recycle it? Show your calculations.
2. From a sustainability standpoint, what should be done with the decommissioned aircraft carrier? List some of the qualitative factors that should enter into this analysis.
3. As a taxpayer, which action would you prefer (sink or recycle)? Defend your answer.

E15-17A Sustainability and budgeting *(Learning Objective 1)*

Liller Beverages manufactures its own soda pop bottles. The bottles are made from polyethylene terephthalate (PET), a lightweight yet strong plastic. The company uses as much PET recycled resin pellets in its bottles as it can, both because using recycled PET helps the company to meet its sustainability goals and because recycled PET is less expensive than virgin PET.

Liller is continuing to search for ways to reduce its costs and its impact on the environment. PET plastic is melted and blown over soda bottle molds to produce the bottles. One idea Liller's engineers have suggested is to retrofit the soda bottle molds and change the plastic formulation slightly so that 25% less PET plastic is used for each bottle. The average kilograms of PET per soda bottle before any redesign is 0.004 kg. The cost of retrofitting the soda bottle molds will result in a one-time charge of $35,947, while the plastic reformulation will cause the average cost per kilogram of PET plastic to change from $4.00 to $4.30.

Liller's management is analyzing whether the change to the bottle molds to reduce PET plastic usage should be made. Management expects the following number of soda bottles to be used in the upcoming year:

	Quarter 1	Quarter 2	Quarter 3	Quarter 4
Number of bottles to be produced	3,200,000	2,600,000	3,000,000	2,900,000

For the upcoming year, management expects the beginning inventory of PET to be 1,280 kilograms, while ending inventory is expected to be 1,690 kilograms. During the first three quarters of the year, management wants to keep the ending inventory of PET at the end of each quarter equal to 10% of the following quarter's PET needs.

Requirements

1. Using the original data (before any redesign of soda bottles), prepare a direct materials budget to calculate the cost of PET purchases in each quarter for the upcoming year and for the year in total.
2. Assume that the company retrofits the soda bottle molds and changes the plastic formulation slightly so that less PET plastic is used in each bottle. Now prepare a direct materials budget to calculate the cost of PET purchases in each quarter for the upcoming year and for the year in total for this possible scenario.
3. Compare the cost of PET plastic for Requirement 1 (original data) and for Requirement 2 (making change to using less PET). What is the direct material cost savings from making the change to using less PET? Compare the total of those savings to the cost of retrofitting the soda bottle molds. Should the company make the change? Explain your rationale.

E15-18A Sustainability and the balanced scorecard *(Learning Objective 1)*

Classify each of the following sustainability key performance indicators (KPIs) according to the balanced scorecard perspective it addresses. Choose from the following five perspectives:

- Financial perspective
- Customer perspective
- Internal business perspective
- Learning and growth perspective
- Community perspective

KPI	Perspective
a. Waste-disposal costs	
b. Energy use per ton of production	
c. Energy use efficiency percentage	
d. CO_2 in metric tons	
e. Environmental fines paid (expense item on income statement)	
f. Wastewater per ton of production	
g. Global in-kind donations as a percentage of total income	
h. Water use per ton of production	
i. Percentage of management with sustainability training	
j. Global charitable contributions as a percent of income	
k. Safety fines paid	
l. Percentage of general staff with sustainability training	
m. Revenue generated through sale of recycled goods	
n. Number of green products	
o. Percent of packaging from products reclaimed and/or recycled	
p. Percentage of total income donated to aid during natural disasters	
q. Direct greenhouse gas emissions	
r. Product safety ratings	

E15-19A Sustainability and standard costing *(Learning Objective 1)*

Wolfe Containers currently uses a recycled plastic to make bottles for the food industry.

Current bottle production information:

The cost and time standards per batch of 10,000 bottles are as follows:

Plastic 220 kilograms at $6.00 per kg
Direct labor 4.0 hours at $20.00 per hour

The variable manufacturing overhead rate is based on total estimated variable manufacturing overhead of $400,000 and estimated total direct labor hours (DLH) of 10,000. The company allocates its variable manufacturing overhead based on direct labor hours.

Proposed changes to bottle design and production process:

The container division manager is considering having both the bottle redesigned and the bottle production process reengineered so that the plastic usage would drop by 25% overall due both to generating less scrap in the manufacturing process and using less plastic in each bottle. In addition to decreasing the amount of plastic used in producing the bottles, the additional following benefits would be realized:

a. Direct labor hours would be reduced by 10% because less scrap would be handled in the production process.

b. Total estimated variable manufacturing overhead would be reduced by 5% because less scrap would need to be hauled away, less electricity would be used in the production process, and less inventory would need to be stocked.

Requirements

1. Calculate the standard cost per batch of 10,000 bottles using the current data (before the company makes any changes). Include direct materials, direct labor, and variable manufacturing overhead in the standard cost per unit.
2. Calculate the standard cost per batch of 10,000 bottles if the company makes the changes to the bottle design and production process so that less plastic is used. Include direct materials, direct labor, and variable manufacturing overhead in the standard cost per unit.
3. Calculate the cost savings per batch by comparing the standard cost per batch under each scenario (current versus proposed change). Assume that the total cost to implement the changes would be $121,100. How many batches of bottles would need to be produced after the change to have the cost savings total equal the cost to make the changes?
4. What other benefits might arise from making this change to using less plastic in the manufacture of the bottles? Are there any risks? What would you recommend the company do?

E15-20A Sustainability and capital investments *(Learning Objective 1)*

Mercado Industries is evaluating investing in solar panels to provide some of the electrical needs of its main office building in Boulder, Colorado. The solar panel project would cost $650,000 and would provide cost savings in its utility bills of $50,000 per year. It is anticipated that the solar panels would have a life of 15 years and would have no residual value.

Requirements

1. Calculate the payback period in years of the solar panel project.
2. If the company uses a discount rate of 12%, what is the net present value of this project?
3. If the company has a rule that no projects will be undertaken that have a payback period of more than five years, would this investment be accepted? If not, what arguments could managers make to get approval for the solar panel project?
4. What would you do if you were in charge of approving capital investment proposals?

E15-21A Sustainability and the statement of cash flows *(Learning Objective 1)*

Webber Plastics is a manufacturer that takes in post-consumer plastics (e.g., empty milk jugs) and recycles those plastics into a variety of building materials. Because the company has a strong focus on sustainability, the company managers try, whenever possible, to use recycled materials and to invest in sustainable projects.

Last year, the company engaged in several sustainable practices that had an impact on its cash flows. For each of the transactions listed below, indicate whether the transaction would have affected the operating, investing, or financing cash flows of the company. Additionally, indicate whether each transaction would have increased (+) or decreased (−) cash.

Transactions:

1. Webber paid off long-term bonds during the year using excess funds.
2. New production equipment that is 40% more energy efficient than the old equipment was purchased for cash.

3. Webber installed a "living roof" on its manufacturing facility. This roof is made mostly from sedum, a drought-resistant perennial grass-like groundcover. The plants help to reduce stormwater runoff and double the expected life of the roof over a conventional roof. The plants also reduce heating and cooling needs by providing an extra layer of insulation. Additionally, the plants absorb carbon dioxide to help to reduce greenhouse gases. The living roof was paid for with cash.
4. A wind turbine was built to power part of Webber's operations. The company paid cash.
5. Engineers at Webber performed research into a new process that injects tiny air bubbles into the plastic to reduce the usage of raw materials (plastics) and to reduce the weight of the finished products.
6. Throughout the year, Webber participated in several trade shows that featured green products for use by the housing construction industry. For each trade show, Webber incurred cash expenses for transportation, registration, meals and lodging, and booth setup.
7. A Honda Civic Hybrid automobile was purchased for use by the sales manager of Webber while on company business. The company paid cash.
8. When the plastic wood is cut into the lengths needed to make trellises, the end pieces cut off are scrap. Webber sold this cutting scrap to another recycler.
9. Webber became a minority partner in a biofuel project by investing $2 million in cash in the project.
10. A fleet of plug-in electric cars was purchased for the sales staff. The company paid cash.

E15-22A Sustainability and external financial reporting *(Learning Objective 1)*

In its 2015 Corporate Social Responsibility Report, the Hershey Company details the results from the steps it has taken to embed a sustainable culture throughout its business operations. In the following list from Hershey's CSR report, categorize each result as to whether it is oriented toward the *economic*, *environmental*, or *social* component of the triple bottom line.

a. Decreased total waste generated in metric tons from 2013 to 2015
b. Partnered with Feeding America to provide financial and volunteer support for six U.S. food banks
c. Had $7.4 billion in net sales during 2015
d. The Monterrey, Mexico, plant saved 16 million gallons of water in 2015 through its new system to remove salt from water
e. 71% of total global production took place in plants that sent zero waste to landfills
f. Decreased lost workday incident rate from 2013 to 2015
g. Decreased greenhouse gas emissions by 23% since 2009
h. Donated more than $20.7 million in cash and products to non-profit organizations in 2015
i. Met 2016 goal to source at least 50% of its cocoa from farms certified to be operating sustainably
j. Granted two paid days off to each employee to allow him or her to volunteer time in his or her community
k. Sponsored Learn to Grow programs in 464 cocoa communities in western Africa that help more than 31,000 farmers

EXERCISES Group B

E15-23B Identify impact of sustainability efforts *(Learning Objective 1)*

Sustainability involves more than just the impact of actions on the environment. The triple bottom line recognizes that a company has to measure its impact on the economy, the environment, and society for its long-term economic and social viability. To follow are examples of green initiatives recently undertaken at Ford Motor Company. For each example, indicate whether the impact of this initiative would be primarily economic, environmental, or social.

a. Made goal to reduce CO_2 emissions in new vehicles by 30%
b. Affiliates of the Ford Volunteer Corps gave over 112,000 volunteer hours to the community, targeting everything from schools to soup kitchens
c. Became national sponsor of the Susan G. Komen Race for the Cure
d. Trained suppliers' workers in human rights via outreach programs, and as a result was ranked first in *CRO Magazine*'s Best Citizens List
e. Expanded global markets to gain market share in more international countries
f. Planned to introduce plug-in hybrid electric vehicles that run on advanced lithium ion batteries
g. Planned to focus on increasing repertoire of small-to-midsize vehicles to respond to consumer demands in an effort to gain market share
h. Product strategy includes advancement of technology in order to reduce greenhouse gas emissions and improved fuel economy
i. Founded Ford Volunteer Corps in response to natural disasters
j. In a recent year, earned its highest net income in a decade
k. During the annual Global Week of Caring, 46,000 hours were contributed to volunteer projects like cleaning up highways
l. Introduced Ford Driving Skills for Life, which educates teens about safe driving practices
m. Planned to aggressively restructure in order to operate profitably at the current rate of consumer demand in light of the difficult economic times and the rising costs of fuel commodities

E15-24B Sustainability and the value chain *(Learning Objective 1)*

Each of the following scenarios describes a sustainability-related cost item for organizations. For each scenario, identify which function of the value chain that cost would represent (R&D, design, purchasing/producing, marketing, distributing, or customer service). *Note: The companies and products used in this exercise are real companies with a strong sustainable practices commitment.*

a. Able Plastics, a plastics production company, has very stringent audits on its carbon emissions and puts a lot of effort into offsetting its carbon emissions. For instance, not only does Able Plastics invest in the Strzelecki Ranges replanting site, but Able Plastics also endeavors to cut emissions by requiring that all electronic devices be fully turned off at night in all company buildings. Able Plastics also uses carbon offsets for its delivery vehicles. The cost of these carbon offsets for delivery vehicles would fall into which function in the value chain?

b. The Coca-Cola Company is currently spotlighting one of its newest innovations in packaging: the PlantBottle. In one of its promotion ads, it is hailed as "The **first ever** recyclable PET plastic beverage bottle made partially from plants . . . and recycles just like traditional PET plastic, but does so with a *lighter footprint* on the planet and its scarce resources." The cost of the research necessary for the Coca-Cola Company's newest foray into greener packaging would fall into which function in the value chain?

c. The Hewlett-Packard Company, a manufacturer of computers and related products, established its own R&R program in 1987. This program enables consumers to return any defective or used electronic goods and ink cartridges, which helps decrease the company's impact on the environment by avoiding landfills and allows the company to recycle the plastics and metals used in these products. The cost of recycling used computer products for consumers would fall into which function in the value chain?

d. The Sharp Corporation manufactures electronics. Sharp purchases recycled plastic parts to use in its products. The costs of this practice would fall into which function in the value chain?

e. Engineered Plastic Systems, LLC, a company that manufactures outdoor furniture, uses plastic lumber that is composed of recycled materials as a wood alternative for building its products. The plastic used is not only eco-friendly, but is also 50% recycled, 10% of which is post-consumer material. In promoting these eco-friendly features, the company is careful to make the distinction that it is not like other companies that falsely inflate their green efforts, stating specifically that it will always back up each of its claims with facts and never mislead the customer about the actual amount of recycled plastic in its products. The cost of such promotions would fall into which function in the value chain?

f. GenPak, LLC, manufactures food packaging and uses plastic in its products that is very conducive to recycling. In fact, much of its products are created from recycled plastic, much of which comes from GenPak's own products' post-consumer usage at the end of the products' life cycle. The cost of designing the process for continuing the life cycle of these products would fall into which function in the value chain?

E15-25B   Sustainability and job costing *(Learning Objective 1)*

Shaker Plastics manufactures custom park furniture and signage from recycled plastics (primarily shredded milk jugs). Many of the company's customers are municipalities that are required by law to purchase goods that meet certain recycled-content guidelines. (Recycled content can include post-consumer waste materials, pre-consumer waste materials, and recovered materials.) As a result, Shaker Plastics includes two types of direct material charges in its job cost for each job: (1) virgin materials (non-recycled) and (2) recycled-content materials. The company also keeps track of the pounds of each type of direct material so that the final recycled-content percentage for the job can be reported to the customer. The company also reports on the percentage of recycled content to total plastic used each month on its own internal reporting system to help encourage managers to use recycled content whenever possible.

The company uses a predetermined manufacturing overhead rate of $8.00 per direct labor hour. Here is a summary of the materials and labor used on a recent job for Osborn County:

Description	Quantity	Cost
Virgin materials	30 pounds	$ 4.00 per pound
Recycled-content materials	70 pounds	$ 3.00 per pound
Direct labor	16 hours	$ 15.00 per hour

Requirements

1. Calculate the total cost of the Osborn County job.
2. Calculate the percentage of recycled-content materials used in the Osborn County job (using pounds). If items purchased by Osborn County are required by county charter to contain at least 50% recycled content, does this job meet that requirement?

E15-26B Sustainability and activity-based costing *(Learning Objective 1)*

Santana Industries manufactures a variety of custom products. The company has traditionally used a plantwide manufacturing overhead rate based on machine hours to allocate manufacturing overhead to its products. The company estimates that it will incur $1,005,000 in total manufacturing overhead costs in the upcoming year and will use 15,000 machine hours.

Up to this point, hazardous waste-disposal fees have been absorbed into the plantwide manufacturing overhead rate and allocated to all products as part of the manufacturing overhead process. Recently, the company has been experiencing significantly increased waste-disposal fees for hazardous waste generated by certain products and, as a result, profit margins on all products have been negatively impacted. Company management wants to implement an activity-based costing system so that managers know the cost of each product, including its hazardous waste disposal costs.

Expected usage and costs for manufacturing overhead activities for the upcoming year are as follows:

Description of cost pool	Estimated cost	Cost driver	Estimated activity for the year
Machine maintenance costs	$ 300,000	Number of machine hours	15,000
Engineering change orders	$ 80,000	Number of change orders	2,000
Hazardous waste disposal	$ 625,000	Pounds of hazardous material generated	2,500
Total overhead cost	$1,005,000		

During the year, Job 356 is started and completed. Usage data for this job are as follows:

> 270 pounds of direct material at $20 per pound
> 70 direct labor hours used at $30 per labor hour
> 130 machine hours used
> 8 change orders
> 60 pounds of hazardous waste generated

Requirements

1. Calculate the cost of Job 356 using the traditional plantwide manufacturing overhead rate based on machine hours.
2. Calculate the cost of Job 356 using activity-based costing.
3. If you were a manager, which cost estimate would provide you more useful information? How might you use this information?

E15-27B Sustainability and process costing *(Learning Objective 1)*

Smigel Industries manufactures plastic bottles for the food industry. On average, Smigel pays $73 per ton for its plastics. Smigel's waste-disposal company has increased its waste-disposal charge to $56 per ton for solid and inert waste. The company generates a total of 500 tons of waste per month.

Smigel's managers have been evaluating the production processes for areas to cut waste. In the process of making plastic bottles, a certain amount of machine "drool" occurs. Machine drool is the excess plastic that drips off the machine between molds. In the past, Smigel has discarded the machine drool. In an average month, 180 tons of machine drool are generated.

Management has arrived at three possible courses of action for the machine drool issue:

1. Do nothing and pay the increased waste-disposal charge.
2. Sell the machine drool waste to a local recycler for $11 per ton.

3. Reengineer the production process at an annual cost of $70,000. This change in the production process would reduce the amount of machine drool generated by 60% each month. The remaining machine drool would then be sold to a local recycler for $11 per ton.

Requirements

1. What is the annual cost of the machine drool currently? Include both the original plastics cost and the waste-disposal cost.
2. How much would the company save per year (net) if the machine drool were to be sold to the local recycler?
3. How much would the company save per year (net) if the production process were to be reengineered?
4. What do you think the company should do? Explain your rationale.

E15-28B Sustainability and cost behavior (Learning Objective 1)

Grant Entertainment is a provider of cable, Internet, and on-demand video services. Grant currently sends monthly bills to its customers via the postal service. Because of a concern for the environment and recent increases in postal rates, company management is considering offering an option to its customers for paperless billing. In addition to saving printing, paper, and postal costs, paperless billing will save energy and water (through reduced paper needs, waste disposal, and transportation needs). While Grant would like to switch to 100% paperless billing, many of its customers are not comfortable with paperless billing or may not have online access, so the paper billing option will remain regardless of whether or not Grant adopts a paperless billing system.

The cost of the paperless billing system would be $101,120 per quarter, with no variable costs since the costs of the system are the salaries of the clerks and the cost of leasing the computer system. The paperless billing system being proposed would be able to handle up to 820,000 bills per quarter (more than 820,000 bills per quarter would require a different computer system and is outside the scope of the current situation at Grant).

The company has gathered its cost data for the past year by quarter for paper, toner cartridges, printer maintenance costs, and postage costs for the billing department. The cost data are as follows:

	Quarter 1	Quarter 2	Quarter 3	Quarter 4
Total paper, toner, printer maintenance, and postage costs	$672,700	$695,000	$800,000	$700,000
Total number of bills mailed	550,000	575,000	740,000	600,000

Requirements

1. Calculate the variable cost per bill mailed under the current paper-based billing system. Use the high-low method.
2. Assume that the company projects that it will have a total of 680,000 bills to mail in the upcoming quarter. If enough customers choose the paperless billing option so that 25% of the mailings can be converted to paperless, how much would the company save from the paperless billing system (be sure to consider the cost of the paperless billing system)?
3. What if only 20% of the mailings are converted to the paperless option (assume a total of 680,000 bills)? Should the company still offer the paperless billing system? Explain your rationale.

E15-29B Sustainability and CVP concepts (Learning Objective 1)

Killian Garage Doors manufactures a premium garage door. Currently, the price and cost data associated with the premium garage door are as follows:

Average selling price per premium garage door	$ 1,800
Average variable manufacturing cost per door	$ 700
Average variable selling cost per door	$ 200
Total annual fixed costs	$ 198,000

Killian Garage Doors has undertaken several sustainability projects over the past few years. Management is currently evaluating whether to develop a comprehensive software control system for its manufacturing operations that would significantly reduce scrap and waste generated during the manufacturing process. If the company were to implement this software control system in its manufacturing operations, use of the software control system would result in an increase of $72,000 in its annual fixed costs, while the average variable manufacturing cost per door would drop by $180.

Requirements

1. What is the company's current breakeven point in units and in dollars?
2. If the company expects to sell 280 premium garage doors in the upcoming year, and it does not develop the software control system, what is its expected operating income from premium garage doors?
3. If the software control system were to be developed and implemented, what would be the company's new breakeven point in units and in dollars?
4. If the company expects to sell 280 premium garage doors in the upcoming year, and it develops the software control system, what is its expected operating income from premium garage doors?
5. If the company expects to sell 280 premium garage doors in the upcoming year, do you think the company should implement the software control system? Why or why not? What factors should the company consider?

E15-30B Sustainability and short-term decision making (Learning Objective 1)

Over the past several years, decommissioned U.S. warships have been turned into artificial reefs in the ocean by towing them out to sea and sinking them. The thinking was that sinking the ship would conveniently dispose of it while providing an artificial reef environment for aquatic life. In reality, some of the sunken ships have released toxins into the ocean and have been costly to decontaminate. Now the U.S. government is taking bids to instead dismantle and recycle ships that have recently been decommissioned (but have not been sunk yet).

Assume that a recently decommissioned aircraft, the USS *Eagle*, is estimated to contain approximately 40 tons of recyclable materials able to be sold for approximately $33.9 million. The low bid for dismantling and transporting the ship materials to appropriate facilities is $36 million. Recycling and dismantling the ship would create about 500 jobs for about a year in the Rust Belt. This geographic area has been experiencing record-high unemployment rates in recent years.

Requirements

1. Is it more financially advantageous to sink the ship (assume that it costs approximately $1.4 million to tow a ship out to sea and sink it) or to dismantle and recycle it? Show your calculations.
2. From a sustainability standpoint, what should be done with the decommissioned aircraft carrier? List some of the qualitative factors that should enter into this analysis.
3. As a taxpayer, which action would you prefer (sink or recycle)? Defend your answer.

E15-31B Sustainability and budgeting (Learning Objective 1)

Danico Beverages manufactures its own soda pop bottles. The bottles are made from polyethylene terephthalate (PET), a lightweight yet strong plastic. The company uses as much PET recycled resin pellets in its bottles as it can, both because using recycled PET helps Danico to meet its sustainability goals and because recycled PET is less expensive than virgin PET.

The company is continuing to search for ways to reduce its costs and its impact on the environment. PET plastic is melted and blown over soda bottle molds to produce the bottles. One idea Danico's engineers have suggested is to retrofit the soda bottle molds and change the plastic formulation slightly so that 20% less PET plastic is used for each bottle. The average kilograms of PET per soda bottle before any redesign is 0.015 kg. The cost of retrofitting the soda bottle molds will result in a one-time charge of $84,856, while the plastic reformulation will cause the average cost per kilogram of PET plastic to change from $4.00 to $4.30.

Danico's management is analyzing whether the change to the bottle molds to reduce PET plastic usage should be made. Management expects the following number of soda bottles to be used in the upcoming year:

	Quarter 1	Quarter 2	Quarter 3	Quarter 4
Number of bottles to be produced	2,800,000	2,000,000	3,000,000	2,300,000

For the upcoming year, management expects the beginning inventory of PET to be 12,600 kilograms, while ending inventory is expected to be 10,880 kilograms. During the first three quarters of the year, management wants to keep the ending inventory of PET at the end of each quarter equal to 30% of the following quarter's PET needs.

Requirements

1. Using the original data (before any redesign of soda bottles), prepare a direct materials budget to calculate the cost of PET purchases in each quarter for the upcoming year and for the year in total.
2. Assume that the company retrofits the soda bottle molds and changes the plastic formulation slightly so that less PET plastic is used in each bottle. Now prepare a direct materials budget to calculate the cost of PET purchases in each quarter for the upcoming year and for the year in total for this possible scenario.
3. Compare the cost of PET plastic for Requirement 1 (original data) and for Requirement 2 (making change to using less PET). What is the direct material cost savings from making the change to using less PET? Compare the total of those savings to the cost of retrofitting the soda bottle molds. Should the company make the change? Explain your rationale.

E15-32B Sustainability and the balanced scorecard (Learning Objective 1)

Classify each of the following sustainability key performance indicators (KPIs) according to the balanced scorecard perspective it addresses. Choose from the following five perspectives:

- Financial perspective
- Customer perspective
- Internal business perspective
- Learning and growth perspective
- Community perspective

KPI	Perspective
a. Percentage of packaging utilizing recycled materials	
b. Number of green products available	
c. Waste pounds generated per ton of production	
d. Percentage of income donated to homeless shelters and food distribution units	
e. Refining costs for recycled goods	
f. Number of employee hours devoted to volunteering for Feeding America	
g. Percentage of packaging reclaimed or recycled after use	
h. Excessive overtime	
i. Percentage of resources purchased from local vendors	
j. Water reclamation costs	
k. Revenue from recycled goods	
l. Number of departments integrating sustainable practices	
m. Waste-removal expense	
n. CO_2 emissions per ton of production	
o. Megawatts of energy consumed	
p. Gas used per ton of production	
q. Percentage of income donated to local after-school programs	
r. Number of sustainability training hours	

E15-33B Sustainability and standard costing *(Learning Objective 1)*

Westerville Containers currently uses a recycled plastic to make bottles for the food industry.

Current bottle production information:

The cost and time standards per batch of 10,000 bottles are as follows:

Plastic 300 kilograms at $11.00 per kg
Direct labor 2.0 hours at $20.00 per hour

The variable manufacturing overhead rate is based on total estimated variable manufacturing overhead of $500,000 and estimated total direct labor hours (DLH) of 10,000. Westerville allocates its variable manufacturing overhead based on direct labor hours.

Proposed changes to bottle design and production process:

The container division manager is considering having both the bottle redesigned and the bottle production process reengineered so that the plastic usage would drop by 30% overall due both to generating less scrap in the manufacturing process and using less plastic in each bottle. In addition to decreasing the amount of plastic used in producing the bottles, the following benefits would be realized:

a. Direct labor hours would be reduced by 20% because less scrap would be handled in the production process.
b. Total estimated variable manufacturing overhead would be reduced by 10% because less scrap would need to be hauled away, less electricity would be used in the production process, and less inventory would need to be stocked.

Requirements

1. Calculate the standard cost per batch of 10,000 bottles using the current data (before the company makes any changes). Include direct materials, direct labor, and variable manufacturing overhead in the standard cost per unit.
2. Calculate the standard cost per batch of 10,000 bottles if the company makes the changes to the bottle design and production process so that less plastic is used. Include direct materials, direct labor, and variable manufacturing overhead in the standard cost per unit.

3. Calculate the cost savings per batch by comparing the standard cost per batch under each scenario (current versus prosed change). Assume that the total cost to implement the changes would be $352,800. How many batches of bottles would need to be produced after the change to have the cost savings total equal the cost to make the changes?
4. What other benefits might arise from making this change to using less plastic in the manufacture of the bottles? Are there any risks? What would you recommend the company do?

E15-34B   Sustainability and capital investments *(Learning Objective 1)*

Jaren Industries is evaluating investing in solar panels to provide some of the electrical needs of its main office building in Phoenix, Arizona. The solar panel project would cost $500,000 and would provide cost savings in its utility bills of $70,000 per year. It is anticipated that the solar panels would have a life of 20 years and would have no residual value.

Requirements

1. Calculate the payback period in years for the solar panel project.
2. If the company uses a discount rate of 8%, what is the net present value of this project?
3. If the company has a rule that no projects will be undertaken that have a payback period of more than five years, would this investment be accepted? If not, what arguments could managers make to get approval for the solar panel project?
4. What would you do if you were in charge of approving capital investment proposals?

E15-35B   Sustainability and the statement of cash flows *(Learning Objective 1)*

Whitman Plastics is a manufacturer that takes in post-consumer plastics (e.g., empty milk jugs) and recycles those plastics into a "plastic lumber" that can be used to build furniture, decking, and a variety of other items. Because Whitman has a strong focus on sustainability, the company managers try, whenever possible, to use recycled materials and to invest in sustainable projects.

Last year, the company engaged in several sustainable practices that had an impact on cash flows. For each of the transactions listed below, indicate whether the transaction would have affected the operating, investing, or financing cash flows of the company. Additionally, indicate whether each transaction would have increased (+) or decreased (–) cash.

Transactions:

1. Whitman built a new office building as its administrative headquarters. The new building is LEED certified and was paid for with cash.
2. Solar panels were installed on the roof of the Whitman manufacturing facility to supply part of the electricity needed for its operations. The company paid cash.
3. A new delivery truck that uses biofuel was purchased for cash.
4. Whitman became a minority partner in a wind-turbine project by investing $1 million in cash in the project.
5. A fleet of Toyota Prius hybrid automobiles was purchased for the use of the sales staff. The company paid cash.
6. Whitman sold plastic scrap generated by its manufacturing process.
7. New production equipment that is 25% more energy efficient than the old equipment was purchased for cash.
8. Throughout the year, Whitman participated in several trade shows that featured green products for use by parks and recreation facilities. For each trade show, Whitman incurred cash expenses for transportation, registration, meals and lodging, and booth setup.
9. Scientists at Whitman performed research into whether another kind of post-consumer plastic not currently used in its plastics extrusion process could be used.
10. Whitman bought its own stock back to use for the company's 401K plan.

E15-36B Sustainability and external financial reporting *(Learning Objective 1)*

In its 2015 Citizenship (CSR) Report, Microsoft Corporation details the results from the steps it has taken to embed a sustainable culture throughout its business operations. In the following list from Microsoft's CSR report, categorize each result as to whether it is oriented toward the *economic*, *environmental*, or *social* component of the triple bottom line.

a. Funded the 110-megawatt Keechi Wind project through a 20-year agreement to purchase 100 % of the power output of the project
b. Made cash donations of $135 million to nonprofit organizations
c. Reduced, reused, or recycled 99% of the waste generated in its Redmond, Washington, dining facilities
d. Donated Microsoft Cloud Services to 50,000 nonprofit organizations in 2015
e. Microsoft's major suppliers averaged a work-related injuries and illness rate of 0.045 compared to an industry benchmark of 1.4
f. Increased cash dividends paid to investors in 2014 and 2015
g. 14.3% of the US Microsoft workforce volunteered their time with nonprofits, as compared to 10.8% in 2013
h. Reduced energy consumption by 15 to 20% in Microsoft's new datacenters through energy-saving design approaches
i. Redesigned packaging for Xbox One and Surface laptop/tablet to reduce use of materials and to replace plastics with paper packaging and materials from sugarcane waste
j. Had net revenue of $93.5 billion in 2015
k. Used renewable energy (electricity) to power 23% of operations

PROBLEMS Group A

P15-37A Sustainability and cost behavior *(Learning Objective 1)*

Miracle Meadow Luxury Resorts has been evaluating how it might expand its sustainability efforts in its hotels. In any given month, an average of 109,500 room days are available in total (this total capacity figure is roughly estimated by taking the total number of hotel rooms in the hotels owned by Miracle Meadow and multiplying by 30 days per month). Management is currently targeting two areas for sustainability projects: Laundry and Housekeeping.

Laundry: Currently, in each hotel room, a small sign is placed beside the bed that informs the hotel guest that the environment will benefit if the guest reuses the linens. The company has experienced some success with the signs; the cost of laundry has decreased slightly over the past several years that the program has been in place. Management is now considering the possibility of giving guests a $1.00 credit on their hotel bill for each day of the stay that the linens in the room are reused rather than laundered.

Housekeeping: Management is also evaluating the possibility of expanding sustainability efforts in housekeeping by providing an incentive of a $1.20 credit on the hotel bill for each day the guest opts to skip a daily room cleaning.

To evaluate these options, management has gathered data for the past year for its laundry costs and housekeeping costs. The costs and occupancy data include:

Month	Monthly Occupancy Percentage	Total Laundry Costs	Total Housekeeping Costs
January	85%	$37,339	$146,456
February	79%	$40,020	$140,540
March	70%	$35,800	$137,180
April	63%	$30,010	$121,430
May	52%	$25,960	$103,870
June	48%	$25,360	$90,610
July	56%	$28,240	$108,190
August	50%	$25,230	$85,850
September	46%	$24,730	$80,400
October	40%	$19,600	$75,500
November	52%	$26,800	$105,040
December	61%	$32,000	$113,090

To satisfy investors, management only wants to implement programs that are cost effective; that is, the benefits of the program must exceed the costs of the program. Sustainability projects are expected to be cost effective.

Requirements

1. Using the high-low method, calculate the cost per guest of laundry per day. (The volume should be the number of room days, which you will have to calculate for each month.)
2. Using the high-low method, calculate the cost per guest of housekeeping per day. (Again, the volume should be the number of room days, which you would have calculated for Requirement 1.)
3. Using the high-low method, evaluate the proposal to give guests a $1.00 per day credit for reusing their room linens. Does it appear to be cost effective to offer this program?
4. Using the high-low method, evaluate the proposal to give guests a $1.20 per day credit for skipping housekeeping services. Does it appear to be cost effective to offer this program?
5. Using regression analysis, calculate the cost per guest of laundry per day. (Again, the volume should be the number of room days, which you would have calculated for Requirement 1.)
6. Using regression analysis, calculate the cost per guest of housekeeping per day. (Again, the volume should be the number of room days, which you would have calculated for Requirement 1.)
7. Using regression analysis, evaluate the proposal to give guests a $1.00 per day credit for skipping housekeeping services. Does it appear to be cost effective to offer this program?
8. Using regression analysis, evaluate the proposal to give guests a $1.20 per day credit for skipping housekeeping services. Does it appear to be cost effective to offer this program?
9. Regarding the two programs, what is your recommendation to management about which program(s) to implement? Provide the rationale for your recommendation.

P15-38A Sustainability and capital investments *(Learning Objective 1)*

A *living roof* is a roof of a building that is completely covered with grass or other vegetation planted over a waterproof layer (to protect the building interior). The Ford Motor Company's Rouge Plant in Dearborn, Michigan, is an example of a successful implementation of a living roof.

There are several benefits associated with a living roof, including the following:

1. Reduce heating and cooling costs for the building.
2. Reduce stormwater runoff.
3. Filter pollution out of air and water.
4. Help to insulate building for sound.
5. Create a habitat for various wildlife.
6. Increase life of roof (as compared to a typical traditional roof).

Anderson Consultants, Inc., is investigating whether it should replace its current roof with a long-lasting composite roof or a living roof. A long-lasting composite roof would cost the company $1,300,000 and would last approximately 25 years. The annual maintenance costs on this composite roof would be approximately $17,000 per year. At the end of its useful life of 25 years, various components of the composite roof could be recycled and sold for $40,000.

The other roofing alternative is a living roof. The costs associated with constructing the living roof total $1,500,000 and include the following: vegetation $330,000, waterproof membrane $135,000, growing medium (dirt) $210,000, living roof expert consultant fee $5,000, construction costs $675,000, and other miscellaneous fees $145,000. Maintenance on the living roof is estimated to be $57,000 per year.

Management estimates that this living roof will last for 25 years. The following savings should result from the living roof:

- Heating and cooling costs will be reduced by $38,000 per year.
- Stormwater treatment costs will be reduced by $4,000 per year.
- Filtering system costs will be reduced by $17,000 per year.

The living roof would have no recyclable components to be sold at the end of its life. The company uses a 12% discount rate in evaluating capital investments.

Requirements

1. Calculate the present value of the composite roof.
2. Calculate the present value of the living roof.
3. From a purely quantitative standpoint, which roof would you recommend?
4. Are there qualitative factors to consider in this decision? What other factors besides financial should be considered in this situation?

PROBLEMS Group B

P15-39B Sustainability and cost behavior *(Learning Objective 1)*

Relaxation Valley Luxury Resorts has been evaluating how it might expand its sustainability efforts in its hotels. In any given month, an average of 109,500 room days are available in total (this total capacity figure is roughly estimated by taking the total number of hotel rooms in the hotels owned by Relaxation Valley and multiplying by 30 days per month). Management is currently targeting two areas for sustainability projects: Laundry and Housekeeping.

Laundry: Currently, in each hotel room, a small sign is placed beside the bed that informs the hotel guest that the environment will benefit if the guest reuses the linens. The company has experienced some success with the signs; the cost of laundry has decreased slightly over the past several years that the program has been in place. Management is now considering the possibility of giving guests a $0.80 credit on their hotel bill for each day of the stay that the linens in the room are reused rather than laundered.

Housekeeping: Management is also evaluating the possibility of expanding sustainability efforts in housekeeping by providing an incentive of a $0.90 credit on the hotel bill for each day the guest opts to skip a daily room cleaning.

To evaluate these options, management has gathered data for the past year for its laundry costs and housekeeping costs. The costs and occupancy data include:

	Monthly Occupancy Percentage	Total Laundry Costs	Total Housekeeping Costs
January	83%	$41,470	$150,051
February	81%	$41,032	$144,096
March	72%	$36,814	$141,097
April	66%	$31,435	$127,202
May	55%	$27,449	$109,858
June	51%	$26,943	$ 96,271
July	59%	$29,745	$113,977
August	53%	$26,739	$ 91,000
September	48%	$25,797	$ 83,891
October	39%	$19,700	$ 81,500
November	55%	$28,336	$111,099
December	64%	$33,572	$118,646

To satisfy investors, management only wants to implement programs that are cost effective; that is, the benefits of the program must exceed the costs of the program. Sustainability projects are expected to be cost effective.

Requirements

1. Using the high-low method, calculate the cost per guest of laundry per day. (The volume should be the number of room days, which you will have to calculate for each month.)
2. Using the high-low method, calculate the cost per guest of housekeeping per day. (Again, the volume should be the number of room days, which you would have calculated for Requirement 1.)
3. Using the high-low method, evaluate the proposal to give guests a $0.80 per day credit for reusing their room linens. Does it appear to be cost effective to offer this program?
4. Using the high-low method, evaluate the proposal to give guests a $0.90 per day credit for skipping housekeeping services. Does it appear to be cost effective to offer this program?
5. Using regression analysis, calculate the cost per guest of laundry per day. (Again, the volume should be the number of room days, which you would have calculated for Requirement 1.)
6. Using regression analysis, calculate the cost per guest of housekeeping per day. (Again, the volume should be the number of room days, which you would have calculated for Requirement 1.)
7. Using regression analysis, evaluate the proposal to give guests a $0.80 per day credit for skipping housekeeping services. Does it appear to be cost effective to offer this program?
8. Using regression analysis, evaluate the proposal to give guests a $0.90 per day credit for skipping housekeeping services. Does it appear to be cost effective to offer this program?
9. Regarding the two programs, what is your recommendation to management about which program(s) to implement? Provide the rationale for your recommendation.

P15-40B Sustainability and capital investments *(Learning Objective 1)*

A *living roof* is a roof of a building that is completely covered with grass or other vegetation planted over a waterproof layer (to protect the building interior). The Ford Motor Company's Rouge Plant in Dearborn, Michigan, is an example of a successful implementation of a living roof.

There are several benefits associated with a living roof, including the following:

1. Reduce heating and cooling costs for the building.
2. Reduce stormwater runoff.
3. Filter pollution out of air and water.
4. Help to insulate building for sound.
5. Create a habitat for various wildlife.
6. Increase life of roof (as compared to a typical traditional roof).

Valley View Consultants, Inc., is investigating whether it should replace its current roof with a long-lasting composite roof or a living roof. A long-lasting composite roof would cost the company $1,500,000 and would last approximately 25 years. The annual maintenance costs on this composite roof would be approximately $21,000 per year. At the end of its useful life of 25 years, various components of the composite roof could be recycled and sold for $45,000.

The other roofing alternative is a living roof. The costs associated with constructing the living roof total $1,750,000 and include the following: vegetation $300,000, waterproof membrane $145,000, growing medium (dirt) $230,000, living roof expert consultant fee $35,000, construction costs $720,000, and other miscellaneous fees $320,000. Maintenance on the living roof is estimated to be $61,000 per year.

Management estimates that this living roof will last for 25 years. The following savings should result from the living roof:

- Heating and cooling costs will be reduced by $35,000 per year.
- Stormwater treatment costs will be reduced by $8,000 per year.
- Filtering system costs will be reduced by $19,000 per year.

The living roof would have no recyclable components to be sold at the end of its life. The company uses a 10% discount rate in evaluating capital investments.

Requirements

1. Calculate the present value of the composite roof.
2. Calculate the present value of the living roof.
3. From a purely quantitative standpoint, which roof would you recommend?
4. Are there qualitative factors to consider in this decision? What other factors besides financial should be considered in this situation?

Serial Case

C15-41 Classify Caesars Entertainment Corporation's sustainability efforts
(Learning Objective 1)

This case is a continuation of the Caesars Entertainment Corporation serial case that began in Chapter 1. Refer to the introductory story in Chapter 1 (see page 43) for additional background. (The components of the Caesars serial case can be completed in any order.)

In 2016, Caesars Entertainment Corporation was recognized by Civic 50, a Points of Light initiative to measure corporate involvement in communities. Caesars' representatives have contributed to the development of Sustainability Accounting Standards Board (SASB) sustainability corporate Form 10-K disclosures for the service sector. Caesars also has a strong track record in sustainability initiatives within the company.

Each year for the past six years, Caesars Entertainment Corporation has issued a Corporate Citizenship Report that details the results of its sustainability efforts. Various highlights from Caesars' 2014–2015 sustainability report include the following list.

a. In 2014, Caesars Foundation committed to an initial gift of $200,000 to the Cleveland Clinic Lou Ruvo Center for Brain Health.
b. In Las Vegas alone, Caesars launders around 24,000 pounds per day including bedding, towels, restaurant linens, and valet uniforms. Caesars has invested in an efficient

laundry facility. The typical laundry load size for Caesars is 250 pounds as compared to 120–125 pounds per load in commercial laundries, enabling Caesars to use less water, energy, and detergent.

c. Hours volunteered by Caesars' employees in their communities increased from 148,080 hours in 2011 to 199,127 hours in 2014.

d. Caesars Foundation has provided 56 vans to Meals on Wheels over its long-time partnership with the non-profit organization.

e. Caesars' employee injury rate per 100 employees decreased from 3.26 in 2011 to 2.24 in 2014.

f. Caesars retrofitted heating and cooling systems in four of its Nevada properties in 2014 to increase energy efficiency.

g. Caesars increased the amount of waste it diverted from landfills by 44.28% in 2014 as compared to 2007.

h. Out of eleven members in total, the number of females on Caesars' board of directors in 2012 through 2014 was zero.

i. Caesars' employee health plan experienced a 2.2% decrease in costs from 2011 to 2014 and saved Caesars millions of dollars.

j. Caesars' greenhouse gas emissions decreased by 22.57% in 2014 as compared to 2007.

k. In 2014, Caesars' housekeepers collected more than 100,000 pounds of soap and toiletries to distribute to impoverished families.

l. Caesars adopted a new corporate anti-money-laundering policy and program in 2014. The company hired a full-time senior manager to ensure that this anti-money-laundering policy is embedded throughout the corporation through training, communications, and risk assessments.

m. Caesars organizes over 15,700 meetings, gatherings, and private events at its venues each year. It has committed to "Responsible Meeting" principles that include paperless online event menus and billing; energy-efficient heating and cooling; china and linen offered in place of disposable plates, cups, and napkins; and water preset on tables only if requested.

n. $2.9 million was gifted to local communities through the Caesars Foundation in 2014.

o. Caesars Foundation has given more than $500,000 to support Teach for America since 2010.

p. Caesars' water use per 1,000 square feet increased by 2.3% in 2014 as compared to 2013.

q. Caesars' consumption of fossil fuel-based energy decreased 21.35% in 2014 as compared to 2007.

r. The employee turnover rate at Caesars increased from 13.80% in 2011 to 21.49% in 2014.

s. Total number of employees trained in Responsible Gaming at Caesars increased from 33,345 in 2011 to 53,825 in 2014.

t. Caesars' water consumption per air-conditioned 1,000 square feet decreased by 16.64% as compared to 2008.

u. LEED certification was achieved for all newly built and expanded properties owned by Caesars since 2011.

v. Caesars increased overall corporate spending on goods or services provided by minority- and women-owned or disadvantaged business enterprises to its highest spending level.

w. The total dollars invested in communities by the Caesars Foundation and its employees (including value of volunteer hours) was $86.9 million in 2011. In 2014, that total dollar amount was $74.53 million.

Requirements

1. Categorize each of the Caesars sustainability results as primarily *environmental*, *social*, or *economic*.
2. Can any of the listed sustainability results have an impact on a second category? Go back through the list and select a second sustainability category (*environmental*, *social*, or *economic*) for as many of the sustainability results as you can.
3. Combining your results from Requirements 1 and 2, what conclusions can you draw about sustainability initiatives at Caesars and in business in general?

CRITICAL THINKING

Discussion & Analysis

A15-42 Discussion Questions

1. Pressure to become more sustainable can usually be categorized into several reasons, including cost reduction and regulatory compliance. Think of an organization you're familiar with. Which reason(s) do you think is(are) strongest in this organization? Which reason do you think is least relevant to this organization?

2. Adding a fifth perspective of "community" to the traditional four balanced scorecard perspectives (financial, customer, internal business, and learning and growth) is sometimes advocated as a way to measure a company's performance in sustainability. Do you think the fifth perspective should be added, or do you think sustainability measures should be integrated into the traditional four perspectives? Provide a rationale for your answer.

3. Information from an environmental management accounting (EMA) system can be used to support managers and their primary responsibilities of planning, directing, and controlling. Think of an organization you're familiar with. Give an example of information from an EMA system that could be useful to a manager in each of these three primary responsibility areas.

4. Find a recent annual report for a publicly held company in which you are interested. Summarize what sustainability information is provided in that annual report. Based on the sustainability information provided in the annual report, what measurements do you think the company might use to track its sustainability efforts? (You can use your imagination here; the actual sustainability measures are unlikely to be in the annual report.)

5. There are three components in the triple bottom line: economic, environmental, and social. Which component do you think is most important? Why?

6. The effect of sustainability on the environment is probably the most visible component of the triple bottom line. For a company with which you are familiar, list two examples of its sustainability efforts related to the planet.

7. One controversial area regarding sustainability is whether organizations should use their sustainability progress and activities in their advertising. Do you think a company should publicize its sustainability efforts? Why or why not?

8. Perform an online search on the terms "carbon offset" and "carbon footprint." What is a carbon footprint? What is a carbon offset? Why would carbon offsets be of interest to a company? What are some companies that offer (sell) carbon offsets?

9. Oftentimes, an investment in sustainable technology is more costly than a comparable investment in traditional technology. What arguments can you make for the investment in sustainable technology? What arguments can you make for the investment in traditional technology? You can use a specific technology or product in your arguments. For example, the hybrid model of a car is usually more expensive to purchase than the comparable gas-engine model.

10. Stakeholders are frequently the reason that companies adopt sustainable practices. Think of an organization with which you are familiar. List as many stakeholders as you can think of for this organization. For each stakeholder listed, describe why that stakeholder would have an interest in the company adopting sustainable practices.

11. The chapter discussed five challenges to implementing an environmental management accounting (EMA) system within an organization. From your viewpoint, which of these challenges seems to be the biggest obstacle to successful implementation? Which challenge is most likely to be easiest to overcome? Provide your rationale for your answers.

12. Where do you think sustainability reporting is heading in the future? Will companies become more transparent, or is sustainability reporting going to be mostly on internal reports? How important do you think this issue is?

Application & Analysis

Mini Cases

A15-43 Corporate Sustainability Reports

Note: In the following activity, the word "sustainability" is used. You may need to search for "green" or "environmental accounting" or other similar terms, depending on the organization and the industry.

Locate an annual report for a company in which you are interested. Look through the annual report for a report on "Corporate Social Responsibility," "Sustainability," "Green," or other similar heading. Also skim the "Chairperson's Letter" or "Letter to Shareholders" for additional information on the organization's sustainability efforts. Additionally, many firms issue Corporate Social Responsibility (CSR) reports; you may use that report if you find that a CSR is available.

Basic Discussion Questions

1. What environmental accounting information does this company report?
2. What environmental goals does this company have for the upcoming five to ten years?
3. Judging from the information in the report(s) from the company, does the company appear to emphasize profits, environment, or society? Or does the company appear to give equal emphasis to each component of the triple bottom line? Justify your answer.
4. What types of EMA information might be reported internally by this company? Make reasonable "guesses"; the annual report will not give this information directly. Use your imagination.
5. Perform an online search to find other sources of information about this company's sustainability efforts other than its own publications. What news articles can you find? Summarize the sustainability news about this company.
6. Perform an online search for sustainability issues in the industry in which this organization operates. Does the company appear to be addressing the sustainability issues of the industry?
7. What is your overall sense of the company's commitment to sustainability from everything you have seen? Be specific and give details to justify your response.

Team Project

A15-44 Sustainability and investment choices

Increasingly, there are calls to manufacture hybrid or electric cars. Businesses and individuals purchase these cars to be environmentally friendly. However, there is an ongoing debate about whether these hybrid or electric cars are truly more environmentally friendly than the traditional gas-engine models and whether the additional upfront cost of the hybrid or electric model is offset by the fuel savings.

Requirements

1. Divide your team into two groups, the Traditional subgroup and the Hybrid subgroup. Select a car that comes in both a traditional gas-engine model and a hybrid model (for example, the Honda Civic comes in both a gas-engine model and a hybrid model). Make the assumption that the vehicle will be driven for five years and the annual miles driven will be 12,000 miles. Also, before going any further, as a group, decide upon an estimate for the cost per gallon of gas.
    a. The Traditional group should investigate the initial cost of the traditional gas-engine model. Include tax and title costs. This group should also estimate the annual fuel cost to operate this vehicle. Calculate the present value of the cost of this vehicle (include the initial cost and the annual fuel costs). Use a discount rate of 6%.
    b. The Hybrid group should investigate the initial cost of the hybrid model. Include tax and title costs. This group should also estimate the annual fuel cost to operate this vehicle. Calculate the present value of the cost of this vehicle (include the initial cost and the annual fuel costs). Use a discount rate of 6%.

2. The groups should compare the costs of the two models. After comparing the costs, each group should:
    a. Research the environmental issues associated with the two car models. Formulate arguments to support your group's car model (either traditional gas-engine or hybrid).
    b. Debate which model is more desirable for businesses to purchase and why. Be specific in your reasoning. Cite your sources.

At the conclusion of the debate, as a team, make a recommendation as to which model of car (traditional gas-engine or hybrid) a typical organization today should purchase and why. Write up your conclusions in a one- to two-page paper.

A15-45 Ethics of internal sustainability reporting *(Learning Objectives 1, 2, & 3)*

ETHICS

Veronica is an intern in the Accounting Department at Kessler Industries, a manufacturer of precision medical instruments. She is anxious to make a good impression because she wants to be offered a full-time position at this company when she has completed her internship.

One of the tasks that Veronica is given is to help prepare the company's internal sustainability report, which is prepared using GRI G4 guidelines. The company does not obtain independent-party assurance on its sustainability report since the report is mainly used for internal purposes and management does not feel that assurance is necessary. Veronica is excited because she is a firm believer in the need for a company to have sustainable practices.

The controller, Andy Thomas, instructs Veronica to skip the report section where the quantity of hazardous waste processed is reported. Andy explains that although this report is intended mainly for internal use, there is always a chance with any written or electronic document that it could make its way into the public's hands. Management feels that there would be public backlash over the hazardous waste, even though the company does not believe the hazardous waste creates any public health risk. The waste is disposed of through legal and responsible channels.

This GRI report goes to the board of directors and to the company's managers. In addition, it is given to the company's bankers.

Veronica protests timidly and says that hazardous waste should probably be recorded and explained if the report is being prepared using the GRI G4 framework. The controller shuts her down promptly, stating that it is not open for debate. Andy points out that the report is only used internally and everyone in the company knows that some hazardous waste is generated, so no harm is done by not stating the obvious. Andy feels that the risk of public disclosure is much greater than any potential harm from not including the hazardous waste on the report.

Veronica is torn about what to do. She really wants to work at this company at the conclusion of her internship. As she considers leaving the hazardous waste figures off the report as instructed, she rationalizes the potential omission by thinking that she will be able to make inroads on the reporting and prepare complete GRI reports in the future when she is a full-time employee. If she's not hired, she will have no opportunity to have a positive impact on this company.

Requirements

1. Using the IMA Statement of Ethical Professional Practice (Exhibit 1-7) as an ethical framework, answer the following questions:
    a. What is(are) the ethical issue(s) in this situation?
    b. What are Veronica's responsibilities as a management accountant?
    c. Are there any mitigating circumstances? Is Veronica's rationalization correct?
2. Discuss the specific steps Veronica should take to resolve the situation. Refer to the IMA Statement of Ethical Professional Practice in your response.

A15-46 FirstEnergy and its sustainability report (Learning Objectives 1, 2, & 3)

FirstEnergy is an electric utility serving markets in the Midwest and Mid-Atlantic regions. It operates an infrastructure of nearly 269,000 miles of distribution lines stretching from the Ohio-Indiana border to the New Jersey shore.

FirstEnergy issued a sustainability report in 2016 entitled "Sustainability report 2016: Focusing our energy on the future." While the report is lengthy (72 pages), FirstEnergy does not indicate the use of GRI reporting guidelines or any other sustainability reporting standards.

Although topics may be listed in FirstEnergy's sustainability report, few actual metrics/data are provided in the report. For example, a core GRI G4 performance indicator, G4-EN3, Energy Consumption within the Organization, is not reported. Dollars invested in selected projects are reported in the sustainability reports, but few other data are provided. Goals for the future are listed in the report, but few current measures are provided. The sustainability report also does not include mention of any independent-party assurance of the report.

Questions

1. What reasons could FirstEnergy have for not using GRI reporting standards (or any other sustainability reporting standards) for its sustainability reporting?
2. What potential issues does a sustainability report prepared without using a standard framework such as GRI raise for stakeholders? Is such a report useful in your opinion? Explain.
3. Do you think that independent-party assurance of a sustainability report is important? Why or why not?
4. What reasons could FirstEnergy have for issuing a sustainability report?

Try It Solutions

page 907:

1. Social: Product responsibility
2. Social: Human rights
3. Environmental
4. Economic
5. Social: Labor practices and decent work
6. Environmental
7. Social: Society
8. Economic

GLOSSARY/INDEX
Combined Glossary/Subject Index

Note: Page references including the letter "n" indicate content appears in a footnote on that page.

5S. A workplace organization system comprised of the following steps: sort, set in order, shine, standardize, and sustain, 202

10-K filings, 842, 849, 859

A

Absorption costing. The costing method where products "absorb" both fixed and variable manufacturing costs, 331–333, 447, 455
  income statement, 334
  reconciling operating income, 338–340
  variable costing vs, 336–338
Account analysis. A method for determining cost behavior that is based on a manager's judgment in classifying each general ledger account as a variable, fixed, or mixed cost, 322
Accounting. *See also specific types of accounting*
  within organizational structure, 9–10
  perception and reality of, 6
Accounting rate of return (ARR). A measure of profitability computed by dividing the average annual operating income from an asset by the initial investment in the asset, 711, 717–719, 739
Accounts payable. *See also* Liabilities
  budgeted balance sheet, 530
  statement of cash flows, 781, 793, 800–801
Accounts receivable. *See also* Sales
  acid-test ratio, 850
  budgeted balance sheet, 529
  cash flow, indirect method, 791
  collection of, 590, 594, 851–852
  financial statement analysis, 841, 851–852
  statement of cash flows, 781, 784, 791, 793, 800
Accounts receivable turnover. Measures a company's ability to collect cash from credit customers. To compute accounts receivable turnover, divide net credit sales by average net accounts receivable, 851, 860
Accrual basis of accounting. Revenues are recorded when they are earned (when the sale takes place) rather than when cash is received on the sale. Likewise, expenses are recorded when they are incurred rather than when they are paid, 784
Accumulated depreciation, 795
Acid-test ratio. Ratio of the sum of cash plus short-term investments plus net current receivables to total current liabilities. It tells whether the entity can pay all of its current liabilities if they come due immediately; also called the *quick ratio*, 850, 860
Activity cost pools, 185
  setting up, 190–191
Activity-based costing (ABC). Focusing on *activities* as the fundamental cost objects. The costs of those activities become building blocks for compiling the indirect costs of products, services, and customers, 184
  to allocate indirect costs, 184–189
  circumstances favoring, 193–194
  results of, 192
  target costing, 452
Activity-based management (ABM). Using activity-based cost information to make decisions that increase profits while satisfying customers' needs, 191

  circumstances favoring, 193–194
  cutting costs, 191–192
  pricing and product mix decisions, 191
  routine planning and control decisions, 192
  using ABC across value chain, 192–193
Actual cost
  direct labor variances, 664–666
  direct materials variances, 660
  manufacturing overhead variances, 671–672
Actual Quantity (AQ), 660–663
Actual Quantity Purchased (AQP), 661–663
Actual Quantity Used (AQU), 661–663
Aggregated accounting information, 911
Air pollution, 910–911. *See also* Sustainability
  environmental management accounting and, 908
Allocate. To assign an indirect cost to a cost object, 56
  ABC and, 184–189
American Institute of Certified Public Accountants (AICPA). The world's largest association representing the accounting profession; together with the Chartered Institute of Management Accountants (CIMA), offers the Chartered Global Management Accountant (CGMA) designation, 11
Amortization expense. *See* Depreciation
Annuity. A stream of equal installments made at equal time intervals, 723
  future value calculations, 726
  internal rate of return, 736–739
  net present value, 732–733
  present value calculations, 727–730
Appraisal costs. Costs incurred to *detect* poor-quality goods or services, 206, 207
Assets
  cash payments and receipts, 800–802
  debt ratio, 852
  investing activities, indirect method, 794–796
  operating activities, indirect method, 788–794
  performance evaluation measures, 596
  profitability, measuring, 853–856
  return on investment, 592–597
  statement of cash flows, 781
  working capital, 849
Assign. To attach a cost to a cost object, 55, 56
Assurance. An independent party's external validation of management's assertions, 906
Attainable standards. Standards based on currently attainable conditions that include allowances for normal amounts of waste and inefficiency. Also known as practical standards, 654
Audit committee. A subcommittee of the board of directors that is responsible for overseeing both the internal audit function and the annual financial statement audit by independent CPAs, 9, 10
Average cost. The total cost divided by the number of units, 74
Average unit costs, 257–258
Avoidable fixed costs. Fixed costs that can be eliminated as a result of taking a particular course of action, 461–462

B

Backflush costing. A simplified accounting system in which production costs are not assigned to the units until they are finished, or even sold, thereby saving the bookkeeping steps of moving the product through the various inventory accounts, 204–205

Bad debt expense, 518
Balance sheet
  budgeted balance sheet, 528–530
  comparative balance sheet, 788, 789
  horizontal analysis, 841
  inventory on, 70
  performance evaluation measures, 596
  vertical analysis, 844–845
Balanced scorecard. A performance evaluation system that integrates financial and operational performance measures along four perspectives: financial, customer, internal business, and learning and growth, 609–615
Batch-level activities. Activities and costs incurred for every batch, regardless of the number of units in the batch, 190
Benchmarking. The practice of comparing a company with other companies or industry averages, 845
  budgets, benefits of, 510
  common-size statements, 845
  standard costs and, 666–667
Benefits, employee. *See also* Labor
  attracting and retaining talent, 901
  job cost record, 114–116
  labor compensation costs, 62
  Manufacturing costs, 60–61
Big data, 18–19
Big Four. The largest four accounting firms in the world: Deloitte, EY, KPMG, and PriceWaterhouseCoopers, 904, 906
Bill of materials. A list of all of the raw materials needed to manufacture a job, 109
Billing rate. The labor rate charged to the customer, which includes both cost and profit components, 145–146
Biofuels, 54
Biomimicry. A means of product design in which a company tries to mimic, or copy, the natural biological process in which dead organisms (plants and animals) become the input for another organism or process, 53–54
Board of Directors. The body elected by shareholders to oversee the company, 9
Book value, gross vs. net, 596, 789–790
Book value per share of common stock. Common stockholders' equity divided by the number of shares of common stock outstanding. It is the recorded amount for each share of common stock outstanding, 858, 861
BP Deepwater Horizon oil spill, 901
Breakeven point. The sales level at which operating income is zero: Total revenues = Total expenses, 386–389
  calculation methods, 386–389, 402–405
  contribution margin ratio, shortcut approach using, 388–389
  cost-volume-profit graphs, 391–392
  fixed cost change, 399–400
  income statement approach, 387, 390
  multiproduct companies, 402–405
  risk indicators, 406–411
  sales price changes, 396
  sales revenue, 404–405
  sales units and, 402–403
  unit contribution margin, shortcut approach using, 388
  variable cost changes, 398–399
  weighted-average contribution margin, 402–405

I-1

Budget. Quantitative expression of a plan that helps managers coordinate and implement the plan, 3. *See also* Capital Budgeting; Master budget
  balance sheet budget, 528–530
  benefits of, 510–511
  budgeted income statement, 519–520
  capital expenditures budget, 524
  cash collections budget, 524–525
  cash payments budget, 525–527
  combined cash budget, 527–528
  credit and debit card sales, impact of, 533–535
  Decision Guidelines, 521, 537
  development process, 508–510
  direct labor budget, 516
  direct materials budget, 515–516
  financial budgets, 511, 524–531
  flexible budgets, 603–608
  manufacturing overhead budget, 517–518
  master budget, 511–512
  merchandising companies, 531–533
  operating budgets, 511
  performance reports and, 588–590
  preparation of, 512–520
  production budget, 513–514
  sales budget, 512–513
  sensitivity analysis and flexible budgeting, 530
  service companies, 531, 532
  standard costs, advantages and disadvantages, 666–667
  starting point for, 509–510
  sustainability and, 536
  uses for, 508
Budget committee. A committee comprised of upper management as well as cross-functional managers that reviews, revises, and approves the final budget, 509
Budgeted balance sheet, 528–530
Budgeted income statement, 519–520
Business activities
  changes in, cost-volume-profit analysis and, 396–405
  types of, 49–53
  in value chain, 51–52
Business decisions
  guidelines on changing, 25
  job cost record for, 119–121
Business managers/management, 8
Business sectors, types of, 49–50
Business trends and regulations, 18–24

C

Cap and trade. *See* Carbon offsets
Capacity. *See* Freed capacity
Capital, attracting, 902
Capital budgeting. The process of making capital investment decisions. Companies make capital investments when they acquire *capital assets*-assets used for a long period of time, 711
  accounting rate of return, 717–719
  Decision Guidelines, 720, 741
  methods compared, 739–740
  net present value, 730–736
  overview of, 711–713
  payback period, 714–717
  present and future value tables, 743–745
  sustainability and, 713–714
  time value of money, 723–730
Capital expenditures, 527
  budget, 524
Capital rationing. Choosing among alternative capital investments due to limited funds, 712, 733–735
Capital turnover. Sales revenue divided by total assets. The capital turnover shows how much sales revenue is generated with every $1.00 of assets, 593–594, 611
Carbon Disclosure Project. A nonprofit organization that collects and disseminates carbon footprint information, 910–911
Carbon emissions, 896, 901

Carbon footprint. A measure of the total emissions of carbon dioxide and other greenhouse gases (GHGs), often expressed for simplicity as tons of equivalent carbon dioxide, 910
Carbon offsets, 54, 911
Cash, acid-test ratio, 850
Cash collections budget, 524–525
Cash equivalents. Very safe, highly liquid assets that are readily convertible into cash, such as money market funds, certificates of deposit that mature in less than three months, and U.S. treasury bills, 781
Cash flow. *See also* Statement of Cash Flows
  accounting rate of return, 717–719
  capital budgeting and, 712
  cash payments and receipts, 800–802
  Decision Guidelines, 803
  direct method, 783–784, 799–802
  indirect presentation of, 784, 788–798
  internal rate of return, 730, 736–739
  investing activities, 794–796
  net present value, 730–736
  operating activities, 781
  payback period, 715–716
  preparing from operating activities, 788–793
  red flags, 858
Cash payments budget, 525–527
Cash position, combined cash budget, 527–528
Certificates of deposit, 781
Certified Management Accountant (CMA). A professional certification issued by the IMA to designate expertise in the areas of managerial accounting, economics, and business finance, 10–11
Certified Public Accountants (CPAs), 4
Chartered Financial Analyst (CFA) Institute, 23
Chartered Global Management Accountant (CGMA). A designation available to qualifying American Institute of Certified Public Accountants (AICPA) members that is meant to recognize the unique business and accounting skill set possessed by those CPAs who work, or have worked, in business, industry, or government, 11
Chartered Institute of Management Accountants (CIMA), 11
Chief Executive Officer (CEO). The position hired by the board of directors to oversee the company on a daily basis, 9–10
Chief Financial Officer (CFO). The position responsible for all of the company's financial concerns, 9, 10
Chief Information Officer, 10
Chief Operating Officer (COO). The position responsible for overseeing the company's operations, 9, 10
Chief Sustainability Officer, 10
Chlorofluorocarbons (CFCs), 901
Clawback rules, 24
Climate Change Act (2008), 901
COD. Collect on Delivery, or Cash on Delivery. A sales term indicating that the inventory must be paid for at the time of delivery, 513, 524–525
Combined cash budget, 527–528
Committed fixed costs. Fixed costs that are locked in because of previous management decisions; management has little or no control over these costs in the short run, 311
Common equity, 858
Common fixed expenses. Expenses that cannot be traced to a particular segment or product line, 463–464, 590
Common stock, cash flow, 797. *See also* Stock
Common-size statement. A financial statement that reports only percentages (no dollar amounts), 845
Communication
  budgets, 510
  EMA and, 911
Compact fluorescent lamp (CFL) lighting, 898

Companion products, discontinuation decisions, 462
Comparative balance sheets. A comparison of the balance sheets from the end of two fiscal periods, usually highlighting the changes in each account, 788–789. *See also* Balance sheet
Compensation, clawback rules, 24. *See also* Salaries
Competence, 13
Competition, globalization and, 20
Compliance issues, 900–901, 909–910
Compound interest. Interest computed on the principal *and* all interest earned to date, 723
Comprehensive report. A GRI-referenced report in which *all indicators* related to each identified material aspect are disclosed, 906
Confidentiality, 13
Conformance costs. The combination of prevention and appraisal costs; the costs incurred to make sure a product or service is not defective and therefore conforms to its intended design, 207
Constraint. A factor that restricts the production or sale of a product, 464–467
Continuous flow, in lean thinking, 202
Contract manufacturers. Manufacturers that make products for other companies, not for themselves, 468
Contribution margin. Sales revenue minus variable expenses, 334, 383–384
  breakeven point calculations, 388–389
  decision making and, 446
  discontinuation decisions, 461–462
  operating leverage factor, 408–409
  outsourcing decisions, 470
  product mix decisions, 465–466, 467
  special order decisions, 453–455
  unit contribution margin, 383–386
Contribution margin income statement. Income statement that organizes costs by *behavior* (variable costs or fixed costs) rather than by *function*; can only be used by internal management, 333–336, 338–340, 383
  breakeven point calculations, 383–384, 387–388
  contribution margin ratio, 385–386
  decision making and, 446, 460
  income statement formats compared, 334–335
  for merchandising company, 336
Contribution margin per unit. The excess of the unit sales price over the variable cost per unit; also called *unit contribution margin*, 384
  sales price changes, 396
  variable cost changes, 398–399
  weighted-average contribution margin, 402–405
Contribution margin ratio. Ratio of contribution margin to sales revenue, 385–386, 388–389
  shortcut approach to breakeven point using, 388–389
Controllable costs. Costs that can be influenced or changed by management, 71
Controller. The position responsible for general financial accounting, managerial accounting, and tax reporting, 9, 10
Controlling. One of management's primary responsibilities; evaluating the results of business operations against the plan and making adjustments to keep the company pressing toward its goals, 3, 4
Conversion costs. The combination of direct labor and manufacturing overhead costs, 61
  equivalent units, 250–251
  process costing, 250
Coordination, budgets and, 510
Core report. A GRI-referenced report in which *at least one* indicator related to each identified material aspect is disclosed, 906
Corporate culture, balanced scorecard, 613
Corporate Social Responsibility (CSR) reports, 22, 70, 859, 902–907. *See also* Sustainability report
Cost allocations. *See also* Activity-based costing; Departmental overhead rates; Plantwide overhead rate
  activity-based costing to allocate, 184–189
  departmental overhead rates for, 179–184

distortion of, 176–177
refining, 176–177
Cost behavior. A behavior that describes how costs change as volume changes, 308
   account analysis to determine, 322
   accounting systems communicating, 331–340
   contribution margin income statement, 333–336
   data concerns, 330
   Decision Guidelines, 320, 341
   fixed costs, 311–313
   high-low method to estimate, 324–326
   managers determining, 322–330
   mixed costs, 314–315
   regression analysis to determine, 326–328
   relevant range, 316–317
   scatterplots to determine, 322–324
   service and merchandising companies, 335–336
   step costs, 317–318
   sustainability, 319
   variable costs, 308–311
   variable vs. absorption costing, 336–338
Cost center. A responsibility center in which managers are responsible for controlling costs, 586, 587
Cost distortion. Overcosting some products while undercosting other products, 177, 194
   comparing allocation systems, 188–189
   plantwide overhead rate causing, 183
Cost driver. The primary factor that causes a cost, 117
Cost equation. A mathematical equation for a straight line that expresses how a cost behaves, 309, 310
Cost hierarchy, 190–191
Cost object. Anything for which managers want to know the cost, 55
Cost of goods manufactured. The cost of manufacturing the goods that were finished during the period, 67–69
Cost of goods sold (CGS), 67–69, 107
   budgeted income statement, 519–520
   job costing vs. process costing, 247–250
Cost of goods sold, inventory, and purchases budget. A merchandiser's budget that computes the cost of goods sold, the amount of desired ending inventory, and amount of merchandise to be purchased, 531–533
Cost per equivalent unit, calculating, 267–268
Cost-benefit analysis. Weighing costs against benefits to help make decisions, 19. *See also* Financial statements, analysis of
   cost of quality reports for, 209
   discontinuation decisions, 460–464
   outsourcing, 469, 471–472
   special order decisions, 453–455
Cost-benefit test, in ABC/ABM system, 193–194
Cost-plus pricing. A pricing approach in which the company adds a desired level of profit to the product's cost; typically used by price-setters, 120, 450–451, 452
Costs. *See also* Absorption costing; Activity-based costing (ABC); Expenses; Job costing; Process costing; Standard costing; *specific types*
   actual cost, 660
   balanced scorecard, 609–611
   cost structure, decisions about, 409–411
   Decision Guidelines, 76
   decision making and, 446–447
   defining, 55–62
   discontinuation decisions, 460–464
   environmental management accounting and, 908, 910
   for external reporting, 57–58
   fixed and variable, 72
   flexible budgets, 603–608
   flow of, in job and process costing, 247–250
   for internal decision making, 57
   manufacturing cost variances, 608
   outsourcing decisions, 469, 471–472
   performance reports, 588–590
   period vs. product, 62
   profit markup added to, 145

   responsibility accounting, 586
   service firms direct costs, 143–144
   service firms indirect costs, 144–145
   special order decisions, 453–455
   sustainability and, 898–899
   target costing, 451–453
   total and average cost calculations, 73–75
   transfer price decisions, 598–599
Costs of quality report. A report that lists the costs incurred by the company related to quality. The costs are categorized as prevention costs, appraisal costs, internal failure costs, and external failure costs, 206
   to aid decisions, 208–209
   Decision Guidelines, 210
   relationship among costs, 207
   reports, 209
   at service and merchandising companies, 207
Costs per equivalent unit, 256
Cost-volume-profit (CVP) analysis. Expresses the relationships among costs, volume, and profit or loss, 382
   breakeven point calculations, 386–389
   changes in business conditions and, 396–405
   contribution margin ratio, 385–386
   cost structure decisions, 409–411
   data and assumptions, 382–383
   Decision Guidelines, 393, 412
   decision making and, 453
   fixed cost changes, 399–400
   graphing of, 391–392
   product mix, changes in, 402–403
   risk indicators, 406–411
   sales price changes, 396–398
   sales volume target decisions, 389–392
   sustainability and, 401–402
   unit contribution margin, 383–386
   variable cost changes, 398–399
   volume changes, 396–398
Credibility, 13
Credit, line of, 528
Credit sales, 524–525
   cash collections budget, 524–525
   growth in, 779
   impact on budget, 533–535
Critical thinking. Improving the quality of thought by skillfully analyzing, assessing, and reconstructing it, 18–19
Cross-functional teams. Corporate teams whose members represent various functions of the organization, such as R&D, design, production, marketing, distribution, and customer service, 10
Current ratio. Current assets divided by current liabilities. It measures the ability to pay current liabilities with current assets, 849–850, 860
Curvilinear costs. A cost behavior that is not linear (not a straight line), 318
Customer perspective, balanced scorecard, 611–612
Customer response time. The time that elapses between receipt of a customer order and delivery of the product or service, 198
Customer satisfaction, balanced scorecard, 611
Customer service. Support provided for customers after the sale, 52, 54, 612
CVP. *See* Cost-volume-profit (CVP) analysis
Cycle times, 202, 203

D

Data, cost-volume-profit analysis, 382–383
Data analytics, 18
Days' sales in receivables. Ratio of average net accounts receivable to one day's sale. It indicates how many days' sales remain in Accounts Receivable awaiting collection, 851–852, 860
Debit card sales, impact on budget, 533–535
Debt
   ability to pay long-term debt, 852–853
   cash flows, indirect method, 796–797

   red flags, 858
   statement of cash flows, 782
Debt ratio. Ratio of total liabilities to total assets. It shows the proportion of a company's assets that is financed with debt, 852, 860
Decentralization, 584
Decentralize. A process where companies split their operations into different operating segments, 584
Decision Guidelines
   balanced scorecard, 615
   building blocks of managerial accounting, 63
   capital budgeting, 720, 741
   cash flows, direct or indirect method, 803
   changing business and regulatory environment, 25
   cost behavior, 320, 341
   costs, 76
   cost-volume-profit analysis, 393, 412
   financial statement analysis, 846, 860–861
   horizontal and vertical analyses, 846
   job costing, 124, 139
   lean operations and costs of quality, 210
   managerial accounting and management accountants, 16
   master budget, 521, 537
   performance evaluation, 600, 615
   process costing, 261
   refined costing systems, 195
   relevant information for decisions, 457
   short-term special business decisions, 474
   standard costs and variances, 668, 676
   statement of cash flows, 786, 803
   sustainability, 913
Decision making. Identifying possible courses of action and choosing among them, 2, 3–4. *See also* Budget; Financial statements, analysis of
   costs, 57–58
   costs of quality reports for, 208–209
   Decision Guidelines, 474
   discontinuation decisions, 460–464
   internal, 57
   outsourcing decisions, 467–472
   pricing decisions, 448–453
   process for, 444–448
   product mix decisions, 464–467
   regular pricing decisions, 448–453
   sell as is or process further, 472–474
   special order decisions, 453–455
Deepwater Horizon oil spill, 901
Defects, 198
Delivery time, balanced scorecard, 611, 612
Departmental cost allocation system, 183
Departmental overhead rates. Separate manufacturing overhead rates established for each department, 180
   to allocate indirect costs, 179–184
   basic steps to compute, 180–182
Depreciation
   accounting rate of return, 719
   accumulated, 795
   book value decisions, 596
   capital expenditures budget, 524
   cash payments budget, 526–527
   discontinuation decisions, 462–464
   investing activities, indirect method, 795
   operating activities, indirect method, 789
   statement of cash flows, 782, 784
Design. Detailed engineering of products and services and the processes for producing them, 52
Differential cost. The difference in cost between two alternative courses of action, 71
Direct cost. A cost that can be traced to a cost object; a cost that is readily identifiable or associated with the cost object, 55, 56, 123, 143–144, 331
Direct fixed expenses. Fixed expenses that can be traced to the segment, 590
Direct labor. The cost of compensating employees who physically convert raw materials into the company's products; labor costs that are directly traceable to the finished product, 60, 61, 132
   budget, 516
   cost of, 526, 655, 680
   recording, 680

Direct labor efficiency variance. This variance tells managers how much of the total labor variance is due to using a greater or lesser amount of time than anticipated. It is calculated as follows: SR × (AH − SHA), 664–666

Direct labor rate variance. This variance tells managers how much of the total labor variance is due to paying a higher or lower hourly wage rate than anticipated. It is calculated as follows: AH × (AR − SR), 664–666

Direct materials. Primary raw materials that become a physical part of a finished product and whose costs are traceable to the finished product, 60, 61, 130–131
   budgeted income statement, 519–520
   direct materials budget, 515–516, 525–526
   recording use of, 679–680
   standard costing, 655, 679–682
   variances, standard costs and, 658–663, 666

Direct materials price variance. This variance tells managers how much of the total direct materials variance is due to paying a higher or lower price than expected for the direct materials it purchased. It is calculated as follows: AQP × (AP − SP), 659, 660–661

Direct materials quantity variance. This variance tells managers how much of the total direct materials variance is due to using a larger or smaller quantity of direct materials than expected. It is calculated as follows: SP × (AQU − SQA), 659, 661

Direct method. A method of presenting cash flows from operating activities that separately lists the receipt and payment of cash for specific operating activities, 783–784, 799–802
   Decision Guidelines, 803

Directing. One of management's primary responsibilities; running the company on a day-to-day basis, 3

Discontinuation decisions, 460–464

Discount rate. Management's minimum desired rate of return on an investment; also called the *hurdle rate* and *required rate of return,* 731

Discounted cash flow methods, 730–736
   capital budgeting methods compared, 739–740

Discounting cash flows, 715–718

Discretionary fixed costs. Fixed costs that are a result of annual management decisions; fixed costs that are controllable in the short run, 311

Distribution. Delivery of products or services to customers, 52, 54

Distribution cost standards, 657

Dividend yield. Ratio of dividends per share of stock to the stock's market price per share. It tells the percentage of a stock's market value that the company returns to stockholders annually as dividends, 857–858, 861

Dividends
   cash flow, indirect method, 796–797
   cash payments budget, 527
   dividend yield, 857–858
   return on equity, 855
   statement of cash flows, 782

Dodd-Frank Wall Street Reform and Consumer Protection Act of 2010, 24

DOWNTIME. An acronym for the eight wastes: defects, overproduction, waiting, not utilizing people to their full potential, transportation, inventory, movement, excess processing, 198–200

E

Earnings per share (EPS). Amount of a company's net income for each share of its outstanding common stock, 611, 856, 861

Earnings per share of common stock, 856, 861

Eco-efficiency. Achieving economic savings by producing goods and services with fewer ecological resources, 898
   examples of, 898–899

Economic category, G4, 905
Economic performance metrics, 70
Economic sustainability, 895
Economic value added (EVA), 596
Economy, shifting, 20
Efficiency variance
   direct labor, 664–666
   manufacturing overhead, 673

Eight wastes. Defects, overproduction, waiting, not utilizing people to their full potential, transportation, inventory, movement, excess processing, 198

Electronic payments, cost behavior, 319

Employees. *See also* Labor; Salaries; Wages
   attracting and retaining talent, 901
   employee capabilities, balanced scorecard, 613
   empowerment of, lean thinking, 201–202
   job cost record, 114–116
   labor compensation costs, 62
   manufacturing costs, 60–61

Energy costs, 711, 898

Enterprise resource planning (ERP). Software systems that can integrate all of a company's worldwide functions, departments, and data into a single system, 18

Entrepreneurs, managerial accounting for, 8

Environmental category, G4, 905

Environmental Management Accounting (EMA). A system used for the identification, collection, analysis, and use of two types of information for internal decision making-monetary and physical information, 895, 908
   future of, 912
   implementation challenges, 911–912
   information for, 908–909
   uses, 909–911

Environmental performance metrics, 70
Environmental Protection Agency (EPA), 900
Environmental sustainability. *See* Sustainability
Environmentalleader.com, 899
Environmental-related overhead costs, 189
Equipment. *See* Property, plant, and equipment (PPE)
Equity shares
   cash flow, indirect method, 796–797
   common equity, 858
   return on equity, 855
   statement of cash flows, 782

Equivalent units. Express the amount of work done during a period in terms of fully completed units of output, 250
   in process costing, 250–251, 266–267

Ethics, 12–15
   dilemma examples, 14–15
   IMA statement, 13
   unethical vs. illegal behavior, 15

Europe, environmental laws in, 901
Evaluating, 4
E-waste, 123

Excel
   horizontal and vertical analysis, 845
   internal rate of return calculations, 739
   net present value calculations, 735
   present value computations, 730
   regression analysis, 326–327, 329
   scatterplots, 324
   time value of money calculations and example solutions, 725, 727, 747–753

Excess processing, 198, 200

Expenses. *See also* Costs; Financial statements, analysis of
   breakeven point calculations, 386–389
   cash payments budget, 525–527
   common fixed expenses, 463–464, 590
   cost-volume-profit graphs, 391–392
   direct fixed expenses, 590
   flexible budgets, 603–608
   noncash expenses, 789
   operating, 58
   operating activities, indirect method, 788–794

   performance reports, 588–590
   SG&A, 58
   statement of cash flows, 782–783

Extended producer responsibility (EPR) laws. Laws that require product manufacturers to "take back" a large percentage of the products they manufacture at the end of the product's life in order to reduce the amount of waste ending up in landfills and the environment, 122–123, 910

External costs. Costs borne by society as a result of a company's operations and the products and services it sells, 896

External failure costs. Costs incurred when the company does not detect poor-quality goods or services until *after* delivery is made to customers, 206, 207

External reporting
   costs for, 57–58
   in EMA systems, 896

F

Facility-level activities. Activities and costs incurred no matter how many units, batches, or products are produced in the plant, 190

Factory overhead. *See* Manufacturing overhead (MOH)

Favorable variance. A variance that causes operating income to be higher than budgeted, 588–589, 607–608

Feedback, 3
   balanced scorecard, 613
   performance evaluation systems, 585

Financial accounting, managerial accounting vs, 4–5
Financial Accounting Standards Board (FASB), cash flow reporting, 784

Financial budgets. The financial budgets include the capital expenditures budget and the cash budget. It culminates in a budgeted balance sheet, 511, 524–531

Financial perspective, balanced scorecard, 611
Financial ratios
   ability to pay current liabilities, 849–850
   ability to pay long-term debt, 852–853
   ability to sell inventory and collect receivables, 850–852
   Decision Guidelines, 860–861
   profitability, 853–856
   stock investments, 857–858

Financial statements. *See also specific statement names*
   product costs and period costs in, 65–70

Financial statements, analysis of
   benchmarking, 845
   common financial ratios, 849–858
   comparing between companies, 845
   Decision Guidelines, 860–861
   horizontal analysis, 839–843
   ratio analysis, 839
   red flags, 858
   sustainability and, 859
   vertical analysis, 839, 843–845

Financing activities. Activities that either generate capital for the company or pay it back, such as issuing stock or long-term debt, paying dividends, and repaying principal amounts on loans; this includes all activities that affect long-term liabilities and owners' equity, 782, 785
   noncash, 783

Finished goods (FG) inventory. Completed goods that have not yet been sold, 50, 107
   job costing vs. process costing, 247–250
   production budget, 513–514
   standard costs, journal entries, 681

First-in, first out (FIFO), 251

Five-step process costing procedure, 272

Fixed costs. Costs that stay constant in total despite wide changes in volume, 72, 311–313. *See also* Cost-volume-profit (CVP) analysis

breakeven point calculations, 386–389
changes in, sensitivity analysis, 399–400
common fixed expenses, 463–464
decision making and, 452
discontinuation decisions, 461–462
equations for, 312–313
flexible budgets, 603–608
manufacturing overhead budget, 517
operating leverage, 407–409
outsourcing decisions, 469, 471
performance reports, 589
product mix decisions, 465–466
transfer price decisions, 599
Fixed operating expenses, 518
Fixed overhead budget variance. This variance measures the difference between the actual fixed overhead costs incurred and the budgeted fixed overhead costs. This variance is sometimes referred to as the fixed overhead spending variance because it specifically looks at whether the company spent more or less than anticipated on fixed overhead costs, 673
Fixed overhead spending variance. Another name for the Fixed Overhead Budget Variance. This variance measures the difference between the actual fixed overhead costs incurred and the budgeted fixed overhead costs, 673
Fixed overhead volume variance. This variance is the difference between the budgeted fixed overhead and the *standard fixed overhead cost* allocated to production. In essence, the fixed overhead volume variance measures the utilization of the fixed capacity costs. If volume is higher than originally anticipated, the variance will be favorable. If volume is lower than originally anticipated, the variance will be unfavorable, 674–675
Flexible budget variance. The difference between the flexible budget and actual results. The flexible budget variances are due to *something other than volume*, 606–608
Flexible budgets. Budgets prepared for different volumes of activity, 530, 603–608, 658
Forecasts, 384–385
Fossil-fuel alternatives, 54, 122
Free cash flow. The amount of excess cash a business generates after taking into consideration the capital expenditures necessary to maintain its business. It is calculated as cash flows from operating activities minus capital expenditures, 798
Freed capacity
discontinuation decisions, 463
outsourcing decisions, 469, 471
Freight-in costs, 59
Future value (FV)
factors, 724–730
table, 745

G

G4 Guidelines, 904–906
Generally Accepted Accounting Principles (GAAP), 4, 331
capital budgeting, 712
EMA and, 912
for external reporting of costs, 57–58
Global Reporting Initiative (GRI). A nonprofit organization whose mission is to make sustainability reporting standard practice by providing guidance and support to organizations. The developer of the G4 Guidelines, 70, 903–904
SASB and, 907
Globalization, 20–21
Goal Congruence. When the goals of the segment managers align with the goals of top management, 585
Goals, balanced scorecard, 609–613. *See also* Performance evaluation; Strategic planning
Green initiatives, 22
Green technologies, investments in, 713–714

Greenwashing. The unfortunate practice of overstating a company's commitment to sustainability, 54
Gross book value. Historical cost of assets, 596
Gross margin percentage, balanced scorecard, 611
Gross profit, 268–269. *See also* Profit
Gross profit percentage. The fraction of each dollar of sales revenue that is gross profit, or markup over the cost of the merchandise, 853–854, 861

H

Hidden costs, 911
High-low method. A method for determining cost behavior that is based on two historical data points: the highest and lowest volume of activity, 324–326
Horizontal analysis. Study of percentage changes in comparative financial statements, 839–843
Decision Guidelines, 846
Human rights, as G4 sub-category, 905
Hurdle rate. Management's minimum desired rate of return on an investment; also called the *discount rate* and *required rate of return*, 731

I

Ideal standards. Standards based on perfect or ideal conditions that do not allow for any waste in the production process, machine breakdown, or other inefficiencies. Also known as perfection standards, 654. *See also* Standard cost
Illegal vs. unethical behavior, 15
Import duties, 59
Income. *See also* Financial statements, analysis of
accrual basis of accounting, 784
breakeven point calculations, 386–389
noncash revenue, 789–790
operating activities, indirect method, 788–794
residual income, 594–596, 597, 611
times-interest-earned ratio, 853
Income statement. *See also* Financial statements, analysis of
breakeven point and, 387, 390
budgeted income statement, 519–520
contribution margin income statement, 383–386, 446, 460
horizontal analysis, 841
product line income statement, 450–451
standard costing, 682
vertical analysis, 843–844
Income taxes, 527, 781, 782, 802
Incremental analysis, short-term decisions, 445–446
Independent Accountants' Review Report, 906
Indifference point. The volume of sales at which a company would be indifferent between alternative cost structures because they would result in the same total cost, 410–411
outsourcing decisions, 470
Indirect cost. A cost that relates to the cost object but cannot be traced specifically to it; a cost that is jointly used or shared by more than one cost object, 55, 56, 143–144, 177–178
Indirect labor. Labor costs that are difficult to trace to specific products, 60, 61, 132
Indirect manufacturing cost. *See* Manufacturing overhead (MOH)
Indirect materials. Materials whose costs are difficult to trace to specific products, 60, 61, 131
Indirect method. A method of presenting the cash flows from operating activities that begins with the company's net income, which is prepared on an accrual basis, and then reconciles it back to the cash basis through a series of adjustments, 784
Decision Guidelines, 803
financing activities, 796–797
information needs for, 788
investing activities, 794–796
operating activities, 788–794

Industrial Revolution, 896
Inflation, cost equations and, 332
Information systems, 613
EMA and, 910, 911
Innovation, 612
Institute of Management Accountants (IMA). The professional organization that promotes the advancement of the management accounting profession, 10
Insurance expense
cash payments, direct method, 801
cash payments budget, 526
manufacturing overhead budget, 517
prepaid insurance, 791
Intangible costs, 908
Integrated reporting (IR). A process resulting in a report that describes how a company is creating value over time using financial, manufactured, intellectual, human, social, and natural capital, 22–23, 859
Integrity, 13
Interest expense
cash flow, indirect method, 792
cash flow, overview, 783
rate of return on total assets, 855
times-interest-earned ratio, 853
Interest income, 783
Interest rate
internal rate of return, 736–739
present and future value tables, 743–745
present value calculations, 728–730
time value of money, 723–730
Interest-coverage ratio. Ratio of income from operations to interest expense. It measures the number of times that operating income can cover interest expense; also called the *times-interest-earned ratio*, 853, 860
Internal Audit Department, professional ethics statement, 13
Internal audit function. The corporate function charged with assessing the effectiveness of the company's internal controls and risk management policies, 9, 10
Internal business perspective, balanced scorecard, 612
Internal costs. Costs that are incurred and paid for by the organization and recorded in GAAP-based accounting records, 896
Internal failure costs. Costs incurred when the company detects and corrects poor-quality goods or services before making delivery to customers, 206, 207
Internal rate of return (IRR). The rate of return (based on discounted cash flows) that a company can expect to earn by investing in a capital asset. The interest rate that makes the NPV of the investment equal to zero, 711, 730, 736–739, 740
Internal Revenue Service (IRS), 331
Internal sales, transfer price, 597–599
International Accounting Standards Board (IASB), 784
International Integrated Reporting Committee (IIRC), 22
International Organization for Standardization (ISO), 909
Inventory, 49, 198, 199. *See also* Finished goods inventory; Raw materials inventory; Work-in-process (WIP) inventory
on balance sheet, 70
cash flow and, 781
cash payments for, 800–801
costing systems showing, 338–340
direct materials budget, 515
indirect cash flow method, 791–792
inventory system types, 66
inventory turnover, 850–851
of manufacturing companies, 50
merchandising companies, 531–533
production budget, 513
red flags, 858
standard costs, 681

I-6   Glossary/Index

Inventory flow, in process costing, 251

Inventory turnover. Ratio of cost of goods sold to average inventory. It indicates how rapidly inventory is sold, 850, 860

Investing activities. Activities that involve buying or selling long-term assets, such as buying or selling property, plant, or equipment; buying or selling stock in other companies (if the stock is meant to be held for the long term); or loaning money to other companies with the goal of earning interest income from the loan, 781

    cash flow, indirect method, 795–796
    noncash, 783
    statement of cash flows, 781
    sustainability and, 784

Investment appraisal, EMA and, 910

Investment center. A responsibility center in which managers are responsible for generating revenues, controlling costs, and efficiently managing the division's assets, 586–587, 590–597

Investment indices, socially responsible, 902

Investments. *See* Capital budgeting

Invoice. Bill from a supplier, 110, 145–146

Irrelevant costs, 71–72

ISO 14000, 909

J

Job cost record. A written or electronic document that lists the direct materials, direct labor, and manufacturing overhead costs assigned to each individual job, 110–112

    for business decisions, 119–121
    custom order bidding, 120–121
    financial statements, 121
    high-volume sales discounts, 120
    labor costs, tracing of, 114–116
    manufacturing overhead allocation, 116–119
    materials costs, tracing of, 112–114
    pricing pressure from competitors, 120
    profitability assessment, 119–120
    reducing future costs, 119

Job costing. A system for assigning costs to products or services that differ in the amount of materials, labor, and overhead required. Typically used by manufacturers that produce unique, or custom-ordered products in small batches; also used by professional service firms, 104, 106

    Decision Guidelines, 124, 139
    for decision making, 121–123
    direct or variable, 123
    flow of inventory through manufacturing system, 107–108
    journal entries in manufacturer's system, 129–138
    manufacturers determining, 107–121
    manufacturing overhead, 118–119
    methods to determine, 105–106
    non-manufacturing costs, 121
    process costing vs, 246–250
    raw materials purchasing, 109–110
    record tracking, 110
    scheduling production, 108
    service firms, 143–146
    special order decisions, 450, 455
    sustainability and, 122–123
    tracing direct materials cost, 112–114
    tracing labor costs, 114–116
    under- and overallocated overhead, 127–129

Journal entries, 191
    job costing, 129–138
    job costing, service firms, 146
    for process costing, 259–260
    in second processing department, 270–271
    standard costing, 679–682

Just in time (JIT). An inventory management philosophy that focuses on purchasing raw materials just in time for production and completing finished goods just in time for delivery to customers, 200

    direct material variances, 662

K

Kaizen. A Japanese word meaning "change for the better." 198

Kaplan, Robert, 609

Key performance indicators (KPIs). Summary performance metrics used to assess how well a company is achieving its goals, 609, 904–905

Knowledge economy, 20

L

Labor. *See also* Employees
    attracting and retaining talent, 901
    budgeted income statement, 519–520
    cash flow, direct method, 801
    cash flow, indirect method, 792–793
    compensation costs, 62
    direct labor (*See* Direct labor)
    direct labor variances, 664–666
    fixed manufacturing overhead variances, 680
    indirect labor, 60, 61, 132
    job cost record, 114–116
    minimum wage, 901
    social responsibility and, 900
    standard cost of, 655, 680
    variable manufacturing overhead variances, 671–672

Labor practices, as G4 sub-category, 905

Labor time record. A written or electronic document that identifies the employee, the amount of time spent on a particular job, and the labor cost charged to a job, 114–116

Lag indicators. Performance indicators that reveal the results of past actions and decisions, 609

Landfills
    extended producer responsibility laws, 910
    zero-waste operations, 899

Lead indicators. Performance measures that predict future performance, 609

Lean operations
    Decision Guidelines, 210
    in service and merchandising companies, 205
    standard costing, 667, 675

Lean thinking. A philosophy and business strategy of operating without waste, 21, 198. *See also* Six Sigma

    5S workplace organization, 202
    backflush costing, 204–205
    characteristics of, 200–205
    continuous flow, 202
    drawbacks, 205
    eight wastes of traditional operations, 198–200
    employee empowerment, 201–202
    JIT, 200
    POUS, 204
    pull system, 202–203
    quality emphasis, 204
    reduced setup times in, 203–204
    self-contained production cells, 201
    in service and merchandising companies, 205
    shorter manufacturing cycle times, 202
    smaller batches, 203
    supply-chain management, 204
    sustainability and, 205
    value stream mapping, 201

Learning and growth, balanced scorecard, 613

Leases, 730n5

LEED certification. LEED, which stands for Leadership in Energy and Environmental Design, is a certification system developed by the U.S. Green Building Council as a way of promoting and evaluating environmentally friendly construction projects, 714

Legal concerns, 900–901

Legal services. *See* Service company

Leverage. Earning more income on borrowed money than the related interest expense, thereby increasing the earnings for the owners of the business; also called *trading on equity*, 856

Liabilities
    ability to pay long-term debt, 852–853
    acid-test ratio, 850
    cash flow, indirect method, 796
    cash payments and receipts, 800–802
    current, measuring ability to pay, 849–850
    investing activities, indirect method, 794–796
    operating activities, indirect method, 788–794
    statement of cash flows, 781–782, 784
    working capital, 849

Life-cycle assessment (LCA). Studying the environmental and social impact of a product or service over its entire life, from "cradle to grave," in attempt to minimize negative environmental consequences throughout the entire lifespan of the product, 53, 896–897, 899

Lifestyles of Health and Sustainability (LOHAS), 54

Light-emitting diode (LED) lighting, 898

Line of credit. A lending arrangement from a bank in which a company is allowed to borrow money as needed, up to a specified maximum amount, yet only pay interest on the portion that is actually borrowed until it is repaid, 528

Litigation risks, 900–901

Low-emission technology, 900

M

Make-or-buy decisions, 467–472

Management accountants
    average salaries of, 12
    Decision Guidelines, 16
    nontechnical competencies, 7
    professional ethics, 12–15
    role of, 6–7
    skills required, 7–8
    technical competencies, 7

Management accounting. A profession that involves partnering in management decision making, devising planning and performance management systems, and providing expertise in financial reporting and control to assist management in the formulation and implementation of an organization's strategy, 2

    as building blocks, 3
    for business management, 8
    business trends and regulations affecting, 18–19
    as career foundation, 8–9
    controlling, 3, 4
    for controlling and evaluating, 4
    Decision Guidelines, 16, 63
    for decision making, 2–3
    for directing, 3
    for entrepreneurs, 8
    financial accounting vs, 4–5
    globalization implications for, 20–21
    integrated reporting, 22–23
    lean thinking, 21
    for marketing and sales, 8–9
    for nonbusiness majors, 8–9
    for planning, 3, 4
    primary responsibilities, 2–3
    for product costing, 3
    professional associations, 10–11
    quality focus, 21
    Sarbanes-Oxley Act of 2002, 23–24
    shifting economy and, 20
    social responsibility, 21–22
    sustainability, 21–22
    triple bottom line, 21–22

Management by exception. A management technique in which managers only investigate budget variances that are relatively large, 589, 608

Managerial accounting
    building blocks of, 63
    financial accounting vs, 4–5
    management accountants and, 16
    for marketing and sales, 8–9

Manufacturing company. A company that uses labor, plant, and equipment to convert raw materials into new finished products, 50, 63. *See also* Job costing; Process costing

budgeted income statement, 519–520
constraints, 464–467
direct labor budget, 516
direct materials budget, 515–516
financial statements, 67–69
job costing determination, 107–121
job costing vs. process costing, 247–250
labor compensation costs, 62
manufacturing overhead budget, 517–518
outsourcing decisions, 467–472
prime and conversion costs, 61
product costs, 60–61
production budget, 513–514
shifting economy influencing, 20
Manufacturing cost, 73
determining, 105–106
variances, 608
Manufacturing cycle time. The time that elapses between the start of production and the product's completion, 202, 203
Manufacturing overhead (MOH). All manufacturing costs other than direct materials and direct labor; also called *factory overhead* and *indirect manufacturing cost*, 60, 61, 177, 331–333
activity-based costing, cost allocation, 184–189
allocating, 116–117, 134–135
budget for, 517–518, 526
budgeted income statement, 519–520
closing, 137–138
costs incurred, 133–134
departmental overhead, cost allocation, 179–184
discontinuation decisions, 463
job costing, 129–138
operating expenses, 137
in process costing journal entries, 260
sale of units, 136
special order decisions, 455
standard cost of, 655, 656–657, 671–675, 680
under- and overallocated, 127–129
variable overhead variances, 671–672
Margin of safety. Excess of expected sales over breakeven sales; the drop in sales a company can absorb without incurring an operating loss, 406–407
Marginal cost. The cost of producing one more unit, 75
Market price, transfer price decisions, 598–599
Market share, 609, 611, 614, 900
Marketing. Promotion and advertising of products or services, 52
with integrity, 54
managerial accounting for, 8–9
Mass customization. Large-scale production of customized product that allows manufacturers to meet a variety of consumer desires, while at the same time achieving the efficiencies of mass production that drive down unit costs, 107
Master budget. The comprehensive planning document for the entire organization. The master budget includes the operating budgets and the financial budgets, 511–512. *See also* Budget
credit and debit card sales, impact of, 533–535
Decision Guidelines, 521, 537
development process, 508–510
financial budgets, 511, 524–531
operating budgets, 511
overview of, 508
sensitivity analysis and flexible budgeting, 530
standard costs, advantages and disadvantages, 666–667
sustainability and budgeting, 536
uses for, 508
Master budget variance. The difference between actual results and the master budget, 603
Materiality. An important concept in CSR reporting defined as those aspects of a business that reflect the organization's significant economic, environmental, and social impacts, or substantively influence the assessments and decisions of stakeholders, 904
Materials cost. *See also* Just in time (JIT)
direct materials budget, 525–526

direct materials price variance, 659, 660–661
direct materials quantity variance, 659, 661
for job costing, 112–114
standard costing, 654–655, 679–682
variances, standard costs and, 660
Materials flow accounting (MFA). An accounting system in which all physical inputs to an organization's operations are reconciled with output generated. The goal is to track where all physical inputs are going, 909
Materials requisition. A written or electronic document requesting that specific materials be transferred from the raw materials inventory storeroom to the production floor, 113
Merchandise inventory, 49
Merchandising company. A company that resells tangible products previously bought from suppliers, 49, 50, 63
budgeting, 531–533
contribution margin income statement for, 336
COQ at, 207
cost behavior, 335–336
cost of goods sold, 335
discontinuation decisions, 464
financial statements, 65–66
lean operations in, 205
product costs, 58–59
using ABC across value chain, 192–193
Microsoft Excel. *See* Excel
Minimum wage, 901
Mixed cost. Costs that change, but *not* in direct proportion to changes in volume. Mixed costs have both variable cost and fixed cost components, 314–315
high-low method, 326–328
manufacturing overhead budget, 517
MOH pool, job costing. *See* Manufacturing overhead (MOH)
Monetary information. The type of information traditionally used in accounting systems, 908
Money market funds, 781
Movement, 198, 199–200
Multiproduct companies, breakeven point, 402–405

N

Negotiated price, transfer price decisions, 598–599
Net book value. The original cost of assets less accumulated depreciation, 596, 789–790
Net cash inflow
accounting rate of return, 718–719
capital budgeting and, 712
internal rate of return, 736–739
net present value, 731–736
payback period, 715–716
Net income. *See also* Financial statements, analysis of
operating activities, 781
profitability measures, 853–856
Net present value (NPV). The *difference* between the present value of the investment's net cash inflows and the investment's cost, 711, 731–736, 740
Non-business ventures, managerial accounting for, 9
Noncash expenses, 789
Noncash financing activities, 783
Noncash investing activities, 783
Noncash revenues, 789–790
Nonconformance costs. The combination of internal failure and external failure costs; the costs incurred when a product is defective and therefore does not conform to its intended design, 207
Nonfinancial factors, decision making, 445
Nonfinancial performance measurement, 609–613
Non-governmental organizations (NGOs). Not-for-profit organizations that serve the public interest, such as Greenpeace and Sierra Club, 70, 896
Non-manufacturing costs, 121

Non-value-added activities. Activities that neither enhance the customer's image of the product or service nor provide a competitive advantage; also known as *waste activities*, 192
Norton, David, 609
Not utilizing full potential, 198, 199

O

Office environment, 901
Offshoring. Having work performed overseas. Offshored work can be performed either by the company itself or by outsourcing the work to another company, 467–468
Oil spills, 901
Operating activities. The day-to-day profit-making activities of the company, such as making or buying inventory, selling inventory, selling services, paying employees, advertising, and so forth; this also includes *any other activity that affects net income* (not just operating income), current assets, or current liabilities, 781
direct method, 783–784, 799–802
indirect method, 784, 788–794
statement of cash flows, 781
sustainability and, 784
Operating budgets. The budgets needed to run the daily operations of the company. The operating budgets culminate in a budgeted income statement, 511. *See also* Budget
Operating cost standards, 657
Operating expenses, 333, 527. *See also* Costs
breakeven point calculations, 386–389
budget for, 518
cash flow, direct method, 802
cash payments budget, 525–527
flexible budget performance reports, 604–607
job costing, journal entries, 137
period costs, 58
Operating income. Earnings generated from the company's primary ongoing operations; the company's earnings before interest and taxes, 65
absorption costing vs. variable costing, 336–338
accounting rate of return, 717–718
performance reports, 588–590
reconciling, between costing systems, 338–340
residual income and, 594–596, 597, 611
return on investment, 592–597
times-interest-earned ratio, 853
Operating income percentage. The percentage of each sales dollar that becomes income from the company's primary business operations before considering interest and income taxes, 854, 861
Operating Leverage. The relative amount of fixed and variable costs that make up a firm's total costs, 407–409
Operating leverage factor. At a given level of sales, the contribution margin divided by operating income; the operating leverage factor indicates the percentage change in operating income that will occur from a 1% change in sales volume, 408–409
Operations, balanced scorecard, 612–613
Opportunity cost. The benefit forgone by choosing a particular alternative course of action, 471
Organization, workplace, 202
Organization chart, 587
Organizational structures, 906
of accounting, 9–10
Organization-wide performance reports, 590
Other indirect manufacturing costs. All manufacturing overhead costs aside from indirect materials and indirect labor, 61
Outliers. Abnormal data points; data points that do not fall in the same general pattern as the other data points, 323, 330
Output, in process costing, 254–255
Outsourcing. Contracting an outside company to produce a product or perform a service. Outsourced work can be done domestically or overseas, 467–472

Overallocated Manufacturing Overhead. The amount of manufacturing overhead allocated to jobs is more than the amount of manufacturing overhead costs actually incurred; results in jobs being overcosted, 127–129

Overhead, plantwide, cost allocation, 177–178. *See also* Manufacturing overhead (MOH)

Overproduction, 198–199

Owners' Equity, 796–797

P

Packaging, 536, 657, 899
   environmentally safe, 53

Paris Agreement, 900, 901

Participative budgeting. Budgeting that involves the participation of many levels of management, 509

Payback period. The length of time it takes to recover, in net cash inflows, the cost of a capital outlay, 711, 714–717, 718, 739
   accounting rate of return and, 719

Percentage change, horizontal analysis, 839–843

Percentage of market share, balanced scorecard, 611

Perfection standards. Standards based on perfect or ideal conditions that do not allow for any waste in the production process, machine breakdown, or other inefficiencies. Also known as ideal standards, 654. *See also* Standard cost

Performance evaluation, 583–614. *See also* Financial statements, analysis of
   balanced scorecard, 609–615
   decentralization and, 584–585
   Decision Guidelines, 600, 615
   environmental management accounting and, 910–911
   flexible budgets and, 603–608
   goal congruence, 585, 595–596
   investment center evaluation, 586–587, 590–597
   limitations of, 597
   measurement issues, 596
   nonfinancial, 609–613
   residual income, 594–596, 597, 611
   responsibility accounting, overview, 586–587
   responsibility center performance reports, 588–590
   return on investment, 592–597
   sales margin and capital turnover, 593–594
   sustainability and, 614
   systems for, 585
   transfer pricing, 597–599

Performance reports. Reports that compare actual results against budgeted figures, 511, 588–590

Performance scorecard or performance dashboard. A report displaying the measurement of KPIs, as well as their short-term and long-term targets, 609–610

Period costs. The costs incurred by the company to operate the business that do *not* get treated as inventory, but rather are expensed immediately in the period in which they are incurred. These costs do *not* relate to manufacturing or purchasing product. Period costs are often called operating expenses or selling, general, and administrative expenses, 57–58
   comparing, 333
   financial statement reporting, 65–70
   product costs vs, 62

Periodic inventory. An inventory system in which Cost of Goods Sold is calculated at the end of the period rather than every time a sale is made, 66

Perpetual inventory. An inventory system in which both Cost of Goods Sold and Inventory are updated every time a sale is made, 66

Physical information. A vital part of environmental management accounting systems. Examples include: quantity of air emissions, tons of solid waste generated, gallons of wastewater generated, pounds of packaging recycled, and total amount of water consumed, 908

Pick. Storeroom workers remove items from raw materials inventory that are needed by production, 113

Planning. One of management's primary responsibilities: setting goals and objectives for the company and deciding how to achieve them, 3, 4
   balanced scorecard, 609–613, 614, 615
   budget, benefits of, 510
   budget process, 508–510
   environmental management accounting and, 909
   G4 Guidelines, 906

Plant. *See* Property, plant, and equipment (PPE)

Plantwide allocation system, 178

Plantwide overhead rate. When overhead is allocated to every product using the same manufacturing overhead rate, 178
   cost allocation, 177–178
   cost distortion caused by, 183
   distortion and, 183
   indirect cost and, 177–178

Point of Use Storage (POUS). A storage system used to reduce the waste of transportation and movement in which tools, materials, and equipment are stored in proximity to where they will be used most frequently, 204

Pollution
   carbon footprint, 910
   environmental management accounting and, 908

Post-audits. Comparing a capital investment's actual net cash inflows to its projected net cash inflows, 713

Post-sales support, balanced scorecard, 612

Practical standards. Standards based on currently attainable conditions that include allowances for normal amounts of waste and inefficiency. Also known as attainable standards, 654

Predetermined manufacturing overhead rate. The rate used to allocate manufacturing overhead to individual jobs; calculated before the year begins as follows: total estimated manufacturing overhead costs divided by total estimated amount of allocation base, 117, 181

Preferred stockholders, 857

Prepaid insurance, 791

Present value, 724–730, 736–739
   tables, 743–744

Present value index. An index that computes the number of dollars returned for every dollar invested, *with all calculations performed in present value dollars.* It is computed as present value of net cash inflows divided by investment; also called *profitability index,* 734

Prevention costs. Costs incurred to *avoid* poor-quality goods or services, 206–209

Price variance, direct materials variances, 659, 660–661

Price/Earnings (P/E) Ratio. Ratio of the market price of a share of common stock to the company's earnings per share. It measures the value that the stock market places on $1 of a company's earnings, 857, 861

Price-setters, 449–450

Price-takers, 449–450, 451

Pricing. *See also* Cost-volume-profit (CVP) analysis; Job costing; Process costing
   breakeven point calculations, 386–389
   cost-plus pricing, 450–451
   decisions about, 448–453
   fixed cost changes, 399–400
   outsourcing price decisions, 470
   regular pricing decisions, 448–453
   sales-price changes, sensitivity analysis, 396
   special order decisions, 453–455
   transfer price, 597–599
   variable cost changes, 398–399
   weighted-average contribution margin, 402–405

Prime costs. The combination of direct material and direct labor costs, 61

Principal, time value of money, 723–730

Principles for Responsible Investment (PRI). Six principles of investing, including a commitment to incorporate environmental, social, and governance issues into investment analysis and decision making, 859, 902

Process costing. A system for assigning costs to a large number of identical units that typically pass through a series of uniform production steps. Costs are averaged over the units produced such that each unit bears the same unit cost, 105–106
   conversion costs, 250
   first processing department, 252–258, 261
   flow in, 254, 266
   inventory flow assumptions, 251
   job costing vs, 246–250
   journal entries needed, 259–260
   overview, 246–250
   second or later processing departments, 264–271
   sustainability and, 258–259
   weighted-average method of, 251, 252–258

Processes, 246

Processing departments, 259

Product costs. The costs incurred by manufacturers to produce their products or incurred by merchandisers to purchase their products. For external financial reporting, GAAP requires that these costs be assigned to inventory until the products are sold, at which point, they are expensed as Cost of Goods Sold, 3, 57
   comparing inventory, 332
   financial statement reporting, 65–70
   manufacturing companies, 60–61
   merchandising companies, 58–59
   period costs vs, 62

Product development, balanced scorecard, 612

Product line income statement. An income statement that shows the operating income of each product line, as well as the company as a whole, 460–461

Product mix, decisions about, 464–467

Product responsibility, as G4 sub-category, 905

Production budget, 513–514

Production cost report. Summarizes a processing department's operations for a period, 269, 272

Production or purchases. Resources used to produce a product or service or to purchase finished merchandise intended for resale, 52

Production schedule. A written or electronic document indicating the quantity and types of inventory that will be manufactured during a specified time frame, 108

Productivity, balanced scorecard, 611

Product-level activities. Activities and costs incurred for a particular product, regardless of the number of units or batches of the product produced, 190

Professional associations, 10–11

Professional billing rate, 145–146

Professional ethics, 12–15

Profit. *See also* Cost-volume-profit (CVP) analysis; Financial statements, analysis of
   accounting rate of return, 717–719
   breakeven point calculations, 386–389
   common-size statements, 845
   contribution margin ratio, 385–386
   cost-volume-profit graphs, 391–392
   decision making and, 446
   discontinuation decisions, 460–464
   fixed cost changes, 399–400
   gross percentage, 853–854, 861
   measuring profitability, 853–856
   payback period calculations, 715–716
   product mix, changes in, 402–403
   product mix, decisions about, 464–467
   regular pricing decisions, 448–453
   residual income, 594–596, 597, 611
   risk indicators, 406–411
   sales volume target decisions, 389–392
   sustainability and, 447
   unit contribution margin, 383–386

Glossary/Index   I-9

Profit center. A responsibility center in which managers are responsible for both revenues and costs, and therefore profits, 586, 587

Profitability index. An index that computes the number of dollars returned for every dollar invested, *with all calculations performed in present value dollars*. Computed as present value of net cash inflows divided by investment; also called *present value index*, 733–735

Property, plant, and equipment (PPE). *See also* Depreciation
    capital expenditures budget, 524
    investing activities, indirect method, 794–796
    manufacturing overhead budget, 517–518
    statement of cash flows, 781

Property taxes
    cash payments budget, 526
    manufacturing overhead budget, 517

Pull system, 202–203

Purchase order. A written or electronic document authorizing the purchase of specific raw materials from a specific supplier, 110

Q

Quality
    balanced scorecard, 609, 611–612
    management accounting and lean thinking, 21

Quality at the source. A term that refers to shifting the responsibility for quality adherence to the operators at each step in the value stream, rather than relying on supervisors or a quality assurance department to catch errors, 204

Quality improvement, 206–209

Quantity variance, 659–664

Quick ratio. Ratio of the sum of cash plus short-term investments plus net current receivables to total current liabilities. It tells whether the entity can pay all its current liabilities if they come due immediately; also called the *acid-test ratio*, 850, 860

R

Rate of return, accounting (ARR), 711, 717–719, 739

Rate of return on common stockholders' equity. Net income minus preferred dividends divided by average common stockholders' equity. It is a measure of profitability; also called *return on equity*, 855–856, 861

Rate of return on net sales. Ratio of net income to net sales. It is a measure of profitability; also called *return on sales*, 854–855, 861

Rate of return on total assets. Net income plus interest expense divided by average total assets. This ratio measures a company's success in using its assets to earn income for the people who finance the business; also called *return on assets*, 855, 861

Ratio analysis. Evaluating the relationships between two or more key components of the financial statements, 839

Raw materials (RM) inventory. All raw materials (direct materials and indirect materials) not yet used in manufacturing, 50, 107. *See also* Direct materials; Just in time (JIT)
    cost variances, 662, 667
    direct materials budget, 515–516, 525–526
    job costing vs. process costing, 247–250
    operating budgets, 509
    purchasing, 109–110, 130
    standard costs, 667, 679–680

Raw materials record. A written or electronic document listing the number and cost of all units used and received, and the balance currently in stock; a separate record is maintained for each type of raw material kept in stock, 109

Receivables. *See* Accounts receivable

Receiving report. A written or electronic document listing the quantity and type of raw materials received in an incoming shipment; the report is typically a duplicate of the purchase order without the quantity pre-listed on the form, 110

Recession, inventory decisions in, 337–338

Recycling, 122–123
    cost-volume-profit analysis, 401–402
    revenue from, 900

Reduced setup times, in lean thinking, 203–204

Refined costing systems
    cost-benefit test, 193–194
    Decision Guidelines, 195
    to improve operations, 191–194
    old systems and distortions, 194
    sustainability and, 189

Regression analysis. A statistical procedure for determining the line that best fits the data by using *all of the historical data points, not just the high and low data points*, 326–328, 329

Regression equation, in scatterplot, 328, 329

Regression line, in scatterplot, 328, 329

Regulatory environment, Decision Guidelines for changing, 25

Regulatory issues, sustainability and, 900–901

Relevant costs, 71–72

Relevant information. Expected *future* data that *differ* among alternatives, 444–445, 457

Relevant range. The band of volume where total fixed costs remain constant at a certain level and where the variable cost *per unit* remains constant at a certain level, 316–317, 382–386, 390–392

Renewable energy, 713–714

Reports
    balanced scorecard, 609, 612, 614
    common-size statements, 845
    Corporate Social Responsibility reports, 902–907
    Independent Accountants' Review Report, 906
    integrated, 859
    responsibility center performance reports, 588–590
    sustainability reports, 902–907

Repurposing, 900

Required rate of return. Management's minimum desired rate of return on an investment; also called the *discount rate* and *hurdle rate*, 731

Research and development (R&D). Researching and developing new or improved products or services or the processes for producing them, 10, 52
    balanced scorecard, 612, 614
    environmental management accounting and, 908

Residual income (RI). Operating income minus the minimum acceptable operating income given the size of the division's assets, 594–596, 597, 611

Residual value, 735

Responsibility accounting. A system for evaluating the performance of each responsibility center and its manager, 585–597

Responsibility center. A part of an organization whose manager is accountable for planning and controlling certain activities, 585

Responsible Electronics Recycling Act, 123

Retail credit cards, 535

Retailer. Merchandising company that sells to consumers, 49. *See also* Merchandising Company

Retained earnings, 797

Return on assets. Net income plus interest expense, divided by average total assets. This ratio measures a company's success in using its assets to earn income for the people who finance the business; also called *rate of return on total assets*, 855, 861

Return on equity. Net income minus preferred dividends, divided by average common stockholders' equity. It is a measure of profitability; also called *rate of return on common stockholders' equity*, 855–856, 861

Return on investment (ROI). Operating income divided by total assets. The ROI measures the profitability of a division relative to the size of its assets, 592–593, 594–597, 910

Return on sales. Ratio of net income to net sales. It is a measure of profitability; also called *rate of return on net sales*, 854–855, 861

Revenue. *See also* Financial statements, analysis of
    balanced scorecard, 609–613
    decision making and, 446
    discontinuation decisions, 460–464
    flexible budgets, 603–608
    noncash revenue, 789–790
    operating activities, indirect method, 788–794
    performance reports, 588–590
    responsibility centers, 585
    sales budget, 512–513
    sustainability and, 899–900

Revenue center. A responsibility center in which managers are responsible for generating revenue, 586, 587

Risk, indicators of, 406–411

Rolling budget. A budget that is continuously updated so that the next 12 months of operations are always budgeted; also known as a *continuous budget*, 509

R-square value, 327–328, 329

S

Safety stock. Extra inventory kept on hand in case demand is higher than expected or problems in the factory slow production, 513

Salaries
    budgeted income statement, 519–520
    cash flow, direct method, 801
    cash flow, indirect method, 792–793
    direct labor budget, 516, 526
    direct labor variances, 664–666
    fixed manufacturing overhead variances, 680
    of management accountants, 12
    minimum wage, 901
    standard cost of direct labor, 655, 680
    variable manufacturing overhead variances, 671–672

Sales. *See also* Cost-volume-profit (CVP) analysis; Financial statements, analysis of
    accounts receivable turnover, 851
    bad debt, 518
    balanced scorecard, 611–612
    breakeven point calculations, 386–389, 402–405
    cash collections budgets, 524–525
    contribution margin ratio, 385–386
    cost structure, decisions about, 409–411
    cost-volume-profit graphs, 391–392
    credit and debit card sales, impact of, 533–535
    days' sales in receivables, 851–852
    discontinuation decisions, 460–464
    flexible budget performance reports, 604–607
    managerial accounting for, 8–9
    product mix, changes in, 402–403
    profitability measures, 853–856
    risk indicators, 406–411
    sales budget, 512–513
    sales price changes, sensitivity analysis, 396
    sales volume target decisions, 389–392
    special order decisions, 453–455
    unit contribution margin, 383–386

Sales margin. Operating income divided by sales revenue. The sales margin shows how much income is generated for every $1.00 of sales, 593–594, 597

Sales mix. The combination of products that make up total sales, 383, 402–403

Sales service, balanced scorecard, 611–612

Sarbanes-Oxley Act of 2002 (SOX). A congressional act that enhances internal control and financial reporting requirements and establishes new regulatory requirements for publicly traded companies and their independent auditors, 23–24

Scatterplot. A graph that plots historical cost and volume data, 322–324, 328

Second or later processing departments, in process costing, 264–271

I-10 Glossary/Index

Securities and Exchange Commission (SEC), 4
    10-K filings, 842, 859
    environmental practices, reporting of, 903

Segment margin. The income resulting from subtracting only the direct fixed costs of a segment from its contribution margin. The segment margin contains no allocation of common fixed costs, 464, 589–590

Segment margin income statement. A product line income statement that contains no allocation of common fixed costs. Only direct fixed costs that can be traced to specific product lines are subtracted from the product line's contribution margin. All common fixed costs remain unallocated and are shown only under the company total, 464

Self-contained production cells, 201

Selling, general, and administrative expenses (SG&A), 58

Sensitivity analysis. A *what-if* technique that asks what a result will be if a predicted amount is not achieved or if an underlying assumption changes, 396, 530, 736

Service company. A company that sells intangible services rather than tangible products, 49, 50, 63
    budgeting, 531, 532
    COQ at, 207
    cost behavior, 335–336
    cost of goods sold, 335
    financial statements, 65
    job costing, 143–146
    lean operations in, 205
    shifting economy influencing, 20
    using ABC across value chain, 192–193

Set in order, in 5S organization, 202

Setup times, in lean thinking, 203–204

Shareholders
    balanced scorecard, 610, 611, 614
    dividends, 527, 782, 796–797, 855, 857–858
    return on equity, 855–856

Shine, in 5S organization, 202

Shortcut approaches, breakeven point
    using contribution margin ratio, 388–389
    using unit contribution margin, 388

Short-term decision making, 443–474
    Decision Guidelines, 474
    discontinuation decisions, 460–464
    keys to making short-term special decisions, 445–446
    outsourcing decisions, 467–472
    pitfalls, 446–448, 455, 463–464, 467, 471
    process for, 444–448
    product mix decisions, 464–467
    regular pricing decisions, 448–453
    sell as is or process further, 472–474
    special order decisions, 453–455
    sustainability, 447

Simple interest. Interest computed *only* on the principal amount, 723

Six Sigma. The goal of producing near perfection, with less than 3.4 defects per million opportunities, 21, 204

Slack. Intentionally overstating budgeted expenses or understating budgeted revenues in order to cope with uncertainty, make performance appear better, or make room for potential budget cuts, 509

Smaller batches, in lean thinking, 203

Social category, G4, 905

Social performance metrics, 70

Social responsibility, 21–22, 585, 614, 895, 900, 902. *See also* Sustainability

Social Return on Investment (SROI). An analytical tool that is used to explain social and environmental value in monetary terms, 910

Socially responsible investment indices, 902

Society, as G4 sub-category, 905

Solar energy use, 713

Sort, in 5S organization, 202

Special orders, decisions about, 453–455

Standard cost. The budget for a single unit of product. Also simply referred to as standards, 653–682
    fixed overhead, 674

Standard cost accounting. Another common name for standard costing, 679

Standard costing. Also known as standard cost accounting. A method of accounting in which product costs are entered into the general ledger inventory accounts at standard cost rather than actual cost. The variances are captured in their own general ledger accounts and displayed on a standard costing income statement prior to being closed out at the end of the period, 679–680, 679–682
    advantages and disadvantages, 666–667
    computing of, 655–658
    Decision Guidelines, 668, 676
    of direct labor, 655, 680
    direct labor variances, 664–666
    of direct materials, 655
    direct materials variances, 658–663, 666
    fixed manufacturing overhead variances, 680
    flexible budgets and, 658
    income statement, 682
    information used to develop and maintain standards, 655
    journal entries, 679–682
    of manufacturing overhead, 656
    of one unit, 656–657
    reengineering, 657
    sustainability and, 657
    systems, 675
    types of, 654
    variable manufacturing overhead variances, 671–672
    variances, computation of, 658–667

Standard hours of time allowed (SHA), 665

Standard Industrial Classification (SIC), 906

Standard Price (SP), 659–661

Standard quantity of materials allowed (SQA), 661

Standardize, in 5S organization, 202

Standards. Another common name for standard costs, 654, 657. *See also* Standard cost

Statement of Accounting Standards (No. 95), 780n1

Statement of cash flows. One of the four basic financial statements; the statement shows the overall increase or decrease in cash during the period as well as how the company generated and used cash during the period, 780. *See also* Cash flow
    Decision Guidelines, 786, 803
    direct method, 783–784, 799–802
    financing activities, 782–783
    function of, 780–781
    indirect method, 784, 788–798
    interpreting, 798
    investing activities, 781
    operating activities, 781, 783–784
    sustainability and, 784–785

Statement of Financial Accounting Standards Number 131 (SFAS 131), 591

Step costs. A cost behavior that is fixed over a small range of activity and then jumps to a different fixed level with moderate changes in volume, 317–318

Stock
    cash flows, indirect method, 796–797
    P/E ratio, 857
    safety, 513
    statement of cash flows, 781–782

Stock exchanges, 902–903

Stock inventory. Products normally kept on hand in order to quickly fill customer orders, 108

Stockholders
    balanced scorecard, 610, 611, 614
    dividend payments, 527, 782, 796–797, 855, 857–858
    profit expectations, 448

Stockholders' equity, return on equity, 855–856

Strategic planning. Setting long-term goals that may extend 5 to 10 years into the future, 508
    balanced scorecard, 609–613, 614, 615
    budget, benefits of, 510–511
    budget process, 508–510
    environmental management accounting and, 909
    G4 Guidelines, 906

Subsidiary ledger. Supporting detail for a general ledger account, 131, 131n4

Sunk cost. A cost that has already been incurred, and therefore cannot be changed regardless of which future action is taken, 72, 446–447

Supply-chain assessment. Making purchase decisions based partially on how well suppliers manage the social and environmental impact of their operations, 900

Supply-chain management, 204

Sustain, in 5S organization, 202

Sustainability. The ability of a system to endure without giving way or to use resources so that they are not depleted or permanently damaged. In business, sustainability is also defined as the ability to meet the needs of the present without compromising the ability of future generations to meet their own needs, 21–22, 895
    budgeting and, 536
    business case for, 897–902
    capital investments and, 713–714
    corporate reporting, 70
    cost behavior, 319
    cost-volume-profit analysis, 401–402
    Decision Guidelines, 913
    environmental management accounting and, 908–912
    financial statement analysis and, 859
    history of, 896–897
    importance of, 895–896
    job costing, 122–123
    lean thinking and, 205
    performance evaluation and, 614
    process costing and, 258–259
    purchasing practices, 54
    refined costing systems and, 189
    short-term decisions and, 447
    standard costs and, 657
    statement of cash flows and, 784–785
    sustainability reports, 902–907
    zero-waste to landfills, 657, 899

Sustainability Accounting Standards Board (SASB), 906–907

Sustainability Consortium, 122

Sustainability profile, 122

Sustainability report. The primary document used for communicating a company's performance on all three pillars of the triple bottom line: economic, environmental, and social. Also known as a Corporate Social Responsibility (CSR) report, 902–907

Sustainability reporting. A process that helps companies set goals, measure performance, and manage change as they move toward an economic model that produces long-term economic profit as well as environmental care and social responsibility, 902–907

T

Take-back laws, 123

Takt time. The rate of production needed to meet customer demand, yet avoid overproduction, 202

Target costing. An approach to pricing used by price-takers; target costing begins with the revenue at market price and subtracts the company's desired profit to arrive at the target total cost, 451–453

Target profit, 448

Target rate of return, 594–595

Taxes
    budgeted income statement, 519, 520
    cash flow, direct method, 802
    cash payments budget, 525–528
    discontinuation decisions, 461, 463
    green investment tax breaks, 714
    income taxes, 527, 782, 802
    property taxes, 517, 526
    statement of cash flows, 782

Technology Makes it Simple. *See also* Excel
    future value computation, 727

Glossary/Index I-11

internal rate of return calculations, 739, 755–756
net present value calculations, 735, 753–755
present value computations, 730
time value of money calculations and example solutions, 725, 727, 747–753

Time Value of Money. The fact that money can be invested to earn income over time, 723

calculation of, 723–730
example solutions, 747–750
future value table, 745
net present value, 730–736
present value tables, 743–744

Times-interest-earned ratio. Ratio of income from operations to interest expense. It measures the number of times operating income can cover interest expense; also called the *interest-coverage ratio*, 853, 860

Total cost. The cost of all resources used throughout the value chain, 57

accounting for, 256
in process costing, 256, 268

Total Quality Management (TQM). A management philosophy of delighting customers with superior products and services by continually setting higher goals and improving the performance of every business function, 206

Trace. To assign a direct cost to a cost object, 55, 56

Trade workers. *See* Service company

Trading on equity. Earning more income on borrowed money than the related interest expense, thereby increasing the earnings for the owners of the business; also called *leverage*, 856

Transaction costs, credit and debit cards, 533–535

Transfer price. The price charged for the internal sale of product between two different divisions of the same company, 597–599

Transferred-in costs. Costs incurred in a previous process that are carried forward as part of the product's cost when it moves to the next process, 264, 272

Transportation, 198, 199
Trash audits, 258, 899, 900

Treasurer. The position responsible for raising the firm's capital and investing funds, 9, 10

Treasury Bills, U.S, 781
Treasury stock, 782

Trend percentages. A form of horizontal analysis in which percentages are computed by selecting a base year as 100% and expressing amounts for the following years as a percentage of the base amount, 841–843

Triple bottom line. Evaluating a company's performance not only by its ability to generate economic profits, but also by its impact on people and on the planet, 21–22, 49, 895

U

Unavoidable fixed costs. Fixed costs that will continue to be incurred even if a particular course of action is taken, 461–462

Uncontrollable costs. Costs that cannot be changed or influenced in the short run by management, 71

Underallocated manufacturing overhead. The amount of manufacturing overhead allocated to jobs is less than the amount of manufacturing overhead costs actually incurred; this results in jobs being undercosted, 127–129

Unethical vs. illegal behavior, 15

Unfavorable variance. A variance that causes operating income to be lower than budgeted, 588–589, 607–608

Unit Contribution Margin. The excess of the unit sales price over the variable cost per unit; also called *contribution margin per unit*, 384

overview of, 383–386
sales price changes, 396

shortcut approach to breakeven point using, 388
variable cost changes, 398–399
weighted-average contribution margin, 402–405

Unit costs, 268–269
special order decisions, 447
standard costing of one unit, 656–657

United Nations, 859, 895

Unit-level activities. Activities and costs incurred for every unit produced, 190

U.S. Treasury Bills, 781

Utilities
discontinuation decisions, 460–464
job costing, 122
manufacturing overhead budget, 517–518
mixed costs, 326–328
value chain and, 55–56

V

Valuation
book value per share of common stock, 858, 861
measurement issues, 596
net book value, 789–790

Value chain. The activities that add value to a firm's products and services; includes R&D, design, production or purchases, marketing, distribution, and customer service, 51

in ABM, 192–193
business activities in, 49–52
coordinating activities, 52–53
sustainability and, 53–54

Value stream mapping (VSM), 201

Value-added activities. Activities for which the customer is willing to pay because these activities add value to the final product or service, 192

Variable costing. The costing method that assigns only *variable* manufacturing costs to products. All fixed manufacturing costs (fixed MOH) are expensed as period costs. Also known as *direct costing*, 123, 331–333

absorption costing vs, 336–338
decision making and, 453
income statement, 334
reconciling operating income, 338–340

Variable costs. Costs that change in total in direct proportion to changes in volume, 72, 308. *See also* Cost-volume-profit (CVP) analysis

breakeven point calculations, 386–389
changes in, sensitivity analysis, 398–399
cost behavior, 308–311
decision making and, 453
manufacturing overhead budget, 517
operating leverage, 407–409
outsourcing decisions, 469

Variable manufacturing overhead variances, 671–672
Variable operating expenses, 518

Variable overhead efficiency variance. This variance tells managers how much of the total variable MOH variance is due to using more or fewer hours of the allocation base (usually machine hours or DL hours) than anticipated for the actual volume of output. It is calculated as follows: SR × (AH − SHA), 672

Variable overhead rate variance. Also called the variable overhead spending variance. This variance tells managers whether more or less was spent on variable overhead than they expected would be spent for the hours worked. It is calculated as follows: AH × (AR − SR), 671–672

Variable overhead spending variance. Another common name for variable overhead rate variance, 671

Variance. The difference between an actual figures and budgeted figures, 511, 588–589. *See also* Standard Costing

budgets, 510
standard costs and, 679–682

Vertical analysis. Analysis of a financial statement that reveals the relationship of each statement item to a specified base, which is the 100% figure, 839, 843–845

Decision Guidelines, 846

Vertical integration. The acquisition of companies within one's supply chain, 597

Volume variance. The difference between the master budget and the flexible budget. The volume variance arises *only* because the actual sales volume differs from the volume originally anticipated in the master budget, 605–606

W

Wages
budgeted income statement, 519–520
cash flow, direct method, 801
cash flow, indirect method, 792–793
direct labor budget, 516, 526
direct labor variances, 664–666
fixed manufacturing overhead variances, 680
minimum wage, 901
standard cost of direct labor, 655, 680
variable manufacturing overhead variances, 671–672

Wages payable
job costing vs. process costing, 247–250
liability, 132–133

Waiting, 198, 199

Warranties
balanced scorecard, 609, 612
sustainability and, 54

Waste
diverting for other uses, 899, 900
eight wastes, 198
environmental management accounting and, 908
e-waste, 123
standard costs, 657
zero-waste to landfills, 258, 657, 899

Waste activities. Activities that neither enhance the customer's image of the product or service nor provide a competitive advantage; also known as non-value-added activities, 192

Waste audits. Studying the stream of waste coming from company operations (solid waste, water discharge, chemicals, etc.) to determine waste that can be avoided and alternative uses for the remaining waste, 258, 899

Water, environmental management accounting and, 908

Water footprint. The total volume of water use associated with the processes and products of a business, 904, 905–906, 911

Weighted-average contribution margin, 402–405

Weighted-average method of process costing. A process costing method that *combines* any beginning inventory units (and costs) with the current period's units (and costs) to get a weighted-average cost, 251, 252–258

Wholesaler. Merchandising companies that buy in bulk from manufacturers, mark up the prices, and then sell those products to retailers, 49

Working capital. Current assets minus current liabilities; measures a business's ability to meet its short-term obligations with its current assets, 849

Work-in-process (WIP) inventory. Goods that are partway through the manufacturing process but not yet complete, 50, 259–260

job costing vs. process costing, 247–250
standard costs, 667, 679–681
total costs, 257

Z

Zero-based budgeting. A budgeting approach in which managers begin with a budget of zero and must justify every dollar put into the budget, 510

Zero-waste to landfills, 258, 657, 899